Handbook of
COGNITIVE
AGING

Dedicated to
John L. Horn
Paul B. Baltes
K. Warner Schaie

Pioneers in the theory and methods of cognitive aging research

Handbook of
COGNITIVE AGING
Interdisciplinary Perspectives

Edited by

Scott M. Hofer
Oregon State University

and

Duane F. Alwin
Pennsylvania State University

SAGE Publications
Los Angeles • London • New Delhi • Singapore

For information:

Sage Publications, Inc.
2455 Teller Road
Thousand Oaks, California 91320
E-mail: order@sagepub.com

Sage Publications Ltd.
1 Oliver's Yard
55 City Road
London EC1Y 1SP
United Kingdom

Sage Publications India Pvt. Ltd.
B 1/I 1 Mohan Cooperative Industrial Area
Mathura Road, New Delhi 110 044
India

Sage Publications Asia-Pacific Pte. Ltd.
33 Pekin Street #02-01
Far East Square
Singapore 048763

Printed in the United States of America.

Library of Congress Cataloging-in-Publication Data

Handbook of cognitive aging: interdisciplinary perspectives/edited by Scott M. Hofer, Duane F. Alwin.
    p. cm.
Includes bibliographical references and indexes.
ISBN 978-1-4129-4105-1 (cloth: alk. paper)
ISBN 978-1-4129-6028-1 (pbk.: alk. paper)
    1. Cognition—Age factors. 2. Aging—Psychological aspects. I. Hofer, Scott M. II. Alwin, Duane F.
(Duane Francis), 1944–

BF724.55.C63H36 2008
155.67'13—dc22   2007039241

This book is printed on acid-free paper.

08 09 10 11 12   10 9 8 7 6 5 4 3 2 1

Acquisitions Editor:	Cheri Dellelo
Editorial Assistant:	Lara Grambling
Production Editor:	Tracy Buyan
Copy Editor:	Kathy Anne Savadel
Typesetter:	C&M Digitals (P) Ltd.
Proofreader:	Penelope Sippel
Indexer:	Kathy Paparchontis
Cover Designers:	Ravi Balasuriya, Cheryl McLean
Marketing Manager:	Stephanie Adams

CONTENTS

FOREWORD

Sometime in the next decade our species will reach a watershed moment. For the first time in human history, people over 60 will outnumber children. The pace with which population aging has occurred is stunning. In less than one century, scientific discoveries and technological advancements resulted in a near doubling of life expectancy in developed regions of the world. Combined with reductions in fertility rates, these same regions began to age at an unprecedented rate.

There is little question that the increase in life expectancy in the 20th century is a remarkable cultural achievement. Yet, myriad questions about the quality of those added years remain unknown. Possible answers leave many uneasy. Whether longevity is a benefit or a burden hinges on the status of long-lived people. To the extent that long-lived people are physically fit, mentally sharp and financially secure, societies will thrive. To the extent that they are frail, dependent on the care of others, and impoverished, the well-being of everyone in a society is diminished.

Among the most, if *the* most, burning questions concern the aging mind. If future generations of the "aged" experience cognitive development like their parents and grandparents, we can expect an increasing prevalence of dementia and other types of low or impaired cognitive functioning in the worlds of the future. Alternatively, to the extent that cognitive decline is influenced by factors such as education, diet, exercise, we may see very different patterns (for better or worse).

The possibilities raise the specter of massive cognitive limitations among the vast numbers of post-65 citizens who will inhabit our future world, but it also raises an entirely different set of possibilities, once we consider several of the differences in cohort-based experiences in how the lives of the future and past aged have played out. What are the projections for low cognitive functioning expected to be when you consider the fact that the "brave new Baby Boomers" are opting to do things in ways different from the past, such as not planning to "retire," continuing to maintain a productive niche, and intending generally to carry on an active lifestyle different from the world of their parents. Does our current knowledge of the post–World War II birth cohorts (e.g., their health, their nutrition, their activities, their work lives) allow us to say something about the future consequences due to the factors predictive of cognitive functioning? And, in addition to knowing what those future lives will be like, does our current knowledge of cognitive aging prepare us to understand the cognitive performance realities of the future?

This handbook addresses these issues. Comprising chapters from a veritable "Who's Who" in cognitive aging, the present collection and the conference on which it was based provide an important indicator of what we know, how we know it, what we need to know, and where we are moving as a field. It draws attention to the need for interdisciplinary research to address the question of the future of cognitive aging. Its publication is a sign of the current interest (among scientists from among a multitude of disciplines) in learning more about the aging mind and creating a better understanding the bio-, neuro-, psycho-, socio-factors that influence processes involved in cognitive aging. Many have challenged the popular notion that mental decline with age is inevitable, progressive, and general, suggesting that research presents a more complex picture. Several of the chapters in the present volume also make the claim that cognitive decline in older age is not inevitable, citing a range of experiential and neuron-pathological risk factors that may produce individual differences in cognitive performance among older adults.

The National Research Council Committee on Future Directions for Cognitive Research on Aging, which I chaired, was encouraged by the Behavioral and Social Science Program of the National Institute on Aging to develop a report on the state of knowledge on cognitive aging. This was published as *The Aging Mind— Opportunities in Cognitive Research* (National Research Council, 2000). In a very real sense, Scott Hofer and Duane Alwin, coeditors of the handbook, extend this work. Through its

emphasis on interdisciplinary and integrative science, the present volume contributes to the understanding of the contributions of both the underlying biological bases of cognitive functions such as attention, language, sensation and sensory function, learning, memory, and other cognitive domains, as well as the experiential and cultural contributions, both independently and through interaction with the former. Cognitive aging involves a complex interplay of multiple layers of potential and experience, and this volume represents a contribution to their understanding. There has never been a time when such understanding was more pressing. Readers are sure to profit from this impressive collection.

Laura L. Carstensen
Professor of Psychology
Director, Stanford Center on Longevity
Stanford University

PREFACE

Although some dimensions of human abilities remain stable over the life span, or in some cases even develop and expand with age and greater maturity (e.g., the ability to exercise good sense and sound judgment), there is general agreement that systematic age-related declines in cognitive functioning occur in midlife and older age across multiple domains, including speed of processing, episodic memory, attention, and verbal fluency. Cognitive function is clearly an essential component of health and well-being across the life span, and understanding the relationship of aging to cognitive function is increasingly a high priority for society because of the realities of population aging and because of its intrinsic relevance to the lives of aging members of society. Moreover, differences in patterns of cognitive aging are crucial to understanding the linkages among socioeconomic, racial/ethnic, gender, and health disparities.

This is an exciting period in which to study the connection between processes of aging and cognitive function; progress is being made on several fronts. This was the conclusion of the National Research Council's (NRC's) Committee on Future Directions for Cognitive Research on Aging, articulated in *The Aging Mind: Opportunities in Cognitive Research.*[1] "Now is a time of great promise for learning more about the aging mind and turning that knowledge to the advantage of older people," the NRC report concluded (2000, p. 8). The committee cited discoveries being made by neuroscientists in understanding the neural basis of many cognitive functions. They concluded that the adult brain "has much greater capacity for

plasticity than previously believed, growing new dendrites and perhaps even new neurons" (p. 7), asserting that neuroscientists "are poised to understand, at the molecular and cellular levels, neural changes that affect the life course of cognitive capabilities" (p. 8). In the area of behavioral science, the committee reported that rapid progress had been made in "classifying types of cognitive functioning, measuring them, tracking changes in particular functions over the life cycle, and documenting declines, maintenance, and improvement in these functions over the life span" (p. 8). They argued that "this research is making it possible to develop behavioral and technological interventions to maintain cognitive performance in older individuals" (p. 8). The committee further observed that "researchers in cognitive science are developing detailed models and theories of cognitive processes that can help make sense of observed patterns of change in functioning and link them to observed changes in neural systems" (p. 8). Finally, they noted that social scientists have demonstrated "the significance of cultural supports and life experiences in shaping cognitive content and processes over the life span" (p. 8). All these developments "are making possible new understandings of how normal processes of aging affect cognitive functioning and new interventions to maintain cognitive performance in older people" (p. 1).

Despite the impressive claims made by the NRC report for knowledge in the field of cognitive aging, it also stressed the need for several major research initiatives that promise to contribute to the improvement of knowledge regarding age-related change in cognitive functioning. One of the central observations articulated in

The Aging Mind was that, although there is "much valuable and promising research" going on across the fields of neuroscience, behavioral (psychological) science, and social science, these "fields do not communicate with each other as much as is probably desirable" and that "what is being learned from each research perspective has not fully penetrated the work of researchers proceeding from other perspectives" (pp. 8–9). The committee argued that the state of our current knowledge about the nature of cognitive aging is encumbered by the failure to develop a comprehensive theoretical framework that incorporates age-related variation in environmental factors, age-related changes in sensory function and health, and the interaction of these factors with neurological changes in development. They proposed a conceptual framework that focused on three interacting systems: "*cognitive structures and processes, neural health, and behavioral context,* including task structure and social, cultural, and technological factors" (pp. 9–11). The implications of this framework for setting the agenda of the future of cognitive aging are far reaching, and we believe they will not go unrecognized by researchers working on these problems across disciplines.

In addition to summarizing the existing knowledge about developments in cognitive aging research, the NRC committee also viewed their task as one of identifying "areas of opportunity in which additional research support from the National Institute on Aging (NIA) would substantially improve understanding of cognitive functioning" (p. 1). They identified a number of serious limitations in research design, data collection, multivariate statistical modeling, and the development of research strategies that adhere to the highest standards for internal and external validity. Indeed, the NRC was quite explicit in the "Research Initiative" section of its report with regard to the requirements of future research on cognitive aging. The report argued that, to achieve the objectives of the recommended research initiatives,

it will be necessary to expand the use of large-scale, multivariate, longitudinal studies . . . to expand and improve on previous longitudinal research by including variables reflecting high-resolution cognitive and neural measures; indicators

of health status and sensory-motor functioning; and measures of relevant life experience. (p. 52)

The report went on to argue that it is also "important to examine a broad representative sample of the population, sometimes oversampling in subgroups whose health status or responses to life experiences are expected to illuminate important theoretical questions, and to encompass a wide age range" (p. 52). Finally, the report argued that "by following individuals into very old age, promising new findings suggesting the existence of unexpected linkages between cognitive functioning and survival could be investigated" (p. 52).

Building in part upon the mandates set by the NRC committee in *The Aging Mind,* the present volume is based on the activities and results of the International Conference on the Future of Cognitive Aging Research (ICFCAR), held at Pennsylvania State University May 20–22, 2005, which was aimed at contributing to a conversation that would confront some of these obstacles to progress in research identified by the NRC committee, with an eye toward developing a shared multidisciplinary agenda for the next few decades of research. The conference was intended in part to employ a somewhat broader compass for the inclusion of cognitive aging researchers in these important discussions. Our recruitment efforts resulted in our gaining the participation of a diverse group of scholars who work in the field of cognitive aging.

The ICFCAR conference was supported in part by a grant award to Pennsylvania State University on behalf of Duane F. Alwin and Scott M. Hofer from the National Institute on Aging (R13-AG02623), and specifically by programs within the Behavioral and Social Research and Neuroscience and Neuropsychology branches of the NIA. The ICFCAR was also cosponsored and supported financially by the Social Science Research Institute, the College of Health and Human Development, and the College of the Liberal Arts, all of Pennsylvania State University, as well as by the Center for Demography of Health and Aging at the University of Wisconsin.

Leading international experts on cognitive aging representing the fields of developmental psychology, psychiatry, neuroscience, behavioral genetics, demography, gerontology, sociology, economics, biostatistics, and epidemiology gathered for a 3-day working conference, focusing on the state of research in the field of cognitive aging and its future. The ICFCAR conference attracted top researchers from Australia, England, Scotland, Germany, Switzerland, Sweden, the Netherlands, and the United States, countries where the majority of research on cognitive aging is done.[2] The five main objectives of the ICFCAR were to explore (1) the current state of the cognitive theorizing as related to processes of aging, (2) present-day empirical assessments of what is known about cognitive aging phenomena in terms of changes and causes, (3) methodological critiques of research designs and measurement models on which our current knowledge base rests, (4) the discussion of alternative designs and innovative lines of interdisciplinary research that promise new insights into the processes of cognitive aging, and (5) the critical issues of the data needs for the future.

More than 60 internationally recognized experts on various aspects cognitive aging were invited to attend the ICFCAR, most of who have made a contribution to the present volume. The following researcher/scholars were in attendance:[3] David M. Almeida (Pennsylvania State University), Kaarin Anstey (Australian National University), Paul Baltes (Max Planck Institute, Germany), Lisa L. Barnes (Rush University Medical Center), Cynthia A. Berg (University of Utah), Fredda Blanchard-Fields (Georgia Institute of Technology), Herman Buschke (Albert Einstein Medical School), Roberto Cabeza (Duke University), Neil Charness (Florida State University), Helen Christensen (Australian National University), Fergus I. M. Craik (University of Toronto, Canada), Dale Dannefer (Case Western Reserve University), Gordon DeJong (Pennsylvania State University), Roger A. Dixon (University of Alberta), Gwenith G. Fisher (University of Michigan), Paul Eslinger (Pennsylvania State University Hershey Medical Center), Jeremy Freese (University of Wisconsin–Madison), Robert M. Hauser (University of Wisconsin–Madison), Steven G. Heeringa (University of Michigan), Christopher Hertzog (Georgia Institute of Technology), Lesa Hoffman (University of Nebraska), John L. Horn (University of Southern California), William J. Hoyer (Syracuse University), Boo Johansson (Göteborg University, Sweden), Susan Kemper (University of Kansas), Shinobu Kitayama (University of Michigan), Margie E. Lachman (Brandeis University), Ulman Lindenberger (Max Planck Institute, Germany), Mary A. Luszcz (Flinders University, Australia), Jennifer Manly (Columbia University), Mike Martin (University of Zurich, Switzerland), John J. McArdle (University of Virginia, now at the University of Southern California), Ryan J. McCammon (University of Michigan), Gerald E. McClearn (Pennsylvania State University), Mark A. McDaniel (University of New Mexico, now at Washington University), Joan M. McDowd (University of Kansas), Peter C. M. Molenaar (University of Amsterdam, The Netherlands; now at Pennsylvania State University), John R. Nesselroade (University of Virginia), Richard E. Nisbett (University of Michigan), Denise C. Park (University of Illinois, Urbana-Champaign, now at University of Texas, Dallas), Andrea M. Piccinin (Pennsylvania State University, now at Oregon State University), Patrick M. A. Rabbitt (Oxford University, England), Naftali Raz (Wayne State University), Patricia Reuter-Lorenz (University of Michigan), Chandra A. Reynolds (University of California, Riverside), Willard L. Rodgers (University of Michigan), Timothy A. Salthouse (University of Virginia), Mary Sano (Columbia University), K. Warner Schaie (Pennsylvania State University), Martin Sliwinski (Syracuse University), Brent J. Small (University of South Florida), Avron Spiro III (Veterans Administration, Boston), Valgeir Thorvaldsson (Göteborg University, Sweden), Paul Verhaeghen (Syracuse University, now at Georgia Institute of Technology), Keith F. Widaman (University of California, Davis), Keith Whitfield (Pennsylvania State University, now at Duke University), Robert J. Willis (University of Michigan), Sherry L. Willis (Pennsylvania State University), Robert S. Wilson (Rush University Medical Center), Linda A. Wray (Pennsylvania State University), and Elizabeth M. Zelinski (University of Southern California). As noted, virtually all of these participants contributed a chapter to the present volume, and of course, we have added several contributors.

We acknowledge the contributions of all these participants at the ICFCAR, plus the many other people who helped make the conference a success, either through their participation or support. This included representatives of the Cognitive Aging programs at the NIA (Jeffrey Elias and Molly Wagster) as well as the Office of Director of the Behavioral and Social Sciences Branch (specifically, Ron Abeles) of the NIA. A number of additional members the NIA Behavioral and Social Sciences Branch staff were invited to attend, as well.

We are also grateful to our respective collegiate administrators, Ray Coward, Dean of the College of Human Development (now Provost at Utah State University); Susan Welch, Dean of the College of the Liberal Arts, Pennsylvania State University; and Mark Hayward, who was then director of the Social Science Research Institute at Pennsylvania State University, the three of whom provided generous support for the conference. We wish to acknowledge our close colleagues at Pennsylvania State University, who served as members of our local organizing committee and who helped introduce speakers and kept the flow of the conference running smoothly, specifically, David M. Almeida, Paul Eslinger, Andrea M. Piccinin, K. Warner Schaie, Keith Whitfield, Sherry L. Willis, and Linda A. Wray. Finally, we wish to thank the Associate Editors and many reviewers of contributions to this handbook for their insightful comments and challenging questions, including Jason C. Allaire, North Carolina State University, Department of Psychology; John Dunlosky, Kent State University, Department of Psychology; Andrea Halpern, Bucknell University, Department of Psychology; Lesa Hoffman, University of Nebraska, Department of Psychology; Diane Howieson, Oregon Health and Science University, Layton Aging and Alzheimer's Disease Center; Susan Kemper, University of Kansas, Department of Psychology; Matthias Kliegel, University of Zurich (Switzerland), Department of Psychology; Donna La Voie, Saint Louis University, Department of Psychology; Cindy A. Lustig, University of Michigan, Department of Psychology; Mike Martin, University of Zurich (Switzerland), Department of Psychology; Ryan J. McCammon, University of Michigan (Ann Arbor), Department of Psychiatry; Gerald E. McClearn, Pennsylvania State University, Department of Biobehavioral Health; Deb McGinnis, Oakland University, Department of Psychology; Jacqueline Mogle, Syracuse University, Department of Psychology; Chandra Reynolds, University of California, Riverside, Department of Psychology; Robert S. Stawski, Pennsylvania State University, Department of Human Development and Family Studies.

The ICFCAR led to the organization of additional activities, some of which are also represented in the present volume. Symposia titled "The Antecedents and Consequences of Cognitive Aging" (co-organized by Duane F. Alwin and Scott M. Hofer) and "Integrative Analysis of Longitudinal Studies: Accounting for Health in Aging-Related Processes" and "Innovative Methods for Describing Developmental Change" (organized by Scott M. Hofer) based on some of the results of this conference, were held at the 59th annual meetings of the Gerontological Society of America, October 2006, in Dallas, Texas. In addition, several of the papers developed for the conference were presented at the annual Cognitive Aging Conference held in Atlanta, Georgia, April 20–23, 2006.

In the present volume, we have put together a set of contributions that span the range of disciplines working on issues related to cognitive aging. We hope this collection will not only contribute to the future of cognitive aging research but also help build a multidisciplinary agenda that will stimulate the improvement of research into the complex set of factors that produce cognitive change in midlife and older age.

Scott M. Hofer, Corvallis, Oregon
Duane F. Alwin, State College, Pennsylvania

NOTES

1. National Research Council. (2000). *The Aging Mind: Opportunities in Cognitive Research.* Committee on Future Directions for Cognitive Research on Aging. Paul C. Stern and Laura L. Carstensen, Eds. Commission on Behavioral and Social Sciences and Education. Washington, DC: National Academy Press.

2. More about the conference can be learned from the conference Web site: http://oregonstate.edu/~hofers/ICFCAR/index.htm

3. In a few instances, final arrangements of schedules made it impossible for invitees to attend, although the vast majority of people on this list were in attendance.

PART I

INTRODUCTION

1

OPPORTUNITIES AND CHALLENGES FOR INTERDISCIPLINARY RESEARCH

DUANE F. ALWIN AND SCOTT M. HOFER

Some years ago, Thomas Kuhn (1962) pointed out that science advances in one of two main ways. First, by focusing on the problems and puzzles defined by existing paradigms, and by training students in the somewhat rigid methods and models of our disciplines, science inevitably makes progress by filling in gaps in knowledge and refuting existing hypotheses. Kuhn referred to this as "normal science," and it constitutes the major mechanism by which scientists produce knowledge that supports contemporary models of the phenomena of interest. Second, in addition to this mode of activity, science progresses by developing fresh approaches, by shifting the paradigms, or by repudiating the past through more dramatic scientific revolutions. Kuhn's work suggests that many of the most important developments in scientific theories and models over past centuries originated through the kind of paradigm shifts implied by this second mechanism.

Innovative advances in science promote the development of new communities that foster change and define progress in new ways. As long as the consensual processes of science accept the validity of given models and dominant theoretical perspectives, the paradigms on which they rest will more or less persist. However, as models

begin to fail in their ability to describe empirical reality, they will eventually fall into disrepute, even when there is strong institutional pressure in support of such models.[1] Moreover, old models are often vulnerable to more careful examination when they are subjected to the scrutiny that is possible with new and more refined methods of measurement and analysis.

ASSESSING PROGRESS IN COGNITIVE AGING RESEARCH

We believe this is a useful model for laying the background for the consideration of the present body of knowledge about cognitive aging and for raising the question about where the field of cognitive aging research is going. How should we measure progress in the field of cognitive aging research? What are the "normal science" paradigms that dominate the area? What is wrong with these paradigms, and what is right with them? What are the standards we should use for assessing the progress and vitality of research on cognitive aging? What are the indications of paradigm shifts, if any, and how should we set priorities for the future of cognitive aging research? In other words, how do we assess what we know, and how we know it, and how do we decide what areas are the most important avenues for future discovery? These are the issues surrounding the chapters of this *Handbook of Cognitive Aging*, and in this regard it is perhaps valuable to place these chapters in a broader context of why these issues are important.

The issues addressed by authors of these chapters are highly relevant to the present historical context, given that major support for research on cognitive aging comes from the federal government, namely the National Institute on Aging (NIA). The NIA places a high priority on supporting research on cognitive aging and has actively stimulated the development and review of research in this area (see National Research Council [NRC], 2000). The National Advisory Council on Aging explicitly mentions cognitive aging as a priority topic area for Behavioral and Social Research (BSR) program activities (NIA, National Advisory Council on Aging, BSR Program Review Committee, 2004), and the NIA Web site contains a number of documents underscoring its commitment to continue support the advancement of cognitive aging research.

At the same time, the NIA itself is taking the lead in examining the question of how to set priorities for funding of research in existing fields. The National Research Committee on Assessing Behavioral and Social Science Research on Aging, at the urging of the NIA, addressed the larger question of priorities for research funding. For example, what are the national priorities that govern the application of societal resources to the development of scientific knowledge? Are such decisions made by implementing any sort of rational evidence-based strategies? Or is it the case that the "decision processes of science agencies are unduly conservative in program and project selection" that fall short in terms of "converting research findings into usable and useful applications" (NRC, 2007, p. 9)? In keeping with these same criteria, the authors of the chapters in this handbook were asked to address the questions of not only "What do we know?" but also "What do we need to know?"

Thus, within the context of addressing the body of knowledge on cognitive aging, and from the point of view of developing funding for future research, it is useful in this context for the NIA to inquire about the priorities across its various initiatives, and specifically about how it might make decisions of funding in the area of cognitive aging research. We ask these questions here not because we plan to explicitly address them but because of their general relevance to the issues posed by the chapters in this book. Given an interest in the future of cognitive aging research, and in anticipation of continuing levels of funding of research on cognitive aging, what are the questions the field should be asking, what kinds of measurement approaches and data resources should be brought to bear on them, and how should data be modeled and explained? Of course, in such an endeavor the first objective is one of summarizing the existing knowledge base and developing recommendations for further research.

Several years ago, the Committee on Future Directions for Cognitive Research on Aging of the NRC made a study of the state of our knowledge about cognitive aging. This study was commissioned by the BSR Program of the NIA, which encouraged the publication of *The Aging Mind: Opportunities in Cognitive Research* (NRC, 2000), edited by Paul Stern and Laura Carstensen. That report was eloquent in its summary of the current state of knowledge in the area of cognitive aging and its recommendations for future research. We return subsequently to a brief discussion of the findings of the Committee on Future Directions for Cognitive Research on Aging and the committee's recommendations, but first we mention some of the reasons for emphasizing the need to focus on a greater understanding of cognitive aging and the importance of considering the future of cognitive aging research. The authors of *The Aging Mind* stressed the need for further investments in new types of research, particularly through a wider-angle interdisciplinary lens, that will enhance our present level of knowledge.

Specifically, there are several areas in which there is a need for greater investments in cognitive aging research and a pressing need to know more. One of the most important phenomena, often used to justify the investment in new knowledge about cognitive aging, is the phenomenon of *population aging*. This refers to the demographic fact of life that for several decades the population has been getting older and the seemingly inevitable prospect that this trend will continue into the first half of the present decade. Within the framework of population change, there are a number of additional questions one can pose regarding the applicability of present generalizations to future cohorts of aging persons (see chap. 4, this volume).

The authors of *The Aging Mind* (NRC, 2000) stressed the fact that behavioral researchers have focused on establishing the classification of types of cognitive functioning and their relationship to age and on the measurement and tracking of these functions over the life span (see, e.g., Salthouse, 1999). At least since Cattell's early publications (1941), and developed further by Horn (1965; Horn & Cattell, 1966), aging researchers have distinguished between two interrelated components of cognitive functioning— fluid and crystallized abilities. The term *fluid abilities* refers to those functions that reflect the capacities for insight into complex problem-solving tasks, independent of sensory modalities and cultural settings, whereas *crystallized abilities* refers to those functions that result from the investment of fluid abilities in experience and culturally defined tasks (Cattell, 1971). The differing relationships to age of fluid and crystallized functions—fluid abilities tend to decline with age after reaching a peak in early life, whereas crystallized abilities tend to remain stable through to very old age—caution one against making broad generalizations about cognitive aging. It is important, therefore, to understand age-related trajectories of performance in terms of what is being measured. There is a great deal of support for the idea that there are several possible trajectories of the life span development of cognitive abilities, and there is clearly a need for more information on the nature of age-related change along multiple dimensions for well-defined populations. In addition, there are several other urgent matters, which we briefly discuss in the following section, involving the inevitability of decline; the nature and patterns of these declines; the relationship between "normal" aging and dementia; the linkage between cognitive aging and several dimensions of health and sensory function; the role of cultural and social factors in cognitive change; and the potential for technological arrangements to assist with adaptation to cognitive change, which especially declines, in older age.

UNDERSTANDING COGNITIVE AGING

Researchers have raised several hypotheses to explain declines in cognitive functioning with increasing age (e.g., see Brown & Park, 2003; Park, 1999; and Park et al., 1996). Taking a somewhat broadly gauged approach, we see three types of theories that account for cognitive aging: (1) psychological theories of cognitive aging that stress underlying common causes accounting for a general cognitive decline with age, such as the hypothesis of generalized slowing or link with sensory acuity (e.g., Baltes & Lindenberger, 1997; Baltes & Mayer, 1999; Birren & Fisher, 1995; Cerella, 1985; Craik & Byrd, 1982; Lindenberger & Baltes, 1994; Myerson, Hale, Wagstaff, Poon, & Smith, 1990; Salthouse, 1993, 1996a, 1996b); (2) biological theories that stress overall age-related declines in organ function, including neurological function, which lead to increases in the onset of illnesses or impairments, and risks of experiencing multiple illnesses or impairments, and which serve as exogenous influences on cognitive function (Waldstein, 2000; Waldstein & Elias, 2001); and (3) sociological theories of disablement (Verbrugge & Jette, 1994) and cumulative disadvantage (Dannefer, 1984, 2003), which posit that social processes account for health (including cognitive functioning) disparities and differences in rates of change. Not only do socioenvironmental inequalities impact individual differences at multiple time points over the life span, but also there is considerable theory suggesting that the residues of these influences in individual differences cumulate over time (Dannefer, 1987, 1988; O'Rand, 1996).

Obviously, these theories complement one another. Although disciplinary biases may tend to emphasize one or the other as relevant theory, an interdisciplinary approach will take all of them as relevant. As noted, the psychological theories attempt to identify and isolate critical unobserved cognitive processes, operations, or constructs that account for between-person differences in rates of cognitive change, whether it is processing speed, a generalized slowing, or declining cognitive reserve. The basic idea is that these underlying processes produce correlated rates of change, and although a number of approaches have been taken to verify these notions, one common approach to the empirical examination of these explanations relies on common factor models. In contrast to the common factor explanations, biological theories rely on explanations involving physical disease processes, which explain between-person differences in rates of change by directly measuring individual differences in the presence of chronic disease (e.g., cardiovascular disease, diabetes, or hypertension). Finally, the explanations that rely on the understanding of the role of social factors focuses on the measurement of between-person differences in social inequalities and the consequences of these for trajectories of cognitive functioning (see Alwin & Wray, 2005).

THE PRESSING NEED TO KNOW MORE

As we noted earlier, the study of cognitive aging is a national priority, not only in the United States but in many other countries as well. There are a number of reasons why the current state of knowledge may not be enough to forecast future levels of cognitive aging for most people who are living today. Prominent among the major rationales for the pressing need to better understand the realities of cognitive aging is the worldwide phenomenon of population aging (Suzman, Willis, & Manton, 1992). Given what is known about the demography of aging—increasing levels of population aging in the 21st century (United Nations, 2002)—the need to understand the population processes that are involved in cognitive aging are ever more pressing (Suzman, 2004).

Population Cognitive Aging

How do processes of population aging impact cognitive aging? Why is this essentially demographic phenomenon relevant to behavioral scientists who study cognitive aging? First, virtually all we know about cognitive aging was learned from studies conducted on persons born in the early part of the last century. If the arguments advanced by Warner Schaie and his colleagues (see Schaie, 1984; Schaie, Willis, &

Pennak, 2005; Willis & Schaie, 2006; also see chap. 23, this volume) are correct—that historical factors influence the nature of cognitive change—then it is reasonable to ask whether our current knowledge is applicable to the cohorts born after World War II (often referred to as the "Baby Boom" cohorts) and whether we can any longer entertain the idea that processes of cognitive aging revealed from past studies apply to these future cohorts. In short, to what populations does our present state of knowledge regarding age-related trajectories of cognitive performance apply?

One of the important components of population aging is declining mortality rates, and thus the naturally occurring question is whether old age can sustain cognitive function as well. Aging is not a disease process, but it does eventually produce both functional decline and increased susceptibility to illness and death from specific diseases. Signs of typical aging, such as short-term memory lapses, wrinkled skin, and gray hair are thus not considered symptoms of disease and need not result in greater susceptibility to death. However, with advanced age also comes weakened ability to fight off diseases such as cancer and infections, even as there is cognitive decline that reduces memory, speed of processing, and the like. When advances are made in curing or forestalling the diseases that tend to result in death to older people, then an even larger proportion of people survive into advanced old age (Finch & Crimmins, 2004; Weiss, 1990).

On the other hand, the population may experience what Vaupel and Yashin (1985) termed an "apparent failure of success" (pp. 181–182). Health advances allow frailer, more susceptible individuals to live longer. Certainly, the best current estimates are that as the rapid growth in the oldest age group continues, so will the prevalence of the dementias, for example, Alzheimer's disease (AD; see Evans et al., 1992). This subpopulation will have a higher dementia rate at a given age than does a more robust subpopulation (consisting of people who would have lived to that age without the advances in health practices). Thus, although one may forestall physical functional decline and the susceptibility to illness and death from specific diseases, there may be no counterpart in the area of cognitive functioning. The question for the student of the future of cognitive aging is: Will changes in cognitive function continue in old age, as our current models predict, or will we be able to develop parallel remedies that cure or forestall cognitive functional decline? Some of the current literature indicates that cognitive impairment in older age is largely not currently preventable and that dementia, particularly AD, will increase in prevalence in future years (Brookmeyer & Gray, 2000; Brookmeyer, Gray, & Kawas, 1998; Evans et al., 1992). Some suggest that the prevalence of AD in the next 50 years is projected to nearly quadruple, "which means that 1 in every 45 Americans will be affected by the disease" (Kawas & Brookmeyer, 2001, p. 1160).

The Inevitability of Cognitive Decline

A second set of related concerns involving the importance of future research on cognitive aging is the question of the inevitability of cognitive decline. Although there is a large and growing theoretical and empirical literature documenting the declines in cognitive functioning across a number of performance domains, there is a great deal of heterogeneity in patterns of change in cognitive functioning as people age, and there is substantial evidence in some cognitive capabilities for stability and even growth. Although the authors of *The Aging Mind* concluded that the overall narrative of cognitive aging is one of decline and loss of function, they challenged the "popular notion that mental decline with age is inevitable, progressive and general," suggesting that "research presents a more complex picture" (NRC, 2000, p. 37). Several of the chapters in the present volume (e.g., chaps. 6, 18, 22, and 34) also make the claim that cognitive decline in older age is not inevitable, citing a range of experiential and neuropathological risk factors that may produce individual differences in cognitive performance among older adults.

Moreover, recent work has suggested that "some cognitive processes decline almost inevitably even in healthy older adults," which has been attributed to "normal aging," but "past experience [in] geriatric research should leave room for skepticism about attribution of any functional decline to 'normal' processes" (Hendrie

et al., 2006, p. 13). Hendrie et al. (2006) argued, for example, that even though "significant cognitive decline" is quite common in the older population, "individuals with cognitive decline are at much greater risk for having dementing disorders" (p. 13). This is a point of view that says there is really no such thing as "normal aging" when it comes to cognitive function. Cognitive declines that occur are instead reflecting some kind of "non-normal" processes that may have the possibility of being treated. The argument is that there is far too much attention placed on cognitive decline in research, rather than on "successful aging" (see Rowe & Kahn, 1998). By reassigning meanings, this approach comes up with the concept of the "healthy aging brain" (Hendrie et al., 2006, p. 13). One of the interdisciplinary challenges that faces cognitive aging researchers involves the relationship among neural health, physical health, and cognitive function. Few, if any, studies have good measures of all three dimensions in longitudinal data.

The Nature and Timing of Cognitive Decline

Although there is admittedly disagreement with respect to the inevitability of cognitive decline, there is certainly heterogeneity in the experience of cognitive aging. Despite this, the overall aggregate trend for many dimensions of human abilities is one of decline. Individual differences aside, there is general agreement that there are systematic age-related declines in cognitive functioning in many performance domains from midlife (in some cases) and into older age. One early debates in the field of cognitive aging—between Paul Baltes and Warner Schaie on the one hand versus John Horn and Gary Donaldson on the other—involved the question of the typical levels of decline in cognitive function and the timing of that decline (see, e.g., Baltes & Schaie, 1976; Horn & Donaldson, 1977, 1980). Baltes and Schaie (1976) argued that much of early theorizing about systematic declines in cognitive abilities from midlife onward were in error and that many cognitive functions remained intact into very old age, challenging what they called the "myth of intellectual decline." Horn and

Donaldson (1977, 1980) argued that this was in part an issue of what is being measured. Recalling the Cattellian duality—the distinction between fluid and crystallized abilities (Cattell, 1971)—and the differing relationship of these two concepts to age, they argued that many fluid intelligence abilities experience declines from early adulthood through to old age. Horn and Donaldson (1980, p. 479) drew the conclusion from their data that with age there is a loss of neurological base for intellectual functions, and that loss is probably reflected most notably in performance measures reflecting fluid intellectual abilities.

Some of the best evidence for the life span development of various cognitive abilities is Schaie's (1996) Seattle Longitudinal Study (SLS; see also Salthouse, 1991), which began tracking a cross-section of the adult population in 1956 at 7-year reinterview intervals. Schaie's early work (1983) concluded, on the basis of 21 years of the SLS, that "reliably replicable age changes in psychometric abilities of more than a trivial magnitude cannot be demonstrated prior to age 60" (Schaie, 1983, p. 127). His more recent work has tended to bear out these conclusions (see Schaie, 1989, 1990, 1994, 1996; see also Hertzog & Schaie, 1986, 1988; Schaie & Hertzog, 1983), and he has made a strong case for stability in many measured abilities over most of the adult life span. Schaie and his colleagues have argued that there is relative stability of mean performance levels throughout most of the life span, with some decline in old age, due to the onset of the dementias and other disease-related impediments to complete cognitive functioning.

However, this seemingly straightforward problem of identifying the age at which change begins and the pattern of change in the population is actually quite complex and has not been fully resolved. Many of these methodological and sampling issues were well described in the early debate over this question of when change begins (Baltes & Schaie, 1976; Horn & Donaldson, 1977, 1980) and are further developed in many of the chapters throughout this handbook. Longitudinal studies, although they provide the essential measurement of within-person change, require repeated exposures to cognitive tests, and this usually results in practice-related gains in performance in the opposite direction of

age-related declines. Valgeir Thorvaldsson et al. (chap. 17) argue that these practice effects cannot be statistically controlled for in most longitudinal studies. Numerous other effects confound simple description of aggregate aging-related change and include cohort differences, differential mortality selection, initial sample selection, and health-related change.

The Linkages Between Health and Cognition

Researchers have raised several hypotheses to explain the apparent decline in cognitive functioning with increased aging. The first of these, which is popular among biological aging specialists, posits that cognitive decline is the result of a more general *process of neurological decline* that affects both cognitive and sensory functioning. A second set of explanatory factors involves *overall age-related declines in organ function* that lead to increases in the onset of illnesses or impairments and risks of experiencing multiple illnesses or impairments. Third, cognitive decline may be related to other age-related functional limitations, particularly in sensory function and physical health. Fourth, as discussed in the section titled "The Role of Social and Cultural Factors in Cognitive Aging," differences among age groups in levels of crystallized intelligence (measured by differences in schooling levels) may account for declines in measures of cognitive functioning and its covariates.

One of the dominant views in the literature, including the view of Paul Baltes and his colleagues, is that the sensory–cognitive function relationship reflects a general common factor underlying the aging process (e.g., Baltes & Lindenberger, 1997; Lindenberger & Baltes, 1994). *Sensory impairments,* particularly vision and hearing, are among the most prevalent age-related functional conditions, with 1 in 7 middle-aged adults and 1 in 4 older adults experiencing at least one impairment (Wray & Blaum, 2001). However, how sensory impairments are related to cognitive test performance (however defined) is not yet clear, and recent research based on longitudinal data has provided very little support for this hypothesis (e.g., Anstey, Hofer, & Luszcz, 2003a, 2003b; Anstey, Luszcz, & Sanchez, 2001). Although vision and hearing appear to take different pathways to impairment, there are social as well as physiological losses to the extent that they diminish a person's ability to interact with his or her surrounding environment. The underlying mechanisms linking sensory and cognitive functioning, in particular, remain inconclusive, because of the sample selection and sample size limitations, overreliance on cross-sectional data (i.e., age differences), definitions of sensory and cognitive impairments, and controls used by the researchers (see Hofer, Berg, & Era, 2003). Nonetheless, the findings are certainly suggestive, and more research is needed that includes precise measures of sensory and cognitive functioning with attention to the measurement commonality of sensory acuity and cognition due to testing material confounds as well as to the broader influences, such as disability and health, that may affect both systems.

In contrast to the common cause theories of cognitive aging, there is a great deal more evidence supporting the *contingent* role of biological factors in cognitive aging (see Waldstein's excellent summary of this literature in NRC, 2000, pp. 189–217). Chronic health conditions reflect serious limitations that may inhibit normal activities that promote the maintenance of cognitive function. Cognitive change has been linked to a number of chronic disease conditions, including cardiovascular disease (Geroldi et al., 2003; Hassing et al., 2002; Pavlik, Hyman, & Doody, 2005), pulmonary function (Anstey, Windsor, Jorm, Christensen, & Rodgers, 2003), type 2 diabetes (Cosway, Strachan, Dougall, Frier, & Deary, 2001; Crooks, Buckwalter, & Petitti, 2003; Hassing, Grant, et al., 2004; Hassing, Hofer, et al., 2004), stroke (Ostir, Raji, Ottenbacher, Markides, & Goodwin, 2003), and depressive symptoms (Wilson, Mendes de Leon, Bennett, Bienias, & Evans, 2004). Longitudinal data clearly are needed to assess the extent to which change in health conditions and disability status are linked to cognitive age-related change. These issues are important in their own right but also as a possible explanation of racial/ethnic and sex differences in cognitive change.

It is also well known that a positive association exists between positive health behaviors and indicators of morbidity and mortality. Cross-sectional research suggests several health-related lifestyle factors are linked to cognitive status, particularly nutrition (Corrêa-Leite, Nicolosi, Cristina, Hauser, & Nappi, 2001), cigarette smoking (Hill, Nilsson, Nyberg, & Bäckman, 2003; Kalmijn et al., 2002; Razani, Boone, Lesser, & Weiss, 2004; Richards, Jarvis, Thompson, & Wadsworth, 2003; Zhou et al., 2003), alcohol consumption (Britton, Singh-Manoux, & Marmot, 2004; Espeland et al., 2005; Harris, Albaugh, Goldman, & Enoch, 2003; Kalmijn, van Boxtel, & Verschuren, 2002; Leroi, Sheppard, & Lyketsos, 2002; Perreira & Sloan, 2002; Schinka, Belanger, Mortimer, & Borenstein-Graves, 2003; Zhang, Heeren, & Ellison, 2005; Zhou et al., 2003), and physical activity (Churchill et al., 2002; Dik, Deeg, Visser, & Jonker, 2003; Emery, Shermer, Hauchk, Hsiao, & MacIntyre, 2003; Heyn, Abreu, & Ottenbacher, 2004; Hillman, Belopolsky, Snook, Kramer, & McAuley, 2004; Schuit, Feskens, Launer, & Kromhout, 2001; Yaffe et al., 2003). Although the research is somewhat mixed, cigarette smoking is a risk factor for healthy cognitive functioning, the relationship of alcohol use seems to favor moderate drinkers, and there is little doubt that a physically active life is good for the brain. Some research ties the factors empirically to cognitive change (e.g., Chen et al., 2003), but in general longitudinal research is lacking. A great deal more research is needed to examine the interplay between cognitive aging and several additional components of health and well-being, particularly chronic disease conditions, lifestyle or health behaviors, and functional status.

Neural Decline Versus Disease Processes

The above-reviewed research dealing with chronic disease and cognitive function has typically not explicitly dealt with neurological disease, as opposed to chronic "physical disease" and lifestyle or health promotion factors. Dementia, particularly AD, is one of the major causes of disability and declining function and quality of life among the oldest in the population (Kawas & Brookmeyer, 2001). It is thought to be the result of a disease process, as are other outcomes classified as resulting from dementia (see Wilson, Bennett, & Swarzendruber, 1997). From a disciplinary perspective, the study of cognitive aging and dementia has proceeded independently. Researchers who study AD and other dementias almost exclusively deal with patient populations that have been diagnosed; little research is aimed at the precursors of the diseases processes that presumably lead to a clinical diagnosis. On the other side, researchers interested in understanding what they consider "normal" or "healthy" aging do not always explicitly deal with neural patterns thought to result from disease processes. Often researchers interested in "normal aging" attempt to eliminate the influence of dementia by screening out impaired individuals with mental status examinations. This strategy is only partially successful, and even in select, highly screened samples of older adults a substantial proportion of older participants may be at the very early stages of preclinical dementia and influence cognitive estimates of cognitive performance and age effects.

This problem of the influence of preclinical dementia would likely be amplified in a more representative sample of elders, compared with self-selected volunteer samples of motivated individuals. Recent studies have shown that the presence of subgroups with preclinical dementia can influence estimates of cognitive change and the covariance of change among cognitive domains (Sliwinski, Hofer, & Hall, 2003; Sliwinski, Hofer, Hall, Bushke, & Lipton, 2003). Moreover, in the absence of dementia and disease (Haan, Shemanski, Jagust, Manolio, & Kuller, 1999; Hall, Lipton, Sliwinski, & Stewart, 2000; Rubin et al., 1998) there is very little evidence of cognitive loss and, if present, is very slight. This problem of preclinical dementia is an illustration of why attempts to study "healthy" populations may be misguided and strongly argues for the simultaneous measurement of neurological and behavioral patterns and processes.

The Role of Social and Cultural Factors in Cognitive Aging

As several of the perspectives articulated in this volume suggest, there are a number of social, cultural, and historical factors—otherwise known as *contextual* factors—that are known to interact with processes of cognitive aging. For example, *The Aging Mind* includes an appendix prepared by Shinobu Kitiyama, which makes an argument about the implications of cultural variations in cognition for the experience of

cognitive aging (NRC, 2000, pp. 218–237). There is little question that social context plays a role in cognitive aging, not only in terms of the average trajectories of cognitive change within contingent conditions of cultural life experience but also with respect to within-culture individual differences in patterns of aging. Kitayama (2000, pp. 219–221) argued that the field of "cultural psychology" has much to offer the study of cognitive aging. The examination of cross-cultural data on age-related change in cognitive function represents one of the important challenges for future research.

In addition to cultural values and definitions of normative changes connected to the life cycle, sociological theories emphasize the processes by which disabilities or disadvantages cumulate over time. Indeed, the life span developmental perspective on social status and health challenges many assumptions about the static nature of the effects of social inequalities on health (Alwin & Wray, 2005). This perspective emphasizes that social status factors (education, economic resources, sex, race/ethnicity) have an impact on health (in this case, cognitive functioning) at multiple points across the life span and that the effects of social inequalities may accumulate over time (Dannefer, 1987, 1988; O'Rand, 1996; Verbrugge & Jette, 1994). Research on social resources and cognitive function shows that there are linkages with social networks, social engagement/activity, and social support (see chap. 36, this volume).

Level of schooling is often taken to be a generalized measure of social resources that condition the development of the level and the degree of change in cognitive functioning. There has been some debate about whether the amount of schooling should be controlled in assessing age-gradients in cognitive functioning. Lorge (1956) and Bandura (1989) have suggested that researchers investigating patterns of cognitive aging may profitably consider the importance of controlling for schooling in examining the nature and patterns of cognitive aging (see also Birren & Morrison, 1961). Salthouse (1991), in contrast, suggested researchers could effectively ignore schooling in the study of cognitive aging. He articulated four reasons for not taking age group differences in schooling into account: (1) schooling is both a cause and a consequence of abilities; (2) units of education have changed their meaning over time; (3) there have been historical changes in the opportunities to acquire more education; and (4) even when age-gradients in cognitive functioning are adjusted for age group differences in schooling, variation in education can account for no more than a small proportion of the age differences observed in certain measures of cognitive functioning (Salthouse, 1991, pp. 74–77). By contrast, the work of Alwin et al. (2008) on cohort effects found that it is important to adjust for differences among cohorts for intercohort differences in schooling; however, doing so accentuates some of the differences among cohorts (see chap. 4, this volume). Cohort differences in schooling act as a suppressor to assessing the true levels and rates of change within cohorts, so by not controlling for both cohort differences and schooling in assessing within-person change one can arrive at a mistaken specification of the aging-related function of cognitive change (see Alwin et al., 2008).

In addition, a literature has developed around the question of whether higher levels of schooling act as a protective factor in cognitive aging by retarding the rate of change in cognitive decline and therefore acting to buffer the processes of normal aging (e.g., see Anstey & Christensen, 2000; Christensen et al., 2001, 1997; Dufouil, Alpérovitch, & Tzourio, 2003). The results of this body of research are mixed, with some studies showing no interaction of schooling and rates of change and others finding such a buffering effect. Alwin et al. (2008) showed, using data from the Health and Retirement Study (HRS), and analyzing this issue separately by cohort, that there is little evidence that schooling significantly affects the rate of cognitive change. This research is summarized in Chapter 26 of this volume.

Technological Supports
for Adaptation to Cognitive Aging

There a need for a great deal more research on the role of social and cultural factors in shaping the environmental influences on the experience of cognitive aging, in part because such research has the potential to lead to experiential interventions that can alter the course of cognitive aging. Indeed, this is one of the primary areas where the NRC report (2000, pp. 35–36) emphasized the need for additional research. The appendix chapter of *The Aging Mind* by Fisher (2000, pp. 166–188) focuses on adaptive technologies that may provide assistance in cognitive functioning. In addition, considerable research has been designed to demonstrate that intervention in the form of cognitive training can produce a salutary change in cognitive functioning (e.g., Willis, 1990; Willis et al., 2006). As Horn and Donaldson (1980, pp. 516–517) advocated, however, such intervention studies require a rigorous approach to assessment and intensive engagement in stimulating activities, and the methodological requirements of such studies are rarely met.

THE INTERDISCIPLINARY CHALLENGE

We believe that the scope of the challenge for future research on cognitive aging involves not only coming to terms with the nature of developmental processes and the social, cultural, and demographic realities of population aging but also the need to foster new interdisciplinary research agendas in the pursuit of knowledge of cognitive aging. The authors of *The Aging Mind* emphasized the need for interdisciplinary approaches that develop a comprehensive theoretical framework that incorporated age-related variation in environmental factors, age-related changes in sensory function and health, and the interaction of these factors with neurological changes in development. They proposed a conceptual system that focused on three interacting systems: "*cognitive structures and processes, neural health,* and *behavioral context,* including task structure and social, cultural, and technological factors" (NRC, 2000, p. 9). The committee summarized the importance of this conceptual system in the following way:

> Older people adapt to changes in their nervous systems and their environments and, at the same time, both types of changes affect their ability to perform cognitive tasks. To separate the various causes of cognitive change, it is necessary to examine inter- and intraindividual differences in cognitive function in both cross-sectionally and over time to identify patterns. Such examinations

should highlight the roles of dynamic adaptive processes, including changes in neuronal structure and function and in behavioral and social factors (e.g., social opportunity structures, the individual's routines and physical environment, the individual's goals, and the use of social and technological supports) that codetermine an individual's ability to function effectively. (NRC, 2000, pp. 10–11)

This is a valuable framework for setting the agenda of the future of cognitive aging, because it highlights the multiple components of the cognitive aging process.

Arguing that the ultimate focus of research on cognitive aging should be on the conjunction of factors that shape performance of activities of living (NRC, 2000, pp. 9–11), the NRC committee articulated the developments in knowledge across different subdisciplines that focus on cognitive aging. However, despite the impressive claims that are made in this report with respect to what is known in the field of cognitive aging, the NRC committee also stressed the need for several major research initiatives that would contribute to the improvement of knowledge regarding age-related change in cognitive functioning. They identified three major areas— neural health, cognition in context, and the structure of the aging mind—in which scientific developments are "creating significant opportunities for breakthroughs," and they urged the NIA to undertake major research initiatives that would (a) build the scientific basis for promoting neural health in the aging brain; (b) to understand the effects of behavioral, social, cultural, and technological context on the cognitive functioning and life performance of aging individuals; (c) to improve the understanding of the structure of the aging mind, including the identification of mechanisms at the behavioral and neural levels that contribute to age-related cognitive change; and (d) build the knowledge needed to intervene effectively in sociocultural contexts to assist individuals' functioning and performance (NRC, 2000).

Cognitive aging is the result of a number of factors working in combination, and the NRC committee stressed the importance of interdisciplinary forms of research. They encouraged the NIA to establish funding mechanisms that would challenge cognitive scientists from a multiplicity of disciplines to work together to solve the problems of understanding how these several factors jointly contribute to cognitive aging. There have been some efforts in these directions, although these developments have been limited in scope and activity. In 2001, the NIA held a workshop on "Cognitive and Emotional Health: The Healthy Brain Workshop," jointly sponsored with the National Institute of Mental Health and the National Institute of Neurological Disorders and Stroke. The purpose of the workshop was to discuss research concerning determinants of cognitive, emotional, and mental health among adults. It brought together selected leaders in the field for substantive discussions about the current status of existing knowledge, the potential value of secondary data analyses of existing data, the need for further instrument development to facilitate future studies, and potential designs of large studies that might be undertaken in the future. An international group of approximately 35 senior investigators attended, together with a large number of staff members from the National Institutes of Health (see Hendrie et al., 2006).[2]

Now known as the *Cognitive and Emotional Health Project*, this project has resulted in several findings and additional recommendations. The goal of this project was to "assess the state of longitudinal and epidemiologic research on demographic, social, and biological determinants of cognitive and emotional health among adults, and to determine how these pathways reciprocally influence each other" (Hendrie et al., 2006, p. 15). The project reports that there are 27 longitudinal data sets that include measurement protocols for both cognitive function and emotional health, meeting certain criteria of substantive and methodological importance (see Hendrie et al., 2006, p. 16). Another strategy for integrating longitudinal studies of aging is through active cross-study collaboration and coordination of analyses (see chaps. 27 and 40 of this volume, which describe the Integrative Analysis of Longitudinal Studies of Aging research network). Finally, the Cognitive and Emotional Health Project assembled an evaluation study committee, which was appointed to assess the state of epidemiological knowledge on the demographic, social, and biological determinants of cognitive and emotional health. This review of the evidence identified several risk factors consistently with cognitive outcomes and considerable overlap in findings across the domains of cognitive function and emotional well-being (Hendrie et al., 2006, pp. 19–21).

THE PRESENT VOLUME

This volume is the result of the International Conference on the Future of Cognitive Aging Research, supported by the NIA, which made an attempt to push for scientific revolutions in the area of cognitive aging research. The conference focused on the present state of knowledge on cognitive aging but stressed the importance of the development of a shared multidisciplinary agenda for future work in this area and the next steps to accomplish this. The questions that were addressed by the conference, and ultimately by the chapters in this volume, were aimed at boldly pushing the limits of what we know about cognitive aging and examining the epistemological basis of "How do we know what we know?" In the remainder of this chapter, we develop a framework for organizing multidisciplinary research on cognitive aging and for coming to terms with the factors that either contribute to or forestall the likelihood of new discoveries in the area of cognitive aging (see NRC, 2007).

By building upon the recommendations of *The Aging Mind*, this handbook explicitly focuses on an examination of the future of cognitive aging research. The chapters contained in this volume push this set of issues further, by critically evaluating the practical, methodological, and theoretical questions involved in translating the report's recommendations into concrete research plans. They were developed against the background of the issues we defined as critical for the future study of cognitive aging as follows:

Where do we want to be as a field in 25 years? What do we need to know about cognitive aging, and what are our plans to meet those needs? What theoretical breakthroughs are needed? How can we encourage those breakthroughs?

What are the interdisciplinary challenges that must be met to accomplish these aims? What novel research opportunities are necessary to link social science, behavioral science, cognitive science, and neuroscience approaches to cognitive aging?

From a demographic perspective, population aging is a fact. What can we predict about the nature of population cognitive aging? Given what we know about cognitive aging, can we predict the prevalence of various types of functional problems? Can we know the parameters of relevant aging functions for populations of interest?

Can we use past research and past models of cognitive aging to make predictions about the cognitive status of individuals and of the population at any point in the future? Are studies focusing on cross-sectional age differences adequate for understanding aging? Can the emerging research literature that focuses on individual-level change be used for making predictions about future cognitive functioning in individuals and the population?

What future research and research designs will be necessary? Are current methods for research adequate for developing the types of knowledge we envision for the future? Is there any good argument for changing the epistemological basis of the ways we have approached building empirical knowledge?

What new types of data are needed to build the kinds of knowledge we anticipate will need to be developed? Is there a need for new databases that can promote the needed developments in the field of cognitive aging?

How can mechanisms for data sharing promote a higher quality of science? Is there a constituency for the development of new models for scientific discourse among cognitive aging researchers?

This list is not exhaustive of issues that were raised by the papers in the conference, but they were the key focus of the papers commissioned for the conference and published in this book. There are a number of more specific methodological issues that are also addressed. For example, there are potentially serious limitations in the dominant methods of research on cognitive aging that pose threats to the validity of projections about the future of cognitive aging in the U.S. population and cross-nationally over the next several decades. The conference aimed to explore each of these domains with an eye toward developing a shared agenda for the next few decades of research on cognitive aging that will begin to implement the recommendations of the NRC report.

Organization and Content

The seven topical divisions around which we have organized the chapters in this volume are as follows: (1) substantive and theoretical reviews of what we know about cognitive aging, with the objective of developing an integrated theoretical perspective; (2) past and future dimensions of cognitive aging (areas covered include attention, memory and encoding, prospective memory, cognitive control, sensory function, everyday problem solving, expertise and knowledge, health and cognitive aging, and behavioral genetic perspectives); (3) biological dimensions of aging and the relationship of health-related processes; (4) historical processes and cultural differences; (5) developments in longitudinal design and measurement of cognitive impairment and functioning; (6) integrating social, demographic, and developmental perspectives; and (7) future directions for research on cognitive aging. Within each of these major sections the themes of the chapters cut across these broad set of issues we discussed in the previous section. Common to all the chapters in this handbook is that they raise concerns critical to the future of cognitive aging research, including theoretical and empirical issues and methodological critiques of design attributes of the current state of research.

Part II: Integrative Theoretical Perspectives

Cognitive function is an essential component of health and well-being across the life span. The understanding of the relationship of aging to cognitive function is a national priority because of its intrinsic relevance to the lives of aging members of society. In this section we have put together several chapters that deal with major theoretical perspectives on age-related changes in cognitive function. The opening chapter, "Theoretical Approaches to the Study of Cognitive Aging: An Individual-Differences Perspective," by Christopher Hertzog, provides a broad perspective on theoretical approaches to cognitive aging. In this chapter, Hertzog argues

that what is needed is "better gerontological theory, along with better integration of such theory with the formulation and testing of explanations for age-related cognitive change." He makes a number of distinctions between concepts that frame research and thus explanatory theories of changes in cognition with age. Throughout this chapter, numerous examples are provided that highlight the interactive role of theory and methods for progress and innovation and the need for interdisciplinary approaches to understanding cognitive aging.

Keith Widaman provides a chapter on "Integrative Perspectives on Cognitive Aging: Measurement and Modeling With Mixtures of Psychological and Biological Variables." In this chapter, Widaman argues that fundamental accounts of cognitive aging, in terms of linking changes in the brain and psychological measures, rests on weak, indirect evidence but that real innovations and advances in understanding age-related changes in terms of biological processes are possible by taking advantage of recent developments in measurement, design, and statistical modeling. Optimal measurement is an essential feature of an integrative science; however, trade-offs are often made, such as the use of short forms, that are detrimental to the goals of linking and understanding complex age-related processes. To move beyond being "theory rich, but data poor" because of our inability to disconfirm theories properly, Widaman encourages an emphasis on the substantive magnitude of results (not just statistical significance), attention to nonlinear trends and complex interaction hypotheses, and increased attention to *both* individual differences and average trends in interdisciplinary integrative research that includes biological process variables.

Chapter 4, "Population Processes and Cognitive Aging," by Duane F. Alwin, Ryan J. McCammon, Linda A. Wray, and Willard L. Rodgers, takes a somewhat different tack. These authors discuss four key issues for research on cognitive aging from a demographic perspective: (1) the need to specify models of aging for well-defined populations, (2) the phenomenon of population aging and its consequences for understanding future population levels of the prevalence of low cognitive functioning, (3) the possibility of cohort effects on estimates of functions that describe typical processes of cognitive aging, and (4) the problem of unmeasured heterogeneity in cohort-specific aging functions resulting from the phenomenon of mortality selection. Drawing examples from their ongoing analyses of cognitive aging in data from the Health and Retirement Study, a national probability sample of cohorts born from pre-1900 to 1947, they report projected increases in levels of prevalence of low cognitive functioning through 2050, resulting from processes linked to population aging (see Alwin et al., 2008). An examination of cohort-specific slopes and intercepts in latent growth curve models of cognitive aging functions suggests the existence of significant differences, net of schooling, in cohort-specific intercepts in functions describing typical patterns of cognitive aging. One explanation for these cohort differences in intercepts is mortality selection, given the heterogeneity among existing cohort survivors in susceptibility to death and disease, a possibility that is explored in the chapter. The authors propose that controlling for cohort differences in expected age at death reduces the observed differences in intercepts and that it may therefore be important to account for heterogeneity in cohort experiences—including not only residues of historical experiences but also variables linked to survivorship, especially mortality selection—in both cross-sectional and longitudinal studies of cognitive aging.

In his chapter on "Consequences of the Ergodic Theorems for Classical Test Theory, Factor Analysis, and the Analysis of Developmental Processes," Peter C. M. Molenaar describes explicitly the required conditions and limitations of an individual-differences approach for building a science of developmental and aging-related processes. In the area of cognitive aging, designs focusing on differences across people varying in age provide the majority of evidence for understanding aging. The concept, and indeed assumption, of ergodicity implicitly underlies inferences from this majority of research on individual age differences and is arguably unlikely to hold in practice given the rigorous conditions that must be met. Molenaar's chapter is inspirational and calls for a refocus on within-person change and variation, the essential and fundamental basis for making inferences regarding aging-related processes.

In the last chapter of Part II, Dale Dannefer and Robin Shura Patterson write from a sociological perspective about the limits and possibilities of cognitive aging research. They provide a critique of the philosophical assumptions often made about the phenomenon of cognitive aging, issues related to its conceptualization, and its even existence. This chapter is a provocative evaluation of both the social construction of aging and the current state of cognitive aging research. Its assessment of the current state of cognitive aging research, undertaken from a sociological perspective, raises a number of questions about the role of a "science of cognitive aging" in a society where "age-ism" is embedded in the institutionalized life course. As Dannefer and Patterson argue, a sociological perspective insists on understanding the origins of cognitive aging not only in organismic terms but also experiential and social terms, especially with regard to how expectations about cognitive aging are developed. The chapter is organized around three main arguments: (1) a consideration about how cohort analysis compels a rethinking of the determinants of cognitive aging; (2) the consideration of the distinctly human dimensions of cognition, including the inherent tendency for flexibility; and (3) a "social constitutive" interpretation of age differences in cognitive functioning. The authors conclude that the study of cognitive aging is at an early point in its development, and they suggest that until a paradigm shift occurs and until "the irrepressible and powerful dynamics" of the "social-constitutionalist paradigm" are recognized and embraced, little progress will be made in the study of cognitive aging.

Part III: Dimensions of Cognitive Aging

One of the most important research questions in the area of cognitive aging involves the nature of the differences among various ability domains in their trajectories of growth and change (Dixon, 1999). The strongest evidence for the link between aging and cognitive declines comes from studies examining declines in perceptual speed and memory in older age. These studies suggest that declines in cognitive performance are probably linked to declines in processing and sensory abilities in older adults, although much of this research has been based on cross-sectional designs. In other areas, such as verbal knowledge, declines appear not to be age related but may be explained by decrements in adaptive sensory function (Park, 1999). The chapters in this section of the book focus on aspects of cognition including attention, speed of processing, memory, encoding, cognitive control, expertise and knowledge, prospective memory, and so on.

The chapter by Joan M. McDowd and Lesa Hoffman, "Challenges in Attention: Measures, Methods, and Applications," provides an account of current knowledge and next steps for measurement development of attentional processes. Attention is fundamental to other cognitive processes and a key factor related to other functional outcomes, such as activities of daily living, in older adults. However, these same studies that demonstrate the importance of attentional processes also provide evidence that more sensitive measures of attention are needed to identify deficits earlier and permitting refined examination of the role of attention in other change processes. McDowd and Hoffman call for an integration of experimental and psychometric approaches for developing precise measures of attentional processes for identifying between-person age differences and within-person age changes and increased application of such assessment tools to real world applications involving aging-related processes and neurological diseases.

In the chapter by Paul Verhaeghen and John Cerella, "Everything We Know About Aging and Response Times: A Meta-Analytic Integration," a broad literature on response times is reviewed through the lens of previous meta-analyses and synthesized. The findings across the many studies of response times are complex but appear to arrange into distinct types of measures exhibiting differential age trends, with lexical tasks showing least effects of age differences, simple response times with modest slowing, and spatial tasks showing the greatest age-related deficit. The insightful and integrative nature of this review and appraisal of results to understanding aging and response times provides a model for theory development in other domains.

Susan R. Old and Moshe Naveh-Benjamin provide a chapter on "Age-Related Changes in Memory: Experimental Approaches" and summarize some of the major empirical evidence for age-related deficits in distinct types of memory performance, providing descriptions of key studies that detail distinct aspects of memory functioning (e.g., implicit vs. explicit memory) and encoding, retention, and retrieval processes. Several theoretical approaches for explaining aging-related deficits in memory performance are discussed, including speed of processing, working memory capacity, and attentional resources. Old and Naveh-Benjamin call for greater integration of basic memory processes and encourage increased emphasis on the practical application of knowledge of both positive and negative factors affecting memory performance from such research.

Mark A. McDaniel and Gilles O. Einstein focus on self-initiated retrieval processes in their chapter, "Prospective Memory and Aging: Old Issues and New Questions." In this chapter, they discuss research on prospective memory, involving the performance of an intended action at an appropriate time or in response to a particular cue in the future. In their view, multiple processes underlie successful prospective memory performance, including strategies that involve controlled monitoring for the target event and spontaneous retrieval mechanisms. McDaniel and Einstein identify challenges and promising avenues for this important area of research that has many real life applications and potential for interventions to maintain functioning in older adults.

Susan Kemper and Joan M. McDowd emphasize task decomposition approaches for understanding frontal lobe function in their chapter, "Dimensions of Cognitive Aging: Executive Function and Verbal Fluency." They describe research that aims to identify a set of component processes of executive function, such as inhibition, updating, time sharing, and switching, that will lead to better measurement of these component processes and permit an examination of how these processes change differentially over the life span and the mapping of these component processes onto other cognitive processes. This approach holds great promise for advancing our understanding of executive function and how aging-related neurological diseases affect semantic and executive functioning processes.

In their chapter, "Executive Function in Cognitive, Neuropsychological, and Clinical Aging," Mary A. Luszcz and Anna P. Lane provide a description of the *frontal hypothesis* of cognitive change with age, emphasizing issues related to measurement and construct validity of neuropsychological measures of executive function. The role of the central executive is fundamental to conceptualizations of cognitive functioning, such as working memory, and is considered to include processes related to control and planning, inhibition, and task switching. Luszcz and Lane provide a succinct account of this approach and discuss challenges and future needs in this research area, particularly in regard to conceptual specification and measurement approaches and links to brain function and dysfunction.

Cynthia A. Berg discusses developments in the assessment of problem-solving capacity in demanding real life situations in her chapter, "Everyday Problem Solving in Context." Berg reviews the literature on this topic and provides succinct accounts of the motivation for this area of research and the theoretical perspectives that guide it, involving the similarity and utility of traditional psychometric tests and cognition in the context of older adults lives. Berg develops an integrative two-process model of everyday problem solving that combines the competency and contextual perspectives. Using this model, she identifies a number of challenges, including the development of a real-world criterion of success for validating measures of everyday problem solving; greater emphasis on intraindividual variability; and the integration of cognitive, affective, interpersonal, and physiological components that are relevant to everyday problem-solving capabilities.

Daniel Zimprich, Mike Martin, and Philippe Rast focus on dynamic aspects of memory performance in their chapter, "Individual Differences in Verbal Learning in Old Age." They discuss early developments in this area of research and the focus on learning curves for modeling performance gains over short intervals. They also describe and contrast a number of alternative formal models for population average and individual-level change in performance over repeated trials and provide an empirical example of such models in the Zurich Longitudinal Study on Cognitive Aging. This chapter provides important perspectives on modeling short-term change processes, with an emphasis on individual differences in learning, that will likely provide insight into cognitive processes affected by aging and health and may serve as more sensitive indicators of long-term change processes.

In their chapter on "Expertise and Knowledge," Neil Charness and Ralf T. Krampe discuss fundamental issues regarding the interplay among aging, knowledge, and expertise. They describe results that show that knowledge, though a strong predictor of performance, is limited by age-related declines on fundamental cognitive processes, such as those measured by speeded tasks. Charness and Krampe highlight several major challenges for research on knowledge and expertise, citing the long and demanding developmental period required for attaining expertise and the lack of congruence of this process to existing quasi-experimental designs used in most studies that would require long-term longitudinal studies of this important research domain.

Part IV: Biological Indicators and Health-Related Processes

Expanding upon the theme that health and cognition are inexorably linked, the chapters in Part IV provide coverage of current empirical and theoretical findings on the relation of biological factors in cognitive and related outcomes, and related physiological changes that are related to cognitive aging, including sensory and health-related changes. Authors of these chapters, as is true throughout this handbook, are the leaders in each respective area and are well versed in what we know and where the work in their area is moving.

Opening this section is a chapter by Avron Spiro III and Christopher B. Brady, "Integrating Health Into Cognitive Aging Research and Theory: Quo Vadis?" Spiro and Brady challenge us to identify health-related explanations for changes with age in cognitive functions—that "age" per se is not the causal factor or a useful approach for understanding or explaining cognitive aging. Although it is understood that the incidence of morbidity and comorbidity is increasingly related to chronological age and cannot be completely disentangled, a number of approaches and recommendations are made to better integrate health into explanations of cognitive change with age. Spiro and Brady advocate the development of better measurement and standards for assessing health within studies on aging and provide several prescriptions for the study of health and cognition and the careful consideration of causal pathways of diseases that affect cognition.

The use of alternative temporal metrics to model and understand individual differences in change is discussed by Valgeir Thorvaldsson, Scott M. Hofer, Linda B. Hassing, and Boo Johansson in their chapter, "Cognitive Change as Conditional on Age Heterogeneity in Onset of Mortality-Related Processes and Repeated Testing Effects." In the study of aging-related changes, years of life remaining, in contrast to years since birth, often provides a better metric for the organization and understanding of individual and population change because of the increasing importance of health-related processes that are causing changes in cognitive and functional outcomes in later life. As in Spiro and Brady's chapter (chap. 16), Thorvaldsson and colleagues encourage analyses that are sensitive to aging and health-related changes simultaneously and point to the necessity of conditioning inferences regarding change to populations defined by both age and survival age. The identification of retesting effects can also confound inference regarding aging-related change, and they discuss important points regarding the design and analysis of longitudinal studies that by definition require repeated exposure to test material and the limitations of current statistical methods for disentangling such effects.

Dementia, particularly AD, is one of the major causes of disability and declining function and quality of life among the oldest in the population (Kawas & Brookmeyer, 2001). From a disciplinary perspective, the study of cognitive aging and dementia has proceeded independently. Researchers interested in understanding "normal" or "healthy" aging attempt to eliminate the influence of dementia by screening out impaired individuals with mental status examinations. This strategy is only partially successful, and even in select, highly screened samples of older adults, a substantial proportion of older participants are in

the very early stages of preclinical dementia and influence cognitive estimates of cognitive performance and age effects (e.g., Sliwinski, Lipton, Buschke, & Stewart, 1996). This problem of the influence of preclinical dementia would likely be amplified in a more representative sample of elders, compared with self-selected volunteer samples of motivated individuals. Recent studies have shown that the presence of subgroups with preclinical dementia can influence estimates of cognitive change and the covariance of change among cognitive domains (Sliwinski, Hofer, Hall, Bushke & Lipton, 2003). Moreover, in the absence of dementia and disease (Haan et al., 1999; Hall et al., 2000; Rubin et al., 1998), there is very little evidence of cognitive loss and, if it is present, is very slight. This problem of preclinical dementia is an illustration of why attempts to study "healthy" populations may be misguided.

In line with these conclusions, Robert S. Wilson argues in his chapter, "Neurological Factors in Cognitive Aging," that age-related cognitive loss is *not* a normal outcome of old age but instead due to an accumulation of neuropathological lesions. He examines the evidence on the differential age-related susceptibility to neuropathologic lesions accumulating in different regions of the brain at different rates and argues against the common assumption that there is something called "normal aging" that is different from "abnormal aging" caused by disease. Instead, cognitive decline in old age results from risk factors linked to age-associated neuropathologic processes. On the assumption that prevention of cognitive loss is possible by tracing the linkage between risk factors and the neuropathologic pathways, he reviews the evidence for a number of neuropathologic lesions and concludes that these lesions, particularly AD pathology, are commonly found in the brains of older people who have no clinically recognizable dementia and that reflect age-related loss of cognition. He calls for the abandonment of the distinction between normal and abnormal cognitive aging and for a better understanding of the biochemical and molecular bases of vulnerability to age-related pathology in new areas of neurodeteriorative age-related change.

One of the strong recommendations of *The Aging Mind* report (NRC, 2000, pp. 14–20) was that the NIA should "undertake a major research initiative to build the scientific basis for promoting neural health in the aging brain." Neuroimaging is a rapidly developing field that continues to provide novel images of physiological indicators of brain function. In the chapter "Imaging Aging: Present and Future," Scott M. Hayes and Roberto Cabeza give a brief history of the study of neuronal loss inferred from cerebral blood flow and review recent advances in neuroimaging methods aimed at understanding the linkage between cognitive and cerebral aging. After reviewing the wide range of neuroimaging methods, including both structural and functional neuroimaging techniques, they conclude with suggestions for methodological integration that will further enhance our understanding of age-related cognitive and cerebral changes in older populations.

Kaarin Anstey's chapter, "Cognitive Aging and Biomarkers: What Do We Know, and Where to From Here?" draws together some of the emerging themes in cognitive aging that have focused on the relationship between cognitive aging and functional biomarkers, focusing primarily on sensory function, structural brain, and biochemical biomarkers. She observes that although some of the theoretical debates in this field tend to be circular and focus on statistical artifacts, the study of biomarkers and cognitive aging may help create bridges across disciplines that focus on differing functional indicators. She argues that multidisciplinary research teams will be required in future research of the linkages between cognitive and sensory change.

In agreement with Robert S. Wilson's conclusions, and responsive to the need for research on this topic, the chapter by Gwenith G. Fisher, Brenda L. Plassman, Steven G. Heeringa, and Kenneth M. Langa, "Assessing the Relationship of Cognitive Aging and Processes of Dementia," describes one ongoing effort that will help assess the relationship between "normal aging" and the clinical assessment of dementia. This is a project conducted by the Institute for Social Research in collaboration with Duke University and the Rand Corporation within the framework of the HRS (see Juster & Suzman, 1995). This study comprises a clinical dementia assessment for a stratified subsample of 856 HRS respondents to identify mild cognitive impairment, dementia, and its severity. This supplement—called the ADAMS (Aging, Demographics and Memory Study) project—represents an effort to combine the strengths of survey-based measurement of cognitive function and the rigors of clinical assessments. The ADAMS project is the first nationally representative population-based study of dementia in the United States. The main goal of this chapter is to show how statistical models can be used to obtain estimates of the probability of dementia in older populations. Although the ADAMS data were not available for use in this chapter, the authors relied on data from the Veterans Study of Memory and Aging, which included a clinical assessment of dementia status, key cognitive status measures, and several demographic variables (e.g., age and schooling). The Veterans Study of Memory and Aging prediction equation was then used for purposes of imputing dementia status in the 1998 HRS sample. The authors speculate about how the clinical data from the ADAMS study will be used to study trajectories of cognitive aging in the HRS data.

Part V: Historical Processes and Cultural Differences

Although research has sought to develop generalizations about aging-related changes in cognitive functioning, it is clear that processes of aging do not occur in a sociohistorical vacuum. There are a number of social, cultural, and historical factors—often labeled *contextual* factors—that are known to interact with processes of aging (e.g., Blanchard-Fields & Hess, 1996; Fiske, Kitiyama, Markus, & Nisbett, 1998). These issues are also addressed by the chapter by Denise C. Park, "Developing a Cultural Cognitive Neuroscience of Aging," in which the author develops a unique contribution focusing on cultural differences in neurocognitive function in old age. She points out that so far the age-related patterns of neural functioning have been observed exclusively with Western samples of adults and that there is a need to investigate whether these neuron patterns are a general phenomenon with respect to culture or whether there are unique culture-specific patterns. She describes some of her preliminary research in this area, suggesting that culture moderates brain function, in that older Westerners have a greater bias for engagement of object areas, whereas older East Asians (from Singapore) focus more attention on background stimuli. This work opens up an entirely new set of exciting questions in the study of aging, culture, and the brain, which bid well to continue so into the future.

One of the important themes in the study of cognitive aging over the past four or five decades is the role of historical and cultural processes that impinge on processes of aging. K. Warner Schaie has pioneered the consideration of historical effects on cognitive functioning (see Schaie, 1984; Schaie, Willis, & Pennak, 2005; Willis & Schaie, 2006). The chapter by Warner Schaie in this volume, "Historical Processes and Patterns of Cognitive Aging," argues that marked cohort and generational differences potentially exist in levels and trajectories of cognitive abilities observed over the past century. The author argues that such patterns exist in the SLS data and that they are accounted for by cohort differences in educational and occupational achievements (see Schaie, 1996). The chapter is organized around the following four major sections: (1) a discussion of four different forms of aging found in the literature— what are called *normal aging*, *successful aging*, *mild cognitive impairment*, and *dementia*; (2) the presentation of a heuristic "co-constructionist" model for patterns of normal aging of cognitive function; (3) the description of historical events that have a bearing on differences in cohort experiences relevant to cognitive development; and (4) the presentation of results for measures of crystallized and fluid abilities that show the impact of historical processes that appear to be most relevant. The chapter concludes with some observations about the future course of changes in levels and rates of cognitive development.

The chapter on "Minority Populations and Cognitive Aging," by Keith Whitfield and Adrienne Aiken Morgan, provides further emphasis to the role of race/ethnicity as a structural force in developing cognitive resources and maintaining them. To understand the nature of race/ethnicity differences, one must develop comprehensive measurement of minority populations in research on cognitive aging. The inclusion of minority populations in studies of cognitive aging is important for several reasons. The demographic shifts toward greater

representations of minority groups in the United States have given greater attention to the relevance of race/ethnicity to studies of health in general. Greater understanding of groups that have heretofore be underrepresented in studies of cognitive aging is important, and there are several challenges reflected in the investigation of minority populations. This chapter outlines many of the theoretical, conceptual, and methodological issues inherent in the study of the unique patterns of cognitive aging among African Americans and other minority populations. The chapter provides an overview of culturally appropriate models for the study of cognitive aging in minority populations and focuses on two key questions: (1) What patterns exist in the changes in cognitive abilities in older African Americans? and (2) what is the nature of variability in cognitive abilities among older African Americans? Factors that impinge upon possible differences of minority populations— for example, health and socioeconomic status— are examined as critical contributions to levels and trajectories of cognitive aging among minority populations.

Finally, in the chapter by Jennifer J. Manly, "Race, Culture, Education, and Cognitive Test Performance Among Older Adults," she argues that assessments of cognitive impairment and daily functioning are susceptible to culturally dependent definitions and are quantified by measures that are sensitive to cultural and educational background. She draws attention to the cultural and educational factors that should be considered when assessing and interpreting cognitive function among older persons who are members of minority groups. She presents evidence from her own work that illustrates the observation that acculturation, quality of education, literacy, and racial socialization are potentially more meaningful than race/ethnicity in adjusting expectations for cognitive test scores and improving specificity of cognitive tests. She identifies specific issues that arise in the recognition of cognitive impairment and measurement of cognitive decline among these populations, including cultural bias in the neuropsychological measurement of cognitive function and differences in presentation of cognitively impaired elders across ethnic and cultural groups. Her work calls for greater clarity in the development of standards and guidelines for cross-cultural research on cognitive aging.

Developing his argument within the framework of environmental factors in cognitive development, the chapter by Duane F. Alwin, "Social Structure and Cognitive Change," introduces the idea that the theoretical consideration of social structure is an essential ingredient in linking cognitive aging to the environment. The concept of structure is central to virtually all schools of social scientific thought as well as many of the theories that are important for understanding processes of aging. It is generally agreed that the concept of social structure reflects a robust and persistent set of resources, opportunities, and constraints that impinge upon behavior and functioning across a wide range of domains relevant to aging. This chapter focuses on the linkage between social structure and cognitive function, particularly as it relates to aging, building on some of the prescient observations of Benjamin Bloom (1964) about the interaction of social environmental influences and cognitive change. Theoretically, differences in patterns of cognitive aging are linked to key elements of social structure. After the development of a theoretical framework that defines critical theoretical constructs—social structure, cognitive function, and aging—Alwin reviews the role of structural factors that contribute to levels and trajectories of change in cognitive function in older age. The principal focus is on the ways in which social structural factors—specifically, educational, socioeconomic, racial/ethnic, and gender factors—produce differences in levels and rates of change in cognitive function. The chapter provides several examples from contemporary research on structural factors and cognitive aging and concludes with some thoughts about how these issues can be usefully pursued in future studies.

Part VI: Longitudinal Measurement and Analysis

Virtually all quantitative social scientists agree that one of the most productive approaches to the study of aging and human development involves the collection and analysis of longitudinal data (see Alwin & Campbell, 2001; Kraemer, Yesavage, Taylor, & Kupfer, 2000). Although the bulk of the evidence on age-related differences in cognitive performance is based on cross-sectional research, an increasing number of studies are longitudinal in design (Schaie & Hofer, 2002). However, most of these studies span a relatively short period of time, often limiting the explanatory variables of cognitive change to static individual-difference variables or retrospective measurements that may be unreliable. More longitudinal research over lengthy periods of time is needed to confirm patterns of cognitive change in middle and older age. When combined with sampling designs that are adequate for the generalization of findings to populations of interests, new longitudinal investigations can take advantage of the significant improvements that have been made in studying change within individuals as they age.

There is an emerging consensus that longitudinal research is essential to the study of cognitive aging, and there are a number of completed and ongoing longitudinal investigations of adult development and aging in North America, Europe, Australia, and elsewhere that are providing important results in this regard. Although results from these studies have been steadily accumulating, the direct comparison of results across studies is often difficult given the variety of study designs, cultural and sampling differences, measurement instruments, and the particular statistical analyses performed. Indeed, meta-analyses of aging-related studies are based primarily on experimental or cross-sectional results with direct cross-study comparison of longitudinal studies only rarely performed. The first chapter in this section, by Andrea M. Piccinin and Scott M. Hofer, "Integrative Analysis of Longitudinal Studies on Aging: Collaborative Research Networks, Meta-Analysis, and Optimizing Future Studies," summarizes collaborative and coordinated efforts that have made use of longitudinal data for the analysis of cognition, health, and aging-related change. In addition to a focus on accumulating and cross-validating findings of within-person aging-related change, this chapter addresses theoretical, measurement, and statistical issues that arise in collaborative and comparative analysis. Piccinin and Hofer describe an international research collaboration, the Integrative Analysis of Longitudinal Studies on Aging, which seeks to optimize future research on cognition and health through careful measurement harmonization and coordinated analysis for cross-national comparison of key hypotheses regarding both between- and within-person aging effects.

Some of the most important quantitative developments in recent years for the study of aging are the advances that have been made in the modeling of growth (and decline) curves that allow researchers to study intraindividual change and its causes. In psychology, growth curve analysis grew out of the tradition of studying change scores. Although there are known problems with studying change scores between two points in time, growth curve approaches focus on trajectories of change across many observations, typically three or more points in time. The application of the growth curve approach now includes the ability to model intraindividual change in latent variables. The basic approach involves modeling the initial levels (or intercepts) and rates of change (or slopes) in a set of observed variables. These models are closely related to multilevel models in that observations over time are nested within individuals (see Collins & Sayer, 2001; Little, Schnabel, & Baumert, 2000), although there are strengths and limitations associated with each approach. Longitudinal research based on representative samples of known populations is needed in order to confirm the conclusions developed on the basis of the extant literature.

Given the diversity of research strategies in the study of cognitive aging, there is a clear need for exchange among investigators who develop inferences about aging functions on the basis of quite different research designs—from those who work within the quasi-experimental tradition, where depth of measurement is viewed as critical but where external validity concerns are minimized, to those whose work is rooted in the demographic tradition of understanding population processes in which a great deal of emphasis is placed on probability methods of sampling but where measurement takes place in interview settings and is therefore relatively limited.

Taking this diversity into account, the chapters in this section focus on methodological developments in measurement and design issues, including the measurement of cognition in large-scale surveys, the potential for cultural bias in testing instruments, and other recent advances. The second chapter in this section, by Martin Sliwinski and Jacqueline Mogle, "Time-Based and Process-Based Approaches to Analysis of Longitudinal Data," provides an overview of different ways in which researchers have conceptualized change—approaching it either from the point of view of between-person differences or from the perspective of within-person change. They make a distinction between two analytical approaches to the analysis of longitudinal data: (1) time-based approaches, which model change as a function of the passage of time (i.e., correlated change), and (2) process-based approaches, which model change as a direct function of a concurrent or lagged effect of another change process (i.e., coupled change). Both of these approaches, based on multivariate growth curves or time-varying predictor models, can be implemented in structural equation modeling or multilevel modeling software, but they lead to different inferences regarding within-person change. Sliwinski and Mogle's chapter critically examines these approaches and contrasts the strengths and limitations of each for explaining aging-related change and encourages greater use of process-based models because these provide a more direct explanation of aging-related changes as a direct function of other aging-related variables.

Another issue of critical concern involves the periodicity of measurement. Most longitudinal aging studies have relied on successive, widely spaced single-shot assessments to estimate changes in cognitive performance. Such longitudinal studies assume that short-term temporal variations in cognitive performance are small relative to long-term temporal changes (i.e., that there is a large signal-to-noise ratio). If short-term temporal variability is moderate to high, then single-shot measurements would fail to produce precise estimates of an individual's average cognitive performance. Although the literature on this topic is scant, sufficient empirical evidence exists that establishes intraindividual cognitive variability as a substantial source of performance variability between people, especially in older adults (Hertzog, Dixon, & Hultsch, 1992; Li, Aggen, Nesselroade, & Baltes, 1998; Strauss, MacDonald, Hunter,

Moll, & Hultsch, 2002). Thus, sampling just one score at each wave could produce observed change indicating substantial decline, improvement, or stability. Alternatively, obtaining multiple, closely spaced performance assessments at each wave allows local temporal smoothing of data for each individual by averaging across multiple assessments. Another way of thinking about this issue involves the implementation of multiple indicators at each wave that permit the modeling of random error components in models that incorporate true change. By improving measurement precision, such designs will increase statistical power to detect cognitive change at both the individual and aggregate sample levels and permit greater understanding of intraindividual processes within and across different time intervals (e.g., Alwin, Hofer, & McCammon, 2006).

Shevaun D. Neupert, Robert S. Stawski, and David M. Almeida discuss the utility of intensive measurement protocols in their chapter, "Considerations for Sampling Time in Research on Aging: Examples From Research on Stress and Cognition." They emphasize the importance of intraindividual change and variation in aging-related processes in addition to between-person differences for understanding short- and long-term processes and discuss how explanatory mechanisms and choices about time sampling are inextricably linked to study results. On the basis of their own work on stress response and measurement of behavioral and biological processes, alternative designs for within-person sampling are critically examined and shown to provide important opportunities and promise for research on aging.

With some important exceptions, cognitive measures are not often included in large-scale survey data collections because it is assumed that reliable assessments are too difficult and time consuming to administer in an interview format using professional interviewers. Instead, most cognitive assessments used in the study of aging have been carried out in a laboratory or clinical setting by trained testers using rather long, time-consuming batteries of questions to assess multiple dimensions of cognitive function. A critical issue of measurement that we believe future studies must address involves the utility and validity of survey measurement of cognitive functioning. If, as we have argued, future research should produce data based on a model of population processes that insists on the use of representative samples of the population, then this raises the question of whether cognitive functioning can be measured in a survey context or whether the survey context must be modified to accommodate the depth of measurement required in psychometric testing. The development of measures of cognitive performance that can be used in survey settings should be given a high priority for research that uses population-based samples. The chapter titled "Cognitive Testing in Large-Scale Surveys: Assessment by Telephone," by Margie E. Lachman and Patricia A. Tun, addresses the set of issues surrounding the assessment of cognitive function in large-scale epidemiological and longitudinal surveys that are more representative of populations of interest than those typically studied in laboratory or clinical settings. These issues focus specifically, among other things, on the advantages and limitations of assessing cognitive function by telephone (see also Herzog & Wallace, 1997; and Folstein, Folstein, & McHugh, 1975). The authors conclude their presentation by reiterating the need to incorporate cognitive assessments into contemporary large-scale surveys of aging, health, and well-being.

The final chapter in this section, by Misha Pavel, Holly Jimison, Tamara Hayes, Jeffrey Kaye, Eric Dishman, Katherine Wild, and Devin Williams, "Continuous, Unobtrusive Monitoring for the Assessment of Cognitive Function," focuses on new designs and measurement protocols for the identification of trends and sensitive detection of changes from normative within-person functioning within natural home environments. The early detection of change processes would enable interventions to be provided early in such processes and help to optimize aging and health-related outcomes. This is a vital, though challenging, area of research that emphasizes physiological and behavioral assessments using new technology for detecting movement and cognitive functioning over the course of normal behaviors. A key idea is that early detection of change must optimally be based on change from a within-person baseline, essentially using individuals as their own controls.

Part VII: Integrative Perspectives on Cognitive Aging

The chapters in Part VII focus on multidisciplinary integration, including life span processes, minority populations, and other factors. The chapter titled "Animal Models of Human Cognitive Aging," by Gerald E. McClearn and David A. Blizard, provides an overview of animal models for understanding basic cognitive processes across the life span. Much of the research on cognition in animals has focused on learning and memory, comparing young and old animals on a variety of tasks. An important feature of animal models is the ability to hold environmental effects relatively constant and to evaluate specific genetic effects and genetic backgrounds in a highly controlled manner. McClearn and Blizard provide insightful perspectives for the use of animal models for identifying complex gene–environment interaction effects in a multivariate context that will surely augment and inform research on human functioning.

The chapter by Chandra A. Reynolds, "Genetic and Environmental Influences on Cognitive Change," describes findings from twin and adoption studies, emphasizing results from studies that have evaluated outcomes of change in cognitive functioning. A number of longitudinal studies of twins and families provide essential data to describe contributions of genetic and environmental influences and permit tests of alternative hypotheses regarding population individual differences. This is an exciting area of research, and Reynolds summarizes future directions, including the identification of candidate genes and specific environmental effects and complex interactions of genes and environments that are essential next steps for understanding aging-related changes.

Brent J. Small and Cathy L. McEvoy take up the issue of lifestyle activities and maintenance of cognitive function in their chapter, "Does Participation in Cognitive Activities Buffer Age-Related Cognitive Decline?" Much of what we know about relationships among lifestyle activities and cognitive functioning comes from cross-sectional studies of individuals who differ in age. Small and McEvoy describe two major theoretical perspectives, one referring to the substantive complexity of environments and one focusing on the development of cognitive reserve related to education and occupational attainment. They evaluate empirical results in the context of these two theories and emphasize the importance of longitudinal findings for the evaluation of this and other important influences on cognitive outcomes with age.

The importance of basic cognitive aging research is high given the fundamental role these processes have in maintaining everyday life. Matthias Kliegel, Peter Rendell, and Mareike Altgassen focus on this interplay of basic and applied science and application in their chapter, "The Added Value of an Applied Perspective in Cognitive Gerontology." They demonstrate how basic research and theorizing, in terms of planning and prospective memory, can benefit from taking implications and findings from applied research and real life aspects of behavior seriously. Their chapter provides an important applied element to the chapters included in this volume—an approach that is beginning to have considerable payoff.

The chapter on "Social Resources and Cognitive Function in Older Persons," by Lisa L. Barnes, Kathleen A. Cagney, and Carlos F. Mendes de Leon, begins with the premise that social integration is linked to better physical and mental health and goes on to review the several research traditions that have developed constructs to assess resources that reflect the salutary effects of the level of social integration. To be more specific, three literatures—social networks, social engagement or activity, and social support—point to such an effect for physical and mental health. Too little attention has been paid to the role of social resources and cognitive function. In addition, it is important to distinguish between individual-level social resources and community-level attributes of the social environment, and these authors present some recent data that estimate the relationships among individual- and community-level social resources to level of cognitive function in a community-based sample. The chapter concludes with the assertion that because social resources are "readily modifiable," this body of research has implications for the cognitive aging of present cohorts. The authors articulate several unresolved issues, including the need for more research on the effects of community- or contextual-level variables on cognitive function and the importance of understanding the mechanisms that mediate or otherwise explain the association of social resources and cognitive function.

Consistent with these themes, the chapter by Fredda Blanchard-Fields, Michelle Horhota, and Andrew Mienaltowski, "Social Context and Cognition," argues that studies of cognitive aging have not examined how social knowledge, emotions, and motivational factors develop in older age. Because of the lack of attention to these variables, past studies may not accurately reflect the potential range of older adults' skills and knowledge. They find that when contextual variables, such as emotions, personal goals, personal beliefs, and interactive milieu, are taken into account, older adults' functioning often remains intact, suggesting that social factors play a highly important role in age-related cognitive change. Among others, one of the literatures covered in this chapter is the work that has been done on *collaborative cognition*, which occurs when two (or more) people work together to solve cognitive tasks. This topic is also covered in depth by the following chapter, by Mike Martin and Melanie Wight, "Dyadic Cognition in Old Age: Paradigms, Findings, and Directions." Focusing on pairs of persons both 60 years of age or older, Martin and Wight discuss the paradigms, observed patterns, and explanatory concepts across several performance domains—dyadic memory, dyadic planning, dyadic decision making, dyadic reasoning, and dyadic comprehension. They conclude that a number of problems and puzzles are still remaining to be solved in this area. For example, it is not completely clear whether "dyadic cognition" is all that much better than individual cognition, and the question of whether older dyads are better or worse than young dyads on certain tasks remains unresolved.

The final chapter in this section, "Midlife Cognition: The Association of Personality With Cognition and Risk of Cognitive Impairment," by Sherry L. Willis and Julie Blaskewicz Boron, remind us that aging begins in midlife, if not earlier. They note that although many trait and personality theories of adult development emphasize the stability of individual differences, levels of change are less pronounced in old age. They argue that an examination of the association of personality and intellective factors during midlife is an interesting topic of research and that research examining early antecedents of cognitive risk in old age has suggested that certain personality dimensions may influence the onset of neuron deterioration that may contribute to cognitive impairment. They review the literature on the potential role of personality (e.g., neuroticism) in creating greater risks of cognitive decline in old age.

Part VIII: Future Directions for Research on Cognitive Aging

In the final section, we provide an overview of promising directions for future research on cognitive aging. Our chapter, "The Future of Cognitive Aging Research," summarizes the issues covered in this handbook for an overall perspective on the priorities that need to be addressed in future work on cognitive aging. Despite the great potential of current theories and methods, there are several serious limitations with the existing data upon which generalizations about cognitive aging rest, raising concerns about projections that may be made about the future of cognitive aging. In fact, the problems with the available data pose a major threat to the credibility of our inferences about age-related differences reported in the social, behavioral, and psychological literatures on cognitive development. Virtually all of our knowledge about age-related changes in cognitive function is based on cross-sectional designs, or on longitudinal studies of relatively short duration from small samples of unknown or questionable representativeness.

Although there are exceptions to this general characterization of the extant literature, most scholars agree that this is a fair description of the state of the current knowledge base. It is therefore critical that we reassess the basis for many of the findings that shape our conclusions about cognitive aging, the optimal designs for studying age-related change, and the kinds of data we will need for studying cognitive aging in the future. Given the many limitations of cross-sectional research emphasizing between-person age differences (Hofer, Flaherty, & Hoffman, 2006; Hofer & Sliwinski, 2001), it is generally agreed that one of the most productive approaches to the study of aging and human development involves the collection and analysis of longitudinal data (see Alwin & Campbell, 2001; Alwin et al., 2006; Hofer & Sliwinski, 2006). Although much of our knowledge and theoretical models have been based on results from cross-sectional research, there are an increasing number of studies that are longitudinal in design (Hofer & Piccinin, 2007; Schaie & Hofer, 2002) that can be used to evaluate current theories and hypotheses and provide a strong foundation for new theoretical developments. However, most of these studies span a relatively short period of time beginning in later life (e.g., age 65), often limiting the explanatory variables of cognitive change to static individual-difference variables or retrospective measurements that may be unreliable. More longitudinal research over broad periods of the life span is needed to confirm patterns of cognitive change in middle and older age and as a function of events and processes earlier in the life span. When combined with sampling designs that are adequate for the generalization of findings to populations of interests, new longitudinal investigations can take advantage of the significant improvements that have been made in studying *change within individuals as they age*. We argue, with the authors of *The Aging Mind* (NRC, 2000), that future research will need to pay closer attention to sampling design issues in order to meet more rigorous standards for generalization to populations of interest and for the sensitive measurement of within-person change.

The NRC committee report on "Future Directions" was quite explicit with regard to the requirements of future research on cognitive aging. To achieve the objectives of the recommended research initiatives, the report argued:

> It will be necessary to expand the use of large-scale multivariate, longitudinal studies . . . to expand and improve on previous longitudinal research by including variables reflecting high-resolution cognitive and neural measures; indicators of health status and sensory-motor functioning; and measures of relevant life experience. (NRC, 2000, p. 52)

Furthermore, it is also "important to examine a broad representative sample of the population, sometimes over-sampling in subgroups whose health status or responses to life experiences are expected to illuminate important theoretical questions, and to encompass a wide age range" (NRC, 2000, p. 53). Finally, the report argued that

> by following individuals into very old age, promising new findings suggesting the existence of unexpected linkages between cognitive functioning and survival could be investigated . . . [and] the conjunction of improved measurement, advances in modeling, and the comprehensive collection of longitudinal data on cognitive functioning and associated factors can have a synergistic effect in advancing knowledge. (NRC, 2000, p. 53)

Our discussion of these issues in the final chapter expands upon these ideas and synthesizes the recommendations made by the many scientists represented in this handbook for the future of cognitive aging research.

NOTES

1. Scientific revolutions can be recognized by two essential characteristics: (1) unprecedented achievements that attract an enduring group of adherents away from competing perspectives and (2) development of new problems and puzzles for new generations of scientists to solve (Kuhn, 1962, p. 10).

2. The Healthy Brain workshop was first held July 9–10, 2001, in Bethesda, MD, and has thereupon held additional meetings (see http://trans.nih.gov/CEHP/workshop.htm).

REFERENCES

Alwin, D. F., et al. (2008). *The aging mind in social and historical context.* Unpublished manuscript, Center on Population Health and Aging, Pennsylvania State University.

Alwin, D. F., & Campbell, R. T. (2001). Longitudinal methods in the study of human development and aging. In R. H. Binstock & L. K. George (Eds.), *Handbook of aging and the social sciences* (pp. 22–43). New York: Academic Press.

Alwin, D. F., Hofer, S. M., & McCammon, R. J. (2006). Modeling the effects of time: Integrating demographic and developmental perspectives.

In R. H. Binstock & L. K. George (Eds.), *Handbook of aging and the social sciences* (pp. 20–38). New York: Academic Press.

Alwin, D. F., & Wray, L. A. (2005). A life-span developmental perspective on social status and health. *Journal of Gerontology: Social Science, 60B*(Special Issue II), 7–14.

Anstey, K. J., & Christensen, H. (2000). Education, activity, health, blood pressure and Apolipoprotein E as predictors of cognitive change in old age: A review. *Gerontology, 46,* 163–177.

Anstey, K. J., Hofer, S. M., & Luszcz, M. A. (2003a). Cross-sectional and longitudinal patterns of dedifferentiation in late life cognitive and sensory function: The effects of age, ability, attrition, and occasions of measurement. *Journal of Experimental Aging Research, 22,* 245–266.

Anstey, K. J., Hofer, S. M., & Luszcz, M. A. (2003b). A latent growth curve analysis of late life cognitive and sensory function over eight years: Evidence for specific and common factors underlying change. *Psychology and Aging, 18,* 714–726.

Anstey, K. J., Luszcz, M. A., & Sanchez, L. (2001). A reevaluation of the common factor theory of shared variance among age, sensory function, and cognitive function in older adults. *Journal of Gerontology: Psychological Sciences, 56B,* P3–P11.

Anstey, K. J., Windsor, T. D., Jorm, A. F., Christensen, H., & Rodgers, B. (2003). Association of pulmonary function with cognitive performance in early, middle, and late adulthood. *Gerontology, 50,* 230–234.

Baltes, P. B., & Lindenberger, U. (1997). Emergence of a powerful connection between sensory and cognitive functions across the adult life span: A new window to the study of cognitive aging. *Psychology and Aging, 12,* 12–21.

Baltes, P. B., & Mayer, K. U. (1999). *The Berlin Aging Study: Aging from 70 to 100.* Cambridge, UK: Cambridge University Press.

Baltes, P. B., & Schaie, K. W. (1976). On the plasticity of intelligence in adulthood and old age: Where Horn and Donaldson fail. *American Psychologist, 31,* 720–725.

Bandura, A. (1989). Regulation of cognitive processes through perceived self-efficacy. *Developmental Psychology, 25,* 729–735.

Birren, J. E., & Fisher, L. M. (1995). Aging and speed of behavior: Possible consequences for psychological functioning. *Annual Review of Psychology, 46,* 329–353.

Birren, J. E., & Morrison, D. F. (1961). Analysis of the WAIS subtests in relation to age and education. *Journal of Gerontology, 16,* 363–369.

Blanchard-Fields, F., & Hess, T. (1996). *Perspectives on cognitive change in adulthood and aging.* Boston: McGraw-Hill.

Bloom, B. S. (1964). *Stability and change in human characteristics.* New York: Wiley.

Britton, A., Singh-Manoux, A., & Marmot, M. (2004). Alcohol consumption and cognitive function in the Whitehall II Study. *American Journal of Epidemiology, 160,* 240–247.

Brookmeyer, R., & Gray, S. (2000). Methods for projecting the incidence and prevalence of chronic diseases in ageing populations: Application to Alzheimer's disease. *Statistics in Medicine, 19,* 1481–1493.

Brookmeyer, R., Gray, S., & Kawas, C. (1998). Projections of Alzheimer's disease in the United States and the public health impact of delaying disease onset. *American Journal of Public Health, 88,* 1337–1342.

Brown, S. C., & Park, D. C. (2003). Theoretical models of cognitive aging and implications for translational research in medicine. *The Gerontologist, 43,* S57–S67.

Cattell, R. B. (1941). Some theoretical issues in adult intelligence testing. *Psychological Bulletin, 38,* 592.

Cattell, R. B. (1971). *Abilities: Their structure, growth and action.* Boston: Houghton Mifflin.

Cerella, J. (1985). Information processing rates in the elderly. *Psychological Bulletin, 98,* 67–83.

Chen, W.-T., Wang, P.-N., Wang, S.-J., Fuh, J.-L., Lin, K.-N., & Liu, H.-C. (2003). Smoking and cognitive performance in the community elderly: A longitudinal study. *Journal of Geriatric Psychiatry and Neurology, 16,* 18–22.

Christensen, H., Hofer, S. M., Mackinnon, A. J., Korten, A. E., Jorm, A. F., & Henderson, A. S. (2001). Age is no kinder to the better educated: Absence of an association investigated using latent growth techniques in a community sample. *Psychological Medicine, 31,* 15–28.

Christensen, H., Korten, A. E., Jorm, A. F., Henderson, A. S., Jacomb, P. A., Rodgers, B., & Mackinnon, A. J. (1997). Education and decline in cognitive performance: Compensatory but not protective. *International Journal of Geriatric Psychiatry, 12,* 323–330.

Churchill, J. D., Galvez, R., Colcombe, S., Swain, R. A., Kramer, A. F., & Greenough, W. T. (2002). Exercise, experience, and the aging brain. *Neurobiology of Aging, 23,* 941–955.

Collins, L. M., & Sayer, A. G. (Eds.). (2001). *New methods for the analysis of change.* Washington, DC: American Psychological Association.

Corrêa-Leite, M. L., Nicolosi, A., Cristina, S., Hauser, W. A., & Nappi, G. (2001). Nutrition and cognitive deficit in the elderly: A population study. *European Journal of Clinical Nutrition, 55,* 1053–1058.

Cosway, R., Strachan, M. W. J., Dougall, A., Frier, B. M., & Deary, I. J. (2001). Cognitive function and information processing in type 2 diabetes. *Diabetic Medicine, 18,* 803–810.

Craik, F., & Byrd, M. (1982). Aging and cognitive deficits: The role of attentional resources. In F. Craik & S. Trehub (Eds.), *Aging and cognitive processes* (pp. 191–211). New York: Plenum.

Crooks, V. C., Buckwalter, J. G., & Petitti, D. B. (2003). Diabetes mellitus and cognitive performance in older women. *Annals of Epidemiology, 13,* 613–619.

Dannefer, W. D. (1984). Adult development and social theory: A paradigmatic reappraisal. *American Sociological Review, 49,* 100–116.

Dannefer, W. D. (1987). Aging as intracohort differentiation: Accentuation, the Matthew effect, and the life course. *Sociological Forum, 2,* 211–236.

Dannefer, W. D. (1988). What's in a name? An account of the neglect of variability in the study of aging. In J. E. Birren & V. L. Bengtson (Eds.), *Emergent theories of aging* (pp. 356–384). New York: Springer.

Dannefer, W. D. (2003). Cumulative advantage/disadvantage and the life course: Cross-fertilizing age and social science theory. *Journal of Gerontology: Social Sciences, 58B,* S327–S357.

Dik, M., Deeg, D. J., Visser, M., & Jonker, C. (2003). Early life physical activity and cognition at old age. *Journal of Clinical and Experimental Neuropsychology, 25,* 643–653.

Dixon, R. A. (1999). The concept of gains in cognitive aging. In D. C. Park & N. Schwarz (Eds.), *Cognition, aging, and self-reports* (pp. 71–92). Philadelphia: Taylor & Francis.

Dufouil, C., Alpérovitch, A., & Tzourio, C. (2003). Influence of education on the relationship between white matter lesions and cognition. *Neurology, 60,* 831–836.

Emery, C. F., Shermer, R. L., Hauchk, E. R., Hsiao, E. T., & MacIntyre, N. R. (2003). Cognitive and psychological outcomes of exercise in a one-year follow-up study of patients with chronic obstructive pulmonary disease. *Health Psychology, 22,* 598–604.

Espeland, M. A., Gu, L., Masaki, K. H., Langer, R. D., Coker, L. H., Stefanick, M. L., et al. (2005). Association between reported alcohol intake and cognition: Results from the Women's Health Initiative Memory Study. *American Journal of Epidemiology, 161,* 228–238.

Evans, D. A., Scherr, P. A., Cook, N. R., Albert, M. S., Funkenstein, H. H., Beckett, L. A., et al. (1992). The impact of Alzheimer's disease in the United States population. In R. M. Suzman, D. P. Willis, & K. G. Manton (Eds.), *The oldest old* (pp. 283–299). New York: Oxford University Press.

Finch, C. E., & Crimmins, E. M. (2004, September 17). Inflammatory exposure and historical changes in human life-spans. *Science, 305,* 1736–1739.

Fisher, D. L. (2000). Cognitive aging and adaptive technologies. In P. C. Stern & L. L. Carstensen (Eds.), *The aging mind: Opportunities in cognitive research* (pp. 166–188). Washington, DC: National Academy Press.

Fiske, A. P., Kitiyama, S., Markus, H. R., & Nisbett, R. E. (1998). The cultural matrix of social psychology. In D. T. Gilbert, S. T. Fiske, & G. Lindzey (Eds.), *The handbook of social psychology* (4th ed., pp. 915–981). Boston: McGraw-Hill.

Folstein, M. F., Folstein, S. E., & McHugh, P. R. (1975). Mini-Mental State: A practical method for grading the cognitive state of patients for the clinician. *Journal of Psychiatric Research, 12,* 189–198.

Geroldi, C., Ferrucci, L., Bandinelli, S., Cavazzini, C., Zanetti, O, Guralnik, J., & Frisoni, G. B. (2003). Mild cognitive deterioration with subcortical features: Prevalence, clinical characteristics, and association with cardiovascular risk factors in community-dwelling older persons (The InCHIANTI Study). *Journal of the American Geriatrics Society, 51,* 1064–1071.

Haan, M., Shemanski, L., Jagust, W., Manolio, T., & Kuller, L. (1999). The role of APOE epsilon 4 modulating effects of other risk factors for cognitive decline in elderly persons. *Journal of the American Medical Association, 282,* 40–46.

Hall, C. B., Lipton, R. B., Sliwinski, M. J., & Stewart, W. F. (2000). A change point model for estimating onset of cognitive decline in preclinical

Alzheimer's disease. *Statistics in Medicine, 19,* 1555–1566.

Harris, C. R., Albaugh, B., Goldman, D., & Enoch, M. A. (2003). Neurocognitive impairment due to chronic alcohol consumption in an American Indian community. *Journal of the Study of Alcohol, 64,* 458–466.

Hassing, L. B., Grant, M. D., Hofer, S. M., Pedersen, N. L., Nilsson, S. E., Berg, S., et al. (2004). Type 2 diabetes mellitus contributes to cognitive change in the oldest old: A longitudinal population-based study. *Journal of the International Neuropsychological Society, 4,* 599–607.

Hassing, L. B., Hofer, S. M., Nilsson, S. E., Berg, S., Pedersen, N. L., McClearn, G. E., & Johansson, B. (2004). Comorbid type 2 diabetes mellitus and hypertension exacerbates cognitive decline: Evidence from a longitudinal study. *Age and Aging, 33,* 355–361.

Hassing, L. B., Johansson, B., Berg, S., Nilsson, S. E., Pedersen, N. L., Hofer, S. M., & McClearn, G. E. (2002). Terminal decline and markers of cerebro- and cardiovascular disease: Findings from a longitudinal study of the oldest old. *Journal of Gerontology: Psychological Sciences, 57B,* P268–P276.

Hendrie, H. C., Albert, M. S., Butters, M. A., Gao, S., Knopman, D. S., Launer, L. J., et al. (2006). The NIH Cognitive and Emotional Health Project: Report of the critical evaluation study committee. *Alzheimer's & Dementia, 2,* 12–32.

Hertzog, C., Dixon, R., & Hultsch, D. (1992). Intraindividual change in text recall of the elderly. *Brain and Language, 42,* 248–269.

Hertzog, C., & Schaie, K. W. (1986). Stability and change in adult intelligence: I. Analysis of longitudinal covariance structures. *Psychology and Aging, 1,* 159–171.

Hertzog, C., & Schaie, K. W. (1988). Stability and change in adult intelligence: 2. Simultaneous Analysis of longitudinal means and covariance structures. *Psychology and Aging, 3,* 122–130.

Herzog, A. R., & Wallace, R. B. (1997). Measures of cognitive functioning in the AHEAD Study. *Journals of Gerontology Series B: Psychological Sciences and Social Sciences, 52B,* 37–48.

Heyn, P., Abreu, B. C., & Ottenbacher, K. J. (2004). The effects of exercise training on elderly persons with cognitive impairment and dementia: A meta-analysis. *Archives of Physical Medicine and Rehabilitation, 85,* 1694–1704.

Hill, R. D., Nilsson, L. G., Nyberg, L., & Bäckman, L. (2003). Cigarette smoking and cognitive performance in healthy Swedish adults. *Age and Ageing, 32,* 548–550.

Hillman, C. H., Belopolsky, A. V., Snook, E. M., Kramer, A. F., & McAuley, E. (2004). Physical activity and executive control: Implications for increased cognitive health during older adulthood. *Research Quarterly for Exercise and Sport, 75,* 176–185.

Hofer, S. M., Berg, S., & Era, P. (2003). Evaluating the interdependence of aging-related changes in visual and auditory acuity, balance, and cognitive functioning. *Psychology and Aging, 18,* 285–305.

Hofer, S. M., Flaherty, B. P., & Hoffman, L. (2006). Cross-sectional analysis of time-dependent data: Problems of mean-induced association in age-heterogeneous samples and an alternative method based on sequential narrow age-cohorts. *Multivariate Behavioral Research, 41,* 165–187.

Hofer, S. M., & Piccinin, A. M. (2007). Longitudinal studies. In J. E. Birren (Ed.), *Encyclopedia of gerontology: Age, aging, and the aged* (2nd ed.). Oxford, UK: Elsevier.

Hofer, S. M., & Sliwinski, M. J. (2001). Understanding ageing: An evaluation of research designs for assessing the interdependence of ageing-related changes. *Gerontology, 47,* 341–352.

Hofer, S. M., & Sliwinski, M. J. (2006). Design and analysis of longitudinal studies of aging. In J. E. Birren & K. W. Schaie (Eds.), *Handbook of the psychology of aging* (6th ed., pp. 15–37). San Diego, CA: Academic Press.

Horn, J. L. (1965). *Fluid and crystallized intelligence: A factor analytic study of the structure among primary mental abilities.* Unpublished doctoral dissertation, University of Illinois.

Horn, J. L., & Cattell, R. B. (1966). Refinement and test of the theory of fluid and crystallized general intelligences. *Journal of Educational Psychology, 57,* 253–270.

Horn, J. L., & Donaldson, G. (1977). Faith is not enough: A response to the Baltes–Schaie claim that intelligence does not wane. *American Psychologist, 32,* 369–373.

Horn, J. L., & Donaldson, G. (1980). Cognitive development in adulthood. In O. G. Brim, Jr. & J. Kagan (Eds.), *Constancy and change in human development* (pp. 445–529). Cambridge, MA: Harvard University Press.

Juster, F. T., & Suzman, R. (1995). An overview of the Health and Retirement Study. *Journal of Human Resources, 30,* S7–S56.

Kalmijn, S., van Boxtel, M. P. J., & Verschuren, M. W. (2002). Cigarette smoking and alcohol consumption in relation to cognitive performance. *American Journal of Epidemiology, 156,* 936–944.

Kawas, C. H., & Brookmeyer, R. (2001). Aging and the public health: Effects of dementia [Editorial]. *New England Journal of Medicine, 344,* 1160–1161.

Kitayama, S. (2000). Cultural variations in cognition: Implications for aging research. In P. C. Stern & L. L. Carstensen (Eds.), *The aging mind: Opportunities in cognitive research* (pp. 218–237). Washington, DC: National Academy Press.

Kraemer, H. C., Yesavage, J. A., Taylor, J. L., & Kupfer, D. (2000). How can we learn about developmental processes from cross-sectional studies, or can we? *American Journal of Psychiatry, 157,* 163–171.

Kuhn, T. S. (1962). *The structure of scientific revolutions.* Chicago: University of Chicago Press.

Leroi, I., Sheppard, J. M., & Lyketsos, C. G. (2002). Cognitive function after 11.5 years of alcohol use. *American Journal of Epidemiology, 156,* 747–752.

Li, S.-C., Aggen, S. H., Nesselroade, J. R., & Baltes, P. B. (1998). Short-term fluctuations in elderly people's sensorimotor functioning predict text and spatial memory performance: The MacArthur Successful Aging Studies. *Gerontology, 47,* 100–116.

Lindenberger, U., & Baltes, P. B. (1994). Sensory functioning and intelligence in old age: A strong connection, *Psychology and Aging, 9,* 339–355.

Little, T. D., Schnabel, K. U., & Baumert, J. (Eds.). (2000). *Modeling longitudinal and multilevel data.* Mahwah, NJ: Lawrence Erlbaum.

Lorge, I. (1956). Aging and intelligence. *Journal of Chronic Diseases, 412,* 131–139.

Myerson, J., Hale, S., Wagstaff, D., Poon, L. W., & Smith, G. A. (1990). The information-loss model: A mathematical theory of age-related cognitive slowing. *Psychological Review, 97,* 475–487.

National Institute on Aging, National Advisory Council on Aging, Behavioral and Social Research (BSR) Program Review Committee.

(2004). *BSR Review Committee report* (revised August 10, 2004). Retrieved August 3, 2007, from http://www.nia.nih.gov/NR/rdonlyres/2EA2 C923-8418-4CF1-8D2A-66B6BEDBB321/2308/ BSRReviewReportFINAL.pdf

National Research Council. (2000). *The aging mind: Opportunities in cognitive research.* Committee on Future Directions for Cognitive Research on Aging. Paul C. Stern and Laura L. Carstensen, Editors. Commission on Behavioral and Social Sciences and Education. Washington, DC: National Academy Press.

National Research Council. (2007). *A strategy for assessing science: Behavioral and social research on aging.* Committee on Assessing Behavioral and Social Science Research on Aging. Irwin Feller and Paul C. Stern, Editors. Center for Studies of Behavior and Development, Division of Behavioral and Social Sciences and Education. Washington, DC: National Academy Press.

O'Rand, A. M. (1996). The precious and the precocious: Understanding cumulative disadvantage and cumulative advantage over the life course. *The Gerontologist, 36,* 230–238.

Ostir, G. V., Raji, M. A., Ottenbacher, K. J., Markides, K. S., & Goodwin, J. S. (2003). Cognitive function and incidence of stroke in older Mexican Americans. *Journal of Gerontology: Medical Sciences, 58A,* 531–535.

Park, D. C. (1999). Cognitive aging, processing resources, and self-report. In N. Schwarz, D. Park, B. Knäuper, & S. Sudman (Eds.), *Cognition, aging, and self-reports* (pp. 45–69). Philadelphia: Psychology Press.

Park, D. C., Smith, A. D., Lautenschlager, G., Earles, J., Frieske, D., Zwahr, M., & Gaines, C. (1996). Mediators of long-term memory performance across the life-span. *Psychology and Aging, 11,* 621–637.

Pavlik, V. N., Hyman, D. J., & Doody, R. (2005). Cardiovascular risk factors and cognitive function in adults 30–59 years of age (NHANES III). *Neuroepidemiology, 24,* 42–50.

Perreira, K. M., & Sloan, F. A. (2002). Excess alcohol consumption and health outcomes: A 6-year follow-up of men over age 50 from the Health and Retirement Study. *Addiction, 97,* 301–310.

Razani, J., Boone, K., Lesser, I., & Weiss, D. (2004). Effects of cigarette smoking history on cognitive functioning in healthy older adults. *American Journal of Geriatric Psychiatry, 12,* 404–411.

Richards, M., Jarvis, M. J., Thompson, N., & Wadsworth, M. E. J. (2003). Cigarette smoking and cognitive decline in midlife: Evidence from a prospective birth cohort study. *American Journal of Public Health, 93,* 994–998.

Rowe, J. W., & Kahn, R. L. (1998). *Successful aging.* New York: Pantheon.

Rubin, E. H., Storandt, M., Miller, J. P., Kinscherf, D. A.,Grant, E. A., Morris, J. C., & Berg, L. (1998). A prospective study of cognitive function and onset of dementia in cognitively healthy elders. *Archives of Neurology, 55,* 395–401.

Salthouse, T. A. (1991). *Theoretical perspectives on cognitive aging.* Hillsdale, NJ: Lawrence Erlbaum.

Salthouse, T. A. (1993). Speed and knowledge as determinants of adult age differences in verbal tasks. *Journal of Gerontology: Psychological Sciences, 48,* P29–P36.

Salthouse, T. A. (1996a). Constraints on theories of cognitive aging. *Psychonomic Bulletin and Review, 3,* 287–299.

Salthouse, T. A. (1996b). The processing-speed theory of adult age differences in cognition. *Psychological Review, 103,* 403–428.

Salthouse, T. A. (1999). Pressing issues in cognitive aging. In D. C. Park & N. Schwarz (Eds.), *Cognition, aging, and self-reports* (pp. 185–198). Philadelphia: Taylor & Francis.

Schaie, K. W. (1983). The Seattle Longitudinal Study: A 21-year exploration of psychometric intelligence in adulthood. In K. W. Schaie (Ed.), *Longitudinal studies of adult psychological development* (pp. 24–49). New York: Guilford Press.

Schaie, K. W. (1984). Historical time and cohort effects. In K. A. McCloskey & H. W. Reese (Eds.), *Life-span developmental psychology: Historical and generational effects* (pp. 1–15). New York: Academic Press.

Schaie, K. W. (1989). Individual differences in rate of cognitive change in adulthood. In V. L. Bengtson & K. W. Schaie (Eds.), *The course of later life: Research and reflections* (pp. 65–85). New York: Springer.

Schaie, K. W. (1990). Intellectual development in adulthood. In J. E. Birren & K. W. Schaie (Eds.), *Handbook of the psychology of aging* (3rd ed., pp. 291–309). San Diego, CA: Academic Press.

Schaie, K. W. (1994). The course of adult intellectual development. *American Psychologist, 49,* 304–313.

Schaie, K. W. (1996). *Intellectual development in adulthood: The Seattle longitudinal study.* Cambridge, UK: Cambridge University Press.

Schaie, K. W., & Hertzog, C. (1983). Fourteen-year cohort-sequential studies of adult intelligence. *Developmental Psychology, 19,* 531–543.

Schaie, K. W., & Hofer, S. M. (2002). Longitudinal studies in aging research. In J. E. Birren & K. W. Schaie (Eds.), *Handbook of the psychology of aging* (5th ed., pp. 53–77). San Diego, CA: Academic Press.

Schaie, K. W., Willis, S. L., & Pennak, S. (2005). An historical framework for cohort differences in intelligence. *Research in Human Development, 2,* 43–67.

Schinka, J. A., Belanger, H., Mortimer, J. A., & Borenstein-Graves, A. (2003). Effects of the use of alcohol and cigarettes on cognition in elderly African American adults. *Journal of International Neuropsychology, 9,* 690–697.

Schuit, A. J., Feskens, E. J., Launer, L. J., & Kromhout, D. (2001). Physical activity and cognitive decline: The role of the apolipoprotein e4 allele. *Medical Science and Sports Exercise, 33,* 772–777.

Sliwinski, M. J., Hofer, S. M., & Hall, C. (2003). Correlated and coupled cognitive change in older adults with and without clinical dementia. *Psychology and Aging, 18,* 672–683.

Sliwinski, M. J., Hofer, S. M., Hall, C., Bushke, H., & Lipton, R. B. (2003). Modeling memory decline in older adults: The importance of pre-clinical dementia, attrition and chronological age. *Psychology and Aging, 18,* 658–671.

Sliwinski, M. J., Lipton, R. B., Buschke, H., & Stewart, W. F. (1996). The effect of pre-clinical dementia on estimates of normal cognitive function in aging. *Journal of Gerontology: Psychological Sciences, 51B,* P217–P225.

Strauss, E., MacDonald, S. W., Hunter, M., Moll, A., & Hultsch, D. F. (2002). Intraindividual variability in cognitive performance in three groups of older adults: Cross-domain links to physical status and self-perceived affect and beliefs. *Journal of the International Neuropsychological Society, 8,* 893–906.

Suzman, R. M. (2004). Research on population aging at NIA: Retrospect and prospect. In L. J. Waite (Ed.), *Aging, health, and public policy: Demographic and economic perspectives* (pp. 239–264; supplement to Vol. 30, *Population and Development Review*). New York: Population Council.

Suzman, R. M., Willis, D. P., & Manton, K. G. (Eds.). (1992). *The oldest old.* New York: Oxford University Press.

United Nations. (2002). *World population ageing: 1950–2050.* New York: Author.

Vaupel, J. W., & Yashin, A. I. (1985). Heterogeneity's ruses: Some surprising effects of selection on population dynamics. *The American Statistician, 39,* 176–185.

Verbrugge, L. M., & Jette, A. M. (1994). The disablement process. *Social Science and Medicine, 38,* 1–14.

Waldstein, S. R. (2000). Health effects on cognitive aging. In P. C. Stern & L. L. Carstensen (Eds.), *The aging mind: Opportunities in cognitive research* (pp. 189–217). Committee on Future Directions for Cognitive Research on Aging, National Research Council. Washington, DC: National Academy Press.

Waldstein, S. R., & Elias, M. F. (Eds.). (2001). *Neuropsychology of cardiovascular disease.* Mahwah, NJ: Lawrence Erlbaum.

Weiss, K. M. (1990). The biodemography of variation in human frailty. *Demography, 27,* 185–206.

Willis, S. L. (1990). Contributions of cognitive training research to understanding late life potential. In M. Perlmutter (Ed.), *Late life potential* (pp. 25–42). Washington, DC: Gerontological Society of America.

Willis, S. L., & Schaie, K. W. (2006). Cognitive functioning in the Baby Boomers: Longitudinal and cohort effects. In S. K. Whitbourne & S. L. Willis (Eds.), *The Baby Boomers grow up: Contemporary perspectives on midlife* (pp. 205–234). Mahwah, NJ: Lawrence Erlbaum.

Willis, S. L., Tennstedt, S. L., Marsiske, M., Ball, K., Elias, J., Koepke, K. M., et al. (2006). Long-term effects of cognitive training on everyday functional outcomes in older adults: The ACTIVE Study. *Journal of the American Medical Association, 296,* 2805–2814.

Wilson, R. S., Bennett, D. A., & Swarzendruber, A. (1997). Age-related change in cognitive function. In P. D. Nussbaum (Ed.), *Handbook of neuropsychology and aging* (pp. 7–14). New York: Plenum.

Wilson, R. S., Mendes de Leon, C. F., Bennett, D. A., Bienias, J. L., & Evans, D. A. (2004). Depressive symptoms and cognitive decline in a community population of older persons. *Journal of Neurology and Neurosurgical Psychiatry, 75,* 126–129.

Wray, L. A., & Blaum, C. S. (2001). Explaining the role of sex on disability: A population-based study. *The Gerontologist, 41,* 499–510.

Yaffe, K., Linquist, K., Penninx, B. W., Simonsick, E. M., Pahor, M., Dritchevsky, S., et al. (2003). Inflammatory markers and cognition in well-functioning African-American and White elders. *Neurology, 61,* 76–80.

Zhang, Y., Heeren, T., & Ellison, R. C. (2005). Education modifies the effect of alcohol on memory impairment: The third National Health and Nutrition Examination Survey. *Neuroepidemiology, 24,* 63–69.

Zhou, H., Deng, J., Li, J., Wang, Y., Zhang, M., & He, H. (2003). Study of the relationship between cigarette smoking, alcohol drinking and cognitive impairment among elderly people in China. *Age and Ageing, 32,* 205–210.

PART II

INTEGRATIVE THEORETICAL PERSPECTIVES

2

THEORETICAL APPROACHES TO THE STUDY OF COGNITIVE AGING

An Individual-Differences Perspective

CHRISTOPHER HERTZOG

Our understanding of aging and its effects on cognition has improved considerably over the last 50 years, as can be seen in a number of reviews (e.g., Craik & Salthouse, 2000; Hoyer & Verhaeghen, 2006). This improvement has occurred despite the fact that it is anything but easy to conduct research on adult cognitive development.

Conducting high-quality research on aging and cognitive development requires knowledge about (a) theory and method in cognitive psychology and (b) theory and method for studying adult development and aging. Questions about cognitive aging are inherently questions about how individuals of different ages or from different subpopulations (e.g., healthy aging vs. Alzheimer's disease) differ from one another and change over time (Baltes, Reese, & Nesselroade, 1988; Hertzog, 1996; Hertzog & Dixon, 1996). Hence, psychologists studying cognitive aging must have at least some degree of knowledge about measurement and assessment of cognitive constructs and must appreciate problems posed by studying individual differences, including methods for sampling

individuals, screening for pathology, and measuring developmental change.

There has been progress in the creation of statistical methods for analyzing multivariate data, including models of developmental change (Hertzog & Nesselroade, 2003; Hofer & Sliwinski, 2006; Wohlwill, 1991). Methods for studying cognitive psychology have also grown in the modern era, and this growth has affected research on adult cognitive development. It is no longer uncommon to see work with aging populations appearing in mainstream cognitive journals, because such studies generate new knowledge about cognition itself (e.g., Jacoby, 1999).

In my view what is needed now to fuel further understanding of adult cognitive development is better gerontological theory, along with better integration of such theory with the formulation and testing of explanations for age-related cognitive change. This integration requires us to grow beyond narrow disciplinary boundaries in both our thinking and our empirical research. Most of us would immediately think of research on aging and cognitive neuroscience as a prototype for multidisciplinary endeavors in our field. I believe that we also need bridges to how to think about adult development from a contextual perspective and to consider how cognition is manifested in social context.

Further progress in integrating theories and methods for the study of cognitive development should be grounded in a perspective on cognition as something that (a) changes within persons in complex ways (e.g., Nesselroade, 1991) and (b) varies between individuals (Hertzog, 1985). Although there are normative changes across the adult life span at biological, psychological, and social levels, there is also diversity in the expression of age-related changes in structures and mechanisms on cognition. Our science should not avoid contemplating such diversity; neither can it shudder at its subtlety and complexity. It should embrace it and understand it for what it is: the crucible in which refinement of our understanding of aging can and must take place.

SIX RELEVANT DISTINCTIONS FOR RESEARCH ON COGNITION AND AGING

To frame current thinking and future needs in this field, I mention and briefly treat six broad distinctions.

1. *Psychometric versus experimental approaches to cognition.* The first distinction is between cognition as understood from a psychometric perspective—that is, a focus on taxonomies of abilities revealed in individual-differences research (Carroll, 1993)—and cognition as revealed by experimental tasks, with focus on microanalysis of cognitive processes and mechanisms (Cronbach, 1957). These two approaches can and should be merged, from my perspective, but for the most part they exist as independent traditions in aging research. Experimental gerontologists typically study cognitive mechanisms in well-crafted experiments with limited age samples (often in extreme age group designs comparing young and old adults; see Hertzog, 1996). The goal is often to detect age interactions with experimental manipulations to observe the effects of aging. Differential psychologists in the gerontological

tradition typically study broad constructs such as fluid or crystallized intelligence in longitudinal or accelerated sequential designs (e.g., McArdle, Ferrer-Caja, Hamagami, & Woodcock, 2002; Schaie, 2005). Studies that combine experimental methods for measuring cognitive processes with differential approaches measuring individual differences or dimensions of age-related change are desirable but rare (e.g., Hultsch, Hertzog, Dixon, & Small, 1998).

2. *Description, explanation, and modification.* The second distinction is among description, explanation, and modification/intervention as goals or targets of research on adult development (e.g., Baltes & Willis, 1977). It is far easier to describe the relationship of age to cognitive constructs than to explain this relationship, or to intervene to change it. Granted, there are methodological issues even in obtaining valid descriptions of age-related variation (e.g., Schaie, 1977). Nevertheless, researchers in the field conduct too much descriptive research. Explanation of cognitive aging does not necessarily require attention to biological mechanisms of the brain, although this level of explanation can be quite illuminating (Cabeza, Nyberg, & Park, 2003). Explanation of cognitive aging can occur at multiple levels of causation (Shadish, Cook, & Campbell, 2002), including the strictly psychological level. For instance, there are exciting theory-grounded trends in cognitive intervention research that deserve continuing attention (Ball et al., 2002; Colcombe & Kramer, 2003; Dunlosky, Hertzog, Kennedy, & Thiede, 2005; Willis, 2001).

3. *Characterizing aggregate (population-level) change in cognition versus variability in cognitive change.* Most gerontological research, especially that derived from experimental approaches, focuses on population-level change, although the population may neither be explicitly defined nor representatively sampled. We know a lot about descriptions of age-related cognitive change, such as the life course trajectories of fluid intelligence and crystallized intelligence (e.g., Horn & Hofer, 1992; Salthouse, 1991; Schaie, 2005). Far greater emphasis should be placed on measuring individual differences in long-term intraindividual change and short-term intraindividual variability

(Nesselroade, 1991), perhaps by what are known as *person-centered* or *idiographic* approaches (Bergman, Magnusson, & El-Khouri, 2003). Fortunately, the field is moving in this direction, linking within-person changes to more traditional dimensions of individual differences (e.g., Ram, Rabbitt, Stollery, & Nesselroade, 2005).

4. *Cognitive mechanisms versus functional or adaptive cognition.* This distinction refers to two fundamentally different goals of research on cognition and aging: (1) to isolate, describe, and explain cognitive mechanisms, on the one hand, and (2) to understand the functional aspects of cognition (what it has evolved to serve, how it operates in ecological contexts; see Dixon & Hertzog, 1988; Park, 1992) on the other hand. Functional aspects of cognition are often relegated to the applied domain, as if one could isolate pure mechanism in the laboratory and then understand how to apply this understanding to the real world. Ecological approaches to cognition, in contrast, emphasize how cognitive mechanisms have evolved in actual environments, requiring attention to environmental demands and to cognition in context (e.g., Gigerenzer, Todd, & The ABC Research Group, 1999; Lawton, 1990). The latter approach takes a functional approach to cognition.

5. *The multiple causal levels of explanations for age-related changes.* Causes of age differences in cognition are not restricted to aging in the biological sense, such as in mechanisms of ontogenesis and senescence. Instead, cognitive psychologists typically observe, to borrow a term from genetics, the *phenotypes* of cognitive aging. Phenotypes are a complex transaction among biological mechanisms, psychological processes, and social contexts (deriving both from macrosocietal influences and microsocial contexts in which individuals' lives are embedded and experienced). Gerontologists acknowledge the multiplicity of causes as a truism, but our acknowledgments rarely have a direct impact on the research done in cognitive aging. Causal analysis of age-related cognitive change can contemplate in a complementary fashion influences at behavioral, neural, and environmental levels of analysis.

6. *Expert versus novice scientific reasoning.* This distinction concerns how scientists think and reason within discipline-bound areas of expertise (usually with considerable sophistication) and how they reason about explanations of cognitive change and variability that lie outside their specialized domain of expertise. The differentiation of science and the knowledge explosion has pushed all of us away from a Renaissance-type of broad understanding of gerontology as a whole, or even a broad view of our own subdiscipline, and drawn us into narrow areas of specialization. This trend has had tremendous benefits for understanding restricted sets of cognitive mechanisms, but it also has tremendous costs for the quality of reasoning about cognitive aging in the broadest sense. Scientists are discipline bound and seek explanations at their preferred level of analysis, commensurate with their expertise. We often make implausible assumptions about causal mechanisms that lie beyond the narrow scope of our own expertise.

In particular, psychologists are wont to resort to simplistic views of aging grounded in an outmoded biomedical worldview. Implicit assumptions of the following type are typical. Because the brain causes behavior, and aging influences the brain, the causes of change in cognitive mechanisms are fundamentally neurological. Or, to the extent that one can map brain changes as a function of aging, one has sufficient information to build an explanatory model of aging and cognition. Or, individual differences in cognitive change are due to individual differences in heredity—receiving good genes for longevity is tantamount to aging gracefully and well. Such static views of aging are consistent with (and may be little more than) lay causal theories about cognitive development (e.g., Berg & Sternberg, 1985). They are inconsistent with transactional views on gene–environment interactions and evidence for gene–environment interactions (e.g., Finkel, Pederson, Plomin, & McClearn, 1998; Gottlieb, 1998), and they do not properly acknowledge the effects of social context and patterns of behavior on patterns of change over the life span. Age differences are not the same as change over time, change is not the same as development, and adult development is not isomorphic with ontogenesis (Wohlwill, 1973).

THE STATE OF COGNITIVE AGING THEORY

Most theories of cognitive aging, as they exist today, fall into one of two classes. They are either (1) broad descriptions of age differences in cognitive tasks (often from a psychometric measurement tradition) or (2) general claims attributing the effects of aging on cognition to a limited number of cognitive mechanisms (usually from a cognitive experimental tradition).

Psychometric Approaches

Many theoretical treatments of cognitive aging are actually grounded in a fundamental phenomenon already well known in the first half of the 20th century—knowledge-based tests show stability or incremental increases across much of the adult life span, whereas measures of reasoning, memory, and other constructs decrease (Horn & Hofer, 1992; Salthouse, 1991). This empirically observed distinction was the basis for the Cattell–Horn theory of fluid and crystallized intelligence (e.g., Horn, 1989). It is also reflected in the theoretical distinction between cognitive mechanics and cognitive pragmatics by Baltes and colleagues (e.g., Baltes, Staudinger, & Lindenberger, 1999). The distinction has also been captured, with greater emphasis on experience-based, domain-specific knowledge structures, by Ackerman and colleagues (e.g., Ackerman & Rolfhus, 1999).

Such a broad generalization based on patterns of mean age differences or changes is certainly parsimonious, but is it accurate and conceptually useful? Psychometric theories of intelligence require a finite but large number of primary abilities and many higher-order factors to account for the structure of the intellect (Carroll, 1993; Horn, 1989), yet aging theorists opt to speak of one class of ability constructs that declines and one that does not. One consequence of this broad bipartite distinction is that one is tempted to view the aging of fluid intelligence or cognitive mechanics in a monolithic fashion.

In my view, the two-factor generalization is so crude as to be almost unhelpful. On the one hand, not all basic cognitive mechanisms with limited links to crystallized intelligence decline with age. For example, aging appears to spare posterior attentional control mechanisms (e.g., Hartley, 1993; Kramer et al., 2006), familiarity mechanisms in recognition memory (Light, Prull, La Voie, & Healy, 2000), and elementary metacognitive monitoring (Hertzog & Hultsch, 2000). On the other hand, the distinction between *available* knowledge and *accessible* knowledge implies that not all the functional benefit of acquired pragmatic skills and knowledge will be accessed or applied by older adults in actual situations. More generally, there is a complex interplay between mechanics and pragmatics in complex cognition, such as reading expository texts or reasoning about ill-structured problems. Of course, a theorist can classify failures to recognize the implicit problem structures and to access relevant solutions based on past experience as failures in cognitive mechanics. However, the risk is that attributions to mechanics as the source of age decline, whenever it is observed, merely reifies the two-factor distinction.

Even if two constructs show similar age-related changes over the life span, this does not imply that these changes share common causes. Spatial visualization is clearly a construct that is distinct from fluid reasoning ability (Horn, 1989) even though it shows similar cross-sectional age gradients (Hertzog, 1989). Perhaps the similarity reflects the age changes in a variable, such as working memory, that influences both constructs (Park et al., 2002; Salthouse, 1991). However, there is no guarantee this is so; stochastic but cumulative effects of aging at multiple neurological loci may produce similar age trends that are caused by different mechanisms.

Experimental/Cognitive Approaches

Most of the theoretical arguments about cognition and aging from an experimental perspective are relatively general and universal. Leading examples include processing resource theory (Salthouse, 1991, 1996), self-initiated processing deficits (Craik & Byrd, 1982), or inhibitory loss (Hasher & Zacks, 1988) as explanations of cognitive aging. We have learned a lot from testing hypotheses derived from such theories. For example, Hasher and Zack's (1988) view of inhibitory loss now focuses more on inhibitory deficits manifested in interactions among attention, working memory, and inhibitory processes (e.g., inhibition of pre-potent responses, resistance to interference), moving away from a more general account that embraces phenomena such as negative priming (e.g., Zacks, Hasher, & Li, 2000).

General slowing theory (e.g., Cerella, 1990) is falling increasingly out of favor today (see Hartley, 2006) because of the intense scrutiny of its theoretical and methodological assumptions (as in the problems associated with Brinley plots) and because research has demonstrated task- and domain-specific slowing that is not consistent with general slowing accounts (e.g., Fisher & Glaser, 1996; Sliwinski & Buschke, 1999). Even its original proponents have acknowledged that there are multiple rates of age-related slowing in response speed (Verhaeghen, Cerella, & Basak, 2006) that are more related to computational complexity and working memory demand than to speed of processing per se. This certainly argues against applying the litmus test that age × complexity interactions can be meaningful only if first adjusted for the effects general slowing (e.g., Cerella, 1990; Salthouse, 1985). This is how progress is achieved in science, by tackling big ideas and showing where they fail.

Other theoretical concepts that have been offered in the field of aging have been very broad in scope (e.g., Welford's [1958] increased neural noise hypothesis) or little more than descriptive generalizations (e.g., Botwinick's [1984] stimulus persistence hypothesis). Stimulus persistence had very little shelf life in the field, but the neural noise hypothesis may still have explanatory potential (Allen, Weber, & May, 1993; Li, 2005). However, theoretical arguments based on such very broad mechanisms may not always be empirically testable.

Cognitive Resources as a Unifying Metaphor

Variants of cognitive resource theory, at least ones that emphasize working memory and attentional resources more than processing speed (Salthouse, 1996), are probably the dominant theoretical approaches in cognitive aging research today (e.g., Hultsch et al., 1998; Salthouse, 1991). One reason the concept of resources may be influential is its relevance to research based on either a psychometric or an experimental perspective. Resources can be seen as an individual-differences characteristic that is relatively general and yet closely related to executive control mechanisms and associated short-term storage systems best assessed by experimental tasks (Kane & Engle, 2003).

Note, however, that aging research in this tradition usually treats the resource concept as a metatheoretical assumption and a conceptual framework for interpreting results (see Salthouse, 1991) and rarely attempts to test some of the implicit assumptions attached to the resource metaphor (e.g., a fixed capacity pool of resources declines with aging). The fixed-capacity metaphor may be especially problematic given research showing that functional capacity in specific task contexts can be malleable, depending on relevance of accessible knowledge and expertise to cognitive processing (e.g., Hoyer & Ingolfsdottir, 2003; Masunaga & Horn, 2001) and the psychological state of the individual (e.g., circadian rhythms; see Hasher, Zacks, & May, 1999). Moreover, typical methods of measuring working memory resources appear to be influenced by the buildup of proactive interference (Lustig, May, & Hasher, 1999), which may challenge the validity of estimated age declines in resources as well as the span-task scaling of the amount of working memory resources available to persons of different ages. Estimates of available resources may be method specific and not generalize fully to resource allocation in actual cognitive tasks.

General Versus Specific Levels of Explanation

Some theoretical views of aging and cognition focus on trying to identify broad, parsimonious explanations of age differences in multiple cognitive tasks (e.g., Salthouse, 1991; Salthouse & Ferrer-Caja, 2003). In contrast, I would argue that progress in our field regarding changes in cognitive processing mechanisms has been most noticeable when theories of cognition and aging are more circumscribed and specific to a domain of cognition, rather than general to all. For example, research on age differences in recognition memory, including false memories, has been greatly influenced by two-process models that emphasize a qualitative difference between recollection and familiarity (e.g., Jacoby, 1999; Jennings & Jacoby, 1997; see Light et al., 2000). By these accounts, one signature of aging is a reduction of recollective experiences but a maintenance of familiarity, so that a greater proportion of older adults' successful recognitions are due to familiarity. Increased reliance on familiarity increases the hazards of false recognition in older adults (Schacter, 1999). This risk can be reduced by instructing older adults to use strategies that emphasize recollection-based mechanisms and avoid the misleading influences of familiarity-based responding (e.g., Dodson & Schacter, 2002). Individual differences in executive control appear to differentiate older adults who are more or less susceptible to such memory illusions (Butler, McDaniel, Dornberg, Price, & Roediger, 2004). Likewise, source monitoring errors in recognition memory are variably associated with a person's age, depending on factors that influence attributions individuals make about retrieval experiences (Johnson & Raye, 2000; Rahhal, May, & Hasher, 2002).

A parsimonious one-process view of aging effects on episodic memory may be consistent with changing levels of memory performance on standardized tests of episodic memory, but it does not help us understand age-related phenomenology of recognition memory processes.

EXTENDING THEORIES OF COGNITIVE AGING

As a field, we tend to reason categorically (e.g., does loss of inhibitory control explain cognitive change?) rather than to ask conditional and probabilistic questions such as: When and under what circumstances is an age-related change in inhibitory control likely to be problematic? In part, this is because our implicit theories about cognition and aging assume normative change, not differential change as a function of contextual influences. We need theories of cognitive aging that are influenced by developmental

perspectives, that acknowledge the multiplicity of levels of causal analysis and causal variables, and that are inherently *probabilistic* (as opposed to categorical) in their views of the role of aging in influencing cognitive processing mechanisms. I believe that, ultimately, successful theories about individual differences in successful cognitive aging will not be theories about cognitive processes alone. Instead, they will embrace a more comprehensive picture of individuals adapting to the constraints and structure of their own environments. In part, such adaptation is required to compensate for the challenges imposed by age-related changes in basic cognitive and perceptual mechanisms.

Selective Optimization With Compensation

One metatheoretical approach that is consonant with this argument is Baltes and Baltes's (1990) selective optimization with compensation (SOC) theory. SOC can be used to characterize and frame developmental change at many levels, including cognition (see also Riediger, Li, & Lindenberger, 2006). A central concept of SOC is that developmental change can be characterized by orchestration of gains and losses over the life span through the processes of selection, optimization, and compensation.

In the cognitive domain, the SOC metatheory has advantages for generating explanatory theories of goal-directed behavior requiring cognition. An SOC perspective embraces, in principle, theoretical statements about age-related constraints on cognitive mechanisms, but it also focuses on how an individual deploys cognitive resources to achieve goals in everyday life. The processes envisaged by SOC are probably important for understanding adult cognitive development, at least as it pertains to goal-directed behavior, the learning of complex skills, investment of cognitive resources in practical pursuits, and so on.

I would argue that an additional general mechanism—encapsulation—is a critical aspect of adult cognition (see Rybash, Hoyer, & Roodin, 1986). *Encapsulation* refers to the creation of highly automatized procedures and conceptual knowledge structures that are needed to govern complex behaviors, including skilled performance (Ericsson & Charness, 1994). SOC theory would treat encapsulation as an aspect of optimization, but in my view it should be elevated to greater prominence as a hallmark of adult cognition.

Routinization and automaticity are critical aspects of human behavior that have both benefits and costs. *Automaticity* characterizes many critical aspects of skilled complex behavior. In a functional sense, automaticity is critical for building an ensemble that does not rely on cognitive control through allocation of processing resources like controlled attention and working memory. *Routinization* involves habitual strategic approaches for engaging in frequently encountered life tasks. As Gigerenzer et al. (1999) pointed out, we learn behavioral heuristics and routines that allow us to reason and act while minimizing cognitive load or effort. We seek to achieve maximum advantage with minimum effort. Moreover, we often rely on familiar procedures that have been effective and shun new ones that cost time, money, and effort to master.

How many of us use old, perhaps even outdated software simply because we already know how to use it? How many of us understand more than the basic set of features of the software we use? Once we develop an automated skill that achieves our primary goals, we stick with it, even when it has become counterproductive to do so. This type of *behavioral inertia* can have profound adaptive benefits, because we can invest time in productive activity rather than in new skill learning. However, it can also create tremendous consequences when shifting environmental contingencies and neurobiological aging render our usual operating procedures ineffective. Orchestration of gains and losses requires understanding when the behavioral repertoire (reliance on tried-and-true behavioral strategies) requires modification due to contextual change or variation. This is not merely reducible to compensation for developmental loss; instead, it can be a function of a well-established learning history clashing with changing environmental contingencies. To the extent that older adults have a longer history of success with a given routine, they may be more resistant to changing their behavioral repertoire.

SOC is a metatheory about development that needs to be instantiated in specific domains of inquiry. In brief, one example of where it appears

to work well is as a metaphor for understanding implicit theories people hold about memory decline and memory control in old age. Existing theories in this area emphasize the value of a control orientation and speak of the hazards of internalizing implicit theories of inevitable decline. However, interview data my colleagues and I have collected suggest that people have a more sophisticated implicit theory about aging and memory. They perceive age-related decline as inevitable but also view their behavior as potentially improving or degrading memory functioning within boundaries established by biological aging. In essence, they perceive the possibility of compensating for biological change to maintain functional capacity.

Embracing the Functional Aspects of Adult Cognition in Context

There is a clear difference between theories and research about cognition that are grounded in understanding structure and mechanism (as is typical for experimental psychologists, who seek to isolate specific mechanisms through experimental control) and functional views of cognition that ask how these mechanisms evolve to serve survival and adaptation in ecological contexts and how they may or may not influence cognition in the wild. There are major hazards in generalizing from experimental research on age differences (or even age changes) in cognitive mechanisms and abilities to expected consequences of any observed age differences for cognition in the ecology. This has long been recognized as an issue in gerontology (e.g., Birren, 1974; Schonfield, 1974), but the practice of overgeneralization from laboratory to life can still be observed today.

Consider the following illustrations. There are substantial changes in fluid intelligence during adulthood. General intelligence has been argued to be a good personnel selection variable (e.g., Gottfredson, 2002). Is it therefore the case that age-related declines in fluid intelligence imply poor job performance by older adults? The answer is: Decidedly not (e.g., Waldman & Avolio, 1986). A study by Colonia-Willner (1998), for example, showed that practical intelligence in the workplace setting (measured in her case in mid-level managers in Brazilian banks) may be a more potent predictor of job performance than fluid intelligence. In real life, pragmatics often trump mechanics when it comes to predicting cognitive performance.

Denise Park, myself, and our colleagues (Hertzog, Park, Morrell, & Martin, 2000; Park et al., 1999) conducted a study of medication adherence in a cross-sectional sample of people with rheumatoid arthritis. Because cognition is required for remembering to take medications, we expected to see age-related declines in adherence behavior. This was not the case. Although cognitive ability predicted adherence, older adults were better at remembering to take medications. When cognitive ability was controlled for, older adults' adherence behavior was remarkably superior. The best predictor of adherence errors was self-reported busy-ness or a lack of a normal, routine daily schedule. A plausible explanation is that older adults anticipate the possibility of memory failure and convert the everyday adherence task to one that is supported by external aids, behavioral routines, and other methods to support remembering to take medications.

Psychologists who use descriptive performance functions on psychometric tests or experimental tasks to predict older adults' success in everyday cognition do so at their own peril. Such generalizations are crudely accurate (the prevalence of people with cognitive impairments that limit activities of daily living increases progressively in old age) but can be highly misleading about the functional capabilities of older adults. Moreover, when cognition predicts everyday function, it may be because it is a proxy for emerging but preclinical pathology, such as with Alzheimer's disease, rather than capturing an effect of normal aging. Finally, we need to understand that cognitive change is functionally problematic only when the decline lowers performance below a threshold that compromises effective functioning. Our theorizing about limitations in functional capacity of older adults may apply to only the oldest-old, not to individuals (arbitrarily) under the age of 80.

INDIVIDUAL DIFFERENCES IN THE EFFECTS OF AGING ON COGNITION

The foregoing discussion of functional aspects of adult cognition raises the issue of individual differences in the structure of cognition and in the effects of aging on cognition. An individual-differences perspective is implicitly central to the way in which gerontologists who do not focus on cognition think about psychological aging. The mission of the National Institute on Aging calls for research focusing on how to optimize the health and well-being, broadly defined, of older adults. Progress in this regard inevitably and inherently requires the understanding of how individuals differ in their level and structure of age-related change (Hertzog, 1985). Moreover, in my experience, most people are primarily concerned with understanding how they can improve their own cognitive functioning and about knowing whether they will be cognitively intact and functioning well in old age. Such views are based on a premise of differential aging: People grow older in different ways and at different rates.

Individual Differences in Rates of Cognitive Change

As Rowe and Kahn (1998) noted, the concept of successful aging implies individual differences in older adults' quality of life as well as longevity. The quest for understanding and isolating the causes of successful cognitive aging—preventing or ameliorating cognitive decline while maximizing opportunities for increasing knowledge and new learning—requires an understanding of the causes and consequences of individual differences in rates of cognitive aging. It also requires us to understand whether there are qualitative differences in (or subtypes of) age-correlated cognitive change. The fundamental problem with the term *cognitive aging* is that it carries an implied link to ontogenesis and a presumption of universal, nomothetic change (Dixon & Hertzog, 1996). Yet most experimental studies of cognitive aging make no attempt to isolate normal aging from pathological aging in contributing to observed age differences in cognition, let alone to explicitly measure antecedent variables that could explain individual differences in rates of cognitive change in adulthood.

From a methodological point of view, longitudinal data are critical to demonstrate that one is studying individual differences in change, not just adjusted cross-sectional age curves (e.g., Baltes & Nesselroade, 1979). Fortunately, longitudinal studies of cognition and related variables have become more common over the last 25 years (Hofer & Sliwinski, 2006). Individual differences in rates of cognitive aging have indeed been demonstrated in a number of different studies (e.g., Hertzog, Dixon, Hultsch, & MacDonald, 2003; Lövdén et al., 2004; Schaie, 2005), and these changes are related across different cognitive constructs in ways that are interpretable (but not always predictable) from cross-sectional results (see Hertzog, 2004; Hertzog et al., 2003). Rates of age-related change are gradual in normal populations, so individuals must be followed for several years for these differences to be measurable (Zelinski & Burnight, 1997).

There are probably multiple causes for individual differences in rates of cognitive change in late life. Even though senescence is a universal phenomenon, individuals may differ in rates of biological aging. Moreover, the distinction between normal aging and age-related pathology matters for cognition in old age. Although there are unresolved issues and controversies surrounding the concept of terminal decline, few question the idea that cognition is compromised by dementia, vascular pathology, and other chronic conditions above and beyond the effects of normal aging per se. Risk factors for onset of dementia vary by age, and the incidence of preclinical dementia, although correlated with age, varies independently of chronological age and contributes to individual differences in rates of cognitive aging (Sliwinski, Hofer, & Hall, 2003).

The Critical Role of Strategic Behavior

Understanding how cognition changes with aging requires an understanding of how individuals use strategies to achieve performance goals. The assessment of strategies matters for at least two reasons. First, strategic behavior is an important influence on individual differences in cognition. Hertzog, Dunlosky, and Robinson (2007) recently showed that spontaneous use of effective encoding strategies in paired-associate learning accounted for about 50% of the variance in associative recall, but none of the age-related variance. Accounting for strategies, then, helped to show that the age deficits could not be attributed to spontaneous strategy production.

On the other hand, spontaneous strategy production was related to fluid intelligence and crystallized intelligence. Such findings are consistent with conceptualizations of central executive functioning, frontal lobe involvement, and strategic behavior—but the relative sparing of strategic behavior in older adults places important constraints on the generality of the assumption that frontal decline accounts for age-related cognitive change.

Second, strategies can lead to qualitative shifts in behavior, and adaptive changes in goal-directed strategic behavior may be critical for understanding effective cognitive functioning. For example, Robinson (2004) found that both older and younger adults shift away from a verbal/analytic strategy in solving spatial reasoning problems to using a visuospatial representation when items become more complex, and they place more working memory demands on the analytic processing approach. Adaptivity is the hallmark of effective strategic compensation. Moreover, different strategies lead to different rates of success and failure for different items or tasks. Years ago, cognitive psychologists demonstrated that use of different strategic approaches can lead to very different patterns of correlations of background abilities with criterion task performance (e.g., Hunt, 1978). These different patterns presumably arise because Strategy A is performed by calling on one set of resources—say, Resource Set A—whereas Strategy B is performed by calling on a different, perhaps overlapping, set cognitive resources—say, Resource Set B. Individual differences within resource sets will tend to shape individual differences in performance using Strategy A or B, shifting the correlations of abilities with performance.

Now, say that it is the case that correlations of cognitive resources, such as working memory, with task performance differ between older and younger adults. Several studies suggest that working memory correlates more strongly with task performance in older adults than for younger adults (e.g., Hultsch et al., 1998). This could happen because of individual differences in rates of decline in working memory, coupled with the importance of working memory as a resource for cognition. However, such shifts could also reflect age differences in the types of strategies used, in relation to reliance on working memory intensive strategies, or some mixture of the two (Hertzog, 1985). Explicit attention to the issue of strategic behavior and measurement of strategies in task contexts is needed to disentangle these two classes of explanations.

Rogers, Hertzog, and Fisk (2000) showed that qualitative differences in strategies in a noun-pair task influenced not only age differences in reaction time (RT) but also patterns of correlations of cognitive tasks with criterion performance on the noun-pair task created by Ackerman and Woltz (1994). The task involves searching a look-up table of paired associates to determine whether a pair of words presented at central fixation is matched by one of the noun pairs in a look-up table shown at the top of the screen. Rates of practice-related performance improvements in the noun-pair task are primarily a function of shifting from visual search (scanning) to memory retrieval (which is enabled by incidental learning of the pairings). More important for our purposes is that large age differences are observed in rates of learning.

Rogers et al. (2000) found that an independent measure of associative learning ability correlated more strongly with noun-pair task performance for older adults than for younger adults, and this was ultimately attributable to older adults' delayed strategy shift. Some older adults relied on memory retrieval, and others did not, even after extensive practice, and this strategic variability increased the degree to which associative learning predicted the rate of improvement in associative learning. When they analyzed only older adults who shift to a retrieval strategy by the end of practice, individual differences in speed of access (retrieval) of information in semantic memory were the best predictor of practice improvements, matching the pattern of prediction in younger adults (who were almost all using the retrieval strategy by the end of practice).

What Causes Successful Cognitive Aging?

One of the major issues in aging research is whether engaging in intellectually stimulating activities can preserve cognitive function in old age. The major problem facing this research is

that this locus of causal influence is impossible to isolate experimentally but instead must be evaluated by correlational research. Although there is evidence consistent with this theory, we need more sustained efforts to test rival hypotheses.

The *cognitive stimulation hypothesis* has strong proponents (e.g., Schooler, Mulatu, & Oates, 1999) and some strong detractors (e.g., Salthouse, 2006). Tests of the hypothesis cannot simply rely on cross-sectional correlations of self-reported activities with cognition, because high levels of ability may lead to different patterns of activity early in life. What is less well appreciated is that there are rival explanations for finding associations of change in these two variables in longitudinal data as well (Hertzog, Hultsch, & Dixon, 1999). Discovering that change in cognition covaries with change in activity patterns could imply that "using it prevents losing it," but it could also reflect a pattern of curtailed activity in the face of cognitive decline. What is needed is critical evaluation of the theory at multiple levels of analysis (e.g., seeking to show enrichment effects at the level of both neuronal and behavior change) as well as measurement of intervening processes and derivative hypotheses. Moreover, we need to attend to methodological issues in evaluating the hypothesis. For instance, long-term longitudinal panel designs are at risk to miss a lot of the observable action regarding such a question, because they measure long-term stability and change in a temporal epoch that is probably out of synchrony with life events and other factors that influence cognitive change, in addition to any enrichment caused by activities.

THE PERFORMANCE–COMPETENCE DISTINCTION IN OLD AGE

Developmental psychologists have long understood the difference between inherent *competence* (what the child can, in principle, do) and *performance* (what the child does in a task environment). The distinction has played a role in gerontological research as well. An emphasis on understanding the processes by which individuals think, reason, and solve problems inevitably leads to the question of whether there are age differences in how cognition is constructed.

Attention to this issue is needed to ensure measurement equivalence (Baltes et al., 1988; Labouvie, 1980), without which we cannot be completely confident that psychometric tests or experimental tasks are measuring the same constructs for persons of different ages. Consider the work my colleague Dayna Touron and I have done studying the noun-pair lookup task described earlier (e.g., Touron & Hertzog, 2004a, 2004b). Some would attribute older adults' delayed strategy shift to age-related loss of the ability to form new associations, and little more. Although age deficits in associative learning undoubtedly contribute to these differences, we have shown that older adults' shift to the retrieval strategy is apparently delayed by other factors, including their metacognitive beliefs, their preferences for being accurate, and their mental model of the task (in terms of whether retrieval ultimately produces better performance). For example, Touron and Hertzog (2004b) showed delayed retrieval shift in older adults *after* individuals learned the pairings to a criterion before being transferred to the noun-pair task. Older adults still showed a delayed shift to the retrieval strategy, which we measured directly with item-level strategy self-reports after each trial. The delayed shift was roughly comparable when lists were mixed with 50% prelearned items and 50% new items, a finding that is inconsistent with a simple associative deficit. We also used interspersed recognition memory probes, in which the table was not shown, forcing people to respond on the basis of memory. Older adults showed a much lower conditional probability of retrieving an item they had previously gotten correct on the last recognition memory probe, suggesting that they were not basing the strategy choice on memory alone. Touron and Hertzog (2004a) showed that increasing the size of the lookup table encouraged older adults to shift more rapidly to retrieval, apparently because of the relative cost of scanning the larger table.

Recent studies indicate a role of beliefs and motivation in the delayed strategy shift. Hertzog and Touron (2006) demonstrated that a deficient mental model (one not appreciating the benefits of the retrieval strategy for faster RTs) correlates with the retrieval shift in both age groups but that older adults are far more likely to fail to appreciate the benefits of the retrieval strategy. Touron, Swaim, and Hertzog (2007) showed that instructions to use the retrieval strategy did not affect age differences in the shift, but providing monetary incentives did, rather dramatically, eliminate much of the age-related delay. In sum, older adults avoid the retrieval strategy, even when they could use it effectively to achieve much faster performance.

This effect is reminiscent of speed–accuracy trade-off issues when evaluating age differences in information-processing speed and, more generally, of work on cautiousness by older individuals in unfamiliar task environments (e.g., Botwinick, 1984). Although some accounts of general slowing emphasize the universality of the phenomenon, and argue for the close linkage between observed rates of slowing and neurobiological substrates (e.g., Cerella, 1990), others have pointed to the formidable problems of separating response criteria from RT in interpreting age differences in slowed speed of response. Recent work by Ratcliff and colleagues, for example (e.g., Ratcliff, Thapar, & McKoon, 2001) has emphasized the importance of response criterion over drift rate as contributing to age differences in speed of response on elementary perceptual and memory tasks.

The larger point is that one cannot treat age differences in RT or in rates of practice improvements in RT as a direct consequence of age changes in the underlying cognitive mechanisms—even when the role of these mechanisms in task performance has face validity. Task performance is generally complex and determined by multiple mechanisms. Older participants bring attitudes and beliefs into the experimental setting, and these variables influence performance whether we like it or not. In fact, without adequate attention to making sure their influence is minimized, they will have more influence on age differences in performance on our tasks than needs to be the case.

Conclusion

Theory and research regarding adult cognitive development must attend to issues of functional use of cognition in actual contexts, recognizing that the processing mechanisms we isolate and study may or may not be relevant to cognition in the wild. We need more attention to the functional impact of cognitive change on everyday cognition, and we cannot assume that observed declines in intellectual abilities or cognitive mechanisms inevitably imply ineffective functional cognition on the part of older adults.

From an individual-differences perspective, there is a clear and compelling need for new explanatory research that ties cognitive mechanisms and processes to antecedent conditions, both within the developing individual and in the larger social context in which that individual changes. We can expect continuing attention to functional brain measures as a class of explanations of age-related cognitive change; however, there is also a need for studies considering a wider range of antecedent conditions, consistent with probabilistic ideas of risk for age-related pathologies or contextual influences. Here, longitudinal studies such as the Seattle Longitudinal Study (Schaie, 2005), the Betula Study (e.g., Lövden et al., 2004), and others provide examples of how to integrate measures of systemic physiological function, genetic markers, lifestyle, family history, and social context into a larger research project. Studies like the Health Retirement Survey demonstrate the potential advantages of embedding cognitive measures in large national surveys that have the potential of understanding the role of cognition in economic decision making and for generating probability sample data on associations of personal characteristics with cognitive change (Herzog & Wallace, 1997).

Finally, more attention needs to be paid to how cognitive performance can be limited by factors that mislead investigators into inferring structural cognitive change on the basis of performance differences. The quality and efficiency of sensory and perceptual processes change with aging, and these can limit the quality of information to which older adults have access when they need it. Likewise, age differences in mental models of tasks, conservative decision criteria, and so on, can be mistaken for ontogenetic change. Gerontologists have been raising such issues for decades, but the problems must be addressed anew in each task paradigm. We cannot allow our well-founded belief that cognitive mechanisms change with aging to reinforce a stereotype of decline when we have not ruled out other explanations for observed age differences. Just as deficient thyroid production can mimic dementia, deficient task strategies and response criteria can masquerade as structural loss. In a sense, these are methodological issues, but they also speak to our theoretical filters and blinders. Research on adult cognitive development may well be headed toward a new golden age of advance, but it can do so only if the subtlety of our thinking matches the complexity of the phenomena we seek to understand.

REFERENCES

Ackerman, P. L., & Rolfhus, E. L. (1999). The locus of adult intelligence: Knowledge, abilities, and nonability traits. *Psychology and Aging, 14,* 314–330.

Ackerman, P. L., & Woltz, D. (1994). Determinants of learning and performance in an associative memory/substitution task: Task constraints, individual differences, volition, and motivation. *Journal of Educational Psychology, 86,* 487–515.

Allen, P. A., Weber, P. A., & May, N. (1993). Age differences in letter and color matching: Selective attention or internal noise? *Journal of Gerontology: Psychological Sciences, 48,* P59–P67.

Ball, K., Berch, D. B., Helmers, K. F., Jobe, J. B., Leveck, M. D., Marsiske, M., et al. (2002). Effects of cognitive training interventions with older adults: A randomized controlled trial. *Journal of the American Medical Association, 288,* 2271–2281.

Baltes, P. B., & Baltes, M. M. (1990). Psychological perspectives on successful aging: The model of selective optimization with compensation. In P. B. Baltes & M. M. Baltes (Eds.), *Successful aging: Perspectives from the behavioral sciences* (pp. 1–34). New York: Cambridge University Press.

Baltes, P. B., & Nesselroade, J. R. (1979). History and rationale of longitudinal research. In J. R. Nesselroade & P. B. Baltes (Eds.), *Longitudinal research in the study of behavior and development* (pp. 1–39). New York: Academic Press.

Baltes, P. B., Reese, H. W., & Nesselroade, J. R. (1988). *Life-span developmental psychology: Introduction to research methods.* Hillsdale, NJ: Lawrence Erlbaum.

Baltes, P. B., Staudinger, U., & Lindenberger, U. (1999). Lifespan psychology: Theory and application to intellectual functioning. *Annual Review of Psychology, 50,* 471–507.

Baltes, P. B., & Willis, S. L. (1977). Toward psychological theories of aging and development. In J. E. Birren & K. W. Schaie (Eds.), *Handbook of the psychology of aging* (pp. 128–154). New York: Van Nostrand Reinhold.

Berg, C. A., & Sternberg, R. J. (1985). A triarchic theory of intellectual development during adulthood. *Developmental Review, 5,* 334–370.

Bergman, L. R., Magnusson, D., & El-Khouri, B. M. (2003). *Studying individual development in an interindividual context: A person-oriented approach.* Mahwah, NJ: Lawrence Erlbaum.

Birren, J. E. (1974). Translations in gerontology: From lab to life. Psychophysiology and speed of response. *American Psychologist, 29,* 808–815.

Botwinick, J. (1984). *Aging and behavior* (3rd ed.). New York: Springer.

Butler, K. M., McDaniel, M. A., Dornberg, C. C., Price, A. L., & Roediger, H. L., III. (2004). Age differences in veridical and false recall are not inevitable: The role of frontal lobe function. *Psychonomic Bulletin and Review, 11,* 921–925.

Cabeza, R., Nyberg, L., & Park, D. C. (Eds.). (2003). *Cognitive neuroscience of aging: Linking cognitive and cerebral aging.* New York: Oxford University Press.

Carroll, J. B. (1993). *Human cognitive abilities: A survey of factor-analytic studies.* New York: Cambridge University Press.

Cerella, J. (1990). Aging and information processing rate. In J. E. Birren & K. W. Schaie (Eds.), *Handbook of the psychology of aging* (3rd ed., pp. 201–221). New York: Academic Press.

Colcombe, S., & Kramer, A. F. (2003). Fitness effects on the cognitive function of older adults: A meta-analytic study. *Psychological Science, 14,* 125–130.

Colonia-Willner, R. (1998). Practical intelligence at work: Relationship between aging and cognitive efficiency among managers in a bank environment. *Psychology and Aging, 23,* 591–614.

Craik, F. I. M., & Byrd, M. (1982). Aging and cognitive deficits: The role of attentional resources. In F. I. M. Craik & S. Trehub (Eds.), *Aging and cognitive processes* (pp. 191–211). New York: Plenum Press.

Craik, F. I. M., & Salthouse, T. A. (Eds.). (2000). *The handbook of aging and cognition.* Mahwah, NJ: Lawrence Erlbaum.

Cronbach, L. J. (1957). The two disciplines of scientific psychology. *American Psychologist, 12,* 671–684.

Dixon, R. A., & Hertzog, C. (1988). A functional approach to memory and metamemory development in adulthood. In F. Weinert & M. Perlmutter (Eds.), *Memory development: Universal changes and individual differences* (pp. 293–330). Hillsdale, NJ: Lawrence Erlbaum.

Dixon, R. A., & Hertzog, C. (1996). Theoretical issues in cognitive aging. In F. Blanchard-Fields & T. Hess (Eds.), *Perspectives on cognitive change in adult development and aging* (pp. 25–65). New York: McGraw-Hill.

Dodson, C. S., & Schacter, D. L. (2002). Aging and strategic retrieval processes: Reducing false memories with a distinctiveness heuristic. *Psychology and Aging, 17,* 405–415.

Dunlosky, J., Hertzog, C., Kennedy, M. R. T., & Thiede, K. W. (2005). The self-monitoring approach for effective learning. *Cognitive Technology, 10,* 4–11.

Ericsson, K. A., & Charness, N. (1994). Expert performance: Its structure and acquisition. *American Psychologist, 49,* 725–747.

Finkel, D., Pederson, N. L., Plomin, R., & McClearn, G. E. (1998). Longitudinal and cross-sectional twin data on cognitive abilities in adulthood: The Swedish Adoption/Twin Study of Aging. *Developmental Psychology, 34,* 1400–1413.

Fisher, D. L., & Glaser, R. A. (1996). Molar and latent models of cognitive slowing: Implications for aging, dementia, depression, development, and intelligence. *Psychonomic Bulletin & Review, 3,* 458–480.

Gigerenzer, G., Todd, P. M., & The ABC Research Group (1999). *Simple heuristics that make us smart.* New York: Oxford University Press.

Gottfredson, L. S. (2002). g: Highly general, highly practical. In R. J. Sternberg & E. S. Grigorenko (Eds.), *The general factor of intelligence: How general is it?* (pp. 331–380). Mahwah, NJ: Lawrence Erlbaum.

Gottlieb, G. (1998). Normally occurring environmental and behavioral influences on gene activity: From central dogma to probabilistic epigenesist. *Psychological Review, 105,* 792–802.

Hartley, A. A. (1993). Evidence for the selective preservation of spatial selective attention in old age. *Psychology and Aging, 8,* 371–379.

Hartley, A. A. (2006). Changing role of the speed of processing construct in the cognitive psychology of human aging. In J. E. Birren & K. W. Schaie (Eds.), *Handbook of the psychology of aging* (6th ed., pp. 183–207). San Diego, CA: Academic Press.

Hasher, L., & Zacks, R. (1988). Working memory, comprehension, and aging: A review and a new view. In G. H. Bower (Ed.), *The psychology of learning and motivation: Advances in research and theory* (Vol. 22, pp. 193–225). San Diego, CA: Academic Press.

Hasher, L., Zacks, R. T., & May, C. P. (1999). Inhibitory control, circadian arousal, and age. In D. Gopher & A. Koriat (Eds.), *Attention and performance XVII: Cognitive regulation of performance* (pp. 653–675). Cambridge, MA: MIT Press.

Hertzog, C. (1985). An individual differences perspective: Implications for cognitive research in gerontology. *Research on Aging, 7,* 7–45.

Hertzog, C. (1989). The influence of cognitive slowing on age differences in intelligence. *Developmental Psychology, 25,* 636–651.

Hertzog, C. (1996). Research design in studies of aging and cognition. In J. E. Birren & K. W. Schaie (Eds.), *Handbook of the psychology of aging* (4th ed., pp. 24–37). New York: Academic Press.

Hertzog, C. (2004). Does longitudinal evidence confirm theories of cognitive aging derived from cross-sectional data? In R. A. Dixon, L. Bäckman, & L.-G. Nilsson (Eds.), *New frontiers for cognitive aging research* (pp. 41–64). Oxford, UK: Oxford University Press.

Hertzog, C., & Dixon, R. A. (1996). Methodological issues in research on cognition and aging. In F. Blanchard-Fields & T. Hess (Eds.), *Perspectives on cognitive change in adult development and aging* (pp. 66–121). New York: McGraw-Hill.

Hertzog, C., Dixon, R. A., Hultsch, D. F., & MacDonald, S. W. S. (2003). Latent change models of adult cognition: Are changes in processing speed and working memory associated with changes in episodic memory? *Psychology and Aging, 18,* 755–769.

Hertzog, C., Dunlosky, J., & Robinson, A. E. (2007). *Intellectual abilities and metacognitive beliefs influence spontaneous use of effective encoding strategies.* Manuscript in preparation.

Hertzog, C., & Hultsch, D. F. (2000). Metacognition in adulthood and old age. In F. I. M. Craik & T. A. Salthouse (Eds.), *The handbook of aging and cognition* (pp. 417–466). Hillsdale, NJ: Lawrence Erlbaum.

Hertzog, C., Hultsch, D. F., & Dixon, R. A. (1999). On the problem of detecting effects of lifestyle on cognitive change in adulthood: Reply to Pushkar et al. *Psychology and Aging, 14,* 528–534.

Hertzog, C., & Nesselroade, J. R. (2003). Assessing psychological change in adulthood: An overview of methodological issues. *Psychology and Aging, 18,* 639–657.

Hertzog, C., Park, D. C., Morrell, R. W., & Martin, M. (2000). Ask and ye shall receive: Behavioral specificity in the accuracy of subjective memory complaints. *Applied Cognitive Psychology, 14,* 257–275.

Hertzog, C., & Touron, D. R. (2006, April). *Aging and individual differences in algorithm to retrieval shift with task practice.* Paper presented at the Cognitive Aging Conference, Atlanta, GA.

Herzog, A. R., & Wallace, R. B. (1997). Measures of cognitive functioning in the AHEAD Study. *Journal of Gerontology: Psychological Sciences, 52,* P37–P48.

Hofer, S. M., & Sliwinski, M. J. (2006). Design and analysis of longitudinal studies on aging. In J. E. Birren & K. W. Schaie (Eds.), *Handbook of the psychology of aging* (6th ed., pp. 15–37). San Diego, CA: Academic Press.

Horn, J. L. (1989). Models of intelligence. In R. L. Linn (Ed.), *Intelligence: Measurement, theory, and public policy* (pp. 29–73). Urbana: University of Illinois Press.

Horn, J. L., & Hofer, S. M. (1992). Major abilities and development in the adult period. In R. J. Sternberg & C. A. Berg (Eds.), *Intellectual development* (pp. 44–99). New York: Cambridge University Press.

Hoyer, W. J., & Ingolfsdottir, D. (2003). Age, skill, and contextual cueing in target detection. *Psychology and Aging, 18,* 210–218.

Hoyer, W. J., & Verhaeghen, P. (2006). Memory aging. In J. E. Birren & K. W. Schaie (Eds.), *Handbook of the psychology of aging* (6th ed., pp. 209–232). San Diego, CA: Academic Press.

Hultsch, D. F., Hertzog, C., Dixon, R. A., & Small, B. J. (1998). *Memory change in the aged*. New York: Cambridge University Press.

Hunt, E. (1978). Mechanics of verbal ability. *Psychological Review, 85,* 109–130.

Jacoby, L. L. (1999). Ironic effects of repetition: Measuring age related differences in memory. *Journal of Experimental Psychology: Learning, Memory, and Cognition, 25,* 3–22.

Jennings, J. M., & Jacoby, L. L. (1997). An opposition procedure for detecting age-related deficits in recollection: Telling effects of repetition. *Psychology and Aging, 12,* 352–361.

Johnson, M. K., & Raye, C. L. (2000). Cognitive and brain mechanisms of false memories and beliefs. In D. L. Schacter & E. Scarry (Eds.), *Memory, brain, and belief* (pp. 35–86). Cambridge, MA: Harvard University Press.

Kane, M. J., & Engle, R. W. (2003). The contributions of goal neglect, response competition, and task set to Stroop interference. *Journal of Experimental Psychology: General, 132,* 47–70.

Kramer, A. F., Boot, W. F., McCarley, J. S., Peterson, M. S., Colcombe, A., & Scialfa, C. T. (2006). Aging, memory, and visual search. *Acta Psychologica, 122,* 288–304.

Labouvie, E. W. (1980). Measurement of individual differences in intraindividual changes. *Psychological Bulletin, 88,* 54–59.

Lawton, M. P. (1990). Residential environment and self-directedness among older people. *American Psychologist, 45,* 638–640.

Li, S.-C. (2005). Neurocomputational perspectives linking neuromodulation, processing noise, representational distinctiveness, and cognitive aging. In R. Cabeza, L. Nyberg, & D. C. Park (Eds.), *Cognitive neuroscience of aging: Linking cognitive and cerebral aging* (pp. 354–379). New York: Oxford University Press.

Light, L. L., Prull, M. W., La Voie, D. J., & Healy, M. R. (2000). Dual-process models of memory in old age. In T. J. Perfect & E. A. Maylor (Eds.), *Models of cognitive aging* (pp. 238–300). New York: Oxford University Press.

Lövdén, M., Rönnlund, M., Wahlin, A., Bäckman, L., Nyberg, L., & Goran-Nilsson, L. (2004). The extent of stability and change in episodic and semantic memory in old age: Demographic predictors of stability and change. *Journal of Gerontology: Psychological Sciences, 59B,* P130–P134.

Lustig, C., May, C. P., & Hasher, L. (1999). Working memory span and the role of proactive interference. *Journal of Experimental Psychology: General, 130,* 199–207.

Masunaga, H., & Horn, J. L. (2001). Expertise and age-related changes in components of intelligence. *Psychology and Aging, 16,* 293–311.

McArdle, J. J., Ferrer-Caja, E., Hamagami, F., & Woodcock, R. W. (2002). Comparative longitudinal structural analyses of the growth and decline of multiple intellectual abilities over the life span. *Developmental Psychology, 38,* 115–142.

Nesselroade, J. R. (1991). The warp and woof of the developmental fabric. In R. Downs, L. Liben, & D. S. Palermo (Eds.), *Visions of development, the environment, and aesthetics: The legacy of Joachim F. Wohlwill* (pp. 213–240). Hillsdale, NJ: Lawrence Erlbaum.

Park, D. C. (1992). Applied cognitive aging research. In F. I. M. Craik & T. A. Salthouse (Eds.), *The handbook of aging and cognition* (pp. 449–493). Hillsdale, NJ: Lawrence Erlbaum.

Park, D. C., Hertzog, C., Leventhal, H., Morrell, R. W., Leventhal, E., Birchmore, D., et al. (1999). Medication adherence in rheumatoid arthritis patients: Older is wiser. *Journal of the American Geriatrics Society, 47,* 172–183.

Park, D. C., Lautenschlager, G., Hedden, T., Davidson, N. S., Smith, A. S., & Smith, P. K. (2002). Models of visuospatial and verbal memory across the adult life span. *Psychology and Aging, 17,* 299–320.

Rahhal, T. A., May, C. P., & Hasher, L. (2002). Truth and character: Sources that older adults can remember. *Psychological Science, 13,* 101–105.

Ram, N., Rabbitt, P. M. A., Stollery, B., & Nesselroade, J. R. (2005). Cognitive performance inconsistency: Intraindividual change and variability. *Psychology and Aging, 20,* 623–633.

Ratcliff, R., Thapar, A., & McKoon, G. (2001). The effects of aging on reaction time in a signal detection task. *Psychology and Aging, 16,* 323–341.

Riedeger, M., Li, S., & Lindenberger, U. (2006). Selection, optimization, and compensation as developmental mechanisms of adaptive resource allocation: Review and preview. In J. E. Birren & K. W. Schaie (Eds.), *Handbook of the psychology of aging* (6th ed., pp. 289–310). San Diego, CA: Academic Press.

Robinson, A. E. (2004). *The role of item complexity, strategies, instructions, and aging in relational deductive reasoning.* Unpublished master's thesis, Georgia Institute of Technology.

Rogers, W. A., Hertzog, C., & Fisk, A. D. (2000). Age-related differences in associative learning: An individual differences analysis of ability and strategy influences. *Journal of Experimental Psychology: Learning, Memory, and Cognition, 26,* 359–394.

Rowe, J. W., & Kahn, R. L. (1998). *Successful aging.* New York: Pantheon.

Rybash, J. M., Hoyer, W. J., & Roodin, P. A. (1986). *Adult cognition and aging: Developmental changes in processing, knowing, and thinking.* New York: Pergamon Press.

Salthouse, T. A. (1985). Speed of behavior and its implications for cognition. In J. E. Birren & K. W. Schaie (Eds.), *Handbook of the psychology of aging* (2nd ed., pp. 400–426). New York: Van Nostrand Reinhold.

Salthouse, T. A. (1991). *Theoretical perspectives on cognitive aging.* Hillsdale, NJ: Lawrence Erlbaum.

Salthouse, T. A. (1996). The processing-speed theory of adult age differences in cognition. *Psychological Review, 103,* 403–428.

Salthouse, T. A. (2006). Mental exercise and mental aging: Evaluating the validity of the "use it or lose it" hypothesis. *Perspectives on Psychological Science, 1,* 68–87.

Salthouse, T. A., & Ferrer-Caja, E. (2003). What needs to be explained to account for age-related effects on multiple cognitive variables? *Psychology and Aging, 18,* 91–110.

Schacter, D. L. (1999). The seven sins of memory: Insights from psychology and cognitive neuroscience. *American Psychologist, 54,* 182–203.

Schaie, K. W. (1977). Quasi-experimental designs in the psychology of aging. In J. E. Birren & K. W. Schaie (Eds.), *Handbook of the psychology of aging* (pp. 39–58). New York: Van Nostrand Reinhold.

Schaie, K. W. (2005). *Developmental influences on adult intelligence.* New York: Oxford University Press.

Schonfield, D. (1974). Translations in gerontology: From lab to life. Utilizing information. *American Psychologist, 29,* 796–801.

Schooler, C., Mulatu, M. S., & Oates, G. (1999). The continuing effects of substantively complex work on the intellectual functioning of older workers. *Psychology and Aging, 14,* 483–506.

Shadish, W., Cook, T. D., & Campbell, D. T. (2002). *Experimental and quasi-experimental designs for generalized causal inference.* Boston: Houghton Mifflin.

Sliwinski, M., & Buschke, H. (1999). Cross-sectional and longitudinal relationships among age, cognition, and processing speed. *Psychology and Aging, 14,* 18–33.

Sliwinski, M. J., Hofer, S. M., & Hall, C. (2003). Correlated and coupled cognitive change in older adults with and without preclinical dementia. *Psychology and Aging, 18,* 672–683.

Touron, D. R., & Hertzog, C. (2004a). Age differences in knowledge, strategy use, and confidence during skill acquisition. *Psychology and Aging, 19,* 452–466.

Touron, D. R., & Hertzog, C. (2004b). Strategy shift affordance and strategy choice in young and older adults. *Memory & Cognition, 32,* 298–310.

Touron, D. R., Swaim, E. T., & Hertzog, C. (2007). Moderation of older adults' retrieval reluctance through task instructions and monetary incentives. *Journal of Gerontology: Psychological Sciences, 62B,* P149–P155.

Verhaeghen, P., Cerella, J., & Basak, C. (2006). Aging, task complexity, and efficiency modes: The influence of working memory involvement on age differences in response times for verbal and visuospatial tasks. *Aging, Neuropsychology, and Cognition, 13,* 254–280.

Waldman, D. A., & Avolio, B. J. (1986). A meta-analysis of age differences in job performance. *Journal of Applied Psychology, 71,* 33–38.

Welford, A. T. (1958). *Ageing and human skill.* Oxford, UK: Oxford University Press.

Willis, S. L. (2001). Methodological issues in behavioral intervention research with the elderly. In J. E. Birren & K. W. Schaie (Eds.), *Handbook of the psychology of aging* (5th ed., pp. 78–108). San Diego, CA: Academic Press.

Wohlwill, J. F. (1973). *The study of behavioral development.* New York: Academic Press.

Wohlwill, J. F. (1991). The partial isomorphism between developmental theory and methods. *Annals of Theoretical Psychology, 6,* 1–43.

Zacks, R., Hasher, L., & Li, K. Z. H. (2000). Human memory. In F. I. M. Craik & T. A. Salthouse (Eds.), *The handbook of aging and cognition* (2nd ed., pp. 293–357). Mahwah, NJ: Lawrence Erlbaum.

Zelinski, E. M., & Burnight, K. P. (1997). Sixteen-year longitudinal and time-lag changes in memory and cognition in older adults. *Psychology and Aging, 12,* 503–513.

3

INTEGRATIVE PERSPECTIVES ON COGNITIVE AGING

Measurement and Modeling With Mixtures of Psychological and Biological Variables

KEITH F. WIDAMAN

Cognitive aging, as a field, is and must be an integrative science, a contention based on any review of the phenomena under study and their likely causal structure. As one example, consider research on cognitive slowing. For over four decades, notions of cognitive slowing have been the object of intense and continuing study. The central claim of theories of cognitive slowing is that the human brain is analogous to the central processor of a computer, that this central processor has a clock that governs the speed at which mental operations can occur and that the speed at which our mental clock "ticks" slows as a function of advancing chronological age. The age-related slowing of this clock speed is reputed to have very general effects on all, or many, forms of cognitive functioning, leading to a general slowing of the processing of information. Many research studies have produced data consistent with the theory of generalized cognitive slowing (cf. Madden, 2001, for a review), although some studies yield data that conflict with the fully general nature of this slowing. For example, Jenkins, Myerson, Joerding, and Hale (2000) found differential age-related slowing on verbal and visuospatial tasks.

More important for the current chapter is the failure to identify definitively the neurocognitive bases of cognitive slowing. This lack of a clear and obvious tie to brain functioning is not unique to research on cognitive slowing. Instead, many domains of research in cognitive aging include theorizing about the biological or brain processes underlying replicated empirical trends on psychological measures, where these empirical trends are based on response measures such as reaction time or percentage correct

AUTHOR'S NOTE: This research was supported by grants from the National Institute of Child Health and Human Development, the National Institute on Drug Abuse, and the National Institute of Mental Health (HD047573, HD051746, and MH051361).

on memory measures. The theoretical bases for these effects on psychological measures often concern changes in brain structure or function. Researchers then rely on general trends in changes in brain structure or function that are verified in other studies (e.g., autopsy studies) to provide the theoretical explanations that underlie and therefore account for the observed, age-related changes in psychological measures. However, if biological measures that reflect brain structure or function are not included in the analytic models in a given empirical study, then the conjecture that brain changes account for or explain the changes on psychological measures is simply that, a conjecture, with little explanatory force other than consistency with results. Such conjectures abound in current literature and are not subject to disconfirmation because analyses are never performed to test the conjectures directly. That this criticism is not unique to cognitive aging, but applies to research in most areas of study in psychology, does not diminish its force in relation to research on cognitive aging.

We are now at an interesting historical point in research on cognitive aging in particular and behavioral science in general, as innovations in measurement and modeling that are becoming available portend advances in integrative approaches to understanding cognitive aging. The primary goals of this chapter are to discuss issues related to measurement and modeling; to describe the implications of choices in measurement or modeling that can impact research on cognitive aging; and then to describe some recent research applications that have incorporated biological, or at least nonpsychological, measures to illuminate age-related trends in cognitive phenomena.

Issues Related to Measurement and Modeling

The main premise of this chapter is that measurement and the modeling of any psychological phenomenon are intimately linked. This link is so close that advances in either measurement or modeling approaches can stimulate and inform the other. New or more accurate measurements in new domains enable researchers to test new theoretical conjectures using current approaches to modeling of data. Indeed, current research in cognitive neuropsychology—through the use of techniques such as structural magnetic resonance imaging (MRI) or functional magnetic resonance imaging (fMRI)—is but one example of a field in which new types of measurement inform researchers of current states of brain structure or function that can be related to traditional psychological measures to test theoretical conjectures. On the other hand, new models or methods of analysis can lead to the testing of relations that would have been impossible previously. This allows the use of standard measurements in new and interesting ways to uncover or represent aging phenomena in illuminating ways.

Measurement

Measurement Theory. Psychological measurement has undergone tremendous development during the past century. In an early contribution, Spearman (1904) introduced many key concepts associated with classical test theory, including the notion of an observed measure being an additive combination of true and error scores. The basic assumption of this approach is that item or test scores are linearly related to the true score underlying the instrument, with a stochastic error term as an additive component. Spearman discussed the correction for attenuation, which provides an estimate of the correlation between the true scores on two measures, as the effects of measurement error on the correlation are eliminated. Within a decade, the Spearman–Brown prophecy formula was developed (Brown, 1910; Spearman, 1910), a formula that expresses the predicted changes in reliability of a measure if the measure were lengthened or shortened a particular number of times. Somewhat later, Kuder and Richardson (1937) provided landmark indices of internal consistency reliability—the KR-20 and KR-21 coefficients embodied in Equations 20 and 21 of their article—and Guttman (1945) and Cronbach (1951) generalized the KR-20 index to coefficient alpha, for internal consistency reliability for data on a more-than-dichotomous scale. By mid-century, Gullickson (1950) summarized classical test theory in a surprisingly complete and modern fashion. Certainly, contributions in the classical test theory vein continue to be made, but most basic procedures associated with classical test theory that are used every day were complete over a half-century ago.

Even as classical test theory was nearing a plateau in fundamental contributions, a new approach—termed *item response theory* (IRT) or *modern test theory*—was initiated. Lord (1952) offered a new and different approach to measurement theory, an approach that has evolved into a wide array of IRT techniques. This new measurement theory was initially designed for dichotomously scored items (i.e., items scored as 1 = passed, 0 = failed). Items that are scored in dichotomous fashion cannot meet the usual assumptions invoked in classical test theory, because errors cannot be normally distributed. Under IRT, item scores and the underlying latent dimension are related through a link function; the most commonly used link function is the logistic. The relation between classical test theory and the newer, modern approaches to test theory were examined in detail by Lord and Novick (1968). Recently, Embretson and Reise (2000) summarized basic research on IRT models at a level accessible to the practicing scientist, so that applied researchers would be able to understand and use IRT methods, and McDonald (1999) provided a very readable account of both classical and modern test theory methods.

Measurement in Practice: Psychometrically Superior Versus "Good Enough" Measures. If psychometric theory has been taken to a relatively advanced state, questions naturally arise regarding the impact of advanced levels of measurement on the testing of psychological theories, or at least the testing of key conjectures based on psychological theories. Any survey of research on cognitive aging would conclude that the clear majority of the measuring instruments are classically designed measures that are identical to or indistinguishable from measures that were developed by Thurstone and his colleagues in the 1930s (e.g., Thurstone, 1938; Thurstone & Thurstone, 1941). For example, the major measures of adult intelligence used by Schaie (2005) in the Seattle Longitudinal Study are closely based on Thurstonian measures that were developed over 70 years ago. This fact is not an indictment of current research on cognitive aging; the

measures developed by Thurstone and others in the 1930s are instruments with very solid psychometric properties. Furthermore, the ability to tie these measurements to results across the ensuing 70 years adds strength to the results of current studies. However, it remains true that little in the way of sophisticated measurement approaches based on modern test theory—or IRT—has found its way into current test batteries.

More problematic is the trend toward reducing the form of measures, such as cutting down the number of items on a scale to create a short form, presuming that newer statistical models can work wonders with "good enough" measures of this sort. Structural equation modeling (SEM) is ever increasing in its application, and researchers are told that the use of multiple indicators of a latent construct in SEM results in latent variables that are represented at an error-free level. Perhaps because of this, some researchers trim down their measures to as small a number of items as possible, presuming that SEM can correct for the slimmed down measurements. Prior to the widespread use of SEM, creating short forms of measures caused problems associated with lowered reliability, including the attenuation of relations with other variables. SEM appears to be a savior in such situations, allowing the inclusion of short-form measures as indicators of a latent construct. But any statistical model, including any structural equation model, is only as good as the manifest variables included in it. Use of short-form versions of standard measures leads to weaker relations between latent and manifest variables, leading to greater uncertainty about the nature of the latent variables identified. Although the use of short-form measures in large studies can be understood, the use of such measures should not be condoned or encouraged.

Efficiency. Efficiency of measurement is always an issue in study design. Researchers strive to assess each individual on as many measures relevant to the theoretical question as can be included reasonably in a research protocol, assuring maximal psychometric properties of measures even as they maximize sample size. Standard measures, such as those employed in the Seattle Longitudinal Study, are very efficient in many ways, and the reliability and validity of the measures are well known. The amount of time to take each test is minimized, because the test formats have been standardized to provide optimal reliability in as short a time as possible. In addition, some researchers use short forms of standard measures, as discussed above, in aiming to assess variables in as efficient a manner as possible.

However, efficiency of measurement can be increased in any number of ways, not always and simply through the use of short-form measures. For example, increased efficiency in measurement could be obtained if advances based on IRT were used in formulating test batteries. Perhaps the greatest increase in efficiency would derive from the use of computerized adaptive testing (CAT). In CAT, an item of middling difficulty is selected randomly from a pool of items as the first item administered to a participant. If the participant gets the item correct, the person presumably has true ability higher than the difficulty of the item, so a more difficult item is selected and administered. On the other hand, if the respondent gets the item incorrect, the person's true level of ability is probably lower than the difficulty of this item, so a less difficult item is selected for administration. Test administration continues in this fashion until the person's true ability is estimated with a prespecified level of accuracy (e.g., a 95% confidence interval around the person's estimated score that is of a given width or less). Typical investigations of CAT find that most respondents need respond to only one third to one half of the usual number of items to achieve a score that has comparable psychometric properties to those for the typical full test or scale. Thus, if CAT approaches were used, testing time for each participant might be cut by half or more with no loss at all in the psychometric properties of resulting scores. Rather than using short-form measures that typically have poor psychometric properties, extant procedures can assure high-quality scores with minimal testing time, and these approaches should be adapted for use in studies of cognitive aging.

Extensive Measurement: Participants Versus Measurements. The design of studies on cognitive aging must also deal with the extensiveness of measurements obtained. By *extensiveness*, I refer to the sheer amount of data collected in a study, which is a function of the number of persons included in the study and the amount of information obtained from each participant on each measure. Any data collection takes time and, as either of these dimensions of extensiveness increases, the time and expense of collecting data increase at least linearly.

One interesting approach to truly extensive sample sizes was discussed by Herbert Toops in the 1930s under the heading of The Standard Million (R. J. Wherry, personal communication, 1977). The idea behind The Standard Million was this: If 1,000 psychologists each were responsible for testing or assessing 1,000 participants, then a total of 1 million persons from across the United States could be assessed each year. Toops argued that the participating psychologists could meet each year at the annual meeting of the American Psychological Association to decide which measures to include in a core battery that all participants in The Standard Million would receive. Then, breakout sessions of smaller numbers of psychologists interested in particular additional substantive domains could be held; each breakout session would add an additional set of measures for the participants assessed. For example, if 100 psychologists were interested in cognitive or intellectual aging, they could meet together and decide on a battery of measures in this domain to be added to the core battery. This would generate a sample of 100,000 participants with scores on the measures of cognitive or intellectual ability, and these participants would also have scores on the core battery administered to all 1 million participants, so one could assess how representative of the entire Standard Million was the sample of 100,000 with cognitive or intellectual ability measures. Needless to say, the idea of The Standard Million never took flight, but ever-increasing opportunities for assessing participants in efficient ways—such as over the Internet—may make The Standard Million more of a possibility now than was formerly the case.

A second approach that is a state-of-the-art suggestion, which has many obvious ties to the Standard Million proposal, is the use of *planned missingness designs* (Graham, Hofer, & MacKinnon, 1996; Graham, Taylor, & Cumsille, 2001; McArdle, 1994). Under planned missingness designs, participants are assigned randomly to one of several data collection protocols, and each protocol includes only some of the measures to be obtained in the study. Consider a simple example in which a protocol can be broken into four sections (S1 through S4). The researcher could then randomly assign participants to one of six conditions, with participants in each condition receiving only one half of the protocol. The six groups would consist of samples that received protocol sections S1 and S2, S1 and S3, S1 and S4, S2 and S3, S2 and S4, and S3 and S4, respectively. Under this approach, the testing time for each participant could be cut in half, reducing substantially the amount of time and effort to collect, code, and clean data. Current state-of-the-art analysis programs can handle quite nicely data from planned missingness designs. Furthermore, under random assignment to groups, missing data are truly missing completely at random, reducing worries about bias in parameter estimates. Simulation studies of the effects of planned missingness on parameter estimates and standard errors reveal that this approach to study design can reduce substantially effort by all concerned and still lead to high-quality results that differ little from results from complete data analyses (see, e.g., Graham et al., 1996, 2001).

"Data Rich, Theory Poor" Versus "Theory Rich, Data Poor." Some research studies amass mounds and mounds of data, in the hopes of engaging in exploratory analyses that will yield a simplified model that can make sense of the data. The hope is that an inductive, data-driven procedure of this sort can yield a reasonable empirically derived theory that is a worthy basis for future research. One approach that, at first blush, appears to fit this characterization is the work by Glymour, Spirtes, Scheines, and colleagues (e.g., Spirtes, Glymour, & Scheines, 1993, 2000). The TETRAD project by Glymour and colleagues was an explicit attempt to develop a computer program that would search a general model space to uncover causal structures that were consistent with data. As discussed by Scheines, Sprites, Glymour, Meek, and Richardson (1998a, 1998b), to argue that the TETRAD project is an attempt to have computers find the causal structure that generated data is misleading and an oversimplification. Instead, the TETRAD approach requires evaluation of the output of model search procedures in the context of background knowledge,

and this background knowledge must be supplied by the scientist with knowledge about how things work. Given this information, a computer program can use any of several algorithms that search for structural models that best fit the data. Of course, different models that fit the data equally well are not all equally useful as summaries of the data or as theoretical accounts of the data. However, the development of multiple, alternative models that fit the data equally well is a useful adjunct to our usual procedures in which we evaluate only those models that are aligned with our theories.

The opposite situation, which can be identified as being "theory rich, but data poor," is almost certainly more common in psychology in general and cognitive aging in particular. In many areas of psychology, theoretical bases are proposed for observed patterns in data. Unfortunately, the theoretical bases for the results are not instantiated in measures in an empirical study. For example, in studies of cognitive aging, various brain processes that exhibit negative changes during adulthood and aging are often posited to be responsible for aging trends on cognitive measures. As is reiterated many times in this chapter, if measures of these brain processes are not included in our statistical models, attributing aging changes to presumed changes in brain structure or function become "just so" stories, impossible to confirm and, more important, impossible to disconfirm.

Modeling

The modeling of data takes many forms, from the simplest forms of correlational analyses to rather more complex structural equation and dynamic approaches to modeling trends in empirical data. In this section, I discuss certain aspects of modeling of data that lead to questions regarding proper use of methods at all levels of sophistication.

Modeling Rich, Measurement Poor: The Cart Before the Horse? One basic and pervasive problem in the modeling of data is captured by the description of "modeling rich, measurement poor." I refer here to attempts to apply highly sophisticated methods of analysis to data that are, in general, not up to the task. Many state-of-the-art modeling techniques require strong assumptions, including linearity of relations between variables and multivariate normality, assumptions that are unlikely to be met by many or any measures included in a particular study. In effect, modeling moves by leaps and bounds, rapidly extending beyond the quality of the measurements to which the models are fit. As a result, researchers must wrestle with measures of model fit that are on the border of acceptability, not because a particular model is far from correct but because the data fail to conform to the assumptions that underlie the approach to modeling the data even though the model is approximately correct. Given the increasing complexity of statistical models, the field of cognitive aging should commit some concerted effort toward improving the measurement or psychometric qualities of measures to ensure that the measures are adequate for sophisticated modeling. The modeling cart often appears to be leading the measurement horse, and researchers should strive to get horse and cart back in the proper order.

At least two additional problems related to weak measurement can be identified. The first of these problems is the use of a small number of indicators to provide the statistical basis for modeling. In SEM, researchers are often advised to have three or more indicators for each latent variable in the model, but this is often either impossible or extremely difficult to obtain. Multiple indicators are impossible for certain latent variables; for example, chronological age is usually best indexed by the single variable of age in years, and additional indicators seem unnecessary or inappropriate. Beyond obvious exceptions of this nature, researchers sometimes use only one or two indicators for a latent variable, when use of three or more indicators could be developed, because the design of a study precluded the collection of a sufficient amount of data to support three or more indicators. Researchers should be encouraged to plan to use three or more indicators for each core latent variable in a model so they can design their studies to meet this stipulation.

The second additional problem is a tendency to use the shortest form of a measure for each indicator in a model. Because this problem was discussed in some detail earlier, I will simply note that optimal forms of modeling data will not be as useful if short-form measures are used as indicators. Short forms may be adequate for asking very basic questions about effects, but asking advanced questions, such as the form of the relation between key constructs, will often be possible only if the indicators are substantial measures. Short forms enable the inclusion of many variables in a study, but the qualities of the answers obtained will be limited by the quality of the measures.

Characterizing Differences. In a seminal paper that deserves to be read with regularity, Tukey (1969) chided the field of psychology for its general approach to data analyses. Tukey argued that our reliance on null hypothesis significance testing leads us to focus on whether a significant difference is present and, if a significance difference is found, the direction of that difference. He followed up this observation by arguing that the field of psychology should move beyond such low-level concerns and begin asking how large a particular difference is. Any comparison of psychology with more mature sciences would demonstrate that our field lags behind other fields in the specificity with which we describe trends in our data. The past 30 years have seen considerable strides in characterizing the magnitudes of differences, with many papers including measures of effect size in standard deviation (e.g., the use of Cohen's d) or explained variance metrics. One can only hope that effect size indicators will become yet more common in psychological research in the future. Only if this occurs will researchers be able to determine whether they are truly replicating and extending prior research or, more importantly, failing either to replicate results from prior research or to confirm theoretical conjectures.

One final concern regarding magnitude of effects derives from concerns about the psychometric qualities of our measures. In short, any index of the magnitude of an effect is meaningful only if measurements are precise. Elementary psychometric theory can be used to demonstrate the attenuation of the relation between two variables as unreliability in each variable increases. The attenuation of the relation is then translated into a smaller index of magnitude of effects using virtually any index of effect size. Thus, effect size estimates are only as good as the measurements on which they are based, emphasizing once again the need for the highest quality measures to be included in our studies.

MEASUREMENT AND MODELING: THE M&Ms OF COGNITIVE AGING

Measurement and modeling are so intimately entwined that we must continually be wary of falling into conceptual traps, limited in our outlook by the measures or the models we employ. To circumvent these traps, we should ask whether our measures and models are adequate for representing the relations we think hold between constructs.

Linearity of Relations

Many of our most popular models in psychology are linear models, whether these are regression, analysis of variance, or structural equation models. With the increasing importance of brain and other physiological processes in understanding cognitive aging, researchers would do well to compare our standard approaches to those used in collateral fields. Perhaps the closest collateral field is biology, and the equations employed in state-of-the-art biological research are not linear; neither are they quadratic. Instead, equations in biological research usually specify nonlinear functional relations among variables, with dynamic systems modeling being increasingly used. Dynamic systems modeling approaches are beginning to appear in psychological research, and we should applaud this trend. But even as we commend the use of these models we should question our general reliance on models that stipulate linear relations among variables.

Nonlinearities

As Widaman (2007) argued, linear models are poor choices for most developmental functions. Linear functions have no lower or upper asymptotes, yet such asymptotes would be posited in almost any behavioral domains. We often assess age-related changes over such a restricted range of the age continuum that little

more than linear relations can be estimated. If a wide span of ages were included in a study, however, then researchers who use only linear models should be prodded for explanations for their analytic approach. Even if nothing more than a linear relation between variables can be estimated in a given study, researchers should caution readers that nonlinearities are likely to appear outside the restricted boundaries of a current study.

A related issue tied to nonlinearity of relations among variables relates back to the properties of our measurements. Nonlinear relations between variables are likely to be replicable and accurate reflections of empirical results only if our measurements have very strong psychometric properties, the sample size is large, and the range of scores on measures is sufficiently broad. Nonlinear relations will be estimated accurately only if the measurements on which they are based have high measurement precision at all points along any relevant continuum (e.g., the age continuum, the range of individual differences on a given trait scale). Because nonlinear models tend to be more sensitive than linear models to influential data points, large and representative samples of participants should be employed. Finally, the full dynamic range of all variables should be employed in a study to ensure that the nonlinear relation obtained did not arise from some form of restricted sampling.

Our Models: Linear (Occasionally Quadratic), Usually Not Interactive

Yet another aspect of our most common models is that, even if we include some nonlinearity in modeled relations among variables, our more sophisticated statistical models often do not contain specifications and tests of interactions among independent variables. The simpler analytic approaches of multiple regression and analysis of variance can easily be adapted for the testing of interactions, but more complex statistical modeling frequently requires more advanced techniques, such as SEM, and the testing of interaction hypotheses with these advanced techniques is difficult. Current improvements to statistical software are making the testing of interactions significantly easier, and the future should see work in this vein with greater frequency.

Importance and Centrality of Individual Differences

Yet another concern that deserves a place at the forefront of methodology in cognitive aging is the centrality of individual differences. Over 30 years ago, Underwood (1975) argued that accounting for individual differences was a "crucible" for cognitive psychology. Traditional experimental designs in cognitive psychology involve the manipulation of conditions and the random assignment of participants to conditions, and research studies that conform to this mold offer convincing demonstrations of the influence of conditions on performance by the average participant. In studies of cognitive aging, participants are not randomly assigned to levels of age, so research studies that include the age variable employ, at best, quasi-experimental designs. Still, the focus of such studies is often on the general aging trend, which reflects the aging of cognition for the "average participant."

However, the presence of marked individual differences is often as striking an aspect of cognitive aging data as is the mean trend. Some individuals exhibit cognitive declines that are much more marked than the mean trend, whereas other individuals seem able to maintain their levels of performance well into old age with little decrement. General trends in brain structure or function can help account for aging trends associated with the general cognitive trend. However, extending the argument to claim that individual differences in changes in brain functioning underlie or account for individual differences in cognitive aging is clearly unwarranted when based only on general or mean trends that coincide. Only by including markers of brain structure or function in statistical models and then testing these conjectures directly will any legitimate arguments be well founded and worthy of extended interest.

This argument can be generalized to a broader indictment of the typical conduct of research in cognitive neuroscience using brain imaging approaches, although such a far-reaching critique is far beyond the scope of the present contribution. But the criticism, sketched hastily, would follow this line: Typical fMRI research presents participants with two or more conditions that differ in the cognitive requirements for successful performance, and mean differences across participants in brain activity between these conditions are then used to argue that the areas that are more active in the test condition than in the control condition are the crucial brain areas uniquely involved in performance of the operations or tasks distinguishing the test condition. In general, I would not dispute this line of reasoning if it went just this far. But at least two things must be kept in mind, things that might diminish the force of the evidence. First, many brain areas that do not exhibit different levels of activation between test and control conditions may be crucial for performance in the test condition; these areas may not exhibit differential activity across conditions because they are required in the control condition as well, and individual differences in activation of these common areas might relate to individual differences in performance in the test condition. So, the failure of any given brain area to exhibit differential activation across conditions should not be used to argue that the area is not crucial to performance in the test condition or that individual differences in activation in this area are unrelated to individual differences in behavioral measures of cognitive aging. Second, merely demonstrating that certain areas exhibit differential activity in test and control conditions does not imply in any way that individual differences in activity in these areas relate to individual differences in behavioral outcomes. In fact, there may be little in the way of individual differences in activity in these areas, which function merely as a gate that must be opened so that a particular form of responding can occur. This gate is unique to the given task, and so is a crucial component of performance, but it may be completely unable to explain any of the marked individual differences in cognitive aging that are a hallmark of research findings in this field.

The solution to this problem is to become more serious about the inclusion of individual-difference information and analyses in research on cognitive aging. Psychometric properties of all measures—including measures derived from fMRI and other forms of brain imaging—should be studied, to ensure that current methods of estimating parameters at the individual level have sufficient precision. This should be followed by appropriate forms of statistical analysis that test directly whether individual differences on the measures of brain structure or function are related to individual differences in more molar, standard measures of cognitive performance.

Measurement Models and Psychological Processes

In this chapter, I have argued that we should strive to use measures of biological or brain structures or processes in our statistical models, instead of merely referring to evidence from other studies to interpret our results. If we include brain-relevant measures in our statistical models, we will be able to test conjectures regarding these measures, rather than merely telling a good story about our results.

One connection between measurement and modeling with brain-related measures can be illustrated using measures of recall and recognition memory. In Figure 3.1, three hypothetical measures of recall memory and three measures of recognition memory are shown. Research on memory initially presumed the presence of a single process underlying all kinds of recall and recognition performance, but various kinds of evidence have proved difficult for single-process theories to explain. As a result, dual-process accounts of memory have been proposed for understanding memory performance.

One set of dual-process accounts are dual-process theories of recall performance. According to such theories, declarative memory, which is based in the hippocampus and surrounding medial temporal brain areas, underlies both recall and recognition memory, and either frontal or prefrontal brain systems contribute to memory search processes that are involved in recall, but not recognition (see, e.g., Moscovitch,

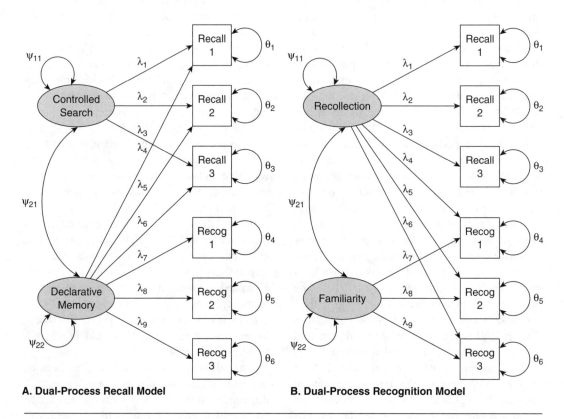

A. Dual-Process Recall Model

B. Dual-Process Recognition Model

Figure 3.1   Hypothetical Structural Models for Distinguishing Between Separable Forms of Explicit Memory

NOTE: Recog = recognition.

1994; Squire & Zola, 1998; Squire & Zola-Morgan, 1991). Also according to these theories, recall is a more complex memory performance, with two separable processes underlying recall, but recognition has a single process supporting it. A confirmatory factor model specification for a dual-process recall model is shown in the left panel of Figure 3.1. There, one can see that one latent variable, labeled *Declarative Memory*, has direct effects on all six manifest measures of recall and recognition memory, whereas a second latent variable, labeled *Controlled Search*, has direct effects only on the manifest measures of recall memory. The former latent variable presumably reflects memory structures in the hippocampus, and the latter latent variable is assumed to represent the operation of frontal or prefrontal control processes.

A separate set of dual-process theories can be termed *dual-process theories of recognition memory*, according to which recognition is the complex memorial process. One set of theories holds that the ability to recollect precise, episodic features resides in the hippocampus. In contrast, the ability to apprehend a stimulus as a familiar one that has been encountered before is supported by the entorhinal cortex or other parahippocampal areas that surround the hippocampus. This position is represented in the right panel of Figure 3.1, with one latent variable, labeled *Recollection*, having direct effects on all six manifest measures of memory and a second latent variable, labeled *Familiarity*, having direct effects on only the three measures of recognition memory.

The special utility of sophisticated methods of modeling in this context is worthy of note. Standard methods of analysis, including regression analysis or analysis of variance, would be unable to separate out the effects hypothesized under either of the models shown in Figure 3.1. Because certain of the manifest variables in each model presumably reflect the influence of two latent processes and the remainder only a single process, typical approaches to analysis would look for some differences across analyses of the two classes of outcome. But the typical analytic methods could not separate statistically the effects of the latent processes. In contrast, SEM can be used to compare the fit of alternative models of these processes in an efficient manner.

Application 1: Effects of Hypoxia on Explicit Memory. In one recent study, Quamme, Yonelinas, Widaman, Kroll, and Sauvé (2004) investigated the effects of hypoxia on memory performance in a group of 56 men who had experienced hypoxia in connection with heart attacks. The sample of participants tended to be in later middle age, with mean age of 61.8 years (*SD* = 11.8 years; range: 35–78 years), had experienced cardiac arrest an average of 2.1 minutes and then experienced comas of moderate duration, with a mean coma duration of 14.9 hours (*SD* = 17.1, range: 0–65 hours). In prior studies of hypoxia, coma duration was linearly related to later extent of memory problems, presumably because hypoxia leads to atrophy of the hippocampus, which is one of the major brain areas involved in explicit memory. Importantly, prior studies had found that hypoxia led to selective damage to the hippocampus, but not to parahippocampal areas such as the entorhinal cortex. The current sample of participants had relatively short cardiac arrest and coma durations, so the effects of hypoxia were likely narrowly confined to the hippocampus. Because the participants had defibrillators, they could not be scanned via magnetic resonance imaging, so the extent of hippocampal atrophy could not be determined. Still, the relatively mild hypoxia experienced by these participants has been found in prior studies to be associated with atrophy primarily of the hippocampus.

The participants in the study were assessed at four points following their hypoxic event, but we used only assessments from the third (12–15 weeks) and fourth (22–25 weeks) measurement occasions, because performance on measures had approximately stabilized by this time. The memory-related outcome measures consisted of a set of three pairs of measures, with one member of each pair from the third time of measurement and the other from the fourth. The three pairs of measures were measures of (1) verbal fluency, (2) recall memory, and (3) recognition memory.

The final model that best fit the data is shown in Figure 3.2. A total of six latent variables are shown in the figure. The first two latent variables—age and coma duration—were single-indicator variables with chronological age in years and coma duration in hours as manifest variables, respectively. Controlled search of long-term memory was specified to affect the two fluency measures, recollection to affect directly all recall and recognition measures, familiarity to have direct effect on only the two measures of recognition, and recovery to affect the measures at the last time of measurement. Given the small sample size, many reasonable constraints on factor loadings were invoked; details are provided by Quamme et al. (2004).

The key findings from this study concern the differential effects of the exogenous variables of age and coma duration on the memory latent variables. Specifically, age had a small and nonsignificant influence on controlled search, a moderate effect on recollection (β = −.41), and no effect at all on familiarity. These findings are consistent with prior research, which has found a negative relation between chronological age and memory task performance in general but no effect on familiarity. The other exogenous variable—coma duration—had an effect of moderate magnitude (β = −.46) only on recollection and had no effect on familiarity. Quamme et al. performed model comparisons to test all paths excluded from the model in Figure 3.2. All of these tests were negative, with path coefficients that were nonsignificant and approximately zero in magnitude.

The upshot of the Quamme et al. (2004) study is support for a dual-process model for recognition, specifically, a model that holds that recollective processes underlie both recall and recognition memory, whereas familiarity contributes selectively to recognition memory. Furthermore, the inclusion of coma duration in the model provides additional support for this

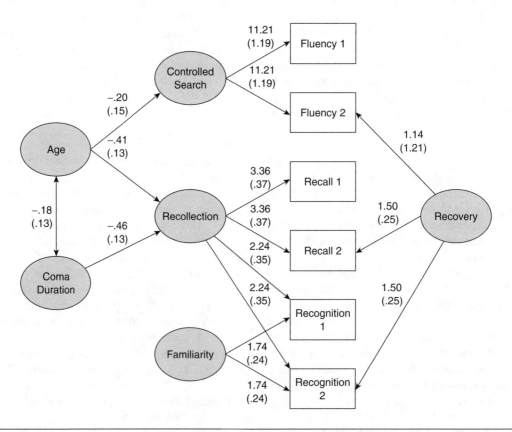

Figure 3.2 Relations Among Age, Coma Duration, and Different Dimensions of Memory in a Sample of Men (*N* = 56) Who Experienced Hypoxia Due to Heart Attack

SOURCE: Adapted from Figure 4 from Quamme, Yonelinas, Widaman, Kroll, & Sauvé (2004), Recall and recognition in mild hypoxia: Using covariance structural modeling to test competing theories of explicit memory, in *Neuropsychologia, 42,* 672–691. Copyright Elsevier (2004).

NOTE: Latent variables were standardized to unit variance; path coefficients are listed, with standard errors in parentheses.

theoretical model because coma duration had an effect only on recollection, not familiarity. The relatively mild hypoxia experienced by participants likely had effects only on hippocampal volumes, which affected the recollective processes centered in the hippocampus. In contrast, the mild hypoxia presumably left the entorhinal cortex unaffected, resulting in no effect of coma duration on the familiarity processes supported by the entorhinal cortex.

Application 2: Age, Brain Structure, and Explicit Memory. The Quamme et al. (2004) study included two brain-relevant variables— age and coma duration—but did not include explicit measures of brain structure or function. In a follow-up study, Yonelinas et al. (in press) sought to extend Quamme et al.'s study by analyzing data on a sample of 157 older, nondemented adults with an age range between 65 and 80 years. The participants had Mini-Mental State Examination scores of 26 or greater, which indicated that they were not demented or at least had no obvious signs of dementia. Among the set of measures administered to the participants was the 12-item Memory Assessment Scale, which includes measures of recall and recognition memory. Given the presence of measures of both recall and recognition memory, Yonelinas et al. were once again able to specify and test dual-process models of recall and recognition to confirm once again the structure of these measures offered by Quamme et al.

More important was the availability of brain volume indices for the hippocampus and the entorhinal cortex for all participants in the Yonelinas et al. (in press) study. Previous research has documented decreases in hippocampal volume as a function of normal aging but little in the way of aging trends in entorhinal cortex volume. An a priori hypothesis would then be that age would be associated negatively with hippocampal volume but unrelated to entorhinal volume. Furthermore, if the hippocampus provides support for recollective processes and the entorhinal cortex supports selectively familiarity-based processing, a double dissociation should be observed in results. This is precisely what was found, with structural relations among the five latent variables shown in Figure 3.3. As shown in Figure 3.3, age had a moderate negative effect on hippocampal volume ($\beta = -.36$) but no direct relation to entorhinal volume. The double dissociation was demonstrated by the remaining relations: Hippocampal volume had a moderate positive effect on recollection ($\beta = .46$) but no significant effect on familiarity; in contrast, entorhinal volume had a moderate effect on familiarity ($\beta = -.53$) but no significant effect on recollection.

In the context of this chapter, the importance of the results reported by Yonelinas et al. (in press) is the demonstration that individual differences in brain measures—in this case, brain volume measures—were related to individual differences in performance on memory measures.

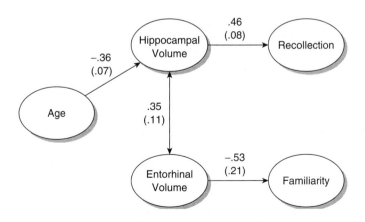

Figure 3.3　　Relations Among Age, Brain Area Volume Measures, and Recollection and Familiarity in an Aging but Nondemented Sample of Men ($N = 157$) Aged 60 to 85 Years

NOTE: Latent variables were standardized to unit variance; path coefficients are listed, with standard errors in parentheses.

Many studies have found negative relations between age and memory performance during the adult years (e.g., Salthouse & Ferrer-Caja, 2003), but these relations have included only test performance by participants. Other studies have documented negative relations between age and hippocampal volumes. Yonelinas et al., however, put these measures in a single analysis that confirmed key theoretical conjectures. Specifically, the model shown in Figure 3.3 is consistent with the theory that advanced age is associated with smaller hippocampal volumes, that these hippocampal volumes are directly related to recollective memory processes, and that age has no additional effect on recollection other than through its effects on hippocampal volumes. Moreover, age is essentially unrelated to entorhinal cortex volume, although entorhinal cortex volume is strongly related to familiarity-based processing. The data in Yonelinas et al. were cross-sectional, so strong causal claims are not justified, and future research using longitudinal measures would provide stronger evidence that age leads to reductions in brain volumes that in turn lead to reductions in recollective memory. Still, the hypothesized relations between brain and memory measures based on the dual-process recognition model were confirmed, and this is a far stronger basis for future research than if the brain measures had not been included in the statistical model.

Finally, one important contribution of the Quamme et al. (2004) and Yonelinas et al. (in press) studies is the demonstration of the key utility of brain-related measures in the testing of conjectures about cognitive aging. In the former study, the brain-related measures included age, a reasonable covariate, and a rather indirect index of likely brain damage, the length of coma after a hypoxic episode. Because damage to the hippocampus could not be imaged because participants had defibrillators, the indirect index of coma duration was the only brain-related measure available. Then, Yonelinas et al. built on Quamme et al.'s study, including measures of the volume of key brain structures thought to underlie memory performance, and the resulting double dissociation was a confirmation of a priori hypotheses regarding the differential operation of the two brain areas to recollection and familiarity. The preceding studies are not unique, because

other interesting applications of modeling with biological variables are appearing. For example, McArdle et al. (2004) recently reported analyses of longitudinal data that demonstrated that a key biological indicator—the size of the lateral cerebral ventricular—was a leading indicator or predictor of later decline in memory, and the reverse direction of causal impact—from memory to size of lateral ventricular—was absent, consistent with a priori hypothesis. The future should see many further investigations of this sort, with brain-related measures at the individual level used to test the relations between brain structure or function and performance on standardized measures used in cognitive aging research.

GENES, BRAINS, BODIES, CONTEXTS, AND BEHAVIORAL AGING

As mentioned earlier, current research on mental abilities, including research on cognitive aging, is at a most interesting point, as new and different ways to investigate phenomena become available seemingly on a daily basis. As we incorporate new brain and genetic information into our statistical models we should continually pay heed to several general considerations, including the importance of the phenomena we study, the complexity of the relations among variables, and the ordering of influences.

Importance of Our Phenomena and Our Models of Phenomena

Research findings in the area of cognitive aging are important for describing mean changes during the time span between adulthood and old age as well as for investigating the role of individual differences in patterns of development. Complete and acceptable theoretical models for cognitive aging will necessarily include explanatory elements at many levels of analysis. The lowest level of explanatory elements, at least for the time being, will lie at the level of genetic material, and the highest level will involve human behaviors and the environments within which individuals exist. Widaman (2007) provided one useful way to think about issues related to contexts of development, complementing much current work that is exploring relations among behavioral phenomena, brain functioning, neuronal activity, and genetic predispositions. Bringing together information and findings across multiple levels of analysis to explain cognitive aging is an exciting goal for the future.

One issue to emphasize in thinking about these matters is to remain open to the fundamental nature of all components at all levels that interact in producing cognitive aging. A great deal of current work is aimed at finding explanations that involve genetic information, seeking Gene × Environment interactions that affect behavioral performance. Cutting-edge work such as this is an ideal way to understand the ways in which genes function within intrapersonal and extrapersonal environments to affect phenotypes. But I would argue that this work also provides elegant support for the claim that the phenomena we study are too important for standard behavior genetic models that lead primarily to estimates of heritability for particular behaviors. Estimating heritability coefficients is a trivialization of the complex interaction of factors at very many levels. Heritability estimates can vary widely if crucial aspects of the environment are altered, and a high heritability does not imply immutability of the phenotype, even if this is the common, if misguided, interpretation. Furthermore, even if genes can be found to have main or interactive relations in affecting behavior, changes in environments can alter these effects. The time appears ripe to discard our old behavior genetic models that estimate proportions of variance of behavioral traits due to genetic sources and focus instead on genetically informed designs that estimate the interactive effects of genes and environments in affecting the phenotype.

Complexity

The complexity of the mechanisms underlying cognitive aging cannot be understated. Investigators search for the simplest explanation of any phenomenon, but all researchers expect that adequate theories will be at least moderately complex. One of the most problematic forms of explanation is *molecular reductionism*, in which phenomena at one level are reduced to or presumably explained by phenomena at a lower level. As one example, molecular reductionism

occurs when researchers argue that brain processes are the fundamental substructure for certain cognitive phenomena (e.g., memory), so the brain processes, encompassing coordinated firings of neurons, account for the higher-level phenomenon. Brain processes certainly constitute the wetware that supports cognitive processes, and brain damage due to stroke or accident or normal aging can severely curtail any particular form of cognitive performance. Evidence of this sort abounds and emphasizes the importance of brain processes as the physical basis that makes cognition possible.

However, acceptance of this statement does not imply that brain processes can explain or account for cognitive phenomena or that brain processes are in any sense more fundamental than the developmental and experiential processes that produced the current brain processes. Evidence continues to accumulate showing that environmental factors, including experience, have fundamental influences on brain development at the neuronal level and even the neurotransmitter level (e.g., Dong & Greenough, 2004; Grossman et al., 2003). This research suggests that, in many fundamental ways, the environment exerts potentially as much influence on brain development as do inherited "programs" that govern the unfolding of brain development. Therefore, we also have a need for *molar reductionism*, which refers to using phenomena at a higher level of abstraction to account for those at a lower level. In this case, we might use differential experience by individuals to account for individual differences in patterns of brain functioning, where the differential experience can arise from a broad array of influences, including nutrition and the degree of challenge or interest in the rearing environment. An overreliance on molecular reductionism, a hallmark of much science during the 20th century, is certain to blind researchers to some of the more interesting aspects of developmental phenomena, which are affected from above, rather than always from below at lower levels of abstraction.

Ordering

One final issue regarding our theories and our statistical models is that of *ordering*, or the presumed patterns of influence among variables. In typical studies of cognitive aging, participants are tested on a single occasion or a small number of occasions, with virtually all information used in statistical models derived from measures during adulthood. In the resulting statistical analyses, relations among variables are estimated under an implicit assumption of autoregressive effects. That is, adults can be measured in middle adulthood, around 50 years of age, and we might use this as a starting point for subsequent modeling. We assume that most important information for predicting later outcomes is present in the assessed adults; developmental processes have brought the individuals to this point in their life, and we use various indicators of current status as predictors of later patterns of aging. One example of such analyses would be growth curve models fit to data on adults in a longitudinal study. If the participants were initially assessed at age 50 years, it is common to center the growth curve at the first time of measurement. That is, the first time of measurement (at age 50) is fixed as the intercept, or zero point, of the growth curve, and the focus of attention is often directed to the substantial individual differences in growth trends after this point.

Initial differences may, however, be extremely important in explaining patterns of aging, and the time point of the crucial initial differences may be far earlier than we have thought. Barker (1998) summarized the results of many studies that support the conjecture that prenatal experience may have strong effects on disease-related outcomes in later life. Barker and his colleagues have concentrated on fetal malnutrition, which leads to the programming of the baby, where *programming* refers to the alteration of bodily organ systems or set points for physiological functioning. Barker argued that fetal malnutrition has clear and sizable effects on blood pressure, cholesterol, non-insulin-dependent diabetes, obesity, and other disease processes in later life, even having notable effects on mortality rates. As Barker concluded, prenatal influences can affect the individual from birth to death, across the entire life span.

If prenatal influences can have profound effects on human physiology and disease processes, we should assume that phenomena in the domain of cognitive aging might also be similarly affected. Barker and his colleagues are pursuing epidemiological research in medical settings, so the foci of their investigations are, quite naturally, in the medical and health domains. But the intimate connection between cognitive aging and the biological substrates that support cognitive functioning suggests that the exploration of the connections between early life experiences, even prenatal experiences, on patterns of aging in late life can and should be the object of study in the future.

Application 3: Intrauterine Environment and Later Developmental Outcomes in Children Born to Mothers With Phenylketonuria. As a third and final application that illustrates some principles outlined above, I refer to findings from the International Maternal PKU Collaborative Study (MPKU Study; see Koch et al., 1999, for a general introduction to the study). *Phenylketonuria*, or *PKU*, refers to an inborn error of metabolism, signaling the inability to convert phenylalanine into tyrosine. If a child has PKU and is not placed on a special diet very early in life, the child will slide from performing at normal levels in early infancy to severe mental retardation (mean IQ = 50) by 2 years of age. This rapid and profound disruption of brain development occurs because of the buildup of phenylalanine (PHE) in the blood or the attendant reduced levels of tyrosine and cannot be remediated. The development in 1962 of a blood test to identify infants with PKU and the presence of a low-PHE diet meant that PKU could be identified very early, affected infants could be placed on an appropriate diet, and these infants developed in essentially normal fashion if kept on the diet throughout the developmental period. This scientific puzzle appeared to have been solved, with infants affected by PKU able to develop normally.

Then, in 1980, Lenke and Levy published a report on over 500 pregnancies by mothers with PKU. These mothers had been on special diets during their own developmental periods, and they had experienced relatively normal development. Then, when these women got pregnant, they did not adhere strictly to the low-PHE diet. As a result, PHE built up in their blood, crossed the placental barrier, and damaged the fetuses. Of mothers with the most severe forms of PKU mutation and therefore the highest levels of blood PHE, 92% of the offspring of mothers with untreated pregnancies had mental retardation.

In response to the Lenke and Levy (1980) findings, the MPKU Study enrolled women between 1984 and 1996, attempting to enroll women prior to conception or at the earliest stage possible. The study was partly an intervention study, as collaborating investigators tried to ensure that the women maintained as careful a diet as possible, given the teratogenic effects to the fetus of exposure to high levels of PHE. But the MPKU Study was also designed to document the relation between prenatal exposure to PHE and an array of physical and psychological outcomes.

One particularly striking outcome of the MPKU Study is the relation between prenatal exposure to PHE and later intellectual outcomes by the offspring. In Figure 3.4, the relation between maternal background variables of maternal education, socioeconomic status, IQ, age, and severity of PKU mutation and average level of PHE in the mother's blood during

pregnancy are shown. Of the maternal background variables, the strongest influence on average PHE during pregnancy was the severity of the mother's genetic mutation—mothers with more severe mutations metabolize less PHE into tyrosine and so tend to have higher levels of PHE in their blood during pregnancy. Having smaller, but still notable effects, mothers who were older, had higher levels of intelligence, and had higher levels of education tended to have lower levels of average PHE—even controlling statistically for the severity of their mutations—presumably because these mothers understood better the need to adhere to a low-PHE diet.

Also shown in Figure 3.4 are the relations between average PHE in the mother's blood during pregnancy and the later intellectual outcomes of Bayley Mental Development Index (MDI) scores at ages 1 year and 2 years, the McCarthy IQ at age 4 years, and the Wechsler Intelligence Scale for Children IQ at age 7 years. Autoregressive

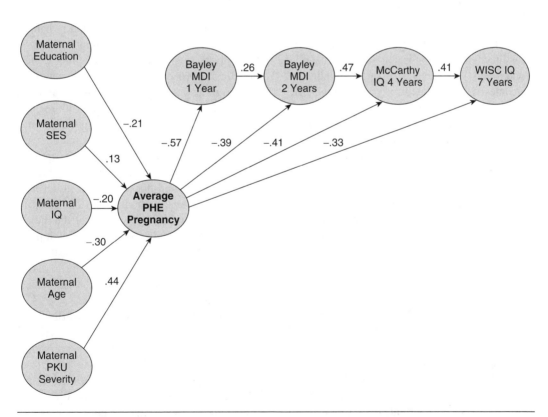

Figure 3.4   Relations Among Maternal Background Measures, Pregnancy Variables, and Later Offspring Intellectual Outcomes Based on the International Maternal PKU Collaborative Study ($N = 413$)

NOTE: MDI = Mental Development Index; WISC = Wechsler Intelligence Scale for Children; SES = socioeconomic status; PKU = phenylketonuria; PHE = phenylalanine.

relations from one time of measurement to the next were specified between the four intelligence outcomes, representing stability of individual differences across time. Average PHE level had a large negative effect on Bayley MDI scores at 1 year ($\beta = -.57$). But even though average PHE level could have had only indirect effects on later intelligence measures given the autoregressive structure of these relations, continued direct effects of average PHE level during pregnancy had to be specified to later intelligence measures. Thus, these direct effects of average PHE level were moderate to strong on Bayley MDI scores at age 2 years ($\beta = -.39$), on McCarthy IQ scores at age 4 years ($\beta = -.41$), and on Wechsler Intelligence Scale for Children IQ scores at age 7 years ($\beta = -.33$).

One notable aspect of the model shown in Figure 3.4 is the absence of direct effects of maternal background variables and the offspring intellectual outcomes. Maternal background variables were correlated significantly with the offspring intellectual outcomes. However, after the effects of average PHE level during pregnancy on intellectual outcomes were estimated, maternal background variables had no significant direct effects. That is, all effects of maternal background variables on offspring intellectual outcomes were mediated fully by average PHE exposure during pregnancy.

At first, inclusion of an analysis of cognitive outcomes through age 7 years in a handbook on cognitive aging may seem rather odd. But the results from the MPKU Study support several claims that are central to this chapter. First, the results are a clear demonstration of an important influence of initial differences on later outcomes, one in which those initial differences arose during the organism's gestation. The continuing importance of these initial differences for the subsequent development of cognition for the offspring in the MPKU Study is unknown, given the ceasing of funding for follow-up of participants. Continued direct effects on intellectual outcomes might be expected. Furthermore, when the offspring participants in the MPKU Study reach old age, it is quite possible that average PHE exposure they experienced during their gestation might have important influences on their patterns of age-related declines. Second, the model in Figure 3.4 includes two biologically related variables—the severity of the mother's

PKU mutation and the average level of PHE in her blood during pregnancy—and these biological measures play a crucial role in understanding the unfolding of intellectual development across the time span of the study. Thus, this analysis is yet another example of the use of nonpsychological variables to explore the biological or physiological underpinnings of the development of behavioral phenomena. Third, this research also suggests that the effects on physical and health outcomes described by Barker (1998) may be only a small part of the story of behavioral development and that similar marked effects of prenatal influences on patterns of cognitive aging might be discovered. We will know about this possibility only if we begin looking at the earliest stages of life, even during prenatal development, for variables that might be useful predictors of aging trends during old age.

CONCLUSION

Measurement and modeling go hand in hand, a truism that is nowhere more important than in the study of cognitive aging. Adapting current modeling approaches or developing new ones are intriguing goals of methodologists, and new and interesting approaches appear with regularity. The flurry of new statistical models is something of a cottage industry for quantitatively oriented psychologists, and keeping up with new methodological contributions is a difficult task. But we should not let interest in developing new statistical methods divert our attention from the measurement properties of the indicators to which these models are fit. Explicit interest in the development of new measurement techniques or the improvement of existing instruments has lagged behind the excitement surrounding new statistical models.

Informative new methods of measuring brain structure and function are also being developed with regularity. Measurement experts should become involved in this research to apply principles of psychological measurement to establish the reliability and validity of these new measurements and suggest changes in operations of measurement, such as lengthening measures, if either reliability or validity is less than adequate. If psychometricians can help validate and even improve these new measurements, practicing scientists will have more faith in the results of modeling these indicators.

In all of this work, we should keep several matters clearly in mind. We should include biological measures in our models when we can, so that we can test, rather than merely hypothesize about, the importance of these variables for our models of phenomena. We should place the study of individual differences in its rightful place as a key approach to analyses that have a unique ability to test many theoretical predictions. We should also resist the enticing urge to engage in molecular reductionism, instead pursuing research and theories that posit upward and downward effects across levels. The most acceptable models we develop will be integrative models that demonstrate the relations between many levels of biological phenomena that interact to influence and be influenced by the molar behavioral trends that embody cognitive aging.

REFERENCES

Barker, D. J. P. (1998). *Mothers, babies and health in later life* (2nd ed.). Edinburgh, UK: Churchill Livingstone.

Brown, W. (1910). Some experimental results in the correlation of mental abilities. *British Journal of Psychology, 3,* 296–322.

Cronbach, L. J. (1951). Coefficient alpha and the internal structure of tests. *Psychometrika, 16,* 297–334.

Dong, W. K., & Greenough, W. T. (2004). Plasticity of nonneuronal brain tissue: Roles in developmental disorders. *Mental Retardation and Developmental Disabilities Research Reviews, 10,* 85–90.

Embretson, S. E., & Reise, S. P. (2000). *Item response theory for psychologists.* Mahwah, NJ: Lawrence Erlbaum.

Graham, J. W., Hofer, S. M., & MacKinnon, D. P. (1996). Maximizing the usefulness of data obtained with planned missing value patterns: An application of maximum likelihood procedures. *Multivariate Behavioral Research, 31,* 197–218.

Graham, J. W., Taylor, B. J., & Cumsille, P. E. (2001). Planned missing-data designs in analysis of change. In L. M. Collins & A. G. Sayer (Eds.), *New methods for the analysis of change* (pp. 335–353). Washington, DC: American Psychological Association.

Grossman, A. W., Churchill, J. D., McKinney, B. C., Kodish, I. M., Otte, S. L., & Greenough, W. T. (2003). Experience effects on brain development: Possible contributions to psychopathology. *Journal of Child Psychology and Psychiatry, 44,* 33–63.

Gullickson, H. (1950). *Theory of mental tests.* New York: Wiley.

Guttman, L. (1945). A basis for analyzing test–retest reliability. *Psychometrika, 10,* 255–282.

Jenkins, L., Myerson, J., Joerding, J. A., & Hale, S. (2000). Converging evidence that visuospatial cognition is more age-sensitive than verbal cognition. *Psychology and Aging, 15,* 157–175.

Koch, R., Friedman, E., Azen, C., Hanley, W., Levy, H., Matalon, R., et al. (1999). The International Collaborative Study of Maternal Phenylketonuria status report 1998. *Mental Retardation and Developmental Disabilities Research Reviews, 5,* 117–121.

Kuder, G. F., & Richardson, M. W. (1937). The theory of the estimation of test reliability. *Psychometrika, 2,* 151–160.

Lenke, R. R., & Levy, H. L. (1980). Maternal phenylketonuria and hyperphenylalaninemia. An international survey of the outcome of untreated and treated pregnancies. *New England Journal of Medicine, 303,* 1202–1208.

Lord, F. M. (1952). A theory of test scores. *Psychometric Monographs,* No. 7.

Lord, F. M., & Novick, M. R. (1968). *Statistical theories of mental test scores.* Reading, MA: Addison-Wesley.

Madden, D. J. (2001). Speed and timing of behavioral processes. In J. E. Birren & K. W. Schaie (Eds.), *Handbook of the psychology of aging* (5th ed., pp. 288–312). San Diego, CA: Academic Press.

McArdle, J. J. (1994). Structural factor analysis experiments with incomplete data. *Multivariate Behavioral Research, 29,* 409–454.

McArdle, J. J., Hamagami, F., Jones, K., Jolesz, F., Kikinis, R., Spiro, A., III, et al. (2004). Structural modeling of dynamic changes in memory and brain structure using longitudinal data from the Normative Aging Study. *Journals of Gerontology, Series B: Psychological Sciences and Social Sciences, 59B,* P294–P304.

McDonald, R. P. (1999). *Test theory.* Mahwah, NJ: Lawrence Erlbaum.

Moscovitch, M. (1994). Memory and working with memory: Evaluation of a component process model and comparisons with other models. In D. L. Schacter & E. Tulving (Eds.), *Memory systems 1994* (pp. 1–59). Cambridge: MIT Press.

Quamme, J. R., Yonelinas, A. P., Widaman, K. F., Kroll, N. E. A., & Suavé, M. J. (2004). Recall and recognition in mild hypoxia: Using covariance structural modeling to test competing theories of explicit memory. *Neuropsychologia, 42,* 672–691.

Salthouse, T. A., & Ferrer-Caja, E. (2003). What needs to be explained to account for age-related effects in multiple cognitive variables? *Psychology and Aging, 18,* 91–110.

Schaie, K. W. (2005). *Developmental influences on adult intelligence: The Seattle longitudinal study.* Oxford, UK: Oxford University Press.

Scheines, R., Spirtes, P., Glymour, C., Meek, C., & Richardson, T. (1998a). Reply to comments. *Multivariate Behavioral Research, 33,* 165–180.

Scheines, R., Spirtes, P., Glymour, C., Meek, C., & Richardson, T. (1998b). The TETRAD project: Constraint based aids to causal model specification. *Multivariate Behavioral Research, 33,* 65–117.

Spearman, C. (1904). The proof and measurement of association between two things. *American Journal of Psychology, 15,* 72–101.

Spearman, C. (1910). Correlation calculated with faulty data. *British Journal of Psychology, 3,* 271–295.

Spirtes, P., Glymour, C., & Scheines, R. (1993). *Causation, prediction, and search.* New York: Springer-Verlag.

Spirtes, P., Glymour, C., & Scheines, R. (2000). *Causation, prediction, and search* (2nd ed.). Cambridge: MIT Press.

Squire, L. R., & Zola, S. M. (1998). Episodic memory, semantic memory, and amnesia. *Hippocampus, 8,* 205–211.

Squire, L. R., & Zola-Morgan, S. (1991, September 20). The medial temporal lobe memory system. *Science, 253,* 1380–1386.

Thurstone, L. L. (1938). Primary mental abilities. *Psychometric Monographs,* No. 1.

Thurstone, L. L., & Thurstone, T. G. (1941). Factorial studies of intelligence. *Psychometric Monographs,* No. 2.

Tukey, J. W. (1969). Analyzing data: Sanctification or detective work? *American Psychologist, 24,* 83–91.

Underwood, B. (1975). Individual differences as a crucible in theory construction. *American Psychologist, 30,* 128–134.

Widaman, K. F. (2007). Intrauterine environment affects infant and child intellectual outcomes: Environment as direct effect. In T. D. Little, J. A. Bovaird, & N. A. Card (Eds.), *Modeling contextual effects in longitudinal studies* (pp. 387–436). Mahwah, NJ: Lawrence Erlbaum.

Yonelinas, A. P., Widaman, K. F., Mungas, D., Reed, B., Weiner, M. W., & Chui, H. C. (in press). Memory in the aging brain: Doubly dissociating the contribution of the hippocampus and entorhinal cortex. *Hippocampus.*

4

POPULATION PROCESSES AND COGNITIVE AGING

DUANE F. ALWIN, RYAN J. MCCAMMON,
LINDA A. WRAY, AND WILLARD L. RODGERS

This chapter argues that research on cognitive aging should be conducted on well-defined populations and that it is important to understand the role of population processes in producing age-related changes in cognitive function. Relying on a demographic perspective, we discuss several related issues that concern the nature of population processes. First, we discuss what it means to say that inferences about processes of cognitive aging should be applied to well-defined populations. Second, we consider the implications of population aging for understanding future population prevalence of low cognitive functioning (LCF). Given what is known about the demography of aging—increasing levels of population aging in the 21st century (United Nations, 2002)—the need to understand the population processes that are involved in cognitive aging are ever more pressing. Third, given that there may be cohort differences in the nature of cognitive aging, we recognize the importance of considering these differences in estimates of functions that

describe population cognitive aging. Finally, we discuss the problem of unmeasured heterogeneity in cohort-specific aging functions resulting from the phenomenon of mortality selection.

In addressing these issues, we draw on examples from our ongoing analyses of cognitive aging in data from the Health and Retirement Study (HRS), a nationally representative probability sample of cohorts born from before 1900 to 1947 (see Alwin et al., 2008). We report projected increases in levels of prevalence of LCF through 2050, resulting from processes linked to population aging. With respect to cohort effects, an examination of cohort-specific slopes and intercepts in latent growth curve models of cognitive aging functions suggests the existence of significant differences, net of schooling, in cohort-specific intercepts in functions describing population cognitive aging. One explanation for these cohort differences in intercepts is mortality selection, given the heterogeneity among existing cohort survivors in susceptibility to death and disease. We propose that controlling for cohort

AUTHORS' NOTE: The research reported here was supported by a grant titled "Latent Growth Models of Cognitive Aging" to Duane Alwin, Willard Rodgers, and Linda Wray from the National Institute on Aging, 2002–2005 (R01-AG021203-03). The authors gratefully acknowledge the research assistance of Paula Tufiş and Pauline Mitchell.

differences in expected age at death reduces the observed differences in intercepts and that it may therefore be important to account for heterogeneity in cohort experiences—including not only residues of historical experiences but also variables linked to survivorship, especially mortality selection—in both cross-sectional and longitudinal studies of cognitive aging.

THE CONCEPT OF POPULATION

The concept of *population* is basic to modern social and behavioral science. From a statistical perspective, "the population" is the universe of generalization, providing a philosophical grounding for drawing inferences from a sample to something broader. From a demographic perspective, the concept of population has substantive meaning. Demography is the human science that focuses on the geographical concept of population, its size, composition, and change, as well as the factors that shape those features of an area's population. Demographic processes—such as fertility, migration, population aging, disease and its transmission, and mortality—that organize human life and around which human lives are constructed, affect society in fundamental ways. The modern science of demography has increasingly focused on other aspects of society that are affected by *population processes* and that can be better informed by taking the study of population into account. Demography as a discipline produces a corpus of empirical findings and theoretical statements about human well-being, using core population concepts, macro- and micro-unit data and measures, and unique quantitative science methodologies (e.g., life tables, cohort analysis, and event history analysis; see De Jong, 2003).

At the same time, developmental sciences are increasingly taking population processes into account, given that the phenomena of interest are often affected by demographic factors. Some early discussions of cohort effects on cognitive performance originated in life span developmental psychology (e.g., Baltes, 1997; Baltes, Cornelius, & Nesselroade, 1979; Baltes & Mayer, 1999; Nesselroade & Baltes, 1974; Schaie, 1984). Future research in the area of cognitive aging will increasingly focus on the integration of the population and developmental sciences. In contrast to many related social, economic, and biological sciences, where structural concepts tend to be dominant, an enduring feature of both population and developmental perspectives is their focus on the processes and mechanisms of change. In the future, we expect that developmental scientists will be exposed to the core concepts, knowledge, and techniques of population science and will be increasingly aware of the need to understand the relationship of aging to differences in population composition and vital rate phenomena. In an empirical context, future research and scholarship necessary to fully understand the processes of aging will require such transdisciplinary integration (see De Jong, 2003; National Research Council, 2000).

In keeping with the emphasis on the integration of demographic and developmental perspectives, this chapter argues that studies of cognitive aging can benefit from an awareness of several demographic issues that affect inferences about estimates of relationships between aging and cognitive performance observed in both cross-sectional and longitudinal studies.

POPULATION CONCEPTS OF COGNITIVE AGING

It is not always clear from the literature on cognitive aging what the population is to which inferences are made. Few studies of cognitive aging, whether cross-sectional or longitudinal, use strategies of sample selection that are developed on the basis of a clear specification of the population of interest and an explicit design for sampling that population (see Alwin & Campbell, 2001; Alwin, Hofer, & McCammon, 2006; Kish, 1965, 1987). Instead, most investigators working on the topic of cognitive aging rely on participant pools composed largely of convenience samples and/or groups of volunteers to minimize the potential problems of external validity (e.g., Hultsch, MacDonald, Hunter, Maitland, & Dixon, 2002).

Regardless of the virtues of convenience samples, variability is often limited in such restricted samples, and standard errors of sample characteristics are not defined. Even the best work in the area of cognitive aging is limited with respect to generalizability. Certainly some of the best evidence for the life span development of various cognitive abilities is Schaie and Willis's Seattle Longitudinal Study, which began tracking a cross-section of the adult population in 1956 at 7-year reinterview intervals (see Schaie, 2005; see also chap. 23, this volume). Although the Seattle Longitudinal Study is still one of the most important and influential studies of age-related cognitive change, even those who work closely with it acknowledge its limitations. For example, the study is based on a nonprobability sample of unknown representativeness, and there are serious potential threats to internal validity due to problems of attrition, as noted by Schaie (1996) himself.

Furthermore, the few studies that use large, representative samples of the U.S. population—both repeated cross-sectional designs and longitudinal designs—are limited in the breadth of their cognitive performance measures (e.g., Alwin, 1991; Alwin & McCammon, 1999, 2001; Alwin, McCammon, Wray, & Rodgers, 2003; Hauser & Huang, 1997; Huang & Hauser, 1998; Wilson & Gove, 1999). Nevertheless, such research has the potential of contributing to the understanding of the nature of cognitive change in adulthood as well as providing information that will be useful in assessing the generalizability of previous findings to middle-aged and older populations in the United States and elsewhere.

Although these ideas are not foreign to researchers studying cognitive aging from a developmental perspective, there is clearly a need for exchange among investigators who develop research within the quasi-experimental tradition where external validity concerns are minimized and those whose work is rooted in the demographic tradition of understanding population processes, which puts a great deal of emphasis on probability methods of survey sampling. The field of demography can contribute to the study of cognitive aging by raising issues related to making generalizations about age-related change in populations of interest, by examining cohort differences in age-related cognitive change, and by considering issues

related to mortality selection in the examination of patterns of cognitive change.

The Importance of Population Concepts

The concept of a "population" is important for three reasons. First, issues related to population composition and related processes urge the clear specification of the population of interest in demographic studies of aging and human development (see Siegel & Swanson, 2004). Second, statistical concerns with inference and generalization emphasize the standard of external validity as a criterion against which to evaluate the quality of statistical inferences, and specification of the relevant population for these inferences and the systematic sampling from that population provide a means to meet that standard (Kish, 1987). Third, substantive questions are almost always linked to a specific population, and the clear definition of the population of interest brings the requirements of research design into sharper relief. The concept of *cohort* as used here—namely, a birth cohort—refers to a central component of population composition. For example, although some studies wish to generalize about the effects of historical events on cohort experiences, this may be futile without data from representative samples of those cohorts for the period studied.

In general, we think of populations as being defined by an event or the aggregation of events, for example, birth, widowhood, retirement, or death. Depending on the substantive question at hand, researchers using longitudinal data may wish to generalize to one of a number of different populations (see Nesselroade, 1988). First, there are several natural groups of interest to aging researchers, for example, nursing home residents, Medicare recipients, or retired persons. Second, the concept of birth cohort is a critical one for the study of population composition. In this case, birth is an event that defines the subpopulation of interest, and typically the division of the population into groups defined by cohort membership is the focus of the analysis (e.g., Alwin & McCammon, 2003). Third, survivorship (e.g., surviving members of birth cohorts) is often a possible basis of inference. Here issues of mortality selection are made explicit in defining the population. Fourth, mortality or death can be considered as a population-defining event—longitudinal data prior to death permit the study of processes linked to time of death.

In some circumstances, it may be desirable to generalize findings to baseline respondents, who, in the case of a total population survey, are themselves a subset of the universe of people ever born. Even in the most inclusive population surveys, the initial sample is frequently bound by geography and is always limited to those individuals alive at the time of sampling. When sampling with age restrictions, the universe of eligible respondents—and, thus, the reference population—is limited to members of the birth cohorts sampled who have survived to the age of study eligibility. Despite this potential censoring, the population of baseline survivors is potentially quite different from another possible population of interest to researchers, namely, endpoint survivors. By this, we typically mean the population of sampling units alive and study eligible at baseline and alive and study eligible at some later occasion of measurement. If one is interested in aging and is willing to put aside the possibility of period and/or cohort differences, this form of survivorship can be thought of as merely referring to those individuals who attained a given chronological age. For example, in the context of modeling longitudinal trajectories of cognitive aging from age 80 to 89, it is not necessary for all respondents to be age 80 at baseline. Instead, if one wishes to generalize to individuals who live to be at least 89, the important factor is that the respondents reach age 89 sometime between $Wave_1$ and $Wave_n$, inclusively.

Population Aging

In 2005, there were an estimated 5,120,394 persons age 85 and over in the United States (3,548,228 women and 1,572,166 men), and these numbers are expected to grow exponentially. We expect that in 2050 there will be more than 20,900,000 persons 85 years and older, a more than fourfold increase in 45 years. Demographers and others have been aware for some years of the growing size of the *oldest-old*, as the population age 85 and over is often called,

but knowledge of this phenomenon is increasingly out of date (see Manton & Suzman, 1992; Suzman, 2004; Suzman, Willis, & Manton, 1992).

Aging clearly is not only an individual matter but also a characteristic of the society at the macro-social level. *Population aging* is the change in the age distribution of the society in which increasing proportions of the population are older than was true for the society at an earlier time (Gavrilov & Heuveline, 2003). Given what is known about the increasing levels of population aging in the 21st century (Hayward & Zhang, 2001; United Nations, 2002), the need to understand the nature of cognitive aging in the future is a high priority.

Let us look at some trends in population composition. In absolute numbers, the older population (those over age 65 years) has tripled over the past 50 years and is expected to triple again in the next 50 years. Figure 4.1 presents the number of the total U.S. population age 65 and older as a percentage of the total population. In 1900, 4% of the U.S. population was 65 and over; in 2000, this figure was roughly 12.5%; and in 2050, about 20.7% of the population is expected be 65 and above. Even by 2030, when the Baby Boomers will mostly all have retired, about 1 in 5 Americans will be eligible for Social Security and Medicare, compared with just 1 in 8 today. Another way of seeing the phenomenon of population aging is to look at the median age of the population. In 1820, the median age of the population was 17; in 1900, it was 23; in 2000; the median age was 36; and in 2050 it is projected to be 38 (see Moody, 2000, p. xxvi).

The percentage figures in Figure 4.1 are broken down into three age categories: 65–74, 75–84, and 85+. All of these groups are growing in size as a percentage of the total population, but the group growing the fastest over this period is the 85+ group. This group constituted 0.2% of the population in 1900; by 1970, this figure was 0.7%; and by 2000, this group comprised 1.5% of the population. The growth in this group is expected to be nonlinear, with the group 85 and older projected to constitute 5% of the population in 2050.

A number of questions can be asked about this phenomenon: Is population aging inevitable? Will it keep on happening? Will the rate at

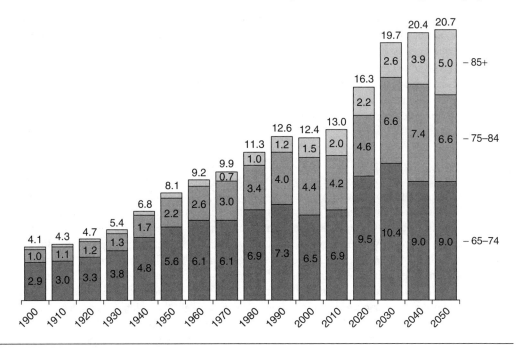

Figure 4.1   Percentage of Total U.S. Population Age 65 and Over, 1900–2050

SOURCES: 1900–2000: Hobbs and Stoops (2002); 2000–2050: U.S. Census Bureau (2004).

which it is happening change? Is American society unique?

These trends are not inevitable, but the demographic transitions being experienced throughout most of the world make them seem so. Populations age because of three demographic phenomena: (1) declining birth rates, (2) increasing life expectancy, and (3) differential migration by age. The first two are the main factors, especially in the United States, but there are some areas in the United States, for example, rural areas, where out-migration of the young is a fact of life. With migration held constant, population aging comes about because of a combination of two sets of population processes: (1) declining fertility and (2) declining mortality. These forces are operating worldwide. On the fertility side, the rising proportion of older people can be in part explained by declines in fertility associated with what is called the *demographic transition* (Caldwell, 1976). In preindustrial societies, both birth rates and death rates remained high, and populations remained stable. In traditional societies, the social structure and cultural values helped maintain high fertility and

reinforced the motivation to produce as many children as possible. Large numbers of children were advantageous because they contributed labor as children and as young adults, they bolstered the family's political and economic position, they ensured survival of the lineage, they undertook necessary religious services for ancestors, and they cared for parents in old age (Caldwell, 1976).

With industrialization and technological advances, mortality rates tended to fall while birth rates remained high for awhile and the population tended to grow. Then, at some point in advanced industrial societies, birth rates began to fall in line with death rates. After industrialization, the costs of having children are high, in terms of the need for parents to invest heavily in their development, with less possibility of an economic or social return on the investment, and the motivation to have children is substantially less (Caldwell, 1982). After the mid-19th century, with improvements in sanitation, nutrition, income, and medical technology, older age mortality began to decline. There are several hypotheses about the processes involved—Finch and Crimmins (2004), for example, argued that because of substantially less exposure to infectious disease in childhood, levels of serum inflammatory proteins (e.g., C-reactive protein), which contribute to the risk of heart attack, stroke, and cancer, have declined in older populations, resulting in delayed mortality.

Population Cognitive Aging

What does any of this have to do with cognitive aging? If there is a process of "typical" or "normative" aging whereby people experience a progressive loss of cognitive functional capacity as they age, and if those processes that keep the older population alive for increasing numbers of years do not reduce their cognitive aging, then it is apparent that the greater numbers of persons 85 and over in future years will bring about the greater prevalence of lower cognitive functioning associated with an aging population.

Let us examine this conclusion more closely. First, we assume that as a biological, neurological, social, and cognitive process, *cognitive aging* can be defined as those time-dependent irreversible changes that lead to progressive loss of functional capacity after a point of maturity. Of course, there is a great deal of heterogeneity in a population, but from this perspective these changes in the conditions of human frailty (e.g., declining respiratory function, hearing, vision, and cognitive function) are to some extent intrinsic within the organism rather than brought about by the outside environment, and they occur in a pattern that is characteristic of all members of a given species (see Weiss, 1990). Studies of cognitive aging should not treat aging as a process that is empirically separable from disease. Instead, to study the causes of cognitive loss in aging individuals, one must directly measure the influence of age-related disease and risk processes. Because our research designs do not usually permit fine-grained analyses of individuals over time, we have examined the effects of dementia (and other diseases, e.g., diabetes) mostly as a between-person variable (present or absent). A more sophisticated treatment would recognize that dementia (like other age-related diseases) is a progressive process that unfolds within individuals over time. Understanding how the progression of dementia and other diseases (in their preclinical stage) influences cognition is an essential step in formulating principled accounts of cognitive aging effects.

However, from a disciplinary perspective, studies of cognitive aging and dementia typically have proceeded independently. Researchers interested in understanding normal or healthy aging attempt to eliminate the influence of dementia by screening out impaired individuals with mental status examinations. This strategy is only partially successful, and even in select, highly screened samples of older adults a substantial proportion of participants are in the very early stages of preclinical dementia and influence estimates of cognitive performance and age effects (e.g., Sliwinski, Lipton, Buschke, & Stewart, 1996). This problem of the influence of preclinical dementia would likely be amplified in a more representative sample of elders, compared with self-selected volunteer samples of motivated individuals. Recent studies have shown that the presence of subgroups with preclinical dementia can influence estimates of cognitive change and the covariance of change among cognitive domains (Sliwinski, Hofer, Hall, Bushke, & Lipton, 2003). Moreover, in the absence of dementia and disease (Haan, Shemanski, Jagust, Manolio, & Kuller, 1999; Hall, Lipton, Sliwinski, & Stewart, 2000; Rubin et al., 1998), there is very little evidence of cognitive loss and if present is very slight. This problem of preclinical dementia is an illustration of why attempts to study "healthy" aging may be misguided (see the discussion of this issue in Chapters 18 and 21, this volume).

Aging is not a disease process, but it does eventually produce both functional decline and increased susceptibility to illness and death from specific diseases. Signs of typical aging, such as short-term memory lapses, wrinkled skin, and gray hair are thus not symptoms of disease and need not result in greater susceptibility to death. However, with advanced age also comes weakened ability to fight off such diseases as cancer and infections, even as there is cognitive decline that reduces memory, speed of processing, and the like.

As noted earlier, one of the important components of population aging is declining mortality rates. When advances are made in curing or forestalling the diseases that tend to result in death to older people, this then means that an even larger proportion of people survive into advanced old age. Thus, although one may forestall physical functional decline, and the susceptibility to illness and death from specific diseases, there may be no counterpart in the area of cognitive functioning. The question for the student of the future of cognitive aging is: Will changes in cognitive function continue in old age, as our current models predict, or will we be able to develop parallel remedies that cure or forestall cognitive functional decline?

To produce some estimates of the nature of LCF over the next half century, we used the Telephone Interview for Cognitive Status (TICS; see Brandt, Spencer, & Folstein, 1988), which is modeled after the Mini-Mental State Examination (Folstein, Folstein, & McHugh, 1975) available in the HRS data. The HRS TICS score we used includes the following tasks (see Herzog & Wallace, 1997): (1) counting backward from 20 for 10 continuous numbers (1 point was given for a correct response), (2) naming the day of the week and the date (1 point for correct day of week, day, month, and year), (3) naming the objects that "people usually use to cut paper" and the "kind of prickly plant that grows in the desert" (1 point for each correct name), and (4) naming the President and Vice President of the United States (1 point for each correct last name). On the basis of these data we constructed a 9-item TICS score (1 point for each of the following: correct backward count; day of week, day, month, year; cactus;

scissors; President; Vice President). The frequency distributions for this score are given in Alwin et al. (2008). For the purpose of (arbitrarily) defining a state of LCF in the community population sampled by the HRS, we used a cutpoint of 5 or less on this composite measure.

Using the distribution of this measure in the 1998 wave of the HRS, and the demographic technique of indirect standardization (see Siegel & Swanson, 2004), we produced a projected distribution of LCF in the United States through 2050, as shown in Figure 4.2. This exercise does not depend on the particular measure used, because we obtained the same result using a number of alternative measurement strategies. In all cases, the results suggest that as the population ages, the levels of LCF in the older ranges of the population will become more prevalent, more than doubling between 2000 and 2050. The interpretation of these estimates is based on several assumptions, which we are willing to concede may invalidate the results presented. Specifically, this assumes that age-specific rates of LCF are constant.

Projecting rates of cognitive impairment requires one to reconcile information about risk factors associated with current rates and making assumptions about the health status of future cohorts of older adults. Much of the current literature indicates that cognitive impairment in older age is largely not preventable, and that

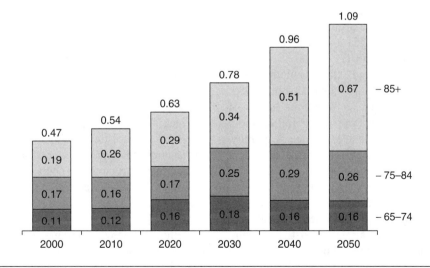

Figure 4.2   Percentage of Total Population That Is Age 65 and Over With Low Cognitive Functioning: 2000–2050

SOURCE: Alwin et al. (2008).

dementia, particularly Alzheimer's disease, will increase in prevalence in the coming years (Brookmeyer & Gray, 2000; Brookmeyer, Gray, & Kawas, 1998; Evans et al., 1992). To cite one recent reference, the prevalence of Alzheimer's disease in the next 50 years is projected to nearly quadruple, "which means that 1 in every 45 Americans will be affected by the disease" (Kawas & Brookmeyer, 2001, p. 1160).

Some research, on the other hand, has suggested that rates of dementia have decreased in recent decades despite increasing population aging (e.g., Corder & Manton, n.d.). It can be argued as well that the decrease may be slowed or even reversed in future decades. Certainly, some risk factors for dementia—smoking and high blood pressure, in particular—have decreased as antismoking campaigns are heeded and blood pressure medications are increasingly prescribed and used. Other lifestyle changes, such as eating a low fat diet, exercising regularly, and maintaining a healthy weight to control high blood pressure and diabetes, may also reduce the risk for vascular dementia and, in turn, Alzheimer's disease (see Kaplan, Haan, & Wallace, 1999). This point of view suggests that the estimates in Figure 4.2 may be too high. However, the projected rising rates of obesity and diabetes in increasingly younger populations as well as concerns about the resurgence of smoking in younger adults warn that these risk factors may erase the positive influences of smoking cessation and blood pressure medications in today's middle-aged and older adults for tomorrow's middle-aged and older adults (see Finch & Crimmins, 2004).

On the other hand, the population may experience what Vaupel and Yashin (1985, pp. 181–182) termed an "apparent failure of success." Health advances allow frailer, more susceptible individuals to live longer. Certainly, the best current estimates are that as the rapid growth in the oldest age group continues, so will the prevalence of the dementias (e.g., Alzheimer's; see Evans et al., 1992). This subpopulation will have a higher dementia rate at a given age than does a more robust subpopulation (consisting of those who would have lived to that age without the advances in health practices). Thus, reduced mortality at younger ages may result in increased morbidity (including

LCF) at older ages, in which case the estimates shown in Figure 4.2 may be too low.

If our projections of greater prevalence of LCF with population aging are correct, the consequences of this estimated greater prevalence of LCF are striking. Future studies of cognitive aging will, we hope, consider the full range of these consequences, specifically the greater burden on caregivers, as well as greater demands on long-term care and the medical system for delivering medical treatment for chronic illnesses linked to aging to persons who experience LCF.

COHORT EFFECTS

Several years ago, Kenneth Gergen (1973), writing about social psychology, made an important set of observations that are relevant in the present context. Gergen (1973) argued that "contemporary" theories of social behavior are "primarily reflections of contemporary history" (p. 309). He suggested we think in terms of a "*continuum of historical durability*, with phenomena highly susceptible to historical influence at one extreme and the more stable processes at the other" (1973, p. 318). Some phenomena may be closely tied to innate and irreversible physiological givens, and many would argue that patterns of cognitive aging are an example of such phenomena. On the other hand, "learned dispositions," Gergen suggested, may in some cases "overcome the strength of some physiological tendencies" (1973, p. 318). In a later essay, elaborating on the same point, Gergen (1980) suggested that evidence of cohort differences in developmental trajectories of a wide range of human characteristics is invariably found among cohorts born in different historical eras within the same culture (Gergen, 1980). He suggested that "depending upon the socio-historical circumstances, differing age-related trajectories are found in value commitments, personality characteristics, *mental capabilities* [italics added], political ideology, communication patterns and so on" (Gergen, 1980, p. 37).

Although Gergen (1980) may have overstated the case somewhat, it is now well accepted that age-related trajectories of cognitive performance observed in samples of individuals from age-heterogeneous populations may be due in part to the spurious effects of historically linked cohort experiences. Historical processes are implicated by the fact that cohort groups differ markedly in their levels of schooling, which are predictive of levels of cognitive performance. In a recent monograph (Alwin et al., 2008), we argued that generalizations about processes of cognitive aging can be improved by examining such issues in broad representative samples of populations of interest and by considering the relevance of demographic processes in estimating aging functions in samples of such populations. We argued that it is important to consider the historical processes of educational expansion and cohort differences in schooling outcomes as they relate to assessments of cognitive functioning in aging populations.

The demographic literature concerned with cohort effects on cognitive functioning has focused primarily on differences between cohorts in levels (or intercepts) of performance (e.g., Alwin, 1991; Alwin & McCammon, 1999, 2001). By contrast, the developmental literature has phrased the issue of cohort variation in terms of the existence (or lack thereof) of "simple age-graded nomothetic and universal patterns of behavioral development" (Baltes et al., 1979, p. 86). As we illustrate below, both of these issues may be investigated within the framework of growth models by explicitly examining the differences between two sets of models—one that posits intraindividual change across all cohorts to follow the same overall age-based trajectory (Bell, 1953, 1954; McArdle & Bell, 2000) and one that allows for potential differences in intercepts and slopes across cohorts (Miyazaki & Raudenbush, 2000). The question for future research on cognitive aging is whether the patterns of cognitive decline witnessed in contemporary data are likely to be observed in similar studies conducted 50 years from now on the cohorts of today's children.

In a related body of work (Alwin et al., 2008), we present a historical framework for understanding cohort differences in cognitive performance, and we briefly summarize the argument here. Cohort experiences can affect cognitive scores (e.g., verbal and quantitative abilities) through several mechanisms. Childhood and youth are periods for learning vast amounts of new information, and this information becomes a resource for further development. Such knowledge may be affected by the distinctiveness of cohort experiences. One of the major mechanisms for the transmission of knowledge is formal schooling, and it is often assumed that greater amounts of time spent in school, as assessed by years of schooling completed, should be related to greater amounts of knowledge across a wide range of domains. More recently born cohorts' greater access to schooling should better prepare them for adult life compared with earlier born cohorts. Indeed, psychometricians have known for a long time that standardized test scores tend to rise from one generation to another. The tendency for test scores on standardized effects to increase over time has been called the *Flynn effect,* named after James Flynn, a political scientist at the University of Otago in New Zealand, who quantified the pervasiveness of the pattern (Flynn, 1984, 1987, 1998; Neisser, 1997, 1998). This is perhaps the most well-documented example of a systematic cohort effect on cognitive test scores. Flynn (1984, p. 48) argued that increased educational levels accounted for much, but far from all, of these IQ gains.

However, the tendency for test scores to rise has not always been the case. During the 1960s and 1970s, there was serious concern expressed about the declining performance by the young on measures of verbal ability. Average verbal scores on standardized tests like the Scholastic Aptitude Test and the American College Testing Service examinations (see Wirtz, Howe, et al., 1977) declined systematically from the mid-1960s through the mid-1980s. There are, of course, serious problems with interpreting changes in college-admissions test scores as if they reflect true aggregate levels of verbal and quantitative skills of high school students, given the changing composition of the test-taking population, but most observers of the test score declines conceded that, net of these compositional shifts, the decline was real (e.g., Blake, 1989). Responding to the need for better information based on national probability samples, Alwin (1991) used data from nine representative samples of the U.S. population in the General Social Survey between 1974 and 1990, showing that there were systematic education-adjusted differences among cohorts in the General Social Survey vocabulary test score, especially beginning with those born subsequent to 1946. He concluded that these differences were a reflection of the same social processes that produced the test score decline of the 1960s and 1970s.

Glenn (1994) confirmed the existence of this intercohort trend in vocabulary knowledge and argued that the trend could be interpreted by reference to intercohort differences in media exposure, that is, television watching and newspaper reading. Since the publication of Alwin's (1991) and Glenn's studies, other work has reinforced the cohort interpretation of the test score decline. Much concern has focused on literacy and what schools are teaching, and recent historical analyses of reading difficulty in student texts are quite revealing. For example, Hayes, Wolfer, and Wolfe (1996) argued that schools have contributed to lower verbal scores because of a progressive simplification of the language used in schoolbooks. Reviewing 800 textbooks used in elementary, middle, and high schools between 1919 and 1991, they found that the vocabulary of the schoolbooks became progressively easier after World War II. They concluded that daily use of simplified textbooks across 11 years of schooling produces "a cumulating deficit in students' knowledge base and advanced verbal skill" (Hayes et al., 1996, p. 493). The systematic dumbing-down of American reading textbooks provides a strong basis for a sociohistorical interpretation of the decline in verbal test scores in the 1960s and 1970s, a decline not experienced to the same extent by the quantitative scores (Chall & Conard 1991, pp. 1–4). Thus, despite the fact that more recent cohorts (post-1946 cohorts) have much higher levels of schooling, according to this argument, they are learning less. (For alternative views, see Wilson & Gove [1999] and Schaie, Willis, & Pennak [2005], and for debate surrounding their arguments, see Alwin & McCammon [1999, 2001] and chap. 23, this volume.)

Are There Cohort Effects on Cognitive Performance in Pre-1947 Cohorts?

To illustrate how cohort effects may have implications for the knowledge and skills relevant to performance on cognitive tasks later in life, we present an example from our ongoing research using the HRS data (see Alwin et al.,

2003, 2008). This example uses the immediate word recall measure from the HRS. The HRS immediate word recall test involves a set of 10 words read to the respondent, who is then asked to recall as many of the words as possible.[1]

Figure 4.3 presents a comparison of two estimates of the aging function for this measure from approximately 50 through 95 years of age based on the following two models: (1) a convergence (or age-based) model in which data from separate cohorts follow the same aging function (McArdle & Bell, 2000), that is, cohort-specific aging functions are constrained to have equivalent intercepts and functional forms, and (2) a free intercepts model in which cohort-specific aging functions have the same functional form within cohorts but different intercepts (Miyazaki & Raudenbush, 2000). Information on statistical fit of the models is given in Table 4.1.

These results strongly suggest that failing to take cohort differences into account in the investigation of patterns of cognitive aging can bias the assessment of rates of cognitive decline in old age. In the example presented in Figure 4.3 the convergence model (solid line) underestimates the rate of change over the age range. Descriptively, the curve is pulled upward at older ages to accommodate intercept differences among cohorts. In contrast, the dashed line illustrates a hypothetical trajectory over the entire age range, using the same quadratic function as the cohort-specific curves. These types of results lead us to reject the more conventional age-based or convergence models that are common in the growth modeling literature, which assume there are no cohort differences in processes of cognitive aging. We believe that the set of models allowing for cohort differences in intercepts and slopes has great promise, and we encourage future students of cognitive aging to reconsider the conventional view in favor of a set of models that are sensitive to cohort differences.

In addition to developing an account of cognitive aging that is sensitive to differences in cohort experiences, our results further suggest that if these processes are examined while controlling for intercohort differences in schooling, the cohort differences are clarified even more. In

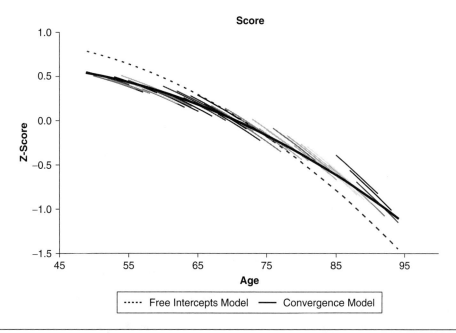

Figure 4.3   Comparison of the Convergence Model With the Free Intercept Model for the Health and Retirement Study Immediate Word Recall Measure

SOURCE: Alwin et al. (2008).

Table 4.1   Goodness of Fit Information for Latent Growth Models for the Health and Retirement Study Immediate Word Recall Measure

Model	Functional form	Free intercepts	Free slopes	Free education slopes	df	CMIN	CMIN/df	p	RMSEA	NFI
1	Quadratic	No	No	N/A	550	949.0	1.73	.000	.006	.925
2	Quadratic	Yes	No	N/A	394	643.4	1.63	.000	.006	.949
3	Quadratic	Yes	Yes	N/A	199	368.8	1.85	.000	.007	.971
1e	Quadratic	No	No	No	749	1,724.6	2.30	.000	.008	.891
2e	Quadratic	Yes	No	No	593	1,349.8	2.28	.000	.008	.915
3e	Quadratic	Yes	Yes	No	398	1,070.9	2.69	.000	.009	.933
4e	Quadratic	Yes	Yes	Yes	359	976.8	2.72	.000	.010	.938

SOURCE: Alwin et al. (2008).

NOTE: $N = 18,881$. Models 1e–4e include years of schooling as a covariate predicting the observed scores. CMIN = minimum value of the discrepancy function; RMSEA = root-mean-square error of approximation; NFI = normed fit index.

the present case, controlling for intercohort differences in schooling appears to accentuate cohort differences in intercepts, as shown in Figure 4.4. The overall results point to a conclusion that, despite greater amounts of schooling, World War II cohorts have scored systematically lower on cognitive tests compared to those born earlier in the century.

This set of results is somewhat puzzling, and even potentially alarming, but it will, we hope, challenge researchers to further explore the patterns observed here. Possible explanations that

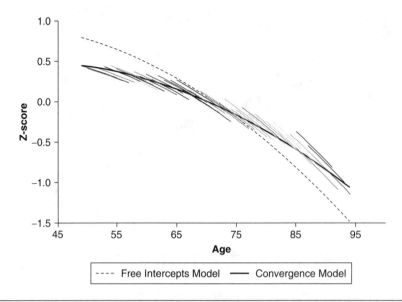

Figure 4.4   Comparison of the Convergence Model With the Free Intercept Model for the Health and
Retirement Study Immediate Word Recall Score, Controlling for Schooling

SOURCE: Alwin et al. (2008).

may account for the cohort-specific differences in intercepts observed in these results include: historical effects on cognitive development via cohort differences in experience and/or mortality selection favoring the earlier born cohorts, such that differential survival of most cognitively fit in the earlier born cohorts are at a comparative advantage relative to the later born cohorts.

Although an argument can be made for differences in the experiences among cohorts in levels of schooling that might account for cohort differences in cognitive test performance, this explanation is counterintuitive in the present case. Our results from the HRS cognitive performance data show the opposite pattern, that is, one in which the intercepts of earlier born cohorts are higher than those of later born cohorts. When intercohort differences in the level of schooling are controlled, the differences in intercepts are accentuated rather than reduced or removed—as shown in Figure 4.5.

This does not mean that controlling for schooling produces a biased set of results, as we would argue that estimates of the effects of aging should control for both cohort and schooling. The cohort differences in intercepts are

observed regardless of whether we adjust for schooling, and the intercept differences favor the earlier born cohorts. However, in order for adjustments for cohort differences in schooling to be undertaken, it is necessary to assume *additivity*, that is, a common education slope across birth cohorts. Without this assumption it is difficult to imagine how we can take schooling into account statistically. At the same time, the meaning of "years of schooling" has changed over this century. A year of schooling measured in the early born cohorts studied here—those born in the early part of the century—is potentially something quite different from a year of schooling measured in the later born cohorts—those born in the early 1940s. In this sense, it may be that any findings resulting from an adjustment for the linear effects of schooling do not really control for schooling or, if they do, they do so in a biased manner.

In our examination of this issue in the HRS data, we estimated a model in which there were systematic differences by cohort in the effects of schooling, that is, in the "cognitive benefit" to a year of schooling. This model (see Model 4e in Table 4.1) frees the effects of schooling on cognitive functioning across cohorts and includes

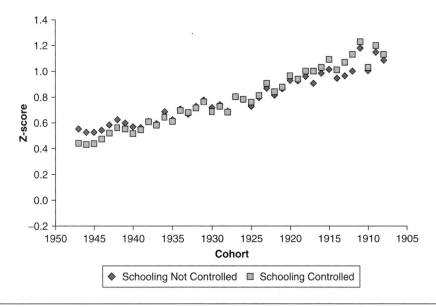

Figure 4.5   Cohort-Specific Intercepts for the Health and Retirement Study Immediate Word Recall With and Without Controls for Schooling

SOURCE: Alwin et al. (2008).

free intercepts and slopes. This model allows us to assess the extent to which the assumption of the homogeneity of schooling slopes across cohorts makes sense. On the basis of the fit statistics given in Table 4.1, it appears that this specification results in only a slight improvement in fit across all measures, and the overall improvement is not large given the number of degrees of freedom involved.

We present the intercohort differences in the education slopes in Figure 4.6, which presents cohort-specific coefficients from the regression of the HRS immediate recall measure on years of schooling (graphed using 3-year moving averages). As these results indicate, there appears to be a systematic increase in these coefficients over cohorts, from earlier to later born cohorts. The main departure from homogeneity occurs among the cohorts born before 1930, where the coefficients appear to be systematically lower. These results remind us of the potential for the waning contributions of schooling, as articulated in the observation made by Lorge (1956, p. 133) that earlier born members of the population are at a disadvantage not only because of their lower levels of schooling but also in part because of

their distance from formal schooling. Of course, to this point in the analysis we have not witnessed the disadvantages that stem from the lower levels of schooling characteristic of the earlier born cohorts.

Given their potentially systematic nature, we believe it is important to be concerned about the possible effects these patterns have on the adjustments we made for schooling. We must consider the possible overadjustments that may occur to the intercepts of the early born cohorts and underadjustments to the later born cohorts when implementing standard statistical controls for individual differences in schooling. At this point, it is not clear how much of an effect this has on our interpretation, but we nonetheless offer caution in accepting the interpretation that there are meaningful differences in the cognitive benefit to years of schooling that favor later born cohorts without further investigation. In addition to the potential consequences of these differences for our statistical adjustments, they may be of inherent substantive interest in that they reflect on the potential for schooling to maintain its influence of cognitive performance, a topic we consider extensively elsewhere (Alwin et al., 2008).

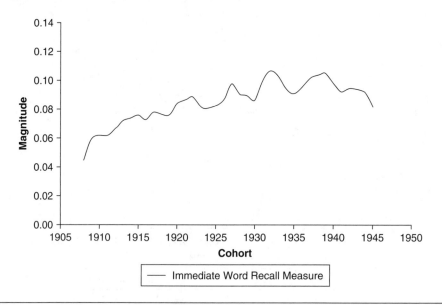

Figure 4.6   Cohort-Specific Coefficients From Regression of the Health and Retirement Study Immediate Recall Measures on Years of Schooling

SOURCE: Alwin et al. (2008).

MORTALITY SELECTION

Perhaps the most plausible explanation of the pattern of intercohort differences in intercepts reported here is the phenomenon of *mortality selection* (e.g., Baltes, 1968; Schaie, Labouvie, & Barrett, 1973). A given birth cohort can be thought of as a collection of subpopulations defined by longevity, and cohorts differ substantially in their representation of these subpopulations. Membership in these subpopulations is not easily discernible prior to death; however, an individual's current age serves as a lower bound. As a result, given stable (or at least proportional) age-specific mortality rates, heterogeneity in longevity decreases with age, meaning that at a given time earlier born cohorts are less heterogeneous with respect to expected age at death than are the later-borns.

Consider the data on age of death presented in Figure 4.7. From these data, one can infer that earlier born cohorts contain substantially less heterogeneity with regard to longevity than do later born cohorts. For persons who live to age 60, total life expectancy in 2002 was roughly 82 years, whereas at age 80 it was about 89 years. Not only is total life expectancy (or expected age at death) higher at age 80, but also there is

considerably less heterogeneity in the expected age at death. Thus, when comparing groups of different ages, one must realize that the younger group contains individuals whose longevity is lower than the lower bound (age) of the older group (Vaupel & Yashin, 1985).

If the variable of interest—in this case, cognitive functioning—is positively related to longevity, then the younger group will necessarily have a lower age-standardized mean than that of the older group, net of any "real" cohort differences.

Mortality is obviously selective, and to the extent that selectivity is linked to factors associated with levels of cognitive performance, then mortality selection is a potential explanation for the above findings. Indeed, it might be the case that such performance-linked selectivity in survivorship might be masking a "true" cohort effect that favors more recently born cohorts. Therefore, a strong argument can be made that differential age-specific mortality rates should be taken into account when examining age differences in cognitive performance, or when comparing cohorts in patterns of age-related within-cohort change.

We can examine the relationship between mortality patterns and age-related trajectories of

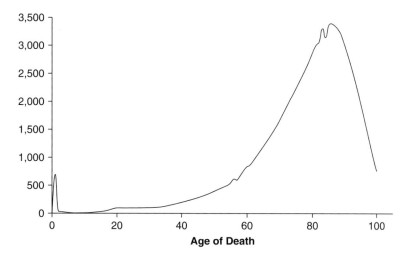

Figure 4.7   Number of Deaths by Age, Out of 100,000 Born Alive: United States, 2002

SOURCE: Arias (2004).

performance using the HRS immediate recall measure, as shown in Table 4.2. For each of several birth cohort groups from the Assets and Health Dynamics (AHEAD) subsample—those born 1890–1908, 1909–1913, 1914–1918, and 1919–1923—this table displays mean levels of the immediate recall measure (in the standardized metric used for the entire HRS sample) for different patterns of mortality, adjusted for differences in schooling (see Alwin et al., 2008). The patterns of mortality displayed in Table 4.2 are for subpopulations defined by longevity, specifically, respondents alive in 1996 who: died prior to 1998, were alive in 1998 and died prior to 2000, were alive in 2000 and died prior to 2002, and were alive in 2002. Note that there is greater heterogeneity in age at death in the fourth group than exists in the first three and that this is borne out in the pattern of group-specific means.

These means are generated separately for each wave, using mortality pattern and age group (birth cohort group) as class variables. Within waves, there is a significant effect for mortality pattern and age group (and education, when it is included), but there is no evidence of an interaction effect between mortality pattern and age group. Similar patterns of results are obtained from all HRS subsamples, but we limit our presentation of findings to the AHEAD cohorts—born pre-1900 to 1923.

There is a clear difference in cognitive performance between members of a given cohort (in this case, a group of cohorts) who are nearer to death in any wave of the study relative to those who prove themselves to have greater longevity. Whatever factors are selective with respect to mortality in these data, they appear to be associated with level of cognitive performance. These results illustrate the phenomena of mortality selection with respect to cognitive performance and strongly suggest that this process is one explanation of the pattern of intercohort differences in intercepts reported in the above analysis.

Given this pattern of cognitive scores among groups defined by patterns of mortality, and given that heterogeneity in longevity decreases with age, the later born cohorts, as a whole, have lower mean levels of cognitive performance than does the subset of these cohorts that will survive to the ages represented by the earlier born cohorts. These results suggest that comparisons of age differences in cognitive performance, particularly when undertaken cross-sectionally, should take age-specific mortality rates into account. We note, however, that if the phenomenon of interest declines with age but is positively related to longevity, then the bias introduced by ignoring mortality selection is conservative; that is, under such circumstances,

Table 4.2 Mean Immediate Word Recall Score by Birth Cohort and Mortality Status: Health and Retirement Study, 1996–2002

Birth cohorts 1919–1923

Mean age / Year of measurement

Mortality pattern	75 / 1996	77 / 1998	79 / 2000	81 / 2002	Total
1000	-0.315				-0.315
1100	-0.404	-0.491			-0.445
1110	-0.277	-0.395	-0.573		-0.409
1111	-0.071	-0.126	-0.280	-0.370	-0.207
Total	-0.267	-0.338	-0.426	-0.370	-0.344

Birth cohorts 1914–1918

Mean age / Year of measurement

Mortality pattern	80 / 1996	82 / 1998	84 / 2000	86 / 2002	Total
1000	-0.610				-0.610
1100	-0.627	-0.695			-0.659
1110	-0.431	-0.543	-0.777		-0.572
1111	-0.209	-0.295	-0.467	-0.529	-0.366
Total	-0.469	-0.511	-0.622	-0.529	-0.525

Birth cohorts 1909–1913

Mean age / Year of measurement

Mortality pattern	85 / 1996	87 / 1998	89 / 2000	91 / 2002	Total
1000	-0.813				-0.813
1100	-0.644	-0.845			-0.736
1110	-0.481	-0.708	-1.065		-0.716
1111	-0.439	-0.515	-0.717	-0.702	-0.581
Total	-0.594	-0.689	-0.891	-0.702	-0.694

Birth cohorts 1890–1908

Mean age / Year of measurement

Mortality pattern	91 / 1996	93 / 1998	95 / 2000	97 / 2002	Total
1000	-1.121				-1.121
1100	-0.808	-1.324			-1.041
1110	-0.687	-1.141	-1.148		-0.969
1111	-0.615	-0.824	-0.955	-1.038	-0.831
Total	-0.808	-1.096	-1.051	-1.038	-0.948

SOURCE: Alwin et al. (2008).

ignoring mortality selection results in an underestimate of age-related decline.

One solution to this is to account for cohort differences in longevity by controlling statistically for intercohort differences in expected age at death. We have used this approach in the example used above for the HRS measure of immediate recall, as shown in Figure 4.8. The objective of this analysis is to account for heterogeneity in cohort experiences in variables linked to survivorship, at least at the cohort level. We know of no research that has attempted to control for individual differences on expected longevity, although the examination of the history of panel respondents who have experienced mortality—which eventually will include all respondents in the HRS—represents an appropriate strategy for analyzing cognitive change in what may be a more informative time metric.

The results in this case confirm the expectation that mortality selection is a plausible explanation for the intercohort differences in the HRS immediate work recall measure reported above. As Figure 4.8 illustrates, after controlling for intercohort differences in expected age at death, the free intercepts model reveals significant differences in cohort-specific intercepts that are consistent with theoretical expectations regarding the historical influences on cohort differences. These results are quite general, extending to other measures of cognitive functioning in the HRS data (Alwin et al., 2008). In brief, these results show that, with statistical adjustments for processes of mortality selection (i.e., controlling for intercohort differences in expected age at death), later born cohorts show significantly higher levels of test performance relative to their earlier born counterparts. In addition, we note that the results in Figure 4.8 reinforce the conclusions advanced earlier, that the free intercepts model appears to reflect a better assessment of the aging function than the more conventional age-based or convergence models that are common in the growth modeling literature, which assume there are no cohort differences in processes of cognitive aging.

CONCLUSION

Long-term declines in fertility and mortality over the past century have contributed to the phenomenon of population aging. With advances in curing or forestalling the diseases that tend to result in death of older people, an even larger proportion of people will survive into advanced

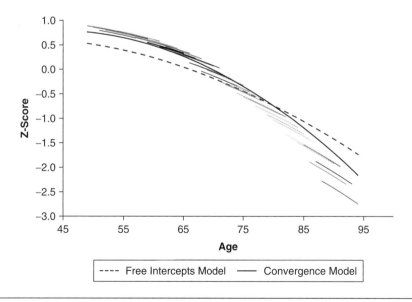

Figure 4.8   Comparison of the Convergence Model With the Free Intercept Model for the Health and Retirement Study Immediate Word Recall Measure, Controlling for Expected Age at Death

SOURCE: Alwin et al. (2008).

old age. The question for the future of cognitive aging is: Will changes in cognitive function continue in old age, as our current models predict, or will we be able to develop parallel remedies that will cure or forestall cognitive functional decline? Will advances in health allow more cognitively fragile persons to live longer, embodying what Vaupel and Yashin (1985, pp. 181–182) termed an "apparent failure of success"? Although we may forestall physical functional decline, and the susceptibility to illness and death from specific diseases, there may be no counterpart in the area of cognitive functioning.

In this chapter, we have argued that to address these questions, future research on cognitive aging will benefit from the cooperation and partnership of the population and developmental sciences. We suggested that future research and scholarship necessary for the complete understanding of processes of cognitive aging will embody a kind of transdisciplinary integration of concepts, data, and methods that is at present lacking. We therefore have emphasized the relevance of concepts involving population processes and certain demographic trends for the understanding of the future of cognitive aging.

On the one hand, one might argue that as a result of these demographic phenomena, the present knowledge we have about cognitive aging may be irrelevant for making projections about how future generations will function in old age. Although there is not a great deal of evidence to date that there are massive intercohort differences in the processes of aging in key dimensions of cognitive functioning, there is a great deal of agreement that the potential for important differences exists. When coupled with the phenomenon of population aging, the idea that cohort differences may exist in cognitive aging functions puts a high premium on gathering new data on new cohorts. However, whether our current levels of knowledge regarding the age trajectories of certain abilities will generalize to future generations remains an open question.

Finally, most would argue that we have evolved as a species primarily for the purpose of reproduction and not for longevity (Baltes, 1997). Although the evolutionary impact of mortality selection on the future of the species can occur any time between the formation of a new zygote to the end of an organism's period of fertility, the fact remains that processes of mortality selection, again in combination with the realities of population aging, create serious problems for the analysis of aging based on the cross-sectional comparison of age differences. Moreover, historical changes in the influence of structural processes on changes in individuals as they age also limit the generalizability of conclusions drawn strictly from longitudinal approaches. It is clear that new data structures and new methods will be required of the future of cognitive aging research in order to avoid many of the puzzles that we currently face with regard to the nature of aging in cognitive function. Aging is a matter of survival, and even as we may entertain ideas about the cognitive patterns of "normal" aging that apply to those who survive, we must also entertain ideas about selective survival and the processes of aging for those parts of the population whose longevity is curtailed in early adulthood and at midlife.

NOTE

1. The survey question was worded as follows: "I'll read a set of 10 words and ask you to recall as many as you can. We have purposely made the list long so that it will be difficult for anyone to recall all the words—most people recall just a few. Please listen carefully as I read the set of words because I cannot repeat them. When I finish, I will ask you to recall aloud as many of the words as you can, in any order. Is this clear?" After reading the list, the interviewer asked, "Now please tell me the words you can recall." An example of the words on one of the lists is as follows: *hotel, river, tree, skin, gold, market, paper, child, king, book.* Four different word lists were used across respondents, and the list used for a given respondent was varied across waves. Up to 2 minutes were allowed to recall the words on the list. For purposes of analysis, we standardized the measure within the list and across waves, using the entire HRS sample.

REFERENCES

Alwin, D. F. (1991). Family of origin and cohort differences in verbal ability. *American Sociological Review, 56,* 625–638.

Alwin, D. F., & Campbell, R. T. (2001). Longitudinal methods in the study of human development and aging. In R. H. Binstock & L. K. George (Eds.),

Handbook of aging and the social sciences (pp. 22–43). New York: Academic Press.

Alwin, D. F., et al. (2008). *The aging mind in social and historical context.* Unpublished manuscript. University Park: Population Research Institute, Pennsylvania State University.

Alwin, D. F., Hofer, S. M., & McCammon, R. J. (2006). Modeling the effects of time: Integrating demographic and developmental perspectives. In R. H. Binstock & L. K. George (Eds.), *Handbook of aging and the social sciences* (6th ed., pp. 20–38). New York: Academic Press.

Alwin, D. F., & McCammon, R. J. (1999). Aging vs. cohort interpretations of intercohort differences in GSS Verbal scores. *American Sociological Review, 64,* 272–286.

Alwin, D. F., & McCammon, R. J. (2001). Aging, cohorts, and verbal ability. *Journal of Gerontology: Social Sciences, 56B,* S1–S11.

Alwin, D. F., & McCammon, R. J. (2003). Generations, cohorts, and social change. In J. T. Mortimer & M. J. Shanahan (Eds.), *Handbook of the life course* (pp. 23–49). New York: Kluwer Academic/Plenum.

Alwin, D. F., McCammon, R. J., Wray, L. A., & Rodgers, W. L. (2003, September). *Populations, cohorts and processes of cognitive aging.* Paper presented at the conference on "The Dynamic Processes in Ageing: The Relationships Among Cognitive, Social, Biological, Health and Economic Factors in Aging," Canberra, Australia.

Arias, E. (2004). *United States life tables, 2002* (National Vital Statistics Reports, Vol. 53, No. 6). Hyattsville, MD: National Center for Health Statistics.

Baltes, P. B. (1968). Longitudinal and cross-sectional sequences in the study of age and generation effects. *Human Development, 11,* 145–171.

Baltes, P. B. (1997). On the incomplete architecture of human ontogeny. *American Psychologist, 52,* 366–380.

Baltes, P. B., Cornelius, S. W., & Nesselroade, J. R. (1979). Cohort effects in developmental psychology. In J. Nesselroade & P. Baltes (Eds.), *Longitudinal research in the study of behavior and development* (pp. 61–87). New York: Academic Press.

Baltes, P. B., & Mayer, K. U. (1999). *The Berlin Aging Study: Aging from 70 to 100.* New York: Cambridge University Press.

Bell, R. Q. (1953). Convergence: An accelerated longitudinal approach. *Child Development, 27,* 45–74.

Bell, R. Q. (1954). An experimental test of the accelerated longitudinal approach. *Child Development, 25,* 281–286.

Blake, J. (1989). *Family size and achievement.* Berkeley: University of California Press.

Brandt, J., Spencer, M., & Folstein, M. (1988). The Telephone Interview of Cognitive Status. *Neuropsychiatry, Neuropsychology, and Behavioral Neurology, 1,* 111–117.

Brookmeyer, R., & Gray, S. (2000). Methods for projecting the incidence and prevalence of chronic diseases in ageing populations: Application to Alzheimer's disease. *Statistics in Medicine, 19,* 1481–1493.

Brookmeyer, R., Gray, S., & Kawas, C. (1998). Projections of Alzheimer's disease in the United States and the public health impact of delaying disease onset. *American Journal of Public Health, 88,* 1337–1342.

Caldwell, J. C. (1976). Toward a restatement of demographic transition theory. *Population and Development Review, 2,* 321–366.

Caldwell, J. C. (1982). *Theory of fertility decline.* New York: Academic Press.

Chall, J. S., & Conard, S. S. (1991). *Should textbooks challenge students? The case for easier or harder books.* New York: Teachers College Press.

Corder, E. H., & Manton, K. G. (n.d.). *Change in the prevalence of severe dementia among older Americans: 1982–1999.* Unpublished manuscript, Center for Demographic Studies, Duke University.

De Jong, G. F. (2003, Spring). Paradigms for graduate training in population studies. *PAA Affairs,* pp. 3–4.

Evans, D. A., Scherr, P. A., Cook, N. R., Albert, M. S., Funkenstein, H. H., Beckett, L. A., et al. (1992). The impact of Alzheimer's disease in the United States population. In R. M. Suzman, D. P. Willis, & K. G. Manton (Eds.), *The oldest old* (pp. 283–299). New York: Oxford University Press.

Finch, C. E., & Crimmins, E. M. (2004, September 17). Inflammatory exposure and historical changes in human life-spans. *Science, 305,* 1736–1739.

Flynn, J. R. (1984). The mean IQ of Americans: Massive gains. *Psychological Bulletin, 95,* 29–51.

Flynn, J. R. (1987). Massive IQ gains in 14 nations: What IQ tests really measure. *Psychological Bulletin, 101,* 171–191.

Flynn, J. R. (1998). IQ gains over time: Toward finding the causes. In U. Neisser (Ed.), *The rising curve: Long-term gains in IQ and related measures* (pp. 25–66). Washington, DC: American Psychological Association.

Folstein, M. F., Folstein, S. E., & McHugh, P. R. (1975). Mini-Mental State: A practical method for grading the cognitive state of patients for the clinician. *Journal of Psychiatric Research, 12,* 189–198.

Gavrilov, L. A., & Heuveline, P. (2003). Aging of population. In P. Demeny & G. McNicoll (Eds.). *The encyclopedia of population* (Vol. 1, pp. 32–37). New York: Macmillan Reference USA.

Gergen, K. J. (1973). Social psychology as history. *Journal of Personality and Social Psychology, 26,* 309–320.

Gergen, K. J. (1980). The emerging crisis in life-span developmental theory. In P. B. Baltes & O. G. Brim, Jr. (Eds.), *Life-span development and behavior* (pp. 32–65). New York: Academic Press.

Glenn, N. D. (1994). Television watching, newspaper reading, and cohort differences in verbal ability. *Sociology of Education, 67,* 216–230.

Haan, M., Shemanski, L., Jagust, W., Manolio, T., & Kuller, L. (1999). The role of APOE epsilon 4 modulating effects of other risk factors for cognitive decline in elderly persons. *Journal of the American Medical Association, 282,* 40–46.

Hall, C. B., Lipton, R. B., Sliwinski, M. J., & Stewart, W. F. (2000). A change point model for estimating onset of cognitive decline in preclinical Alzheimer's disease. *Statistics in Medicine, 19,* 1555–1566.

Hauser, R. M., & Huang, M.-H. (1997). Verbal ability and socioeconomic success: A trend analysis. *Social Science Research, 26,* 331–376.

Hayes, D., Wolfer, L., & Wolfe, M. (1996). Schoolbook simplification and its relation to the decline in SAT-Verbal scores. *American Educational Research Journal, 33,* 489–508.

Hayward, M. D., & Zhang, Z. (2001). Demography of aging: A century of global change, 1950–2050. In R. H. Binstock & L. K. George (Eds.), *Handbook of aging and the social sciences* (pp. 69–85). New York: Academic Press.

Herzog, A. R., & Wallace, R. B. (1997). Measures of cognitive functioning in the AHEAD Study. *Journals of Gerontology: Series B, 52B,* 37–48.

Hobbs, F., & Stoops, N. (2002). *Demographic trends in the 20th century* (U.S. Census Bureau, Census 2000 Special Reports, Series CENSR-4). Washington, DC: U.S. Government Printing Office.

Huang, M.-H., & Hauser, R. M. (1998). Trends in Black–White test score differentials II: The WORDSUM Vocabulary Test. In U. Neisser (Ed.), *The rising curve: Long-term gains in IQ and related measures* (pp. 303–332). Washington, DC: American Psychological Association.

Hultsch, D. F., MacDonald, S. W. S., Hunter, M. A., Maitland, S. B., & Dixon, R. A. (2002). Sampling and generalizability in developmental research: Comparison of random and convenience samples of older adults. *International Journal of Behavioral Development, 26,* 345–359.

Kaplan, G. A., Haan, M. N., & Wallace, R. B. (1999). Understanding changing risk factor associations with increasing age in adults. *Annual Review of Public Health, 20,* 89–108.

Kawas, C. H., & Brookmeyer, R. (2001). Editorial— Aging and the public health: Effects of dementia. *New England Journal of Medicine, 344,* 1160–1161.

Kish, L. (1965). *Survey sampling.* New York: Wiley.

Kish, L. (1987). *Statistical design for research.* New York: Wiley.

Lorge, I. (1956). Aging and intelligence. *Journal of Chronic Diseases, 412,* 131–139.

Manton, K. G., & Suzman, R. M. (1992). Conceptual issues in the design and analysis of longitudinal surveys of the health and functioning of the oldest old. In R. M. Suzman, D. P. Willis, & K. G. Manton (Eds.), *The oldest old* (pp. 89–122). New York: Oxford University Press.

McArdle, J. J., & Bell, R. Q. (2000). An introduction to latent growth models for developmental data analysis. In T. D. Little, K. U. Schnabel, & J. Baumert (Eds.), *Modeling longitudinal and multilevel data* (pp. 69–107). London: Lawrence Erlbaum.

Miyazaki, Y., & Raudenbush, S. W. (2000). Tests for linkage of multiple cohorts in an accelerated longitudinal design. *Psychological Methods, 5,* 544–563.

Moody, H. R. (2000). *Aging: Concepts and controversies* (3rd ed.). Thousand Oaks, CA: Pine Forge Press.

National Research Council. (2000). *The aging mind: Opportunities in cognitive research.* Committee on Future Directions for Cognitive Research on Aging. Paul C. Stern & Laura L. Carstensen, Editors. Commission on Behavioral and Social Sciences and Education. Washington, DC: National Academy Press.

Neisser, U. (1997). Rising scores on intelligence tests. *American Scientist, 85,* 440–447.

Neisser, U. (1998). Introduction: Rising test scores and what they mean. In U. Neisser (Ed.), *The rising curve: Long-term gains in IQ and related measures* (pp. 3–22). Washington, DC: American Psychological Association.

Nesselroade, J. R. (1988). Sampling and generalizability: Adult development and aging research issues examined within the general methodological framework of selection. In K. W. Schaie, R. T. Campbell, W. Meredith, & S. C. Rawlings (Eds.), *Methodological issues in aging research* (pp. 13–42). New York: Springer.

Nesselroade, J. R., & Baltes, P. B. (1974). Adolescent personality development and historical change: 1970–1972. *Monographs of the Society for Research on Child Development, 39*(No. 1, Serial No. 154).

Rubin, E. H., Storandt, M., Miller, J. P., Kinscherf, D. A., Grant, E. A., Morris, J. C., & Berg, L. (1998). A prospective study of cognitive function and onset of dementia in cognitively healthy elders. *Archives of Neurology, 55,* 395–401.

Schaie, K. W. (1984). Historical time and cohort effects. In K. A. McCloskey & H. W. Reese (Eds.), *Life-span developmental psychology: Historical and generational effects* (pp. 1–15). New York: Academic Press.

Schaie, K. W. (1996). *Intellectual development in adulthood: The Seattle Longitudinal Study.* Cambridge, UK: Cambridge University Press.

Schaie, K. W. (2005). *Developmental influences on adult intelligence: The Seattle Longitudinal Study.* New York: Oxford University Press.

Schaie, K. W., Labouvie, G. V., & Barrett, T. J. (1973). Selective attrition effects in a fourteen-year study of adult intelligence. *Journal of Gerontology, 28,* 328–334.

Schaie, K. W., Willis, S. L., & Pennak, S. (2005). An historical framework for cohort differences in

intelligence. *Research in Human Development, 2,* 43–67.

Siegel, J. S., & Swanson, D. A. (2004). *The methods and materials of demography* (2nd ed.). New York: Elsevier Academic Press.

Sliwinski, M. J., Hofer, S. M., Hall, C., Bushke, H., & Lipton, R. B. (2003). Modeling memory decline in older adults: The importance of preclinical dementia, attrition and chronological age. *Psychology and Aging, 18,* 658–671.

Sliwinski, M. J., Lipton, R. B., Buschke, H., & Stewart, W. F. (1996). The effect of pre-clinical dementia on estimates of normal cognitive function in aging. *Journals of Gerontology: Psychological Sciences, 51B,* P217–P225.

Suzman, R. M. (2004). Research on population aging at NIA: Retrospect and prospect. In L. J. Waite (Ed.), *Population and Development Review, Supplement to Vol. 30: Aging, health, and public policy: Demographic and economic perspectives* (pp. 239–264). New York: Population Council.

Suzman, R. M., Willis, D. P., & Manton, K. G. (Eds.). (1992). *The oldest old.* New York: Oxford University Press.

United Nations. (2002). *World population ageing: 1950–2050.* New York: Author.

U.S. Census Bureau. (2004). *U.S. interim projections by age, sex, race and Hispanic origin.* Retrieved August 26, 2004, from http://www.census.gov/ipc/www/usinterimproj/

Vaupel, J. W., & Yashin, A. I. (1985). Heterogeneity's ruses: Some surprising effects of selection on population dynamics. *The American Statistician, 39,* 176–185.

Weiss, K. M. (1990). The biodemography of variation in human frailty. *Demography, 27,* 185–206.

Wilson, J., & Gove, W. (1999). The intercohort decline in verbal ability: Does it exist? *American Sociological Review, 64,* 253–266.

Wirtz, W., Howe, H., II, Watson, B. C., Tyler, R. W., Tucker, L. R., Tom, V. H. T., et al. (1977). *On further examination: Report of the Advisory Panel on the Scholastic Aptitude Test Score Decline.* New York: College Entrance Examination Board.

5

CONSEQUENCES OF THE ERGODIC THEOREMS FOR CLASSICAL TEST THEORY, FACTOR ANALYSIS, AND THE ANALYSIS OF DEVELOPMENTAL PROCESSES

PETER C. M. MOLENAAR

The currently dominant approach to statistical analysis in psychology and biomedicine is based on analysis of interindividual variation. Differences between subjects, drawn from a population of subjects, provide the information for making inferences about states of affairs at the population level (e.g., mean and/or covariance structure). This approach underlies all standard statistical analysis techniques, such as analysis of variance, regression analysis, path analysis, factor analysis, cluster analysis, and multilevel modeling techniques. Whether the data are obtained in cross-sectional or longitudinal designs (or more elaborated designs, such as sequential designs), the statistical analysis always is focused on the structure of interindividual variation. Parameters and statistics of interest are estimated by pooling across subjects, where these subjects are assumed to be homogeneous in all relevant respects. This is the hallmark of analysis of interindividual variation: The sums defining the estimators in statistical analysis are taken over different subjects randomly drawn from a population of presumably homogeneous subjects. In mixed modeling the population is considered to be composed of different subpopulations, but within each subpopulation subjects again are assumed to be homogeneous.

In the next section, definitions will be given of interindividual variation and homogeneity of a population of subjects, but the intuitive content of these concepts is clear. These intuitions would seem to imply that inferences about states of affairs at the population level obtained by pooling across subjects constitute general findings that apply to each subject in the homogeneous population. Yet in general this is not the case; that is, in general it is not true that inferences about states of affairs at the population level based on analysis of interindividual variation apply to any of the individual subjects making up the population. This negative result is a direct implication of a set of mathematical–statistical theorems, the so-called *classical ergodic theorems* (cf. Molenaar, 2004). A concise heuristic description of the classical ergodic theorems will be given below. The main focus of this chapter, however, is on some of the implications of these theorems. For instance, it will be shown that classical test theory is based on assumptions that violate the classical ergodic theorems, and hence, in a precise sense to be defined later, the results of classical test theory do not apply in individual assessments. This, of course, is a serious shortcoming of classical test theory, because many psychological tests have been constructed and standardized according to classical test theory and are applied in the assessment of individual subjects.

Special emphasis will be given to the fact that developmental systems constitute prime examples of nonergodic systems having age-dependent statistical characteristics (mean trends and sequential dependencies). Therefore, the statistical analysis of developmental processes has to be based not on interindividual variation, as now is the standard approach, but on intraindividual variation (the latter type of variation will be defined in the next section). It will be indicated that the insistence that developmental processes be studied at the individual level has a long history in theoretical developmental psychology. The classical ergodic theorems provide a definite vindication of this theoretical line of thought.

At the close of this chapter, a new statistical modeling technique will be presented with which it is possible to analyze developmental processes with age-dependent statistical characteristics at the required intraindividual level. This modeling technique is based on advanced engineering methods for the analysis of complex dynamic systems. It will be shown that the new modeling technique allows for the optimal guidance of ongoing developmental processes at the intraindividual level. Evidently, this opens up entirely new possibilities for applied developmental psychological science.

PRELIMINARIES

In this section, definitions will be given of the main concepts used in this chapter. The given definition of (non-)ergodicity is heuristic; selected references will be given to the vast literature on ergodic theory for more formal elaborations.

Unit of Analysis

Each actually existing human being can be conceived of as a high-dimensional integrated system whose behavior evolves as function of place and time. In psychology, one usually does not consider place, leaving time as the dimension of main interest. The system includes important functional subsystems, such as the perceptual, emotional, cognitive, and physiological systems, as well as their dynamic interrelationships. The complete set of measurable time-dependent variables characterizing the system's behavior can be represented as the coordinates of a high-dimensional space (cf. Nayfeh & Balachandran, 1995, chap. 1), which will be called the *behavior space*. According to De Groot (1954), the behavior space contains all the scientifically relevant information about a person.

The realized values of all measurable variables for a particular individual at consecutive time points constitute a trajectory (life history) in behavior space. This trajectory in behavior space is our basic unit of analysis. Accordingly, the complete set of life histories of a population of humans can be represented as an ensemble of trajectories in the same behavior space.

Inter- and Intraindividual Variation

A standard dictionary definition of *variation* is: "the degree to which something differs, for example, from a former state or value, from others of the same type, or from a standard." The degree to which something differs implies a comparison, either between different replicates of the same type of entity (interindividual variation) or else between consecutive temporal states of the same individual entity (intraindividual variation). On the basis of this dictionary definition and using the construct of an ensemble of life trajectories defined in the previous section, it is possible to give appropriate definitions of inter- and intraindividual variation. The following definitions are inspired by Cattell's (1952) notion of the Data Box.

With respect to an ensemble of trajectories in behavior space, interindividual variation is defined as follows: (a) select a fixed subset of variables; (b) select one or more fixed time points as measurement occasions, (c) determine the variation of the scores on the selected variables at the selected time points by pooling across subjects. Analysis of interindividual variation thus defined was called *R-technique* by Cattell (1952). In contrast, intraindividual variation is defined as follows: (a) select a fixed subset of variables, (b) select a fixed subject, (c) determine the variation of the scores of the single subject on the selected variables by pooling across time points. Analysis of intraindividual variation thus defined was called *P-technique* by Cattell.

Ergodicity

We now can present a heuristic definition of ergodicity in terms of the concepts defined in the previous sections. Ergodicity addresses the following foundational question: Given the same set of selected variables (of Cattell's [1952] Data Box), under which conditions will an analysis of interindividual variation yield the same results as an analysis of intraindividual variation? To illustrate this question: Under which conditions will factor analysis of interindividual covariation yield a factor solution that is equal to factor analysis of intraindividual covariation? The latter illustration can be rephrased in terms of Cattell's Data Box in the following way: Under which conditions will R-technique factor analysis of interindividual covariation yield a solution that equals the analogous P-technique factor solution of intraindividual covariation?

The general answer to this question is provided by the classical ergodic theorems (cf. Molenaar, 2003, chap. 3; Molenaar, 2004). The answer is: Only if the ensemble of time-dependent trajectories in behavior space obeys two rigorous conditions will an analysis of interindividual variation yield the same results as an analysis of intraindividual variation. The two conditions concerned are the following. First, the trajectory of each subject in the ensemble has to obey exactly the same dynamical laws (homogeneity of the ensemble). Second, each trajectory should have constant statistical characteristics in time (*stationarity*, i.e., constant mean level and serial dependencies).

In case either one (or both) of these two conditions is not met, the psychological process concerned is nonergodic, that is, its structure of interindividual variation will differ from its structure of intraindividual variation. For a nonergodic process, the results obtained in standard analysis of interindividual variation do not apply at the individual level of intraindividual variation.

The meaning of the homogeneity and stationarity assumptions will be elaborated more fully in later sections, starting with the section on classical test theory below. The requirement that each subject in the ensemble should obey the same dynamical laws is expressed in the language of ergodic theory, which has its roots in the theoretical foundations of statistical mechanics. Statistical mechanics arose as the attempt by Boltzmann to explain the equilibrium characteristics of a homogeneous gas kept under constant pressure and temperature in a container, where the atoms of the homogeneous gas each obey the Newton laws of motion (cf. Sklar, 1993). Nowadays, ergodic theory is an independent mathematical discipline; standard introductions are Petersen (1983) and Walters (1982). An excellent recent monograph is Choe (2005). The theorem which for the ensuing discussion is the most important one in the set of classical ergodic theorems has been proven by Birkhoff (1931).

THE NONERGODICITY OF CLASSICAL TEST THEORY

Many of the psychological tests currently in use have been constructed according to the principles of classical test theory. The basic concept in classical test theory is the concept of *true score*: Each observed score is conceived of as a linear combination of a true score and an error score. In their authoritative book on classical test theory, Lord and Novick (1968) defined the concept of true score as follows. They consider a fixed person P; that is, P is not randomly drawn from some population but is the given person for which the true score is to be defined. The true score of P is defined as the expected value of the propensity distribution of P's observed scores. The propensity distribution is characterized as a "distribution function defined over repeated statistically independent measurements on the same person" (Lord & Novick, 1968, p. 30). The concept of error score then follows straight-forwardly: The error score is the difference between the observed score and the true score.

Several aspects of this definition of true score are noteworthy. The definition is based on the intraindividual variation characterizing a fixed person *P*. Repeated administration of the same test to *P* yields a time series of scores of *P*, the mean level of which is defined to be *P*'s true score. Hence this definition of true score does not involve any comparison with other persons and therefore is not at all dependent on interindividual variation. The single-subject repeated measures design used to obtain *P*'s time series of observed scores is akin to stan-dard psychophysical measurement designs (e.g., Gescheider, 1997). Lord and Novick (1968) required that the repeated measurements are independent. This implies that the time series of *P*'s scores should lack any sequential dependen-cies (autocorrelation). At the close of this sec-tion, I will further discuss the requirement that repeated measurements have to be independent.

Lord and Novick (1968) did not further elab-orate their original definition of true score in the context of intraindividual variation because: "it is not possible in psychology to obtain more than a few independent observations" (p. 30). Instead of considering an arbitrary large number of replicated measurements of a single fixed person *P*, Lord and Novick shifted attention to an alternative scheme in which an arbitrary large number of persons is measured at a single fixed time: "Primarily, test theory treats individual differences or, equivalently, the distribution of measurements over people" (p. 32). Apparently, it is expected that if one uses an individual-differences approach, valid information can be obtained about the distinct propensity distribu-tions underlying individual true scores. We will see shortly that this expectation is unwarranted.

Before focusing in the remainder of their book solely on the latter definition of true score based on interindividual variation, Lord and Novick (1968) made the following interesting comment about their initial definition of true score based on intraindividual variation:

> The true and error scores defined above [based on intraindividual variation] are not those primarily considered in test theory . . . They are, however, those that would be of interest to a theory that deals with individuals, rather than with groups (counseling rather than selection). (p. 32)

This is a remarkable, though somewhat oblique, statement. What is clear is that Lord and Novick consider a test theory based on their ini-tial concept of true score, defined as the mean of the intraindividual variation characterizing a fixed person *P* to be "of interest to a theory that deals with individuals"; that is, they consider such a test theory based on intraindividual varia-tion to be important in the context of individual assessment. But what is not clear is whether they also consider the alternative concept of true score based on interindividual variation (individ-ual differences) to be *not* of interest to a theory that deals with individuals; that is, do they imply that classical test theory as we know it is appro-priate only for the assessment of groups and not for individuals? It will be shown that classical test theory indeed is inappropriate for individual assessment.

To summarize the discussion thus far, Lord and Novick (1968) defined the concept of true score as the expected value of the propensity distribution of the observed scores of a given individual person *P*. This definition of true score based on intraindividual variation then is used in an interindividual context focused on individual differences, that is, classical test theory as we know it. This raises the all-important question of whether the information provided by individual differences (interindividual variation) is able to determine the individual propensity distribu-tions to a degree that is sufficient to apply the concept of true score based on intraindividual variation. Note that this is exactly the question concerning the ergodicity of the psychological process concerned: For a given test, will an analysis of interindividual variation of test scores yield the same results as an analysis of intraindividual variation of test scores? To answer this question it has to be established that the psychological process presumed by classical test theory to underlie the generation of test scores obeys the two criteria for ergodicity.

The psychological process that according to classical test theory underlies the generation of test scores is very simple. It is implicit in the definition of *true score* given by Lord and Novick (1968). Each individual person P is assumed to generate a time series of independent scores in response to repeated administration of the same test. Each observed score of P's time series constitutes an independent random sample drawn from P's propensity distribution. Hence there exists a one-to-one relationship between the time series of P's observed test scores and P's propensity distribution. The psychological process underlying P's time series of observed scores therefore is characterized, according to classical test theory, by P's propensity distribution. Statistical analysis of P's intraindividual variation boils down to statistical analysis based on P's propensity distribution. Classical test theory considers only the first two central moments of P's propensity distribution (its mean and its variance).

According to classical test theory, the propensity distributions of different persons have different means and different variances. The true score of person P_1 (i.e., the mean of the propensity distribution of P_1) will in general differ from the true score of person P_2. Also, the variance of P_1's observed scores will in general differ from the variance of P_2's observed scores. Hence, given the one-to-one correspondence between individual time series and individual propensity distributions noted above, the ensemble involving persons P_i, $i = 1, 2, \ldots$, is populated by time series (propensity distributions) that have different mean levels (means of the propensity distributions) and different variances. Clearly, such an ensemble is entirely heterogeneous: The psychological process according to which P_i's time series of observed scores is generated is different from the psychological process according to which P_k's time series of observed scores is generated because, for $i \neq k$, the underlying propensity distribution of P_i has mean and variance different from P_k's propensity distribution. Consequently, the ensemble of time series (propensity distributions) violates at least one of the two criteria for ergodicity: The trajectories (time series) in the ensemble do not obey the homogeneity criterion for ergodity; that is, trajectories associated with different persons do not obey exactly the same dynamical laws. Stated more specifically, the random motion characterizing time series of observed scores in the ensemble has different mean level and variance

for different persons. Consequently, the psychological process that according to classical test theory underlies the generation of test scores is nonergodic; that is, it follows from the classical ergodic theorems that results obtained in an analysis of interindividual variation (individual differences) of test scores based on classical test theory do not apply at the individual level of intraindividual variation. In short, the results obtained with classical test theory do not apply in the context of individual assessment.

SOME FORMAL ELABORATIONS

I now present some simple formal elaborations showing the invalidity of classical test theory for individual assessment. In particular, I focus on the concept of reliability as defined in classical test theory, show how estimation of an individual's true score in classical test theory depends upon the reliability of the test, and indicate why this leads to invalid inferences. In what follows, equations related to classical test theory are based on Lord and Novick (1968).

Consider first the situation with respect to the definition of true score based on intraindividual variation. A particular test has been selected (it will be understood in the rest of this section that the same test is being considered). Also, a particular person P is given. Let $y(P, t)$, $t = 1, 2, \ldots$ denote the time series of P's scores obtained by repeatedly administering the test. The number of repeated measurements is left undefined: It is understood that this number can be taken to be arbitrarily large. Then the true score of P, $\mu(P)$, is defined as the expected value (mean) of $y(P, t)$ across all repeated measurements t. Notice that $\mu(P)$ is a constant. The variance of $y(P, t)$ across all repeated measurements is denoted by $\sigma^2(P)$. The variance $\sigma^2(P)$ is a measure of the reliability of a single score $y(P, t = T)$, which is obtained at the Tth repeated measurement (T arbitrary), conceived of as an indicator of P's true score, $\mu(P)$. If $\sigma^2(P)$ is large, $y(P, t = T)$ can be very different from $\mu(P)$, whereas if $\sigma^2(P)$ is small its value will be close to $\mu(P)$.

To reiterate, in classical test theory one does not consider an arbitrary large number of repeated measurements of a single person P, but instead one considers an arbitrary large number of persons measured at a single time T. This is the shift from an intraindividual variation perspective underlying the concept of true score to an interindividual variation perspective underlying classical test theory as we know it. Accordingly, we consider an ensemble of time series of test scores associated with different persons P_i, $i = 1, 2, \ldots$, where the number of persons can be taken as arbitrarily large. Associated with each distinct person P_i is a distinct propensity distribution that has, as explained above, a one-to-one relationship with the psychological process according to which P_i generates his or her time series of observed test scores. The mean (true score) of the propensity distribution of P_i is $\mu(P_i)$, and the observed score of P_i is $y(P, t = T)$, where T is arbitrary but fixed. To ease the presentation, $\mu(P_i)$ will be denoted as μ_i and $y(P_i, t = T)$ as y_i. The error score associated with $y(P_i, t = T) = y_i$ is $\varepsilon(P_i, t = T)$ and will be denoted as $\varepsilon(P_i, t = T) = \varepsilon_i$.

We now are ready to express the basic relationships of classical test theory:

$$y_i = \mu_i + \varepsilon_i, \; i = 1, 2, \ldots \qquad (1a)$$

$$\text{var}[y_i] = \text{var}[\mu_i] + \text{var}[\varepsilon_i]. \qquad (1b)$$

According to 1a, the observed score y_i of a randomly selected person P_i is a linear combination of the true score μ_i and the error score ε_i of P_i. According to Equation 1b, the variance of observed scores across persons consists of a linear combination of the variance of the true scores across persons and the variance of the error scores across persons. The reliability ρ of the test then is defined as:

$$\rho = \text{var}[\mu_i] \, / \, \{\text{var}[\mu_i] + \text{var}[\varepsilon_i]\}. \qquad (1c)$$

Hence the reliability ρ is the proportion of true score variance across persons in the total variance of observed scores across persons.

Now suppose that the reliability ρ of our test is given and that also is given the observed score y_i of person P_i. Then the following so-called Kelly estimator of the true score μ_i of P_i can be defined (cf. Lord & Novick, 1968, p. 65, formula 3.7.2a):

$$\text{est}[\mu_i \,|\, y_i] = \rho y_i + (1 - \rho)\mu, \qquad (2a)$$

where μ is the mean of observed scores across persons. The error variance associated with the Kelly estimator 2a is (Lord & Novick, 1968, p. 68, formula 3.8.4a):

$$\text{var}\{\text{est}[\mu_i \,|\, y_i]\} = \text{var}[y_i](1 - \rho)\rho. \qquad (2b)$$

Equations 2a and 2b show that the estimate and associated standard error of a person's true score in classical test theory are a direct function of the test reliability ρ. The reliability itself is, according to 1c, a direct function of the variance of error scores $\text{var}[\varepsilon_i]$ across persons. Hence the Kelly estimate 2a of a person's true score is a direct function of the error variance $\text{var}[\varepsilon_i]$ across persons.

We have reached the conclusion that in classical test theory based on analysis of interindividual variation (individual differences), the estimate of a person's true score as well as the standard error of this estimated true score depend directly upon the reliability ρ of the test. In contrast, it was indicated at the beginning of this section that the variance $\sigma^2(P)$ of the propensity distribution describing P's intraindividual variation is a measure of the reliability of a single score $y(P, t = T)$ estimating P's true score $\mu(P)$. Hence we have two different concepts of reliability: (1) an intraindividual definition in which the reliability is given by $\sigma^2(P)$ and (2) an interindividual definition in which the reliability is a direct function of $\text{var}[\varepsilon_i]$. Given that the definition of true score as the mean of a person P's propensity distribution is the starting point of both concepts of reliability, the definition of reliability in terms of the intraindividual variance $\sigma^2(P)$ is basic. The question then arises whether the classical test theoretical definition of reliability in terms of the interindividual error variance $\text{var}[\varepsilon_i]$ is a good approximation of $\sigma^2(P)$. The answer to this question is given by the following equation (Lord & Novick, 1968, p. 35, formula 2.6.4):

$$\text{var}[\varepsilon_i] = E_i[\sigma^2(P_i)], \qquad (3)$$

where E_i denotes the expectation taken over persons P_i, $i = 1, 2, \ldots$. Equation 3 states that the interindividual error variance $\text{var}[\varepsilon_i]$ is the mean of the intraindividual variances of individual propensity distributions across persons P_i, $i = 1, 2, \ldots$.

So, coming to our final verdict, how good an approximation is Equation 3 for each of the individual variances $\sigma^2(P_i)$, $i = 1, 2, \ldots$? Given that the number of persons in the ensemble is taken to be arbitrarily large, and given that the $\sigma^2(P_i)$, $i = 1, 2, \ldots$ can differ arbitrarily according to classical test theory, it is immediately clear that in general Equation 3 bears no relationship to any of the variances of the individual propensity distributions. Hence, Equation 3 is a poor approximation to the variances $\sigma^2(P_i)$ of the individual propensity distributions. Suppose that Equation 3 is small, which implies that the (interindividual) reliability ρ is high. This leaves entirely open the possibility that the variance $\sigma^2(P)$ of a given person P's propensity distribution is arbitrarily large (the psychological process generating test scores is heterogeneous and hence nonergodic). Estimation of P's true score by means of the Kelly estimator 2a then will yield a severely biased result. Also the standard error (2b) of this estimate will be severely biased, suggesting an illusory high precision of the Kelly estimate. Only the actual value of $\sigma^2(P)$ will provide the correct precision of taking P's observed score as an estimate of P's true score. The true value of $\sigma^2(P)$ can be estimated only in an analysis of P's intraindividual variation. That is, the test should be repeatedly administered to P, yielding a time series of P's observed scores. The mean of P's time series of observed scores constitutes an unbiased estimate of P's true score, and the standard deviation of P's time series of observed scores provides an unbiased estimate of the precision of P's estimated true score.

Fundamental Reasons or Contingent Circumstances

This section presents a critical discussion of the reasons why Lord and Novick (1968), after having defined the concept of true score in terms of intraindividual variation, do not further pursue an intraindividual foundation for test theory and turn instead to an interindividual perspective. It will be argued that their reasons for doing so are not fundamental, but pertain to contingent circumstances that can be dealt with by means of appropriate statistical–methodological techniques.

The key remark leading up to the rejection of the possibility of a test theory based on intraindividual variation is the following: Characterizing the propensity distribution associated with the time series of a given person P's observed test scores, Lord and Novick (1968) required that the "distribution function [is] defined over repeated statistically independent measurements on the same person" (p. 30). The important qualification is that the repeated measurements should be statistically independent. This implies the requirement that P's time series of observed test scores should lack sequential dependencies (e.g., autocorrelation).

After having postulated the requirement of obtaining statistically independent observed scores, Lord and Novick (1968) concluded: "It is not possible in psychology to obtain more than a few independent observations" (p. 30). This is the reason why they did not consider the possibility of a test theory based on intraindividual variation to be feasible. In general, test scores obtained in a single-subject time series design will be sequentially dependent, that is, have significant autocorrelation. Moreover, the statistical properties of the psychological process according to which test scores are generated may change in time. For instance, the process concerned may be vulnerable to learning and habituation influences that induce time-dependent changes in the way test scores are being generated.

Before scrutinizing the details of Lord and Novick's (1968) requirement that repeated measurements of the same person P should be statistically independent, I first consider their reason not to pursue a test theory based on intraindividual variation. Because the basic concept underlying classical test theory, the concept of true score, is defined at the level of intraindividual variation, one would expect that the reason to leave that level and move to a different level of interindividual variation would have to be a fundamental reason. One would expect to be given an argument involving issues of logical necessity or impossibility. Yet the actual argument given by Lord and Novick concerns more an issue of contingent character: Repeated measurement of the same person P yields test scores that are in general not statistically independent. Indeed, all psychometricians will agree. But the statistical analysis techniques used to determine

P's propensity distribution can accommodate the presence of sequential dependencies, and then we still can have a test theory that is directly based on the concept of true score as defined by Lord and Novick; that is, a test theory based on intraindividual variation that would be of interest for individual assessment and counseling. The reason Lord and Novick gave for not further pursuing such a test theory is not fundamental and does not prove the impossibility of such a theory.

I now turn to discussion of the requirement that repeatedly measuring the same person *P* should yield a time series of statistically independent scores. To reiterate, no psychometrician will expect this to occur: Repeated measurement of the same person generally will yield a time series of sequentially dependent scores. But is this problematic? The time series of scores provides the information to determine the propensity distribution characterizing person *P*. In particular, the mean and variance of *P*'s propensity distribution have to be determined. This is a standard problem in the statistical analysis of time series that has been completely solved in case the time series is stationary (cf. Anderson, 1971). Hence, the important requirement is not that *P*'s time series should consist of statistically independent scores but that the time series is stationary. Stationarity of a time series implies that the series has constant mean level and that its autocorrelation depends only upon the relative distance (lag) between measurement occasions.

The alternative requirement that a time series has to be stationary can be tested for in several ways (cf. Priestley, 1988). In case such tests indicate that the series is nonstationary, it can be analyzed by means of special techniques, such as evolutionary spectrum analysis (Priestley, 1988) or wavelet analysis (e.g., Hogan & Lakey, 2005; Houtveen & Molenaar, 2001). At the close of this chapter, a new modeling technique for multivariate nonstationary time series will be presented. Hence, from a statistical analytic point of view, nonstationary time series can be handled satisfactorily. Yet from the point of view of a test theory based on intraindividual variation, a person *P*'s time series of test scores should be stationary to allow estimation of the constant mean and constant variance of *P*'s time-invariant propensity distribution. In case

P's time series of test scores is nonstationary, the mean and/or variance of the series will in general be time varying. Lord and Novick's (1968) definition of true score, however, does not pertain to time-varying propensity distributions with time-varying means and/or variances.

Hence, either methodological or statistical techniques have to be invoked to guarantee that *P*'s time series of test scores is stationary. Only then can the (constant) mean and variance of *P*'s time series be used as estimates of the mean and variance of *P*'s propensity distribution. Methodological techniques can be used to guarantee that nonstationarity due to learning and habituation is avoided. For instance, using a common approach in reaction time research, registration of *P*'s time series of test scores should begin only if *P* has reached a steady state after an initial transient state due to novelty effects. This will require the availability of a pool of many parallel test items in order to avoid learning effects. Statistical techniques can be used a posteriori to remove transient effects due to habituation and learning from *P*'s time series of test scores (e.g., Molenaar & Roelofs, 1987). Almost certainly, new methodological and statistical techniques will have to be developed to accommodate the intricacies due to nonstationarity and fully exploit the possibilities of a test theory based on intraindividual variation. Until now, these possibilities have not been pursued systematically, for the wrong reasons, as has been argued in this section. Given that the psychological process underlying the generation of test scores is nonergodic according to classical test theory based on analysis of interindividual variation, psychometricians will have to seriously reconsider their reasons for not pursuing a test theory based on intraindividual variation.

One promising psychological paradigm that allows for straightforward determination of person-specific propensity distributions is *mental chronometry*. In his excellent monograph on mental chronometry, Jensen (2006) stated:

The main reasons for the usefulness of chronometry are not only the advantages of its absolute scale properties, but also its sensitivity and precision for measuring small changes in cognitive functioning, *the unlimited repeatability of measurements under identical procedures* [italics added], the adaptability of chronometric techniques for measuring a variety of cognitive processes, and the possibility of obtaining the same measurements with consistently identical tasks and procedures over an extremely wide age range. (p. 96)

The possibility to obtain unlimited repeated measurements under identical procedures will allow for the determination of person-specific reaction time propensity distributions with arbitrary precision. Jensen presented impressive empirical results showing the importance of not only the intraindividual means of person-specific reaction time distributions but also their intraindividual variances in assessing cognitive status and development (e.g., in the context of the so-called *neural noise hypothesis*; Jensen, 2006, pp. 122 ff.). Consequently, I conjecture that mental chronometry provides a very interesting approach to pursue a test theory based on intraindividual variation.

Additional Thoughts

The impact of the fact that the ensemble of time series underlying classical test theory is nonergodic is enormous. Psychological tests are applied for individual assessment in all kinds of settings. Using the population average expressed by Equation 3 as an estimate of the intraindividual variance $\sigma^2(P)$ of a given person P can lead to entirely erroneous conclusions. To give an arbitrary example: Suppose that the norm μ of a test is $\mu = 100$, that the interindividual reliability ρ of the test is $\rho = 0.9$, and that the between-subjects variance of test scores is $\text{var}[y_i] = 25$. Suppose also that a true score that is larger than $y_C = 120$ is considered reason for special treatment (clinical, educational, or otherwise). Finally, suppose that person P has observed score $y_P = y(P, t = T) = 126$. Then the Kelly estimate (2a) of P's true score μ_P is: $\text{est}[\mu_P \,|\, y_P] = 0.9 \times 126 + (1 - 0.9) \times 100 = 123.4$. According to 2b, the error variance of this estimated true score is: $\text{var}\{\text{est}[\mu_P \,|\, y_P]\} = 25 \times (1 - 0.9) \times 0.9 = 2.25$. Hence, the standard error is 1.5, and a commonly used confidence interval about the estimated true score is: $123.4 \pm 2 \times 1.5$, yielding $120.4 < \text{est}[\mu_P \,|\, y_P] < 126.4$. This confidence interval is entirely located above the criterion score $y_C = 120$, hence it is concluded that P needs special treatment. Suppose, however, that the intraindividual variance $\sigma^2(P)$ of P's propensity distribution is $\sigma^2(P) = 36$. Then the difference between P's observed score, $y_P = 126$, and the criterion score for special treatment, $y_C = 120$, is only 1 standard deviation, which according to standard statistical criteria would *not* indicate that P needs special treatment.

Numerical exercises such as the one given above can be carried out in a variety of formats, using Monte Carlo simulation techniques and alternative settings. I intend to report the results of one such a simulation study in a separate publication. But the overall message should be clear: Using the (interindividual) population value of the error variance (based on the interindividual reliability) as approximation for the intraindividual variance of a person P's propensity distribution is vulnerable to lead to erroneous conclusions about P's true score and, consequently, to erroneous decisions about the necessity to apply special treatment to P. The fundamental reason for the invalidity of Equation 3 as approximation for $\sigma^2(P)$ is because the ensemble of time series of observed scores is nonergodic.

HIDDEN HETEROGENEITY

In the previous section, I discussed heterogeneity with respect to the means and variances of the propensity distributions underlying classical test theory. That kind of heterogeneity can be considered to be a special instance of a much wider class of heterogeneous phenomena, including also qualitative heterogeneity. An important example of qualitative heterogeneity concerns individual differences in the loadings in a factor model. The standard factor model of interindividual covariation is (using boldface lowercase letters for vectors and boldface uppercase letters for matrices):

$$\mathbf{y}_i = \mathbf{\Lambda}\mathbf{\eta}_i + \mathbf{\varepsilon}_i, \; i = 1, 2, \ldots, \qquad (4)$$

where

$\mathbf{y}_i = [y_{1i}, y_{2i}, \ldots, y_{pi}]'$ is the p-variate vector of observed scores of a randomly drawn subject i (the apostrophe denotes transposition),

$\mathbf{\eta}_i = [\eta_{1i}, \eta_{2i}, \ldots, \eta_{qi}]'$ is the *q*-variate vector of factor scores of subject *i*,

$\mathbf{\varepsilon}_i = [\varepsilon_{1i}, \varepsilon_{2i}, \ldots, \varepsilon_{pi}]'$ is the *p*-variate vector of measurement errors for subject *i*, and

$\mathbf{\Lambda}$ is the (p, q)-dimensional matrix of factor loadings.

The factor model of interindividual covariation not only underlies classical test theory but also is of central importance in much of psychology. The factor model can be heuristically characterized as follows. In the context of the behavior space introduced in the "Unit of analysis" section, choose a fixed time and a select a set of *p* variables **y** that are considered to be indicators of a *q*-variate latent factor **η**. Then the factor loadings **Λ** represent the regression coefficients in the linear relationships between the *p* indicators and the *q*-variate latent factor **η**. It is an essential assumption underlying the factor model that the factor loadings are invariant across subjects. That is, **Λ** does not depend upon *i*, where the subscript *i* stands for subject *i* in the population; $i = 1, 2, \ldots$. Hence the assumption is that each individual person *i* in the population has a person-specific *q*-variate factor score $\mathbf{\eta}_i$ and person-specific *p*-variate error score $\mathbf{\varepsilon}_i$, but the factor model for each person in the population has the same (p, q)-dimensional matrix of factor loadings **Λ**.

Suppose now that we carry out a simulation experiment in which each person has not only a person-specific *q*-variate factor score and *p*-variate error score but also a person-specific set of values for the factor loadings $\mathbf{\Lambda}_i$, $i = 1, 2, \ldots$. Hence each person has a person-specific factor model:

$$\mathbf{y}_i = \mathbf{\Lambda}_i \mathbf{\eta}_i + \mathbf{\varepsilon}_i, \quad i = 1, 2, \ldots. \tag{5}$$

This heterogeneity of factor loadings $\mathbf{\Lambda}_i$, $i = 1, 2, \ldots$, constitutes a severe violation of an important assumption underlying the standard factor model, namely, the assumption that the matrix of factor loadings should be invariant (fixed) across subjects. The fact that the matrix of factor loadings in Equation 5 is subject specific implies that the way in which factors are expressed in the observed scores is qualitatively different for different subjects. These interindividual differences in the values of factor scores

are called *qualitative* because the substantial interpretation (semantic labeling) of factors is based on these loading values.

Despite the fact that Equation 5 involves a severe violation of the qualitative homogeneity assumption (invariance of factor loadings across subjects) underlying the standard factor model 4, it was shown in a number of simulation studies that factor analysis of interindividual covariation appears to be insensitive to this violation. The typical setup of these simulation studies was to generate data according to the person-specific (qualitatively heterogeneous) Factor Model 5 and then fit the standard Factor Model 4 to the simulated data. Although one would expect the fit of Model 4 to be poor because the simulated data violate the assumption of qualitative homogeneity underlying Model 4, it turns out that this is not at all the case. The general finding in these simulation studies is that (variants of) Factor Model 4 provide(s) satisfactory fits to data generated according to (variants of) Factor Model 5. Satisfactory fits, that is, according to all usual criteria of goodness of fit, such as the chi-square likelihood ratio test, standardized root-mean-square residual, and root-mean-square error of approximation (cf. Brown, 2006, for definitions and discussion of these criteria). Nowhere in the obtained (maximum likelihood) solutions is a flag waving indicating that something is fundamentally wrong. These simulation studies were based on the cross-sectional factor model (Molenaar, 1997), the longitudinal factor model (Molenaar, 1999), and the behavior genetical factor model for multivariate phenotypes of monozygotic and dizygotic twins (Molenaar, Huizenga, & Nesselroade, 2003). A mathematical–statistical proof of the insensitivity of the factor model of interindividual covariation to the qualitative heterogeneity of the factor loadings is given in Kelderman and Molenaar (in press).

The finding that the standard factor model of interindividual covariation evidently is insensitive to the presence of extreme qualitative heterogeneity in the population of subjects, created by the person-specific matrices of factor loadings $\mathbf{\Lambda}_i$, $i = 1, 2, \ldots$, in Model 5, raises serious questions. To reiterate, nothing in the results obtained with the standard factor analyses based on Model 4 indicates that the true state of affairs is in severe violation of the assumptions underlying this model. The standard factor models yield satisfactory fits to the data generated according to Model 5. Consequently, the presence of substantial qualitative heterogeneity in the simulated data remains entirely hidden in the standard factor analyses based on interindividual covariation. Before I discuss some of the consequences of this finding, note that there exist a priori reasons to expect that widespread qualitative heterogeneity actually exists in human populations. The reasons have to do with the way in which cortical neural networks grow and adapt during the life span, namely, by means of self-organizing epigenetic processes (cf. Molenaar, Boomsma, & Dolan, 1993). Self-organizing growth and adaptation give rise to emergent endogenous variation in neural network connections, even between homologous structures located at the left and right sides of the brain within the same subject (cf. Edelman, 1987). Insofar as cognitive information processing is associated with cortical neural activity, one can expect that these endogenously generated differences in neural network architectures will become discernable as qualitative heterogeneity of the structure of observed behavior of different subjects (see Molenaar, in press, for further elaboration and mathematical–biological modeling of these epigenetic processes).

One direct consequence of the fact that standard factor analysis of interindividual covariation is insensitive to qualitative heterogeneity is the following. Suppose that the standard q-factor Model 4 yields a satisfactory fit to the data obtained with a test composed of p subtests (e.g., items). Let est[Λ] denote the estimated (p, q)-dimensional matrix of factor loadings thus obtained. Suppose also that in reality qualitative heterogeneity is present in the population of subjects, so that the true (p, q)-dimensional matrix of factor loadings Λ_P for a given subject P differs substantially from the nominal loading matrix est[Λ]. For instance, several of the p subtests have negative or zero loadings in Λ_P, whereas the analogous loadings in est[Λ] are high and positive. Of course, Λ_P is unknown in the context of standard factor analysis of interindividual variation. The estimate of P's factor score, est[η_P], is based on the nominal loading matrix est[Λ] and, because est[Λ] is a poor approximation of the true Λ_P, this estimate est[η_P] will be substantially biased. For quantitative details about this bias,

the reader is referred to the publications mentioned above (Kelderman & Molenaar, in press; Molenaar, 1999; Molenaar et al., 2003).

Another consequence of the insensitivity of standard factor analysis of intraindividual variation to qualitative heterogeneity concerns the fact that the semantic interpretation of factors thus obtained is inappropriate at the person-specific level. Suppose that standard factor analysis of personality test scores yields the expected pattern of factor loadings in est[Λ] corresponding to the Big Five theory (cf. Borkenau & Ostendorf, 1998). Then, if qualitative heterogeneity is present, the factor loadings in Λ_P for a particular person P may not at all conform to the Big Five pattern, and hence the semantic interpretation of the factors for P will be different. Stated more specifically, the nominal semantic interpretation of the five factors obtained in standard factor analysis is inappropriate for P. The reader is referred to Hamaker, Dolan, and Molenaar (2005) for an elaborate illustration based on empirical personality test scores.

Heterogeneity in Time

To reiterate, a (psychological) process should obey two criteria in order to qualify as an ergodic process. First, the trajectory of each subject in the ensemble should conform to exactly the same dynamical laws (homogeneity of the ensemble). Second, each trajectory should have constant statistical characteristics in time (stationarity, i.e., constant mean level and serial dependencies which depend only upon relative time differences). In the previous sections, attention has been confined to psychological processes which are nonergodic because they violate the first criterion, that is, heterogeneity of different trajectories in the ensemble. Whereas the first criterion involves a comparison between different trajectories, the second stationarity criterion involves comparison of the same trajectory at different times. In this section I consider psychological processes which are nonergodic because they violate the second criterion, that is, they are nonstationary.

In general, nonstationarity implies that parameters of a dynamic system are time varying. Prime examples of nonstationary systems are developmental systems which typically have time-varying parameters such as waxing and/or waning factor loadings. For this reason, developmental systems are nonergodic, and their analysis should be based on intraindividual variation. There exists a long tradition in theoretical developmental psychology in which it is argued that developmental processes should be analyzed at the level of intraindividual variation (time series data). The general denotation for this tradition is developmental systems theory. Important contributions to developmental systems theory include Wohlwill's (1973) monograph on the concept of developmental functions describing intraindividual variation, Ford and Lerner's (1992) integrative approach based on the interplay between intraindividual variation and interindividual variation and change, and Gottlieb's (1992, 2003) theoretical work on probabilistic epigenetic development.

Intraindividual analysis of nonstationary multivariate time series requires the availability of sophisticated statistical modeling techniques. Such a technique has been developed based on a systems model with arbitrarily time-varying parameters (Molenaar, 1994; Molenaar & Newell, 2003). The model can be conceived of as a suitably generalized factor model for nonstationary p-variate time series $y(t)$, $t = 1, 2, \ldots,$ T. Its schematic form is:

$$y(t) = \Lambda[\theta(t)]\eta(t) + \varepsilon(t) \tag{6a}$$

$$\eta(t + 1) = B[\theta(t)]\eta(t) + \zeta(t + 1) \tag{6b}$$

$$\theta(t + 1) = \theta(t) + \xi(t + 1). \tag{6c}$$

In 6a, $y(t)$ denotes the observed p-variate time series, $\eta(t)$ is the q-variate latent factor series (system state process), and $\varepsilon(t)$ is the p-variate measurement error process. The factor loadings in $\Lambda[\theta(t)]$ depend upon the r-variate time-varying parameter vector $\theta(t)$. Equation 6b describes the evolution of the latent factor series $\eta(t)$ by means of a q-variate stochastic difference equation (autoregression) relating $\eta(t + 1)$ to $\eta(t)$, where $\zeta(t + 1)$ denotes the q-variate residual process. The (q,q)-dimensional matrix of regression weights $B[\theta(t)]$ depends upon the r-variate time-varying parameter vector $\theta(t)$. Equation 6c describes the time-dependent variation of the unknown parameters. The r-variate parameter vector process $\theta(t)$ obeys a special

stochastic difference equation: a random walk with r-variate innovations process $\xi(t)$.

The system of equations (6a, 6b, and 6c) allows for the modeling of a large class of multivariate nonstationary (nonergodic) processes. Equations 6a and 6b have the same formal structure as the well-known interindividual longitudinal q-factor model, which helps in their interpretation. Yet the system of Equations 6a, 6b, and 6c is applied to analyze the structure of intraindividual variation underlying the observed p-variate time series $y(t)$ obtained with a single subject. Generalization of this model to accommodate multivariate time series obtained in a replicated time series design is straightforward. Extension of the model with arbitrary mean trend functions and covariate processes having time-varying effects also is straightforward.

The fit of Equations 6a, 6b, and 6c to an observed p-variate time series $y(t)$, $t = 1, 2, \ldots, T$, where T is the number of repeated measurements obtained with a single subject P, is based on advanced statistical analysis techniques taken from the engineering sciences (Bar-Shalom, Li, & Kirubarajan, 2001; Ristic, Arulampalam, & Gordon, 2004). It consists of a combination of recursive estimation (filtering), smoothing, and iteration (EKFIS: extended Kalman filter with iteration and smoothing). The EKFIS yields a time series (trajectory) of estimated values for each of the r parameters in $\theta(t)$: $\theta_k(t)$, $t = 1, 2, \ldots, T$; $k = 1, 2, \ldots, r$.

To illustrate the performance of the EKFIS, the following small simulation study has been carried out. A four-variate ($p = 4$) time series $y(t)$ has been generated by means of the state-space model with time-varying parameters 6a, 6b, and 6c. The model has a univariate ($q = 1$) latent state process $\eta(t)$. The autoregressive coefficient $B[\theta(t)] = b(t)$ in the process model 6b for the latent state increases linearly from 0.0 to 0.9 over the observation interval comprising $T = 100$ time points: $b(t) = 9t/1000, t = 1, 2, \ldots,$ 100. Hence the sequential dependence (autocorrelation) of the latent state process (latent factor series) increases from zero to 0.9 across 100 time points and therefore is highly time varying (nonstationary, hence nonergodic). Depicted in Figure 5.1 is the estimate of this autoregressive weight $b(t)$ obtained by means of the EKFIS based on a single-subject time series $y(t)$, $t = 1, 2, \ldots, 100$. It is clear that the estimated

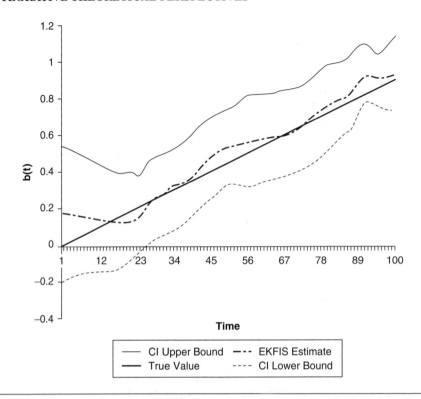

Figure 5.1   EKFIS (Extended Kalman Filter With Iteration and Smoothing) Estimate of Time-Varying
Coefficient $B(T)$ in the Autoregressive Model for the Latent Factor Scores

NOTE: CI = Confidence Interval.

trajectory closely tracks the true time-varying
path of this parameter.

CONCLUSION

In this chapter, some of the implications of the
classical ergodic theorems have been considered
in the contexts of classical test theory, factor
analysis of interindividual covariation, and
the analysis of nonstationary developmental
processes. In each of these contexts the classical
ergodic theorems imply that instead of using
standard statistical approaches based on analysis
of interindividual variation, it is necessary to use
single-subject time series analysis of intraindividual variation. This conclusion holds for individual assessment based on classical test theory,
for testing the assumption of homogeneity (fixed
factor loadings across subjects) in factor analysis
of interindividual covariation, and for the analysis of nonstationary processes such as learning
and developmental processes.

The consequences of the classical ergodic
theorems in these and many other contexts in
psychology imply that time series designs and
time series analysis techniques will have to be
assigned a much more prominent place than is
currently the case in psychological methodology. The overall aim of scientific research
in psychology still should be to arrive at general
(nomothetic) laws that hold for all subjects in a
well-defined population. But the inductive tools
to arrive at such general laws have to be fundamentally different from the currently standard
approaches for psychological processes that are
nonergodic. Only if a psychological process is
ergodic, that is, obeys the two criteria of homogeneity and stationarity, can results obtained by
means of analysis of interindividual variation be
generalized to the level of intraindividual variation. But the two criteria for ergodicity are
very strict, and many psychological processes
of interest will fail to obey these criteria.
Psychologists have to understand that ergodicity
is the special case, whereas nonergodicity is the

rule. For nonergodic psychological processes, analysis of interindividual variation yields results that may not apply to any of the individual subjects in the population of subjects.

In conclusion, the inductive tools necessary to arrive at general (nomothetic) laws for nonergodic processes involve the search for communalities between single-subject process models fitted to time series data obtained in replicated time series designs. The latter search for communalities between single-subject process models can be based on standard mixed modeling techniques (see the excellent textbook of Demidenko, 2004).

Having available appropriate time series models for each individual subject opens up possibilities which are entirely new in psychology. These possibilities involve the optimal control of ongoing psychological processes. For instance, consider the following special instance of the system of Equations 6a and 6b:

$$\mathbf{y}(t) = \mathbf{\Lambda}\mathbf{\eta}(t) + \mathbf{\varepsilon}(t) \tag{7a}$$

$$\mathbf{\eta}(t + 1) = \mathbf{B}\mathbf{\eta}(t) + \mathbf{\Gamma}\mathbf{u}(t) + \mathbf{\zeta}(t + 1). \tag{7b}$$

Here the same definitions apply as for Equations 6a and 6b. Notice that in 7a and 7b the (p,q)-dimensional matrix of factor loadings $\mathbf{\Lambda}$ and the (q,q)-dimensional matrix of regression weights $\mathbf{B}$ are assumed to be constant in time. This is to ease the presentation; generalization of what follows to the nonstationary model given by 6a, 6b, and 6c is straightforward. Notice also that 7b contains a new component: $\mathbf{\Gamma}\mathbf{u}(t)$. The s-variate process $\mathbf{u}(t)$ represents a known process that can be manipulated; for instance, dose of medication or environmental stimulation. $\mathbf{\Gamma}$ is a (q, s)-dimensional matrix of regression weights.

Suppose that 7a and 7b provide a faithful description of the p-variate time series $\mathbf{y}(t)$ for subject P. It then is possible to determine $\mathbf{u}(t)$ in such a way that the state process $\mathbf{\eta}(t)$ is steered to its desired level $\mathbf{\eta}^{\#}$, where $\mathbf{\eta}^{\#}$ is chosen by the controller. The optimal input $\mathbf{u}^{@}(t)$ is determined according to the following schematic feedback function:

$$\mathbf{u}^{@}(t) = \mathbf{F}[\mathbf{y}(t), t], \tag{8}$$

where $\mathbf{F}[.]$ denotes an (s,p)-dimensional nonlinear feedback function. Application of $\mathbf{u}^{@}(t)$ at time t guarantees that the state process $\mathbf{\eta}(t + 1)$ at the next time point $t + 1$ will be as close as possible to the desired level $\mathbf{\eta}^{\#}$.

Optimal control is an important field of research in the engineering sciences. There exists a vast literature on many different variants of optimal control (cf. Kwon, 2005, for a thorough explanation of the currently most advanced approaches). These control techniques can be applied straightforwardly in analyses of intraindividual variation in order to steer psychological processes in desired directions (cf. Molenaar, 1987, for an application to the optimal control of a psychotherapeutic process). This opens up an entirely new promising field of applied psychology: person-specific modeling and adaptive control of ongoing psychological processes.

REFERENCES

Anderson, T. W. (1971). *The statistical analysis of time series*. New York: Wiley.

Bar-Shalom, Y., Li, X. R., & Kirubarajan, T. (2001). *Estimation with applications to tracking and navigation*. New York: Wiley.

Birkhoff, G. D. (1931). Proof of the ergodic theorem. *Proceedings of the National Academy of Sciences USA, 17,* 656–660.

Borkenau, P., & F. Ostendorf, F. (1998). The Big Five as states: How useful is the five-factor model to describe intra-individual variations over time? *Journal of Personality Research, 32,* 202–221.

Brown, T. A. (2006). *Confirmatory factor analysis for applied research*. New York: Guilford Press.

Cattell, R. B. (1952). The three basic factor-analytic designs—Their interrelations and derivatives. *Psychological Bulletin, 49,* 499–520.

Choe, G. H. (2005). *Computational ergodic theory*. Berlin: Springer.

De Groot, A. D. (1954). Scientific personality diagnosis. *Acta Psychologica, 10,* 220–241.

Demidenko, E. (2004). *Mixed models: Theory and applications*. Hoboken, NJ: Wiley.

Edelman, G. M. (1987). *Neural Darwinism: The theory of neuronal group selection*. New York: Basic Books.

Ford, D. H., & Lerner, R. M. (1992). *Developmental systems theory*. Newbury Park, CA: Sage.

Gescheider, G. A. (1997). *Psychophysics: The fundamentals*. Mahwah, NJ: Lawrence Erlbaum.

Gottlieb, G. (1992). *Individual development and evolution: The genesis of novel behavior*. New York: Oxford University Press.

Gottlieb, G. (2003). On making behavioral genetics truly developmental. *Human Development, 46,* 337–355.

Hamaker, E. L., Dolan, C. V., & Molenaar, P. C. M. (2005). Statistical modeling of the individual: Rationale and application of multivariate time series analysis. *Multivariate Behavioral Research, 40,* 207–233.

Hogan, J. A., & Lakey, J. D. (2005). *Time-frequency and time-scale methods: Adaptive decompositions, uncertainty principles, and sampling*. Boston: Birkhäuser.

Houtveen, J. H., & Molenaar, P. C. M. (2001). Comparison between the Fourier and wavelet methods of spectral analysis applied to stationary and non-stationary heart period data. *Psychophysiology, 38,* 729–735.

Kelderman, H., & Molenaar, P. C. M. (in press). The effect of individual differences in factor loadings on the standard factor model. *Multivariate Behavioral Research*.

Jensen, A. R. (2006). *Clocking the mind: Mental chronometry and individual differences*. Amsterdam: Elsevier.

Kwon, W. H. (2005). *Receding horizon control: Model predictive control for state models*. London: Springer.

Lord, F. M., & Novick, M. R. (1968). *Statistical theories of mental test scores*. Reading, MA: Addison-Wesley.

Molenaar, P. C. M. (1987). Dynamic assessment and adaptive optimization of the therapeutic process. *Behavioral Assessment, 9,* 389–416.

Molenaar, P. C. M. (1994). Dynamic latent variable models in developmental psychology. In A. von Eye & C. C. Clogg (Eds.), *Analysis of latent variables in developmental research* (pp. 155–180). Thousand Oaks, CA: Sage.

Molenaar, P. C. M. (1997). Time series analysis and its relationship with longitudinal analysis. *International Journal of Sports Medicine, 19,* 232–237.

Molenaar, P. C. M. (1999). Longitudinal analysis. In H. J. Ader & G. J. Mellenbergh (Eds.), *Research methodology in the social, behavioral and life sciences* (pp. 143–167). London: Sage.

Molenaar, P. C. M. (2003). *State space techniques in structural equation modeling: Transformation of latent variables in and out of latent variable models*. Retrieved from http://www.hhdev.psu.edu/hdfs/faculty/molenaar.html

Molenaar, P. C. M. (2004). A manifesto on psychology as idiographic science: Bringing the person back into scientific psychology, this time forever. *Measurement, 2,* 201–218.

Molenaar, P. C. M. (in press). On the implications of the classic ergodic theorems: Analysis of developmental processes has to focus on intra-individual variation. *Developmental Psychobiology*.

Molenaar, P. C. M., Boomsma, D. I., & Dolan, C. V. (1993). A third source of developmental differences. *Behavior Genetics, 23,* 519–524.

Molenaar, P. C. M., Huizenga, H. M., & Nesselroade, J. R. (2003). The relationship between the structure of interindividual and intraindividual variability: A theoretical and empirical vindication of developmental systems theory. In U. M. Staudinger & U. Lindenberger (Eds.), *Understanding human development: Dialogues with life-span psychology* (pp. 339–360). Dordrecht, The Netherlands: Kluwer.

Molenaar, P. C. M., & Newell, K. M. (2003). Direct fit of a theoretical model of phase transition in oscillatory finger motions. *British Journal of Mathematical and Statistical Psychology, 56,* 199–214.

Molenaar, P. C. M., & Roelofs, J. W. (1987). The analysis of multiple habituation profiles of single trial evoked potentials. *Biological Psychology, 24,* 1–21.

Nayfeh, A. H., & Balachandran, B. (1995). *Applied nonlinear dynamics: Analytical, computational, and experimental methods*. New York: Wiley.

Petersen, K. (1983). *Ergodic theory*. Cambridge, UK: Cambridge University Press.

Priestley, M. B. (1988). *Non-linear and non-stationary time series analysis*. London: Academic Press.

Ristic, B., Arulampalam, S., & Gordon, N. (2004). *Beyond the Kalman filter: Particle filters for tracking applications*. London: Artech House.

Sklar, L. (1993). *Physics and chance: Philosophical issues in the foundations of statistical mechanics*. Cambridge, UK: Cambridge University Press.

Walters, P. (1982). *An introduction to ergodic theory* (2nd ed.). New York: Springer.

Wohlwill, J. F. (1973). *The study of behavioral development*. New York: Academic Press.

6

THE MISSING PERSON

Some Limitations in the Contemporary Study of Cognitive Aging

DALE DANNEFER AND ROBIN SHURA PATTERSON

This chapter offers a sociological perspective on cognition, human development, and aging. The sociological lens brings into focus several questions that receive relatively little attention in the prevailing discourses of cognitive aging yet are fundamental to an adequate understanding of age, cognition, and their interrelationship. These questions concern both the *explanandum* (the phenomenon to be explained, in this case, cognitive aging) and the *explanans* (the explanations—the causal forces that must be taken into account in understanding cognitive aging). A sociological perspective contends that the explanans of cognitive age-related outcomes cannot be understood without a systematic consideration of both *social structure* and *human action,* as we discuss in the first section. In the second section, we relate these considerations to the concept of ergodicity. In the third section, we consider the implications of a sociological perspective for considering the explananda—the range of phemomena that comprise the subject

matter of cognitive aging that includes some distinctly human dimensions of cognitive performance. These issues have implications for research questions and thus for the kinds of data and evidence that are marshaled for assessing cognitive aging. Our intent is to encourage a reconsideration and clarification of some of the basic premises and objectives of the field.

THE CONSTITUTION OF AGE: DIMENSIONS OF THE SOCIAL

The genuine mark of an empirical science is to respect the nature of its empirical world.
—Herbert Blumer

It will not be news to readers of this volume that a revolution occurred in the study of human aging four decades ago, when cohort analysis was introduced independently, and almost simultaneously, in psychology and sociology. In

AUTHORS' NOTE: We thank Judith Harris for research assistance. We thank Merlin Donald, Gunhild Hagestad, Paul Stein, the editors of the *Handbook of Cognitive Aging,* and an anonymous reviewer for helpful comments and criticisms on a draft of this chapter.

psychology, this happened through the work of Schaie and Baltes (Baltes, 1968; Baltes & Reinert, 1969; Schaie, 1965). In sociology, Ryder's (1965) classic paper introducing the concept of cohort was followed by the influential work of Riley and associates (Riley, 1973; Riley & Foner, 1968; Riley, Johnson, & Foner, 1972). It is interesting that in both cases the initial work was focused not on age but on other problems. Schaie's initial concerns were heavily methodological, and Ryder—writing in the context of the youth activism of the 1960s—focused on the dynamics of generational change, as had Mannheim's (1952) earlier paper. As Riley and associates made clear, the paradigm of cohort analysis as practiced in the social and behavioral sciences originated still elsewhere, in epidemiology (e.g., Frost, 1939; MacMahon, Pugh, & Ipson, 1960; Riley et al., 1972). In the work of Baltes and Schaie in psychology and Riley and Foner in sociology, the relevance of cohort analysis for the study of aging in the social and behavioral sciences became rapidly apparent.

In this section, we discuss cohort analysis, scholarly reactions to it, and its implications for the study of age in general and cognitive age in particular. As we will show, the implications of cohort analysis are not limited to matters of intercohort variation. Cohort analysis also opens up the more general problem of the contingency of age-related outcomes on social forces. To understand age-related change requires consideration of broader ways in which age is socially constituted (Baars, 1991) and of the developmental principles that underlie the central role that social forces play in human aging.

Cohort Analysis

A *cohort* can be defined as the aggregate of individuals who enter a social system in the same time period (see Riley et al., 1972). In studies of age, birth is typically the entry event. Because human societies inevitably involve technical and cultural change, members of a birth cohort (typically defined in 5- or 10-year intervals) experience a common set of societal circumstances that may cause them to develop and age in distinct ways.

Cohort analysis demonstrated that age-related patterns are not fixed but variable and contingent, in a range of properties, including personality development (e.g., Baltes, Cornelius, & Nesselroade, 1979) and lifestyle preferences, as well as cognitive performance (e.g., Alwin, Hofer, & McCammon, 2006; Alwin & McCammon, 1999; Schaie, 2005; Schaie, Willis, & Pennak, 2005). Especially under conditions of rapid change, the differentiated experience of members of succeeding cohorts produced differentiated patterns of cohort aging on multiple characteristics (Elder, 1998; Elder, Johnson, & Crosnoe, 2003). One of the most familiar demonstrations of the contingency of age-related patterns focuses on the impact of educational expansion over the 20th century in the United States and other late modern societies. Educational expansion, it was argued, created a steady trend of increase in related performance capabilities (including test taking) for succeeding cohorts. From this perspective, when cross-sectional age differences indicate increased performance in cognitive test performance by younger respondents, this may be in substantial part an artifact of cohort differences in educational opportunity and experience. Such an interpretation has recently been called into question by Alwin and colleagues, who have reported inferior performance in younger cohorts (e.g., Alwin, 1991; Alwin & McCammon, 1999, 2001). What is not at issue from either of these perspectives is that cohort effects are real and consequential.

Longitudinal analyses have shown that cross-sectional studies that had previously been widely assumed to represent natural processes of chronological aging are not that at all: They instead represent the piling up of multiple cohorts at a single point in time—cohorts that differ not only in age but also in experience. Each cohort possesses its own collectively shared experience as well as its members' historically unique life histories. As Matilda Riley frequently reminded us, individuals who are 75 today are not at all the same as were the 75-year-olds of a century ago, or as will be those of 2045. She termed the common practice of using cross-sectional data to make inferences about individual change the *life-course fallacy* (e.g., Riley, 1973; Riley et al., 1972). As the tradition of longitudinal research developed, it became recognized that cross-sectional age patterns could no longer be treated as reliable indicators of the actual life course trajectory of a given characteristic.

The impact of this multidisciplinary appreciation of cohort analysis sparked a revolution for the study of age in the social and behavioral sciences. As a result, the enterprise of life span psychology was born (Baltes, 1968; Schaie 1967), as was the modern sociology of age (Riley & Foner, 1968; Riley et al., 1972) and the life course (Elder, 1975). It established the necessity of longitudinal research in the study of age and helped fuel the development of quality longitudinal data sets and of analytical techniques to deal with such complex data. Nevertheless, the full implications of cohort analysis for understanding aging have yet to become part of the mainstream scientific discourse in social and behavioral science approaches to age.

The Response to the Challenge of Cohort Analysis

It is informative to consider responses within the behavioral and social sciences to the challenges posed by cohort analysis and the realization it brought—that patterns of development and aging that had been generally taken for granted and assumed to be universal were actually quite contingent on life course experience. We focus on two alternative responses: (1) paradigm change and (2) damage control. *Paradigm change* is, at least from a sociological perspective, the logically required response. It encompasses a number of dimensions and principles that require detailed exploration. *Damage control* warrants attention because it describes what has been the major reaction within social and behavioral sciences generally, including the study of cognitive aging.

Paradigm Change: Rethinking Basic Assumptions

To the extent that human aging is historically and socially contingent, it cannot be a matter of transcultural, transhistorical universality. That human aging has been shown to have such contingencies on many dimensions is the premise on which the need for paradigm change is founded. This has been a matter of some debate in the study of life span development (Baltes & Nesselroade, 1984; Dannefer, 1984a, 1984b, 1999a; Lerner, 2002) and gerontology (Baars, Dannefer, Phillipson, & Walker, 2006). Paradigm change entails a rejection of the idea of normal aging as it is described by the major intellectual traditions of human development. These include not only the classic organismic model with its strong assumptions of universal, sequential patterns of age-related change (see, e.g., Gutmann, 1994; Reese & Overton, 1970) but also its nuanced variants that give some attention to contextual factors, such as life span development and developmental contextualism (Baltes, 1979; Baltes & Smith, 2004; Featherman & Lerner, 1985; Lerner, 1991). Although such approaches indicate positive movement toward an appreciation of context, they remain constricted by their reliance on traditional models (Dannefer, 1984a; Dannefer & Perlmutter, 1990; Morss, 1990, 1995). An apprehension of human aging requires a recognition of the limits of such assumptions, and the introduction of a set of principles that will countenance these contingencies, which we term the *social-constitutionalist* (SC) paradigm (Baars, 1991; Baars et al., 2006).

Cohort analysis reveals that numerous aspects of human aging are contingent on experience in a particular social context. Yet logic requires that "cohort effects" stand not as the central problem but merely as a symptom of larger unresolved problems and issues of how and why sociohistorical contexts influence the lifelong development of human beings. From this broader perspective, cohort effects have been important not only in their own right but also because they open a window onto more fundamental questions: What exactly is it about the nature of the subject matter—the life form and species-being of *homo sapiens*—that permits such inordinate variability in the way that its members age? In what other ways is aging socially organized? The source of cohort differences is in the differentiated circumstances and environmental contingencies experienced by succeeding cohorts as they age, yet it must be acknowledged that social and environmental contingencies vary within cohorts as well as between them, generating intracohort variation that is patterned and systemic, as well as intercohort variation. The SC paradigm thus reveals that the cohort problematic is only the tip of the iceberg in the exploration of social *explanans* of cognitive aging. Social forces that shape patterns of aging are not limited to issues of social change and intercohort variability; they apply equally to conditions of social stability and intercohort homogeneity. Thus, rather than encapsulating or being synonymous with environmental effects on aging, cohort differences comprise only a *first opening* to a new horizon of inquiry, a horizon that is predicated on the recognition of a distinctly human problem of age-related change.

In order to grasp the significance of this opening, it is necessary to move from the level of cohorts and populations to the level of the aging individual. "The genuine mark of an empirical science," Blumer asserted, "is to respect the nature of its empirical world" (1969, p. 48). The subject matter of cognitive aging is, of course, age-related change in individual human beings. Therefore, the question is: What is it about the developing and aging individual—about human nature—that allows for the diversity of age-related outcomes observed across cohorts and between members of the same cohorts?

Homo Sapiens: Hard-Wired for Flexibility. To begin to confront these questions will require a systematic consideration of the features of the human organism and human development that permit open-ended outcomes and a variable range of responses. It will compel an acknowledgment that the developmental processes that govern age-related change within the human organism itself are, in Barbara Rogoff's (2003) apt phrase, "hard-wired for flexibility." This is evident in infancy and early childhood in the uniquely human condition of *exterogestation* (Berger & Luckmann, 1967; Dannefer, 1999b; Gould, 1977a; Hrdy, 2000), which refers to the relatively extended portion of neonatal human development that occurs after birth, immersed in a social environment. Human development is thus fundamentally contingent on social and interactional influences. Exterogestation helps explain the plasticity and "world-open" character of human development from infancy onward. A companion principle, *neoteny* (Bromhall, 2003; Dannefer, 1999b; Gould, 1977b; Montagu, 1989), refers to the lifelong potentials for growth,

learning, responsiveness and change that in other species are largely the province of childhood. In homo sapiens, such potentials are evident through the life course, including old age (Baltes & Willis, 1982; Langer, 1989, 2005; Langer & Rodin, 1999; Schaie, 2005; Yang, Krampe, & Baltes, 2006). The recognition of these species-unique, evolutionarily selected, and hard-wired features of human development require a replacement of the organismic model—with its strong assumptions of age-related sequences of universal change—with an interactionist approach that apprehends and incorporates processes occurring in the social environment into the model of age-related individual change, including cognitive change.

Beyond Cohort Effects: The Social Organization of Cognitive Aging. In addition to these developmental principles of flexibility and potentials for change, a range of other explanatory principles must be considered as aspects of the social organization of aging. We have discussed elsewhere (Dannefer, 1987, 1999b; Dannefer & Patterson, 2007; Dannefer & Uhlenberg, 1999; Hagestad & Dannefer, 2001) several such principles relevant for age-related outcomes. Here we focus on three in particular: (1) the *intra-cohort variability principle*, (2) the *intercohort stability principle*, and (3) the *naturalization principle*. Because of space limitations, the discussion will necessarily be brief.

1. Sociogenesis of intracohort variation. Over the past several years, increasing attention has been given to the phenomenon of the diversity of the aged on a wide range of characteristics, especially to the tendency for intracohort variability and inequality to increase with age. This has been a theme in both the psychology of aging (e.g., Baltes, 1993; Rowe & Kahn, 1987, 1998) and the sociology of age (Crystal & Waehrer, 1996; Dannefer, 1988). As noted elsewhere, if increasing intracohort diversity is a regular feature of cohort aging, it is misleading to focus only on measures of central tendency and to ignore the problems introduced by systematic changes in diversity over the life course (Dannefer, 1987). To the extent that such a pattern exists, it warrants focused analysis and interpretation as an enduring aspect of the social reality of aging. The robust tendency of systematically increasing differentiation also raises obvious new questions of explanation and interpretation. Unless it is treated as error variation, intra-age variability logically compels the question of causality in a new way: If systematic *age-related changes in the amount of interindividual variability* recur, the cause cannot be age alone.

2. Sociogenesis of intercohort homogeneity. A persistent tendency within life span and life course literatures has been to equate "contextual effects" with the phenomenon of social change, implying that stability across cohorts plays little role in the production of age-related outcomes (Dannefer & Uhlenberg, 1999; Hagestad & Dannefer, 2001). An implication of the above considerations is the recognition that the effects of social forces do not depend on change: Effects of social forces may be especially evident in times of change, but in times of stability they are no less present, and indeed may be even more potent because they go unnoticed. Stability across cohorts does not entitle researchers to presume that the recurrent pattern represents an absence of environmental effects, or the presence of an ontogenetic human universal of aging and development.

One of the underappreciated insights of Riley's original age stratification paradigm is the naming of age as a feature not only of individuals but also of social structure, which is embedded in language and cultural systems of normative expectations. The very concept of age, when it becomes an integrated, normative feature of social structure, takes on a facticity of its own and becomes an independent influence on the aging of individuals. As a social fact, age is a coercive and constraining feature both of social structure and of micro-interaction and thus has an influence on individuals and groups that is not reducible to ontogenetic processes of organismic aging.

When social practices that rely on age as a primary basis of social organization remain stable over a sustained period of time, they may generate a relatively high degree of stability across cohorts in patterns of aging. This is precisely what occurred with the establishment of the institutionalized life course in late modern societies in the 20th century (Kohli & Meyer, 1986). The institutionalized life course, which has produced both increasing intracohort and intercohort homogeneity of timing of life transitions, is a result of a constellation of socially emergent age-graded policies and practices, including age-graded homogeneity in school experience and in the transition to adulthood as well as career and retirement experiences. The effects of such social processes can extend beyond role structures to influence individual identity and other psychological characteristics. For example, these processes may be hypothesized to account for findings of stability of individual differences over time in attitudes or personality (e.g., Alwin, 1994; Alwin, Cohen, & Newcomb, 1991; Costa & MacRae, 1980), because research reporting personality stability has generally been based on samples of respondents living in the relatively stable social orders of late modernity.

3. The principle of naturalization: The social organization of the idea of age. When the significance of age as a basis of social organization and feature of social structure remains stable over a sustained period of time, it may not only generate a relatively high degree of stability across cohorts in empirical patterns of aging, but also may lend plausibility to the idea of age as a naturally unfolding reality. A concomitant of the establishment of the institutionalized life course has been the emergence of age norms as a powerful aspect of social structure and as a guide for personal life (e.g., Chudacoff, 1989). Despite their historical recency and obvious social sources, age norms have become taken-for-granted, definitional aspects of age. This cohort-centric misattribution of a socially organized patterning of age as something that is natural and inevitable comprises an example of naturalization—mistaking humanly produced and socially specific phenomena for natural ones (Dannefer, 1999b). Of course, this is not to suggest that all patterned, age-correlated individual outcomes are social in origin. Yet the extent to which such patterns reflect general, organismically based processes of aging cannot be understood without considering the role of historically specific, socially contingent conditions such as the bureaucratization and naturalization of age that have occurred over the past 150 years in industrial societies. Without an understanding of the social organization of age or of the ways in which social organization interacts with ontogenetic features of aging, the ability to provide an explanation of the processes underlying age-related cognitive outcomes will remain severely limited. It is for this reason that a paradigm change—a reformulated model of human nature and a reformulated set of research assumptions and questions—is required to move the task of explanation of cognitive aging forward.

Damage Control: Defending Orthodoxy

From a sociological perspective, it is clear that paradigm change comprises at least one necessary condition for meaningful advance to occur in the study of cognitive aging. Equally clear, however, is that paradigm change has not been the primary mode of response to the vast array of evidence of social influences on age-related processes. The dominant response to the challenge of cohort analysis in the social and behavioral sciences has not been to confront the full theoretical and empirical implications of the challenge but to adopt an intellectual posture that has the effect of minimizing, containing, and ignoring those implications. This has been a long-standing practice, and we are not the first to note it. It was noted by Irving Rosow (1978), and the legitimacy of his concern was subsequently acknowledged by Schaie:

> Developmentalists have often treated historical time and generational effects as confounds to be controlled and explained away. Thus, it is not without a good deal of justification that Rosow (1978) could argue that [varieties of cohort analysis] treated the effects other than age as nuisances and that any information developed on them was at best incidental. (1984, pp. 1–2)

We term this posture *damage control*. The logic of damage control is roughly as follows: The discovery of cohort differences in patterns of aging clearly makes the task of defining the true character of aging more complex, but it does not eliminate the truth that aging is ultimately a universal and internally governed process. In terms of empirical research practices, a damage control perspective seeks to treat cohort analysis and any other social factors as essentially noise to be controlled in the quest to understand true aging processes. From a damage control perspective, it is important to get a handle on such factors as cohort effects, in order to get such extraneous variation under control so that the "true age" pattern that is present in the population, lying beneath the annoyance posed by cohort effects, can be discovered. Indeed, to give too much ground to cohort analysis may seem to threaten the very idea of a science of development and aging, because it diminishes the predictive power and explanatory claims of age. Damage control continues to be a frequent mode of response to the problems raised by the SC approach. We consider two modes of damage control: (1) containment and (2) abandonment.

Containment. Containment can take two forms: (1) limiting attention to social forces on aging to those associated with social change, namely, dramatic social–historical events or times of pronounced or rapid social change ("cohort effects" proper), and (2) focusing on nomothetic, central-tendency patterns within each cohort, thereby ignoring the problem of intracohort variability.

1. Equating social forces and social change. The first form of containment—equating the importance of social forces with social change—derives from the close linkages between cohort analysis, the life course and life span perspectives, and macro-social change. In innumerable programmatic statements and paradigmatic formulations across these perspectives, scholars have emphasized social change as a basis for the need to analyze life course patterns of discrete cohorts (e.g., Baltes, 1979; Elder, 1998; Riley, 1973; Riley & Foner, 1968).

The close connection between social change and cohort differences ultimately compels the logical question: "What if there were no change? Would the power of social and environmental forces to alter the path of human aging be any different?" In a hypothetical society of great demographic and cultural stability, cohort effects might be nil. However, in view of the known mechanisms of human development discussed above, such a circumstance clearly would not imply a reduction to zero of social effects on aging. It would simply mean that in order to understand the extent to which social influences are regulating the aging process, it will be necessary to go beyond the study of historically unique events and to investigate more subtle yet pervasive aspects of the social organization of aging (Dannefer & Uhlenberg, 1999; Hagestad & Dannefer, 2001).

2. *Focusing on nomothetic patterns.* The second form of containment is the tendency to *focus on nomothetic patterns and central tendency measures* while treating intra-age variability as uninteresting and unimportant error variation. This has been extensively discussed elsewhere (Dannefer, 1987, 1988, 2003; Maddox & Lawton, 1988). Both forms of containment deflect attention from examining the extent to which intra-age variation is socially organized through mechanisms of resource allocation operating, for example, in labor and marriage markets, education and health care policy, and other aspects of opportunity structures through which advantage and disadvantage accumulate. As noted earlier, the likelihood that intracohort variation in cognitive test performance is organized by opportunity structures and other social factors has been supported by numerous empirical analyses (e.g., chap. 26, this volume; Schmitz-Scherzer & Thomae, 1983).

Abandonment. Abandonment is the second significant form of damage control and entails the movement away from cohort analysis and other forms of longitudinal research. It is true that the initial wave of enthusiasm for cohort analyses lasted some time, fueling not only influential conceptual frameworks in the 1970s but also significant new enterprises of longitudinal research. Yet, looking back over the past two decades of work, it appears increasingly that such longitudinal databases may be of more interest to health researchers than to researchers focusing on cognitive performance, personality, or other mental characteristics. Our review of recent published analyses of age-related change in cognition suggests a continuing preference for cross-sectional designs (details available from the authors at robin.patterson@case.edu).

Taken together, we regard these various aspects of damage control as reflecting a long and established tradition of research practices founded on the logic of the organismic model. As an indication of the scope of this legacy, it is interesting to recall that disinclination toward longitudinal data predates cohort analysis and was sometimes based on remarkably felicitous reasoning, with its own latent implications. In his classic analyses of intelligence, David Wechsler (1958) acknowledged the value of longitudinal data yet vigorously defended his cross-sectional analyses. A main thrust of his defense provides remarkable testimony to the power of the organismic paradigm and the logic of damage control, because of its unwittingly back-handed use of sociological logic:

> Actually, only a few longitudinal studies have been reported, and the two most frequently cited . . . were done on special population samples . . . in that the subjects for the studies were individuals of superior intelligence . . . college students with estimated IQ's of 110 and above . . . (and) . . . the parents of gifted children. . . . Now it is well known that intelligence test scores of persons of superior intellectual ability tend to hold up or even improve for some time beyond the age of 25. . . . The subjects of the Bayley study were individuals engaged in vocations and professions (teaching, etc.) whose day to day activity might well exercise or involve some practice in the kinds of ability called for by the tests. (Wechsler, 1958, p. 138)

Ironically, what Wechsler is describing here is precisely the social organization of intelligence. Anticipating the findings of later research, Wechsler recognizes that (1) the age-based declines are not universal but vary essentially along social class lines, and (2) test performance is substantially influenced by one's work and other experiences (Manly et al., 1999).

The resistance to paradigm change has clear intellectual costs for limiting researchers' abilities to recognize the social contingency of age-related declines in individual lives. Not surprisingly, these costs can also impede theoretical progress along the very cutting edge of cognitive aging research.

DAMAGE CONTROL, PARADIGM CHANGE, AND ERGODICITY

From a sociological perspective, continued efforts at damage control inhibit the advance of sociological understanding of cognition, while the embrace of a paradigm change that recognizes the social contingencies of cognitive development and change can further advancement in the field. In relation to age, recent work on heterogeneity and cumulative dis/advantage has provided one example of the benefits of an SC paradigm for understanding age-related processes (Dannefer, 2003). The exploding body of work in cognitive science and brain imaging that demonstrates how experience and context affect brain growth and development in adulthood as well as in childhood provides another powerful example (e.g., Donald, 2001; Maguire et al., 2000).

As an additional example, consider the value, as yet unrealized, of the SC paradigm for the study of ergodicity. The proposition that change processes in human individuals and populations are nonergodic is consistent with the logic of the SC paradigm. Part of the challenge of ergodicity concerns what appears to be the uniqueness of individual trajectories over time, when viewed against the pattern of the cohort. As Molenaar (2004) put it:

> Each person is initially conceived of as a possibly unique system of interacting dynamic processes, the unfolding of which gives rise to an individual life trajectory in a high-dimensional psychological space. Most psychological processes will have to be considered to be nonergodic. For nonergodic processes, an analysis of the structure of IEV [interindividual variation] will yield results that differ from results obtained in an analogous analysis of IAV [intraindividual variation]. Hence, for the class of nonergodic processes (which include all developmental processes, learning processes, adaptive processes, and many more), explicit analyses of IAV for their own sakes are required to obtain valid results concerning individual development, learning performance, and so forth. The foundational issue at stake concerns the relation between the structure of IEV and the structure of IAV. (p. 202)

The SC paradigm can make important contributions to this challenge. By recognizing the role of social forces in organizing aspects of individual cognitive resources and processes and their change over time, some of the "unique" variation in individual trajectories can be understood as not unique at all but as socially patterned. Recent research on cortical plasticity is making clear that the effects of experience are as dramatically evident in physiological as in psychological terms. For instance, London taxi drivers have been shown to grow larger hippocampi based on their learning and practice in knowing London streets (Hartley, Maguire, Spiers, & Burgess, 2003; Maguire et al., 2000; Maguire et al., 2003). Changes in the somatosensory system have been shown to occur because of extended guitar practice or violin playing, or many other tasks requiring fine motor skills (e.g., Levitin, 2006; Rencanzone, Schreiner, & Merzenich, 1993). It is reasonable to expect, then, that some of the apparent uniqueness in intraindividual variation (IAV) over time can be reinterpreted as a pattern of change that will be shared across individuals (interindividual variation) who share strong commonalities in daily experience (whether driving a London cab or playing classical violin). Of course, the likelihood of becoming a cab driver or violinist (or a psychiatrist, street gang leader, or stewardess) is not random. It is a likelihood that is related to social origins, to education and labor market circumstances, and to other socially organized contingencies an individual encounters across time through particular historical and biographical moments. Thus, experientially patterned commonalities in intraindividual change may be linked to broader influences of social location, social relationships, and social opportunity. It may be fruitful for scholars of ergodicity to consider the social context of individuals whose IAV is studied and its influence on IAV patterns.

This suggests the hypothesis that, by consideration of social processes that organize individual opportunity and cognitive experience (e.g., the system of occupational stratification and its norms and expectations around characteristics like age and gender), one can reduce dramatically the proportion of IAV that must be treated as a matter of individual uniqueness. Such a strategy can provide a new set of ordering principles—principles of social structure that organize populations, which includes the role structure that organizes opportunities for learning and change. Thus, ergodicity may benefit from the addition of a sociodynamic level of analysis between the discrete (but only partly unique) individual and the aggregate of a cohort or population. This approach would further the goal of understanding, shared with and in agreement with ergodic analysis, by demonstrating that although age-related change is nonergodic it is nevertheless a systemic, orderly phenomenon, one that is governed by the forces of social life. The SC approach agrees that many of the processes leading to IAV are unique and "self-organizing" (Molenaar, 2004, p. 211), but emphasizes that self-organization is a socially located and socially driven process. The learning of cab drivers can in some respects be thought of as self-organizing, but it is a process that is dictated by the imperatives of their life situation in a particular social structure, the rules of the road. Self-organization is dependent on social organization. An SC approach allows for the possibility that the trajectory of "each single participant obeys a different factor model" (Molenaar, 2004, p. 210), but it goes further in postulating that the different factor models in question are likely to be obeying the dictates of opportunity in a historically specific, socially organized structure of opportunity, desire, constraint, and legitimacy.

THE MISSING PERSON: DISTINCTLY HUMAN DIMENSIONS OF COGNITION

Minimalist settings produce Minimalist people.

—Merlin Donald

As noted, a sociological perspective requires a reconsideration not only of the *explanans*—the postulated explanations and conceptual models proposed to account for age-related cognitive outcomes—but also of the *explananda*—the phenomenon of cognitive aging itself. Such an approach must begin with an acknowledgment of distinctly human aspects of cognition.

Paul Baltes (1993) concluded his Kleemeier Award address to the Gerontological Society of America with this statement: "When I was 28, I was a fool. But I had an excellent memory." Baltes thus juxtaposed the distinction between two fundamentally different properties of cognitive functioning—wisdom and judgment on one hand, speed and memory on the other.

These two dimensions are not equally represented in the psychology of aging. The study of wisdom and practical intelligence remain undernourished stepchildren in the field of human cognition. Thus, the study of cognitive aging has yet to capture adequately those aspects of cognition that are most distinctly human, notably imagination, creativity, and innovation. These are not esoteric or occasionally occurring characteristics, and they are not the exclusive province of successful inventors and artists. The use of imagination and creativity and the devising of innovation are integral to human activity in everyday life, occurring routinely in ordinary mundane situations that require practical everyday problem solving (Lave & Wenger, 1991). Without broad consideration of these uniquely human aspects of cognition, the science of cognitive aging is "missing the person" that is its true subject matter.

In the lived experience of everyday life, human cognition is constantly applied to world-construction—the generation and maintenance of social relationships that provide the context of one's own sense of self and personhood. In the course of the everyday, human actors generate novel ideas, contrive new forms of terrorism and new defenses against it, practice powers of persuasion (whether for the purpose of selling appliances, getting out the vote, or rechanneling the motives of children or consociates) and engage in empathy (choosing with great care and precision the words, pacing, and tone of speech, and accompanying nonverbal gestures). We devise creative ways to keep students engaged in a late afternoon class and devise methods and measures to distinguish fluid from crystallized intelligence, and so on. These capabilities are fundamental to the very condition of human personhood, both because creativity is always socially grounded (Langer, 2005; Russ, 2000–2001) and because the constitution of social relationships happens only through a purposeful, intentional, and ultimately creative process.

Although properties like memory, processing speed, and abstract reasoning are clearly not irrelevant to such endeavors, they represent only a small subset of the dimensions that are germane to understand the workings of human cognition and cognitive aging. To focus on such characteristics alone may be compared to conducting the road test of a new automobile by focusing only on the luggage capacity and steering ratio while ignoring more central features to its quality and performance, such as torque, center of gravity and the responsiveness of its suspension, and its overall structural integrity.

From this perspective, the study of cognition and aging has been, in neuropsychologist Merlin Donald's (2001) term, *minimalist*:

> Experimental psychologists, like me, tend to examine people in stripped-down Minimalist settings. And Minimalist settings produce Minimalist people. . . . In the laboratory, we objectify humans in the same way that we do rats and insects. (pp. 16–17)

Donald (2001) offered this observation as both a defense of the laboratory method, and also a critique of its limits:

> When people are removed from their familiar settings—work, school, home, city, street—and subjected to bare-knuckled scrutiny, their conscious capacity reveals its severe limitations. This includes everyone. (p. 18)

Of course, questions of the degree to which such laboratory exercises can be extrapolated to real world activities, and the extent to which they rely on matters like the motivation of the respondent (which is likely not age neutral), remain especially relevant in judging their utility in studies of age. Practical everyday tasks undertaken in the service of an often consequential goal or outcome are, at least in principle, measurable as well as "real." To develop comparatively meaningful, standardized assessments of these outcomes obviously is a daunting task, but it is a required task if the science of cognitive aging is to be true to its subject matter. This argument implies the need to develop new and more complex kinds of cognitive assessments and measurement. Moreover, it has been shown that when older people are tested on tasks that have personal relevance to them, they often perform dramatically better. This suggests the need for a broadened lens of inquiry and measures of a wider range of dimensions, to capture the essence of the distinct character of human cognition and its relationship to aging.

If research on cognitive aging largely considers a limited range of dimensions of human cognition, and utilizes a limited set of measures of

cognitive ability, the resultant conclusions of such research will also have limited scope and value. Important as these properties may be, human cognitive ability is not reducible to scores on intelligence tests, dementia screening tools, or quickness and accuracy of vocabulary recall. It must be acknowledged that the subject matter of human cognition is complex, elusive, and dauntingly difficult to measure. Yet the dictates of science require that the task of measuring or otherwise characterizing the phenomenon of interest is determined first of all by the phenomenon itself, and not by the preconceptions, traditions, and measures inherited or imported from the study of some other subject matter. "The genuine mark of an empirical science is to respect the nature of its empirical world"—Blumer's dictum applies here as well. Thus we must confront the question: To what extent is the subject matter of human cognition and cognitive aging adequately respected by studies that focus on the narrowly defined performance, speed, or memory capabilities?

CONCLUSION: SOCIAL FORCES, THE MISSING PERSON, AND THE FUTURE OF COGNITIVE AGING

Citizens of late modernity are born into and live out their lives immersed in a society and culture that systematically denigrates old age. It is a society comprised of institutional forms that systematically exclude elders from full social participation and that focus on perceived decrements and debilities of advancing age while failing to ask questions of (a) the social sources of these perceived decrements and (b) the specific individual characteristics upon which the perception is based. Instead, observed age-related differences in behavior and in performance are naturalized, and one of the central roots of social beliefs in inevitable decline with age— pervasive ageism within society—remains unnoticed and unnamed. When a social context is one that systematically and pervasively denigrates old age and glorifies youth, it is a context that may be capable, all by itself, of producing negative age-related trajectories of intellectual performance and physical health.

In terms of life history and circumstances, behavioral and social scientists are not insulated from the realities of ageism: For us, too, ageism is an integral, constant part of everyday life, with its pervasive tendencies toward the naturalization of age-associated behavior. Yet developing an adequate understanding of the relationship of age and cognition obviously requires an interrogation not only of the immediate performance capabilities of individuals but also of the causal factors that contribute to those outcomes, not only of the dimensions of human cognition for which established measures have been developed but also of uniquely human cognitive abilities, like imagination and creativity, that are even more daunting to measure. It requires not only the refinement of technical procedures of measurement but also a scrutiny of how those particular measures were chosen in the first place. Such considerations, in our view, add further to the reasons to question the assumption of general slowing that has often been regarded as an integral part of normal aging and to constitute a general null hypothesis in numerous studies of aging (e.g., Perfect & Maylor, 2000).

Recently, evidence challenging the "general slowing hypothesis" has been accumulating, even in studies that rely on cross-sectional data and focus on narrowly defined performance measures (e.g., Kliegl, Mayr, & Krampe, 1994; Verhaeghen et al., chap. 8, this volume), leaving space for doubt about the generality of general slowing with age, even under such "minimalist" conditions where it has most clearly been established. When age differences are found on less difficult tasks but not on more complex tasks, and when they erode asymptotically, possibly indicating a learning effect (Verhaeghen, 2002), the credibility of general slowing as a substantively meaningful, universal human process is called further into question. Slowing, it may be suggested, is in some cases not general but is socially organized and socially specific. In this volume, for example, Berg's chapter (chap. 13) illustrates a growing body of work on practical reasoning that provides clear relief from the mantra of decline, by reporting an age trajectory of positive improvement. This is, of course, what might be expected from the known divergence in the trajectories of fluid versus crystallized intelligence.

Shifting to the domains of everyday life, with the practical demands and opportunities for creative micro-solutions that are integral to it, there is even greater reason to doubt that general slowing with age is a general human process. In everyday life, it has been demonstrated that performance is related to life history and circumstantial conditions. There is also evidence to suggest that an individual's test performance and the mental and physical conditions that underlie it are related to ageism. In a cleverly designed set of experiments, Langer and associates (Langer, 1989, 2005; Langer & Rodin, 1999) have shown that when elders are removed from the oppressiveness of an ageist societal context, their performance can improve significantly.

In this chapter, we have suggested that the study of cognitive aging is at an early point in developing an adequate understanding of age and that such understanding can be advanced by drawing on the perspectives offered by the SC paradigm. Like the study of aging more generally, the study of cognitive aging to a large extent has accepted the pervasive, implicit assumptions— the "hidden curriculum"—of the culture of ageism as representative of human nature rather than analyzing the social sources of age-related change, and has too often focused on a restrictively narrow set of outcomes that define age-related differences in terms set by modernity and ageism, outcomes that do not capture higher-level cognitive functions that are the unique province of homo sapiens. Thus much of the field of cognitive aging implicitly embraces the conditions produced by modernity and constructs its problematic in such a way that those conditions cannot be interrogated.

In sum, we suggest that progress in advancing understanding of the relation of cognition and age will depend on attention to both the explanans and the explananda of cognitive aging. Regarding the explanans, the study of cognitive aging will be advanced to the extent that the irrepressible and powerful dynamics that are adumbrated by the SC paradigm are recognized and embraced as an integral aspect of research design. Regarding the explananda, we suggest that advance will be inhibited as long as the study of cognitive aging focuses on measures that capture only a small and constricted subset of the range of human cognitive capabilities. By facing such problems, the study of cognitive aging can contribute to generating ideas and findings that clarify the extent to which age-related outcomes are the result of the institutionalized life course of late modernity, rather than continuing to report findings that legitimate and render invisible the structures of the institutionalized life course as well as the culture of ageism and their influences on various cognitive outcomes. On the other hand, without facing such problems, the field of cognitive aging risks legitimating not only structures but also definitions of aging and old age that delimit opportunities available to elders and that are destructive to the self-understanding, self-definition, and identity of aging individuals.

Again, this is not to contend that all age-related decrements are due to the ageism embedded in the institutionalized life course. We recognize that experiential and social forces interact with obdurate, organismic processes that involve diminishing capacities and that may directly and indirectly affect cognitive performance (Baltes & Lindenberger, 1997; Dannefer & Patterson, 2007; Dannefer & Perlmutter, 1990). Our concern is not to deny the existence of domains in which there may be unavoidable decline but to point to two broadly important truths about age-related cognition that make a wholesale embrace of phenomena such as "general slowing" untenable. First, to some unknown yet substantial degree, age-related decrements have their source in social practices, not in organismic processes; and second, there are vast domains of cognitive performance—often consisting of dimensions that are difficult to study—that may not follow a common, age-linked trajectory of decrement. Until these problems and possibilities are directly confronted, the study of aging, including cognitive aging, will continue to be a source of legitimation of the institutionalized life course and ageism rather than a means of understanding the extent to which the institutionalized life course and ageism are sources of what is mistaken for natural reality of aging.

REFERENCES

Alwin, D. F. (1991). Family of origin and cohort differences in verbal ability. *American Sociological Review, 56,* 625–638.

Alwin, D. F. (1994). Aging, personality and social change: The stability of individual differences over the adult life span. In D. L. Featherman, R. M. Lerner, & M. Perlman (Eds.), *Life span development and behavior* (Vol. 12, pp. 135–185). Hillsdale, NJ: Lawrence Erlbaum.

Alwin, D. F., Cohen, R. L., & Newcomb, T. M. (1991). *Political attitudes over the life span: The Bennington women after fifty years.* Madison: University of Wisconsin Press.

Alwin, D. F., Hofer, S. M., & McCammon, R. J. (2006). Modeling the effects of time: Integrating demographic and developmental perspectives. In R. H. Binstock & L. K. George (Eds.), *Handbook of aging and the social sciences* (6th ed., pp. 20–38). San Diego, CA: Elsevier.

Alwin, D. F., & McCammon, R. J. (1999). Aging vs. cohort interpretations of intercohort differences in GSS verbal scores. *American Sociological Review, 64,* 272–286.

Alwin, D. F., & McCammon, R. J. (2001). Aging, cohorts and verbal ability. *Journal of Gerontology: Social Sciences, 56B,* S1–S11.

Baars, J. (1991). The challenge of critical gerontology: The problem of social constitution. *Journal of Aging Studies, 3,* 219–243.

Baars, J., Dannefer, D., Phillipson, C., & Walker, A. (2006). *Aging, globalization and inequality: The new critical gerontology.* Amityville, NY: Baywood.

Baltes, P. B. (1968). Longitudinal and cross-sectional sequences in the study of age and generation effects. *Human Development, 11,* 145–171.

Baltes, P. B. (1979). Life-span development psychology: Some converging observations on history and theory. In P. B. Baltes & O. G. Brim, Jr. (Eds.), *Life-span development and behavior* (Vol. 2, pp. 255–279). New York: Academic Press.

Baltes, P. B. (1993). The aging mind: Potential and limits. *The Gerontologist, 33,* 580–594.

Baltes, P. B., Cornelius, S. W., & Nesselroade, J. R. (1979). Cohort effects in developmental psychology. In J. R. Nesselroade & P. B. Baltes (Eds.), *Longitudinal research in the study of behavior and development* (pp. 61–87). New York: Academic Press.

Baltes, P. B., & Lindenberger, U. (1997). Emergence of a powerful connection between sensory and cognitive functions across the adult life span: A new window to the study of cognitive aging? *Psychology and Aging, 12,* 12–21.

Baltes, P. B., & Nesselroade, J. R. (1984). Paradigm lost and paradigm regained: Critique of Dannefer's portrayal of life-span developmental psychology. *American Sociological Review, 49,* 841–846.

Baltes, P. B., & Reinert, G. (1969). Cohort effects in cognitive development of children as revealed by cross-sectional sequences. *Developmental Psychology, 1,* 169–177.

Baltes, P. B., & Smith, J. (2004). Lifespan psychology: From developmental contextualism to developmental biocultural co-constructivism. *Research on Human Development, 1,* 123–143.

Baltes, P. B., & Willis, S. L. (1982). Plasticity and enhancement of intellectual functioning in old age. In F. I. M. Craik & E. E. Trehub (Eds.), *Aging and cognitive processes* (pp. 353–389). New York: Plenum.

Berger, P. L., & Luckmann, T. (1967). *The social construction of reality.* New York: Anchor.

Blumer, H. (1969). *Symbolic interactionism: Perspective and method.* Englewood Cliffs, NJ: Prentice Hall.

Bromhall, C. (2003). *The eternal child: How evolution has made children of us all.* London: Ebury Press.

Chudacoff, H. (1989). *How old are you? Age consciousness in America.* Princeton, NJ: Princeton University Press.

Costa, P. T., & McCrae, R. (1980). Still stable after all these years: Personality as a key to some issues in adulthood and old age. In P. B. Baltes & O. G. Brim (Eds.), *Life-span development and behavior* (Vol. 3, pp. 65–102). New York: Academic Press.

Crystal, S., & Waehrer, K. (1996). Late life economic inequality in longitudinal perspective. *Journal of Gerontology: Social Sciences, 51B,* S307–S318.

Dannefer, D. (1984a). Adult development and social theory: A paradigmatic reappraisal. *American Sociological Review, 49,* 100–116.

Dannefer, D. (1984b). The role of the social in life-span developmental psychology, past and future: Rejoinder to Baltes and Nesselroade. *American Sociological Review, 49,* 847–850.

Dannefer, D. (1987). Aging as intracohort differentiation: Accentuation, the Matthew effect, and the life course. *Sociological Forum, 2,* 211–236.

Dannefer, D. (1988). Differential aging and the stratified life course: Conceptual and methodological issues. In G. L. Maddox & M. P. Lawton (Eds.), *Annual review of gerontology* (Vol. 8, pp. 3–36). New York: Springer.

Dannefer, D. (1999a). Freedom isn't free: Power, alienation and the consequences of action. In J. Brandtstädter & R. M. Lerner (Eds.), *Action and development: Origins and functions of intentional self development* (pp. 105–131). New York: Springer.

Dannefer, D. (1999b). Neoteny, naturalization and other constituents of human development. In C. Ryff & V. W. Marshall (Eds.), *Self and society in aging processes* (pp. 67–93). New York: Springer.

Dannefer, D. (2003). Cumulative advantage/disadvantage and the life courses: Cross-fertilizing age and social science theory. *Journals of Gerontology, Series B: Psychological and Social Sciences, 58B,* S327–S337.

Dannefer, D., & Patterson, R. S. (2007). The second demographic transition, aging families, and the aging of the institutionalized life course. In P. Uhlenberg & K. W. Schaie (Eds.), *Impact of demographic changes on health and wellbeing in the elderly* (pp. 212–229). New York: Springer.

Dannefer, D., & Perlmutter, M. (1990). Development as a multidimensional process: Individual and social constituents. *Human Development, 33,* 108–137.

Dannefer, D., & Uhlenberg, P. (1999). Paths of the life course: A typology. In V. L. Bengtson & K. W. Schaie (Eds.), *Handbook of theories of aging* (pp. 306–326). New York: Springer.

Donald, M. (2001). *A mind so rare: The evolution of human consciousness.* New York: W. W. Norton.

Elder, G. H., Jr. (1975). Age differentiation and the life course. In A. Inkeles, J. Coleman, & N. Smelser (Eds.), *Annual review of sociology* (pp. 165–190). Palo Alto, CA: Annual Reviews.

Elder, G. H., Jr. (1998). *Children of the Great Depression: Social change in life experience.* Boulder, CO: Westview Press.

Elder, G. H., Jr., Johnson, M. K., & Crosnoe, R. (2003). The emergence and development of the life course. In J. T. Mortimer & M. J. Shanahan (Eds.), *Handbook of the life course* (pp. 3–19). New York: Plenum.

Featherman, D. L., & Lerner, R. M. (1985). Ontogenesis and sociogenesis: Problematics for theory and research about development and socialization across the lifespan *American Sociological Review, 50,* 659–676.

Frost, W. H. (1939). The age selection of mortality from tuberculosis in successive decades. *American Journal of Hygiene, Section A, 30,* 91–96.

Gould, S. J. (1977a). Human babies as embryos. In S. J. Gould (Ed.), *Ever since Darwin: Reflections on natural history* (pp. 70–75). New York: Norton.

Gould, S. J. (1977b). *Ontogeny and phylogeny.* Cambridge, MA: Belknap Harvard.

Gutmann, D. (1994). *Reclaimed powers: Men and women in later life*. Evanston, IL: Northwestern University Press.

Hagestad, G. O., & Dannefer, D. (2001). Concepts and theories of aging: Beyond microfication in social science approaches. In R. H. Binstock & L. K. George (Eds.), *Handbook of aging and the social sciences* (pp. 3–21). New York: Academic Press.

Hartley, T., Maguire, E. A., Spiers, H. J., & Burgess, N. (2003). The well-worn route and the path less traveled: Distinct neural bases of route following and wayfinding in humans. *Neuron, 37,* 877–888.

Hrdy, S. B. (2000). *Mother Nature*. London: Vintage.

Kliegl, R., Mayr, U., & Krampe, R. T. (1994). Time-accuracy functions for determining process and person differences: An application to cognitive aging. *Cognitive Psychology, 26,* 134–164.

Kohli, M., & Meyer, J. W. (1986). Social structure and social construction of life stages. *Human Development, 29,* 145–149.

Langer, E. J. (1989). *Mindfulness*. Reading, MA: Addison-Wesley.

Langer, E. J. (2005). *On becoming an artist: Reinventing yourself through mindful creativity*. New York: Ballantine.

Langer, E. J., & Rodin, J. (1999). In control and glad of it! The effects of choice and enhanced personal responsibility for the aged: A field experiment in an institutional setting. In R. R. Hock (Ed.), *Forty studies that changed psychology: Explorations into the history of psychological research* (pp. 148–155). Upper Saddle River, NJ: Prentice Hall.

Lave, J., & Wenger, E. (1991). *Situated learning: Legitimate peripheral participation*. New York: Cambridge University Press.

Lerner, R. M. (1991). Changing organism–context relations as the basic process of development: A developmental contextual perspective. *Developmental Psychology, 27,* 27–32.

Lerner, R. M. (2002). *Concepts and theories of human development* (3rd ed.). Mahwah, NJ: Lawrence Erlbaum.

Levitin, D. J. (2006). *This is your brain on music: The science of a human obsession*. New York: Dutton Adult.

MacMahon, B., Pugh, T. F., & Ipson, J. (1960). *Epidemiologic methods*. Boston: Little, Brown.

Maddox, G. L., & Lawton, M. P. (1988). *Annual review of gerontology and geriatrics: Varieties of aging* (Vol. 8). New York: Springer.

Maguire, E. A., Gadian, D. G., Johnsrude, I. S., Good, C. D., Ashburner, J., Frackowiak, R. S. J., et al. (2000). Navigation-related structural change in the hippocampi of taxi drivers. *Proceedings of the National Academy of Sciences, USA, 97,* 4398–4403.

Maguire, E. A., Spiers, H. J., Good, C. D., Hartley, T., Frackowiak, R. S. J., & Burgess, N. (2003). Navigation expertise and the human hippocampus: a structural brain imaging analysis. *Hippocampus, 13,* 208–217.

Manly, J. J., Jacobs, D. M., Sano, M., Merchant, C. A., Small, S. A., & Stern, Y. (1999). Effect of literacy on neuropsychological test performance in non-demented, education-matched elders. *Journal of the International Neuropsychological Society, 5,* 191–202.

Mannheim, K. (1952). The problem of generations. In P. Kecskemetia (Ed.), *Essays in the sociology of knowledge* (pp. 276–322). Boston: Routledge & Kegan Paul. (Original work published 1927)

Molenaar, P. C. M. (2004). A manifesto on psychology as idiographic science: Bringing the person back into scientific psychology, this time forever. *Measurement, 2,* 201–218.

Montagu, A. (1989). *Growing young* (2nd ed.). Granby, MA: Bergin & Garvey.

Morss, J. (1990). *The biologising of childhood: Developmental psychology and the Darwinian myth*. New York: Psychology Press.

Morss, J. (1995). *Growing critical*. London: Routledge.

Perfect, T. J., & Maylor, E. (2000). *Models of cognitive aging*. Oxford, UK: Oxford University Press.

Reese, H. W., & Overton, W. F. (1970). Models of development and theories of development. In L. R. Goulet & P. B. Baltes (Eds.), *Life-span developmental psychology: Research and theory* (pp. 115–145). New York: Academic Press.

Rencanzone, G., Schreiner, C. E., & Merzenich, M. (1993). Plasticity in the frequency representation of primary auditory cortex following discrimination training in adult owl monkeys. *Journal of Neuroscience, 13,* 87–103.

Riley, M. W. (1973). Aging and cohort succession: Interpretations and misinterpretations. *Public Opinion Quarterly, 37,* 35–49.

Riley, M. W., & Foner, A. (1968). *Aging and the society, Vol. I: An inventory of research findings*. New York: Russell Sage Foundation.

Riley, M. W., Johnson, M. E., & Foner, A. (1972). *Aging and the society, Vol. III: A sociology of age stratification.* New York: Russell Sage Foundation.

Rogoff, B. (2003). *The cultural nature of human development.* Oxford, UK: Oxford University Press.

Rosow, I. (1978). What is a cohort and why? *Human Development, 21,* 65–75.

Rowe, J. W., & Kahn, R. L. (1987, July 10). Human aging: Usual and successful. *Science, 237,* 143–149.

Rowe, J. W., & Kahn, R. L. (1998). *Successful aging.* New York: Pantheon.

Russ, S. (2000–2001). Primary process thinking and creativity: Affect and cognition. *Creativity Research Journal, 13,* 27–35.

Ryder, N. (1965). The cohort as a concept in the study of social change. *American Sociological Review, 30,* 843–861.

Schaie, K. W. (1965). A general model for the study of development problems. *Psychological Bulletin, 64,* 92–107.

Schaie, K. W. (1967). Age changes and age differences. *The Gerontologist, 7,* 128–132.

Schaie, K. W. (1984). Historical time and cohort effects. In K. A. McCluskey & H. W. Reese (Eds.), *Life-span developmental psychology: Historical and generational effects* (pp. 1–15). Orlando, FL: Academic Press.

Schaie, K. W. (2005). *Developmental influences on adult intelligence: The Seattle Longitudinal Study.* New York: Oxford University Press.

Schaie, K. W., Willis, S. L., & Pennak, S. (2005). An historical framework for cohort differences in intelligence. *Research in Human Development, 2,* 43–67.

Schmitz-Scherzer, R., & Thomae, H. (1983). Constancy and change of behavior in old age: Findings from the Bonn Longitudinal Study. In K. W. Schaie (Ed.), *Longitudinal studies of adult psychological development* (pp. 191–221). New York: Guilford Press.

Verhaeghen, P. (2002). Age differences in efficiency and effectiveness of encoding for visual search and memory search: A time-accuracy study. *Aging, Neuropsychology, and Cognition, 9,* 114–126.

Wechsler, D. (1958). *The measurement and appraisal of adult intelligence* (4th ed.). Baltimore: Williams & Wilkins.

Yang, L., Krampe, R. T., & Baltes, P. B. (2006). Basic forms of cognitive plasticity extended into the oldest-old: Retest learning, age, and cognitive functioning. *Psychology and Aging, 21,* 372–378.

PART III

DIMENSIONS OF COGNITIVE AGING

7

CHALLENGES IN ATTENTION

Measures, Methods, and Applications

JOAN M. McDOWD AND LESA HOFFMAN

The history of gerontology indicates that the study of cognitive aging had its beginnings in applied science. In the late 1920s, the issue of the older worker in industry prompted the study of age differences in sensory and motor abilities. In the 1950s, Welford's work (e.g., Welford, 1958) in human skill and its application to understanding the older worker further contributed to awareness of the importance of understanding cognitive aging as well as to the empirical database documenting cognitive aging. The work of Birren and Botwinick in the 1950s and 1960s (e.g., Birren & Botwinick, 1955) continued the development of knowledge regarding perception and speed of processing in cognitive aging. Then came Canestrari, Eisdorfer, Arenberg, Hulicka, Talland, Craik, and Rabbitt, among others, and the study of cognitive aging was soon growing exponentially (see Riegel, 1977).

Given this history, it is interesting that the executive summary of the National Research Council's (2000) report *The Aging Mind* states that "*Now* [italics added] is a time of great promise for learning more about the aging mind and *turning that knowledge to the advantage of older people* [italics added]" (p. 1). Thus the emphasis is on obtaining information and then translating that information into useful prescriptions for maintaining and improving quality of life among older adults. Indeed, the report goes on to urge the National Institute on Aging to develop "the knowledge needed to design effective technologies . . . to support adaptivity in older people" (p. 3). In this chapter, we address the question of how the study of attentional ability in aging can contribute to this goal as well as outline some more general approaches of measurement that are likely to become increasingly important in the future of cognitive aging research.

ATTENTION AND FUNCTIONAL STATUS

Attention, or control of attention as regulated via executive function, is increasingly recognized as an important factor in the functional status of older adults. This association has been observed in both clinical and nursing home populations (Rochester et al., 2004; Royall, Mahurin, & Gray, 1992; Swanberg, Tractenberg, Mohs, Thal, & Commings, 2004) and generally healthy community-dwelling older adults (e.g., Carlson et al., 1999; Grigsby, Kaye, Baxter, Shetterly, & Hamman, 1998; Royall, Palmer, Chiodo, & Polk,

2004). For example, an association between attentional functioning and functional status was reported by Carlson et al. (1999). They assessed functional ability and what they called "executive attention" in a large sample of women from the Women's Health in Aging Study II. Their functional assessment included both activities of daily living (walking speed, dressing) and instrumental activities of daily living (dial a phone; using a key in a deadbolt lock). Executive attention measures included the Hopkins Attention Screening Test, "measuring temporal sequencing ability" (Carlson et al., 1999, p. S264), which uses a series of lights and tones in a task similar to the children's game Simon Says; the Trail Making Test (A and B); and the Brief Test of Attention, which requires monitoring and counting letters or numbers in an auditory sequence. They found that "executive tests of planning, organization, and flexibility were selectively associated with the performance of IADLs in a physically high-functioning, cognitively intact, community-dwelling sample of older women" (Carlson et al., 1999, p. S268). They further found that the Trail Making Test B accounted for the greatest proportion of variance among the cognitive tests. They concluded that "mental flexibility, rather than fine motor agility, is the attentional component critical to efficiently completing many complex, everyday activities" (Carlson et al., 1999, p. S268).

The same sort of association has been observed in clinical populations, such as people with Alzheimer's or Parkinson's disease. For example, Swanberg et al. (2004) assessed attention in patients with Alzheimer's disease using a cancellation task to test "the subject's ability to concentrate and use appropriate search strategies" and a maze task to test "impulse resistance, planning, reasoning, and foresight" (p. 557). They then split their sample of patients with Alzheimer's disease into two groups: (1) those with attention deficits (defined as scores 1.5 *SD* or more below the mean scores of a healthy comparison group) and (2) those without deficits, and compared their functional status using the Alzheimer's Disease Cooperative Study Activities of Daily Living Inventory, which assesses both basic and instrumental activities. They found that the group with attention deficits had significantly worse functional scores than those without attention deficits and concluded

that the patients with attention impairments "had poorer everyday and community function" (Swanberg et al., 2004, p. 559). Rochester et al. (2004) examined the role of attention in walking performance of people with Parkinson's disease; they concluded that impaired attentional function increases walking difficulty for people with Parkinson's disease.

Together, these studies indicate a significant role for attention abilities in functional status. Future studies could work toward identifying the specific attentional processes that are responsible for the association and in that way be able to inform intervention and care planning strategies. McDowd, Filion, Pohl, Richards, and Stiers (2003) did some initial work along these lines in the area of stroke recovery. Their project was motivated both by the literature on stroke that was increasingly documenting cognitive deficits and their role in recovery, as well as a series of focus groups conducted with stroke survivors. In those focus groups, the issue of attention and memory problems was raised repeatedly as a significant concern affecting stroke survivors in their everyday lives. In light of this, McDowd et al. designed a project to test a group of stroke survivors who were at least 6 months poststroke, along with a group of older adults without stroke, on a series of experimental tests of attention: divided attention, switching attention, and sustained attention. In addition, they used a stroke-specific measure of everyday function, the Stroke Impact Scale (Duncan et al., 1999), to assess the relation between the cognitive measures and functional status among these individuals.

The findings indicated that, relative to individuals without stroke, stroke survivors were less able to maintain the simultaneous performance of two tasks (divided attention), were more slowed by the requirement to switch attention between stimulus features, and were less able to sustain attention across time. To assess the relevance of these differences observed in the laboratory, McDowd et al. (2003) estimated correlations between the attention measures and the five subscales of the SIS: (1) Physical Functioning, (2) Emotional Control, (3) Communication, (4) Memory, and (5) Social Participation. They observed several moderate associations. Stroke survivors' performance on the memory task under divided-attention conditions was correlated with the Physical Functioning, Memory, and Social Participation subscales. Performance on the alternating-attention task was correlated with the Social Participation subscale, and performance on the sustained-attention task was correlated with scores on the Physical Functioning subscale and the Social Participation subscale. These findings indicate that the level of ability measured in the laboratory was related to people's perceptions of their own everyday abilities. The promise of these data is that measures of attentional ability may be useful in predicting outcome following stroke and may contribute to the planning for accommodations necessary to maximize independence and quality of life. Part of this may involve tailoring rehabilitation interventions to match the needs and abilities of the person receiving services. In addition, these data raise the question of whether attention training might have a positive influence on outcome following stroke. This would seem to be an interesting and important avenue for future research.

Another domain in which attention has been studied relates to the attentional requirements of gait and balance. Investigators interested in balance and gait have frequently used dual-task methodology to understand group differences. In these studies, a secondary task is used to assess the attentional requirements of gait or balance under various conditions. The secondary task typically is of little interest except as a consumer of attention. The primary interest is in what happens to gait or balance under divided-attention conditions. The tables are easily turned, however; Kemper, McDowd, Pohl, Herman, and Jackson (2006) carried out a study of "walking and talking" in which they used the motor task as an attention consumer instead of as a primary task, because they were most interested in language function in the presence of other attentional demands. The participants were a group of 10 stroke survivors who were judged to be highly recovered based on a set of standard assessments including both motor and cognitive items. In particular, none of the participants was deemed aphasic on the basis of their performance on the Aphasia Diagnostic Profile (Goodglass, Kaplan, & Barresi, 2000). However, Kemper et al.'s hypothesis was that dual-task conditions would reveal the presence of significant residual cognitive deficits that

were not detected under single-task conditions. Thus, they were predicting that the dual-task assessments would be more sensitive to cognitive deficits than standard assessments against which stroke recovery is judged. Participants were asked to respond to items such as "What is the most important invention in the 20th century?" or "Describe a recent vacation that you enjoyed" for 3 to 5 minutes, while also performing finger-tapping, walking, or no secondary task. Language samples and motor task performance were recorded for off-line analysis.

Motor task performance was significantly affected by dual-task requirements; time on task, tapping, and walking rates were each negatively affected by concurrent talking. In the case of language performance, Kemper et al. (2006) examined indexes of language fluency, complexity, and content. In each case, stroke survivors were more negatively affected by the requirement to divide attention than was a comparison group of older adults without stroke. In some cases the effect was quite dramatic, as either speech or motor performance stopped completely while the participant performed the other task. Thus, although participants had normal language as measured by the Aphasia Diagnostic Profile, they "became aphasic" when task demands were significantly increased. Therefore, the extent of cognitive deficits is not always immediately obvious. Practically speaking, these findings suggest that rehabilitation therapies might be administered in both optimal and suboptimal conditions in order to mimic performance with real life demands. In terms of advancing theory and knowledge about attentional abilities in aging, this study makes obvious that very sensitive measures are required to assess more subtle deficits. Accordingly, further exploration of how individual differences in attention relate to functional outcomes is likely to require new measurement tools that are both theoretically meaningful and psychometrically viable.

MEASURING ATTENTION

In our view, an important and productive avenue for developing psychometrically and theoretically sound measures of attention utilizes the collaboration of experimental and psychometric approaches. In a typical experimental study of attention, differences between younger and older adults in performance of carefully controlled tasks are evaluated at the group level. Accordingly, any individual differences observed within experimental studies are regarded as error—a nuisance to be eliminated as much as possible. However, it is just these individual differences in attentional abilities that are likely to be relevant in evaluating many different cognitive and functional outcomes in aging individuals. The removal of driving privileges, placement into assisted-care facilities, and other similar concerns are serious decisions that require the utmost precision of measurement in order to minimize misdiagnosis and mislabeling. Thus, individual differences in attention represent an important factor to be conceptualized, measured, and explored in the context of both theoretical examinations of cognition and in everyday life.

Therefore, in addition to experimental approaches, the study of attention could also be informed by employing correlational approaches from the other side of the methodological spectrum. Large-scale individual-differences studies of persons varying in age are common within the study of cognitive aging, often with an emphasis on the extent to which age-related differences are common or unique across perceptual and cognitive abilities (e.g., Anstey, Hofer, & Luszcz, 2003; Anstey, Luszcz, & Sanchez, 2001; Baltes & Lindenberger, 1997; Salthouse & Czaja, 2000; Salthouse & Ferrer-Caja, 2003). In contrast to other primary abilities, such as working memory or processing speed, however, examination of individual differences in attentional ability is exceedingly rare in correlational studies. The most likely reason for this lack of attention to the construct of attention is a lack of measurement tools with which attentional abilities can be assessed.

Investigators seeking to understand relationships among individual differences in cognitive processes often administer existing instruments used in neuropsychology (e.g., Wisconsin Card Sorting Test; Heaton, 1981) or the study of intelligence (e.g., the Wechsler Adult Intelligence Scale subscales; Wechsler, 1997). Although such measures may not be ideal, they are convenient for the study of individual differences in that they can be administered quickly and often

without specialized equipment. Further, because they are commonly used, direct comparisons can be made with findings from other studies as well as with published norms. In comparison, investigators interested in relating individual differences in attention with those of other constructs frequently have resorted to ad hoc measures of individual mean response times from study-specific attention-based experimental tasks (e.g., D'Aloisio & Klein, 1990; Pringle, Kramer, & Irwin, 2004; Stankov, 1988). The use of mean response times or response time differences as direct indicators of individual ability may be appropriate within a single study, in which only the rank order of participants is of interest as it relates to their rank order on another outcome. However, the direct use of experimental tasks as psychometric instruments falls short of many goals of measurement. Despite their intuitive appeal, the limitations of such approaches preclude any meaningful interpretation of individual differences across samples or across time, and they offer little evidence of construct validity of the task as a measure of individual differences in attentional ability. The reasons for these limitations, as well as the solutions proposed by the use of explanatory latent trait modeling, are presented next.

Benefits of Explanatory Latent Trait Methods in the Measurement of Attention

The scoring of many popular cognitive tests has its roots in classical test theory (i.e., true score theory; Gulliksen, 1950), in which the same group of functionally identical items or trials are typically administered to each person, and an aggregate score across items (e.g., percentage correct, mean across items) is thought to provide the best of estimate of each person's true ability. The core assumption in aggregating across items is that the items are equivalent to each other in terms of their *difficulty*, or in their location along the latent continuum of ability to be measured, and in terms of their *discrimination*, or in the strength of their relation to the underlying ability measured by the test. Item aggregation has two undesirable consequences. First, because the overall score depends on the exact set of items administered, scores from different forms of the instrument (i.e., with items added or removed) cannot be directly compared. Second, the individual scores have meaning only in relation to the other scores from the sample. The same aggregate score could place a given person in the 90th or 40th percentile depending on the scores of the persons to whom he or she was being referenced. Large norming samples are thus needed to interpret the score of a given person, but such norm-based scores are still somewhat arbitrary in that they have little direct relation to what a given person can actually do (i.e., how he or she is likely to answer a given item).

A fundamentally different perspective is taken within latent trait theory (i.e., item response and Rasch models; De Boeck & Wilson, 2004; Embretson & Reise, 2000). For ease of exposition, we consider models in which accuracy is the response. The measurement model for a latent trait includes differences in the abilities of the persons being measured as well as differences in the difficulty of the items being answered. This separation of persons and items (within Rasch models in particular) is called *specific objectivity*: Person ability estimates do not depend on the particular items administered, and item difficulty estimates do not depend on the particular persons responding to the items. Person abilities and item difficulties are located on a common underlying or latent continuum. A person's ability is the latent trait level that is most likely to have given rise to the observed responses and is the item difficulty location at which he or she has a 50% probability of a correct response. A latent trait estimate is directly informative as to the most likely response to an item of any given difficulty. It is important to note that because latent trait estimates are interpreted relative to the items rather than to the sample, they are directly comparable across different combinations of items (i.e., test versions).

An additional issue concerns the measurement properties of ability scores within each framework. Latent trait estimates of ability have interval measurement properties; in other words, the latent trait metric is continuous, with unlimited points, and differences in latent abilities have the same meaning across the latent metric. On the other hand, because aggregate observed scores from classical test theory are likely to be compressed at the extreme ability levels, they are likely to be nonlinearly related to the underlying latent trait and thus ordinal rather than interval (Maxwell & Delaney, 1985). Although common, the use of ordinal outcomes in statistical analyses that assume interval measurement has been shown to result in greater bias and Type I error rates for estimates of group mean differences, group interactions, and regression coefficients than when analyzing interval-level latent ability outcomes. These problems worsen with a greater mismatch between the distributions of person ability and item difficulty, as is probable when groups that differ widely on ability are administered the same test (i.e., younger vs. older adults; Embretson, 1996; Kang & Waller, 2005). Although the extent of this mismatch can be evaluated within latent trait models, there is no basis for its evaluation within classical test theory.

The two frameworks also differ in terms of assessing reliability of measurement (see Smith, 2001). Reliability in classical test theory is assumed to be a static property that applies equally across all persons in the sample. Yet because items are often selected in order to be maximally sensitive at the mid-range of ability (i.e., a proportion passing of 50%), the range over which ability can be measured reliably is likely to be compressed. As a result, the obtained estimate of reliability may not be applicable for persons of extreme abilities, for whom many items may be too easy or too difficult and thus for whom little information is available with which to measure their abilities. In evaluating persons with attentional impairments, this lack of sensitivity at extreme ability levels can be problematic.

In contrast, in latent trait theory reliability differs across persons, such that the precision with which persons at a given ability level are measured depends directly on the availability of items of comparable difficulty. Measurement precision at each ability level can be evaluated explicitly; to the extent that the distributions of person ability and item difficulty are well matched (i.e., an adequate number of items for each ability level), then reliability will be high. It is thus desirable to include items that differ broadly in difficulty in order to achieve good coverage of the range of abilities in the population to be measured. One way to achieve a broad range of item difficulty is to design items that differ in their levels of the features believed to relate to the process being measured. Items can be designed systematically with features that produce targeted levels of difficulty, filling in any gaps along the ability–difficulty continuum and thus improving measurement precision. This advantage is significant when measuring change in aging individuals, because floor effects can be avoided by adding easier items at each occasion. Yet given precalibration of the properties of the potential pool of items, individual abilities can still be compared across time because they are in reference to the underlying common metric of item difficulty and person ability, rather than an aggregate score without a direct interpretation outside the sample at hand.

In addition to providing a means with which to improve measurement precision, decomposition of item difficulty also provides evidence for task validity. Specifically, the extent to which item difficulty relates to these item design features provides evidence for *construct representation*, or the underlying meaning of the construct measured by the test (see Embretson, 1983, 1998). For example, what do we mean by *attention*? How can one observe attentional processes, or how can one observe their limits? It is in this step that the rich experimental tradition can be most helpful. Items or tasks can be constructed to tap theoretically motivated aspects of attentional processing, and multiple dimensions of processing can be assessed independently through careful instrument design. Furthermore, as substantive theories of attentional processing undergo revision, so too can an instrument measuring attention (e.g., by incorporating new sources of difficulty). This represents a most exciting possibility—that individual-differences measures of attention (and of other processes as well) can become not only a tool with which to conduct research on cognitive aging but also a continually evolving reflection of that research.

A final issue concerns how *nomothetic span*, or a test's utility in measuring individual differences, can be evaluated within each framework. In addition to static estimates of reliability, psychometric evaluations in classical test theory are almost exclusively based on evidence of predictive and concurrent validity, or the extent to which the scores on the test relate to the scores from other tests in an anticipated direction. Such relationships do not unequivocally support construct representation, and they are not informative as to the sensitivity of the test in distinguishing individuals of different ability levels or detecting changes in ability. As discussed previously, precision of measurement across ability levels can be explicitly evaluated and potentially improved through the use of latent trait modeling, and this improvement in reliability is then likely in turn to improve the power with which relations of individual differences across constructs can be detected.

To summarize, the decomposition of difficulty within explanatory latent trait modeling provides the basis for developing psychometric instruments that are theoretically informed; sensitive over a wide range of abilities; and, most important, that are modifiable as needed while retaining comparability across samples or occasions. These modeling techniques provide important guidance for developing new instruments with which to assess individual differences in attention, as well as in evaluating current measures of attention.

Current Approaches in Measuring Attention

One such measure is the Useful Field of View Test (UFOV), developed by Ball, Owsley, and colleagues (Ball & Owsley, 1993; Owsley, Ball, Sloane, Roenker, & Bruni, 1991) on the basis of earlier work (Mackworth, 1965; Sanders, 1970). The UFOV has three subtests designed to assess the spatial extent of the attentional window in older adults in the context of predicting automobile accident risk and is sold commercially (by Harcourt Assessment) for that purpose. The Processing Speed subtest requires the discrimination of a central car or truck subtending $3° \times 5°$ visual angle. The Divided Attention subtest pairs the same central discrimination task with a concurrent peripheral localization task, in which a car is also presented on one of eight radial spokes at a fixed eccentricity of $30°$. In the Selective Attention subtest the central discrimination and peripheral localization tasks are performed in the presence of 47 triangles across the $30°$ visual field. Thus, in both the Divided Attention and the Selective Attention subtests, attention must be distributed in order to perform both tasks correctly, whereas attention must only be allocated centrally in the Processing Speed subtest.

Presentation time is increased after incorrect responses and decreased after correct responses, and the time needed to achieve 75% accuracy is the ability score for each subtest. Although the subtests have distinct attentional requirements, their thresholds are nevertheless combined into a single score, interpreted as the percentage reduction in the visual field. In the PC version of the UFOV as described, the eccentricity of the peripheral target is fixed, and thus "shrinkage" can be evaluated at only two levels, "near" or "far." In the original version of the UFOV, however, the eccentricity of the peripheral target was varied instead of presentation time. Scores between the original and PC versions have shown adequate correspondence (attenuation-corrected $rs \approx .7$), and each have shown adequate test–retest reliability over short intervals (corrected $rs \approx .7$ after < 1 year; Edwards et al., 2005). However, psychometric evaluation of the UFOV has mostly been limited to its utility in predicting accident risk. The UFOV has shown good sensitivity and specificity in predicting accident risk when participants are heavily oversampled for visual impairment and history of previous accidents (Ball & Owsley, 1993; Owsley et al., 1991). However, comparable levels of sensitivity and specificity have not been reported when participants are not oversampled for history of previous accidents (Brown, Greaney, & Mitchel, 1993, cited in Harris, 1999; Hennessey, 1995, cited in Staplin, Lococo, Stewart, & Decina, 1999; Hoffman, McDowd, Atchley, & Dubinsky, 2005).

A second measure of attention, the Attention Network Test (ANT; Fan, McCandliss, Sommer, Raz, & Posner, 2002; Fan, Wu, Fossella, & Posner, 2001; Fossella, Posner, Fan, Swanson, & Pfaff, 2002), was developed for use with children, adults, or animals and is available online. The ANT was derived on the basis of neurological evidence for the existence of three distinct functions of attention: (1) Alerting (achieving and maintaining an alert state), (2) Orienting (selection of information from sensory input), and (3) Executive Control (resolution of conflict among responses). Ability estimates in each function are obtained through the subtraction of mean response times in different conditions of a single task, a fixed-choice discrimination of the direction of central target (left or right arrow) flanked by response-neutral, incompatible, or compatible distracter arrows. Before each target is either no cue, an alerting cue (i.e., single or double nondirectional cue), or a valid spatial cue. For Alerting, double-alerting-cue mean response time is subtracted from no-cue mean response time. For Orienting, spatial-cue mean response time is subtracted from single-alerting-cue mean response time. For Executive Control, congruent-response mean response time is subtracted from incongruent-response mean response time. Subtraction scores were uncorrelated across functions in 40 adults ages 20 through 44, suggesting orthogonal functions of attention, although the effect of incongruent responses was slightly greater in the alerting-cue condition. One-hour test–retest correlations for the subtraction scores ranged from .5 to .7 (Fan et al., 2002).

A third measure of attention, DriverScan, illustrates how experimental findings can be translated into components of difficulty within a psychometric instrument for measuring attentional ability in aging individuals (Hoffman et al., 2005; Hoffman, Yang, Bovaird, & Embretson, 2006). DriverScan uses a change detection task (Rensink, O'Regan, & Clark, 1997) in which original (A) and modified (A') digital photographs of driving scenes are presented for 280 milliseconds, while blank screens are interspersed for 80 milliseconds as follows: A, blank, A, blank, A', blank, A', blank . . . , for 45 seconds or until the change is detected, whichever comes first. With this method of presentation, search for a change between repeated presentations of an otherwise-identical scene must be conducted through controlled processing, given that local luminance cues at the change location are unable to direct attention in the presence of a global luminance change (the blank screen). It often takes considerably longer to notice even large, salient changes than when such changes are presented without interruption (i.e., *change blindness*). The primary measure of performance is a combination of accuracy and response time to detect the change, including categories of *immediate response* (< 8 seconds), *delayed response* (8–45 seconds), or *no response* (a time out of the trial), and a Rasch version of a graded response model was used to estimate latent traits as an index of attentional search ability.

Previous research has suggested that both endogenous (goal-directed) and exogenous (stimulus-driven) orienting can be utilized to facilitate change detection (e.g., Hollingworth & Henderson, 2000; Scholl, 2000; Werner & Thies, 2000; Williams & Simons, 2000). The DriverScan items were designed to vary along three dimensions in order to tap into these types of search processes, and subjective ratings for each dimension for each item were obtained during test development. Stimulus-driven attentional search was represented through the dimensions of *visual clutter* (i.e., the overall level of congestion of the scene) and *change brightness* (i.e., the overall conspicuity of the change), whereas goal-directed attention search was represented through *change relevance*, or how important the change would be to the driver in the scene. Each dimension was shown to significantly predict item difficulty, such that items were more difficult when they included a scene with a greater amount of visual clutter and featured a change of less brightness and less relevance to driving. Thus, a deficit in any one of these areas would be related to less efficient search performance in the task (Hoffman et al., 2006). Furthermore, DriverScan performance was shown to be related to the Divided and Selection Attention subtests of the UFOV and was shown to independently predict simulated driving performance in older adults over and above the contributions of visual functioning and the UFOV subtests (Hoffman et al., 2005).

Evaluating Current Approaches to Measuring Attention

The principles of latent trait modeling can serve as a guide for evaluating the strengths and weaknesses of each of aforementioned measures of attention. Furthermore, these principles can also inform the development of new measures of attention through the integration of experimental and psychometric approaches.

The first consideration of instrument design is the response to be modeled. In the ANT, the outcome is the difference in mean response time across trials that have different functional requirements. Because only response times from correct trials are included, to the extent that accuracy differs across items or across persons, response time will be misleading as the sole indicator of ability. The response times of persons

with low ability may also be less reliable because fewer trials were answered correctly to be included in their means. Furthermore, large response times may be obtained from persons who lack the ability needed to solve the items of from persons with sufficient ability but who deliberately respond more slowly.

A different problem with the response outcome is encountered in the UFOV, in which the outcome for each subtest is the presentation time needed to achieve 75% accuracy. In the Divided Attention and Selective Attention subtests, if the central task is performed incorrectly, then that trial is not counted, and another trial is administered. Thus, observers are differentially receiving practice on these tasks, or "speed of processing training" (e.g., Ball et al., 2002), while being measured. As a result, persons of lower abilities may have artificially improved scores relative to persons who perform the central task more accurately to begin with.

Yet another problem with the response outcome is encountered in DriverScan. Because response times were censored by accuracy, the response time distribution was divided at admittedly arbitrary points to approximate an ordinal variable that best describes the combination of speed and accuracy. This is not an ideal solution, because there is no empirical basis with which to evaluate the quality of the cut-points.

In short, the problem of speed–accuracy dependency is likely to arise whenever response times are the primary outcome and accuracy is not at ceiling, or when accuracy is the primary outcome but response time is still informative as to individual differences in the process under study. A possible resolution lies in the conversion of time to an independent variable, or as another design feature along which items can vary (e.g., Verhaeghen, 2000). Accuracy for a given presentation time would then be the sole outcome measure. The manipulation of time as a design feature has been applied in many experimental paradigms and in the UFOV test and is also a natural manner in which the range of difficulty covered in a test can be extended to measure extreme levels of ability more reliably.

A second consideration of instrument design is variation in the difficulty levels of the test items and the resulting precision of measurement across ability levels. To the extent that the factors manipulated to produce trials of differential difficulty have very few distinct levels, the capacity of the test to reliably distinguish individuals of different abilities will be severely limited. For example, in the ANT, Alerting is measured by contrasting trials with two types of precues; differences of distractor type across trials are ignored. Executive Control is measured by contrasting trials with two types of distractors; differences of precue type across trials are ignored. In the UFOV, although subtraction of thresholds is not explicitly conducted as in the ANT, Selective Attention is essentially measured by two types of trials: with or without distractors, and Divided Attention ability is also measured by two types of trials: "near" or "far" targets. Even though the incremental varying of presentation time should help matters, just as instructors would not expect to obtain reliable estimates of achievement from a test with two questions, a researcher cannot expect to obtain reliable estimates of attentional ability from a task with limited variation in its trials. Instead, the levels of the factors thought to relate to task difficulty should vary more continuously from one another rather than discretely. Although completely contrary to the traditional experimental mindset, factors that vary more continuously will be helpful in obtaining the range of item difficulty necessary for precise measurement of individual differences. However, it is important that the levels of the factors be independently verifiable and meaningful, rather than based on subjective ratings (i.e., as was used in DriverScan).

Finally, the process of instrument design must consider the generalizability of performance in experimental tasks to real world abilities. Research on attention has primarily relied on tightly controlled and thus necessarily contrived experimental tasks, yet accurate, responsible assessment of attentional functioning requires that we move beyond artificial laboratory manipulations into a more realistic and ultimately applicable depiction of what the result of attentional declines may be for an older person. Because attention is thought to support higher-order cognitive processing, it is essential to assess attentional abilities in the contexts in which they operate. Previous research has demonstrated that older adults are able to make use of environmental supports to guide attention,

yet neither the UFOV nor the ANT include a real world context in which to perform their tasks. Thus, the extent to which any deficits observed in these tasks would be evidenced in more contextually driven and ecologically valid tasks is an open question, one with significant implications for real world decisions. Kramer and Kray (2006) also noted the "relatively sparse literature" comparing performance under laboratory and "real-world" situations (pp. 65–66), observing that such comparisons will be an important part of future research.

Although DriverScan does feature a real world context (i.e., of driving), the use of real world scenes directly as test items presents a new problem, in that the items cannot be meaningfully readministered at later points in time (i.e., because they are likely to be recognized). One solution for this problem within longitudinal studies is to create an item bank of natural scenes and manipulated scene changes and administer only some of the items at a given occasion. This solution may not be practically feasible, however, given that natural scenes will vary in multiple unknown dimensions and thus would not be directly comparable, even after controlling for key design features. A better solution would be to make use of the identified sources of difficulty to computer-generate new items as needed online. As discussed earlier, these design features could then provide the structure for an infinite number of items that vary along the dimensions that underlie item difficulty.

CONCLUSION

Although the studies described here have operationalized attentional performance in different ways, they are by no means exhaustive. Indeed, one of the thorniest problems researchers interested in studying and measuring attention must face is the multifaceted nature of the construct. The integral nature of attention in cognitive processing makes it difficult to construct what is ultimately needed: an independent definition and conceptualization of attention that could be the basis of one or more psychometric instruments. Continued development of measures and methods for examining individual differences in attention is critical to the future success of theoretical investigations of cognitive aging as well as real world assessments of ability and disability.

Research on attention thus far has been largely based on experimental designs, with very little emphasis on individual differences. Yet the measurement of attention and other cognitive processes could be well informed by traditions common in the educational testing fields, namely, the use of model-based measurement procedures. Specifically, we believe a latent trait approach as presented here shows great promise for developing and evaluating meaningful and reliable psychometric instruments with which to assess ability and change in ability. Indeed, by carefully considering the properties of both items and persons, we can construct measures that are most efficient and most accurate and yet retain the possibility of comparing across samples or time points within an individual. Furthermore, as substantive theories of attentional processing in aging are continually refined, through an understanding of the origins of item difficulty, so too can measures of individual differences.

The study of attentional processes in older age has had a rich history, a tradition that will no doubt continue. But the time has come to ask more of our research in order to answer the challenges of the world outside the laboratory. Meeting these challenges will likely require research teams who bring varied methodological and disciplinary expertise to the problem of understanding attention in aging and age-related neurological disease. This "problem" is an important one, having implications for cognitive aging theory as well as laying the groundwork for translating empirical findings into assessment tools that can be used to maximize quality of life among older adults.

REFERENCES

Anstey, K. J., Hofer, S. M., & Luszcz, M. A. (2003). Cross-sectional and longitudinal patterns of dedifferentiation in late-life cognitive and sensory function: The effects of age, ability, attrition, and occasion of measurement. *Journal of Experimental Psychology: General, 132,* 470–487.

Anstey, K. J., Luszcz, M. A., & Sanchez, L. (2001). A reevaluation of the common factor theory of shared variance among age, sensory function, and cognitive function in older adults. *Journal of Gerontology: Psychological Sciences, 56B,* P3–P11.

Ball, K., Berch, D. B., Helmers, K. F., Jobe, J. B., Leveck, M. D., Marsiske, M., et al. (2002). Effects of cognitive training interventions with older adults: A randomized controlled trial. *Journal of the American Medical Association, 288,* 2271–2281.

Ball, K. K., & Owsley, C. (1993). The Useful Field of View Test: A new technique for evaluating age-related declines in visual function. *Journal of the American Optomological Association, 63,* 71–79.

Baltes, P. B., & Lindenberger, U. (1997). Emergence of a powerful connection between sensory and cognitive functions across the adult life span: A new window to the study of cognitive aging? *Psychology and Aging, 12,* 12–21.

Birren, J. E., & Botwinick, J. (1955). Age differences in finger, jaw, and foot reaction time to auditory stimuli. *Journal of Gerontology, 10,* 429–432.

Carlson, M., Fried, L., Xue, Q., Bandeen-Roche, K., Zeger, S., & Brandt, J. (1999). Association between executive attention and physical functioning performance in community-dwelling older women. *Journal of Gerontology: Social Sciences, 54B,* 262–270.

D'Aloisio, A., & Klein, R. M. (1990). Aging and the deployment of visual attention. In J. T. Enns (Ed.), *The development of attention: Research and theory* (pp. 447–465). New York: Elsevier North-Holland.

De Boeck, P., & Wilson, M. (2004). *Explanatory item response models.* New York: Springer.

Duncan, P. W., Wallace, D., Lai, S. M., Johnson, D., Embretson, S., & Laster, L. J. (1999). The Stroke Impact Scale version 2.0: Evaluation of reliability, validity, and sensitivity to change. *Stroke, 30,* 2131–2140.

Edwards, J. D., Vance, D. E., Wadley, V. G., Cissell, G. M., Roenker, D. L., & Ball, K. K. (2005). Reliability and validity of Useful Field of View Test scores as administered by personal computer. *Journal of Clinical and Experimental Neuropsychology, 27,* 529–543.

Embretson, S. E. (1983). Construct validity: Construct representation versus nomothetic span. *Psychological Bulletin, 93,* 179–197.

Embretson, S. E. (1996). Item response theory models and spurious interaction effects in factorial ANOVA designs. *Applied Psychological Measurement, 20,* 201–212.

Embretson, S. E. (1998). A cognitive design system approach to generating valid tests: Application to abstract reasoning. *Psychological Methods, 3,* 380–396.

Embretson, S. E., & Reise, S. P. (2000). *Item response theory for psychologists.* Mahwah, NJ: Lawrence Erlbaum.

Fan, J. I., McCandliss, B. D., Sommer, T., Raz, A., & Posner, M. I. (2002). Testing the efficiency and independence of attentional networks. *Journal of Cognitive Neuroscience, 14,* 340–347.

Fan, J., Wu, Y., Fossella, J., & Posner, M. I. (2001). Assessing the heritability of attentional networks. *BioMed Central Neuroscience, 2,* 14.

Fossella, J., Posner, M. I., Fan, J., Swanson, J. M., & Pfaff, D. W. (2002). Attentional phenotypes for the analysis of higher mental function. *Scientific World, 2,* 217–223.

Goodglass, H., Kaplan, E., & Barresi, B. (2000). *Boston Diagnostic Aphasia Examination* (3rd ed.). Austin, TX: Pro-Ed.

Grigsby, J., Kaye, K., Baxter, J., Shetterly, S., & Hamman, R. (1998). Executive cognitive abilities and functional status among community-dwelling older persons in the San Luis Valley Health and Aging Study. *Journal of the American Geriatrics Society, 46,* 590–596.

Gulliksen, H. (1950). *Theory of mental tests.* New York: Wiley.

Harris, P. (1999). Vision and driving in the elderly. *Journal of Optometric Vision Development, 30,* 188–197.

Heaton, R. K. (1981). *A manual for the Wisconsin Card Sorting Test.* Odessa, FL: Psychological Assessment Resources.

Hoffman, L., McDowd, J. M., Atchley, P., & Dubinsky, R. A. (2005). The role of visual attention in predicting driving impairment in older adults. *Psychology and Aging, 20,* 610–622.

Hoffman, L., Yang, X., Bovaird, J. A., & Embretson, S. E. (2006). Measuring attention in older adults: Development and psychometric evaluation of DriverScan. *Educational and Psychological Measurement, 66,* 984–1000.

Hollingworth, A., & Henderson, J. M. (2000). Semantic informativeness indicates the detection of changes in natural scenes. *Visual Cognition, 7*(1/2/3), 213–235.

Kang, S. M., & Waller, N. G. (2005). Moderated multiple regression, spurious interaction effects, and IRT. *Applied Psychological Measurement, 29,* 87–105.

Kemper, S., McDowd, J., Pohl, P., Herman, R., & Jackson, S. (2006). Revealing language deficits after stroke: The costs of doing two things at once. *Aging, Neuropsychology, and Cognition, 13,* 113–139.

Kramer, A. F., & Kray, J. (2006). Aging and attention. In E. Bialystock & F. I. M. Craik (Eds.), *Lifespan cognition: Mechanisms of change* (pp. 57–69). Oxford, UK: Oxford University Press.

Mackworth, N. H. (1965). Visual noise causes tunnel vision. *Psychonomic Science, 3,* 67–68.

Maxwell, S. E., & Delaney, H. D. (1985). Measurement and statistics: An examination of construct validity. *Psychological Bulletin, 97,* 85–93.

McDowd, J., Filion, D., Pohl, P., Richards, L., & Stiers, W. (2003). Attentional abilities and functional outcome following stroke. *Journal of Gerontology: Psychological Sciences, 58B,* P45–P53.

National Research Council. (2000). *The aging mind: Opportunities in cognitive research.* Washington, DC: National Academy Press.

Owsley, C., Ball, K. K., Sloane, M. E., Roenker, D. L., & Bruni, J. R. (1991). Visual/cognitive correlates of vehicle accidents in older drivers. *Psychology and Aging, 6,* 403–415.

Pringle, H. L., Kramer, A. F., & Irwin, D. E. (2004). Individual differences in the visual representation of scenes. In D. T. Levin (Ed.), *Thinking and seeing: Visual metacognition in adults and children* (pp. 165–186). Westport, CT: Greenwood/Praeger.

Rensink, R. A., O'Regan, J. K., & Clark, J. J. (1997). To see or not to see: The need for attention to perceive changes in scenes. *Psychological Science, 8,* 368–373.

Riegel, K. F. (1977). History of psychological gerontology. In J. E. Birren & K. W. Schaie (Eds.), *Handbook of the psychology of aging* (pp. 70–102). New York: Van Nostrand Reinhold.

Rochester, L., Hetherington, V., Jones, D., Nieuwboer, A., Willems, A., Kwakkel, G., et al. (2004). Attending to the task: Interference effects of functional tasks on walking in Parkinson's disease and the roles of cognition, depression, fatigue, and balance. *Archives of Physical Medicine and Rehabilitation, 85,* 1578–1585.

Royall, D. R., Mahurin, R. K., & Gray, K. (1992). Bedside assessment of executive impairment: The Executive Interview (EXIT). *Journal of the American Geriatrics Society, 40,* 1221–1226.

Royall, D. R., Palmer, R., Chiodo, L., & Polk, M. (2004). Declining executive control in normal aging predicts change in functional status: The Freedom House study. *Journal of the American Geriatrics Society, 52,* 346–352.

Salthouse, T. A., & Czaja, S. J. (2000). Structural constraints on process explanations in cognitive aging. *Psychology and Aging, 15,* 44–55.

Salthouse, T. A., & Ferrer-Caja, E. (2003). What needs to be explained to account for age-related effects on multiple cognitive variables? *Psychology and Aging, 18,* 91–110.

Sanders, A. F. (1970). Some aspects of the selective process in the functional visual field. *Ergonomics, 13,* 101–117.

Scholl, B. J. (2000). Attenuated change blindness for exogenously attended items in a flicker paradigm. *Visual Cognition, 7*(1/2/3), 377–396.

Smith, E. V., Jr. (2001). Evidence for the reliability of measures and validity of measure interpretation: A Rasch measurement perspective. *Journal of Applied Measurement, 2,* 281–311.

Stankov, L. (1988). Aging, attention, and intelligence. *Psychology and Aging, 3,* 59–74.

Staplin, L. S., Lococo, K. H., Stewart, J., & Decina, L. E. (1999). *Safe mobility for older people notebook* (DOT HS 808-853). Washington, DC: National Highway Traffic Safety Administration. Retrieved September 8, 2006, from http://www.nhtsa.dot.gov/people/injury/olddrive/safe/safe-toc.htm

Swanberg, M. M., Tractenberg, R. E., Mohs, R., Thal, L. J., & Cummings, J. L. (2004). Executive dysfunction in Alzheimer disease. *Archives of Neurology, 61,* 556–560.

Verhaeghen, P. (2000). The parallels in beauty's brow: Time–accuracy functions and their implications for cognitive aging theories. In T. J. Perfect & E. A. Maylor (Eds.), *Models of cognitive aging* (pp. 50–85). Oxford, UK: Oxford University Press.

Wechsler, D. (1997). *Wechsler Adult Intelligence Scale—Third edition.* San Antonio, TX: Harcourt Assessment.

Welford, A. T. (1958). *Aging and human skill.* London: Methuen.

Werner, S., & Thies, B. (2000). Is "change blindness" attenuated by domain-specific expertise? An expert–novice comparison of change detection in football images. *Visual Cognition, 7*(1/2/3), 163–173.

Williams, P., & Simons, D. J. (2000). Detecting changes in novel, complex three-dimensional objects. *Visual Cognition, 7*(1/2/3), 297–322.

8

EVERYTHING WE KNOW ABOUT AGING AND RESPONSE TIMES

A Meta-Analytic Integration

PAUL VERHAEGHEN AND JOHN CERELLA

Older adults take longer to process information than younger adults. It has long been known that the increase in response time (RT) is monotonic with adult age. In a large meta-analysis of studies using continuous age samples, Verhaeghen and Salthouse (1997) reported an age–speed correlation of −.52, and Welford (1977) estimated that each additional year of adult age increases choice reaction time by 1.5 ms. Cerella and Hale (1994) estimated that the average 70-year-old functions at the speed of the average 8-year-old—a large effect.

It also appears that this age-related slowing occurs in a wide variety of tasks, implicating a wide variety of cognitive systems: Memory search, visual search, lexical decision, mental rotation, speech discrimination, digit–symbol substitution are but a few of the tasks that have consistently been found to yield age-related deficits in RTs (see Kausler, 1991, and Salthouse,

1991, for excellent reviews of the deficits observed in the literature). A key and still unsettled question in the field of cognitive aging is: How many explanatory mechanisms or dimensions are necessary for an adequate description of age-related slowing?

A first school of thought tends toward strong reductionism. A monograph that best exemplifies this tendency is Salthouse's 1991 *Theoretical Perspectives on Cognitive Aging.* This research program seeks to establish a single mechanism as governing aging, identified as either processing speed (e.g., Salthouse, 1996), the neuromodulation effects underlying it (Braver & Barch, 2002; Li, Lindenberger, & Frensch, 2000), or even a common cause linking cognitive change to perceptual/motor processes (e.g., Lindenberger & Baltes, 1997). Researchers working in this framework have favored a correlational, individual-differences approach in which a set of antecedent variables—often

AUTHORS' NOTE: This research was supported in part by a grant from the National Institute on Aging (AG-16201). We thank Lieve De Meersman, Martin Sliwinski, David Steitz, and Christina Wasylyshyn for their contributions to the original research.

measured by a small set of tasks assumed to tap a relatively broad psychometric factor—is used to predict age differences (in a cross-sectional design) or age changes (in a longitudinal design) in some aspect of cognition. The current aspiration among reductionists is of cross-level unification, building explanations for cognitive aging from the bottom up, starting with gross changes in brain structure or neuronal functioning (see, e.g., the strong claims in Li et al., 2000, and Park, Polk, Mikels, Taylor, & Marshuetz, 2001).

A second school of thought is well represented by Kausler's 1991 monograph *Experimental Psychology, Cognition, and Human Aging*. The explanatory preference here is toward high precision, leading researchers to measure aging at the level of information-processing components. The emergent current in this process-oriented camp is computational—starting with mathematical models from cognitive psychology, the goal is to isolate those parameters whose modification reproduces the observed pattern of age effects (see, e.g., the strong positions taken by Byrne, 1998; Kahana, Howard, Zaromb, & Wingfield, 2002; Meyer, Glass, Mueller, Seymour, & Kieras, 2001; and Ratcliff, Spieler, & McKoon, 2000). The preferred data are experimental, comparing performance (latency or accuracy) between a baseline task and a version in which the process of interest is manipulated.

These two approaches to cognitive aging are opposite in many ways. One broadcasts its effects at a macro-level and aims at breadth; the other focuses its effects at a micro-level and aims at depth. The first engenders the impression that cognitive aging is orderly and simple; the second that it is diverse and messy. A third orientation has evolved at a meso-level: Aging is conceptualized in more detail than in macro-research but at a resolution coarser than obtained in micro-research (e.g., Hale & Myerson, 1996; Verhaeghen et al., 2002). The approach here has been to examine large data sets for communalities in the age effects from tasks thought to represent similar kinds of processes, and for dissimilarities in the age effects from tasks differing in kind. Communalities are expressed as common "slowing factors" for related tasks; dissimilarities are seen in distinct slowing factors for dissimilar tasks; outcomes of the latter sort are often called *dissociations* (e.g., Perfect &

Maylor, 2000). Dissociation research grew out of early attempts to expose regularities in young–old RT data through the use of Brinley plots (e.g., Brinley, 1965; Cerella, Poon, & Williams, 1980). Historically, such plots were a primary impetus for reductionist theories. Their refinement led directly from the extreme reductionism noted above to the moderate reductionism of our own views. Given its central role in our argument, this unique way of portraying age outcomes must be understood by the reader.

THE TOOLS: BRINLEY PLOTS AND DISSOCIATIONS

Figure 8.1 (upper left panel) shows data from an experiment conducted in our laboratory (Verhaeghen, Cerella, & Basak, 2006). The task was mental arithmetic (We will show data from several other tasks in this experiment as we go along): Addition problems consisting of four, five, six, or seven signed digits were displayed on a screen, and participants had to determine whether the indicated sum was correct or off by one unit (e.g., $5 + 2 - 3 - 2 + 6 - 3 = 5$). The figure shows the mean RTs for both age groups as a function of problem size or load. Not surprisingly, solution times increased as a linear function of problem size. This is characteristic of iterative tasks, in which difficulty is manipulated by varying the number of processing steps. The slopes of linear load functions offer a precise measurement of the mental-processing rate of the iterated operation—single-digit addition in this case. The load function for the older participants is slightly steeper than the load function for the younger participants, with slopes of 1,533 ms/digit and 1,320 ms/digit, respectively. These measures allow a conclusion as precise as any micro-research: the addition rate in elderly participants was slowed by a factor of 1533/1320 = 1.16, or 16%.

Figure 8.1 (upper right panel) shows the same data reconfigured as a Brinley plot. Where there are eight points in the load functions (four points for the older participants, and four points for the younger participants), the Brinley function has only four points, one point for each load level. The data for each level can be construed as an (X, Y) pair, defined by (RT[young], RT[old]). These pairs are entered in a scatter

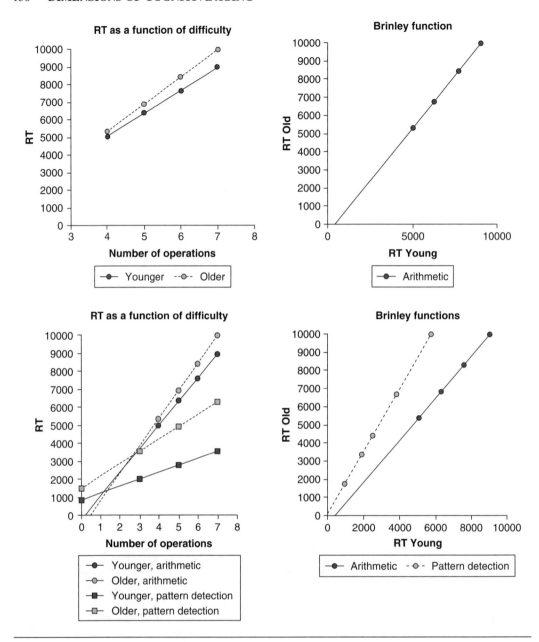

Figure 8.1 From Load Functions (Left Panels) to Brinley Functions (Right Panels) in an Arithmetic Task (Top Panels) and an Arithmetic and a Pattern Detection Task (Bottom Panels)

SOURCE: Data from Verhaeghen, Cerella, and Basak (2006).

NOTE: RT = response time.

plot, with RT(young) values composed along the abscissa and RT(old) values along the ordinate. It can be demonstrated both analytically and empirically that when the load functions are linear, the Brinley function will also be linear (as can be seen in the right panel), and further,

that the slope of the Brinley function will be equal to the ratio of the slopes of the component load functions (1.16 in this case; Myerson, Adams, Hale, & Jenkins, 2003). Thus the slowing factor for mental arithmetic can be read off the slope of the Brinley function.

In the case of mental arithmetic, this exercise gains us nothing—the aging outcome is given in a more insightful form in the load functions themselves. In the fields of cognitive aging, however, and of cognition itself, iterative tasks are rare. Most experiments involve comparisons between conditions unrelated by any quantitative parameter from which load functions might be constructed. These data can still, however, be plotted as a Brinley function. The value of the Brinley plot then arises from the fact that it can be constructed from any ensemble of conditions that yield paired young–old data points. Indeed, data sets need not be restricted to individual experiments. A Brinley plot provides a convenient format for combining data across studies; from the onset, meta-analyses of age and RTs have adopted this methodology.

The first of those meta-analyses was published by Cerella et al. (1980), based on 99 data points taken from 18 studies. Their result was striking—the locus of points was highly linear, described by the regression equation RT(old) = 1.36 RT(young) – 70 ms with an R^2 of .95. (We note that this R^2 value reflects the amount of variance in condition means of older adults that can be explained from condition means of younger adults; this obviously neglects a large portion of the total variance in RT. In other words, we can explain the condition means of older adults very well, but that does not necessarily imply high predictability at the individual level.) Subsequent data sets showed a similar pattern (e.g., Cerella, 1985, 1990; Myerson, Hale, Wagstaff, Poon, & Smith, 1990). The regularity of this outcome gave rise to the idea that, from the perspective of cognitive aging, performance on a wide variety of tasks could be viewed as the outcome of a single processing stream. The stream differs in content from task to task, and in duration from condition to condition—differences of a sort that may be exposed by micro-theories but are irrelevant to a macro-theory. A linear Brinley function puts strong constraints on the processing stream of older adults: First, it must correspond, step by step, to the young adult stream; and second, the stream rate, whatever its value in the young adult for a particular task, is slowed by a constant proportion in older adults (Cerella, 1994). The claim that all computational processes in older adults are slowed to the same degree, indexed by the

slope of the Brinley function (the slope of 1.36 from the Cerella et al. [1980] meta-analysis indicates 36% slowing), is known as the *generalized slowing hypothesis*.

AGING IN THREE DIMENSIONS: AGE-RELATED DISSOCIATIONS BY TASK DOMAIN

Verhaeghen (2006) offers a recent update of the classical meta-analyses just cited, including a total of 1,354 young–old RT pairs from 190 studies (with the stipulation that RT[young] ≤ 2,000 ms; this meta-analysis also investigated accuracy, but this aspect of the analysis will not be summarized here). The RT results (which we will revisit in more detail below) are shown in Figure 8.2. A single linear function fitted the full data set well (RT[old] = 1.46 RT[young] – 74 ms, R^2 = .79), with values that replicated the 1980 Cerella et al. result closely (46% slowing).

Despite the fact that a single line describes the data fairly well, the scatter in Figure 8.2 is conspicuous and raises the possibility that the degree of slowing may be less than uniform from task to task. This impression was reinforced by a multilevel regression (Sliwinski & Hall, 1998) that assessed the linear trend within each of the 190 studies. This analysis exposed significant heterogeneity in slope values. In such a broad database the causes of heterogeneity may be uninteresting: differences in the absolute age of the participant samples (sexagenarians, octogenarians), in the populations sampled (in college, out of college; independently living, institutionalized), in the experimental methodology (paper-and-pencil, computer), in modality (visual, auditory), in the amount of practice (disuse effects; Baron & Cerella, 1993), and so on. Beginning with the first meta-analysis of Cerella et al. (1980), heterogeneity has been attributed to far more interesting differences, those of task domain.

Figure 8.1 (lower left panel, square symbols) shows data from another task in the Verhaeghen and Cerella (2002) experiment that illustrates heterogeneity in slowing due to task domain. Participants performed a pattern-detection task; 4, 7, 9, or 11 dots were scattered over the screen, and participants had to determine if four of the dots occupied the corners of a possible square.

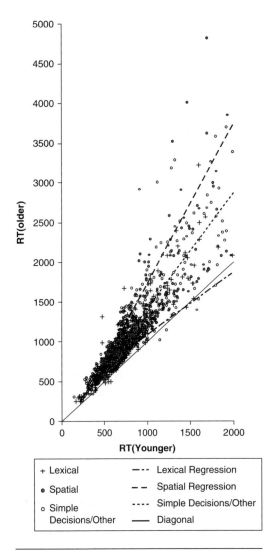

Figure 8.2   Brinley Plot From 1,354 Data Points From 190 Studies, as a Function of Task Type

SOURCE: Verhaeghen (2006).

NOTE: RT = response time.

Like the arithmetic data (which are lifted from the upper panel and duplicated in the lower panel, depicted by round symbols), detection RTs were a linear function of the load parameter (the number of foils in the display was 0, 3, 5, or 7). This task was easier than mental arithmetic—the load functions were considerably shallower, with slopes of 392 ms/foil (younger participants) and 679 ms/foil (older participants). But the slowing factor defined by these processing rates, 679/392 = 1.73, was considerably greater than arithmetic slowing (73% vs. 16%). Here then is a difference in age outcome due to a difference in task domain, with other variables, such as participant sample and amount of practice, and so on, held constant. In the lower right panel, data from both tasks are combined in a Brinley plot—two lines are needed for an adequate description of this data set; one line is not sufficient. This is a direct consequence of the fact that processing in the two tasks is slowed by different factors. These data echo similar data obtained from meta-analytic Brinley plots that suggest that verbally or semantically based tasks are bound by a common slowing factor that is less than the factor that governs spatially based tasks (Lima, Hale, & Myerson, 1991; Myerson & Hale, 1993), with a slope around 1.5 for the verbal trend and around 2.0 for the spatial trend.

The verbal–spatial distinction is one of two that have arisen in meso-research. The other is the distinction between peripheral (i.e., perceptual and motor processes), and central (i.e., computational and decision) processes (Cerella, 1985; Cerella et al., 1980). This distinction followed experimental findings that tasks with minimal computational demands show lesser deficits than heavily computational tasks, with a slope around 1.2 for the sensory-motor trend and around 1.5 for the computational trend.

Guided by these meso-theories, tasks in the Verhaeghen (2006) survey were divided into four classes as follows:

1. *Simple Decisions* (104 observations): single RTs, choice RTs, saccadic RTs, digit–digit RTs, vocal RTs, initiation time for single RTs, preparation times for target detection, attentional capture, and mouse movement times (this class comes closest to a peripheral or sensory-motor class)

2. *Lexical* (252 observations): letter reading, lexical decision, word naming, picture naming, semantic category judgment, semantic matching, semanticity judgment, synonym matching, synonym–antonym production, reading rates, speech discrimination, spoken word identification, grammatical judgment, and generating an appropriate verb for a noun

3. *Spatial* (646 observations): visual search, visual marking, location discrimination or detection, line length discrimination, orientation detection, shape classification, pattern detection, shape identity judgment, distance judgment, matrix scanning, pro-saccade tasks and the Simon task

4. *All Other* (352 observations): enumeration, arithmetic, alphabet arithmetic, memory retrieval, letter cancellation, digit–symbol substitution, auditory classification of consonants, color naming, odd/even judgments on digits, Stroop or other kinds of response inhibition, and the like (Note that some tasks examined below under the heading of "executive control" are grouped here).

A multilevel regression analysis was applied to the data set to determine which, if any, classes were governed by distinct slowing factors. Its outcome defines the "dimensionality" of simple tasks from the perspective of cognitive aging (conditional, of course, on the classification scheme in force).

The outcome is presented in Figure 8.2. Three distinct slowing factors were obtained, with the trifurcation emanating from a common origin at (470, 640). The lowest limb of the trifurcation was defined by lexical tasks, which exhibited not age-related slowing, but an age-related speed-up, by a factor of 0.8. This striking result is in line with the finding that older adults in modern aging studies typically show an age advantage in standardized tasks that require active or passive retrieval from the lexicon (Verhaeghen, 2003). Simple-decision tasks and unclassified tasks clustered together on the middle limb of the trifurcation, with a slowing factor of 1.5. Spatial tasks occupied the highest limb, with a slowing factor of 2.0. Altogether the trifurcation explained 92% of the within-study variance in condition means, compared to 83% when only RT (young) was used as a predictor.

The cause of these dissociations is as yet unclear. We cite one small observation: Bopp (2003) found that processing times for verbal items in working memory showed less slowing than processing times for visuospatial items cast as exact analogues to the verbal items. Thus the stimulus type seemed to force a dissociation while the task remained the same: The type of material (verbal vs. visual) may be more important than the type of processing.

One unanticipated result was that many cognitive tasks—those falling under the ill-defined category of "other"—displayed no more slowing than was observed for simple decisions. Thus many tasks that are commonly assumed to demonstrate age-related "cognitive" slowing may in fact be affected no more than any simple decision—slowing in sensory-motor and response selection processes. In this light, researchers would do well to include a simple decision of some sort as a control in their aging designs. We would argue that aging effects in cognitive tasks are truly interesting only if they exceed the simple-decision deficit.

We would like to point out another methodological consequence of these findings, namely, its implications for the analysis of Age × Condition interactions (see Cerella, 1995, and Faust, Balota, & Spieler, & Ferraro, 1999, for earlier and more exhaustive treatments of this problem). The relationship between RTs of younger and older adults is near-multiplicative. This implies that with increasing task duration, even within each of the domains proposed here, the absolute difference between RTs of younger and older participants will increase as well (with the exception of lexical tasks). Conventional techniques for assessing Age × Condition interactions (analysis of variance [ANOVA], first and foremost) test for this absolute difference and can therefore be expected to generate false positives. An example illustrates this. Our best estimate of the equation relating the RTs of young and old adults in spatial tasks is RT(older) = 2 × RT(young) – 270 (Verhaeghen, 2006). Assume that groups of young and old adults perform a task such as visual search with five distractors. Young adults take 1,000 ms in this condition; then we would expect older adults to take 2 × 1,000 – 270 ms, or 1,730 ms. The absolute age difference is 730 ms. We then make the task more difficult by increasing the number of distractors, so that the young adults now take 2,000 ms. The expected value for older adults in the harder condition is 2 × 2,000 – 270 ms, or 3,730 ms. The absolute age difference is now 1,730 ms, much larger than in the easier condition. If the data are at all reliable, an ANOVA will flag the Age × Condition interaction as significant, and the researcher might conclude that older adults have particular difficulty with larger displays.

From the perspective of a macro- or meso-theory, however, the same slowing factor is operating in the two conditions; no additional mechanism needs to be invoked to explain the increase in the absolute age difference between conditions.

AGING IN ONE ADDITIONAL DIMENSION: AGE-RELATED DISSOCIATIONS IN TASKS REQUIRING EXECUTIVE CONTROL

We turn now from tasks that can be defined by a single processing stream to tasks involving multiple processing streams. Let us call single-stream tasks *simple*; multiple-stream tasks will be referred to as *compound*. Interest in compound tasks arises from the control processes they are thought to necessitate: the need to suppress (as with the Stroop) or else to maintain and coordinate (as with dual and switching tasks) two processing streams.

Control processes are measured indirectly, by means of experimental designs that contrast the duration of a task component executed in two contexts: (1) the simple-task context, or baseline, and (2) the compound-task context. For example ink-color naming latencies may be measured with the neutral stimulus XXXX, and with conflicting color words, BLUE, RED, and so on; or parity judgments ("Is the digit 7 odd or even?") may be measured in same-task blocks of trials, and in mixed-task blocks alternated with magnitude judgments ("Is the digit 7 greater than or less than 5?"). We will refer to the context manipulation as the *compounding* of a task or component. In most cases, compounding leads to an increase in RT over the baseline. The primary literature is predicated on the assumption that the RT increase reflects the intrusion of control processes. Theories of control processes stand or fall depending on the magnitude of the increase in various situations.

This somewhat elaborate data structure, the contrast between a set of compound tasks and the corresponding simple tasks, is complicated further in an aging study. We are then seeking to compare the age deficit in the compound tasks with the age deficit in the simple tasks. The comparison will expose a deficit specific to the control process, if any exists. In the meso-theoretic framework this maps neatly onto a test for dissociation between the compound tasks and the simple tasks in a Brinley analysis. This is the methodology we bring to bear in what follows. As noted earlier, this approach avoids the hazard of false positives arising from the use of an ANOVA on raw RTs, a hazard that pervades the aging literature.

Control Costs

A complicating factor is that the effects of executive control are themselves not well understood. The common (often implicit) assumption is that compounding adds an extra stage to the processing stream (task-switching studies provide the clearest examples of this interpretation; e.g., Allport, Styles, & Hsieh, 1994; Pashler, 2000). In that case, the cost of executive intervention can be calculated by subtracting the simple RTs from the compound RTs. An often-unrecognized possibility is that the control cost may be expressed nonadditively. For instance, executive oversight may prolong each step of a processing stream by a constant multiple. An astute test for age deficits in control must first resolve the form of its influence on the processing stream and explore the consequences for a Brinley analysis.

To quantify the influence of control processes an adjunct to the Brinley plot is useful and is called a *state-space plot* (Mayr, Kliegl, & Krampe, 1996). In state space, performance on a set of compound tasks is plotted as a function of performance on the corresponding simple tasks. The resulting locus of points is the state trace. Thus the state trace follows the performance of a single subject group across conditions. In an aging study, data from the young will define one trace, and data from the old will define another trace.

Endless configurations of Brinley functions and state traces are possible. Here we present a framework within which a number of canonical configurations are open to straightforward interpretation (see Verhaeghen, Steitz, Sliwinski, & Cerella, 2002, Appendix A, for a formal mathematical treatment), namely, the cases of additive and multiplicative complexity.

One effect of compounding may be to add an extra processing stage to a task, perhaps by imposing a fixed overhead cost or "setup charge." We call this type of compounding *additive*, because its effect is to add a constant interval to the simple RT. This outcome is illustrated in the top row of Figure 8.3, which shows data from another task from Verhaeghen et al. (2006). In the simple conditions, 6, 7, 8, or 9 Xs were scattered over the screen; the task was to count the Xs. In the compound conditions, several Os appeared as distractors among the Xs. As seen in the left panel, the effect of this manipulation was to elevate the compound load function above the simple load function—bypassing the distractors apparently added a step to the processing stream but did not reduce the counting rate. As seen in the center panel, the resulting state trace is a line elevated above and parallel to the diagonal. This figure also shows that the state trace for the old participants is elevated above and parallel to that of the young participants. This will be true regardless of the age-related slowing factors. The corresponding Brinley plot, however, can have two parallel lines or one, depending on whether age-related slowing is larger in the compounded condition than in the baseline condition. The obtained Brinley function in Verhaeghen et al. (2006) is given in the right panel. It shows two lines rather than one; thus compounding induces a dissociation in the Brinley plot for this task. This two-part analysis allows us to conclude that (a) counting-with-distractors leads to an additive cost in RT and that (b) the age difference in counting-with-distractors was proportionally larger than that observed in counting per se.

Alternately in our framework, compounding may prolong each step in the original processing stream. We call this type of compounding *multiplicative*, because it induces multiplicative effects in the state trace. This outcome is illustrated in the bottom row of Figure 8.3. The round symbols in the left panel repeat data from the mental arithmetic task already seen in Figure 8.1. The square symbols show data from a "bracketed" version of the task (e.g., [5 – (1 + 2)] + [(2 + 6) – 3] = 7). This kind of compounding forced participants to store intermediate results and to reorder operations. As can be seen in the lower left panel, the compounded load functions were steeper than the simple load functions—negotiating the brackets slowed the rate of the addition process itself. The state trace in the lower center panel is a line steeper than the diagonal; the multiplicative cost is given directly by the slope of this line. The state trace

of old adults will either overlay the state trace of the young adults or else will diverge from it, depending on whether the multiplicative cost in the old is equal to or greater than the multiplicative cost in the young. The Brinley functions follow the state traces and will dissociate or not depending on whether the control cost in the old is equal to or greater than the control cost in the young. In the case of mental arithmetic, both the state traces and the Brinley functions point to an age deficit in the multiplicative cost associated with bracketed arithmetic.

In our view, then, an answer to two questions is critical to establishing an age-related deficit specific to executive-control manipulations: (1) Is the control manipulation associated with an additive compounding effect, a multiplicative compounding effect, or both? and (2) Can an age deficit specific to this effect be reliably observed?

Age Claims

The three "compounding" paradigms mentioned at the outset, Stroop, dual-task, and task-switching, have been studied intensively in cognitive aging. Results have led to claims of age declines in executive processes in all three cases (for a recent overview, see McDowd & Shaw, 2000; for our classification of control processes, we used Miyake, Friedman, Emerson, Witzki, & Howerter, 2000):

1. *Resistance to interference*, also known as *inhibitory control*, has been a central explanatory construct in aging theories throughout the 1990s (e.g., Hasher & Zacks, 1988; Hasher, Zacks, & May, 1999; for a computational approach, see Braver & Barch, 2002). A loss of inhibitory control would lead to mental clutter in older adults' working memory, thereby limiting its functional capacity and perhaps also its speed of operation.

2. Age-related deficits have been posited in the ability to *coordinate* multiple tasks or processing streams. Much of the relevant literature pertains to dual-task performance (e.g., Hartley & Little, 1999; McDowd & Shaw, 2000), but this type of deficit has also been raised in the working memory literature (e.g., Mayr & Kliegl, 1993). Losses in coordination

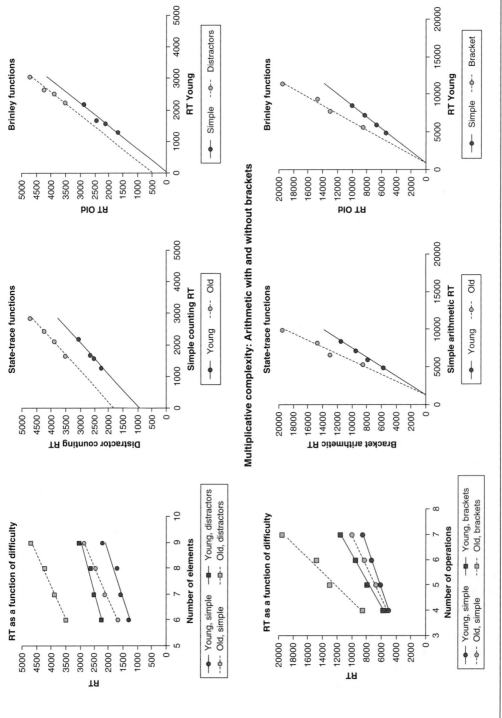

Figure 8.3 Illustration of Additive and Multiplicative Complexity Effects in Two Experimental Tasks: Reaction Time (RT) as a Function of Difficulty, Brinley Plots, and State Traces

SOURCE: Based on data from Verhaeghen and Cerella (2002).

NOTE: In the latter two graphs, the diagonal is indicated by a full line.

appear to be necessary to explain age differences in compound contexts in excess of those projected on the basis of mere slowing.

3. Age and *task-switching* deficiencies have been targeted in a surge of publications from the late 1990s and early 2000s (e.g., Mayr, Spieler, & Kliegl, 2001). Much like the coordination theories, this work considers age declines in task-switching efficiency as additional to other deficits that may exist in the cognitive system.

4. A fourth control process, working memory *updating*, has been investigated relatively rarely in cognitive aging (e.g., Van der Linden, Brédart, & Beerten, 1994); the sparsity of data does not allow for its inclusion in our analyses.

In the sections that follow we assess these several claims, reviewing the conclusions of a number of meta-analyses conducted in our laboratory (We draw heavily on a previous review paper; Verhaeghen & Cerella, 2002). If any or all of these control deficits are sustained, they will add to the dimensionality or explanatory mechanisms necessary for a full account of age changes in RTs.

Aging and Resistance to Interference

The Stroop task and negative priming are the procedures most often used to test for age differences in resistance to interference. In the Stroop task, participants are presented with colored stimuli and have to report the color. RTs from a baseline condition where the stimulus is neutral (e.g., a series of colored Xs) are compared with RTs from a critical condition in which the stimulus is itself a word denoting a color (e.g., the word *yellow* printed in red). RTs are slower in that case, because of interference from the meaning of the word. In the negative-priming task, participants are shown two stimuli simultaneously, one of which is the stimulus to be evaluated (the target), the other is the stimulus to be ignored (the distractor). For instance, the participant can be asked to name a red letter in a display that also contains a superimposed green letter. If the distractor on one trial becomes the target on the next (the critical, negative-priming condition), RT is slower than in a neutral condition where none of the stimuli are repeated (the baseline condition). Note that this effect is counterintuitive: Higher levels of inhibition are associated with larger costs.

Results from two meta-analyses (Verhaeghen & De Meersman, 1998a, 1998b) are presented in Figure 8.4 (surveying 20 studies for Stroop and 21 studies for negative priming). Each data point represents a result from an independent participant sample. Gamboz, Russo, and Fox (2002) updated the negative-priming analysis by adding more recent studies; Verhaeghen (2006) updated both the Stroop and the negative-priming analyses by adding more recent studies and by applying multilevel modeling to the data (i.e., by taking into account that conditions are nested within studies). The pattern of results from these recent updates was unchanged from that showing in the figure.

Both Stroop interference and negative priming induced multiplicative control effects, signaled by slopes greater than unity in the state traces. This indicates that in these two tasks, the need to resist interference inflates central processing. Although both effects were multiplicative, they differed in magnitude. The inflation factor in the Stroop tasks (a slope of 1.9, indicating 90% inflation) was much larger than in the negative priming tasks (a slope of 1.1, indicating 10% inflation). The difference may be due to the temporal dynamics of the two tasks. The Stroop task involves selection of one of two information sources that are present simultaneously; negative priming involves reactivating a stimulus that was deactivated on the previous trial. The time delay alone may explain the smaller effect in negative priming.

The second result to observe in Figure 8.4 is the absence of age deficits specific to the interference effects in either task. A single line sufficed to capture the inflation of central processes in both young and old state traces; so too a single line was sufficient to capture both baseline and critical conditions in the Brinley plot.

Like the inflation factor, the age-related slowing factor was larger for color naming (with or without interference, the slope of the Brinley function was 1.8) than for negative priming (with or without priming, the slope of the Brinley function was 1.04). This difference most likely reflects the nature of the baseline tasks. The typical task involved in baseline negative-priming conditions is the sounding of letters or the naming of depicted objects; both of these are lexical tasks, and so little or no slowing is expected. The baseline Stroop task involves color naming; it is possible that the

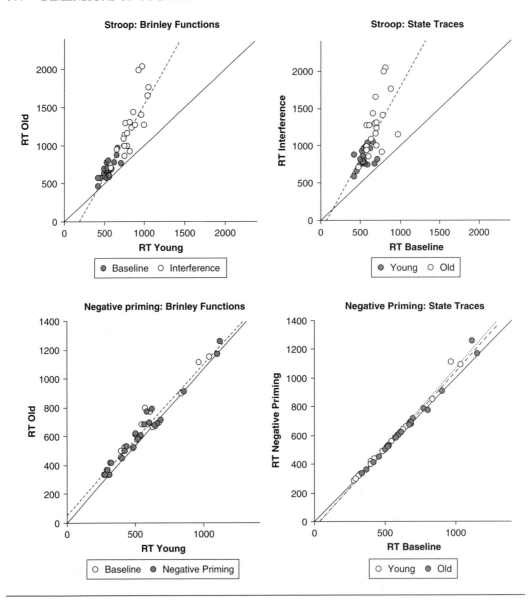

Figure 8.4   Brinley Plots and State Traces for Two Tasks for Resistance to Interference (Stroop and Negative Priming)

SOURCE: Based on data from Verhaeghen and Cerella (2002).

NOTES: The diagonal is indicated by a full line. RT = response time.

large slope indicates that color naming is by nature a spatial-type task.

Aging and Coordination

Coordinative ability is typically appraised in a dual-task paradigm in which performance on a single task is compared to performance on the same task when a second task has to be performed concurrently (e.g., a visual RT task with or without a concurrent auditory reaction time task). Verhaeghen et al. (2003) reported a meta-analysis of 33 dual-task studies that included age as a design factor. The results of their multilevel analysis are given in the top row of Figure 8.5.

The pattern in Figure 8.5 differs markedly from that in Figure 8.4. First, the state traces,

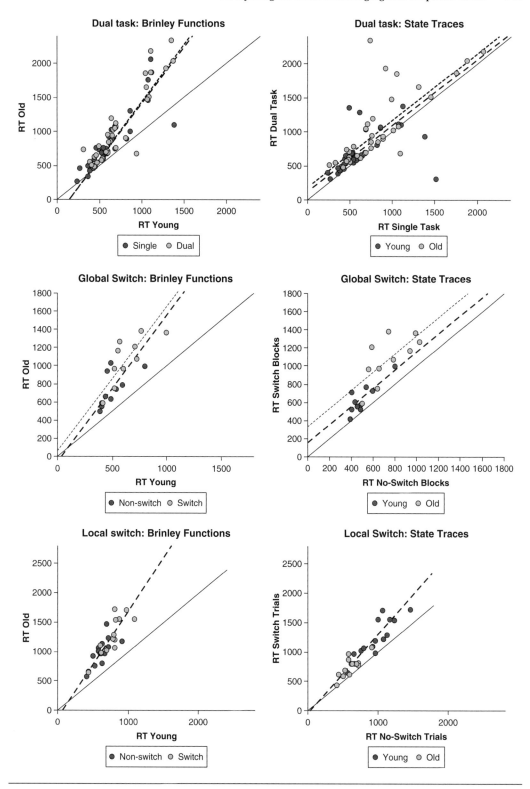

Figure 8.5 Brinley Plots and State Traces for Dual-Task Performance and Global and Local Task Switching

SOURCE: Based on data from Verhaeghen and Cerella (2002).

NOTES: The diagonal is indicated by a full line. RT = response time.

having positive intercepts and slopes of unity, show an additive effect. This indicates that dual-tasking involves a setup cost that does not permeate the computational processes involved in the baseline task. Second, the lines for single and dual separate out in the Brinley plot, indicating that the coordination process is slowed by a larger amount than the central computational process.

Several moderators of the dual-task effect were examined by Verhaeghen et al. (2003): the peripheral versus central locus of the primary task; the lexical versus nonlexical status of the task; its modality, visual versus auditory; and the match in modality between the primary and the secondary task. None of the moderators interacted reliably with age. Therefore, the age-sensitivity of coordination seems to arise from the control process itself and not to how it happens to be implemented under different task conditions. Note, however, that the age effect is a small one. The slowing factor in the baseline task was 1.6 (this is the slope of the baseline Brinley function). The degree of slowing in the dual-task effect was estimated by the old:young ratio of the difference in intercepts. This factor had a value of 1.8, an increase of 20% over baseline slowing (80% − 60%).

Aging and Task Switching

A more recent paradigm, called *task switching* (e.g., Allport et al., 1994), studies the maintenance and scheduling of two mental task sets performed in succession. In task-switching research, the participant is shown a series of stimuli and has to perform one of two possible tasks on each, the required task being indicated by the experimenter. For example, a series of digits may be shown: If the number is printed in red, the participant must report its parity; if the number is printed in blue, the participant must report its relative magnitude. The switch in task can be predictable or not; in the former case, it can be explicitly cued (e.g., by the color coding just described) or not.

Two types of task-switching costs can be calculated. First, one can compare RTs from pure, single-task blocks with RTs from mixed, multiple-task blocks. This is the *global task-switching cost*; it is thought to indicate the setup cost

associated with maintaining and scheduling two mental task sets. This cost is similar to a dual-task cost, where performance on a block of dual-task trials is compared to performance on a block of single-task trials. The two paradigms—dual-task performance and global task switching—differ mainly in their temporal dynamics: In task switching, Task A and Task B are performed in succession; in dual tasking, they are performed concurrently.

A second type of task-switching cost involves the comparison, within a mixed block, between trials in which a switch is actually required, with nonswitch or repeat trials. This *local task-switching cost* is an indication of the control process associated with the actual switching.

Wasylyshyn, Verhaeghen, and Sliwinski (2003) reported a multilevel meta-analysis of age and task switching based on 10 studies for global switching and 15 studies for local switching. Their results are presented in Figure 8.5, middle and bottom rows. For global task switching, the compounding effect was additive; for local task switching, the compounding effect was multiplicative. Global task switching was clearly age sensitive: In state space, the lines for younger and older adults separate out reliably, as do the lines for switch and nonswitch blocks in the Brinley plot. The degree of slowing in the global task-switching cost was 2.2 (the old:young ratio of the intercept difference between mixed blocks and pure blocks), compared to a slowing factor of 1.6 in the baseline task. Local task switching was found to be age-constant: One line described the data adequately in both the state space and the Brinley plot. Again, several moderator variables were examined, but none yielded reliable interactions with age.

Aging and Executive Control: Summary and Outlook

Two kinds of outcomes arise from our meta-analyses of aging and executive control. Tasks involving resistance to interference (Stroop and negative priming) showed a multiplicative compounding effect of the same magnitude in young and old. This was also true of local task switching. On the other hand, global task switching yielded an additive compounding effect, and the effect was larger for older adults than would be projected from their baseline slowing. The latter pattern was also observed for coordination (dual-task performance).

Accepting our mathematical framework, these findings can be summarized as follows. Age deficits in control were never observed when compounding costs were multiplicative, that is, when the central-processing rate was reduced. When compounding costs were additive, that is, when the processing stream was extended by an additional step but unchanged in rate, age deficits in the inserted step were found, and those deficits were larger than the ones extrapolated from the baseline tasks.

The same findings can be restated closer to the psychology of the tasks. We found that control-specific deficits did not emerge in tasks that involved active selection of relevant information, such as determining the ink color of words (Stroop), actively ignoring or inhibiting a stimulus (negative priming), or relinquishing attention from one aspect of the stimulus to reattach it to a different aspect (local task switching). In those cases the selection requirement rescaled the entire processing sequence, but the rescaling was no greater in older adults than in younger adults. On the other hand, age differences emerged in tasks that involved the maintenance of two distinct mental task sets, as in dual-task performance or global task switching. The costs of maintaining such dual states of mind were additive—some step was added or prolonged. The duration of the added step was greater for older adults than that extrapolated from the surrounding steps.

From these meta-analyses we conclude that, contrary to many claims in the literature, there is no age-related deficit specific to inhibitory control. Multiple task set maintenance, on the other hand, does lead to an age-related deficit over and beyond the effects of general slowing in the relevant task domain. Multiple task set maintenance could challenge the control system in several ways. The deficit could arise from the logic implemented in the coordination step itself (the most natural interpretation). But it is also possible that an age-related deficit in the capacity of working memory may be responsible for the difficulty in maintaining multiple sets (for a meta-analysis of age and working memory, see

Bopp & Verhaeghen, 2005). In that case, the underlying problem would arise from a structural limit rather than from a specific control process (Verhaeghen, Cerella, Bopp, & Basak, 2005, expanded on this point).

From our meso-theoretic perspective, control processes are not all of a kind. Some are spared by age, and others are disproportionately damaged. The identification of such differential effects in this set of basic control processes is an important step forward in our understanding of cognitive aging deficits, a step that may have implications for a broader class of more complex tasks.

Conclusion

Reviewing all the meta-analyses presented here, we are led to offer a modest proposal: The aging of RTs unfolds in three-plus-one dimensions. Lexical tasks are largely spared from the ill effects of aging; simple decisions show modest age-related slowing; spatial tasks are slowed to a greater degree. Dual-task-set maintenance adds another dimension, orthogonal to the three content-based domains, a degree of slowing that exceeds the baseline domain. Contrary to received opinion, other control processes (resistance to interference, local task switching) appear to be age constant—the deficits reported in the primary literature may be due to insufficient statistical control for baseline slowing. The picture of cognitive aging that emerges from our analyses is both simpler and more positive than that painted in typical review articles: Apart from spatial processes and tasks demanding dual task set maintenance, no cognitive tasks appear to show deficits beyond those seen in simple decisions.

More work needs to be done. We do not know what drives the trifurcation into three dimensions; we do not know how lexical tasks apparently circumvent the restrictions on simple decisions; we know hardly anything at all about the process of working memory updating. We trust that our simple three-plus-one scheme will soon prove naïve, and are looking forward to more astute theorizing. To that end, we advocate that researchers in the field include simple-decision control conditions in their experiments and carefully control for the effects of general slowing in their baseline measures.

REFERENCES

Allport, A., Styles, E. A., & Hsieh, S. (1994). Shifting intentional set: Exploring the dynamic control of tasks. In C. Umilta & M. Moscovitch (Eds.), *Attention and Performance IV* (pp. 421–452). Cambridge, MA: MIT Press.

Baron, J. A., & Cerella, J. (1993). Laboratory tests of the disuse account of cognitive decline. In J. Cerella, J. M. Rybash, W. J. Hoyer, & M. Commons (1993). *Adult information processing: Limits on loss* (pp. 175–203). San Diego, CA: Academic Press.

Bopp, K. L. (2003). *Exploration of age-related differences in executive control processes of verbal and visuo-spatial working memory: Evidence from the repetition detection paradigm.* Unpublished doctoral dissertation, Syracuse University, Syracuse, New York.

Bopp, K. L., & Verhaeghen, P. (2005). Aging and verbal memory span: A meta-analysis. *Journal of Gerontology: Psychological Sciences, 60B,* 223–233.

Braver, T. S., Barch, D. M. (2002). A theory of cognitive control, aging cognition, and neuromodulation. *Neuroscience and Biobehavioral Reviews, 26,* 809–817.

Brinley, J. F. (1965). Cognitive sets, speed and accuracy of performance in the elderly. In A. T. Welford & J. E. Birren (Eds.), *Behavior, aging and the nervous system* (pp. 114–149). Springfield, IL: Charles C Thomas.

Byrne, M. D. (1998). Taking a computational approach to aging: The SPAN theory of working memory. *Psychology and Aging, 13,* 309–322.

Cerella, J. (1985). Information processing rates in the elderly. *Psychological Bulletin, 98,* 67–83.

Cerella, J. (1990). Aging and information processing rate. In J. E. Birren & K. W. Schaie (Eds.), *Handbook of the psychology of aging* (3rd ed., pp. 201–221). San Diego, CA: Academic Press.

Cerella, J. (1994). Generalized slowing in Brinley plots. *Journal of Gerontology: Psychological Sciences, 49,* P65–P71.

Cerella, J., & Hale, S. (1994). The rise and fall in information-processing rates over the life span. *Acta Psychologica, 86,* 109–197.

Cerella, J., Poon, L. W., & Williams, D. H. (1980). Age and the complexity hypothesis. In L. W. Poon (Ed.), *Aging in the 1980s* (pp. 332–340). Washington, DC: American Psychological Association.

Faust, M. E., Balota, D. A., Spieler, D. H., & Ferraro, F. R. (1999). Individual differences in information-processing rate and amount: Implications for group differences in response latency. *Psychological Bulletin, 125,* 777–799.

Gamboz, N., Russo, R., & Fox, E. (2002). Age differences and the negative priming effect: An updated meta-analysis. *Psychology and Aging, 17,* 525–531.

Hale, S., & Myerson, J. (1996). Experimental evidence for differential slowing in the lexical and nonlexical domains. *Aging, Neuropsychology, and Cognition, 3,* 154–165.

Hartley, A. A., & Little, D. M. (1999). Age-related differences and similarities in dual task interference. *Journal of Experimental Psychology: General, 128,* 416–449.

Hasher, L., & Zacks, R. T. (1988). Working memory, comprehension, and aging: A review and a new view. In G. H. Bower (Ed.), *The psychology of learning and motivation* (Vol. 22, pp. 193–225). San Diego, CA: Academic Press.

Hasher, L., Zacks, R. T., & May, C. P. (1999). *Inhibitory control, circadian arousal, and age.* In D. Gopher & A. Koriat (Eds.), *Attention & Performance XVII. Cognitive regulation of performance: Interaction of theory and application* (pp. 653–675). Cambridge: MIT Press.

Kahana, M. J., Howard, M. W., Zaromb, F., & Wingfield, A. (2002). Age dissociates recency and lag recency effects in free recall. *Journal of Experimental Research: Learning, Memory, and Cognition, 28,* 530–540.

Kausler, D. H. (1991). *Experimental psychology, cognition, and human aging* (2nd ed.). New York: Springer-Verlag.

Li, S.-C., Lindenberger, U., & Frensch, P. (2000). Unifying cognitive aging: From neuromodulation to representation to cognition. *Neurocomputing, 32–33,* 879–890.

Lima, S. D, Hale, S., Myerson, J. (1991). How general is general slowing? Evidence from the lexical domain. *Psychology and Aging, 6,* 416–425.

Lindenberger, U., & Baltes, P. B. (1997). Intellectual functioning in old and very old age: Cross-sectional results from the Berlin Aging Study. *Psychology and Aging, 12,* 410–432.

Mayr, U., & Kliegl, R. (1993). Sequential and coordinative complexity: Age-based processing limitations in figural transformations. *Journal of Experimental Psychology: Learning, Memory, and Cognition, 19,* 1297–1320.

Mayr, U., Kliegl, R., & Krampe, R. (1996). Sequential and coordinative processing dynamics in figural transformation across the life span. *Cognition, 59,* 61–90.

Mayr, U., Spieler, D. H., & Kliegl, R. (2001). *Aging and executive control.* New York: Routledge.

McDowd, J. M., & Shaw, R. J. (2000). Attention and aging: A functional perspective. In F. I. M. Craik & T. A. Salthouse (Eds.), *The handbook of aging and cognition* (2nd ed., pp. 221–292). Mahwah, NJ: Lawrence Erlbaum.

Meyer, D. E., Glass, J. M., Mueller, S. T., Seymour, T. L., & Kieras, D. E. (2001). Executive-process interactive control: A unified computational theory for answering 20 questions (and more) about cognitive aging. *European Journal of Cognitive Psychology, 13,* 123–164.

Miyake, A., Friedman, N. P., Emerson, M. J., Witzki, A. H., & Howerter, A. (2000). The unity and diversity of executive functions and their contributions to complex "frontal lobe" tasks: A latent variable analysis. *Cognitive Psychology, 41,* 49–100.

Myerson, J., Adams, D. R., Hale, S., & Jenkins, L. (2003). Analysis of group differences in processing speed: Brinley plots, Q–Q plots, and other conspiracies. *Psychonomic Bulletin and Review, 10,* 224–237.

Myerson, J., & Hale, S. (1993). General slowing and age invariance in cognitive processing: The other side of the coin. In J. Cerella, J. Rybash, W. Hoyer, & M. L. Commons (Eds.), *Adult information processing: Limits on loss* (pp. 115–141). San Diego, CA: Academic Press.

Myerson, J., Hale, S., Wagstaff, D., Poon, L. W., & Smith, G. A. (1990). The information-loss model: A mathematical theory of age-related cognitive slowing. *Psychological Review, 97,* 475–487.

Park, D. C., Polk, T. A., Mikels, J. A., Taylor, S. F., & Marshuetz, C. (2001). Cerebral aging: Integration of brain and behavioral models of cognitive function. *Dialogues in Clinical Neuroscience, 3,* 151–165.

Pashler, H. (2000). Task switching and multitask performance. In S. Monsell & Driver, J. (Eds.), *Attention and performance XVIII: Control of mental processes* (pp. 277–307). Cambridge, MA: MIT Press.

Perfect, T. J., & Maylor, E. A. (2000). Rejecting the dull hypothesis: The relation between method and theory in cognitive aging research. In T. J. Perfect & E. A. Maylor (Eds.), *Models of cognitive aging* (pp. 1–18). Oxford, UK: Oxford University Press.

Ratcliff, R., Spieler, D., & McKoon, G. (2000). Explicitly modeling the effects of aging on response time. *Psychonomic Bulletin and Review, 7,* 1–25.

Salthouse, T. A. (1991). *Theoretical perspectives on cognitive aging.* Hillsdale, NJ: Lawrence Erlbaum.

Salthouse, T. A. (1996). The processing-speed theory of adult age differences in cognition. *Psychological Review, 103,* 403–428.

Sliwinski, M., & Hall, C. B. (1998). Constraints on general slowing: A meta-analysis using hierarchical linear models with random coefficients. *Psychology and Aging, 13,* 164–175.

Van der Linden, M., Brédart, S., & Beerten, A. (1994). Age-related differences in updating working memory. *British Journal of Psychology, 85,* 145–152.

Verhaeghen, P. (2003). Aging and vocabulary scores: A meta-analysis. *Psychology and Aging, 18,* 332–339.

Verhaeghen, P. (2006). *Cognitive aging in three-plus-one dimensions: A meta-analysis of age-related dissociations in response times.* Unpublished manuscript.

Verhaeghen, P., & Cerella, J. (2002). Aging, executive control, and attention: A review of meta-analyses. *Neuroscience and Biobehavioral Reviews, 26,* 849–857.

Verhaeghen, P., Cerella, J., & Basak, C. (2006). Aging, task complexity, and efficiency modes: The influence of working memory involvement on age differences in response times for verbal and visuospatial tasks. *Aging, Neuropsychology, and Cognition, 13,* 254–280.

Verhaeghen, P., Cerella, J., Bopp, K. L., & Basak, C. (2005). Aging and varieties of cognitive control: A review of meta-analyses on resistance to interference, coordination and task switching, and an experimental exploration of age-sensitivity in the newly identified process of focus switching. In R. W. Engle, G. Sedek, U. von Hecker, & D. N. McIntosh (Eds.), *Cognitive limitations in aging and psychopathology: Attention, working memory, and executive functions* (pp. 160–189). Cambridge, MA: Cambridge University Press.

Verhaeghen, P., Cerella, J., Semenec, S. C., Leo, M. E., Bopp, K. L., & Steitz, D. W. (2002). Cognitive efficiency modes in old age: Performance on sequential and coordinative verbal and visuo-spatial tasks. *Psychology and Aging, 17,* 558–570.

Verhaeghen, P., & De Meersman, L. (1998a). Aging and negative priming: A meta-analysis. *Psychology and Aging, 13,* 435–444.

Verhaeghen, P., & De Meersman, L. (1998b). Aging and the Stroop effect: A meta-analysis. *Psychology and Aging, 13,* 120–126.

Verhaeghen, P., & Salthouse, T. A. (1997). Meta-analyses of age–cognition relations in adulthood: Estimates of linear and non-linear age effects and structural models. *Psychological Bulletin, 122,* 231–249.

Verhaeghen, P., Steitz, D. W., Sliwinski, M. J., & Cerella, J. (2003). Aging and dual-task performance: A meta-analysis. *Psychology and Aging, 18,* 443–460.

Washylyshyn, C., Verhaeghen, P., & Sliwinski, M. J. (2003). *Aging and task switching: A meta-analysis.* Unpublished manuscript.

Welford, A. T. (1977). Motor performance. In J. E. Birren & K. W. Schaie (Eds.), *Handbook of the psychology of aging* (pp. 450–496). New York: Van Nostrand Reinhold.

9

AGE-RELATED CHANGES IN MEMORY

Experimental Approaches

SUSAN R. OLD AND MOSHE NAVEH-BENJAMIN

It is commonly thought that aging leads to an overall decline in memory performance. It is interesting, however, that the effects of age are highly dependent upon the type of memory task being administered, with some tasks showing large impairment yet others showing no decline or even improvement into old age. An important goal of research on memory and aging is to explain this variability. In the first section of this chapter, we review empirical findings regarding age-related differences in several domains of memory performance, distinguishing between short- and long-term memory, explicit and implicit memory, and semantic and episodic memory. We also examine age-related differences in specific processes involved in episodic memory—encoding, retention, and retrieval—as well as various other manifestations of age-related episodic memory differences. Next, we discuss several general theoretical approaches that have been offered to explain age-related cognitive changes, examining how these approaches can explain age-related differences in memory performance. Finally, we note ways in which future researchers can use empirical findings to generate memory-preserving interventions for older adults, and we address the need for the integration of various lines of research.

EMPIRICAL EVIDENCE

Numerous studies have been carried out in the different domains of memory and aging. Because we cannot review all of those studies, we have chosen to first present relevant meta-analytical findings, when such findings are available. Meta-analyses provide quantitative summaries of a large number of studies on a given topic, thus allowing researchers to reach generalizable conclusions. After citing such meta-analytical studies in each domain, we provide examples of representative empirical works, in order to describe typical methods and results in that area of study. Most of these examples employ cross-sectional designs, in which different age groups of adults (usually, young ones in their 20s, and older ones, in good health, between 65 and 85 years of age) are tested at a given point in time. The cross-sectional approach allows researchers to determine overall age differences on a variety of tasks. It should be noted, however, that it is also important to investigate intraindividual variability in the effects of age on memory (see, e.g., Lindenberger & von Oertzen, 2006; see also chaps. 27 and 28, this volume, for a discussion of longitudinal designs in aging research, which can determine changes in single individuals across time). Furthermore, it is important to address individual differences in change across middle adulthood (e.g., Martin & Zimprich, 2005); it has been suggested, for example, that there are subtypes of "stables," "decliners," and "gainers" in terms of memory performance in middle age (see Willis & Schaie, 2005). Despite the limitations of the cross-sectional approach, it does provide advantages, such as controlled conditions and a relatively brief time commitment. Readers interested in individual differences in cognitive aging are referred to chapter 2 in this volume.

Short-Term Memory and Working Memory

Short-term memory (STM) involves the ability to retain a recently experienced event for a brief period of time, such as repeating a phone number until it can be dialed. The original conceptualization of STM was based on a mechanism that allows temporary storage of information (Atkinson & Shiffrin, 1968). The later concept of *working memory* (WM; Baddeley & Hitch, 1974) involves the simultaneous maintenance and active manipulation of information. For example, when multiplying two 2-digit numbers, you must maintain some of the digits and products while multiplying other digits. Thus, whereas STM requires only maintenance, WM requires both maintenance and processing.

Aging seems to affect WM more negatively than STM. For example, a meta-analysis by Bopp and Verhaeghen (2005) examined age differences in several verbal tasks and indicated relatively small age differences in tasks requiring simple temporary maintenance of materials. Forward digit span, for instance, showed modest age-related differences ($d = -0.53$, where d is the mean effect size in terms of unit standard deviations over all the studies included). As a processing component was added to the task, however, and as processing became more dominant relative to the maintenance component, age

differences became much larger ($ds = -1.01$, -1.27, and -1.54 for sentence span, listening span, and computation span tasks, respectively).

One relevant empirical work was conducted by Park et al. (2002), who asked 345 people, ranging in age from 20 to 92 years, to complete a series of tasks involving visuospatial and verbal measures of both STM and WM. STM tasks included Corsi blocks tasks, in which participants tried to replicate patterns tapped out on raised blocks by the experimenter, as well as a digit span task, in which strings of presented digits were to be recalled in order. WM tasks included reading span and computation span tasks, in which participants answered series of questions or math problems, respectively. Following an entire series, they were asked to recall the last word from each question or the last number from each math problem. Results showed that, whereas all measures of WM and STM declined with age, this decline was larger in the WM than in the STM tasks. It seems, then, that older adults are more impaired on tasks that require both processing and storage than on tasks requiring only storage and that age-related differences increase as the processing required becomes more demanding.

Implicit/Indirect Memory Versus Explicit/Direct Memory

Another notable distinction made by memory researchers is that between *explicit* (or *declarative/direct*) and *implicit* (or *nondeclarative/indirect*) memory systems (e.g., Squire, 1986). The former is involved when conscious intentional retrieval is used (e.g., trying to remember an address that was given to you yesterday), whereas the latter involves memories that can be inferred by subsequent behavior without any intention of memory retrieval (e.g., responding quickly to a familiar face). Research conducted during the last 20 years shows that aging affects these two forms of memory differently. A meta-analysis carried out by Light and La Voie (1993), for example, concluded that age-related declines on implicit memory measures ($d = -0.18$) are much smaller than those on explicit measures, such as recognition or recall, which, in other meta-analytical studies, reviewed below, show d values ranging from -0.5 to -1.5.

Such a pattern was obtained by D. B. Mitchell and Bruss (2003). In their study, young, middle-aged, and older adults named a combination of presented words and pictures, unaware of the implicit and explicit memory tests they would be given at a later point. In one of the implicit tests, participants were given a category name and were asked to name six exemplars from that category. Words and pictures from the previous list fit into some of the categories, but participants were not aware of this and therefore did not intentionally try to report previously named items (targets). Implicit memory could therefore be measured by comparing participants' reporting of targets to a baseline measure produced by people who had not been exposed to the initial list of words and pictures. Participants also took part in an explicit memory task, in which they were asked to recall the two words and two pictures from the original list that belonged to a given category. The results indicated no significant age differences in the implicit memory tasks—in fact, age was slightly related to an improvement in this measure—whereas the explicit test showed significant age-related declines (see also Light & Albertson, 1989; Light & Singh, 1987).

The major conclusion based upon such studies is that older adults are impaired more on explicit than on implicit memory measures. Hence, in order to assess and predict potential age-related changes, it is important to take into account the degree to which a given task involves intentional and nonintentional memory retrieval.

Long-Term Memory: Episodic Versus Semantic Memory

Within the declarative memory system, a distinction has been made (Tulving, 1972) between *episodic memory*, which involves one's personal memories tied to a particular time and place (e.g., remembering who came to your recent birthday party), and *semantic memory*, which involves knowledge of general facts not related to a specific time and place (e.g., naming the capital of Germany or defining a given word). Like the explicit/implicit distinction discussed above, episodic and semantic memory seem to be affected differently by aging.

In one study, Rönnlund, Nyberg, Bäckman, and Nilsson (2005) analyzed data collected from 1,000 participants between 35 and 80 years of age, on two occasions separated by 5 years. Episodic memory measures included recall of self-performed and other-performed actions, recall of nouns, and recall of statements. Semantic measures included tests of general knowledge, vocabulary, and word fluency. After the researchers adjusted the results for practice effects and education levels, the longitudinal and cross-sectional data led to converging conclusions. Episodic memory stayed fairly stable until around the age of 55–60, at which point there was a large decline in performance. Semantic memory performance, on the other hand, increased between the ages of 35 and 55, leveled off, then declined beginning around the age of 65; this decline, however, was less substantial than that for episodic memory (see also Park et al., 2002).

Using other episodic and semantic memory tasks in a cross-sectional design, Spaniol, Madden, and Voss (2006) asked older and younger adults to judge the pleasantness of a series of words, half of which described living things. After a 1-minute retention interval, each participant took part in either an episodic test, in which they indicated whether a given word was from the study list, or a semantic memory test, in which they decided if a given word described a living or nonliving thing. In both tests, they were asked to respond as quickly as possible. Results indicated that older adults performed less accurately than younger adults on the episodic task, but not on the semantic task. Furthermore, response time data showed that, although both age groups were slower to respond to the episodic than to the semantic task, this difference was larger in the older than the younger adults.

This finding of differential effects of age on episodic and semantic memory seems to be a robust finding. For example, it applies not only to explicit memory, as described above, but also to implicit memory, with older adults showing semantic priming effects comparable to—and often larger than—those of younger adults (e.g., Laver & Burke, 1993; Madden, 1988). Overall, then, it seems that semantic memory is relatively spared of age-related decline. Episodic memory, however, can be quite impaired with advancing age; we will discuss this impairment in more detail in the following section.

Episodic Memory

In this section, we examine research on several factors that affect age-related changes in episodic memory. We have classified many of those factors as occurring at encoding (i.e., the changing of outside information into an internal representation), at retention/maintenance, or at retrieval (i.e., accessing from memory), of the information. We also highlight various other manifestations of age-related differences in episodic memory.

Encoding Processes and Age-Related Memory Changes

One distinction frequently used to address both theoretical and applied questions is that between incidental and intentional learning. In the context of aging, the question is whether the magnitude of age-related differences is similar when information is learned without expectation of later memory tests (e.g., when witnessing a crime) as when learning occurs with the knowledge that this information will be required at a later time (e.g., when trying to commit to memory a phone number for future use). A meta-analysis by Spencer and Raz (1995) addressed this issue and found larger age effects in studies involving memory for intentionally learned ($d = -0.62$) than incidentally learned ($d = -0.41$) materials. R. E. Johnson (2003) reached a similar conclusion in a meta-analysis of memory for text ($d = -0.85$ with advance knowledge of an upcoming test, and $d = -0.55$ when this information was withheld).

One relevant study was conducted by Troyer, Häfliger, Cadieux, and Craik (2006), who compared age-related differences in incidental and intentional learning of names. Older and younger adults viewed a series of surnames and were told that they would need to remember only specified names. Before each presented name, participants were given encoding instructions that involved *physical processing* (stating the first letter of the surname), *phonemic processing* (stating a word that rhymed with the name), *semantic processing* (defining or creating an association with the name), or *intentional learning* (simply trying to remember the name for a later test). Whether testing involved recall or recognition, younger adults outperformed older adults in memory for intentionally learned names, but there were no significant age differences in any of the other encoding conditions for either test form (i.e., for incidentally learned names).

Such results indicate that older adults can encode information incidentally quite well but that they are highly impaired when intentional learning is required. One possible reason for this finding, supported by Dunlosky and Hertzog (2001), is that older adults do not spontaneously use strategies that are as effective as those employed by younger adults at encoding and at retrieval.

Retention Processes and Age-Related Memory Changes

Whereas the differential effects of encoding instructions on age-related memory differences are largely consistent, the picture regarding forgetting rates is much less clear. A meta-analysis by Verhaeghen, Marcoen, and Goossens (1993) found similar age differences on immediate as on delayed memory measures; this applies to tests of list recall ($ds = -1.01$ and -0.83 for immediate and delayed recall, respectively), paired-associate recall ($ds = -0.84$ and -0.97), and prose recall ($ds = -0.66$ and -0.85). R. E. Johnson (2003), however, conducted a meta-analysis of studies involving memory for text and found that age differences were significantly larger when testing occurred between 1 and 10 minutes after study ($d = -0.97$, with one mean effect size per study), compared to both immediate testing ($d = -0.78$) and testing after more than 10 minutes ($d = -0.70$). Thus, the breakdown of retention intervals seems to be an important factor in these investigations.

This lack of converging evidence is shown by specific empirical studies as well. Park, Royal, Dudley, and Morrell (1988) conducted a study to determine if there are age differences in rates of forgetting picture information over an extended period of time. Older and younger adults studied a series of line drawings. Each participant took recognition tests over the drawings 3 minutes, 48 hours, 1 week, 2 weeks, and 4 weeks after study, with no stimulus appearing in more than one test. Results supported previous work (e.g., Rybarczyk, Hart, & Harkins, 1987) in that there was no age-related difference in forgetting rates when testing occurred within 48 hours of study.

However, older adults exhibited larger forgetting rates than younger adults beyond this 48-hour interval. These findings point to the importance of the retention intervals studied and offer one explanation for why only some studies find differential effects of age on forgetting.

Another suggested reason for discrepant findings was put forth by Wheeler (2000), who tested word recall of older and younger adults either 3 minutes or 1 hour after incidental learning took place. Whether testing occurred between or within subjects, results showed larger rates of forgetting in the older than in the younger participants. However, although age differences were consistent in these experiments, effect sizes were quite modest; thus, Wheeler offered this as an explanation for why many previous studies have found similar rates of forgetting in younger and older adults. It seems likely that age differences do increase along with retention intervals but that this effect is small and may differ according to the precise retention intervals being tested.

Retrieval From Memory

Test Type. For explicit memory tasks, processes involved in accessing information when it is needed—that is, *retrieving* it—are as important as those involved in the encoding of information. One factor that affects age-related memory differences is the degree to which a test employs retrieval cues. For example, free-recall tasks provide no cues to participants, whereas cued-recall tasks do provide cuing. In recognition tests, participants receive copies of original stimuli as cues; thus recognition involves a greater degree of cuing than either free recall or cued recall. By comparing age-related differences on each type of test, it is possible to determine the degree to which older and younger adults utilize these cues.

Spencer and Raz (1995), in their meta-analysis mentioned above, found larger age differences in tests of recall ($d = -1.01$, which includes both free and cued recall) than in recognition tests ($d = -0.57$). Similarly, in a meta-analysis involving memory for text, R. E. Johnson (2003) showed that age effects were smaller in recognition tests ($d = -0.67$) than in free recall ($d = -0.82$) or cued recall ($d = -0.88$) tests. Such an effect is exemplified by the aforementioned study by Troyer et al. (2006; Experiment

1). At study, older and younger participants were presented with surnames. In a recall test, participants were simply asked to write down all of the names they could remember. In a recognition test, they responded as to whether a presented name had appeared in the study list. Results showed an age-related impairment in the ability to recall names, but there was no significant age difference in terms of recognition test performance.

Cued recall also seems to be more impaired with age than is recognition. For example, Craik and McDowd (1987) reported a large age-related deficit in the ability to use a cue phrase (e.g., "a body of water") to recall a target word (e.g., *pond*) following study of the phrase–target word pairs. However, there were no significant age differences in the ability to make yes–no responses to target and distractor words.

One proposed explanation for this differential effect of test type on age-related memory differences involves Craik's (1986) notion of *self-initiated operations*. According to this idea, older adults have difficulty carrying out tasks that require a high degree of self-initiated processing—that is, tasks not accompanied by sufficient environmental support. Because recognition tasks include more environmental support than recall tasks, and cued-recall tasks include more environmental support than free recall, Craik's idea is supported by empirical evidence such as that mentioned above. A related explanation for such findings is the idea that aging has a more negative impact on tasks requiring controlled, effortful processes than on tasks mediated by more automatic processes (Hasher & Zacks, 1979).

Recollection and Familiarity. There has been a recent distinction made between two types of retrieval processes (e.g., Yonelinas, 2002). The first, *recollection*, requires retrieval of contextual details of an episode, whereas the second, *familiarity*, is based on a feeling of having previously experienced an event without remembering any specific contextual details. Three major paradigms used to measure recollection and familiarity are the *process dissociation procedure* (PDP), the *Remember/Know* (R/K) method, and the assessment of *receiver operating characteristics* (ROC) curves.

Studies using the PDP (Jacoby, 1991) show an age-related decline in retrievals based on recollection but not on familiarity (e.g., Hay & Jacoby, 1999). One experiment using this method was conducted by Jennings and Jacoby (1993, Experiment 2). In the first phase of the study, older and younger adults read a list of words, unaware that memory for the words would later be tested. In the next phase, participants were told to remember auditorily presented words for a later test. Finally, in each of two tests, participants were presented with a word from one of the previous phases and a new word. In the *exclusion test*, participants were falsely told that all test pairs included one auditorily presented word and that they should choose that word; because no word had been presented in both study lists, recollecting that one of the test words had appeared in the visual phase would lead participants to choose the other word in the test pair. Thus, incorrectly choosing a visually presented word would indicate familiarity in the absence of recollection. In the *inclusion test*, participants were correctly informed that each word pair included one old and one new word and were asked to choose the old word. With these instructions, choosing words from the visual phase could indicate either recollection or familiarity without recollection. The researchers used performance on the tests to calculate estimates of recollection and familiarity. Younger adults' recollection estimates were higher than those for older adults, whereas there were no significant age differences in familiarity estimates. The authors thus concluded that aging impairs recollection but leaves familiarity intact. Variations of the PDP have been developed in more recent studies (e.g., Toth & Parks, 2006).

The R/K method makes use of participants' reports of whether they "remember" a particular stimulus (indicating recollection) or simply feel or "know" that the stimulus was previously presented (representing familiarity). The ROC curves method involves plotting hit rates against false alarm rates at various levels of confidence. Like the PDP method, studies using these two methods show a definite age-related decline in recollection. The picture regarding familiarity is less clear, however. Prull, Dawes, Martin, Rosenberg, and Light (2006) used all three procedures discussed here; the PDP method found no age-related deficit in familiarity, but the R/K and ROC methods did show such a deficit. This finding is consistent with other studies that have used R/K (e.g., Light, Prull, La Voie, & Healy, 2000) and ROC (e.g., Healy, Light, & Chung, 2005) methods.

Overall, then, although age-related patterns in familiarity seem to depend on the measurement method used, there is a great deal of evidence that recollection declines with age. It has been claimed (e.g., Jacoby, Jennings, & Hay, 1996) that this recollection deficit—an inability during retrieval to access the details of an episode—is largely responsible for older adults' memory deficit. This notion can explain the relatively adequate performance of older adults in tasks involving implicit or semantic memory, because such tasks do not require detailed conscious recollection of an original event.

Other Manifestations of Age-Related Episodic Memory Change

Memory for Content Versus Context–Source. A defining characteristic of episodic memory is that it is tied to a time and place. If you are asked whom you met last Thanksgiving, you can use various contextual aspects of the episode—for example, perhaps the time (Thanksgiving dinner) and the place (your brother's house) where you had the festive dinner—in order to retrieve the relevant information about the people you have met there. Studies show that older adults demonstrate poor memory for such contextual elements, including the external source of presented information (e.g., the voice in which information was presented) and whether it was presented or imagined (e.g., M. K. Johnson, Hashtroudi, & Lindsay, 1993), relative to their memory for the content of the event (e.g., what was said or presented). Spencer and Raz (1995) reviewed evidence from 46 studies involving both young and old participants and found larger age-related differences in memory for context ($d = -0.90$) than for content ($d = -0.72$).

A representative study was conducted by Simons, Dodson, Bell, and Schacter (2004). Older and younger adults heard a series of sentences read by one of four speakers (two male and two female) while viewing the written sentence and a photograph of the speaker. A surprise test indicated that older adults were just as able as young adults to distinguish between old and new sentences. However, they were less able, compared to younger participants, to identify the speaker of earlier presented sentences. The authors concluded that although older adults can remember information presented in sentences (content), they are impaired in the ability to remember the source (voice and face) associated with that sentence. Similar results have been reported in memory for words and their spatial locations (Puglisi, Park, Smith, & Hill, 1985) and for words and the case (upper- or lowercase) in which they appeared at study (Kausler & Puckett, 1980).

This age-related contextual-source memory deficit may explain many aspects of older adults' memory decline (e.g., Kausler & Puckett, 1980; Naveh-Benjamin & Craik, 1995; Spencer & Raz, 1995). Contextual details, if remembered, can serve as retrieval cues when relevant information must be recalled. Without such cues, memory suffers. Furthermore, the contextual-source deficit suggestion is in line with findings discussed earlier in this chapter. For example, episodic memory and tests of recall depend heavily on contextual information and are more impacted by age than are semantic memory and recognition memory, which rely less on context.

Memory for Items Versus Associations. Another distinction related to episodic memory involves the difference between item and associative memory (e.g., Naveh-Benjamin, 2000; Naveh-Benjamin, Guez, Kilb, & Reedy, 2004; Naveh-Benjamin, Hussain, Guez, & Bar-On, 2003). Item information may involve a single contextual feature, such as remembering that a certain voice has been heard before, or basic content information, such as recalling a word. Associative information, on the other hand, involves the binding together of two or more items (e.g., a name and a face) or contexts, or an item and its context, such as remembering that a specific word was heard in a particular voice.

It has been shown that age-related memory deficits are much larger when associative information is tested than when item information is tested. For example, Naveh-Benjamin (2000; Experiment 2) presented younger and older adults with a series of unrelated pairs of words, with instructions to remember either the words

or their pairings. All participants then took both item and associative recognition tests. In the item test, they indicated whether they had seen a given word during study. In the associative test, they were presented with word pairs as they had appeared at study and with pairs consisting of two words taken from different studied pairs, and indicated which pairs were the same as at study. Results revealed that, in each of the study instruction conditions, age differences in performance were larger on the associative than on the item test.

Older adults' particular difficulty in binding components of an episode into a cohesive unit has led to the suggestion that this age-related associative deficit can partially explain overall age differences in memory (Chalfonte & Johnson, 1996; K. J. Mitchell, Johnson, Raye, Mather, & D'Esposito, 2000; Naveh-Benjamin, 2000). Naveh-Benjamin termed this idea the *associative-deficit hypothesis.* Such an age-related impairment in the ability to associate or bind together units of information can accommodate several of the results reviewed earlier. For example, semantic memory does not require the specific binding of information to a place and time and should therefore be less affected by aging than is episodic memory; this is in alignment with results discussed earlier. It is interesting to note that the associative-deficit hypothesis may partially reflect similar age-related deficits as the recollection- and context-deficit hypotheses discussed previously in this chapter, in that all three ideas attribute older adults' episodic memory impairment to the inefficient episodic encoding and retrieval of detailed bound pieces of information.

Autobiographical Memory. Episodic memory can also be assessed by asking people of different ages to remember events in their personal pasts. In contrast to events presented for study in the laboratory, researchers cannot verify the accuracy of these memories. Nevertheless, the study of autobiographical memory can indicate a great deal about the aging process. Research on this topic indicates that the age at which memories are established is quite important. Not surprisingly, people tend to remember recent events. More interesting is that there seems to be an increase in memory for events that happened between the ages of 10 and 30—an effect known as the *reminiscence bump*. This bump is quite robust and has been found using various stimuli as cues. For example, in a study by Willander and Larsson (2006), older adults between the ages of 65 and 80 years were presented with retrieval cues that could take the form of odors, words, or pictures, and were asked to retrieve an autobiographical memory evoked by each cue. Results showed a reminiscence bump in the second decade of life in response to picture cues and word cues. There was also an odor-evoked reminiscence bump, but this occurred during the first decade of life.

One explanation for the reminiscence bump, proposed by Holmes and Conway (1999) is that *privileged encoding* occurs for events that are especially important within one's state of development. For example, identification with society occurs during childhood, whereas a focus on personal relationships occurs during adolescence and early adulthood. In support of this idea, the researchers found that the reminiscence bump in reported public events occurred during the first decade of life, whereas that in reported personal events occurred during the second decade.

False Memory. Another line of research focuses on the memory errors that people commit. A review article by Jacoby and Rhodes (2006) concludes that older adults are more susceptible than younger adults to misinformation—that is, to incorporating new materials into their memory for an original event—although, it is interesting to note, they are more confident than younger adults in the accuracy of these false memories. Karpel, Hoyer, and Toglia (2001), for example, showed that older adults were more likely than younger adults to incorporate misinformation, presented in a questionnaire, into their memories for a crime viewed in slides, yet were highly confident in these false memories.

False memories are not always externally generated but may be internally generated as well. Watson, Balota, and Sergent-Marshall (2001), for example, asked older and younger adults to learn lists of words presented on a screen. Each list consisted of words that were associated—either semantically or phonetically—with an unpresented critical lure. After the presentation of a list, participants were asked to freely recall all the words they could remember from that list. Results showed that older adults falsely recalled more critical lures than the younger group in each relatedness condition. This study aligns with and extends findings based on the Deese–Roediger–McDermott paradigm (Deese, 1959; Roediger & McDermott, 1995), which elicits false memories of critical lures that are semantically related to a given list of words.

One suggested reason for the increase in false memories by older adults (e.g., Smith, Lozito, & Bayen, 2005) involves the inability to link content information to its context. This may lead older adults to experience difficulty in remembering whether a familiar item was externally presented or internally generated (Hashtroudi, Johnson, Vnek, & Ferguson, 1994), or in remembering the sources of conflicting pieces of information. Such a notion is in alignment with the recollection deficit, contextual-deficit, and associative-deficit hypotheses discussed earlier in this chapter.

Emotional Materials. Some recent studies indicate that older adults tend to remember positively valenced information quite well; this is true for both working memory (e.g., Mikels, Larkin, Reuter-Lorenz, & Carstensen, 2005) and long-term episodic memory (see Carstensen, Mikels, & Mather, 2006, for a review). For example, Charles, Mather, and Carstensen (2003) asked young, middle-aged, and older adults to view a series of 32 images—some neutral in valence and others positive or negative. When later asked to recall the images, middle-aged and older adults remembered more positive than negative images, whereas the young adults reported equal numbers of images from those two valences. On a recognition test, younger adults performed better on the negative stimuli than on the positive or neutral stimuli, whereas the middle-aged and older adults performed similarly across all three valence levels. Thus, age-related memory deficits seem to be reduced when positive stimuli are involved.

One suggestion raised to explain this effect (e.g., Carstensen, Isaacowitz, & Charles, 1999) is that, as people approach the end of life, emotional goals—as opposed to knowledge-based goals—become increasingly salient. This, in turn, leads to successful encoding and retrieval of emotional—especially positive—information in older adults.

EXPLAINING AGE-RELATED MEMORY CHANGES USING GENERAL THEORETICAL APPROACHES

Several theoretical frameworks and hypotheses have been suggested to explain empirical findings regarding cognitive aging in general. In this section, we discuss briefly how these ideas may apply to age-related changes in memory.

Speed of Processing

Several researchers have proposed that the execution of mental processes slows down in old age (e.g., Birren, 1965). Salthouse (1996), for example, holds that older adults' slowing of processing speed is a major factor involved in general cognitive decline. According to his processing-speed theory, there are two separate mechanisms contributing to the speed–cognition relationship. The *limited time mechanism* involves slowing at an early stage of basic information processing, which leaves less available time for later processing. The *simultaneity mechanism* involves the notion that products formed early in processing are lost before later processing is finished. When multiplying two 2-digit numbers together, for example, slow performance of late operations may lead to the forgetting of products found earlier.

Salthouse (1996) analyzed the outcomes of several studies in order to show the relationship between speed and various measures of memory performance, including free recall, associative learning, and working memory. After controlling for reaction-time speed, age-related variance on the memory tasks was reduced by over 75%. Furthermore, Verhaeghen and Salthouse (1997) conducted a meta-analysis of cross-sectional studies and found that speed can account for over 70% of age-related variance in episodic memory measures. Thus, processing speed seems to be a key factor involved in age-related memory impairment.

Working Memory Capacity

Several researchers (e.g., Hasher & Zacks, 1988; Welford, 1980) claim that reduced WM capacity is a major factor in the age-related declines in many cognitive tasks, including memory tasks. To effectively encode information, such as spoken sentences, one must use WM to store previously learned information while simultaneously processing and integrating new information into a cohesive meaningful event (Baddeley, 1986). According to one suggestion, older adults do not possess the control processes necessary to switch between processing and storage tasks (e.g., Light & Albertson, 1988). For example, Hogan, Kelly, and Craik (2006) presented older and younger adults with a set of words, with instructions to report either the color of each word or whether the word described a living or nonliving thing. After six to nine words had appeared with the same instructions, the instructions changed to the other task. Results showed that older adults were more impaired than younger adults by this task switch, both in terms of accuracy and response time to the encoding task.

Other executive processes involved in WM may also help to account for episodic memory decline in older adults. Hasher and Zacks (1988) and Hasher, Zacks, and May (1999) have claimed that older adults have trouble using inhibitory processes to block irrelevant information from entering WM. For example, Hartman and Hasher (1991) found that older adults tend to hold disconfirmed information in WM to a greater extent than do young adults. This notion extends to long-term episodic memory as well; Salthouse, Siedlecki, and Krueger (2006) found that older adults were quite impaired in recall of items they had been instructed to remember but were just as able as younger particip~~ recall items they had been told t~

Attentional l

There have
decline in attent.
of resources avai.
in old age and t
changes in a va
(Craik, 1986; Craik

this notion, older adults lack the attentional resources required to effectively perform certain tasks—especially difficult tasks, which are highly demanding of resources. Evidence is consistent with this idea (e.g., Craik, 1986; Craik & Byrd, 1982; Craik & McDowd, 1987).

One relevant line of research involves the effects of divided attention (DA) on memory. There have been several studies using memory tasks that indicate a larger reduction in overall performance of older than younger adults when under DA conditions (e.g., Anderson, Craik, & Naveh-Benjamin, 1998). Furthermore, studies have shown that young people whose attentional resources are reduced through use of DA conditions exhibit a pattern of memory performance decline similar to that of older adults (e.g., Craik & Byrd, 1982; Jennings & Jacoby, 1993), suggesting that older adults' resources are in fact depleted even without a secondary task.

This suggestion of a possible mediating role of reduced attentional resources is in line with the age-related patterns of memory performance described earlier. For example, explicit memory requires more attentional resources than does implicit memory, and the age-related impairment is larger on explicit tasks. Likewise, the larger effect of age on recall than on recognition measures could be due to the substantial amount of resources needed to search for a target stimulus. Thus, although there have been criticisms of the reduced attentional resources notion on the grounds of vagueness (e.g., Salthouse, 1988), it provides a heuristic functional explanation of age-related differences in memory performance.

FUTURE DIRECTIONS

The empirical evidence reviewed in this chapter points to interesting differential effects of aging on memory. In the following section, we discuss some issues reflecting ways in which these findings can be applied. For example, researchers should actively search for factors that positively or negatively affect older adults' memory performance in order to develop practical measures to improve memory functioning in old age. In this respect, various lines of research must be unified so as to determine the causes of age-related memory loss and ways to avoid such loss.

Practical Applications

Maximizing Older Adults' Episodic Memory Strengths

One issue that should be pursued in future research deals with the factors that reduce older adults' declines in memory performance. One area of study showing some positive effects of age involves prospective memory (PM; i.e., the ability to remember to perform a future action; see chap. 10 for an in-depth discussion of PM and aging). Although older adults are impaired in laboratory-based PM tasks, they seem to outperform younger adults on naturalistic PM tasks, such as remembering to make phone calls or to take medications, even when participants are asked not to use external aids (e.g., Henry, MacLeod, Phillips, & Crawford, 2004). Perhaps future researchers will be able to determine the precise mechanisms behind this effect and to help older adults apply those mechanisms to retrospective memory tasks. Seniors might be trained, for example, to make new information highly personally relevant, as with naturalistic PM tasks, to see if this aids retrospective memory performance.

Another area of memory in which older adults are relatively unimpaired is semantic memory, as discussed earlier (e.g., Park et al., 2002). An important question is whether they can use this semantic knowledge to improve episodic memory performance. There is some evidence that this is the case. For example, a meta-analysis by Verhaeghen et al. (1993) provides an indication that increasing categorizability (the ability to group information into previously learned semantic categories) of episodically to-be-remembered information leads to a decrease in age differences. Furthermore, Naveh-Benjamin (2000) found larger age differences in memory for unrelated than for related word pairs, suggesting that older adults can use previously learned semantic information to support new episodic knowledge, thus reducing age-related deficits in episodic memory (see also Naveh-Benjamin, Craik, Guez, & Kreuger, 2005). Thus, various factors rather than purely mechanistic ones can affect older adults' memory performance. By focusing not just on memory impairment but on factors positively related to memory and aging, future research may discover ways in which the findings can be practically applied.

*Minimizing Negative Influences on Older
Adults' Episodic Memory Performance*

One factor associated with older adults' memory impairment involves stereotype threat; that is, older adults may not perform at their best because they are aware of (and threatened by) the common notion that aging impairs memory abilities. Hess, Auman, Colcombe, and Rahhal (2003), for example, examined free-recall performance of older and younger adults who had just read articles indicating either positive or negative effects of aging on memory. Whereas the younger adults were unaffected by the stereotype threat manipulation, the older adults were quite impaired in the negative, relative to the positive stereotype condition. Manipulations presumably eliciting stereotype threat, or the related feelings of anxiety, may also be surprisingly subtle. For example, Rahhal, Hasher, and Colcombe (2001) found that age differences in memory were eliminated when the terms *memory* and *testing* were completely omitted from task instructions.

Although without further assumptions, anxiety and stereotype threat may not be able to explain interaction effects (i.e., cases in which age deficits are larger on one episodic task than on another), these factors can increase the overall differences observed between young and old. Thus, one practical way to reduce age-related episodic memory impairment in the laboratory is to take measures to reduce older adults' anxiety and to alleviate stereotype threat. Such measures should be extended to naturalistic settings, to aid older adults' memory performance in their everyday lives.

The above sections provide a sample from the wealth of research investigating some of the factors that are positively and negatively associated with older adults' memory functioning, but more work is needed to shape the results into a more applicable form. Future researchers should integrate the results of this basic research into effective interventions for older adults.

*Effects of Training on Older
Adults' Episodic Memory Performance*

One especially applicable area of research involves the effects of special training on older adults' memory performance. Results of past studies seem to be quite promising. Verhaeghen, Marcoen, and Goossens (1992), for example, conducted a meta-analysis of studies comparing pre- and postmnemonic training performance of older adults. Groups receiving this training improved significantly more than those not receiving training ($d = 0.73$ for trained groups, compared to ds = 0.38 and 0.37 for control and placebo groups, respectively); all types of mnemonic training (method of loci, name–face, and organization) were equally effective. The authors concluded that "even in old age memory remains plastic" (Verhaeghen et al., 1992, p. 248).

An example of an empirical study involving memory training was conducted by Cavallini, Pagnin, and Vecchi (2003), who compared pre- and posttraining performance of young (20–35 years), younger elderly (60–70 years), and older elderly (70–80 years) participants. First, participants completed a test battery, which included various ecological tasks, such as recalling a short story after reading it, studying and then recalling items from a shopping list, and remembering names paired with faces. Next, each participant underwent one of two types of memory training, which were completed in five separate sessions. Some participants received training in the loci mnemonic, associating images along a familiar route with to-be-remembered items. The remaining participants underwent "strategic training," in which they learned a variety of memory techniques and were taught to choose the method most appropriate for a given task. After finishing all training sessions, the participants completed a test battery similar to the one from the pretraining session. Results showed that the types of training had similar effects on memory performance. Importantly, all age groups improved to a similar extent. On one task—recall of stories— trained older adults were actually able to improve their performance to the levels of untrained young adults.

There is also evidence that older adults maintain a benefit of memory training over long periods. For example, Derwinger, Neely, and Bäckman (2005) found that, 8 months after being trained to generate memory strategies, older adults maintained a boost in performance. There are some indications, however, that although older adults benefit greatly from intense mnemonic training, their "developmental reserve capacity," found through testing the upper limits of training benefits, is relatively small (see, e.g., Baltes & Kliegl, 1992; Kliegl, Smith, & Baltes, 1989). Thus, memory training may be one highly useful tool through which researchers and practitioners can work to improve older adults' memories, but training is unlikely to completely remove age differences. Training that is used should teach older adults how to create and evaluate their own memory strategies, because this creates lasting benefits (Derwinger et al., 2005).

Integration of Research: Combining Perspectives

To create useful interventions as mentioned above, various lines of research must be brought together. In a narrow sense, this involves the integration of findings regarding aging's effects on various specific aspects of memory. This has already been done to some extent; for example, researchers have noted that aging negatively impacts episodic memory but does not greatly affect semantic memory (e.g., Park et al., 2002). Such comparisons can help to determine the precise mechanisms behind age-related memory impairment.

In more broad terms, researchers should also strive to establish causal links between various factors, such as health issues, and memory performance. Work on this task, too, has already begun. Factors such as physical exercise, diet, and stress levels have been suggested to influence the degree to which memory declines with age (e.g., Small, 2002). For example, data from the Nurses' Health Study showed that self-reported physical activity was positively associated with performance on immediate and delayed recall of 10-word lists and East Boston Memory Tests (Weuve et al., 2004) in women between 70 and 81 years of age. It is also important for researchers to consider disease as a potential contributor to memory decline. Diabetes, for example, appears to impair performance on a variety of memory tasks (Bent, Rabbitt, & Metcalfe, 2000). By considering physiologically related changes and their relationship to memory performance, it may be possible to determine new ways to reduce age-related memory deficits through simple lifestyle changes (see chap. 16 for more on the relationship between health and cognition). Although this is a monumental task, future researchers should seek to integrate information provided from diverse areas of study.

The Relationship Between Age-Related Memory Changes and Cognitive Changes in General

The preceding few paragraphs provide a brief review of approaches needed to demonstrate the effects of various factors on memory and aging. We would now like to examine in greater detail the relationship between age-related changes in memory and in general cognition. The question is whether there is uniqueness in changes that occur in memory as people age or whether these changes are just a manifestation of more general changes in cognition.

Certain statistical approaches are quite valuable in the assessment of this question, especially because relevant studies tend to involve correlation rather than manipulation. Salthouse, Berish, and Miles (2002) assessed performance of different age groups on several variables, some related to memory and others to other cognitive tasks. After statistically controlling the variance in some non-memory-related tasks, the proportion of age-related variance in free-recall memory performance was greatly reduced, implying that age-related effects on memory measures and on other cognitive variables are not independent of each other. Similar results have been obtained for source memory and other episodic memory measures (e.g., Salthouse et al., 2006; Siedlecki, Salthouse, & Berish, 2005).

The above results raise interesting questions regarding different research approaches in the study of age-related changes in memory. The main approach discussed in this chapter involves the effects of various experimental manipulations on memory performance and reveals a variety of differential effects of those manipulations on the memory performance of younger and older adults. The other approach discussed here looks simultaneously at relationships between age and several memory and cognitive indexes, and often shows, as in the examples above, that the effects of age on memory are not unique but are shared with other cognitive factors. If this is the case, then it is crucial for future researchers to integrate findings from these experimental and psychometric approaches. This would provide a better understanding of the absolute age-related changes in different tasks as well as the degree to which these changes are independent from those in other areas.

The issues raised in this section regarding the applicability of memory research for older adults, as well as the integration of various approaches and statistical methods used in this research, should be further investigated. Consideration of these issues and approaches will help researchers to better understand the phenomena involved in the effects of aging on memory processes. Finally, although the empirical work described throughout this chapter has proven valuable in the search for mechanisms behind age-related memory change, there is clearly a need for greater theoretical development (see, e.g., chap. 2, this volume). Such advancement may be generated, in part, through the integration of various lines of research.

CONCLUSION

In this chapter, we first reviewed empirical evidence for differential patterns of age-related declines in memory. Certain types of tasks, especially those involving the encoding, retention, and explicit retrieval of detailed, bound episodic information, seem to be quite impaired in old age. In contrast, implicit and semantic memory processes remain relatively intact. We also described several theoretical approaches to the study of general cognitive change and showed how each of these perspectives can be applied more specifically to age-related changes in memory performance. Finally, we discussed directions for future research on memory and aging, including the practical application of findings involving factors that positively and negatively affect older adults' episodic memory performance, as well as the integration of diverse lines of research. Such directions should allow researchers to progress in the understanding of developmental changes that occur in memory.

REFERENCES

Anderson, N. D., Craik, F. I. M., & Naveh-Benjamin, M. (1998). The attentional demands of encoding and retrieval in younger and older adults: 1. Evidence from divided attention costs. *Psychology and Aging, 13,* 405–423.

Atkinson, R. C., & Shiffrin, R. M. (1968). Human memory: A proposed system and its control processes. In K. W. Spence & J. T. Spence (Eds.), *The psychology of learning and motivation* (Vol. 2, pp. 89–105). New York: Academic Press.

Baddeley, A. (1986). *Working memory.* New York: Clarendon Press/Oxford University Press.

Baddeley, A. D., & Hitch, G. (1974). Working memory. In G. H. Bower (Ed.), *The psychology of learning and motivation: Advances in research and theory* (Vol. 8, pp. 47–89). New York: Academic Press.

Baltes, P. B., & Kliegl, R. (1992). Further testing of limits of cognitive plasticity: Negative age differences in a mnemonic skill are robust. *Developmental Psychology, 28,* 121–125.

Bent, N., Rabbitt, P., & Metcalfe, D. (2000). Diabetes mellitus and the rate of cognitive ageing. *British Journal of Clinical Psychology, 39,* 349–362.

Birren, J. E. (1965). Age changes in speed of behavior: Its central nature and physiological correlates. In A. T. Welford & J. E. Birren (Eds.), *Behavior, aging, and the nervous system: Biological determinants of speed of behavior and its changes with age* (pp. 191–216). Springfield, IL: Charles C Thomas.

Bopp, K. L., & Verhaeghen, P. (2005). Aging and verbal memory span: A meta-analysis. *Journal of Gerontology: Psychological Sciences, 60B,* P223–P233.

Carstensen, L. L., Isaacowitz, D. M., & Charles, S. T. (1999). Taking time seriously: A theory of socioemotional selectivity. *American Psychologist, 54,* 165–181.

Carstensen, L. L., Mikels, J. A., & Mather, M. (2006). Aging and the intersection of cognition, motivation, and emotion. In J. E. Birren & K. W. Schaie (Eds.), *Handbook of the psychology of aging* (pp. 343–362). Amsterdam: Elsevier.

Cavallini, E., Pagnin, A., & Vecchi, T. (2003). Aging and everyday memory: The beneficial effect of memory training. *Archives of Gerontology and Geriatrics, 37,* 241–257.

Chalfonte, B. L., & Johnson, M. K. (1996). Feature memory and binding in young and older adults. *Memory & Cognition, 24,* 403–416.

Charles, S. T., Mather, M., & Carstensen, L. L. (2003). Aging and emotional memory: The forgettable nature of negative images for older adults. *Journal of Experimental Psychology: General, 132,* 310–324.

Craik, F. I. M. (1986). A functional account of age differences in memory. In F. Klix & H. Hagendorf (Eds.), *Human memory and cognitive capabilities, mechanisms and performance* (pp. 409–422). Amsterdam: North-Holland and Elsevier.

Craik, F. I. M., & Byrd, M. (1982). Aging and cognitive deficits: The role of attentional resources. In F. I. M. Craik & S. E. Trehub (Eds.), *Aging and cognitive processes* (pp. 191–211). New York: Plenum.

Craik, F. I. M., & McDowd, J. M. (1987). Age differences in recall and recognition. *Journal of Experimental Psychology: Learning, Memory, and Cognition, 13,* 474–479.

Deese, J. (1959). On the prediction of occurrence of particular verbal intrusions in immediate recall. *Journal of Experimental Psychology, 58,* 17–22.

Derwinger, A., Neely, A. S., & Bäckman, L. (2005). Design your own memory strategies! Self-generated strategy training versus mnemonic training in old age: An 8-month follow-up. *Neuropsychological Rehabilitation, 15,* 37–54.

Dunlosky, J., & Hertzog, C. (2001). Measuring strategy production during associative learning: The relative utility of concurrent versus retrospective reports. *Memory & Cognition, 29,* 247–253.

Hartman, M., & Hasher, L. (1991). Aging and suppression: Memory for previously relevant information. *Psychology and Aging, 6,* 587–594.

Hasher, L., & Zacks, R. T. (1979). Automatic and effortful processes in memory. *Journal of Experimental Psychology: General, 108,* 356–388.

Hasher, L., & Zacks, R. T. (1988). Working memory, comprehension, and aging: A review and a new view. In G. H. Bower (Ed.). *The psychology of learning and motivation: Advances in research and theory* (Vol. 22, pp. 193–225). San Diego, CA: Academic Press.

Hasher, L., Zacks, R. T., & May, C. P. (1999). Inhibitory control, circadian arousal, and age. In D. Gopher (Ed.), *Attention and performance XVII: Cognitive regulation of performance: Interaction of theory and application* (pp. 653–675). Cambridge: MIT Press.

Hashtroudi, S., Johnson, M. K., Vnek, N., & Ferguson, S. A. (1994). Aging and the effects of

affective and factual focus on source monitoring and recall. *Psychology and Aging, 9,* 160–170.

Hay, J. F., & Jacoby, L. L. (1999). Separating habit and recollection in young and older adults: Effects of elaborative processing and distinctiveness. *Psychology and Aging, 14,* 122–134.

Healy, M. R., Light, L. L., & Chung, C. (2005). Dual-process models of associative recognition in young and older adults: Evidence from receiver operating characteristics. *Journal of Experimental Psychology: Learning, Memory, and Cognition, 31,* 768–788.

Henry, J. D., MacLeod, M. S., Phillips, L. H., & Crawford, J. R. (2004). A meta-analytic review of prospective memory and aging. *Psychology and Aging, 19,* 27–39.

Hess, T. M., Auman, C., Colcombe, S. J., & Rahhal, T. A. (2003). The impact of stereotype threat on age differences in memory performance. *Journal of Gerontology: Psychological Sciences, 58B,* P3–P11.

Hogan, M. J., Kelly, C. A. M., & Craik, F. I. M. (2006). The effects of attention switching on encoding and retrieval of words in younger and older adults. *Experimental Aging Research, 32,* 153–183.

Holmes, A., & Conway, M. A. (1999). Generation identity and the reminiscence bump: Memory for public and private events. *Journal of Adult Development, 6,* 21–34.

Jacoby, L. L. (1991). A process dissociation framework: Separating automatic from intentional uses of memory. *Journal of Memory and Language, 30,* 513–541.

Jacoby, L. L., Jennings, J. M., & Hay, J. F. (1996). Dissociating automatic and consciously-controlled processes: Implications for diagnosis and rehabilitation of memory deficits. In D. J. Herrmann, C. L. McEvoy, C. Hertzog, P. Hertel, & M. K. Johnson (Eds.), *Basic and applied memory research: Theory in context* (Vol. 1, pp. 161–193). Hillsdale, NJ: Lawrence Erlbaum.

Jacoby, L. L., & Rhodes, M. G. (2006). False remembering in the aged. *Current Directions in Psychological Science, 15,* 49–53.

Jennings, J. M., & Jacoby, L. L. (1993). Automatic versus intentional uses of memory: Aging, attention, and control. *Psychology and Aging, 8,* 283–293.

Johnson, R. E. (2003). Aging and the remembering of text. *Developmental Review, 23,* 261–346.

Johnson, M. K., Hashtroudi, S., & Lindsay, D. S. (1993). Source monitoring. *Psychological Bulletin, 114,* 3–28.

Karpel, M. E., Hoyer, W. J., & Toglia, M. P. (2001). Accuracy and qualities of real and suggested memories: Nonspecific age differences. *Journal of Gerontology: Psychological Sciences, 56B,* P103–P110.

Kausler, D. H., & Puckett, J. M. (1980). Adult age differences in recognition memory for a nonsemantic attribute. *Experimental Aging Research, 6,* 349–355.

Kliegl, R., Smith, J., & Baltes, P. B. (1989). Testing-the-limits and the study of adult age differences in cognitive plasticity of a mnemonic skill. *Developmental Psychology, 25,* 247–256.

Laver, G. D., & Burke, D. M. (1993). Why do semantic priming effects increase in old age? A meta-analysis. *Psychology and Aging, 8,* 34–43.

Light, L. L., & Albertson, S. A. (1988). Comprehension of pragmatic implications in young and older adults. In L. L. Light & D. M. Burke (Eds.), *Language, memory and aging* (pp. 133–153). New York: Cambridge University Press.

Light, L. L., & Albertson, S. A. (1989). Direct and indirect tests of memory for category exemplars in young and older adults. *Psychology and Aging, 4,* 487–492.

Light, L. L., & La Voie, D. (1993). Direct and indirect measures of memory in old age. In P. Graf & M. E. J. Masson (Eds.), *Implicit memory: New directions in cognition, development, and neuropsychology* (pp. 207–230). Hillsdale, NJ: Lawrence Erlbaum.

Light, L. L., Prull, M. W., La Voie, D. J., & Healy, M. R. (2000). Dual-process theories of memory in old age. In T. J. Perfect & E. A. Maylor (Eds.), *Models of cognitive aging* (pp. 238–300). New York: Oxford University Press.

Light, L. L., & Singh, A. (1987). Implicit and explicit memory in young and older adults. *Journal of Experimental Psychology: Learning, Memory, and Cognition, 13,* 531–541.

Lindenberger, U., & von Oertzen, T. (2006). Variability in cognitive aging: From taxonomy to theory. In E. Bialystok & F. I. M. Craik (Eds.), *Lifespan cognition: Mechanisms of change* (pp. 297–314). New York: Oxford University Press.

Madden, D. J. (1988). Adult age differences in the effects of sentence context and stimulus degradation during visual word recognition. *Psychology and Aging, 3,* 167–172.

Martin, M., & Zimprich, D. (2005). Cognitive development in midlife. In S. L. Willis & M. Martin (Eds.), *Middle adulthood: A lifespan perspective* (pp. 179–206). Thousand Oaks, CA: Sage.

Mikels, J., Larkin, G. R., Reuter-Lorenz, P. A., & Carstensen, L. L. (2005). Divergent trajectories in the aging mind: Changes in working memory for affective versus visual information with age. *Psychology and Aging, 20,* 542–553.

Mitchell, D. B., & Bruss, P. J. (2003). Age differences in implicit memory: Conceptual, perceptual, or methodological? *Psychology and Aging, 18,* 807–822.

Mitchell, K. J., Johnson, M. K., Raye, C. L., Mather, M., & D'Esposito, M. (2000). Aging and reflective processes of working memory: Binding and test load deficits. *Psychology and Aging, 15,* 527–541.

Naveh-Benjamin, M. (2000). Adult age differences in memory performance: Tests of an associative deficit hypothesis. *Journal of Experimental Psychology: Learning, Memory, and Cognition, 26,* 1170–1187.

Naveh-Benjamin, M., & Craik, F. I. M. (1995). Memory for context and its use in item memory: Comparisons of younger and older persons. *Psychology and Aging, 10,* 284–293.

Naveh-Benjamin, M., Craik, F. I. M., Guez, J., & Kreuger, S. (2005). Divided attention in younger and older adults: Effects of strategy and relatedness on memory performance and secondary task costs. *Journal of Experimental Psychology: Learning, Memory, and Cognition, 31,* 520–537.

Naveh-Benjamin, M., Guez, J., Kilb, A., & Reedy, S. (2004). The associative memory deficit of older adults: Further support using face–name associations. *Psychology and Aging, 19,* 541–546.

Naveh-Benjamin, M., Hussain, Z., Guez, J., & Bar-On, M. (2003). Adult age differences in episodic memory: Further support for an associative-deficit hypothesis. *Journal of Experimental Psychology: Learning, Memory, and Cognition, 29,* 826–837.

Park, D. C., Lautenschlager, G., Hedden, T., Davidson, N. S., Smith, A. D., & Smith, P. K. (2002). Models of visuospatial and verbal memory across the adult life span. *Psychology and Aging, 17,* 299–320.

Park, D. C., Royal, D., Dudley, W., & Morrell, R. (1988). Forgetting of pictures over a long retention interval in young and older adults. *Psychology and Aging, 3,* 94–95.

Prull, M. W., Dawes, L. L. C., Martin, A. M., III, Rosenberg, H. F., & Light, L. L. (2006). Recollection and familiarity in recognition memory: Adult age differences and neuropsychological test correlates. *Psychology and Aging, 21,* 107–118.

Puglisi, J. T., Park, D. C., Smith, A. D., & Hill, G. W. (1985). Memory for two types of spatial location: Effects of instructions, age, and format. *American Journal of Psychology, 98,* 101–118.

Rahhal, T. A., Hasher, L., & Colcombe, S. J. (2001). Instructional manipulations and age differences in memory: Now you see them, now you don't. *Psychology and Aging, 16,* 697–706.

Roediger, H. L., III, & McDermott, K. B. (1995). Creating false memories: Remembering words not presented in lists. *Journal of Experimental Psychology: Learning, Memory, and Cognition, 21,* 803–814.

Rönnlund, M., Nyberg, L., Bäckman, L., & Nilsson, L.-G. (2005). Stability, growth, and decline in adult life span development of declarative memory: Cross-sectional and longitudinal data from a population-based study. *Psychology and Aging, 20,* 3–18.

Rybarczyk, B. D., Hart, R. P., & Harkins, S. W. (1987). Age and forgetting rate with pictorial stimuli. *Psychology and Aging, 2,* 404–406.

Salthouse, T. A. (1988). Resource-reduction interpretations of cognitive aging. *Developmental Review, 8,* 238–272.

Salthouse, T. A. (1996). The processing-speed theory of adult age differences in cognition. *Psychological Review, 103,* 403–428.

Salthouse, T. A., Berish, D. E., & Miles, J. D. (2002). The role of cognitive stimulation on the relations between age and cognitive functioning. *Psychology and Aging, 17,* 548–557.

Salthouse, T. A., Siedlecki, K. L., & Krueger, L. E. (2006). An individual differences analysis of memory control. *Journal of Memory and Language, 55,* 102–125.

Siedlecki, K. L., Salthouse, T. A., & Berish, D. E. (2005). Is there anything special about the aging of source memory? *Psychology and Aging, 20,* 19–32.

Simons, J. S., Dodson, C. S., Bell, D., & Schacter, D. L. (2004). Specific- and partial-source memory: Effects of aging. *Psychology and Aging, 19,* 689–694.

Small, G. W. (2002). What we need to know about age related memory loss. *British Medical Journal, 324,* 1502–1505.

Smith, R. E., Lozito, J. P., & Bayen, U. J. (2005). Adult age differences in distinctive processing: The modality effect on false recall. *Psychology and Aging, 20,* 486–492.

Spaniol, J., Madden, D. J., & Voss, A. (2006). A diffusion model analysis of adult age differences in episodic and semantic long-term memory retrieval. *Journal of Experimental Psychology: Learning, Memory, and Cognition, 32,* 101–117.

Spencer, W. D., & Raz, N. (1995). Differential effects of aging on memory for content and context: A meta-analysis. *Psychology and Aging, 10,* 527–539.

Squire, L. R. (1986, June 27). Mechanisms of memory. *Science, 232,* 1612–1619.

Toth, J. P., & Parks, C. M. (2006). Effects of age on estimated familiarity in the process dissociation procedure: The role of noncriterial recollection. *Memory & Cognition, 34,* 527–537.

Troyer, A. K., Häfliger, A., Cadieux, M. J., & Craik, F. I. M. (2006). Name and face learning in older adults: Effects of level of processing, self-generation, and intention to learn. *Journal of Gerontology: Psychological Sciences, 61B,* P67–P74.

Tulving, E. (1972). Episodic and semantic memory. In E. Tulving & W. Donaldson (Eds.), *Organization of memory* (pp. 381–403). Oxford, UK: Academic Press.

Verhaeghen, P., Marcoen, A., & Goossens, L. (1992). Improving memory performance in the aged through mnemonic training: A meta-analytic study. *Psychology and Aging, 7,* 242–251.

Verhaeghen, P., Marcoen, A., & Goossens, L. (1993). Facts and fiction about memory aging: A quantitative integration of research findings. *Journal of Gerontology: Psychological Sciences, 48,* P157–P171.

Verhaeghen, P., & Salthouse, T. A. (1997). Meta-analyses of age–cognition relations in adulthood: Estimates of linear and nonlinear age effects and structural models. *Psychological Bulletin, 122,* 231–249.

Watson, J. M., Balota, D. A., & Sergent-Marshall, S. D. (2001). Semantic, phonological, and hybrid veridical and false memories in healthy older adults and in individuals with dementia of the Alzheimer type. *Neuropsychology, 15,* 254–267.

Welford, A. T. (1980). Memory and age: A perspective view. In L. W. Poon, J. L. Fozard, L. Cermak,

D. Arenberg, & L. W. Thompson (Eds.), *New directions in memory and aging: Proceedings of the George A. Talland Memorial Conference* (pp. 1–17). Hillsdale, NJ: Lawrence Erlbaum.

Weuve, J., Kang, J. H., Manson, J. E., Breteler, M. M., Ware, J. H., & Grodstein, F. (2004). Physical activity, including walking, and cognitive function in older women. *Journal of the American Medical Association, 292,* 1454–1461.

Wheeler, M. A. (2000). A comparison of forgetting rates in older and younger adults. *Aging, Neuropsychology, and Cognition, 7,* 179–193.

Willander, J., & Larsson, M. (2006). Smell your way back to childhood: Autobiographical odor memory. *Psychonomic Bulletin & Review, 13,* 240–244.

Willis, S. L., & Schaie, K. W. (2005). Cognitive trajectories in midlife and cognitive functioning in old age. In S. L. Willis & M. Martin (Eds.), *Middle adulthood: A lifespan perspective* (pp. 243–275). Thousand Oaks, CA: Sage.

Yonelinas, A. P. (2002). The nature of recollection and familiarity: A review of 30 years of research. *Journal of Memory and Language, 46,* 441–517.

10

PROSPECTIVE MEMORY AND AGING

Old Issues and New Questions

MARK A. McDANIEL AND GILLES O. EINSTEIN

The topic of aging and cognition has been considered by scholars for the past 2,300 years, with most if not all approaches focused on noting and accounting for age-related decline in memory and cognitive function. Examples include Aristotle and Cicero from 1 to 300 BC, Tetens in the 18th century, and Angell and Miles in the early 20th century (see Surprenant, Bireta, & Farley, 2007, for an extended review). Until recently, however, aging researchers had not considered prospective memory. *Prospective memory* refers to remembering to execute an intended action at some appropriate moment in the future. This kind of memory task is ubiquitous in our everyday lives and none less so for older adults. Even minimal reflection underscores the importance of prospective memory tasks for maintaining the fabric of older adults' lives. These tasks range from remembering to send a grandchild or a friend a birthday card, to remembering to pay bills, to remembering to take medication (cf. McDaniel & Einstein, 2007a). Indeed, significant problems in remembering to carry out tasks such as paying bills and taking medication can threaten independent living.

Research on prospective memory and aging has been conducted only within the past 20 years, but already different theoretical approaches and apparently diverging empirical findings make it evident that prospective memory is a complex topic and that much remains to be learned. In this chapter, we summarize the current theoretical perspectives on prospective memory and aging, emphasize patterns of findings that are puzzling from these perspectives, and highlight challenges for future work. Along the way, we suggest possibly fruitful directions for cognitive aging research in prospective memory.

THEORETICAL PERSPECTIVES

In a seminal analysis, Craik (1986) noted that prospective memory involves not only remembering the intended action but also remembering to remember that action. So, for example, in a free-recall task, the experimenter at some point prompts you to begin recall. In the prospective memory task of remembering to give someone a

AUTHORS' NOTE: Preparation of this chapter was supported in part by National Institute of Aging Grant AG 17481 to Mark A. McDaniel. We thank Matthias Kliegel for his helpful comments on an earlier version of this chapter.

message, however, there is no one there to remind you to search memory when you encounter the person (target event). Consequently, Craik suggested that prospective memory requires more self-initiated retrieval than any retrospective memory task. According to the view that self-initiated retrieval processes decline with age, this perspective anticipates that prospective memory should be especially at risk for older adults. Echoing this theme, Smith (2003; see also Smith & Bayen, 2006) proposed that prospective memory retrieval requires preparatory attentional resources to evaluate the environment for the presence of signals indicating the moment to perform the intended action (for purposes of exposition, we refer to these attention demanding processes as *monitoring*). The idea here is that as a person moves from one event to the next (e.g., a trial in an experiment), he or she evaluates (either consciously or non-consciously) whether the event is the appropriate marker for initiating the intended action. As applied to aging, this view also anticipates age-related decline in prospective memory because of reduced attentional resources in older adults (Smith & Bayen).

A sharply divergent view was prompted by initial laboratory-based findings. Einstein and McDaniel (1990) developed a paradigm to study prospective memory and aging under carefully controlled laboratory situations. Our general approach was to parallel the typical everyday situation in which a person encodes an intention to perform an action at some point in the future, subsequent activity occupies the person's attention so that the prospective memory intention is no longer in awareness, and the person is busily engaged in ongoing activity at the point when the intended action must be executed. These elements were implemented in the laboratory paradigm by engaging participants in an ongoing activity (e.g., short-term recall of short lists of words). During the initial instructions the experimenter also asked the participants to perform a task (e.g., press a designated function key on the keyboard) if they should encounter a particular word in the short-term memory trials (e.g., *rake*). Another activity was interleaved between the prospective memory instruction and the main ongoing activity, and the experimenter made no further mention of the prospective

memory task throughout the experiment. To avoid the prospective memory task becoming a focus for the participant (again, paralleling many everyday prospective memory situations), the prospective memory cue word was presented only three times in the experiment. Additionally, in one condition participants were given materials to generate memory aids for themselves if they so elected.

Figure 10.1 shows the prospective memory responses for younger and older adults. In stark contrast to the view that aging should be accompanied by robust decrements in prospective memory, older adults performed just as well as younger adults. Was this sample of older adults an extremely high-functioning group in which memory decrements were spared? The answer is "no." On free-recall and recognition tasks these older participants performed significantly more poorly than the younger participants. Thus, this initial research suggested that prospective memory is "an exciting exception to typically found age-related decrements in memory" (Einstein & McDaniel, 1990, p. 724). As we shall see, the emerging picture is much more complex.

EVENT-BASED PROSPECTIVE MEMORY AND SPONTANEOUS RETRIEVAL

We (Einstein & McDaniel, 1990) suggested that prospective memory tasks vary in the degree of self-initiated retrieval required and accordingly will vary in the degree to which age-related declines are observed. In *time-based* prospective memory tasks, the appropriate moment for executing the prospective memory intention is a particular time of day (a doctor's appointment) or the passage of a particular amount of time (taking cookies out of the oven in 10 minutes). These tasks arguably have no concrete environmental cue (unless, of course, one sets a timer or uses some other external reminder) to signal the appropriateness of the intended action and consequently require high levels of self-initiated retrieval (e.g., for checking and being aware of time). Consistent with our analysis, time-based laboratory prospective memory tasks typically produce age-related deficits (see Henry, MacLeod, Phillips, & Crawford's, 2004, meta-analytic review).

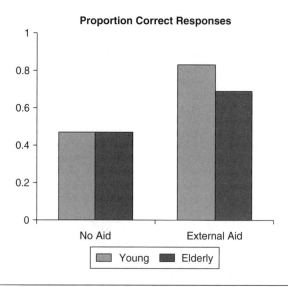

Figure 10.1   Mean Proportion of Correct Prospective Memory Responses in Einstein and McDaniel's (1990, Experiment 1) Study

In contrast, our (Einstein & McDaniel, 1990) finding of an absence of age differences was obtained with an *event-based* prospective memory task. Here, an environmental event serves as the memory cue that may prompt retrieval of the intended action. Examples are remembering to give a friend a message when you see her and remembering to buy bread when you pass the grocery store. We (Einstein & McDaniel, 1996; McDaniel & Einstein, 1993, 2000, 2007a, 2007c) have proposed that retrieval in these prospective-memory situations can be spontaneous, thereby requiring minimal self-initiated retrieval. By *spontaneous retrieval* we refer to conditions in which no attempt is made to voluntarily retrieve the intention at the moment that the target event occurs (i.e., no resources are devoted to preparing or monitoring for the prospective memory target) and yet the presence of a relevant cue triggers recollection of the intended action. We have sometimes in the past referred to this as *automatic* retrieval but we now prefer the more theoretically neutral term *spontaneous* retrieval (see McDaniel, Guynn, Einstein, & Breneiser, 2004, for a detailed discussion of processes that mediate spontaneous retrieval). This preference is based on our suspicion that spontaneous retrieval processes are relatively automatic but may require some resources for successful realization of the intention (cf. Einstein, Smith, McDaniel, &

Shaw, 1997; Kvavilashvili & Mandler, 2004; Mandler, 1994).

On the assumption that spontaneous retrieval processes are not at risk with age, older adults should not exhibit declines on these event-based prospective memory tasks. Subsequent conceptual replications of Einstein and McDaniel (1990) have borne out this expectation (Cherry & LeCompte, 1999; Einstein, Holland, McDaniel, & Guynn, 1992; Einstein, McDaniel, Richardson, Guynn, & Cunfer, 1995). Thus, the common assumption that prospective memory is especially problematic for older adults may not be uniformly true. Indeed, naturalistic-based studies of prospective memory and aging consistently do not find age differences or find that older adults show performance superior to that of younger adults (e.g., Devolder, Brigham, & Pressley, 1990; Moscovitch, 1982; Rendell & Thomson, 1999). Confirming this impression, Henry et al.'s (2004) meta-analysis reported that, for naturalistic studies, there is a significant positive relation between age and prospective memory performance.

However, there is a central puzzle that looms prominently and raises a critical issue for future work. A substantial number of laboratory studies of event-based prospective memory report significant age-related declines in prospective memory performance (e.g., d'Ydewalle, Luwel,

& Brunfaut, 1999; Maylor, 1996; Park, Hertzog, Kidder, Morrell, & Mayhorn, 1997). In their recent meta-analytic review, Henry et al. (2004) identified 48 laboratory event-based experiments, the sum of which showed a moderate-sized age decrement on these prospective memory tasks. Given the ubiquity of prospective memory tasks in everyday life, and an increasingly aging society, it is paramount to understand the reasons for opposing patterns of age-related deficits with many laboratory event-based tasks in contrast to spared age-related performance in other laboratory event-based tasks and when prospective memory is examined in more naturalistic contexts.

Initial explorations of prospective and aging have understandably been oriented toward documenting age-related changes in prospective memory. *Our first general recommendation for future work is that research designs and accompanying theoretical work expand toward the more complicated objective of specifying the conditions and reasons under which prospective memory does and does not decline with age.* We believe that several key themes may be fruitful in this regard: more refined theoretical analyses of prospective memory and its application to aging, increase in experimental paradigms that identify and directly manipulate variables that appear to be candidates for modulating age effects in prospective memory, development of laboratory-based paradigms that attempt to better mimic naturalistic contexts, and identification of individual differences in older adults that affect prospective memory. We illustrate these themes in turn with selected examples from very recent ongoing work.

NEW THEORETICAL ANALYSES

Approaches to prospective memory have embraced or proposed a single process or sequence of processes to account for how prospective memory retrieval is achieved. We think this kind of orientation fails to appreciate the importance of prospective memory to human behavior. Prospective memory demands are ubiquitous in everyday life. Also, because prospective memory is involved in planning and carrying out future actions, it is important for survival and for independent living. Our proposal is that the cognitive system exploits several cognitive processes for solving the prospective memory problem (i.e., remembering to perform an action at an appropriate moment in the future without an explicit request to remember). This multiprocess framework (see McDaniel & Einstein, 2000, 2007a, for a complete description of the framework and processes) assumes that there is a general bias to rely on spontaneous retrieval processes. However, people are likely to reinforce spontaneous retrieval processes with strategic monitoring under certain conditions (cf. Marsh, Hicks, & Watson, 2002).

It is even likely that a mix of strategies is used in remembering a single prospective memory task. For instance, consider the task of remembering to buy bread on the way home from work. Given the demanding dual-task nature of monitoring, it is likely that we do not rehearse or monitor this intention throughout the day but rather spontaneously retrieve it later in the day when we are driving home. At that point, given the brief delay between our retrieval and the presence of the supermarket, it may, depending on other factors, such as the importance of remembering the bread, be worthwhile to augment spontaneous retrieval processes with a monitoring process to help ensure retrieval. The idea is that prospective remembering is successful in a variety of situations by having a flexible system that relies on several cognitive processes.

As applied to aging, the multiprocess model anticipates that age-related changes in prospective memory will be a function of (a) how each of these several cognitive processes fare with age and (b) the conditions under which each of these processes are most prominent in supporting prospective memory. Specifically, we assume that spontaneous retrieval processes are relatively spared in normal aging, whereas strategic monitoring requires attentional resources that decline with age (Craik & Byrd, 1982). Before illustrating how this model lends understanding to aging and prospective memory, we remark on its more general implications.

Most if not all cognitive tasks of interest depend on a number of processes, with some of these processes likely declining with age and others being spared with age. Accordingly, *our second general challenge for future research on aging is to unravel the mix of cognitive processes that support particular cognitive tasks, with the objective of identifying those processes that are at risk with age and those processes that are spared.* In several arenas—language comprehension (e.g., Wingfield, 2005) and retrospective memory, to name just two—research is revealing that although age-related decline may be apparent, some underlying component processes are spared. The applied potential of this approach is enormous, because gerontologists can implement a dual-pronged approach to (1) pinpoint spared processes to help older adults retain function and increase success of rehabilitation and (2) target at-risk processes for training interventions (for further elaboration, see McDaniel, Einstein, & Jacoby, in press). We see great promise for work in this vein in which basic researchers collaborate with applied gerontologists and rehabilitation therapists to more successfully design interventions and engineer environments that articulate with spared cognitive processes (see chap. 35, this volume, for additional discussion). Next, we provide a concrete example in prospective memory and aging for the potential of such an approach.

FOCAL AND NONFOCAL PROSPECTIVE MEMORY CUES

One prediction of our multiprocess theory is that the nature of the target cue in event-based prospective memory influences the degree to which spontaneous retrieval and monitoring processes are involved in prospective remembering, which in turn influences the degree to which age-related declines will occur. We (McDaniel & Einstein, 2000) made a distinction between target cues that overlap with the information constellation relevant to performing the ongoing task in which a person is engaged (we label these *focal* cues) versus those cues that are present in the environment but not part of the information being considered by the person (labeled *nonfocal* cues). An example of a focal cue would be encountering and pausing to converse with the friend to whom you intend to give a message. An example of a nonfocal cue would be a grocery store (for buying bread) located a bit off the road when you are traveling in rush hour traffic (and

thus attending to the traffic; see Einstein & McDaniel, 2005, for other examples).

We further proposed that focal cues can stimulate a relatively automatic spontaneous retrieval of the intended action. On the basis of the assumption that spontaneous retrieval processes are preserved in older adults (e.g., Craik, 1986), we have suggested that older adults should show relatively intact remembering (compared with young adults) when the prospective memory task involves a focal event-based cue. Nonfocal cues, in contrast, require more strategic attentional resources to monitor for the cue signaling the appropriateness of performing the intended action. Thus, older adults should be challenged by nonfocal cues (because these cues place more demands on attentional resources—e.g., for monitoring for the cue—that presumably decline with age). Because of these resource challenges, age-related declines in prospective memory should be prevalent for nonfocal cues (see also Maylor, 1996).

The foregoing analysis is consistent with the literature. When focal cues are used, typically age differences in prospective memory are less pronounced and sometimes eliminated (Kliegel, Jäger, & Phillips, in press). For example, in Cherry and LeCompte's (1999) and Einstein and McDaniel's (1990) research, the target cue was the appearance of a particular word and the ongoing task was remembering a set of presented words (see also Einstein et al., 1995, Experiments 2 and 3). When nonfocal target cues are used, robust age differences are typically reported. For instance, Park et al. (1997) found age differences in a study in which the ongoing task involved remembering items, and the target cue was a particular background pattern on which the to-be-remembered items for the ongoing task were displayed. More directly, recent experiments have contrasted focal and nonfocal cues across younger and older adults, and the finding is that age-related declines are significantly more robust for nonfocal than for focal cues (Maylor, Darby, Logie, Della Sala, & Smith, 2002; Rendell, McDaniel, Forbes, & Einstein, 2007, Experiment 1).

It should be noted that the focal–nonfocal distinction is only one dimension that is important to determining whether people depend on spontaneous retrieval or monitoring in prospective memory situations. For example, research shows that people are less likely to rely on spontaneous retrieval processes with a large number (e.g., 6) of different target events (Einstein et al., 2005; Smith & Bayen, 2006) and when there is high emphasis on the prospective memory task (Einstein et al., 2005).

These basic findings lead to clear recommendations for enhancing prospective memory performance in older (and also younger) adults. In line with the orientation sketched above, one would want to find ways to increase the involvement of spontaneous retrieval processes in older adults' prospective memory tasks, processes that seem to be relatively spared in aging. Thus, event-based cues, especially focal cues, could be integrated into older adults' challenging prospective memory tasks, such as time-based prospective memory tasks. For instance, older adults might be advised to reconceptualize their time-based medication-taking prospective memory task into an event-based task that is signaled by a prominent daily event. To remember to take medication in the morning, one might think of taking the medication while drinking juice at breakfast (see McDaniel & Einstein, 2007b).

EMPHASIS ON EVERYDAY FUNCTIONING

The medication-taking example highlights our third general challenge for future research: Convene multidisciplinary workshops, and initiate interdisciplinary research centers and institutes targeted at central everyday challenges faced by older adults. The idea is to expand the perspectives of basic researchers, gerontologists, behavioral medicine specialists, human factors engineers, and technology experts and by so doing increase the fruitfulness of research and development efforts in aging. After attending a multidisciplinary workshop several years ago on medication adherence in older adults (see Park & Liu, 2007), we became more sensitive to the nuances of real world prospective memory demands and failures in this critically important domain. We also became more aware of developing technologies that might benefit older adults as well as pose new challenges.

These realizations ideally can help stimulate basic laboratory paradigms that are more representative of the parameters and processes involved in everyday functioning. As prospective memory

and aging research has steadily increased in popularity among students and memory researchers, new laboratory prospective memory paradigms are proliferating. Without thoughtful consideration of the everyday tasks researchers are trying to understand, we see a danger that some laboratory paradigms could potentially misdirect our energies to effects and processes that are unique to special characteristics of the laboratory task. For instance, some paradigms present relatively frequent prospective memory trials over the course of a 30- to 60-minute laboratory task. This kind of paradigm might allow efficient data collection procedures and more power to detect effects, but one can reasonably question whether the processes stimulated in this task accurately reflect the processes that underlie prospective memory tasks in the real world, tasks that aren't repeated a dozen times within an hour, and indeed may be performed only once (with the possible exception of habitual prospective memory tasks, which may be repeated but over the course of days and months, rather than minutes). So, a corollary of our third challenge, perhaps especially for future development of prospective memory research, is to develop paradigms that better capture the critical features of naturalistic tasks (e.g., Craik & Bialystok, 2006).

Thinking back to the workshop on medication adherence, in a similar vein we hope that applied psychologists and medical personnel attending the workshop better appreciated that prospective memory is not a single process that is invariably at risk in older adults but that certain aspects of prospective memory tasks are more problematic than other aspects for older adults. That is, the prospective memory aspect of medication adherence involves a number of components, and failure to remember to take medication might be due to any one of these components. Successful intervention depends on accurately identifying the causes of the prospective memory failure.

DELAYING EXECUTION OF RETRIEVED INTENTIONS

As just one example, consider that retrieval of the intention to take your medication may *not* be a relatively severe problem in the real world. Real world medication taking is often prompted by external support, such as calendars, pill-boxes, notes, physical signs from aches and pains, and the habitual nature of many medication-taking tasks. We have suggested that a more problematic aspect of remembering to take medication for older adults occurs after retrieval of the intention to take the medication (McDaniel & Einstein, 2007b). A typical feature of laboratory prospective memory paradigms, however, is that participants are asked to perform the action as soon as a target event occurs.

By contrast, in everyday life after retrieving an intention, we often have to delay the action until the conditions are appropriate for performing it. For instance, you might retrieve the intention to take your medication while in the kitchen (downstairs) but then have to delay its execution until you get to the bathroom where you keep your pills (upstairs). It may not be uncommon that in walking upstairs to the bathroom, you are interrupted by a telephone call, by the dog barking, or by a book sitting in the den that catches your attention (indeed, one senior psychologist shared with us just such an example of his or her own prospective memory failure). A story that recently was being passed over electronic mail suggests that for older adults, distraction can critically interfere with executing intended actions:

> This is how it goes: I decide to wash the car; I start toward the garage and notice the mail on the table. OK, I'm going to wash the car. But first, I'm going to go through the mail. I lay the keys down on the desk, discard the junk mail and I notice the trash can is full. OK, I will just put the bills on the desk and take the trash can out, but since I'm going to be near the mailbox anyway, I'll pay the bills first. Now where is my checkbook? Oops, there's only one check left. My extra checks are in my desk. Oh there is the Coke that I was drinking. I am going to look for those checks. But first I need to put my Coke further away from the computer, oh maybe I'll pop it into the fridge to keep it cold for a while. I head toward the kitchen and my flowers catch my eye, they need some water. I set the Coke on the counter and uh oh! There are my glasses. I was looking for them all morning! I better put them away first. End of day: The car isn't washed, the bills aren't paid, the Coke is sitting on the kitchen counter, the flowers are half-watered, and the checkbook still only has one check in it.

In light of these considerations, we recently developed a prospective memory task in which people had to briefly delay (5–30 seconds) the execution of the intended response after retrieving the intention (Einstein, McDaniel, Manzi, Cochran, & Baker, 2000; McDaniel, Einstein, Stout, & Morgan, 2003). Of interest for present purposes is whether this *delayed-execute* component of prospective remembering would show significant age-related declines. A priori, the outcome was uncertain. The delays were brief, and in some cases there was little activity filling the delays. Under these conditions, older adults might easily initiate rehearsal strategies to maintain the intended action in working memory. Alternatively, given age-related decrements in working memory (Park et al., 2002), it might be difficult for older adults to actively maintain an intention while also attending to demands of an ongoing task.

In brief, participants were engaged in comprehending three-sentence paragraphs, followed by a 10- to 30-second delay that was either filled with performing a synonym task or unfilled. Next, two unrelated trivia questions were presented, and then two multiple-choice comprehension questions about the preceding paragraph completed the trial. There were 20 of these trials (Figure 10.2 shows the flow of tasks in the paradigm from Einstein et al., 2000). After participants were instructed on these tasks, we told them that we had an additional interest in their ability to remember to perform an action in the future. They were told that whenever they saw the words *TECHNIQUE* or *SYSTEM,* they should press the F1 key on the keyboard, but not until they reached the trivia questions. The target words occurred on 8 of the 20 trials, and they were presented in the third sentence of a paragraph. Thus, participants had to delay execution of the intended action for 10 to 30 seconds until they reached the trivia questions. The idea here was to try to approximate the real world situation in which an intention is retrieved but its execution must be briefly delayed for one reason or another.

An important methodological point is that we purposely created distinctive target events: *TECHNIQUE* and *SYSTEM* were presented in capital letters, whereas the other words were in lowercase letters. We wanted to ensure that

Sequence of Events

1. Paragraph-comprehension task instructions

2. Prospective memory instructions: If *technique* or *system* in paragraph, then press "1" key but not until trivia phase

3. One practice trial of all tasks (in # 5 below), excluding prospective memory.

4. Mill Hill Vocabulary Test

5. Paragraph comprehension subsequence

    a. 3-sentence paragraph presented

    b. Synonym or Break period lasting either 5 or 15 s (1 synonym item for 5 s period; 3 synonym items for 15 s period)

    c. Two trivia questions for 10 s each

    d. Paragraph comprehension questions

6. Repeat the paragraph comprehension subsequence for 20 paragraphs

Figure 10.2   Structure of the Delayed-Execute Prospective Memory Paradigm

SOURCE: From "Aging and Maintaining Intentions Over Delays: Do It or Lose It," by M. A. McDaniel, G. O. Einstein, A. C. Stout, and Z. Morgan, 2003, *Psychology and Aging, 18,* p. 835. Copyright 2003 by the American Psychological Association. Reprinted with permission.

participants retrieved the intention. To verify this occurred, two immediate control groups (young and older) were asked to press the key immediately on seeing either of the two target events. Except for 1 older participant who failed to press the key on most trials, performance was nearly perfect for both younger and older participants (97% and 95% correct, respectively). Thus, participants were retrieving the intention to press the key when the target events occurred. The central question is, how successfully is this retrieved intention maintained over the brief delays?

Figure 10.3 shows the results reported by Einstein et al. (2000). Younger participants, regardless of the length of the delay or whether the delay was filled with activity (the synonym task), did very well on the delayed-execute task, remembering on about 82% of the trials. By contrast, older adults showed robust declines, with performance dropping to 47% relative to the 95% displayed when they could respond immediately. It is especially noteworthy that older adults performed poorly even in what would seem to be the easiest condition—a 10-second, unfilled delay.

McDaniel et al. (2003, Experiment 1) extended this result using 5-second delays. Reinforcing the finding that even with brief delays older adults are especially challenged by delaying execution of retrieved intentions, performance after a 5-second, unfilled delay was only 45%! (However, in a variant of this paradigm, Kliegel & Jäger [in press] observed this extremely low level of performance only for older adults in the 80- to 91-year-old range.)

As another example of the importance of identifying the components of prospective memory tasks that are most at risk from aging, consider a habitual prospective memory task in which the response needs to be performed repeatedly at regular intervals (as would be the case when taking medication on a daily basis over a period of weeks or months). When studying this type of prospective memory situation in the laboratory, we and our colleagues (Einstein, McDaniel, Smith, & Shaw, 1998) found that after several trials older adults did not have problems remembering to initiate actions at the appropriate times. Instead, the deficit for older adults emerged in remembering whether they had recently performed the action. Thus, older adults were much more likely to mistakenly repeat an action (i.e., the equivalent of repeating a dose in a medication situation) in this type of habitual prospective memory task (see Marsh, Hicks, Cook, & Mayhorn, 2007, for a similar finding using a different paradigm).

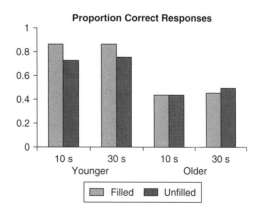

Figure 10.3   Mean Proportion of Correct Prospective Memory Responses in Einstein et al. (2000, Experiment 2)

To return to the main themes of this chapter, the just-summarized results underscore the importance of understanding the component processes of functional tasks (in this case, prospective memory), uncovering those component processes that are spared with aging (spontaneous retrieval of intentions with focal events), and identifying those that are dramatically at risk with aging (maintaining the intention over brief delays). Laboratory findings can accordingly highlight contexts of special challenge to older adults, thereby alerting gerontologists and practitioners to problematic situations for these adults. Moreover, development of these findings in an interdisciplinary context potentially promotes more refined understanding of age-related decline in everyday settings, better analysis of what aspects need to be targeted for intervention, and perhaps development of new technology. The potential fruitfulness of linking basic theory with interdisciplinary thrusts is more concretely illustrated in our final section.

PROSPECTIVE MEMORY IN PATHOLOGICAL AGING

Conversations with professionals in occupational therapy at Washington University have indicated that memory and cognitive difficulties sometimes outweigh physical difficulties in reducing quality of life for their patients. More specifically, with Parkinson's patients, caretakers express that prospective memory failures create frustrations and contribute to reduced quality of life. Yet there are no more than several published studies on prospective memory in Parkinson's patients. Given that Parkinson's is characterized by dopamine-related decline in frontal areas, and given a general assumption that prospective memory must be frontally mediated (presumably because prospective memory has been characterized as relying on strategic monitoring or self-initiation), the expectation by Parkinson's researchers is that Parkinson's patients should show prospective memory deficits (cf. Katai, Maruyama, & Ikeda, 2003).

By contrast, linking our multiprocess model to this issue suggests that Parkinson's patients may not be especially at risk for prospective

memory tasks that involve spontaneous retrieval. Such prospective memory tasks would include those with focal target events and for which the person has formed a good associative encoding between the target event and the intended action (McDaniel et al., 2004; see Kliegel, Phillips, Lemke, & Kopp, 2005, for evidence that Parkinson's disease may challenge encoding of the intention in some prospective memory situations). This expectation is based on the notion that spontaneous retrieval is supported by medial temporal structures, not frontal structures (Moscovitch, 1994). On the other hand, Parkinson's patients should be at risk for prospective memory tasks for which frontal systems are involved, such as time-based prospective memory tasks and event-based prospective memory tasks with nonfocal target events (but see Katai et al., 2003, for a different pattern). Laboratory paradigms that isolate effects of focal and nonfocal cues (e.g., Einstein et al., 2005, which was outlined earlier) can be applied to directly test these refined predictions. Erin Foster, a researcher in the occupational therapy program at Washington University, is conducting a study with Parkinson's patients along these lines. The results have potential to further inform theory, develop neuropsychological understanding of prospective memory, and more clearly illuminate prospective memory challenges for Parkinson's patients. Interventions then could better target the prospective memory tasks that particularly challenge Parkinson's patients and perhaps help individuals convert these tasks into focal event-based tasks that might be spared in Parkinson's disease.

As a final example, preliminary findings are suggesting that integrating prospective memory research (and, more generally, other cognitive processes) into behavioral genetics may provide dramatic advances. Several years ago, we became interested in the possible influence of the apolipoprotein E (APOE) gene on prospective memory. The presence of just one e4 allele of the APOE gene confers an estimated fourfold risk for developing Alzheimer's disease (AD), as well as earlier age of onset for AD (see Small, Rosnick, Fratiglioni, & Bäckman, 2004). One issue in this arena is the extent to which exaggerated memory decline might be evidenced in older APOE e4 carriers who as yet do not display

AD. Because of a favorable interdisciplinary atmosphere at the University of New Mexico medical school, we (Driscoll, McDaniel, & Guynn, 2005) were able to explore prospective memory performance in an ongoing study involving aging and nutritional issues, bone density, lipid functioning, and various genetic polymorphisms (including APOE). Existing work on memory impairment in nondemented APOE e4 carriers had found mixed results, with general trends suggesting limited e4-related impairments in episodic memory performance (small effect sizes) on standard episodic memory tasks such as recall and recognition (Small et al., 2004). Prospective memory tasks were noticeably missing from these experimental studies, however.

Driscoll et al. (2005) tested APOE e4 carriers and noncarriers on one of our standard event-based prospective memory tasks (e.g., McDaniel et al., 2004). The ongoing task was to rate characteristics of words on one of four dimensions (concreteness, pleasantness, meaningfulness, or vividness). The prospective memory task was to remember to write down a specified word if a particular target word appeared. To minimize the retrospective memory demands of this task (so that possible retrospective memory impairments would not cloud interpretation of the results), in some conditions the response word was highly associated with the target word. For example, the intended response for the target *spaghetti* was *sauce*, and the intended response for the target *steeple* was *church*. (Each participant was given only one target word, but four were used across participants for purposes of generality.) Postexperimental testing verified that 100% of the e4 carriers (and the noncarriers) remembered the intended response for the target word.

As expected on the basis of our previous findings with normally aging older adults and the multiprocess theory, the noncarriers displayed good prospective memory performance, with correct responding on 85% of trials (out of three trials). The APOE e4 carriers showed a dramatic divergence from this pattern. APOE e4 carriers remembered to respond on only 25% of the trials. Examination of individual performances confirmed the substantial decline in prospective memory for the carriers. Seventy percent of the carriers failed to respond on any of these prospective memory trials, whereas just

12% of the noncarriers failed to respond on any of the trials. These effect sizes were robust enough to be considered a large effect, in striking contrast to the small effect sizes reported when normally aging APOE e4 carriers are contrasted with noncarriers on other episodic memory tasks (Small et al., 2004).

Did the carriers tend to be individuals who were already in early stages of Alzheimer's disease? Perhaps (see, e.g., Duchek, Balota, & Cortese, 2006, for APOE e4 related declines in prospective memory that are associated with early stages of Alzheimer's disease) but, if so, then the prospective memory decline was the only behavioral marker we observed that showed a significant difference between the two groups of older adults. The groups did not significantly differ in performance on the modified Mini-Mental State Examination (Folstein, Folstein, & McHugh, 1975), the Fuld Object-Memory Evaluation (Fuld, 1977), Color Trails A and B (D'Elia, Satz, Uchiyama, & White, 1997), and the Clock Test (Tuokko, Hadjistavropoulos, Miller, Horton, & Beattie, 1992). Assuming these patterns are stable and replicable, and if the carriers were for the most part in an early stage of AD, then a simple laboratory prospective memory task could potentially become an important diagnostic marker for early detection of AD.

Perhaps, though, most of the individuals in the APOE e4 group were not in early stages of AD. If so, then prospective memory could turn out to be an easily obtained behavioral footprint of a genetic susceptibility to AD. In either case, prospective memory could potentially be a valuable cognitive marker that could allow earlier detection and treatment of genetically related decline in older adults. Certainly, the results suggest fruitful future directions.

Another provocative implication is that the prospective memory deficits reported above may reflect declines in spontaneous retrieval processes associated with APOE e4 (in contrast to the more strategically based prospective memory processes that might be deficient in Parkinson's patients). This idea is based on the observation that AD devastates medial–temporal systems, the very systems that are presumed to support spontaneous retrieval (Moscovitch, 1994). Moreover, the interventions indicated for a spontaneous retrieval deficit may focus more on retrieval-based processes rather than attentional processes. The spaced-retrieval technique developed by Camp and colleagues (Camp, Foss, Stevens, & O'Hanlon, 1996) that is successful with AD patients is one such example.

CONCLUSION

Prospective memory is self-initiated in the sense that one needs to remember to remember on her or his own. Unlike typically studied retrospective memory tasks such as cued recall, where the experimenter presents a cue along with an explicit request to remember, successful prospective memory requires that the occurrence of a target time or cue produces retrieval in the absence of an external request to remember. We believe that prospective memory retrieval can be accomplished through multiple processes, ranging from controlled monitoring of the environment for the target event to spontaneous retrieval for the intended action when encountering the appropriate target cue, and that different processes are prominent in different situations (see McDaniel & Einstein, 2007a, for details). Thus, to better understand the kinds of prospective memory tasks that are especially difficult for older adults and how to improve prospective remembering, we believe that it is critical to carefully analyze three things: (1) the component processes that are needed for successful prospective memory retrieval in different kinds of prospective memory tasks, (2) the extent to which aging compromises each of these processes and the willingness to use them, and (3) how various age-related disorders as well as genetic constitutions affect these processes. The existing literature is promising in suggesting spared component processes that can serve as the basis for successful interventions in older adults.

REFERENCES

Camp, C. J., Foss, J. W., Stevens, A. B., & O'Hanlon, A. M. (1996). Improving prospective memory task performance in persons with Alzheimer's disease. In M. Brandimonte, G. O. Einstein, & M. A. McDaniel (Eds.), *Prospective memory: Theory and applications* (pp. 351–367). Mahwah, NJ: Lawrence Erlbaum.

Cherry, K. E., & LeCompte, D. C. (1999). Age and individual differences influence prospective memory. *Psychology and Aging, 14,* 60–76.

Craik, F. I. M. (1986). A functional account of age differences in memory. In F. Klix & H. Hagendorf (Eds.), *Human memory and cognitive capabilities: Mechanisms and performances* (pp. 409–422). Amsterdam: Elsevier Science.

Craik, F. I. M., & Bialystok, E. (2006). Planning and task management in older adults: Cooking breakfast. *Memory & Cognition, 34,* 1236–1249.

Craik, F. I. M., & Byrd, M. (1982). Aging and cognitive deficits: The role of attentional resources. In F. I. M. Craik & S. Trehub (Eds.), *Advances in the study of communication and affect: Vol. 8. Aging and cognitive processes* (pp. 191–211). New York: Plenum.

D'Elia, L. F., Satz, P., Uchiyama, C. L., & White, T. (1997). *Color Trails Test Manual*. Odessa, FL: Psychological Assessment Resources.

Devolder, P. A., Brigham, M. C., & Pressley, M. (1990). Memory performance awareness in younger and older adults. *Psychology and Aging, 5,* 291–303.

Driscoll, I., McDaniel, M. A., & Guynn, M. J. (2005). Apolipoprotein E and prospective memory in normally aging adults. *Neuropsychology, 19,* 28–34.

Duchek, J. M., Balota, D. A., & Cortese, M. (2006). Prospective memory and apolipoprotein E in healthy aging and early stage Alzheimer's disease. *Neuropsychology, 20,* 633–644.

d'Ydewalle, G., Luwel, K., & Brunfaut, E. (1999). The importance of on-going concurrent activities as a function of age in time- and event-based prospective memory. *European Journal of Cognitive Psychology, 11,* 219–237.

Einstein, G. O., Holland, L. J., McDaniel, M. A., & Guynn, M. J. (1992). Age-related deficits in prospective memory: The influence of task complexity. *Psychology and Aging, 7,* 471–478.

Einstein, G. O., & McDaniel, M. A. (1990). Normal aging and prospective memory. *Journal of Experimental Psychology: Learning, Memory, and Cognition, 16,* 717–726.

Einstein, G. O., & McDaniel, M. A. (1996). Retrieval processes in prospective memory: Theoretical approaches and some new empirical findings. In M. Brandimonte, G. O. Einstein, & M. A. McDaniel (Eds.), *Prospective memory: Theory and applications* (pp. 115–141). Mahwah, NJ: Lawrence Erlbaum.

Einstein, G. O., & McDaniel, M. A. (2005). Prospective memory: Multiple retrieval processes. *Current Directions in Psychological Science, 14*, 286–290.

Einstein, G. O., McDaniel, M. A., Manzi, M., Cochran, B., & Baker, M. (2000). Prospective memory and aging: Forgetting intentions over short delays. *Psychology and Aging, 15*, 671–683.

Einstein, G. O., McDaniel, M. A., Richardson, S. L., Guynn, M. J., & Cunfer, A. R. (1995). Aging and prospective memory: Examining the influences of self-initiated retrieval processes. *Journal of Experimental Psychology: Learning, Memory, and Cognition, 21*, 996– 1007.

Einstein, G. O., McDaniel, M. A., Smith, R. E., & Shaw, P. (1998). Habitual prospective memory and aging: Remembering intentions and forgetting actions. *Psychological Sciences, 9*, 284–288.

Einstein, G. O., McDaniel, M. A., Thomas, R., Mayfield, S., Shank, H., Morrisette, N., & Breneiser, J. (2005). Multiple processes in prospective memory retrieval: Factors determining monitoring versus spontaneous retrieval. *Journal of Experimental Psychology: General, 134*, 327–342.

Einstein, G. O., Smith, R. E., McDaniel, M. A., & Shaw, P. (1997). Aging and prospective memory: The influence of increased task demands at encoding and retrieval. *Psychology and Aging, 12*, 479–488.

Folstein, M. F., Folstein, S. F., & McHugh, P. R. (1975). Mini-Mental State: A practical method for grading the cognitive state of patients for the clinician. *Journal of Psychiatric Research, 12*, 189–198.

Fuld, P. A. (1977). *Fuld Object-Memory Evaluation manual*. Wood Dale, IL: Stoelting.

Henry, J. D., MacLeod, M. S., Phillips, L. H., & Crawford, J. R. (2004). A meta-analytic review of prospective memory and aging. *Psychology and Aging, 19*, 27–39.

Katai, S., Maruyama, T., & Ikeda, S. (2003). Event based and time based prospective memory in Parkinson's disease. *Journal of Neurological and Neurosurgical Psychiatry, 74*, 704–709.

Kliegel, M., & Jäger, T. (in press). Delayed-execute prospective memory performance: The effects of age and working memory. *Developmental Neuropsychology*.

Kliegel, M., Jäger, T., & Phillips, L. H. (in press). Adult age differences in event-based prospective memory: A meta-analysis on the role of focal versus nonfocal cues. *Psychology and Aging*.

Kliegel, M., Phillips, L. H., Lemke, U., & Kopp, U. A. (2005). Planning and realisation of complex intentions in patients with Parkinson's disease. *Journal of Neurology, Neurosurgery, and Psychiatry, 76*, 1501–1505.

Kvavilashvili, L., & Mandler, G. (2004). Out of one's mind: A study of involuntary semantic memories. *Cognitive Psychology, 48*, 47–94.

Mandler, G. (1994). Hypermnesia, incubation, and mind popping: On remembering without really trying. In C. Umilta & M. Moscovitch (Eds.), *Attention and performance XV* (pp. 3–33). Cambridge, MA: MIT Press.

Marsh, R. L., Hicks, J. L., Cook, G. I., & Mayhorn, C. B. (2007). Comparing older and younger adults in an event-based prospective memory paradigm containing an output monitoring component. *Aging, Neuropsychology, and Cognition, 14*, 168–188.

Marsh, R. L., Hicks, J. L., & Watson, V. (2002). The dynamics of intention retrieval and coordination of action in event-based prospective memory. *Journal of Experimental Psychology: Learning, Memory, and Cognition, 28*, 652–660.

Maylor, E. A. (1996). Age-related impairment in an event-based prospective memory task. *Psychology and Aging, 11*, 74–78.

Maylor, E. A., Darby, R. J., Logie, R., Della Sala, S., & Smith, G. (2002). Prospective memory across the lifespan. In P. Graf & N. Ohta (Eds.), *Lifespan development of human memory* (pp. 235–256). Cambridge, MA: MIT Press.

McDaniel, M. A., & Einstein, G. O. (1993). The importance of cue familiarity and distinctiveness in prospective memory. *Memory, 1*, 23–41.

McDaniel, M. A., & Einstein, G. O. (2000). Strategic and automatic processes in prospective memory retrieval: A multiprocess framework. *Applied Cognitive Psychology, 14*, S127–S144.

McDaniel, M. A., & Einstein, G. O. (2007a). *Prospective memory: An overview and synthesis of an emerging field*. Thousand Oaks, CA: Sage.

McDaniel, M. A., & Einstein, G. O. (2007b). Prospective memory components most at risk for older adults and implications for medication adherence. In D. C. Park & L. Liu (Eds.), *Medical adherence and aging: Social and cognitive perspectives* (pp. 49–75). Washington, DC: American Psychological Association.

McDaniel, M. A., & Einstein, G. O. (2007c). Spontaneous retrieval in prospective memory. In J. Nairne (Ed.), *The foundations of remembering: Essays in honor of Henry L. Roediger III* (pp. 227–242). Hove, UK: Psychology Press.

McDaniel, M. A., Einstein, G. O., & Jacoby, L. L. (in press). New considerations in aging and memory: The glass may be half full. In F. Craik & T. Salthouse (Eds.), *The handbook of aging and cognition* (3rd ed.). Mahwah, NJ: Lawrence Erlbaum.

McDaniel, M. A., Einstein, G. O., Stout, A. C., & Morgan, Z. (2003). Aging and maintaining intentions over delays: Do it or lose it. *Psychology and Aging, 18,* 823–835.

McDaniel, M. A., Guynn, M. J., Einstein, G. O., & Breneiser, J. (2004). Cue-focused and reflexive-associative processes in prospective memory retrieval. *Journal of Experimental Psychology: Learning, Memory, and Cognition, 30,* 605–614.

Moscovitch, M. (1982). A neuropsychological approach to memory and perception in normal and pathological aging. In F. I. M. Craik & S. Trehub (Eds.), *Aging and cognitive processes* (pp. 55–78). New York: Plenum.

Moscovitch, M. (1994). Memory and working with memory: Evaluation of a component process model and comparisons with other models. In D. L. Schacter & E. Tulving (Eds.), *Memory Systems* (pp. 269–310). Cambridge: MIT Press.

Park, D. C., Hertzog, C., Kidder, D. P., Morell, R. W. & Mayhorn, C. B. (1997). Effect of age on event-based and time-based prospective memory. *Psychology and Aging, 12,* 314–327.

Park, D. C., Lautenschlager, G., Hedden, T., Davidson, N. S., Smith, A. D., & Smith, P. K. (2002). Models of visuospatial and verbal memory across the adult life span. *Psychology and Aging, 17,* 299–320.

Park, D. C., & Liu, L. (Eds.). (2007). *Medical adherence and aging: Social and cognitive perspectives.* Washington, DC: American Psychological Association.

Rendell, P. G., McDaniel, M. A., Forbes, R. D., & Einstein, G. O. (2007). Age-related effects in prospective memory are modulated by ongoing task complexity and relation to target cue. *Aging, Neuropsychology, and Cognition, 14,* 236–256.

Rendell, P. G., & Thompson, D. M. (1999). Aging and prospective memory: Differences between naturalistic and laboratory tasks. *Journal of Gerontology: Psychological Sciences, 54B,* P256–P269.

Small, B. J., Rosnick, C. B., Fratiglioni, L., & Bäckman, L. (2004). Apolipoprotein E and cognitive performance: A meta-analysis. *Psychology and Aging, 19,* 592–600.

Smith, R. E. (2003). The cost of remembering to remember in event-based prospective memory: Investigating the capacity demands of delayed intention performance. *Journal of Experimental Psychology: Learning, Memory, and Cognition, 29,* 347–361.

Smith, R. E., & Bayen, U. J. (2006). The source of adult age differences in event-based prospective memory: A multinomial modeling approach. *Journal of Experimental Psychology: Learning, Memory, and Cognition, 32,* 623–635.

Surprenant, A. M., Bireta, T. J., & Farley, L. A. (2007). A brief history of memory and aging. In J. S. Nairne (Ed.), *The foundations of remembering: Essays in honor of Henry L. Roediger III* (pp. 107–123). Hove, UK: Psychology Press.

Tuokko, H., Hadjistavropoulos, T., Miller, J. A., Horton, A., & Beattie, B. L. (1992). A sensitive measure to differentiate normal elderly from those with Alzheimer disease. *Journal of the American Geriatrics Society, 40,* 579–584.

Wingfield, A. (2005, April). *Spoken language comprehension in adult aging: How the bumble bee can fly.* Colloquium presented at Washington University, St. Louis, MO.

11

DIMENSIONS OF COGNITIVE AGING

Executive Function and Verbal Fluency

SUSAN KEMPER AND JOAN M. McDOWD

A persistent issue in cognitive aging is whether all aspects of cognition are equivalently affected by developmental processes or whether some are differentially spared from developmental decline (Zelinski & Lewis, 2003). This argument has been nowhere more contentious than in debates concerning the effects of aging and age-associated diseases such as Alzheimer's disease (AD) and Parkinson's disease (PD) on language use. Linguistic tasks are commonly used to assess cognitive status and neuropsychological impairments; they include tests of verbal fluency, vocabulary, and prose comprehension and recall. A related concern has been whether these tests measure discrete, autonomous linguistic abilities (Fodor, 1982; Waters & Caplan, 1996) or composite abilities that draw on multiple cognitive domains, including working memory and executive function (Just & Carpenter, 1992). In particular, impairments of executive function (EF)

have been implicated as contributing to a wide range of linguistic and cognitive abilities; for example, verbal fluency involves not only semantic knowledge of lexical items and the ability to search semantic memory using phonological or categorical rules but also "executive" skills required to track prior responses and block intrusions from other semantic categories. Complicating this question has been the problem of defining and measuring EF.

Measures of EF have proliferated over the past half-century. In their review of executive function, Royall et al. (2002, Table 11.3) listed 46 studies conducted between 1983 and 2001 that involve factor analyses of EF. These studies employed 34 different measures of EF and report factor structures ranging from one to four independent EF factors. This summary indicates that there is little consensus regarding appropriate measures of EF or about the underlying structure of EF. Some of this heterogeneity

AUTHORS' NOTE: We thank Laura Berman, Pat Laubinger, Kelly Lyons, Alicia MacKay, and Kim Metcalf for their assistance with data collection. This research was supported in part by grants from the National Institutes of Health to the University of Kansas through the Mental Retardation and Developmental Disabilities Research Center (Grant P30 HD-002528); and the Center for Biobehavioral Neurosciences in Communication Disorders (Grant P30 DC-005803); as well as by Grants RO1 AG06319, K04 AG000443, P30 AG10182, RO1 AG09952, RO1 AG18892, and RO1 AG025906 from the National Institute on Aging. Its contents are solely the responsibility of the authors and do not necessarily represent the official views of the National Institutes of Health.

comes from the use of different populations (e.g., people with schizophrenia, children, college students, older adults, individuals with AD) both within and between studies. For example, Kanne, Balota, and Storandt (1998) found that people with AD had a different EF factor structure than did the elderly control participants. In that study, the normal older adults showed a single-factor structure for EF, whereas the patients with AD showed a three-factor structure with mental control, verbal memory, and visuospatial factors. In contrast, a study involving only people with AD produced a single factor structure (Loewenstein et al., 2001). Likely relevant is the fact that Loewenstein et al. (2001) administered only three measures of EF, and Kanne et al. administered five; only two tasks overlapped in the two studies. A further contrast is provided by a study healthy aging adults by Royall, Chiodo, and Polk (2003); they reported a three-factor structure: (1) Procedural Control, (2) Abstraction, and (3) Attention Switching. Together, these studies point to important questions that remain to be answered: What is the cognitive structure underlying the construct of EF? Does the structure vary with age or clinical population? What are the best measures of EF?

Two recent studies highlight the continuing need to resolve these issues. Salthouse, Atkinson, and Berish (2003), noting the complexity and breadth of notions of EF, undertook an examination of the construct validity of EF in a sample of 261 adults ranging in age from 18 to 84 years. Their approach was to examine convergent and discriminant validity among a set of neuropsychological and cognitive tasks typically associated with EF and a set of psychometric tasks. The neuropsychological tasks in their battery included the Wisconsin Card Sorting Test; the Connections test (based on the Trail-Making Test), the Tower of Hanoi, verbal fluency, and figural fluency. Three additional sets of tasks designed to assess component (cognitive) processes of EF included measures of time sharing, updating, and inhibitory processes. Psychometric measures included indices of verbal ability, fluid intelligence, episodic memory, and perceptual speed. A series of structural equation analyses were then conducted to look at the relations among these sets of variables. Salthouse et al. identified verbal fluency as the

"best" neuropsychological measure of EF based on factor loadings and the Stroop task as the best measure of inhibition, a keeping track task as the best measure of updating, and a paired-associate learning task combined with keeping track task as the best measure of time sharing. However, their results indicated that the various neuropsychological measures were not very highly related to one another (i.e., had low convergent validity) and were fairly highly related to other variables, particularly fluid intelligence, indicating low discriminant validity. The same pattern of results was reported for the cognitive process variables: little convergent or discriminant validity for inhibition, updating, or time-sharing abilities. All were fairly highly correlated with fluid intelligence. The authors concluded that individual differences in measures of EF may in fact reflect differences in much broader abilities, such as fluid intelligence.

Miyake and colleagues (Friedman & Miyake, 2004; Miyake, Emerson, & Friedman, 2000; Miyake et al., 2000) have addressed similar questions but take a somewhat different approach and reach different conclusions. For example, Miyake, Friedman, et al. (2000) noted that descriptions of task requirements underlying the same EF measure may vary widely, and perhaps rightly so because such measures are typically complex and may require several cognitive processes to carry out successfully. At the same time, different EF measures may require different cognitive processes for good performance. To address these issues, Miyake, Friedman, et al. (2000) reported a study addressing "the unity and diversity of executive functions" (p. 49) using confirmatory factor analysis and structural equation modeling. Like the Salthouse et al. study, Miyake, Friedman, et al. identified a set of EF tasks used in neuropsychological studies: the Wisconsin Card Sorting Test, the Tower of Hanoi, a random number generation test, the operation span task, and a dual task. They also identified a set of tasks designed to measure three subtypes of EF: (1) shifting, (2) updating, and (3) inhibition. To address the question of unity and/or diversity of functions, they first conducted confirmatory factor analyses using data from 137 college students performing the EF subtype measures. They found that a three-factor solution fit the data better than any of the one- or two-factor solutions, indicating that there are separable dimensions of EF. They identified their letter memory and keeping track tasks as the best measure of updating, the plus/minus and number/letter tasks as the best measures of shifting, and the antisaccade and Stroop tasks as the best measures of inhibition. In addition to these analyses, Miyake, Friedman, et al. (2000) also tested a series of structural equation models to examine the contribution of these separable factors to the more complex neuropsychological EF tasks. Using structural equation modeling, they reported that the shifting factor is most relevant for Wisconsin Card Sorting Test performance, the inhibition factor is most relevant for the Tower of Hanoi, and that both inhibition and updating are relevant for the random number generation task. The authors concluded from this study that the three EF functions they measured (updating, shifting, and inhibition) are "clearly distinguishable" and that each plays a different role in more complex EF measures, such as the Wisconsin Card Sorting Test and the Tower of Hanoi.

Given these conflicting conclusions, there is a clear need to resolve this controversy regarding the structure of EF. Furthermore, neither of these studies directly addresses how aging affects EF, and they leave unresolved how best to assess EF in clinical populations. The Miyake, Friedman, et al. (2000) study involved only young adults, and the question remains whether the same pattern of results would be obtained with a sample of older adults. Indeed, in a partial replication of Miyake, Friedman, et al.'s study with adults 20 to 81 years of age, Fisk and Sharp (2004) found support for four factors: three corresponding to Miyake, Friedman, et al.'s updating, inhibition, and shifting components and a fourth, word fluency factor. Salthouse et al.'s (2003) study involved both young and old adults, but the age groups were not analyzed separately, and, based on the arguments of Hofer and Sliwinski (2001) and Hofer, Flaherty, and Hoffman (2007), there is some reason to predict that the pattern of results might be different for the two groups. Finally, neither study examined EF in clinical populations. We can only echo Rabbitt's (1997) lament: "Life would be simpler if there were generally agreed paradigmatic 'executive' tasks available for rigorous empirical analysis" (p. 8).

A second issue concerns the task impurity problem (e.g., Miyake, Friedman, et al., 2000). Many measures of EF are relatively complex, involve a variety of component processes that may or may not be part of EF, and are sometimes also used to assess other cognitive processes. One example of such a task is verbal fluency. Verbal fluency tasks, sometimes termed *generative naming*, typically require the person to generate as many words as possible meeting a criteria in a set amount of time. Many variations of the standard letter fluency task have been developed including generating words beginning with a target letter, words belonging to a semantic category, items occurring in a supermarket, and so on. Counts of valid responses and various types of errors (e.g., perseverations and intrusions) are typically assessed.

First introduced by Borkowski, Benton, and Spreen (1967) and Benton (1968), measures of verbal fluency are frequently part of batteries designed to assess EF in adults and children and diagnosis mild cognitive impairment and dementia due to AD, PD, HIV/AIDs, or other disorders; verbal fluency measures are also used to assess semantic memory or word knowledge and the impact of strokes and other closed head injuries, developmental disorders, and clinical conditions on semantic processes.

Verbal fluency was traditionally assumed to correspond to more general notions of discourse fluency, although there is no widely agreed-on definition or measure of discourse fluency. *Discourse fluency* is commonly assumed to involve word retrieval, sentence formulation, and articulation processes and to be subject to lapses of attention, memory limitations, and motor and articulatory control problems. Discourse is marked by many types of dysfluencies: interjections, filled and unfilled pauses, and sentence fragments. *Fillers*, defined as speech serving to fill gaps in the speech flow, include both lexical and nonlexical fillers. Fillers may serve pragmatic and discourse functions (Fox Tree, 1995) or reflect word finding problems or other breakdowns in semantic retrieval, syntactic planning, or sentence production. Nonlexical fillers, such as "uh," "umm," "duh," and so on, are also common (Bortfield, Leon, Bloom, Schober, & Brennan, 2000; Brennan & Schober, 2001; Ferber, 1991) and are generally considered to reflect problems in sentence and discourse planning.

Some forms of dysfluency, such as unfilled pauses; circumlocutions; "empty speech," such as pronouns lacking clear referents; and substitution errors (substituting *he* for *she*) during spontaneous speech have also been noted in older adults and may reflect age-related impairments in accessing and retrieving lexical information (Obler, 1980; Ulatowska, Cannito, Hayashi, & Fleming, 1985). Burke, Worthley, and Martin (1988) observed that word finding problems are common in the speech of older adults and often result in tip-of-the-tongue experiences. Burke and her colleagues (Burke & Laver, 1990; Burke, MacKay, Worthley, & Wade, 1991) suggest that aging affects the ability to retrieve complete phonological information about words, resulting in the retrieval of partial phonological information characteristic of tip-of-the-tongue experiences.

Kemper and Sumner (2001) compared measures of verbal ability, including initial letter and category fluency measures, obtained from a group of young adults, 18 to 27 years of age, and a group of older adults, 63 to 88 years of age. For older adults, Kemper and Sumner found that initial letter fluency and category fluency were related to other measures of processing efficiency, such as reading rate. Processing efficiency appeared to impose general limitations on task performance by older adults, affecting how efficiently they can search their mental lexicon for words with the appropriate initial letter and how efficiently they can search their memory for answers to comprehension questions. In contrast, young adults' performance on the fluency tasks appeared to be constrained by their knowledge of lexical items as measured by vocabulary tests. Hence, verbal fluency tasks may measure semantic knowledge in young adults but processing efficiency or EF in older adults.

Mayr and Kliegl (2000) recently developed an approach to disentangle the semantic and executive components of fluency performance. In their task, fluency performance is audio-recorded. Interword response intervals are computed and modeled as a function of retrieval position: $t_n = c + s \times n$, where t_n is the time between the recall of word $n - 1$ and word n, c is a constant representing EF, and s is the slope representing the time

increment with every additional word recalled. According to Mayr and Kliegl's reasoning, the constant (intercept) of this function represents executive functions that support or enable semantic retrieval processes—such as systematic searching and avoiding perseverations and noncategory intrusions. The slope parameter represents semantic retrieval processes.

They tested their view with a fluency task that included a manipulation of semantic retrieval difficulty by varying the frequency and familiarity of the categories and a manipulation of demands on EF by including both normal and "switching" versions of fluency tasks. This switching manipulation was motivated by a suggestion (Troyer, Moscovitch, & Winocur, 1997) that executive processes are particularly relevant in memory retrieval tasks that require switching between semantic clusters. Thus, participants were asked to produce category exemplars, either blocked by category in the typical way (e.g., animal, animal, animal, etc.) or alternating between two categories (e.g., animal, tool, animal, tool, animal, tool, etc.). They hypothesized that the category difficulty manipulation should affect the slope parameter, and the switching manipulations should affect the constant parameter. They also hypothesized that age differences in the constant parameter would indicate age differences in EF in fluency tasks, whereas age differences in the slope parameter would indicate age differences in semantic processes.

Mayr and Kliegl (2000) observed no age differences for the no-switch condition in the slope parameter, although the difficulty manipulation did affect slope as expected, but equally so for young and old adults. In contrast, there was a significant age difference in the constant parameter, assumed to reflect EF. "This pattern [supports] the assumption of no age effects in semantic processing (i.e., the slope parameter), but age sensitivity in non-semantic, executive processes" (Mayr & Kliegl, 2000, p. 36). These findings illustrate the importance of separating component processes in order to identify the ones underlying group differences in task performance. In the case of older adults in Mayr and Kliegl's study, EF appears to be responsible for the group differences in fluency performance.

It is interesting that the switch condition did not produce larger age differences in the constant parameter than the no-switch condition. Mayr and Kliegl (2000) concluded that EF impairment specific to switching is not the source of age differences in fluency performance. They suggested that updating and set maintenance may be more likely candidates for age-impaired EF functions.

In summary, Mayr and Kliegl's (2000) approach and findings illustrate two important points. First, there are significant interpretive problems when task components are poorly understood, and task performance could be affected by any of them. Second, separate analysis of task components is very useful in identifying specific deficits. In the case of normal aging, fluency task performance deficits appear to be due more to EF deficits than to semantic memory differences. A somewhat different approach to disentangling semantic function and EF in verbal fluency has been taken by Troyer and her colleagues (Troyer et al., 1997; Troyer, Moscovitch, Winocur, Alexander, & Suss, 1998; Troyer, Moscovitch, Winocur, Leach, & Freedman, 1998; but see Mayr, 2002; Troster et al., 1998).

To demonstrate the feasibility of Mayr and Kliegl's (2000) approach to the analysis of fluency tasks, we have conducted a series of small pilot studies using available participant pools from the Parkinson's Center and the Center for Brain Aging at the University of Kansas Medical Center. Our first study was a small pilot study with 10 healthy older adults (mean age: 73.4 years; mean education: 15.2 years) and 10 older adults with Parkinson's disease (mean age: 72.8 years; mean education: 16.1 years). All participants with PD were taking Carbidopa-Levodopa; all were 5 to 6 years postinitial diagnosis and had Hoehn and Yahr (1967) scores of 1 or 2. None of the participants had a history of heart disease, cancer, neurological disorders, or alcoholism. All were native speakers of English. None were taking anticholinergics, antidepressants, or anxiolytics. There were 7 women and 3 men in the group of healthy older adults and 6 women and 4 men in the group with PD.

All participants were given four versions of a category verbal fluency test, modeled after those of Mayr and Kliegl (2000). They were: (1) an easy version requiring participants to name exemplars of familiar categories (e.g., birds, clothes, body parts, and colors), (2) a hard version requiring

participants to name exemplars of unfamiliar categories (e.g., insects, writing utensils, fabrics, fluids), (3) an easy switching version requiring participants to name exemplars of two categories (e.g., birds alternating with body parts), and (4) a hard switching version requiring participants to name exemplars of two categories (e.g., writing utensils and fluids). Instructions and procedures followed those of Mayr and Kliegl with the exception that categories were presented on cue cards placed before the participants rather than on a computer monitor. All responses were digitally recorded for later analysis.

The results are summarized in Figures 11.1 and 11.2. The critical dependent measure is the interword response interval, timed from the offset of one response to the onset of the next response. Slopes and constant parameters from a linear regression analysis of these data are also presented.

Mayr and Kliegl (2000) argued that the slope of these functions represents semantic search; we found that the slopes increased with task difficulty and that the slopes were greater for the participants with PD than for the healthy older adults, suggesting that PD does affect the efficiency of semantic processing. Mayr and Kliegl also argued that the constants represent nonsemantic EF; our results show that the constants increased with task difficulty and were greater for the participants with PD than the group of healthy older adults, suggesting executive functions also contribute to group differences in fluency performance.

To further explore this approach, we conducted a second pilot study with 30 healthy older adults and 30 older adults with PD. This study was designed to test the validity of Mayr and Kliegl's (2000) interpretation of slope and constant parameters. In this pilot, we regressed the participants' slopes and constants from the category fluency tests onto measures of EF and verbal ability. The selection of tests was dictated by individuals currently assessed by the Parkinson's Center; they do not provide an ideal test of our hypotheses. We hypothesized that the constant parameter should be associated with EF; that is, participants who score poorly on EF tests should have higher constants, if the constants reflect executive function. From the tests available, we selected the Wisconsin Card

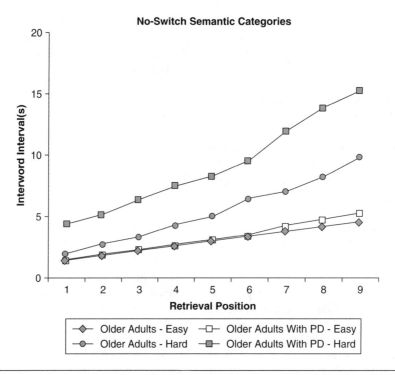

Figure 11.1   Interword Response Times for Easy and Hard Verbal Fluency Tests Administered to Healthy Older Adults and Older Adults With Parkinson's Disease: No-Switch Condition

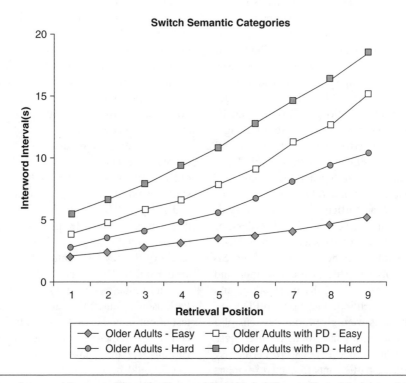

Figure 11.2   Interword Response Times for Easy and Hard Verbal Fluency Tests Administered to Healthy Older Adults and Older Adults With Parkinson's Disease: Switching Condition

Sorting test (Heaton et al., 1993) and the FAS fluency test (Spreen & Benton, 1977) as the measures of EF. In addition, the slope parameter might be expected to be related to vocabulary scores, which typically is indexed by verbal ability. Scores on the Shipley Institute of Living Scale vocabulary subtest (Shipley & Zachary, 1940), as well as years of formal education, were available for use as measures of verbal ability. In addition, a backward digit span test had been administered, and we considered this to be a measure of working memory. These hypotheses were tested in a group of 20 older adults and 8 older adults with PD. Mean performance levels on demographic, verbal ability, and EF variables are shown in Table 11.1.

Participants were tested on the easy and hard category fluency tests, described above, in both no-switching and switching conditions. The results are summarized in Table 11.2. Consistent with our previous findings, we found slope differences between easy and hard categories, reflecting ease of semantic retrieval; furthermore, slopes for healthy older adults were lower than those for individuals with PD, suggesting that PD does affect the efficiency of semantic retrieval.

We also found that the constants were greater for the switch conditions than for the no-switch conditions and greater for individuals with PD than for the healthy older adults, suggesting a breakdown of EF with PD.

We then defined a first-order factor for EF by loading scores for the FAS and Wisconsin Card Sorting tests onto a single factor. Two sets of regression analyses were then performed. In a test of our hypothesis that EF should be related to the constant parameter, we regressed the slopes and constants for the switching conditions onto the EF factor scores in Step 1 and then entered the verbal ability covariates (Shipley vocabulary score and years of education) in Step 2. In Step 3, we entered the working memory measure (backward digit span) and age.

The results are summarized in Table 11.3. The results of Step 1 indicate that individual variation in EF accounts for 6% to 18% (for healthy older adults) and 42% to 58% (for adults with PD) of the variance in the constants for the switching conditions but little ($< .01–.04$) of the variance in the slopes. Adding verbal ability to the regression models in Step 2 accounts for little additional variance in the constants (.02% – .05% increase in R^2) but adds to the prediction of individual variation in the slopes; verbal ability accounts for a 10% to 60% increase in R^2. Adding the remaining covariates in Step 3 provided no additional increase in the fit of the regression equations. We also reversed the order of entry, entering the verbal ability measures in Step 1 and the EF measures in Step 2, with similar results: The verbal ability measures accounted for 25% to 35% of the variance in the slopes for the switching trials in Step 1 but only

Table 11.1 Comparison of the Healthy Older Adults and Older Adults With Parkinson's Disease Who Participated in the First Pilot Study

	Healthy older adults		*Older adults with Parkinson's disease*	
	M	*SD*	*M*	*SD*
Variable				
Age	75.7	4.3	73.3	5.7
Education	17.2	3.2	14.6	2.3
Shipley Vocabulary	32.9	5.2	29.6	6.8
Backward digit span	6.9	2.1	7.0	1.2
FAS Verbal Fluency	36.4	14.5	38.2	12.8
Wisconsin Card Sorting				
Categories	2.5	1.5	1.3	1.5
Total errors	21.2	10.4	29.5	13.1

Table 11.2 Comparison of the Easy and Hard Verbal Fluency Tests Administered to Healthy Older Adults and Older Adults With Parkinson's Disease and Alzheimer's Disease

| | Slopes | | | | Constants | | | |
| | No switch | | Switch | | No switch | | Switch | |
	Easy	Hard	Easy	Hard	Easy	Hard	Easy	Hard
Participant								
Healthy older adults	0.69	1.95	0.43	1.36	−1.00	−0.16	0.46	0.74
Older adults with Parkinson's disease	1.16	2.39	0.17	2.56	−1.90	−0.41	0.43	2.74
Older adults with Alzheimer's disease	1.74	4.12	2.10	5.54	1.76	2.22	1.95	3.88

Table 11.3 Results of the Regression Analysis (Total R^2) of the Slopes and Constants Obtained From the Easy and Hard Switching Fluency Tests

| | Healthy older adults | | Older adults with Parkinson's disease | |
	Slope	Constant	Slope	Constant
Step				
Step 1: Executive function				
Easy categories	.06	.06	.02	.42
Hard categories	.14	.18	0.8	.58
Step 2: Verbal ability				
Easy categories	.27	.10	.03	.52
Hard categories	.41	.22	.13	.61

0% to 8% of the variance in the constants, and the EF measures accounted for 15% to 46% additional variance in the constants in Step 2 but only 2% to 5% additional variance in the slopes.

We also conducted a third pilot study with 8 AD patients recruited from the Brain Aging Center. All participants with AD were taking Aricept, and 5 of the 8 were also taking Nemenda; all were judged to have mild to moderate AD. None of the participants had a history of heart disease, cancer, other neurological disorders, or alcoholism. All were native speakers of English. None were taking anticholinergics, antidepressants, or anxiolytics. We administered the same easy and hard category fluency tests given in our second pilot study; however, we were constrained in our choice of covariates to those currently assessed by the Brain Aging Center. The Wisconsin Card Sorting task was not administered; however, the Trail Making Test (Reitan & Wolfson, 1995) was administered, so we used the proportional difference score (Test A – Test B/Test A) as a measure of EF ($M = -0.68$, $SD = 0.55$). The Boston Naming Test (Kaplan, Goodglass, & Weintraub, 2001; $M = 11.63$, $SD = 16.69$), rather than the Shipley vocabulary test, was available as a measure of verbal ability, along with education ($M = 17.4$, $SD = 3.2$). Backward digit span scores ($M = 5.4$, $SD = 1.5$) and age ($M = 76.0$, $SD = 6.7$), as well as an overall rating of dementia severity (Mini-Mental Status Examination [Folstein, Folstein, & McHugh, 1975]; $M = 24.5$, $SD = 5.3$) were also available and entered in Step 3.

The slopes and constants from the category fluency tests for the older adults with AD are also presented in Table 11.2. The slopes for older adults with AD were greater than those for healthy older adults as well as those for older adults with PD, confirming our hypothesis that AD affects the efficiency of semantic retrieval. We also found an effect of AD on the constants, indicating that AD also affects the efficiency of EF (see Ullman et al., 1997).

The results of the regression analysis are summarized in Table 11.4. In Step 1, we entered the EF measure, the proportional difference score from the Trail Making Test. In Step 2, we entered the verbal ability measures, the Boston Naming Test and education. In Step 3, we entered age, backward digit span, and Mini-Mental State Examination score. The results of Step 1 indicate that individual variation in EF accounts for much (48%–75%) of the variance in the constants for the switching conditions but less (24%–28%) of the variance in the slopes. Adding verbal ability to the regression models in Step 2 accounts for little additional variance in the constants but adds to the prediction of individual variation in the slopes; verbal ability accounts for a 10% to 60% increase in R^2. Adding the remaining covariates in Step 3 provided little additional increase in the fit of the regression equations. We also reversed

Table 11.4 Results of the Regression Analysis (Total R^2) of the Slopes and Constants Obtained From the Easy and Hard Switching Fluency Tests: Older Adults With Alzheimer's Disease

Step	*Slope*	*Constant*
Step 1: Executive function		
Easy categories	.28	.48
Hard categories	.24	.73
Step 2: Verbal ability		
Easy categories	.38	.59
Hard categories	.74	.75

the order of entry, entering the verbal ability measures in Step 1 and the EF measures in Step 2, with similar results: The verbal ability measures accounted for much (49%–74%) of the variance in the slopes for the switching trials in Step 1 but only 10% to 15% of the variance in the constants, and the EF measures accounted for 38% to 54% additional variance in the constants in Step 2 but only 3% to 16% additional variance in the slopes.

In comparing the results of our regression analysis of fluency task performance by individuals with AD and PD we note that the EF and verbal abilities covariates account for considerably more variance in the performance of the older adults with AD on the switch trials than for the older adults with PD. Much of the variance in the constants for the older adults with PD remains unexplained. It is likely that unmeasured variance in the severity of PD may contribute to the variance in the slopes on the switch trials.

Together, this series of pilot studies supports the validity of Mayr and Kliegl's (2000) analysis of the components of fluency tasks; although very preliminary, our findings indicate a dissociation of verbal and executive functions in fluency task performance in terms of their relation to the slope and intercept parameters derived from the fluency task data. In addition, these results show that this approach of decomposing EF tasks, in this case fluency tasks, can lead to a better understanding of the component cognitive processes that affect performance in those tasks. These results also demonstrate how this approach will advance our understanding of AD and PD by revealing how these age-associated diseases affect semantic processes and EF.

CONCLUSION

Decomposing fluency tasks into their component processes may provide an answer to Rabbitt's (1997) lament (see p. 183, this chapter): Life would be easier.

Life would be easier because verbal fluency tasks may be sensitive tests of EF for use in clinical contexts as well as for population-based assessments of cognition. Impairments of EF have been linked to functional impairments (Cahn-Weiner, Malloy, Boyle, Marran, & Salloway,

2000; Carlson et al., 1999; Farias, Harrell, Neumann, & Houtz, 2003; Grigsby, Kaye, Baxter, Shetterly, & Hamman, 1998; Royall, Palmer, Chiodo, & Polk, 2004), although the lack of an easily administered "gold standard" for EF has hindered research on this issue.

The traditional FAS verbal fluency test is commonly included with the Wisconsin Card Sorting Task and the Trail Making Test in neuropsychological test batteries. Although the Wisconsin Card Sorting Task has been used extensively, it is time consuming to administer and score, although computerized versions are available. The Trail Making Test is also widely used, and it is easily administered. However, both Wisconsin Card Sorting Task and Trail Making Test lack convergent and discriminant validity. No-switching and switching fluency tests could be easily automated using existing voice recognition techniques, making these tests suitable for administration in clinical settings using only an audio- or video-recorder. Our pilot studies suggest that the decomposition of interword response times, particularly on switching trials, may discriminate among the effects of aging, PD, and AD on semantic and executive processes.

Life would also be easier because this approach provides a significant guidepost to the future of cognitive aging studies. For far too long we have relied on cognitive and neuropsychological tests of dubious construct validity. We have failed to bring to bear the vast armature of contemporary cognitive psychology to the task of decomposing these tasks into their component processes. Parameterizing task performance—into slopes and intercepts, time–accuracy functions, Rasch scaling, or other techniques—will yield a new generation of tests that can provide insights into the differential effects of aging and clinical conditions; clarify neuroimaging findings regarding brain–behavior linkages; and advance our understanding of functional status, care needs, and rehabilitation outcomes.

Life would be easier because parameterized verbal fluency tests could add a new level of sophistication to large, population-based studies of health and cognition. Currently, cognition is assessed by tests such as immediate and delayed word recall, counting backward, identifying words from definitions, and subtracting 7s. Switching and no-switching fluency tests

coupled with the automated analysis of interword response times could help identify how population demographics and health status affect verbal/semantic processes versus EF. Indeed, automatic speech recognition could add a new dimension to existing test batteries by permitting automatic scoring of verbal responses as well as the measurement of response times. The Center for Spoken Language Understanding makes available a toolkit of techniques to map speech input onto text output. Using these techniques, it is possible to approximate human speech recognition under ideal circumstances with around 90% accuracy; higher rates of accuracy can be obtained by training the systems on the acoustic characteristics of individual speakers, groups of speakers (e.g., elderly speakers) or models of accented speech. Further accuracy can be gained by limited word or response sequences and lexical inventories and limited environmental or system noise. These techniques are now capable of running in real time on desktop computers. It is further possible to develop add-ons that measure pause duration and interword response times (Hosom, Shriberg, & Green, 2004). Tools such as the Coh-Mex system of Graesser, McNamara, Louwerse, and Chai (2004) are now available to perform extensive text-based analyses, statistical analyses of word frequencies, extract measures of coherence, syntactic complexity, and semantic content. These technologies are now available, and their application could open up new approaches to clinical and population-based assessments of health and cognition.

REFERENCES

Benton, A. L. (1968). Differential behavioral effects of frontal lobe disease. *Neuropsychologia, 6,* 53–60.

Borkowski, J., Benton, A., & Spreen, O. (1967). Word fluency and brain damage. *Neuropsychologia, 5,* 135–140.

Bortfield, H., Leon, S. D., Bloom, J. E., Schober, M. F., & Brennan, S. E. (2000). Disfluency rates in spontaneous speech: Effects of age, relationship, topic, role, and gender. *Memory and Language, 44,* 123–147.

Brennan, S. E., & Schober, M. F. (2001). How listeners compensate for disfluencies in spontaneous speech. *Memory and Language, 45,* 274–296.

Burke, D. M., & Laver, G. D. (1990). Aging and word retrieval: Selective age deficits in language. In

E. A. Lovelace (Ed.), *Aging and cognition: Mental processes, self-awareness, and interventions* (pp. 281–300). New York: Elsevier–North Holland.

Burke, D. M., MacKay, D. G., Worthley, J. S., & Wade, E. (1991). On the tip of the tongue: What causes word finding failures in young and older adults. *Journal of Memory and Language, 30,* 542–579.

Burke, D., Worthley, J., & Martin, J. (1988). I'll never forget what's-her-name: Aging and the tip of the tongue experience in everyday life. In M. M. Gruneberg, P. Morris, & R. N. Sykes (Eds.), *Practical aspects of memory: Current research and theory* (Vol. 2, pp. 113–118). Chichester, UK: Wiley.

Cahn-Weiner, D. A., Malloy, P. F., Boyle, P. A., Marran, M., & Salloway, S. (2000). Prediction of functional status from neuropsychological tests in community-dwelling elderly individuals. *The Clinical Neuropsychologist, 14,* 187–195.

Carlson, M., Fried, L., Xue, Q., Bandeen-Roche, K., Zeger, S., & Brandt, J. (1999). Association between executive attention and physical functioning performance in community-dwelling older women. *Journal of Gerontology: Social Sciences, 54B,* 262–270.

Farias, S., Harrell, E., Neumann, C., & Houtz, A. (2003). The relationship between neuropsychological performance and daily functioning in individuals with Alzheimer's disease: Ecological validity of neuropsychological tests. *Archives of Clinical Neuropsychology, 18,* 655–672.

Ferber, R. (1991). Slip of the tongue or slip of the ear? On the perception and transcription of naturalistic slips of the tongue. *Journal of Psycholinguistic Research, 20,* 105–122.

Fisk, J. E., & Sharp, C. A. (2004). Age-related impairment in executive functioning: Updating, inhibition, shifting, and access. *Journal of Clinical and Experimental Neuropsychology, 26,* 874–890.

Fodor, J. A. (1982). *Modularity of mind.* Cambridge: MIT Press.

Folstein, M. F., Folstein, S. E., & McHugh, P. R. (1975). *Mini-Mental State Examination.* Lutz, FL: Psychological Assessment Resources.

Fox Tree, J. E. (1995). The effects of false starts and repetitions on the processing of subsequent words in spontaneous speech. *Journal of Memory and Language, 34,* 709–738.

Friedman, N. P., & Miyake, A. (2004). The relations among inhibition and interference control functions: A latent-variable analysis. *Journal of Experimental Psychology: General, 133,* 101–135.

Graesser, A. C., McNamara, D. S., Louwerse, M. M., & Chai, Z. (2004). Coh-Metrix: Analysis of text cohesion and language. *Behavior Research Methods, Instruments, and Computers, 36,* 193–202.

Grigsby, J., Kaye, K., Baxter, J., Shetterly, S., & Hamman, R. (1998). Executive cognitive abilities and functional status among community-dwelling older persons in the San Luis Valley Health and Aging Study. *Journal of the American Geriatrics Society, 46,* 590–596.

Heaton, R. K., Chelune, G. J., Talley, J. L., Kay, G. G., & Curtis, G. (1993). *Wisconsin Card Sorting Test (WCST) manual, revised and expanded.* Odessa, FL: Psychological Assessment Resources.

Hoehn, M., & Yahr, M. (1967) Parkinsonism, onset, progression and mortality. *Neurology, 17,* 427–442.

Hofer, S. M., Flaherty, B. P., & Hoffman, L. A. (2007). Cross-sectional analysis of time-dependent data: Mean-induced association in age-heterogeneous samples and an alternative method based on sequential narrow age-cohort samples. *Multivariate Behavioral Research, 41,* 165–187.

Hofer, S. M., & Sliwinski, M. J. (2001). Understanding ageing: An evaluation of research designs for assessing the interdependence of ageing-related changes. *Gerontology, 47,* 341–352.

Hosom, J. P., Shriberg, L., & Green, J. R. (2004). Diagnostic assessment of childhood apraxia of speech using automatic speech recognition (ASR) methods. *Journal of Medical Speech-Language Pathology, 12,* 167–171.

Just, M. A., & Carpenter, P. A. (1992). A capacity theory of comprehension: Individual differences in working memory. *Psychological Review, 99,* 122–149.

Kanne, S. M., Balota, D. A., & Storandt, M. (1998). Relating anatomy to function in Alzheimer's disease: Neuropsychological profiles predicting regional neuropathology 5 years later. *Neurology, 50,* 979–985.

Kaplan, E. F. Goodglass, H., & Weintraub, S. (2001). *The Boston Naming Test* (2nd ed.). Philadelphia: Lippincott Williams, & Wilkins.

Kemper, S., & Sumner, A. (2001). The structure of verbal abilities in young and older adults. *Psychology and Aging, 16,* 312–322.

Loewenstein, D. A., Ownby, R., Schram, L., Acevedo, A., Rubert, M., & Argueelles, T. (2001). An evaluation of the NINCDA–ADRDA neuropsychological criteria for the assessment of Alzheimer's disease: A confirmatory factor analysis of single versus multi-factor models. *Journal of Clinical and Experimental Neuropsychology, 23,* 274–284.

Mayr, U. (2002). On the dissociation between clustering and switching in verbal fluency: Comment on Troyer, Moscovitch, Winocur, Alexander, and Stuss. *Neuropsychologia, 40,* 562–566.

Mayr, U., & Kliegl, R. (2000). Complex semantic processing in old age: Does it stay or does it go? *Psychology and Aging, 15,* 29–43.

Miyake, A., Emerson, M. J., & Friedman, N. P. (2000). Assessment of executive functions in clinical settings: Problems and recommendations. *Seminars in Speech and Language, 21,* 169–183.

Miyake, A., Friedman, N. P., Emerson, M. J., Witzki, A. H., Howerter, A., & Wager, T. D. (2000). The unity and diversity of executive functions and their contributions to complex "frontal lobe" tasks: A latent variable analysis. *Cognitive Psychology, 41,* 49–100.

Obler, L. K. (1980). Narrative discourse style in the elderly. In L. K. Obler & M. L. Albert (Eds.), *Language and communication in the elderly* (pp. 75–90). Lexington, MA: Heath.

Rabbitt, P. (1997) Introduction: Methodologies and models in the study of executive function. In P. Rabbitt (Ed.), *Methodology of frontal and executive function* (pp. 1–38). Hove, UK: Psychology Press.

Reitan, R. M., & Wolfson, D. (1995). Category Test and Trail Making Test as measures of frontal lobe functions. *Clinical Neuropsychologist, 9,* 50–56.

Royall, D. R., Chiodo, L. K., & Polk, M. J. (2003). Executive dyscontrol in normal aging: Normative data, factor structure, and clinical correlates. *Current Neurology and Neuroscience Reports, 3,* 487–493.

Royall, D. R., Lauterbach, E. C., Cummings, J. L., Reeve, A., Rummans, T. A., Kaufer, D. I., et al. (2002). Executive control function: A review of its promise and challenges for clinical research. *Journal of Neuropsychiatry and Clinical Neuroscience, 14,* 377–405.

Royall, D. R., Palmer, R., Chiodo, L., & Polk, M. (2004). Declining executive control in normal aging predicts change in functional status: The Freedom House study. *Journal of the American Geriatrics Society, 52,* 346–352.

Salthouse, T. A., Atkinson, T. M., & Berish, D. E. (2003). Executive functioning as a potential mediator of age-related cognitive decline in normal adults. *Journal of Experimental Psychology: General, 132,* 566–594.

Shipley, W. C., & Zachary, R. A. (1940). *Shipley Institute of Living Scale.* Los Angeles: Western Psychological Services.

Spreen, O., & Benton, A. L. (1977). *Neurosensory Center Comprehensive Examination for Aphasia.* Victoria, BC: Neuropsychology Laboratory, University of Victoria.

Troster, A., Fields, J. A., Testa, J. A., Paul, R. H., Blanko, C. R., Hames, K. A., et al. (1998). Cortical and subcortical influences on clustering and switching in the performance of verbal fluency tasks. *Neuropsychologia, 36,* 295–304.

Troyer, A. K., Moscovitch, M., & Winocur, G. (1997). Clustering and switching as two components of verbal fluency: Evidence from younger and older healthy adults. *Neuropsychology, 11,* 138–146.

Troyer, A. K., Moscovitch, M., Winocur, G., Alexander, M. P., & Suss, D. (1998). Clustering and switching on verbal fluency: The effects of focal, frontal- and temporal-lobe lesions. *Neuropsychologia, 36,* 499–504.

Troyer, A. K., Moscovitch, M., Winocur, G., Leach, L., & Freedman, M. (1998). Clustering and switching on verbal fluency tests in Alzheimer's and Parkinson's disease. *Journal of the International Neuropsychological Society, 4,* 137–143.

Ulatowska, H. K., Cannito, M. P., Hayashi, M. M., & Fleming, S. G. (1985). Language abilities in the elderly. In H. K. Ulatowska (Ed.), *The aging brain: Communication in the elderly* (pp. 125–139). San Diego, CA: College-Hill.

Ullman, M. T., Corkin, S., Coppola, M., Hickok, G., Growdon, J. H., Koroshetz, W. J., et al. (1997). A neural dissociation within language: Evidence that the mental dictionary is part of declarative memory, and that grammatical rules are processed by the procedural system. *Journal of Cognitive Neuroscience, 9,* 266–276.

Waters, G. S., & Caplan, D. (1996). The capacity theory of sentence comprehension: Critique of Just and Carpenter (1992). *Psychological Review, 103,* 761–772.

Zelinski, E. M., & Lewis, K. L. (2003). Adult age differences in multiple cognitive functions: Differentiation, dedifferentiation, or process-specific change? *Psychology and Aging, 18,* 727–745.

12

EXECUTIVE FUNCTION IN COGNITIVE, NEUROPSYCHOLOGICAL, AND CLINICAL AGING

MARY A. LUSZCZ AND ANNA P. LANE

Executive functioning (EF) has become an increasingly popular cognitive construct in its own right, and it is often invoked to understand and explain cognitive changes that accompany aging. It has been considered, along with speed, as a possible *cognitive primitive* that constitutes a basic change responsible for declines on a variety of tasks (see Luszcz & Bryan, 1999, and associated commentaries by Anstey, 1999; Salthouse, 1999; and Sliwinski & Hofer, 1999). Indeed, geropsychologists interested in both cognitive aging and the neuropsychology of aging have embraced the construct, and its use with older adults in clinical settings is increasing. Conceptualizations of EF within these specializations vary widely; in this chapter, we attempt to capture this diversity and elucidate the complexity of EF. However, it is not the intention to provide a comprehensive review of EF (others have already contributed to this effort, e.g., Rabbitt, 1997; chap. 11, this volume; and Daniels, Toth, and Jacoby, 2006, also complement information covered in this chapter); instead, we highlight some of the contrasting viewpoints and controversies surrounding EF. The innovative features of this chapter will be to give a flavor of the kind of research that may assist in resolving validity issues of the construct or addressing its capacity as a mediator of other cognitive activities and to capture the breadth of application of the construct.

We begin this chapter with a discussion of the *frontal hypothesis* of cognitive aging on which EF is framed and the varying disciplinary conceptualizations of EF, followed by some comments on how EF can be measured. We then turn our attention to empirical work on construct validity and mediation. Original empirical work from the Australian Longitudinal Study of Ageing (Luszcz, Bryan, & Kent, 1997) is presented, along with additional issues that pertain to the study of EF within individuals over time. Finally, some of its actual or potential clinical implications or applications are canvassed. We conclude the chapter by recapitulating the key challenges for future work.

The primary challenge for future research is to resolve the myriad theoretical and methodological dilemmas posed by EF as well as its role as an explanatory mechanism in cognitive aging. Depending on which portion of the growing literature one reads, EF could be the "all or the nothing" of cognitive aging.

FRONTAL HYPOTHESIS OF COGNITIVE AGING

Very generally, the frontal lobe hypothesis of cognitive aging states that cognitive functions supported by the frontal lobes—or, more specifically, the prefrontal cortex—are more susceptible (or susceptible at an earlier time) to the effects of aging than are functions that rely on other areas of the brain (Daigneault, Braun, & Whitaker, 1992; Dempster, 1992; Duncan, 2005; West, 1996). Furthermore, "decrements in frontally mediated executive control processes can account for many of the age-related [cognitive] changes observed" (Hogan, 2004, p. 98).

The frontal lobe hypothesis is founded on complementary, multidisciplinary sources of evidence. First, studies using brain imaging techniques have shown that the structure of the frontal lobes, compared with other areas of the brain, undergoes early and progressive change with advancing age (Albert & Kaplan, 1980; Raz, 2000). Similarly, neuropsychological studies have shown that older adults perform more poorly than younger adults on batteries of tests that were originally developed by neuropsychologists to detect frontal or *executive* dysfunction in clinical patients. Finally, there are parallels between the types of cognitive impairments found in healthy older adults and patients with frontal lobe damage (Moscovitch & Winocur, 1992; Perfect, 1997). Together these lines of reasoning concur with a model of cognitive aging that relates specifically to changes in the frontal lobe of the brain.

Both West (1996) and Hogan (2004) have pointed out, however, that a major theoretical shortcoming in the frontal lobe hypothesis is its failure to account for age-related erosion of memory. Hogan also pointed out that neurological models of cognitive aging must also be able to explain changes at a lower level in the information-processing system (e.g., speed of processing and variability). In a compelling review, he suggested the frontal lobe hypothesis must be augmented by consideration of the supportive role of the cerebellum. He emphasized that, apart from volumetric studies of the cerebellum aimed at assessing its early shrinkage, few studies have directly examined its role in age-related reductions in information-processing efficiency. Nonetheless, the cerebellum plays a central modulating role in sensorimotor and cognitive functions (see chap. 20, this volume, for more on the interplay of sensorimotor and cognitive aging), with projections to motor, language, and cognitive areas of the frontal lobe (Schmahmann, 1996; Schmahmann & Pandya, 1997). It also supports three fundamental components of information processing: (1) timing, (2) speed of processing, and (3) automaticity, suggesting that its functional role in cognitive aging warrants further investigation. Hence a further challenge for the future of cognitive aging is to pursue the fronto-cerebellar aging hypothesis with empirical research designed to demonstrate its contribution. Most crucial in this pursuit is determination of fronto-cerebellar involvement in elemental information-processing activities and the higher-order abilities they serve, particularly EFs.

INTERFACE OF COGNITIVE AND NEUROPSYCHOLOGICAL CONCEPTUALIZATIONS AND PERSPECTIVES OF EXECUTIVE FUNCTION

Defining Executive Function

The relatively recent application of EF to age-related cognitive decline emerged from the confluence of neuropsychology and cognitive aging (Daniels et al., 2006; Luszcz & Bryan, 1999). Although it is generally agreed that *executive functioning* broadly refers to the control of complex thought and the regulation of behavior, conceptualizations, and thus the use of the term *EF* by geropsychologists within and across these fields, varies widely. Next, we highlight some key distinctions within these fields before going on to examine how EF may be captured through traditional psychometric or purpose-designed tasks.

From a neuropsychological perspective, the focus is on *executive dysfunction*: impairment in behavior or cognitive performance that is a direct consequence of neurological damage to the frontal lobe. The neuropsychologist's fundamental task of formally capturing the behavioral features of executive dysfunction has proved difficult. With this problem in mind, Crawford and Henry (2005) provided a balanced and well-informed distillation of the utility of various instruments, their ecological validity, and psychometric properties. In a different vein, Burgess et al. (2006) articulated a compelling case for a next generation of ecologically valid neuropsychological tests of EF (e.g., the Multiple Errands or Six Elements test) that flow from function to construct, rather than the reverse, which characterizes the currently observed approach. Finally, Daniels et al. (2006) identified limitations with the tasks used and the issue of multiple EFs from the vantage point of both neuropsychology and cognitive psychology.

From a cognitive perspective, *executive function* refers to a range of mental processes associated with neurological integrity of the brain. These processes are of interest in their own right and in terms of the extent to which they could serve as mediators or links between aging and other aspects of cognition. Within the cognitive literature, most contemporary definitions of EF include three broad processes or mechanisms for controlling cognition, namely, (1) coordination and monitoring (or working memory), (2) inhibitory control, and (3) task switching (Verhaeghen & Cerella, 2002). Historically, the term can be linked to the basic distinction made decades ago by Atkinson and Shiffrin (1968) between *structural* and *control processes* in the memory system. More recently, Daniels et al. (2006) explicitly defined "*cognitive control* in the context of dual-processes theories as being coextensive with *executive processes*" (p. 100), a view at which the current authors independently arrived.

When viewed as a system of control processes, EF may be "responsible for planning, assembling, coordinating, sequencing, and monitoring other cognitive operations" (Salthouse, Atkinson, & Berish, 2003, p. 566). Others have added to the definition the coordination of complex goal-directed behavior (Royall et al., 2002) or have emphasized the (lapses of) intentionality

associated with executive control (West, Murphy, Armilio, Craik, & Stuss, 2002) or goal maintenance (Daniels et al., 2006). Verhaeghen's work (e.g., Verhaeghen & Cerella, 2002; chap. 8, this volume) also follows this tradition.

Baddeley's (2001) notion of a *central executive* within his working memory model also bears resemblance to EF and has possibly contributed to its adoption within neuropsychological studies of executive dysfunction. When invoked here, EF is characterized loosely as a collection of higher-order, strategic cognitive activity that controls and integrates other cognitive actions (Baddeley, 1990; Luria, 1973; Shallice, 1982; Temple, 1997) or functions that "allow people to plan and organize themselves over long periods of time; make complex high-level and abstract judgments; and organize and control their memory processes" (Burgess & Simons, 2005, p. 212).

It is clear from this small sample of definitions that use of the term *EF* is diverse and ranges from very micro-level, fractionated processes (see chap. 11, this volume) to a macro-level and homunculus-like regulator of cognition. As foreshadowed at the outset, the primary challenge for future research is to resolve, or progress, the conceptualization of EF. This is crucial to enhancing cohesion in the field and congruence in the nature of the entity being investigated in, assessed for, or applied to, older adults. Alternatively, because EF means many things to many people, it is important for those working in the area to specify their conceptualization of the construct and its operational definition. Problems with conceptualization are inextricably linked to the way EFs are measured or assessed, and indeed, the understanding of EFs has been obstructed by both conceptual and methodological issues. Some examples are presented in the next section.

Measuring (Assessing) Executive Functioning

A number of studies have directly investigated EF as a mechanism of cognitive aging. Accordingly, discussions about the exact nature of the EF construct and how best to assess it have maintained center stage in the cognitive aging literature (see, e.g., Bryan & Luszcz, 2000a; Daniels et al., 2006; Miyake, Friedman,

Emerson, Witzki, Howerter, & Wager, 2000; Phillips, 1997, 2005; Rabbitt, 1997).

Because of the association between EF and the frontal lobes, neuropsychological tests known to be sensitive to frontal lobe damage are commonly used to measure EF (e.g., Stroop, Wisconsin Card Sorting Test, verbal fluency tasks, variants of the Trail Making Test). However, as pointed out by Phillips (1997; see also Bryan & Luszcz, 2000a), tests are often deemed tests of EFs simply because they are sensitive to frontal lobe damage, not because they have been devised to assess the theoretical construct of EF (for a detailed discussion of the uncertain validity of executive tests, see Rabbitt, 1997).

Cognitive psychologists prototypically assess EF using tasks that require switching during the task (e.g., n-back tasks, antisaccade tasks, or choice reaction tasks with strings of digits or numbers). Verhaeghen and Cerella (2002) conducted a series of meta-analyses on aging, executive control, and attention. Global switching tasks and those that required multiple task sets to be held in memory (i.e., dual tasks) were most sensitive to aging effects. In chapter 8 of this volume, Verhaeghen describes in detail the nature of several of these tasks and how executive intervention may alter computational processes required for accurate performance.

A key difference in the tasks used by neuropsychologists compared with cognitive psychologists pertains to the level at which EF is operationalized (Daniels et al., 2006). Neuropsychologists, and much of the correlational research done by cognitive aging researchers, use psychometric tests that are likely to be multifaceted and hence driven by, or reliant on, multiple aspects of EF. Thus, they are assessing EF at a macro-level. Cognitive psychologists adopting experimental methods adopt a more fine-grained componential approach, studying EF at a more micro-level. In this case, the attempt is to identify the particular facet of EF that is operative or sensitive to aging, or likely to mediate relationships between aging and whatever aspect of cognitive function is under scrutiny. It is in this context that the issue of construct validity is of paramount importance.

A number of researchers have discussed the limitations to the *task-based approach* to assessing EFs (Burgess, 1997; Daniels et al., 2006; Phillips, 1997; Rabbitt, 1997). The two key problems espoused are (1) that executive tasks are not process pure in the sense that performance may be determined not only by the target executive process but also by nonexecutive processes, and (2) there is the possibility that performance on an executive task may reflect a multitude of executive processes. Miyake et al. (2000) sought to address these problems by using latent-variable techniques (which examine the relations between multiple tasks), whereas Daniels et al. (2006) reported convincing process-dissociation results that separate multiple executive and nonexecutive processes within a task before examining the relations of such processes to each other and to age. This micro-analytic approach has much to commend it, with its newest "I told you . . ." paradigm likely to lend theoretical traction and practical import to the study of EF.

In contrast, for the purposes of this chapter, we emphasize EF at a more macro-level. This not only complements information presented elsewhere and in this volume but also reflects a top-down approach that is in wide use in the field, often with little indication of an appreciation of the limitations of such an approach. In this context, the third challenge arises, namely, to determine what is unique about the EF construct in comparison to other cognitive ability constructs. This challenge and the controversy surrounding it are clearly at the forefront of contemporary research agendas of both experimentalists (e.g., Salthouse, 2005; Verhaeghen & Cerella, 2002) and clinicians (e.g., Burgess et al., 2006), and efforts to resolve it are likely to extend for a considerable period into the future.

THE UNIQUENESS OF THE EXECUTIVE FUNCTION CONSTRUCT

This conundrum pertains to the specificity or uniqueness of the EF construct relative to other cognitive abilities (Salthouse, 2005) and, from a neuropsychological perspective, the analogous notion of whether executive dysfunction constitutes a differential deficit relative to other cognitive abilities (Crawford, Bryan, Luszcz, Obonsawin, & Stewart, 2000).

Establishing the uniqueness of a construct (i.e., its construct validity) relies on assessment of both its convergent and discriminant validity.

In the case of convergent validity, we would expect to see moderate to strong correlations among various measures of EF. Discriminant validity, on the other hand, is observed when EF and measures of other cognitive constructs are virtually uncorrelated or when EF can predict a third variable, after taking into account (or removing the variance associated with) the other cognitive constructs. Little work has been done to examine the construct validity of EF. A major exception is the work of Salthouse and his colleagues (Salthouse, 2005, in press; Salthouse et al., 2003).

Salthouse (2005, in press) has theorized that if a variable truly represents the EF construct, and this construct is distinct from the other cognitive constructs, then the relationship between the constructs and the variable should be relatively small. In addition, that variable should have a significant direct relationship with age, if the frontal hypothesis of cognitive aging is to be supported. Using this rationale, Salthouse (2005) carefully examined the validity of various neuropsychological measures of EF (e.g., Wisconsin Card Sorting Test, verbal fluency tasks, a variant of the Trail Making Test) by examining the pattern of relationship with other established cognitive abilities (e.g., perceptual speed, reasoning, spatial visualization, episodic memory, and vocabulary), for adults spanning a wide age range (see also chap. 11, this volume, for a discussion of this issue).

Salthouse (2005) found that many of the hypothesized EF measures were strongly related to other cognitive abilities, especially perceptual speed abilities. Furthermore, he found that very few measures had any unique relations with age, after taking into consideration the relations of age through the cognitive abilities. In other words, most of the variance shared between the EF variables and age overlapped with the variance in other established cognitive abilities. This is not consistent with an argument that the EF variables represent a distinct construct. This reasoning led Salthouse to the conclusion that neuropsychological tests currently used to assess EF tap into the same dimensions of differences assessed by more traditional cognitive tests. These tests are essentially tests of fluid ability, which demonstrably have superior psychometric properties. His findings are consistent with others who have also purported that EF and "g" (i.e., general intelligence) is essentially the same construct (Duncan, 2005).

Other studies have also failed to find age-related effects on tasks purported to measure EF (e.g., Boone, Miller, Lesser, Hill, & D'Elia, 1990). Many studies have examined the extent to which age-related differences in EF explain age-related differences in cognitive performances (e.g., Bryan & Luszcz, 2000b; Bryan, Luszcz, & Pointer, 1999; Bunce & Macready, 2005; Crawford, Bryan, Luszcz, Obonsawin, & Stewart, 2000; Salthouse et al., 2003; Schretlen et al., 2000; Troyer, Graves, & Cullum, 1994). Although some positive results have been reported, observed effects often were eliminated when performance on perceptual speed or general ability tasks are taken into account (e.g., Bryan & Luszcz, 2000b; Parkin & Java, 1999). Studies showing a role for EF were often flawed by not also including other measures to exclude construct overlap with fluid ability or perceptual speed.

Weak construct validity (either discriminant or convergent) may be a key reason for this. At the least, the equivocal findings imply that it may be premature to assert that EF is a distinct cognitive phenomenon, highly sensitive to age differences or constituting a unique cognitive primitive to account for them. On the other hand, the equivocal findings, and lack of discriminant validity in particular, may also stem from either a mismatch between the criterion tasks and the elements of EF measured to predict them or a failure to measure other aspects of cognition that may influence both EF and outcome measures. Some of our work has attempted to address this possibility.

UTILITY OF EXECUTIVE FUNCTION FOR COGNITIVE AGING AND CLINICAL GEROPSYCHOLOGY

Executive Function as a Mediator of Memory Aging

As mentioned previously, myriad abilities are encompassed under the umbrella of EF. Theoretically, the successful performance on any cognitive task will be significantly influenced by those specific abilities of (executive) function on which the cognitive task depends. We have used mediational analyses to understand cognitive and noncognitive contributors to the relationship between aging and memory (e.g., Luszcz et al., 1997). More recently, our attention has turned to the extent to which the age–memory relationship can be (partially) explained by EF (e.g., Bryan & Luszcz, 2000b).

The essence of this macro-analytic approach (Bryan & Luszcz, 2000b; Luszcz & Bryan, 1999) has been to adopt as exemplars of EF, tests that tap into component processes of executive abilities thought to map onto processes purported to underlie the cognitive task in question. For instance, the "gold standard" frontal task of verbal fluency (Crawford & Henry, 2005; Crawford et al., 2000) relies at least in part on strategic retrieval search of a lexicon or semantic memory. Likewise, successfully completing an *incidental* recall memory task requires effortful retrieval strategies because, during encoding, memory has not been anticipated. In this example, both the EF task (verbal fluency) and the memory task (incidental recall) call on the same process (strategic retrieval search). Under these conditions, one might expect that because the component of EF that is most prominent in the verbal fluency task is functionally similar to the retrieval process on which incidental memory relies, EF might explain individual differences in incidental memory beyond that attributable to other cognitive abilities. Furthermore, if EF is particularly important in explaining memory aging, then it should also account for a significant portion of the variance in incidental memory. We now look in detail at some studies performed in our cognitive aging laboratory that have applied this logic.

Cross-Sectional Findings From the Australian Longitudinal Study of Ageing

Using data from the Australian Longitudinal Study of Ageing (Bryan & Luszcz, 2000b; Luszcz et al., 1997), we examined EF cross-sectionally as a mediator of incidental memory among a large population-based sample of community-dwelling older adults ($n = 565$) ranging from 75 to 92 years of age. We argued that strategic retrieval search is both the principal memory process thought to underlie successful incidental memory performance (recollection) and an EF that is reliably indexed by measures of fluency.

Three measures of fluency were used to predict incidental recall. The measures were initial letter (generate as many unique words beginning with, e.g., "f," in 60 seconds), excluded letter (generate as many unique words that do *not* contain, e.g., "a," in 60 seconds), and ideational fluency (Uses for Objects [Guilford, Christensen, Merrifield, & Wilson, 1978]: generate as many novel uses for, say, a brick, in 60 seconds). These three tasks have previously been shown by us to conform to a hierarchy of reliance on goal-directed strategic retrieval (see Bryan, Luszcz, & Crawford, 1997, for details).

In keeping with the logic of discriminant validity outlined above, if the executive decline hypothesis is to be upheld—that is, if fluency is to make a unique contribution to explaining age-related variance in incidental memory—it is essential to establish that measures of EF mediate the relationship between age and memory performance *after* controlling for general cognitive ability or tasks that tap other cognitive functions. Hence, other variables included in multiple regression analyses were perceptual speed (Digit Symbol Subscale from Wechsler, 1977), because of its status as a cognitive primitive and its strong mediational role in memory aging, and verbal knowledge (National Adult Reading Test; Crawford & Henry, 2005), to take into account the reliance of fluency tasks on the internal lexicon and/or semantic memory (Bryan et al., 1997).

Initial results showed that fluency measures accounted for age-related variance in incidental recall. However, further analyses in which we added speed and verbal knowledge prior to entry of the EF measures showed that not only did speed emerge as the best predictor of incidental memory but also that initial- and excluded-letter fluency no longer were significant. Nonetheless, ideational fluency continued to account for age-related variance in recall. The latter result is consistent with the idea that ideational fluency is the most reliant on strategic retrieval of the three fluency tasks. It may also be that emphasis on the element of novelty in the retrieval required of EF tasks (Uses for Objects and excluded letter) plays an important role in memory, particularly when it is a by-product of other processing requirements.

In summary, these initial cross-sectional results show mixed support for EF as indexed by fluency as a mediator of incidental recall memory in adults over age 70 years. It has to be recognized that these results are essentially correlational, because all cognitive measures were gathered on the same occasion. Another limitation of this report is the failure to include a measure of fluid ability among the cognitive covariates. If included, it may have absorbed the 3% of age-related variance associated with the ideational fluency task and again cast doubt on the frontal hypothesis of cognitive aging. Finally, there is the possibility that cognitive processes accounting for variance associated with age at one point in time may not capture the developmental dynamics of change over time.

Longitudinal Findings From the Australian Longitudinal Study of Ageing

Given the equivocal support for the primary hypotheses and other limitations of the cross-sectional study (Bryan & Luszcz, 2000b), data presented in this chapter provide the first prospective study of the unique contribution of fluency as a predictor of change in memory over a 6-year period. Behavioral data again come from the population-based sample of the Australian Longitudinal Study of Ageing (n = 349), measured on two occasions, 6 years apart (1994: mean age = 80, SD = 6.5; 2000: mean age = 84, SD = 5.6; range: 72–101). Measures of EF included the same three variants of fluency tasks and composite incidental immediate word and symbol recall; speed was again indexed by the digit symbol task. Measures of fluid ability (similarities) and crystallized ability (vocabulary) were added. Noncognitive contextual variables with possible confounding effects on memory change included depression (Center for Epidemiologic Studies Depression scale; Radloff, 1977), gender, and self-rated health. To facilitate comparison of results with those of Bryan and Luszcz (2000b), multiple regression analyses were again employed. The results are shown in Tables 12.1 to 12.4.

The first set of analyses (see Tables 12.1 and 12.2) were designed to assess age-related variance in memory change over the 6 years by first entering recall at Time 1 (Recall W3) and then age at time of testing. Although initial recall accounted for a significant 26% of the variance

in Time 2 recall, there was no age-related variance in memory change in this sample of very old adults. This is problematic for identifying EF as crucial to mediating age-related variance in the change in incidental memory over 6 years. However, this finding does not preclude further examination of the question of the discriminant validity, that is, the extent to which EF (fluency) independently contributes to individual differences in memory change per se. The second set of analyses examined this question.

Table 12.3 shows significant results for all models. A total of 41% of the variance was explained by depression, gender, speed, and excluded-letter fluency. There was no significant change in R^2 for the model (Model 4) in which fluid and crystallized intelligence were entered or the one in which age was entered (Model 6). Table 12.4 reveals perceptual speed as the strongest contributor, followed by excluded-letter fluency. Note that the failure of the fluid ability measure to contribute to memory performance casts doubt on its equivalence to EF. This calls into question claims that nothing is to be gained from assessing EF that cannot be derived from assessing fluid ability. It must be borne in mind, however, that, as with EF, this is only one marker of fluid ability, and it may not adequately assess this domain. Nonetheless, finding that EF contributes to memory performance, after taking into account baseline performance and processing efficiency, lends some support to the discriminant validity of the EF construct as a mediator of memory change.

We also found that being female and having relatively few depressive symptoms were associated with less change in memory over 6 years. This finding illustrates the importance of taking into account noncognitive factors that have been related to memory performance.

Taken together, these two studies from the Australian Longitudinal Study of Ageing provide some evidence in favor of EF as a mediator of memory and memory change in late life. The absence of a significant component of age-related variance in memory change leaves open the aspect of the frontal hypothesis of cognitive aging that suggests that EF has a crucial role to play in explaining aging of other cognitive activities, in this case, remembering. Alternatively, it may be that the age range of the cohort under

Table 12.1 Summary of Multiple Regression Model Examining Age-Related Variance in Memory Change Over 6 Years

Model and Variables Entered	R	R^2	Adj R^2	SE	Change Startistics				Model ANOVA	
					R^2 Change	F Change	df	p	F Overall	p
1 Recall T1	.512	.262	.260	3.417	.262	122.281	1,344	.000	122.28	.000
2 (1) + Age	.515	.265	.261	3.416	.003	1.259	1,343	.263	61.81	.000

NOTE: Adj = adjusted; ANOVA = analysis of variance; T1 = Time 1.

Table 12.2 Unstandardized and Standardized Coefficients for Multiple Regression Model Examining Age-Related Variance in Memory Change Over 6 Years

Model		Unstandardized Coefficients		Standardized Coefficients			Correlations		
		B	SE	β	t	p	Zero-Order	Partial	Part
1	(Constant)	5.350	.617		8.669	.000			
	Recall T1	.558	.051	.512	11.058	.000	.512	.512	.512
2	(Constant)	8.853	3.182		2.782	.006			
	Recall T1	.538	.054	.494	10.040	.000	.512	.477	.465
	Age	−.039	.035	−.055	−1.122	.263	−.221	−.060	−.052

NOTE: T1 = Time 1.

Table 12.3 Summary of Multiple Regression Model Examining Variance in Memory Change Over 6 Years Explained by All Variables

Model	R	R^2	Adj R^2	SE	Change Statistics				Model ANOVA	
					R^2 Change	F Change	df	p	F Overall	p
1 Recall T1	.512	.262	.260	3.417	.262	120.148	1,338	.000	120.148	.000
2 (1) + CES–D, Sex, SRH	.543	.295	.287	3.355	.033	5.177	3,335	.002	35.033	.000
3 (2) + Speed	.626	.392	.383	3.121	.097	53.220	1,334	.000	43.039	.000
4 (3) + Gc, Gf	.629	.396	.383	3.120	.004	1.059	2,332	.348	31.055	.000
5 (4) + ILF, Uses, ELF	.651	.423	.406	3.062	.028	5.268	3,329	.001	24.157	.000
6 (5) + Age	.653	.426	.407	3.060	.003	1.476	1,328	.225	22.127	.000

NOTE: Adj = adjusted, ANOVA = analysis of variance, T1 = Time 1, SRH = self-rated health, CES–D = Center for Epidemiologic Studies Depression scale, Gc = Crystallized Ability (Definitions), Gf = Fluid Ability (Similarities), ILF = Initial Letter Fluency, Uses = Uses for Objects, ELF = Excluded Letter Fluency.

Table 12.4   Unstandardized and Standardized Coefficients for Multiple Regression Model Variance in Memory Change Over 6 Years Explained by All Variables

Model	Unstandardized Coefficients		Standardized Coefficients			Correlations		
	B	*SE*	*β*	*t*	*p*	*Zero-Order*	*Partial*	*Part*
1 Predictor (Constant)	−1.055	3.531		−.315	.753			
Recall T1	.491	.056	.450	8.689	.000	.512	.433	.363
2 Sex	.810	.342	.102	2.367	.019	.181	.130	.099
SRH	−.180	.178	−.047	−1.010	.313	.086	−.056	−.042
CESD	−.083	.028	−.139	−2.936	.004	−.143	−.160	−.123
3 Speed	.155	.020	.406	7.847	.000	.488	.398	.328
4 Similarities	.327	.229	.064	1.430	.154	.244	.079	.060
Definitions	.072	.133	.025	.542	.588	.192	.030	.023
5 Initial Fluency	.014	.030	.026	.477	.634	.215	.026	.020
Excluded Fluency	−.125	.037	−.194	−3.387	.001	.204	−.184	−.142
Uses for Objects	−.044	.051	−.044	−.872	.384	.233	−.048	−.036
6 Age	.042	.034	.059	1.215	.225	−.221	.067	.051

NOTE: SRH = self-rated health, CES–D = Center for Epidemiologic Studies Depression scale.

investigation was too narrow to identify age-related variance. However, if EF reputedly comes into its own as a marker or mediator of cognitive change in late life, then one could argue that a 30-year range at this time of life should provide ample scope for capturing age-related variance and hence the capacity to identify mediators of this source of variation. Future longitudinal research is required that covers a wider age range of older adulthood and examines a broader range of EF and memory tasks.

Methodological Considerations for Measuring EF Longitudinally

Examining the role of EF in memory change introduces a range of additional methodological issues regarding the most appropriate EF tasks to include. It was argued that one criterion for selecting tasks is that the mediating EF task and the criterion memory task rely on analogous subcomponents of EF (Luszcz & Bryan, 1999). The goals of the research and the specific research question being addressed will dictate

selection of EF tasks in practice, so it is not possible to recommend a single EF task or even a small subset of EF tasks that are optimal for detecting age-related change in them or the extent to which they may mediate age-related change in memory. We have previously made recommendations for EF tasks most likely to detect the relatively mild executive dysfunction in subcomponents or processes of EF that occurs with normal aging (Bryan & Luszcz, 2000a). For repeated assessments of memory it is also important to keep in mind the importance of the element of novelty inherent in many definitions of EF. For this reason, paradigms such as those introduced by Daniels et al. (2006) may be well suited to longitudinal research. The excluded-letter fluency task used in our research is also a strong contender, both because of its demonstrated efficacy in detecting differential performance and vis à vis its face validity stemming from a long history of using fluency measures for neuropsychological assessment of frontal lobe damage. A final suggestion is alternating versions of the Connections Test

(Salthouse et al., 2000) developed as a variant of the Trail Making Test. These tasks lend themselves to alternative forms, so that, on the one hand, performance over time can be compared, but on the other hand, an element of novelty is retained in the specific version of the task used.

This brings us to a consideration of ways in which EF is currently being invoked and implemented within clinical geropsychology. Function-led tasks being developed in this area (Burgess et al., 2006) may also be well suited to longitudinal studies of EF.

Executive Function as an Element of Clinical Practice in Geropsychology

To reiterate, notions of EF have been embraced not only within cognitive aging but also within neuropsychology, clinical psychology, and cognitive and behavioral rehabilitation programs involving older adults. Hence, the final area we cover in this chapter highlights clinical applications of EF.

EF has been examined extensively as a mediator of functional outcomes in clinical settings (e.g., Allen, Jain, Ragab, & Malik, 2003; Bell-McGinty, Podell, Franzen, Baird, & Williams, 2002; Cahn-Weiner, Boyle, & Malloy, 2002; Insel, Morrow, Brewer, & Figueredo, 2006; Mohlman & Gorman, 2005; Nathan, Wilkinson, Stammers, & Low, 2001; Rapp & Reischies, 2005; Royall, Palmer, Chiodo, & Polk, 2004), particularly in relation to depression (Channon & Green, 1999). We discuss a few of these studies in detail to give a flavor of this research and to illustrate the potential utility of the EF construct for applied work.

Insel et al. (2006) investigated the efficacy of EF and working memory as predictors of medication adherence over an 8-week period among a sample of 95 community-dwelling older adults (mean age = 78). The theoretical rationale behind the study was that "because taking medicines consistently involves developing and implementing a plan to adhere; remembering to adhere . . . ; and remembering whether the medicine was taken as desired" (p. 102), adhering to medicines should evoke the recruitment of processes subsumed under the construct of EF.

A simultaneous regression analysis showed that a composite measure of EF and working memory emerged as the only significant predictor of medication adherence ($\beta = .44$). After controlling for age, score on the Mini-Mental State Examination (which has been construed as a crude index of fluid ability; Hill & Bäckman, 1995), education, illness severity, financial well-being, and depression, the EF/working memory score explained an additional 9% of the variance in medical adherence. Insel et al. (2006) concluded that valid and reliable measures of self-care capacity must include tests of EF. However, because the significant measure was a *composite* of EF and working memory, it is not clear that this conclusion is warranted. It may have been the working memory component that was driving the effect observed.

Mohlman and Gorman (2005) examined the role of EF as a potential mediator of cognitive–behavioral therapy (CBT) outcomes in a pilot study with 32 anxious older adults (mean age = 68, $SD = 5.6$). They argued that CBT success is dependent on cognitive abilities that can be subsumed under the EF construct (e.g., self-monitoring, attention, problem solving). Hence, treatment success theoretically should be dependent in part on EF. Their results indicated that some, but not all, older adults with executive dysfunction showed decreased benefit from CBT, leading them to conclude that "CBT may not be an effective anxiety treatment for a subset of older adults" (Mohlman & Gorman, 2005, p. 461).

Royall et al. (2004) assessed the relationship between EF, as measured by the Executive Interview (EXIT25)[1] and functional status, as indexed by instrumental activities of daily living (IADL). The study used data from 547 retirees (mean age = 80, $SD = 5$, at baseline) from the Freedom House Study, living in noninstitutionalized levels of care. Participants were evaluated at three separate points over 3 years. Their results show that the rate of change in EXIT25 was strongly correlated with change in IADL ($r = -.57$) and remained significant after adjusting for baseline EXIT25 scores, IADL, age, comorbid disease, and level of care. Hence, Royall et al. (2004) concluded that EF is a "significant and independent correlate of functional status in normal aging" (p. 346).

These three articles are illustrative only. They demonstrate the heuristic and potential practical value of EF for understanding functioning and well-being in late life. Nonetheless, the same problems with construct validity, nomenclature, and choice of tasks apply here as in the cognitive and neuropsychological literature.

Burgess et al. (2006) recently developed a case that challenges the utility of the construct–driven approach characteristic of experimental neuropsychology (e.g. Salthouse, 2005; Salthouse et al., 2003) when developing measures of EF. They purported that many of the widely used tests of EF (e.g., Wisconsin Card Sorting Test, Stroop) are adaptations of outdated conceptual and experimental frameworks, which may be less than optimal for clinical purposes. They advocated instead an approach that is "function led" and better reflects the interaction between an individual and the situational context in which demands are made on EF. Theirs is an interesting approach that may foreshadow the next generation of EF tasks that are more ecologically valid and explicitly address clinical needs. The Multiple Errands (e.g., Knight, Alderman, & Burgess, 2002) and Six Element (Emslie, Wilson, Burden, Nimmo-Smith, & Wilson, 2003) tests are provided as examples.

CONCLUSION

The frontal hypothesis of cognitive aging and the related construct of EF provide a neurobiological basis for understanding or explaining age-related cognitive declines or clinical dysfunction in late life. The primary challenge in this area is better specification of the conceptual, definitional, and methodological approach adopted by researchers. At the neuroanotomical level, there is a challenge to determine fronto-cerebellar involvement in elemental information-processing activities and the higher-order abilities they serve, particularly EFs. Interrelated challenges pertain to what is unique about the EF construct in comparison to other cognitive ability constructs and how to distinguish its constituent components. The work of Daniels et al. (2006) and Kemper and McDowd (chap. 11, this volume) is particularly relevant here. Burgess et al.'s (2006) function-led approach to task development also shows promise, especially in pursuit of specifying ways in which EF can assist in understanding normative cognitive aging as well as amelioration of clinical conditions.

A novel feature of this chapter is an attempt to capture the penetration of the concept of EF not only in cognitive aging but also in the neuropsychology and clinical psychology of aging. Variants on the challenges outlined above confront each of these areas, and there is much to be gained from deliberate cross-fertilization of these intradisciplinary fields of geropsychology.

A substantial amount of further theoretical and empirical development will be required before a consensus can be achieved in resolving these challenges. It is clear from the extant and emerging body of work on this construct that it will remain on the future research agendas of clinical and experimental geropsychologists and neuropsychologists and provide a dynamic field of inquiry for many years to come. Controversy and heuristic appeal bode well for extending the longevity of this aspect of cognitive aging.

NOTE

1. The EXIT25 (Royall et al., 1992) provides a standardized clinical assessment of executive control. Items assess clinical signs associated with frontal dysfunction.

REFERENCES

Albert, M. S., & Kaplan, E. (1980). Organic implications of neuropsychological deficits in the elderly. In L. W. Poon, L. S. Fozard, L. S. Cermak, D. Arenberg, & L. W. Thompson (Eds.), *New directions in memory and aging: Proceedings of the George A. Talland Memorial Conference* (pp. 403–432). Hillsdale, NJ: Lawrence Erlbaum.

Allen, S. C., Jain, M., Ragab, S., & Malik, N. (2003). Acquisition and short-term retention of inhaler techniques require intact executive function in elderly subjects. *Age and Ageing, 32,* 299–302.

Anstey, K. (1999). Construct overlap in resource theories of memory aging: Commentary. *Gerontology, 45,* 348–350.

Atkinson, R. C., & Shiffrin, R. M. (1968). Human memory: A proposed system and its control processes. In K. Spence & J. Spence (Eds.), *The psychology of learning and motivation* (Vol. 2, pp. 89–195). New York: Academic Press.

Baddeley, A. D. (1990). *Human memory: Theory and practice*. London: Lawrence Erlbaum.

Baddeley, A. D. (2001). Is working memory still working? *American Psychologist, 56,* 851–864.

Bell-McGinty, S., Podell, K., Franzen, M., Baird, A. D., & Williams, M. J. (2002). Standard measures of executive function in predicting instrumental activities of daily living in older adults. *International Journal of Geriatric Psychiatry, 17,* 828–834.

Boone, K. B., Miller, B. L., Lesser, I. M., Hill, E., & D'Elia, L. (1990). Performance on frontal lobe tests in healthy older adults. *Developmental Neuropsychology, 6,* 215–223.

Bryan, J., & Luszcz, M .A. (2000a). Measurement of executive function: Considerations for detecting adult age differences. *Journal of Clinical and Experimental Neuropsychology, 22,* 40–55.

Bryan, J., & Luszcz, M. A. (2000b). Measures of fluency as predictors of incidental memory among older adults. *Psychology and Aging, 15,* 483–489.

Bryan, J., Luszcz, M. A., & Crawford, J. R. (1997). Verbal knowledge and speed of information processing as mediators of age differences in verbal fluency performance among older adults. *Psychology and Aging, 12,* 473–478.

Bryan, J., Luszcz, M. A., & Pointer, S. (1999). Executive function and processing resources as predictors of adult age differences in the implementation of encoding strategies. *Aging, Neuropsychology, and Cognition, 6,* 273–287.

Bunce, D., & Macready, A. (2005). Processing speed, executive function, and age differences in remembering and knowing. *Quarterly Journal of Experimental Psychology: Section A, 58,* 155–168.

Burgess, P. W. (1997). Theory and methodology in executive function. In P. Rabbitt (Ed.), *Methodology of frontal and executive function* (pp. 81–116). Hove, UK: Psychology Press.

Burgess, P. W., Alderman, N., Forbes, C., Costello, A., Coates, L. M-A., Dawson, D. R., et al. (2006). The case for the development and use of "ecologically valid" measures of executive function in experimental and clinical neuropsychology. *Journal of the International Neuropsychological Society, 12,* 194–209.

Burgess, P. W., & Simons, J. S. (2005). Theories of frontal lobe executive function: Clinical applications. In P. W. Halligan & D. T. Wade (Eds.), *Effectiveness of rehabilitation for cognitive deficits* (pp. 211–232). Oxford, UK: Oxford University Press.

Cahn-Weiner, D. A., Boyle, P. A., & Malloy, P. F. (2002). Tests of executive function predict instrumental activities of daily living in community-dwelling older individuals. *Applied Neuropsychology, 9,* 187–191.

Channon, S., & Green, P. S. S. (1999). Executive function in depression: The role of performance strategies in aiding depressed and non-depressed participants. *Journal of Neurology, Neurosurgery and Psychiatry, 66,* 162–171.

Crawford, J. R., Bryan, J., Luszcz, M. A., Obonsawin, M. C., & Stewart, L. (2000). Executive decline hypothesis of cognitive aging: Do executive deficits qualify as differential deficits and do they mediate age-related memory decline? *Aging, Neuropsychology, and Cognition, 7,* 9–31.

Crawford, J., & Henry, J. (2005). Assessment of executive dysfunction. In P. W. Halligan & D. T. Wade (Eds.), *Effectiveness of rehabilitation for cognitive deficits* (pp. 233–245). Oxford, UK: Oxford University Press.

Daigneault, S., Braun, M. J., & Whitaker, H. A. (1992). Early effects of normal aging on perseverative and non-perseverative prefrontal measures. *Developmental Neuropsychology, 8,* 99–114.

Daniels, K., Toth, J., & Jacoby, L. (2006). The aging of executive functions. In E. Bialystock & F. I. M. Craik (Eds.), *Lifespan cognition: Mechanisms of change* (pp. 96–111). New York: Oxford University Press.

Dempster, F. N. (1992). The rise and fall of the inhibitory mechanism: Toward a unified theory of cognitive development and aging. *Developmental Review, 12,* 45–75.

Duncan, J. (2005). Frontal lobe function and general intelligence: Why it matters. *Cortex, 41,* 215–217.

Emslie, H., Wilson, F. C., Burden, V., Nimmo-Smith, I., & Wilson, B. A. (2003). *Behavioural Assessment of the Dysexecutive Syndrome in Children (BADS-C).* London: Harcourt Assessment.

Guilford, J. P., Christensen, P. R., Merrifield, P. R., & Wilson, R. C. (1978). *Alternate Uses: Manual of instructions and interpretation.* Orange, CA: Sheridan Psychological Services.

Hill, R. D., & Bäckman, L. (1995). The relationship between the Mini-Mental State Examination and cognitive functioning in normal elderly adults: A componential analysis. *Age and Ageing, 24,* 440–446.

Hogan, M. J. (2004). The cerebellum in thought and action: A fronto-cerebellar aging hypothesis. *New Ideas in Psychology, 22,* 97–125.

Insel, K., Morrow, D., Brewer, B., & Figueredo, A. (2006). Executive function, working memory, and medication adherence among older adults. *Journals of Journals of Gerontology: Series B: Psychological Sciences and Social Sciences, 61,* P102–P107.

Luria, A. R. (1973). *The working brain.* New York: Basic Books.

Luszcz, M. A., & Bryan, J. (1999). Towards an understanding of age-related memory loss in late adulthood. *Gerontology, 45,* 2–9.

Luszcz, M. A., Bryan, J., & Kent, P. (1997). Predicting episodic memory performance of very old men and women: Contributions from age, depression, activity, cognitive ability, and speed. *Psychology and Aging, 12,* 340–351.

Knight, C., Alderman, N., & Burgess, P. W. (2002). Development of a simplified version of the Multiple Errands Test for use in hospital settings. *Neuropsychological Rehabilitation, 12,* 231–255.

Miyake, A., Friedman, N. P., Emerson, M. J., Witzkik, A. H., Howerter, A., & Wager, T. D. (2000). The unity and diversity of executive functions and their contributions to complex "frontal lobe" tasks: A latent variable analysis. *Cognitive Psychology, 41,* 49–100.

Mohlman, J., & Gorman, J. M. (2005). The role of executive functioning in CBT: A pilot study with anxious older adults. *Behaviour Research and Therapy, 43,* 447–465.

Moscovitch, M., & Winocur, G. (1992). The neuropsychology of memory and aging. In F. I. M. Craik & T. A. Salthouse (Eds.), *The handbook of aging and cognition* (pp. 315–372). Hillsdale, NJ: Lawrence Erlbaum.

Nathan, J., Wilkinson, D., Stammers, S., & Low, J. L. (2001). Role of tests of frontal executive function in the detection of mild dementia. *International Journal of Geriatric Psychiatry, 16,* 18–26.

Parkin, A. J., & Java, R. I. (1999). Deterioration of frontal lobe function in normal aging: Influences of fluid intelligence versus perceptual speed. *Neuropsychology, 13,* 539–545.

Perfect, T. J. (1997). Memory aging as frontal lobe dysfunction. In M. A. Conway (Ed.), *Cognitive models of memory* (pp. 315–339). Cambridge, MA: MIT Press.

Phillips, L. H. (1997). Do "frontal tests" measure executive function? Issues of assessment and evidence from fluency tests. In P. Rabbitt (Ed.),

Methodology of frontal and executive function (pp. 191–213). London: Psychology Press.

Phillips, L. (2005). Both specific functions and general ability can be useful: But it depends what type of research question you ask. *Cortex, 41,* 236–237.

Rabbitt, P. (1997). Introduction: Methodologies and models in the study of executive function. In P. Rabbitt (Ed.), *Methodology of frontal and executive function* (pp. 1–38). London: Psychology Press.

Radloff, L. S. (1977). The CES–D Scale: A self report depression scale for research in the general population. *Applied Psychological Measurement, 1,* 385–401.

Rapp, M. A., & Reischies, F. M. (2005). Attention and executive control predict Alzheimer disease in late life: Results from the Berlin Aging Study (BASE). *American Journal of Geriatric Psychiatry, 13,* 134–141.

Raz, N. (2000). Aging of the brain and its impact on cognitive performance: Integration of structural and functional findings. In F. I. M. Craik & T. A. Salthouse (Eds.), *Handbook of aging and cognition* (pp. 1–90). Mahwah, NJ: Lawrence Erlbaum.

Royall, D. R., Lauterbach, E. C., Cummings, J. L., Reeve, A., Rummans, T. A., Kaufer, D. I., et al. (2002). Executive control function: A review of its promise and challenges for clinical research. *Journal of Neuropsychiatry and Clinical Neuroscience, 14,* 377–405.

Royall, D. R., Mahurin, R. K., & Gray, K. F. (1992). Bedside assessment of executive cognitive impairment: The Executive Interview. *Journal of the American Geriatrics Society, 40,* 1221–1226.

Royall, D. R., Palmer, R., Chiodo, L. K., & Polk, M. J. (2004). Declining executive control in normal aging predicts change in functional status: The Freedom House Study. *Journal of the American Geriatrics Society, 52,* 346–352.

Salthouse, T. A. (1999). From the present to the future: Commentary on Luszcz and Bryan. *Gerontology, 45,* 345–347.

Salthouse, T. A. (2005). Relations between cognitive abilities and measures of executive functioning. *Neuropsychology, 19,* 532–545.

Salthouse, T. A. (in press). Executive functioning. In D. C. Park & N. Schwarz (Eds.), *Cognitive aging: A primer.* Washington, DC: Psychology Press.

Salthouse, T. A., Atkinson, T. M., & Berish, D. E. (2003). Executive functioning as a potential mediator of age-related cognitive decline in normal adults. *Journal of Experimental Psychology: General, 132,* 566–594.

Salthouse, T. A., Toth, J., Daniels, K., Parks, C., Pak, R., Wolbrette, M., et al. (2000). Effects of aging on efficiency of task switching in a variant of the Trail Making Test. *Neuropsychology, 14,* 102–111.

Schmahmann, J. D. (1996). From movement to thought: Anatomic substrates of the cerebellar contribution to cognitive processing. *Human Brain Mapping, 4,* 174–198.

Schmahmann, J. D., & Pandya, D. N. (1997). The cerebrocerebellar system. In J. D. Schmahmann (Ed.), *The cerebellum and cognition: International review of neurobiology* (Vol. 41, pp. 31–60). San Diego, CA: Academic Press.

Schretlen, D., Pearlson, G. D., Anthony, J. C., Aylward, E. H., Augustine, A. M., Davis, A., et al. (2000). Elucidating the contributions of processing speed, executive ability, and frontal lobe volume to normal age-related differences in fluid intelligence. *Journal of the International Neuropsychological Society, 6,* 52–61.

Shallice, T. (1982). Specific impairments in planning. Philosophical Transactions of the Royal Society of London: Series B, Biological Sciences, 298, 199–209.

Sliwinski, M., & Hofer, S. M. (1999). How strong is the evidence for mediational hypotheses of age-related memory loss? Commentary. *Gerontology, 45,* 351–354.

Temple, C. M. (1997). *Developmental cognitive neuropsychology.* Hove, UK: Psychology Press.

Troyer, A. K., Graves, R. E., & Cullum, C. M. (1994). Executive functioning as a mediator of the relationship between age and episodic memory in healthy aging. *Aging and Cognition, 1,* 45–53.

Verhaeghen, P., & Cerella, J. (2002). Aging, executive control, and attention: A review of meta-analyses. *Neuroscience and Biobehavioral Reviews, 26,* 849–857.

Wechsler, D. (1977). *Wechsler Adult Intelligence Scale—Third edition.* San Antonio, TX: Psychological Corporation.

West, R. L. (1996). An application of prefrontal cortex function theory to cognitive aging. *Psychological Bulletin, 120,* 272–292.

West, R., Murphy, K. J., Armilio, M. L., Craik, F. I., & Stuss, D. T. (2002). Lapses of intention and performance variability reveal age-related increases in fluctuations of executive control. *Brain and Cognition, 49,* 409–419.

13

EVERYDAY PROBLEM SOLVING IN CONTEXT

CYNTHIA A. BERG

In the last 20 years or more, the field of everyday problem solving has examined how individuals use their cognitive skills to solve "practical" problems that individuals face on an "everyday" basis. This field grew out of dissatisfaction with the use of traditional measures of intelligence to capture the intelligence of adults, who were no longer in the academic environment (Demming & Pressey, 1957; Labouvie-Vief, 1982). Intelligence tests were designed to predict the academic success of children, and scholars argued that these tests were ill devised to assess the intelligence of adults, for whom the prediction of academic success was no longer a relevant goal. Instead, measures of adult intelligence should assess the cognitive skills that adults need to adapt to their everyday environments (Berg & Sternberg, 1985). Thus, the field was guided by the question "What everyday problem-solving abilities are needed to adapt to the unique demands and opportunities of adult development?" The challenge for the field was not only to find alternative measures of everyday problem solving used by adults but also to find measures of adult success that would replace the outcome of academic success.

Measuring everyday problem solving was also consistent with a growing interest in contextualist approaches to intelligence (P. Baltes, Dittmann-Kohli, & Dixon, 1984; Dixon, 1992; Sternberg, 1984), which viewed intelligence as adaptation to the intellectual demands of one's environment. A central tenet of this perspective is that intellectual development will be disparate across groups of individuals who are situated within different contexts (Laboratory of Comparative Human Cognition, 1982). The implication for adult development is that if the context of late adulthood sets up different constraints and opportunities for cognitive function than at other epochs of development, then intellectual development should also look different. Although a comprehensive depiction of the changing context of adult intelligence has not been achieved, the context of older adults differs in several ways from that of young adults (decreased contact with school and work environments, increased salience of problems dealing with health). Thus, as P. Baltes et al. (1984) described, "with

AUTHOR'S NOTE: Some of the research reported in this article was supported by a grant from the National Institute of Aging (R01 AG 18903) awarded to Timothy Smith (Principal Investigator) and Cynthia A. Berg (Co-Principal Investigator).

aging . . . domains of psychological functioning other than performance on intelligence tests gain in relative significance" (p. 50).

These diverse beginnings of the field have certainly contributed to the multiplicity of terms used to describe this general field: *everyday competence* (M. Baltes, Mayr, Borchelt, Maas, & Wilms, 1993; Diehl, 1998; Willis, 1991), *everyday problem solving* (Berg, Strough, Calderone, Sansone, & Weir, 1998; Blanchard-Fields, Jahnke, & Camp, 1995; Denney, 1989; Diehl, Willis, & Schaie, 1995; Marsiske & Willis, 1995; Sinnott, 1989), *everyday cognition* (Allaire & Marsiske, 2002; Poon, Rubin, & Wilson, 1989; Rogoff & Lave, 1984), *practical problem solving* (Scribner, 1986), *everyday reasoning and decision making* (Johnson, 1990; Klaczynski, 2000), and *practical intelligence* (Sternberg & Wagner, 1986). Throughout this chapter, the term *everyday problem solving* is used, because it is the term most commonly applied in the cognitive aging literature. Similar to the diversity of terms used to describe this field, there are numerous views of what defines everyday problem solving, guided in part by different theoretical positions on the field. Most definitions involve distinctions between everyday problem solving and the type of intelligence required to perform well on traditional intelligence measures (i.e., "academic intelligence"; Neisser, 1976; Wagner, 1986). All perspectives to everyday problem solving agree that the content of everyday problems (e.g., problems dealing with finances, interpersonal relationships, reading medication labels) are much more familiar and experienced on a more routine basis than are the items on an intelligence test.

In this chapter, the review of the past literature and comments regarding the future of everyday problem solving are organized around the question that led to the formation of the field of everyday problem solving: "How does everyday problem solving predict adaptation to everyday environments?" The vast majority of past research has focused on the question "What is everyday problem solving, and how does it differ from traditional measures of intelligence?" which is only a part of the original question guiding the field. Two dominant theoretical perspectives have guided work on everyday problem solving: (1) the *competency perspective* and (2) the *contextual perspective*

(Berg & Klaczynski, 1996). These two perspectives make very different predictions regarding the relation of everyday problem solving to more traditional intellectual abilities and have been guided by quite different questions for the field. These perspectives are used to guide a brief review of the literature of everyday problem solving, describing current empirical work. Next, an integrative model of everyday problem solving is introduced that represents a potential rapprochement of these two perspectives. This model also provides an excellent framework for the next 25 years of the field that may move us closer to models addressing how everyday problem solving is associated with successful real world adaptation. Understanding how adults successfully solve everyday problems in context will likely involve complex models that require cognitive psychologists to understand the integration of cognition with emotion, social interaction, and physiological processes (Berg, Skinner, & Ko, in press).

THEORETICAL POSITIONS GUIDING WORK ON EVERYDAY PROBLEM SOLVING

Two quite different theoretical positions have guided work on everyday problem solving (Berg & Klaczynski, 1996): (1) the competency perspective and (2) the contextual perspective. The competency perspective views everyday problem solving as solving problems that are ecologically valid (i.e., experienced in one's daily life) but that are well defined in that the problems contain a single correct answer (Allaire & Marsiske, 2002; Willis & Schaie, 1986). Problem solving is frequently assessed in a fairly decontextualized environment where problems are presented within a particular setting and a single correct answer is chosen. The contextual perspective views everyday problems as ill defined (as opposed to well defined) in that there is more than one "right answer" and multiple paths toward the solution of the problem (Berg et al., 1998; Blanchard-Fields et al., 1995). These ill-defined problems frequently exist (a) in a complex web of interpersonal relationships that can both facilitate and derail problem solution (Gould, Kurzman, & Dixon, 1994; Meacham & Emont, 1989; Meegan & Berg,

2002; Strough & Margrett, 2002); (b) over an extended time frame of days, weeks, and months; and (c) with high emotional salience, requiring that one integrate emotion and cognition (Blanchard-Fields et al., 1995; Labouvie-Vief, 2003). These two theoretical perspectives have come to quite different conclusions regarding the relationship between everyday problem solving and traditional measures of intelligence and the developmental function of age differences across the adult life span.

THE COMPETENCY PERSPECTIVE

The competency perspective views everyday problem solving as a manifestation of underlying intellectual abilities. For instance, Willis and Schaie (1986) stated that

> We shall use the term "intelligence" to denote those genotypic ability factors commonly identified with the psychometric approach to the study of structural intelligence. In contrast, practical intelligence will be viewed as the phenotypic expression of the combination of genotypic factors that, given minimally acceptable levels of motivation, will permit adaptive behavior within a specific situation or class of situations. (p. 240)

Because traditional intellectual abilities are thought to underlie everyday problem solving, empirical research from this perspective has been oriented toward addressing (a) the relation between everyday problem solving and intelligence and (b) whether the developmental trajectory of performance on everyday measures is the same or different from the trajectory for traditional measures of intelligence.

The competency approach has been fruitfully involved in designing measures of everyday problem solving. These measures typically involve a revision of psychometric measures of intelligence to include items that reflect problems one might experience in daily life (e.g., understanding information on a medication label; reading and using forms such as an income tax return form; understanding and utilizing nutritional facts regarding fat and calorie content of foods). The primary "everyday" feature of this approach is that the problems are

familiar, rather than unfamiliar. However, measures designed within this perspective share many features with traditional measures of intelligence in that the problems have one correct answer, they are solved individually, and the problems occur over a limited time frame.

Across multiple studies, the results obtained using these measures indicate that everyday problem-solving performance is quite similar to measures of traditional intellectual performance (Allaire & Marsiske, 1999; Marsiske & Willis, 1995; Willis & Schaie, 1986; see Thornton & Dumke, 2005, for a review). For instance, Allaire and Marsiske (1999) devised everyday analogues of inductive reasoning, knowledge, declarative memory, and working memory and compared these measures to traditional measures of these constructs. Correlations between each cognitive analogue were high (ranging from $r = .26$ to $r = .74$), suggesting that everyday problem solving is quite related to traditional measures of intelligence (see also Willis & Schaie, 1986). In addition, age differences in the everyday analogues were similar to those found for fluid intelligence, suggesting again substantial overlap in what these measures are tapping.

A second approach within this perspective recasts the distinction between traditional and everyday problem solving measures as a focus on unpracticed versus practiced abilities (Denney, 1989). Traditional intelligence tests are posited to be relatively unexercised, whereas everyday problem-solving measures reflect exercised potential. Because the relatively exercised abilities draw on the unexercised abilities, exercised potential is always at a higher level than unexercised potential and declines later developmentally. Within this perspective, the primary measure of everyday problem solving involves presenting individuals with ill-structured problems (e.g., A 67-year-old man with limited finances has a heart condition and his yard needs to be mowed) and asking them to generate as many strategies as possible to deal with the problem. The number of safe and effective solutions is typically the measure of everyday problem-solving performance. This measure enlarges the scope of everyday problem solving beyond simply relatively familiar problems to include multiple solutions and an extended time frame. In several studies, Denney and her colleagues

(Denney & Palmer, 1981; Denney & Pearce, 1989; Denney, Pearce, & Palmer, 1982) have found that problem-solving performance increased up to middle age and declined during later adulthood.

Thus, the view from the competency perspective is that everyday problem solving derives from a set of more basic cognitive abilities. In addition, because traditional cognitive abilities underlie everyday problem-solving performance, the developmental trajectory of performance is similar across these two types of abilities, although decline may be delayed when everyday problems are constructed to be more ill defined, such that multiple correct solutions are possible.

THE CONTEXTUAL PERSPECTIVE

The contextual perspective greatly enlarges the scope of what constitutes everyday problem solving. Everyday problem solving is examined as the cognitive, social, motivational, and cultural factors that influence adaptation to specific contexts (Berg & Klaczynski, 2002; Blanchard-Fields & Chen, 1996). Cognitive abilities are only one of many abilities that individuals may use to provide a closer fit between themselves and their environment (Hartley, 1989). Individuals may also draw on their abilities to regulate emotions (Blanchard-Fields et al., 1995), use the social context to facilitate problem solving (Berg et al., 1998; Meegan & Berg, 2002), and draw on broader styles of coping with life stressors (Blanchard-Fields, Chen, & Norris, 1997; Cornelius & Caspi, 1987).

Because of the similarity of everyday problems with the daily hassles examined in the coping literature, this approach often examines strategies by drawing on the distinctions laid out within the coping literature (Folkman, Lazarus, Pimley, & Novacek, 1987), such as problem-focused coping, passive dependent behavior, cognitive reappraisal, and avoidant thinking and denial. Two predominant approaches to measurement exist within this perspective. First, individuals are presented with hypothetical problems experienced in daily life, and participants rate the efficacy of different coping strategies. Second, individuals describe a recently experienced everyday problem and how they solved the problem, with qualitative coding of the problem-solving strategies (e.g., Berg et al., 1998; Blanchard-Fields et al., 1995). Multiple criteria exist across these different measures. Some studies rely on the fit between strategies selected and some standard of optimal performance derived from those occupying the context (e.g., Cornelius & Caspi, 1987). Others rely on the participants' own subjective appraisal of strategy effectiveness (Berg et al., 1998) or the extent of contextual fit between strategies and goals (Berg et al., 1998).

The research generated within this perspective yields a substantially different picture of everyday problem solving than that gained by the competency perspective. First, the relation between performance on measures of everyday problem solving and traditional measures of intelligence is far more modest ($rs = .27–.29$ in Cornelius & Caspi, 1987; see also Blanchard-Fields et al., 1997) than that revealed by the competency perspective, suggesting that everyday problem solving is rather distinct from traditional measures of intelligence. Second, age differences in everyday problem-solving performance have revealed higher overall effectiveness with age (Cornelius & Caspi, 1987), increases in ability to deal with the inevitable emotions present in everyday problem-solving situations (e.g., Blanchard-Fields et al., 1995), a preference to combine strategies dealing with the problem and the emotions of the problem (Blanchard-Fields et al., 1997; Watson & Blanchard-Fields, 1998), and an enhanced ability to make use of the interpersonal context by working with collaborative partners (Gould et al., 1994). Thus, there is considerable evidence that everyday problem solving is far more distinct from traditional measures of intelligence than revealed by the competency perspective.

A key feature of the contextual perspective to everyday problem solving is that domains of problem solving (e.g., consumer, health, friends, and family) may pose different opportunities and constraints for problem solving at different ages. This is important, because the normative context of everyday problem solving likely varies across adult development (Berg & Calderone, 1994) such that during late adulthood everyday problem solving occurs more frequently in domains such as health and family than at other periods of the life span (Sansone & Berg, 1993). Thus, in contrast to the competency perspective, which holds that everyday problem-solving competencies transcend the particulars of problems, according to the contextual perspective strategies that are effective in one context may be much less effective in another context and at different developmental time periods. A particularly important contextual distinction has been between problems that are *instrumental* (involving competence concerns) and those that are *interpersonal* (involving social/interpersonal concerns; see Berg et al., 1998; Blanchard-Fields et al., 1997). These contexts are associated with different goals and strategies (Berg et al., 1998; Blanchard-Fields et al., 1997; Cornelius & Caspi, 1987), perceived controllability (Blanchard-Fields et al., 1997), perceived efficacy (Artistico, Cervone, & Pezzuti, 2003), and attenuated patterns of age differences (Thornton & Dumke, 2005).

The contextual perspective substantially broadens the view of everyday problem solving beyond traditional intellectual abilities to include a diverse set of skills that individuals use to adapt to their everyday environments. Within this perspective, everyday problem solving is viewed as fairly distinct from intellectual abilities, and age differences in everyday problem solving often reveal that older adults use their skills more effectively to adapt to everyday problem-solving situations than do younger adults. The field currently is beginning to address the multidimensional landscape of everyday problem solving, which may involve a rapprochement of the competency and contextual perspectives.

INTEGRATION OF THE COMPETENCY AND CONTEXTUAL PERSPECTIVES

Several recent investigations of everyday problem solving suggest a sort of rapprochement between the competency and contextual perspectives; that is, investigators acknowledge that everyday problem solving may involve solving some problems where there is a "single" correct answer (e.g., What is the correct amount of taxes to pay per year? What is the daily dose of medication that you have been prescribed?) and others that do not (What do you do when you cannot pay your bills? What sort of treatment decision should you make in response to prostate cancer?). Many of these investigations use measures of everyday problem solving from both theoretical traditions (e.g., competency and contextual). The evidence coming from research using well- and ill-defined measures reveals (a) that well-defined and ill-defined measures are distinct and cannot be captured under a single construct of "everyday problem solving," (b) that both types of measures uniquely predict measures of everyday functioning, and (c) that age-related differences in these measures suggest two different sorts of trajectories.

Evidence that well-defined and ill-defined measures are distinct constructs comes from the work of Allaire and Marsiske (2002). They compared performance on their everyday analogues of inductive reasoning, knowledge, declarative memory, and working memory with performance on ill-defined problems (excluding problems that contained social content, often an important component of ill-defined measures). For ill-defined problems, they used the scoring procedures of Denney and colleagues (e.g., Denney & Pearce, 1989) involving the number of safe and effective solutions participants generated, and they had a separate group of "experts" rate the quality of the solution. Correlations among measures indicated that the well-defined measures of everyday cognition (analogues of traditional intelligence tests) correlated most strongly with the measure of solution quality rated by experts. It is interesting that, for the same ill-defined task, two measures of performance (quality of the solution and number of strategies generated) were not significantly correlated ($r = .17$). Marsiske and Willis (1995) found similar low relations among different measures of everyday problem solving varying along the well-defined and ill-defined dimension. This work strongly suggests that not only is everyday problem solving multidimensional in terms of the cognitive processes involved but that even for the same task, multiple facets of problem solving exist. Allaire and Marsiske (2002) also found that well-defined and ill-defined measures of everyday problem solving made independent contributions in predicting individuals' perceptions of their instrumental activities of daily living (long considered an important measure of daily functioning; Lawton & Brody, 1969).

Additional support for the idea of the multidimensionality of everyday problem solving comes from findings that the pattern of age-related differences in everyday problem-solving performance varies across different measures of everyday problem solving. Marsiske and Willis (1995) found age differences only for well-defined measures (the Everyday Problem Test). Thornton and Dumke (2005), in a meta-analysis of everyday problem-solving studies, found evidence for important moderators of age differences in everyday problem-solving performance. Greater age differences were found on well-defined measures of everyday problem solving where performance criteria transcend context as opposed to ill-defined problems, where criteria are fit to the context (e.g., participant-rated effectiveness).

These results indicate that the types of measures of everyday problem solving used by researchers coming from the competency and contextual perspective are different and predict different facets of real world performance. In daily life, it is likely that we experience everyday problems that include both well-defined (what is the balance in the checkbook?) and ill-defined problems (how much overdraft protection should we have attached to our checking account?), even within the same content area. In addition, the well- and ill-defined nature of everyday problems may lie not simply in the content or structure of the problem but in the appraisal of the problem (Klaczynski, 2000). The task for the future of everyday problem solving is to understand the process by which adults solve both well- and ill-defined everyday problems and how successful solution of both types of problems relates to real world adaptation. Current models in the decision-making field that integrate the analytic and heuristic nature of cognitive processing (Epstein, 1994; Kahneman, Slovic, & Tversky, 1982; Klaczynski, 2000; Stanovich, 1999) will be used to understand how adults solve both well- and ill-defined everyday problems.

THE TWO-PROCESS MODEL OF EVERYDAY PROBLEM SOLVING

A key issue coming from the research within competency and contextual perspectives is to understand performance differences across well- and ill-defined everyday problems. Older adults perform more poorly relative to younger individuals on well-defined everyday problems, but not necessarily on ill-defined problems, and the relation between performances on well- and ill-defined problems is quite modest. Two-process theories of decision making have been used in the child development and social psychological literature to address the variability seen across individuals in everyday reasoning tasks as well as the variability within individuals across specific problems (Klaczynski, 2005; Stavonich & West, 1999). In this section, I apply these models to research on well- and ill-defined everyday problems, using this framework to address where the field of everyday problem solving should go in the future.

In two-process theories, decision making and problem solving are a factor of two ongoing cognitive systems: (1) an analytical system and (2) an experiential or heuristic system. Analytical processing is somewhat decontextualized, encoded in abstract components, and is more likely to be activated when a particular task is stripped down of specific contextual features. For instance, the deductive reasoning problems presented on many traditional intelligence tests and the everyday analogues used by Allaire and Marsiske (2002) are most likely to be solved by means of an analytical processing system. The problems are presented in a testlike multiple-choice format (which strongly indicates that there is one correct answer) and that analysis is required. In contrast, experiential processing is a highly contextualized process that operates on problems that are highly contextualized, familiar, and activate existing beliefs and schemas (Stanovich & West, 1997). Processing is affectively driven and rapid, requiring little cognitive effort and oriented toward taking direct action (Epstein, 1994). The types of problems examined within the contextual perspective frequently contain interpersonal and emotional components that likely activate the experiential system (e.g., what to do with a landlord who will not pay for expensive repairs, from the Everyday Problem Solving Inventory; Cornelius & Caspi, 1987). Multiple aspects of the problem context (familiarity of the task, contextual details) as well as the individual (e.g., beliefs relevant to the problem, age) transact to push processing toward one system or the other on a particular problem.

The two-process theories of cognition may be helpful in understanding how everyday problem solving involves both analytical and experiential processing not only across the well-defined and ill-defined problems but also on a problem-to-problem basis. Klaczynski and Robinson (2000) showed that adults switched between these two systems across problems that were either consistent or inconsistent with one's beliefs (in their case, beliefs regarding religion and political preferences). Heuristic processing was used when the information presented was consistent with one's beliefs; however, analytical processing was used to reason about problems that were inconsistent with one's beliefs. Middle-aged and older adults used more heuristic reasoning in relation to belief-consistent problems than did younger adults. This contextual specificity of reasoning is particularly interesting because Blanchard-Fields et al. (1997) found that older adults' strategies are more contextually specific than are young and middle-aged adults' strategies. Furthermore, Blanchard-Fields, Chen, Schocke, and Hertzog (1998) found that this contextual specificity is evoked by different attitudes, beliefs, and values present in everyday situations, consistent with Klaczynski and Robinson's (2000) research showing that the two systems are activated depending on personal theories and beliefs. This might suggest that middle-aged and older adults activate the experiential or heuristic processing system more frequently in solving everyday problems (Klaczynski & Robinson, 2000; Meyer, Russo, & Talbot, 1995; Sinnott, 1989) than do younger adults. Coordination of the two systems may reflect a higher order goal of cognitive development during adulthood in light of the fact that the integration of the cognitive and affective systems is a component of postformal operational thought (Labouvie-Vief, 1992).

The activation of the experiential system occurs through rich contextualized representations that draw on affective (Epstein, 1994) and potentially interpersonal regulatory systems. Thus, especially for problems that are approached by means of the experiential mode of processing, the ability to regulate one's emotions and use the interpersonal context to facilitate problem solving may be important to successfully solve such

problems. Developmental differences exist in the ability to regulate emotions, such that older adults may be better able to regulate their emotions, particularly in the context of social interaction (Blanchard-Fields et al., 1997; Carstensen, Isaacowitz, & Charles, 1999). In late adulthood, however, there appears to be a decline in affect complexity and differentiation (Labouvie-Vief, 2003) that may limit older adults' abilities to analyze emotions at high levels of complexity and experience ambiguity in emotional experience (i.e., the focus in late adulthood is simply to focus on the positive and minimize the negative).

In sum, this two-process framework to everyday problem solving promises to integrate some of the previous research in the field oriented around well-defined and ill-defined problems. Problems coming from the well-defined tradition may by the very nature of their abstract presentation activate the analytical processing system, a system that appears to be tied to traditional abstract reasoning tasks (Willis, 1996) and declines with advancing age. Problems coming from the ill-defined tradition come with detailed contextual information rich with beliefs and emotions that may activate the experiential processing system. Although it has been suggested that different types of problems activate different processes, it is also the case that for the same problem, the analytical system may be activated for one individual and the heuristic for another, depending on the activation of beliefs and emotion. I now use this two-process system to address the question of how both analytical and heuristic cognition may predict everyday problem solving in real world contexts.

THE FUTURE OF EVERYDAY PROBLEM SOLVING

The two-process model of cognition helps to address the existing issues in the field focused on understanding what everyday problem solving is and how it is distinguished from traditional intelligence. From this perspective, everyday cognition involves both analytical processing as well as more experiential or heuristic strategies. However, as described above, this is only part of the challenge with which the field first began. A key question guiding the formation of the field was "How can everyday problem solving help us understand crucial measures of problem-solving success that are important in adulthood?" This question is still very important and has yet to be fully addressed, because the vast majority of the literature has not linked measures of everyday problem solving to important real world outcomes crucial for better adaptation. Thus, although the field has numerous measures of everyday problem solving, in only a limited number of cases do we understand whether they are important in predicting markers of successful everyday adaptation (Allaire & Marsiske, 2002; Diehl et al., 1995).

This mapping of everyday problem-solving skills to real world adaptive outcomes is what remains as the challenge ahead for the field of everyday problem solving (see also Marsiske & Margrett, 2006). The challenge involves (a) an exploration of the real world outcomes that are crucial for adult success and how analytical and heuristic processing of everyday problems relate to those outcomes, (b) how analytical and heuristic processing may relate to the variability that exists in cognition in daily life, and (c) how, especially for problems solved by means of the heuristic system, adults integrate cognition with affective and interpersonal processes (e.g., Heckhausen & Schulz, 1995; Labouvie-Vief, 2003) to achieve better success. Although linking everyday problem-solving measures to real world adaptational success is a rather daunting challenge, such work may provide a rather unique opportunity in the field of adult development to put what are sometimes deemed separate psychological aspects of the older adult back together again. Everyday problem solving draws on individuals' cognitive, social, emotional, and coping skills as they deal with complex problems that change over time. However, the areas of cognition, social problem solving, emotional regulation, and coping are not always examined together as individuals approach problems and potentially work with close relationship partners (for a treatment of these issues, see Berg, Skinner, & Ko, in press, and Berg, Smith, et al., 2007). A crucial role for the field of everyday problem solving is to put these components together so that we can understand how adults adapt to their changing environments across the life span. This integrative challenge will require several crucial steps, which I now outline.

Challenge No. 1: Development of Real World Markers of Successful Everyday Problem Solving

The field is posed to address how everyday analytical and heuristic problem solving are related to an adult's ability to adapt to his or her everyday world, by validating everyday problem-solving measures with real world outcomes of success. The field of everyday problem solving has been dominated by the use of hypothetical problem sets and strategies (Berg, Meegan, & Klaczynski, 1999; Blanchard-Fields et al., 1997; Cornelius & Caspi, 1987; Denney & Pearce, 1989). Such problem sets use problems that individuals might experience as they deal with finances, friends, family, home, work, and being a consumer. In constructing such problems researchers have been attentive to issues of ecological validity and occasionally measure the extent to which individuals experience the problems regularly. However, results often indicate that the problems designed to be reflective of "everyday" problems are in fact experienced by individuals very infrequently (Berg et al., 1999; Cornelius & Caspi, 1987). Furthermore, rarely are such measures validated by comparing everyday problem-solving performance to real world performance (see Diehl et al., 1995, and Diehl et al., 2005, for excellent illustrations of such comparisons).

We know much less than we should at this point in the field's development in addressing whether our measures of everyday problem solving predict some aspects of adult success; that is, just as the field of intelligence examined how intelligence tests predict academic success, we need to know whether measures of everyday problem solving predict aspects of everyday success. For example, Willis (1996) argued that everyday problem-solving performance should be compared with the ability to deal with seven crucial domains of daily living (food preparation, medication use and health behaviors, telephone use, shopping and consumerism, financial management, housekeeping and laundry, and transportation) such as those measured on assessments of instrumental activities of daily living (Lawton & Brody, 1969). This approach has revealed that both everyday well-defined and ill-defined measures are important for predicting self-reported daily functioning (Allaire & Marsiske, 2002). This approach is perhaps most fruitful in understanding adaptation in very late adulthood, when these domains of life are challenged. However, it is unclear how everyday problems predict real world outcomes in middle adulthood or young adulthood. From our own database of problems that adults report experiencing across the life span (Sansone & Berg, 1993), in middle adulthood, and young-old age, problems such as time management (e.g., managing demands of work and family), keeping one's emotion in check during difficult family problems, and assisting adult children in solving everyday problems may be key domains of everyday problemsolving with corresponding real world outcomes, including measures such as job success, parent self-efficacy, and measures of general well-being.

This effort could be approached by focusing on very specific everyday problem-solving tasks and outcomes that are important for daily living. An illustration of this approach is work by Diehl et al. (1995) that compared everyday problem-solving tasks to observational measures of such tasks (modifying cake mix instructions, loading a pill reminder box). In addition, Wagner and Sternberg (1986) examined the tacit knowledge that is required of particular jobs relating measures to actual measures of job success (e.g., financial success, managerial success).

Such work would benefit by examining analytic and heuristic processing within a single domain, holding knowledge and expertise somewhat more constant, and following problem solving across time as adults adapt to new constraints and opportunities presented in the problem environment. Consider the domain of health decision making (see Park & Liu, 2007; Willis, Dolan, & Betrand, 1999) and the specific challenges of dealing with prostate cancer (Berg et al., 2007; Meyer, Talbot, & Ranalli, 2007) or breast cancer (Meyer et al., 1995), arguably important contexts for problem solving that are crucial for everyday successful adaptation. Adults are presented with numerous problems, such as adjusting medical treatments; combining risk and benefit information; and deciding on the best treatment, weighing the value of mortality

and quality of life (Mazur & Merz, 1996) as well as the needs and desires of close relationship partners (Echlin & Rees, 2002). Such problems can be solved by means of either the analytical or experiential processing system. There is some evidence that older adults may differentially solve such problems with the experiential system. For example, Meyer et al. (1995) found that older women making decisions about either hypothetical or actual treatment decisions for breast cancer used less information to make the decision, although no age differences existed in the final treatment selected for breast cancer. Thus, although older women use what appears to be more experiential or heuristic processing, this does not affect their adaptational outcome. Such research would benefit by including measures that activate the analytical processing system as well (e.g., combining risk and benefit information) to see how analytical versus experiential processing predict adaptational outcomes. By holding context constant and examining problem solving that is analytical versus heuristic we may better understand developmental differences in the ways that adults adapt to their everyday environments.

Several tasks within the decision-making field provide excellent candidates to begin a focused examination of the relation between measures of everyday decision making and real world outcomes. The field of decision making has only recently been integrated within the everyday problem-solving arena (Marsiske & Margrett, 2006; Thornton & Demke, 2005). The decision-making field in cognitive aging has examined a range of decisions that are potentially "everyday" in nature: purchasing cars (Johnson, 1990) and over-the-counter medications (Johnson & Drungle, 2000), deciding where to go on a vacation (Berg, Johnson, Meegan, & Strough, 2003), making medical treatment decisions (Meyer et al., 1995; Zwahr, Park, & Shifren, 1999), and making financial decisions (Chen & Sun, 2003; Walsh & Hershey, 1993). Such tasks are ready made to examine whether a more analytical versus heuristic approach is taken to the task in that algorithms have been established for when heuristics are used (see Johnson, 1990). These tasks also lend themselves well to the development of real world adaptational outcomes regarding the success of making medical decisions, financial investments, and purchasing decisions.

To select tasks that are important markers of everyday success, the field needs to adequately depict the landscape of everyday problem solving and how it may change across the adult life span. Such work will benefit from careful ethnographic type work such as that conducted by Margret Baltes and her colleagues in 1990, depicting the daily life of elderly Germans. Baltes, Wahl, and Schmid-Furstoss (1990) described finding "an almost complete lack of reliable data describing the everyday lives of the elderly" (p. P173). A similar statement could be made about our current understanding of the everyday problem-solving lives of adults across the life span, especially during middle adulthood. From some of the stress and coping research we know that domains such as balancing work and family (Almeida & Kessler, 1998), midlife career transitions, and changes in parenting (Morfei, Hooker, Fiese, & Corderio, 2001) may be important contexts to examine. Markers of success within these domains will be important to establish. This work detailing everyday cognition in context could benefit from the detailed ethnographic work of Scribner (1986) and Lave (1988), who have explored how everyday cognition is transformed through cognitive shortcuts to the specific features of the context.

Challenge No. 2: Understanding Both Inter- and Intraindividual Variability

As researchers in the field begin to examine the relation between hypothetical everyday problem solving and real-world indicators of problem-solving success, we must be mindful of past research that indicates that such relations may be modest at best (see Berg & Klaczynski, 2002, for a review). For example, both Scribner (1986) and Lave (1988) have shown that basic arithmetic operations (e.g., multiplication and addition) are substantially different across contexts such as abstract story problems and real world contexts (e.g., milk processing plant, grocery store). The two-process theory of cognition has the promise to address this intraindividual variability in response to different problems even within a single domain (Blanchard-Fields et al., 1997, 1998; Cornelius & Caspi, 1987).

Different problems may activate a different set of beliefs that evoke either the analytical or experiential processing system. Even within a single system, such as the experiential system, problem interpretations and goals (Berg et al., 1998), theory-guided motivations (Klaczynski & Robinson, 2000), and social rules (Blanchard-Fields et al., 1998) may be activated that lead to variability in strategies to everyday problems. Older adults' strategies may be more variable across different problems than young or middle-aged adults' strategies (Blanchard-Fields et al., 1997). An important challenge facing the everyday problem-solving field will be to understand this variability and whether variability is related to success or failure in adaptation to everyday environments.

In examining variability, the field must understand whether intraindividual variability is a positive or negative factor in the development of everyday problem solving. Researchers who use the criteria "number of safe and effective solutions," used extensively by Denney and colleagues (Denney, 1989), imply that variability is a good thing. Within the contextual perspective, variability may reflect the process whereby individuals fit their strategies to the specific contexts, goals, and emotional salience of problem situations (Berg & Calderone, 1994; Blanchard-Fields et al., 1997). Klaczynski and Robinson (2000) found that variability in everyday reasoning is found on a problem-to-problem basis, such that reasoners use sophisticated normative strategies when problems violate their beliefs but less sophisticated heuristic strategies when faced with arguments that are belief consistent. Such variability was associated not with intellectual ability but with metacognitive skills that recognize the motivated nature of reasoning (Klaczynski, 2000). However, within the field of cognitive aging more broadly variability has been identified as a sign of compromised functioning in the system (Hultsch, MacDonald, Hunter, Levy-Bencheton, & Strauss, 2000; Murtha, Cismaru, Waechter, & Chertkow, 2002).

The field now has an array of methodological and statistical tools that can be used to address the issue of day-to-day variability. Current use of daily diary methods (Bolger, Davis, & Rafaeli, 2003), experience sampling techniques (Stone, Kessler, & Haythornthwaite, 1991), and the associated statistical tools of hierarchical linear modeling can assist us in this effort (Bryk & Raudenbush, 1992). By following individuals across time as they deal with ongoing problems experienced in various domains (work, home, health) and tracking how they solve everyday problems, we can see whether consistency in analytical or experiential processing is detrimental or more effective for success in these domains.

Challenge No. 3: Solving Everyday Problems Involves an Integration of Cognitive, Affective, Interpersonal, and Physiological Components

As the field identifies adaptation outcomes relevant for understanding adult success, we must acknowledge that such outcomes may not simply be cognitive in kind. This may be especially true for problems that activate the experiential processing system. A characteristic feature of everyday problem solving nominated by researchers (Meacham & Emont, 1989) and laypeople alike (Hartley, 1989) is that it involves the regulation of emotion, reading social cues, coping with stress, and integrating these components together with cognition. This suggests that relevant outcomes in understanding success may involve measures of psychological well-being (and perhaps emotional intelligence) and social functioning (Lang & Baltes, 1997; Weitzman & Weitzman, 2001) in addition to measures of cognitive functioning. This notion is quite consistent with neo-Piagetian views of what defines postformal thinking during adulthood (Labouvie-Vief, 1992). To illustrate the importance of understanding these outcomes as individuals deal with daily problems consider the following everyday problem that a woman described in one of our studies:

I quit my job and got my son in Job Corps up in Oregon because he has been in trouble in Salt Lake. Well job [corps] called and said "Oh Kurt can't make it" so they shipped him back home and so we said "Well you have to get a job and these are things you have to do" because he doesn't like to do those things because he likes Mom to take care of him. So, we gave him a car and told him there were certain things he would have to get done. He would still come home at 4:30 in the morning, sleep all day, none of the job hunting. So we changed the locks as of Saturday, on the door and told him he had to find a place to live.

These problems and others within our database indicate that everyday problems do occur over an extended time frame and draw on an individual's cognitive, coping, and social resources, guided by larger developmental goals (e.g., creating independence in adult children) and perhaps even physiological resources (see Berg, Skinner, & Ko, in press; Uchino, Berg, Smith, Pearce, & Skinner, 2006). Models of everyday problem solving must integrate relevant outcomes for the solution of such problems such as understanding how one's sense of solving adult parent–child problems is related to psychological well-being and life-satisfaction (Ryff, Lee, Essex, & Schmutte, 1994). Broader models of successful aging may be useful to consider, because adaptation outcomes include success in the health, cognitive, and social arenas (Rowe & Kahn, 1998); mature coping defenses (Labouvie-Vief, Hakim-Larson, & Hobart, 1987); and successful life span strategies of selective optimization with compensation (P. B. Baltes & Baltes, 1990) and adjustment of goals (Brandstädter & Greve, 1994; Heckhausen & Schulz, 1995).

Furthermore, because so many everyday problems occur in a social context (Berg et al., 1998; Blanchard-Fields et al., 1997), everyday problems are solved not solely by an individual but rather by individuals in conjunction with each other (Dixon & Gould, 1996; Meegan & Berg, 2002; Strough & Margrett, 2002). Individuals may frequently appraise specific everyday problems as shared, especially with another close relationship partner (Berg et al., 2007; Wiebe et al., 2005). Many of the everyday problems that adults experience (e.g., consumer, finances, medical decision making) are ones that individuals share with a spouse, another family member, or a close friend. Appraising a problem as shared may initiate a process of collaborative problem solving (Dixon, 1992; Meegan & Berg, 2002; Strough & Margrett, 2002) in which dyads or small groups optimize the problem solving of members of the group (Johansson, Andersson, & Ronnberg, 2000; Wegner, Erber, & Raymond, 1991). Such collaborative problem solving may initially involve appraising the specific parameters of the problem, which may involve some discussion as to whether the problem should be solved analytically or experientially. For example, in our own work couples frequently discuss the parameters of a hypothetical errand running task by staying within the parameters of the task as given to accomplish 12 errands in the shortest distance possible or embellishing the task so that it fits closer within their own experience. Collaborative problem solving may require new outcomes that are based on the dyad as the unit of analysis rather than individual outcomes.

In our own research, my colleagues and I have examined the cognitive and emotional factors involved in how adults collaboratively solve hypothetical problems in the laboratory (Berg et al., 2007; Smith et al., 2006) as well as approach everyday stressors throughout their daily lives (Uchino et al., 2006). Our results indicate that part of the process of solving everyday problems involves dealing with emotions evoked, interpersonal processes in working with others, and physiological processes. As couples collaborate in the laboratory on an errand running task, performance is affected by cognitive abilities and the interpersonal interactions that couples use to fit their interpersonal control over the task to the cognitive abilities of self and spouse (Berg, Smith, et al., 2007). Couples do best when the individual who is cognitively more capable is taking more control over the task. In the laboratory context, older adults experience more emotional arousal, particularly anxiety, in the task than do middle-aged adults, and older men experience more physiological arousal than all other groups. In daily life, however, older adults experience less negative affect than middle-aged adults when daily stressful experiences occur, but they do experience greater increases in blood pressure (Uchino et al., 2006).

These results indicate that everyday problem solving draws not only on the cognitive abilities of adults but also on their emotional, interpersonal, and physiological regulatory systems. The field is really in its infancy in understanding how adults approach everyday problems. Although emotional and interpersonal factors may be more frequently activated for ill-defined problems that are solved by means of heuristic processing, such factors are also important for well-defined problems solved by means of the abstract processing system (Berg, Smith, et al., 2007).

CONCLUSION

The field of everyday problem solving was guided by the question "What cognitive skills are needed to adapt to the unique demands and opportunities of adult development?" The early years of the field were spent developing measures of everyday problem solving and distinguishing it from measures of traditional intelligence. The field was approached through two quite different perspectives that examined different types of everyday problems. The competency perspective viewed everyday problem solving as a manifestation of intelligence and examined problem solving on well-defined problems where a single correct answer was possible. The contextual perspective viewed everyday problem solving as providing a better fit between the problem-solver and the environmental context and examined everyday problem solving on ill-defined problems, rich with contextual details and multiple solutions and strategies. The field currently acknowledges that everyday problem solving involves both the solution of well-defined problems (e.g., how much diabetes medication to take in order to follow my prescription) as well as ill-defined problems (e.g., how to follow my exercise and diet regimen and maintain quality of life).

A two-process model of cognition was used to integrate the competency and contextual perspectives that acknowledges that adults frequently switch between an analytical versus experiential processing mode when approaching everyday problems. This model was used to identify future challenges for the field of everyday problem solving that revolve around addressing the question with which the field first began, that of understanding how everyday problem solving predicts adaptation to real world contexts. The challenges for the field lie in identifying real world markers of everyday adaptation success; understanding the variability in everyday problem solving that may lead to such success; and broadening our approach to everyday problem solving outcomes beyond simply the cognitive to include affective, interpersonal, and physiological processes. Understanding how adults successfully solve everyday problems in context holds the promise to integrate cognition, emotion, social interaction, and physiological processes.

REFERENCES

Allaire, J. C., & Marsiske, M. (1999). Everyday cognition: Age and intellectual ability correlates. *Psychology and Aging, 14,* 627–644.

Allaire, J. C., & Marsiske, M. (2002). Well- and ill-defined measures of everyday cognition: Relationship to older adults' intellectual ability and functional status. *Psychology and Aging, 17,* 101–115.

Almeida, D. M., & Kessler, R. C. (1998). Everyday stressors and gender differences in daily distress. *Journal of Personality and Social Psychology, 75,* 670–680.

Artistico, D., Cervone, D., & Pezzuti, L. (2003). Perceived self-efficacy and everyday problem solving among young and older adults. *Psychology and Aging, 18,* 68–79.

Baltes, M. M., Mayr, U., Borchelt, M., Maas, I., & Wilms, H.-U. (1993). Everyday competence in old and very old age. An interdisciplinary perspective. *Ageing and Society, 13,* 657–680.

Baltes, M. M., Wahl, H. W., & Schmid-Furstoss, U. S. (1990). The daily life of elderly Germans: Activity patterns, personal control, and functional health. *Journal of Gerontology: Psychological Sciences, 45,* P173–P179.

Baltes, P. B., & Baltes, M. M. (1990). Psychological perspectives on successful aging: The model of selective optimization with compensation. In P. B. Baltes & M. M. Baltes (Eds.), *Successful aging: Perspectives from the behavioral sciences* (pp. 1–34). New York: Cambridge University Press.

Baltes, P. B., Dittmann-Kohli, F., & Dixon, R. A. (1984). New perspectives on the development of intelligence in adulthood: Toward a dual-process conception and a model of selective optimization with compensation. In P. B. Baltes & O. G. Brim, Jr. (Eds.), *Life-span development and behavior* (Vol. 6, pp. 33–76). New York: Academic Press.

Berg, C. A., & Calderone, K. S. (1994). The role of problem interpretations in understanding the development of everyday problem solving. In R. J. Sternberg & R. K. Wagner (Eds.), *Mind in context: Interactionist perspectives on human intelligence* (pp. 105–132). New York: Cambridge University Press.

Berg, C. A., Johnson, M. M. S., Meegan, S. P., & Strough, J. (2003). Collaborative problem-solving interaction in young and old married couples. *Discourse Processes, 35,* 33–58.

Berg, C. A., & Klaczynski, P. (1996). Practical intelligence and problem solving: Searching for perspectives. In F. Blanchard-Fields & T. M. Hess (Eds.), *Perspectives on cognition in adulthood and aging* (pp. 323–357). New York: McGraw-Hill.

Berg, C. A., & Klaczynski, P. A., (2002). Contextual variability in the expression and meaning of intelligence. In R. J. Sternberg & E. L. Grigorenko (Eds.), *The general factor of intelligence: How general is it?* (pp. 381–412). Mahwah, NJ: Lawrence Erlbaum.

Berg, C. A., Meegan, S. P., & Klaczynski, P. (1999). Age and experiential differences in strategy generation and information requests for solving everyday problems. *International Journal of Behavioral Development, 23,* 615–639.

Berg, C. A., Skinner, M., Ko, K. K. (in press). An integrative model of everyday problem solving across the adult life span. In M. C. Smith (Ed.), *Handbook of research on adult learning and development.* Mahwah, NJ: Lawrence Erlbaum.

Berg, C. A., Smith, T. W., Ko, K., Story, N., Beveridge, R., Allen, N., et al. (2007). Task control and cognitive abilities of self and spouse in collaboration in middle-aged and older couples. *Psychology and Aging, 22,* 420–427.

Berg, C. A., & Sternberg, R. J. (1985). A triarchic theory of intellectual development during adulthood. *Developmental Review, 5,* 334–370.

Berg, C. A., Strough, J., Calderone, K. S., Sansone, C., & Weir, C. (1998). The role of problem definitions in understanding age and context effects on strategies for solving everyday problems. *Psychology and Aging, 5,* 334–370.

Berg, C. A., Wiebe, D. J., Beveridge, R. M., Palmer, D. L., Korbel, C. D., Upchurch, R., et al. (2007). Appraised involvement in coping and emotional adjustment in children with diabetes and their mothers. *Journal of Pediatric Psychology, 32,* 995–1005.

Berg, C. A., Wiebe, D. J., Butner, J., Bloor, L., Bradstreet, C., Upchurch, R., et al. (2007).

Collaborative coping and daily mood in couples dealing with prostate cancer. Under review.

Blanchard-Fields, F., & Chen, Y. (1996). Adaptive cognition and aging. *American Behavioral Scientist, 39,* 231–248.

Blanchard-Fields, F., Chen, Y., & Norris, L. (1997). Everyday problem solving across the life span: Influence of domain specificity and cognitive appraisal. *Psychology and Aging, 12,* 684–693.

Blanchard-Fields, F., Chen, Y., Schocke, M., & Hertzog, C. (1998). Evidence for content-specificity of causal attributions across the adult life span. *Aging, Neuropsychology, and Cognition, 5,* 241–263.

Blanchard-Fields, F., Jahnke, H. C., & Camp, C. (1995). Age differences in problem-solving style: The role of emotional salience. *Psychology and Aging, 10,* 173–180.

Bolger, N., Davis, A., & Rafaeli, E. (2003). Diary methods: Capturing life as it is lived. *Annual Review of Psychology, 54,* 579–616.

Brandtstädter, J., & Greve, W. (1994). The aging self: Stabilizing and protective processes. *Developmental Review, 14,* 52–80.

Bryk, A. S., & Raudenbush, S. W. (1992). *Hierarchical linear models: Applications and data analysis methods.* Thousand Oaks, CA: Sage.

Carstensen, L., Isaacowitz, D. M., & Charles, C. T. (1999). Taking time seriously: A theory of socioemotional selectivity. *American Psychologist, 54,* 165–181.

Chen, Y., & Sun, Y. (2003). Age differences in financial decision-making: Using simple heuristics. *Educational Gerontology, 29,* 627–635.

Cornelius, S. W., & Caspi, A. (1987). Everyday problem solving in adulthood and old age. *Psychology and Aging, 2,* 144–153.

Demming, J. A., & Pressey, S. L. (1957). Tests "indigenous" to adult and older years. *Journal of Counseling Psychology, 4,* 144–148.

Denney, N. W. (1989). Everyday problem solving: Methodological issues, research findings, and a model. In L. W. Poon, D. C. Rubin, & B. A. Wilson (Eds.), *Everyday cognition in adulthood and late life* (pp. 330–351). New York: Cambridge University Press.

Denney, N. W., & Palmer, A. M. (1981). Adult age differences on traditional and practical problem-solving measures. *Journal of Gerontology, 36,* 323–328.

Denney, N. W., & Pearce, K. A. (1989). A developmental study of practical problem solving in adults. *Psychology and Aging, 4,* 438–442.

Denney, N. W., Pearce, K. A., & Palmer, A. M. (1982). A developmental study of adults' performance on traditional and practical problem-solving tasks. *Experimental Aging Research, 8,* 115–118.

Diehl, M. (1998). Everyday competence in later life: Current status and future directions. *The Gerontologist, 38,* 422–433.

Diehl, M., Marsiske, M., Horgas, A. L., Rosenberg, A., Saczynski, J. S., & Willis, S. L. (2005). The revised observed tasks of daily living: A performance-based assessment of everyday problem solving in older adults. *Journal of Applied Gerontology, 24,* 211–230.

Diehl, M., Willis, S. L., & Schaie, K. W. (1995). Everyday problem solving in older adults: Observational assessment and cognitive correlates. *Psychology and Aging, 10,* 478–491.

Dixon, R. (1992). Contextual approaches to adult intellectual development. In R. J. Sternberg & C. A. Berg (Eds.), *Intellectual development* (pp. 350–380). New York: Cambridge University Press.

Dixon, R. A., & Gould, O. N. (1996). Adults telling and retelling stories collaboratively. In P. B. Baltes & U. M. Staudinger (Eds.), *Interactive minds: Life-span perspective on the social foundation of cognition* (pp. 221–241). New York: Cambridge University Press.

Echlin, K. N., & Rees, C. (2002). Information needs and information-seeking behaviors of men with prostate cancer and their partners: A review of the literature. *Cancer Nursing, 25,* 35–41.

Epstein, S. (1994). Integration of the cognitive and the psychodynamic unconscious. *American Psychologist, 49,* 709–724.

Folkman, S., Lazarus, R. S., Pimley, S., & Novacek, J. (1987). Age differences in stress and coping processes. *Psychology and Aging, 2,* 171–184.

Gould, O. N., Kurzman, D., & Dixon, R. A. (1994). Communication during prose recall conversations by young and old dyads. *Discourse Processes, 17,* 149–165.

Hartley, A. A. (1989). The cognitive ecology of problem solving. In L. W. Poon, D. C. Rubin, & B. A. Wilson (Eds.), *Everyday cognition in adulthood and late life* (pp. 300–329). New York: Cambridge University Press.

Heckhausen, J., & Schulz, R. (1995). A life-span theory of control. *Psychological Review, 102,* 284–304.

Hultsch, D. F., MacDonald, S. W. S., Hunter, M. A., Levy-Bencheton, J., & Strauss, E. (2000).

Intraindividual variability in cognitive performance in older adults: Comparison of adults with mild dementia, adults with arthritis, and healthy adults. *Neuropsychology, 14,* 588–598.

Johansson, O., Andersson, J., & Ronnberg, J. (2000). Do elderly couples have a better prospective memory than other elderly people when they collaborate? *Applied Cognitive Psychology, 14,* 121–133.

Johnson, M. M. S. (1990). Age differences in decision making: A process methodology for examining strategic information processing. *Journal of Gerontology, 45,* 75–78.

Johnson, M. M. S., & Drungle, S. C. (2000). Purchasing over-the-counter medications: The influence of age and familiarity. *Experimental Aging Research, 26,* 245–261.

Kahneman, D., Slovic, P., & Tversky, A. (1982). *Judgment under uncertainty: Heuristics and biases.* New York: Cambridge University Press.

Klaczynski, P. A. (2000). Motivated scientific reasoning biases, epistemological beliefs, and theory polarization: A two-process approach to adolescent cognition. *Child Development, 71,* 1347–1366.

Klaczynski, P. A. (2005). Metacognition and cognitive variability: A dual-process model of decision making and its development. In J. E. Jacobs & P. A. Klaczynski (Eds.), *The development of judgment and decision making in children and adolescents* (pp. 39–76). Mahwah, NJ: Lawrence Erlbaum.

Klaczynski, P. A., & Robinson, B. (2000). Personal theories, intellectual ability, and epistemological beliefs: Adult age differences in everyday reasoning biases. *Psychology and Aging, 15,* 400–416.

Laboratory of Comparative Human Cognition. (1982). Culture and intelligence. In R. J. Sternberg (Ed.), *Handbook of human intelligence* (pp. 642–719). Cambridge, UK: Cambridge University Press.

Labouvie-Vief, G. (1982). Dynamic development and mature autonomy: A theoretical prologue. *Human Development, 25,* 161–191.

Labouvie-Vief, G. (1992). A neo-Piagetian perspective on adult cognitive development. In R. J. Sternberg & C. A. Berg (Eds.), *Intellectual developmental* (pp. 197–228). New York: Cambridge University Press.

Labouvie-Vief, G. (2003). Dynamic integration: Affect, cognition, and the self in adulthood. *Current Directions in Psychological Science, 12,* 201–206.

Labouvie-Vief, G., Hakim-Larson, J., & Hobart, C. J. (1987). Age, ego level, and the life-span development of coping and defense processes. *Psychology and Aging, 2,* 286–293.

Lang, F. R., & Baltes, M. M. (1997). Being with people and being alone in late life: Costs and benefits for everyday functioning. *International Journal of Behavioral Development, 21,* 729–746.

Lave, J. (1988). *Cognition in practice.* New York: Cambridge University Press.

Lawton, M. P., & Brody, E. M. (1969). Assessment of older people: Self-maintaining and instrumental activities of daily living. *The Gerontologist, 9,* 179–185.

Marsiske, J. A., & Margrett, J. (2006). Everyday problem solving and decision making. In J. E. Birren & K. W. Schaie (Eds.), *Handbook of the psychology of aging* (6th ed., pp. 315–342). Burlington, MA: Academic Press.

Marsiske, M., & Willis, S. L. (1995). Dimensionality of everyday problem solving in older adults. *Psychology and Aging, 10,* 269–283.

Mazur, D. J., & Merz, J. F. (1996). How older patients' treatment preferences are influenced by disclosures about therapeutic uncertainty: Surgery versus expectant management for localized prostate cancer. *Journal of the American Geriatrics Society, 44,* 934–937.

Meacham, J. A., & Emont, N. C. (1989). The interpersonal basis of everyday problem solving. In J. D. Sinnott (Ed.), *Everyday problem solving: Theory and applications* (pp. 7–23). New York: Praeger.

Meegan, S. P., & Berg, C. A. (2002). Contexts, functions, forms, and processes of collaborative everyday problem solving in older adulthood. *International Journal of Behavioral Development, 26,* 6–15.

Meyer, B. J. F., Russo, C., & Talbot, A. (1995). Discourse comprehension and problem solving: Decisions about the treatment of breast cancer by women across the life-span. *Psychology and Aging, 10,* 84–103.

Meyer, B. J. F., Talbot, A. P., & Ranalli, C. (2007). Why older adults make more immediate treatment decisions about cancer than younger adults. *Psychology and Aging, 22,* 505–524.

Morfei, M. Z., Hooker, K., Fiese, B. H., & Corderio, A. M. (2001). Continuity and change in parenting possible selves: A longitudinal follow-up. *Basic and Applied Social Psychology, 23,* 217–223.

Murtha, S., Cismaru, R., Waechter, R., & Chertkow, H. (2002). Increased variability accompanies frontal lobe damage in dementia. *Journal of the International Neuropsychological Society, 8,* 360–372.

Neisser, U. (1976). General, academic, and artificial intelligence. In L. B. Resnick (Ed.), *The nature of intelligence* (pp. 135–144). Hillsdale, NJ: Lawrence Erlbaum.

Park, D. C., & Liu, L. L. (2007). *Medical adherence and aging.* Washington, DC: American Psychological Association.

Poon, L. W., Rubin, D. C., & Wilson, B. A. (1989). *Everyday cognition in adulthood and late life.* Cambridge, UK: Cambridge University Press.

Rogoff, B., & Lave, J. (Eds.). (1984). *Everyday cognition: Its development in social context.* Cambridge, MA: Harvard University Press.

Rowe, J., & Kahn, R. (1998). *Successful aging.* New York: Random House.

Ryff, C. D., Lee, Y. H., Essex, M. J., & Schmutte, P. S. (1994). My children and me: Midlife evaluations of grown children and of self. *Psychology and Aging, 9,* 195–205.

Sansone, C., & Berg, C. A. (1993). Adapting to the environment across the life span: Different process or different inputs? *International Journal of Behavioral Development, 16,* 215–241.

Scribner, S. (1986). Thinking in action: Some characteristics of practical thought. In R. J. Sternberg & R. Wagner (Eds.), *Practical intelligence: Origins of competence in the everyday world* (pp. 143–162). New York: Cambridge University Press.

Sinnott, J. D. (Ed.). (1989). *Everyday problem solving: Theory and applications.* New York: Praeger.

Smith, T. W., Berg, C. A., Uchino, B. N., Florsheim, P., Pearce, G., Hawkins, M., et al. (2006). *Conflict and collaboration in middle-aged and older married couples: Sex, age, and interaction context as moderators of cardiovascular response.* Unpublished manuscript.

Stanovich, K. E. (1999). *Who is rational?: Studies of individual differences in reasoning.* Mahwah, NJ: Lawrence Erlbaum.

Stanovich, K. E., & West, R. F. (1997). Reasoning independently of prior belief and individual differences in actively open-minded thinking. *Journal of Educational Psychology, 89,* 342.

Stanovich, K. E., & West, R. F. (1999). Discrepancies between normative and descriptive models of decision making and the understanding/ acceptance principle. *Cognitive Psychology, 38,* 349.

Sternberg, R. J. (1984). A contextual view of the nature of intelligence. In P. S. Fry (Ed.), *Changing conceptions of intelligence and intellectual functioning: Current theory and* research (pp. 7–34). Amsterdam: North-Holland.

Sternberg, R. J., & Wagner, R. K. (Eds.). (1986). *Practical intelligence.* New York: Cambridge University Press.

Stone, A. A., Kessler, R. C., & Haythornthwaite, J. A. (1991). Measuring daily events and experiences: Decisions for the researcher. *Journal of Personality, 59,* 575–607.

Strough, J., & Margrett, J. (2002). Overview of the special section on collaborative cognition in later adulthood. *International Journal of Behavioral Development, 26,* 2–5.

Thornton, W. J. L., & Dumke, H. A. (2005). Age differences in everyday problem-solving and decision-making effectiveness: A meta-analytic review. *Psychology and Aging, 20,* 85–99.

Uchino, B. N., Berg, C. A., Smith, T. W., Pearce, G., & Skinner, M. (2006). Age-related differences in ambulatory blood pressure during daily stress: Evidence for greater blood pressure reactivity with age. *Psychology and Aging, 21,* 321–239.

Wagner, R. K. (1986). The search for extraterrestrial intelligence. In R. J. Sternberg & R. K. Wagner (Eds.), *Practical intelligence: Origins of competence in the everyday world* (pp. 361–378). New York: Academic Press.

Wagner, R. K., & Sternberg, R. J. (1986). Tacit knowledge and intelligence in the everyday world. In R. J. Sternberg & R. K. Wagner (Eds.), *Practical intelligence.* New York: Cambridge University Press.

Walsh, D. A., & Hershey, D. A. (1993). Mental models and the maintenance of complex problem solving skills into old age. In J. Cerella & W. Hoyer (Eds.), *Adult information processing: limits on loss* (pp. 553–584). New York: Academic Press.

Watson, T. L., & Blanchard-Fields, F. (1998). Thinking with your head and your heart: Age differences in everyday problem-solving strategy preferences. *Aging, Neuropsychology, and Cognition, 5,* 225–240.

Wegner, D. M., Erber, R., & Raymond, P. (1991). Transactive memory in close relationships. *Journal of Personality and Social Psychology, 61,* 923–929.

Weitzman, P. F., & Weitzman, E. A. (2001). Everyday interpersonal conflicts of middle-aged women: An examination of strategies and their contextual correlates. *International Journal of Aging and Human Development, 52,* 281–295.

Wiebe, D. J., Berg, C. A., Korbel, C. D., Palmer, D. L., Beveridge, R. M., Upchurch, R., et al. (2005). Children's appraisals of maternal involvement in diabetes care: Enhancing our understanding of quality of life, adherence, and metabolic control across adolescence. *Journal of Pediatric Psychology, 30,* 167–178.

Willis, S. L. (1991). Cognition and everyday competence. In K. W. Schaie (Ed.), *Annual review of gerontology and geriatrics* (Vol. 11, pp. 80–109). New York: Springer.

Willis, S. L. (1996). Everyday problem solving. In J. E. Birren & K. W. Schaie (Eds.), *Handbook of the psychology of aging* (4th ed., pp. 287–307). New York: Academic Press.

Willis, S. L., Dolan, M., & Betrand, R. (1999). Problem solving on health-related tasks of daily living. In D. C. Park, R. W. Morrell, & K. Shifren (Eds.), *Processing of medical information in aging patients: Cognitive and human factors perspectives* (pp. 199–219). Mahwah, NJ: Lawrence Erlbaum.

Willis, S. L., & Schaie, K. W. (1986). Practical intelligence in later adulthood. In R. J. Sternberg & R. K. Wagner (Eds.), *Practical intelligence: Nature and origins of competence in the everyday world* (pp. 236–268). New York: Cambridge University Press.

Zwahr, M. D., Park, D. C., & Shifren, K. (1999). Judgments about estrogen replacement therapy: The role of age, cognitive abilities, and beliefs. *Psychology and Aging, 14,* 179–191.

14

Individual Differences in Verbal Learning in Old Age

Daniel Zimprich, Philippe Rast, and Mike Martin

Until not too long ago, the psychological study of how people learn and remember verbal material has kept a number of eminent thinkers, scholars, researchers, and students occupied. Beginning in the 1950s, a variety of rather formalized statistical models of verbal learning emerged that were doing relatively well in capturing empirical data, mostly average learning curves (e.g., Bush & Mosteller, 1955; Estes, 1950). Despite their success, the work of these scientists by and large now stands there, unread, gathering dust on the shelves of many university libraries. The main reason for this might be that most of these models were formulated in a stimulus–response framework, which went out of style at the end of the 1960s and was replaced by the concepts and vocabulary of information processing. With this replacement, the term *learning* lost much of the popularity it had in conjunction with verbal memory phenomena, while at the same time *memory* became the more often-used notion (Nelson & Narens, 1994). However, because verbal learning necessarily entails acquisition, storage, and retrieval, verbal learning and memory research are in fact so closely connected that

any distinction between these two parts of a bipartite field might be considered arbitrary. As Tulving and Madigan (1970) pointed out at the beginning of the cognitive era of psychology, verbal learning and memory research might be described as two intertwined subcultures that share a common goal but talk different languages and use different methods.

Similarly, Craik (1977, p. 385) argued that research into memory mainly uses once-presented material and one single recall trial, whereas examining verbal learning usually requires multiple presentations of material and several or multitrial recall cycles. With a grain of salt, then, one might assert that verbal learning captures the "dynamic" aspects of memory, that is, systematic changes in verbal memory performance due to repeated practice.

Taking up such a working distinction between verbal learning and memory, one has to diagnose that the bulk of research on verbal memory phenomena today is conducted using single recall trials; that is, it represents memory research. This holds also and is especially true for the investigation and comparison of memory performance in different age groups. A glimpse into

AUTHORS' NOTE: Parts of the preparation of this chapter were supported by the Swiss National Science Foundation, Grant SNSF-100013-103525.

the references section of Kausler's (1994) benchmark monograph on learning and memory in older adults shows that the majority of research on age differences in verbal learning, that is, multitrial free recall, was performed before 1980. Although we do not present any exact numbers here, we suspect that this situation has not changed very much since the publication of Kausler's book; that is, interest in examining verbal learning in younger and older adults—as opposed to investigating their verbal memory—appears to have become minimal, apart from, for example, issues in diagnosing dementia (Schoenberg et al., 2006). Such an unbalanced situation might not be without reasons (see above) but appears unwarranted in light of the fact that many naturalistic learning situations do not comprise only one study cycle but rather involve several trials until a desired level of mastery is reached (cf. Nelson & Narens, 1994). This is even more true with respect to older adults, where the importance of learning for maintaining cognitive performance has been frequently stressed as providing an enormous preventive potential (e.g., Hultsch, Hertzog, Dixon, & Small, 1998; Martin & Zimprich, 2005; Stern, 2002; Willis & Schaie, 2005) and is becoming more and more of an issue in cognitive aging research (e.g., Willis et al., 2006).

Facing this state of affairs, we felt it timely to revive interest in verbal learning in old age. Such an effort should, of course, not be interpreted as an attempt to discredit memory research in the elderly but rather to complement and enrich it by taking a closer look at individual differences in learning in old age. Our approach to verbal learning in old age differs from previous ones that have demonstrated that older adults show decrements in verbal learning (cf. Kausler, 1994). Instead of focusing on group-based data and, thus, the average learning curve, our goal was to reinstate the individual into the learning curve. More specifically, we aimed at modeling individual differences in learning in old age. Such an individual-centered perspective represents a fundamental shift from and extension of traditional verbal learning research, because it is less focused on the question of why older people learn at all but instead asks why different older people learn differentially, that is, why older people differ in their amount and rate of verbal

learning. Note that a similar shift from group-based to individual-specific approaches has taken place in developmental aging research, where, during the last 10 years, a number of studies began to emerge that provided new insights into cognitive aging by taking into account individual differences in change (e.g., Hofer & Sliwinski, 2006; Martin & Zimprich, 2005; Zimprich, 2002; Zimprich & Martin, 2002). After having thus clarified the setting and aims of our research, we begin by introducing some formal models of the learning curve.

FORMALIZING LEARNING IN OLD AGE

Performance on a task typically improves with repetition. However, with every repetition the amount of performance improvement decreases. As a consequence of these two constituents, performance improvement or learning of a task may be described as a process that benefits from investing in further practice, but with diminishing returns. If performance is diagrammed as a function of the number of practice repetitions, the so-called learning curve emerges that follows a gradually increasing, albeit negatively accelerated trajectory (cf. Ritter & Schooler, 2001). The relation between performance improvement and repeated practice as described in the learning curve is so ubiquitous that it applies to a broad variety of performance increments in human behavior, for example, acquisition of new skills (e.g., Ackerman, 1988), gaining knowledge of statistics (e.g., Smith, 1998), and of course verbal learning (Tulving, 1964).

As noted above, learning curves describe the change in performance over trials t ($t = 1, \ldots, n$). More formally, if learning is monotonically increasing, learning curves can be described using the following equation:

$$f(t) = \alpha - (\alpha - \beta) \cdot g(t), \qquad (14.1)$$

where α is the upper asymptote of the curve and β is the initial value of performance.[1] These two parameters act as boundaries, because the lower performance limit is given by β and the upper performance limit is given by α. The function $g(t)$ describes the type of curvature present in the learning curve across the n trials. As such, $g(t)$ might be called the *core* of the learning curve and is usually a function of a third parameter, a learning rate parameter γ (cf. Paul, 1994). A psychological interpretation of the three parameters is straightforward. The parameter β represents performance after the first trial, that is, after the first learning cycle is finished. Thus, it may be interpreted as an initial performance level that closely resembles the performance that is measured using typical, one-trial memory tasks (cf. Hultsch et al., 1998). The presence of an upper asymptote (α) in Equation 14.1 suggests that learning tasks have natural ceilings or limits on performance. These asymptotes may be determined by the experimenter's choice of task material, for example, list length in free recall. Note that the asymptote is not necessarily reached within a given range of trials but instead, as a limiting value, should be interpreted as potential maximum performance, that is, a prediction of a subject's performance after an infinite amount of training (cf. Browne, 1993; Browne & Du Toit, 1991; Mazur & Hastie, 1978; Meredith & Tisak, 1990; Richards, 1959). Eventually, the learning rate γ denotes the rate of approach from initial level to potential maximum performance. Larger values of γ correspond to faster rates of learning, that is, higher quantums of improvement in performance.

As candidates for $g(t)$, different authors have suggested different core functions. For example, Heathcote, Brown, and Mewhort (2000) advocated the exponential curve, the core function of which is given as $g_{ex}(t) = \exp(-\{t-1\}\gamma_{ex})$, which, after substituting into Equation 14.1, leads to

$$f_{ex}(t) = \alpha_{ex} - (\alpha_{ex} - \beta_{ex})\exp(-\{t-1\}\gamma_{ex}). \quad (14.2)$$

As a viable alternative, Mazur and Hastie (1978) proposed a hyperbolic function, the core function of which is $g_{hy}(t) = \frac{t-1}{-t+1-\gamma_{hy}^{-1}} + 1$. Combined with Equation 14.1, this gives

$$f(t) = \alpha_{hy} - (\alpha_{hy} - \beta_{hy})\left(\frac{t-1}{-t+1-\gamma_{hy}^{-1}} + 1\right). \quad (14.3)$$

As a third function describing learning, a power curve has been forwarded by, for example, Logan (1988, 1995) and, in its more general form, by A. Newell and Rosenbloom (1981). The core function of the simple power curve is $g_{po}(t) = t^{-\gamma_{po}}$, whereas for the general power curve it is $g_{gpo}(t) = (t + \delta)^{-\gamma_{gpo}}$, where the additional parameter δ takes into account learning prior to the beginning of the task. If the core function of the simple power curve is substituted into Equation 14.1, we have

$$f_{po}(t) = \alpha_{po} - (\alpha_{po} - \beta_{po})t^{-\gamma_{po}}. \quad (14.4)$$

The different core functions mentioned above not only affect the curvature of learning trajectories but also have important theoretical implications. For example, as detailed by Restle and Greeno (1970), the exponential curve may be interpreted as being based on a *replacement model* of learning, which suggests that learning is a process through which incorrect response tendencies are replaced by more and more correct response tendencies. As an exponential curve, the replacement model implies a constant learning rate relative to the amount left to be learned; that is, the replacement process is assumed to occur at a constant rate. As such, the exponential learning model fits nicely into the theories of Estes (1950) and Bush and Mosteller (1955).

By contrast, as Restle and Greeno (1970) pointed out, the hyperbolic curve is based on an *accumulation model* of learning. According to the accumulation model, learning is a process by which correct response tendencies increase steadily with practice and compete with incorrect response tendencies, which remain constant across trials. Unlike the exponential model, the amount of accumulation per trial is considered a constant proportion of the amount or duration of the study. The accumulation model was first introduced by L. L. Thurstone (1919) in his monograph on the learning curve.

Finally, the power curve is based on the assumption that "some mechanism is slowing down the rate of learning" (A. Newell & Rosenbloom, 1981, p. 18). Thus, if learning follows a power law, then learning slows down across trials. This slowing, however, is not proportional to the amount left to be learned or the duration of study. ACT–R (Adaptive Control of Thought—Rational; Anderson & Lebiere, 1998) and SOAR (A. Newell, 1990), two cognitive architectures, generally predict a power law of learning, albeit for different reasons. ACT-R posits that rules and memory traces are strengthened across trials according to a power law based on the assumption that the cognitive system is adapted to the statistical structure of the environment (Anderson & Schooler, 1991). Several models in SOAR have been created that model the power law (e.g., Nerb, Ritter, & Krems, 1999; A. Newell, 1990). These models explain the power law as arising out of mechanisms such as hierarchical learning (i.e., learning parts of the environment or internal goal structures) that initially comprise low-level actions that are very common and, thus, useful. With further practice, even more valuable, larger patterns of actions that occur less frequently are learned.

The purpose of this chapter is not, however, to decide which type of learning curve is the "true" one for verbal learning in old age. In the end, the issue of which core function describes learning most adequately—be it in the elderly or other age groups—is still controversial (e.g., Heathcote et al., 2000; Logan, 1995; Mazur & Hastie, 1978; K. M. Newell, Liu, & Mayer-Kress, 2001; A. Newell & Rosenbloom, 1981).[2] Instead, in preparing this chapter we aimed at extending the examination of learning curves in old age by a thus-far neglected dimension: Whereas previously, learning curves have almost exclusively been investigated using averaged data (e.g., Logan, 1988), we wanted to bring the individual back into the investigation of learning curves. Specifically, we intended to model individual differences in the three parameters governing learning curves in old age as described in Equations 14.2, 14.3, and 14.4. In our opinion, it seems unwise to leave information regarding individuals unused in examining learning curves, a point that has similarly been made with respect to developmental changes in elderly persons (cf. Hofer & Sliwinski, 2001, 2006; Zimprich, 2002; Zimprich & Martin, 2002).

Assessing the amount of verbal learning across a number of practice trials necessarily requires repeated measurements. In this respect, the examination of systematic performance changes due to learning bears similarities to investigating developmental changes over time. However, although the study of developmental changes has benefited from novel statistical analysis techniques that reach beyond the traditional analysis of variance approach—for example, growth curve models that distinguish

between fixed or average effects and random or individual effects (cf. Bryk & Raudenbush, 1992, chap. 6; Goldstein, 1995, chap. 6; McArdle & Anderson, 1990)—the same has not happened regarding learning curves. Note that a key feature of these comparatively recent statistical approaches is that by including random effects they allow for the modeling of interindividual differences in intraindividual change and the inclusion of explanatory variables that may account for the diversity in longitudinal trajectories (e.g., Zimprich, 2002; Zimprich & Martin, 2002). By contrast, the analysis of age differences in learning curves is still dominated by statistical approaches that rely mainly on means, that is, average performance changes, where individual differences in memory performance increments are treated as a nuisance (cf. Davis et al., 2003).

Formally, an individual-specific approach requires an expansion of the fixed effects verbal learning curves as expressed in Equations 14.2, 14.3, and 14.4 by random effects. If we denote random effects by Latin letters—as opposed to fixed effects, which are typically referred to by Greek letters—the hyperbolic learning curve, for example, given in Equation 14.3, of individual *i* becomes

$$y_{,i}(t) = \{\alpha_{hy} + a_i\} - (\{\alpha_{hy} + a_i\} - \{\beta_{hy} + b_i\}) \left(\frac{t-1}{-t+1-\{\gamma_{hy} + g_i\}^{-1}} + 1 \right), \quad (14.5)$$

which looks rather formidable. However, under standard assumptions about random effects (zero mean, normality), Equation 14.5 represents a model that belongs to a general class of estimable latent curve models (cf. Meredith & Tisak, 1990; Richards, 1959). Yet, to the best of our knowledge, growth curve type models including random effects have not been used in the examination of verbal learning curves. Part of the problem might be that learning curves usually are inherently nonlinear, which renders standard (i.e., linear or quadratic) growth models inappropriate. Although nonlinear growth models have also been elaborated (see Cudeck & Harring, 2007; Davidian & Giltinan, 1995; Molenberghs & Verbeke, 2005, chap. 20), both the specification and estimation of such models become complex, especially in large samples.

As a viable alternative, Browne (1993; Browne & Du Toit, 1991) suggested applying *structured latent curve models* for learning data, which impose specific nonlinear constraints on the pattern matrix of otherwise-standard latent growth curve models. This more manageable and tractable approach was followed in the present investigation to model individual differences in verbal learning.

Note that focusing on individual learning curves instead of drawing mainly from grouped data is not an entirely new idea. Heathcote and colleagues (2000), for example, fitted nonlinear functions directly to individual data. Such an approach, however, holds the shortcoming that it requires a two-step procedure if inferences about population parameters shall be drawn: In a first step, individual learning curves are estimated, which in the second step represent the raw data of further analyses (e.g., in modeling the average learning curve). By contrast, our approach allows for simultaneously estimating individual parameters *and* parameters that characterize the whole sample. This not only has the advantage of resulting in correct standard errors of parameters estimates but, also, in estimating the parameters characterizing one specific individual, it allows for borrowing strength (i.e., use information) from other individuals whose trajectory of verbal learning is similar (see Bryk & Raudenbush, 1992; Goldstein, 1995; Molenberghs & Verbeke, 2005). This is not to say that the description of average changes is invaluable. To the contrary, as is common for mixed-effects models, our approach relies on the assumption that individual learning curves follow the same functional form as the average learning curve (cf. Davidian & Giltinan, 1995). At the same time, modeling the average learning curve above all provides a means to an end to bring the (older) individual back into learning curves, which is why we do not attempt to review previous findings on age-related differences in verbal learning here. Suffice it to say that previous work on verbal learning has demonstrated that older adults, on average, take longer to learn the same amount of new material than do younger adults (cf. Cerella, Onyper, & Hoyer, 2006; Kausler, 1994).

In what follows, we try to demonstrate the fruitfulness of the individual-centered approach on verbal learning in old age outlined above. In a first step, we intended to find the most adequate representation of verbal learning data stemming from the Zurich Longitudinal Study on Cognitive Aging (ZULU; Zimprich et al., in press) by testing different growth curve models based on different nonlinear functions. After selecting the best fitting model (the hyperbolic function), we modeled the linkages of the learning parameters initial performance level (β), potential maximum performance (α), and rate of learning (γ) to age and processing speed. The inclusion of this cognitive ability was motivated by the fact that processing speed represents a major explanatory variable of cognitive aging (Salthouse, 1991, 1996). We subsequently included memory as an outcome variable; that is, parameters of verbal learning (β, α, γ) were used as predictor variables of memory performance in old age. In light of the duality of learning and memory phenomena, memory performance represents an obvious and extensively studied outcome variable in cognitive aging research (Craik, 1977; Hultsch et al., 1998; Kausler, 1994). In the complete model, the verbal learning parameters initial performance level (β), potential maximum performance (α), and rate of learning (γ) thus acted as mediating variables between processing speed and memory.

An Empirical Analysis of Verbal Learning in Old Age

The data used in the sequel come from ZULU, an ongoing longitudinal study on cognitive and learning abilities of elderly persons in Switzerland (Zimprich et al., in press). At the first measurement occasion (2005), the ZULU sample comprised 364 participants between 65 and 80 years of age (mean age: 73 years, $SD = 4.4$ years, 46% women). The majority of the sample was married and resided with others. On average, participants reported about 13 years of formal education. There were no signs of cognitive impairments or pronounced depressive affect in the sample. The majority of participants judged their health as "good," and no participant reported any severe hearing or vision difficulties. Part of the cognitive testing protocol in ZULU were three measures of processing speed (Number Comparison, Identical Pictures, and

Letter Digit Substitution), a verbal learning measure that comprised five trials of a word list recall task, and three measures of memory (Paired Associates, Story Recall, and Picture Memory).

The Number Comparison task (Ekstrom, French, Harman, & Derman, 1976) required participants to compare as rapidly as possible whether two numbers presented on the computer screen were identical. The number of correct answers, which could range between 0 and 60, was scored. After two practice items during the instruction phase, participants had 90 seconds to work on the task. The Identical Pictures task (Ekstrom et al., 1976) required participants to choose one out of five objects that was identical to a reference object as rapidly as possible. The number of correctly answered items, which could range from 0 to 60, was scored. After two practice items during the instruction phase, participants had 90 seconds to work on the task. Letter Digit Substitution consisted of 75 items. For each item, a table that assigned five different letters to the numbers 1 to 5 was displayed on the top of the computer screen. Below the table, a single letter was presented together with a question mark. Participants were supposed to press the number that belonged to the single letter according to the presented coding table. For each item, there was a different coding table. The number of correctly answered items, which could range from 0 to 75, was scored. After two practice items, participants had 90 seconds to work on the task.

Verbal Learning was assessed by five consecutive trials of a word list recall task. The task comprised 27 meaningful but unrelated words that were taken from the German version of the Rey Auditory Verbal Learning Test (Helmstädter, Lendt, & Lux, 2001). The 27 words appeared on a computer screen at a rate of 2 seconds each, and participants were required to read them aloud.

After the presentation of all 27 words, participants were asked to recall as many words as possible, in any order. This procedure was repeated five times, with the order of words being different for each trial. At each trial, the number of correctly recalled words was scored; scores could range between 0 and 27.

The Paired Associates task comprised 12 semantically unrelated word pairs taken from the German version of the Wechsler Memory

Scale—Revised (Härting et al., 2000) and from the Munich Verbal Memory Test (Ilmberger, 1988). After two examples during instruction, word pairs were presented for 4 seconds each, and participants had to read them aloud. After a pause of 1 second, the next word pair was displayed. After presentation of all 12 word pairs, only the first word of a pair appeared on the screen as a cue, and the second one was replaced by a question mark (e.g., salad–?), using a different order than during encoding. The number of correctly recalled target words, which could range from 0 to 12, was scored. Story Recall consisted of Story A of the Logical Memory subtest of the German version of the Wechsler Memory Scale—Revised. The 66-word story was read by the experimenter during 60 seconds. Participants were asked to listen closely and, when the story was finished, to immediately recall as many details as possible. The number of correctly recalled propositions, which could range from 0 to 25, was scored. Finally, the Picture Memory task encompassed 12 pictures taken from the Nuremberg Age Inventory (Nürnberger-Alters-Inventar; Oswald & Fleischmann, 1999). For each item, a picture of a simple object was shown for 2.75 seconds, and participants were required to name the shown object aloud (e.g., "apple"). After a pause of 1 second, the next picture was displayed. Immediately after presentation of all 12 pictures, participants were asked to verbally recall as many of the seen objects as possible. The number of correctly recalled objects, which could range between 0 and 12, was scored. All analyses reported below were conducted using Mx (Neale, Boker, Xie, & Maes, 2003). Nonlinear learning models were specified as structured growth models (Browne, 1993; Browne & Du Toit, 1991). The absolute goodness of fit of models was evaluated using the chi-square test and two additional criteria: (1) the Comparative Fit Index (CFI) and (2) the Root-Mean-Square Error of Approximation (RMSEA). Values of the CFI above .95 are considered to be adequate, whereas for the RMSEA values less than .06 indicate an acceptable model fit (cf. Hu & Bentler, 1999). In comparing the relative fit of nested models, we used the chi-square difference test where appropriate. Because of its dependency on sample size and because we also wanted to compare non-nested models, we mainly relied on calculating 90% RMSEA confidence intervals for the models estimated (MacCallum, Browne, & Sugawara, 1996). Because the RMSEA is virtually independent of sample size, the comparison of RMSEA confidence intervals (i.e., whether they do or do not overlap), provides an effective, alternative method of assessing relative model fit of nested and non-nested models. Throughout, we refer to a significance level of $p < .05$ if a parameter estimate is denoted as statistically significant.

EMPIRICAL FINDINGS

Descriptive statistics of the 11 manifest cognitive variables and age together with their intercorrelations are shown in Table 14.1. For the means of the verbal learning indicators, a typical learning curve emerged, that is, a gradually increasing but negatively accelerated trajectory. Raw data were checked for departures from both univariate and multivariate normality. Skewness and kurtosis estimates of the 11 manifest cognitive variables did not exceed 1 or –1 (average skewness: .08; average kurtosis: .25), whereas the distribution of age, for which the sample had been stratified, was platykurtic. The normalized estimate of Mardia's coefficient of multivariate kurtosis was .65. Thus, with the limitation that the distribution of age was inconsistent with univariate normality, the multivariate distributional properties of the 11 manifest cognitive variables and age warranted the use of maximum likelihood parameter estimation.

MODELS OF VERBAL LEARNING IN OLD AGE

In a first model (VL1), changes in verbal learning performance were fitted by a growth curve comprising level, linear slope, and quadratic slope. As can be seen in Table 14.2, Model VL1 evinced a satisfactory fit as indexed by the CFI, although not as judged by the statistically significant chi-square value and the RMSEA. On average, 82% of variance was explained in the verbal learning indicators. For the latent level variable, a mean of 5.34 was estimated, and for

linear slope and quadratic slope means were 4.43 and –0.45, respectively. Variances were estimated as 3.93 (level), 4.46 (linear slope), and 0.06 (quadratic slope). These variances were all statistically significant, implying that there were reliable individual differences in initial performance level, linear change across trials, and negative acceleration of performance changes across trials. Level and linear slope were significantly related ($r = .29$), as were level and quadratic slope ($r = -.30$) and linear and quadratic slope ($r = -.91$).[3] Thus, participants who started out at a higher level had a somewhat higher linear performance increase and a more pronounced negative acceleration in performance changes. Also, those with a high linear performance increase showed a much stronger flatting out of performance improvements. In sum, the quadratic growth model appeared to capture important aspects of verbal learning, but it did not fit acceptably.

In a second model (VL2), exponential learning curves as described by Equation 14.2 in the introductory section were imposed. Model VL2 had an acceptable fit (see Table 14.2), with the chi-square value indicating no statistically significant differences between the moments predicted by Model VL3 and actual moments of the data. Although a chi-square difference comparison of Model VL2 with Model VL1 is impossible because both models have the same degrees of freedom, the CFI as well as the RMSEA clearly favored Model VL2. Note, however, that the RMSEA confidence intervals overlapped somewhat, indicating that difference in fit was not statistically significant. The amount of explained variance in the verbal learning indicators was 84%, on average. The latent variable representing initial performance level (β_{ex}) had a mean of 5.29, and the latent variable reflecting potential maximum or asymptotic performance (α_{ex}) was 19.23, on average. Mean rate of learning (γ_{ex}) was estimated as 0.358. The statistically significant variances were 4.11 ($SE = 0.69$) for initial performance, 29.35 ($SE = 7.60$) for potential maximum or asymptotic performance, and 0.029 ($SE = 0.012$) for rate of learning. The correlation between initial performance level and potential maximum performance reached statistical significance ($r = .43$), implying that participants who started out at a higher level of

Table 14.1   Descriptive Statistics and Sample Correlations of Cognitive Variables and Age

	M	SD	1	2	3	4	5	6	7	8	9	10	11
1. Number Comparison	17.15	4.30	—										
2. Identical Pictures	21.38	4.54	.49	—									
3. Letter Digit Substitution	31.86	6.62	.64	.63	—								
4. Verbal learning, Trial 1	5.27	2.24	.18	.24	.29	—							
5. Verbal learning, Trial 2	9.62	3.15	.28	.31	.36	.68	—						
6. Verbal learning, Trial 3	12.33	3.72	.31	.29	.41	.62	.81	—					
7. Verbal learning, Trial 4	14.38	4.03	.29	.29	.41	.57	.77	.85	—				
8. Verbal learning, Trial 5	16.01	4.47	.23	.25	.35	.53	.73	.81	.85	—			
9. Paired Associates	2.99	2.35	.14	.15	.21	.23	.38	.46	.45	.44	—		
10. Story Recall	14.52	4.12	.15	.15	.25	.21	.28	.33	.33	.28	.33	—	
11. Picture Memory	6.84	1.57	.23	.29	.34	.33	.44	.46	.45	.43	.23	.23	—
12. Age	72.98	4.43	-.25	-.35	-.37	-.12	-.16	-.20	-.17	-.12	-.18	-.07	-.21

NOTES: $N = 364$. Correlations larger than $r = .09$ in absolute size are statistically significant at $p < .05$, one-tailed.

memory performance also tended to show a higher asymptotic memory performance after five learning trials. By contrast, the associations between initial performance level and rate of learning ($r = -.22$), and between rate of learning and potential maximum performance ($r = .15$), were statistically not significant. Taken together, the exponential learning curve model seemed to adequately describe the verbal learning data.

As an alternative to exponential verbal learning, we also fitted a hyperbolic model (VL3) of verbal learning as described by Equation 14.3 in the introductory section. The fit of Model VL3 was excellent (see Table 14.2). Again, a chi-square difference comparison with the previous model (VL2) was impossible, but both the CFI and RMSEA showed a better fit of Model VL3. At the same time, the overlapping RMSEA confidence intervals indicated that the difference in model fit was not statistically significant. However, RMSEA confidence intervals compared with Model VL1 did not overlap, denoting that Model VL3 fit significantly better than Model VL1. On average, 84% of variance were explained in the five manifest indicators of verbal learning. For the latent variable capturing initial performance level (β_{hy}), a mean of 5.28 emerged. The latent variable representing potential maximum performance (α_{hy}) had a mean of

26.58. Note that this estimate was much closer to the actual list length (27), that is, the maximum number of words that could be recalled, than in the exponential model (19.23). The mean rate of learning (γ_{hy}) was 0.251. Variances (of the learning parameters were 4.23 ($SE = 0.87$) for initial level, 84.83 ($SE = 28.78$) for potential maximum performance, and 0.026 ($SE = 0.012$) for the rate of learning. Hence, with respect to all three parameters there were reliable interindividual differences. The nonsignificant correlations of initial performance with potential maximum performance and with rate of learning were $r = .25$ and $r = .10$, respectively. The statistically significant correlation between potential maximum performance and rate of learning was $r = -.65$, indicating that participants with a higher asymptotic performance had a slower rate of learning; that is, they needed more trials to achieve their potential maximum performance. In sum, the hyperbolic model of learning captured the data very well.

Eventually a power model of learning as given by Equation 14.4 eventually was estimated. However, we were unable to arrive at a solution that led to a stable estimate of potential maximum performance (α_{po}), which was estimated as being 133. As a consequence of these estimation difficulties, a number of parameters

Table 14.2   Sequence of Estimated Models and Fit Statistics

Model[a]	χ^2	df	p	CFI	RMSEA	90% CI
VL1 (Quadratic learning)	30.90	6	<.05	.984	.107	.071, .145
VL2 (Exponential learning)	8.37	6	>.20	.999	.033	.000, .081
VL3 (Hyperbolic learning)	3.28	6	>.77	1.000	.000	.000, .046
AVL1 (VL3 & age)	5.64	8	>.69	1.000	.000	.000, .048
AVL2 (VL3 & equal age)	9.23	10	>.51	1.000	.000	.000, .054
SVL1 (AVL1 & speed)	21.73	22	>.47	1.000	.000	.000, .043
SVL2 (SVL1 & equal speed)	28.88	27	>.36	.999	.014	.000, .044
SVLM1 (SVL1 & memory)	56.26	47	>.17	.996	.023	.000, .043
SVLM2 (SVLM1—direct effects)	62.05	49	>.10	.994	.027	.000, .046

NOTES: $N = 364$. CFI = Comparative Fit Index; RMSEA = Root-Mean-Square Error of Approximation; CI = confidence interval; VL = verbal learning; VL1 = Model 1; VL2 = Model 2; VL3 = Model 3.

[a]See text for a more detailed description of the estimated models.

became statistically nonsignificant. More specifically, upon inspection, the power curve fitted excellently within the range of the five trials providing data, but afterward it hardly changed its slope, which led to the formally correct but unstable estimate of α_{po} and its variance. With some more trials, we probably would have been able to estimate α_{po} consistently. On the basis of these difficulties in estimation, however, we decided to skip the power model of learning from further analyses.

To summarize, it appeared that a hyperbolic model represented the ZULU verbal learning data best, because it showed the best point estimates of model fit. In addition, the fit of the hyperbolic model was significantly better than that of the quadratic model. Hence, we decided to accept and retain the hyperbolic model for the analyses to follow. Note, however, that because of the very similar form of the trajectories in the first five trials, we cannot safely conclude that the hyperbolic model outperforms the exponential model. Thus, using the ZULU data, it was impossible to distinguish between the replacement and accumulation models of verbal learning, because neither one of them did clearly outperform the other in terms of model fit.

Figure 14.1 depicts the predicted trajectories as based on Model VL3. Shown are seven randomly selected model-based trajectories (thin lines) and the mean trajectory (thick line); dots denote observed values, and circles denote observed means. As can be seen, Model VL3 does very well not only in describing the mean learning curve but also in capturing individual learning curves.

COVARIATES OF LEARNING IN OLD AGE

As a first extension of the hyperbolic learning model, age was included as a predictor of individual differences in the three learning parameters of initial level (β_{hy}), potential maximum performance (α_{hy}), and rate of learning (γ_{hy}). This extended model (AVL1) achieved an excellent model fit (see Table 14.2), which was virtually identical to that of Model VL3, implying that age effects on the manifest indicator variables of verbal learning were mediated completely by the three learning parameters. The

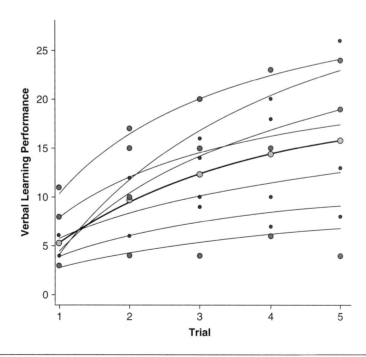

Figure 14.1   Model-Based Trajectories of Verbal Learning

NOTES: Shown are seven randomly selected model-based trajectories. The thick black line denotes the mean profile. Predicted values are based on the hyperbolic model (VL3); dots represent observed values.

standardized effect of age on β_{hy} was –.13 and statistically significant, accounting for approximately 2% of variance in initial level—a small effect in terms of the standards recommended by Cohen (1988). By contrast, the standardized regression of α_{hy} on age was .07, a value so small that it did not reach statistical significance. Accordingly, age explained approximately 0.5% of variance in potential maximum performance. The significant standardized age effect in γ_{hy} was estimated as –.23, which amounted to 5% of explained variance (or an effect of medium size) in rate of learning. Thus, it appeared that age accounted mainly for individual differences in rate of learning, followed by the effect on initial performance level. Effects were in the medium to small range, however, indicating that individual differences among participants of the same age by far outweighed the age-related differences.

In an attempt to more rigorously test for differences in the regression of the three learning parameters on age, in the next model (AVL2) the standardized regression coefficients were constrained to be equal. As shown in Table 14.2, imposing these constraints hardly reduced model fit. Although the point estimates in Model AVL1 indicated different age-related effects, these differences were not reliable. The constrained standardized regression parameter was –.08 and statistically significant. On the basis of the ZULU data, one may not safely conclude that age had a differential effect on initial level, potential maximum performance, and rate of learning. An explanation for this lack of statistical power is that differences in age-related effects were small, which, after taking into account the sample size of 364, made it virtually impossible to differentiate Model AVL2 from AVL1—in fact, as calculated using the procedure suggested by MacCallum et al. (1996), power was .02 only.

Next, for Model SVL1, processing speed was included as an additional predictor of the three learning parameters into the AVL1 model. Processing speed was measured by three manifest variables, namely Number Comparison, Identical Pictures, and Letter Digit Substitution. Standardized factor loadings on the common speed factor were .69 (Number Comparison), .70 (Identical Pictures), and .91 (Letter Digit

Substitution), indicating large amounts of shared variance of the three indicator variables of speed of information processing. The standardized regression of processing speed on age was –.42, with the latter accounting for 17% of variance in the former. As displayed in Table 14.2, Model SVL1 fit the data excellently. Processing speed showed statistically significant effects on initial performance level (β_{hy}), followed by learning rate (γ_{hy}), with standardized regression coefficients of .34 and .25, respectively; that is, participants who processed information more rapidly remembered more words at the beginning of the verbal learning test and showed a more pronounced learning rate compared with individuals with low processing speed. By contrast, the effect of processing speed on potential maximum performance (α_{hy}) was not significant (.13). At the same time, the effects of age on the three learning parameters were attenuated to statistical nonsignificance; specifically, processing speed mediated 87% of the age-related effects in initial performance, 42% in potential maximum performance, and 43% in rate of learning. The correlation between potential maximum and learning rate increased slightly to $r = –.66$ and remained statistically significant. The amount of variance processing speed and age accounted for ranged, in terms of effect size, from small to medium, with 11% in β_{hy}, 2% in α_{hy}, and 10% in γ_{hy}. Together, processing speed and age thus exerted medium effects on initial performance level and learning rate, whereas potential maximum performance seemed largely unaffected.

As with the effects of age (see Model AVL2), one may wonder whether the effects of processing speed on β_{hy}, α_{hy}, and γ_{hy} were significantly different. Hence, after removing the nonsignificant direct effects of age on initial level, potential maximum, and learning rate, we constrained the standardized effects of processing speed on the three learning parameters to be equal in Model SVL2. Table 14.2 shows that doing so did not lead to a substantial decrement in model fit. The constrained regression parameter was .31 and statistically significant. Processing speed explained approximately 9% of variance in initial performance level, potential maximum performance, and rate of learning. As a consequence, one should not consider the effects of processing speed on β_{hy}, α_{hy}, and γ_{hy} as being statistically different in the population. However, taking into account the small differences in model fit and the ZULU sample size, it was practically impossible to differentiate Model SVL2 from SVL1: Statistical power was only .05.

The next step was to include memory as an outcome variable of verbal learning (SVLM1). Memory was assessed by three manifest variables: Paired Associates, Story Recall, and Picture Memory. The standardized factor loadings on the Memory factor were .54 (Paired Associates), .42 (Story Recall), and .54 (Picture Memory), showing that memory indicators shared substantial amounts of variance, albeit less than the processing speed indicators did. Model SVLM1 evinced an excellent model fit (see Table 14.2). The strongest effect on memory was exerted by the learning rate, with a standardized regression coefficient of .84, followed closely by potential maximum performance (.83) and initial performance level (.21). Hence, participants with a higher rate of learning showed better memory performance, which was also true for those with a higher potential maximum of verbal learning and, albeit to a much lesser extent, for those high in initial performance level. Note that memory was assessed by three one-trial tests, from which one might have expected that initial verbal learning performance (β), which, in terms of its definition, is most similar to memory, should emerge as the strongest predictor. However, initial performance level turned out to be the least predictive learning parameter. The standardized effect of age on memory (–.11) did not reach statistical significance; neither did the effect of processing speed (.13). Note that Model SVLM1 can be regarded as a mediational model, in which verbal learning mediated the effects of processing speed on memory. More specifically, the three learning parameters mediated approximately 70% of the effect of processing speed on memory. Together, age, processing speed, and the three learning parameters β_{hy}, α_{hy}, and γ_{hy} accounted for sizable 85% of variance in memory.

Next, for Model SVLM2, the nonsignificant direct effects of age and processing speed on memory were removed. Table 14.2 shows that Model SVLM2 achieved an excellent fit, which, compared with Model SVLM1, was not statistically significant, $\Delta\chi^2(2) = 5.79$, $p > .05$. At the same time, the effects of processing speed on β_{hy}, α_{hy}, and γ_{hy} changed somewhat in proceeding from Model SVLM1 to SVLM2: Although the explained variance in the three learning parameters remained virtually unchanged in initial level and potential maximum performance, it increased to 28% in the learning rate; that is, the three learning parameters acting as mediating variables affected also the association strength between processing speed and learning—a result that might appear counterintuitive but represents a statistical necessity (cf. Pedhazur, 1982). The correlation between potential maximum and initial performance reached statistical significance ($r = .29$), whereas the correlation between potential maximum performance and learning rate was not significant any longer and decreased to $r = -.43$. In Model SVLM2, the standardized effect β on memory was unaltered, while the standardized effect of α decreased somewhat (.63) and that of the learning rate increased slightly (.85). The amount of explained variance in memory increased to 92%.

We selected Model SVLM2 as representing the interrelations among age, processing speed, memory, and the three parameters of verbal learning adequately, while being as parsimonious as possible. Model SVLM2 is depicted in Figure 14.2.

CONCLUSION

In this investigation, we set out to bring the individual back into the verbal learning curve, an issue that in our opinion has been neglected. Focusing on the average learning curve only, and thus relegating individual differences in verbal learning to a nuisance parameter appears to be antithetical to a science of development. Before we turn to the substantive implications of this individual-focused approach, a short discussion of methods for capturing individual learning curves seems in order.

The fact that the average learning curve can be different and can even have a different functional form than the majority of individual curves represents a well-known result (e.g., Sidman, 1952). The situation becomes more complicated if one acknowledges that learning performance can be

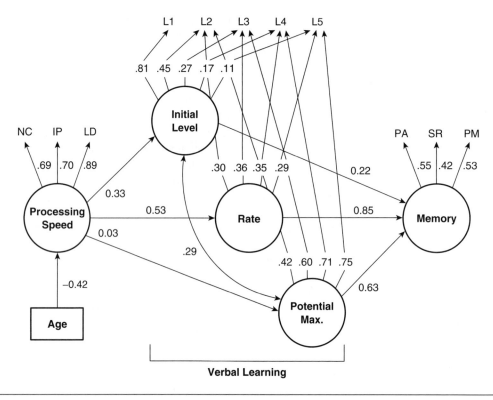

Figure 14.2 Accepted Structural Model of Speed, Verbal Learning, and Memory (Model SVLM2)

NOTES: N = 364. All parameters are standardized. L1–L5 = verbal learning indicators; NC = Number Comparison; IP = Identical Pictures; LD = Letter Digit Substitution; PA = Paired Associates; SR = Story Recall; PM = Picture memory; Max. = maximum.

averaged across persons, across blocks of trials, or both, and that each way of summarizing data gives rise to specific difficulties (Brown & Heathcote, 2003; Cousineau, Hélie, & Lefebvre, 2003). Hence, a curve that describes grouped data must not necessarily be representative of any individual person. One way to bring back the individual into learning curves is thus to focus on individual data, that is, model learning directly for single persons. Heathcote and colleagues (2000), for example, did so in investigating whether the exponential or the power function is more appropriate in describing learning data from a variety of studies. This approach, however, holds the shortcoming that standard errors of parameters may be biased. Also, in estimating individual parameters it does not use information provided by other individuals, whose trajectory is similar. A natural way to strike a balance between grouped data and individual data is to borrow strength from both sides.

For this reason, we chose a structured growth curve approach. In this sense, our perspective on learning curves resembles nonlinear mixed effects models as described in Davidian and Giltinan (1995) and Molenberghs and Verbeke (2005, chap. 20), although for actually fitting curves to data we used structured latent curve models as developed by Browne (1993; Browne & Du Toit, 1991), which allows for fitting nonlinear growth curves belonging to the Richards (1959) family as structural equation models. From the perspective of developmental research in old age, extending the investigation of learning curves in old age to models incorporating individual effects is only natural.

Some years ago, developmental aging researchers became aware of individuals again, based on the pioneering work of methodologists who in the late 1980s and early 1990s provided developmentalists with the tools needed to model individual differences (Bryk &

Raudenbush, 1992; Goldstein, 1995; McArdle & Anderson, 1990). This has resulted in new insights into the process of aging and at the same time raised new questions about development that require theoretical elaboration.

After having clarified these methodological points, we turn to the substantive issues regarding verbal learning in old age. What have we learned about verbal learning in old age by bringing back the individual into the learning curve? Among the four functions applied, the hyperbolic learning curve seemed to best describe the evolution of performance across the five trials. Each of the three parameters of the hyperbolic curve can be interpreted in a different way: Whereas β_{hy} denotes the initial level in learning performance, α_{hy} is a more theoretical value because it is formulated as the upper asymptote or limiting value. Hence, it can only be approached, but never achieved within a given range of trials. Finally, γ_{hy} defines the curvature of the learning trajectory; that is, a high learning rate leads to a steep increase in learning performance across the first trials, whereas a low rate leads to a flatter trajectory and a more evenly distributed increase in learning (Browne, 1993; Browne & Du Toit, 1991; Meredith & Tisak, 1990). The hyperbolic function would, strictly speaking, also mean that the amount of accumulation per trial is a constant proportion relative to the trials completed (Mazur & Hastie, 1978). In the ZULU sample, however, the fit of the hyperbolic and the exponential function was statistically indistinguishable, which leaves the question of whether learning follows an accumulative or a replacement process an open issue.

Note that the excellent model fit implied that *both* the average learning curve *and* the individual ones were captured by the hyperbolic equation—albeit with varying parameter values; that is, in the verbal learning data we analyzed, the average curve and individual curves were of the same functional form. Fitting the hyperbolic model thus allowed us to confirm that verbal learning showed reliable interindividual differences in old age. To compare the magnitude of individual differences in the parameters β_{hy}, α_{hy}, and γ_{hy}, we calculated the coefficient of variation (CV) of each parameter. These amounted to CV (β_{hy}) = .39, CV (α_{hy}) = .35, and CV(γ_{hy}) = .64, implying that individual

differences were most pronounced in rate of learning. Hence, older people tended to show more pronounced individual differences in the rate of acquisition than in initial level or total potential maximum performance. The random effects of potential maximum performance (α_{hy}) and rate of learning (γ_{hy}) were negatively correlated, implying that participants with a higher upper limit of learning performance needed more trials to bridge the performance gap between initial performance level and maximum performance. We acknowledge, though, that this latter finding might also be indicative of a ceiling effect, although our list comprised 27 words, which, together with the fact that the mean number of recalled words was 16 at Trial 5 (see Table 14.1), renders strong ceiling effects unlikely. Still, more detailed analyses are required in this regard, for example, by excluding participants with a performance close to the maximum number of words.

Next, we examined the relations between aging and the three verbal learning parameters. The finding that aging negatively affected verbal learning performance as a whole is not new (see Kausler, 1994), but because of the latent growth curve approach we were able to refine Kausler's (1994) observations in several respects. According to the point estimates of effects, aging mainly affects the verbal learning rate, followed by the effect on initial performance, whereas potential maximum performance was practically unrelated to age. Thus, with increasing age, more learning experiences were needed to attain the same level of mastery. These findings would imply that age differences in verbal learning are due to a flattening of the learning curve as one grows older, which also has the effect that the (predicted) learning curves of some individuals look almost linear (see Figure 14.1). One has to take into account, however, that the ZULU sample consists of elderly persons only and that age-related effects were in the small-to-medium range. It remains an open issue at present whether larger age-related effects in verbal learning parameters would have been found using a broader age range. We certainly would expect this to happen for initial performance level, because this parameter closely mirrors the typical one-trial memory assessments shown to follow a decline trajectory in old age (Craik, 1977; Davis et al., 2003; Hultsch et al., 1998; Kausler, 1994). At present, however, we do not know how much variance age might account for in α and γ in a life span sample. A more age-heterogeneous sample—and, thus, potentially stronger age-related effects—might also help overcoming the lack of statistical power we faced in our analyses when age effects were constrained to be equal (cf. MacCallum et al., 1996). Thus, we think that it is important to follow this research path further, because it might confirm what corresponds to a common lay impression of aging: Older persons take longer to learn, but they can, given enough effort and time, reach the same level of mastery as younger adults. Having said this, the small age-related effects in verbal learning necessarily mean that, in the ZULU data, individual differences among persons of the same age by far outweighed age-related differences in β, α, and γ. As an alternative research avenue—and more in line with the focus of this chapter—we would thus like to encourage researchers to focus on individual differences orthogonal to cross-sectional age (cf. Zimprich et al., in press). In line with this, another fruitful approach would be to analyze the development of the three parameters longitudinally (Hofer & Sliwinski, 2001, 2006).

Processing speed was subsequently included as an additional predictor of verbal learning. On the basis of the assumption that speed of information processing is more basic than other cognitive abilities, and hence represents a resource for higher order cognitive functions (Salthouse, 1991), it appeared instructive to examine which of the three learning parameters was most strongly affected by speed. It turned out that processing speed had positive, medium-sized effects on initial performance level and learning rate, whereas the effect on potential maximum performance was small.

Thus, elderly persons higher in mental speed started out at a higher level and, more important, showed a steeper increase in their verbal learning trajectories. These findings underline the importance of being able to process information rapidly for remembering new material after one trial—a finding that is well established in the literature on memory aging (e.g., Hultsch et al., 1998). In addition, processing speed appeared even more important for the number of trials needed to attain one's potential maximum learning performance (i.e., rate of learning). A more stringent test of the equality of processing speed effects on learning parameters showed that they were statistically indistinguishable, but this might be the consequence of our medium-sized sample. Hence, we believe that in a larger sample these effects may prove to be distinct.

After including speed, the age effects on learning were no longer statistically significant, implying that the age effects in verbal learning were mediated by speed, which is in line with Salthouse's (1996) processing speed theory. However, one has to keep in mind that, as Hofer and Sliwinski (2001) argued, tests of mediational hypotheses in models of cognitive aging might be problematic if they rely on cross-sectional (between-person variance) methods instead of longitudinal (within-person variance) methods, because the provide only a weak basis for drawing conclusions about correlated within-person age changes (see also Cole & Maxwell, 2003).

An important insight we gained from the learning parameters was the finding that learning rate, followed by potential maximum performance, had the strongest effect on memory. In terms of its definition, one would have expected β to be the strongest predictor of memory, because both are defined as the recall performance after one learning trial. Instead, initial learning displayed the smallest effect. This finding is even more intriguing if one considers the task proximity of the indicators for memory, especially Picture Memory or Paired Associates, which were procedurally and conceptually very similar to the verbal learning task (cf. Kausler, 1994). Unexpectedly, then, our results suggest that learning rate and potential maximum performance can be regarded as memory-inherent and highly predictive of memory performance. Regarding learning rate, a possible explanation might be that it is highly relevant for initial performance level as well, because learning, of course, already takes place before the first recall trial. Other parameterizations of the learning curve, which do not include a parameter for initial level, describe this situation of learning (with individually differing rates) right from the start more adequately than the ones we applied (see Mazur & Hastie, 1978).

With respect to potential maximum performance, one might argue that verbal learning and testing-the-limits (see, e.g., Lindenberger & Baltes, 1995) share some commonalities: Across trials, participants get closer to their specific performance limits, which increases individual differences. At the same time, these increasing individual differences can be mapped more exactly, because the full range of the measurement scale of 27 words is better used from trial to trial. Together with the assumption that closer to the limit, chance or unsystematic influences on performance become smaller, the reliability of measuring interindividual differences should increase, which should lead to stronger correlations with other variables (e.g., memory). We also demonstrated that verbal learning mediated the direct effect of processing speed on memory to a considerable extent (70%). This finding might at first glance appear surprising, but in light of the fact that verbal learning almost completely accounted for the variance in memory, this strong mediational effect represents nearly a necessity.

Future Perspectives

We think we have demonstrated in the preceding sections the usefulness of an individual-centered analysis of verbal learning. The analysis of short-term repeated measures data by means of the hyperbolic equation including random effects we presented offers researchers new possibilities to examine seemingly well-established relations between cognitive constructs such as, for example, verbal learning, speed, and memory (cf. Cudeck & Harring, 2007). We would argue that individual differences in verbal learning parameters as provided by the hyperbolic function are psychologically meaningful in that they capture between-person variability in within-person performance changes occurring at different stages of learning. Moreover, all three learning parameters exhibited substantial individual differences, implying that individual learning trajectories should not be collapsed across individuals because this would discount both theoretically and practically relevant information. Of course, our understanding of learning in old age would also benefit from transferring the analyses presented herein to other types of material and other types

of learning, for example, skill acquisition (Ackerman, 1988; Cerella et al., 2006; Wisher et al., 1995).

Individual differences in verbal learning, however, require more elaborated conceptual models to explain and predict individual learning trajectories. We acknowledge that it is important to ask how and why people learn in old age (cf. Bush & Mosteller, 1955; Estes, 1950; Kausler, 1994) but would suggest complementing this question by asking how and why people learn differentially in old age. Although we would expect that theoretical approaches aiming to answer each question show a large overlap, they would still focus on different aspects. An advantage of a differential perspective on learning is that a number of explanatory variables, be it from the cognitive domain or from other domains, can easily be included as individual-differences variables. This also allows for a shift from analysis of variance-type models to regression-type models. For example, one might expect that older persons high in typical intellectual engagement show superior learning compared with older adults being intellectually less active (Dellenbach & Zimprich, in press). Also, the investigation of learning bears the potential to bridge the gap between objective cognitive performance and subjective judgments of one's cognitive performance, because learning may constitute a more naturalistic measure of memory (Rast, Zimprich, van Boxtel, & Jolles, in press; Zimprich, Martin, & Kliegel, 2003).

The investigation of individual differences in learning is attractive also from a conceptual perspective of development: One might speculate that learning represents *microdevelopment*, that is, development within a short time frame, as opposed to *macrodevelopment*, which typically covers development over longer time spans. Lindenberger and Baltes (1995) conjectured that the mechanisms underlying learning might be the same or very similar to those underlying cognitive development, thus turning the study of learning into a showcase of examining cognitive development. Although development and learning are often treated as a dichotomy, they are both characterized by a persistent change of behavior over time, although time scales are different (cf. K. M. Newell et al., 2001). In accordance with such a link between learning and development, Zimprich, Hofer, and Aartsen (2004) demonstrated that, in old age, learning at first measurement occasion is positively associated with the amount of longitudinal change in cognitive functioning. Integrating the examination of learning and development would thus bring together two research avenues that, once their different time horizons are taken into account, may turn out to be very similar.

In the same context, the analysis of learning curves as presented in this chapter may be useful in describing retest effects in longitudinal studies (cf. Hofer & Sliwinski, 2006). To date, retest effects have oftentimes been taken into account in the form of comparatively unrealistic models, for example, by assuming that learning due to retest is linear or constant (e.g., Lövdén, Ghisletta, & Lindenberger, 2004). However, to disentangle two superimposed change processes in old age—one developmental process resulting in decline and one learning process leading to performance improvements—one would either need specialized designs with, for example, independent samples, which constitutes what has been done hitherto regarding retest effects. Alternatively, strong, testable hypotheses about the nature and form of the two processes at hand, development and learning, could be examined. To us, the latter approach now seems much more traceable: On the basis of the methods and analyses presented herein, it appears possible, if not timely, to revisit retest effects in longitudinal studies with a much stronger emphasis on learning than previously. Learning is not something to get rid of in longitudinal studies but rather contains vital information about the cognitive aging process that awaits being utilized.

In closing, if one considers the verbal learning and memory duality a pendulum, we would encourage researchers to give this pendulum a new momentum such that it swings back into the direction of verbal learning. In the end, remembering new material is a dynamic process that oftentimes involves more than just one static learning cycle (cf. Nelson & Narens, 1994). In a broader sense, the study described in this chapter illustrates the capabilities of nonlinear growth curve models as an analytical framework for linking both theoretical and methodological considerations in examining verbal learning and memory.

NOTES

1. As an aside, we note that counterexamples to a smooth, monotonic, concave-upward function predicted by this general model are abundant. If learning, for example, occurs in bursts of insight, there may be "jumps" in the according learning curve, a phenomenon that typically occurs in problem solving (e.g., Jones, 2003). Also, learning curves for, as an example, copying of Morse code often contain plateaus where little progress is made, only to be followed by new increases in learning rate with further practice (e.g., Wisher, Sabol, & Kern, 1995).

2. During the 1950s, different models of learning (Bush & Mosteller, 1955; Estes, 1950) oftentimes fit the data almost equally well. The reason for this was that empirical predictions derived from the various models were rather similar. A similar problem may be observed in distinguishing among the exponential, hyperbolic, and power functions using only limited amounts of data.

3. Note that the strong correlation between linear and quadratic slope represents a statistical necessity and could be reduced by using, for example, orthogonal polynomial contrasts. Biesanz, Deeb-Sossa, Papadaki, Bollen, and Curran (2004), however, cautioned against doing so, because interpretation of parameters then may become meaningless.

REFERENCES

Ackerman, P. L. (1988). Determinants of individual differences during skill acquisition: Cognitive abilities and information processing. *Journal of Experimental Psychology: General, 117,* 288–318.

Anderson, J. R., & Lebiere, C. (1998). *The atomic components of thought.* Mahwah, NJ: Lawrence Erlbaum.

Anderson, J. R., & Schooler, L. J. (1991). Reflections of the environment in memory. *Psychological Science, 2,* 396–408.

Biesanz, J. C., Deeb-Sossa, N., Papadaki, A. A., Bollen, K. A., & Curran, P. J. (2004). The role of coding time in estimating and interpreting growth curve models. *Psychological Methods, 9,* 30–52.

Brown, S., & Heathcote, A. (2003). Averaging learning curves across and within participants. *Behavior Research Methods, Instruments, and Computers, 35,* 11–21.

Browne, M. W. (1993). Structured latent curve models. In C. M. Cuadras & C. R. Rao (Eds.), *Multivariate analysis: Future directions* (pp. 171–198). Amsterdam: North-Holland.

Browne, M. W., & Du Toit, S. H. C. (1991). Models for learning data. In L. M. Collins & J. L. Horn (Eds.), *Best methods for the analysis of change* (pp. 47–68). Washington, DC: American Psychological Association.

Bryk, A. S., & Raudenbush, S. W. (1992). *Hierarchical linear models*. Newbury Park, CA: Sage.

Bush, R. R., & Mosteller, F. (1955). *Stochastic models for learning*. New York: Wiley.

Cerella, J., Onyper, S. V., & Hoyer, W. J. (2006). The associative-memory basis of cognitive skill learning: Adult age differences. *Psychology and Aging, 21,* 483–498.

Cohen, J. (1988). *Statistical power analysis for the behavioral sciences* (2nd ed.). Hillsdale, NJ: Lawrence Erlbaum.

Cole, D. A., & Maxwell, S. E. (2003). Testing mediational models with longitudinal data: Questions and tips in the use of structural equation modeling. *Journal of Abnormal Psychology, 112,* 558–577.

Cousineau, D., Hélie, S., & Lefebvre, C. (2003). Testing curvatures of learning functions on individual trial and block average data. *Behavior Research Methods, Instruments, and Computers, 35,* 493–503.

Craik, F. I. M. (1977). Age differences in human memory. In J. E. Birren & K. W. Schaie (Eds.), *Handbook of the psychology of aging* (pp. 384–420). New York: Van Nostrand Reinhold.

Cudeck, R., & Harring, J. R. (2007). The analysis of nonlinear patterns of change with random coefficient models. *Annual Review of Psychology, 58,* 615–637.

Davidian, M., & Giltinan, D. M. (1995). *Nonlinear models for repeated measurement data*. New York: Chapman & Hall.

Davis, H. P., Small, S. A., Stern, Y., Mayeux, R., Feldstein, S. N., & Keller, F. R. (2003). Acquisition, recall, and forgetting of verbal information in long-term memory by young, middle-aged and elderly individuals. *Cortex, 39,* 1063–1091.

Dellenbach, M., & Zimprich, D. (in press). Typical intellectual engagement and cognition in old age. *Aging, Neuropsychology, and Cognition.*

Ekstrom, R. B., French, J. W., Harman, H. H., & Dermen, D. (1976). *Manual for kit of factor-referenced cognitive tests*. Princeton, NJ: Educational Testing Service.

Estes, W. K. (1950). Toward a statistical theory of learning. *Psychological Review, 57,* 94–107.

Goldstein, H. (1995). *Multilevel statistical models* (2nd ed.). London: Arnold.

Härting, C., Markowitsch, H. J., Neufeld, H., Calabrese, P., Deisinger, K., & Kessler, J. (Eds.). (2000). *Wechsler Gedächtnistest—Revidierte Fassung* [Wechsler Memory Scale—Revised]. Bern, Switzerland: Huber.

Heathcote, A., Brown, S., & Mewhort, D. J. K. (2000). The power law repealed: The case for an exponential law of practice. *Psychonomic Bulletin and Review, 7,* 185–207.

Helmstädter, C., Lendt, M., & Lux, S. (2001). *Verbaler Lern und Merkfähigkeitstest* [Rey Auditory Verbal Learning Test]. Göttingen, Germany: Lelitz.

Hofer, S. M., & Sliwinski, M. J. (2001). Understanding ageing: An evaluation of research designs for assessing the interdependence of ageing-related changes. *Gerontology, 47,* 341–352.

Hofer, S. M., & Sliwinski, M. J. (2006). Design and analysis of longitudinal studies on aging. In K. W. Schaie & J. E. Birren (Eds.), *Handbook of the psychology of aging* (6th ed., pp. 15–37). San Diego, CA: Academic Press.

Hu, L., & Bentler, P. M. (1999). Cutoff criteria for fit indexes in covariance structure analysis: Conventional criteria versus new alternatives. *Structural Equation Modeling, 6,* 1–55.

Hultsch, D. F., Hertzog, C., Dixon, R. A., & Small, B. J. (1998). *Memory change in the aged.* Cambridge, UK: Cambridge University Press.

Ilmberger, J. (1988). *Münchner Verbaler Gedächtnistest* [Munich Verbal Memory Test].München, Germany: Institut für Medizinische Psychologie.

Jones, G. (2003). Testing two cognitive theories of insight. *Journal of Experimental Psychology: Learning, Memory, and Cognition, 29,* 1017–1027.

Kausler, D. H. (1994). *Learning and memory in normal aging*. San Diego, CA: Academic Press.

Lindenberger, U., & Baltes, P. B. (1995). Testing-the-limits and experimental simulation: Two methods to explicate the role of learning in development. *Human Development, 38,* 349–360.

Logan, G. D. (1988). Toward an instance theory of automatization. *Psychological Review, 95,* 492–527.

Logan, G. D. (1995). The Weibull distribution, the power law, and the instance theory of automaticity. *Psychological Review, 102,* 751–756.

Lövdén, M., Ghisletta, P., & Lindenberger, U. (2004). Cognition in the Berlin Aging Study (BASE): The first ten years. *Aging, Neuropsychology, and Cognition, 11,* 104–133.

MacCallum, R. C., Browne, M. W., & Sugawara, H. M. (1996). Power analysis and determination of sample size for covariance structure modeling. *Psychological Methods, 1,* 130–149.

Martin, M., & Zimprich, D. (2005). Cognitive development in midlife. In S. L. Willis & M. Martin (Eds.), *Middle adulthood: A lifespan perspective* (pp. 179–206). Thousand Oaks, CA: Sage.

Mazur, J. E., & Hastie, R. (1978). Learning as accumulation: A reexamination of the learning curve. *Psychological Bulletin, 85,* 1256–1274.

McArdle, J. J., & Anderson, E. (1990). Latent variable growth models for research on aging. In J. E. Birren & K. W. Schaie (Eds.), *Handbook of the psychology of aging* (3rd ed., pp. 310–319). San Diego, CA: Academic Press.

Meredith, W., & Tisak, J. (1990). Latent curve analysis. *Psychometrika, 55,* 107–122.

Molenberghs, G., & Verbeke, G. (2005). *Models for discrete longitudinal data.* New York: Springer.

Neale, M. C., Boker, S. M., Xie, G., & Maes, H. H. (2003). *Mx: Statistical modeling* (6th ed.). (Available from Department of Psychiatry, VCU Box 900126, Richmond, VA 23298.)

Nelson, T. O., & Narens, L. (1994). Why investigate metacognition? In J. Metcalfe & A. P. Shimamura (Eds.), *Metacognition: Knowing about knowing* (pp. 1–25). Cambridge: MIT Press.

Nerb, J., Ritter, F. E., & Krems, J. (1999). Knowledge level learning and the power law: A Soar model of skill acquisition in scheduling. *Kognitionswissenschaft, 8,* 20–29.

Newell, A. (1990). *Unified theories of cognition.* Cambridge, MA: Harvard University Press.

Newell, A., & Rosenbloom, P. S. (1981). Mechanisms of skill acquisition and the law of practice. In J. R. Anderson (Ed.), *Cognitive skills and their acquisition* (pp. 1–51). Hillsdale, NJ: Lawrence Erlbaum.

Newell, K. M., Liu, Y.-T., & Mayer-Kress, G. (2001). Time scales in motor learning and development. *Psychological Review, 108,* 57–82.

Oswald, W. D., & Fleischmann, U. M. (1999). *Nürnberger-Alters-Inventar,* 4 [Nuremberg Age Inventory]. Göttingen, Germany: Hogrefe.

Paul, L. M. (1994). Making interpretable forgetting comparisons: Explicit versus hidden assumptions. *Journal of Experimental Psychology: Learning, Memory, and Cognition, 20,* 992–999.

Pedhazur, E. (1982). *Multiple regression in behavioural research: Explanation and prediction.* New York: Rinehart and Winston.

Rast, P., Zimprich, D., van Boxtel, M., & Jolles, J. (2006). *Factorial structure and measurement invariance of the Cognitive Failures Questionnaire across the adult life-span.* Manuscript submitted for publication.

Restle, F., & Greeno, J. G. (1970). *Introduction to mathematical psychology.* Reading, MA: Addison-Wesley.

Richards, F. J. (1959). A flexible growth function for empirical use. *Journal of Experimental Botany, 10,* 290–300.

Ritter, F. E., & Schooler, L. J. (2001). The learning curve. In N. J. Smelser & P. B. Baltes (Eds.), *International encyclopedia of the social and behavioral sciences* (pp. 8602–8605). Cambridge, UK: Cambridge University Press.

Salthouse, T. A. (1991). *Theoretical perspectives on cognitive aging.* Hillsdale, NJ: Lawrence Erlbaum.

Salthouse, T. A. (1996). The processing-speed theory of adult age differences in cognition. *Psychological Review, 103,* 403–428.

Schoenberg, M. R., Dawson, K. A., Duff, K., Patton, D., Scott, J. G., & Adams, R. L. (2006). Test performance and classification statistics for the Rey Auditory Verbal Learning Test in selected clinical samples. *Archives in Clinical Neuropsychology, 21,* 693–703.

Sidman, M. (1952). A note on functional relations obtained from group data. *Psychological Bulletin, 49,* 263–269.

Smith, G. (1998). Learning statistics by doing statistics. *Journal of Statistics Education, 6.* Retrieved February 22, 2007, from http://www.amstat .org/publications/jse/v6n3/smith.html

Stern, Y. (2002). What is cognitive reserve? Theory and research application of the reserve concept. *Journal of the International Neuropsychological Society, 8,* 448–460.

Thurstone, L. L. (1919). The learning curve equation. *Psychological Monographs, 26,* 1–51.

Tulving, E. (1964). Intratrial and intertrial retention: Notes towards a theory of free recall verbal learning. *Psychological Review, 71,* 219–237.

Tulving, E., & Madigan, S. A. (1970). Memory and verbal learning. *Annual Review of Psychology, 21,* 437–484.

Willis, S. L., & Schaie, K. W. (2005). Cognitive trajectories in midlife and cognitive functioning in old age. In S. L. Willis & M. Martin (Eds.), *Middle adulthood: A lifespan perspective* (pp. 243–276). Thousand Oaks, CA: Sage.

Willis, S. L., Tennstedt, S. L., Marsiske, M., Ball, K., Elias, J., Mann Koepke, K., et al. (2006). Long-term effects of cognitive training on everyday functional outcomes in older adults. *Journal of the American Medical Association, 296,* 2805–2814.

Wisher, R. A., Sabol, M. A., & Kern, R. P. (1995). Modeling acquisition of an advanced skill: The case of Morse code copying. *Instructional Science, 23,* 381–403.

Zimprich, D. (2002). Cross-sectionally and longitudinally balanced effects of processing speed on intellectual abilities. *Experimental Aging Research, 28,* 231–251.

Zimprich, D., Hofer, S. M., & Aartsen, M. J. (2004). Short-term versus long-term longitudinal changes in processing speed. *Gerontology, 50,* 17–21.

Zimprich, D., & Martin, M. (2002). Can longitudinal changes in processing speed explain longitudinal age changes in fluid intelligence? *Psychology and Aging, 17,* 690–695.

Zimprich, D., Martin, M., & Kliegel, M. (2003). Subjective cognitive complaints, memory performance, and depressive affect in old age: A change-oriented approach. *International Journal of Aging and Human Development, 57,* 341–368.

Zimprich, D., Martin, M., Kliegel, M., Dellenbach, M., Rast, P., & Zeintl, M. (in press). Cognitive abilities in old age: Results from the Zurich Longitudinal Study on Cognitive Aging. *Swiss Journal of Psychology.*

15

EXPERTISE AND KNOWLEDGE

NEIL CHARNESS AND RALF T. KRAMPE

The goal of this chapter is to examine how age, knowledge, and expertise interrelate by addressing definitions of terms, exploring measurement issues, and discussing some of the fundamental issues that the field is trying to address. Questions about the relation of age and human performance have a relatively long history (e.g., Quetelet, 1842/1969). A specific focus on the relation between aging and expertise is provided in reviews such as Bosman and Charness (1996), Krampe and Baltes (2003), Krampe and Charness (2006), and Salthouse (1990).

The field of expertise research is primarily concerned with how people develop and maintain high levels of performance in a given domain of human endeavor. Experts are important to society because they typically quickly find excellent solutions to what are considered to be very difficult problems.

Before we can assess the interrelations of age, knowledge, and expertise, we need to address some definition and measurement issues.

DEFINITIONS

Age

The definition of *age* is near universal, tied to time elapsed since birth measured in years (though some Asian cultures count time from conception). Alternatives to chronological age have been proposed, such as *functional age*: a mixture of psychological and physiological markers relative to a chronological age norm group. However, it too references back to chronological age for norm groups.

Knowledge

A functional definition of *knowledge* was given by Charness and Schultetus (1999): "acquired information that can be activated in a timely fashion in order to generate an appropriate response" (p. 61). Knowledge allows people to respond adaptively to their environment. Our species' name, *Homo sapiens* (wise/knowing man), indicates the high degree of regard given

AUTHORS' NOTE: This work was conducted while the first author was supported by a grant from National Institute on Aging (1 P01 AG17211). We thank Michael Tuffiash, Katinka Dijkstra, and an anonymous reviewer for comments on a draft of this chapter.

by biologists and anthropologists to our ability to acquire knowledge.

Expertise

Ericsson and Charness (1994) suggested that *expertise* can be characterized as consistently superior performance on representative tasks from a domain, where *superior* represents performance that is at least 2 standard deviations above the mean of the population. Experts are seen as "outliers." It takes them thousands of hours (e.g., Charness, Tuffiash, Krampe, Reingold, & Vasyukova, 2005; Chase & Simon, 1973a, 1973b) of engaging in *deliberate practice* (Ericsson, 2006; Ericsson, Krampe, & Tesch-Römer, 1993) to acquire the mechanisms, including domain-specific knowledge, that support expert performance.

WHY EXPERTISE IS IMPORTANT: THE 80/20 RULE FOR PRODUCTIVITY

Villfredo Pareto (1848–1923) is credited with being the first to generate the observation (principle, rule) that 80% of the land/wealth of a country is owned/created by 20% of the population. Management gurus such as Joseph Juran proposed in the 1930s that there is an 80/20 principle for many things, such as 80% of defects coming from 20% of a product line and 80% of a company's sales coming from 20% of the sales force.

The first author checked the 2005 publication figures for his department (in a research-oriented university), which has 42 members, and found that the Pareto/Juran estimate doesn't fit all that well—the top 20% produced only about 60% of the (161) publications. This may mean that competitive market forces and an oversupply of labor are resulting in more pruning out of the bottom of the distribution.

Still, 60% of publications is a substantial contribution by a relatively small number of department members ($n = 9$). Should we extend such an analysis out to all psychologists in academic positions (who average about 1.2 publications/year; Joy, 2006), we suspect that we would more closely approximate this "rule."

In short, as a society, we probably do need to accord more attention to the performers who rank in the top 20%, given their very high contribution rates.

Expertise research typically concerns itself with the top 5% or fewer of a target population. Now, why worry about such outliers? After all, they are already overprivileged with respect to their level of accomplishments, and even later in life they will be performing well above the level of the average young adult. The reason is that they are aging too, and we need to consider how to safeguard their productivity from expected age-related decline (e.g., Salthouse, 2006).

Many people have contributed over the years to understanding the relation among age, career age, and productivity, starting with Quetelet (1842/1969), continuing with Lehman (1953) and Dennis (1966), and extended most intensively by Simonton (1997).

THE RELATION BETWEEN KNOWLEDGE AND EXPERTISE

The decisive role of specialized knowledge for the development of expertise has been a cornerstone of extant conceptions since the work on chess published by de Groot (1946/1978) and Chase and Simon (1973a, 1973b). Although chess is seen as the "drosophila" of expertise-research (Charness, 1992) the field has explored many other domains, such as music, sports, or creative writing (e.g., see the collection of chapters in Ericsson, 1996, and in Ericsson, Charness, Feltovich, & Hoffman, 2006). Naturally, domains differ with respect to the role of abstract knowledge. Expert musical performance, for example, involves elaborate knowledge about musical styles, expressive means, and the historical context of a certain oeuvre. At the same time, virtuoso performances rest on cognitive–motor skills at the limits of the musicians' biomechanical capacities. Whereas some sports emphasize strategic competencies (e.g., team sports or golf), others rest predominantly on athletic strength or endurance (e.g., triathlon). The relative importance of knowledge for a given expertise compared with physical strength or the speed of mental processes presumably determines the duration of acquisition processes, peak-performance ages, and the degree to which expertise can be maintained in later adulthood. This proposition is supported by analyses of historical records for peak-performance ages for a variety of academic and artistic professions (Lehman, 1953; Simonton, 1988, 1991, 1996) as well as between different disciplines in sports (Ericsson, 1990; Schulz & Curnow, 1988).

Models of expertise following the Chase and Simon (1973a, 1973b) tradition typically emphasize the role of specialized knowledge that helps experts to circumvent the processing limitations (e.g., for memory span; Chase & Ericsson, 1982) of "normal" individuals but shows little transfer to other domains or general cognitive abilities. Intelligence research takes a slightly different stance in that knowledge and knowledge acquisition are assumed to reflect general (i.e., psychometric) intelligence. This relation indeed holds for general knowledge domains, such as those assessed in school or academic performance. In contrast, training and expertise research suggests that general intelligence benefits initial acquisition of novel skills (e.g., Ackerman, 1988), but general and specific capacities are gradually decoupled when the individual progresses to higher levels of performance (Krampe & Baltes, 2003; Krampe & Charness, 2006). Decoupling of expertise- and domain-general memory capacities can be observed at early stages of development. Child-expert chess players, while excelling in their skill domain and surpassing less skilled adults, show the same memory span limitations relative to (novice and expert) adults as their peers (Chi & Ceci, 1987; Schneider, Gruber, Gold, & Opwis, 1993).

Related findings have revitalized attempts to incorporate aspects of real life expertise into a revised notion of intelligence (Horn & Masunaga, 2000; Krampe & Baltes, 2003; Sternberg, 1999). One framework that is oriented toward the particulars of age-related changes in knowledge-related intelligence is the dual-process model proposed by Baltes, Staudinger, and Lindenberger (1999). At the core of their model is a distinction of two dimensions of intellectual functioning, namely mechanics and pragmatics. The category of mechanics relates to basic (i.e., content-poor) information processing, such as being able to react to stimuli by simple motor responses, rehearse information in working memory, or the ability to learn associations from contingencies in the environment (as in the case of simple conditioning). The content-rich dimension of pragmatics refers to culture-based knowledge and skills that are acquired through cultural learning and experience (e.g., language acquisition, daily problem solving, or the acquisition of a professional expertise). The heuristic usefulness of the mechanic–pragmatic distinction was recently demonstrated in a study by Li and colleagues (2004), who assessed intellectual functioning on both dimensions in a sample of participants aged between 6 and 89 years. The authors observed differential life span trajectories (from cross-sectional data) for the two dimensions: Relative to pragmatics, mechanics showed an earlier rise in efficiency with age; however, there was also an earlier and sharper drop of mechanics compared with pragmatics during later adulthood. Li and her colleagues attributed the differences during childhood to rapid brain maturation (mechanics), combined with the relatively slower accumulation of knowledge (pragmatics) during the first two life decades (certain brain areas, like the frontal lobes, complete their maturation as late as the onset of puberty). Following the dual-process model of intelligence, mechanic capacities are "invested" into the acquisition of pragmatic skills, such as expertise. Thus, the development of mechanics must necessarily lead the way relative to the pragmatics. On the other hand, losses in biological functioning during late adulthood presumably affected the mechanics earlier while continued cultural support and maintenance provided for a gentler decline of pragmatics at older ages.

The different developmental trajectories for mechanic and pragmatic components of intellectual functioning illustrate the above argument of a decoupling of expertise-related skills from general abilities at a larger scope. They also point to the possibility of compensatory benefits through acquired expert knowledge. We now examine two representative expertise domains in more detail to investigate the interplay of expertise developments and age-related changes in general abilities.

Sample Expertise Domains: Chess and Music

Chess

In Figure 15.1, we show longitudinal chess performance data collected by Elo (1965), who examined Grandmaster chess players.

The function relating age to performance is scaled in standard deviation units scaled around the player's performance at age 21. The rapid rise in the teenage years to a peak in the 30s followed by a slow decline is a characteristic function in many professions (e.g., Simonton, 1997).

The decisive power of acquired knowledge over and above domain-general abilities is already evident at early stages of expertise acquisition and in childhood. While excelling in their skill domain, child-expert chess players show the same limitations in memory span relative to adults as their novice peers (Chi & Ceci, 1987; Schneider et al., 1993). An interesting trend noted in chess expertise is the move toward younger and younger ages for attaining high-level play, such as achieving the Grandmaster designation or even becoming World Champion (e.g., Ruslan Ponomariov became FIDE World Champion in 2001 at age 18). Lehman (1953) noted a similar generational shift to earlier achievement in his classic book on age and achievement. Some attribute this shift to the availability of computer systems with large databases of chess games paired with extremely strong chess programs. Players (of all ages) can access all games played by high-level players and can prepare much more easily than was the case in the past; that is, they have already compiled knowledge sources. They can also develop and test their tactical skills against virtually perfect opponents (chess programs).

It is also plausible that lifetime performance trajectories depend somewhat on how skilled someone is when he or she enters the rating pool as well as his or her age at time of entry. Roring and Charness (2007) used multilevel modeling to examine trajectories for a very large group (~5,000) of elite internationally rated chess players for whom archival ratings were available. Both peak age of performance and degree of age-related decline depended on initial skill levels. Age was somewhat kinder to the initially more able, with a less steep descent from peak for the initially more highly skilled players. Also, age of peak performance occurred later in the sample as a whole (age 44) than in Elo's (1965) very small sample of players (see Figure 15.1), although it occurred very slightly (though not significantly) earlier for more skilled players. Elo restricted his analysis to the very top performers.

Why would peak performance for an intellectually demanding game such as chess occur so late in life? After all, intellectual abilities appear to peak in the 20s or 30s for the "mechanics" of intelligence (tapped by tests that involve solving novel problems). As discussed earlier, the "pragmatics" of intellectual ability

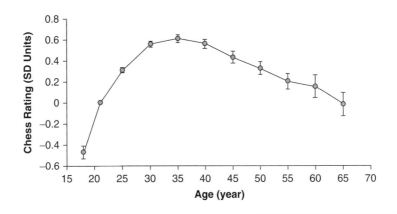

Figure 15.1   Chess Ratings for Grandmasters Across Their Life Span

SOURCE: Based on data from Elo (1965).

NOTE: Error bars are +/−1 SE unit.

(knowledge-dependent abilities tapped by tests of information or vocabulary) tend to show slight increases with age until the 50s. So, it may be that even in chess, where correctly anticipating future moves and their consequences is necessary, having a large vocabulary of patterns linked to plausible moves can compensate for age-related declines in fluid abilities. However, Jastrzembski, Charness, and Vasyukova (2006) showed that although the ability to react to patterns or to anticipate moves was positively related to skill level, the speed with which older players could carry out these mental operations was inferior to that of equivalently skilled younger ones.

Degree of age-related slowing is a strong predictor of many aspects of cognitive performance (Salthouse, 1996). In fast-paced environments, such as tournament chess, in which there is only about 3 minutes available on average to make each move, slowing may hamper players' access to critical knowledge. Slight age-related slowing in information processing may make a bigger difference in performance where players function at the limits of human adaptation, the very top competitive levels.

Given the easy accessibility of encyclopedic knowledge sources, and of computerized sparring partners, why would one expect any change in chess skill with age? Motivational changes may be a source for age-related declines in chess performance past the 50s. Although the case is much stronger for music (see next section), it appears that elite performers may not be willing or able to maintain the very taxing training schedules necessary to prepare adequately for tournament play. However, evidence in favor of such an explanation is currently lacking. Charness et al. (2005) showed essentially a zero correlation ($r = -.06$, $r = .13$) between age and solitary study alone in two large samples ($n = 200$, $n = 164$) of chess players.

Music

Music has several advantages as a subject of study in the context of expertise and knowledge development. First, music performance comprises a wide spectrum of component skills, including superior motor skills (e.g., finger dexterity in pianists; Keele & Hawkins, 1982) as well as knowledge about musical interpretation, that can be represented in abstract plans and rules guiding actual performance (Palmer, 1989) Second, individuals at all ages and levels of accomplishment engage in musical performances, and the relatively distinct characteristics of related activities allow some assessment of practice efforts (Ericsson et al., 1993). Finally, although there have been considerable historical changes in the level of technical skills and the size of repertoire expected from professional musicians (e.g., Lehmann & Ericsson, 1998), there is also a largely stable tradition of pieces and their continued interpretation, mostly in classical music. A potential disadvantage is, of course, that the quality of a musical interpretation remains an aesthetic issue that may ultimately escape the precision of assessment we rely on in chess or most sports.

Research on musical expertise, a traditional talent domain, has largely supported the role of individual practice efforts. Ericsson et al. (1993) used self-report and diary data recording to assess past and current time investments in deliberate practice activities in skilled and top-level violinists. They showed that adult levels of accomplishment were correlated to past amounts of practice. At the level of brain functioning, a correlation between musical practice and the extent of cortical representation for relevant limbs (i.e., left-hand fingers in string players) had earlier been established by Elbert and colleagues (Elbert, Pantev, Wienbruch, Rockstroh, & Taub, 1995). The superior role of long-term training over innate dispositions in music has also received some support from twin studies. Whereas levels of performance as well as initial learning rates show a heritable component during short-term trainings in a novel skill (Fox, Hershberger, & Bouchard, 1996), heritability estimates decline dramatically as a result of long-term training, as demonstrated by Coon and Carey (1989), who assessed musical abilities in twins.

As in the earlier described example with chess players, the power of conceptual knowledge for musical performance can be observed at early ages. Palmer and Meyer (2000) showed that advanced pianists (12-year-old children as well as young adults) were able to transfer conceptual (melodic) relations from an earlier practiced piece to a new piece, even if the motor requirements changed. In contrast, novice pianists in either age group showed successful transfer only for identical motor patterns. These findings nicely illustrate that broader benefits of expert knowledge emerge only at higher levels of skill.

The role of expert knowledge in music and its effects at different ages were also evident in a study by Krampe and Ericsson (1996), who tested expertise-related skills and general intellectual abilities in adult expert and amateur pianists from two different age groups. Older professional pianists showed normal age-related declines in measures of general processing speed, such as choice reaction time and speed of digit–symbol substitution. Age effects within the amateur group with regard to expertise-related measures of multiple-finger coordination speed were similar to those pertaining to the general speed measures (e.g., choice reaction time). However, effects in skill-related tasks were reduced or fully absent in the expert sample. The extent to which levels of performance in speeded expertise tasks were maintained in old age depended on the amounts of deliberate practice invested at the later stages of life, namely in the 5th and 6th decades. Age effects in the expert group in Krampe and Ericsson's study were significantly reduced when pianists performed complex sequences from memory compared with a condition in which they sight-read the tasks, suggesting that older professionals benefited from their vast knowledge related to harmonic relations or melodic patterns during encoding. In addition, older experts and older amateurs showed levels of performance similar to those of their age-matched controls in a musical interpretation task, which involved a piece that posed little challenge in terms of speed or technical virtuosity. This latter finding suggests that skills with a stronger knowledge component can be more easily maintained at advancing ages. Experts in both age groups naturally showed performance in this task superior to that of both amateur groups, assessed by expert ratings of tape-recordings as well as through analyses of consistencies in expressive phrasing.

Age, Knowledge, and Compensation

Those holding a life span developmental perspective see aging as a process with both losses and gains that requires selective optimization and compensation (e.g., Baltes & Baltes, 1990). The compelling questions in age, expertise, and knowledge revolve around the extent to which acquired knowledge can compensate (e.g., Bäckman & Dixon, 1992) for age-related changes in general cognitive abilities.

Some of the earliest work in this area was driven by the paradoxical finding that although basic abilities thought to support high-level domain performance, such as tapping rate in typists or memory for patterns in chess, showed age-related decline, older typists and chess players were able to perform expertly (at transcription typing: Salthouse, 1984; or at choosing good chess moves: Charness, 1981). Although the mechanism for compensation in typing was identified, a greater eye–hand span for older typists than equivalently skilled younger ones (e.g., Bosman, 1993; Salthouse, 1984), compensatory mechanisms in chess were not identified, although they were presumed to rely on greater knowledge, and later simulation work with neural net models showed that this was indeed plausible (Mireles & Charness, 2002).

The basis for understanding potential age–skill trade-off effects can be developed from a classic finding in expertise research. Experts are usually not privileged in terms of superior general cognitive abilities. The classic demonstration of the domain specificity of skill can be seen in the oft-replicated skilled memory effect, first demonstrated by Chase and Simon (1973a, 1973b). They showed chessboard positions taken from unfamiliar real chess games to novice, intermediate, and expert chess players for 5 seconds. Recall depended heavily on the player's level of skill. When the same pieces were quasi-randomly distributed around the board and the position shown for 5 seconds, the skilled memory effect vanished. Skilled chess players do not seem to have superior visuospatial memory (e.g., Waters, Gobet, & Leyden, 2002). Expertise may represent the ultimate case in adaptive specialization where highly specific knowledge and procedures determine performance.

This issue of age–skill trade-off has been investigated within a diverse set of research questions and paradigms that include traditional cross-sectional investigations of skilled performers, such as aircraft pilots (e.g., Taylor,

O'Hara, Mumenthaler, Rosen, & Yesavage, 2005; Morrow, Leirer, Altieri, & Fitzsimmons, 1994; Morrow et al., 2003); game experts, such as bridge players (e.g., Charness, 1983), GO players (Masunaga & Horn, 2001), and crossword puzzle experts (Hambrick, Salthouse, & Meinz, 1999; Rabbitt, 1993).

Another facet to understanding age–knowledge trade-off has involved checks on whether abilities such as speed of processing or working memory limit knowledge acquisition in later life. Perceptual speed losses seem to limit the acquisition of new vocabulary in late life (Ghisletta & Lindenberger, 2003), and lesser working memory capacity independently affects the acquisition of new baseball knowledge from baseball broadcasts (Hambrick & Engle, 2002). However, in most of these cases knowledge is usually the strongest predictor of performance, consistent with the "Matthew effect": the rich get richer, or "knowledge is power."

Yet another important facet of understanding trade-offs has involved formal modeling, such as computer simulation of age and knowledge trade-off using neural nets (e.g., Hannon & Hoyer, 1994; Li, Lindenberger, & Frensch, 2000; Mireles & Charness, 2002; Salthouse, 1988). Such studies have shown the sufficiency of knowledge to counteract normative age-related decline in basic abilities. However, such studies do not adequately address the necessity of knowledge for compensation and will require supplementation by intervention studies, discussed below.

Finally, researchers have mined epidemiological data on education and occupation influences to assess whether people can build up brain reserve capacity to hinder the progression of dementia (reviewed in Charness, 2006).

Perhaps the most compelling real world evidence in favor of compensation effects can be seen in the very different pattern of results shown in laboratory research and in job performance. Many cognitive processes (e.g., speed measures, working memory measures) show strong cross-sectional decline trends from the decade of the 20s (Verhaeghen & Salthouse, 1997). In contrast, meta-analyses on age and job performance show correlations between age and performance that are close to zero (e.g., McEvoy & Cascio, 1989; Waldman & Avolio, 1986) or slightly positive (Sturman, 2004). It is assumed that acquired knowledge enables older workers to maintain work performance equivalent to younger ones, although the narrow age ranges investigated in the latter research, together with the sometimes-questionable outcome measures (peer ratings, supervisor ratings), make the issue difficult to resolve (Salthouse & Maurer, 1996).

What is clear from the expertise literature is that a very significant investment is required before high-level performance can be reached (e.g., thousands of hours; Charness et al., 2005). However, our increasing longevity is providing many of us with the opportunity to become highly skilled in more than one field of human endeavor, assuming that we remain highly motivated to do so. And we do need high motivation (e.g., Charness, Tuffiash, & Jastrzembski, 2004), given that, even to maintain performance efficiency in old age, continued deliberate practice is a necessary component (e.g., for musicians playing piano pieces: Krampe & Ericsson, 1996). Furthermore, as we increase in age we have to cope with a slowed rate of acquiring new information (e.g., Charness, Kelley, Bosman, & Mottram, 2001), making it that much more difficult to reach the summit of performance compared with younger competitors.

Measurement Issues

Measuring Expertise

There are many concerns in trying to understand the relation among knowledge, expertise, and age. Foremost is measuring performance in the domain of interest. Many psychological studies of the relation between age and performance rely on cross-sectional investigations, in which people from different birth cohorts are compared at one point in time. A classic problem with letting interindividual differences (age differences) proxy for intraindividual change (aging) is that there may be important generational trends that can obscure the underlying function.

It is fairly apparent that the population living in the United States is aging better. This can be seen both in terms of longevity (life expectancy) and in disability-free longevity for physical functioning (Manton, Stallard, & Corder, 1995). But what are the trends in cognitive functioning? One striking example is the *Flynn effect* (Dickens & Flynn, 2001; Flynn, 1987), which shows strong (+1 *SD*) generational improvement in intelligence test performance. Other trends, some up, some down, can be seen in the classic work reported by the Seattle Longitudinal Study on Aging, where different cohorts show varying trends across time depending on the particular measure of cognitive ability (Schaie, 1994). Similar positive trends have been uncovered by expertise researchers.

Nowhere is a positive generational effect more evident than in the field of sports expertise, where changes in equipment and, particularly, in training, have resulted in ever-improving world championship performances. For instance, mere qualifying times for entry to events such as the Boston Marathon for 18- to 34-year-old men (3 hours, 10 minutes)[1] are set at the level of the original world championship record time for the 1896 Olympics (2 hours, 58 minutes, 50 seconds)[2]. That first Olympics race used a considerably shorter distance of 24.85 miles compared with the standard adopted in 1908 of 26 miles, 385 yards. The 2006 Boston Marathon winner ran the race in 2 hours, 7 minutes, and 14 seconds.[3]

Similarly, today's typical college music performance student is likely far superior to 19th-century virtuoso performers (Lehmann & Ericsson, 1998). As well, in the past century, error rates (blunders) in move selection have declined steeply during world chess championship matches (Roring & Ericsson, in preparation).

A caveat from these historical trends is that age differences in performance may be overestimated when relying on cross-sectional comparisons. An older expert could be improving throughout his or her lifetime in terms of personal performance yet fall farther and farther behind the current record holders with each passing year if the expert's performance gain function is less steep than that of current (younger) competitors. So, ideally, longitudinal data are needed to try to assess the true trajectory for age and performance. If there are longitudinal data available (in some domains there are archival sources), it may be possible to scale cross-sectional performance relative to cohort trends.

Measuring Knowledge

The definition of *knowledge* given earlier maps well to cognitive psychology constructs of declarative ("knowing that") and procedural ("knowing how") memory. However, the earliest systematic approach to measuring knowledge originated within the field of intelligence testing. For instance, tests of vocabulary and information date back to the earliest work on intelligence testing of children by Binet in the 19th century. Modern tests, such as the Wechsler Adult Intelligence Scale (WAIS; Wechsler, 1997), have continued that tradition but have representative sampling of the adult population so that people can be compared with their peers, especially age peers. Cross-sectional age plots of psychometric measures such as WAIS vocabulary and information scores (raw data rather than age-normed data) typically show a slightly rising function through the decade of the 50s with minor dropoff thereafter.

However, there also have been attempts to infer quantity of knowledge. A good example is work by Oldfield (1963). He attempted to establish the size of the English vocabulary of college undergraduates by testing them with entries from a large dictionary. He bounded their lexical (word) knowledge to about 50,000 entries. Another interesting attempt to bound knowledge was taken by Landauer (1986). Using a variety of techniques based on results from learning experiments, he estimated that people over a lifetime would acquire about 10^9 bits of information (several hundred megabytes).

A hybrid version of psychometric and quantitative attempts to understand knowledge extent, particularly with regard to age differences, is represented by the work of Ackerman and colleagues (e.g., Ackerman & Rolfhus, 1999; Beier & Ackerman, 2001, 2005). Their theory of knowledge involves multiple components: intelligence-as-process, personality, interests, intelligence-as-knowledge. However, they attempt to sample knowledge much more broadly (e.g., 20 or more domains) than does the typical psychometric intelligence test such as the WAIS. In contrast to performance on non-knowledge components of intelligence tests (fluid abilities), middle-aged adults show better performance than young adults on such domain knowledge tests. Also, domain knowledge is a strong predictor of ability to acquire further information from the domain (Beier & Ackerman, 2005). Such age-related knowledge differences have been shown to be mediated by exposure to knowledge sources, such as print (Stanovich, West, & Harrison, 1995).

There have been several other attempts to bound knowledge in specific domains. In chess, a computer simulation experiment led Simon and Gilmartin (1973) to estimate that a strong Master chess player possessed a vocabulary of chess patterns in the range of 50,000 entries. Later simulation work by Gobet suggested a much higher estimate: about 300,000 patterns (see the review by Gobet & Charness, 2006).

Such estimates suggest that, to the extent that expert performance relies on knowledge, given the relatively slow learning rate of humans—about 5 to 10 seconds to consolidate a new chunk of information (Simon, 1974)—many thousands of hours are necessary to acquire expert-level domain knowledge. From the perspective of understanding aging, there have apparently not been many systematic attempts to quantify knowledge in older experts using such simulation techniques.

FUTURE DIRECTIONS

Measurement Challenges

Psychometric approaches and multilevel modeling offer promising techniques for trying to quantify life span trajectories in intellectual abilities (e.g., Roring & Charness, 2007). However, as pointed out above, measures of intellectual ability do not usually seem to relate very strongly to measures of expert performance, and all too often measures of expertise are not that easily available in many domains. As well, there are probably generational trends toward improvement making it difficult to compare older and younger performers from different eras. So, one useful approach to measurement would be to try to find derivative measures that could allow for absolute scaling.

In chess playing, Elo (1965, 1986) developed an interval-level rating scale for assessing performance of then-current top players, Grandmasters, and bootstrapped his way backward in time to assess past performers. Others with access to better historical data and to computers have continued to tinker with his approach and improve on it (e.g., Sonas; see, e.g., http://www.chessbase .com/newsdetail.asp?newsid=562).[4] Elo's rating system has also been extended to other competitive domains, such as the game of Scrabble. Of course, since widespread adoption of Elo's rating scale we now have access to a very extensive database of the ratings of current performers. Garry Kasparov, who just announced his retirement from tournament chess in 2005, was probably the top-rated player in history, holding that position for about 20 years. If one assumes that the rating scale is stable over time, we can also see that current top players are much better than past ones. However, we can argue over whether the scale is relative or absolute when stepping back in time. We also have to note that many more players play chess today than at earlier times. Simple statistical models predict that Kasparov, history's current most extreme performer, can be expected to be more highly rated than the most extreme performer in past eras (Charness & Gerchak, 1996).

As many have noted, the vast majority of measures in cognitive research fall into two categories: (1) speed and (2) accuracy. We can't go back in time and retrieve information about speed, but we can do so for accuracy when records are sound. Roring and Ericsson (in preparation), using a technique first introduced by Chabris and Hearst (2003), examined world championship matches over the past two centuries. They employed a strong chess playing program, Fritz, to search for tactical errors. Each move of each game is compared with the one picked by Fritz to see whether it falls below a cutoff score. Not too surprisingly, past world championship games had many more such tactical errors than current ones, indicating that the quality of play has improved significantly over the past century. Although the technique for searching for flaws in expert performance may not work well in all domains, it is a potentially valuable tool.

Simulation and Intervention Study Challenges

Expertise, like age, is an individual-difference variable. Typical research designs in expertise tend to parallel ones seen in aging: mainly cross-sectional ones looking at skill differences and longitudinal ones looking at skill changes, although, of course, all are really quasi-experimental studies. In the former, people at different skill levels are compared to assess processes or knowledge that might explain performance differences. In longitudinal studies, the usual practice is to follow a relatively small sample ($n = 1$ or 2) across an extended period of time as the sample members are trained in performing a specific task. A good example is the classic study about the making of a digit span expert (Ericsson, Chase, & Faloon, 1980). A relatively ordinary undergraduate improved from a digit span of about 7 random digits to about 80 digits with about 100 hours of practice. All of these designs are quite familiar in aging research, and some of the more interesting ones combine both skill and age variables (e.g., in word span, learning by means of the method of loci; Kliegl, Smith, & Baltes, 1989).

One of the interesting trends in expertise research is the use of simulation models to unpack the cognitive processes seen as necessary for explaining skill differences. Again, for digit span, a good example is the symbolic computer simulation by Richman, Staszewski, and Simon (1995), which provides a mechanism to explain the development of the long-term working memory structures (Ericsson & Kintsch, 1995) necessary to encode random digits. Using a different architecture, neural net simulation, Mireles and Charness (2002) attempted to explain how knowledge might moderate or mediate age-related decline in memory for opening move sequences in chess. Although mathematical models and computer simulations are not that popular in cognitive aging research, they are potentially very useful tools for theory development, although they can speak only to the sufficiency of mechanisms, such as acquired knowledge, to compensate for age-related decline in other processes and abilities.

However, the most underutilized instrument in the toolbox of cognitive aging research is the intervention study. Intervention studies address the necessity and sufficiency of knowledge acquisition to compensate for decline in other processes. It is one thing to show, under carefully controlled laboratory conditions, that a theoretically motivated manipulation can minimize (or eliminate) age differences in cognitive performance. It is quite another to take that manipulation out of the laboratory and demonstrate an impact on the life of an older adult. Examples are infrequent even in expertise research (e.g., Williams, Ward, Knowles, & Smeeton, 2002, in sports).

There have been attempts to improve intellectual functioning for those undergoing aging changes (e.g., Schaie & Willis, 1986) and even a randomized clinical trial to examine how cognitive training impacts the performance of older adults (the Advanced Cognitive Training for Independent and Vital Elderly [ACTIVE] trial training memory, reasoning, speed of processing; Ball et al., 2002), although, to be frank, the results thus far are somewhat disappointing in terms of providing much benefit outside the trained skill. (The trained skill itself improved at the level of an effect equivalent to 7–14 years of expected cognitive decline.) Nearly 100 years of research on expertise predicts narrow transfer of training, so the expectation of broad improvement was misplaced. Still, demonstrating a laboratory-to-life linkage is probably the most promising approach to showing the effectiveness and efficiency of cognitive aging research.

CONCLUSION

Can acquired knowledge compensate for age-related decline in general intellectual functioning when considering expert performance? Although knowledge is probably the strongest predictor of performance, age-related declines in basic abilities seem to set some limits on its expression, particularly with respect to speeded tasks. However, we need additional progress in ruling out confounds for the age–expertise relationship, such as accounting for generational improvements and understanding whether declines are mediated by changes in deliberate practice.

Expertise research concerns itself with trying to understand extreme adaptation effects. Aging research is typically concerned with understanding life span development, which often is seen as a mixture of losses and gains. Lives in developed countries now approach 80 years in duration. A typical laboratory experiment in cognitive aging lasts about 1 hour. In comparison, turning fast-twitch muscle fiber to slow-twitch fiber takes on the order of 6 to 8 weeks of strenuous exercise

(Ericsson & Charness, 1994). The time constraint for turning a novice into a world-class expert is somewhere between 1,000 and 10,000 hours of deliberate practice (Charness et al., 2005). In short, our typical methods for conducting experimental research (cross-sectional comparisons) leave us many orders of magnitude away from the phenomena we seek to identify and explain. Of course, there are pragmatic reasons why we typically require only about an hour of time from participants. Few participants in our research studies are as motivated as those seeking to become experts. Nonetheless, if we hope to bridge the gap between our current knowledge state and an ideal one, we need to adopt longitudinal research methods more frequently within cognitive aging studies. Such studies may be difficult to fund but are a necessary adjunct to our current cross-sectional efforts.

NOTES

1. http://media.baa.org/BostonMarathon/Qualifying.asp

2. http://www.marathonguide.com/history/

3. http://media.baa.org/BostonMarathon/PastChampions.asp

4. http://db.chessmetrics.com/

REFERENCES

Ackerman, P. L. (1988). Determinants of individual differences during skill acquisition: Cognitive abilities and information processing. *Journal of Experimental Psychology: General, 117,* 288–318.

Ackerman, P. L., & Rolfhus, E. L. (1999). The locus of adult intelligence: Knowledge, abilities, and non-ability traits. *Psychology and Aging, 14,* 314–330.

Bäckman, L., & Dixon, R. A. (1992). Psychological compensation: A theoretical framework. *Psychological Bulletin, 112,* 259–283.

Ball, K., Berch, D. B., Helmers, K. F., Jobe, J. B., Leveck, M. D., Marsiske, M., et al. (2002). Effects of cognitive training interventions with older adults: A randomized control trial. *Journal of the American Medical Association, 288,* 2271–2281.

Baltes, P. B., & Baltes, M. M. (1990). Psychological perspectives on successful aging: The model of selective optimization with compensation. In P. B. Baltes & M. M. Baltes (Eds.), *Successful aging: Perspectives from the behavioral sciences* (pp. 1–34). Cambridge, MA: Cambridge University Press.

Baltes, P. B., Staudinger, U. M., & Lindenberger, U. (1999). Lifespan psychology: Theory and application to intellectual functioning. *Annual Review of Psychology, 50,* 471–507.

Beier, M. E., & Ackerman, P. L. (2001). Current-events knowledge in adults: An investigation of age, intelligence, and nonability determinants. *Psychology and Aging, 16,* 615–628.

Beier, M. E., & Ackerman, P. L. (2005). Age, ability, and the role of prior knowledge on the acquisition of new domain knowledge: Promising results in a real-world learning environment. *Psychology and Aging, 20,* 341–355.

Bosman, E. A. (1993). Age-related differences in motoric aspects of transcription typing skill. *Psychology and Aging, 8,* 87–102.

Bosman, E. A., & Charness, N. (1996). Age differences in skilled performance and skill acquisition. In T. Hess & F. Blanchard-Fields (Eds.), *Perspectives on cognitive change in adulthood and aging* (pp. 428–453). New York: McGraw-Hill.

Chabris, C. F., & Hearst, E. S. (2003). Visualization, pattern recognition, and forward search: Effects of playing speed and sight of the position on grandmaster chess errors. *Cognitive Science, 27,* 637–648.

Charness, N. (1981). Aging and skilled problem solving. *Journal of Experimental Psychology: General, 110,* 21–38.

Charness, N. (1983). Age, skill, and bridge bidding: A chronometric analysis. *Journal of Verbal Learning and Verbal Behavior, 22,* 406–416.

Charness, N. (1992). The impact of chess research on cognitive science. *Psychological Research, 54,* 4–9.

Charness, N. (2006). The influence of work and occupation on brain development. In P. B. Baltes, F. Rösler, & P. Reuter-Lorenz (Eds.). *Lifespan development and the brain: The perspective of biocultural co-constructivism* (pp. 306–325). New York: Cambridge University Press.

Charness, N., & Gerchak, Y. (1996). Participation rates and maximal performance: A Log-linear explanation for group differences, such as Russian and male dominance in chess. *Psychological Science, 7,* 46–51.

Charness, N., Kelley, C. L., Bosman, E. A., & Mottram, M. (2001). Word processing training and retraining: Effects of adult age, experience, and interface. *Psychology and Aging, 16,* 110–127.

Charness, N., & Schultetus, R. S. (1999). Knowledge and expertise. In F. T. Durso, R. S. Nickerson, R. W. Schvaneveldt, S. T. Dumais, D. S. Lindsay, & M. T. H. Chi (Eds.), *Handbook of applied cognition* (pp. 57–81). Chichester, UK: Wiley.

Charness, N., Tuffiash, M., & Jastrzembski, T. (2004). Motivation, emotion, and expert skill acquisition. In D. Dai & R. J. Sternberg (Eds.) *Motivation, emotion, and cognition: Integrative perspectives* (pp. 299–319). Mahwah, NJ: Lawrence Erlbaum.

Charness, N., Tuffiash, M., Krampe, R., Reingold, E. M., & Vasyukova, E. (2005). The role of deliberate practice in chess expertise. *Applied Cognitive Psychology, 19,* 151–165.

Chase, W. G., & Ericsson, K. A. (1982). Skill and working memory. In G. H. Bower (Ed.), *The psychology of learning and motivation* (Vol. 16, pp. 1–58). San Diego, CA: Academic Press.

Chase, W. G., & Simon, H. A. (1973a). The mind's eye in chess. In W. G. Chase (Ed.), *Visual information processing* (pp. 215–281). San Diego, CA: Academic Press.

Chase, W. G., & Simon, H. A. (1973b). Perception in chess. *Cognitive Psychology, 4,* 55–81.

Chi, M. T. H., & Ceci, S. J. (1987). Content knowledge: Its role, representation, and restructuring in memory development. *Advances in Child Development and Behavior, 20,* 91–142.

Coon, H., & Carey, G. (1989). Genetic and environmental determinants of musical ability in twins. *Behavioral Genetics, 19,* 183–193.

de Groot, A. (1978). *Thought and choice in chess* (2nd ed.). The Hague, The Netherlands: Mouton. (Original work published 1946)

Dennis, W. (1966). Creative productivity between ages of 20 and 80 years. *Journal of Gerontology, 21,* 1–8.

Dickens, W. T., & Flynn, J. R. (2001). Heritability estimates versus large environmental effects: The IQ paradox resolved. *Psychological Review, 108,* 346–369.

Elbert, T., Pantev, C., Wienbruch, C., Rockstroh, B., & Taub, E. (1995, October 13). Increased cortical representation of the fingers of the left hand in string players. *Science, 270,* 305–307.

Elo, A. E. (1965). Age changes in master chess performances. *Journal of Gerontology, 20,* 289–299.

Elo, A. E. (1986). *The rating of chessplayers, past and present* (2nd ed.). New York: Arco.

Ericsson, K. A. (1990). Peak performance and age: An examination of peak performance in sports. In P. B. Baltes & M. M. Baltes (Eds.), *Successful aging: Perspectives from the behavioral sciences* (pp. 164–196). New York: Cambridge University Press.

Ericsson, K. A. (Ed.). (1996). *The road to excellence: The acquisition of expert performance in the arts, sciences, sports and games.* Mahwah, NJ: Lawrence Erlbaum.

Ericsson, K. A. (2006). The influence of experience and deliberate practice on the development of superior expert performance. In K. A. Ericsson, N. Charness, P. Feltovich, & R. Hoffman (Eds.), *Cambridge handbook of expertise and expert performance* (pp. 683–704). Cambridge, UK: Cambridge University Press.

Ericsson, K. A., & Charness, N. (1994). Expert performance: Its structure and acquisition. *American Psychologist, 49,* 725–747.

Ericsson, K. A., Charness, N., Feltovich, P., & Hoffman, R. (Eds.). (2006). *Cambridge handbook of expertise and expert performance.* Cambridge, UK: Cambridge University Press.

Ericsson, K. A., Chase, W. G., & Faloon, S. (1980, June 6). Acquisition of a memory skill. *Science, 208,* 1181–1182.

Ericsson, K. A., & Kintsch, W. (1995). Long-term working memory. *Psychological Review, 102,* 211–245.

Ericsson, K. A., Krampe, R. T., & Tesch-Römer, C. (1993). The role of deliberate practice in the acquisition of expert performance. *Psychological Review, 100,* 363–406.

Flynn, J. R. (1987). Massive gains in 14 nations: What IQ tests really measure. *Psychological Bulletin, 101,* 171–191.

Fox, P. W., Hershberger, S. L., & Bouchard, T. J. (1996, November 28). Genetic and environmental contributions to the acquisition of a motor skill. *Nature, 384,* 356–358.

Ghisletta, P., & Lindenberger, U. (2003). Age-based structural dynamics between perceptual speed and knowledge in the Berlin Aging Study: Direct evidence for ability dedifferentiation in old age. *Psychology and Aging, 18,* 696–713.

Gobet, F., & Charness, N. (2006). Expertise in chess. In K. A. Ericsson, N. Charness, P. Feltovich, & R. Hoffman (Eds.), *Cambridge handbook of expertise and expert performance* (pp. 523–538). New York: Cambridge University Press.

Hambrick, D. Z., & Engle, R. W. (2002). Effects of domain knowledge, working memory capacity, and age on cognitive performance: An investigation of the knowledge-is-power hypothesis. *Cognitive Psychology, 44*, 339–387.

Hambrick, D. Z., Salthouse, T. A., & Meinz, E. J. (1999). Predictors of crossword puzzle proficiency and moderators of age–cognition relations. *Journal of Experimental Psychology: General, 128*, 131–164.

Hannon, D. J., & Hoyer, W. J. (1994). Mechanisms of visual-cognitive aging: A neural network account. *Aging and Cognition, 1*, 105–119.

Horn, J. L., & Masunaga, H. (2000). New directions for research into aging and intelligence: The development of expertise. In T. J. Perfect & E. A. Maylor (Eds.), *Models of cognitive aging: Debates in psychology* (pp. 125–159). New York: Oxford University Press.

Jastrzembski, T., Charness, N., & Vasyukova, C. (2006). Expertise and age effects on knowledge activation in chess. *Psychology and Aging, 21*, 401–405.

Joy, S. (2006). What should I be doing, and where are they doing it? Scholarly productivity of academic psychologists. *Perspectives on Psychological Science, 1*, 346–364.

Keele, S. W., & Hawkins, H. L. (1982). Explorations of individual differences relevant to high level skill. *Journal of Motor Behavior, 14*, 3–23.

Kliegl, R., Smith, J., & Baltes, P. B. (1989). Testing-the-limits and the study of adult age differences in cognitive plasticity of a mnemonic skill. *Developmental Psychology, 25*, 247–256.

Krampe, R. T., & Baltes, P. B. (2003). Intelligence as adaptive resource development and resource allocation: A new look through the lenses of SOC and expertise. In R. J. Sternberg & E. L. Grigorenko (Eds.), *The psychology of abilities, competencies, and expertise* (pp. 31–69). New York: Cambridge University Press.

Krampe, R. T., & Charness, N. (2006). Aging and expertise. In K. A. Ericsson, N. Charness, P. Feltovich, & R. Hoffman (Eds.), *Cambridge handbook of expertise and expert performance* (pp. 723–742). Cambridge, UK: Cambridge University Press.

Krampe, R. T., & Ericsson, K. A. (1996). Maintaining excellence: Deliberate practice and elite

performance in young and older pianists. *Journal of Experimental Psychology: General, 125*, 331–359.

Landauer, T. K. (1986). How much do people remember? Some estimates of the quantity of learned information in long-term memory. *Cognitive Science, 10*, 477–493.

Lehman, H. C. (1953). *Age and achievement*. Princeton, NJ: Princeton University Press.

Lehmann, A., & Ericsson, K. A. (1998). The historical development of domains of expertise: Performance standards and innovations in music. In A. Steptoe (Ed.), *Genius and the mind: Studies of creativity and temperament in the historical record* (pp. 67–94). New York: Oxford University Press.

Li, S., Lindenberger, U., & Frensch, P. (2000). Unifying cognitive aging: From neuromodulation to representation to cognition. *Neurocomputing: An International Journal, 32–33*, 879–890.

Li, S.-C., Lindenberger, U., Hommel, B., Aschersleben, G., Prinz, W., & Baltes, P. B. (2004). Transformations in the couplings among intellectual abilities and constituent cognitive processes across the life span. *Psychological Science, 15*, 155–163.

Manton, K. G., Stallard, E., & Corder, L. (1995). Changes in morbidity and chronic disability in the U.S. elderly population: Evidence from the 1982, 1984, and 1989 National Long Term Care Surveys. *Journal of Gerontology: Social Sciences, 50*, S194–S204.

Masunaga, H., & Horn, J. (2001). Expertise and age-related changes in components of intelligence. *Psychology and Aging, 16*, 293–311.

McEvoy, G. M., & Cascio, W. F. (1989). Cumulative evidence of the relationship between employee age and job performance. *Journal of Applied Psychology, 74*, 11–17.

Mireles, D. E., & Charness, N. (2002). Computational explorations of the influence of structured knowledge on age-related cognitive decline. *Psychology and Aging, 17*, 245–259.

Morrow, D., Leirer, V., Altieri, P., & Fitzsimmons, C. (1994). When expertise reduces age differences in performance. *Psychology and Aging, 9*, 134–148.

Morrow, D. G., Ridolfo, H. E., Menard, W. E., Sanborn, A., Stine-Morrow, E. A. L., Magnor, C., et al. (2003). Environmental support promotes expertise-based mitigation of age differences on pilot communication tasks. *Psychology and Aging, 18,* 268–284.

Oldfield, R. C. (1963). Individual vocabulary and semantic currency: A preliminary study. *British Journal of Social and Clinical Psychology, 2,* 122–130.

Palmer, C. (1989). Mapping musical thought to musical performance. *Journal of Experimental Psychology: Human Perception and Performance, 12,* 331–346.

Palmer, C., & Meyer, R. K. (2000). Conceptual and motor learning in music performance. *Psychological Science, 11,* 63-68.

Quetelet, L. A. J. (1969). *A treatise on man and the development of his faculties.* Gainesville, FL: Scholars' Facsimiles and Reprints. (Original work published 1842)

Rabbitt, P. M. A. (1993). Crystal quest: A search for the basis of maintenance of practised skills into old age. In A. Baddeley & L. Weiskrantz (Eds.), *Attention: Selection, awareness, and control* (pp. 188–230). Oxford, UK: Clarendon Press.

Richman, H. B., Staszewski, J. J., & Simon, H. A. (1995). Simulation of expert memory using EPAM IV. *Psychological Review, 102,* 305–330.

Roring, R.W., & Charness, N. (2007). A multilevel model analysis of expertise in chess across the lifespan. *Psychology and Aging, 22,* 291–299.

Roring, R., & Ericsson, K. A. (in preparation). *The measurement of the highest levels of productive thought: an application to elite performance in chess.* Manuscript in preparation.

Salthouse, T. A. (1984). Effects of age and skill in typing. *Journal of Experimental Psychology: General, 13,* 345–371.

Salthouse, T. A. (1988). Initiating the formalization of theories of cognitive aging. *Psychology and Aging, 3,* 3–16.

Salthouse, T. A. (1990). Cognitive competence and expertise in aging. In J. E. Birren & K. W. Schaie (Eds.). *Handbook of the psychology of aging* (3rd ed., pp. 310–319). San Diego, CA: Academic Press.

Salthouse, T. A. (1996). The processing-speed theory of adult age differences in cognition. *Psychological Review, 103,* 403–428.

Salthouse, T. A. (2006). Mental exercise and mental aging: Evaluating the validity of the "use it or lose it" hypothesis. *Perspectives on Psychological Science, 1,* 68–87.

Salthouse, T. A., & Maurer, J. J. (1996). Aging, job performance, and career development. In J. E. Birren & K. W. Schaie (Eds.), *Handbook of the psychology of aging* (4th ed., pp. 353–364). New York: Academic Press.

Schaie, K. W. (1994). The course of adult intellectual development. *American Psychologist, 49,* 304–313.

Schaie, K. W., & Willis, S. L. (1986). Can decline in adult intellectual functioning be reversed? *Developmental Psychology, 22,* 223–232.

Schneider, W., Gruber, H., Gold, A., & Opwis, K. (1993). Chess expertise and memory for chess positions in children and adults. *Journal of Experimental Child Psychology, 56,* 328–349.

Schulz, R., & Curnow, C. (1988). Peak performance and age among superathletes: Track and field, swimming, baseball, tennis and golf. *Journal of Gerontology: Psychological Sciences, 43,* 113–120.

Simon, H. A. (1974, February 8). How big is a chunk? *Science, 183,* 482–488.

Simon, H. A., & Gilmartin, K. (1973). A simulation of memory for chess positions. *Cognitive Psychology, 5,* 29–46.

Simonton, D. K. (1988). Age and outstanding achievement: What do we know after a century of research? *Psychological Bulletin, 104,* 251–267.

Simonton, D. K. (1991). Career landmarks in science: Individual differences and interdisciplinary contrasts. *Developmental Psychology, 27,* 119–130.

Simonton, D. K. (1996). Creative expertise: A lifespan developmental perspective. In K. A. Ericsson (Ed.), *The road to excellence* (pp. 227–253). Mahwah, NJ: Lawrence Erlbaum.

Simonton, D. K. (1997). Creative productivity: A predictive and explanatory model of career trajectories and landmarks. *Psychological Review, 104,* 66–89.

Stanovich, K. E., West, R. F., & Harrison, M. R. (1995). Knowledge growth and maintenance across the life span: The role of print exposure. *Developmental Psychology, 31,* 811–826.

Sternberg, R. J. (1999). Intelligence as developing expertise. *Contemporary Educational Psychology, 24,* 359–375.

Sturman, M. C. (2004). Searching for the inverted u-shaped relationship between time and performance: Meta-analyses of the experience/performance, tenure/performance, and age/performance relationships. *Journal of Management, 29,* 609–640.

Taylor, J. L., O'Hara, R., Mumenthaler, M. S., Rosen, A. C., & Yesavage, J. A. (2005). Cognitive ability, expertise, and age differences in following air-traffic control instructions. *Psychology and Aging, 20,* 117–133.

Verhaeghen, P., & Salthouse, T. A. (1997). Meta-analyses of age–cognition relations in adulthood: Estimates of linear and non-linear age effects and structural models. *Psychological Bulletin, 122,* 231–249.

Waldman, D. A., & Avolio, B. J. (1986). A meta-analysis of age differences in job performance. *Journal of Applied Psychology, 71,* 33–38.

Waters, A. J., Gobet, F., & Leyden, G. (2002). Visuospatial abilities of chess players. *British Journal of Psychology, 93,* 557–565.

Wechsler, D. (1997). *Wechsler Adult Intelligence Scale—Third edition.* San Antonio, TX: Harcourt Assessment.

Williams, A. M., Ward, P., Knowles, J., & Smeeton, N. (2002). Anticipation skill in "real-world" tasks: Measurement, training and transfer. *Journal of Experimental Psychology: Applied, 8,* 259–270.

PART IV

BIOLOGICAL INDICATORS AND HEALTH-RELATED PROCESSES

16

INTEGRATING HEALTH INTO COGNITIVE AGING RESEARCH AND THEORY

Quo Vadis?

AVRON SPIRO III AND CHRISTOPHER B. BRADY

As people age, the likelihood of cognitive impairment and dementia increase, although they are far from inevitable. Both are associated with increased morbidity, mortality, and health care costs and with worsening quality of life. Improving our understanding of the risk factors for cognitive impairment, and determining whether these same risk factors are also associated with dementia, has become increasingly important as the population ages. Although extensive research documents the nature and extent of cognitive impairment and dementia, much less is known about the etiology of age-related cognitive decline (i.e., cognitive *change* with age). As Bennett (2000) noted, less is known about predictors of cognitive decline than about many other chronic conditions of aging.

AUTHORS' NOTES: An earlier version of this chapter was presented at the International Conference on the Future of Cognitive Aging, Pennsylvania State University, May 20–22, 2005.

The Cognition and Health in Aging Men Project has been supported by U.S. Department of Veterans Affairs Merit Reviews to Avron Spiro III and Christopher B. Brady and by grants from the National Institutes of Health (AA08941, AG13006, AG14345, AG18436, DK071292, ES05947, ES0525) and the U.S. Department of Agriculture (ARS Contract 53-K06-510). The VA Normative Aging Study is supported by the Cooperative Studies Program/ERIC of the U.S. Department of Veterans Affairs and is a research component of the Massachusetts Veterans Epidemiology Research and Information Center (MAVERIC). The views expressed in this chapter are those of the authors and do not necessarily represent the views of the U.S. Department of Veterans Affairs.

We thank Martin L. Albert, J. Michael Gaziano, and Pantel S. Vokonas for their contributions to our thinking, as well as our other colleagues at the Normative Aging Study, Language and Aging Brain Laboratory, MAVERIC, and the Geriatric Research, Education, and Clinical Center at VA Boston Healthcare System and Boston and Harvard Universities.

One implication of this lack of knowledge is that a substantial portion of cognitive decline seen in nondemented older adults may be preventable or modifiable. Another is that factors associated with cognitive decline may begin to exert their influence many years before impairment or dementia are observed. Thus, it is of particular importance to determine whether there are aspects of age-related cognitive decline that are due to preventable or modifiable factors (e.g., risk factors or disease onset) because of the possibility that treatment might reduce or delay the impact of these factors. Such a delay in cognitive decline would greatly improve the quality of life of nondemented older adults and perhaps prolong the time until onset of more severe impairment. The benefits of increased cognitive health to older adults and their families are obvious; furthermore, this increased cognitive longevity would represent substantial reduction in health care costs.

We begin this chapter with a couple of observations, and then we offer a thesis. We then pose several questions about health and cognitive aging and attempt to develop them in support of our thesis. Rather than provide definitive answers, we offer instead our own views, developed over the last decade as we have studied the effects of health on cognitive aging. In brief, our view is that (a) in later life, cognitive decline happens; (b) aging is not a cause of this decline; (c) hence the term *cognitive aging* is somewhat of a misnomer; and (d) we must seek other causal explanations for cognitive decline with age. We propose health, specifically vascular disease and its risk factors, as a candidate explanation.

Our first observation is that cognition (in some domains) declines during later life (for some persons). The second observation is that age is often called upon to serve as an "explanation" for this finding (hence the term *cognitive aging*). However, Wohlwill (1973) noted some time ago that age (i.e., time since birth) is not an explanatory variable but rather a descriptive one, a temporal axis along which developmental phenomena can be arrayed. As first noted by Riegel and Riegel (1972), for some outcomes, time until an event may sometimes be preferable to time since birth (cf. also Sliwinski, Stawski, Katz, Verghese, & Lipton, 2006). Thus, we are faced with the question, What, other than aging

(which, according to Peto & Doll [1997], does not exist), might explain cognitive decline in later life?

The answer to this question that we propose cognitive psychologists should seriously consider is health. Our thesis is that the study of cognitive aging (used here as a shorthand term for "quantitative decline in some cognitive functions that typically occurs with age for some persons") would benefit from an increased appreciation of, focus on, and commitment to integrating health (and disease) into its theories, studies, and measures. More specifically, we believe that the *vascular hypothesis* (e.g., Bowler, 2005; Chui, 2006; O'Brien et al., 2003) deserves consideration as an explanation for cognitive aging. The vascular hypothesis proposes that vascular diseases (cardiovascular or cerebrovascular diseases [CVDs], including coronary heart disease, atherosclerosis, and stroke), as well as vascular disease risk factors (e.g., hypertension, diabetes), affect minds as well as hearts. Through their actions on the brain, particularly in frontal systems and their associated white matter tracts, CVDs seem to affect frontal system cognitive functions in particular. We mention this pattern of CVD-related cognitive dysfunction because of the recent debate about whether frontal systems dysfunction plays a causal role in cognitive aging (e.g., Burke, 1997; Greenwood, 2000; Hasher & Zacks, 1988, McDowd, 1997; Moscovitch & Winocur, 1992; West, 1996, 2000). We believe that this debate would be clarified substantially by better assessing the vascular health of older adults.

To support our thesis, we pose, and then discuss, the following questions:

1. WHY should we consider health in cognitive aging?

2. Where are we NOW (descriptive)?

3. Where SHOULD we be heading (prescriptive)?

WHY CONSIDER HEALTH?

Most of the explanations for decline offered by cognitive agers derive from the cognitive domain (e.g., slowing or resource reduction). But this seems to take a rather restricted view of things, somewhat like the alcohol-impaired individual who looks for his car keys under the streetlight because the light is better. Instead, we should consider as explanations those variables that are likely to drive cognitive change, rather than those that are easy to understand or to measure. Thus, in this chapter, we sketch our view of what it would mean to consider health as an explanation of cognitive aging, at both the individual and the population levels.

What we mean when we state that cognitive aging would benefit from an increased appreciation of health is twofold. First, an increased understanding and study of disease, in its various aspects (e.g., incidence, severity, progression, treatment) must be considered in any study of cognitive aging. What we propose is that health should become one of the "usual suspects," joining age, gender, and education, that are included in the set of variables considered in relation to cognition. Second, this increased focus can serve as a means to reduce cognitive decline and optimize cognitive function in later life by means of prevention or remediation of some diseases. At the individual level, this would lead to a longer life without cognitive impairment or, to paraphrase Fries (1983/2005), to a compression of cognitive impairment. At the population level, even a modest delay of the onset of impairment in a fraction of the population could have large implications for society in terms of health care use, medical and long-term case costs, and improved quality of life (Alzheimer's Association, 2007).

As an aside, we should note that much of our discussion is directed primarily toward psychologists who study cognitive aging, because of their frequent failure to adequately consider disease processes and their role in cognitive changes with age. Too often "health" is measured by ratings or self-reports and used to screen or describe participants. Sometimes it is included as a covariate (e.g., self-assessed health status, number of medications or conditions), to control for differences among persons. Regardless, all too often health is ignored by most cognitive psychologists as a potential explanation for between-person differences or within-person changes. (For some exceptions, see Elias et al., 2003; Raz, Rodrigue, & Acker, 2003; Wahlin, MacDonald, deFrias, Nilsson, & Dixon, 2006; Waldstein, Giggey, Thayer, & Zonderman, 2005.)

In contrast to most cognitive aging psychologists, others (e.g., epidemiologists and neurologists; cf. Hendrie et al., 2006), often working with large-population studies, are more seriously examining the influence of health and disease on cognitive change. Rather than operating within psychology departments, they work primarily within medical settings, and although we have disagreements with certain aspects of their approach (e.g., use of limited cognitive assessments), we admire their focus on health. On the other hand, those who approach cognitive aging from such a biomedical perspective could benefit from an increased concern with issues championed by psychologists, such as the use of conceptually based multidimensional measurements of cognition. We believe that by combining the best of both approaches, psychological and biomedical, we can develop studies that best have the potential to unlock the secrets of cognitive aging. Such multidisciplinary research has been recently identified as a priority at the National Institutes of Health, as part of the Cognitive and Emotional Health Project (http://trans.nih.gov/cehp).

We consider health to be important in understanding cognitive aging for several reasons. First, we believe that aging per se is not a useful explanation for developmental change in general, or cognitive change in particular (Peto & Doll, 1997; Wohlwill, 1973). Once aging is removed from the explanatory arena, health becomes much more salient as a potential explanation. By ignoring health as an explanation of cognitive change, many sources of heterogeneity among older persons are ignored; in essence, health becomes a "hidden variable." This tends to result in variability that is due to health, especially to age-dependent diseases such as CVDs and diabetes (cf. Masoro, 2006), being misattributed to age. The result of such misattribution is that the role of aging is overstated, and important sources of variation are ignored. Second, the question of whether Alzheimer's disease is a vascular disease is currently controversial in the biomedical literature (e.g., Bowler, 2005; Casserly & Topol, 2004; Chui, 2006; O'Brien et al., 2003) and has major implications for prevention and treatment. This relates to the third reason that, if disease, particularly vascular disease, is responsible for some portion of cognitive decline with age, then there are safe and effective treatments for reducing vascular disease and its risks, and these might offer additional motivation for elders to engage in health promotion and disease prevention practices.

In sum, the problem is that we use aging to explain cognitive decline, without a thorough consideration of what other age-related factors, such as disease, might provide further explanatory power. With advancing age, health as well as cognition typically decline within persons. To attribute such declines simply to the passage of time is improper; instead, it is likely that with the passing of time, one or more of several things occur: diseases progress from asymptomatic or subclinical to overt, new diseases occur, or diseases accumulate and interact to have clinically meaningful effects on cognition. In other words, both cognitive decline and health decline are related to, but not caused by, aging. This is certainly the case at the population level, where age and decline are merely correlated. However, at the individual level it is less clear whether aging "causes" cognitive decline; it depends in part on whether one accepts aging as a single underlying biological process (Hayflick, 2004; Martin, 2006). Regardless, even within a person, the correlation of aging and cognitive decline often seems clear; what remains to be determined is whether aging is a causal process or merely a temporal axis along which other changes occur that cause such declines.

What Is the Health of the Elderly?

Among the elderly (aged 65+), chronic diseases are prevalent, many risk factors are elevated, and medication use is common. All of these can affect the brain, heart, vasculature, and other organ systems (e.g., renal) that are related to cognition. Functional (i.e., sensory, physical) limitations, such as hearing and vision loss or arthritis, are also prevalent and can also affect cognitive performance indirectly.

Table 16.1 shows the prevalence of selected diseases, conditions, and symptoms among older persons aged 65+ (Federal Interagency Forum on Aging-Related Statistics, 2006). The prevalence of many of these among the elderly are relatively high. Heart disease affects about one third of elders; the most serious condition,

stroke, is least frequent, with a prevalence of 8% to 10%. Diabetes, a risk factor for heart disease, stroke, blindness, and kidney disease, affects 15% to 20% of elders. Conditions such as arthritis are quite common, affecting 43% of men and 55% of women. Hearing impairment is also common; vision, memory impairment, and depression less so. Despite the relatively high prevalence of these and other diseases and conditions, only one quarter of adults rate their overall health as fair or poor.

Even for common conditions, such as diabetes or hypertension, perhaps because of their initially asymptomatic nature, underdiagnosis and undertreatment are common (see Table 16.2, which presents data from several studies that used nationally representative data from the Third National Health and Nutrition Examination Survey; http://www.cdc.gov/nchs/nhanes.htm). Although diabetes is diagnosed in 15% to 20% of elders, another 4% to 8% meet criteria for diabetes yet are unaware of it (Cowie et al., 2006). In many cases, the diagnosis of diabetes is preceded by 5 years of elevated insulin and 2.5 years of elevated glucose (Hara, Egusa, & Yamakido, 1996), both of which have been associated with reduced cognitive function (Awad, Gagnon, & Messier, 2004). Nearly half of men and over one third of women have impaired fasting glucose, a precursor of diabetes,

Table 16.1   Prevalence (%) of Selected Diseases and Conditions Among U.S. Adults Aged 65+

Disease or condition	Men	Women
Heart disease	37	28
Hypertension	48	55
Stroke	10	8
Diabetes	20	15
Arthritis	43	55
Trouble hearing	48	34
Trouble seeing	14	19
Memory impairment	13	11
Depression	11	18
Fair/poor self-rated health	27	26

SOURCE: Data are adapted from Tables 15–17 and Table 20 of Federal Interagency Forum (2006).

and almost half of those over age 60 are affected by the metabolic syndrome, a risk factor for developing diabetes and cardiovascular disease (Ford, Giles, & Dietz, 2002).

Hypertension may be the most prevalent disease of the elderly, affecting 63%. However, a substantial proportion (31%) of the elderly with hypertension are unaware that they have it; among those who are aware and seek treatment, only about 20% succeed in controlling their blood pressure (Hyman & Pavlik, 2001). As Table 16.2 shows, the situation is similar for the U.S. population aged 18+ (Hajjar & Kotchen, 2003)

Perhaps of greater concern is the reservoir of undiagnosed or subclinical disease among the elderly. Subclinical cardiovascular disease (Kuller et al., 1994) affects over one third of elders (Chaves, Kuller, O'Leary, Manolio, & Newman, 2004). Taking into account that one third of elders have a diagnosed cardiovascular disease, this implies that about 62% of those presumed to be disease free have subclinical cardiovascular disease (Kuller et al., 2006). Subclinical cardiovascular disease is not benign; it substantially increases the risk of heart disease and mortality (Chaves et al., 2004; Kuller et al.,

2006). Brain imaging has shown that as many as one third of elders who are free of stroke and transient ischemic attack nonetheless have significant lesions or white matter hyperintensities suggestive of disease (Bryan et al., 1999; Chaves et al., 2004; Longstreth et al., 1996; Vermeer, Koudstaal, Oudkerk, Hofman, & Bretler, 2002). These infarcts are associated with hypertension; those with poorly controlled hypertension have the greatest risk of severe white matter lesions (van Dijk et al., 2004). In turn, white matter lesions have been related to greater risk of CVDs, cognitive impairments, and greater cognitive decline (Au et al., 2006; Peters, 2006; Price et al., 1997; Soderlund et al., 2006; Vermeer et al., 2003; White, 1996).

Even if a disease is recognized by both the patient and his or her medical provider, treatment is not always sought nor given; neither is it always effective, because compliance can be less than optimal or because of individual variations in response to treatment (Kravitz, Duan, & Breslow, 2004). Table 16.3 presents data from a 2003 survey of Medicare beneficiaries (Safran et al., 2005). The majority of elders (nearly 90%) use some prescription medication, and the

Table 16.2   Prevalence of Undiagnosed and Untreated Diseases Among the Elderly

		Prevalence (%)		
Disease	*Subgroup*	*Men*	*Women*	*Pooled*
Diabetes, age 65+ (Cowie et al., 2006)				
	Diagnosed	15.8	15.9	
	Undiagnosed	7.9	4.2	
	Impaired fasting glucose	43.2	36.0	
Hypertension, age 65+ (Hyman & Pavlik, 2001)				
	Prevalence			63
	Unaware			31
	Aware, not treated			12
	Treated, not controlled			37
	Treated & controlled			19
Hypertension, U.S. population 18+ (Hajjar & Kotchen, 2003)				
	Prevalence	27.1	30.1	
	Aware	66.3	71.2	69.8
	Treated	54.3	62.0	62.7
	Controlled (among all treated)	59.9	47.8	43.9
	Controlled (among all hypertensive)	32.6	29.6	27.4

average number of medications per person in this survey was over 4. However, nonadherence is common, with over 40% reporting it in the past 12 months, due either to cost or other factors. Even among those with known chronic conditions, such as hypertension or diabetes, 40% reported nonadherence in the past 12 months.

Given the information in these tables, it should be clear why self-ratings of health cannot be used to assess health and disease in the elderly. Many people have conditions, sometimes serious ones, that can affect cognition, yet they are often unaware of them. This is particularly true of conditions that may be asymptomatic (e.g., diabetes, hypertension) at some point during their course. Some symptomatic conditions that can affect cognition can be relatively easily assessed by self-report (e.g., arthritis, sensory limitations). However, our concern is that the typical samples of the elderly included in most psychological studies of

cognitive aging are compromised by the inadvertent inclusion of persons with substantial disease burden. And when this disease burden includes vascular diseases that affect the brain and cognition, we should be concerned about the validity of conclusions drawn from such samples.

On the other hand, attempting to understand aging as a cause of cognitive decline by excluding older adults with disease will further obfuscate a meaningful understanding of age-related cognitive decline. Masoro (2006) provided an excellent discussion of whether excluding persons free of disease actually yields a disease-free sample, in part because of the prevalence of undiagnosed disease that we illustrate above. Masoro noted that with better medical technology, the number of "disease-free" older participants will continue to be reduced. Therefore, if *age-dependent* diseases are an integral part of aging, a corollary of this would be to embrace the assessment of disease rather than to incorrectly attempt to exclude it

Table 16.3 Prescription Medication Use in the United States, 2003

			Percentage
Prescription medication use			
	Any	89.2	
	1–2 meds		*25.6*
	3–4 meds		*28.4*
	5+		*46.1*
	Mean no. meds	4.7	
Nonadherence (past 12 months)			
	Overall	40.1	
	Due to cost	26.3	
	Skipped dose		*15.8*
	Took smaller dose		*12.4*
	Due to other factors	24.5	
	Made me feel worse		*18.5*
	Not helping		*17.8*
	Due to self-assessed need	14.5	
	Not think needed		*12.2*
	Taking too many meds		*8.9*
Nonadherence by disease (past 12 months)			
	Hypertension	40.1	
	Diabetes	42.1	

SOURCE: Data from Safran et al. (2005).

NOTE: Italicized numbers in the right-hand column are subgroups of the numbers in the left-hand column.

from cognitive aging research. Alternatively, excluding persons with disease would lead to a larger number of older persons being excluded, and the resulting sample ever more positively selected for good health (and, concomitantly, less representative of the cohort) at older ages.

Thus, the question arises, what is the population of the elderly to which we wish to generalize? In other words, if we study only healthy people at older ages (e.g., 75 and older), are we studying "normally aging" older adults, or "optimally aging" ones? Both are legitimate populations; however, we should be explicit about which is of interest in a given investigation and why, and then obtain a relevant sample.

Assessing Health

We use the term *health* to refer to a continuum, anchored on the positive end by health and on the negative end by disease. We view health from a biomedical rather than a psychosocial perspective, one that focuses on a physiological level rather than considering health in the sense of global assessments, self-ratings, or functional limitations. Furthermore, by health (or disease), we intend to imply a more objective assessment than would be obtained simply by means of the commonly used self-rating (e.g., "How would you rate your health?"). In other words, health in the sense we use it includes symptoms, conditions, and diagnoses, as well as physiological measures and biomarkers.

Figure 16.1 offers a hierarchical model of health proposed by Spiro (2001, 2007), based on Elinson (1988) and Hernandez, Durch, Blazer, and Hoverman (1999). Various dimensions of health are ordered from physiological to psychosocial. In terms of this model, most cognitive aging research focuses on Levels 5 or 8, using participant reports to characterize health. Dimensions 1 through 4 are more likely to be obtained in medical than in academic settings, although there are a number of projects defining health at these levels, for example, work on stress hormones and memory (Li et al., 2006), heart rate variability and cognition (Wood, Maraj, Lee, & Reyes, 2002), or brain imaging (Colcombe et al., 2006; Raz et al., 2003).

Although self-ratings of health are useful in some psychological contexts (e.g., prediction of mortality; Idler & Benyamini, 1997), they are not especially helpful in understanding cognitive decline with age. There are several reasons for this, including their global nature, lack of variability (most folks rate their health as excellent or good; see Table 16.1), and their lack of specificity (many with diseases rate their health as good, if not excellent).

Information on health (e.g., symptoms, conditions, and diagnoses) can be obtained by self-report, in a reasonably reliable and valid manner (Wahlin, 2004). For example, national surveys such as the National Health Interview Study (Edwards et al., 1994) or Medicare's Health Outcomes Survey (Miller, Rogers, Spiro, & Kazis, 2003) have found reasonably high agreement between some symptomatic diseases or conditions (e.g., diabetes, stroke) and diagnoses from administrative data. Self-reports of disease are particularly useful when the nature or scope of the study make it difficult to have medical evaluations conducted by appropriately trained personnel.

WHERE ARE WE NOW?

A review of recent research by psychologists on age-related cognitive changes suggests that we have a long way to go if we are to integrate health into cognitive aging. We reviewed 44 studies on cognitive aging published in 2006 in one of the premier aging journals. Less than half reported the health of their participants, with only 3 using some type of objective health assessment and 18 using self-ratings. The use of self-ratings for assessing health is inadequate for several reasons, as noted above. For example, Nilsson et al. (1997) found that subjective health measures exhibited little relationship with memory performance, whereas objective measures (e.g., systolic blood pressure) accounted for 62% of age-related variance in memory performance (vs. 34% attributable to age alone). Thus, there is much yet to be done; here we offer some suggestions on how to better assess health (and cognition) in studies of cognitive aging. For a broader discussion of the role of health in cognitive aging, see Anstey and Christensen (2000), Wahlin (2004), or Waldstein and Elias (2001).

1. Tissue alterations (e.g., atherosclerosis, carcinoma)

2. Laboratory assays or physiological parameters (e.g., glucose)

3. Records produced by physiologic measuring equipment (e.g., electrocardiogram; imaging)

4. Judgments rendered by clinicians in the form of a diagnosis (e.g., coronary heart disease)

5. Self-reports of conditions or diagnoses:
   • Presence of a given disease (e.g., "I have a bad heart")
   • Doctor diagnosis (e.g., "Has a doctor ever told you that you have had a heart attack?")

6. Self-reports of objectively observable symptoms (e.g., rash, sweating, swelling, lumps)

7. Self-reports of sensations, feelings, or thoughts not directly observable by others (e.g., headache, anger, hallucinations)

8. Self-ratings (e.g., "How would you rate your health?")
   • Global ratings (e.g., How would you rate your health?)
   • Multidimensional measures of functional status (e.g., Short Form-36 Health Survey [Ware, 2000], Veterans Rand 36-item Health Survey [Kazis et al., 2004])

Figure 16.1   Dimensions of Health: Physiological to Psychosocial

Assessing Cognition and Health

We take for granted that cognition changes (often, it declines) with age. Different aspects of cognition evidence different trajectories of change (some increase or remain stable); people vary in their trajectories. Although these changes occur with age, the extent to which they are the *result* of aging per se is debatable.

Cognition can be assessed using a variety of approaches and measures, for example, screening tools (e.g., the Mini-Mental State Examination [MMSE]; Folstein, Folstein, & McHugh, 1975); self-reports (e.g., Stewart, Ware, Sherbourne, & Wells, 1992); or performance measures derived from several perspectives, including psychometric (Carroll, 1993; Cattell, 1971), neuropsychological (Lezak, Howieson, Loring, Hannay, & Fischer, 2004), or ecological (Poon, Rubin, & Wilson, 1989). The choice of cognitive measures depends on the aims and constraints of a given study, as well as the investigators' preferences. In epidemiological studies, global measures such as the MMSE are widely used, largely because these studies were designed to address broader goals than the study of cognitive aging and have limited time to devote to cognitive assessment. In contrast, many cognitive aging studies use measures like the MMSE to screen participants; once enrolled, they are given detailed batteries based on psychometric or neuropsychological

perspectives. Unfortunately, in either case, little effort is devoted toward consideration of a standardized battery. Much could be gained if different studies adopted a common set of measures, which would simplify comparisons across different populations. Recently, Hachinski et al. (2006) proposed a harmonized battery for assessing vascular cognitive impairment (VCI); in addition to the full 60-minute cognitive version, they also proposed reduced versions requiring 30 or 5 minutes.

In contrast to the thoughtfulness psychologists generally apply to selecting cognitive measures, most cognitive aging research collects a limited set of health data, which are then used in relatively limited ways: to screen participants for inclusion, to describe the sample, or as a nuisance covariate to be adjusted statistically in the analysis (and not considered as substantively relevant). At best, the typical cognitive aging study collects a number of self-report health items and uses them to determine which respondents to include in the study. Some of these health items are then used to describe the remaining sample. However, as shown above, many people are unaware that they have certain conditions, or choose not to report them. Subclinical disease is not always diagnosed but can have important effects on cognition. Thus, use of ratings or self-reports to screen participants in cognitive aging studies can be misleading. The resulting inclusion of unhealthy participants, who are often older, can result in increased variance being mistakenly associated with age rather than with disease, thus overestimating the effects of age on cognitive change.

Often, these same self-report items, global ratings, or summary indices (e.g., number of conditions reported, medications taken, or doctor visits reported) are used to adjust statistically for the effects of health. Although these measures may more or less accurately indicate that one participant is "sicker" than another, this approach does not advance the theoretical integration of disease processes in cognitive aging. We have discussed the limitations of ratings above; summary indices also have their limitations. In particular, these additive measures can mask the impact of specific diseases, such that a person who reports having had one heart attack or stroke being counted as "less severe" than someone who has both arthritis and skin cancer.

On the basis of the results of studies using these approaches, many seem to believe that there is little evidence indicating that health is related to cognition. The evidence that leads them to this conclusion, however, suffers from a number of limitations, including the following:

1. Overreliance on self-ratings of health (as opposed to use of validated self-reports or diagnoses).

2. Inadequate measures of cognition (e.g., global measures, such as the MMSE, or a limited selection of ad hoc measures that cannot be compared across studies).

3. Use of cross-sectional rather than prospective or longitudinal designs.

4. Lack of theoretical rationale for selecting samples of persons and measures (of both cognition and health).

5. Use of convenience samples, often inadequately screened for health, with an unclear relation to the population of interest.

6. Overcontrol of health effects by adjusting for variables on health–cognition pathways (e.g., adjusting for obesity in a study of the effects of diabetes on cognition), which leads to an underestimate of health's effects. More studies should use causal modeling to allow testing of pathways, rather than using regression which removes the effects of intermediate variables (Spiro, 2007).

7. Failure to adequately consider and model the effects of modifiers of health's effects, for example, genetics, presence of comorbid conditions, or medication use.

When these limitations are taken into account, the evidence suggests otherwise, that health and disease account for some portion of age-related cognitive declines (e.g., Anstey & Christensen, 2000; M. F. Elias et al., 2003; Waldstein & Elias, 2001).

As noted above, there is a distinction between within-person processes over time and cross-sectional relations within a population. At the population level, the associations between health and cognition are likely quite different than those within a given person.

The lack of an adequate consideration of health is a limitation we must overcome. What is required is that we focus on models of relations between health and cognition; improve our measurements of both; and conduct studies that better assess, model, and reveal these complex relations. We advocate, strongly, that cognitive psychologists study health in a meaningful way, rather than relying solely on ratings or self-reports to assess their participants' health. There is ample precedent for this, dating from the 1960s and 1970s, including, for example, the work of Birren and Spieth (1962); Wilkie and Eisdorfer (1971); Spieth (1964); Hertzog, Schaie, and Gribbin (1978); and M. F. Elias and Streeten (1980). Despite these important early works, most of the major reference works on adult development and aging during the 1970s and 1980s (e.g., Eisdorfer & Lawton, 1973; Poon, Fozard, Cermak, Arenberg, & Thompson, 1980; Salthouse, 1991), including the first *Handbooks of the Psychology of Aging* (Birren & Schaie, 1977, 1985) largely ignored health as an influence on cognitive aging. Perhaps this was due to the experimental origins of much of the early literature on cognitive aging, which was conducted in laboratories using volunteer participants who at most were asked to provide self-ratings of health. At the same time, however, the National Institute on Aging initiated a research program focused on Alzheimer's disease, largely conducted at medical centers, and perhaps this dichotomization of resources resulted in a divorce of between health and cognitive aging. Recently, a number of cardiovascular studies funded by the National Health, Lung and Blood Institute began assessing cognition (e.g., Framingham [M. F. Elias et al., 2004], Cardiovascular Health Study [Kuller et al., 1998], Honolulu–Asia Aging Study [Launer et al., 2000], Atherosclerosis Risk in Communities [Knopman et al., 2001]). This work is exemplary in many ways of what we suggest should be the model of how to study health and its effects on cognition, although we believe that psychologists would have proposed better assessments of cognition than are used in some of these studies.

We advocate a reintegration of health into the study of cognitive aging. There are several ways this can be done, as the above examples demonstrated. Whether tested in a laboratory or in their own home, health can be assessed using medical examinations, physiological recordings, biomarkers, and so on. In addition to the cardiovascular health studies mentioned above, a number of other long-standing epidemiological studies of aging based in medical settings (e.g., the VA Normative Aging Study [NAS]) have added cognitive measures to their biomedical protocols. Several long-term cognitive aging studies (e.g., Seattle Longitudinal Study, Victoria Longitudinal Study) have added medical assessments to their cognitive protocols (Hultsch, 2004). New studies have been initiated to study relations between cognition and health, such as the Canadian Study of Health and Aging (http://www.csha.ca). Even a national study such as the Health and Retirement Study (http://hrsonline.isr.umich.edu), which conducts cognitive assessment via telephone, has begun an in-home biomedical examination (Willis, 2006). We believe that in order to advance, we need to adopt a multidisciplinary approach to cognitive aging, which encompasses other potential classes of explanatory factors, such as health and disease.

The Vascular Hypothesis of Cognitive Aging

To illustrate the arguments made above, we devote the remainder of the chapter to reviewing some work that we and others are conducting on the effects of vascular diseases and their risk factors (VDRF) on cognition. We believe that this will help to demonstrate the usefulness of considering health substantively in cognitive aging research. Such consideration will, we believe, inform some of the current debates in cognitive aging.

One such debate is about the role of the inhibitory/executive/prefrontal cortex dysfunction in cognitive aging (e.g., Band, Ridderinkhof, & Segalowitz, 2002; Burke, 1997; Dempster, 1992; Greenwood, 2000; Hasher & Zacks, 1988; McDowd, 1997; Moscovitch & Winocur, 1992; Shimamura, 1990; West, 1996, 2000). This debate has arisen, in part, because of inconsistent findings regarding age differences on tests of executive function. Some have found age-related changes on classical tests of executive function such as the Wisconsin Card Sorting Test and verbal fluency (e.g., Daigneault, Braun, & Whitaker, 1992; Dywan, Segalowitz, & Unsal, 1992; Haaland, Vranes, Goodwin, & Garry, 1987; Parkin & Walter, 1991; Troyer, Moskovitch, & Winocur, 1997; Whelihan & Lesher, 1985), whereas others have not (e.g., Boone, Miller, Lesser, Hill, & D'Elia, 1990; Salthouse, Fristoe, & Rhee, 1996). Others have suggested that age deficits are larger on executive function tests than on tests of other domains (Mittenberg, Seidenberg, O'Leary, & DiGiulio, 1989), whereas some have argued against this (Salthouse et al., 1996). Several cognitive aging models have proposed executive/frontal systems dysfunction as a mediator of cognitive aging (Dempster, 1992; Moscovitch & Winocur, 1992; West, 1996), but these models have been challenged (Greenwood, 2000; Salthouse et al., 1996).

Some of our data were consistent with each side of this debate. For example, we examined the pervasiveness of frontal systems dysfunction in older adults (Brady & Spiro, 2007) by analyzing a neuropsychological battery administered to a well-screened sample of 88 younger (mean age = 19.6, SD = 2.1) and 88 older (mean age = 71.3, SD = 6.3) adults. Factor analyses suggested that the older adults exhibited larger age differences on an executive function factor (composed of Wisconsin Card Sorting Test measures) relative to the other factors, similar to previous research. Subsequent cluster analyses, however, revealed that only 43% of the older sample exhibited this pattern of performance, whereas 57% exhibited relatively intact performance (Cluster 1; see Figure 16.2). Although relatively greater executive dysfunction was demonstrated in some older adults, not all experienced this deficit, suggesting that executive dysfunction may have been related to factors other than age. Because we did not collect health information other than to screen these participants, this study suffered from the same limitations that we have been discussing to this point. This, and findings from the literature on the effects of hypertension and other VDRFs on cognition, were the impetus for our subsequent research, which explicitly incorporated health measures into cognitive aging research.

Research on VCI (e.g., Bowler, 2005) and vascular dementia (e.g., Roman et al., 1993) is relevant. For example, Hachinski et al. (2006) characterized VCI thus:

The pattern of VCI cognitive deficits may include all cognitive domains, but there is likely to be a preponderance of so-called "executive" dysfunction, such as slowed information processing, impairments in the ability to shift from one task to another, and deficits in the ability to hold and manipulate information (i.e., working memory). (p. 2222)

The pattern of cognitive impairment seen in VCI, with relatively greater impairment in frontally mediated cognitive functions, parallels that being debated in the "normal" cognitive aging literature.

Our view is that the psychological literature on frontal systems dysfunction in "normal" cognitive aging would benefit from broader consideration of the literature on VCI (e.g., Hachinski et al., 2006). For example, we and others (e.g., M. F. Elias et al., 2003, 2004; Raz et al., 2003; Waldstein et al., 2005) have been examining the effects of age, vascular disease risk, and individual risk factors (e.g., hypertension) on cognition. The overarching hypothesis of our research is that the effects of age on cognition are related, at least in part, to vascular disease and VDRFs that selectively affect frontal systems function.

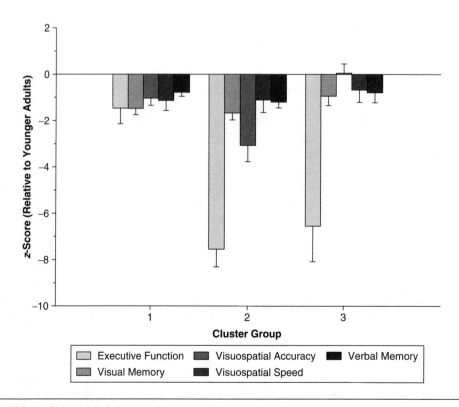

Figure 16.2   Older Adult Subgroups Based on Cluster Analysis

The VA NAS began in 1963 as a longitudinal study of health and aging among a sample of initially healthy men (Spiro & Vokonas, 2006). Every 3 years, men report to the VA clinic for a standardized medical examination, including a physical examination, medical history, and blood workup. Beginning in 1993, we began testing the vascular hypothesis by adding a brief (20-minute) cognitive assessment to the ongoing biomedical exam. The measures we selected included the Consortium to Establish a Registry for Alzheimer's Disease battery (Morris et al., 1989; Welsh et al., 1994), supplemented with some additional tests (Payton, Riggs, Spiro, Weiss, & Hu, 1998; Riggs, Spiro, Tucker, & Rush, 1996). The Consortium to Establish a Registry for Alzheimer's Disease battery is relatively short; widely used; and assesses a broad selection of cognitive functions that change with age, including the MMSE, verbal fluency (animals), a word list task with immediate and delayed recall and recognition, figure copying, and a short version of the Boston Naming Test (Goodglass & Kaplan, 2000). We also administered the WAIS–R (Wechsler, 1981) backward digit span, some additional figures for copying from the Developmental Test of Visual-Motor Integration (Beery, 1989), and a measure of perceptual speed and attention (Pattern Comparison from the Neurobehavioral Evaluation System— 2; Letz, 1991).

By embedding this battery within the ongoing NAS examination, we have been able to collect longitudinal cognitive data on over 1,100 men with a well-characterized health profile, based on the results of medical examinations; blood assays; health histories; medication use; and, in some cases, selected genetic polymorphisms. Through questionnaires, we also assess self-reports of diseases, health ratings, and mental health. The addition of the cognitive battery allowed us not only to consider cognition as an outcome of the prior 30 years of health data but also to collect 15 years of concomitant medical and cognitive data. Furthermore, this brief cognitive examination allows us to select and screen participants for enrollment in collaborating studies (e.g., Weisskopf et al., 2007).

Our subsequent studies in the NAS have specifically addressed the role of vascular disease risk in the "age effects" seen on tests of frontal system functions. The relationship between overall stroke risk and cognitive decline was examined in 235 healthy older men (mean age = 66.4) from the NAS (Brady, Spiro, McGlinchey-Berroth, Milberg, & Gaziano, 2001). These men received a thorough medical examination and neuropsychological tests on two occasions separated by a 3-year interval. Based on the initial medical examination, 10-year stroke risk was calculated using a modified version of the Framingham Stroke Risk Profile originally developed by D'Agostino, Wolf, Belanger, and Kannel (1994). Verbal fluency was used as a measure of executive function. Digit span backward (WAIS–R) and a word list learning test with both immediate and delayed recall trials were used to measure memory function. A speeded pattern comparison test served as a measure of visuospatial function. Regression was used to assess relations between stroke risk and cognitive changes; age and education were also included to assess their relations with change in cognitive function. Results showed that whereas increasing age was associated with decline in all cognitive functions, increasing stroke risk was associated only with decline in executive function. Furthermore, the relation between stroke risk and executive decline was nearly (80%) as large as the relation between age and executive decline. These results suggested that overall stroke risk in relatively healthy older men exerted specific effects on decline in executive function but not on memory or visuospatial functions and that the magnitude of these effects rivaled those of age effects.

In an extension of these findings, Brady, Spiro, and Gaziano (2005) examined the effect of a *specific* stroke risk factor, hypertension, on frontal system functions. We examined the influence of age and hypertensive status on several cognitive tests in 357 nondemented older men (mean age = 67) whose hypertensive status was stable over 3 years and had no comorbid disease. On the basis of multiple regression analyses, age was negatively associated with performance on all but one test. Age interacted with hypertensive status on verbal fluency (see Figure 16.3, left panel) and word list immediate recall (Figure 16.3, right panel); older uncontrolled hypertensives exhibited significantly larger age differences on these tests compared with normotensives. These findings suggested that uncontrolled hypertension produces specific cognitive deficits on frontal system functions (i.e., retrieval processes involved in verbal fluency and memory retrieval) beyond those attributable to age alone.

We examined whether there were cognitive differences across classes of antihypertensive medications. Eggen (2005) studied nearly 500 NAS men who had a consistent diagnosis of hypertension at two successive examinations and were free of coronary disease, stroke, dementia, and diabetes. Similar to Brady et al. (2005), they were divided into three groups: (1) untreated hypertensives, (2) uncontrolled hypertensives, and (3) controlled hypertensives (normotensives were not considered). Adjusting for age, education, and years since diagnosis of hypertension, performance on two of the seven cognitive tasks examined varied by type of antihypertensive. Men taking calcium-channel blockers had lower scores (about 2.8 words) on semantic fluency than did men on ACE (angiotensin-converting enzyme) inhibitors; on pattern comparison, response time was slower (about 700 milliseconds) in men on calcium-channel blockers or on no medication than those on beta-blockers.

Our findings from the NAS are largely consistent with the literature, which suggests that hypertension has specific effects on frontal system functions. Other measures of vascular health (e.g., cardiac output) also show specific effects on executive function (Jefferson, Poppas, Paul, & Cohen, 2007); however, VDRFs may be associated with other cognitive impairments. For example, Type 2 diabetes is linked to consistent deficits in verbal memory and processing speed, as well as less consistent deficits in nonverbal memory and executive function (Awad et al., 2004; Cukierman, Gerstein, & Williamson, 2005). Furthermore, comorbid hypertension and diabetes have independent and synergistic effects on cognition. For example, P. K. Elias et al. (1997) showed that hypertension was related to impaired verbal fluency and memory recall and that diabetes was related to impaired memory recall and reasoning; however, persons with hypertension and diabetes had additional impairments in visual memory and overall cognition. Therefore, comorbidity among VDRFs is important to consider, and we expect that the timing of the onset of each condition will also be shown to be important. For a recent discussion of some of the complexities of comorbidity, see Karlamangla et al. (2007) and Yancik et al. (2007).

In our current work with the NAS, we are using information on disease (based on an integration of physician examination, self-report of diagnoses, physiological measurements, and medications) to distinguish among profiles of cognitive change. In particular, we are examining differences in cognitive changes among persons with different vascular diseases. We know that all

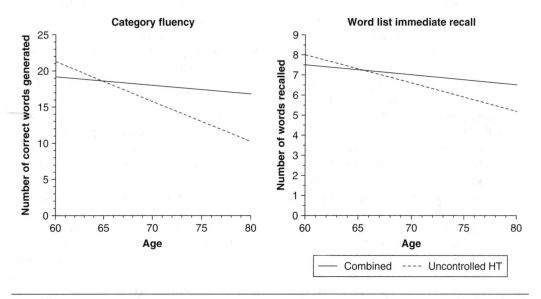

Figure 16.3 Predicted Score by Age: Men With Uncontrolled Hypertension (HT) Versus Others

persons do not show similar changes with age; perhaps by taking disease into account (e.g., stratification) we can account for some of this variability. As an example, we examined MMSE scores, adjusted for age (both linear and quadratic) and years of education for men aged 50 to 90 at their first examination. We stratified by which of several vascular conditions (angina [*n* = 32], myocardial infarction [*n* = 151], hypertension [*n* = 169]) occurred first; for comparison, 722 men with no vascular disease were included, and men with prior stroke were excluded. Within each of these four groups, predicted means were estimated for each year of age; these means were then smoothed using a parametric spline function (SAS Institute, 1990). For comparison, the MMSE means were also computed for each year of age for the total sample.

Figure 16.4 shows that MMSE trajectories across age differ as a function of first vascular disease. Men with hypertension are similar to those with no disease but are lower on average at younger (<60) and older (>70) ages. Men with angina are better than average, and similar to men with no coronary heart disease. Men with myocardial infarction perform the worst through age 73 or so; after that, men with hypertension have the lowest means.

Figure 16.5 shows corresponding MMSE trajectories stratified by level of self-rated health. At their baseline cognitive examination, 199 men rated their health as excellent, 467 as good, 117 as fair, and 110 as poor or very poor. As might be expected, men who rated their health as excellent had higher means than men who rated it as good. It is surprising, however, that men who rated their health as fair had a trajectory indicating lower scores with age than any other group, even than those who rated their health as poor or very poor.

These data suggest that health, even self-rated health, can be used to distinguish among

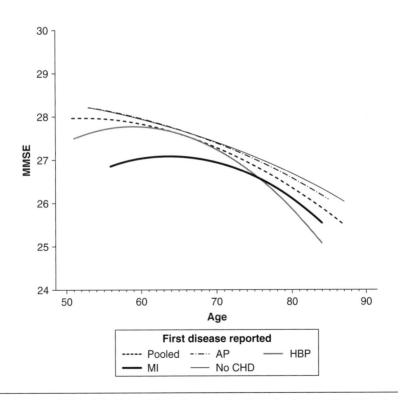

Figure 16.4   Predicted Mean Mini-Mental State Examination Score by Age and First Vascular Disease

NOTE: AP = angina pectoris; HBP = high blood pressure; MI = myocardial infarction; CHD = coronary heart disease.

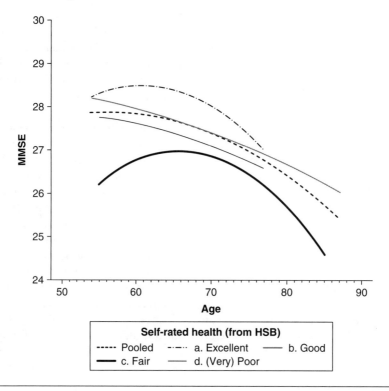

Figure 16.5   Predicted Mean Mini-Mental State Examination Score by Age and Self-Rated Health

NOTE: HSB = Health and Social Behavior Survey.

patterns of cognitive change. However, it should be noted that measures of disease provide a more useful perspective, because in these data the mean levels of self-rated health did not differ among men with different diseases.

Additional evidence of the link between VDRFs and cognition comes from studies showing that cognitive decline and associated brain changes may be related to vascular health (Raz et al., 2007), that tighter glycemic control appears to attenuate cognitive deficits in type 2 diabetes (Awad et al., 2004), and that aerobic exercise increased volume in both gray and white matter primarily located in prefrontal and temporal cortices (Colcombe et al., 2006). Such work illustrates that we should assess not only health but also its treatment. Furthermore, other variables, such as physical activity, will also be relevant, perhaps through its effects on blood flow.

As discussed above, there is considerable overlap between the largely distinct literatures on cognitive aging and VCI with respect to frontal systems dysfunction. Where "normal" VDRF-related frontal systems dysfunction in "healthy" cognitive aging ends and where VCI begins—if indeed there is a clear distinction—is unknown. As long as these two literatures, one studying normal cognitive aging using psychological approaches and another focusing on vascular cognitive impairment from a medical perspective, remain largely distinct, the situation is unlikely to change. A marriage of these two approaches, or even a long-term engagement, would offer hope to those in both families who believe that a successful union could advance the concerns of all.

WHERE SHOULD WE BE GOING?

One could make a compelling argument that a good deal of "normal" age-related cognitive change/decline is the result of vascular phenomena. If true, then measures of vascular disease and VDRFs should be incorporated into the analyses of cognitive studies, where they could help to explain some of the "age-related" cognitive variance that remains unexplained. We and others believe that including VRDFs as explanatory variables will provide better understanding of the etiology of age-related cognitive decline, which may perhaps be better defined as health-related cognitive decline. Once we accept the need to measure both cognition and health, it would be advantageous for the field, in the sense of generating cumulative knowledge, if we could agree, at least broadly, on what and how to measure both cognition and health.

1. We should adopt, as a first step, consensus models of cognition and health, to serve a function similar to the Big Five in personality. We need a taxonomy of each, which can serve as the starting point in testing models of their interrelations. Only when we mean the same thing by *hypertension* or *executive function* can we investigate the influence of the former on the latter.

   a. Taxonomies and methodologies for assessing health and disease are available (Elinson, 1988; Hernandez et al., 1999; Spiro, 2007). A recent special section of the *Journals of Gerontology* (e.g., Karlamangla et al., 2007; Yancik et al., 2007) discusses relevant issues on how to assess onset, duration, and severity of comorbid conditions.

   b. Adoption of diagnostic criteria such as those of the Joint National Committee on Prevention, Detection, Evaluation and Treatment of High Blood Pressure (Chobanian et al., 2003) for blood pressure would allow measurements to become standardized across studies. For example, a single measurement of blood pressure is about as informative a measure of hypertension or blood pressure as is asking someone to remember three words would be a measure of memory. As in cognitive assessment, multiple measures increase reliability and validity.

2. A priority should be the development of standards for making health assessment an integral part of cognitive aging research. Accomplishing this goal should not be difficult, because other scientific literatures have developed and adopted such standards.

   a. The National Institute for Neurological Disorders and Stroke and the Canadian Stroke Network recently suggested standardized assessment procedures for the study of VCI (Hachinski et al., 2006). Incorporating some or all of the approaches suggested in this guideline would be directly useful to the cognitive aging literature, because the pattern of cognitive impairment seen in VCI, with relatively greater impairment in frontally mediated cognitive functions (e.g., executive/inhibitory and retrieval functions), is similar to that seen in "normal" cognitive aging.

   b. Regularly consulting biomedical journals, such as *Hypertension*, *Stroke*, *Journal of Gerontology: Medical Sciences*, or *Journal of the American Geriatrics Society*, provides numerous examples of how biomedical data and analytic techniques can be incorporated with cognitive data.

On the basis of our experience, we offer several prescriptions for the study of health and its influence on cognition.

Health

1. Use self-report measures of health as you would self-report measures of cognition, that is, cautiously (if at all) and with due consideration of their limitations. If you must rely on self-report measures of health, it is better to ask, for example, "Has a doctor ever told you that you have . . . ?" and use questions from national survey studies (e.g., National Health Interview Study or Behavioral Risk Factor Surveillance System [http://www.cdc.gov/brfss]), or to adopt standardized and validated self-report measures (e.g., the Rose questionnaire for assessing angina; LaCroix, Haynes, Savage, & Havlik, 1989]). The advantage of such measures is that one can in the former case compare a given sample to national reference data, and in the latter case to other samples that have been assessed using such standardized measures.

2. Avoid health rating or summary measures such as counts of diseases or medications. Such indices often blur distinct differences in health and can obscure the impact of specific diseases on cognitive functions.

3. Recognize the trade-off between excluding participants with any health problems versus including sufficient health-related variability. Unless they are the focus of investigation, we would recommend excluding persons who have conditions that affect cognition directly, such as strokes, head injuries, psychiatric disorders, or that might prevent accurate assessment, such as severe sensory impairments.

4. Consider carefully the issue of causal pathways between health and cognition. In particular, it is important not to control for confounders that are on the health–cognition pathway under study. For example, adjusting for hypertension in a study examining the effects of diabetes on cognition runs the risk of overadjustment, because of the comorbidity between these diseases. On the other hand, omitting steps on the causal pathway of disease (e.g., excluding persons with stroke or kidney disease from an investigation of the impact of hypertension on cognition) can result in underestimates of the effect of the disease by removing those with more severe forms.

Cognition

1. We recently celebrated the centennial of Spearman's work on factor analysis, developed to study intelligence. Cattell (1971), Horn and Noll (1997), and Carroll (1993) have presented taxonomies of psychometric approaches to cognition; Lezak et al. (2004) summarized neuropsychological approaches. In personality research, the Big Five is increasing useful as a "Rosetta Stone" (Wiggins, 1996); we should adopt such a taxonomy for both cognition and health (Hachinski et al., 2006; Hendrie et al., 2006).

2. Dementia tests are appropriately used to assess cognition in clinical or at-risk samples, or to screen community samples. They should not be used to assess cognition in community or convenience samples. The issue of floor and ceiling effects should be considered carefully in selecting cognitive measures.

3. We should discourage the use of global measures such as the MMSE to make inferences regarding cognitive aging. Instead, a broad selection of cognitive processes relevant to the questions under study should be selected, and preferably measures that have known measurement properties.

4. There is more to the study of cognition than examining (a) "normal" performance of volunteers in laboratories and (b) persons diagnosed with or suspected of having Alzheimer's. There is more to cognition in the elderly, including VCI; other dementias; as well as "usual" aging of persons with a variety of diseases, conditions, and other concerns. As noted above, the extent to which Alzheimer's can be considered distinct from vascular dementia and other vascular diseases is currently the subject of some debate. Likewise, we believe that the distinction between VCI and "normal" cognitive aging may also be unclear.

We can implement many of these suggestions by thinking more broadly. Hendrie et al. (2006) suggested more secondary analysis of large longitudinal studies of health (e.g., Health and Retirement Study, Cardiovascular Health Study, Atherosclerosis Risk in Communities, Framingham). Indeed, over the past decade, many of these long-term epidemiologic studies have added measures of cognition to their assessments; cognitive psychologists should actively seek other studies in which to implement such assessments, as we have done with the NAS. Another approach is to develop consortia to conduct collaborative or pooled analyses of existing data; such approaches are common in medical sciences (e.g., CASCADE [Cardiovascular Determinants of Dementia; Soderlund et al., 2006; van Dijk et al., 2004], EURODEM [European Community Concerted Action Epidemiology of Dementia; Launer et al., 1999]). Increasingly, randomized controlled trials of vascular interventions are adding cognitive assessments as outcomes to test whether reduction of blood pressure, for example, would reduce cognitive decline; cognitive psychologists should seek to become more involved in such efforts (Resnick et al., 2004; Williamson et al., 2007).

Cognitive psychologists should increase collaborations with biomedical scientists. NIH supports 78 general clinical research centers (GCRCs; now known as Clinical and Translational Science Awards [http://www.ctsaweb.org]) across the United States, in 33 states; they are designed and funded to support collaborative research (http://www.ncrr.nih.gov/clinical/cr_gcrc.asp). The Department of Veterans Affairs supports 21 GRECCs (Geriatric Research, Education, and Clinical Centers) across the United States (http://www1.va.gov/grecc/) that serve a similar function.

The costs of studying health as we have proposed are high. So, too, are the consequences of ignoring health, or of measuring it poorly. Much could be learned by including some relatively simple health measures, for example, blood pressure measurements and standardized disease questionnaires. Access to health records (e.g., conducting studies of health plan members) might provide another affordable approach. Regardless of which measures of health are used, there should be a clear theoretical rationale for their inclusion, based on consideration of their potential role in cognitive change.

Conclusion

Our chapter has been an extended attempt to argue that the study of cognitive aging should be about health and disease as well as about aging. To understand cognitive aging, it is necessary to study both hearts and minds. Only when cognitive aging incorporates health and disease into both its theories and its research can it reach its full potential to change lives. We must also recognize that aging per se is not a cause of cognitive decline but a concomitant at best, or at worst, a dimension along which to observe changes. Only when we consider health as an explanation of cognitive change will be on a path toward true understanding.

REFERENCES

Alzheimer's Association. (2007). *Alzheimer's disease facts and figures 2007*. Retrieved April 16, 2007, from http://www.alz.org/national/documents/Report_2007FactsAndFigures.pdf

Anstey, K., & Christensen, H. (2000). Education, activity, health, blood pressure and apolipoprotein E as predictors of cognitive change in old age: A review. *Gerontology, 46,* 163–177.

Au, R., Massaro, J. M., Wolf, P. A., Young, M. E., Beiser, A., Seshadri, S., et al. (2006). Association of white matter hyperintensity volume with decreased cognitive functioning: The Framingham Heart Study. *Archives of Neurology, 63,* 246–250.

Awad, N., Gagnon, M., & Messier, C. (2004). The relationship between impaired glucose tolerance, type 2 diabetes, and cognitive function. *Journal of Clinical and Experimental Neuropsychology, 26,* 1044–1080.

Band, G. P. H., Ridderinkhof, K. R., & Segalowitz, S. (2002). Explaining neurocognitive aging: Is one factor enough? *Brain and Cognition, 49,* 259–267.

Beery, K. E. (1989). *The Developmental Test of Visual-Motor Integration manual* (rev. ed.). Cleveland, OH: Modern Curriculum Press.

Bennett, D. A. (2000). Diabetes and change in cognitive function [Editorial]. *Archives of Internal Medicine, 160,* 141–143.

Birren, J. E., & Schaie, K. W. (Eds.). (1977). *Handbook of the psychology of aging.* New York: Van Nostrand Reinhold.

Birren, J. E., & Schaie, K. W. (Eds.). (1985). *Handbook of the psychology of aging* (2nd ed.). New York: Van Nostrand Reinhold.

Birren, J. E., & Spieth, W. (1962). Age, response speed, and cardiovascular functions. *Journal of Gerontology, 17,* 390–391.

Boone, K. B., Miller, B. L., Lesser, I. M., Hill, E., & D'Elia, L. F. (1990). Performance on frontal lobe tests in healthy, older individuals. *Developmental Neuropsychology, 6,* 215–224.

Bowler, J. V. (2005). Vascular cognitive impairment. *Journal of Neurology, Neurosurgery, and Psychiatry, 76*(V), V35–V44.

Brady, C. B., & Spiro, A. III (2007). *How pervasive is executive dysfunction in healthy aging? Patterns of cognitive performance and the implications for cognitive aging research.* Manuscript in preparation.

Brady, C. B., Spiro, A., III, & Gaziano, J. M. (2005). Effects of age and hypertension status on cognition: The Veterans Affairs Normative Aging Study. *Neuropsychology, 19,* 770–777.

Brady, C. B., Spiro, A., McGlinchey-Berroth, R., Milberg, W., & Gaziano, J. M. (2001). Stroke risk predicts verbal fluency decline in healthy older men: Evidence from the normative aging study. *Journal of Gerontology: Psychological Sciences, 56B*, P340–P346.

Bryan, R. N., Cai, J., Burke, G., Hutchinson, R. G., Liao, D., Toole, J. F., et al. (1999). Prevalence and anatomic characteristics of infarct-like lesions on MR images of middle-aged adults: The Atherosclerosis Risk in Communities Study. *American Journal of Neuroradiology, 20*, 1273–1280.

Burke, D. M. (1997). Language, aging, and inhibitory deficits: Evaluation of a theory. *Journal of Gerontology: Psychological Sciences, 52B*, P254–P264.

Carroll, J. B. (1993). *Human cognitive abilities: A survey of factor-analytic studies*. New York: Cambridge University Press.

Casserly, I., & Topol, E. (2004). Convergence of atherosclerosis and Alzheimer's disease: Inflammation, cholesterol, and misfolded proteins. *The Lancet, 363*, 1139–1146.

Cattell, R. B. (1971). *Abilities: Their structure, growth, and action*. New York: Houghton Mifflin.

Chaves, P. H., Kuller, L. H., O'Leary, D. H., Manolio, T. A., & Newman, A. B. (2004). Subclinical cardiovascular disease in older adults: insights from the Cardiovascular Health Study. *American Journal of Geriatric Cardiology, 13*, 137–151.

Chobanian, A. V., Bakris, G. L., Black, H. R., Cushman, W. C., Green, L. A., Izzo, J. L., Jr., et al. (2003). The seventh report of the Joint National Committee on Prevention, Detection, Evaluation, and Treatment of High Blood Pressure: The JNC 7 report. *Journal of the American Medical Association, 289*, 2560–2572.

Chui, H. C. (2006). Vascular cognitive impairment: Today and tomorrow. *Alzheimer's and Dementia, 2*, 185–194.

Colcombe, S. J., Erickson, K. I., Scalf, P. E., Kim, J. S., Prakash, R., McAuley E., et al. (2006). Aerobic exercise training increases brain volume in aging humans. *Journals of Gerontology Series A: Biological Sciences and Medical Sciences, 61*, 1166–1170.

Cowie, C. C., Rust, K. F., Byrd-Holt, D. D., Eberhardt, M. S., Flegal, K. M., Engelgau, M. M., et al. (2006). Prevalence of diabetes and impaired fasting glucose in adults in the U.S. population: National Health and Nutrition Examination Survey 1999–2002. *Diabetes Care, 29*, 1263–1268.

Cukierman, T., Gerstein, H. C., & Williamson, J. D. (2005). Cognitive decline and dementia in diabetes: Systematic overview of prospective observational studies. *Diabetologia, 48*, 2460–2469.

D'Agostino, R., Wolf, P. A., Belanger, A. J., & Kannel, W. B. (1994). Stroke risk profile: Adjustment for anti-hypertensive medication. *Stroke, 25*, 40–43.

Daigneault, S., Braun, C. M. J., & Whitaker, H. A. (1992). Early effects of normal aging in perseverative and nonperseverative prefrontal measures. *Developmental Neuropsychology, 8*, 99–114.

Dempster, F. N. (1992). The rise and fall of the inhibitory mechanism: Toward a unified theory of cognitive development and aging. *Developmental Review, 12*, 47–75.

Dywan, J., Segalowitz, S. J., & Unsal, A. (1992). Speed of information processing, health, and cognitive performance in older adults. *Developmental Neuropsychology, 8*, 473–490.

Edwards, W. S., Winn, D. M., Kurlantzick, V., Sheridan, S., Berk, M. L., Retchin, S., & Collins, J. G. (1994). Evaluation of National Health Interview Survey diagnostic reporting. National Center for Health Statistics. *Vital Health Stat* 2(120), DHS Publication No. (PHS)94-1394. Available at http://www.cdc.gov/nchs/data/series/sr_02/sr02_120.pdf

Eggen, M. (2005). *Effects of anti-hypertensive treatment on cognition: Evidence from the VA Normative Aging Study*. Unpublished master's thesis, Boston University School of Medicine, Department of Graduate Medical Sciences.

Eisdorfer, C., & Lawton, M. P. (Eds.). (1973). *The psychology of adult development and aging*. Washington, DC: American Psychological Association.

Elias, M. F., Robbins, M. A., Budge, M. M., Elias, P. K., Hermann, B. A., & Dore, G. A. (2003). Studies of aging, hypertension, and cognitive functioning: With contributions from the Maine–Syracuse study. In P. Costa & I. C. Siegler (Eds.), *Advances in cell aging and gerontology* (Vol. 15, pp. 89–131). New York: Elsevier.

Elias, M. F., & Streeten, D. H. P. (Eds.). (1980). *Hypertension and cognitive processes*. Mt. Desert, ME: Beech Hill.

Elias, M. F., Sullivan, L. M., D'Agostino, R. B., Elias, P. K., Beiser, A., Au, R., et al. (2004). Framingham stroke risk profile and lowered cognitive performance. *Stroke, 35,* 404–409.

Elias, P. K., Elias, M. F., D'Agostino, R. B., Cupples, L. A., Wilson, P. W., Silbershatz, H., & Wolf, P. A. (1997). NIDDM and blood pressure as risk factors for poor cognitive performance. *Diabetes Care, 20,* 1388–1395.

Elinson, J. (1988). Defining and measuring health and illness. In K. W. Schaie, R. T. Campbell, W. Meredith, & S. C. Rawlings (Eds.), *Methodological issues in aging research* (pp. 231–248). New York: Springer.

Federal Interagency Forum on Aging-Related Statistics. (2006, May). *Older Americans Update 2006: Key indicators of well-being.* Washington, DC: U.S. Government Printing Office. Retrieved July 31, 2006, from http://agingstats.gov/update 2006/default.htm

Folstein, M. F., Folstein, S. E., & McHugh, P. R. (1975). Mini-Mental State: A practical method for grading the cognitive state of patients for the clinician. *Journal of Psychiatric Research, 12,* 189–198.

Ford, E. S., Giles, W. H., & Dietz, W. H. (2002). Prevalence of the metabolic syndrome among US adults: Findings from the third National Health and Nutrition Examination Survey. *Journal of the American Medical Association, 287,* 356–359.

Fries, J. F. (2005). The compression of morbidity. *Milbank Quarterly, 83,* 801–223. (Original work published 1983)

Goodglass, H., & Kaplan, E. (2000). *Boston Naming Test.* Philadelphia: Lippincott Williams & Wilkins.

Greenwood, P. M. (2000). The frontal aging hypothesis evaluated. *Journal of the International Neuropsychological Society, 6,* 705–726.

Haaland, K. Y., Vranes, L. R., Goodwin, F. S., & Garry, P. J. (1987). Wisconsin Card Sort Test performance in a healthy elderly population. *Journal of Gerontology, 42,* 345–346.

Hachinski, V., Iadecola, C., Petersen, R. C., Breteler, M. M., Nyenhuis, D. L., Black, S. E., et al. (2006). National Institute of Neurological Disorders and Stroke–Canadian Stroke Network vascular cognitive impairment harmonization standards. *Stroke, 37,* 2220–2241.

Hajjar, I., & Kotchen, T. A. (2003). Trends in prevalence, awareness, treatment, and control of hypertension in the United States, 1988–2000. *Journal of the American Medical Association, 290,* 199–206.

Hara, H., Egusa, G., & Yamakido, M. (1996). Incidence of non-insulin-dependent diabetes mellitus and its risk factors in Japanese-Americans living in Hawaii and Los Angeles. *Diabetic Medicine, 13,* S133–S142.

Hasher, L., & Zacks, R. T. (1988). Working memory, comprehension, and aging: A review and a new view. In G. H. Bower (Ed.), *The psychology of learning and motivation* (Vol. 22, pp. 193–225). San Diego, CA: Academic Press.

Hayflick, L. (2004). The not-so-close relationship between biological aging and age-associated pathologies in humans. *Journal of Gerontology: Biological Sciences, 59A,* 547–550.

Hendrie, H. C., Albert, M. S., Butters, M. A., Gao, S., Knopman, D. S., Launer, L. J., et al. (2006). The NIH Cognitive and Emotional Health Project: Report of the critical evaluation study committee. *Alzheimer's and Dementia, 2,* 12–32. Available at http://trans.nih.gov/cehp/

Hernandez, L. M., Durch, J. S., Blazer, D. G., & Hoverman, I. V. (Eds.). (1999). *Gulf war veterans: Measuring health.* Washington, DC: Institute of Medicine.

Hertzog, C., Schaie, K. W., & Gribbin, K. (1978). Cardiovascular disease and changes in intellectual functioning from middle to old age. *Journal of Gerontology, 33,* 872–883.

Horn, J. L., & Noll, J. (1997). Human cognitive capabilities: Gf-Gc theory. In D. P. Flanagan, J. L. Genshaft, & P. L. Harrison (Eds.), *Contemporary intellectual assessment: Theories, tests and issues* (pp. 53–91). New York: Guilford Press.

Hultsch, D. (Ed.). (2004). Introduction to Special Issue on longitudinal studies of cognitive aging. *Aging, Neuropsychology, and Cognition, 11*(2–3).

Hyman, D. J., & Pavlik, V. N. (2001). Characteristics of patients with uncontrolled hypertension in the United States. *New England Journal of Medicine, 345,* 479–486. Erratum in: *New England Journal of Medicine* (2002), *346,* 544.

Idler, E. L., & Benyamini, Y. (1997). Self-rated health and mortality: A review of twenty-seven community studies. *Journal of Health and Social Behavior, 38,* 21–37.

Jefferson, A. L., Poppas, A., Paul, R. H., & Cohen, R. A. (2007). Systemic hypoperfusion is associated with executive dysfunction in geriatric cardiac patients. *Neurobiology of Aging, 28,* 477–483.

Karlamangla, A., Tinetti, M., Guralnick, J., Studenski, S., Wetle, T., & Reuben, D. (2007). Comorbidity in older adults: Nosology of impairment, diseases, and conditions. *Journal of Gerontology: Medical Sciences, 62A,* 296–300.

Kazis, L. E., Miller, D. R., Clark, J. A., Skinner, K. M., Lee, A., Ren, X. S., et al. (2004). Improving the response choices on the veterans SF-36 Health Survey role functioning scales: Results from the Veterans Health Study. *Journal of Ambulatory Care Management, 27,* 263–280.

Knopman, D., Boland, L. L., Mosley, T., Howard, G., Liao, D., Szklo, M., et al. (2001). Cardiovascular risk factors and cognitive decline in middle-aged adults. *Neurology, 56,* 42–48.

Kravitz, R. L., Duan, N., & Braslow, J. (2004). Evidence-based medicine, heterogeneity of treatment effects, and the trouble with averages. *Milbank Quarterly, 82,* 661–687.

Kuller, L. H., Arnold, A. M., Psaty, B. M., Robbins, J. A., O'Leary, D. H., Tracy, R. P., et al. (2006). 10-year follow-up of subclinical cardiovascular disease and risk of coronary heart disease in the Cardiovascular Health Study. *Archives of Internal Medicine, 166,* 71–78.

Kuller, L., Borhani, N., Furberg, C., Gardin, J., Manolio, T., O'Leary, D., et al. (1994). Prevalence of subclinical atherosclerosis and cardiovascular disease and association with risk factors in the Cardiovascular Health Study. *American Journal of Epidemiology, 139,* 1164–1179.

Kuller, L. H., Shemanski, L., Manolio, T., Haan, M., Fried, L., Bryan, N., et al. (1998). Relationship between ApoE, MRI findings, and cognitive function in the Cardiovascular Health Study. *Stroke, 29,* 388–398.

LaCroix, A. Z., Haynes, S. G., Savage, D. D., & Havlik, R. J. (1989). Rose Questionnaire angina among United States Black, White, and Mexican-American women and men: Prevalence and correlates from The Second National and Hispanic Health and Nutrition Examination Surveys. *American Journal of Epidemiology, 129,* 669–686.

Launer, L. J., Andersen, K., Dewey, M. E., Letenneur, L., Ott, A., Amaducci, L. A., et al. (1999). Rates and risk factors for dementia and Alzheimer's disease: Results from Eurodem pooled analyses. *Neurology, 52,* 78–84.

Launer, L. J., Ross, G. W., Petrovitch, H., Masaki, K., Foley, D., White, L. R., & Havlik, R. J. (2000). Midlife blood pressure and dementia: The Honolulu–Asia Aging Study. *Neurobiology of Aging, 21,* 49–55.

Letz, R. (1991). *NES–2 user's manual* (Version 4.4). Winchester, MA: Neurobehavioral Systems.

Lezak, M. D., Howieson, D. B., Loring, D. W., Hannay, H. J., & Fischer, J. S. (2004). *Neuropsychological assessment* (4th ed.). New York: Oxford University Press.

Li, G., Cherrier, M. M., Tsuang, D. W., Petrie, E. C., Colasurdo, E. A., Craft, S., et al. (2006). Salivary cortisol and memory function in human aging. *Neurobiology of Aging, 27,* 1705–1714.

Longstreth, W. T. Jr., Manolio, T. A., Arnold, A., Burke, G. L., Bryan, N., Jungreis, C. A., et al. (1996). Clinical correlates of white matter findings on cranial magnetic resonance imaging of 3301 elderly people. The Cardiovascular Health Study. *Stroke, 27,* 1274–1282.

Martin, G. M. (2006). Keynote lecture: An update on the what, why and how questions of ageing. *Experimental Gerontology, 41,* 460–463.

Masoro, E. J. (2006). Are age-associated diseases an integral part of aging? In E. Masoro & S. Austad (Eds.), *Handbook of the biology of aging* (6th ed., pp. 43–62). New York: Academic Press.

McDowd, J. M. (1997). Inhibition in attention and aging. *Journals of Gerontology: Psychological Sciences & Social Sciences, 52B,* 256–273.

Miller, D. R., Rogers, W. H., Spiro, A., III, & Kazis, L. E. (2003, December). *Evaluation of disease status based on patient self-report in the Medicare Health Outcomes Survey: Using linked data from surveys and computerized medical data from the Veterans Health Administration.* Retrieved February 1, 2006, from http://www.hosonline.org/surveys/hos/download/HOS_Evaluation_Self-Report_Disease_Status.pdf

Mittenberg, W., Seidenberg, M., O'Leary, D. S., & DiGiulio, D. V. (1989). Changes in cerebral functioning associated with normal aging. *Journal of Clinical and Experimental Neuropsychology, 11,* 918–932.

Morris, J. C., Heyman, A., Mohs, R. C., Hughes, J. P., van Belle, G., Fillenbaum, G., et al. (1989). The Consortium to Establish a Registry for Alzheimer's Disease (CERAD), I. Clinical and neuropsychological assessment of Alzheimer's disease. *Neurology, 39,* 1159–1165.

Moscovitch, M., & Winocur, G. (1992). The neuropsychology of memory and aging. In F. I. M. Craik & T. A. Salthouse (Eds.), *The handbook of aging and cognition* (pp. 315–372). Hillsdale, NJ: Lawrence Erlbaum.

Nilsson, L.-G., Baeckman, L., Nyberg, L., Erngrund, K., Adolfsson, R., Bucht, G., et al. (1997). The Betula prospective cohort study: Memory, health, and aging. *Aging, Neuropsychology & Cognition, 4,* 1–32.

O'Brien, J. T., Erkinjuntti T., Reisberg B., Roman, G., Sawada, T., Pantoni, L., et al. (2003). Vascular cognitive impairment. *Lancet Neurology, 2,* 89–98.

Parkin, A. J., & Walter, B. M. (1991). Aging, short-term memory, and frontal dysfunction. *Psychobiology, 19,* 175–179.

Payton, M., Riggs, K., Spiro, A., III, Weiss, S. T., & Hu, H. (1998). Effects of low-level lead exposure on cognitive function in aging men. *Neurotoxicology and Teratology, 20,* 19–27.

Peters, R. (2006). Ageing and the brain. *Postgraduate Medical Journal, 82,* 84–88.

Peto, R., & Doll, R. (1997). There is no such thing as aging. *British Medical Journal, 315,* 1030–1032.

Poon, L. W., Fozard, J. L., Cermak, L. S., Arenberg, D., & Thompson, L. W. (Eds.). (1980). *Aging in the 1980's: Psychological issues.* Washington, DC: American Psychological Association.

Poon, L. W., Rubin, D. C., & Wilson, B. A. (Eds.). (1989). *Everyday cognition in adulthood and late life.* Cambridge, UK: Cambridge University Press.

Price, T. R., Manolio, T. A., Kronmal, R. A., Kittner, S. J., Yue, N. C., Robbins, J., et al. (1997). Silent brain infarction on magnetic resonance imaging and neurological abnormalities in community-dwelling older adults. The Cardiovascular Health Study. *Stroke, 28,* 1158–1164.

Raz, N., Rodrigue, K. M., & Acker, J. D. (2003). Hypertension and the brain: Vulnerability of the prefrontal regions and executive functions. *Behavioral Neuroscience, 117,* 1169–1180.

Raz, N., Rodrigue, K. M., Kennedy, K. M., & Acker, J. D. (2007). Vascular health and longitudinal changes in brain and cognition in middle-aged and older adults. *Neuropsychology, 21,* 149–157.

Resnick, S. M., Coker, L. H., Makia, P. M., Rapp, S. R., Espeland, M. A., & Shumaker, S. A. (2004). The Women's Health Initiative Study of Cognitive Aging (WHISCA): A randomized clinical trial of the effects of hormone therapy on age-associated cognitive decline. *Clinical Trials, 1,* 440–450.

Riegel, K. F., & Riegel, R. M. (1972). Development, drop, and death. *Developmental Psychology, 6,* 306–319.

Riggs, K. M., Spiro, A., III, Tucker, K., & Rush, D. (1996). Vitamins B-12, B-6 and folate and homocysteine and cognitive performance in the Normative Aging Study. *American Journal of Clinical Nutrition, 63,* 306–314.

Roman, G. C., Tatemichi, T. K., Erkinjuntti, T., Cummings, J. L., Masdeu, J. C., Garcia, J. H., et al. (1993). Vascular dementia: Diagnostic criteria for research studies. Report of the NINDS–AIREN International Workshop. *Neurology, 43,* 250–260.

Safran, D. G., Neuman, P., Schoen, C., Kitchman, M. S., Wilson, I. B., Cooper, B., et al. (2005). Prescription drug coverage and seniors: Findings from a 2003 national survey. *Health Affairs,* Supplemental Web Exclusives: W5-152–W5-166. Retrieved February 6, 2007, from http://content.healthaffairs.org/cgi/content/abstract/hlthaff.w5.152v1

Salthouse, T. (1991). *Theoretical perspectives on cognitive aging.* Hillsdale, NJ: Lawrence Erlbaum.

Salthouse, T. A., Fristoe, N., & Rhee, S. H. (1996). How localized are age-related effects on neuropsychological measures? *Neuropsychology, 10,* 272–285.

SAS Institute. (1990). SAS/Graph (Version 6, 1st ed.) [Computer software]. Cary, NC: Author.

Shimamura, A. P. (1990). Aging and memory disorders: A neuropsychological analysis. In M. L. Howe, M. J. Stones, & J. Brainerd (Eds.), *Cognitive and behavioral performance factors in atypical aging* (pp. 37–65). New York: Springer-Verlag.

Sliwinski, M. J., Stawski, R. S., Katz, M., Verghese, J., & Lipton, R. (2006). Distinguishing pre-terminal and terminal cognitive decline. *European Psychologist, 11,* 172–181.

Soderlund, H., Nilsson, L. G., Berger, K., Breteler, M. M., Dufouil, C., Fuhrer, R., et al. (2006). Cerebral changes on MRI and cognitive function: The CASCADE study. *Neurobiology of Aging, 27,* 16–23.

Spieth, W. (1964). Cardiovascular health status, age, and psychological performance. *Journal of Gerontology, 19,* 277–284.

Spiro, A., III. (2001). Health in midlife: Toward a lifespan view. In M. E. Lachman (Ed.), *Handbook of midlife development* (pp. 156–187). New York: Wiley.

Spiro, A., III. (2007). The relevance of a lifespan developmental approach to health. In C. M. Aldwin, C. L. Park, & A. Spiro III (Eds.), *Handbook of health psychology and aging* (pp. 75–93). New York: Guilford Press.

Spiro, A., III, & Vokonas, P. S. (2006). The Normative Aging Study. In R. Schulz (Ed.), *Encyclopedia of aging* (4th ed., pp. 838–839). New York: Springer.

Stewart, A. L., Ware, J. E., Sherbourne, C. D., & Wells, K. B. (1992). Psychological distress/well-being and cognitive functioning measures. In A. L. Stewart & J. E. Ware (Eds.), *Measuring functioning and well-being: The Medical Outcomes Study approach* (pp. 102–142). Durham, NC: Duke University Press.

Troyer, A. K., Moscovitch, M., & Winocur, G. (1997). Clustering and switching as two components of verbal fluency: Evidence from younger and older healthy adults. *Neuropsychology, 11,* 138–146.

van Dijk, E. J., Breteler, M. M., Schmidt, R., Berger, K., Nilsson, L. G., Oudkerk, M., et al. (2004). The association between blood pressure, hypertension, and cerebral white matter lesions: Cardiovascular determinants of dementia study. *Hypertension, 44,* 625–630.

Vermeer, S. E., Koudstaal, P. J., Oudkerk, M., Hofman, A., & Breteler, M. M. (2002). Prevalence and risk factors of silent brain infarcts in the population-based Rotterdam Scan Study. *Stroke, 33,* 21–25.

Vermeer, S. E., Prins, N. D., den Heijer, T., Hofman, A., Koudstaal, P. J., & Breteler, M. M. (2003). Silent brain infarcts and the risk of dementia and cognitive decline. *New England Journal of Medicine, 348,* 1215–1222.

Wahlin, A. (2004). Health, disease, and cognitive functioning in old age. In R. A. Dixon, L. Bäckman, & L. G. Nilsson (Eds.), *New frontiers in cognitive aging* (pp. 279–302). New York: Oxford University Press.

Wahlin, A., MacDonald, S. W., deFrias, C. M., Nilsson, L. G., & Dixon, R. A. (2006). How do health and biological age influence chronological age and sex differences in cognitive aging: Moderating, mediating, or both? *Psychology and Aging, 21,* 318–332.

Waldstein, S. R., & Elias, M. F. (Eds.). (2001). *Neuropsychology of cardiovascular disease.* Mahwah, NJ: Lawrence Erlbaum.

Waldstein, S. R., Giggey, P. P., Thayer, J. F., & Zonderman, A. B. (2005). Nonlinear relations of blood pressure to cognitive function: The Baltimore Longitudinal Study of Aging. *Hypertension, 45,* 374–379.

Ware, J. E., Jr. (2000). SF-36 Health Survey update. *Spine, 25,* 3130–3139.

Wechsler, D. (1981). *Wechsler Adult Intelligence Scale—Revised manual.* San Antonio, TX: The Psychological Corporation.

Weisskopf, M. G., Proctor, S., Wright, R. O., Schwartz, J., Spiro, A., III, Sparrow, D., et al. (2007). Prospective study of cumulative lead exposure and cognitive test scores among elderly men: The VA Normative Aging Study. *Epidemiology, 18,* 59–66.

Welsh, K. A., Butters, N., Mohs, R. C., Beekly, D., Edland, S., Fillenbaum, G., & Heyman, A. (1994). The Consortium to Establish a Registry for Alzheimer's Disease (CERAD). Part V. A normative study of the neuropsychological battery. *Neurology, 44,* 609–614.

West, R. L. (1996). An application of prefrontal cortex function theory to cognitive aging. *Psychological Bulletin, 120,* 272–292.

West, R. L. (2000). In defense of the frontal lobe hypothesis of cognitive aging. *Journal of the International Neuropsychological Society, 6,* 727–729.

Whelihan, W. M., & Lesher, E. L. (1985). Neuropsychological changes in frontal functions with aging. *Developmental Neuropsychology, 1,* 371–380.

White L. (1996). Is silent cerebrovascular disease an important cause of late-life cognitive decline? *Journal of the American Geriatrics Society, 44,* 328–330.

Wiggins, J. (Ed.). (1996). *The five-factor model of personality.* New York: Guilford Press.

Wilkie, F., & Eisdorfer, C. (1971, May 28). Intelligence and blood pressure in the aged. *Science, 172,* 959–962.

Williamson, J., Miller, M. E., Bryan, N., Lazar, R. M., Coker, L. H., Johnson, J., et al. (2007). The Action to Control Cardiovascular Risk in Diabetes Memory in Diabetes Study (ACCORD-MIND): Rationale, design, and methods. *American Journal of Cardiology, 99*(Suppl.), 112i–122i.

Willis, R. J. (2006). *Aging in the US: The Health and Retirement Study*. Paper presented at Longitudinal Social and Health Surveys in an International Perspective, McGill University, Montreal, PQ, Canada. Retrieved March 10, 2007, from http://www.ciqss.umontreal.ca/Longit/Doc/Robert_Willis.pdf

Wohlwill, J. F. (1973). *The study of behavioral development*. New York: Academic Press.

Wood, R., Maraj, B., Lee, C. M., & Reyes, R. (2002). Short-term heart rate variability during a cognitive challenge in young and older adults. *Age and Ageing, 31,* 131–135.

Yancik, R., Ershler, W., Satariano, W., Hazzard, W., Cohen, H. J., & Ferrucci, L. (2007). Report of the National Institute on Aging Task Force on Comorbidity. *Journal of Gerontology: Medical Sciences, 62A,* 275–280.

17

Cognitive Change as Conditional on Age Heterogeneity in Onset of Mortality-Related Processes and Repeated Testing Effects

Valgeir Thorvaldsson, Scott M. Hofer,
Linda B. Hassing, and Boo Johansson

Chronological age is only one of many alternative time metrics for describing aging-related change and variability, and it may not always be the most useful one. An age-based modeling approach assumes that within-person change is well described by the average (or aggregate) age trend in the population. However, in later life this is unlikely to be the case because changes at both the individual and population level can often be traced to pathological processes (i.e., morbidity and comorbidity) that, although often linked to chronological age, are not necessarily related strongly to chronological age. In other words, years to a critical event (i.e., disease diagnosis, death) may be a better metric to organize both individual and population change in later life than years from birth. Changes in later life are likely to be idiosyncratic and are unlikely to be well described by population average age change. The distinction between *normative* and *non-normative* (i.e., disease-based) processes (Baltes & Nesselroade, 1979; Sliwinski, Hofer, & Hall, 2003) is important to consider for understanding within-person change as well as population change. From an individual perspective, one or several causes can produce changes within individuals. However, given the high degree of heterogeneity among potential causes, ages of onset, and multiplicity of outcomes, these same causes may account for only small proportions of individual differences in the population. This perspective has ramifications for how we approach the study of aging and how we analyze data from longitudinal studies on aging.

In this chapter, we discuss the need to account for heterogeneity in age of onset and rate of change in pathological processes for understanding aging-related change in cognitive outcomes in later life. We further propose that within-person longitudinal analysis, as conditional on terminal decline (see reviews by Berg, 1996; Bosworth & Siegler, 2002; Siegler, 1975; Small & Bäckman, 1999), provides a useful temporal metric to structure individual differences and to account for change processes associated with individual differences in cognitive and other functional outcomes. The analysis of terminal decline essentially entails the recalibration of within-person change in a population relative to remaining years of life (i.e., proximity to death), in contrast to the typical metric of age since birth (or time in study conditional on chronological age). Because longitudinal studies provide the prerequisite basis for analysis of within-person change and inference to defined populations of aging individuals and behaviors, we discuss retest effects in longitudinal studies of cognitive aging with widely spaced assessments and the related issues of internal validity and generalizability.

POPULATION MORTALITY SELECTION AND COGNITION

An essential characteristic of human aging populations is the substantial heterogeneity in age of onset of biological devitalization and pathology producing disabilities in various functional outcomes and later mortality. The consequence of age-related heterogeneity in morbidity and later mortality are changes to the population composition, with selectivity compounded in subsequent age-graded populations given the continued selection on mortality-related processes (e.g., Nesselroade, 1988; Riegel & Riegel, 1972; Vaupel & Yashin, 1985). Cognition represents a highly important functional domain and is indeed selected in this manner. Cognition is a functional outcome of the underlying processes leading to mortality (Batty, Deary, & Gottfredson, 2007). Numerous studies have suggested strong associations among level and rate of change of cognitive functions and mortality (e.g., Berg, 1987; Bosworth & Schaie, 1999; Bosworth, Schaie, & Willis, 1999; Deeg, Hofman, & van Zonneveld, 1990; Ghisletta, McArdle, & Lindenberger, 2006; Johansson & Berg, 1989; Kleemeier, 1962; Rabbitt et al., 2002; Riegel & Riegel, 1972;

Riegel, Riegel, & Meyer, 1967; Small & Bäckman, 1997; Small, Fratiglioni, von Strauss, & Bäckman, 2003; Wilson, Beckett, Bienias, Evans, & Bennett, 2003). These associations are generally termed *terminal decline* or *terminal drop*, where *decline* refers to an accelerated trend prior to death and *drop* refers to an acute precipitous decline immediately preceding death (see Palmore & Cleveland, 1976). With few exceptions (e.g., Harel, Hofer, Hoffman, Pedersen, & Johansson, 2007; Johansson et al., 2004), the effects of terminal decline, or drop, and population composition changes have still not been well integrated into analyses of cognitive aging in longitudinal studies. Generalizations to populations of aging individuals require that inferences be made conditional on survival in a population (DuFouil, Brayne, & Clayton, 2004; Harel et al., 2007; Hofer & Hoffman, 2007).

Most of the modern approaches used to analyze longitudinal cognitive aging data aggregate individual trajectories according to a particular time metric (i.e., chronological age or time in study) to obtain estimates of the population parameters of interest (see reviews by Hertzog & Nesselroade, 2003; Hofer & Sliwinski, 2006; McArdle & Nesselroade, 2003). Interpretation, and generalizability, of within- and between-person estimates in these models are conditioned on the time-related aggregation (e.g., Sliwinski, Hofer, & Hall, 2003; Sliwinski, Hofer, Hall, Buschke, & Lipton, 2003). Time-related aggregation structured by years of life remaining (i.e., terminal decline, time to death) is supported by the notion that various health-related factors (e.g., dementia, stroke, diabetes), previously associated with cognitive change, are correlated with mortality (e.g., Ferraro & Kelley-Moore, 2001; Jagger et al., 2000; Schulz et al., 2000). Organizing the analysis according to years of life remaining might therefore provide a less biased estimate of between-person differences in the pathological process of interest, because age-related heterogeneity in time of onset and rate of change will presumably be better accounted for. Naturally, the representation of change relative to mortality may provide only a crude representation of individual change because of the heterogeneity in various health-related conditions (e.g., disease prevalence and severity). Nevertheless, conditioning change on mortality will reflect aggregate pathological processes found in an aging population (Nilsson, Johansson, Berg, Karlsson, & McClearn, 2001) and permit inference to defined populations, conditional on both age and age at death. Of course, whenever possible, an even better approach would be to model change based on information from comprehensive health examinations with diagnoses (e.g., Alzheimer's disease; Hall, Lipton, Sliwinski, & Stewart, 2000) or time-based severity rating of the cumulative effects of disease processes or other valid markers of biological health and functioning. Such alternative time metrics can better account for aggregate within-person change if the disease process in question truly underlies the observed pattern of change. Understanding the utility of modeling terminal decline or terminal drop is perhaps best explained by evaluating how this phenomenon has been addressed in previous studies.

UNDERSTANDING TERMINAL DECLINE

Cognitive change is a within-person phenomenon that manifests itself over a particular time period, with potential individual differences in initial status, onset of change, pattern, and rate of change. Consequently, a high priority in terminal decline analyses should be to separate mortality-related variability at the individual level from other sources of within- and between-person variation (e.g., normative age change, cohort effects, non-mortality-related selective attrition). Optimally, understanding changes in functioning in late life associated with mortality-related processes (i.e., terminal decline) should start at the descriptive level of individual change trajectories before attempts are made to aggregate these estimates across individuals and draw inferences about between-person differences (Baltes & Nesselroade, 1979). Only recently, however, have we started to witness the emergence of such an analytical route using available longitudinal data (see Hofer & Piccinin, 2007).

Reviews of the methodological approaches used to examine terminal decline typically distinguish between cross-sectional and longitudinal estimates (e.g., Siegler, 1975; Small & Bäckman, 1999). *Cross-sectional estimates* are analyses that compare cognitive performance of survivors and the deceased at a single time point by using the average group differences or the cognitive test scores as predictors of survival status. The deceased are then often further categorized into subgroups based on distance to death from a certain time point of measurement. Results based on these types of analyses typically indicate lower levels of functioning across groups of individuals assessed more proximal to death (Ljungquist, Berg, & Steen, 1995; Neale, Brayne, & Johnson, 2001). Although this approach can provide valuable information about level of performance as a predictor of survival status, it has been argued (e.g., Baltes, Reese, & Nesselroade, 1977; Berg, 1996) that this method confounds possible lifelong individual differences (e.g., lifelong IQ; Deary, Whiteman, Starr, Whalley, & Fox, 2004) with change estimates. This design can therefore be considered only an indirect test of the hypothesis of a relationship among cognitive function, life span age, and mortality-related change.

Longitudinal analyses of terminal decline focus not merely on level of performance as a predictor of mortality but also on how various cognitive change estimates are associated with proximity to death. These analyses can be separated into three general categories: (1) studies that compare average cognitive changes across samples of survivors and deceased (or subgroups of deceased; e.g., Berg, 1987; Hassing, Johansson, et al., 2002; Hassing, Small, von Strauss, Fratiglioni, & Bäckman, 2002; Johansson & Berg 1989); (2) studies that estimate cognitive changes for each individual and then aggregate them across slopes as a conditional function of study occasions, or chronological age, and use time to death, or age of death, as within- and between-person predictors of the level and change estimates (e.g., Johansson et al., 2004); and (3) studies that model individual cognitive change, and between-person differences in these changes, as a direct conditional function of time to death (e.g., Sliwinski, Hofer, Hall, et al., 2003).

All three approaches have provided insights into the nature of the phenomenon of terminal decline. However, in terms of an optimal dissociation of different sources of within-person change and between-person differences, none of the aforementioned approaches can fully claim to provide a satisfactory solution. For example, average cognitive change estimates in the first longitudinal approach can confound within- and between-person information, and right censoring of the data (i.e., lack of information about age of death) often presents difficulties when the aim is to infer within-person terminal change based on group differences. The second longitudinal approach, although directly addressing individual differences in change, can confound these estimates with age of decline onset or time in the study. The third approach, although directly addressing within-person changes and between-person differences as a conditional function of terminal decline, can confound within-person normative and non-normative cognitive change (see Sliwinski et al., 2006).

To our knowledge, only two studies have so far attempted to disentangle normative and non-normative changes at the individual level in the analysis of terminal decline. Both studies relied on different versions of the *change point model approach* (Hall et al., 2000). This is essentially a modeling procedure in which a series of piecewise linear slopes are fit to the data and the likelihood function is maximized to determine the best fit of a change point at particular points in time as defined in the model (e.g., time prior to diagnosis or years of life remaining). This change point reflects the time at which an acceleration of change occurs, based on the two-slope linear change model. In their analyses of a subsample of data with known age of death from the Religious Orders Study, Wilson et al. (2003) reported a cross-cognitive domain span of average break points ranging from 2.75 years before death (for perceptual speed) to 6 years before death (for visuospatial ability) and an estimated average change point for global cognition at 3.6 years before death in their sample of an initially relatively healthy group of older Catholic nuns, priests, and brothers. Sliwinski et al. (2006), however, reported a much longer terminal decline interval (8.4 years before death) in episodic memory based on analyses of an initially nondemented community sample from the Bronx Aging Study.

Perhaps the most important findings from the Sliwinski et al. (2006) and Wilson et al. (2003) research is that both studies provide evidence that the variation in previous estimates of terminal decline is likely to be the result of differences in the onset of terminal decline processes. Methodological solutions that allow direct estimates of between-person variability in the terminal decline break points are recently starting to emerge (e.g., Hall, Ying, Kuo, & Lipton, 2003; Jacqmin-Gadda, Commenges, & Dartigues, 2006). However, the power of these analyses to detect individual change points is rather low in most longitudinal studies given the constraints of minimal within-person information before and after the putative change points. As is well known, between-person information is not a substitute for within-person information (e.g., Hofer & Sliwinski, 2001, 2006; Molenaar, Huizenga, & Nesselroade, 2003), particularly for understanding individual-level change in morbidity and mortality-related processes. This fact should encourage efforts for more measurement-intensive data collections that capitalize even further on ontogenetic information in designing data collection for powerful and informative cognitive aging studies.

An informative demonstration of how to embed change estimates as predictors of survival functions was recently presented by Ghisletta et al. (2006) in the Berlin Aging Study (for a similar approach but in the context of predicting diagnoses of Alzheimer's disease, see McArdle, Small, Bäckman, & Fratiglioni, 2005). Their findings were generally in support of the terminal decline hypotheses, indicating a robust relation between cognitive changes and mortality across different cognitive abilities.

ACCOUNTING FOR POPULATION CHANGES

In an influential article, Riegel and Riegel (1972) presented cross-sectional findings from a German sample demonstrating larger average verbal ability difference between survivors (over a 10-year period) and decedents in younger ages (55–65 years old) than in older ages (above 65). Their interpretation of these findings was that

> age differences in the predictability of survival indicate that at the earlier ages death strikes subjects who are psychologically distinctly different from survivors, that is, less able. At the higher age

levels death strikes more randomly and psychological difference between survivors and nonsurvivors are less marked. (p. 308)

Riegel and Riegel's longitudinal analyses over a 5-year period support this notion by demonstrating larger differences in average change scores between groups of survivors and decedents at younger ages compared with older ages. However, Riegel and Riegel seem to have mainly been concerned with between-person differences across groups based on survival and how chronological age moderates these differences. This might, in some instances, seem self-evident because of lifelong accumulation of age-related causal factors in the older groups (see Rabbitt, Lunn, & Wong, 2006) but has less to do with age-related moderation of terminal decline. In fact, these are two important but distinct research questions.

When analyzing the potential role of age at death as a moderator of terminal decline, it is important to make a distinction between two fundamental questions. The first can be stated as: "Do individual differences in cognitive changes (or level) across survivors and decedents vary as a function of age?" The second question is "Do individuals vary in cognitive terminal change as a function of age?" Analyses of the former type of question refer to identification of age-related moderation of between-person differences between survivors and decedents, whereas analyses of the latter type refer to identification of age-related moderation of between-person differences in terminal change and provide the opportunity to account for the population selection in either age-heterogeneous or age-homogeneous samples. Both questions are informative concerning the nature of between-person differences in terminal decline in an aging population, but they do provide different answers. For example, it could be that age differences in the combination of normative and non-normative causal factors (see Brayne, 2007) are responsible for age-related interaction in survivor and nonsurvivor differences (e.g., normative aging brain change in the survivors), whereas non-normative factors are mainly responsible for terminal decline at the individual level but interact as a function of age of onset. Population mortality selection can

have a major impact on the comparability of survivors and decedents across the adult age span, but these effects can be accounted for directly in within-person analyses of change (e.g., Thorvaldsson, Hofer, & Johansson, 2006).

TERMINAL DECLINE ACROSS DISTINCT COGNITIVE CAPABILITIES

A theoretically intriguing aspect of terminal decline relates to the specificity of the phenomenon across distinct types of cognitive abilities and is related to how specific pathologies differentially affect various domains of cognitive function. Is it the case, as White and Cunningham (1988) once proposed, that the phenomenon of terminal decline might be specific to those particular cognitive abilities that are relatively unaffected by age? The existing evidence seems to contradict that claim. Most studies report terminal decline effects across a wide variety of fluid abilities assumed to be affected with age (Berg, 1987; Deeg et al., 1990; Hassing, Johansson, et al., 2002; Johansson & Berg, 1989; Johansson et al., 2004; Maier & Smith, 1999; Smith, Deeg, Kriegsman, & Schmand, 1999). The current view is therefore that terminal decline is pervasive across various cognitive abilities. However, the validity of this conclusion may be questioned by the fact that this hypothesis is essentially a hypothesis of association among within-person terminal cognitive changes, although it has mainly been estimated by similarities of age-related population-based curves (see chap. 28, this volume).

Analysis of associations among within-person cognitive changes has mainly been conducted among estimates of age- or occasion-related between-person differences in rates of change (Anstey, Hofer, & Luszcz, 2003; Christensen et al., 2004; Hertzog, Dixon, Hultsch, & MacDonald, 2003; Mackinnon, Christensen, Hofer, Korten, & Jorm, 2003; Wilson et al., 2002; Zimprich & Martin, 2002). These findings suggest moderate correlations among cognitive changes in old age. For example, Anstey et al. (2003) reported a correlation of .61 among latent growth curve changes in memory and speed and that these estimates were relatively robust to various covariate adjustments. Wilson et al. (2002) reported correlated changes ranging from .37 to .78 among seven different cognitive domains, and Christensen et al. (2004) suggested moderate correlated latent growth curve changes among memory and reaction time (.42) and memory and processing speed (.56). However, evaluation of correlations among within- and between-person differences in within-person changes can be expected to be conditional on the time-related aggregation of the individual change trajectories (Sliwinski, Hofer, & Hall, 2003). Estimates of correlations among within-person terminal changes and correlation among between-person differences in within-person terminal changes largely remain to be conducted conditional on survival age.

Although the evidence seems to suggest that the terminal decline pattern is relatively robust across various cognitive abilities (e.g., Johansson et al., 2004), it is entirely possible that the length of the terminal decline interval as well as the magnitude of the terminal effects may vary across the different cognitive abilities and individual characteristics. Wilson et al. (2003), for example, reported that whereas the longest terminal decline interval was for a measure of visuospatial ability, the strongest magnitude of terminal decline effects, on both level of performance and change, was found for a measure of perceptual speed. These findings should, however, be interpreted cautiously because of the contingency of these estimates to the estimate of onset of terminal change. Ghisletta et al. (2006) reported that level of performance and change in perceptual speed and verbal fluency predicted mortality, whereas only level of performance was significant for episodic memory and verbal knowledge. These findings underline the notion that terminal decline may be expected across the full spectrum of cognitive abilities but that the onset of decline and rate of change may vary across distinct types of cognitive capabilities.

CAUSES OF MORTALITY-RELATED CHANGE

Researchers attempting to explain individual differences in cognitive change over the life span should consider health-related factors leading to an accelerated change in cognitive functions in the years preceding death. The mechanism underlying the cognition–mortality relations obviously should include factors associated with neurodegenerative pathology and general systemic decline. These factors could either be in the form of normative biological aging, such as the loss of grey matter integrity or neuromodulatory regulations (e.g., Bäckman & Farde, 2005), or they could relate to specific type of disease pathology, such as Alzheimer's disease, cerebro/cardiovascular diseases (Hassing, Johansson, et al., 2002), or type 2 diabetes mellitus (Hassing et al., 2004).

Concerning the framework of explanations behind the terminal decline phenomenon, Berg (1996) suggested two basic but interrelated explanatory categories. The first type relates to various diseases and comorbidity, and the second type relates to a more general biological system breakdown due to basic aging processes that results in decreased organic reserve capacity and failure in the homeostatic system. This is in close agreement with the basic ideas of a limited brain reserve capacity and threshold models of the cognitive aging process (Stern, 2003). The breakdown point is likely to vary considerably across individuals and cognitive domains depending on various genetic, pathological, and lifestyle factors and is therefore unlikely to be highly dependent on chronological age in an aging population.

Laukka, MacDonald, and Bäckman (2006) recently argued how preclinical dementia might be responsible for a larger part of the terminal decline phenomenon. Other studies, such as Johansson et al. (2004), have indicated that terminal decline may be expected even in a nondemented sample on a variety of cognitive outcomes. Both studies emphasize the importance of accounting for individual differences in dementia pathology in retrospective analyses of longitudinal data. This can be done by excluding individuals from the data analysis, or a sometimes-better alternative is to directly model the different disease processes separately and therefore capitalize on the statistical power of the study.

Given the extent to which comorbidity manifests itself in an aging population (Fillenbaum, Pieper, Cohen, Cornoni-Huntley, & Guralnik, 2000; Nilsson et al., 2001), and to the extent to which pathological and nonpathological influences interact in a complex manner, it is unlikely that a single factor (normative or non-normative) would be responsible for the terminal decline pattern in any single individual. Even in the case of Alzheimer's disease and other types of dementia, a clear pattern of individual differences in the pathological processes can be observed indicating an interaction of pathology and other normative or/and non-normative aging factors. Indeed, as has been argued elsewhere (e.g., Evans, 1988), the categorical distinction between normative/primary and non-normative/secondary aging becomes increasingly blurred in late life.

In a recent review of 47 studies on cognition–mortality relations in patients with stroke, coronary heart disease, and cancer, Anstey, Mack, and von Sanden (2006) concluded that the results generally demonstrated that, within each one of these clinical groups, both cognitive performance and cognitive impairment predicted subsequent mortality. The review provides further support for the ubiquity of the terminal decline hypothesis and that these types of change pattern may be expected within different disease processes. For example, Small et al. (2003) reported that causes of death (i.e., cerebro/cardiovascular disease and noncerebro/cardiovascular disease) failed to modify terminal decline, either within a cross-sectional or longitudinal framework. A further indication of the robustness of the terminal decline pattern across individuals are Sliwinski et al.'s (2006) finding that 89% of the sample was estimated to decline (i.e., have a negative slope) on the postchange point terminal decline phase after accounting for within- and between-person differences in age-based decline.

Available evidence seems to indicate that a relative few individuals may be expected to remain stable on functional variables in old age preceding death (see, e.g., Rabbitt et al., 2006). Heterogeneity in age of onset, rate of change, and combination of declining functions may be expected. Concerning diversity of the explanatory factors, Bäckman and MacDonald (2006) stated:

> Hence, bold versions of either a disease mediation or biological vitality notion fail to account for the available evidence. Rather, it would seem that the truth lies somewhere in between, with both a deterioration of global biological vitality as well

as specific disease mediation playing a contributing role; this view is consistent with the premise that terminal cognitive decline is a multidetermined phenomenon. (p. 225)

We agree with this line of argumentation and further emphasize the perspective of individual differences, and we suggest along with others that early-life factors and heritability might provide a significant contribution to the multidimensionality of the phenomenon and in the end also part of the explanation of terminal decline.

EFFECTS OF REPEATED TESTING ON ESTIMATES OF CHANGE

In addition to population inference related to mortality selection, the identification of change with chronological age or years of life remaining must also deal with other design issues, most notably that of retest or practice effects. The main justifications for spending considerable time and resources for conducting longitudinal studies of cognitive aging is to allow direct inference of change within individuals as well as to examine between-person differences in such changes in a well-defined population. Under most natural circumstances, an aging individual will learn and acquire experience over time. This learning potential (i.e., cognitive plasticity) becomes manifest in the population as between-person differences in within-person change (e.g., Mahncke, Bronstone, & Merzenich, 2006). In fact, it can be argued that between-person differences in change in learning behavior (i.e., cognition) is essentially what researchers in cognitive aging are interested in and are attempting to explain. However, considerable effort has been devoted by some researchers to develop procedures aiming to "strip longitudinal cognitive aging data" from information about within-person changes in learning potentials. This has been done in the name of retest effects (i.e., practice effects, effects of repeated testing), defined as an internal validity threat that obscures inferences about a "true" cognitive aging trajectory using quasi-experimental longitudinal panels. However, a central problem in this regard is how one can identify and interpret, at the individual level, a true cognitive aging trajectory, because such trajectories can generally not be identified without repeated measurements. Between-person comparisons have essential confounds with factors such as mortality selection, selective attrition, cohort effects, and effect of time of sampling. We view this general problem as a design issue that is difficult to remedy through post hoc statistical analysis.

Schaie (1965) and Baltes (1968) early identified retest effects as an essential confound of change estimates in longitudinal studies with widely spaced assessments. They proposed a design-based approach to identify retest effects as between-group average difference of previous participants and a representative resampling group. This method is essentially based on the assumption that the number of test occasions to which individuals are exposed reflects retest effects and that these effects are identical across individuals. A few recent studies have employed this approach. Rönnlund, Nyberg, Bäckman, and Nilsson (2005) reported estimates of 5-year retest effects, over two measurement occasions, in episodic memory and semantic memory based on analyses from an age-heterogeneous (35–80 years) sample drawn from the Betula Study. They found small (in semantic memory) to modest (in episodic memory) group differences (i.e., retest effects) in both younger and older samples. Similar findings were reported by Schaie (1988). Another study reported retest effect estimates on both level and change estimates in various fluid and crystallized abilities based on analyses from an age-homogeneous sample. The main finding was that of modest retest effects on level of cognitive performance in two out of five cognitive abilities but an overall nonsignificant retest effect on change estimates (Thorvaldsson, Hofer, Berg, & Johansson, 2006).

A somewhat different design-based approach was proposed by McArdle and Woodcock (1997). Instead of relying on random manipulation of the frequency of test occasion assigned to participants, and holding the length of the time intervals between testing occasions relatively constant, they proposed randomly assigning the length of time intervals between testing occasions and holding the frequency of test occasions constant. This approach is based on the assumption that length of time between testing occasions reflects retest effects that will

diminish, or vanish, over time. Both design-based approaches can be combined by randomly manipulating both frequency of test occasions and length of time intervals across participants in the same study. This approach assumes that within-person effects are fixed (i.e., average) effects that can be obtained from aggregate between-person differences. To our knowledge, this combination has not yet been applied in cognitive aging research. In essence, both approaches provide information about the magnitude of retest effects on the between-person level, either by comparing previous participants and a resampling group or by comparing participants with short time intervals and long time intervals. Retest effects are, however, by definition, a within-person phenomenon that can vary substantially across individuals.

A related approach to identify retest effects in longitudinal cognitive aging studies relies on multilevel statistical modeling (e.g., McArdle, Ferrer-Caja, Hamagami, & Woodcock, 2002; Rabbitt, Diggle, Smith, Holland, & McInnes, 2001). In this approach, retest effects are identified as the number of occasions on which a participant has been previously exposed to a cognitive test at a particular time point in the longitudinal study. Age-related between-person differences then represent the core information used to estimate the aging effects. This approach, however, cannot claim to fully separate retest effects from other cognitive changes at the within-person level, because there is no independent index that allows the separation of these processes (i.e., retest effects are often very highly correlated with time in study or chronological age). In fact, an independent index that allows separation of retest effects from cognitive change at the within-person level is generally not obtainable in typical longitudinal designs. Within-person cognitive changes cannot be estimated without repeated observations of the same individual, which is the same index used to identify within-person retest effects. An exception is the *measurement burst design*, in which the time index is significantly different for learning effects (e.g., days) and long-term effects of aging (years), which may permit the opportunity for disentangling learning and learning-decay functions from long-term within-person change.

The general idea of identifying retest effects, as a potential internal validity threat of inferences to level or change in a cognitive ability, is basically drawn from the idea that it is possible to infer sample estimates of level or change on a particular behavior to a population that in fact has not been previously exposed to a situation requiring that particular cognitive behavior. There are other issues related to retest effects that are concerned with generalizability, or predictive validity, of the level or change estimates. The population of interest encounters many cognitively demanding tasks in their everyday lives where a proper solution requires that individuals know what to do and how to perform. These individuals will often repeatedly encounter similar situations and tasks for which previous exposure will be beneficial. Individual differences in performance on such tasks may be largely determined by the individual's ability to learn what to do and how to perform. Learning is always embedded in cognitive behavior and may in fact be the essential cognitive behavior of interest in aging research.

A principal aim for cognitive aging scientists is to infer a population change in cognitive behavior that essentially requires the individual to know what to do and how to perform. An important question that aging scientists who advocate a principal distinction between retest effects and "true" cognitive trajectories is "How does a true latent cognitive aging trajectory manifest itself within an individual irrespective of a cognitive system that has a potential for learning?" (Hofer & Sliwinski, 2006). Perhaps a more meaningful understanding of retest effects in cognitive aging studies might be derived from the dynamic testing tradition (see the review by Grigorenko & Sternberg, 1998) that identifies learning as an informative and naturally embedded part of cognitive function. An approach along these lines can also be found in the cognitive aging literature and is represented by attempts to quantify learning potentials (e.g., Kliegl, Smith, & Baltes, 1989).

It has been suggested that retest effects might contribute to overestimation of within-person mortality-related change, because frail and unhealthy individuals in the process of terminal decline learn to a lesser degree than the healthy survivors. However, the identification of terminal decline should be conducted at the individual level and not be based on comparisons between survivors and nonsurvivors. Individuals in the process of terminal decline, by definition, exhibit poorer cognitive performance relative to their performance earlier in life (otherwise they would not be in the process of terminal decline). Learning what to do and how to perform typically requires a variety of cognitive behaviors (i.e., perceiving instructions, semantic representation, execution and control of response, etc.). The identification of gain and decline across different cognitive behaviors at the individual level and within the same testing conditions is difficult, particularly in designs with few repeated measurements and long intervals between test occasions, which is typical in most longitudinal studies.

CONCLUSION

Age-related between-person differences in onset and rate of mortality-related pathological processes will produce heterogeneity in onset and rate of change in cognitive and associated functional outcomes. These processes will result in population selection and become manifest in changes in the age-based population composition. With age, the population will be more selective in terms of the mortality-related variables, but at the same time the remaining individuals are more likely to decline in function. The discrepancy between population composition changes and individual changes must be reflected in both sampling and research design as well as in the analyses of cognitive aging data. Valid inference of population parameters is essentially determined by the nature of the target population, which in cognitive aging research is generally one that must be conditional on both chronological age and survival age (Diehr & Patrick, 2003; Diehr, Williamson, Burke, & Psaty, 2002; DuFouil et al., 2004; Hofer & Hoffman, 2007; Hofer & Sliwinski, 2006; Nesselroade, 1988).

A related issue concerns estimates of moderating and mediating factors of within-person changes and between-person differences in within-person changes. There are substantial age-related increases in comorbidity in old age (e.g., Fillenbaum et al., 2000; Nilsson et al., 2001), and interactions across health-related influences are the major source of age-related between-person differences in onset and rate of cognitive change (see Baltes, Reese, & Lipsitt, 1980). Although complete control of confounding factors in quasi-experimental longitudinal cognitive aging designs is never possible (Schaie, 1977), control should be optimized whenever possible. Biasing influences of age-related heterogeneity in onset of pathological processes leading to cognitive decline can be partly accounted for when estimating moderating and mediating effects of these changes by relying on within-person changes and variability as conditioned on mortality.

For the analysis of longitudinal cognitive data, we recommend the inclusion of terminal decline as an alternative to occasion-based or age-based analyses, not only because it accounts for known population composition changes in terms of cognitive selectivity but also because it accounts in part for the biasing effects of age of onset in estimates of moderating and mediating factors of within-person change and between-person differences in change. Only after a proper identification of cognitive change at the within-person level, and subsequent identification of between-person differences, can hypotheses of moderating and mediating factors of terminal decline be successfully tested. Studies of overall change patterns should, however, be supplemented by micro-studies, such as case control, to identify specific hypotheses of the cognitive effects of certain pathological processes and diseases (e.g., diabetes, hypertension, stroke) or by the more common disease constellations manifest in late life comorbidity (e.g., metabolic syndrome).

REFERENCES

Anstey, K. J., Hofer, S. M., & Luszcz, M. A. (2003). A latent growth curve analysis of late-life sensory and cognitive function over 8 years: Evidence for specific and common factors underlying change. *Psychology and Aging, 18,* 714–726.

Anstey, K. J., Mack, H. A., & von Sanden, C. (2006). The relationship between cognition and mortality in patients with stroke, coronary heart disease, or cancer. *European Psychologist, 11,* 182–195.

Bäckman, L., & Farde, L. (2005). The role of dopamine systems in cognitive aging. In R. Cabeza, L. Nyberg, & D. Park (Eds.), *Cognitive neuroscience of aging: Linking cognitive and cerebral aging* (pp. 58–84). New York: Oxford University Press.

Bäckman, L., & MacDonald, S. W. S. (2006). Death and cognition: Synthesis and outlook. *European Psychologist, 11,* 224–235.

Baltes, P. B. (1968). Longitudinal and cross-sectional sequences in the study of age and generation effects. *Human Development, 11,* 145–171.

Baltes, P. B., & Nesselroade, J. R. (1979). History and rationale of longitudinal research. In J. R. Nesselroade & P. B. Baltes (Eds.), *Longitudinal research in the study of behavior and development* (pp. 1–39). New York: Academic Press.

Baltes, P. B., Reese, H. W., & Lipsitt, L. P. (1980). Life-span developmental psychology. *Annual Review of Psychology, 31,* 65–110.

Baltes, P. B., Reese, H. W., & Nesselroade, J. R. (1977). *Life-span developmental psychology: Introduction to research methods.* Monterey, CA: Brooks/Cole.

Batty, G. D., Deary, I. J., & Gottfredson, L. S. (2007). Premorbid (early life) IQ and later mortality risk: Systematic review. *Annals of Epidemiology, 17,* 278–288.

Berg, S. (1987). Intelligence and terminal decline. In G. L. Maddox & E. W. Busse (Eds.), *Aging: The universal human experience* (pp. 411–416). New York: Springer.

Berg, S. (1996). Aging, behavior, and terminal decline. In J. E. Birren & K. W. Schaie (Eds.), *Handbook of the psychology of aging* (4th ed., pp. 323–337). San Diego, CA: Academic Press.

Bosworth, H. B., & Schaie, K. W. (1999). Survival effects in cognitive function, cognitive style, and sociodemographic variables in the Seattle Longitudinal Study. *Experimental Aging Research, 25,* 121–139.

Bosworth, H. B., Schaie, K. W., & Willis, S. L. (1999). Cognitive and sociodemographic risk factors for mortality in the Seattle Longitudinal Study. *Journal of Gerontology: Psychological Sciences, 54B,* P273–P282.

Bosworth, H. B., & Siegler, I. C. (2002). Terminal change in cognitive function: An updated review of longitudinal studies. *Experimental Aging Research, 28,* 299–315.

Brayne, C. (2007). The elephant in the room— Healthy brains in later life, epidemiology and public health. *Nature Reviews and Neuroscience, 8,* 223–239.

Christensen, H., Mackinnon, A., Jorm, A. F., Korten, A., Jacomb, P., Hofer, S. M., et al. (2004). The Canberra Longitudinal Study: Design, aims, methodology, outcomes and recent empirical investigations. *Aging, Neuropsychology, and Cognition, 11,* 169–195.

Deary, I. J., Whiteman, M. C., Starr, J. M., Whalley, L. J., & Fox, H. C. (2004). The impact of childhood intelligence on later life: Following up the Scottish Mental Surveys of 1932 and 1947. *Journal of Personality and Social Psychology, 86,* 130–147.

Deeg, D. J. H., Hofman, A., & van Zonneveld, R. J. (1990). The association between change in cognitive function and longevity in Dutch elderly. *American Journal of Epidemiology, 132,* 973–982.

Diehr, P., & Patrick, D. L. (2003). Trajectories of health for older adults over time: Accounting fully for death. *Annals of Internal Medicine, 139,* 416–421.

Diehr, P., Williamson, J., Burke, G. L., & Psaty, B. M. (2002). The aging and dying processes and the health of older adults. *Journal of Clinical Epidemiology, 55,* 269–278.

DuFouil, C., Brayne, C., & Clayton, D. (2004). Analysis of longitudinal studies with death and drop-out: A case study. *Statistics in Medicine, 23,* 2215–2226.

Evans, J. G. (1988). Ageing and disease. *Ciba Foundation Symposium, 134,* 38–57.

Ferraro, K. F., & Kelley-Moore, J. A. (2001). Self-rated health and mortality among black and white adults: Examining the dynamic evaluation thesis. *Journal of Gerontology: Social Sciences, 56B,* S195–S205.

Fillenbaum, G. G., Pieper, C. F., Cohen, H. J., Cornoni-Huntley, J. C., & Guralnik, J. M. (2000). Comorbidity of five chronic health conditions in elderly community residents: Determinants and impact on mortality. *Journal of Gerontology: Medical Sciences, 55A,* M84–M89.

Ghisletta, P., McArdle, J. J., & Lindenberger, U. (2006). Longitudinal cognition–survival relations in old and very old age. *European Psychologist, 11,* 204–223.

Grigorenko, E. L., & Sternberg, R. J. (1998). Dynamic testing. *Psychological Bulletin, 124,* 75–111.

Hall, C. B., Lipton, R. B., Sliwinski, M., & Stewart, W. F. (2000). A change point model for estimating the onset of cognitive decline in preclinical Alzheimer's disease. *Statistics in Medicine, 19,* 1555–1566.

Hall, C. B., Ying, J., Kuo, L., & Lipton, R. B. (2003). Bayesian and profile likelihood change point methods for modeling cognitive function over time. *Computational Statistics & Data Analysis, 42,* 91–109.

Harel, O., Hofer, S. M., Hoffman, L., Pedersen, N. L., & Johansson, B. (2007). Population inference with mortality and attrition in longitudinal studies on aging: A two-stage multiple imputation method. *Experimental Aging Research, 33,* 187–203.

Hassing, L. B., Grant, M. D., Hofer, S. M., Pedersen, N. L., Nilsson, S. E., Berg, S., et al. (2004). Type 2 diabetes mellitus contributes to cognitive change in old age: A longitudinal population-based study. *Journal of the International Neuropsychological Society, 10,* 599–607.

Hassing, L. B., Johansson, B., Berg, S., Nilsson, S. E., Pedersen, N. L., Hofer, S. M., et al. (2002). Terminal decline and markers of cerebrovascular and cardiovascular disease: Findings from a longitudinal study of the oldest old. *Journal of Gerontology: Psychological Sciences, 57B,* P268–P276.

Hassing, L. B., Small, J. B., von Strauss, E., Fratiglioni, L., & Bäckman, L. (2002). Mortality-related differences and changes in episodic memory among the oldest old: Evidence from a population-based sample of nonagenarians. *Aging, Neuropsychology, and Cognition, 9,* 11–20.

Hertzog, C., Dixon, R. A., Hultsch, D. F., & MacDonald, S. W. S. (2003). Latent change models of adult cognition: Are changes in processing speed and working memory associated with changes in episodic memory? *Psychology and Aging, 18,* 755–769.

Hertzog, C., & Nesselroade, J. R. (2003). Assessing psychological change in adulthood: An overview of methodological issues. *Psychology and Aging, 18,* 639–657.

Hofer, S. M., & Hoffman, L. (2007). Statistical analysis with incomplete data: A developmental perspective. In T. D. Little, J. A. Bovaird, & N. A. Card (Eds.), *Modeling contextual effects in longitudinal studies of human development* (pp. 13–32). Mahwah, NJ: Lawrence Erlbaum.

Hofer, S. M., & Piccinin, A. M. (2007). Longitudinal studies. In J. E. Birren (Ed.), *Encyclopedia of gerontology: Age, aging, and the aged* (2nd ed., pp. 341–352). Oxford, UK: Elsevier Ltd.

Hofer, S. M., & Sliwinski, M. J. (2001). Understanding ageing: An evaluation of research designs for assessing the interdependence of ageing-related changes. *Gerontology, 47,* 341–352.

Hofer, S. M., & Sliwinski, M. J. (2006). Design and analysis of longitudinal studies of aging. In J. E. Birren & K. W. Schaie (Eds.), *Handbook of the psychology of aging* (6th ed., pp. 15–37). San Diego, CA: Academic Press.

Jacqmin-Gadda, H., Commenges, D., & Dartigues, J.-F. (2006). Random changepoint model for joint modeling of cognitive decline and dementia. *Biometrics, 62,* 254–260.

Jagger, C., Andersen, K., Breteler, M. M., Copeland, J. R., Helmer, C., Baldereschi, M., et al. (2000). Prognosis with dementia in Europe: A collaborative study of population-based cohorts. Neurologic diseases in the elderly research group. *Neurology, 54,* S16–S20.

Johansson, B., & Berg, S. (1989). The robustness of the terminal decline phenomenon: Longitudinal data from the Digit-Span Memory Test. *Journal of Gerontology: Psychological Sciences, 44,* P184–P186.

Johansson, B., Hofer, S. M., Allaire, J. C., Maldonado-Molina, M. M., Piccinin, A. M., Berg, S., et al. (2004). Change in cognitive capabilities in the oldest old: The effects of proximity to death in genetically related individuals over a 6-year period. *Psychology and Aging, 19,* 145–156.

Kleemeier, R. W. (1962). Intellectual change in the senium. *Proceedings of the American Statistical Association, 1,* 290–295.

Kliegl, R., Smith, J., & Baltes, P. B. (1989). Testing-the-limits and the study of adult age differences in cognitive plasticity of a mnemonic skill. *Developmental Psychology, 25,* 247–256.

Laukka, E. J., MacDonald, S. W. S., & Bäckman, L. (2006). Contrasting cognitive trajectories of impending death and preclinical dementia in the very old. *Neurology, 66,* 833–838.

Ljungquist, B., Berg, S., & Steen, B. (1995). Prediction of survival in 70-year olds. *Archives of Gerontology and Geriatrics, 20,* 295–307.

Mackinnon, A., Christensen, H., Hofer, S. M., Korten, A. E., & Jorm, A. F. (2003). Use it and still lose it? The association between activity and cognitive performance established using latent growth techniques in a community sample. *Aging, Neuropsychology, and Cognition, 10,* 215–229.

Mahncke, J. W., Bronstone, A., & Merzenich, M. M. (2006). Brain plasticity and functional losses in the aged: Scientific bases for a novel intervention. *Progress in Brain Research, 157,* 81–109.

Maier, H., & Smith, J. (1999). Psychological predictors of mortality in old age. *Journal of Gerontology: Psychological Sciences, 54B,* P44–P54.

McArdle, J. J., Ferrer-Caja, E., Hamagami, F., & Woodcock, R. W. (2002). Comparative longitudinal structural analyses of the growth and decline of multiple intellectual abilities over the life span. *Developmental Psychology, 38,* 115–142.

McArdle, J. J., & Nesselroade, J. R. (2003). Growth curve analysis in contemporary psychological research. In J. Schinka & W. Velicer (Eds.), *Comprehensive handbook of psychology: Vol. 2. Research methods in psychology* (pp. 447–480). New York: Pergamon Press.

McArdle, J. J., Small, B. J., Bäckman, L., & Fratiglioni, L. (2005). Longitudinal models of growth and survival applied to the early detection of Alzheimer's disease. *Journal of Geriatric Psychiatry and Neurology, 18,* 234–241.

McArdle, J. J., & Woodcock, R. W. (1997). Expanding test–retest designs to include developmental time-lag components. *Psychological Methods, 2,* 403–435.

Molenaar, P. C. M., Huizenga, H. M., & Nesselroade, J. R. (2003). The relationship between the structure of interindividual and intraindividual variability: A theoretical and empirical vindication of developmental system theory. In U. M. Staudinger & U. Lindenberger (Eds.), *Understanding human development: Dialogues with lifespan psychology* (pp. 339–360). Dordrecht, The Netherlands: Kluwer Academic.

Neale, R., Brayne, C., & Johnson, A. L. (2001). Cognition and survival: An exploration in a large multicentre study of the population aged 65 years and over. *International Journal of Epidemiology, 30,* 1383–1388.

Nesselroade, J. R. (1988). Sampling and generalizability: Adult development and aging research issues examined within the general methodological framework of selection. In K. W. Schaie, R. T. Campbell, W. Meredith, & S. C. Rawlings

(Eds.), *Methodological issues in aging research* (pp. 13–42). New York: Springer.

Nilsson, S. E., Johansson, B., Berg, S., Karlsson, D., & McClearn, G. E. (2001). A comparison of diagnosis capture from medical records, self-reports, and drug registrations: A study in individuals 80 years and older. *Aging, Clinical and Experimental Research, 14,* 178–184.

Palmore, E., & Cleveland, W. (1976). Aging, terminal decline, and terminal drop. *Journal of Gerontology, 31,* 76–81.

Rabbitt, P., Diggle, P., Smith, D., Holland, F., & McInnes, L. (2001). Identifying and separating the effects of practice and of cognitive ageing during a large longitudinal study of elderly community residents. *Neuropsychologia, 39,* 532–543.

Rabbitt, P., Lunn, M., & Wong, D. (2006). Understanding terminal decline in cognition and risk of death: Methodological and theoretical implications of practice and dropout effects. *European Psychologist, 11,* 164–171.

Rabbitt, P., Watson, P., Donlan, C., McInnes, L., Horan, M., Pendleton, N., et al. (2002). Effects of death within 11 years on cognitive performance in old age. *Psychology and Aging, 17,* 468–481.

Riegel, K. F., & Riegel, R. M. (1972). Development, drop, and death. *Developmental Psychology, 6,* 306–319.

Riegel, K. F., Riegel, R. M., & Meyer, G. (1967). A study of the dropout rates in longitudinal research on aging and the prediction of death. *Journal of Personality and Social Psychology, 5,* 342–348.

Rönnlund, M., Nyberg, L., Bäckman, L., & Nilsson, L.-G. (2005). Stability, growth, and decline in adult life span development of declarative memory: Cross-sectional and longitudinal data from a population-based study. *Psychology and Aging, 20,* 3–18.

Schaie, K. W. (1965). A general model for the study of developmental problems. *Psychological Bulletin, 64,* 92–107.

Schaie, K. W. (1977). Quasi-experimental designs in the psychology of aging. In J. E. Birren & K. W. Schaie (Eds.), *Handbook of the psychology of aging* (pp. 39–58). New York: Van Nostrand Reinhold.

Schaie, K. W. (1988). Internal validity threats in studies of adult cognitive development. In M. L. Howe & C. J. Brainard (Eds.), *Cognitive development in adulthood: Progress in cognitive*

development research (pp. 241–272). New York: Springer-Verlag.

Schulz, R., Beach, S. R., Ives, D. G., Martire, L. M., Ariyo, A. A., & Kop, W. J. (2000). Association between depression and mortality in older adults: The Cardiovascular Health Study. *Archives of International Medicine, 160,* 1761–1768.

Siegler, I. C. (1975). The terminal drop hypothesis: Fact or artifact? *Experimental Aging Research, 1,* 169–185.

Sliwinski, M. J., Hofer, S. M., & Hall, C. (2003). Correlated and coupled cognitive change in older adults with and without preclinical dementia. *Psychology and Aging, 18,* 672–683.

Sliwinski, M. J., Hofer, S. M., Hall, C., Buschke, H., & Lipton, R. B. (2003). Modeling memory decline in older adults: The importance of preclinical dementia, attrition, and chronological age. *Psychology and Aging, 18,* 658–671.

Sliwinski, M. J., Stawski, R. S., Hall, C. B., Katz, M., Verghese, J., & Lipton, R. (2006). Distinguishing preterminal and terminal cognitive decline. *European Psychologist, 11,* 172–181.

Small, B. J., & Bäckman, L. (1997). Cognitive correlates of mortality: Evidence from a population-based sample of very old adults. *Psychology and Aging, 12,* 309–313.

Small, B. J., & Bäckman, L. (1999). Time to death and cognitive performance. *Current Directions in Psychological Science, 8,* 168–172.

Small, B. J., Fratiglioni, L., von Strauss, E., & Bäckman, L. (2003). Terminal decline and cognitive performance in very old age: Does cause of death matter? *Psychology and Aging, 18,* 193–202.

Smith, C. H. M., Deeg, D. J. H., Kriegsman, D. M. W., & Schmand, B. (1999). Cognitive functioning and health as determinants of mortality in an older population. *American Journal of Epidemiology, 150,* 978–986.

Stern, Y. (2003). The concept of cognitive reserve: A catalyst for research. *Journal of Clinical and Experimental Neuropsychology, 25,* 589–593.

Thorvaldsson, V., Hofer, S. M., Berg, S., & Johansson, B. (2006). Effects of repeated testing in a longitudinal age-homogeneous study of cognitive aging. *Journal of Gerontology: Psychological Sciences, 61B,* P348–P354.

Thorvaldsson, V., Hofer, S. M., & Johansson, B. (2006). Aging and late-life terminal decline in perceptual speed. *European Psychologist, 11,* 196–203.

Vaupel, J. W., & Yashin, A. (1985). Heterogeneity's ruses: Some surprising effects of selection on population dynamics. *American Statistician, 39,* 176–185.

White, N., & Cunningham, W. R. (1988). Is terminal drop pervasive or specific? *Journal of Gerontology, 43,* P141–P144.

Wilson, R. S., Beckett, L. A., Barnes, L. L., Schneider, J. A., Bach, J., Evans, D. A., et al. (2002). Individual differences in rate of change in cognitive abilities in older persons. *Psychology and Aging, 17,* 179–193.

Wilson, R. S., Beckett, L. A., Bienias, J. L., Evans, D. A., & Bennett, D. A. (2003). Terminal decline in cognitive function. *Neurology, 60,* 1782–1787.

Zimprich, D., & Martin, M. (2002). Can longitudinal change in processing speed explain longitudinal age changes in fluid intelligence? *Psychology and Aging, 17,* 690–695.

18

NEUROLOGICAL FACTORS IN COGNITIVE AGING

ROBERT S. WILSON

In the past century, average life expectancy in the United States increased by approximately 30 years, primarily because of reduced mortality from common conditions in early and midlife. As a result, there has been a substantial increase in the proportion of older people in the population, and this proportion is expected to further increase in the first half of the current century as the post–World War II generation ages. With the aging of the population, common chronic conditions of old age have come to pose an increasing public health burden. In particular, cognition-impairing conditions such as Alzheimer's disease that are relatively uncommon before age 65 have now become leading causes of morbidity and mortality. Therefore, identifying factors that may prevent or delay age-related cognitive decline is of great public health importance.

The central premise of this chapter is that age-related cognitive decline represents the interaction of experiential and genetic risk factors with multiple age-associated neuropathologic processes taking place in brains with differing structural and functional characteristics prior to old age. According to this view, age-related loss of cognition is not a normal developmental process or an inevitable outcome of old age but rather the result of different age-related neuropathologic lesions accumulating at different rates in different brain regions of individuals with differing vulnerabilities to the lesions; that is, risk factors may contribute to loss of cognition either by affecting the accumulation of common neuropathologic lesions or by somehow affecting the ability to maintain function despite accumulating pathology. To the extent that this view is valid, understanding the neurobiologic pathways linking risk factors to age-related loss of cognition is likely to be critical to research on prevention.

The remainder of this chapter is divided into three parts. In the first section, I describe four neuropathologic lesions that are common findings on postmortem examinations of the brains of old people and discuss their distribution and relation to cognition in people with and without dementia. In the second section, I consider selected predictors of age-related cognitive decline and propose different neurobiologic bases for the associations. In the final section,

AUTHOR'S NOTE: This work was supported by National Institute on Aging Grants R01 AG024871, R01 AG15819, R01 AG17917, and P30 AG10161.

I summarize the preceding sections and consider implications for future research.

AGE-RELATED NEUROPATHOLOGY

Alzheimer's disease is the most common cause of cognitive decline and dementia in old age. It has two defining pathologic features, first described by Alzheimer about 100 years ago: neuritic plaques, which accumulate outside neurons and mainly consist of a protein called *amyloid-beta*, and neurofibrillary tangles, which are found inside neurons, primarily consist of a protein called *tau* and appear as a tangled mass of filaments under a microscope. Both of these lesions are commonly found on postmortem examination of the brains of people who died in old age. The pathologic diagnosis of Alzheimer's disease is determined by the severity of this pathology, with the Consortium to Establish a Registry for Alzheimer's Disease criteria based on estimates of neuritic plaque density (Mirra et al., 1991), the Braak staging system based on neurofibrillary pathology (Braak & Braak, 1991), and the National Institute on Aging research criteria based on both plaques and tangles ("Consensus recommendations," 1997).

Plaques and tangles are not the only forms of pathology contributing to late life cognitive impairment. Cerebral infarction is common. Thus, in the Religious Orders Study (Wilson, Bienias, Evans, & Bennett, 2004), a longitudinal clinical–pathologic study of Catholic clergy members with a mean age at death of about 85, more than one third had one or more chronic cerebral infarctions on brain autopsy (Schneider, Wilson, Bienias, Evans, & Bennett, 2004; Schneider et al., 2003). Both infarction and Alzheimer's disease pathology were negatively associated with level of cognitive function proximate to death, and these associations were independent, meaning the negative effects were additive. In a subsequent study of this same cohort, Lewy bodies were present in about 15% and associated with cognitive impairment, and only 2 brains out of more than 200 autopsies showed no evidence of Alzheimer's disease, cerebral infarction, or Lewy bodies (Wilson, Arnold, Schneider, Li, & Bennett, 2007).

Although these neuropathologic lesions are common in old age and known to be correlated with age-related cognitive impairment, the correlation is far from perfect; that is, some people show little or no cognitive impairment despite substantial pathology while others have profound cognitive impairment despite minimal pathology. In the Religious Orders Study, for example, measures of amyloid, tangles, Lewy bodies, and cerebral infarction together accounted for 26.9% of the variance in a measure of global cognition proximate to death, after accounting for the effects of age at death, sex, and education (Wilson, Arnold, et al., 2007). That a substantial proportion of the variance in late life cognitive function is not associated with the leading causes of late life dementia suggests that other factors are involved, either other lesions whose pathologic footprint we do not yet recognize or structural or functional properties of neural systems that render them more or less able to effectively adapt to changes caused by age-related pathology.

A common idea in aging research is that normal aging can and should be distinguished from abnormal aging. This idea assumes that the factors contributing to late life dementia are different from the factors contributing to subtle changes in memory and cognition seen in old people without dementia. Recent clinical–pathologic research suggests that this assumption is incorrect. A substantial number of older persons exhibit some cognitive dysfunction but do not meet criteria for dementia, and the term *mild cognitive impairment* is increasingly being used to designate this border zone between normal cognition and dementia. In persons with mild cognitive impairment proximate to death, levels of Alzheimer's disease pathology (Bennett, Schneider, Wilson, et al., 2005; Petersen et al., 2006) and cerebral infarction (Bennett, Schneider, Wilson, et al., 2005) have been shown to be intermediate between levels in persons with no cognitive impairment and those with dementia. Neurofibrillary pathology in particular has been proposed as the pathologic substrate of mild cognitive impairment (Guillozet, Weintraub, Mash, & Mesulam, 2003; Riley, Snowden, & Markesbery, 2002) and, from a neuropathologic standpoint, mild cognitive impairment has been characterized as early

Alzheimer's disease (Markesbery et al., 2006). Neither is the impact of age-related neuropathology confined to persons with mild cognitive impairment. In one clinical–pathologic study with detailed annual cognitive testing and clinical evaluation, all those with mild cognitive impairment or dementia were excluded, leaving 134 persons who died without any evidence of cognitive impairment proximate to death (Bennett, Schneider, Arvanitakis, et al., 2006). More than one third met pathologic criteria for Alzheimer's disease (and more than one fifth had cerebral infarctions, and more than one eighth had Lewy bodies), and meeting Alzheimer's disease criteria was associated with lower episodic memory performance. Indeed, the correlation of Alzheimer's disease pathology with cognition does not appear to vary across the spectrum from dementia to mild cognitive impairment to no cognitive impairment (Bennett, Schneider, Wilson, et al., 2005).

If most old people have at least some Alzheimer's disease pathology and it negatively affects cognitive functioning across the full spectrum of cognitive ability, we may ask when these deleterious effects begin. Dementia due to Alzheimer's disease is strongly age related (Evans et al., 2003; Evans et al., 1989; Zhang et al., 1990), and the diagnosis is relatively uncommon in those aged less than 65. Yet the onset of dementia in Alzheimer's disease is difficult to pinpoint, and it is typically preceded by years of subtle impairments in cognition and other neurobehavioral functions. Studies of persons who eventually developed Alzheimer's disease suggest a prodromal period of several years duration marked by cognitive decline and atrophic changes in the medial temporal lobe (Twamley, Ropacki, & Bondi, 2006). Neuropathologic research also suggests that the medial temporal lobe is among the first sites of Alzheimer's disease pathologic changes (Braak & Braak, 1991; Hyman, Van Hoesen, Kromer, & Damasio, 1984). In the Braak model of the natural history of Alzheimer's disease, neurofibrillary pathology is confined to transentorhinal and entorhinal cortices during a long clinically silent phase of the disease followed by a spread of pathology to other limbic structures and the appearance of prodromal clinical symptoms during a subsequent limbic phase (Braak & Braak, 1991). A remarkable feature of the autopsy series of Braak and Braak (1991), based on 2,661 brains obtained from three German universities, is that neurofibrillary pathology was relatively common prior to old age, with one third of those under the age of 50 showing at least some tangles in the entorhinal cortex (though only 6% showed evidence of amyloid-beta accumulation at this age). Further evidence that Alzheimer's disease may begin in middle age comes from studies of persons genetically at risk for the disease. Thus, healthy persons in their 50s with two copies of the apolipoprotein E ε4 allele have been shown to exhibit subtle deficits in visual attention and working memory (Greenwood, Lambert, Sunderland, & Parasuraman, 2005) which progressively worsen (Greenwood, Sunderland, Putnam, Levy, & Parasuraman, 2005).

PREDICTORS OF AGE-RELATED LOSS OF COGNITION

In the past decade, a wide array of genetic, clinical, and lifestyle variables has been associated with cognitive decline and dementia in prospective observational studies. Developing effective strategies to prevent or delay age-related cognitive decline is likely to depend in part on understanding the neurobiologic mechanisms linking these variables to late life cognitive function. As shown in the preceding section of this chapter, the long prodromal period in Alzheimer's disease and individual differences in the ability to tolerate its pathology complicate efforts to identify these mechanisms. In this section, I consider four possible mechanisms and provide examples of each.

Early Signs of Neuropathology

Given the long prodromal period in Alzheimer's disease, it is likely that some variables that predict cognitive decline are not true risk factors but subtle early signs of its pathology. Thus, difficulty identifying familiar odors is associated with more rapid cognitive decline (Graves et al., 1999; Wilson, Arnold, Tang, & Bennett, 2006) and with the transitions from no cognitive impairment to mild cognitive impairment (Wilson, Schneider, Arnold, et al., 2007) and from mild cognitive impairment to Alzheimer's disease (Devanand et al., 2000; Tabert et al., 2005; Wilson, Schneider, Arnold, et al., 2007). These correlations are likely due in large part to a robust association of olfactory identification with neurofibrillary pathology in the entorhinal cortex, hippocampus, and other central olfactory regions (Wilson, Arnold, Schneider, Tang, & Bennett, 2007). Similarly, Parkinsonian gait dysfunction has been associated with risk of dementia (Louis, Tang, & Mayeux, 2004; Wilson, Schneider, Bienias, Evans, & Bennett, 2003) and with neurofibrillary pathology in the substantia nigra (Schneider et al., 2006), and loss of body mass is associated with cognitive decline (Buchman et al., 2005) and Alzheimer's disease pathology (Buchman, Schneider, Wilson, Bienias, & Bennett, 2006).

Factors Associated With Accumulation of Neuropathology

Given the prevalance in old age of neuropathologic lesions associated with cognitive impairment, it is not surprising that some factors appear to predict age-related cognitive decline by virtue of an association with neuropathology. Thus, possession of at least one copy of the apolipoprotein E ε4 allele, a well-established risk factor for cognitive decline and Alzheimer's disease (Corder et al., 1993; Evans et al., 2003), has been associated with amyloid deposition in the brain (Polvikoski et al., 1995; Schmechel et al., 1993). In clinical–pathologic analyses in the Religious Orders Study (Bennett, Schneider, Wilson, et al., 2005), possession of an ε4 allele was associated with lower level of cognitive function proximate to death. After controlling for a composite measure of amyloid burden based on tissue from eight brain regions, this association was reduced by about 60% and was no longer significant. The ε4 allele was also related to a measure of tangle density, but the association was eliminated after controlling for amyloid load. The ε4 allele has also been associated with increased likelihood of cerebral infarction (Schneider et al., 2005). These data suggest that the association of ε4 with cognitive impairment is largely mediated by its association with neuropathologic lesions known to contribute to cognitive impairment in old age.

Diabetes mellitus affects about one fifth of persons aged 65 years or older in the United States (National Institute of Diabetes and Digestive and Kidney Diseases, 2002). Large prospective studies have found persons with diabetes to experience more rapid cognitive decline (Arvanitakis, Wilson, Bienias, Evans, & Bennett, 2004; Kanaya, Barrett-Conner, Gildengorin, & Yaffe, 2004; Logroscino, Kang, & Grodstein, 2004) and an increased risk of dementia (Arvanitakis et al., 2004; Leibson et al., 1997; Ott et al., 1999) compared to persons without diabetes. In clinical–pathologic analyses from the Religious Orders Study (Arvanitakis et al., 2006), diabetes was associated with the presence of cerebral infarction on postmortem examination but not with composite measures of amyloid load or tangle density, suggesting that diabetes is associated with age-related cognitive decline by virtue of an association with cerebral infarction.

Factors Modifying the Association of Neuropathology With Cognition

Several large epidemiologic studies have found that people with higher levels of educational or occupational attainment have a decreased risk of late life dementia compared to persons with lower levels of attainment (Evans et al., 1997; Stern et al., 1994; Wilson, Bennett, et al., 2002). Because few investigators believed that education or occupation were associated with the pathology underlying dementia, the observation suggested that education might be a marker of brain's ability to tolerate age-related neuropathology. Support for this idea comes from analyses of clinical and pathologic data from the Religious Orders Study (Bennett et al., 2003). Among those who died and underwent brain autopsy, the negative association of Alzheimer's disease pathology with cognitive function proximate to death was reduced in participants with higher levels of schooling compared to those with lower levels; that is, it took about 5 times more pathology to reduce cognition by a fixed amount in a person with a high level of education relative to a person with a low level, consistent with the neural reserve hypothesis.

Having a large social network has been associated with reduced risk of cognitive decline and dementia (L. L. Barnes, Mendes de Leon, Wilson, Bienias, & Evans, 2004; Fratiglioni, Wang, Ericsson, Maytan, & Winblad, 2000;

Zunzunegui, Alvarado, Del Ser, & Otero, 2003), although negative results have also been reported (Wilson, Krueger, et al., 2007). In a recent clinical–pathologic study, social network size modified the association of neurofibrillary pathology with cognitive function proximate to death (Bennett, Schneider, Tang, et al., 2006). As social network size increased, the negative correlation of tangles with cognition decreased, suggesting that neural systems involved in developing and maintaining a large social network may help the brain function despite increasing neurofibrillary changes, possibly by facilitating recruitment of additional neural systems during cognitive processing.

Factors Operating Through Other Mechanisms

For many factors that have been found to predict age-related loss of cognition, the neurobiologic basis of the association is uncertain, and in some cases novel mechanisms have been hypothesized. A case in point is depressive symptomatology. With relatively few exceptions, longitudinal studies have found higher level of depressive symptoms in old age to be associated with loss of cognition in the form of higher incidence of mild cognitive impairment (D. E. Barnes, Alexopoulos, Lopez, Williamson, & Yaffe, 2006: Geda et al., 2006; Wilson, Schneider, Boyle, et al., 2007) or dementia (Berger, Fratiglioni, Forsell, Winblad, & Bäckman, 1999; Devanand et al., 1996; Gatz, Tyas, St. John, & Montgomery, 2005; Modrego & Ferrández, 2004; Wilson, Barnes, et al., 2002; Wilson, Krueger, et al., 2007) or more rapid cognitive decline (Paterniti, Verdier-Tillefer, Dufouil, & Alperovitch, 2002; Sachs-Ericsson, Joiner, Plant, & Blazer, 2005; Wilson, Barnes, et al., 2002; Wilson, Mendes de Leon, Bennett, Bienias, & Evans, 2004; Yaffe et al., 1999). One interpretation of these data is that depressive symptoms are an early sign of the pathology associated with dementia. Yet longitudinal studies do not suggest that depressive symptoms worsen in old age (Barefoot, Mortensen, Helms, Avlund, & Schroll, 2001; Davey, Halverson, Zonderman, & Costa, 2004; Haynie, Berg, Johansson, Gatz, & Zarit, 2001; Pitkälä, Kähönen-Väre, Valvanne, Strandberg, & Tilvis, 2003;

Skarupski et al., 2005; Wallace & O'Hara, 1992) when neuropathology is accumulating in the brain, unlike other established signs that predict cognitive decline (i.e., olfactory identification, body mass, gait). Furthermore, in the Religious Orders Study, the level of depressive symptoms was not related to cerebral infarction or composite measures of amyloid load, tangle density, or Lewy bodies and did not modify the relation of pathology to cognition. However, depressive symptomatology was related to likelihood of dementia and level of cognitive function proximate to death, even after controlling for all forms of neuropathology (Wilson, Arnold, et al., 2007). These data suggest that the association of depressive symptoms with age-related loss of cognition may be independent of the neuropathology traditionally associated with dementia and that novel pathologic changes may be involved. Animal models of chronic stress have described a spectrum of limbic system changes, particularly in portions of the hippocampal formation and medial prefrontal cortex, including dendritic atrophy, downregulation of glucocorticoid receptors, and reduced expression of brain-derived neurotrophic factor and its tyrosine kinase B receptor, accompanied by impaired learning and memory (Johren, Flugge, & Fuchs, 1994; Magarinos, McEwan, Flugge, & Fuchs, 1996; Radley et al., 2004; Smith Makino, Kvetnansky, & Post, 1995; Sousa, Lukoyanov, Madeira, Almeida, & Paula-Barbosa, 2000). That these models might have relevance to humans is suggested by neuroimaging evidence of reduced volume of the hippocampus and prefrontal cortex in major depression (Drevets et al., 1997; Sheline, Wang, Gado, Csernansky, & Vannier, 1996) and postmortem evidence of reduced glucocorticoid receptor mRNA in the hippocampus and frontal cortex in persons with mood disorders (Webster, Knable, O'Grady, Orthman, & Weickert, 2002) and reduced expression of brain-derived neurotrophic factor in suicide victims (Dwivedi et al., 2003).

CONCLUSION

In this chapter, I have discussed the neuropathologic lesions associated with Alzheimer's disease, stroke, and Parkinson's disease, common age-related conditions that impair cognitive function. I have tried to make two main points. First, these lesions, particularly Alzheimer's disease pathology, are commonly found in the brains of older people without dementia and are known to adversely affect cognition in this subgroup, suggesting that the distinction between normal and abnormal cognitive aging is artificial and constrains thinking about the bases of age-related loss of cognition. Second, these common neuropathologies do not account for all of the heterogeneity in age-related loss of cognition, implying that other neurobiologic mechanisms are involved, possibly by somehow modifying the association of pathology with cognition or by an association with currently unrecognized neurodeteriorative changes.

Future research on age-related loss of cognition faces many challenges, two in particular. First, knowledge of the natural history of Alzheimer's disease is sketchy, but current data suggest that the initial pathological changes in the brain may precede the first clinical manifestations of the disease by many years. Better understanding of this long period may help to inform strategies for delaying symptom onset and for identifying people with the disease before debilitating pathologic and cognitive changes have taken place. A second challenge is to clarify the structural, biochemical, and molecular bases of individual differences in vulnerability to age-related pathology, which may suggest novel preventive strategies.

REFERENCES

Arvanitakis, Z., Schneider, J. A., Wilson, R. S., Li, Y., Arnold, S. E., Wang, Z., et al. (2006). Diabetes is related to cerebral infarction but not to AD pathology in older persons. *Neurology, 67,* 1960–1965.

Arvanitakis, Z., Wilson, R. S., Bienias, J. L., Evans, D. A., & Bennett, D. A. (2004). Diabetes mellitus and risk of Alzheimer's disease and decline in cognitive function. *Archives of Neurology, 61,* 661–666.

Barefoot, J. C., Mortensen, E. L., Helms, M. J., Avlund, K., & Schroll, M. (2001). A longitudinal study of gender differences in depressive symptoms from age 50 to 80. *Psychology and Aging, 16,* 342–345.

Barnes, D. E., Alexopoulos, G. S., Lopez, O. L., Williamson, J. D., & Yaffe, K. (2006). Depressive symptoms, vascular disease, and mild cognitive impairment. *Archives of General Psychiatry, 63,* 273–280.

Barnes, L. L., Mendes de Leon, C. F., Wilson, R. S., Bienias, J. L., & Evans, D. A. (2004). Social resources and cognitive decline in a population of older African Americans and whites. *Neurology, 63,* 2322–2326.

Bennett, D. A., Schneider, J. A., Arvanitakis, Z., Kelly, J. F., Aggarwal, N. T., Shah, R. C., et al. (2006). Neuropathology of older persons without cognitive impairment from two community-based studies. *Neurology, 66,* 1837–1844.

Bennett, D. A., Schneider, J. A., Tang, Y., Arnold, S. E., & Wilson, R. S. (2006). The effect of social networks on the relation between Alzheimer's disease pathology and level of cognitive function in old people: A longitudinal cohort study. *Lancet Neurology, 5,* 406–412.

Bennett, D. A., Schneider, J. A., Wilson, R. S., Bienias, J. L., Berry-Kravis, E., & Arnold, S. E. (2005). Amyloid mediates the association of apolipoprotein E ε4 allele to cognitive function in older people. *Journal of Neurology, Neurosurgery, and Psychiatry, 76,* 1194–1199.

Bennett, D. A., Wilson, R. S., Schneider, J. A., Evans, D. A., Mendes de Leon, C. F., Arnold, S. E., et al. (2003). Education modifies the relation of AD pathology to level of cognitive function in older persons. *Neurology, 60,* 1909–1915.

Berger, A. K., Fratiglioni, L., Forsell, Y., Winblad, B., & Bäckman, L. (1999). The occurrence of depressive symptoms in the preclinical phase of AD: A population-based study. *Neurology, 53,* 1998–2002.

Braak, H., & Braak, E. (1991). Neuropathological staging of Alzheimer-related changes. *Acta Neuropathologica, 82,* 239–259.

Buchman, A. S., Schneider, J. A., Wilson, R. S., Bienias, J. L., & Bennett, D. A. (2006). Body mass index in older persons is associated with Alzheimer's disease pathology. *Neurology, 67,* 1949–1954.

Buchman, A. S., Wilson, R. S., Bienias, J. L., Shah, R. C., Evans, D. A., & Bennett, D. A. (2005). Change in body mass index (BMI) and risk of incident Alzheimer's disease. *Neurology, 65,* 892–897.

Consensus recommendations for the postmortem diagnosis of Alzheimer's disease. The National Institute on Aging, and Reagen Institute

Working Group on Diagnostic Criteria for the Neuropathological Assessment of Alzheimer's Disease. (1997). *Neurobiology of Aging, 18*(4, Suppl.), S1–S2.

Corder, E. H., Saunders, A. M., Strittmatter, W. J., Schmechel, D. E., Gaskell, P. C., Small, G. W., et al. (1993, August 13). Gene dose of apolipoprotein E type 4 allele and the risk of Alzheimer's disease in late onset families. *Science, 261,* 921–923.

Davey, A., Halverson, C. F., Zonderman, A. B., & Costa, P. T. (2004). Change in depressive symptoms in the Baltimore Longitudinal Study of Aging. *Journal of Gerontology: Psychological Sciences, 59B,* P270–P277.

Devanand, D. P., Michaels-Marston, K. S., Liu, X., Pelton, G. H., Padilla, M., Marder, K., et al. (2000). Olfactory deficits in patients with mild cognitive impairment predict Alzheimer's disease at follow-up. *American Journal of Psychiatry, 157,* 1399–1405.

Devanand, D. P., Sano, M., Tang, M. X., Taylor, S., Gurland, B. J., Wilder, D., et al. (1996). Depressed mood and the incidence of Alzheimer's disease in the elderly living in the community. *Archives of General Psychiatry, 53,* 175–182.

Drevets, W. C., Price, J. L., Simpson, J. R., Todd, R. D., Reich, T., Vannier, M., et al. (1997, April 24). Subgenual prefrontal cortex abnormalitites in mood disorders. *Nature, 386,* 824–827.

Dwivedi, Y., Rizavi, H. S., Conley, R. R., Roberts, R. C., Tamminga, C. A., & Pandey, G. N. (2003). Altered gene expression of brain-derived neurotrophic factor and receptor tyrosine kinase B in post-mortem brain of suicide subjects. *Archives of General Psychiatry, 60,* 804–815.

Evans, D. A., Bennett, D. A., Wilson, R. S., Bienias, J. L., Morris, M. C., Scherr, P. A., et al. (2003). Incidence of Alzheimer's disease in a biracial urban community: Relation to apolipoprotein E allele status. *Archives of Neurology, 60,* 185–189.

Evans, D. A., Funkenstein, H. H., Albert, M. S., Scherr, P. A., Cook, N. R., Chown, M. J., et al. (1989). Prevalance of Alzheimer's disease in a community population of older persons. Higher than previously reported. *Journal of the American Medical Association, 262,* 2551–2556.

Evans, D. A., Hebert, L. E., Beckett, L. A., Scherr, P. A., Albert, M. S., Chown, M. J., et al. (1997). Education and other measures of socioeconomic

status and risk of incident Alzheimer's disease in a defined population of older persons. *Archives of Neurology, 54,* 1399–1405.

Fratiglioni, L., Wang, H. X., Ericsson, K., Maytan, M., & Winblad, B. (2000). Influence of social network on occurrence of dementia: A community-based longitudinal study. *The Lancet, 355,* 1315–1319.

Gatz, J. L., Tyas, S. L., St. John, P., & Montgomery, P. (2005). Do depressive symptoms predict Alzheimer's disease and dementia? *Journal of Gerontology: Medical Sciences, 60A,* 744–747.

Geda, Y. E., Knopman, D. S., Mrazek, D. A., Jicha, G. A., Smith, X. X., Negash, S., et al. (2006). Depression, apolipoprotein E genotype, and the incidence of mild cognitive impairment. *Archives of Neurology, 63,* 435–440.

Graves, A. B., Bowen, J. D., Rajaram, L., McCormick, W. C., McCurry, S. M., Schellenberg, G. D., et al. (1999). Impaired olfaction as a marker for cognitive decline: Interaction with apolipoprotein E ε4 status. *Neurology, 53,* 1480–1487.

Greenwood, P. M., Lambert, C., Sunderland, T., & Parasuraman, R. (2005). Effects of apolipoprotein E genotype on spatial attention, working memory, and their interaction in healthy, middle-aged adults: Results from the National Institute of Mental Health's BIOCARD study. *Neuropsychology, 19,* 199–211.

Greenwood, P. M., Sunderland, T., Putnam, K., Levy, J., & Parasuraman, R. (2005). Scaling of visuospatial attention undergoes differential longitudinal change as a function of APOE genotype prior to old age: Results from the NIMH BIOCARD study. *Neuropsychology, 19,* 830–840.

Guillozet, A. L., Weintraub, S., Mash, D. C., & Mesulam, M. M. (2003). Neurofibrillary tangles, amyloid, and memory in aging and mild cognitive impairment. *Archives of Neurology, 60,* 729–736.

Haynie, D. A., Berg, S., Johansson, B., Gatz, M., & Zarit, S. H. (2001). Symptoms of depression in the oldest old: A longitudinal study. *Journal of Gerontology: Psychological Sciences, 56B,* P111–P118.

Hyman, B. T., Van Hoesen, G. W., Kromer, C., & Damasio, A. (1984, September 14). Alzheimer's disease: Cell specific pathology isolates the hippocampal formation. *Science, 225,* 1168–1170.

Johren, O., Flugge, G., & Fuchs, E. (1994). Hippocampal glucocorticoid receptor expression in the tree shrew: Regulation by psychosocial conflict. *Cellular and Molecular Neurobiology, 14,* 281–296.

Kanaya, A. M., Barrett-Conner, E., Gildengorin, G., & Yaffe, K. (2004). Change in cognitive function by glucose tolerance status in older adults: A 4-year prospective study of the Rancho Bernardo study cohort. *Archives of Internal Medicine, 184,* 1327–1333.

Leibson, C. L., Rocca, W. A., Hanson, V. A., Cha, R., Kokmen, E., O'Brien, P. C., et al. (1997). Risk of dementia among persons with diabetes mellitus: A population-based cohort study. *American Journal of Epidemiology, 145,* 301–308.

Logroscino, G., Kang, J. H., & Grodstein, F. (2004). Prospective study of type 2 diabetes and cognitive decline in women aged 70–81 years. *British Medical Journal, 328,* 548–551.

Louis, E. D., Tang, M. X., & Mayeux, R. (2004). Parkinsonian signs in older people in a community-based study: Risk of incident dementia. *Archives of Neurology, 61,* 1273–1276.

Magarinos, A. M., McEwan, B. S., Flugge, G., & Fuchs, E. (1996). Chronic psychosocial stress causes apical dendrite atrophy of hippocampal CA3 pyramidal neurons in subordinate tree shrews. *Journal of Neuroscience, 6,* 3534–3540.

Markesbery, W. R., Schmitt, F. A., Kryscio, R. J., Davis, D. G., Smith, C. D., & Wekstein, D. R. (2006). Neuropathologic substrate of mild cognitive impairment. *Archives of Neurology, 63,* 38–46.

Mirra, S. S., Heyman, A., McKeel, D., Sumi, S. M., Crain, B. J., Brownlee, L. M., et al. (1991). The Consortium to Establish a Registry for Alzheimer's Disease (CERAD). Part II: Standardization of the neuropathologic assessment of Alzheimer's disease. *Neurology, 41,* 479–486.

Modrego, P. J., & Ferrández, J. (2004). Depression in patients with mild cognitive impairment increases the risk of developing dementia of Alzheimer type. *Archives of Neurology, 61,* 1290–1293.

National Institute of Diabetes and Digestive and Kidney Diseases. (2002). *National diabetes statistics fact sheet: General information and national estimates on diabetes in the United States, 2000.* Bethesda, MD: U.S. Department of Health and Human Services, National Institutes of Health.

Ott, A., Stolk, R. P., van Harskamp, F., Pols, H. A., Hofman, A., & Breteler, M. M. (1999). Diabetes mellitus and the risk of dementia: The Rotterdam Study. *Neurology, 53,* 1937–1942.

Paterniti, S., Verdier-Taillefer, M.-H., Dufouil, C., & Alperovitch, A. (2002). Depressive symptoms and cognitive decline in elderly people. *British Journal of Psychiatry, 181,* 404–410.

Petersen, R. C., Parisi, J. E., Dickson, D. W., Johnson, K. A., Knopman, D. S., Boeve, B. F., et al. (2006). Neuropathologic features of amnestic mild cognitive impairment. *Archives of Neurology, 63,* 665–672.

Pitkälä, K., Kähönen-Väre, M., Valvanne, J., Strandberg, R. S., & Tilvis, R. S. (2003). Long-term changes in mood of an aged population: Repeated Zung-tests during a 10-year follow-up. *Archives of Gerontology and Geriatrics, 36,* 185–195.

Polvikoski, T., Sulkava, R., Haltia., M., Kainulainen, K., Vuorio, A., Verkkoniemi, A., et al. (1995). Apolipoprotein E, dementia, and cortical deposition of beta-amyloid protein. *New England Journal of Medicine, 333,* 1242–1247.

Radley, J. J., Sisti, H. M., Hao, J., Rocher, A. B., McCall, T., Hof, P. R., et al. (2004). Chronic behavioral stress induces apical dendritic reorganization in pyramidal neurons of the medial prefrontal cortex. *Neuroscience, 125,* 1–6.

Riley, K. P., Snowden, D. A., & Markesbery, W. R. (2002). Alzheimer's neurofibrillary pathology and the spectrum of cognitive function: Findings from The Nun Study. *Annals of Neurology, 51,* 567–577.

Sachs-Ericsson, N., Joiner, T., Plant, E. A., & Blazer, D. G. (2005). The influence of depression on cognitive decline in community-dwelling elderly persons. *American Journal of Geriatric Psychiatry, 5,* 402–408.

Schmechel, D. E., Saunders, A. M., Strittmatter, W. J., Crain, B. J, Hulette, C. M., Joo, S. H., et al. (1993). Increased amyloid beta-peptide deposition in cerebral cortex as a consequence of apolopoprotein E genotype in late-onset Alzheimer's disease. *Proceedings of the National Academy of Sciences, USA, 90,* 9649–9653.

Schneider, J. A., Bienias, J. L., Wilson, R. S., Berry-Kravis, E., Evans, D. A., & Bennett, D. A. (2005). The apolipoprotein E ε4 allele increases odds of chronic cerebral infarction detected at autopsy in older persons. *Stroke, 36,* 954–959.

Schneider, J. A., Li, J. L., Li, Y., Wilson, R. S., Kordower, J. H., & Bennett, D. A. (2006).

Neurofibrillary tangles in the substantia nigra are related to gait impairment in older persons. *Annals of Neurology, 59,* 166–173.

Schneider, J. A., Wilson, R. S., Bienias, J. L., Evans, D. A., & Bennett, D. A. (2004). Cerebral infarctions and the likelihood of dementia from Alzheimer's disease pathology. *Neurology, 62,* 1148–1155.

Schneider, J. A., Wilson, R. S., Bienias, J. L., Evans, D. A., Cochran, E. J., Arnold, S. E., et al. (2003). Relation of cerebral infarctions to dementia and cognitive function in older persons. *Neurology, 60,* 1082–1088.

Sheline, Y. I., Wang, P. W., Gado, M. H., Csernansky, J. G., & Vannier, M. W. (1996). Hippocampal atrophy in recurrent major depression. *Proceedings of the National Academy of Sciences, USA, 93,* 3908–3913.

Skarupski, K., Mendes de Leon, C. F., Bienias, J. L., Barnes, L. L., Everson-Rose, S. A., Wilson, R. S., et al. (2005). Black–white differences in depressive symptoms among older adults over time. *Journal of Gerontology: Psychological Sciences, 60B,* P136–P142.

Smith, M. A., Makino, S., Kvetnansky, R., & Post, M. (1995). Stress and glucocorticoids affect the expression of brain-derived neurotrophic factor and neurotrophin-3 mRNAs in the hippocampus. *Journal of Neuroscience, 15,* 1768–1777.

Sousa, N., Lukoyanov, N. V., Madeira, M. D., Almeida, O. F. X., & Paula-Barbosa, M. M. (2000). Reorganization of the morphology of the hippocampal neurites and synapses after stress-induced damage correlates with behavioral improvements. *Neuroscience, 97,* 253–266.

Stern, Y., Gurland, B., Tatemichi, T., Tang, M. X., Wilder, D., & Mayeux, R. (1994). Influence of education and occupation on the incidence of Alzheimer's disease. *Journal of the American Medical Association, 271,* 1004–1010.

Tabert, M. H., Liu, X., Doty, R. L., Serby, M., Zamora, D., Pelton, G. H., et al. (2005). A 10-item smell identification scale related to risk for Alzheimer's disease. *Annals of Neurology, 58,* 155–160.

Twamley, E. W., Ropacki, S. A. L., & Bondi, M. W. (2006). Neuropsychological and neuroimaging changes in preclinical Alzheimer's disease. *Journal of the International Neuropsychological Society, 12,* 707–735.

Wallace, J., & O'Hara, M. W. (1992). Increases in depressive symptomatology in the rural elderly: Results from a cross-sectional and longitudinal study. *Journal of Abnormal Psychology, 101,* 398–404.

Webster, M. J., Knable, M. B., O'Grady, J., Orthman, J., & Weickert, C. S. (2002). Regional specificity of brain glucocorticoid receptor mRNA alterations in subjects with schizophrenia and mood disorders. *Molecular Psychiatry, 7,* 985–994.

Wilson, R. S., Arnold, S. E., Schneider, J. A., Li, Y., & Bennett, D. A. (2007). Chronic distress, age-related neuropathology, and late life dementia. *Psychosomatic Medicine, 69,* 47–53.

Wilson, R. S., Arnold, S. E., Schneider, J. A., Tang, Y., & Bennett, D. A. (2007). The relation of cerebral Alzheimer's disease pathology to odor identification in old age. *Journal of Neurology, Neurosurgery, and Psychiatry, 78,* 30–35.

Wilson, R. S., Arnold, S. E., Tang, Y., & Bennett, D. A. (2006). Odor identification and decline in different cognitive domains in old age. *Neuroepidemiology, 26,* 61–67.

Wilson, R. S., Barnes, L. L., Mendes de Leon, C. F., Aggarwal, N. T., Schneider, J. A., Bach, J., et al. (2002). Depressive symptoms, cognitive decline, and risk of AD in older persons. *Neurology, 59,* 364–370.

Wilson, R. S., Bennett, D. A., Bienias, J. L., Aggarwal, N. T., Mendes de Leon, C. F., Morris, M. C., et al. (2002). Cognitive activity and incident AD in a population-based sample of older persons. *Neurology, 59,* 1910–1914.

Wilson, R. S., Bienias, J. L., Evans, D. A., & Bennett, D. A. (2004). Religious Orders Study: Overview and change in cognitive and motor speed. *Journal of Aging, Neuropsychology, and Cognition, 11,* 281–303.

Wilson, R. S., Krueger, K. R., Arnold, S. E., Schneider, J. A., Kelly, J. F., Barnes, L. L., et al. (2007). Loneliness and risk of Alzheimer's disease. *Archives of General Psychiatry, 64,* 234–240.

Wilson, R. S., Mendes de Leon, C. F., Bennett, D. A., Bienias, J. L., & Evans, D. A. (2004). Depressive symptoms and cognitive decline in a community population of older persons. *Journal of Neurology, Neurosurgery, and Psychiatry, 75,* 126–129.

Wilson, R. S., Schneider, J. A., Arnold, S. E., Tang, Y., Boyle, P. A., & Bennett, D. A. (2007). Olfactory identification and incidence of mild cognitive impairment in old age. *Archives of General Psychiatry, 64,* 802–808.

Wilson, R. S., Schneider, J. A., Bienias, J. L., Evans, D. A., & Bennett, D. A. (2003). Parkinsonian-like signs and incident Alzheimer's disease in older persons. *Archives of Neurology, 60,* 539–544.

Wilson, R. S., Schneider, J. A., Boyle, P. A., Arnold, S. E., Tang, Y., & Bennett, D. A. (2007). Chronic distress and incidence of mild cognitive impairment. *Neurology, 68,* 2085–2092.

Yaffe, K., Blackwell, T., Gore, R., Sands, L., Reus, V., & Browner, W. S. (1999). Depressive symptoms and cognitive decline in nondemented elderly women. *Archives of General Psychiatry, 56,* 425–430.

Zhang, M. Y., Katzman, R., Salmon, D., Jin, H., Cai, G. J., Wang, Z. Y., et al. (1990). The prevalence of dementia and Alzheimer's disease in Shanghai, China: Impact of age, gender, and education. *Annals of Neurology, 27,* 428–437.

Zunzunegui, M. V., Alvarado, B. E., Del Ser, T., & Otero, A. (2003). Social networks, social integration, and social engagement determine cognitive decline in community-dwelling Spanish older adults. *Journal of Gerontology: Social Sciences, 58B,* S93–S100.

19

IMAGING AGING

Present and Future

SCOTT M. HAYES AND ROBERTO CABEZA

Traditionally, cognitive aging research has been based on behavioral measures of cognitive performance such as response time and accuracy. Data have indicated that age-related decline occurs in multiple cognitive functions (e.g., speed of processing, attention, episodic memory), whereas others remain relatively well preserved (e.g., semantic knowledge). Given that cognitive processes depend on brain anatomy and physiology, previously observed behavioral changes in aging are likely intimately linked to changes in the integrity of cerebral architecture and function. As novel imaging techniques have been developed, application to age-related issues typically occurs shortly thereafter. For instance, over 60 years ago, cerebral blood flow in humans was assessed by having research participants inhale nitrous oxide and measuring the difference in nitrous oxide concentration in blood samples simultaneously collected with needles inserted in the femoral artery and in the jugular vein (Kety & Schmidt, 1945, 1948). The application

of this technique to address age-related issues followed shortly thereafter (Freyhan, Woodford, & Kety, 1951; Kety, 1956), with authors suggesting that observed reductions in cerebral blood flow in older adults reflected neuronal loss. Despite these early attempts to link cerebral changes to aging, neuroimaging of aging studies have only recently proliferated, with the development of less invasive imaging techniques, leading to significant advances in cognitive aging research.

Within the last 25 years, neuroimaging of age-related changes has typically correlated behavioral with structural neuroimaging measures, such as magnetic resonance imaging (MRI) or resting functional neuroimaging measures, such as positron emission tomography (PET), which measures blood flow and metabolism. For example, cross-sectional structural MRI studies have revealed a negative relationship between age and hippocampal volume (for a review, see Raz, 2000), and age-related hippocampal atrophy has been typically associated

AUTHORS' NOTE: This work was supported by Grants R01AG19731 and RO1AG023770 from the National Institute of Aging, awarded to Roberto Cabeza, primary investigator, and by Grant F32AG029738, awarded to Scott M. Hayes.

with reductions in episodic memory performance (Raz, Gunning-Dixon, Head, Dupuis, & Acker, 1998), although these results are not always consistent across studies (for a review, see Van Petten, 2004).

Within the last 15 years, activation neuroimaging techniques, such as functional MRI (fMRI), which measure brain activity during cognitive task performance, have continued to elucidate the relationship between cognitive aging and cerebral aging. Activation neuroimaging studies have associated aging not only with *decreases* but also with *increases* in brain activity. Whereas age-related decreases in activation are usually attributed to neurocognitive decline, age-related increases in activation are typically attributed to functional compensation. Activation imaging studies have yielded two consistent aging effects across different cognitive domains. The first effect is known as *Hemispheric Asymmetry Reduction in Older Adults* (HAROLD; Cabeza, 2002) and refers to an age-related increase in the hemisphere less activated by young adults (YA), leading to a more bilateral activation pattern in older adults (OA) than YA. The second effect is known as *Posterior–Anterior Shift in Aging* (PASA; Dennis, Daselaar, & Cabeza, 2006) and refers to an age-related reduction in occipital activity coupled with an age-related increased in prefrontal cortex (PFC) activity. Both the contralateral recruitment in HAROLD and the PFC recruitment in PASA have been attributed to compensatory mechanisms in the aging brain, an idea that has received substantial support (e.g., Cabeza, Anderson, Locantore, & McIntosh, 2002; Davis, Dennis, Daselaar, Fleck, & Cabeza, 2007).

The goal of this chapter is to briefly review recent advances in neuroimaging methods and analysis that will continue to shed light on cognitive and cerebral aging. Topics were selected on the basis of novelty and potential to elucidate age-related changes in cognition and cerebral function. We first consider advances in structural and functional neuroimaging, followed by novel imaging domains. Finally, we conclude with suggestions for methodological integration to further our understanding of the relationship between age-related cognitive and cerebral changes.

DEVELOPMENTS IN STRUCTURAL NEUROIMAGING

Longitudinal Neuroimaging

The majority of age-related structural neuroimaging studies have used a cross-sectional approach (for a review, see Raz, 2000), which is insensitive to individual differences and susceptible to cohort effects. A handful of longitudinal structural MRI studies have recently begun to address these limitations (Persson et al., 2006; Pfefferbaum, Sullivan, Rosenbloom, & Mathalon, 1998; Resnick, Pham, Kraut, Zonderman, & Davatzikos, 2003; Scahill et al., 2003). For example, in a series of studies by Raz and colleagues, healthy adults (age range at baseline: 20–77 years) were scanned 5 years apart. Differential reductions in volume of basal ganglia structures were observed (Raz et al., 2003). Although decreases in volume of the caudate nucleus and putamen were predicted, the reductions in volume were larger than expected based on previous cross-sectional estimates. Furthermore, although previous cross-sectional studies suggested that the volume of the globus pallidus was stable, significant reductions in palladium volume were observed. Finally, the results indicated that shrinkage in the basal ganglia was not restricted to OA: Shrinkage was linear across the life span.

In contrast to the basal ganglia, medial temporal regions show differential rates of shrinkage across the life span (Raz, Rodrigue, Head, Kennedy, & Acker, 2004). In adults over age 50, clear annualized reductions in volume were observed in the hippocampus and entorhinal cortex. In adults less than 50 years old, less severe annualized volume reductions were observed in the hippocampus, and there was essentially no loss of entorhinal cortex volume. Furthermore, the results indicated strikingly greater atrophy in the hippocampus relative to the entorhinal cortex. Finally, Rodrigue and Raz (2004) reported that although greater annualized volume reductions were observed in the hippocampus and PFC relative to entorhinal cortex, only change in entorhinal cortex volume predicted episodic memory performance, results that are relatively consistent with a previous resting PET study (de Leon et al., 2001).

The aforementioned longitudinal studies highlight age-related changes, as opposed to age differences (cross-sectional comparisons of YA vs. OA). It should be noted that longitudinal studies have weaknesses as well. Data collected in longitudinal aging studies are typically derived from the healthiest portion of the population, because follow-up data collection is negatively impacted by mortality in OA, morbidity in middle-aged adults, and mobility in YA (the "three M's"; see Raz, 2005, for additional discussion). Despite this potential selection bias, differential rates of volume reduction among brain regions and across the life span were identified. These results raise interesting questions about the aging brain, such as whether functional compensation can occur in the face of structural degradation. It will be important for future studies to continue to address the relationship between longitudinal changes in cognitive function and neural structure.

Diffusion Tensor Imaging

The development of diffusion tensor imaging (DTI) represents a significant advance in neuroimaging white matter in the brain (Basser, Mattiello, & LeBihan, 1994). White matter was previously presented on MRI as a relatively homogeneous structure. With DTI, direction (e.g., anterior–posterior, superior–inferior, right–left) of white matter structures can be determined and, furthermore, specific white matter tracts (e.g., cingulum bundle) can be identified. DTI reflects water diffusion, which in the brain is restricted by axons, cell bodies, and myelin (for technical review of diffusion properties and MRI, see Beaulieu, 2002, and LeBihan, 2003). In regard to white matter, less diffusion reflects greater white matter integrity. Two measures of diffusion, fractional anisotropy (FA) and the apparent diffusion coefficient, are commonly reported. FA measures the directionality of movement of water molecules, with values ranging between 0 and 1. Higher FA (closer to 1) is assumed to reflect greater white matter integrity. The apparent diffusion coefficient measures the diffusion of water, and in this case, lower values are assumed to reflect greater white matter integrity.

In healthy OA, reductions in FA appear to follow an anterior-to-posterior gradient in the brain (Head et al., 2004; Madden et al., 2007; Pfefferbaum et al., 2000; Salat et al., 2005). This trend fits with the idea of "last in, first out": Frontal lobe white matter is the latest to mature, increasing in volume into the early 40s, and it is the first one to show the deleterious effects of aging (Bartzokis et al., 2003). Decreases in indicators of frontal lobe white matter (e.g., FA values) have been associated with measures of processing speed and reasoning (Stebbins, Carillo, et al., 2001; Stebbins, Poldrack, et al., 2001). Madden, Whiting, et al. (2004) found that decreased reaction time was predicted by FA in the splenium of YA, but in the anterior limb of the internal capsule in OA, suggesting that performance in OA is more dependent on the integrity of fronto-striatal circuitry rather than the frontal circuitry alone.

To date, most DTI studies of aging have used a regions-of-interest approach whereby FA or apparent diffusion coefficient are measured within a white matter volume that is crossed by several different tracts (for a review, see Moseley, 2002). Whereas the regions-of-interest approach does not provide independent measures for the various fiber tracts passing through a region-of-interest, these measures can be provided by the technique of quantitative fiber tracking (Corouge, Gouttard, & Gerig, 2004; Mori & van Zijil, 2002; Xu, Mori, Solaiyappan, van Zijl, & Davatzikos, 2002). Using this method, FA or apparent diffusion coefficient values for different groups of individuals (YA vs. OA) can be compared across the entire fiber or for sections of the fiber and can be correlated with cognitive performance. For example, the effects of aging on cross-hemispheric genu fibers, which connect left and right anterior PFC regions, are obvious even in individual participants (see Figure 19.1 inset). Mean FA can be separately extracted for segments of the fiber, and the effects of aging can be assessed (see Figure 19.1). The effects of aging on each segment of each fiber can be linked to the effects of aging on behavior by means of correlations and regression analyses. Of course, these analyses can be performed on multiple fibers, such as the cingulum bundle, uncinate fasciculus, and so on.

There are several limitations to DTI. First, the spatial resolution of DTI (millimeters) is poor compared with postmortem tract tracers

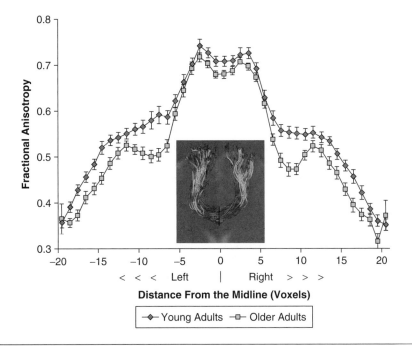

Figure 19.1   Results of Cross-Genu Fiber Tracking in Young and Older Adults

The image inset displays multiple fibers identified by quantitative fiber tracking in a single individual, with the black bar in the center of the fibers representing the midline. The graph represents fractional anisotropy values in a group of young and older adults. X-axis units correspond to voxel distance to the left (negative values) and to the right (positive values) of the midline ($x = 0$) of cross-genu fibers. Voxel size was 2 mm³.

(μm), which can identify single axons. Indeed, the spatial resolution of voxels using DTI consists of a large number of axons. Furthermore, DTI cannot distinguish between efferent and afferent projections. Nevertheless, the potential of DTI to inform cognitive aging has yet to be fully tapped, because few studies have applied quantitative fiber tracking to age-related issues.

DEVELOPMENTS IN FUNCTIONAL NEUROIMAGING

Hybrid Designs

The first generation of functional neuroimaging studies used *blocked designs*, in which trials belonging to different experimental conditions had to be presented in different blocks or scans. About a decade ago, functional neuroimaging studies started using *event-related designs*, in which trials from different conditions could be randomly intermixed. Blocked and event-related designs sometimes yield different results, not only because of differences in cognitive strategies but also because of differences in sustained versus transient neural activity. *Sustained activations* persist across several trials of the same kind and tend to reflect mental states associated with the task, whereas *transient activations* decay between trials and tend to reflect cognitive operations specific to each trial. Given that blocked designs emphasize sustained activations and event-related designs, transient activations, the results of these two kinds of designs do not need to be identical.

A few years ago, researchers developed a new kind of design known as *hybrid designs* (e.g., Donaldson, 2004; Otten, Henson, & Rugg, 2002; Visscher et al., 2003), which essentially combine the features of blocked and event-related designs and allow simultaneous measures of sustained and transient activations (see Figure 19.2). Similar to blocked designs, hybrid designs consist of blocks separated by interblock intervals (represented in Figure 19.2 by the large + symbols) and, similar to event-related designs, the trials within the blocks are separated by jittered intertrial intervals (represented in Figure 19.2 by small + symbols). In a hybrid design, sustained activity is identified by comparing block activity to interblock activity, and transient activity is identified by comparing trial activity to intertrial activity.

The use of a hybrid design provides a within-subject method for reconciling conflicting results between blocked and event-related studies of cognitive aging. For example, whereas most of the blocked PET and fMRI studies of episodic encoding have found age-related *decreases* in PFC (Anderson, Iidaka et al., 2000; Cabeza, Grady, et al., 1997; Grady, Bernstein, Beig, & Siegenthaler, 2002; Grady et al., 1995; Logan, Sanders, Snyder, Morris, & Buckner, 2002; Schiavetto, Kohler, Grady, Winocur, & Moscovitch, 2002), the few event-related fMRI studies in this domain have found age-related *increases* in PFC activity (Gutchess et al., 2005; Morcom, Good, Frackowiak, & Rugg, 2003). Although this inconsistency may reflect differences between general encoding activity and successful encoding activity, an intriguing possibility is that it reflects differences between the effects of aging on sustained versus transient activity.

This possibility was investigated in a recent study from our laboratory that used a quasi-hybrid design that included rests between trials but not between blocks (Dennis et al., 2006). This study yielded a dissociation between the effects of aging on sustained versus transient activity: Aging reduced sustained encoding activity in right PFC but increased transient encoding activity in left PFC. One possible explanation of these effects is that OA have a deficit in sustained encoding activity, possibly due to a decline in sustained attention, for which they attempt to compensate by recruiting additional transient activity. More generally, this finding suggests a possible solution for observed inconsistencies between blocked and event-related functional neuroimaging studies of encoding and aging.

Hybrid designs may also clarify age-related changes in the default network. Functional neuroimaging studies have revealed a network of brain regions, including anterior and posterior midline cortices and lateral parietal cortex, that are consistently deactivated during attentionally demanding cognitive tasks compared with resting baseline (Greicius, Krasnow, Reiss, & Menon, 2003; McKiernan, Kaufman, Kucera-Thompson, & Binder, 2003). Raichle and colleagues have suggested these regions comprise a *default network*, which is normally active during conscious rest but must be able to temporarily shut down or

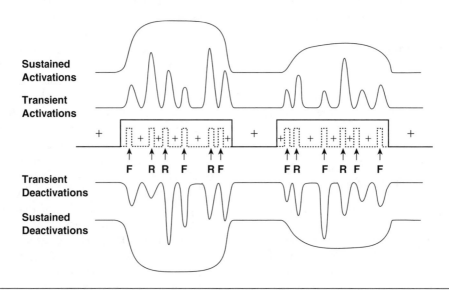

Figure 19.2   Schematic of Hybrid Blocked/Event-Related Design, Illustrating, in This Example, Modeled Responses of Sustained and Transient Activations and Deactivations in a Memory Paradigm

NOTES: Large plus signs (+) indicate between block fixation/rest periods, whereas smaller plus signs (+) indicate variable duration intertrial fixation/rest events (i.e., jitter) that allow for the deconvolution of the hemodynamic response. F = forgotten trials; R = remembered trials.

deactivate during demanding cognitive tasks, when resources are needed for efficient cognitive performance (Gusnard & Raichle, 2001; Raichle et al., 2001). Daselaar, Prince, and Cabeza (2004) found that regions of the default network, such as posterior parietal and posterior midline cortices, showed greater deactivations during encoding for stimuli that were subsequently remembered than for those that were subsequently forgotten. Regarding aging, there is evidence that deactivations of the default network during encoding are attenuated in healthy OA and even more so in adults diagnosed with mild cognitive impairment and Alzheimer's disease (AD; Celone et al., 2006; Lustig et al., 2003; Rombouts, Barkhof, Goekoop, Stam, & Scheltens, 2005). It is very tempting to link these two lines of evidence and suggest that a failure to deactivate the default network during encoding contributes to encoding deficits in healthy and pathological aging. However, the link we found between deactivations and successful encoding was observed for transient deactivations in an event-related design, whereas the link between aging and deactivation failure was observed for sustained deactivations in a blocked design. Thus, to link these findings it will be critical to measure both transient and sustained deactivations using a hybrid design.

Single-Trial Analysis

Single- or *individual-trial analysis* is a technique in which each trial (or phases within a trial) is entered as its own regressor in the statistical analyses, as opposed to averaging trials across conditions (Rissman, Gazzaley, & D'Esposito, 2004). Thus, single-trial analysis yields an activation measure (parameter estimate) for each trial for every individual participant, which can then be linked within participants with their performance on the corresponding trial. These data can then be entered into a regression model and used to predict memory performance at the individual-trial level (Daselaar, Fleck, & Cabeza, 2006; Daselaar, Fleck, Dobbins, Madden, & Cabeza, 2006).

For instance, results of a recent event-related fMRI study compared the effects of aging on recollection-related versus familiarity-related brain activity during an episodic recognition task (Daselaar, Fleck, Dobbins, et al., 2006). The effects of aging yielded a double dissociation within the medial temporal lobe: Whereas recollection-related activity in the hippocampus was reduced by aging, familiarity-related activity in rhinal cortex was increased by aging. These results suggested that OA compensated for deficits in recollection by relying more on familiarity. Results of single-trial analysis revealed that recognition responses were determined only by hippocampal activity in YA but by hippocampal and rhinal activity in OA (see Figure 19.3), providing converging evidence for an age-related shift from recollection to familiarity-based processing in OA.

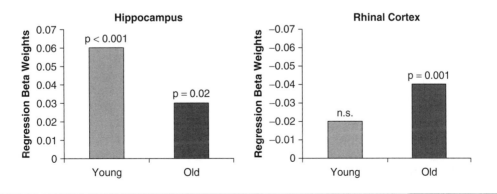

Figure 19.3   Results of Single-Trial Analysis

The results revealed that recognition responses were predicted only by hippocampal activity in young adults but by hippocampal and rhinal activity in older adults, providing evidence for an age-related shift from recollection to familiarity-based memory processing in older adults.

Functional Connectivity Analysis

It is obvious that cognition depends not only on the functions of various brain regions but also on their interactions, yet the vast majority of functional neuroimaging studies have focused on brain regions activated during a cognitive task, with very few studies addressing the issue of functional connectivity. The situation is similar among functional neuroimaging studies of cognitive aging, although it is clear that age-related cognitive decline may reflect a combination of deficits in particular regions and deficits in communications between regions. The latter idea has been described as the disconnection hypothesis (Bartzokis et al., 2004; O'Sullivan et al., 2001) and can be investigated using functional connectivity analyses.

Functional connectivity analyses also can be used to investigate compensatory mechanisms in the aging brain. For example, using functional connectivity analysis, Cabeza, McIntosh, Tulving, Nyberg, and Grady (1997) demonstrated a difference in neural networks in YA and OA, because more bilateral PFC interactions were observed in OA during episodic recall relative to YA (HAROLD pattern). In the aforementioned study by Daselaar, Fleck, Dobbins, et al. (2006), data from parametric and single-trial analyses indicated that OA rely more heavily on familiarity than recollection during a word recognition task, suggesting a top-down modulation from PFC on rhinal cortex. To explore this possibility, a functional connectivity analysis was performed in which single-trial hippocampal and rhinal activations were correlated with activations in the rest of the brain for the corresponding trials. Whereas YA showed greater correlations between the hippocampus and posterior regions (retrosplenial cortex and left parieto-temporal) that were also associated with recollection, OA showed greater connectivity between rhinal cortex and bilateral PFC regions (see Figure 19.4). The results of the functional connectivity analysis support the hypothesis that OA compensate for hippocampal deficits by relying more on rhinal cortex, possibly mediated via top-down modulation from PFC. Additional studies using functional connectivity analysis highlight the difference in effective connectivity between the hippocampus

and other brain regions in YA and OA, even under circumstances in which behavioral performance and hippocampal activation are similar (Cabeza, McIntosh, Grady, et al., 1997; Della-Maggiore et al., 2000; Grady, McIntosh, & Craik, 2003).

NOVEL IMAGING DOMAINS

Neurotransmitter Imaging

Imaging of neurotransmitter systems has become more prevalent with advances in PET radioligand development. Early neurotransmitter imaging studies, while representing significant methodological advances, suffered from cross-binding with multiple receptors, for example, serotonin (5-HT) and dopamine (DA; Iyo & Yamasaki, 1993; Wong et al., 1984). Although deficits in cholinergic function in aging and AD are well documented (e.g., Davies & Maloney, 1976; Strong, 1998), few *in vivo* neuroimaging studies have addressed the issue. Two PET studies have reported negative relationships between age and serotonin receptor density (Meltzer et al., 1998; Rosier et al., 1996). A more recent report found no correlation between cognitive function and serotonin receptor density (Borg, Andree, Lundberg, Halldin, & Farde, 2006). Because of limited data, in this section we focus primarily on imaging the DA system.

DA systems are critical for higher-order cognitive functions. For example, cognitive deficits are often observed in Parkinson's disease patients, whose DA deficit is attributed to cell loss in the substantia nigra, a major source of DA production. The role of DA in cognition is also supported by ontogenetic (Pendleton, Rasheed, Roychowdhury, & Hillman, 1998) and phylogenetic evidence (for a discussion of the role of DA in the evolution of human intelligence, see Previc, 1999) and by computational models (Li, Lindenberger, & Sikstrom, 2001). There are two main families of DA receptors, D_1 and D_2. In the presynaptic terminal, the DA transporter (DAT) protein regulates synaptic DA concentration. Radioligands have been developed to bind to the D_1 (e.g., Farde, Halldin, Stone-Elander, & Sedvall, 1987) or D_2 (Farde,

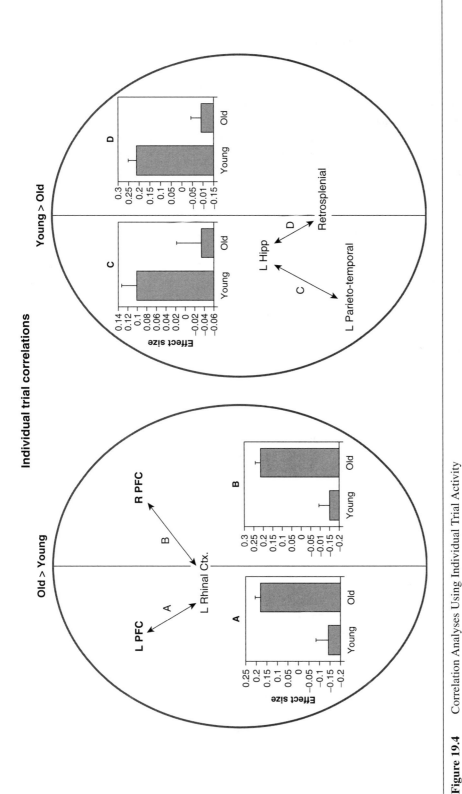

Figure 19.4 Correlation Analyses Using Individual Trial Activity

The analyses showed an age-related increase in functional connectivity within a rhinal–bilateral frontal network (A, B) coupled with an age-related decrease in connectivity within a hippocampal–retrosplenial/parietotemporal network (C, D).

SOURCE: From "Effects of Healthy Aging on Hippocampal and Rhinal Memory Functions: An Event-Related fMRI Study," by S. M. Daselaar, M. S. Fleck, I. G. Dobbins, D. J. Madden, and R. Cabeza, 2006, *Cerebral Cortex, 16*, p. 1779. Copyright 2006 by Oxford University Press. Adapted with permission.

NOTE: L = left; R = right; PFC = prefrontal cortex; Ctx. = cortex; Hipp = hippocampus.

Hall, Ehrin, & Sedvall, 1986) receptor and DAT (Erixon-Lindroth et al., 2005; for a recent review of DA imaging, see Brooks, 2006).

In vivo studies using PET and single photon emission computed tomography (SPECT) have found loss of striatal D_1 and D_2 receptor binding across adulthood, with age-related decreases ranging between 7% and 10% per decade (Antonini & Leenders, 1993; Ichise et al., 1998; Suhara et al., 1991; Wang et al., 1998) and, in striatal DAT binding, with rates of decline of 4.4% to 8% per decade (Rinne, Sahlberg, Ruottinen, Nagren, & Lehikoinen, 1998; van Dyck et al., 1995). DA loss has been observed in frontal, temporal, and occipital cortices as well as the hippocampus and thalamus (Inoue et al., 2001; Kaasinen et al., 2000). Given the role of fronto-striatal circuits in cognition (Cummings, 1993), striatal DA deficits could account for age-related cognitive deficits associated with PFC dysfunction. Indeed, age-related deficits in striatal DA have been associated with reductions in episodic memory (Bäckman et al., 2000; Erixon-Lindroth et al., 2005), executive function (Erixon-Lindroth et al., 2005; Mozley, Gur, et al., 2001; Volkow, Gur, et al., 1998), and motor performance (Mozley, Gur, et al., 2001; Wang et al., 1998), and striatal DA markers have been shown to predict cognitive performance after controlling for the effects of age (Bäckman et al., 2000; Volkow, Gur, et al., 1998). Furthermore, reductions in striatal DA function have been shown to mediate age-related cognitive deficits (Erixon-Lindroth et al., 2005).

Future research in DA imaging will continue to address neurochemical relationships to cognitive function. One issue that remains to be addressed is the lack of differential age or neuroanatomical effects between D_1 and D_2 imaging, despite differences in preferential localization of D_1 and D_2 within striatal circuitry. Research with larger sample sizes, comparative DA imaging, and inclusion of cognitive measures may elucidate age-related changes within specific striatal circuits.

Imaging Alzheimer's Disease Biomarkers

AD is characterized by the presence of beta-amyloid plaques and tau neurofibrillary tangles. Because of recent advances in radioligand development (for a review, see Mathis, Wang, & Klunk, 2004), *in vivo* neuroimaging of AD neuropathology is now possible (see Figure 19.5; for review of AD neuropathology imaging technologies, see Bacskai, Klunk, Mathis, & Hyman, 2002). Thus far in humans, *in vivo* imaging of AD biomarkers has used PET, and primarily two radioligand tracers, either Pittsburgh Compound B (PIB) or FDDNP (for a conceptual discussion of quantification of amyloid burden, see Shoghi-Jadid et al., 2005). PIB and FDDNP differ on the basis of whether the tracer binds only beta-amyloid (PIB) or whether it binds beta-amyloid plaques and tau neurofibrillary tangles (FDDNP). Imaging results are typically reported in terms of residence time or standard uptake value, which are based on ratios of the amount of tracer detected in a given brain region relative to a region typically unaffected by AD, such as the pons or cerebellum. Longer residence times or greater standard uptake values indicate binding of the tracer and are assumed to reflect greater density of AD neuropathology.

At present, we are aware of only four AD biomarker imaging studies in humans. The initial report used PET with FDDNP, which is reported to bind beta-amyloid plaques and tau neurofibrillary tangles (Shoghi-Jadid et al., 2002). The results indicated increased residence time of the probe in medial temporal lobe (MTL) regions of probable AD patients relative to control participants, and residence times correlated with scores on the Mini-Mental State Exam, immediate verbal recall, and delayed figure recall. Brain regions exhibiting increased residence times appeared to match those showing glucose hypometabolism as measured by FDG (glucose) PET. In another study, Klunk et al. (2004) reported increased retention of a beta-amyloid probe (PIB) in association cortices of AD patients relative to control participants, corresponding to postmortem assessments of plaque accumulation in AD. Equivalent probe retention was observed in brain regions typically preserved in AD. Furthermore, probe retention was inversely correlated with glucose metabolism, consistent with the observations of Shoghi-Jadid et al. (2002). Using a novel beta-amyloid tracer and PIB, Verhoeff et al. (2004) reported results consistent with those of Klunk et al. (2004).

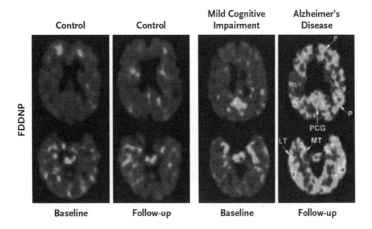

Figure 19.5 Example of FDDNP–Positron Emission Tomography Scans in a Representative Control Participant at Baseline and 2-Year Follow-Up and a Patient With Mild Cognitive Impairment Who Developed Alzheimer's Disease

SOURCE: Adapted from Small, G. W., Kepe, V., Ercoli, L. M., Siddarth, P., Bookheimer, S. Y., Miller, K. J., et al. (2006). PET of brain amyloid and tau in mild cognitive impairment. *New England Journal of Medicine, 355*(25), 2652–2663. Copyright © 2006 Massachusetts Medical Society. All rights reserved.

NOTE: Light gray areas correspond to high FDDNP values. F = frontal; P = parietal; PCG = posterior cingulate; LT = lateral temporal; MT = medial temporal.

In the most comprehensive AD biomarker imaging study to date, structural MRI, FDG (glucose) PET, and FDDNP PET were performed on participants (age range: 49–84 years) classified as normal, with mild cognitive impairment, or with AD, on the basis of comprehensive neuropsychological testing (Small et al., 2006). Results indicated that FDDNP PET more accurately distinguished among unimpaired participants, those with mild cognitive impairment, and those with AD than FDG PET and MRI (volume of the medial temporal lobes). In the only participant for whom postmortem data were available, binding of FDDNP PET corresponded well to beta-amyloid and tau immunohistochemical staining. Finally, in a small subset of participants for whom follow-up data (mean duration: 2 years) were available, the three participants exhibiting cognitive deterioration also exhibited increases in FDDNP binding from 5.5% to 11%, whereas minimal increases in FDDNP binding (less than 3%) were observed in 9 cognitively stable control participants.

There are several challenges facing the utility of amyloid imaging, namely development of a probe that crosses the blood–brain barrier and binds selectively to AD neuropathology (Nichols, Pike, Cai, & Innis, 2006). Accumulation of the radioligand is typically not specific to beta-amyloid, because the probe initially accumulates the most in the pons, an area typically unaffected by AD, and least in the hippocampus, one of the areas most affected by AD. Over time, however, the pattern reverses, as the probe clears from the pons yet remains in the hippocampus. Concerns regarding the ratio of the imaging probe in the hippocampus relative to the pons remain (Bacskai et al., 2002), and current methods may not be sensitive to identification of AD in the prodromal phase. The current promise of amyloid imaging resides in *in vivo* assessment of drug efficacy for medications designed to reduce plaque and/or tangle burden in AD patients.

Imaging Genetics

Genetic information and neuroimaging have been used to identify brain-related changes in individuals at risk for disease, with most age-relevant research to date focusing on apolipoprotein E (APOE) status, a gene in which the ε4 allele shows a dose-related effect on risk and age of onset of AD (Corder et al., 1993; Saunders et al., 1993). In a landmark study, Reiman and colleagues (1996) observed reductions in glucose metabolism in posterior cingulate, parietal, temporal and PFC of cognitively intact adults (50–65 years old) at risk for AD (homozygous APOE ε4 allele), the same regions exhibiting reductions in glucose metabolism in probable AD patients (Alexander, Chen, Pietrini, Rapoport, & Reiman, 2002; Minoshima, Frey, Foster, & Kuhl, 1995). A similar pattern of abnormal glucose reductions was observed in younger adults (20–39 years old) at risk for AD (one APOE ε4 allele; Reiman et al., 2004), and APOE ε4 gene dose (homozygotes > heterozygotes > noncarriers) has been shown to correlate with lower glucose metabolism in posterior cingulate, precuneus, and parietotemporal and frontal cortex (Reiman et al., 2005).

In addition to changes in glucose metabolism, differences in patterns of fMRI activation between APOE ε4 and homozygous ε3 carriers have been observed while scanning during an active memory task (Bookheimer et al., 2000). Despite equivalent behavioral performance (as measured outside the scanner), increased activation in the medial temporal lobes (hippocampus and parahippocampal gyrus) and PFC was observed during episodic memory encoding and recall in ε4 carriers relative to homozygous ε3 carriers. In a subset of adults tested 2 years later, subsequent verbal memory decline was associated with increased activation in the left hemisphere at baseline, which was attributed to a compensatory response. An additional report indicated that the compensatory response was specific to the requirements of the episodic memory task, because a difference in activation pattern was not observed in ε4 carriers and homozygous ε3 carriers on a working memory task (Burggren, Small, Sabb, & Bookheimer, 2002).

Whereas imaging genetics of healthy and pathological aging has primarily focused on APOE, the future of age-related imaging genetics will likely incorporate other candidate genes associated with episodic memory performance, hippocampal function, or PFC function. For example, the Ser allele of the disrupted-in-schizophrenia 1

(DISC1) gene, which is primarily expressed in the hippocampus, has been associated with reductions in hippocampal volume. Moreover, decreased hippocampal activation has been observed during a working memory (n-back) task and during episodic encoding and retrieval of neutral scenes in healthy participants with homozygous Ser alleles relative to participants with homozygous Cys alleles (Callicott et al., 2005).

The COMT (catechol-o-methyltransferase) gene has received a great deal of attention in schizophrenia research because of its role in metabolism of DA and associated deficits in DA and prefrontal function in schizophrenia. The Val allele of COMT catabolizes DA approximately four times faster than the Met allele, leading to the hypothesis that individuals with Val/Val alleles on the COMT gene would have lower levels of prefrontal DA and therefore experience inefficient prefrontal function and deficits on tasks of executive function. During a working memory task, increased fMRI activation (greater inefficiency) in dorsolateral PFC and anterior cingulate was observed in individuals with homozygous Val on the COMT gene relative to Val/Met individuals (Egan et al., 2001). Moreover, Val/Met COMT individuals had greater activation than Met/Met COMT. Because DA plays a critical role in cognitive function, as previously discussed, the COMT gene has implications for aging as well.

Genetic variation in brain-derived neurotrophic factor (BDNF) has also been associated with differential patterns of cognitive performance and brain activation. Decreased episodic memory performance was observed in individuals with Val/Met BDNF relative to Val/Val (Egan et al., 2003). Furthermore, Val/Met BDNF individuals failed to deactivate the hippocampus during a working memory task, whereas Val/Val BDNF patterns exhibited normal activity.

Imaging genetics studies highlight the potential utility of combining genotype and neuroimaging. In each of the aforementioned studies, groups were matched for age, education, gender, and behavioral performance, yet differences in brain activity, as measured by PET or fMRI, were associated with allelic variation. Despite equivalent cognitive task performance, functional neuroimaging can reveal biological effects of genetic variability, even when relatively small sample sizes ($n < 20$) are used. Because of complex interactions between genes and between genes and the environment, these studies represent the beginning of a promising research endeavor. Indeed, many relatively basic questions remain unaddressed. For example, genetic variations within APOE, COMT, and BDNF, when considered in isolation, have implications for hippocampal function and episodic memory. Thus far, they have not been considered in relation to one another. Do genetic variants of COMT and BDNF elicit further inefficient processing within the hippocampus or increase risk for AD in APOE ε4 carriers? Indeed, as imaging genetics continues to develop, more elegant neuroimaging designs and more sophisticated questions will be addressed.

CONCLUSION

Technological advances have enabled the *in vivo* assessment of cerebral structure and function, leading to a new field of aging research, the cognitive neuroscience of aging (see Cabeza, Nyberg, & Park, 2005). As indicated in Figure 19.6, neural structure is a prerequisite for resting neural function, which in turn is a prerequisite for cognition-related activity. The imaging tools (identified in italics in the figure) provide measures of different but interconnected aspects of the neural basis of cognitive aging (identified in boldface in the figure). Indicators of neuropathological disease processes, such as plaques and tangles, are also identified in Figure 19.6, as are factors that can influence their expression, such as genotype and environment, all of which can impact cognitive function.

Clarification of brain structure–function–cognition relationships will require the integration of multiple imaging techniques, such as DTI and fMRI data. Indeed, several reports integrating DTI and fMRI were published recently (Madden et al., 2007; Oleson, Nagy, Westerberg, & Klingberg, 2003; Persson et al., 2006; Takahashi, Ohki, & Kim, 2007). Persson et al. (2006) provide a particularly nice example of multimethod imaging as they reported fMRI, DTI, structural MRI, and longitudinal data. They compared FA in regions of the corpus callosum and fMRI activation in OA whose episodic memory performance declined across a decade relative to those whose memory performance remained stable. In memory-stable and memory-declining OA, equivalent levels of fMRI activation were found in left prefrontal regions. However, increased activation was observed in right ventral PFC in memory-declining relative to -stable OA. In the genu of the corpus callosum, FA was significantly lower in the memory decline relative to stable OA. Furthermore, FA in the genu correlated negatively with right ventral prefrontal activity; that is, decreased white matter integrity in the genu was associated with increased ventral prefrontal activity. Finally, Persson et al. (2006) reported reductions in hippocampal volume in memory-declining OA. This study highlights the richness of data that can be acquired and simultaneously assessed in a single neuroimaging study and the multiple measures that can be associated with age-related memory changes within subjects.

Although not reported by Persson et al. (2006), integration of functional connectivity analysis, which measures the relations of activations within the brain (Daselaar, Fleck, Dobbins, et al., 2006; McIntosh, 1999), with DTI tractography, could offer structurally constrained and biologically plausible models of neural networks. Combining fMRI and DTI allows one to assess the structural integrity of white matter tracts that presumably connect regions of activation identified by functional connectivity analyses.

Turning to genetic imaging, consideration of multiple genes and age-related changes represents an interesting step forward and could provide informative data into theoretical debate regarding age-related changes in cognitive function. For instance, if hippocampal dysfunction (as measured by fMRI) is observed in individuals with the Ser/Ser allele of DISC1, is hippocampal dysfunction attenuated by the Met/Met variant of COMT, which is associated with enhanced PFC function? Are individuals with the Met/Met variant of COMT more likely to exhibit neural compensation in the form of HAROLD or PASA pattern due to enhanced PFC function? Future studies aimed at addressing age-related compensation and dedifferentiation will need to address these questions.

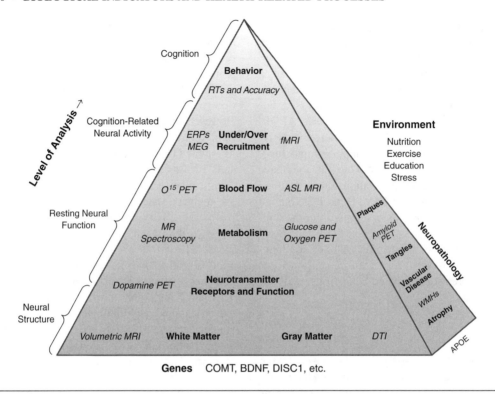

Figure 19.6   Imaging Techniques Measure Different Levels of Neural Phenomena

NOTES: Imaging tools are presented in italics type, whereas the phenomena they measure are presented in boldface type. The level of analysis is noted on the left in a hierarchical fashion, although a degree of codependence among levels is noted (e.g., gray matter structural integrity is dependent on blood flow). RT = response time; ERPs = event-related potentials; MEG = magnetoencephalography; fMRI = functional magnetic resonance imaging; PET = positron emission tomography; ASL MRI = arterial spin labeling magnetic resonance imaging; MR = magnetic resonance; DTI = diffusion tensor imaging; WMH = white matter hyperintensities; APOE = apolipoprotein E; COMT = catechol-*o*-methyltransferase; BDNF = brain-derived neurotrophic factor; DISC1 = disrupted-in-schizophrenia 1 gene.

In addition, although we have discussed age-related changes and resting DA imaging studies, DA activation imaging studies have yet to be applied to issues regarding healthy aging. Thus far, DA activation imaging studies have measured DA release while playing a video game (Koepp et al., 1998), learning a motor sequencing task (Lawrence & Brooks, 1999), and performing a rewarded or unrewarded visual search task (Sawamoto et al., 2006). Advances in the cognitive neuroscience of aging will likely include application of DA activation imaging studies to age-related issues. An obvious important integration of techniques would be the incorporation of assessment of allelic variation of the COMT gene, which is associated with enhanced PFC function, to resting and activation DA imaging studies.

Multiple noninvasive *in vivo* neuroimaging techniques are available to assess the integrity of the human brain across the life span. Neuroimaging remains a rapidly developing field, with breakthroughs in PET and MRI methods and design continuing to provide novel images of physiological indicators of brain function. Data derived from structural, resting functional, activation, neuropathological, and genetic imaging methods have revealed significant age-related changes throughout the brain. Based on the level of the neural indicator that each technique measures, these imaging methods have complementary strengths and weaknesses. The major challenge for the field of cognitive neuroscience of aging will be the simultaneous assessment of data collected from these various imaging techniques to identify the causal relationship between changes in cerebral and cognitive function. One way to address this issue is through the use of a combination of imaging techniques and, furthermore, to interpret the results of imaging studies within a given modality in relation to those attained from complementary imaging modalities.

REFERENCES

Alexander, G. E., Chen, K., Pietrini, P., Rapoport, S. I., & Reiman, E. M. (2002). Longitudinal PET evaluation of cerebral metabolic decline in dementia: A potential outcome measure in Alzheimer's disease treatment studies. *American Journal of Psychiatry, 159,* 738–745.

Anderson, N. D., Iidaka, T., Cabeza, R., Kapur, S., McIntosh, A. R., & Craik, F. I. (2000). The effects of divided attention on encoding- and retrieval-related brain activity: A PET study of younger and older adults. *Journal of Cognitive Neuroscience, 12,* 775–792.

Antonini, A., & Leenders, K. L. (1993). Dopamine D2 receptors in normal human brain—Effect of age measured by positron emission tomography (PET) and [C-11] raclopride. In *Alzheimer's disease: Amyloid precursor proteins, signal transduction, and neuronal transplantation* (pp. 81–85). New York: New York Academy of Sciences.

Bäckman, L., Ginovart, N., Dixon, R. A., Wahlin, T. B. R., Wahlin, A., Halldin, C., et al. (2000). Age-related cognitive deficits mediated by changes in the striatal dopamine system. *American Journal of Psychiatry, 157,* 635–637.

Bacskai, B. J., Klunk, W. E., Mathis, C. A., & Hyman, B. T. (2002). Imaging amyloid-beta deposits in vivo. *Journal of Cerebral Blood Flow and Metabolism, 22,* 1035–1041.

Bartzokis, G., Cummings, J. L., Sultzer, D., Henderson, V. W., Nuechterlein, K. H., & Mintz, J. (2003). White matter structural integrity in healthy aging adults and patients with Alzheimer disease—A magnetic resonance imaging study. *Archives of Neurology, 60,* 393–398.

Bartzokis, G., Sultzer, D., Lu, P. H., Neuchterlein, K. H., Mintz, J., & Cummings, J. L. (2004). Heterogeneous age-related breakdown of white matter structural integrity: Implications for cortical "disconnection" in aging and Alzheimer's disease. *Neurobiology of Aging, 25,* 843–851.

Basser, P. J., Mattiello, J., & LeBihan, D. (1994). MR diffusion tensor spectroscopy and imaging. *Biophysical Journal, 66,* 259–267.

Beaulieu, C. (2002). The basis of anisotropic water diffusion in the nervous system—A technical review. *NMR in Biomedicine, 15,* 435–455.

Bookheimer, S. Y., Strojwas, M. H., Cohen, M. S., Saunders, A. M., Pericak-Vance, M. A., Mazziotta, J. C., et al. (2000). Patterns of brain activation in people at risk for Alzheimer's disease. *New England Journal of Medicine, 343,* 450–456.

Borg, J., Andree, B., Lundberg, J., Halldin, C., & Farde, L. (2006). Search for correlations between serotonin 5-HT1A receptor expression and cognitive functions—A strategy in translational psychopharmacology. *Psychopharmacology, 185,* 389–394.

Brooks, D. J. (2006). Dopaminergic action beyond its effects on motor function: Imaging studies. *Journal of Neurology, 253,* 8–15.

Burggren, A. C., Small, G. W., Sabb, F. W., & Bookheimer, S. Y. (2002). Specificity of brain activation patterns in people at genetic risk for Alzheimer disease. *American Journal of Geriatric Psychiatry, 10,* 44–51.

Cabeza, R. (2002). Hemispheric asymmetry reduction in older adults: The HAROLD model. *Psychology and Aging, 17,* 85–100.

Cabeza, R., Anderson, N. D., Locantore, J. K., & McIntosh, A. R. (2002). Aging gracefully: Compensatory brain activity in high-performing older adults. *Neuroimage, 17,* 1394–1402.

Cabeza, R., Grady, C. L., Nyberg, L., McIntosh, A. R., Tulving, E., Kapur, S., et al. (1997). Age-related differences in neural activity during memory encoding and retrieval: A positron emission tomography study. *Journal of Neuroscience, 17,* 391–400.

Cabeza, R., McIntosh, A. R., Grady, C. L., Nyberg, L., Houle, S., & Tulving, E. (1997). Age-related changes in neural interactions during memory encoding and retrieval: A network analysis of PET data. *Brain and Cognition, 35,* 369–372.

Cabeza, R., McIntosh, A. R., Tulving, E., Nyberg, L., & Grady, C. L. (1997). Age-related differences in effective neural connectivity during encoding and recall. *Neuroreport, 8,* 3479–3483.

Cabeza, R., Nyberg, L., & Park, D. C. (Eds.). (2005). *Cognitive neuroscience of aging: linking cognitive and cerebral aging.* New York: Oxford University Press.

Callicott, J. H., Straub, R. E., Pezawas, L., Egan, M. F., Mattay, V. S., Hariri, A. R., et al. (2005). Variation in DISC1 affects hippocampal structure and function and increases risk for schizophrenia. *Proceedings of the National Academy of Sciences, USA, 102,* 8627–8632.

Celone, K. A., Calhoun, V. D., Dickerson, B. C., Atri, A., Chua, E. F., Miller, S. L., et al. (2006). Alterations in memory networks in mild cognitive impairment and Alzheimer's disease: An independent component analysis. *Journal of Neuroscience, 26,* 10222–10231.

Corder, E. H., Saunders, A. M., Strittmatter, W. J., Schmechel, D. E., Gaskell, P. C., Small, G. W., et al. (1993, August 13). Gene dose of apolipoprotein-E type-4 allele and the risk of Alzheimer's disease in late-onset families. *Science, 261,* 921–923.

Corouge, I., Gouttard, S., & Gerig, G. (2004). A statistical shape model of individual fiber tracts extracted from diffusion tensor MRI. In D. R. Haynor, P. Hellier, C. Barillot (Eds.), *Medical Image Computing and Computer-Assisted Intervention—MICCAI 2004: 7th International Conference Saint-Malo, France, September 26-29, 2004, Proceedings, Part II* (pp. 671–679). Berlin: Springer-Verlag.

Cummings, J. L. (1993). Frontal-subcortical circuits and human behavior. *Archives of Neurology, 50,* 873–880.

Daselaar, S. M., Fleck, M. S., & Cabeza, R. (2006). Triple dissociation in the medial temporal lobes: Recollection, familiarity, and novelty. *Journal of Neurophysiology, 96,* 1902–1911.

Daselaar, S. M., Fleck, M. S., Dobbins, I. G., Madden, D. J., & Cabeza, R. (2006). Effects of healthy aging on hippocampal and rhinal memory functions: An event-related fMRI study. *Cerebral Cortex, 16,* 1771–1782.

Daselaar, S. M., Prince, S. E., & Cabeza, R. (2004). When less means more: Deactivations during encoding that predict subsequent memory. *Neuroimage, 23,* 921–927.

Davies, P., & Maloney, A. J. F. (1976). Selective loss of central cholinergic neurons in Alzheimer's disease. *The Lancet, 2,* 1403.

Davis, S., Dennis, N. A., Daselaar, S., Fleck, M. S., & Cabeza, R. (2007). Que PASA? The posterior–anterior shift in aging. *Cerebral Cortex* Advance Access, October 8, 2007. Retrieved from doi 10.1093/cercor/bhm155

de Leon, M. J., Convit, A., Wolf, O. T., Tarshish, C. Y., DeSanti, S., Rusinek, H., et al. (2001). Prediction of cognitive decline in normal elderly subjects with 2-[F-18]fluoro-2-deoxy-D-glucose/positron-emission tomography (FDG/PET). *Proceedings of the National Academy of Sciences USA, 98,* 10966–10971.

Della-Maggiore, V., Sekuler, A. B., Grady, C. L., Bennett, P. J., Sekuler, R., & McIntosh, A. R. (2000). Corticolimbic interactions associated with performance on a short-term memory task are modified by age. *Journal of Neuroscience, 20,* 8410–8416.

Dennis, N. A., Daselaar, S., & Cabeza, R. (2006). Effects of aging on transient and sustained successful memory encoding activity. *Neurobiology of Aging, 28*(11), 1749–1758.

Donaldson, D. I. (2004). Parsing brain activity with fMRI and mixed designs: What kind of a state is neuroimaging in? *Trends in Neurosciences, 27,* 442–444.

Egan, M. F., Goldberg, T. E., Kolachana, B. S., Callicott, J. H., Mazzanti, C. M., Straub, R. E., et al. (2001). Effect of COMT Val(108/158) Met genotype on frontal lobe function and risk for schizophrenia. *Proceedings of the National Academy of Sciences, USA, 98,* 6917–6922.

Egan, M. F., Kojima, M., Callicott, J. H., Goldberg, T. E., Kolachana, B. S., Bertolino, A., et al. (2003). The BDNF val66met polymorphism affects activity-dependent secretion of BDNF and human memory and hippocampal function. *Cell, 112,* 257–269.

Erixon-Lindroth, N., Farde, L., Wahlin, T. B. R., Sovago, J., Halldin, C., & Bäckman, L. (2005). The role of the striatal dopamine transporter in cognitive aging. *Psychiatry Research: Neuroimaging, 138,* 1–12.

Farde, L., Hall, H., Ehrin, E., & Sedvall, G. (1986, January 17). Quantitative-analysis of D2 dopamine receptor-binding in the living human brain by PET. *Science, 231,* 258–261.

Farde, L., Halldin, C., Stone-Elander, S., & Sedvall, G. (1987). PET analysis of human dopamine receptor subtypes using C-11 SCH 23390 and C-11 raclopride. *Psychopharmacology, 92,* 278–284.

Freyhan, F. A., Woodford, R. B., & Kety, S. S. (1951). Cerebral blood flow and metabolism in psychoses of senility. *Journal of Nervous and Mental Disease, 113,* 449–456.

Grady, C. L., Bernstein, L. J., Beig, S., & Siegenthaler, A. L. (2002). The effects of encoding task on age-related differences in the functional neuroanatomy of face memory. *Psychology and Aging, 17,* 7–23.

Grady, C. L., McIntosh, A. R., & Craik, F. I. M. (2003). Age-related differences in the functional connectivity of the hippocampus during memory encoding. *Hippocampus, 13,* 572–586.

Grady, C. L., McIntosh, A. R., Horwitz, B., Maisog, J. M., Ungerleider, L. G., Mentis, M. J., et al. (1995, July 14). Age-related reductions in human recognition memory due to impaired encoding. *Science, 269,* 218–221.

Greicius, M. D., Krasnow, B., Reiss, A. L., & Menon, V. (2003). Functional connectivity in the resting brain: A network analysis of the default mode hypothesis. *Proceedings of the National Academy of Sciences, USA, 100,* 253–258.

Gusnard, D. A., & Raichle, M. E. (2001). Searching for a baseline: Functional imaging and the resting human brain. *Nature Reviews Neuroscience, 2,* 685–694.

Gutchess, A. H., Welsh, R. C., Hedden, T., Bangert, A., Minear, M., Liu, L. L., et al. (2005). Aging and the neural correlates of successful picture encoding: Frontal activations compensate for decreased medial-temporal activity. *Journal of Cognitive Neuroscience, 17,* 84–96.

Head, D., Buckner, R. L., Shimony, J. S., Williams, L. E., Akbudak, E., Conturo, T. E., et al. (2004). Differential vulnerability of anterior white matter in nondemented aging with minimal acceleration in dementia of the Alzheimer type: Evidence from diffusion tensor imaging. *Cerebral Cortex, 14,* 410–423.

Ichise, M., Ballinger, J. R., Tanaka, F., Moscovitch, M., St. George-Hyslop, P. H., Raphael, D., et al. (1998). Age-related changes in D2 receptor binding with iodine-123-iodobenzofuran SPECT. *Journal of Nuclear Medicine, 39,* 1511–1518.

Inoue, M., Suhara, T., Sudo, Y., Okubo, Y., Yasuno, F., Kishimoto, T., et al. (2001). Age-related reduction of extrastriatal dopamine D2 receptor measured by PET. *Life Sciences, 69,* 1079–1084.

Iyo, M., & Yamasaki, T. (1993). The detection of age-related decrease of dopamine-D1, dopamine D-2 and serotonin 5-HT2 receptors in living human brain. *Progress in Neuro-Psychopharmacology & Biological Psychiatry, 17,* 415–421.

Kaasinen, V., Vilkman, H., Hietala, J., Nagren, K., Helenius, H., Olsson, H., et al. (2000). Age-related dopamine D2/D3 receptor loss in extrastriatal regions of the human brain. *Neurobiology of Aging, 21,* 683–688.

Kety, S. S. (1956). Human cerebral blood flow and oxygen consumption as related to aging. *Journal of Chronic Disease, 3,* 478–486.

Kety, S. S., & Schmidt, C. F. (1945). The determination of cerebral blood flow in man by the use of nitrous oxide in low concentrations. *American Journal of Physiology, 143,* 53–66.

Kety, S. S., & Schmidt, C. F. (1948). The nitrous oxide method for the quantitative determination of cerebral blood flow in man—Theory, procedure and normal values. *Journal of Clinical Investigation, 27,* 476–483.

Klunk, W. E., Engler, H., Nordberg, A., Wang, Y. M., Blomqvist, G., Holt, D. P., et al. (2004). Imaging brain amyloid in Alzheimer's disease with Pittsburgh Compound-B. *Annals of Neurology, 55,* 306–319.

Koepp, M. J., Gunn, R. N., Lawrence, A. D., Cunningham, V. J., Dagher, A., Jones, T., et al. (1998, July 16). Evidence for striatal dopamine release during a video game. *Nature, 393,* 266–268.

Lawrence, A. D., & Brooks, D. J. (1999). Neural correlates of reward processing in the human brain: A PET study. *Neurology, 52*(Suppl 2), A307.

LeBihan, D. (2003). Looking into the functional architecture of the brain with diffusion MRI. *Nature Reviews Neuroscience, 4,* 469–480.

Li, S. C., Lindenberger, U., & Sikstrom, S. (2001). Aging cognition: From neuromodulation to representation. *Trends in Cognitive Sciences, 5,* 479–486.

Logan, J. M., Sanders, A. L., Snyder, A. Z., Morris, J. C., & Buckner, R. L. (2002). Under-recruitment and nonselective recruitment: Dissociable neural mechanisms associated with aging. *Neuron, 33,* 827–840.

Lustig, C., Snyder, A. Z., Bhakta, M., O'Brien, K. C., McAvoy, M., Raichle, M. E., et al. (2003). Functional deactivations: Change with age and dementia of the Alzheimer type. *Proceedings of the National Academy of Sciences, USA, 100,* 14504–14509.

Madden, D. J., Spaniol, J., Whiting, W. L., Bucur, B., Provenzale, J. M., Cabeza, R., et al. (2007). Adult age differences in the functional neuroanatomy of visual attention: A combined fMRI and DTI study. *Neurobiology of Aging, 28*(3), 459–476.

Madden, D. J., Whiting, W. L., Huettel, S. A., White, L. E., MacFall, J. R., & Provenzale, J. M. (2004). Diffusion tensor imaging of adult age differences in cerebral white matter: Relation to response time. *Neuroimage, 21,* 1174–1181.

Mathis, C. A., Wang, Y., & Klunk, W. E. (2004). Imaging beta-amyloid plaques and neurofibrillary tangles in the aging human brain. *Current Pharmaceutical Design, 10,* 1469–1492.

McIntosh, A. R. (1999). Mapping cognition to the brain through neural interactions. *Memory, 7,* 523–548.

McKiernan, K. A., Kaufman, J. N., Kucera-Thompson, J., & Binder, J. R. (2003). A parametric manipulation of factors affecting task-induced deactivation in functional neuroimaging. *Journal of Cognitive Neuroscience, 15,* 394–408.

Meltzer, C. C., Smith, G., Price, J. C., Reynolds, C. F., Mathis, C. A., Greer, P., et al. (1998). Reduced binding of [F-18]altanserin to serotonin type 2A receptors in aging: Persistence of effect after partial volume correction. *Brain Research, 813,* 167–171.

Minoshima, S., Frey, K. A., Foster, N. L., & Kuhl, D. E. (1995). Preserved pontine glucose-metabolism in Alzheimer-disease—A reference region for functional brain image (PET) analysis. *Journal of Computer Assisted Tomography, 19,* 541–547.

Morcom, A. M., Good, C. D., Frackowiak, R. S. J., & Rugg, M. D. (2003). Age effects on the neural correlates of successful memory encoding. *Brain, 126,* 213–229.

Mori, S., & van Zijl, P. C. M. (2002). Fiber tracking: Principles and strategies—A technical review. *NMR in Biomedicine, 15,* 468–480.

Moseley, M. (2002). Diffusion tensor imaging and aging—A review. *NMR in Biomedicine, 15,* 553–560.

Mozley, L. H., Gur, R. C., Mozley, P. D., & Gur, R. E. (2001). Striatal dopamine transporters and cognitive functioning in healthy men and women. *American Journal of Psychiatry, 158,* 1492–1499.

Nichols, L., Pike, V. W., Cai, L. S., & Innis, R. B. (2006). Imaging and in vivo quantitation of beta-amyloid: An exemplary biomarker for Alzheimer's disease? *Biological Psychiatry, 59,* 940–947.

Olesen, P. J., Nagy, Z., Westerberg, H., & Klingberg, T. (2003). Combined analysis of DTI and fMRI data reveals a joint maturation of white and grey matter in a fronto-parietal network. *Cognitive Brain Research, 18,* 48–57.

O'Sullivan, M., Jones, D. K., Summers, P. E., Morris, R. G., Williams, S. C. R., & Markus, H. S. (2001). Evidence for cortical "disconnection" as a mechanism of age-related cognitive decline. *Neurology, 57,* 632–638.

Otten, L. J., Henson, R. N., & Rugg, M. D. (2002). State-related and item-related neural correlates of successful memory encoding. *Nature Neuroscience, 5,* 1339–1344.

Pendleton, R. G., Rasheed, A., Roychowdhury, R., & Hillman, R. (1998). A new role for catecholamines: ontogenesis. *Trends in Pharmacological Sciences, 19,* 248–251.

Persson, J., Nyberg, L., Lind, J., Larsson, A., Nilsson, L. G., Ingvar, M., et al. (2006). Structure-function correlates of cognitive decline in aging. *Cerebral Cortex, 16,* 907–915.

Pfefferbaum, A., Sullivan, E. V., Hedehus, M., Lim, K. O., Adalsteinsson, E., & Moseley, M. (2000). Age-related decline in brain white matter anisotropy measured with spatially corrected echo-planar diffusion tensor imaging. *Magnetic Resonance in Medicine, 44,* 259–268.

Pfefferbaum, A., Sullivan, E. V., Rosenbloom, M. J., Mathalon, H., & Lim, K. O. (1998). A controlled study of cortical gray matter and ventricular changes in alcoholic men over a 5-year interval. *Archives of General Psychiatry, 55,* 905–912.

Previc, F. H. (1999). Dopamine and the origins of human intelligence. *Brain and Cognition, 41,* 299–350.

Raichle, M. E., MacLeod, A. M., Snyder, A. Z., Powers, W. J., Gusnard, D. A., & Shulman, G. L. (2001). A default mode of brain function. *Proceedings of the National Academy of Sciences, USA, 98,* 676–682.

Raz, N. (2000). Aging of the brain and its impact on cognitive performance: Integration of structural and functional findings. In F. I. Craik & T. A. Salthouse (Eds.), *The handbook of aging and cognition* (pp. 1–90). Mahwah, NJ: Lawrence Erlbaum.

Raz, N. (2005). The aging brain observed *in vivo*: Differential changes and their modifiers. In R. Cabeza, L. Nyberg, & D. C. Park (Eds.), *Cognitive neuroscience of aging: linking cognitive and cerebral aging* (pp. 19–57). New York: Oxford University Press.

Raz, N., Gunning-Dixon, F. M., Head, D., Dupuis, J. H., & Acker, J. D. (1998). Neuroanatomical correlates of cognitive aging: Evidence from structural magnetic resonance imaging. *Neuropsychology, 12,* 95–114.

Raz, N., Rodrigue, K. M., Head, D., Kennedy, K. M., & Acker, J. D. (2004). Differential aging of the medial temporal lobe—A study of a five-year change. *Neurology, 62,* 433–438.

Raz, N., Rodrigue, K. M., Kennedy, K. M., Head, D., Gunning-Dixon, F., & Acker, J. D. (2003). Differential aging of the human striatum: Longitudinal evidence. *American Journal of Neuroradiology, 24,* 1849–1856.

Reiman, E. M., Caselli, R. J., Yun, L. S., Chen, K. W., Bandy, D., Minoshima, S., et al. (1996). Preclinical evidence of Alzheimer's disease in persons homozygous for the epsilon 4 allele for apolipoprotein E. *New England Journal of Medicine, 334,* 752–758.

Reiman, E. M., Chen, K. W., Alexander, G. E., Caselli, R. J., Bandy, D., Osborne, D., et al. (2004). Functional brain abnormalities in young adults at genetic risk for late-onset Alzheimer's dementia. *Proceedings of the National Academy of Sciences, USA, 101,* 284–289.

Reiman, E. M., Chen, K. W., Alexander, G. E., Caselli, R. J., Bandy, D., Osborne, D., et al. (2005). Correlations between apolipoprotein E epsilon 4 gene dose and brain-imaging measurements of regional hypometabolism. *Proceedings of the National Academy of Sciences, USA, 102,* 8299–8302.

Resnick, S. M., Pham, D. L., Kraut, M. A., Zonderman, A. B., & Davatzikos, C. (2003). Longitudinal magnetic resonance imaging studies of older adults: A shrinking brain. *Journal of Neuroscience, 23,* 3295–3301.

Rinne, J. O., Sahlberg, N., Ruottinen, H., Nagren, K., & Lehikoinen, P. (1998). Striatal uptake of the dopamine reuptake ligand [11C]beta-CFT is reduced in Alzheimer's disease assessed by positron emission tomography. *Neurology, 50,* 152–156.

Rissman, J., Gazzaley, A., & D'Esposito, M. (2004). Measuring functional connectivity during distinct stages of a cognitive task. *Neuroimage, 23,* 752–763.

Rodrigue, K. M., & Raz, N. (2004). Shrinkage of the entorhinal cortex over five years predicts memory performance in healthy adults. *Journal of Neuroscience, 24,* 956–963.

Rombouts, S., Barkhof, F., Goekoop, R., Stam, C. J., & Scheltens, P. (2005). Altered resting state networks in mild cognitive impairment and mild Alzheimer's disease: An fMRI study. *Human Brain Mapping, 26,* 231–239.

Rosier, A., Dupont, P., Peuskens, J., Bormans, G., Vandenberghe, R., Maes, M., et al. (1996). Visualisation of loss of 5-HT2A receptors with age in healthy volunteers using [F-18]altanserin and positron emission tomographic imaging. *Psychiatry Research: Neuroimaging, 68,* 11–22.

Salat, D. H., Tuch, D. S., Hevelone, N. D., Fischl, B., Corkin, S., Rosas, H. D., et al. (2005). Age-related changes in prefrontal white IF matter measured by diffusion tensor imaging. In J. L. Ulmer, L. Parsons, M. Moseley, & J. Gabrieli (Eds.), *White matter in cognitive neuroscience: Advances in diffusion tensor imaging and its applications* (pp. 37–49). New York: New York Academy of Sciences.

Saunders, A. M., Strittmatter, W. J., Schmechel, D., Georgehyslop, P. H. S., Pericak-Vance, M. A., Joo, S. H., et al. (1993). Association of apolipoprotein-E allele epsilon-4 with late-onset familial and sporadic Alzheimers disease. *Neurology, 43,* 1467–1472.

Sawamoto, N., Hotton, G., Pavese, N., Thielemans, K., Piccini, P., & Brooks, D. J. (2006). Neurobiological mechanism underlying decreased motivation in Parkinson's disease: A C-11-raclopride positron emission tomography study. *Neurology, 66,* A113–A113.

Scahill, R. I., Frost, C., Jenkins, R., Whitwell, J. L., Rossor, M. N., & Fox, N. C. (2003). A longitudinal study of brain volume changes in normal aging using serial registered magnetic resonance imaging. *Archives of Neurology, 60,* 989–994.

Schiavetto, A., Kohler, S., Grady, C. L., Winocur, G., & Moscovitch, M. (2002). Neural correlates of memory for object identity and object location: effects of aging. *Neuropsychologia, 40,* 1428–1442.

Shoghi-Jadid, K., Barrio, J. R., Kepe, V., Wu, H. M., Small, G. W., Phelps, M. E., et al. (2005). Imaging beta-amyloid fibrils in Alzheimer's disease: A critical analysis through simulation of amyloid fibril polymerization. *Nuclear Medicine and Biology, 32,* 337–351.

Shoghi-Jadid, K., Small, G. W., Agdeppa, E. D., Kepe, V., Ercoli, L. M., Siddarth, P., et al. (2002). Localization of neurofibrillary tangles and beta-amyloid plaques in the brains of living patients with Alzheimer disease. *American Journal of Geriatric Psychiatry, 10,* 24–35.

Small, G. W., Kepe, V., Ercoli, L. M., Siddarth, P., Bookheimer, S. Y., Miller, K. J., et al. (2006). PET of brain amyloid and tau in mild cognitive impairment. *New England Journal of Medicine, 355,* 2652–2663.

Stebbins, G. T., Carillo, M. C., Medina, D., deToledo-Morrell, L., Klingberg, T., Poldrack, R. A., et al. (2001). Frontal white matter integrity in aging and its role in reasoning performance: A diffusion tensor imaging study. *Society for Neuroscience Abstracts, 456,* 3.

Stebbins, G. T., Poldrack, R. A., Klingberg, T., Carrillo, M. C., Desmond, J. E., Moseley, M. E., et al. (2001). Aging effects on white matter integrity and processing speed: A diffusion tensor imaging study. *Neurology, 56,* A374–A375.

Strong, R. (1998). Neurochemical changes in the aging human brain: Implications for behavioral impairment and neurodegenerative disease. *Geriatrics, 53,* S9–S12.

Suhara, T., Fukuda, H., Inoue, O., Itoh, T., Suzuki, K., Yamasaki, T., et al. (1991). Age-related changes in human D1 dopamine receptors measured by positron emission tomography. *Psychopharmacology, 103,* 41–45.

Takahashi, E., Ohki, K., & Kim, D. S. (2007). Diffusion tensor studies dissociated two fronto-temporal pathways in the human memory system. *Neuroimage, 34,* 827–838.

van Dyck, C. H., Seibyl, J. P., Malison, R. T., Laruelle, M., Wallace, E., Zoghbi, S. S., et al. (1995). Age-related decline in striatal dopamine transporter binding with iodine-123-beta-CITSPECT. *Journal of Nuclear Medicine, 36,* 1175–1181.

Van Petten, C. (2004). Relationship between hippocampal volume and memory ability in healthy individuals across the lifespan: Review and meta-analysis. *Neuropsychologia, 42,* 1394–1413.

Verhoeff, N., Wilson, A. A., Takeshita, S., Trop, L., Hussey, D., Singh, K., et al. (2004). In-vivo imaging of Alzheimer disease beta-amyloid with [C-11]SB-13 PET. *American Journal of Geriatric Psychiatry, 12,* 584–595.

Visscher, K. M., Miezin, F. M., Kelly, J. E., Buckner, R. L., Donaldson, D. I., McAvoy, M. P., et al. (2003). Mixed blocked/event-related designs separate transient and sustained activity in fMRI. *Neuroimage, 19,* 1694–1708.

Volkow, N. D., Gur, R. C., Wang, G. J., Fowler, J. S., Moberg, P. J., Ding, Y. S., et al. (1998). Association between decline in brain dopamine activity with age and cognitive and motor impairment in healthy individuals. *American Journal of Psychiatry, 155,* 344–349.

Wang, Y., Chan, G. L., Holden, J. E., Dobko, T., Mak, E., Schulzer, M., et al. (1998). Age-dependent decline of dopamine D1 receptors in human brain: A PET study. *Synapse, 30,* 56–61.

Wong, D. F., Wagner, H. N., Dannals, R. F., Links, J. M., Frost, J. J., Ravert, H. T., et al. (1984, December 21). Effects of age on dopamine and serotonin receptors measured by positron emission tomography in the living human-brain. *Science, 226,* 1393–1396.

Xu, D. R., Mori, S., Solaiyappan, M., van Zijl, P. C. M., & Davatzikos, C. (2002). A framework for callosal fiber distribution analysis. *Neuroimage, 17,* 1131–1143.

20

COGNITIVE AGING AND FUNCTIONAL BIOMARKERS

What Do We Know, and Where to From Here?

KAARIN ANSTEY

WHAT DO WE KNOW?

Functional Biomarker Research and Its Relevance to Cognitive Aging

In the broader biomarker literature there has been much debate about the definition of *biomarkers* (Butler et al., 2004; Hofer, Berg, & Era, 2003) and how they relate to physiological aging and chronological age. This is complicated by several issues, including the overlap between aging and disease processes; debate about whether aging is caused by a single cause or multiple cause; and the use of animal models in biomarker research, which may not necessarily translate to humans. The discovery of biological factors that define the mechanism of aging should ultimately predict the same outcomes as functional biomarkers. However, the role of environment and adaptation by the organism means that no single type of variable will perfectly index biological aging.

While acknowledging that the vast literature on biomarkers from basic science is highly relevant to the ultimate goals of understanding cognitive aging, the scope of this chapter is restricted to biomarkers involving sensory function and, to a lesser extent, the nonsensory function, such as muscle strength, lung capacity, gait, and balance (K. Z. Li & Lindenberger, 2002; Lindenberger & Baltes, 1994; Lord & Fitzpatrick, 2001). These *functional biomarkers* are used to predict functional outcomes in everyday life, such as mobility, injury, and driving. For example, measures of sensorimotor function (vision, muscle strength, balance, reaction time, forced expiratory volume) are associated with falling in late life (Anstey, Lord, & Smith, 1996; Butler et al., 2004; Lord, Ward, Williams, & Anstey, 1994). Functional biomarkers involve measuring behavior or perception and are hence relevant to psychologists and psychological outcomes. Measures of muscle strength and lung capacity involve behaviors that test the limits of function, through behavioral tasks such as grasping a dynamometer as tightly as possible or breathing out with as much force as possible. From a broader perspective, it is also clear that cognition is another functional biomarker. Fluid cognition has similar relationships with several major functional outcomes; it declines in normal aging, and it predicts mortality (Anstey, Luszcz,

Giles, & Andrews, 2001). The underlying theoretical question driving research on functional biomarkers from the perspective of cognitive aging is whether there is a common causal factor that determines aging of sensorimotor and functional decline, and cognitive decline (Lindenberger & Baltes, 1994). Attempts to answer this question have led to a reappraisal of methodological approaches (e.g., Hofer & Sliwinski, 2001) and stimulated much research over the past decade.

The Unique Role of Sensory Biomarkers

Sensory variables are functional biomarkers of aging but also have unique effects on cognition because they influence perception (Schneider & Pichora-Fuller, 2000). There is also evidence of shared central factors that influence aging of both vision and memory and possibly other pairs of sensory and cognitive abilities (Anstey, Hofer, & Luszcz, 2003b; Lindenberger, Scherer, & Baltes, 2001). Therefore, among functional biomarkers, measures of sensory abilities have a special role in relation to cognitive aging in comparison to biomarkers such as grip strength and measures of lung function.

Cross-Sectional Research

Several decades of research have now shown that measures of sensory function, muscle strength, and lung function are associated with cognitive performance in cross-sectional studies (Chown & Heron, 1965; Heron & Chown, 1961). In the last 10 to 15 years, in the cognitive aging literature, a number of studies from Finland, the United States, Germany, Australia, the United Kingdom, and other countries have shown that a range of noncognitive variables explain age differences in cognition (Allen et al., 2001; Baltes & Lindenberger, 1997; Christensen, Mackinnon, Korten, & Jorm, 2001; Lindenberger & Baltes, 1994; Salthouse, Hambrick, & McGuthry, 1998; Salthouse, Hancock, Meinz, & Hambrick, 1996). A number of studies have shown that these variables load onto a common factor and that in cross-sectional studies they explain age differences in memory, speed, and fluid abilities (Anstey & Smith, 1999; Christensen et al., 2001; Salthouse et al., 1998). The size of the correlations

between biomarkers and cognitive variables ranges from about $r = .1$ to $r = .5$, depending on the variables and the age range of the sample. The size of the associations between biomarkers and cognition is often similar to the size of associations among cognitive variables.

The main difficulty in interpreting these associations has been the possibility that the association is mostly due to the variables' joint association with chronological age and that the observation is a *third-variable effect* (Hofer et al., 2003; Mackinnon, Christensen, & Jorm, 2006). Although this problem occurs in all cross-sectional research (Hofer & Sliwinski, 2001), particularly in models that use multiple regression (Lindenberger & Potter, 1998), it has been especially problematic in the field of gerontology, where the focus of most research questions is on explaining within-person change yet the design of most studies is cross-sectional.

Several avenues have been followed to determine the extent to which the association is "real" or meaningful from the point of view of cognitive psychologists. Statistical methods that partial out age from the associations between biomarkers and cognition have generally shown that although the relationships are reduced in size, they remain significant. For example, Anstey, Dain, Andrews, and Drobny (2002) showed that, even after partialing out age, significant correlations remained between Matrices and visual acuity, between Stroop Color Word performance and visual acuity, and between contrast sensitivity and color vision (see Table 20.1).

Structural equation models have also been used to assess the problem of interpreting the correlations among this diverse range of variables (Allen et al., 2001; Anstey, Luszcz, & Sanchez, 2001a; Christensen et al., 2001) and to test alternative configurations of the relationships among chronological age, biomarkers, and cognitive test performance.

Narrow age cohort designs eliminate the potential problem of age differences influencing the observed associations among variables and have been advocated as a means of overcoming the problem of mean age trends influencing correlations among cognitive and noncognitive variables (Hofer & Sliwinski, 2001). The PATH (Personality and Total Health) Through Life Study is a narrow age cohort design including

Table 20.1 Correlations Between Cognitive Measures and Visual Measures/Age-Partialed Correlations Between Cognitive Measures and Visual Measures (n = 92)

Measure	Bailey–Lovie[a]	Landolt C	MET	D15	HRR
Matrices[b]	−.32/−.21	−.42/−.29	.24/.08	.02/.06	.03/−.06
DSB	−.07/.00	−.14/−.06	.15/.04	.13/.05	.02/−.09
Similarities[c]	−.18/−.07	−.19/−.04	.14/−.01	.08/−.02	.16/.06
StroopC	.05/−.01	.22/.20	−.08/.05	−.40/.04	−.10/.07
StroopCW	−.38/−.26	−.46/.32	.39/.26	.52/.43	.26/.12
Face recognition[d]	−.18/−.05	−.02/−.09	.10/−.08	.05/−.01	.09/.00

NOTES: Correlations > .21 are significant at .05. MET = Melbourne Edge Test (Verbaken & Johnson, 1986); D15 = Farnsworth–Munsell Panel Test (Farnsworth, 1943); HRR = American Optical Hardy–Rand–Rittler Pseudoisochromatic Plates (Hardy, Rand, & Rittler, 1954); DSB = Digit Span Backward (Wechsler, 1945); StroopC = Stroop Color Test (Trenerry, Crosson, DeBoe, & Leber, 1999); Stroop CW = Stroop Color Word Test (Trenerry et al., 1999).

a. Bailey and Lovie (1976); b. Raven (1940); c. Wechsler (1981); d. Wechsler (1997).

three age groups of 20–24, 40–44, and 60–64 (Jorm, Anstey, Christensen, & Rodgers, 2004). This study includes a range of cognitive and psychosocial measures as well as biomarkers and neuroimaging and genetic indices. It therefore provides an opportunity to determine whether relationships among these variables are observed when the "problem" of chronological age has been controlled for in the design of the study. Table 20.2 shows the correlations between cognitive variables and biomarkers within each age group. Significant associations were observed among biomarkers and cognitive variables, even in the 20- to 24-year-old group. The associations were small in size, but they appear reliable. This provides evidence that biomarkers are independently associated with cognitive test performance, in addition to sharing age-related variance in cognitive test performance.

It is important to note that even if the association between biomarkers and cognition is due to their joint association with age, this may still be an important finding, indicating a parallel trajectory among these variables. If a reliable parallel trajectory can be established among certain variables (e.g., episodic memory and visual decline), then this would have clinical implications, because change in one ability would indicate change in another. Dismissing findings after statistical correction for age may lead researchers inadvertently to dismiss associations

that are functionally or clinically important. However, an even more powerful finding would be one where we could establish some causal relationship between age-related change in biomarkers and age-related change in cognition, or if we could identify brain changes that lead to both. Clinical studies have also sought to determine how sensory impairment is related to cognitive function, and vice versa. For example, results from the Leiden 85+ study found that visual impairment is associated with cognitive function but that hearing impairment is not (Gussekloo, de Craen, Oduber, van Boxtel, & Westendorp, 2005).

Another important consideration is the distinction between *peripheral* and *central* changes that affect sensory function. Although in practice it is difficult to distinguish peripheral and central factors without using simulation studies that do not necessarily emulate the true aging processes, one possible explanation for the association between visual function and cognitive function is that most cognitive tests are presented visually, and hence peripheral visual factors influence test performance (Hofer et al., 2003). There are several means of testing this, including examining cross-domain associations between sensory function and cognitive function. For example, Drobny, Anstey, and Andrews (2005) correlated visual tests with measures of both visual and verbal memory. They

Table 20.2   Correlations Between Cognitive Variables and Biomarkers in Three Narrow Age Bands

Age Group	Measures				
	SDMT	*DSB*	*IMREC*	*RT*	*SPOTWORD*
20+[a]					
Vision	**.06**	.01	.01	−.03	.00
Grip	**−.07**	**.07**	**−.13**	**−.21**	.01
FEV	.02	**.10**	−.05	**−.18**	**.12**
SBP	−.02	.02	**−.10**	**−.16**	.03
40+[b]					
Vision	**.10**	**.06**	**.06**	**−.11**	**.07**
Grip	−.00	**.08**	**−.10**	**−.20**	**.08**
FEV	**.05**	**.11**	−.01	**−.15**	**.19**
SBP	−.02	−.01	**−.06**	−.04	.03
60+[c]					
Vision	**.17**	**.11**	**.11**	**−.10**	**.11**
Grip	**.08**	**.11**	**−.08**	**−.27**	**.09**
FEV	**.14**	**.15**	−.04	**−.21**	**.15**
SBP	−.02	−.01	−.04	**−.06**	.01

NOTES: Correlations significant at $p < .05$ are in boldface type. SDMT = Symbol Digit Modalities Test (Smith, 1982); DSB = Digit Span Backwards (Wechsler, 1945); IMREC = Immediate Recall (Delis, Kramer, Kaplan, & Ober, 1987); RT = Reaction Time (Anstey, Dear, Christensen, & Jorm, 2005); SPOTWORD = Spot-the-Word Test (Baddeley, Emslie, & Nimmo-Smith, 1992); FEV = forced expiratory volume; SBP = systolic blood pressure.

a. $n = 2{,}269–2{,}388$; b. $n = 2{,}363–2{,}519$; c. $n = 2{,}419–2{,}547$.

found that visual function was associated with memory tested in both domains and concluded that the association between visual function and visual memory in late life was not due to peripheral visual changes. Likewise, in a previous study including measures of vision and hearing, and visually and aurally presented reaction time tests, Anstey (1999) found cross-domain associations for all reaction time measures, suggesting that sensory modality was not the key common factor explaining associations among sensory function and reaction time.

Longitudinal and Experimental Approaches

Another means of investigating the peripheral versus central explanations for the observed association between sensory function and cognition is to manipulate visual function peripherally. My colleagues and I recently conducted a randomized

controlled trial of cataract surgery to see whether removal of cataract would improve neuropsychological test performance (Anstey, Lord, et al., 2006), but we found no benefit of cataract surgery. However, we did find that reducing the contrast of test stimuli in an experimental study with older adults resulted in slower information processing and associative memory and that test performance was also associated with static visual contrast sensitivity (Anstey, Butterworth, Borzycki, & Andrews, 2006).

There are now a few reports from longitudinal studies examining how sensory and cognitive variables are interrelated over time. One is the Australian Longitudinal Study of Aging (ALSA), in which analyses were conducted over 8 years and three occasions of measurement to see whether sensory and cognitive decline shared variance (Anstey, Hofer, & Luszcz, 2003a, 2003b; Anstey, Luszcz, & Sanchez, 2001b). Although trajectories of decline in vision, hearing, memory, and processing speed were similar, there was no shared variance between sensory measures and decline in processing speed. There was some shared variance between decline in visual acuity and decline in episodic memory.

Results from the Maastricht Longitudinal Aging Study also revealed that change in visual acuity was associated with change in memory (Valentijn et al., 2005). This study also found that change in auditory acuity predicted change in memory performance but, consistent with the Australian results (i.e., ALSA), found that visual decline was a more important predictor of memory decline. It is likely that this is because much hearing loss is associated with occupational and environmental exposure and hence hearing loss is a less reliable correlate of brain aging than visual loss. However, analyses conducted on the Maastricht Longitudinal Aging Study did not evaluate whether rates of decline shared variance. Sensory and cognitive aging were also studied in the Study of Osteoporotic Fractures (Lin et al., 2004) in a sample of 1,668 adults aged 69 and older over a period of 2 years. Consistent with the findings from ALSA, this study showed that visual function was associated with subsequent decline but that hearing was not. Results from the Hispanic Populations for Epidemiological Studies of the Elderly also showed that hearing was not associated with cognitive decline but indicated that near vision impairment (not distance vision) was associated with cognitive decline (Reyes-Ortiz et al., 2005).

Results from longitudinal studies clearly indicate that visual decline is predictive of cognitive decline, but the extent to which we are observing a set of parallel aging processes compared with a causally interrelated set of associations remains unclear. Examination of correlations among rates of change in ALSA suggested that most of what we are observing is parallel rates of change but that there is some causally interrelated change in vision and memory.

Another longitudinal approach to evaluating the degree to which sensory and cognitive aging may be causally related is to examine de-differentiation among cognitive and sensory abilities longitudinally. If the associations among sensory and cognitive variables increase in aging, then this would suggest a convergence of abilites, possibly driven by a general factor. De-differentiation among cognitive and sensory factors was not observed in ALSA over an 8-year period, after adjusting for gender, depression, physical health, self-rated health, and sample attrition (Anstey et al., 2003a).

FACTORS TO WHICH WE MAY HAVE NOT PAID ENOUGH ATTENTION IN COGNITIVE AGING RESEARCH

Differentiation of Impairment From Normal Aging

It is possible that some of the lack of clarity in research on biomarkers more generally, (Butler et al., 2004), and in this field specifically, stems from a lack of distinction between impairment in sensory and cognitive function and normal aging. Pathological processes may underlie more rapid decline in visual and memory aging, as is seen in Alzheimer's disease (AD) and, more recently, in mild cognitive impairment. Focusing on clinical groups may prove beneficial for disentangling the causal from the correlational associations observed between sensory and cognitive function. Many longitudinal aging studies may include individuals with sensory or cognitive deficits or with preclinical syndromes that may contribute to observed associations at the population level. Participants may be in a preclinical stage of a disease that is not obvious on initial testing. In ALSA, we identified groups who showed rapid visual and auditory decline over 2 years, and we investigated whether these groups also showed marked cognitive decline. We found that marked visual decline was associated with memory decline, but not decline in processing speed. Decline in hearing was not associated with cognitive decline (Anstey et al., 2001b). It is possible that the participants identified in this study were in the preclinical stage of dementia.

Cognitive aging studies often exclude individuals with low scores on the Mini-Mental State Examination or with dementia. It is possible that excluding these individuals is denying us important information about the sources of joint associations among sensory and cognitive factors.

The Circularity of Resource and Common Factor Explanations

Even longitudinal analyses do not necessarily overcome the problem of circularity in attempting to explain associations between biomarkers and cognitive aging. If two variables are aging in parallel, then any cross-lagged analysis will indicate that they predict decline in each other, or that rate of change in one predicts rate of change in another. Therefore, longitudinal analysis will not always enable us to overcome the circularity that plagues cross-sectional research. There are several possible avenues to moving beyond some of the explanatory difficulties in this field. Two of these include the following:

1. Seeking pathological processes that underlie decline in both an individual biomarker and a type of cognitive ability

2. Identifying third variables that are linked to both biomarkers and cognition and a lifestyle, disease, or pathological process. For example, brain atrophy or homocysteine level may be linked to both cognitive function and other functional biomarkers and have been associated with medical conditions (Sachdev, 2004). Physical activity has been linked to cognition and brain function and structure.

Underlying Pathological Processes: Visual and Cognitive Impairment in Alzheimer's Disease

There is growing evidence of visual deficits in AD (Cronin-Golomb & Hof, 2004). Accumulation of neurofibrillary tangles and senile plaques may disconnect certain cortico-cortical pathways, which may in turn affect visual function (von Gunten, Giannakopoulos, Bouras, & Hof, 2004). Visual symptoms are often present in the initial presentation of AD patients, and there are some patients for whom visual and visuospatial difficulties are prominent in their clinical presentation. In typical AD, the visual association areas contain high densities of senile plaques and neurofibrillary tangles, and a reduction of choline acetyltransferase activity has been found in primary visual cortex (Ikonomovic, Mufson, Wuu, Bennett, & DeKosky, 2005). They are also found in the primary visual association cortex in some patients. It is possible that different patterns of neuropathology lead to a diversity in the clinical manifestations of visual problems in AD. Measures of visual function used in epidemiological studies usually include basic visual acuity. The hypothesis proposed here is that the joint association between visual and memory aging observed in the longitudinal aging studies reflects neuropathological changes associated with pre-clinical dementia.

Third Variables That Are Not Chronological Age: Brain Atrophy, Homocysteine Levels, and White Matter Hyperintensities

Further progress in understanding the interrelationships among functional biomarkers and cognitive aging is being made in the field of neuroimaging. Identification of neurological factors that underlie pairs or groups of variables will allow us to develop better articulated theories of the underlying processes of cognitive aging. In the PATH Through Life study, my colleagues and I have examined forced expiratory volume and other biomarkers in relation to cognition (Anstey, Windsor, Jorm, Christensen, & Rodgers, 2004) and brain aging. Analysis of structural magnetic resonance imaging in a subsample of 478 60- to 64-year-olds revealed that lung function was also associated with brain atrophy and periventricular white matter hyperintensity (WMH) level in the total brain (Sachdev et al., 2006). Further analyses showed that vision was associated with the proportion of total WMHs as a function of total white matter volume and right ventricular volume. Grip strength was associated with corpus callosum area, and total WMH in women. Higher systolic blood pressure was associated with more cortical cerebrospinal fluid and more WMH. Homocysteine was associated with weaker grip, greater atrophy, and worse lung function in men but was not associated with poorer cognitive function in the sample, although other studies have shown this association (Schafer et al., 2005). Of all the biomarkers, the strongest associations in the PATH Through Life study were found between measures of lung function and brain structures. Statistical modeling of these relationships, first cross-sectionally and then

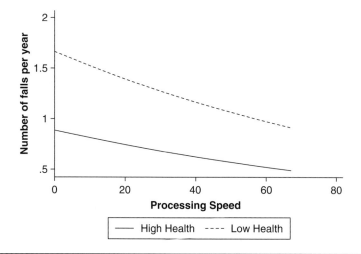

Figure 20.1   Predicted Number of Falls per Year Over 8 Years According to Baseline Processing Speed

longitudinally as we follow our sample, will allow us to relate measures of human performance and function to neuropathology.

APPLYING WHAT WE KNOW ABOUT COGNITIVE AND SENSORY AGING

There is much potential for work on the interrelationships among cognitive and sensory aging to be applied to clinical and functional outcomes in late life. There is growing evidence that neuropsychological factors are associated with falls, as are balance, visual function, and muscle strength (Lord, Clark, & Webster, 1991; Lord & Fitzpatrick, 2001). Recent results from ALSA showed that, within individuals, decline in verbal ability, processing speed, and immediate memory were associated with increased rates of falling and fall risk over 8 years (Anstey, von Sanden, & Luszcz, 2006). For example, Figure 20.1 shows results for two 80-year-old women with 9 years of education. High health was defined as no hypertension, no psychotropic medication, and being a nonsmoker, and low health was defined as being a hypertensive smoker taking psychotropic medication. The association between processing speed and fall risk was significant (Anstey, von Sanden, & Luszcz, 2006). Recent research shows that both cognitive and visual functions are associated with preferred walking speed in adults aged 72

to 92 (Patel, Coshall, Rudd, & Wolfe, 2002). Experimental studies have shown how tasks that challenge balance, or dual tasks involving maintaining postural control while conducting a secondary activity, influence cognitive performance (K. Z. Li, Lindenberger, Freund, & Baltes, 2001; Shumway-Cook & Woollacott, 2000). Likewise, cognitive ability has been shown to influence performance on a complex stepping task (Alexander, Ashton-Miller, Giordani, Guire, & Schultz, 2005), and sensory function contributes to the capacity to conduct everyday cognitive activities (Marsiske, Klumb, & Baltes, 1997).

The interaction between visual and cognitive aging has implications for safe driving in older adults and decision making in relation to driving behavior. A recent review of the literature on cognitive and sensorimotor predictors of on-road driving and crashes in older adults (Anstey, Wood, Lord, & Walker, 2005) found that measures of cognitive function had the strongest association with driving performance, followed by measures of visual function. It is interesting that other biomarkers, such as grip strength, had minimal associations with driving performance.

Visual selective attention has been identified as one of the key areas of cognitive ability that affects driving performance in aging (Ball, Owsley, Sloane, Roenker, & Bruni, 1993) and has also been identified as impaired in mild cognitive impairment (Tales, Haworth, Nelson, Snowder, & Wilcock, 2005). There is also recent evidence of visually processed measures of executive function predicting motor vehicle accidents (Ball et al., 2006). Ball and colleagues found that the Trail Making Test B, visual closure, and a subtest of the Useful Field of View task predicted subsequent at-fault involvement in motor vision collisions, in a sample of 1,910 adults aged 55 to 96.

Biomarkers and cognitive test performance also have the commonality of predicting mortality (Anstey, Luszcz, et al., 2001). In this area, the issue of the distinction between biomarkers and cognition measuring normal aging versus disease processes is especially pertinent (Anstey, Mack, & von Sanden, 2006). It is now well established that cognitive performance predicts mortality both within samples of elders and samples of young and middle-aged adults (Andersen et al., 2002; Geerlings et al., 1999; Neale, Brayne, & Johnson, 2001). There is also evidence that visual impairment predicts mortality (Lee, Gomez-Marin, Lam, & Zheng, 2002), as does pulmonary function (Schunemann, Dorn, Grant, Winkelstein, & Trevisan, 2000). Public health interventions are increasingly targeting factors that influence these biomarkers, such as physical activity leading to better lung function.

FUTURE DIRECTIONS IN THE FIELD OF FUNCTIONAL BIOMARKERS AND COGNITIVE AGING

Further research in this important field needs to incorporate both basic science and functional applications.

Scientific Issues Involving Vision and Cognitive Decline

The basic questions in visual and cognitive aging involve two key themes. The first of these is determining how neuropathological changes in the aging brain may jointly affect visual and cognitive function. This requires neuroimaging and neuropathological work to be conducted on samples of patients with varying degrees of dementia and cognitive impairment. Animal models may assist in understanding how damage to particular neural pathways may jointly affect

vision and cognition. The second theme involves determining how the aging eye (including cataract, lens thickening, etc.) affects perception and how this may slow information processing (Scialfa, 2002) and affect visual attention (Atchley & Hoffman, 2004). Understanding peripheral changes and their effect on cognitive performance is essential for disentangling the complex relationships among sensory and cognitive abilities.

Experimental approaches and simulation studies are required to tease out the relative contribution of different aspects of visual aging to slowing of information processing and reduction in attention. Increased intraindividual variability in reaction time has been associated with stimulus degradation (Macdonald, Hultsch, & Bunce, 2006).

Scientific Issues Involving Other Functional Biomarkers in Relation to Cognitive Aging

Conceptually, it is more difficult to see links between biomarkers such as pulmonary function and muscle strength and cognition. These capacities may reflect general central nervous system function and integrity and general health and lifestyle. For example, physical fitness is associated with muscle strength, muscle mass, and cardiopulmonary output. Studies have also shown fitness to be associated with maintenance of cognitive abilities (Kramer et al., 2003). Basic scientific research is required to identify the biological connections between these variables and cognition. For example, functional magnetic resonance imaging studies of brain activation after a randomized controlled trial of an exercise intervention may indicate how brain function may be enhanced or maintained by physical activity (Kramer et al., 2003). Fitness and pulmonary function may be linked to measures of brain blood oxygenation, which in turn may be associated with cognitive performance.

We need to relate other aspects of cognitive aging, such as intraindividual variability, to levels of biomarkers (e.g., homocysteine, brain atrophy, or forced expiratory volume) and to lifestyle or disease variables that may jointly influence these associations. However, the extent to which intraindividual variability reflects pathological (Christensen et al., 2005; Hultsch, MacDonald, Hunter, Levy-Bencheton, & Strauss, 2000) as opposed to normal cognitive decline (Hultsch, MacDonald, & Dixon, 2002; S. C. Li, Brehmer, Shing, Werkle-Bergner, & Lindenberger, 2006) remains unclear. It is especially important to examine intraindividual change in biomarkers in case assumptions about biomarkers based on between-person analyses do not hold within persons (Hofer & Sliwinski, 2001; Martin & Hofer, 2004). Likewise, short-term changes within individuals may not be distinct from long-term change (S. C. Li, Lindenberger, & Sikstrom, 2001).

Research Applications

Further work needs to examine the effects of visual aging on neuropsychological assessment. Work from our laboratory has shown that, for most older adults, standard tests of visual memory are unaffected by visual aging (Drobny, Anstey, & Andrews, 2005). However, my colleagues and I have found that Stroop performance is affected by age-related changes in color vision (Anstey et al., 2002), and thus we do not recommend this test for use in very old adults or in any adult with color vision deficits. Another major application of work in this area is in developing interventions to maintain mobility and risk assessment tools to prevent injury. Evaluation of how cognitive decline interacts with functional decline is required. Many current risk assessment tools for falls do not include cognitive measures. In the field of driving, there is room to develop risk assessment tools that incorporate both cognitive measures and functional biomarkers. Another area where future research may be directed is in the use of technology to compensate for functional and cognitive decline (Scheiber, 2003). A broadening of the theory of "environmental support" to encompass cognitive declines other than memory and sensory and physical deficits will provide a framework for using technology to enable maintenance of independence. A tangible example of this is in the area of smart car technology, where early warning systems may be developed to improve sign recognition by older drivers (Walker, Barnes, & Anstey, 2006).

Conclusion

Although some of the theoretical debates in this field have tended to be circular and possibly arise from focus on statistical artifacts, it is clear that the applications of research into biomarkers and cognitive aging will have a major impact on ensuring that older adults age productively and can adapt optimally to inevitable sensory and cognitive change. Research in the field of biomarkers and cognitive aging has sometimes lacked strong theoretical underpinning. This is changing as recent developments in neuroscience are leading to theoretical models that promise to link age-related declines in functional and cognitive systems (Bäckman, Nyberg, Lindenberger, Li, & Farde, 2006; S. C. Li et al., 2006). A greater understanding of the genetic and environmental factors causing brain aging will also further our understanding of the relationships between functional biomarkers and cognition (Barzilai, Atzmon, Derby, Bauman, & Lipton, 2006; Bufill & Carbonell, 2006; Levin, Perraut, Pollard, & Freedman, 2006; Payton, 2006). Bridging the gap between disciplines will contribute to the development of theories that incorporate the range of variables and systems involved in late life functional decline and its prevention.

REFERENCES

Alexander, N. B., Ashton-Miller, J. A., Giordani, B., Guire, K., & Schultz, A. B. (2005). Age differences in timed accurate stepping with increasing cognitive and visual demand: A walking trail making test. *Journals of Gerontology Series A, Biological Sciences and Medical Sciences, 60,* 1558–1562.

Allen, P. A., Hall, R. J., Druley, J. A., Smith, A. F., Sanders, R. E., & Murphy, M. D. (2001). How shared are age-related influences on cognitive and noncognitive variables? *Psychology and Aging, 16,* 532–549.

Andersen, K., Nybo, H., Gaist, D., Petersen, H. C., McGue, M., Jeune, B., et al. (2002). Cognitive impairment and mortality among nonagenarians: The Danish 1905 cohort survey. *Dementia and Geriatric Cognitive Disorders, 13,* 156–163.

Anstey, K. J. (1999). Sensorimotor variables and forced expiratory volume as correlates of speed, accuracy, and variability in reaction time performance in late adulthood. *Aging, Neuropsychology, and Cognition, 6,* 84–95.

Anstey, K. J., Butterworth, P., Borzycki, M., & Andrews, S. (2006). Between- and within-individual effects of visual contrast sensitivity on perceptual matching, processing speed, and associative memory in older adults. *Gerontology, 52,* 124–130.

Anstey, K. J., Dain, S., Andrews, S., & Drobny, J. (2002). Visual abilities in older adults explain age differences in Stroop and fluid intelligence but not face recognition: Implications for the vision–cognition connection. *Aging, Neuropsychology, and Cognition, 9,* 253–265.

Anstey, K. J., Dear, K., Christensen, H., & Jorm, A. F. (2005). Biomarkers, health, lifestyle and demographic variables as correlates of reaction time performance in early, middle and late adulthood. *Quarterly Journal of Experimental Psychology, 58A,* 5–21.

Anstey, K. J., Hofer, S. M., & Luszcz, M. A. (2003a). Cross-sectional and longitudinal patterns of dedifferentiation in late-life cognitive and sensory function: The effects of age, ability, attrition, and occasion of measurement. *Journal of Experimental Psychology: General, 132,* 470–487.

Anstey, K. J., Hofer, S. M., & Luszcz, M. A. (2003b). A latent growth curve analysis of late-life sensory and cognitive function over 8 years: Evidence for specific and common factors underlying change. *Psychology and Aging, 18,* 714–726.

Anstey, K. J., Lord, S. R., Hennessy, M., Mitchell, P., Mill, K., & von Sanden, C. (2006). The effect of cataract surgery on neuropsychological test performance: A randomized controlled trial. *Journal of the International Neuropsychological Society, 12,* 632–639.

Anstey, K. J., Lord, S. R., & Smith, G. A. (1996). Measuring human functional age: A review of empirical findings. *Experimental Aging Research, 22,* 245–266.

Anstey, K. J., Luszcz, M. A., Giles, L. C., & Andrews, G. R. (2001). Demographic, health, cognitive, and sensory variables as predictors of mortality in very old adults. *Psychology and Aging, 16,* 3–11.

Anstey, K. J., Luszcz, M. A., & Sanchez, L. (2001a). A reevaluation of the common factor theory of shared variance among age, sensory function, and cognitive function in older adults. *Journals of Gerontology Series B: Psychological Sciences and Social Sciences, 56,* P3–P11.

Anstey, K. J., Luszcz, M. A., & Sanchez, L. (2001b). Two-year decline in vision but not hearing is associated with memory decline in very old adults in a population-based sample. *Gerontology, 47,* 289–293.

Anstey, K. J., Mack, H., & von Sanden, C. (2006). The relationship between cognition and mortality in patients with stroke, coronary heart disease or cancer. *European Psychologist, 11,* 182–195.

Anstey, K. J., & Smith, G. A. (1999). Interrelationships among biological markers of aging, health, activity, acculturation, and cognitive performance in late adulthood. *Psychology and Aging, 14,* 605–618.

Anstey, K. J., von Sanden, C., & Luszcz, M. A. (2006). An 8-year prospective study of the relationship between cognitive performance and falling in very old adults. *Journal of the American Geriatrics Society, 54,* 1169–1176.

Anstey, K. J., Windsor, T. D., Jorm, A. F., Christensen, H., & Rodgers, B. (2004). Association of pulmonary function with cognitive performance in early, middle and late adulthood. *Gerontology, 50,* 230–234.

Anstey, K. J., Wood, J., Lord, S., & Walker, J. G. (2005). Cognitive, sensory and physical factors enabling driving safety in older adults. *Clinical Psychology Review, 25,* 45–65.

Atchley, P., & Hoffman, L. (2004). Aging and visual masking: Sensory and attentional factors. *Psychology and Aging, 19,* 57–67.

Bäckman, L., Nyberg, L., Lindenberger, U., Li, S. C., & Farde, L. (2006). The correlative triad among aging, dopamine, and cognition: Current status and future prospects. *Neuroscience and Biobehavioral Reviews, 30,* 791–807.

Baddeley, A., Emslie, H., & Nimmo-Smith, I. (1992). *The Spot-the-Word Test.* Bury St. Edmunds, UK: Thames Valley Test Company.

Bailey, J. L., & Lovie, J. K. (1976). New design for visual acuity letter charts. *American Journal of Optometry and Physiological Optics, 53,* 740–745.

Ball, K., Owsley, C., Sloane, M. E., Roenker, D. L., & Bruni, J. R. (1993). Visual attention problems as a predictor of vehicle crashes in older drivers. *Investigative Ophthalmology and Visual Science, 34,* 3110–3123.

Ball, K. K., Roenker, D. L., Wadley, V. G., Edwards, J. D., Roth, D. L., McGwin, G., Jr., et al. (2006).

Can high-risk older drivers be identified through performance-based measures in a Department of Motor Vehicles setting? *Journal of the American Geriatrics Society, 54,* 77–84.

Baltes, P. B., & Lindenberger, U. (1997). Emergence of a powerful connection between sensory and cognitive functions across the adult life span: A new window to the study of cognitive aging? *Psychology and Aging, 12,* 12–21.

Barzilai, N., Atzmon, G., Derby, C. A., Bauman, J. M., & Lipton, R. B. (2006). A genotype of exceptional longevity is associated with preservation of cognitive function. *Neurology, 67,* 2170–2175.

Bufill, E., & Carbonell, E. (2006). Apolipoprotein E polymorphism and neuronal plasticity. *American Journal of Human Biology, 18,* 556–558.

Butler, R. N., Sprott, R., Warner, H., Bland, J., Feuers, R., Forster, M., et al. (2004). Biomarkers of aging: From primitive organisms to humans. *Journals of Gerontology Series A: Biological Sciences and Medical Sciences, 59,* B560–B567.

Chown, S. M., & Heron, A. (1965). Psychological aspects of ageing in man. *Annual Review of Psychology, 16,* 417–450.

Christensen, H., Dear, K. B., Anstey, K. J., Parslow, R. A., Sachdev, P., & Jorm, A. F. (2005). Within-occasion intraindividual variability and preclinical diagnostic status: Is intraindividual variability an indicator of mild cognitive impairment? *Neuropsychology, 19,* 309–317.

Christensen, H., Mackinnon, A. J., Korten, A., & Jorm, A. F. (2001). The "common cause hypothesis" of cognitive aging: Evidence for not only a common factor but also specific associations of age with vision and grip strength in a cross-sectional analysis. *Psychology and Aging, 16,* 588–599.

Cronin-Golomb, A., & Hof, R. R. (Eds.). (2004). *Vision in Alzheimer's disease.* Basel, Switzerland: Karger.

Delis, D. C., Kramer, J. H., Kaplan, E., & Ober, B. A. (1987). *California Verbal Learning Test.* San Antonio, TX: The Psychological Corporation/ Harcourt Brace Jovanovich.

Drobny, J., Anstey, K. J., & Andrews, S. (2005). Visual memory testing in older adults with age-related visual decline: A measure of memory or visual functioning? *Journal of Clinical and Experimental Neuropsychology, 27,* 425–435.

Farnsworth, D. (1943). Farnsworth 100 Hue and Dichotomous Tests. *Journal of the Optometrical Society of America, 33,* 568–578.

Geerlings, M. I., Deeg, D. J., Penninx, B. W., Schmand, B., Jonker, C., Bouter, L. M., & van Tilburg, W. (1999). Cognitive reserve and mortality in dementia: The role of cognition, functional ability and depression. *Psychological Medicine, 29,* 1219–1226.

Gussekloo, J., de Craen, A. J., Oduber, C., van Boxtel, M. P., & Westendorp, R. G. (2005). Sensory impairment and cognitive functioning in oldest-old subjects: The Leiden 85+ Study. *American Journal of Geriatric Psychiatry, 13,* 781–786.

Hardy, L. H., Rand, G., & Rittler, M. C. (1954). The H-R-R Polychromatic Plates. *Journal of the Optometrical Society of America, 44,* 509–523.

Heron, A., & Chown, S. M. (1961). Ageing and the semi-skilled: A survey in manufacturing industry on Merseyside. *Medical Research Council Annual Report, 40,* 1–59.

Hofer, S. M., Berg, S., & Era, P. (2003). Evaluating the interdependence of aging-related changes in visual and auditory acuity, balance, and cognitive functioning. *Psychology and Aging, 18,* 285–305.

Hofer, S. M., & Sliwinski, M. J. (2001). Understanding ageing: An evaluation of research designs for assessing the interdependence of ageing-related changes. *Gerontology, 47,* 341–352.

Hultsch, D. F., MacDonald, S. W., & Dixon, R. A. (2002). Variability in reaction time performance of younger and older adults. *Journals of Gerontology Series B: Psychological Sciences and Social Sciences, 57,* P101–P115.

Hultsch, D. F., MacDonald, S. W., Hunter, M. A., Levy-Bencheton, J., & Strauss, E. (2000). Intraindividual variability in cognitive performance in older adults: Comparison of adults with mild dementia, adults with arthritis, and healthy adults. *Neuropsychology, 14,* 588–598.

Ikonomovic, M. D., Mufson, E. J., Wuu, J., Bennett, D. A., & DeKosky, S. T. (2005). Reduction of choline acetyltransferase activity in primary visual cortex in mild to moderate Alzheimer's disease. *Archives of Neurology, 62,* 425–430.

Jorm, A. F., Anstey, K. J., Christensen, H., & Rodgers, B. (2004). Gender differences in cognitive abilities: The mediating role of health state and health habits. *Intelligence, 32,* 7–23.

Kramer, A. F., Colcombe, S. J., McAuley, E., Eriksen, K. I., Scalf, P., Jerome, G. J., et al. (2003). Enhancing brain and cognitive function of older adults through fitness training. *Journal of Molecular Neuroscience, 20,* 213–221.

Lee, D. J., Gomez-Marin, O., Lam, B. L., & Zheng, D. D. (2002). Visual acuity impairment and mortality in US adults. *Archives of Ophthalmology, 120,* 1544–1550.

Levin, E. D., Perraut, C., Pollard, N., & Freedman, J. H. (2006). Metallothionein expression and neurocognitive function in mice. *Physiology and Behavior, 87,* 513–518.

Li, K. Z., & Lindenberger, U. (2002). Relations between aging sensory/sensorimotor and cognitive functions. *Neuroscience and Biobehavioral Reviews, 26,* 777–783.

Li, K. Z., Lindenberger, U., Freund, A. M., & Baltes, P. B. (2001). Walking while memorizing: Age-related differences in compensatory behavior. *Psychological Science, 12,* 230–237.

Li, S. C., Brehmer, Y., Shing, Y. L., Werkle-Bergner, M., & Lindenberger, U. (2006). Neuromodulation of associative and organizational plasticity across the life span: Empirical evidence and neurocomputational modeling. *Neuroscience and Biobehavioral Reviews, 30,* 775–790.

Li, S. C., Lindenberger, U., & Sikstrom, S. (2001). Aging cognition: From neuromodulation to representation. *Trends in Cognitive Science, 5,* 479–486.

Lin, M. Y., Gutierrez, P. R., Stone, K. L., Yaffe, K., Ensrud, K. E., Fink, H. A., et al. (2004). Vision impairment and combined vision and hearing impairment predict cognitive and functional decline in older women. *Journal of the American Geriatrics Society, 52,* 1996–2002.

Lindenberger, U., & Baltes, P. B. (1994). Sensory functioning and intelligence in old age: A strong connection. *Psychology and Aging, 9,* 339–355.

Lindenberger, U., & Potter, U. (1998). The complex nature of unique and shared effects in hierarchical linear regression: Implications for developmental psychology. *Psychological Methods, 3,* 218–230.

Lindenberger, U., Scherer, H., & Baltes, P. B. (2001). The strong connection between sensory and cognitive performance in old age: Not due to sensory acuity reductions operating during cognitive assessment. *Psychology and Aging, 16,* 196–205.

Lord, S. R., Clark, R. D., & Webster, I. W. (1991). Visual acuity and contrast sensitivity in relation to falls in an elderly population. *Age and Ageing, 20,* 175–181.

Lord, S. R., & Fitzpatrick, R. C. (2001). Choice stepping reaction time: A composite measure of falls risk in older people. *Journals of Gerontology Series A: Biological Sciences and Medical Sciences, 56,* M627–M632.

Lord, S. R., Ward, J. A., Williams, P., & Anstey, K. J. (1994). Physiological factors associated with falls in older community-dwelling women. *Journal of the American Geriatrics Society, 42,* 1110–1117.

Macdonald, S. W. A., Hultsch, D., & Bunce, D. (2006). Intraindividual variability in vigilance performance: Does degrading visual stimuli mimic age-related "neural noise"? *Journal of Clinical and Experimental Neuropsychology, 22,* 655–675.

Mackinnon, A., Christensen, H., & Jorm, A. F. (2006). Search for a common cause factor amongst cognitive, speed and biological variables using narrow age cohorts. *Gerontology, 52,* 243–257.

Marsiske, M., Klumb, P., & Baltes, M. M. (1997). Everyday activity patterns and sensory functioning in old age. *Psychology and Aging, 12,* 444–457.

Martin, M., & Hofer, S. M. (2004). Intraindividual variability, change, and aging: Conceptual and analytical issues. *Gerontology, 50,* 7–11.

Neale, R., Brayne, C., & Johnson, A. L. (2001). Cognition and survival: An exploration in a large multicentre study of the population aged 65 years and over. *International Journal of Epidemiology, 30,* 1383–1388.

Patel, M. D., Coshall, C., Rudd, A. G., & Wolfe, C. D. (2002). Cognitive impairment after stroke: Clinical determinants and its associations with long-term stroke outcomes. *Journal of the American Geriatrics Society, 50,* 700–706.

Payton, A. (2006). Investigating cognitive genetics and its implications for the treatment of cognitive deficit. *Genes, Brain, and Behavior, 5*(Suppl. 1), 44–53.

Raven, J. C. (1940). Matrix tests. *Mental Health, 1,* 10–18.

Reyes-Ortiz, C. A., Kuo, Y. F., DiNuzzo, A. R., Ray, L. A., Raji, M. A., & Markides, K. S. (2005). Near vision impairment predicts cognitive decline: Data from the Hispanic Established Populations for Epidemiologic Studies of the Elderly. *Journal of the American Geriatrics Society, 53,* 681–686.

Sachdev, P. (2004). Homocysteine, cerebrovascular disease and brain atrophy. *Journal of the Neurological Sciences, 226,* 25–29.

Sachdev, P. S., Anstey, K. J., Parslow, R. A., Wen, W., Maller, J., Kumar, R., et al. (2006). Pulmonary function, cognitive impairment and brain atrophy in a middle-aged community sample. *Dementia and Geriatric Cognitive Disorders, 21,* 300–308.

Salthouse, T. A., Hambrick, D. Z., & McGuthry, K. E. (1998). Shared age-related influences on cognitive and noncognitive variables. *Psychology and Aging, 13,* 486–500.

Salthouse, T. A., Hancock, H. E., Meinz, E. J., & Hambrick, D. Z. (1996). Interrelations of age, visual acuity, and cognitive functioning. *Journals of Gerontology Series B: Psychological Sciences and Social Sciences, 51,* P317–P330.

Schafer, J. H., Glass, T. A., Bolla, K. I., Mintz, M., Jedlicka, A. E., & Schwartz, B. S. (2005). Homocysteine and cognitive function in a population-based study of older adults. *Journal of the American Geriatrics Society, 53,* 381–388.

Scheiber, F. (2003). Human factors and aging: Identifying and compensating for age-related deficits in sensory and cognitive function. In N. Charness & K. W. Schaie (Eds.), *Impact of technology on successful aging* (pp. 42–84). New York: Springer.

Schneider, B., & Pichora-Fuller, M. (2000). Implications of perceptual deterioration for cognitive ageing research. In F. I. M. Craik & T. A. Salthouse (Eds.), *The handbook of aging and cognition* (pp. 155–219). Mahwah, NJ: Lawrence Erlbaum.

Schunemann, H. J., Dorn, J., Grant, B. J., Winkelstein, W., Jr., & Trevisan, M. (2000). Pulmonary function is a long-term predictor of mortality in the general population: 29-year follow-up of the Buffalo Health Study. *Chest, 118,* 656–664.

Scialfa, C. T. (2002). The role of sensory factors in cognitive ageing research. *Canadian Journal of Experimental Psychology, 56,* 153–163.

Shumway-Cook, A., & Woollacott, M. (2000). Attentional demands and postural control: The effect of sensory context. *Journals of Gerontology Series A: Biological Sciences and Medical Sciences, 55,* M10–M16.

Smith, A. (1982). *Symbol Digit Modalities Test (SDMT) manual.* Los Angeles: Western Psychological Services.

Tales, A., Haworth, J., Nelson, S., Snowder, R. J., & Wilcock, G. (2005). Abnormal visual search in mild cognitive impairment and Alzheimer's disease. *Neurocase, 11,* 80–84.

Trenerry, M. R., Crosson, B. C., DeBoe, J., & Leber, W. R. (1999). *Stroop Neuropsychological Screening Test.* San Antonio, TX: The Psychological Corporation.

Valentijn, S. A., van Boxtel, M. P., van Hooren, S. A., Bosma, H., Beckers, H. J., Ponds, R. W., et al. (2005). Change in sensory functioning predicts change in cognitive functioning: Results from a 6-year follow-up in the Maastricht Aging Study. *Journal of the American Geriatrics Society, 53,* 374–380.

Verbaken, J. H., & Johnson, A. W. (1986). Population norms for edge contrast sensitivity. *American Journal of Optometry and Physiological Optics, 63,* 724–732.

von Gunten, A., Giannakopoulos, P., Bouras, C., & Hof, P. R. (2004). Neuropathological changes in visuospatial systems in Alzheimer's disease. In A. Cronin-Golomb & P. R. Hof (Eds.), *Vision in Alzheimer's disease* (pp. 30–61). Basel, Switzerland: Karger.

Walker, J. G., Barnes, N., & Anstey, K. (2006, December). *Sign detection and driving competency for older drivers with impaired vision.* Paper presented at the Australasian Conference on Robotics and Automation, Auckland, New Zealand.

Wechsler, D. (1945). A standardized memory scale for clinical use. *Journal of Psychology, 19,* 87–95.

Wechsler, D. (1981). *Manual for the Wechsler Adult Intelligence Scale—Revised.* San Antonio, TX: The Psychological Corporation.

Wechsler, D. (1997). *The Wechsler Memory Scale—Third edition.* San Antonio, TX: The Psychological Corporation.

21

Assessing the Relationship of Cognitive Aging and Processes of Dementia

Gwenith G. Fisher, Brenda L. Plassman,
Steven G. Heeringa, and Kenneth M. Langa

Distinguishing between cognitive changes present in healthy aging and those related to a neuropathological process in late life has challenged researchers for some time. These "normal" and pathological aging processes typically have been viewed as two distinct pathways toward different endpoints. On the basis of this fundamental perspective, many cognitive aging studies have sought to exclude individuals with dementia. However, in this chapter we present several lines of evidence suggesting it is not realistic to expect to be able to segregate these two groups. For example, Alzheimer's disease (AD) and likely other subtypes of dementia have a protracted period in which the individual is asymptomatic or exhibits only mild cognitive impairment.

Recently, cognitive aging researchers (e.g., Sliwinski, Hofer, Hall, Buschke, & Lipton, 2003) have emphasized the need to focus on the processes that distinguish between what Baltes and Nesselroade (1979) labeled *normative age-graded* and *non-normative developmental influences* of aging. *Normative aging* refers to changes that all adults experience and occur with chronological age. Non-normative changes, on the other hand, are not necessarily experienced by all individuals, although they may be more frequent, intense, or severe as one's age increases. Dementia is an example of a non-normative aging process and a prevalent condition that must be addressed in the study of cognitive aging. As the editors of this volume have mentioned, prior research has sought to study normal aging and dementia as separate processes. However, we concur with the editors that cognitive functioning falls on a continuum, and it behooves us to consider dementia processes as a part of cognitive aging, especially in light of preclinical dementia or the

AUTHORS' NOTE: Partial support for the work on this chapter was provided by the National Institute on Aging, R01 AG027010 (Kenneth M. Langa, Principal Investigator). The National Institute on Aging provided funding for the Health and Retirement Study and the Aging, Demographics, and Memory Study (U01 AG09740). In addition, we thank the editors, reviewers, and Bill Rodgers for their very helpful comments.

middle ground of "cognitively impaired but not demented."

Given that different profiles of cognitive performance in dementia and normal aging have been reported (Sliwinski et al., 2003), the inclusion of these individuals likely affects the estimates of the pattern and extent of cognitive change in normal aging; however, the degree to which they affect the results is not clear. In this chapter, we further discuss some of the challenges of distinguishing normal cognitive aging from dementia processes. We then propose another approach to handling these challenges to study the trajectories of cognitive aging. Finally, we describe how the Aging, Demographics and Memory Study (ADAMS), a substudy of the Health and Retirement Study (HRS), may be used to investigate some of these issues.

Cognitive Aging Due to Dementia Processes

Implicit in the concept of normal cognitive aging is the premise that the majority of individuals experience normal cognitive aging. However, research evidence does not necessarily support this. For example, in the case of AD, by far the most common type of dementia, there has long been a debate about whether every person will get the disease if he or she just lives long enough (Khachaturian, Gallo, & Breitner, 2000). This suggests that dementia is part of the normative aging process. However, some studies offer a somewhat more positive outlook and have suggested that possibly 25% to 30% (still a minority) of the population remains cognitively intact and thus may be invulnerable to AD (Khachaturian, Zandi, Breitner, Corcoran, & Mayer, 2004) and other dementias (Andersen-Ranberg, Vasegaard, & Jeune, 2001) over an extended life span approaching 100 years.

Identifying the minority of individuals who may not be susceptible to AD is difficult given the extensive evidence of a long preclinical or latent phase of AD during which time there are typically only mild, if any, overt clinical symptoms. The evidence supporting the presence of an extended latent phase of AD is strongest among those at genetic risk for the disease, but it by no means is limited to this group of individuals. The evidence includes the presence of extracellular beta amyloid plaques, one of the hallmark neuropathological markers of AD, found postmortem in the brain tissue of individuals who died as early as age 30 (Braak & Braak, 1997). Further evidence comes from neuroimaging studies that report a thinning of the medial temporal lobe gray matter shown on magnetic resonance imaging several years prior to detection of overt dementia symptoms (Breitner et al., 1995; Erkinjuntti et al., 1993; Golomb et al., 1996; Graham et al., 1997; Levy, 1994; Petersen, Smith, Waring, Ivnik, Tangalos, & Kokmen, 1999). Positron emission tomography studies use fluoro-deoxyglucose to show regional brain hypometabolism in nondemented individuals at risk for AD in a pattern similar to that observed in AD (Reiman et al., 1996; G. W. Small et al., 2000). Finally, some neuropsychological studies show relatively subtle differences between nondemented individuals genetically at risk for AD and those with no known genetic risk for the disease (B. J. Small, Rosnick, Fratiglioni, & Bäckman, 2004). Others have shown that small differences on cognitive tests are present 7 years prior to dementia onset in individuals who later develop dementia and those who do not (Hall, Lipton, Sliwinski, & Stewart, 2000). It is noteworthy that not all studies have reported consistent findings with regard to cognitive performance, which may be due to differences in methodology, sample characteristics, and the sensitivity of the measures used.

In addition, the association between the pathophysiological changes associated with AD and cognitive change are not well understood. Further complicating the issue is the fact that there are limits to the sensitivity and specificity of the measures used to detect cognitive change. In other words, although test results from neuroimaging, neuropathology, and neuropsychological testing discriminate reliably between individuals with AD and those who do not have AD, these assessment methods do not accurately distinguish between these groups 100% of the time. As a result, the sensitivity and specificity of these measures are limited and eliminated as optimal candidates for diagnostic tests for preclinical dementia.

COGNITIVE IMPAIRMENT BUT NOT DEMENTIA

The challenge of distinguishing "normal" aging from preclinical dementia is further compounded by the proposed middle ground between normal aging and overt dementia in which mild impairment insufficient to call dementia is present. The definition for this group has been operationalized in a number of different ways and has used varied nomenclature, for example, *cognitive impairment, not dementia* (CIND; Graham et al., 1997), *mild cognitive impairment* (MCI; Petersen et al., 1999), age-associated cognitive decline (Levy, 1994), and mild-ambiguous (Breitner et al., 1995). All of these diagnostic categories have been defined on the basis of mild impairment in one or more cognitive domains (often emphasizing memory impairment) to identify a group of individuals who are thought to be at increased risk of progressing to dementia. In this chapter, we use the term *CIND,* which has typically been used to encompass cognitive or functional impairment in any of the cognitive domains (and not necessarily limited to memory impairment) that is due to a number of different etiologies (e.g., prodromal AD, cerebrovascular disease, medications or medical conditions, and sensory impairment). In the context, the often-used term *mild cognitive impairment* is considered a subtype of CIND.

The few studies reporting prevalence of CIND have suggested that CIND occurs twice as frequently as dementia (Graham et al., 1997; Lopez et al., 2006). Studies that have included longitudinal follow-up of clinical samples have estimated that the presence of mild impairment increases the likelihood of subsequent progression to dementia to a rate of 10% to 15% per year compared to about 1% to 2% among individuals with normal cognitive function (Bowen et al., 1997; Daly, Zaitchik, Copeland, Schmahmann, Gunter, & Albert, 2000; Petersen, Kokmen, Tangalos, Smith, & Ivnik, 1994; Smith et al., 1996). However, not all individuals do progress to dementia, and some studies report that a sizable minority (up to 44%) of the mildly impaired also revert to normal cognition (Ganguli, Dodge, Shen, & DeKosky, 2004; Ritchie, 2004). Recent reports suggest that mildly impaired persons as a group show neuropathological changes postmortem intermediate to those with normal cognition and AD (Bennett et al., 2005; Markesbery et al., 2006; Petersen et al., 1999). The interpretation of these data differs among researchers such that some propose to label this group as having *mild AD* (Markesbery et al., 2006; Morris, 2006), whereas others caution restraint pending improved specificity in the diagnosis of the boundary cognitive zone between normal cognition and dementia and a better understanding of the association between the cognitive and neuropathological findings (Petersen et al., 1999).

In summary, mild impairment has been the focus of much recent research, because it is not clear whether this middle ground represents an extension of normal aging; the prodrome of dementia; or a third option, which includes some individuals from both groups. At the other end of the cognitive spectrum, the threshold for discriminating between mild impairment and dementia differs among diagnosticians, thus making it even more difficult to ensure that the demented are excluded from the normal aging group. At the very least, the cumulative data on the mildly impaired suggest this group may represent an overlap between normal elderly persons at the low end of the cognitive distribution (those who do not progress or improve over time) and elderly persons with preclinical dementia (those who do progress).

OTHER FACTORS RELATED TO COGNITIVE ASSESSMENT

One of the criteria for the diagnosis of both dementia and CIND is the presence of decrements in cognitive functioning. In the absence of actual baseline measurement of cognition, one must estimate baseline ability on the basis of demographic variables, such as education, or performance on tests that are relatively impervious to the dementing process (at least in the early stages of the disease), such as reading and vocabulary tests. The aim of this methodology is to differentiate between actual decline in cognitive functioning and lifelong stable cognitive weaknesses. In other words, the goal is to be able to make a distinction between individuals who experienced an actual decline in ability and those who never developed the ability early on. This can be particularly challenging to accomplish among individuals with low levels of literacy, poor education quality, and differences in acculturation that may make accurate interpretation of test scores difficult (Manly et al., 1998).

In addition, performance on neuropsychological tests may also be adversely impacted by auditory, visual, or motor impairment; medical illnesses; and medication effects. Similar to dementia, the prevalence of these potential confounds increases with age and comorbidity, making it difficult to differentiate the effect of each confound on cognitive performance. The challenges of interpreting performance on neuropsychological tests are increased in epidemiological samples given the greater heterogeneity in these samples compared with most clinical samples (Kokmen, O'Brien, Rocca, Ozsarfati, & Beard, 1996).

SUMMARY AND IMPLICATIONS

All of this information combined suggests that the premise that individuals exhibiting normal cognitive aging can be accurately identified may be unfounded. Given the long course of pathological AD-related changes and the many factors that contribute to the variability in cognitive performance, our current diagnostic criteria and assessment methods lack the sensitivity and specificity to distinguish between individuals with preclinical dementia (or who will progress to dementia) and those who will live out their life with "normal" cognition.

One interim solution to this dilemma may be to prospectively assess cognition at multiple time points beginning at the age when individuals are at increased risk of developing AD. To assess large, heterogeneous groups fully representative of the population, one would likely need to limit the assessment to brief cognitive status measures because of the logistics and cost of doing more extensive testing in such samples. A limitation of brief cognitive status measures is that they are not suitable for diagnosing dementia because obtaining good sensitivity for dementia requires that the cut-point on the

screening measure be set relatively low. Given the trade-off between specificity (i.e., false positives) and sensitivity (i.e., false negatives) of the measures, this typically results in low specificity. Furthermore, another limitation of brief measures is that they do not differentiate among the causes of impairment, because test performance can be affected by many factors other than dementia, such as medical illness, medications, visual or hearing impairment, and lifelong educational and cultural advantages and disadvantages. For example, one such study (Breitner et al., 1999) reported a sensitivity of 98.4% and specificity of 69.1% for dementia (Z. S. Khachaturian, 2000). This resulted in a positive predictive value of only 25% because of the large number of false positive screens that resulted from the low specificity of the screening test. Similar results have been reported for other studies (Canadian Study of Health and Aging Working Group, 1994; Gallo & Breitner, 1995).

Performance in the impaired range on such brief cognitive screens does not, in itself, represent dementia, because poor performance may be due to other factors. However, a more thorough assessment may be conducted among a subset of individuals following the initial screening. When a diagnosis of dementia is then assigned on the basis of further clinical evaluation, cognition (and its various components) could be modeled as a function of disease progression by aligning individuals at the estimated point at which they crossed the threshold of dementia based on the longitudinal cognitive data. One could then compare performance between and within individuals at, for example, 6 years prior to crossing the threshold for dementia. This method assumes that individuals are at comparable stages when detected and that the disease progresses in a consistent manner across individuals. We next describe an ongoing study that facilitates this approach.

THE AGING, DEMOGRAPHICS, AND MEMORY STUDY

The ADAMS is the first nationally representative population-based study of dementia in the United States. In an effort to explore the health and economic implications of dementia in the United States, the HRS, which began in 1992, launched the ADAMS in 2001. The HRS is a cooperative agreement between the National Institute on Aging and the Survey Research Center at the University of Michigan to study health transitions in the second half of life and their impact on health care expenditures; claims on structured programs such as Social Security, Medicare, and Medicaid; informal assistance from family members; and, ultimately, economic status. Because of its nationally representative sample; its longitudinal design; and its detailed measures relating to health, health care utilization, help patterns, and economic resources and behavior, the HRS offers a number of unique features for interdisciplinary investigations of dementia and cognitive aging in the population. Although the HRS administers biennial brief cognitive status tests to participants, it lacks a true clinical assessment of dementia. Such a trade-off between national representativeness of cost information and refinement of diagnostic information is common in studies of dementia costs (Taylor, Schenkman, Zhou, & Sloan, 2001).

To conduct the ADAMS, a team of HRS investigators at the University of Michigan partnered with a team at Duke University Medical Center that has a wealth of experience with conducting community-based epidemiological studies of dementia (including ongoing studies, e.g., the Duke University–National Academy of Science–National Research Council Collaborative Twins Study, the Veterans Study of Memory and Aging, and the Cache County [Utah] Study of Memory and Aging). A total of 856 individuals participated in the ADAMS and were assigned a diagnosis of dementia, CIND, or normal cognition (Langa et al., 2005). Within the categories of dementia and CIND, subtypes were diagnosed to reflect the etiology of the impairment. The ADAMS sought to combine the advantages of clinical and epidemiological approaches to dementia diagnosis. To this end, it included a single standardized diagnostic protocol to assess dementia, and the sample spanned an age range from 70 to 110 from multiple ethnic groups. (See Langa et al., 2005, for additional details regarding the study design and methods.)

As the first nationally representative population-based study of dementia that includes participants from all regions of the United States, the ADAMS is an excellent source for estimating the national prevalence of AD and other dementia subtypes (Plassman et al., 2007). Another way that the data from the ADAMS can be examined is to use a multiple-imputation procedure to model the probability of dementia among a comparable age cohort among the larger HRS sample. This process is explained below.

MODELING THE PROBABILITY OF DEMENTIA FOR THE OLDER AGE HEALTH AND RETIREMENT STUDY COHORTS

Diagnostic classifications of disease (e.g., dementia) are subject to uncertainties that arise from a number of factors (Ohayon, 1993). Faced with this inherent uncertainty, physicians and other medical professionals often must use diagnostic tools and expert judgment to place patients in discrete categories for purposes of patient management or treatment. Wainwright, Surtees, and Gilks (1997) and Surtees, Wainwright, Gilks, and Brugha (1997) have demonstrated that for epidemiological research designed to study disease prevalence, disease risk models, or disease-related outcomes in large population samples, such discrete classifications of individuals are neither necessary nor optimal. These authors employed maximum likelihood methods for latent class analysis of symptom scale counts to assign each study participant a probability of belonging to one of four depression event classifications: (1) no event, (2) mild, (3) moderate, or (4) severe. They demonstrated the use of the probability measures in estimating simple prevalence as well as odds ratios from multivariate models of factors related to depression and its severity.

We conducted a test of a related method in which HRS longitudinal data on cognition were integrated with supplemental data that included both measures of cognition and a consensus diagnosis of dementia status. The objectives of this test were to demonstrate (a) the feasibility of imputing a probability of dementia diagnosis "score" to individual HRS participants and (b) the utility of the imputed probability values for studying the population-averaged impact of dementia on health and economic outcomes. With appropriate caution to the reader concerning the exploratory nature of this exercise, we describe the method and present a set of illustrative results.

Because the ADAMS is based on a stratified random subsample of the actual HRS panel, it would have been ideal to conduct the test using the ADAMS cognition data and diagnostic assessments using the ADAMS data. However, ADAMS data were not yet available for the first trial of the method. Therefore, the data used to develop the diagnostic model for this methodological test were obtained from a previous study, the Veterans Study of Memory and Aging (VSMA; Plassman et al., 2000) conducted by the Epidemiology of Dementia Program at the Duke University Medical Center. The VSMA data set included the Duke project teams' clinical assessment of dementia status (yes/no), basic demographic data (age, education), and key cognitive self-report and proxy measures for a total sample of 1,990 male veterans aged 67 to 90 years.

Two dementia prediction models were fit to the VSMA diagnostic data—one using a score based on a set of cognition measures and one for proxy reports of cognition status. In each model, the logit of the probability of a positive dementia diagnosis (1 = yes, 0 = no) was modeled as a simple function of the uncentered values for the participant's age in years, education in grades completed, and cognition score. The general form of each prediction model was:

$$logit[p(\text{dementia dx})|x] = \beta_0 + \beta_1 \cdot \text{age(years)} + \beta_2 \cdot \text{education(years)} + \beta_3 \cdot \text{cognition\_score}.$$

The cognition score used in modeling dementia probability for the VSMA participants who were capable of responding on their own behalf (self-reporters) was an index based on 10 cognitive test items used in both the VSMA and the HRS (Herzog & Wallace, 1997; Ofstedal, Fisher, & Herzog, 2005). The Informant Questionnaire on Cognitive Decline in the Elderly measure (Jorm, 1994) was used as the predictor of cognitive status in modeling the probability of dementia for participants whose information was supplied by a proxy. Figure 21.1

illustrates the typical nonlinear form of the predicted probability function derived from the estimated logistic model for the VSMA proxy reports. The estimated probability function illustrated in this figure corresponds to an individual who is age 80 and has a 12th-grade education. In addition to the predicted probabilities of dementia, Figure 21.1 illustrates the 95% lower and upper confidence bounds for the predicted probabilities over the range of Informant Questionnaire on Cognitive Decline in the Elderly scores.

The VSMA dementia probability self- and proxy reporter models were used in conjunction with the 1998 HRS sample data on demographics, cognition, and other characteristics to develop multiple imputations (Little & Rubin, 2002) of the probability of dementia for each 1998 HRS panel member who was born prior to 1924—those approximately age 75 years and older in 1998. Ten independent multiple imputations of the individual dementia probability were developed for each 1998 HRS respondent over age 70. Each multiple imputation ($m = 1, \ldots, 10$) for the ith respondent involved two steps:

1. A stochastic draw of the coefficient values:

$$\hat{\beta}_{(m)} = (\hat{\beta}_{(m)0}, \hat{\beta}_{(m)1}, \hat{\beta}_{(m)2}, \hat{\beta}_{(m)3})$$

   from the distribution of the logistic model coefficients estimated from the VSMA data, and

2. Application of the coefficient value "draws" to the observed age, education level, and cognition score data from the 1998 HRS data to create an imputed dementia probability value:

$$\hat{p}_{(m),i} = \frac{e^{X_i \hat{\beta}_{(m)}}}{1 + e^{X_i \hat{\beta}_{(m)}}}.$$

The multiple-imputation method was used to correctly reflect two sources of stochastic variability that are introduced in the construction of the dementia probability variables for HRS respondents: (1) the uncertainty due to the sampling error in the parameter estimates of the VSMA-based prediction models and (2) the uncertainty associated with the individual prediction "draws" from the conditional probability distributions corresponding to the estimated regression models for self and proxy reporters.

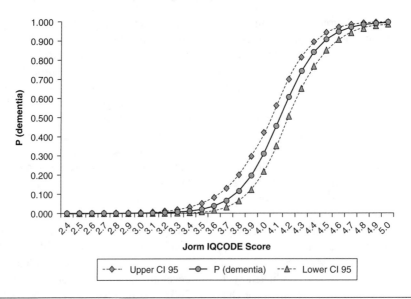

Figure 21.1   Predicted Probability (P) of Dementia

SOURCE: This model was estimated on the basis of Veterans Study of Memory and Aging data (Plassman et al., 2000).

NOTE: CI = confidence interval; IQCODE = Informant Questionnaire on Cognitive Decline in the Elderly (Jorm, 1994).

Tables 21.1 and 21.2 provide illustrative results that demonstrate how such multiple imputations of dementia probability could be used to study population outcomes of dementia, including serious falls and annual medical costs. Table 21.1 presents results of an exploratory logistic regression analysis using the 1998 HRS data, augmented with predicted dementia probabilities from the VSMA models, to study the relationship of dementia probability and other covariates to the likelihood of a serious fall within the past two years. The multiple-imputation analysis results for this model suggest that the model-based predictions of dementia probability are a strong predictor of falls. Table 21.2 presents simple logistic regression results that model the probability that eligible respondent's annual medical costs exceeded selected thresholds (>$5,000, >$25,000) as a function of the predicted dementia probability and the age, gender, and race of the HRS participant. These test results clearly suggest that a higher probability of dementia is strongly related to high annual medical costs.

Data collection for the ADAMS is now complete, and we are moving ahead with a formal evaluation of the utility of the multiple-imputation method based on that data set. The simple test based on the VSMA prediction model showed promise, but key questions remain to be answered. Some of these questions pertain to what constitute the optimal statistical approaches to the dementia probability modeling and the multiple-imputation process. One important empirical question is: "Will augmentation of the full HRS sample of older-age adults ($n \sim 7,000$) with imputations based on models derived from the smaller sample of ADAMS cases ($n \sim 856$) significantly increase the precision of analyses (relative to simpler, direct analysis of the ADAMS sample itself)?" These and related questions will be the focus of future research on statistical methodology for the ADAMS data set.

FUTURE RESEARCH

The inclusion of cognitive measures as part of many national longitudinal studies is an asset and excellent resource for researchers examining cognitive aging phenomena. The data collected for the ADAMS provide not only a diagnosis of dementia or CIND based on a clinical evaluation of the 856 respondents in the ADAMS sample but also a wealth of information on the clinical,

Table 21.1 Estimated Relationship Between Probability of Dementia and Having a Serious Fall Within the Past 2 Years

Variable	Coefficient	SE	Odds ratio (OR)	OR 95% CI
Intercept	−5.4893	0.7265	2.3681	1.7946, 3.1250
P-dementia	0.8621	0.1415	1.0482	1.0305, 1.0663
Age	0.0471	0.0463	0.4988	0.4147, 0.6000
Male	−0.6995	0.0942	0.5767	0.04635, 0.7175
African American	−0.5505	0.1115		

SOURCE: The dementia probability model was estimated from the Duke University Veteran's Study of Memory and Aging. The illustrative analysis was done using the 1998 Health and Retirement Study data.

NOTE: P = probability; CI = confidence interval.

Table 21.2 Estimated Relationship Between Probability of Dementia and Annual Medical Costs

Variable	Medical cost > $5,000		Medical cost > $25,000	
	Coefficient	SE	Coefficient	SE
Intercept	−1.9829	0.5792	−.49759	0.6594
P-dementia	0.9906	0.1397	1.2228	0.1354
Age	0.0157	0.0069	0.0365	0.0081
Male	0.2043	0.0764	0.1894	0.1053
African American	−0.1833	0.1105	−0.1013	0.1598
	Odds ratio (OR)	OR 95% CI	OR	OR 95% CI
P-dementia	2.6928	2.0478, 3.5410	3.3967	2.6050, 4.4290
Age	1.0158	1.0022, 1.0297	1.0372	1.0208, 1.0538
Male	1.2267	1.0561, 1.4248	1.2085	0.9832, 1.4856
African American	0.8325	0.6704, 1.0338	0.9037	0.6607, 1.2360

SOURCE: The dementia probability model was estimated from the Duke University Veteran's Study of Memory and Aging. The illustrative analysis was done using the 1998 Health and Retirement Study data.

NOTE: P = probability; CI = confidence interval.

medical, and family history of those individuals. The unique characteristics of this study, such as its nationally representative sample and the availability of the extensive longitudinal information collected as part of the HRS, make this data set a rich analytic opportunity for researchers in a myriad of disciplines.

The ADAMS will be particularly useful for studying trajectories of cognitive aging and shedding light on the distinction between normal and dementia processes in cognitive aging. The detailed neuropsychological test data and dementia diagnoses available in the ADAMS data set can be merged with the brief HRS cognitive screening measures (Herzog & Wallace, 1997; Ofstedal et al., 2005) available in all waves of the HRS, including waves before as well as after the ADAMS dementia diagnoses were assigned. At the time this chapter was written, a second wave of follow-up assessments was being conducted with original ADAMS participants, which will provide additional cognitive data to facilitate longitudinal analysis. Specifically, these data will be instrumental in further investigations of cognitive trajectories over age and time.

The illustration of a multiple-imputation procedure to develop a dementia probability model and to apply that model to study other variables, including covariates and dementia outcomes, provides an example of how analysts can use dementia diagnoses from a subset of respondents to study many topics among a larger sample. The HRS/ADAMS data lend themselves well to this technique. Altogether, it is our hope that the ADAMS and HRS data sets can be used together to provide the interdisciplinary research community with a wealth of data to further study cognitive trajectories and individual differences related to cognitive functioning to further develop knowledge and theory of cognitive aging.

REFERENCES

Andersen-Ranberg, K., Vasegaard, L., & Jeune, B. (2001). Dementia is not inevitable: A population-based study of Danish centenarians. *Journals of Gerontology Series B: Psychological Sciences and Social Sciences, 56,* P152–P159.

Baltes, P., & Nesselroade, J. R. (1979). History and rationale of longitudinal research. In P. Baltes & J. R. Nesselroade (Eds.), *Longitudinal research in the study of behavior and development* (pp. 1–39). San Diego, CA: Academic Press.

Bennett, D. A., Schneider, J. A., Wilson, R. S., Bienias, J. L., Berry-Kravis, E., & Arnold, S. E. (2005). Amyloid mediates the association of apolipoprotein E e4 allele to cognitive function in older people. *Journal of Neurology, Neurosurgery, and Psychiatry, 76,* 1194–1199.

Bowen, J., Teri, L., Kukull, W., McCormick, W., McCurry, S. M., & Larson, E. B. (1997). Progression to dementia in patients with isolated memory loss. *The Lancet, 349,* 763–765.

Braak, H., & Braak, E. (1997). Frequency of stages of Alzheimer-related lesions in different age categories. *Neurobiology of Aging, 18,* 351–357.

Breitner, J. C. S., Welsh, K. A., Gau, B. A., McDonald, W. M., Steffens, D. C., Saunders, A. M., et al. (1995). Alzheimer's disease in the National Academy of Sciences–National Research Council Registry of Aging Twin Veterans. III. Detection of cases, longitudinal results, and observations on twin concordance. *Archives of Neurology, 52,* 763–771.

Breitner, J. C. S., Wyse, B. W., Anthony, J. C., Welsh-Bohmer, K. A., Steffens, D. C., Norton, M. C., et al. (1999). APOE-epsilon4 count predicts age when prevalence of AD increases, then declines: The Cache County Study. *Neurology, 53,* 321–331.

Canadian Study of Health and Aging Working Group. (1994). Canadian Study of Health and Aging: Study methods and prevalence of dementia. *Canadian Medical Association Journal, 150,* 899–913.

Daly, E., Zaitchik, D., Copeland, M., Schmahmann, J., Gunther, J., & Albert, M. (2000). Predicting conversion to Alzheimer disease using standardized clinical information. *Archives of Neurology, 57,* 675–680.

Erkinjuntti, T., Lee, D. H., Gao, F., Steenhuis, R., Eliasziw, M., Fry, R., et al. (1993). Temporal lobe atrophy on magnetic resonance imaging in the diagnosis of early Alzheimer's disease. *Archives of Neurology, 50,* 305–310.

Gallo, J. J., & Breitner, J. C. S. (1995). Alzheimer's disease in the N.A.S.–N.R.C. Registry of aging twin veterans. IV. Performance characteristics of a two-stage telephone screening procedure for Alzheimer's dementia. *Psychological Medicine, 25,* 1211–1219.

Ganguli, M., Dodge, H. H., Shen, C., & DeKosky, S. T. (2004). Mild cognitive impairment, amnestic type: An epidemiologic study. *Neurology, 63,* 115–121.

Golomb, J., Kluger, A., de Leon, M. J., Ferris, S. H., Mittelman, M., Cohen, J., et al. (1996). Hippocampal formation size predicts declining memory performance in normal aging. *Neurology, 47,* 810–813.

Graham, J. E., Rockwood, K., Beattie, B. L., Eastwood, R., Gauthier, S., Tuokko, H., et al. (1997). Prevalence and severity of cognitive impairment with and without dementia in an elderly population. *The Lancet, 349,* 1793–1796.

Hall, C. B., Lipton, R. B., Sliwinski, M. J., & Stewart, W. F. (2000). A change point model for estimating onset of cognitive decline in preclinical Alzheimer's disease. *Statistics in Medicine, 19,* 1555–1566.

Herzog, A. R., & Wallace, R. B. (1997). Measures of cognitive functioning in the AHEAD study. *Journals of Gerontology Series B, 52B,* 37–48.

Jorm, A. F. (1994). A short form of the Informant Questionnaire on Cognitive Decline in the Elderly (IQCODE): Development and cross-validation. *Psychological Medicine, 24,* 145–153.

Khachaturian, A. S. (2000). Toward a comprehensive theory of Alzheimer's disease—Challenges, caveats, parameters. In A.-M. Cantwell, E. Friedlander, & M. Tramm (Eds.), *Annals of the New York Academy of Sciences: Vol. 925. Ethics and anthropology: Facing future issues in human biology, globalism, and cultural property* (pp. 184–193). New York: New York Academy of Sciences.

Khachaturian, A. S., Gallo, J. J., & Breitner, J. C. S. (2000). Performance characteristics of a two-stage dementia screen in a population sample. *Journal of Clinical Epidemiology, 53,* 531–540.

Khachaturian, A. S., Zandi, P. P., Breitner, J. C. S., Corcoran, C. D., & Mayer, L. S. (2004). Apolipoprotein E epsilon4 count affects age at onset of Alzheimer disease, but not lifetime susceptibility: The Cache County Study. *Archives of General Psychiatry, 61,* 518–524.

Kokmen, E., O'Brien, P. C., Rocca, W. A., Ozsarfati, Y., & Beard, C. M. (1996). Impact of referral bias on clinical and epidemiologic studies of Alzheimer's disease. *Journal of Clinical Epidemiology, 49,* 79–83.

Langa, K., Plassman, B., Wallace, R., Herzog, A. R., Heeringa, S., Ofstedal, M. B., et al. (2005). The Aging, Demographics and Memory Study: Study design and methods. *Neuroepidemiology, 25,* 181–191.

Levy, R. (1994). Aging-associated cognitive decline. *International Psychogeriatrics, 6,* 63–68.

Little, R. J. A., & Rubin, D. B. (2002). *Statistical analysis with missing data.* Hoboken, NJ: Wiley.

Lopez, O. L., Becker, J. T., Jagust, W. J., Fitzpatrick, A., Carlson, M. C., DeKosky, S. T., et al. (2006). Neuropsychological characteristics of mild cognitive impairment subgroups. *Journal of Neurology, Neurosurgery & Psychiatry, 77,* 159–165.

Manly, J. J., Jacobs, D. M., Sano, M., Bell, K., Merchant, C. A., Small, S. A., et al. (1998). Cognitive test performance among nondemented elderly African Americans and Whites. *Neurology, 50,* 1238–1245.

Markesbery, W. R., Davis, D. G., Smith, C. D., Schmitt, F. A., Kryscio, R. J., & Wekstein, D. R. (2006). Neuropathologic substrate of mild cognitive impairment. *Archives of Neurology, 63,* 38–46.

Morris, J. C. (2006). Mild cognitive impairment is early AD: Time to revise diagnostic criteria. *Archives of Neurology, 63,* 15–16.

Ofstedal, M. B., Fisher, G. G., & Herzog, A. R., (2005). *Documentation of cognitive functioning measures in the Health and Retirement Study* (HRS/AHEAD Documentation Report DR-006). Available through the Survey Research Center at the Institute for Social Research, University of Michigan (http://hrsonline.isr.umich.edu/docs/userg/dr-006.pdf).

Ohayon, M. M. (1993). Utilization of expert systems in psychiatry. *Canadian Journal of Psychiatry, 38,* 203–211.

Petersen, R. C., Kokmen, E., Tangalos, E. G., Smith, G. E., & Ivnik, R. J. (1994). Memory function in very early Alzheimer's Disease. *Neurology, 44,* 867–872.

Petersen, R. C., Smith, G. E., Waring, S. C., Ivnik, R. J., Tangalos, E. G., & Kokmen, E. (1999). Mild cognitive impairment: Clinical characterization and outcome. *Archives of Neurology, 56,* 303–308.

Plassman, B. L., Havlik, R. J., Steffens, D. C., Helms, M. J., Newman, T. N., Drosdick, D., et al. (2000). Documented head injury in early adulthood and risk of Alzheimer's disease and other dementias. *Neurology, 55,* 1158–1166.

Plassman, B. L., Langa, K. M., Fisher, G. G., Heeringa, S. G., Weir, D. R., et al. (2007). Prevalence of dementia in the United States: The Aging, Demographics, and Memory Study. *Neuroepidemiology, 29,* 125–132.

Reiman, E. M., Caselli, R. J., Yun, L. S., Chen, K., Bandy, D., Minoshima, S., et al. (1996). Preclinical evidence of Alzheimer's disease in persons homozygous for the epsilon 4 allele for apolipoprotein E. *New England Journal of Medicine, 334,* 752–758.

Ritchie, K. (2004). Mild cognitive impairment: An epidemiological perspective. *Dialogues in Clinical Neuroscience, 6,* 401–408.

Sliwinski, M. J., Hofer, S. M., Hall, C., Buschke, H., & Lipton, R. B. (2003). Modeling memory decline in older adults: The importance of preclinical dementia, attrition, and chronological age. *Psychology of Aging, 18,* 658–671.

Small, B. J., Rosnick, C. B., Fratiglioni, L., & Bäckman, L. (2004). Apolipoprotein E and cognitive performance: A meta-analysis. *Psychology and Aging, 19,* 592–600.

Small, G. W., Ercoli, L. M., Silverman, D. H., Huang, S. C., Komo, S., Bookheimer, S. Y., et al. (2000). Cerebral metabolic and cognitive decline in persons at genetic risk for Alzheimer's disease. *Proceedings of the National Academy of Sciences, USA, 97,* 6037–6042.

Smith, G. E., Petersen, R. C., Parisi, J. E., Ivnik, R. J., Kokmen, E., Tangalos, E. G., et al. (1996). Definition, course, and outcome of mild cognitive impairment. *Aging, Neuropsychology, and Cognition, 3,* 141–147.

Surtees, P. G., Wainwright, N. W. J., Gilks, W. R., & Brugha, T. S. (1997). Diagnostic boundaries, reasoning and depressive disorder: II. Application of a probabilistic model to the OPCS general population survey of psychiatric morbidity in Great Britain. *Psychological Medicine, 27,* 847–860.

Taylor, D. H., Schenkman, M., Zhou, J., & Sloan, F. A. (2001). The relative effect of Alzheimer's disease and related dementias, disability, and comorbidities on cost of care for elderly persons. *Journals of Gerontology Series B: Psychological Sciences and Social Sciences, 56B,* 285–293.

Wainwright, N. W. J, Surtees, P. G., & Gilks, W. R. (1997). Diagnostic boundaries, reasoning and depressive disorder: I. Development of a probabilistic morbidity model for public health psychiatry. *Psychological Medicine, 27,* 835–845.

PART V

HISTORICAL PROCESSES AND CULTURAL DIFFERENCES

22

DEVELOPING A CULTURAL COGNITIVE NEUROSCIENCE OF AGING

DENISE C. PARK

The overarching goal of this chapter is to understand how neurocognitive function in old age is simultaneously modified by two forces: contextual factors and neurobiology. There is evidence from many sources that, with age, there is a decrease in many fundamental cognitive processes (Park et al., 2002) and that these declines are universal, because they are manifested in both high- and low-functioning older adults (Baltes & Lindenberger, 1988) as well as across cultures (Hedden et al., 2002). The breadth and reliability of these findings suggest that such declines are biological concomitants of human aging. Recent evidence suggests that linear age-related decline in cognitive function is not accompanied by a corresponding linear decrease in neural response. Instead, the brain reorganizes with age, with many lines of evidence suggesting that aging results in (a) increased frontal activation more broadly distributed across neural sites (Cabeza, 2002; Grady et al., 1994; Gutchess et al., in press; Park

et al., 2003; Reuter-Lorenz, 2002; Reuter-Lorenz et al., 2001), (b) less selective or de-differentiated response in ventral visual cortex to different classes of stimuli (Chee et al., 2006; Park et al., 2004), and (c) decreased activation of hippocampal sites (Gutchess, Welsh, et al., 2006; Park et al., 2003). Thus far, these age-specific patterns of neural recruitment have been observed exclusively in Western samples of older adults, and it is not clear whether these neural patterns are a general characteristic of aging or a pattern typical of only Western cultures.

When aged brains show broad similarities across cultures in terms of neural recruitment patterns and structural integrity, we can be almost certain that these changes, relative to young brains, represent biological aging. If older adults, however, exhibit differences in neural circuitry and activation as a function of culture, this is likely due to experience and provides us with a window into the plasticity of the aging neurocognitive system. Similarly, at the behavioral

AUTHOR'S NOTE: Preparation of this chapter was supported by grants from the National Institute on Aging to the author (AGO60625-15 and AGO-15047). The author thanks Joshua Goh, Andy Hebrank, and Lucas Jenkins for assistance in manuscript preparation.

level, we can assume that broad similarities across cultures in patterns of gain and decline that occur with cognitive aging are due to biological changes that occur with age, whereas culturally unique patterns of cognitive aging suggest domains that are plastic and affected by experience (Park & Gutchess, 2002, 2006; Park, Nisbett, & Hedden, 1999). The study of the cognitive neuroscience of aging and culture provides a unique method for understanding of the role of experience in shaping basic neurocognitive circuitry as well as the malleability of such neurocognitive circuitry across the life span. The inquiry into how culture affects fundamental cognitive processes is one of the most rapidly growing domains of knowledge in psychology. In this chapter, I examine how cultural influences on behavior may be particularly informative in helping us understand what components of cognitive aging are primarily biologically determined and what components are due more to social constraints and environments. The focus is primarily on two cultures: East Asian and Western, because this is where a significant body of knowledge has developed. First, I review a framework for understanding cultural differences in cognition, followed by key findings from the neurocognitive aging literature, and then I integrate these two topics. I close with some methodological issues that must be addressed in conducting sound cross-cultural research on cognitive aging.

LIFE EXPERIENCES AND CULTURE SCULPT NEUROCOGNITIVE FUNCTION

Every individual is enmeshed in a culture, and the influences of culture on behavior are often transparent to the individual, so deeply is he or she enmeshed in society. Thus, the notion that cultural influences affect cognitive and neural function may not be as intuitively obvious as the possibility that other life experiences affect neurocognitive function. Although the extant data suggesting that culture influences neural function are quite limited at this time, the hypothesis that culture exerts such influences is credible, because there is clear and growing evidence indicating that a broad range of life experiences influence cortical structure and function. For example,

there is evidence that letter recognition is neurally segregated from digit recognition in a region near left fusiform gyrus. Because letters and digits are arbitrarily prescribed symbolic systems, this segregation of function had to result from the experience of differentially processing the two classes of symbols throughout one's life (Polk et al., 2002; Puce, Allison, Asgari, Gore, & McCarthy, 1996). Another example of everyday experiences influencing neural organization is the finding that taxicab drivers' extensive experience with spatial navigation increases hippocampal volume. The fact that the size of the hippocampus correlates positively with length of time as a London taxi driver suggests experience effects aggregate across the life span (Maguire et al., 2000). In a similar vein, Draganski et al. (2004) reported that after merely 3 months of juggling training, skilled participants show increased gray matter relative to nonjugglers in the vicinity of V5 bilaterally and in left posterior intraparietal. With regard to aging and experience, evidence for plasticity in neural function in older adults was reported by Colcombe et al. (2004), who found functional changes in frontal cortex as a result of sustained aerobic exercise in sedentary older adults. Finally, there is an extensive animal literature that indicates clearly that exposure of elderly rats to enriched information-processing environments leads to birth of new neurons (neurogenesis) in the hippocampus, as well as volumetric increases in this structure (Kempermann, Kuhn, & Gage, 1998).

Although there are considerable data indicating that different types of experiences affect neurocognitive function, there are relatively little data on the role of culture in affecting neural function (Park & Gutchess, 2006). There is, however, a wealth of evidence that culture influences cognitive behavioral function (Nisbett, 2003; Nisbett, Peng, Choi, & Norenzayan, 2001). Nisbett (2003) proposed that, beginning in ancient times, Western thought (characterized by the Greeks) and Eastern thought (characterized by the Chinese) had fundamentally different philosophical views of the world that have persisted into the present and subtly shape perception, memory, and higher-order cognition, as well as social relationships (Nisbett & Masuda, 2003). In brief, Western thought is grounded in an analytic focus on objects and categories, with rules that define objects' properties and function. In contrast, Eastern thought is grounded in a holistic focus where objects are part of a larger whole and central and contextual elements of information are given equal focus. Nisbett al. (2001) noted that the social systems of the two cultures reflect these biases, because Western cultures tend to focus on the individual with an independent self that is largely unconnected to others, whereas East Asian cultures (e.g., Chinese, Japanese, Singaporean, Korean, Thai, etc.) are based on complex interdependent social relationships with the self being defined by relationships to, and function of, a social group (Markus & Kitayama, 1991). The East Asian tendency to focus on others in the group results in a tendency to monitor context and relationships and to treat complex systems in a relatively unitary, holistic fashion. Unlike East Asians, Westerners tend to process information in an object-based, analytic fashion because of their individualistic bias and relatively unconnected selves. These tendencies result in biases to prioritize different types of information for processing, with East Asians attending relatively more to contextual, relational information than Westerners and Westerners focusing relatively more attention on objects and their properties.

Evidence that sociocultural context exerts top-down effects that mold cognitive function, with East Asians showing more sensitivity to contextual information, comes from multiple lines of research. In initial work on perceptual processes, Ji, Peng, and Nisbett (2000) demonstrated that East Asians were more field dependent than Westerners on the Witkin Rod and Frame Test (Witkin & Berry, 1975), and Kitayama, Duffy, Kawamura, and Larsen (2003) recently found in two experiments that Japanese and Americans differed in use of context to judge line length. Westerners were more accurate than Japanese when they had to make judgments of the absolute length of a line without reference to a frame. Japanese, however, were more accurate in estimating line length when they were required to estimate how large a line was relative to a frame, incorporating context into their perceptual judgment. These effects are not limited to the visual domain, because East Asians experience more interference on an emotional Stroop task presented in the auditory

modality in which research participants heard words presented in emotional tones incongruent with the word meaning (e.g., "joy" in an angry tone) and had to judge the pleasantness of the word without regard to the tone (Ishii, Reyes, & Kitayama, 2003; Kitayama & Ishii, 2002). The difficulty of this task for East Asians suggests a culturally driven inability to separate target words from their context.

Other studies have focused on culture differences not only in perception but also on the incorporation of context into memory and reasoning. Masuda and Nisbett (2001) presented East Asians and Westerners with target pictures against a complex background and reported that when backgrounds were changed at recognition, East Asians were more sensitive to this disruption. A host of studies have shown that context is more salient in reasoning for East Asians, in that they are more likely to invoke context as an explanatory construct for an individual's behavior, whereas Westerners are more likely to believe an individual behaved as he or she did because of stable, dispositional traits (Cha & Nam, 1985; Choi & Nisbett, 1998; Morris & Peng, 1994). There is also evidence that East Asians are more relationship based rather than category based when making judgments about objects. Chiu (1972) reported that Chinese children were more likely to group pictures together based on relations ("Mothers take care of babies and these go together"), whereas American children grouped based on features ("These objects all have a motor"). Norenzayan, Smith, Kim, and Nisbett (2002) reported that Asians performed more poorly than Americans when required to use formal categorization rules to classify cartoon animals based on the animals' physical attributes, but they performed similarly when an implicit technique for acquiring the category was used. Ji, Zhang, and Nisbett (2004) found that category membership played a greater role in judgments of similarity for Americans than for East Asians.

To summarize, I have presented compelling data suggesting that experiences affect neural structure and organization in systematic and observable ways. Furthermore, behavioral data suggest clearly that cultural experiences subtly but specifically shape perception, memory, and decision-making processes, with East Asians more sensitive than Americans to contextual relationships in perceptual, memory, and reasoning tasks. This combination of experience-based neural effects and culturally based behavioral effects leads to the hypothesis that there will be differences in neural engagement and possibly even neural organization between cultures. Moreover, because sustained exposure to culture increases with advanced age, the effects of cultural biases on cognition and neural function may be more prevalent in older adults. Such cultural differences in cognitive function provide insight into components of cognitive aging shaped more by experience than neurobiology.

PATTERNS OF NEUROCOGNITIVE AGING

Before considering the interaction of culture with age, I provide a brief snapshot of major neurocognitive effects associated with aging. As individuals age, there is behavioral evidence that cognitive processes become slower (Salthouse, 1996), working memory capacity decreases (Park et al., 1996, 2002), and the ability to inhibit irrelevant information (Hasher & Zacks, 1988; Zacks & Hasher, 1997) and switch between cognitive operations (Kray & Lindenberger, 2000) is diminished. At the same time that these declines are experienced, individuals continue to store new experiences and show stability and even growth in world knowledge (Park et al., 2002). These patterns of reliable decline with age in many behavioral measures of cognitive function are not paralleled in neural activations. There are now considerable data demonstrating that older adults show greater distribution of activation across prefrontal cortex compared with young adults when performing equivalently to young adults, or even when performing somewhat more poorly than young adults. These effects have been demonstrated during encoding and retrieval of information in both working and long-term memory (Bäckman et al., 1997; Cabeza, 2002; Cabeza et al., 1997; Grady, Bernstein, Beig, & Siegenthaler, 2002; Gutchess et al., in press; Logan, Sanders, Snyder, Morris, & Buckner, 2002; Madden et al., 1999; Morcom, Good, Frackowiak, & Rugg, 2003; Park et al., 2003; Reuter-Lorenz et al., 2000; Rosen et al., 2002). In particular, there is evidence that older adults show bilateral activation in homologous prefrontal areas on tasks where young adults show unilateral activation patterns, such as a word encoding task (Cabeza et al., 1997; Madden et al., 1999).

A major question in the neurocognitive aging literature is whether the increased activation that occurs in elderly in the face of behavioral decline reflects a compensatory response to a deteriorating neural system or whether the increased activation is dysfunctional and merely reflects deterioration (Cabeza, 2002; Grady et al., 1994; Park & Gutchess, 2005; Park, Polk, Mikels, Taylor, & Marshuetz, 2001; Reuter-Lorenz, 2002). In a recent review of the literature, Park and Gutchess (2005) noted that such increased frontal activations in older adults relative to young adults occur most reliably in the context of decreased hippocampal activations and are likely compensatory for deficient hippocampal activations. Many others have reported similar evidence for increased frontal/decreased hippocampal function with age (Daselaar, Veltman, Rombouts, Raaijmakers, & Jonker, 2003; Grady et al., 2002; Grady, McIntosh, & Craik, 2003; Gutchess, Welsh, et al., 2006; Park et al., 2003). Of particular interest are the strong negative correlations reported by Gutchess, Welsh, et al. (2006) between frontal and hippocampal activations that occurred for old but not young adults. Moreover, in this same study, increased frontal and decreased hippocampal activations were associated only with remembered items in elderly participants, adding confidence to the argument that the additional frontal activations were compensatory.

It is against this backdrop of declining processing efficiency in concert with heightened, but more distributed, neural activations with age that I consider (a) cultural differences and similarities in behavioral studies of knowledge and executive processes associated with cognitive aging and (b) patterns of neural differences resulting from age and culture.

DIFFERENCES IN KNOWLEDGE STRUCTURES AS A FUNCTION OF AGE AND CULTURE

One of the first issues that should be considered in embarking on an in-depth understanding of cultural differences is the importance of using stimuli that are cross-culturally sensitive and equally familiar to both ages and cultures. In an effort to develop stimuli that were appropriate for life span cross-cultural studies of cognition, I and my colleagues (Yoon, Feinberg, Luo, et al., 2004) examined how readily old and young adults in the Unites States and in Beijing, China, could name the item portrayed in simple line drawings of everyday objects developed by Snodgrass and Vanderwart (1980) for the study of cognitive processes associated with pictures. We found that, of the set of 260 pictures, there was agreement across age and culture for the specific name of 57 (22%) of the pictures (Yoon, Feinberg, Luo, et al., 2004). An additional 29 pictures (11%) were given names from the same category across cultures and ages. The remaining 67% of the pictures differed in the label applied as a function of age, culture, or both. The cultural differences were much larger than the age differences, but it was also quite surprising to learn that name agreement had changed for 33% of the pictures originally normed by Snodgrass and Vanderwart in 1980. The corpus of data suggests how critical it is to use stimuli that are equally familiar to both cultures before making inferences about cultural differences in memory, category structure, or other cognitive processes. The complete norms for the pictures may be downloaded for use by all researchers from the following Web site: http://agingmind.cns.uiuc.edu/Pict_Norms or from http://www.psychnomic.org/archive/.

In another study, my colleagues and I (Yoon, Feinberg, Hu, et al., 2004) considered evidence reported by Chiu (1972) and Choi, Nisbett, and Smith (1997) suggesting that East Asians focus more on functional relationships than hierarchical categories. We considered that this finding might have been due to the fact that studies suggesting unusual uses of categorical information in Asian cultures have been based on Western category norms. In an effort to develop categorical stimuli that are cross-culturally sensitive, we conducted a very ambitious study on category structure in young and old Chinese and Americans. We collected data on 105 categories drawn from published Western norms (Battig & Montague, 1969; McEvoy & Nelson, 1982), or that were generated by the research team. We tested 423 individuals (a minimum of 100

participants in each of the groups created by crossing age (young or old) with culture (Chinese in Beijing and Americans in Ann Arbor, Michigan). Participants received booklets with category names (e.g., farm animal, bicycle parts, body parts) and were instructed to list five items belonging to that category in the order in which the items came to mind. To determine differences and similarities across categories, we employed a team of bilingual researchers for scoring and then used a series of statistical techniques, including rank-ordered logit modeling and Hellinger Affinity methods to measure the degree of between group differences for each category. Overall, we found that the vast majority of category membership was not shared between the two cultures. Of the original 105 categories studied, there were only 13 for which there were no significant age or culture differences and that would be suitable for use in cross-cultural work. Examples of such categories include units of time, seasons, internal organs, and parts of a face. We also determined that 96 out of 105 categories showed high levels of agreement between young and old Americans, whereas young and old Chinese shared 89 out of 105 categories. These data may be used by researchers to develop age- and culture-appropriate categorized stimuli and are available at http://agingmind.cns.uiuc.edu/Cat_Norms/. Presented on this Web site are over 10,000 unique items responses, translations, and similarity measures, organized in a database that can readily be used by other researchers. Overall, data on knowledge structures of East Asians and Westerners suggest that the cultural differences are very substantial and even that age differences within a culture are far from inconsequential. Hence, researchers interested in studying cultural differences need to consider the nature of the stimuli they use very carefully.

DIFFERENCES IN SPEED, WORKING MEMORY, AND BINDING OPERATIONS AS A FUNCTION OF AGE AND CULTURE

Besides focusing on stimulus development, our initial work in understanding differences in cognitive aging across cultures focused on understanding whether the basic "hardware of the mind" differed as a function of culture. Basic processes that are fundamentally important in human cognition include speed of processing (Salthouse, 1996), working memory capacity (Park et al., 2002), binding operations (Chalfonte & Johnson, 1996; Hedden & Park, 2001), and long-term memory (Park et al., 1996, 2002). Age differences have been demonstrated in all of these domains. Thus, in an initial study, Hedden et al. (2002) attempted to assess whether cultural differences did exist in measures of speed and working memory, as well as whether age differences in these measures were equivalent across cultures. Hedden et al. tested young and old adults from the United States and China who were matched within each age group on education and vocabulary. As shown in Figure 22.1, they found evidence that there were large age effects, but no culture differences on visuospatial measures of speed (Pattern Comparison) and working memory (Corsi Blocks-Backwards). In contrast, on digit-based measures of speed and working memory, there was a significant Age × Culture interaction on both measures, caused primarily by a superiority of young Chinese in contrast to young Americans. Hedden et al. concluded that they had isolated a culture-invariant measure of speed of processing and working memory that could be useful for measurement of individual differences in cognitive function between the two cultures. Hedden et al. suggested that they observed culture differences in digit-based measures due to linguistic differences in spoken Chinese (Mandarin) versus spoken English. Chinese syllables are less dense and pronounced more quickly than English syllables, resulting in a more rapid articulation rate for Chinese. Hedden et al. also noted that cultural differences between the younger groups were not always maintained in the older groups. They suggested that this finding is congruent with theorizing by Park et al. (1999), who proposed that neurobiological declines associated with aging may impose constraints on an older adult's ability to apply strategies that are culturally specific when task demands are high. Thus, the linguistic advantage conferred by the Mandarin language might be smaller for older compared with younger Chinese. In general, this work suggests that (a) age differences on the speed and working memory tasks were much larger than culture

differences; (b) but culture differences do occur on digit-based tasks, so that such tasks are not likely a good estimate of cognitive function between cultures, and (c) culturally invariant visuospatial tasks are available that do provide accurate measurement of age differences across cultures.

Another critically important cognitive process that differs between old and young adults is the ability to bind a target to a source. As people age, the deficits that occur in memory are much more pronounced for the context or source in which they learned information (e.g., the voice or gender of a speaker) relative to the target information (Hedden & Park, 2003; Johnson, De Leonardis, Hashtroudi, & Ferguson, 1995; Spencer & Raz, 1995). Because there is clear evidence that East Asians attend more to contextual information (Nisbett, 2003; Nisbett et al., 2001) than Westerners, Chua, Chen, and Park (2006) hypothesized that East Asians might be superior at binding a source to a context. Moreover, they considered that Chinese older adults would not decline as steeply as older Americans, if the bias to process contextual information is an automatic, culturally determined process. They presented old and young adults from the United States and Beijing with a series of trivia statements, such as "Bats are the only mammals capable of flying," that were normed to be of moderate and equal familiarity to both cultures and ages. Research participants viewed a video of four different speakers reading statements, with each statement presented only once by one of the speakers. The four speakers were young versus old men and women, with the cultural identity of the speakers mapped to the participants' cultures. Results yielded clear evidence for age effects on memory for speaker as well as for facts, with the age effect much larger for speaker (source) memory, as expected. There was no evidence for cultural differences in either age group, suggesting that binding processes operate similarly across cultures, at least when the relationship of the target to the context is arbitrary, as occurred in this case. In sum, the finding that there were equivalent age differences in source memory in both cultures across two different experiments suggests that decreased memory of context is characteristic of cognitive aging across cultures and

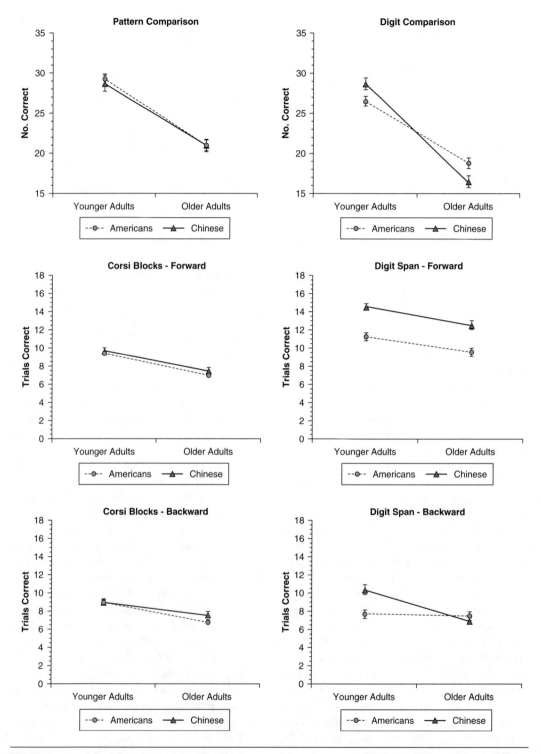

Figure 22.1   Measures of Visuospatial Speed (Pattern Comparison) and Working Memory (Corsi Blocks)

SOURCE: From "Cultural Variation in Verbal Versus Spatial Neuropsychological Function Across the Life Span," by T. Hedden, D. C. Park, R. Nisbett, L. Ji, Q. Jing, & S. Jiao, 2002, *Neuropsychology, 16,* p. 70. Copyright 2002 by the American Psychological Association. Reprinted with permission.

likely represents a fundamental neurobiological signature of cognitive aging.

The impact of aging and culture on long-term memory and a memory strategy was studied by Gutchess, Yoon, et al. (2006), who presented young and old American and Chinese with a list of words for study. In Experiment 1, participants received a list of unrelated words and another list of words that were strong associates of several categories. Older adults from both cultures recalled less, but Chinese elderly showed less categorical clustering, consistent with the prediction that older Chinese would rely less on categorization than Americans. Young Chinese, however, used categorical clustering as much as young Americans when the category relationships were strong. In a second experiment, weaker associates of categories were presented for free recall, and under these conditions both young and old Chinese categorized less relative to their American age counterparts. The emergence of cultural differences in old adults on the highly related lists provides evidence to support Park et al.'s (1999) hypothesis that prolonged absorption of a culture can lead to greater expression of cultural biases in information processing. When a categorization strategy as a basis for recall was less obvious (as was the case for the weakly associated list), neither young nor old Asians used the clustering strategy, because it was inconsistent with their cultural bias to rely on functional relationships. We should note that the use of items from Yoon, Feinberg, Hu, et al.'s (2004) norms resulted in stimulus lists where the exemplars from each category were equally familiar to both cultures and ages, so that the tendency to cluster less was unrelated to differences in category organization as a function of either age or culture. Future work on this topic would be useful that demonstrated organizational strategies preferred by old Chinese relative to old Americans, so that a deeper understanding of the interplay between culturally based knowledge and neurobiological aging could emerge.

To summarize, the behavioral work on cognitive aging demonstrates subtle differences between old adults from East Asian and Western cultures in strategy use, but speed of processing, working memory function, and binding processes appear to differ little between the cultures, unless culturally biased stimuli (e.g., the digit-based tasks, which have a faster articulation rate in Mandarin) are used. At the same time, the magnitude of age effects are large and reliable across cultures on basic information-processing tasks, suggesting that neurobiological aging, rather than cultural experiences, is the primary contributor to differences observed in these studies.

AGE, CULTURE, AND NEURAL FUNCTION

There is substantial evidence in young adults for functional specialization of neural response in ventral visual cortex. Different parts of ventral visual cortex respond maximally to faces (Kanwisher, McDermott, & Chun, 1997), to places (Epstein & Kanwisher, 1998), to objects, and to orthography (Polk et al., 2002). This specialization of ventral visual cortex provides an ideal medium for studying both age and culture differences in cortical specialization. Baltes and Lindenberger (1997) argued that with age, sensory and cognitive functions become *de-differentiated*, that is, cognitive and sensory functions are both degraded with age and intercorrelate. Such an argument is consistent with the possibility that ventral visual cortex may be less specialized for recognition of particular categories with age. Moreover, Nisbett's (2003) hypothesis that East Asians pay more attention to backgrounds and Westerners to objects suggests that Westerners may show more specialization in object areas and East Asians in background (place) areas. Finally, the interaction of age with culture in terms of neural specialization addresses the interplay between sustained cultural experiences and biological aging (Park & Gutchess, 2002).

What might the joint impact of age and culture be on neural specialization? One could imagine that with age, because of sustained experience in a culture, differences in neural circuitry that are culturally prescribed (e.g., an object area in Westerners) might become larger (Park et al., 1999). Alternatively, cultural differences in neural circuitry that are pronounced in young adults could become less differentiated with age, due to the profound effect that neurobiological aging has on neural circuitry (the *biological leveling hypothesis*, proposed by Park et al., 1999).

In an initial study, Park et al. (2004) investigated how specialized ventral visual cortex was in young and old adults. They hypothesized that the neural activity elicited by different categories of visual stimuli (e.g., faces, places, and words) would be less distinctive in old compared with young adults. In a functional magnetic resonance imaging (fMRI) study, Park et al. (2004) scanned young and old adults while they looked at gray-scale pictures from four categories: (1) faces, (2) places (pictures of houses), (3) chairs, and (4) pseudowords. They reported clear evidence for more neural specificity in young adults compared with old adults, when viewing each category. Figure 22.2 shows the activity of the most active voxels in the face area to the other categories. The figure clearly demonstrates that younger adults' face-specific voxels showed little activation to the other categories of stimuli. In contrast, older adults showed markedly less selectivity across all categories. In other words, voxels that were highly active to faces for older adults also showed considerable activity to other categories. Overall, these results provide striking evidence for a decrease in the category-specificity of neural response in ventral visual cortex with age,

providing strong evidence for dedifferentiation of neural response in older adults.

Given the relatively striking differences Park et al. (2004) found in ventral visual cortex with age, and given that culture effects in the behavioral domain are primarily perceptual (e.g., the greater attention to object stimuli in Westerners and to contextual information in East Asians), it makes sense to focus efforts to understand neurocultural differences in the ventral visual area. In an initial functional imaging study of culture, Gutchess, Welsh, et al. (2006) presented young adults who were either East Asian or Western with a series of photographs (displayed in Figure 22.3) that were of three types: (1) a relatively simple target object, such as an elephant or an airplane; (2) a complex scene with no discernible central object, such as a picture of a jungle or lake; or a (3) target object against a meaningful background scene (e.g., an elephant in a jungle). Through a series of contrasts, we were able to isolate areas uniquely associated with object processing and areas uniquely associated with contextual or background processing in the ventral visual areas. Of central importance was the finding of evidence for heightened activation of object processing areas in Americans, in regions including

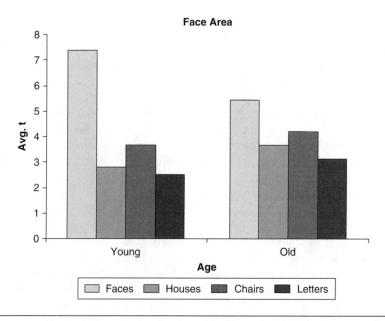

Figure 22.2   Mean *t* Values for the 15 Most Activated Voxels (Task Condition Minus Control Contrast) in the Face Area for Young and Old Age Groups

SOURCE: Based on Park et al. (2004).

NOTE: Avg. = average.

middle temporal gyrus, as the culture hypothesis would predict. We saw less evidence for cultural differences in context processing, although we did observe a slight bias for more activation of context areas in East Asians, as cultural theorists would predict.

On the basis of this initial evidence that there were differences in neural specialization for object areas as a function of culture, we further explored neural specialization of object processing, background processing, and binding in the ventral visual cortex in young and old adults from East Asian and Western cultures using a neural adaptation paradigm. In the first study, Goh et al. (2004) presented young adults with quartets of pictures. For some quartets, no aspect of the picture was changes, whereas in other quartets only the central object or the background of the picture varied (see Figure 22.4). By examining in what part of the brain the fMRI blood-oxygen-level-dependent signal becomes progressively less activated when a pictorial element is repeated, we can map neural/anatomical specialization for different stimulus components (see Grill-Spector & Malach [2001] for a detailed discussion of the adaptation technique). For example, in the second row in Figure 22.4, when the object was repeated and the background changed, a diminished blood-oxygen-level-dependent response was observed in the lateral occipital complex (LOC; Grill-Spector, Kourtzi, & Kanwisher, 2001; Malach et al., 1995) in both hemispheres. This suggests that the LOC was selectively engaged for processing objects and showed an "adapted" response as the objects repeated across the quartets. Similarly, in Row 3 in Figure 22.4,

where the object changed and the background was held constant, bilateral parahippocampal place areas (Epstein, Graham, & Downing, 2003; Epstein & Kanwisher, 1998) showed adaptation, suggesting these areas were specialized for background processing. Finally, binding areas in a bilateral parahippocampal gyrus (separate from the parahippocampal place areas) and right hippocampus showed adaptation when both elements were repeated, but not when both were varied, suggesting that these areas were important for contextually binding a target object to a scene (Henke, Buck, Weber, & Wieser, 1997). This was the first study that showed binding-related processing when research participants passively viewed scenes rather than actively attempted to bind scene elements.

In a second study, Chee, Lee, Soon, Westphal, and Venkatraman (2003) compared the performance of young and old East Asian adults using the procedures described above. They found evidence that the background processing area in the parahippocampus was intact in the older Asian adults, but both the binding area and object processing area were greatly diminished with age. The finding of a diminished object processing background in the older East Asians was congruent with the hypothesis that East Asians show less object processing, and led me and my colleagues to conduct a third study in which we used the adaptation procedure shown in Figure 22.4 to test 80 research participants: young and old Americans and East Asians (Singaporeans of Chinese descent), 20 in each group (Goh et al., in press). There were three major findings from this third study. First,

Object-Only Picture   Background-Only   Combined Picture

Figure 22.3   Examples of Target, Background, and Combined Stimuli

SOURCE: From "Cultural Differences in Neural Function Associated With Object Processing," by A. H. Gutchess, R. C. Welsh, A. Boduroglu, and D. C. Park, 2006, *Cognitive, Affective, & Behavioral Neuroscience, 6,* p. 103. Copyright 2006 by the Psychonomic Society. Adapted with permission.

Figure 22.4   Examples of Stimulus Quartets for Four Experimental Conditions: (1) Same Object, Same Background (OO); (2) Same Object, Different Background (ON); (3) Different Object, Same Background (NO); and (4) Different Object, Different Background (NN)

SOURCE: Reprinted with permission from Goh et al., 2004. *The Journal of Neuroscience, 24*(45), 10223–10228.

NOTE: P1 = Photograph 1, and so on.

there were no differences in patterns of neural activation in young Asians and Americans. Second, old adults in both cultures showed evidence for a diminished object-processing area in the LOC. Third, the object area was significantly more diminished in the older East Asians compared to the older Americans. In fact, the old East Asians showed almost no adaptation in the object area whatsoever. This pattern of finding provides neuroimaging evidence for cultural biases in perceptual processing of objects and is in agreement with Gutchess, Welsh, et al. (2006), who reported greater neural engagement for object processing regions in a picture recognition task, albeit for young Westerners compared with young East Asians.

Perhaps because the adaptation paradigm is comparatively subtle, cultural differences were not observed in young and were apparent only in old participants who have had more exposure to their respective cultural environments than young participants. The notion that length of exposure to culture affects neurocultural effects is a plausible explanation because there is substantial evidence that neuroanatomical changes in the brain are related to the length of time individuals spend being engaged in specific behavioral practices and sensory environments. In a structural magnetic resonance imaging (MRI) study, posterior hippocampal volume was positively correlated with the amount of experience with spatial navigation in London taxicab drivers compared with controls (Maguire et al., 2000). I should also note that my colleagues and I have conducted additional studies on this paradigm using eye tracking devices to examine where the different cultural groups looked on the pictures. We have found that both young and old East Asians spend more time looking at backgrounds (Goh et al., 2007), whereas young and old Westerners spend more time looking at objects (Wang & Park, 2007). Thus, the eye tracking measures have supported the neural and behavioral data, demonstrating that East Asians are particularly disadvantaged in processing objects and, furthermore, that older adults from both cultures show less object processing than young adults.

METHODOLOGICAL ISSUES IN NEUROIMAGING AGE AND CULTURAL DIFFERENCES

For behavioral studies of cultures, the best strategy is to use some of the cross-culturally appropriate cognitive tasks isolated by Hedden et al. (2002) to equate samples. At the same time, it is important to recognize that conducting neuroimaging studies across cultures has the added issue of examining between-culture neural activations (Park & Gutchess, 2002). The greatest concern in conducting cross-cultural neuroimaging studies (beyond normal population and cohort differences) is the ability to scan individuals from different cultures at different MRI sites and be assured that magnet stability and hemodynamic response measurement is the same at multiple sites. An alternative approach is to find old and young cross-cultural populations available at a single site with access to a magnet. The difficulties of recruiting a young and old East Asian and Western population in nearly any country is quite daunting—so the second approach, scanning cultures in two different places, seems more feasible.

Given that the scientific utility of functional MRI relies on the ability to reproduce results of studies, there is an emerging literature on reproducibility of results across sessions, sites, and imaging techniques. A review of the literature suggests that scanning at two sites to make inferences about cultural differences was feasible. Assessing the issue of within-subject stability, Cohen and DuBois (1999) reported that regression coefficients exhibited very little between-session and between-subject variability on visual and motor tasks. Also regarding within-subject reproducibility, Specht, Willmes, Shah, and Jaencke (2003) examined three measures on a visual attention modulation task with multiple sessions per participant. First, they made scatter plots of t scores from different scanning sessions and calculated a correlation coefficient between the t scores. Voxels active during either of the runs were included for the correlation coefficient calculation to limit effects from noise. Second, they made maps of intraclass correlation coefficients that compared the within-subject variance to the between-subject variance. Finally, they counted percentage overlap of activated voxels. All of these measures showed a high degree of reproducibility of results within subjects. Other research has investigated reproducibility within subjects in a study of the word frequency effect (Chee et al., 2003), in which they found that signal change

and voxel counting measures reliably detected the effect at the group level.

Other studies addressed comparability of fMRI results across different sites, different types of magnets, and even multiple neuroimaging techniques. Ojemann et al. (1998) compared activations in groups acquired through fMRI results versus results acquired via positron emission tomography on a word stem completion task. The fMRI results used were acquired at two different institutions, using MRI scanners from two manufacturers with different pulse sequences, and were analyzed with two different techniques. Despite all of these differences, they found that the fMRI results were highly reproducible in areas of activation across magnets and sites and that the fMRI data agreed well with positron emission tomography data. Similarly, Casey et al. (1998) reported reliable activation patterns on a spatial working memory task performed at four institutions with different scanners, pulse sequences, and analysis techniques and reported strong evidence for reproducibility of results.

Taken together, these results suggest that it should be feasible to study cross-cultural differences in neural activations between sites. In our own cross-cultural research, my colleagues and I use magnets that are identical at two sites (one in Singapore and one in the United States). We routinely scan the same individuals at both sites (typically members of our research teams who travel to both sites) and have demonstrated a remarkable comparability of the magnets between the sites. A great deal of effort is expended to assess stability of signal across sites, with frequent checks of stability between the two sites.

CONCLUSION

The study of age and cultural neuroscience is just beginning. There is clear evidence that culture moderates engagement of the ventral visual cortex with age, such that old Westerners have a greater bias for engagement of object areas compared with old East Asians. At this point, little is known about cultural differences in brain structure with age or about patterns of neural recruitment in frontal and medial temporal structures. Another important question is whether observed cultural differences in neural structure become "hard-wired" over time or rather merely reflect perceptual and strategic biases than can readily be modified by switching attention or strategy. Although there are more questions than answers at this stage, it seems clear that the study of cultural differences in neural function across the life span have the potential to provide an important mechanism for examining domains where neurobiological aging is universal versus those areas where experience and culture modify neurocognitive function.

REFERENCES

Bäckman, L., Almkvist, O., Andersson, J., Nordberg, A., Winblad, B., Reineck, R., et al. (1997). Brain activation in young and older adults during implicit and explicit retrieval. *Journal of Cognitive Neuroscience, 9,* 378–391.

Baltes, P. B., & Lindenberger, U. (1988). On the range of cognitive plasticity in old age as a function of experience: 15 years of intervention research. *Behavior Therapy, 19,* 283–300.

Baltes, P. B., & Lindenberger, U. (1997). Emergence of a powerful connection between sensory and cognitive functions across the adult life span: A new window to the study of cognitive aging? *Psychology and Aging, 12,* 12–21.

Battig, W., & Montague, W. (1969). Category norms for verbal items in 56 categories. *Journal of Experimental Psychology: Learning, Memory, and Cognition, 80*(3, Pt. 2), 1–46.

Cabeza, R. (2002). Hemispheric asymmetry reduction in older adults: The HAROLD model. *Psychology and Aging, 17,* 85–100.

Cabeza, R., Grady, C. L., Nyberg, L., McIntosh, A. R., Tulving, E., Kapur, S., et al. (1997). Age-related differences in neural activity during memory encoding and retrieval: A positron emission tomography study. *Journal of Neuroscience, 17,* 391–400.

Casey, B., Cohen, J. D., O'Craven, K., Davidson, R. J., Irwin, W., Nelson, C. A., et al. (1998). Reproducibility of fMRI results across four institutions using a spatial working memory task. *NeuroImage, 8,* 249–261.

Cha, J., & Nam, K. (1985). A test of Kelley's cube theory of attribution: A cross-cultural replication of McArthur's study. *Korean Social Science Journal, 12,* 151–180.

Chalfonte, B. L., & Johnson, M. K. (1996). Feature memory and binding in young and older adults. *Memory & Cognition, 24,* 403–416.

Chee, M. W. L., Goh, J. O. S., Venkatraman, V., Chow Tan, J., Gutchess, A., Sutton, B., et al. (2006). Age-related changes in object processing and contextual binding revealed using fMR adaptation. *Journal of Cognitive Neuroscience, 18,* 495–507.

Chee, M. W., Lee, H. L., Soon, C. S., Westphal, C., & Venkatraman, V. (2003). Reproducibility of the word frequency effect: Comparison of signal change and voxel counting. *NeuroImage, 18,* 468–482.

Chiu, L. H. (1972). A cross-cultural comparison of cognitive styles in Chinese and American children. *International Journal of Psychology, 7,* 235–242.

Choi, I., & Nisbett, R. E. (1998). Situational salience and cultural differences in the correspondence bias and actor–observer bias. *Personality and Social Psychology Bulletin, 24,* 949.

Choi, I., Nisbett, R., & Smith, E. (1997). Culture, categorization and inductive reasoning. *Cognition, 65,* 15–32.

Chua, H. F., Chen, W., & Park, D. C. (2006). Source memory, aging and culture. *Gerontology, 52,* 306–313.

Cohen, M. S., & DuBois, R. M. (1999). Stability, repeatability, and the expression of signal magnitude in functional magnetic resonance imaging. *Journal of Magnetic Resonance Imaging, 10,* 33–40.

Colcombe, S. J., Kramer, A. F., Erickson, K. I., Scalf, P., McAuley, E., Cohen, N. J., et al. (2004). Cardiovascular fitness, cortical plasticity, and aging. *Proceedings of the National Academy of Sciences, USA, 101,* 3316–3321.

Daselaar, S., Veltman, D., Rombouts, S., Raaijmakers, J., & Jonker, C. (2003). Neuroanatomical correlates of episodic encoding and retrieval in young and elderly subjects. *Brain, 126,* 43.

Draganski, B., Gaser, C., Busch, V., Schuierer, G., Bogdahn, U., & May, A. (2004, January 22). Neuroplasticity: Changes in grey matter induced by training. *Nature, 427,* 311–312.

Epstein, R., Graham, K. S., & Downing, P. E. (2003). Viewpoint-specific scene representations in human parahippocampal cortex. *Neuron, 37,* 865–876.

Epstein, R., & Kanwisher, N. (1998, April 9). A cortical representation of the local visual environment. *Nature, 392,* 598–601.

Goh, J., Chee, M., Tan, J., Venkatraman, V., Hebrank, A., Leshikar, E., et al. (2007). Age and culture modulate object processing and object-scene binding in the ventral visual area. *Cognitive, Affective, & Behavioral Neuroscience. 7, 44-52.*

Goh, J. O., Siong, S. C., Park, D. C., Gutchess, A., Hebrank, A., & Chee, M. W. (2004). Cortical areas involved in object, background, and object-background processing revealed with functional magnetic resonance adaptation. *Journal of Neuroscience, 24,* 10223–10228.

Grady, C. L., Bernstein, L. J., Beig, S., & Siegenthaler, A. L. (2002). The effects of encoding task on age-related differences in the functional neuroanatomy of face memory. *Psychology and Aging, 17,* 7–23.

Grady, C. L., McIntosh, A. R., & Craik, F. I. M. (2003). Age-related differences in the functional connectivity of the hippocampus during memory encoding. *Hippocampus, 13,* 572–586.

Grady, C. L., Maisog, J. M., Horwitz, B., Ungerleider, L. G., Mentis, M. J., Salerno, J. A., et al. (1994). Age-related changes in cortical blood flow activation during visual processing of faces and location. *Journal of Neuroscience, 14*(3, Pt. 2), 1450–1462.

Grill-Spector, K., Kourtzi, Z., & Kanwisher, N. (2001). The lateral occipital complex and its role in object recognition. *Vision Research, 41,* 1409–1422.

Grill-Spector, K., & Malach, R. (2001). fMR-Adaptation: A tool for studying the functional properties of human cortical neurons. *Acta Psychologica, 107,* 293–321.

Gutchess, A. H., Hebrank, A., Sutton, B., Leshikar, E., Chee, M., Tan, J. C., et al. (in press). Contextual interference in recognition memory with age. *NeuroImage.*

Gutchess, A. H., Welsh, R. C., Boduroglu, A., & Park, D. C. (2006). Cultural differences in neural function associated with object processing. *Cognitive, Affective, & Behavioral Neuroscience, 6,* 102–109.

Gutchess, A. H., Yoon, C., Luo, T., Feinberg, F., Hedden, T., Jing, Q., et al. (2006). Categorical organization in free recall across culture and age. *Gerontology, 52,* 314–323.

Hasher, L., & Zacks, R. T. (1988). Working memory, comprehension, and aging: A review and a new view. In G. H. Bower (Ed.), *Psychology of learning and motivation* (Vol. 22, pp. 193–225). New York: Academic Press.

Hedden, T., & Park, D. C. (2001). Culture, aging, and cognitive aspects of communication. In N. Charness, D. C. Park, & B. Sabel (Eds.), *Communication, technology, and aging* (pp. 81–108). New York: Springer.

Hedden, T., & Park, D. C. (2003). Contributions of source and inhibitory mechanisms to age-related retroactive interference in verbal. *Journal of Experimental Psychology: General, 132,* 93–112.

Hedden, T., Park, D. C., Nisbett, R., Ji, L., Jing, Q., & Jiao, S. (2002). Cultural variation in verbal versus spatial neuropsychological function across the life span. *Neuropsychology, 16,* 65–73.

Henke, K., Buck, A., Weber, B., & Wieser, H. G. (1997). Human hippocampus establishes associations in memory. *Hippocampus, 7,* 249–256.

Ishii, K., Reyes, J. A., & Kitayama, S. (2003). Spontaneous attention to word content versus emotional tone: Differences among three cultures. *Psychological Science, 14,* 39–46.

Ji, L. J., Peng, K., & Nisbett, R. E. (2000). Culture, control, and perception of relationships in the environment. *Journal of Personality and Social Psychology, 78,* 943–955.

Ji, L. J., Zhang, Z., & Nisbett, R. E. (2004). Is it culture or is it language? Examination of language effects in cross-cultural research on categorization. *Journal of Personality and Social Psychology, 87,* 57–65.

Johnson, M. K., De Leonardis, D. M., Hashtroudi, S., & Ferguson, S. A. (1995). Aging and single versus multiple cues in source monitoring. *Psychology and Aging, 10,* 507–517.

Kanwisher, N., McDermott, J., & Chun, M. M. (1997). The fusiform face area: A module in human extrastriate cortex specialized for face perception. *Journal of Neuroscience, 17,* 4302–4311.

Kempermann, G., Kuhn, H. G., & Gage, F. H. (1998). Experience-induced neurogenesis in the senescent dentate gyrus. *Journal of Neuroscience, 18,* 3206–3212.

Kitayama, S., Duffy, S., Kawamura, T., & Larsen, J. (2003). Perceiving an object and its context in different cultures: A cultural look at new look. *Psychological Science, 14,* 201–206.

Kitayama, S., & Ishii, K. (2002). Word and voice: Spontaneous attention to emotional speech in two cultures. *Cognition & Emotion, 16,* 29–59.

Kray, J., & Lindenberger, U. (2000). Adult age differences in task switching. *Psychology and Aging, 15,* 126–147.

Logan, J. M., Sanders, A. L., Snyder, A. Z., Morris, J. C., & Buckner, R. L. (2002). Under-recruitment and nonselective recruitment dissociable neural mechanisms associated with aging. *Neuron, 33,* 827–840.

Madden, D. J., Turkington, T. G., Provenzale, J. M., Denny, L. L., Hawk, T. C., Gottlob, L. R., et al. (1999). Adult age differences in the functional neuroanatomy of verbal recognition memory. *Human Brain Mapping, 7,* 115–135.

Maguire, E. A., Gadian, D. G., Johnsrude, I. S., Good, C. D., Ashburner, J., Frackowiak, R. S. J., et al. (2000). Navigation-related structural change in the hippocampi of taxi drivers. *Proceedings of the National Academy of Sciences, USA, 97,* 4398–4403.

Malach, R., Reppas, J., Benson, R., Kwong, K., Jiang, H., Kennedy, W., et al. (1995). Object-related activity revealed by functional magnetic resonance imaging in human occipital cortex. *Proceedings of the National Academy of Sciences, USA, 92,* 8135–8139.

Markus, H. R., & Kitayama, S. (1991). Culture and the self: Implications for cognition, emotion, and motivation. *Psychological Review, 98,* 224–253.

Masuda, T., & Nisbett, R. (2001). Attending holistically versus analytically: Comparing the context sensitivity of Japanese and Americans. *Journal of Personality and Social Psychology, 81,* 922–934.

McEvoy, C. L., & Nelson, D. L. (1982). Category name and instance norms for 106 categories of various sizes. *American Journal of Psychology, 95,* 581–634.

Morcom, A. M., Good, C. D., Frackowiak, R. S. J., & Rugg, M. D. (2003). Age effects on the neural correlates of successful memory encoding. *Brain, 126,* 213–229.

Morris, M. W., & Peng, K. (1994). Culture and cause: American and Chinese attributions for social and physical events. *Journal of Personality and Social Psychology, 67,* 949–971.

Nisbett, R. E. (2003). *The geography of thought: How Asians and Westerners think differently—and why.* New York: Free Press.

Nisbett, R. E., & Masuda, T. (2003). Culture and point of view. *Proceedings of the National Academy of Sciences, USA, 100,* 11163–11170.

Nisbett, R. E., Peng, K., Choi, I., & Norenzayan, A. (2001). Culture and systems of thought: Holistic versus analytic cognition. *Psychological Review, 108,* 291–310.

Norenzayan, A., Smith, E. E., Kim, B. J., & Nisbett, R. E. (2002). Cultural preferences for formal versus intuitive reasoning. *Cognitive Science, 26,* 653–684.

Ojemann, J. G., Buckner, R. L., Akbudak, E., Snyder, A. Z., Ollinger, J. M., McKinstry, R. C., et al. (1998). Functional MRI studies of word-stem completion: Reliability across laboratories and comparison to blood flow imaging with PET. *Human Brain Mapping, 6,* 203–215.

Park, D. C., & Gutchess, A. H. (2002). Aging, cognition, and culture: A neuroscientific perspective. *Neuroscience and Biobehavioral Reviews, 26,* 859–867.

Park, D. C., & Gutchess, A. H. (2005). Long-term memory and aging: A cognitive neuroscience perspective. In R. Cabeza, L. Nyberg, & D. C. Park (Eds.), *Cognitive neuroscience of aging: Linking cognitive and cerebral aging* (pp. 218–245). New York: Oxford University Press.

Park, D. C., & Gutchess, A. (2006). The cognitive neuroscience of aging and culture. *Current Directions in Psychological Science, 15,* 105–108.

Park, D. C., Lautenschlager, G., Hedden, T., Davidson, N. S., Smith, A. D., & Smith, P. K. (2002). Models of visuospatial and verbal memory across the adult life span. *Psychology and Aging, 17,* 299–320.

Park, D. C., Nisbett, R., & Hedden, T. (1999). Aging, culture, and cognition. *Journals of Gerontology Series B: Psychological Sciences and Social Sciences, 54,* P75–P84.

Park, D. C., Polk, T. A., Mikels, J. A., Taylor, S. F., & Marshuetz, C. (2001). Cerebral aging: Integration of brain and behavioral models of cognitive function. *Dialogues in Clinical Neuroscience: Cerebral Aging, 3,* 151–165.

Park, D. C., Polk, T. A., Park, R., Minear, M., Savage, A., & Smith, M. R. (2004). Aging reduces neural specialization in ventral visual cortex. *Proceedings of the National Academy of Sciences, USA, 101,* 13091–13095.

Park, D. C., Smith, A. D., Lautenschlager, G., Earles, J. L., Frieske, D., Zwahr, M., et al. (1996). Mediators of long-term memory performance across the life span. *Psychology and Aging, 11,* 621–637.

Park, D. C., Welsh, R. C., Marshuetz, C., Gutchess, A. H., Mikels, J., Polk, T. A., et al. (2003). Working memory for complex scenes: Age differences in frontal and hippocampal activations. *Journal of Cognitive Neuroscience, 15,* 1122–1134.

Polk, T. A., Stallcup, M., Aguirre, G. K., Alsop, D. C., D'Esposito, M., Detre, J. A., et al. (2002). Neural specialization for letter recognition. *Journal of Cognitive Neuroscience, 14,* 145–159.

Puce, A., Allison, T., Asgari, M., Gore, J. C., & McCarthy, G. (1996). Differential sensitivity of human visual cortex to faces, letterstrings, and textures: A functional magnetic resonance imaging study. *Journal of Neuroscience, 16,* 5205–5215.

Reuter-Lorenz, P. A. (2002). New visions of the aging mind and brain. *Trends in Cognitive Sciences, 6,* 394–400.

Reuter-Lorenz, P. A., Jonides, J., Smith, E. E., Hartley, A., Miller, A., Marshuetz, C., et al. (2000). Age differences in the frontal lateralization of verbal and spatial working memory revealed by PET. *Journal of Cognitive Neuroscience, 12,* 174–187.

Reuter-Lorenz, P. A., Marshuetz, C., Jonides, J., Smith, E. E., Hartley, A., & Koeppe, R. (2001). Neurocognitive ageing of storage and executive processes. *European Journal of Cognitive Psychology, 13,* 257–278.

Rosen, A. C., Prull, M. W., O'Hara, R., Race, E. A., Desmond, J. E., Glover, G. H., et al. (2002). Variable effects of aging on frontal lobe contributions to memory. *Neuroreport, 13,* 2425–2428.

Salthouse, T. (1996). The processing-speed theory of adult age differences in cognition. *Psychological Review, 103,* 403–428.

Snodgrass, J. G., & Vanderwart, M. (1980). A standardized set of 260 pictures: Norms for name agreement, image agreement, familiarity, and visual complexity. *Journal of Experimental Psychology, 6,* 174–215.

Specht, K., Willmes, K., Shah, N. J., & Jaencke, L. (2003). Assessment of reliability in functional imaging studies. *Journal of Magnetic Resonance Imaging, 17,* 463–471.

Spencer, W. D., & Raz, N. (1995). Differential effects of aging on memory for content and context: A meta-analysis. *Psychology and Aging, 10,* 527–539.

Wang, W., & Park, D. C. (2007). *Age differences in eye movements associated with objects and backgrounds.* Unpublished manuscript.

Witkin, H. A., & Berry, J. W. (1975). *Psychological differentiation in cross-cultural perspective.* Princeton, NJ: Educational Testing Service.

Yoon, C., Feinberg, F., Hu, P., Gutchess, A. H., Hedden, T., Chen, H. Y., et al. (2004). Category norms as a function of culture and age: Comparisons of item responses to 105 categories by American and Chinese adults. *Psychology and Aging, 19,* 379–393.

Yoon, C., Feinberg, F., Luo, T., Hedden, T., Gutchess, A. H., Chen, H. Y., et al. (2004). A cross-culturally standardized set of pictures for younger and older adults: American and Chinese norms for name agreement, concept agreement, and familiarity. *Behavior Research Methods, Instruments, & Computers, 36,* 639–649.

Zacks, R., & Hasher, L. (1997). Cognitive gerontology and attentional inhibition: A reply to Burke and McDowd. *Journals of Gerontology Series B: Psychological Sciences and Social Sciences, 52,* 274–283.

23

HISTORICAL PROCESSES AND PATTERNS OF COGNITIVE AGING

K. WARNER SCHAIE

I n this chapter I comment on some of the historical influences that contribute to the marked cohort and generational differences in levels and trajectories of cognitive abilities that have been observed over the past century. I then use data from the Seattle Longitudinal Study (SLS; Schaie, 2005) to show how changes in educational attainment and occupational status have served as mediating variables for these changes.

Because I have investigated these processes primarily in a normal community-dwelling population sample, I need to begin by dealing with a number of definitional issues. First, I want to be specific in distinguishing between different forms of aging that can be found in the literature (cf. Schaie, 2006). I then try to embed normal age trends within a co-constructionist heuristic model of cognition (cf. Willis & Schaie, 2006).

Next, I describe some of the historical events that have bearing on differences in cognitive development across the cohorts for which I present relevant data. I discuss exemplars of events that seem to me to have mediating properties for

changes in cognitive trajectories across cohorts. Finally, I provide specific data for a crystallized and a fluid ability to show the impact of historical processes that appear to be most relevant. This last section also includes speculations about the future course of changes over time in level and rate of cognitive development in adulthood.

FORMS OF COGNITIVE AGING

Scrutiny of a variety of longitudinal studies of cognitive aging (cf. Schaie & Hofer, 2001) suggests most of the observed differences in cognitive trajectories can be described by four major patterns. Most individuals can be classified as (1) those who age normally, (2) the supernormals (those who are said to age successfully), (3) those who develop mild cognitive impairment, and (4) those who eventually become clinically diagnosed as suffering from dementia. I would like to suggest that historical processes are likely to have a differential impact on these patterns.

AUTHOR'S NOTE: Parts of the content of this chapter were first presented at the International Conference on the Future of Cognitive Aging research at Pennsylvania State University, University Park, March 2005. I would like to acknowledge the assistance of Sarah Pennak in assembling the historical data included in this chapter. Preparation of this chapter was supported in part by Grants AG008055 and AG024102 from the National Institute on Aging.

Normal Aging. The most frequently observed pattern is what most researchers would describe as the *normal aging* of cognitive abilities. In this pattern most individuals reach an asymptote in their 30s or early 40s, maintain a plateau until the late 50s or early 60s, and then show modest decline on most abilities through the early 80s. For the survivors of this group, more marked decline occurs in the years prior to death (cf. Bosworth, Schaie, Willies, & Siegler, 1999). Among those whose cognitive aging can be described as normal, we can distinguish two subgroups. The first includes those individuals who reach a relatively high level of cognitive functioning, who even if they become physically frail can remain independent until close to their demise. Individuals in the second group, who reach only a modest asymptote in cognitive development, on the other hand, may in old age require greater support and be more likely to experience a period of institutional care. It is apparent from our own analyses and those of others (cf. Dickens & Flynn, 2001) that the first group has benefited from favorable societal advantages while the second represents those left behind because of more limited gains in environmental support.

Successful Aging. A small number of adults experience what is often described as *successful aging* (Fillit et al., 2002; Rowe & Kahn, 1987). Members of this group are usually genetically and socioeconomically advantaged; they tend to continue cognitive development later than most and typically do not reach their cognitive asymptotes until late midlife. This group also shows some very modest decline on highly speeded tasks, but they are likely to maintain their overall asymptotic level of cognitive functioning until shortly before their demise. This group contains those fortunate individuals for whom the mortality curve has been virtually squared and whose active life expectancy closely approaches their actual life expectancy. There is reason to believe that this is the group that has particularly benefited from the cumulative effects of historical changes in educational opportunities and occupational structures.

Mild Cognitive Impairment. A third pattern, *mild cognitive impairment* (MCI; Petersen et al., 1999), characterizes that group of individuals who, typically in early old age, experience greater than normative cognitive declines. Different definitions, mostly statistical, have been proposed to assign individuals to membership in this group. Some have argued for a criterion of 1 standard deviation of performance compared with the young adult average, whereas others have proposed a rating of 0.5 on a clinical dementia rating scale, where 0 is normal and 1.0 is probable dementia. The identification of MCI originally required the presence of significant memory loss. More recently, the diagnosis has been extended to include decline in cognitive abilities other than memory. It is still an unresolved question whether individuals with the diagnosis of MCI inevitably progress to dementia or whether this group of individuals represents a unique entity, perhaps one could that could be denoted as the *unsuccessful aging* (cf. Petersen, 2003). Definitions of membership in this group are too recent to determine to what extent historical processes may have impacted this group.

Dementia. All of the above patterns are clearly distinct from the fourth group, which includes those individuals who in early or advanced old age are diagnosed as suffering from *dementia*. Regardless of the specific cause of the dementia, these individuals have in common dramatic impairment in cognitive functioning. However, the pattern of cognitive change, particularly in those whose postmortem diagnosis turns out to be Alzheimer's disease, may be very different from that experienced by the normally aging. When followed longitudinally, at least some of these individuals show earlier decline, perhaps starting in midlife (cf. Willis & Schaie, 2005). Again, it is not clear at this point to what extent changes in the proportion of those who will eventually be diagnosed as suffering from clinically diagnosable dementia has increased over time, but one may speculate that the cumulative advantages of the normal and successful aging will serve to more clearly identify those at eventual risk for dementia at earlier ages than has been true in the past.

Although all of these forms of aging are likely to be impacted by historical processes, in this chapter I address primarily the historical influences that most clearly seem to affect adults who follow patterns of normative aging.

HISTORICAL EVENTS THAT MAY INFLUENCE CHANGES IN COGNITIVE TRAJECTORIES ACROSS COHORTS

Understanding the historical context of cohort differences requires the examination of the political, sociocultural, and educational events that occurred within a cohort's lifetime. In general, one would select events or processes that would be considered high watermarks in American history or major shifts in the prevailing practices (also see Schaie, Willis, & Pennak, 2005). Seven major life stages in a cohort's lifetime are considered in relation to these events and trends: Childhood (0–14 years), Adolescence (15–21 years), Young Adulthood (22–35 years), Early Middle Age (36–49 years), Late Middle Age (50–63 years), Young-Old Age (64–77 years), and Old Age (78+ years). The particular years used to frame these life stages were chosen specifically to match the cohorts used in the SLS (see Table 23.1; cf. Schaie, 2005).

Calendar years were then applied to each cohort's life stage to yield a time frame for the historical context (see Table 23.1). For example, members of the oldest cohort in the SLS (cohort = 1) were young adults between 1911 and 1924, thus making the males eligible for World War I military duty. As adolescents between 1904 and 1910, many in this cohort did not have the opportunity to attend high school because American public education typically ended after the eighth grade prior to 1900 (Mondale & Patton, 2001).

Political Influences

Political events affecting the United States have had an overarching influence on education processes as well as sociocultural trends (see Table 23.1). American military involvements in particular appear to have had the most far-reaching impact. For example, intelligence testing by the U.S. Army in World War I led to intelligence testing in American public schools. During World War II, women entered the workforce in unprecedented numbers, Black workers had new opportunities, and returning veterans found greater access to higher education (GI Bill; cf. Laub & Sampson, 2005; Sampson & Laub, 1996). The Cold War of the 1960s and America's obsession with beating the Soviets in space led to significant changes in public education, with a curriculum focus on sciences and technology.

Political events other than war also shaped health policies, education, and American culture. In the 1930s, the Great Depression had a direct impact on educational practices. President Lyndon Johnson's Great Society provided social interventions such as Medicare (1965) and Head Start (1964). In 1965, Johnson first used the term *affirmative action* regarding employment, but by the mid-1970s this policy had opened doors in education for minorities and women as well.

Educational Events

Perhaps one of the greatest environmental influences on cognitive abilities is the shift in the educational processes (see Table 23.3) by which one is taught to problem-solve and learn. Over the past century, these educational processes have undergone several trends—from the basics to "progressive" to "tracking" and back to basics time and again. In the late 1800s, education was a structured curriculum that included rigid recitations of the 3 R's—reading, writing, and arithmetic. High schools were not typical, and most children ended their education after 8 years. Kindergarten did not become the norm until the 1920s.

At the turn of the century, John Dewey at the University of Chicago, and the schools in Gary, Indiana, began to promote a "progressive," less rigid curriculum that was popularly termed "Learning by Doing." In addition to teaching the

Table 23.1   Mean Birth Years for the 7-Year Cohorts in the Seattle Longitudinal Study

Cohort	1	2	3	4	5	6	7	8	10	11	12	13
Mean birth year	1889	1896	1903	1910	1917	1924	1931	1938	1945	1952	1959	1966

Table 23.2   U.S. Political Events by Seattle Longitudinal Study Cohort and Life Stage

Event	Childhood 0–14	Adolescence 15–21	Young Adult 22–35	Early Midlife 36–49	Late Midlife 50–63	Young-Old 64–77	Old 78+
Labor violence (1892–1917)	1 2 3 4 (5)	1 2	1				
World War I (US: 1917–1918)	[3] (4)	[2] (3)	1 2				
Women's vote (1919)	4 5	3	1 2				
Prohibition (1920–1933)	4 5 6 (7)	3 4 (5)	1 2 3 (4)	1 (2)			
Great Depression (1929–1941)	5 6 7 (8)	4 5 (6)	[2] 3 4 (5)	1 2 (3)	1		
New Deal (1933–1938)	6 7 (8)	5 (6)	3 4 (5)	[1] 2 (3)	(1)		
Pearl Harbor/World War II (1941–1945)	7 8 (9)	6 (7)	4 5 (6)	[2] 3 (4)	1 (2)		
Korean War (1950–1953)	8 9 10	7 8	5 6 7	4 5	1 2 3	1	
JFK assassinated (1963)	10 11	9	7 8	5 6	3 4	1 2	
Civil Rights (1954–1971)	9 10 11 12	8 9 10	6 7 8 9	4 5 6 7	2 3 4 5	1 2 3	1
Great Society (1964–1969+)	10 11 12 (13)	9 10 (11)	7 8 9	5 6 7 (8)	3 4 5 (6)	1 2 3 5	1 (2)
Space race (1957–1969)	9 10 11 12	8 9 10	6 7 8 9	4 5 6 7	2 3 4 5	1 2 3	1
Vietnam War (1963–1973)	10 11 12 (13)	9 10 (11)	7 8 9 (10)	5 6 7 (8)	3 4 5 (6)	1 2 3 (4)	1 (2)
Cold War/nukes: Cuban Missile Crisis (1962)	10 11	9	7 8	5 6	3 4	1 2	
Watergate (1972–1974)	[11] 12 (13)	[10] (11)	[8] 9 (10)	[6] 7 (8)	[4] 5 (6)	[2] 3 (4)	1 (2)
Abortion rights: Roe v. Wade (1973)	[11] 12 (13)	[10] (11)	[8] 9 (10)	[6] 7 (8)	[4] 5 (6)	[2] 3 (4)	1 (2)
Dotcom economy 1992–2000		13	11 12 13	9 10 11	7 8 9	5 6 7	2 3 4 5

NOTE: ( ) = leading edge of cohort; [ ] = trailing edge of cohort.

Table 23.3 Educational Trends in the United States by Cohort and Life Stage

Trend	Childhood 0–14	Adolescence 15–21	Young Adult 22–35	Early Midlife 36–49	Late Midlife 50–63	Young-Old 64–77	Old 78+
Grades 1–8: 3 R's, "Learning by doing," reciting (1890–1910)	1 2 (3)	1	(1)				
High schools (1910–1930)*	[2] 3 4 (5)	[1] 2 3 4	1 2 3	[1] (2)			
IQ testing to track students (1917–1930)*	[3] 4 5 6 (7)	[2] 3 4 (5)	1 2 3	1 (2)			
Junior highs and kindergarten (1920s)* Child labor laws; required	[3] 4 5 6 (7)	3 4 (5)	1 2 3	1 (2)			
School attendance (1930s)*	[5] 6 (7)	[4] 5 (6)	[2] 3 (4)	1 2 (3)	(1)		
Curriculum: college prep vs. voc tec (1940s)*	7 8 9 (10)	[5] 6 7 (8)	[3] 4 5 6	[1] 2 3 4	1 2	(1)	
SATs (1945)*	[7] 8 9	[6] (7)	[4] 5 (6)	2 3 (4)	1 (2)		
GI Bill (1945–1957)*	[7] 8 9 10 (11)	[6] 7 8	[4] 5 6 7	2 3 4 5	1 2 3	1 (2)	
Dick & Jane (1950–1965)	8 9 10 11	7 8 9 (10)	5 6 7	3 4 5 6 (7)	1 2 3 4 (5)	1 2 (3)	(1)
Cold War/space race curriculum (1958–1970s)	9 10 11 12 13	8 9 10 11	6 7 8 9 10	4 5 6 7 8	1 2 3 4 5	1 2 3 4	1 2
Desegregation acts (1964, 1965)	10 11 (12)	9 (10)	7 8 (9)	5 6 (7)	3 4 (5)	1 2 (3)	(1)
Head Start (1964)	10 11	9	7 8	5 6	3 4	1 2	
Equality acts: busing (1971), Title IX (1972), ESL (1974)	11 12 13	10 11	[8] 9 10	6 7 (8)	4 5 (6)	2 3 (4)	1 (2)
Alternative schools (1970s)*	11 12 13	10 11 (12)	8 9 10	6 7 8	4 5 6	2 3 4	1 2
Computers in school (1980s)	[12] 13	[11] 12 13	[9] 10 11 12	[7] 8 10	[5] 6 7 8	[3] 4 5 6	1 2 3 4

NOTES: Asterisks denote year(s) when shift began and/or trend became widespread. ( ) = leading edge of cohort; [ ] = trailing edge of cohort; prep = preparatory; voc tech = vocational/technical training; ESL = English as a second language.

basics, these curricula included field trips; nature studies; exercise; changing classrooms throughout the day; working with machinery; and lessons in health, manners, and cooking.

In the 1920s, intelligence testing began to be used more frequently to handle the increasing number of students and to more efficiently place students in an appropriate education "track" based on their aptitude. Administered in English, IQ testing was heavily biased against the thousands of immigrant children attending urban public schools. By the 1930s, when greater numbers of children attended school because of the Depression, IQ tests became more frequently used despite criticisms of their cultural bias.

Tracking continued through the 1940s, and the curriculum became even more split between college preparatory classes and industrial training. By the end of World War II, the Scholastic Aptitude Test (SAT) was beginning to replace the IQ tests for college admissions, and its use continues to this day. The Scholastic Aptitude Test was similarly biased against minorities and immigrant children who did not have the same level of language skills or experience the same culture as the White, middle-, and upper-middle class students. The Cold War caused another major shift in American public schools. Progressive curricula had evolved into "life adjustment" courses by the early 1950s. When the Soviets launched *Sputnik* in 1957, however, the reaction was a swift National Defense Education Act (1958) to ensure that American public education would be competitive with the Soviets in math and physics. Advanced students were now being tracked away from English and history to be trained in science and technology.

In the 1950s, the leading edge of the Baby Boomer population created an enormous impact on resources for teachers, classrooms, and the educational system. Although first-graders had been reading Dick and Jane textbooks since the Depression, vast numbers of Baby Boomers were now learning to read, making Dick and Jane the icons of the American Dream. Dick, Jane, Spot, and Sally reflected the perfect all-American family in the suburbs where Father worked and Mother stayed home.

Despite this portrayal of the American Dream, equal opportunities for education were becoming significant social issues, and civil rights violence erupted in schools during the 1950s and early 1960s. The Civil Rights Act of 1964 and the Elementary and Secondary Education Act (1965) forced desegregation in American public schools, and in 1971 the Supreme Court ruled that busing was lawful. Title IX (1972) afforded equal opportunities for young women, and the Civil Rights Act was extended to children with disabilities in 1976.

In 1969, "Sesame Street" premiered on television. Although destined to become a cultural icon, its primary intent was, and still is, to educate while entertaining toddlers and preschoolers. Positive effects attributed to "Sesame Street" include increased letter and number literacy when children enter school (Rice, Huston, Truglio, & Wright, 1990), as well as increased social skills (Bankart & Anderson, 1979).

As the urban decay of the 1970s progressed and "white flight" from mandatory busing created better tax bases in the suburbs, public school districts in American cities fought back with alternative programs and magnet schools. By the 1980s, these schools not only managed to attract the best students but also enabled their students to gain admissions to good colleges. The 1980s also introduced computers and calculators into the classroom, creating new skills in technology but at the possible risk of losing basic arithmetic abilities, as shown in negative cohort differences for this ability in the SLS.

Sociocultural Events and Trends

American culture has been rich and diverse over the past 110 years that the SLS cohorts have lived (see Table 23.4). For the two oldest cohorts, the 1890s were a cultural decade of teddy bears, Frank Lloyd Wright architecture, Buffalo Bill Wild West shows, zippers, John Phillip Sousa band music, and Joplin ragtime. It was also a decade that witnessed Jim Crow laws, lynching of Blacks, and the Financial Panic of 1893.

The turn of the 20th century and its first decade could best be described by a single term—*mass*. Mass transportation and mass media had increased the public's political awareness and decreased the geographic landscape. In 1907, the Wright Brothers flew at Kitty Hawk, and America's automobile culture

Table 23.4 Sociocultural Historic Events by Cohort and Life Stage

Event	Childhood 0–14	Adolescence 15–21	Young Adult 22–35	Early Midlife 36–49	Late Midlife 50–63	Young-Old 64–77	Old 78+
American frontier "closes" (1890s)	1 2						
Transportation: mass transit (1890s), flight (1907), automobile culture (1907)	1 2 3	1 (2)					
Segregation (1890–1920)	1 2 3 4 5	1 2 3	1 2				
Immigration peaks (1907)	2 3	1					
Roaring 20s: "speakeasies"	4 5 6	3 4	1 2 3				
Globalization of American culture: literature & film (1920–1940)	4 5 6 7 (8)	3 4 5 (6)	1 2 3 4 (5)	1 2 (3)	(1)		
Women in the workforce and military (1940s)	[6] 7 8 9	6 7	[3] 4 5 6	[1] 2 3 4	1 2		
Baby Boom* 1946–64	[7] 8 **9 10 11 12**	[6] 7 8 **9**	[4] 5 6 7 8	[2] 3 4 5 6	1 2 3 4	1 2	
Suburbia (1945–65)	[7] 8 9 10 11 12	[6] 7 8 9	[4] 5 6 7 8	[2] 3 4 5 6	1 2 3 4	1 2	
"All-American" ideals (1950s)	8 9 10 (11)	7 8 (9)	5 6 7 (8)	3 4 5 (6)	1 2 3 (4)	1 (2)	
TV: "The vast wasteland" (1961)	[9] 10 11	[8] 9	[6] 7 8	[4] 5 6	[2] 3 4	1 2	
Social Crisis 1965–1970s	10 11 12 13	9 10 11	[7] 8 9 10	[5] 6 7 8	[3] 4 5 6	1 2 3 4	1 2
Women's lib & gay rights (1963–1972)	10 11 (12)	9 10 (11)	7 8 9 (10)	5 6 7 (8)	3 4 5 (6)	1 2 3 (4)	1 (2)
"Me" generation (1980s)	[12] 13	[11] 12 (13)	[9] 10 11 12	[7] 8 9 (10)	[5] 6 7 (8)	[3] 4 5 (6)	1 2 3 (4)
PCs (1985–1990s)	13	12 13	10 11 12 13	8 9 10 11	6 7 8 9	4 5 6 7	[1] 2 3 4 5
Internet/www.com (1990s)		13	11 12 13	9 10 11	7 8 9	5 6 7	2 3 4 5

NOTES: Cohorts with Baby Boom birth years are in boldface type. ( ) = leading edge of cohort; [ ] = trailing edge of cohort.

374

was born when Ford began to mass-produce the Model T. Mass immigration peaked by 1907, and cities became public health disasters, with bubonic plague; massive numbers of deaths related to industrial accidents; and upper respiratory diseases such as pneumonia, tuberculosis, and influenza.

Although the Roaring Twenties with its "speakeasies," dance marathons, and mob activities would give way to the Great Depression, it was also the decade of innovations that would affect American culture for the rest of the century and beyond. Sound motion pictures became the norm, and the invention of frozen food (1925) and television (1926) would someday lead to the confluence of the frozen TV dinner as each evolved over the next three decades.

With the onset of World War II, women again found themselves in new cultural territory as they worked in factories, joined the military, and even formed a professional baseball league. Once their husbands returned from war, however, they retreated to their traditional roles that not only marked the beginning of the Baby Boom but also created the suburban streetscape and a new American social environment.

During the 1950s, the interstate highway system, constructed by the U.S. government for military logistics, increased America's love affair with the car while convenience foods and new household appliances made life at home less labor intensive. Pediatrician Dr. Spock, television, Cold War paranoia, and rock 'n' roll music influenced raising of the Baby Boomers in the 1950s.

American culture shifted dramatically in the 1960s with the assassinations of John F. Kennedy, Robert Kennedy, and Martin Luther King. The Civil Rights movement kept company with movements for women's liberation and gay rights. Continued escalation in the Vietnam War eventually created a cultural revolution in America with its anti-war protests. Although the Vietnam War ended in 1973, American culture was still influenced by political events. Television satirized politics and social mores with *Saturday Night Live* and *All in the Family*'s Archie Bunker. The children's educational television show *Sesame Street* became a cultural icon while gas shortages and long lines at the pump created by OPEC's oil embargo created new attitudes about the environment and

reliance on fossil fuels. The microchip processor and technology advances in the 1970s would eventually lead to the personal computers of the 1980s and the Internet culture from the 1990s onward.

A CO-CONSTRUCTIONIST MODEL FOR THE IMPACT OF HISTORICAL PROCESSES ON COGNITIVE DEVELOPMENT IN ADULTHOOD

How are we to relate the historical processes described above to understand cohort trends in cognitive development across adulthood? I next describe a co-constructive model for adult development that has recently been explicated in more detail elsewhere (Willis & Schaie, 2006). This model is informed by two life span perspectives: (1) the dual-intelligence perspective proposed by Horn and Cattell (1966) and (2) the more recent co-constructionist perspective of Baltes and colleagues (Baltes, 1997; Li, 2003; Li & Freund, 2005).

The Co-Constructive Perspective. Coevolutionary theorists have long maintained that both biological and cultural evolution has occurred and that recent, cohort-related advances in human development in domains such as intelligence can be attributed largely to cumulative cultural evolution (Cavalli-Sforza & Feldman, 1981; Dunham, 1991; Tomasello, 1999). Cultural activities impact the environment, thereby allowing humans to codirect their own evolution (Cavalli-Sforza & Feldman, 1981; Dunham, 1991). The co-constructionist approach advocated by Baltes and his colleagues further imposes a life span developmental perspective on coevolutionary theory. It provides principles for the timing of the varying contributions of neurobiology and culture at different developmental periods and across different domains of functioning. Of particular importance for understanding the impact of historical processes is the principle that continuing advances in human development depend on ever-increasing cultural resources. Increases in cultural resources have occurred through cumulative cultural evolution and have resulted in humans reaching higher levels of functioning. At the individual level, this implies that increasing cultural resources will be required at older ages to prevent age-related losses or to make possible further development.

The Dual-Intelligence Perspective. The co-construction perspective described above can be applied to the dual-component model of intelligence. Horn and Cattell (1966) described a hierarchical model of psychometric intelligence organizing mental abilities into the supraordinate domains of fluid and crystallized intelligence. Neurobiological influences impact particularly fluid intelligence, and experience and culture-based knowledge influence crystallized intelligence. Fluid intelligence is thought to develop and decline earlier in the life span, whereas the more culture-based crystallized abilities are maintained well into old age. Psychometric abilities, such as inductive reasoning, spatial orientation, and memory processes, were considered more fluid like, whereas verbal, numerical, and social knowledge skills were thought to be crystallized. Note, however, that the Horn–Cattell model is concerned primarily with intraindividual change and does not offer any specific hypotheses with respect to secular trends in intelligence.

Implications for Adult Cognitive Development. The effects of historical processes described above determine changes in both neurobiological and sociocultural influences. The mechanisms through which cognition is affected include the accumulation of societal resources in knowledge, values, and material artifacts that are transmitted to future generations; these resources continue to develop and change through cumulative cultural evolution (Tomasello, 1999). With respect to cognition, these accumulated cultural resources are represented specifically by structural variables such as educational level, occupational status, and ability level. Thus, advances in cognition as represented by cohort and generational effects may be seen as being primarily due to an accumulation of cultural resources and knowledge across time (cf. Willis & Schaie, 2006, for further details).

Sociocultural and neurobiological influences vary in the timing of their impact in the early and later half of adulthood. Sociocultural resources such as educational level, occupational status, and ability level are acquired and accumulated primarily during the first half of adulthood. Social processes impact current activities, habits, and beliefs of the individual, represented by activities in domains such as health behaviors, cognitive engagement, and the complexity of one's work tasks. Neurobiological influences such as chronic diseases and biomarkers impact cognitive change primarily in later adulthood. A schematic of the model is provided in Figure 23.1. The solid lines indicate strong directional relationships, and the dashed lines indicate weaker relationships.

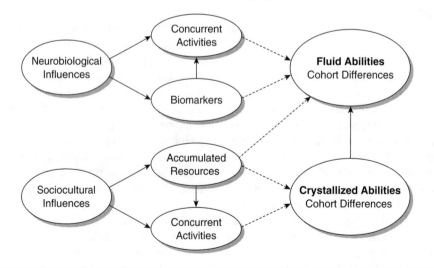

Figure 23.1   The Co-Constructionist Model Applied to Cohort Differences in Fluid and Crystallized Abilities

The model proposes that cohort differences in fluid abilities are mediated also, in a time-lagged manner, by cohort differences in crystallized abilities; that is, the acquisition of higher levels of sociocultural knowledge and skills will increase the likelihood of the adoption of lifestyles that provide the infrastructure for cohort-related increase in fluid abilities.

GENERATIONAL DIFFERENCES IN COGNITION

The co-constructionist model suggests that historical processes that allow the positive accumulation of resources and the increased mastery of deleterious neurobiological influences should lead to increased levels of cognitive functions across generations, but I would also predict positive changes in the shape of cognitive trajectories. These should prevail for both fluid and crystallized intelligence in the first half of adulthood due to the cumulative impact of accumulated cultural resources (e.g., cohort-related increases in educational level). With regard to later adulthood, a cohort-related increase in prevalence of positive trajectories is predicted to occur for crystallized but not for fluid intelligence. Sociocultural influences are expected to have the greater impact on positive crystallized trajectories in the second half of adulthood. The increasingly positive crystallized trajectories may be impacted primarily by current cultural activities (e.g., cognitive engagement), which should become more frequent across cohorts because of gains in accumulated resources that have occurred for more recent cohorts early in adulthood. The deleterious effects of neurobiological influences will limit the impact of cultural advances in relation to fluid intelligence in old age. However, given the delayed onset of chronic disease in more recent cohorts and the increased use of prophylactic medications (e.g., anti-hypertensives), the impact of neurobiological influences such as chronic disease should decrease in more recent cohorts as they reach advanced ages.

I now focus on the impact of sociocultural influences in particular, using examples from the SLS for the crystallized ability of verbal meaning and the fluid ability of inductive reasoning. The two sociocultural influences to be addressed for this purpose will be (1) years of educational attainment and (2) occupational status.

Figure 23.2 shows the observed longitudinal age gradients for the crystallized verbal meaning ability (comprehension of word meaning) for 12 successive cohorts with average birth years from 1889 to 1966, over the age range from 25 to

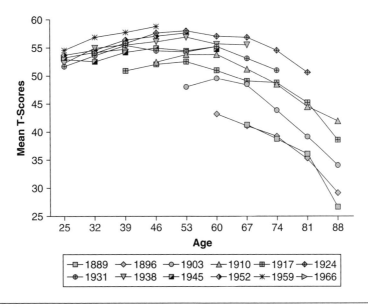

Figure 23.2 Intracohort Trajectories for the Crystallized Ability of Verbal Meaning for 12 Successive Cohorts Born From 1889 to 1966

88 years, for those ages when the specific cohorts were in the study from 1956 to 2005. These data are based on longitudinal changes within each cohort for individuals available over each 7-year interval, anchored on the mean values when cohorts first entered the study.

Substantial increases were observed across successive cohorts at all ages. The available cohort comparisons at the same ages are most noteworthy in late middle and early old age (approximately 2 *SD*). They still amount to 0.7 *SD* over the most recent cohorts in young adulthood and to about 1.5 *SD* even in advanced old age. Similar findings for the fluid ability of inductive reasoning are shown in Figure 23.3. It should be noted also that the slopes of the intracohort trajectories, particularly in early old age, have become shallower (a decrease in rate of aging) for the crystallized ability but not for the fluid ability examined here.

COHORT DIFFERENCES IN SOCIOCULTURAL INFLUENCES

We must ask, then, what historical influences may be implicated in these dramatic changes in level and slope (for verbal meaning). Direct data for the samples for which cognitive data are

shown can be examined for the two demographic indicators of (1) education and (2) occupational attainment.

Educational Attainment

As discussed above, there have been substantial changes in both duration of average educational experiences as well as shifts from rote learning to discovery learning and other participatory educational strategies. We have no direct data on qualitative differences in our study participants' education, but we do have data on the level of education attained. Figure 23.4 indicates the distribution of educational attainment across cohorts in the SLS by proportion of persons whose education was limited to grade school and high school or who attended college and graduate school. Although our data come from a geographical area with unusually high educational attainment, the shift across cohorts appears to be quite representative of the general U.S. pattern of cohort shift.

The increasing proportion of the population with high educational attainment also has significant implications for level and slope of cognitive trajectories across the adult life span. To show these consequences, I next present data in Figures 23.5 and 23.6 on longitudinal changes

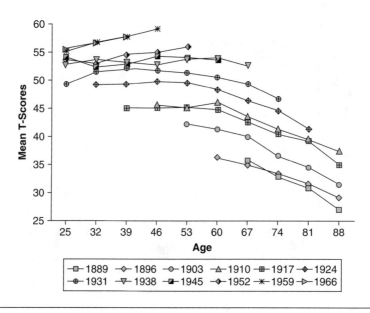

Figure 23.3 Intracohort Trajectories for the Fluid Ability of Inductive Reasoning for 12 Successive Cohorts Born From 1889 to 1966

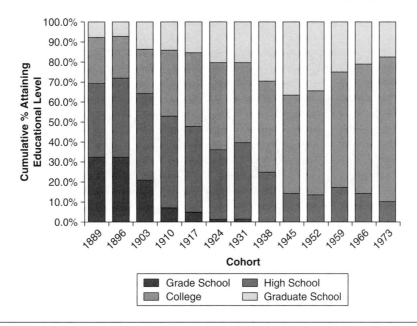

Figure 23.4   Cumulative Proportions of Educational Attainment for 13 Successive Cohorts Born From
1889 to 1973

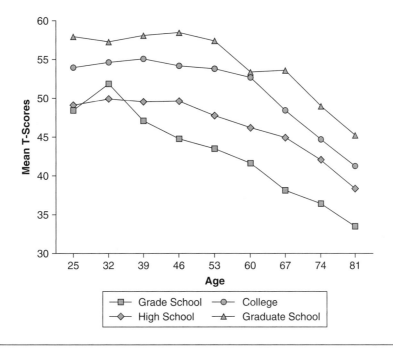

Figure 23.5   Longitudinal Trajectories for the Crystallized Ability of Verbal Meaning by Level of
Educational Attainment

SOURCE: From Schaie, K. W. (2006). Societal influences on cognition in historical context. In K. W. Schaie & L. L.
Carstensen (Eds.), *Social structures, aging and self-regulation in the elderly* (p. 19). New York. Springer Publishing Co.
Reproduced by permission.

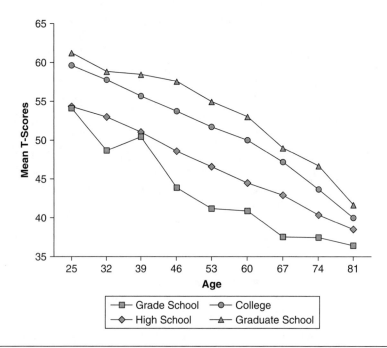

Figure 23.6   Longitudinal Trajectories for the Fluid Ability of Inductive Reasoning by Level of Educational Attainment

SOURCE: From Schaie, K. W. (2006). Societal influences on cognition in historical context. In K. W. Schaie & L. L. Carstensen (Eds.), *Social structures, aging and self-regulation in the elderly* (p. 19). New York. Springer Publishing Co. Reproduced by permission.

in cognitive trajectories for the two abilities I am using as exemplars in this chapter. For the crystallized ability of verbal meaning there are substantial differences in level and slope that are largest in early old age. These differences may indicate that more recent cohorts may be able to work longer in occupations involving primarily verbal skills (see "Occupational Status" section). For the fluid ability of inductive reasoning we find primarily differences in level, converging somewhat at very old ages. Here too, more recent cohorts would be at an advantage by virtue of their higher educational attainment.

Occupational Status

Another historical process that provides an important influence on cohort differences in cognitive abilities is the changing occupational structure in our working population. To examine these changes in our longitudinal samples, I have examined the cumulative proportion of individuals who were retired, or employed in unskilled, skilled, and professional occupations

at age 60, for seven successive cohorts. As shown in Figure 23.7, there were virtually no retirees at age 60 prior to the cohorts born in 1910; from then, their proportion has increased, although there is recent trend for some to remain longer in the workforce. More important is that there has been a significant decrease in the proportion of persons in unskilled occupations from the earlier cohorts and a steady move toward a greater proportion in professional occupations.

Similar to the influence of increasing levels of educational attainment, the increasing proportion of the population with higher occupational status has significant implications for level and slope of cognitive trajectories across the adult life span. The consequences of these trends are presented in Figures 23.8 and 23.9. For the crystallized ability of verbal meaning there are substantial differences in both level and slope. Note the substantial difference in favor of those with professional occupations. For the fluid ability of inductive reasoning, there are also significant differences in level and a flatter slope for those with professional occupations; at least until age

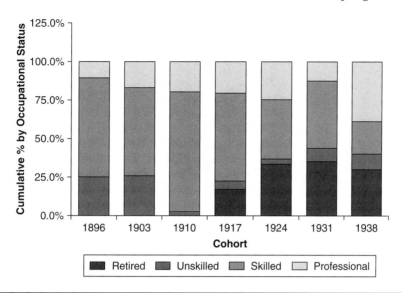

Figure 23.7　　Cumulative Proportions of Educational Attainment for Seven Successive Cohorts at Age 60 Born From 1896 to 1938

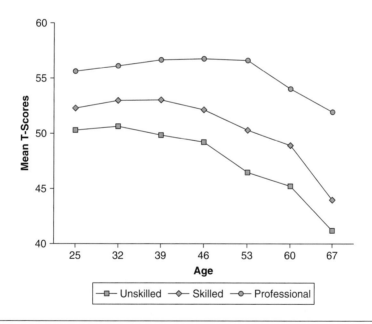

Figure 23.8　　Longitudinal Trajectories for the Crystallized Ability of Verbal Meaning by Level of Occupational Status

SOURCE: From Schaie, K. W. (2006). Societal influences on cognition in historical context. In K. W. Schaie & L. L. Carstensen (Eds.), *Social structures, aging and self-regulation in the elderly* (p. 19). New York. Springer Publishing Co. Reproduced by permission.

60 is reached. Again, the cohort trend reveals the cumulative advantage obtained by successive cohorts via an increase of the population proportion employed in occupational pursuits that seem to mediate maintenance of cognitive functions into old age.

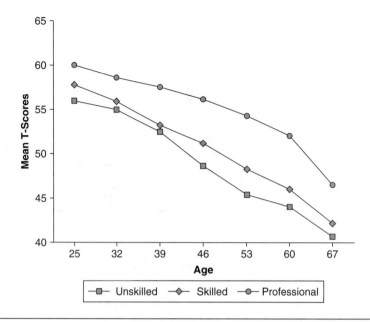

Figure 23.9 Longitudinal Trajectories for the Fluid Ability of Inductive Reasoning by Level of Occupational Status

SOURCE: From Schaie, K. W. (2006). Societal influences on cognition in historical context. In K. W. Schaie & L. L. Carstensen (Eds.), *Social structures, aging and self-regulation in the elderly* (p. 20). New York. Springer Publishing Co. Reproduced by permission.

CONCLUSION

In this chapter, I have described generational differences in cognitive trajectories and have reviewed some of the influences of historical change that affect level and slope of cognitive trajectories through adulthood. I also suggested the relevance of the co-constructive model in understanding the impact of neurobiological and sociocultural influences on adult cognitive development. I then provided data from the SLS to document cohort trends in both cognitive abilities and sociocultural influences that affect them. From these data, I conclude that future generations are likely to display more positive cognitive trajectories than their parents and grandparents. One of the major reasons for this trend is that sociocultural influences are at work to ensure that advances in educational attainment in shifts in the occupational structure will result in protective factors, sometimes called *cognitive reserve*, will compensate for many cognitive risks associated with neurobiological losses associated with increasing longevity.

REFERENCES

Baltes, P. B. (1997). On the incomplete architecture of human ontogeny: Selection, optimization and compensation as foundation of developmental theory. *American Psychologist, 52,* 366–380.

Bankart, C. P., & Anderson, C. C. (1979). Short-term effects of prosocial television viewing on play of preschool boys and girls. *Psychological Reports, 44,* 935–941.

Bosworth, H. B., Schaie, K. W., Willis, S. L., & Siegler, I. C. (1999). Age and distance to death in the Seattle Longitudinal Study. *Research on Aging, 21,* 723–738.

Cavalli-Sforza, L. L., & Feldman, M. W. (1981). *Cultural transmission and evolution: A quantitative approach.* Princeton, NJ: Princeton University Press.

Dickens, W. T., & Flynn, J. R. (2001). Heritability estimates versus large environmental effects: The IQ paradox resolved. *Psychological Review, 108,* 346–369.

Dunham, W. H. (1991). *Co-evolution: Genes, culture, and human diversity.* Palo Alto, CA: Stanford University Press.

Fillit, H. M., Butler, R. N., O'Connell, A. W., Albert, M. S., Birren, J. E., Cotman, C. W., et al. (2002). Achieving and maintaining cognitive vitality with aging. *Mayo Clinic Proceedings, 7,* 681–696.

Horn, J. L., & Cattell, R. B. (1966). Refinement and test of the theory of fluid and crystallized intelligence. *Journal of Educational Psychology, 57,* 253–270.

Laub, J. H., & Sampson, R. J. (2005). Coming of age in wartime: How World War II and the Korean War changed lives. In K. W. Schaie & G. H. Elder, Jr. (Eds.), *Historical influences on lives and aging* (pp. 208–228). New York: Springer.

Li, S.-C. (2003). Biocultural orchestration of developmental plasticity across levels: The interplay of biology and culture in shaping the mind and behavior across the life span. *Psychological Bulletin, 129,* 171–194.

Li, S.-C., & Freund, A. M. (2005). Advances in lifespan psychology: A focus on biocultural and personal influences. *Research in Human Development, 2,* 1–23.

Mondale, S., & Patton, S. B. (Eds.). (2001). *School: The story of American public education.* Boston: Beacon Press.

Petersen, R. C. (2003). Conceptual overview. In R. C. Petersen (Ed.), *Mild cognitive impairment: Aging to Alzheimer's disease* (pp. 1–14). New York: Oxford University Press.

Petersen, R. C., Smith, G. E, Waring, S. C., Ivnik, R. J., Tangalos, E. G., & Kokmen, E. (1999). Mild cognitive impairment: Clinical characterization and outcome. *Archives of Neurology, 5,* 303–308.

Rice, M. L., Huston, A. C., Truglio, R., & Wright, J. C. (1990). Words from *Sesame Street*: Learning vocabulary while viewing. *Developmental Psychology, 26,* 421–428.

Rowe, J. W., & Kahn, R. L. (1987, July 10). Human aging: Usual and successful. *Science, 237,* 143–149.

Sampson, R. J., & Laub, J. H. (1996). Socioeconomic achievement in the life course of disadvantaged men: Military service as a turning point, circa 1940–1965. *American Sociological Review, 61,* 347–367.

Schaie, K. W. (2005). *Developmental influences on adult intelligence: The Seattle Longitudinal Study.* New York: Oxford University Press.

Schaie, K. W. (2006). Societal influences on cognition in historical context. In K. W. Schaie & L. L. Carstensen (Eds.), *Social structures, self-regulation and aging* (pp. 13–24). New York: Springer.

Schaie, K. W., & Hofer, S. M. (2001). Longitudinal studies in research on aging. In J. E. Birren & K. W. Schaie (Eds.), *Handbook of the psychology of aging* (5th ed., pp. 55–77). San Diego, CA: Academic Press.

Schaie, K. W., Willis, S. L., & Pennak, S. (2005). A historical framework for cohort differences in intelligence. *Research in Human Development, 2,* 43–67.

Tomasello, M. (1999). *The cultural origins of human cognition.* Cambridge, MA: Harvard University Press.

Willis, S. L., & Schaie, K. W. (2005). Cognitive trajectories in midlife and cognitive functioning in old age. In S. L. Willis & M. Martin (Eds.), *Middle adulthood: A lifespan perspective* (pp. 243–276). Thousand Oaks, CA: Sage.

Willis, S. L., & Schaie, K. W. (2006). A co-constructionist view of the third age: The case of cognition. *Annual Review of Gerontology and Geriatrics, 26,* 131–152.

24

MINORITY POPULATIONS AND COGNITIVE AGING

KEITH WHITFIELD AND ADRIENNE AIKEN MORGAN

Current projections suggest that by 2050, the total number of non-Hispanic Whites age 65 and older will double, the number of African Americans age 65 and older will more than triple, and the number of Hispanics will increase elevenfold (Angel & Hogan, 2004). Conversely, there is a significant dearth of information about the factors that create unique features of cognitive aging process for most minority groups. The predicted explosion in demographic shift toward ethnic minorities representing a greater proportion of the United States has made the science of studying race an unavoidable consideration. The National Institutes of Health have made several recent revisions to their guidelines for human subject treatment. One of the central points of change in policy are the strong statements and rules about the necessity of the inclusion of minorities in federally funded research projects. Some scientists believe that this is being done for social reasons and has no grounding in basic science. Others argue, however, that if researchers are to adequately and thoroughly test hypotheses and provide answers to America's health concerns, they must formulate answers based on data from all who might be affected. Regardless, every application for National Institutes of Health funding must address the inclusion of minorities or face reviews that are less than favorable. Although this may be increasing the amount of research that includes ethnic groups other than Caucasians, often the results are not discussed relative to race. When race is discussed, it is presented only as a main effect, even though there are obvious interactions between other variables (e.g., health, income, education) and race. From these accounts, race is being added only as a nuisance variable and not as a central factor of importance. From some perspectives, if the research questions are not focused on race, this is an acceptable omission, compared with the standards set for the study of other variables. The question then logically arises: "Should every study have as its central question the issue of race?" Of course not. When it is important, however, race is often conceptualized as Caucasians and others.

Further understanding of understudied groups offers the possibility to promote healthy aging for the entire nation. One could imagine learning about a situation or factor that is overrepresented

AUTHORS' NOTE: This work was supported by National Institutes of Health Grants NIA-AG13662 and NIA-AG24108.

in a subpopulation but that also impacts the aging population in general. We discuss examples of this type of relationship later in this chapter. In this chapter, information on minorities and cognitive aging are discussed, but the majority of examples focus on cognitive aging among African Americans. The study of other minority groups presents similar challenges that we outline in this chapter. The aim of this chapter is to demonstrate the challenges in understanding cognitive aging among minorities. We hope to provide some examples of culturally appropriate models and suggest some of the ways minority populations provide an understanding of cognitive aging in unique ways.

In advancing knowledge about cognitive aging in minorities, research design is important. Although cross-group research has generated literature on cognitive aging in African Americans, it has not provided insights on the degree to which within-group variability contributes to observed differences between groups (see Burton & Bengston, 1982). Unique dimensions of psychological, social, and health factors in the history of African American life in the United States likely contribute to individual differences among seniors. Using current theories concerning intellectual abilities in late life, one might predict that decline is a prevalent and pervasive change as part of the normal aging process in ethnic minority elders. However, questions such as "What patterns exist in the changes of cognitive abilities in older African Americans?" or "What is the nature of variability in cognitive abilities among older African Americans?" have not been systematically addressed.

CONCEPTUAL MODELS

Caucasians often are seen as the comparison group necessary to decipher the importance of the findings from research on an ethnic minority group. Caucasians have been described as the *control group*, or the standard by which an understanding of minorities is gained from observing differences. There are some difficulties inherent to this perspective. First, there is a long history of research that does not include ethnic groups other than Caucasians. The validity of this research is never questioned. Second,

Caucasians are sometimes thought to be needed in an analysis of ethnic minorities to assess differences. There is an assumption of differences, but differences from what? The assumption seems to be that Caucasians represent a standard from which ethnic minorities deviate. These kinds of conceptualizations about racial differences research were discussed by Cauce, Cornado, and Watson (1998), who described three models typically used in thinking about and interpreting results from cross-cultural research that exemplify the issue of misinterpretation. These models are (1) the *cultural deviance model*, (2) the *cultural equivalence model*, and (3) the *cultural variant model*.

The cultural deviance model characterizes differences or deviations between groups as deviant and inferior. An example might involve racial group differences in cognitive aging. An interpretation based on this model might suggest that African Americans perform more poorly on cognitive tests because they lack the ability to do the tests. The cultural equivalence model is an improvement over the cultural deviance model in that it proposes that superior socioeconomic status (SES) provides advantages that create superior performance. Using this model, differences in performance on cognitive aging would be described differently. An interpretation might suggest that lack of opportunities to obtain education due to segregation hampered educational opportunities and achievement, which accounts for a large portion of the differences found between African Americans and Caucasians on tests of cognitive performance. The cultural equivalence model attributes advantages or superior performance to culture. Putting the onus on culture blames a group for not having the same ideals, resources, attitudes, and beliefs as the majority culture. Placing culpability on SES shifts the responsibility to social structures that are inherently unbalanced in their distribution of resources. The cultural variant model describes differences as adaptations to external forces, exemplifying resilience in the face of oppression. Differences are explained not in relation to a majority/superior group but as culturally rooted internal explanations. This third model, by definition, allows an appreciation for between-group differences and challenges one to explore within group heterogeneity. Using our example of racial differences in cognitive aging, an interpretation of the differences might include discussion about how culture fair stimuli were not used or based on unique experiences of African Americans. Thus, African Americans' performance was due to a different knowledge base, or perhaps because expectations were high among earlier cohorts for leaving the educational system to support their family financially, especially if the respondents lived in rural areas where education was an option rather than mandatory.

Examples of each of these models can be found in the current literature. We predict that as knowledge about ethnic minorities grows, use of cultural variant models to explain differences will also increase. The cultural variant model is important not only for the design and interpretation of research but also for the translation of research. The presentation of findings in a manner that accurately depicts ethnic minority elders will be more informative for older minorities and more openly received by them. At some level, minority elders know about the phenomena researchers study, and they make interpretations of their own. It is doubtful that they see themselves as deviant.

ANALYTIC STRATEGIES

Between-Group Methodology

Following traditional experimental methods, most cross-cultural research involving comparisons typically uses statistical analyses that involve comparison of group means. One central assumption in these types of analyses is homogeneity of variance. Meeting this assumption may be very difficult in cross-cultural comparisons of cognitive functioning across ethnic groups. As mentioned earlier, ethnic minorities possess unique attributes by virtue of their language, lifestyle, SES, and historical experiences. These attributes create different degrees of variability within groups that may violate assumptions of homogeneity of variance. An empirical example may be found in data from the American Changing Lives Study (House, Landis, & Umberson, 1988). The heterogeneity between Caucasians and African Americans can be observed in the scatter plots provided in Figure 24.1, which

are based on a composite of verbal IQ scores and items from the Short Portable Mental Status Questionnaire (Pfeiffer, 1975). As this figure shows, there is greater variability in the African American sample relative to the Caucasian sample. Statistical analyses of homogeneity of variance reveal a significant difference in the patterns of variability between the groups.

The same measures that have been standardized on Caucasians are often used when studying minority elders, without attention to reliability and, even more important, to validity issues. If existing measures are to be used or cross-cultural comparisons to be made, multiple levels of equivalence should be achieved. Cauce et al. (1998) not only discussed the conceptual models used in cross-group research but also offered standards for equating measures across groups so accurate group differences can be assessed. They suggested that there are five levels or kinds of measurement equivalence: (1) cultural, (2) conceptual, (3) linguistic, (4) functional, and (5) scalar. *Cultural equivalence* is described by the extent to which a measure has the same internal structure and meanings within and across groups. *Conceptual equivalence* is defined as the item content being defined similarly across groups. This suggests that the items are equally familiar across groups. *Linguistic equivalence* is having the language of items understood the same across groups. *Functional equivalence* is when scores have similar correlates across groups. Last, *scalar equivalence* is when scores reflect the same level of the construct across groups

Within-Group Approaches

Past research on culture has focused on distinguishable qualities by addressing the significant differences among ethnic groups. This conceptual–methodological approach has generated a considerable body of literature in the area of racially comparative research on elders. Social scientists initially argued that although ethnic minority elders may in fact have some distinctive attributes by virtue of their language, lifestyle, SES, and historical experiences in the United States, those attributes were best captured in comparative research between groups. Contemporary researchers cite several limitations in these

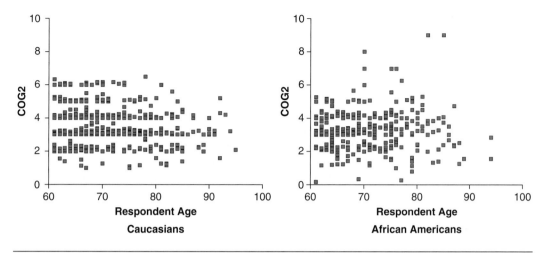

Figure 24.1 Heterogeneity Between Groups

NOTE: COG2 = cognitive composite.

cross-ethnic comparisons, which preclude a full appreciation of the distinctiveness of the groups under study (Markides, Liang, & Jackson, 1990). One limitation in applying comparative research to questions of aging is its lack of insight into the degree of within-group variability. For example, a Hispanic subgroup might include Mexican Americans, Latin Americans, and Puerto Ricans. Each of these cultural subgroups reflects some unique and varying historical culture and levels of assimilation, which may bear on cognitive processes affected by aging. These individual groups are inherently different; collapsing the groups under one ethnic umbrella and then comparing them with Caucasians eliminates important distinctions within each group. These lost distinctions may be very important in interpreting differences in research on cognitive aging across various cultural groups. To this end, advances in cognitive aging research must depart from the exclusive use of between-subjects designs.

Including race as a between-subjects variable assesses the variability due to the categorization of individuals by race. However, it does not assess the possible dynamic effect of ethnicity on the variables in the model being tested. Race implies only a biological differentiation while ignoring other possible sources of variability in cross-cultural comparisons, such as lifestyle, beliefs about aging, language, and historical experiences. Race, then, is not an adequate proxy for the synergistic effects present in studies

designed to address ethnic diversity. To this end, an important point to remember in developing research questions is that *factors that account for between-group variability do not necessarily account for within-group variability* (Whitfield & Baker-Thomas, 1999). Furthermore, there may be good grounds for using ethnicity instead of race when culturally relevant behavior is the focus of an investigation.

If we are to grasp a cross-cultural understanding of cognitive functioning, we must be willing to reconceptualize some of our starting points. For example, ample evidence suggests significant individual differences in cognitive aging in studies of Caucasians (e.g., Rapp & Amaral, 1992). In particular, the rate of cognitive decline varies among individuals. Decline in cognitive functioning does not occur in a linear manner (e.g., Schaie, 1990; Willis, 1991). In addition, the results of longitudinal investigations of cognitive abilities have shown that very few individuals exhibit decline in all or most abilities (Schaie, 1989a). Some abilities are maintained into late life. Fluid abilities are thought to be innate and less influenced by culture or education; however, they are vulnerable to decline with advancing age (Horn, 1982; Schaie, 1989a). Crystallized abilities, on the other hand, are thought to be dependent on and developed from cultural influences and resistant to changes with advancing age (Hertzog & Schaie, 1988; Schaie, 1983; Schaie & Hertzog,

1983, 1986); however, crystallized abilities show a steeper decrement after age 70. What do these individual differences mean within ethnic minority groups?

The impact of SES and cultural and contextual factors may coalesce to create even greater heterogeneity within than between groups in examinations of cognitive abilities. Using the previously cited example, it may be inappropriate to use measures that connote the conceptual dimensions of crystallized and fluid cognitive abilities in the study of older ethnic minorities because of the inherent nature of crystallized abilities (which are believed to be significantly influenced by culture (Cattell, 1963). Because such typically used measures were standardized on Caucasian populations, using them with other cultural groups should be done cautiously; making comparisons is not likely to be appropriate without understanding sources of within-group variability.

One strategy for overcoming the performance bias in comparisons of different cultural groups is to study each group as its own heterogeneous population first and investigate the appropriateness of the measure and its items for each population under study. Then, examine the mean and, perhaps more important, variances and error variances between groups. Another approach is to use an acculturation measure as a covariate in between-group analyses. In this way, basic cognitive processes, devoid of the impact of culture, can be examined appropriately.

It is not sufficient to propose that within-group analyses be done and have no concrete suggestions for the kind of analytical issues and strategies that should be used. Within-group designs provide the opportunity to examine how meaningful social variables contribute to variability. For example, SES is thought to be one of the most important stratifying variables in social science literature (Adler 2004). Stratifying by SES may be an important approach to understanding within-group variability by more closely examining how demographic variables, such as education and income, contribute to social and psychological variables. Techniques such as tests of invariance (Alwin, 1988; Meredith, 1993; Meredith & Horn, 2001) could be highly useful in shedding light on the variability within ethnic groups and lead to an understanding of how variables differ in their contribution to psychological processes. Furthermore, these types of studies can provide critical information about subprocesses occurring and lost in racially comparative analyses and identify where there may be measurement and epistemological differences in the processes under study.

Accelerated Cognitive Aging

Although cross-sectional research has provided data on normative levels of functioning for populations by gender, race, and age, these studies cannot address the issue of positive and negative trajectories and the determinants for such paths in the process of aging. Longitudinal studies provide the ability to identify factors that are involved in the progression of cognitive processes during aging (Schaie, 1989a, 1989b; Schaie & Hertzog, 1983; Schaie & Hofer, 2001). From this research, patterns evolve to show the course of cognitive aging. In addition, mediating and moderating factors that cause diversions from the "normal course" of cognitive aging have also been identified.

Implicit in this body of research is that the presence of identifiable risk factors may contribute to changes in the trajectory of change in cognitive processes. Proposed here is the concept of *accelerated cognitive aging*, which is defined as the premature and rapid (rapid as compared with age norms) decline of normal cognitive functioning to a state of impairment functioning. Accelerated cognitive aging is hypothesized to appear from the presence of one or more risk factors. These characteristics involve health indexes and disease processes, demographic factors, and characteristics related to ability. Perhaps much of the between-group differences found for Caucasians and African Americans is due in fact to the "early" aging of African Americans (Whitfield, 2004). African Americans at the population level have more of these risk factors than other ethnic groups. If this hypothesis is true, then there should be significant numbers of African Americans who decline over short periods of time.

FACTORS CONTRIBUTING TO COGNITIVE AGING IN MINORITY POPULATIONS

Possible differences in the sources of individual variability between Caucasians and African

Americans (social, psychological, health, etc.) restrict the ability to make assumptions of parallelism in cognitive functioning in late life, without empirical support. Thus, it is important to understand significant contributors to individual variation in cognitive aging within ethnic groups. Conceptual issues around within-group studies have been discussed. Whitfield (1996) discussed the paucity of studies of cognitive aging that have included African Americans and described the challenge to define conceptual starting points for investigations of cognitive aging. Although numerous variables have been found to correlate with and account for performance in cognitive abilities in older adults (e.g., occupation, education, age, health, emotional status), he suggested two conceptual issues that have been important in past research on cognitive aging in Caucasians and of importance in past studies of African American elderly as starting points: (1) health and (2) social factors, such as SES.

Health

One variable of possible importance in initial investigations of cognition in minority populations, particularly in elderly African Americans, is physical health. Investigating links between cognition and physical health indexes is an important step in understanding cognitive aging in African Americans, for several reasons. In several studies, health appears to be an important mediator in adult intellectual functioning (e.g., Barrett & Watkins, 1986; Elias, Elias, & Elias, 1990; Perlmutter et al., 1988; Perlmutter & Nyquist, 1990; Rosano et al., 2005; Schaie, 1994; Weuve et al., 2004; Ylikoski et al., 2000). It has been proposed that fluid abilities are affected by experiential determinants and other influences that directly influence physiological processes and structures on which intellectual development is based (see Horn & Donaldson, 1980).

Health problems have been shown to negatively influence cognitive functioning and are more prevalent in the elderly (e.g., Perlmutter et al., 1988). There is evidence of the relationship between cognition and health from studies that have examined self-rated health, cardiovascular disease, hypertension, and mortality.

There is a considerable body of research on self-rated health as a significant predictor of cognition (e.g., Anstey, Luszcz, Giles, & Andrews, 2001; Field, Schaie, & Leino, 1988; Hultsch, Hammer, & Small, 1993; Perlmutter et al., 1988; Perlmutter & Nyquist, 1990; Salthouse, Kausler, & Saults, 1990), with the opposite being true as well (Leinonen, Heikkinen, & Jylha, 2001). For example, Perlmutter and Nyquist (1990) found that self-reported health accounted for a significant proportion of the variance in cognitive performance, even after age-related differences in health were statistically controlled. They found that, for their sample, self-reported health accounted for significant proportions of variance in digit span and fluid intelligence. Anstey et al. (2001) found that poor performance on nearly all the cognitive variables included in their study was associated with mortality, but many of these effects were explained by measures of self-rated health and disease. So, even in contrast to mortality, self-rated health is a significant predictor of cognitive performance.

In addition to self-rated health, two chronic diseases that have been related to lower cognitive functioning include cardiovascular disease and hypertension. Much of the research on associations between cognition and hypertension has focused on neuropsychological assessments of cognition (for a review, see Waldstein, 1995). In summary, this extensive body of research suggests that high blood pressure levels are adversely related to cognitive functioning, particularly when normotensives are compared with hypertensives. This relationship has recently been examined in analyses within (e.g., Izquierdo-Porrera & Waldstein, 2002) and across race (Bohannon, Fillenbaum, Pieper, Hanlon, & Blazer, 2002) in studies involving African Americans, and similar results have been found. Thus, hypertension is an important risk factor for cardiovascular disease as well as cognitive functioning.

The presence of cardiovascular disease has also been shown to have a negative impact on cognitive functioning (e.g., Ylikoski et al., 2000). Heart disease continues to be the leading cause of death in the United States (for a review, see Whitfield, Weidner, Clark, & Anderson, 2002). Recent trends suggest that heart disease is decreasing among Caucasian men but may be increasing in African American men (e.g., Hames & Greenlund, 1996). African Americans experience significantly higher age-adjusted mortality rates from and poorer trends for coronary heart disease than Caucasians (e.g., Barnett & Halverson, 2001).

A number of studies have examined the relationship between mortality and cognitive performance. These studies tend to suggest that lower cognitive performance is an important predictor of mortality in older adults (e.g., Deeg, Hofman, & van Zonneveld, 1990; Evans et al., 1991; Kliegel, Moor, & Rott, 2004; Liu, LaCroix, & White, 1990; Swan, Carmelli, & LaRue, 1995). Kliegel and colleagues (2004) analyzed cognitive change over a 1.5-year period, and their findings suggest that the terminal decline or drop in cognitive functioning decreases in very old age. Given the well-observed earlier mortality by African Americans compared with Caucasians (for a review, see Whitfield & Hayward, 2003; Whitfield et al., 2002), the impact of chronic conditions on cognitive aging among this vulnerable population may be significant.

If the link between cognitive functioning and health operates similarly in African Americans and Caucasians, then there are important public health considerations for this population. There is growing evidence of low availability and utilization of health care and previous findings of high rates of chronic illnesses (e.g., hypertension, diabetes mellitus, and coronary heart disease) among African Americans (Ferraro & Farmer, 1996; Harper & Alexander, 1990; Marquis & Long, 1996; Miles & Bernard, 1992). These conditions may be important factors in increased susceptibility to the development of vascular dementia (Folstein, Anthony, & Parhad, 1985) and accelerated declines in cognition in African Americans.

Whitfield and colleagues (1997) examined associations between cognition and indexes of health in 224 elderly African Americans using data from the MacArthur Studies of Successful Aging (Berkman et al., 1993). Using cross-sectional and longitudinal data, they examined relationships between seven different indexes of health and cognitive functioning. The results indicated that greater average peak expiratory flow was predictive of better cognitive performance at the first interview. A longitudinal analysis of the first and second interviews (28 months ±4 months between interviews) showed that gender was the only significant predictor of change (when the change in performance on the cognitive measure was treated as a continuous variable), with women tending to maintain and improve their cognitive performance. When change was treated as a dichotomous variable (e.g., a decline of 6 or more points), lower levels of average peak expiratory flow and education were predictive of decline. To the contrary, positive self-ratings of current health and changes in health in the past year were important factors in the maintenance of cognitive performance. Although these results greatly contribute to our understanding of within-group variability (by means of cross-sectional and longitudinal designs) in African Americans, the applicability of this study to understanding cognitive aging has limitations similar to Albert et al.'s (1995) study: It is limited by the selective nature of sample.

Whitfield et al. (2000) also published research using the MacArthur data set that shows that controlling for health and the interactions between health and ethnicity are important for understanding differences across ethnic groups. Specifically, their analyses showed that after controlling for health (including interactions of health and ethnicity) among successfully aging Caucasians and African Americans, the original racial differences in the identification of items on the Boston Naming Task (a knowledge-based task) were not ameliorated. However, in examining the task as an incidental memory task, after controlling for health, there were no ethnic differences. These results also suggest that the model of cognitive functioning differed between the two racial groups. Some of these differences reflected alternative ways of operationalizing a particular concept, such as health status. For instance, various measures of health status were included in the analysis. Of these, peak expiratory flow helped explain the performance of Caucasians, whereas the number of chronic conditions was important in explaining the performance of African Americans. These results suggest that African Americans may have unique patterns of cognitive aging, due in part to health status. Although these results are compelling support for different patterns of aging and the factors that impact the process, they are limited in that the sample is highly selective.

Social Factors

Social and sociodemographic factors have potential direct and mediated effects on cognitive functioning. Mediated effects conceptually arise from measures of social support affecting health that also affect cognition. Previous research suggests that socioeconomic indicators are strong candidates for sources of direct effects on cognitive functioning. Both SES and social support may play an important role in cognitive functioning in African Americans.

Social support is broadly defined as the resources one has available through social ties to other individuals and groups (Billings & Moos, 1984; Lin, Ensel, Simeone, & Kuo, 1979). These resources may serve as buffers against the effects of stress (Caplan, 1974; Cassel, 1976; Cobbs, 1976; Payne & Jones, 1987) and/or mechanisms for assisting one in meeting daily needs and the fundamental needs for human attachment (Barrera, 1981; Kahn & Antonucci, 1980; Unger & Wandersman, 1985). A summary of the literature on social support among African Americans reveals deficits in social networks but also shows compensatory effects of cultural factors, such as religion (J. S. Jackson, Antonucci, & Gibson, 1990). J. S. Jackson et al. (1990) suggested that demographic variables such as SES, marital status, age, and sex are particularly important in the study of religious behavior in African Americans. For many older African Americans, the church can serve as an alternative source of support to that of family and friends (Ortega, Crutchfield, & Rushing, 1983).

Individual variability in cognition may also be influenced by social factors that are related to health in African Americans. Social factors, such as social support (e.g., Cohen & Syme, 1985; Dressler, Dos-Santos, & Viteri, 1986; House et al., 1988; Strogatz & James, 1986) and religious participation (Livingston, Levine, & Moore, 1991), have been found to be important predictors of health outcomes. Thus, links that exist between health and cognition may reflect a set of complex relationships that directly and/or indirectly involve social and psychological factors. For example, some previous research suggests that there are associations between cardiovascular health and social support in African Americans (e.g., J. J. Jackson, 1988; J. S. Jackson et al., 1990; James, 1984). From this research, three conclusions can be drawn: (1) social disorganization is related to elevated stroke mortality rates, (2) individuals within cohesive families are at reduced risk for elevated blood pressure, and (3) social ties and support play a positive role in reducing elevated blood pressure (J. S. Jackson et al., 1990; James, 1984). We discussed the relationship between blood pressure and cardiovascular disease with cognitive functioning earlier. In this way, the potential indirect link between social support and cognitive functioning may be mediated through health factors in African Americans.

SES as a composite variable is important in the study of cognitive aging. The variables typically included in the conceptualization of SES consist of education, employment, and income (see Gibson, 1993). Each of these variables is a significant factor in the study of cognition (e.g., Arbuckle, Gold, & Andres, 1986; Gribbon, Schaie, & Parham, 1980; Owens, 1966; Schaie, 1983). As a consequence, SES may account for significant proportions of variability in the performance of elderly African Americans on cognitive tasks.

Of the variables that comprise SES, education may be the most integral to the study of cognition. The relationship between intellectual abilities and education has a long history (e.g., Birren & Morrison, 1961; Blum & Jarvik, 1974; Denny & Palmer, 1981; Green, 1969; Kesler, Denny, & Whitney, 1976; Ripple & Jaquish, 1981; Selzer & Denny, 1980). A measure of years of education or some assessment of educational attainment is common in most studies of cognition in the elderly. Summarizing the results of these studies, we find that as education increases so does performance on many cognitive tasks. Individual differences in performance by elderly Caucasians on measures of cognition due to variability in educational attainment underscore the need to characterize the educational factors involved in individual differences for a prospective study of cognition in elderly African Americans.

African Americans have an important history-graded influence that may impact the relative contribution of education to cognitive functioning. The *Brown v. Board of Education* ruling in 1954 established desegregated schools in three cities: (1) New York; (2) Washington, District of Columbia; and (3) Baltimore, Maryland. The idea was to make education equal for Caucasians and African Americans. If this were the impact on education for African Americans, then there should be a difference in cognitive aging between those who attended desegregated schools and those who attended segregated schools. To examine the potential influence of quality of education on cognitive aging among African Americans, Whitfield and Wiggins (2003) used one of the most common conceptualizations of cognition: fluid and crystallized abilities (Horn, 1982, 1986). Measures of fluid abilities included in the study were spatial orientation and inductive reasoning, and crystallized abilities were assessed by verbal meanings (vocabulary) and numerical concepts. Data were collected from 201 participants, 40% of whom had attended segregated schools. The results demonstrated that the desegregated-school group had significantly higher mean cognitive scores compared with the segregated-school group. However, after accounting for age and years of education, significant mean differences between the schooling groups for either the fluid or crystallized composite dimensions were not found. Also, no group differences on the specific measures of numerical concepts and inductive reasoning were found, but mean differences were found for measures of verbal meanings and spatial orientation. This study involved one of the first cohorts to attend desegregated schools. Any improvement in educational quality due to desegregation that would lead to better cognitive aging appears to have been diminished by other aspects of the school environment, such as racism by students or by teachers. With this in mind, any differences in school attendance might be observed only in future cohorts.

One of the difficulties in gaining knowledge from comparisons between Caucasian and African American elderly on tests of intellectual abilities involves group mean differences in the level of educational attainment. It is well documented that African American elderly are more likely to have less formal education on average than elderly Caucasians (Harper & Alexander, 1990). These race differences are in addition to cohort differences that exist in educational achievement (Adams-Price, 1993). The existing variability in the education that African American elders received as children is also an important factor that has not been an inherent element in discussions of the origins of racial differences in intellectual abilities. One of the

results of African Americans being restricted in their access to formal education is that the spoken word was heavily relied on by older cohorts for the exchange of information. For example, story telling is a major component of African American culture for purposes of obtaining general knowledge as well as passing on family histories and legacies. There is great variability in how much families and individuals currently rely on story telling to communicate information (this ability might be assessed using a measure of verbal memory). This may be associated with education and variability in intellectual abilities among African Americans. For example, in part as a function of differential access to education, it has been argued that many elderly Caucasians obtained a higher *quantity and quality* of education than most African Americans did during childhood (e.g., Beady & Hansel, 1981; Bruno & Doscher, 1981; Massey, Scott, & Dornbusch, 1975; Walker, 1996). In comparing Caucasians and African Americans with an eighth-grade education, the level of attainment may be the same, but the groups may possess different knowledge bases, skills, and learning strategies from which to perform psychometric or laboratory-based cognitive tests. These different skills may be what cause differential outcomes or perceived deficits in performance on measures of cognitive ability. Manly, Jacobs, Touradji, Small, and Stern (2002) observed race differences in neuropsychological test performance. However, after adjusting the scores for literacy using Wide Range Achievement Test—3 reading scores, racial differences on several neuropsychological tests (except category fluency and a drawing measure) were nonsignificant.

The cognitive skills and strategies that have been provided to older African Americans in their educational training may not be adequately tapped by standard cognitive tests. Elderly African Americans appear to posses strengths for solving problems relevant to their existence and may possess yet-unidentified abilities that well serve them for tasks and challenges particular to their environment (Whitfield, 1996). Conversely, there is a significant proportion of African Americans who perform comparable to Caucasians on standard psychometric tasks. Thus, as a basic starting point for understanding cognitive aging in African Americans, it is just as important and meaningful to understand what factors create variability within African Americans as it is to conduct between-group comparisons. In essence, a within-group strategy allows one to first compare apples to apples and not apples to oranges (Whitfield & Baker, 1999).

Identifying factors relevant to African Americans and related to the decline or stability of cognitive functioning in African Americans contributes to our understanding of cognitive aging for all elderly. The relative impact of factors that are perhaps differentially prevalent in other cultures (e.g., hypertension, social support, and low education levels) can be examined in relation to these factors' potential to affect cognition in late life across different elderly populations.

CONCLUSION

The inclusion of ethnic minorities challenges researchers to broaden research questions and examine within-group variability. The move to research on cognitive aging that uses appropriate designs and questions in describing the entire population will be a useful advance in knowledge about the context of cognitive functioning. Much work is needed to understand the origin of differences between and variability within ethnic groups on cognitive functioning. Not only is there a need for more research on minorities, but also the research needs to encompass ethnic groups other than African Americans. Hispanics are predicted to increase in numbers even greater than African Americans, but little research has examined cognitive aging among these populations. This is an important missed opportunity for understanding the critical features of individual variability in cognitive aging. In particular, the effect of bilingualism may be important for understanding risk and protective factors for cognitive aging, but it has received only scant attention. There is evidence that bilingualism can be a protective effect for cognitive aging. Bialystok, Craik, Klein, and Viswanathan (2004) found that bilingualism compensated for age-related losses in certain executive processes.

In sum, improvements in measurement, standardization of assessments, conducting complex but appropriate data analyses, and accurate interpretations of data in ethnically diverse samples will significantly improve our understanding of cognitive aging universally.

REFERENCES

Adams-Price, C. E. (1993). Age, education, and literacy skills of adult Mississippians. *The Gerontologist, 33,* 741–746.

Adler, N. E. (2004). Socioeconomic status and health. In N. B. Anderson (Ed.), *Encyclopedia of health and behavior* (pp. 768–770). Thousand Oaks, CA: Sage.

Albert, M. S., Jones, K., Savage, C. R., Berkman, L., Seeman, T., Blazer, D., et al. (1995). Predictors of cognitive change in older persons: MacArthur Studies of Successful Aging. *Psychology and Aging, 10,* 578–589.

Alwin, D. F. (1988). Structural equation models in research on human development and aging. In K. W. Schaie, R. T. Campbell, W. Meredith, & S. C. Rawlings (Eds.), *Methodological issues in aging research* (pp. 71–170). New York: Springer.

Angel, J., & Hogan, D. (2004). Population aging and diversity in a new era. In K. E. Whitfield (Ed.), *Closing the gap: Improving the health of minority elders in the new millennium* (pp. 1–12). Washington, DC: Gerontological Society of America.

Anstey, K. J., Luszcz, M. A., Giles, L. C., & Andrews, G. R. (2001). Demographic, health, cognitive, and sensory variables as predictors of mortality in very old adults. *Psychology of Aging, 16,* 3–11.

Arbuckle, T. Y., Gold, D., & Andres, D. (1986). Cognitive functioning of older people in relation to social and personality variables. *Psychology and Aging, 1,* 55–62.

Barnett, E., & Halverson, J. (2001). Local increases in coronary heart disease mortality among Blacks and Whites in the United States, 1985–1995. *American Journal of Public Health, 91,* 1499–1506.

Barrera, M. (1981). Social support in the adjustment of pregnant adolescents. In B. H. Gottlieb (Ed.), *Social networks and social support* (pp. 69–96). Beverly Hills, CA: Sage.

Barrett, T. R., & Watkins, S. K. (1986). Word familiarity and cardiovascular health as determinants of age-related recall differences. *Journal of Gerontology, 41,* 222–224.

Beady, C. H., & Hansel, S. (1981). Teacher race and expectations for student achievement. *American Education Research Journal, 18,* 191–206.

Berkman, L. F., Seeman, T. E., Albert, M., Blazer, D., Kahn, R., Mohs, R., et al. (1993). High, usual and impaired functioning in community-dwelling older men and women: Findings from the MacArthur Foundation Research Network on Successful Aging. *Journal of Clinical Epidemiology, 46,* 1129–1140.

Bialystok, E., Craik, F.I. M., Klein, R., & Viswanathan, M. (2004). Bilingualism, aging, and cognitive control: Evidence from the Simon task. *Psychology and Aging, 19,* 290–303.

Billings, A. G., & Moos, R. H. (1984). Coping, stress, and social resources among adults with unipolar depression. *Journal of Personality and Social Psychology, 46,* 877–891.

Birren, J. E., & Morrison, D. F. (1961). Analysis of the WAIS subtests in relation to age and education. *Journal of Gerontology, 16,* 363–369.

Blum, J. E., & Jarvik, L. F. (1974). Intellectual performance of octogenarians as a function of education and initial ability. *Human Development, 17,* 364–375.

Bohannon, A. D., Fillenbaum, G. G., Pieper, C. F., Hanlon, J. T., & Blazer, D. G. (2002). Relationship of race/ethnicity and blood pressure to change in cognitive function. *Journal of the American Geriatrics Society, 50,* 424–429.

Bruno, J. D., & Doscher, M. L. (1981). Contributing to the harms of racial isolation: Analysis of a quest for teacher transfer in a large urban school district. *Educational Administration Quarterly, 17,* 93–108.

Burton, L. M., & Bengston, V. L. (1982). Research in elderly minority communities: Problems and potentials. In R. C. Manuel (Ed.), *Minority aging: Sociological and social psychological issues* (pp. 215–222). Westport, CT: Greenwood Press.

Caplan, C. (1974). *Support systems and community mental health.* New York: Behavioral Publications.

Cassel, J. (1976). Psychosocial processes and stress: Theoretical formulation. *International Journal of Health Services, 4,* 471–482.

Cattell, R. B. (1963). Theory of fluid and crystallized intelligence: A critical experiment. *Journal of Educational Psychology, 54,* 1–22.

Cauce, A. M., Coronado, N., & Watson, J. (1998). Conceptual, methodological and statistical issues in culturally competent research. In M. Hernandez & M. R. Isaacs (Eds.), *Promoting cultural competence in children's mental health services* (pp. 305–331). Baltimore: Paul H. Brookes.

Cobbs, S. (1976). Social support as a moderator of life stress. *Psychosomatic Medicine, 38,* 300–314.

Cohen, S., & Syme, S. L. (1985). *Social support and health.* San Francisco: Academic Press.

Deeg, D. J. H., Hofman, A., & van Zonneveld, R. J. (1990). The association between change in cognitive function and longevity in Dutch elderly. *American Journal of Epidemiology, 132,* 973–982.

Denny, N. W., & Palmer, A. M. (1981). Adult age differences on traditional and practical problem-solving measures. *Journal of Gerontology, 36,* 323–328.

Dressler, W. W., Dos-Santos, J. E., & Viteri, F. E. (1986). Blood pressure, ethnicity, and psychosocial resources. *Psychosomatic Medicine, 48,* 509–519.

Elias, M. F., Elias, J. W., & Elias, P. K. (1990). Biological and health influences on behavior. In J. E. Birren & K. W. Schaie (Eds.), *Handbook of the psychology of aging* (pp. 70–102). New York: Academic Press.

Evans, D. A., Smith, L. A., Scherr, P. A., Albert, M. S., Funkenstein, H. H., & Hebert, L. E. (1991). Risk of death from Alzheimer's disease in a community population of older persons. *American Journal of Epidemiology, 134,* 403–412.

Ferraro, K. F., & Farmer, M. M. (1996). Double jeopardy to health hypothesis for African Americans: Analysis and critique. *Journal of Health and Social Behavior, 37,* 27–43.

Field, D., Schaie, K. W., & Leino, E. V. (1988). Continuity in intellectual functioning: The role of self-reported health. *Psychology and Aging, 3,* 385–392.

Folstein, M. S., Anthony, J. C., & Parhad, L. (1985). The meaning of cognitive impairment in the elderly. *Journal of the American Geriatrics Society, 33,* 228–235.

Gibson, R. C. (1993). The Black American retirement experience. In J. S. Jackson, L. M. Chatters, & R. T. Taylor (Eds.), *Aging in Black America* (pp. 277–300). Newbury Park, CA: Sage.

Green, R. F. (1969). Age–intelligence relationship between ages sixteen and sixty-four: A rising trend. *Developmental Psychology, 34,* 404–414.

Gribbon, K., Schaie, K. W., & Parham, I. (1980). Complexity of life style and maintenance of intellectual abilities. *Journal of Social Issues, 36,* 47–67.

Hames, C. G., & Greenlund, K. J. (1996). Ethnicity and cardiovascular disease: The Evans County Heart Study. *American Journal of the Medical Sciences, 311,* 130–134.

Harper, M. S., & Alexander, C. D. (1990). Profile of the Black elderly. In M. S. Harper (Ed.), *Minority aging: Essential curricula content for selected health and allied health professions* (DHHS Publication No. HRS-P-DV 90-4, pp. 193–222). Washington, DC: U.S. Department of Health and Human Services.

Hertzog, C., & Schaie, K. W. (1988). Stability and change in adult intelligence: Simultaneous analysis of longitudinal means and covariance structures. *Psychology and Aging, 3,* 122–130.

Horn, J. L. (1982). The theory of fluid and crystallized intelligence in relation to concepts of cognitive psychology and aging in adulthood. In F. I. M. Craik & S. Trehub (Eds.), *Aging and cognitive processes* (pp. 237–278). New York: Plenum.

Horn, J. L. (1986). Intellectual ability concepts. In R. J. Sternberg (Ed.), *Advances in the psychology of human intelligence* (Vol. 3, pp. 35–78). Hillsdale, NJ: Lawrence Erlbaum.

Horn, J. L., & Donaldson, G. (1980). Cognitive development in adulthood. In G. G. Brim & J. Kagan (Eds.), *Constancy and change in human development* (pp. 445–529). Cambridge, MA: Harvard University Press.

House, J., Landis, K., & Umberson, D. (1988, July 29). Social relationships and health. *Science, 241,* 540–545.

Hultsch, D. F., Hammer, M., & Small, B. J. (1993). Age differences in cognitive performance in later life: Relationships to self-reported health and activity style. *Journal of Gerontology: Psychological Sciences, 48,* P1–11.

Izquierdo-Porrera, A. M., & Waldstein, S. R. (2002). Cardiovascular risk factors and cognitive function in African Americans. *Journal of Gerontology Series B: Psychological Sciences and Social Sciences, 57,* P377–P380.

Jackson, J. J. (1988). Social determinants of the health of aging Black populations in the United States. In J. Jackson (Ed.), *The Black American elderly: Research on physical and psychosocial health* (pp. 69–98). New York: Springer.

Jackson, J. S., Antonucci, T. C., & Gibson, R. C. (1990). Cultural, racial, and ethnic minority influences on aging. In J. E. Birren & K. W. Schaie (Eds.), *Handbook of the psychology of aging* (pp. 103–123). San Diego, CA: Academic Press.

James, S. A. (1984). Socioeconomic influences on coronary heart disease in Black populations. *American Heart Journal, 108*(3, Pt. 2), 669–672.

Kahn, R. L., & Antonucci, T. C. (1980). Convoys over the life course: Attachment, roles, and social support. In P. Baltes & O. Brim (Eds.), *Life-span development and behavior* (pp. 253–286). New York: Academic Press.

Kesler, M. S., Denny, N. W., & Whitney, S. E. (1976). Factors influencing problem solving in middle-aged and elderly adults. *Human Development, 19,* 310–320.

Kliegel, M., Moor, C., & Rott, C. (2004). Cognitive status and development in the oldest old: A longitudinal analysis from the Heidelberg Centenarian Study. *Archives of Gerontology and Geriatrics, 39,* 143–156.

Leinonen, R., Heikkinen, E., & Jylha, M. (2001). A pattern of long-term predictors of health ratings among older people. *Aging, 13,* 454–464.

Lin, N., Ensel, W. M., Simeone, R. S., & Kuo, W. (1979). Social support, stressful live events, and illness: A model and empirical test. *Journal of Health and Social Behavior, 20,* 108–119.

Liu, I. Y., LaCroix, A. Z., & White, L. R. (1990). Cognitive impairment and mortality: A study of possible confounders. *American Journal of Epidemiology, 132,* 136–143.

Livingston, I. L., Levine, D. M., & Moore, R. D. (1991). Social integration and Black intraracial variation in blood pressure. *Ethnicity and Disease, 1,* 135–149.

Manly, J. J., Jacobs, D. M., Touradji, P., Small, S. A., & Stern, Y. (2002). Reading level attenuates differences in neuropsychological test performance between African American and White elders. *Journal of the International Neuropsychological Society, 8,* 341–348.

Markides, K. S., Liang, J., & Jackson, J. S. (1990). Race, ethnicity, and aging: Conceptual and methodological issues. In R. H. Binstock & L. K. George (Eds.), *Handbook of aging and social sciences* (pp. 112–129). New York: Van Nostrand Reinhold.

Marquis, M. S., & Long, S. H. (1996). Reconsidering the effect of Medicaid on health care services use. *Health Services Research, 30,* 791–808.

Massey, G. C., Scott, M. V., & Dornbusch, S. M. (1975). Racism without racists: Institution racism in urban schools. *The Black Scholar, 7,* 10–19.

Meredith, L. (1993). Measurement, factor analysis, and factorial invariance. *Psychometrika, 58,* 525–543.

Meredith, L., & Horn, J. (2001). The role of factorial invariance in modeling growth and change. In L. M. Collins & A. G. Sayer (Eds.), *New methods for the analysis of change* (pp. 201–240). Washington, DC: American Psychological Association.

Miles, T. P., & Bernard, M. A. (1992). Health status of Black American elderly. *Journal of the American Geriatrics Society, 40,* 1047–1054.

Ortega, S. T., Crutchfield, R. D., & Rushing, W. A. (1983). Race differences in elderly personal well-being: Friendship, family, and church. *Research on Aging, 5,* 101–118.

Owens, W. A. (1966). Age and mental abilities: A second adult follow-up. *Journal of Educational Psychology, 57,* 311–325.

Payne, R. L., & Jones, G. J. (1987). Measurements and methodological issues in social support. In S. V. Kasl & C. L. Cooper (Eds.), *Stress and health: Issues in research methodology* (pp. 167–205). New York: Wiley.

Perlmutter, M., Adams, C., Berry, J., Kaplan, M., Persons, D., & Verdonik, F. (1988). Memory and aging. In K. W. Schaie (Ed.), *Annual review of gerontology and geriatrics* (pp. 57–92). New York: Springer.

Perlmutter, M., & Nyquist, L. (1990). Relationships between self-reported physical and mental health and intelligence performance across adulthood. *Journal of Gerontology, 45,* 145–155.

Pfeiffer, E. (1975). A short portable mental status questionnaire for the assessment of organic brain deficit in elderly patients. *Journal of American Geriatrics Society, 23,* 433–441.

Rapp, P. R., & Amaral, D. G. (1992). Individual differences in the cognitive and neurobiological consequences of normal aging. *Trends in Neuroscience, 15,* 340–345.

Ripple, R. E., & Jaquish, G. A. (1981). Fluency, flexibility, and originality in later adulthood. *Educational Gerontology, 7,* 1–10.

Rosano, C., Simonsick, E. M., Harris, T. B., Kritchevsky, S. B., Brach, J., Visser, M., et al. (2005). Association between physical and cognitive function in healthy elderly: The Health, Aging and Body Composition Study. *Neuroepidemiology, 24,* 8–14.

Salthouse, T. A., Kausler, D. H., & Saults, J. S. (1990). Age, self-assessed health status, and cognition. *Journal of Gerontology, 45,* 156–160.

Schaie, K. W. (1983). The Seattle Longitudinal Study: A twenty-one year exploration of psychometric intelligence in adulthood. In K. W. Schaie (Ed.), *Longitudinal studies of adult psychological development* (pp. 64–135). New York: Guilford Press.

Schaie, K. W. (1989a). Individual differences in rate of cognitive change in adulthood. In V. L. Bengston & K. W. Schaie (Eds.), *The course of latter life: Research and reflections* (pp. 68–83). New York: Springer.

Schaie, K. W. (1989b). Perceptual speed in adulthood: Cross-sectional and longitudinal studies. *Psychology and Aging, 4,* 443–453.

Schaie, K. W. (1990). Intellectual development in adulthood. In J. E. Birren & K. W. Schaie (Eds.), *Handbook of the psychology of aging* (pp. 291–310). San Diego, CA: Academic Press.

Schaie, K. W. (1994). The course of adult intellectual development. *American Psychologist, 49,* 304–313.

Schaie, K. W., & Hertzog, C. (1983). Fourteen-year cohort-sequential studies of adult intelligence. *Developmental Psychology, 19,* 531–543.

Schaie, K. W., & Hertzog, C. (1986). Toward a comprehensive model of adult intellectual development: Contributions of the Seattle Longitudinal Study. In R. J. Sternberg (Ed.), *Advances in human intelligence* (Vol. 3, pp. 79–119). Hillsdale, NJ: Lawrence Erlbaum.

Schaie, K. W., & Hofer, S. M. (2001). Longitudinal studies in aging research. In J. E. Birren (Ed.), *Handbook of the psychology of aging* (5th ed., pp. 53–77). San Diego, CA: Academic Press.

Selzer, S. C., & Denny, N. W. (1980). Conservation abilities among middle aged and elderly adults. *International Journal of Aging and Human Development, 11,* 135–146.

Strogatz, D. S., & James, S. A. (1986). Social support and hypertension among Blacks and Whites in a rural southern community. *American Journal of Epidemiology, 124,* 949–956.

Swan, G. E., Carmelli, D., & LaRue, A. (1995). Performance on the Digit Symbol Substitution test and 5 year mortality in the Western Collaborative Group Study. *American Journal of Epidemiology, 141,* 32–40.

Unger, D. G., & Wandersman, L. P. (1985). Social support and adolescent mothers: Action research contributions to theory and application. *Journal of Social Issues, 41,* 29–43.

Waldstein, S. R. (1995). Hypertension and neuropsychological function: A lifespan perspective. *Experimental Aging Research, 21,* 321–352.

Walker, V. S. (1996). *Their highest potential: An African American school community in the segregated south.* Chapel Hill: University of North Carolina Press.

Weuve, J., Kang, J. H., Manson, J. E., Breteler, M. M., Ware, J. H., & Grodstein, F. (2004). Physical activity, including walking, and cognitive function in older women. *Journal of the American Medical Association, 292,* 1454–1461.

Whitfield, K. E. (1996). Studying cognition in older African Americans: Some conceptual considerations. *Journal of Aging and Ethnicity, 1,* 35–45.

Whitfield, K. E. (2004). Accelerated cognitive aging: A hypothesis to account for racial differences. *African American Perspectives, 10*(1), 120–129.

Whitfield, K. E., & Baker-Thomas, T. A. (1999). Individual differences in aging among African-Americans. *International Journal of Aging and Human Development, 48,* 73–79.

Whitfield, K. E., Fillenbaum, G., Peiper, C., Seeman, T. E., Albert, M. S., Berkman, L. F., et al. (2000). The effect of race and health related factors on naming and memory: The MacArthur Studies of Successful Aging. *Journal of Aging and Health, 12,* 69–89.

Whitfield, K., & Hayward, M. (2003). The landscape of health disparities in older adults. *Public Policy and Aging Report, 13*(3).

Whitfield, K. E., Seeman, T. E., Miles, T. P., Albert, M. S., Berkman, L. F., Blazer, D. G., et al. (1997). Health indices as predictors of cognition among older African Americans: MacArthur Studies of Successful Aging. *Ethnicity and Disease, 7,* 127–136.

Whitfield, K. E., Weidner, G., Clark, R., & Anderson, N. B. (2002). Sociodemographic diversity and behavioral medicine. *Journal of Consulting and Clinical Psychology, 70,* 463–481.

Whitfield, K. E., & Wiggins, S. A. (2003). Educational influences on cognitive aging among African Americans: Quantity and quality. *Journal of Black Psychology, 2,* 275–291.

Willis, S. L. (1991). Cognition and everyday competence. In K. W. Schaie & M. F. Lawton (Eds.), *Annual review of gerontology and geriatrics* (Vol. 11, pp. 80–109). New York: Springer.

Ylikoski, R., Ylikoski, A., Raininko, R., Keskivaara, P., Sulkava, R., Tilvis, R., et al. (2000). Cardiovascular diseases, health status, brain imaging findings and neuropsychological functioning in neurologically healthy elderly individuals. *Archives of Gerontological Geriatrics, 30,* 115–130.

25

RACE, CULTURE, EDUCATION, AND COGNITIVE TEST PERFORMANCE AMONG OLDER ADULTS

JENNIFER J. MANLY

Over the next few decades, there will be significant changes in the ethnic and racial landscape among the older adults in the United States. The U.S. Census Bureau estimates that the proportion of people age 65 and older who are White and non-Hispanic will decline from 85.3% (in 2000) to 67% in 2050. By the year 2010, the population of Hispanic elders is expected to double from that in 1990, and will be 11 times greater by 2050. Of the 86.7 million people age 65 and older projected for 2050, 10.4 million (12%) will be African American, as compared to 8.5% in 2005. The growth in diversity of older adults in the United States presents a unique opportunity for cognitive psychologists and neuropsychologists to study the role of race, culture, and ethnicity in recognition, diagnosis, and treatment of age-related cognitive impairment and dementia.

Cognitive aging researchers must contend with the fact that assessments of cognitive impairment and daily functioning are susceptible to culturally dependent definitions and are quantified by measures that are sensitive to cultural and educational background. In the absence of a substantial scientific body of literature that provides clear standards, guidelines, and aspirations for cross-cultural research on cognitive aging, in this chapter I present a discussion of cultural and educational factors that should be systematically considered when assessing cognitive function among ethnic minority elders. I present evidence that acculturation, quality of education, literacy, and racial socialization are more meaningful than race/ethnicity in adjusting expectations for cognitive test scores and improving specificity of cognitive tests. I identify specific issues in the recognition of cognitive impairment and measurement of cognitive decline among these populations, including cultural bias in the neuropsychological measurement of cognitive function and differences in presentation of cognitively impaired elders across ethnic and cultural groups. Within this discussion, I use some examples from my own work to highlight the issues and make recommendations for future research.

COGNITIVE TEST PERFORMANCE AMONG OLDER ETHNIC MINORITIES

On the basis of neuropsychological test performance, ethnic minority elders are judged to be cognitively impaired more often than non-Hispanic White persons. Use of the standard cutoff of 23 on the Mini-Mental Status Examination (MMSE; Folstein, Folstein, & McHugh, 1975) leads to overdiagnosis of dementia among African Americans, even after controlling for years of education (Bohnstedt, Fox, & Kohatsu, 1994). Racial, ethnic, and cultural differences have been found on MMSE performance and other screening measures before (Mast, Fitzgerald, Steinberg, MacNeill, & Lichtenberg, 2001; Unverzagt, Hall, Torke, & Rediger, 1996) and after adjusting for education (Escobar et al., 1986; Fillenbaum, Hughes, Heyman, George, & Blazer, 1988; Kuller et al., 1998; Salmon et al., 1989; Teresi, Albert, Holmes, & Mayeux, 1999; Welsh et al., 1995).

Difficulties in interpreting cognitive scores among ethnic minority elders are not limited to brief screening instruments; several studies have indicated that ethnic or cultural factors have a substantial effect on neuropsychological batteries (Adams, Boake, & Crain, 1982; Overall & Levin, 1978). Roberts and Hamsher (1984) found that neurologically intact Whites obtained significantly higher scores on a measure of visual naming ability than did neurologically intact African Americans, even after correcting for education level. Several other studies also have reported ethnic differences in performance on tests of visual confrontation naming (Carlson, Brandt, Carson, & Kawas, 1998; Ross, Lichtenberg, & Christensen, 1995; Welsh et al., 1995). Batteries of tests designed to detect dementia also show ethnic differences (Fillenbaum, Heyman, Huber, Ganguli, & Unverzagt, 2001; Manly, Jacobs, et al., 1998b; Unverzagt et al., 1996).

Ethnic differences have been reported on measures of nonverbal abilities as well (Bernard, 1989; Brown et al., 1991; Campbell et al., 1996; Heverly, Isaac, & Hynd, 1986; Miller, Bing, Selnes, Wesch, & Becker, 1993). One study (Jacobs et al., 1997) found that Spanish-speaking elders scored significantly lower than age- and education-matched English-speaking elders on a measure of nonverbal abstraction (i.e., the Identities and Oddities subtest from the Mattis Dementia Rating Scale); multiple-choice matching and recognition formats of the Benton Visual Retention Test; and measures of category fluency and comprehension. In another study, healthy Spanish-speaking Mexicans and Mexican Americans who lived near a U.S.–Mexico Border (*n* = 200) were compared with residents of Madrid, Spain (*n* = 218). After accounting for education, borderland residents obtained significantly lower scores on measures of recognition discriminability for stories and figures, learned fewer details from a story over five trials, and made more perseverative responses on the Wisconsin Card Sorting Task (Artiola i Fortuny, Heaton, & Hermosillo, 1998). There were some interactions between years of education and place of birth, suggesting that among those with high levels of education, borderland and Spanish participants performed similarly on several measures.

POSSIBLE EXPLANATIONS FOR RACIAL/ETHNIC DIFFERENCES ON COGNITIVE TESTS

There are three overall categories of possible explanations for racial/ethnic differences in cognitive test performance. The first argues that cognitive tests lack construct validity when used among ethnic minorities. The second focus is on confounding factors that influence test performance and interact with ethnic group status; a discussion of the possible role of the multiple factors does not assume that the cognitive measures themselves are valid among ethnic minorities. The final category of explanations concentrate on genetic, biologic, and physiological causes of ethnic group differences in cognitive test performance; these arguments make sense only when the measures are assumed to be valid and the effects of confounds are controlled or null. Because each of these categories of explanations are relevant to research on cognitive aging, I now explore these alternatives in more detail.

Poor Construct Validity of Cognitive Measures Across Ethnic Groups

A measure has *construct validity* when it is measuring the construct it claims to be measuring (Nunnally, 1994). Several researchers have reported attenuated specificity of verbal and nonverbal cognitive tests, such that cognitively normal ethnic minorities are more likely to be misdiagnosed as impaired as compared to Whites (Ford-Booker et al., 1993; Hilliard, 1979; Klusman, Moulton, Hornbostle, Picano, & Beattie, 1991; Manly, Jacobs, et al., 1998b; Stern et al., 1992; van de Vijver, 1997; Welsh et al., 1995; R. L. Williams, 1971, 1974). These findings indicate that not all tasks are functionally equivalent (Helms, 1992; Ratcliff et al., 1998). In other words, although performance on a cognitive test may not reflect the same underlying construct across all racial and ethnic groups, many assume that test scores provide valid indicators of cognitive ability regardless of cultural background (Nell, 2000). Research on Western intelligence test performance (e.g., Wechsler Scales of Intelligence) and other tests of cognitive ability (e.g., tests of reasoning, abstraction, and speed of information processing) among several indigenous groups in Africa, Asia, and North America have led investigators to conclude that "the abilities of mankind may be captured in western tests, but they are not fully expressed in them" (Irvine & Berry, 1988, p. 29). Our field has not yet demonstrated that, using the majority of measures in cognitive aging research, equivalent scores (or performance below a common, race-independent cutoff) mean the same thing across race, ethnicity, and geographic region. Whether common, race-independent test cutoffs have similar longitudinal health outcomes across race has not yet been fully investigated. Evaluating the construct validity of commonly used instruments in cognitive aging research is thus clearly an important direction for future research.

Factors That Confound the Relationship of Ability to Test Performance Among Ethnic Minorities

I now focus on variables that are related to cognitive test performance, differ within and between race/ethnicity, and are thought to interact with racial/ethnic group on cognitive test performance. Because of these interactions, performance on cognitive measures cannot be properly interpreted unless confounding factors are accurately measured and accounted for, and ethnic group differences could at least in part be explained by these variables. A small subset of these factors is discussed in the next section.

Regional Differences in Cognitive Test Performance

The geographic region in which an individual resides, or was born and raised, appears to interact with racial/ethnic group on cognitive test performance. Much of the research on geographic region in cognitive test performance has been conducted among children and has used IQ measures as the key outcome variables. One study found that in the standardization sample of the Wechsler Preschool and Primary Scale of Intelligence—Revised (Wechsler, 1989), geographic region (Northeast, Midwest, South, and West) effects on scores were small but significant (Sellers, Burns, & Guyrke, 2002). Furthermore, there were a number of Region × Ethnicity interactions on a measures of Full Scale IQ, such that in the West and Northeast scores of African Americans were not significantly lower than those of Whites, whereas they were in the South and Midwest. Among adults, the effect of geographic region is significant enough that test developers continue to sample by region in their standardization cohorts (Wechsler, 1997). Furthermore, a widely used formula applied in the estimation of premorbid IQ on the Wechsler Adult Intelligence Scale—Revised (Wechsler, 1981) included geographic region and urban versus rural residence as two of the predictor variables, along with age, sex, years of education, and occupation (Barona, Reynolds, & Chastain, 1984). It is possible that these regional differences reflect underlying differences in nutrition (Lynn, 1998), occupational status (Schooler, 1998), exposure to technology and urbanization (Wheeler, 1970), and socialization practices that improve performance on cognitive measures. Residence in urban areas in the North and West could be associated with increased exposure in schools to "teaching to the test" and increased test sophistication (W. Williams, 1998), such as guessing skills and persevering through difficult items (Brand, 1987). If a region is serving as a proxy for these factors, one might expect that the effect size of geographic region on cognition will differ depending on the age cohort under study, just as discrepancies in mortality rates across race have differed by region and year (Geronimus, Bound, & Waidmann, 1999).

Rural residence has been reported to have a modest effect on risk for developing Alzheimer's disease (AD) in some studies outside the United States (Hall et al., 1998; Liu et al., 1995; Prince, Cullen, & Mann, 1994; Rocca et al., 1990; Tsolaki, Fountoulakis, Chantzi, & Kazis, 1997). One study among African Americans reported that childhood rural residence, along with low education, was a risk factor for prevalence of AD (Hall, Gao, Unverzagt, & Hendrie, 2000). This was reported in Indianapolis, Indiana, where many African Americans were born and raised in the rural South and moved north or west during the "Great Migration" between 1915 and 1950, when African Americans moved to northern states to secure better paying jobs, live in better neighborhoods, and escape extreme racism in the South (Lemann, 1992; Scott, 1920).

*Relationship of Acculturation
to Cognitive Test Performance*

Most previous research on ethnic differences on cognitive tests has classified participants on the basis of physical appearance or self-identified racial/ethnic classification instead of measuring the cultural variables that accompany ethnic group membership. However, as Helms (1992) suggested, specification of experiential, attitudinal, or behavioral variables that distinguish those belonging to different ethnic groups, and that also vary among individuals within an ethnic group, may allow investigators to understand better the underlying reasons for the relationship between ethnic background and cognitive test performance. Level of acculturation is one way in which social scientists have operationalized within-group cultural variability. *Acculturation* is defined as the level at which an individual participates in the values, language, and practices of his or her own ethnic community versus those of the

dominant culture (Landrine & Klonoff, 1996; Padilla, 1980). Previous studies have identified ideologies, beliefs, expectations, and attitudes as important components of acculturation, as well as cognitive and behavioral characteristics, such as language and customs (Berry, 1976; Moyerman & Forman, 1992; Negy & Woods, 1992; Padilla, 1980). Arnold, Montgomery, Castaneda, and Longoria (1994) found a relationship between Hispanic acculturation and performance on selected tests of the Halstead–Reitan Battery among college students. Several studies show that African American acculturation (as measured by the African American Acculturation Scale (Landrine & Klonoff, 1994, 1995) is related to cognitive test performance (Kennepohl, Shore, Nabors, & Hanks, 2004; Lucas, 1998; Manly, Jacobs, et al., 1998a; Manly, Miller, et al., 1998), even after accounting for age, years of education, and sex. However when quality of education (which I discuss in more detail below) is included as a covariate, the predictive power of acculturation is weakened, as in a study of 503 African Americans age 65 and older (Manly, Byrd, Touradji, & Stern, 2004). In this study, acculturation was a significant but weak correlate of measures of verbal and nonverbal ability, accounting for no more than 6% of variance on any measure, and after accounting for age, years of education, sex, and reading level, acculturation remained a unique predictor of only performance on a drawing test. Taken together, investigations of acculturation level suggest that there are cultural differences within elders of the same ethnicity that relate to neuropsychological measures of verbal and nonverbal skills and that accounting for acculturation may improve the accuracy of certain cognitive tests. Although previous research has focused on ethnic minority elders in the United States, it is likely that within-group cultural differences are also significant factors in the test performance of American elders who identify themselves as White or Caucasian, as well as groups outside the United States.

Socioeconomic Status and Cognitive Aging

In most studies comparing cognitive test performance across groups of ethnically, culturally, or racially diverse groups of older adults, differences persist despite correcting for indicators of socioeconomic status, such as years of education, income, or occupational attainment (Jacobs et al., 1997; A. S. Kaufman, McLean, & Reynolds, 1988; Manly, Jacobs, et al., 1998b; Reynolds, Chastain, Kaufman, & McLean, 1987). However, a number of studies have found no discrepancies in test performance between racial, ethnic, or cultural groups after participants were matched on years of education (Carlson et al., 1998; Ford, Haley, Thrower, West, & Harrell, 1996), after statistically adjusting for education (Loewenstein, Ardila, Rosselli, & Hayden, 1992; Marcopulos, McLain, & Giuliano, 1997; Mungas, Marshall, Weldon, Haan, & Reed, 1996), or after cut-scores were adjusted for individuals with low education (Murden, McRae, Kaner, & Bucknam, 1991). However, the statistical power to detect a significant difference in several of these studies was limited by the small sample sizes of non-White participants. For example, there were no significant ethnic differences among a small number of African Americans ($n = 11$) and Whites ($n = 32$) with AD on measures of naming, picture vocabulary, verbal abstraction, verbal list learning, and pragmatic language use after controlling for MMSE score and years of education (Ripich, Carpenter, & Ziol, 1997). Another study found that, among 18 African American and 114 White participants who met NINCDS–ADRDA criteria for AD, there were no significant differences by race on decline in MMSE score over an average 2.5-year period, whereas left-handedness, more years of education, and family history of dementia were associated with more rapid decline (Rasmusson, Carson, Brookmeyer, Kawas, & Brandt, 1996). Therefore, the majority of prior research on cognitive test performance across diverse groups of older adults in the United States reveals that discrepancies in scores persist, despite equating groups on traditional indicators of socioeconomic background, such as income and years of school, or adjusting for differences in prevalence of medical disorders such as cardiovascular disease.

It is important to note that the impact of socioeconomic factors on cognitive aging may be moderated by racial/ethnic status. Empirical studies on racial/ethnic differences in the relationship of socioeconomic class to cognitive aging are lacking; however, there is a growing body of literature on more general health outcomes. These studies indicate that individuals with more resources are better prepared for the stress of everyday life and can meet a range of material needs, and thus they have better health outcomes (Adler, Boyce, Chesney, Folkman, & Syme, 1993). However, middle-class status does not provide African Americans with the normally expected reductions of several health risks (D. R. Williams, 1997). Several investigators have posited that the link between wealth and health breaks down among African Americans because they may undergo more stressful life experiences than their White counterparts because of their minority status (Jackson & Stewart, 2004). As compared to Whites, middle-class African Americans may face more support requests from friends or family members who may not be able to reciprocate because of their own economic hardship (Taylor & Chatters, 1989). Also notable is that the economic status of middle-class African Americans is more unstable than their White peers, because status is based on current income rather than wealth attainment or inherited wealth (Collins, 1997; Oliver & Shapiro, 1997; D. R. Williams, Yu, Jackson, & Anderson, 1997). College-educated African Americans are four times more likely than Whites to experience unemployment (Wilhelm, 1987) and are less likely to translate higher economic status into advantageous neighborhood and housing conditions (Alba, Logan, & Stults, 2000). One study found that White suburban residents were at lower risk for mortality, whereas mortality risks were notably elevated among suburban African Americans (House, Lepkowski, & Williams, 2000). In addition, chronic strain may be increased among college-educated African Americans because investment in education does not provide the expected parallel gains in income (Anderson, 1999).

Quality of Education

Extreme differences in educational level are often found between ethnic minorities and Whites. Illiteracy rates in the United States are highest among people age 65 and over but are especially elevated among ethnic minority elders (Kirsch, Jungeblut, Jenkins, & Kolstad, 1993). In the studies cited earlier, covariance, matching procedures, or education-corrected norms were used to "equate" ethnic groups on years of education before interpretations of neuropsychological test performance were made. However, disparate school experiences could explain why many ethnic minorities obtain lower scores on cognitive measures even after controlling for years of education. Table 25.1 provides examples of expenditures in selected states for African American and White schools in 1935, and Figure 25.1 shows length of school year by race for several states.

The data shown in Table 25.1 are complemented by the results of one of the first studies on

quality of education and cognitive test performance, which showed that African American Army recruits schooled in northern states obtained higher average scores on the Army Alpha test than did Whites schooled in southern states, and African Americans' scores increased for every year they stayed in northern cities (Klineberg, 1935). These data suggest that even if an investigator "adjusts" for years of school, we cannot assume that the effect of educational experience has been removed from an analysis of ethnic and racial group differences in cognitive test performance. Because of the disparities in quality of education, matching on quantity of formal education does not necessarily mean that the quality of education received by each racial/ethnic group is comparable (J. S. Kaufman, Cooper, & McGee, 1997; Loewenstein, Arguelles, Arguelles, & Linn-Fuentes, 1994; Whitfield & Baker-Thomas, 1999). The variable "years of education" systematically differs between African Americans and Whites (Margo, 1985). If this variable is not commensurate between racial groups, residual confounding will occur, and spurious racial differences will be interpreted despite matching of groups on years of education.

Reading level and literacy can serve as estimates of quality of education among older people. Reading level is a very powerful predictor of cognitive test performance, independent of years of education, age, or ethnicity (Ardila,

Table 25.1   Per-Pupil Expenditures by State in 1935

State	African American	White	Ratio
Alabama	17.50	53.18	.33
Florida	17.71	39.80	.45
Maryland	80.63	102.84	.78
Mississippi	13.36	58.61	.23
North Carolina	32.92	51.43	.64
South Carolina	18.62	67.74	.28
Virginia	33.05	63.81	.52
New York	110.97		
Pennsylvania	75.74		

SOURCE: Blose and Caliver (1938).

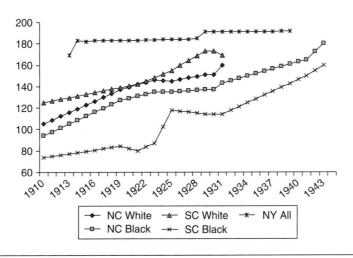

Figure 25.1   Length of School Year by Race and Year for North Carolina (NC), South Carolina (SC), and New York (NY)

SOURCE: U.S. Office of Education (1917–1956).

Rosselli, & Rosas, 1989; Lecours et al., 1987; Manly et al., 1999; Matute, Leal, Zaraboso, Robles, & Cedillo, 1997; Reis, Guerreiro, & Castro-Caldas, 1994; Rosselli, Ardila, & Rosas, 1990; Scribner & Cole, 1981; Weiss, Reed, Kligman, & Abyad, 1995). My colleagues and I recently reported a study that sought to determine whether discrepancies in quality of education could explain differences in cognitive test scores between African American and White elders matched on years of education (Manly, Jacobs, Touradji, Small, & Stern, 2002). A comprehensive neuropsychological battery was administered to a sample of nondemented African American and non-Hispanic White participants in an epidemiological study of normal aging and dementia in the northern Manhattan (New York) community. The Reading Recognition subtest from the Wide Range Achievement Test—3 (Wilkinson, 1993) was used as an estimate of quality of education. African American elders obtained significantly lower scores than Whites on measures of word list learning and memory, figure memory, abstract reasoning, fluency, and visuospatial skill, even though the groups were matched on years of education. However, after adjusting the scores for Wide Range Achievement Test—3 reading subtest, the overall effect of race was greatly reduced, and racial differences on all tests (except category fluency and a drawing measure) became nonsignificant.

These findings suggest that the full extent of discrepancies in educational experience between African Americans and Whites are not captured by a simple highest-grade attained variable, and thus residual confounding may explain findings of "persistent" race effects after matching groups on years of education. Nevertheless, despite the clear improvement in specificity that is provided by adjusting cognitive test scores for differences in educational experience across ethnic groups, some researchers caution against controlling for educational variables in studies of dementia, because low education may itself be a risk factor for disease. I discuss this further in the section titled "Cognitive Reserve."

Stereotype Threat

Level of comfort and confidence during the testing session may also differentially affect the cognitive test performance of older ethnic minorities (Katz, 1964). The concept of stereotype threat has been described as a factor that may attenuate the performance of racial minorities on cognitive tests. Stereotype threat describes the effect of attention diverting from the task at hand to the concern that one's performance will confirm a negative stereotype about one's group. Steele and his colleagues (Steele, 1997; Steele & Aronson, 1995) demonstrated that when a test consisting of difficult verbal Graduate Record Examination items was described as measuring intellectual ability, African American undergraduates at Stanford University performed worse than SAT–score matched Whites. However, when the same test was described as a "laboratory problem-solving task" or a "challenging test" that was unrelated to intellectual ability, scores of African Americans matched those of White students. Using similar methods, another study showed an effect of stereotype threat on Ravens Progressive Matrices performance (McKay, 2003). Researchers have also shown that when gender differences in math ability were invoked, stereotype threat undermined performance of women on math tests (Spencer, Steele, & Quinn, 1999) and among White males (when comparisons to Asians were invoked; Aronson et al., 1999). The role of stereotype threat in the neuropsychological test performance of African Americans and Hispanics has not been investigated to date. In addition, it is possible that the salience of negative stereotypes within ethnic minorities differs by age and education cohorts, and therefore stereotype threat may affect some test takers more than others.

Explaining Racial/Ethnic Differences in Cognitive Aging With Biological Causes

Using biological factors such as genetics, early life nutritional status, neural reserve, toxic exposures, and access to health care to explain racial/ethnic differences in cognitive test performance requires an assumption that cognitive measures are equally valid across groups. Because several authors have challenged this validity for measures of intellectual and neuropsychological function (Ardila, 1995; Gould, 1996; Helms, 1992, 1997; Hilliard, 1979, 1994;

Manly, Jacobs, et al., 1998b), biological factors should be considered only if the validity of the measures has been proven.

Genetic Causes of Racial/Ethnic Differences in Cognitive Aging

There is an extensive, well-known history of publications regarding genetic/biological theories of intelligence, which emphasize the heritability of cognitive ability and implicate genetic factors as a large contributor to the differences in IQ test performance across different ethnic groups (Herrnstein & Murray, 1994; Jensen, 1972; Jensen & Miele, 2002; Lynn, 2002). Advocates of genetic/biological theories propose that genetic variation in mental abilities across races has occurred because of divergent evolutionary trends and that IQ test performance has the same meaning for people of different racial/ethnic backgrounds, because test scores have similar predictive validity (e.g., for future income, occupational status, academic success, etc.) among groups. Characterizing the numerous responses to this work, which question the assumptions embedded in the tests, the scientific rigor of the work on which these theories are based, and the biological basis of race itself (Cooper, 2005; Gould, 1996; Helms, 1992, 1997; Hilliard, 1994, 1979; Neisser et al., 1996), is beyond the scope of this chapter. Nevertheless, it is important to consider the history and wide-ranging impact of this topic on the study of cognitive aging among ethnic minorities.

Much of the contemporary research on genetic causes that may explain ethnic differences in rates of cognitive decline in aging has focused on apolipoprotein E (APOE ε4). The association between APOE ε4 and cognitive decline and AD in African Americans remains unclear. Several studies show little to no increase in the risk of AD among African Americans with the APOE ε4 allele (Evans et al., 2003; Farrer et al., 1997; Hendrie et al., 1995; Tang et al., 1998). In contrast, investigators in Alabama, Florida, Georgia, Massachusetts, and South Carolina have found an association between APOE ε4 and AD in African Americans similar to that observed in patients of European descent (Graff-Radford et al., 2002). Each study had a different design. The studies reporting no association

have focused on representative samples of unrelated African Americans, whereas studies that have found an association are family based or clinic based (Devi et al., 1999; Green et al., 2002). The frequency of the APOE ε4 allele in the patients assembled in these studies was nearly double that observed in prior reports (Hendrie et al., 1995; Tang et al., 1998). In contrast, APOE ε4 frequency among control participants was similar. This suggests that studies reporting the increase in risk were mainly from families in which both AD and APOE ε4 were likely to have been enriched. Differential survival among older patient groups may also have contributed to these differences (Lee et al., 2001). Because variability in APOE genotypic risks has not been apparent in studies involving other ethnic groups, this issue is ripe for further examination. It is possible that issues with accuracy of diagnosis of AD have affected the strength of the relationship between APOE 4 allele and AD.

Cerebrovascular Causes of Racial/Ethnic Differences in Cognitive Aging

The prevalence of several risk factors for cerebrovascular disease, such as hypertension and diabetes, is higher in African Americans than in Whites and may be related to higher rates of cognitive decline and risk for dementia as well as increased morbidity and mortality from cerebrovascular disease (Sundquist, Winkleby, & Pudaric, 2001). It is well established that African Americans are at greater risk for the development of clinical strokes than are White Americans (Gorelick, 1998). The rate of mortality due to stroke in African Americans is at least twice as great as in Whites (Morgenstern, Spears, Goff, Grotta, & Nichaman, 1997). Atherosclerotic risk factors are primary contributors to the development of stroke or cerebral white matter vascular disease (Awad, Spetzler, Hodak, Awad, & Carey, 1986; Bots et al., 1993) and are more prevalent among African Americans (Fox et al., 2005) than among non-Hispanic Whites (Kase et al., 1989). Similarly, the prevalence of subclinical "silent" stroke in the Atherosclerosis Risk in Communities' (ARIC) community-based sample of African Americans (17%; Fox et al., 2005) was notably greater than that reported in the predominantly White

Framingham Heart Study cohort (10%; Kase et al., 1989). In a report from the ARIC cohort, in which severity of white matter disease was compared between ethnic groups, African Americans had a significantly higher proportion of severe white matter disease than European Americans (Liao et al., 1997). There is a surprising dearth of studies that have explicitly examined the prevalence or severity of white matter hyperintensity as a function of race. However, the identified risk factors for white matter disease (e.g., hypertension, low socioeconomic status) are strong correlates of race (Longstreth et al., 2000).

Racial discrepancies in risks for cerebrovascular disease are particularly relevant given the growing evidence that cerebrovascular disease and modifiable risk factors, such as hypertension, diabetes, the insulin resistance syndrome, obesity/overweight, and hyperlipidemia, increase the risk of cognitive decline and dementia, particularly when present at midlife and when risk factors persist from midlife to older ages (Carmelli et al., 1998; Elkins et al., 2004; Kilander, Nyman, Boberg, Hansson, & Lithell, 1998; Kivipelto et al., 2001a, 2001b; Knopman et al., 2001; Swan, Carmelli, & Larue, 1998; Swan et al., 1998). Increases in blood pressure have been shown to affect psychomotor speed, visual constructive ability, learning, memory, and executive function (Alves de Moraes, Szklo, Knopman, & Sato, 2002; Elias, 1998; Elias, Robbins, Elias, & Streeten, 1998). A meta-analysis of 34 papers suggested that hypertension, low educational level, and other markers of cardiovascular health were risk factors for poor cognitive performance (Antsey & Christensen, 2000). In the ARIC study of middle-aged White and African American men and women, participants with uncontrolled hypertension had greater declines on the Digit Symbol subtest of the Wechsler Adult Intelligence Scale—Revised than did normotensive participants (Alves de Moraes et al., 2002). In the same cohort, the presence of diabetes and hypertension were independently associated with greater decline in scores on both the Digit Symbol subtest and in word fluency (Knopman et al., 2001). Diabetes and the *metabolic syndrome*, a cluster of impaired glucose tolerance, hypertension, and dyslipidemia associated with hyperinsulinemia, have been found to increase risk for cognitive and functional decline and cognitive dysfunction in a number of studies (Kumari, Brunner, & Fuhrer, 2000; Wu et al., 2003a, 2003b).

Cognitive Reserve

The cognitive reserve theory is another biologically based potential explanation for the relationship between race/ethnicity and cognitive aging. Multiple studies in and outside of the United States have shown higher prevalence and incidence of AD and dementia among elders with low levels of education (Bonaiuto et al., 1990; Bowirrat, Treves, Friedland, & Korczyn, 2001; Callahan et al., 1996; Caramelli et al., 1997; Dartigues et al., 1991; Evans et al., 1993; Fratiglioni et al., 1991; Gatz et al., 2001; Gurland et al., 1995; Hill et al., 1993; Korczyn, Kahana, & Galper, 1991; Letenneur, Commenges, Dartigues, & Barberger-Gateau, 1994; Mortel, Meyer, Herod, & Thornby, 1995; Ott et al., 1995; Prencipe et al., 1996; Stern et al., 1994; Sulkava et al., 1985; White et al., 1994; Zhang et al., 1990). Cognitive decline appears to be faster (Stern, Albert, Tang, & Tsai, 1999; Teri, McCurry, Edland, Kukull, & Larson, 1995; Unverzagt, Hui, Farlow, Hall, & Hendrie, 1998) and associated with increased risk of mortality (Stern, Tang, Denaro, & Mayeux, 1995) among highly educated minorities with AD, which suggests that the level of brain pathology is greater by the time well-educated individuals show the signs of dementia. Several studies of normal aging have reported more rapid cognitive and functional decline among individuals with lower educational attainment (Albert et al., 1995; Butler, Ashford, & Snowdon, 1996; Chodosh, Reuben, Albert, & Seeman, 2002; Christensen et al., 1997; Farmer, Kittner, Rae, Bartko, & Regier, 1995; Finley, Ardila, & Roselli, 1991; Snowdon, Ostwald, & Kane, 1989). These studies suggest that the same education-related factors that delay the onset of dementia also allow individuals to cope more effectively with changes encountered in normal aging.

Cognitive reserve theory has been suggested as the mechanism for the link between low education and higher risk of dementia and cognitive decline observed in these studies (Mortimer, 1988; Satz et al., 1993; Stern, 2002). *Reserve*, or the brain's ability to tolerate the effects of dementia pathology, may result from native ability or from the effects of lifetime experience. Years of education may serve as a proxy for reserve whether it results from ability or experience. In passive models of reserve (Stern, 2002), education would be a proxy for the brain's capacity (synaptic density or complexity) to tolerate either gradual or sudden insult. In active models, years of education would be an indicator of the brain's ability to compensate for pathology through more efficient use of existing cognitive networks or recruitment of alternate networks.

There are cases in which the relationship between education and risk for cognitive impairment or dementia is weakened or absent. Two large international studies of incident dementia found that illiteracy or low levels of education did not increase the risk of AD among elders in India (Chandra et al., 2001) and West Africa (Hall et al., 1998; Hendrie, 2001). In fact, these studies had the lowest prevalence and incidence rates of dementia observed to date despite the fact that a large proportion of the populations lacked formal schooling or literacy training. In environments where there is little opportunity to obtain schooling and/or literacy, persons with high native intellect may not have been able to achieve academic success commensurate with their ability. High and low literacy groups would thus not differ in innate intellect or in the resistance to pathology it may confer (Gatz et al., 2001). Studies that find that levels of dementia remain low in areas where illiteracy rates are high (also finding no relationship between literacy and dementia) support the theory that reserve is the result of innate traits rather than acquired through education.

Reserve is measured using proxy variables such as years of education, occupational level, or IQ measures, but there are a number of ways in which cultural, racial, and economic factors may affect the predictive power of these proxies. First, it is possible that race- and income-based limits on educational opportunity weaken the relationship between years of education and native ability, leading to underestimates of the relationship between education and cognitive decline. Minorities with strong intellectual abilities may not achieve high levels of academic or occupational status because their opportunities are limited by societal forces (e.g., racism, poverty) unrelated to their native intellect or drive to succeed. Although such individuals may be powerful or influential in their communities, their abilities

may not be reflected in years of schooling or traditional indicators of occupational status. Alternatively, rather than a reflection of innate ability, years of education could be an indicator of lifetime experiences that change the brain during childhood or adult life and thus create a reserve against disease pathology. However, use of years of education to represent a direct effect of experience on the brain or cognition is also problematic when used among ethnic minorities and immigrants because of the increased discordance between years of education and quality of education among these groups.

To determine whether literacy was a stronger predictor of memory decline (and thus a more sensitive indicator of reserve) than years of education or racial/ethnic classification, a study was designed to explore the relationship of literacy level to change in memory ability over time among a sample of English-speaking African American and Caucasian nondemented older adults (Manly, Touradji, Tang, & Stern, 2003). The analyses focused on immediate and delayed recall measures from a verbal word list learning task, because these measures are sensitive to age-related memory decline and the earliest signs of AD. Elders with both high and low levels of literacy declined in immediate and delayed memory over time; however, the decline was more rapid among low literacy elders. This suggests that high literacy skills provide not complete preservation of memory skills but rather a slowing of age-related decline. Literacy was the only factor besides age that interacted with time to influence rate of decline; race and years of school did not influence rate of memory change when literacy was in the model.

CONCLUSION

Because of the dramatic increase in diversity among older adults in the United States, and because of the exciting potential of cross-cultural and cross-national research, researchers will need to prepare for assessment of cognitive abilities among people with disparate cultural, racial, and linguistic experiences. Cognitive tests currently have poor specificity among minority populations and cannot reliably differentiate subtle impairment associated with the early stages of dementia from the effects of normal aging. Misdiagnosis of cognitive impairment and dementia is thus more likely among cognitively normal ethnic minorities as compared to non-Hispanic Whites. This problem is intimately linked to the construct validity of our tests and whether they accurately assess the abilities that we have designed them to measure. It is clear that the construct validity of our measures should be evaluated across culturally diverse groups using more sophisticated methodology such as structural equation modeling (Salthouse, 2001).

Once construct validity is established, factors that may interact with group status should be evaluated. In essence, this is the process of breaking down traditional racial/ethnic classifications into more meaningful variables that are explicitly measured and related to test performance both cross-sectionally and longitudinally. This approach recognizes that racial classifications change over time and by geographical region; are of little use for the growing number of individuals who self-identify within multiple racial categories; and overlook important differences in linguistic, geographic, economic, and educational experiences and level of exposure to the dominant culture. One important aspect of these variables is that they may be useful even in studies that do not include culturally diverse participants because, regardless of ethnicity, these factors may explain significant variance in test score and thus should guide adjustment of expectations of performance before interpreting scores, just as years of education and gender are now routinely taken into account. Researchers who examine cognition across the life span take care to match their old and young participants on non-age demographics (e.g., years of school) and health characteristics. Research on quality of education indicates that perhaps this construct is a more important reflection of the educational experience across age cohorts than years of schooling.

In this chapter, I have reviewed prior work relating socioeconomic status, racial socialization, cultural experience, literacy, and quality of education to cognitive test performance among older adults, but this is only a sampling of the potential variables that could be examined. The most obvious gap in this review is the complex and critical subject of language use, the structural and functional differences across languages, and bilingualism. Research on the effect of region of birth and current residence on cognitive function among ethnic minorities is badly needed but will require large multisite cohorts. This is true not only of elders born in the United States but also among immigrant groups. For example, it is of practical and theoretical interest to characterize any differences that may exist among Spanish speakers by not only acculturation level and bilingualism but also nationality. Finally, the effect of race and racism on neuropsychological test performance of ethnic minority elders should not be ignored or underestimated. The operationalization of racism for the purposes of research on cognitive function among elders is an area that is ripe for exploration.

Although biological and genetic factors may in fact play a role in ethnic differences in cognitive test performance, this line of work can produce meaningful results only if these variables must be measured rather than assumed. Furthermore, the critical period during which chronic diseases such as diabetes and hypertension have an effect on cognitive function in aging and risk for dementia may occur in midlife; therefore, studies of the relationship of cardiovascular disease and cognitive aging must include longitudinal designs and enroll ethnically diverse people in their fourth and fifth decades of life.

Recruitment of large numbers of older, nondemented ethnic minority adults into longitudinal research studies is a difficult task that has had spotty success, at best. Nevertheless, responsible and comprehensive examination of the relationships discussed in this chapter is impossible without achieving this goal.

REFERENCES

Adams, R. L., Boake, C., & Crain, C. (1982). Bias in a neuropsychological test classification related to age, education and ethnicity. *Journal of Consulting and Clinical Psychology, 50*, 143–145.

Adler, N. E., Boyce, W. T., Chesney, M. A., Folkman, S., & Syme, S. L. (1993). Socioeconomic inequalities in health: No easy solution. *Journal of the American Medical Association, 269*, 3140–3145.

Alba, R. D., Logan, J. R., & Stults, B. J. (2000). How segregated are middle-class African Americans? *Social Problems, 47*, 543–558.

Albert, M. S., Jones, K., Savage, C. R., Berkman, L., Seeman, T., Blazer, D., et al. (1995). Predictors of cognitive change in older persons: MacArthur Studies of Successful Aging. *Psychology and Aging, 10,* 578–589.

Alves de Moraes, S., Szklo, M., Knopman, D., & Sato, R. (2002). The relationship between temporal changes in blood pressure and changes in cognitive function: Atherosclerosis Risk in Communities (ARIC) Study. *Preventive Medicine, 35,* 258–263.

Anderson, E. (1999). The social situation of the Black executive: Black and White identities in the corporate world. In M. Lamont (Ed.), *The Cultural territories of race: Black and White boundaries* (pp. 3–29). Chicago: University of Chicago Press.

Antsey, K., & Christensen, H. (2000). Education, activity, health, blood pressure and apolipoprotein E as predictors of cognitive change in old age: A review. *Gerontology, 46,* 163–177.

Ardila, A. (1995). Directions of research in cross-cultural neuropsychology. *Journal of Clinical and Experimental Neuropsychology, 17,* 143–150.

Ardila, A., Rosselli, M., & Rosas, P. (1989). Neuropsychological assessment in illiterates: Visuospatial and memory abilities. *Brain and Cognition, 11,* 147–166.

Arnold, B. R., Montgomery, G. T., Castaneda, I., & Longoria, R. (1994). Acculturation and performance of Hispanics on selected Halstead–Reitan neuropsychological tests. *Assessment, 1,* 239–248.

Aronson, J., Lustina, M. J., Good, C., Keough, K., Steele, C. M., & Brown, J. (1999). When White men can't do math: Necessary and sufficient factors in stereotype threat. *Journal of Experimental and Social Psychology, 35,* 29–46.

Artiola i Fortuny, L., Heaton, R. K., & Hermosillo, D. (1998). Neuropsychological comparisons of Spanish-speaking participants from the U.S.–Mexico border region versus Spain. *Journal of the International Neuropsychological Society, 4,* 363–379.

Awad, I. A., Spetzler, R. F., Hodak, J. A., Awad, C. A., & Carey, R. (1986). Incidental subcortical lesions identified on magnetic resonance imaging in the elderly: I. Correlation with age and cerebrovascular risk factors. *Stroke, 17,* 1084–1089.

Barona, A., Reynolds, C., & Chastain, R. L. (1984). A demographically based index of premorbid intelligence for the WAIS–R. *Journal of Consulting and Clinical Psychology, 52,* 885–887.

Bernard, L. (1989). Halstead–Reitan neuropsychological test performance of Black, Hispanic, and White young adult males from poor academic backgrounds. *Archives of Clinical Neuropsychology, 4,* 267–274.

Berry, J. W. (1976). *Human ecology and cognitive style.* New York: Sage–Halstead.

Blose, D., & Caliver, A. (1938). *Statistics of the education of Negroes, 1933–34 and 1935–36* (U.S. Office of Education Bulletin No. 13). Washington, DC: U.S. Government Printing Office.

Bohnstedt, M., Fox, P. J., & Kohatsu, N. D. (1994). Correlates of Mini-Mental Status Examination scores among elderly demented patients: The influence of race–ethnicity. *Journal of Clinical Epidemiology, 47,* 1381–1387.

Bonaiuto, S., Rocca, W. A., Lippi, A., Luciani, P., Turtu, F., Cavarzeran, F., et al. (1990). Impact of education and occupation on prevalence of Alzheimer's disease (AD) and multi-infarct dementia (MID) in Appignano, Macerata Province, Italy. *Neurology, 40*(Suppl. 1), 346.

Bots, M. L., van Swieten, J. C., Breteler, M. M., de Jong, P. T., van Gijn, J., Hofman, A., et al. (1993). Cerebral white matter lesions and atherosclerosis in the Rotterdam Study. *The Lancet, 341,* 1232–1237.

Bowirrat, A., Treves, T., Friedland, R. P., & Korczyn, A. D. (2001). Prevalence of Alzheimer's type dementia in an elderly Arab population. *European Journal of Epidemiology, 8,* 119–123.

Brand, C. (1987, July 9). Bryter still and bryter? *Nature, 328,* 110.

Brown, A., Campbell, A., Wood, D., Hastings, A., Lewis-Jack, O., Dennis, G., et al. (1991). Neuropsychological studies of Blacks with cerebrovascular disorders: A preliminary investigation. *Journal of the National Medical Association, 83,* 217–229.

Butler, S. M., Ashford, J. W., & Snowdon, D. A. (1996). Age, education, and changes in the Mini-Mental State Exam scores of older women: Findings from the Nun Study. *Journal of the American Geriatrics Society, 44,* 675–681.

Callahan, C. M., Hall, K. S., Hui, S. L., Musick, B. S., Unverzagt, F. W., & Hendrie, H. C. (1996). Relationship of age, education, and occupation with dementia among a community-based sample of African Americans. *Archives of Neurology, 53,* 134–140.

Campbell, A., Rorie, K., Dennis, G., Wood, D., Combs, S., Hearn, L., et al. (1996). Neuropsychological assessment of African Americans: Conceptual and methodological considerations. In R. Jones (Ed.), *Handbook of tests and measurement for Black populations* (Vol. 2, pp. 75–84). Berkeley, CA: Cobb and Henry.

Caramelli, P., Poissant, A., Gauthier, S., Bellavance, A., Gauvreau, D., Lecours, A. R., et al. (1997). Educational level and neuropsychological heterogeneity in dementia of the Alzheimer type. *Alzheimer Disease and Associated Disorders, 11,* 9–15.

Carlson, M. C., Brandt, J., Carson, K. A., & Kawas, C. H. (1998). Lack of relation between race and cognitive test performance in Alzheimer's disease. *Neurology, 50,* 1499–1501.

Carmelli, D., Swan, G. E., Reed, T., Miller, B., Wolf, P. A., Jarvik, G. P., et al. (1998). Midlife cardiovascular risk factors, ApoE, and cognitive decline in elderly male twins. *Neurology, 50,* 1580–1585.

Chandra, V., Pandav, R., Dodge, H. H., Johnston, J. M., Belle, S. H., DeKosky, S. T., et al. (2001). Incidence of Alzheimer's disease in a rural community in India: The Indo–US study. *Neurology, 57,* 985–989.

Chodosh, J., Reuben, D. B., Albert, M. S., & Seeman, T. E. (2002). Predicting cognitive impairment in high-functioning community-dwelling older persons: MacArthur Studies of Successful Aging. *Journal of the American Geriatrics Society, 50,* 1051–1060.

Christensen, H., Korten, A. E., Jorm, A. F., Henderson, A. S., Jacomb, P. A., Rodgers, B., et al. (1997). Education and decline in cognitive performance: Compensatory but not protective. *International Journal of Geriatric Psychiatry, 12,* 323–330.

Collins, S. M. (1997). Black mobility in White corporations: Up the corporate ladder but out on a limb. *Social Problems, 44,* 55–67.

Cooper, R. S. (2005). Race and IQ: Molecular genetics as *deus ex machina*. *American Psychologist, 60,* 71–76.

Dartigues, J. F., Gagnon, M., Michel, P., Letenneur, L., Commenges, D., Barberger-Gateau, P., et al. (1991). Le programme de recherche paquid sur l'epidemiologie de la demence: methodes et resultats initiaux [The PAQUID research program on the epidemiology of dementia: Methods and initial results]. *Revue Neurologique (Paris), 147,* 225–230.

Devi, G., Ottman, R., Tang, M., Marder, K., Stern, Y., Tycko, B., et al. (1999). Influence of APOE genotype on familial aggregation of AD in an urban population. *Neurology, 53,* 789–794.

Elias, M. F. (1998). Effects of chronic hypertension on cognitive functioning. *Geriatrics, 53,* S49–S52.

Elias, M. F., Robbins, M. A., Elias, P. K., & Streeten, D. H. (1998). A longitudinal study of blood pressure in relation to performance on the Wechsler Adult Intelligence Scale. *Health Psychology, 17,* 486–493.

Elkins, J. S., O'Meara, E. S., Longstreth, W. T., Jr., Carlson, M. C., Manolio, T. A., & Johnston, S. C. (2004). Stroke risk factors and loss of high cognitive function. *Neurology, 63,* 793–799.

Escobar, J. I., Burnam, A., Karno, M., Forsythe, A., Landsverk, J., & Golding, J. M. (1986). Use of the Mini-Mental State Examination (MMSE) in a community population of mixed ethnicity: Cultural and linguistic artifacts. *Journal of Nervous and Mental Disease, 174,* 607–614.

Evans, D. A., Beckett, L. A., Albert, M. S., Hebert, L. E., Scherr, P. A., Funkenstein, H. H., et al. (1993). Level of education and change in cognitive function in a community population of older persons. *Annals of Epidemiology, 3,* 71–77.

Evans, D. A., Bennett, D. A., Wilson, R. S., Bienias, J. L., Morris, M. C., Scherr, P. A., et al. (2003). Incidence of Alzheimer disease in a biracial urban community: Relation to apolipoprotein E allele status. *Archives of Neurology, 60,* 185–189.

Farmer, M. E., Kittner, S. J., Rae, D. S., Bartko, J. J., & Regier, D. A. (1995). Education and change in cognitive function: The Epidemiologic Catchment Area Study. *Annals of Epidemiology, 5,* 1–7.

Farrer, L. A., Cupples, L. A., Haines, J. L., Hyman, B., Kukull, W. A., Mayeux, R., et al. (1997). Effects of age, sex, and ethnicity on the association between apolipoprotein E genotype and Alzheimer disease. A meta-analysis. *Journal of the American Medical Association, 278,* 1349–1356.

Fillenbaum, G. G., Heyman, A., Huber, M. S., Ganguli, M., & Unverzagt, F. W. (2001). Performance of elderly African American and White community residents on the CERAD Neuropsychological Battery. *Journal of the International Neuropsychological Society, 7,* 502–509.

Fillenbaum, G. G., Hughes, D. C., Heyman, A., George, L. K., & Blazer, D. G. (1988). Relationship of health and demographic characteristics to Mini-Mental State Examination score among community residents. *Psychological Medicine, 18,* 719–726.

Finley, G. E., Ardila, A., & Roselli, M. (1991). Cognitive aging in illiterate Colombian adults: A reversal of the classical aging pattern? *Revista Interamericana de Psicologia, 25,* 103–105.

Folstein, M. F., Folstein, S. E., & McHugh, P. R. (1975). *Mini-Mental State Examination.* Lutz, FL: Psychological Assessment Resources.

Ford, G. R., Haley, W. E., Thrower, S. L., West, C. A. C., & Harrell, L. E. (1996). Utility of Mini-Mental State Exam scores in predicting functional impairment among White and African American dementia patients. *Journals of Gerontology Series A: Biological Sciences and Medical Sciences, 51,* 185–188.

Ford-Booker, P., Campbell, A., Combs, S., Lewis, S., Ocampo, C., Brown, A., et al. (1993). The predictive accuracy of neuropsychological tests in a normal population of African Americans. *Journal of Clinical and Experimental Neuropsychology, 15,* 64.

Fox, E. R., Taylor, H. A., Jr., Benjamin, E. J., Ding, J., Liebson, P. R., Arnett, D., et al. (2005). Left ventricular mass indexed to height and prevalent MRI cerebrovascular disease in an African American cohort: The Atherosclerotic Risk in Communities Study. *Stroke, 36,* 546–550.

Fratiglioni, L., Grut, M., Forsell, Y., Viitanen, M., Grafstrom, M., Holmen, K., et al. (1991). Prevalence of Alzheimer's disease and other dementias in an elderly urban population: Relationship with age, sex and education. *Neurology, 41,* 1886–1892.

Gatz, M., Svedberg, P., Pederson, N. L., Mortimer, J. A., Berg, S., & Johansson, B. (2001). Education and the risk of Alzheimer's disease: Findings from the study of dementia in Swedish twins. *Journals of Gerontology Series B: Psychological Sciences and Social Sciences, 56B,* 292–300.

Geronimus, A. T., Bound, J., & Waidmann, T. A. (1999). Poverty, time, and place: Variation in excess mortality across selected US populations, 1980–1990. *Journal of Epidemiology and Community Health, 53,* 325–334.

Gorelick, P. B. (1998). Cerebrovascular disease in African Americans. *Stroke, 29,* 2656–2664.

Gould, S. J. (1996). *The mismeasure of man.* New York: W. W. Norton.

Graff-Radford, N. R., Green, R. C., Go, R. C. P., Hutton, M. L., Edeki, T., Bachman, D., et al. (2002). Association between Apolipoprotein E genotype and Alzheimer disease in African American subjects. *Archives of Neurology, 59,* 594–600.

Green, R. C., Cupples, L. A., Go, R., Benke, K. S., Edeki, T., Griffith, P. A,. et al. (2002). Risk of dementia among White and African American relatives of patients with Alzheimer disease. *Journal of the American Medical Association, 287,* 329–336.

Gurland, B. J., Wilder, D., Cross, P., Lantigua, R., Teresi, J. A., Barret, V., et al. (1995). Relative rates of dementia by multiple case definitions, over two prevalence periods, in three cultural groups. *American Journal of Geriatric Psychiatry, 3,* 6–20.

Hall, K. S., Gao, S., Unverzagt, F. W., & Hendrie, H. C. (2000). Low education and childhood rural residence: Risk for Alzheimer's disease in African Americans. *Neurology, 54,* 95–99.

Hall, K. S., Gureje, O., Gao, S., Ogunniyi, A., Hui, S. L., Baiyewu, O., et al. (1998). Risk factors and Alzheimer's disease: A comparative study of two communities. *Australian and New Zealand Journal of Psychiatry, 32,* 698–706.

Helms, J. E. (1992). Why is there no study of cultural equivalence in standardized cognitive ability testing? *American Psychologist, 47,* 1083–1101.

Helms, J. E. (1997). The triple quandary of race, culture, and social class in standardized cognitive ability testing. In D. P. Flanagan, J. L. Genshaft, & P. L. Harrison (Eds.), *Contemporary intellectual assessment: Theories, tests, and issues* (pp. 517–532). New York: Guilford Press.

Hendrie, H. C. (2001). Exploration of environmental and genetic risk factors for Alzheimer's disease: The value of cross cultural studies. *Current Directions in Psychological Science, 10,* 98–101.

Hendrie, H. C., Hall, K. S., Hui, S., Unverzagt, F. W., Yu, C. E., Lahiri, D. K., et al. (1995). Apolipoprotein E genotypes and Alzheimer's disease in a community study of elderly African Americans. *Annals of Neurology, 37,* 118–120.

Herrnstein, R. J., & Murray, C. A. (1994). *The bell curve: Intelligence and class structure in American life.* New York: Free Press.

Heverly, L. L., Isaac, W., & Hynd, G. W. (1986). Neurodevelopmental and racial differences in tactile–visual (cross-modal) discrimination in normal Black and White children. *Archives of Clinical Neuropsychology, 1,* 139–145.

Hill, L. R., Klauber, M. R., Salmon, D. P., Yu, E. S. H., Liu, W. T., Zhang, M., et al. (1993). Functional status, education, and the diagnosis of dementia in the Shanghai survey. *Neurology, 43,* 138–145.

Hilliard, A. G. (1979). Standardization and cultural bias impediments to the scientific study and validation of "intelligence." *Journal of Research and Development in Education, 12,* 47–58.

Hilliard, A. G. (1994). What good is this thing called intelligence and why bother to measure it? *Journal of Black Psychology, 20,* 430–444.

House, J. S., Lepkowski, J. M., & Williams, D. R. (2000). Excess mortality among urban residents: How much, for whom, and why? *American Journal of Public Health, 90,* 1898–1904.

Irvine, S. H., & Berry, J. W. (1988). *The abilities of mankind: A reevaluation.* Cambridge, UK: Cambridge University Press.

Jackson, P. B., & Stewart, Q. (2004). A research agenda for the Black middle class: Work stress, survival strategies, and mental health. *Journal of Health & Social Behavior, 44,* 442–455.

Jacobs, D. M., Sano, M., Albert, S., Schofield, P., Dooneief, G., & Stern, Y. (1997). Cross-cultural neuropsychological assessment: A comparison of randomly selected, demographically matched cohorts of English- and Spanish-speaking older adults. *Journal of Clinical & Experimental Neuropsychology, 19,* 331–339.

Jensen, A. R. (1972). *Genetics and education.* New York: Harper & Row.

Jensen, A. R., & Miele, F. (2002). *Intelligence, race and genetics: Conversations with Arthur R. Jensen.* Boulder, CO: Westview Press.

Kase, C. S., Wolf, P. A., Chodosh, E. H., Zacker, H. B., Kelly-Hayes, M., Kannel, W. B., et al. (1989). Prevalence of silent stroke in patients presenting with initial stroke: The Framingham Study. *Stroke, 20,* 850–852.

Katz, I. (1964). Review of evidence relating to effects of desegregation on the intellectual performance of Negroes. *American Psychologist, 19,* 381–399.

Kaufman, A. S., McLean, J. E., & Reynolds, C. R. (1988). Sex, race, residence, region, and education differences on the 11 WAIS–R subtests. *Journal of Clinical Psychology, 44,* 231–248.

Kaufman, J. S., Cooper, R. S., & McGee, D. L. (1997). Socioeconomic status and health in Blacks and Whites: The problem of residual confounding and the resilience of race. *Epidemiology, 8,* 621–628.

Kennepohl, S., Shore, D., Nabors, N., & Hanks, R. (2004). African American acculturation and neuropsychological test performance following traumatic brain injury. *Journal of the International Neuropsychological Society, 10,* 566–577.

Kilander, L., Nyman, H., Boberg, M., Hansson, L., & Lithell, H. (1998). Hypertension is related to cognitive impairment: A 20-year follow-up of 999 men. *Hypertension, 31,* 780–786.

Kirsch, I. S., Jungeblut, A., Jenkins, L., & Kolstad, A. (1993). *Adult literacy in America: The National Adult Literacy Survey.* Washington, DC: U.S. Government Printing Office.

Kivipelto, M., Helkala, E. L., Hanninen, T., Laakso, M. P., Hallikainen, M., Alhainen, K., et al. (2001a). Midlife vascular risk factors and late-life mild cognitive impairment: A population-based study. *Neurology, 56,* 1683–1689.

Kivipelto, M., Helkala, E. L., Laakso, M. P., Hanninen, T., Hallikainen, M., Alhainen, K., et al. (2001b). Midlife vascular risk factors and Alzheimer's disease in later life: longitudinal, population based study. *British Medical Journal, 322,* 1447–1451.

Klineberg, O. (1935). *Race differences.* New York: Harper & Brothers.

Klusman, L. E., Moulton, J. M., Hornbostle, L. K., Picano, J. J., & Beattie, M. T. (1991). Neuropsychological abnormalities in asymptomatic HIV seropositive military personnel. *Journal of Neuropsychological and Clinical Neurosciences, 3,* 422–428.

Knopman, D., Boland, L. L., Mosley, T., Howard, G., Liao, D., Szklo, M., et al. (2001). Cardiovascular risk factors and cognitive decline in middle-aged adults. *Neurology, 56,* 42–48.

Korczyn, A. D., Kahana, E., & Galper, Y. (1991). Epidemiology of dementia in Ashkelon, Israel. *Neuroepidemiology, 10,* 100.

Kuller, L. H., Shemanski, L., Manolio, T., Haan, M., Fried, L., Bryan, N., et al. (1998). Relationship between ApoE, MRI findings, and cognitive function in the Cardiovascular Health Study. *Stroke, 29,* 388–398.

Kumari, M., Brunner, E., & Fuhrer, R. (2000). Minireview: Mechanisms by which the metabolic syndrome and diabetes impair memory. *Journals of Gerontology Series A: Biological Sciences and Medical Sciences, 55,* B228–B232.

Landrine, H., & Klonoff, E. A. (1994). The African American Acculturation Scale: Development, reliability, and validity. *Journal of Black Psychology, 20,* 104–127.

Landrine, H., & Klonoff, E. A. (1995). The African American Acculturation Scale II: Cross-validation and short form. *Journal of Black Psychology, 21,* 124–152.

Landrine, H., & Klonoff, E. A. (1996). *African American acculturation: Deconstructing race and reviving culture.* Thousand Oaks, CA: Sage.

Lecours, A. R., Mehler, J., Parente, M. A., Caldeira, A., Cary, L., Castro, M. J., et al. (1987). Illiteracy and brain damage: 1. Aphasia testing in culturally contrasted populations (control subjects). *Neuropsychologia, 25,* 231–245.

Lee, J. H., Tang, M. X., Schupf, N., Stern, Y., Jacobs, D. M., Tycko, B., et al. (2001). Mortality and apolipoprotein E in Hispanic, African-American, and Caucasian elders. *American Journal of Medical Genetics, 103,* 121–127.

Lemann, N. (1992). *The promised land: The great Black migration and how it changed America.* New York: Vintage Books.

Letenneur, L., Commenges, D., Dartigues, J. F., & Barberger-Gateau, P. (1994). Incidence of dementia and Alzheimer's disease in elderly community residents of south-western France. *International Journal of Epidemiology, 23,* 1256–1261.

Liao, D., Cooper, L., Cai, J., Toole, J., Bryan, N., Burke, G., et al. (1997). The prevalence and severity of white matter lesions, their relationship with age, ethnicity, gender, and cardiovascular disease risk factors: The ARIC Study. *Neuroepidemiology, 16,* 149–162.

Liu, H. C., Lin, K.-N., Teng, E. L., Wang, S.-J., Fuh, J. L., Guo, N., et al. (1995). Prevalence and subtypes of dementia in Taiwan: A community survey of 5,297 individuals. *Journal of the American Geriatrics Society, 43,* 144–149.

Loewenstein, D. A., Ardila, A., Rosselli, M., & Hayden, S. (1992). A comparative analysis of functional status among Spanish- and English-speaking patients with dementia. *Journals of Gerontology, 47,* 389–394.

Loewenstein, D. A., Arguelles, T., Arguelles, S., & Linn-Fuentes, P. (1994). Potential cultural bias in the neuropsychological assessment of the older adult. *Journal of Clinical and Experimental Neuropsychology, 16,* 623–629.

Longstreth, W. T., Jr., Arnold, A. M., Manolio, T. A., Burke, G. L., Bryan, N., Jungreis, C. A., et al. (2000). Clinical correlates of ventricular and sulcal size on cranial magnetic resonance imaging of 3,301 elderly people. The Cardiovascular Health Study. *Neuroepidemiology, 19,* 30–42.

Lucas, J. A. (1998). Acculturation and neuropsychological test performance in elderly African Americans. *Journal of the International Neuropsychological Society, 4,* 77.

Lynn, R. (1998). In support of the nutrition theory. In U. Neisser (Ed.), *The rising curve: Long-term gains in IQ and related measures* (pp. 207–218). Washington, DC: American Psychological Association.

Lynn, R. (2002). Skin color and intelligence in African Americans. *Population & Environment, 23,* 365–375.

Manly, J. J., Byrd, D., Touradji, P., & Stern, Y. (2004). Acculturation, reading level, and neuropsychological test performance among African American elders. *Applied Neuropsychology, 11,* 37–46.

Manly, J. J., Jacobs, D. M., Sano, M., Bell, K., Merchant, C. A., Small, S. A., et al. (1998a). African American acculturation and neuropsychological test performance among nondemented community elders. *Journal of the International Neuropsychological Society, 4,* 77.

Manly, J. J., Jacobs, D. M., Sano, M., Bell, K., Merchant, C. A., Small, S. A., et al. (1998b). Cognitive test performance among nondemented elderly African Americans and Whites. *Neurology, 50,* 1238–1245.

Manly, J. J., Jacobs, D. M., Sano, M., Bell, K., Merchant, C. A., Small, S. A., et al. (1999). Effect of literacy on neuropsychological test performance in nondemented, education-matched elders. *Journal of the International Neuropsychological Society, 5,* 191–202.

Manly, J. J., Jacobs, D. M., Touradji, P., Small, S. A., & Stern, Y. (2002). Reading level attenuates differences in neuropsychological test performance between African American and White elders. *Journal of the International Neuropsychological Society, 8,* 341–348.

Manly, J. J., Miller, S. W., Heaton, R. K., Byrd, D., Reilly, J., Velasquez, R. J., et al. (1998). The effect of African-American acculturation on neuropsychological test performance in normal and HIV positive individuals. *Journal of the International Neuropsychological Society, 4,* 291–302.

Manly, J. J., Touradji, P., Tang, M.-X., & Stern, Y. (2003). Literacy and memory decline among ethnically diverse elders. *Journal of Clinical and Experimental Neuropsychology, 5,* 680–690.

Marcopulos, B. A., McLain, C. A., & Giuliano, A. J. (1997). Cognitive impairment or inadequate norms: A study of healthy, rural, older adults with limited education. *Clinical Neuropsychologist, 11,* 111–131.

Margo, R. A. (1985). *Disenfranchisement, school finance, and the economics of segregated schools in the United States south, 1980–1910.* New York: Garland.

Mast, B. T., Fitzgerald, J., Steinberg, J., MacNeill, S. E., & Lichtenberg, P. A. (2001). Effective screening for Alzheimer's disease among older African Americans. *Clinical Neuropsychologist, 15,* 196–202.

Matute, E., Leal, F., Zaraboso, A., Robles, A., & Cedillo, C. (1997). Influence of literacy level on stick constructions in non-brain-damaged subjects. *Journal of the International Neuropsychological Society, 3,* 32.

McKay, P. F. (2003). The effects of demographic variables and stereotype threat on Black/White differences in cognitive ability test performance. *Journal of Business and Psychology, 18,* 1–14.

Miller, E. N., Bing, E. G., Selnes, O. A., Wesch, J., & Becker, J. T. (1993). The effects of sociodemographic factors on reaction time and speed of information processing. *Journal of Clinical and Experimental Neuropsychology 15,* 66.

Morgenstern, L. B., Spears, W. D., Goff, D. C., Grotta, J. C., & Nichaman, M. Z. (1997). African Americans and women have the highest stroke mortality in Texas. *Stroke, 28,* 15–18.

Mortel, K. F., Meyer, J. S., Herod, B., & Thornby, J. (1995). Education and occupation as risk factors for dementia of the Alzheimer and ischemic vascular types. *Dementia, 6,* 55–62.

Mortimer, J. A. (1988). Do psychosocial risk factors contribute to Alzheimer's disease? In A. S. Henderson & J. H. Henderson (Eds.), *Etiology of dementia of Alzheimer's type* (pp. 39–52). Chichester, UK: Wiley.

Moyerman, D. R., & Forman, B. D. (1992). Acculturation and adjustment—A meta-analytic study. *Hispanic Journal of Behavioral Sciences, 14,* 163–200.

Mungas, D., Marshall, S. C., Weldon, M., Haan, M., & Reed, B. R. (1996). Age and education correction of Mini-Mental State Examination for English and Spanish-speaking elderly. *Neurology, 46,* 700–706.

Murden, R. A., McRae, T. D., Kaner, S., & Bucknam, M. E. (1991). Mini-Mental State Exam scores vary with education in Blacks and Whites. *Journal of the American Geriatrics Society, 39,* 149–155.

Negy, C., & Woods, D. J. (1992). The importance of acculturation in understanding research with Hispanic-Americans. *Hispanic Journal of Behavioral Sciences, 14,* 224–247.

Neisser, U., Boodoo, G., Bouchard, T. J. J., Boykin, A. W., Brody, N., Ceci, S. J., et al. (1996). Intelligence: Knowns and unknowns. *American Psychologist, 51,* 77–101.

Nell, V. (2000). *Cross cultural neuropsychological assessment: Theory and practice.* Mahwah, NJ: Lawrence Erlbaum.

Nunnally, J. C. (1994). *Psychometric theory* (3rd ed.). New York: McGraw-Hill.

Oliver, M. L., & Shapiro, T. M. (1997). *Black wealth/White wealth: A new perspective on racial inequality.* New York: Routledge.

Ott, A., Breteler, M. M., van Harskamp, F., Claus, J. J., van der Cammen, T. J., Grobbee, D. E., et al. (1995). Prevalence of Alzheimer's disease and vascular dementia: Association with education. The Rotterdam study. *British Medical Journal, 310,* 970–973.

Overall, J. E., & Levin, H. S. (1978). Correcting for cultural factors in evaluating intellectual deficit on the WAIS. *Journal of Clinical Psychology, 34,* 910–915.

Padilla, A. M. (1980). *Acculturation: theory, models, and some new findings.* Boulder, CO: Westview Press.

Prencipe, M., Casini, A. R., Ferretti, C., Lattanzio, M. T., Fiorelli, M., & Culasso, F. (1996). Prevalence of dementia in an elderly rural population: Effects of age, sex, and education. *Journal of Neurology, Neurosurgery & Psychiatry, 60,* 628–633.

Prince, M., Cullen, M., & Mann, A. (1994). Risk factors for Alzheimer's disease and dementia: A case-control study based on the MRC elderly hypertension trial. *Neurology, 44,* 97–104.

Rasmusson, D. X., Carson, K. A., Brookmeyer, R., Kawas, C., & Brandt, J. (1996). Predicting rate of cognitive decline in probable Alzheimer's disease. *Brain & Cognition, 31,* 133–147.

Ratcliff, G., Ganguli, M., Chandra, V., Sharma, S., Belle, S., Seaberg, E., et al. (1998). Effects of literacy and education on measures of word fluency. *Brain and Language, 61,* 115–122.

Reis, A., Guerreiro, M., & Castro-Caldas, A. (1994). Influence of educational level of non brain-damaged subjects on visual naming capacities. *Journal of Clinical and Experimental Neuropsychology, 16,* 939–942.

Reynolds, C. R., Chastain, R. L., Kaufman, A. S., & McLean, J. E. (1987). Demographic characteristics and IQ among adults: Analysis of the WAIS–R standardization sample as a function of the stratification variables. *Journal of School Psychology, 23,* 323–342.

Ripich, D. N., Carpenter, B., & Ziol, E. (1997). Comparison of African-American and White persons with Alzheimer's disease on language measures. *Neurology, 48,* 781–783.

Roberts, R. J., & Hamsher, K. D. (1984). Effects of minority status on facial recognition and naming performance. *Journal of Clinical Psychology, 40,* 539–545.

Rocca, W. A., Bonaiuto, S., Lippi, A., Luciani, P., Turtu, F., Cavarzeran, F., et al. (1990). Prevalence of clinically diagnosed Alzheimer's disease and other dementing disorders: A door-to-door survey in Appignano, Macerata Province, Italy. *Neurology, 40,* 626–631.

Ross, T. P., Lichtenberg, P. A., & Christensen, B. K. (1995). Normative data on the Boston Naming Test for elderly adults in a demographically diverse medical sample. *Clinical Neuropsychologist, 9,* 321–325.

Rosselli, M., Ardila, A., & Rosas, P. (1990). Neuropsychological assessment in illiterates: II. Language and praxic abilities. *Brain and Cognition, 12,* 281–296.

Salmon, D. P., Riekkinen, P. J., Katzman, R., Zhang, M. Y., Jin, H., & Yu, E. (1989). Cross-cultural studies of dementia: A comparison of Mini-Mental State Examination performance in Finland and China. *Archives of Neurology, 46,* 769–772.

Salthouse, T. A. (2001). A research strategy for investigating group differences in a cognitive construct: Application to ageing and executive

processes. *European Journal of Cognitive Psychology, 13,* 29–46.

Satz, P., Morgenstern, H., Miller, E. N., Selnes, O. A., McArthur, J. C., Cohen, B. A., et al. (1993). Low education as a possible risk factor for cognitive abnormalities in HIV-1: Findings from the Multicenter AIDS Cohort Study (MACS). *Journal of Acquired Immune Deficiency Syndromes, 6,* 503–511.

Schooler, C. (1998). Environmental complexity and the Flynn Effect. In U. Neisser (Ed.), *The rising curve: Long-term gains in IQ and related measures* (pp. 67–79). Washington, DC: American Psychological Association.

Scott, E. J. (1920). *Negro migration during the war.* New York: Oxford University Press.

Scribner, S., & Cole, M. (1981). *The psychology of literacy.* Cambridge, MA: Harvard University Press.

Sellers, A. H., Burns, W. J., & Guyrke, J. (2002). Differences in young children's IQs on the Wechsler Preschool and Primary Scale of Intelligence—Revised as a function of stratification variables. *Applied Neuropsychology, 9,* 65–73.

Snowdon, D. A., Ostwald, S. K., & Kane, R. L. (1989). Education, survival and independence in elderly Catholic sisters, 1936–1988. *American Journal of Epidemiology, 130,* 999–1012.

Spencer, S. J., Steele, C. M., & Quinn, D. M. (1999). Stereotype threat and women's math performance. *Journal of Experimental and Social Psychology, 35,* 4–28.

Steele, C. M. (1997). A threat in the air: How stereotypes shape intellectual identity and performance. *American Psychologist, 52,* 613–629.

Steele, C. M., & Aronson, J. (1995). Stereotype threat and the intellectual test performance of African Americans. *Journal of Personality and Social Psychology, 69,* 797–811.

Stern, Y. (2002). What is cognitive reserve? Theory and research application of the reserve concept. *Journal of the International Neuropsychological Society, 8,* 448–460.

Stern, Y., Albert, S., Tang, M.-X., & Tsai, W.-Y. (1999). Rate of memory decline in AD is related to education and occupation: Cognitive reserve? *Neurology, 53,* 1942–1947.

Stern, Y., Andrews, H., Pittman, J., Sano, M., Tatemichi, T., Lantigua, R., et al. (1992). Diagnosis of dementia in a heterogeneous population: Development of a neuropsychological paradigm-based diagnosis of dementia and quantified correction for the effects of education. *Archives of Neurology, 49,* 453–460.

Stern, Y., Gurland, B., Tatemichi, T. K., Tang, M. X., Wilder, D., & Mayeux, R. (1994). Influence of education and occupation on the incidence of Alzheimer's disease. *Journal of the American Medical Association, 271,* 1004–1010.

Stern, Y., Tang, M. X., Denaro, J., & Mayeux, R. (1995). Increased risk of mortality in Alzheimer's disease patients with more advanced educational and occupational attainment. *Annals of Neurology, 37,* 590–595.

Sulkava, R., Wikstrom, J., Aromaa, A., Raitasalo, R., Lahtinen, V., Lahtela, K., et al. (1985). Prevalence of severe dementia in Finland. *Neurology, 35,* 1025–1029.

Sundquist, J., Winkleby, M. A., & Pudaric, S. (2001). Cardiovascular disease risk factors among older Black, Mexican-American, and White women and men: An analysis of NHANES III, 1988–1994. *Journal of the American Geriatrics Society, 49,* 109–116.

Swan, G. E., Carmelli, D., & Larue, A. (1998). Systolic blood pressure tracking over 25 to 30 years and cognitive performance in older adults. *Stroke, 29,* 2334–2340.

Swan, G. E., DeCarli, C., Miller, B. L., Reed, T., Wolf, P. A., Jack, L. M., et al. (1998). Association of midlife blood pressure to late-life cognitive decline and brain morphology. *Neurology, 51,* 986–993.

Tang, M.-X., Stern, Y., Marder, K., Bell, K., Gurland, B., Lantigua, R., et al. (1998). The APOE-e4 allele and the risk of Alzheimer's disease among African Americans, Whites, and Hispanics. *Journal of the American Medical Association, 279,* 751–755.

Taylor, R. J., & Chatters, L. M. (1989). Family, friend, and church support networks of Black Americans. In R. L. Jones (Ed.), *Black adult development and aging* (pp. 245–271). Berkeley, CA: Cobb and Henry.

Teresi, J. A., Albert, S. M., Holmes, D., & Mayeux, R. (1999). Use of latent class analyses for the estimation of prevalence of cognitive impairment, and signs of stroke and Parkinson's disease among African-American elderly of central Harlem: Results of the Harlem Aging Project. *Neuroepidemiology, 18,* 309–321.

Teri, L., McCurry, S. M., Edland, S. D., Kukull, W. A., & Larson, E. B. (1995). Cognitive decline in Alzheimer's disease: A longitudinal investigation of risk factors for accelerated decline. *Journals of Gerontology Series A: Biological Sciences and Medical Sciences, 50A,* M49–M55.

Tsolaki, M., Fountoulakis, K., Chantzi, E., & Kazis, A. (1997). Risk factors for clinically diagnosed Alzheimer's disease. *International Psychogeriatrics, 9,* 327–341.

Unverzagt, F. W., Hall, K. S., Torke, A. M., & Rediger, J. D. (1996). Effects of age, education and gender on CERAD neuropsychological test performance in an African American sample. *Clinical Neuropsychologist, 10,* 180–190.

Unverzagt, F. W., Hui, S. L., Farlow, M. R., Hall, K. S., & Hendrie, H. C. (1998). Cognitive decline and education in mild dementia. *Neurology, 50,* 181–185.

U.S. Office of Education. (1917–1956). *Biennial survey of education in the United States.* Washington, DC: U.S. Government Printing Office.

van de Vijver, F. (1997). Meta-analysis of cross-cultural comparisons of cognitive test performance. *Journal of Cross-Cultural Psychology, 28,* 678–709.

Wechsler, D. (1981). *Wechsler Adult Intelligence Scale—Revised.* San Antonio, TX: The Psychological Corporation.

Wechsler, D. (1989). *Wechsler Preschool and Primary Scale of Intelligence—Revised.* San Antonio, TX: The Psychological Corporation.

Wechsler, D. (1997). *Wechsler Adult Intelligence Scale—III.* San Antonio, TX: The Psychological Corporation.

Weiss, B. D., Reed, R., Kligman, E. W., & Abyad, A. (1995). Literacy and performance on the Mini-Mental State Examination. *Journal of the American Geriatrics Society, 43,* 807–810.

Welsh, K. A., Fillenbaum, G., Wilkinson, W., Heyman, A., Mohs, R. C., Stern, Y., et al. (1995). Neuropsychological test performance in African-American and White patients with Alzheimer's disease. *Neurology, 45,* 2207–2211.

Wheeler, L. R. (1970). A trans-decade comparison of the IQ's of Tennessee mountain children. In I. Al-Issa & W. Dennis (Eds.), *Cross-cultural studies of behavior* (pp. 120–133). New York: Holt, Rinehart & Winston.

White, L., Katzman, R., Losonczy, K., Salive, M., Wallace, R., Berkman, L., et al. (1994).

Association of education with incidence of cognitive impairment in three established populations for epidemiological studies of the elderly. *Journal of Clinical Epidemiology, 47,* 363–374.

Whitfield, K. E., & Baker-Thomas, T. (1999). Individual differences in aging minorities. *International Journal of Aging and Human Development, 48,* 73–79.

Wilhelm, S. M. (1987). Economic demise of Blacks in America: A prelude to genocide? *Journal of Black Studies, 17,* 201–254.

Wilkinson, G. S. (1993). *Wide Range Achievement Test—3.* Lutz, FL: Psychological Assessment Resources.

Williams, D. R. (1997). Race and health: Basic questions, emerging directions. *Annals of Epidemiology, 7,* 322–333.

Williams, D. R., Yu, Y., Jackson, J. S., & Anderson, N. B. (1997). Racial differences in physical and mental health. *Journal of Health Psychology, 2,* 335–351.

Williams, R. L. (1971). Abuses and misuses in testing Black children. *The Counseling Psychologist, 2*(3), 62–73.

Williams, R. L. (1974). Scientific racism and IQ: The silent mugging of the Black community. *Psychology Today, 7*(12), 32–41.

Williams, W. (1998). Are we raising smarter children today? School and home related influences on IQ. In U. Neisser (Ed.), *The rising curve: Long-term gains in IQ and related measures* (pp. 125–154). Washington, DC: American Psychological Association.

Wu, J. H., Haan, M. N., Liang, J., Ghosh, D., Gonzalez, H. M., & Herman, W. H. (2003a). Diabetes as a predictor of change in functional status among older Mexican Americans: A population-based cohort study. *Diabetes Care, 26,* 314–319.

Wu, J. H., Haan, M. N., Liang, J., Ghosh, D., Gonzalez, H. M., & Herman, W. H. (2003b). Impact of diabetes on cognitive function among older Latinos: A population-based cohort study. *Journal of Clinical Epidemiology, 56,* 686–693.

Zhang, M., Katzman, R., Salmon, D., Jin, H., Cai, G., Wang, Z., et al. (1990). The prevalence of dementia and Alzheimer's disease in Shanghai, China: Impact of age, gender and education. *Annals of Neurology, 27,* 428–437.

26

SOCIAL STRUCTURE AND COGNITIVE CHANGE

DUANE F. ALWIN

The authors of the National Research Council (2000) report *The Aging Mind* emphasized the fact that the state of our current knowledge about cognitive aging is encumbered in part by the failure to develop a comprehensive theoretical framework incorporating age-related variation in environmental factors together with age-related changes in sensory function and health, and the interaction of these factors with age-related neurological changes in cognitive development. In an effort to supply such a comprehensive framework, they highlighted a narrative of human adaptation, involving

> dynamic adaptive processes, including changes in neuronal structure and function and in behavioral and social factors (e.g., social opportunity structures, the individual's routines and physical environment, the individual's goals, and the use of social and technological supports) that codetermine an individual's ability to function effectively. (National Research Council, 2000, pp. 9–11)

Little is known about these dynamic adaptive processes, but *The Aging Mind* was correct in calling for a multidimensional and multidisciplinary approach in the understanding of cognitive change in adulthood.

Despite the urgent need for this type of multidisciplinary theoretical framework, individuals who conduct research on human development and cognitive functioning generally do so in the absence of a well-established and consensually based multidimensional theoretical framework to guide their work. To be blunt, a theoretical framework that specifies the role of the social environment in cognitive development and change in the older ages is remarkably absent in virtually all research on cognitive aging. In general, research on age-related cognitive change is not informed by the kinds of multidimensional thinking emphasized by the authors of *The Aging Mind*—namely, a foundational consideration of the interaction between the environment and development, within a model that accounts for changes in this relationship

AUTHOR'S NOTE: The research reported in this chapter was supported in part by grants from the National Institute on Aging (R01-AG-021203 and R13-AG026231). The author acknowledges helpful discussions with Ryan McCammon and Linda Wray during the writing of this chapter and the comments of Brent Small and Scott Hofer on a previous version. The author takes full responsibility for the use of their ideas and suggestions. The assistance of Paula Tufis and Alyson Otto is greatly appreciated.

and its impact on levels of and change in cognitive functioning.

Indeed, I think it is a fair assessment that, rather than being theoretically driven, the vast majority of research on cognitive change is unabashedly descriptive and mainly informed by "normal science" paradigms that are motivated by single-disciplinary understandings (see, e.g., Salthouse, 1999) rather than being multidisciplinary in its pursuit of knowledge. This tendency is not necessarily limited to any one discipline; it is generally characteristic of contemporary research across the disciplinary spectrum. Research in this area typically focuses on empirical regularities that lead to inferences regarding expected levels of change in cognitive function (usually declines, but also gains) across major periods of the life cycle, especially later adulthood, and it generally does not theorize as to their causes or the sources of change or, if it does, it typically assumes maturational or ontogenic factors work alone.[1]

Using a life span developmental perspective, in this chapter I examine the relationship between social structure and cognitive change over the entire life span, within a comprehensive framework that considers cognitive change as resulting from social and environmental factors as well as neurological and maturational changes.[2] The chapter is organized as follows. First, I briefly review the state of present theory and discuss the need for an interdisciplinary approach to understanding the relationship between *cognitive function* and *socioenvironmental* factors over the life span. I argue on the basis of this review that present theoretical perspectives are enormously valuable from the point of view of orientation to the problem but that they are inadequate with respect to the specification of research strategies for studying the joint influences of maturational and environmental factors in cognitive function across the life span. Second, I lay the conceptual groundwork for the development of an alternative perspective that specifies the role of structural features of society and life course events in cognitive change. I define what I mean by the key concepts of cognitive function, social environment, social structure, and the dynamics of cognitive change. Next, I present the rudiments of a research strategy for understanding the relationship between social structural factors and the development of cognitive function and its change

over the life span, suggesting a model for examining the elements of this theory. After developing a theoretical framework that defines critical theoretical constructs—for example, social structure and cognitive function—I then briefly review some of what is known (and what is missing) about the role of structural factors that contribute to levels, trajectories, and of change across the life span in cognitive function, particularly with respect to older age. The principal focus is to conceptualize the ways in which individual statuses derived from social structural factors—such as educational, socioeconomic, racial/ethnic, and gender factors—produce differences in *levels*, *trajectories*, and *rates of change* in cognitive function.

It is *not* the purpose of this chapter to argue that cognitive aging researchers have entirely ignored the importance of the environment. That would be the wrong impression to draw from my comments above. Indeed, later in the chapter I review some of the important contributions that have discussed the importance of socioenvironmental covariation with cognitive functioning or age-related change. Neither do I contend that researchers have ignored a life span developmental approach, because there have been several researchers who have examined the effects of early life experiences and their lasting effects on cognitive function later in adulthood, even into later life (e.g., Kuh & The New Dynamics of Ageing [NDA] Preparatory Network, 2007; Richards & Deary, 2005; Snowdon et al., 1996). The early influences of the social environment have been established as a strong component of life span development. What is less well understood are the influences of the environment later on in life. Hardly anyone disagrees that the environment is important in cognitive function, but what is not known is the *timing of that influence* from a life span developmental perspective, as well as the *persistence of that influence*. There also appears, from a life span developmental perspective, to be little disagreement that the greatest impact of differences in the social environment come in the early part of the life cycle. Differences between individuals in skill levels applicable to cognitive tasks are established in childhood, adolescence, and the young adult years.

One objective of the chapter is, then, to raise the question of the *nature* of the role of differences in the social environment across the life span, and particularly the *timing* of the influence of the environment on cognitive development. For example, is the influence of the social environment equally important across the entire life span, or are there critical years in which the bulk of the impact of differences in the environment matter? Is it possible that old age in any way replicates the experiences of the young with respect to increasing levels of environmental influence, or does the influence of the environment on individual differences in cognitive function primarily result from structural factors arising early in life? Thus, I examine last in this chapter empirical evidence that is pertinent to the key elements of a theoretical model that is sensitive to the experiential conditions of differing stages in the life cycle. I use a *synthetic cohort approach* to the evaluation of life span differences in susceptibility of influence from the environment. I conclude the chapter with a summary of my thoughts on how this model can be applied in future research on cognitive change across the life span in ways that will inform the future of cognitive aging.

PRESENT THEORY

It is not as though there is a complete absence of life span theoretical development in this area. There are in fact several highly influential and widely cited theoretical statements about human development in adulthood to which one can turn, which stress the multicausal nature of development. However, it is only within the past 30 years that the field of cognitive aging has become a major field of research endeavor. The subdiscipline of human development became aware of the importance of the *life span developmental perspective*, and that perspective has guided substantial amounts of research on cognitive change in the older years. This perspective conceptualizes human development across the entire life span in terms of multicausal, multidimensional, and multidirectional change (e.g., Baltes, 1987, 1997; Baltes & Mayer, 1999; Baltes, Staudinger, & Lindenberger, 1999; Featherman & Lerner, 1985; Schaie, 1983, 1989, 1990, 1994, 1996). Development, according to this perspective, is embedded in multiple contexts and is conceived of as a dynamic

process in which the ontogeny of development interacts with the social environment, a set of interconnected social settings, embedded in a multilayered social and cultural context (e.g., Bronfenbrenner, 1979).

The main theoretical argument resulting from this perspective can be found in Baltes's (1997) address to the American Psychological Association, in which he drew upon both evolutionary and ontogenetic ideas about development and theorized about the contribution of biological–genetic factors and the social–cultural arrangements to what he called the "architecture of human development." Baltes (1997) posited "three foundational (constraining) principles of the life span architecture of human ontogeny," which can be applied to the phenomenon of cognitive aging. He first argued that there is a negative relationship between the benefits resulting from evolutionary selection and chronological age. As many others have suggested, evolutionary pressures have emphasized reproduction rather than longevity (e.g., Finch & Kirkwood, 2000). Humans have evolved to reproduce themselves and experienced the greatest protection from their biological and genetic architecture in the younger years. Consequently, the human genome in older ages contains, in Baltes's (1997) words, "an increasingly larger number of deleterious genes and dysfunctional gene expressions" (p. 367) compared with younger ages. In short, "reproduction fitness" trumps "longevity fitness." As an illustration of what he was talking about is the existence of the dementias, such as Alzheimer's disease, but there are many others as well (see Martin, Austad, & Johnson, 1996), wherein the chronic condition does not manifest itself until age 70 and prevalence rates increase exponentially (see Brookmeyer & Gray, 2000; Brookmeyer, Gray, & Kawas, 1998). Reproductive fitness, in the broad evolutionary schema, is neutral with respect to the diseases of old age.

In addition to the adaptive conditions afforded humans by the neglect occasioned by their evolutionary circumstances, humans also experience the phenomena associated with biological (or ontological) processes of aging, which produce a number of age-associated mechanisms involving biological loss. In Baltes's (1997) words, "evolution and biology are not good friends of old age" (p. 368)—biological losses amplify the "evolutionary neglect of old age." There is, according to Baltes (1997), an "unfinished architecture" of life span development created by the course of evolutionary selection and biological ontogeny. These processes work together to produce a parallel phenomenon, which Baltes (1997) referred to as "the second cornerstone of a life span architecture of human ontogenesis (or development)," namely, that "there is an age-related increase in the need or demand for culture" (p. 368). By *culture* Baltes (1997) referred to "the entirety of psychological, social, material, and symbolic (knowledge-based) resources" that promote human development. In the case of cognitive functioning, this refers to the set of factors I discuss below under the headings of "social environment" and "social structure" and all of the factors contained therein (e.g., social resources, social capital, and social status). The argument is that, with age, largely because of principles of evolutionary and biological ontogeny, there is an increased demand or need for culture to play a role. Social environmental resources play an increasingly important role in cognitive functioning in older age (see, e.g., Rowe & Kahn, 1998). As evidence of this need, one can point to improvements in life expectancy in industrialized societies over the 20th century (see chap. 4, this volume).

The third foundational principle of life span development articulated in Baltes's (1997) essay is that over the course of time "there is an age-related loss in the effectiveness or efficiency of cultural factors and resources" largely conditioned by the "negative biological trajectory of the life course" (p. 368). Baltes (1997) argued for the view that there continues to be a great deal of flexibility or plasticity in development in older age and that the extent of this potential for change may in fact be greater than normally believed, that the "scope of plasticity of the human organism declines with age" (Baltes, 1997, p. 368). He used cognitive learning in old age as an example of this phenomenon. He cited the common finding of declining speed of processing in older age (e.g., Craik & Salthouse, 1992), which strongly suggests that when it comes to high levels of performance, older adults may never be able to reach the same levels of functioning as younger adults, even after extensive training (Baltes, 1997, pp. 368–369; see also Baltes & Kliegl, 1992; Kliegl, Mayr, &

Krampe, 1994; Kliegl, Smith, & Baltes, 1989; Magnusson, 1996; Salthouse, 1993, 1996a, 1996b).

Baltes's (1997) architecture of the life span dynamics between biology and culture forms a general framework within which human (cognitive) development is embedded and the contours for his *selective optimization with compensation (SOC) model* (see Baltes & Baltes, 1980, 1990; Staudinger, Marsiske, & Baltes, 1995), which involves the consideration of three general functions or outcomes of development: (1) growth, (2) maintenance, and (3) regulation of loss. According to Baltes and his colleagues, there is over the life span a systematic shift in the relative allocation of resources to these three functions. In his words:

> In childhood, the primary allocation is directed toward growth; during adulthood, the predominant allocation is toward maintenance and recovery (resilience). In old age, more and more resources are directed toward regulation or management of loss. . . . (Note) that the reallocation of resources toward maintenance of functioning and regulation of loss is facilitated by the tendency of individuals to prefer avoidance of loss over enhancement of gains. (Baltes, 1997, p. 370)

I do not dwell on the intricacies of Baltes's SOC framework here, because they are stated eloquently in the above citations, except to note that the theory is not accompanied by the specification of methods for studying the joint influences of maturational and environmental factors in cognitive function across the life span. At a general level, the SOC framework is useful in terms of orienting one to the general considerations necessary for studying cognitive aging as an adaptive process involving cognitive, neural, and environmental resources. It lacks specificity, however, regarding research strategies for studying the changing role of the social environment in the development, maintenance, and decline of cognitive functioning.

The False Debate About Ontogenesis Versus Sociogenesis

As I suggest in this chapter, little research has empirically addressed the changing role of the social environment in the development of cognitive function over the life span. There are clearly several important contributions to the understanding of the early influences on adult development. For example, the ideas advocated by the cognitive reserve perspective highlight the importance of initial environment on late life cognitive changes (Richards & Deary, 2005; Stern, 2007). The work of Schooler (1984, 1987) on environmental complexity, an outgrowth of his work with Kohn and their colleagues (e.g., see Kohn & Slomcyznski, 1990), is an illustration of how environmental factors assessed across the life span help shape levels of cognitive complexity. There is also some evidence, for example, linking social resources and social network ties on later life cognitive functioning. Fratiglioni, Paillard-Borg, and Winblad's (2004) review article on this topic highlights the role of social integration as a predictor of dementia (see also chap. 36, this volume). Similarly, the epidemiological literature on social engagement underscores the importance of social factors in shaping cognitive change (Bassuk, Glass, & Berkman, 1999). In this chapter I redress the relative neglect of these issues by considering the impact of variations in the social environment on levels, trajectories, and rates of change in cognitive function *over the entire life span*, with special attention to the development and change in cognitive function in older age.

Although the life span developmental perspective has dominated research on cognitive change, there is an "ontogenic mirage" surrounding much of this theoretical development, allowing it to be viewed as strictly emphasizing *only* the developmental and/or maturational sources of change (i.e., ontogenic, or organic factors) and minimizing the social factors involved. The life span perspective has been criticized for viewing the environment as simply a vessel in which cognitive development takes place, rather than an independent source of variation in individual differences in outcomes. Hence, the life span developmental perspective, though certainly alert to the realities of social causation, is not necessarily shared universally, and there are important points of contention between that view and one that is more social constructionist in nature (e.g., Dannefer, 1984; Gergen, 1980; chap. 6, this volume).

I do not take sides on the relative importance of ontogeny and the environment. To be sure,

distinguishing between social causes and ontogenic causes is as risky as making the distinction between nature and nurture, and it is notoriously unhelpful if too rigidly drawn (see Musgrove, 1977). One cannot happen without the other, and most informed researchers doing empirical work on cognitive change agree that development (or change) occurs because of both social and biological factors (see chap. 33, this volume). It is true that in the work of Paul Baltes (e.g., Baltes, 1997) summarized above there is clearly a bias toward finding that evolutionary and ontological (biological) factors are the root cause of age-related adaptive phenomena. Regardless of emphasis, there is little question that social factors play an environmental role in the development, maintenance, and change in cognitive function across the entire life span, even as organic or biological changes produce predictable patterns. We cannot settle the relative contributions of these various sources of variation in cognitive function here, but we can contribute to the growing debate about the ways in which ontogenic and environmental sources of variation combine to produce patterns of cognitive aging over the entire life span.

COGNITIVE FUNCTION AND SOCIETY

Cognitive functioning obviously does not occur in a social vacuum—it happens within a configuration of opportunities and constraints linked to social roles, institutional arrangements, and interpersonal relationships. *Mind*, according to George Herbert Mead (1934), "resides in the ability of the organism to indicate (those elements in the social environment) which answer to his responses" and through this ability, "to control those responses in various ways" (p. 132). Mind, however, "presupposes and is a product of the social process," wrote Mead, because it is "through language and play the young child enters society by 'taking the role of the other,'" an essential ingredient in learning (p. 161). Following the "behaviorist" approach of Mead, I here define *cognitive function* as the human ability to manipulate the environment in such ways as to solve both simple and complex problems posed by that (primarily external) environment. These processes condition the formation, maintenance, and expression of cognitive abilities across the entire life span.

Modern psychology considers the attributes of "mind" to be basic, in the sense that they are assumed to be laid down in childhood and adolescence through interaction with the environment. *Socialization* is the process by which humans are molded by their environments and the particular social groups to which they belong, and cognitive function is one of those dimensions of human life that is so molded. Those aspects of the environment that organize behavior, which are external to the individual, become part of the individual through the process of socialization, and with developmental changes come changes in the complexity of the environment (Kohn & Schooler, 1983; Kohn & Slomczynski, 1990; Schooler, 1987). Obviously, ontological factors are involved as well, because a level of biological maturation is required in order to acquire information from the environment (e.g., Piaget, 1970). The complexities of the environment become incorporated into the cognitive function of the individual through a sequence of increasingly complex activities, interpersonal structures, and linked micro-settings (i.e., meso-environments; see Bronfenbrenner, 1979, pp. 56–65; Bronfenbrenner & Ceci, 1994). The study of the linkage between these complexities of mind and environmental structures clearly is necessary if we are to understand the nature of cognitive aging.

Sociologists typically make a distinction between *primary socialization* and *secondary socialization*. Primary socialization happens early in life, mainly in the family and school, whereas secondary socialization involves learning roles relevant to occupation and family. There are obvious connections between skills captured in early parts of the life span and those required for adult roles. Some sociologists even go so far as to say that the occupational structure defines the key social roles in which performance is variable, with the quality of performance being the basis of the assignment of social status (Duncan, Featherman, & Duncan, 1972, pp. 77–79). The criteria that are used to test for role performance in the schools at an early age (e.g., cognitive or intelligence test scores) are often linked abstractly to notions of mental or cognitive function (see preceding definition) associated with the concept of intelligence. This concept, as well as those that are highly linked to it, such as Kohn and Slomczynski's (1990) concept of *intellectual flexibility*, or others, are an important component of what students of cognitive aging investigate, although the aging years are often studied separately.

What Is Social Structure?

The concept of structure is central to virtually all schools of social scientific thought as well as to many of the theories that are important for understanding processes of aging. As a concept, *social structure* is a venerable tool of social scientific analysis and the subject of sociological discourse at least over the last few centuries (see Merton, 1949). Although often misunderstood, the concept of social structure is "one of the most important and most elusive terms in the vocabulary of current social sciences" (Sewell, 1992, p. 1).[3]

In this chapter, I use the concept of social structure to refer to opportunities and constraints within networks of roles, relationships, and communication patterns, which are relatively patterned and persisting (see R. M. Williams, 1960). The concept is applicable to large structures as well as small ones. In this sense, *structure* may refer, on the one hand, to large organic institutional structures, such as bureaucracies, which organize and orient human activities, or it may refer, at the other extreme, to a set of dyadic norms negotiated between two individuals for purposes of social exchange (Alwin, 1995, p. 219). This approach is consistent with definitions of the concept in current literature, although there are some differences.

Researchers often reify individual-level variables, such as educational level or occupational status, as aspects of social structure. These are not measures of social structure per se but individual-level resources that result from structural relations. Bronfenbrenner and Crouter (1983) considered such approaches to be limited in that they focused on the "social address" of the individual and criticized their failure to undertake a thorough conceptualization of the linkage between structural elements at the societal or group level and the individual (see also Bronfenbrenner, 1986; Bronfenbrenner & Ceci,

1994). Individual-level properties (e.g., level of education) may be useful indicators of the resources the individual receives from his or her location in the network of positions that define social structure, but in terms of measuring social structure the idea of capturing the "social address" as a means of getting at the true nature of social structure hits wide of the mark (Alwin, 1995, p. 218). Structural variables are defined at the group level rather than the individual level, and it is important to maintain a distinction in levels of analysis. Structural variables are assumed to exist apart from the aggregation of individual attributes. Structural arrangements produce benefits or advantages to some and fewer benefits or disadvantages to others—and it is those individual-level properties, such as gender, race/ethnicity, and level of education—that reflect these environmental exposures. These individual-level attributes of individuals may be thought of as remnants of socially structured arrangements that shape and organize the experiences of individuals, but they are not measures of social structure per se.

Conceptual Parallels

The concepts of social structure and cognitive ability both involve the foundational concept of *resources* that are available for the conduct of simple and complex tasks, a concept that ties them together in the process of socialization. Cognitive function is considered to be a set of resources, applied in the process of adapting to environmental demands, that are an essential component of social functioning across the life span. Similarly, it is generally agreed that the concept of social structure reflects a robust and persistent set of social arrangements that provide resources, opportunities, and constraints that impinge upon behavior and functioning of individuals across a wide range of domains relevant to human development. It is therefore useful to examine differences in patterns of cognitive resources that are linked theoretically and empirically to key elements of social structure, as well as the manner in which these linkages change over the life span.

At a minimum, the concept of social structure is used to understand the opportunities and constraints posed by social relationships, for example, a set of organizational role relationships (see Kohn & Slomczynski, 1990). This is the key set of factors that are the focus of this chapter. There is strong social science theory that suggests structural factors impinge on the aging process and that their influence needs to be understood with respect to cognitive aging. Some of the themes developed in this chapter converge with some of those discussed in other chapters (see, e.g., chaps. 6, 24, and 36, this volume). From the point of view of this chapter, the critical question is not *whether,* or even *how much*, social structural factors matter for the production of individual differences in cognitive function. The overriding question for this chapter is: *When and in what manner* do social environmental factors matter?

Cumulative Advantage and Disadvantage

Few doubt that the social environment is an important element in the development of cognitive functioning, but sociologists argue that cognitive function is shaped by differences in structural opportunities and other factors. In fact, one of the prevailing assumptions is that it is both the early and later environments that contribute independently to the development of intellectual resources in childhood (see Alwin & Thornton, 1984). The argument is typically extended further to suggest there is a compounding of the influences of the social environment over time. Not only do socioenvironmental inequalities impact individual differences at multiple time points over the life span, but also there is considerable theory suggesting that the residues of these influences in individual differences cumulate over time (Dannefer, 1987, 1988, 2003; O'Rand, 1996).

Although there is some evidence of the declining significance of genetic differences in affecting health outcomes in older age (see Rowe & Kahn, 1998), research on the relationship of social status factors and physical health consistently finds inequalities in health across the life span (Dannefer, 1987, 1988; O'Rand, 1996; O'Rand & Hamil-Luker, 2005). Despite this persistence and the growing strength of the relationship between social status and health with increasing age, the level of the association is generally found to diminish in older age (e.g., House et al., 1992; House, Lantz, & Herd, 2005; House et al., 1994; Marmot & Shipley, 1996; Robert & House, 1996). Such findings are hard to account for on the basis of the premises of cumulative advantage/disadvantage theory, in that one would expect the socioeconomic gradient to become steeper with time—that is, "The rich get richer and the poor get poorer" or, in the words of the Gospel writer, "Those who have, get more" (see Matthew 25:14–30). One would expect that those higher-status, cognitively advantaged individuals would actually increase their advantage over time, although as far as we can tell there is hardly any evidence for it in the case of cognitive abilities. Beckett (2000) tested the hypothesis that the convergence in health inequalities in older age resulted from mortality selection, concluding that selection biases do not account for the declining levels of association between social status and health. If mortality selection cannot account for this pattern, then this may be seen as an even greater setback for cumulative advantage/disadvantage theory (see the discussion of mortality selection in chap. 4, this volume).

At the same time, there is some evidence from the gerontological literature that cognitive decline is a risk factor for mortality (e.g., Bosworth, Schaie, & Willis, 1999). To the extent that mortality is selective on factors related to cognitive function, either with respect to levels or to rates of change, then any assessment of the changing role of social status factors in cognitive functioning (i.e., an age-related pattern to the social status–cognition relationship) will need to temper its conclusions against the possibility of mortality selection (see chap. 4, this volume). Until we better understand the relative contributions of environmental influences and population processes to assessed levels of associations of socioenvironmental factors to cognitive outcomes, both levels and rates of change, it is perhaps best to counsel prudence in interpreting such findings (see Alwin & Wray, 2005, p.14).

UNDERSTANDING THE LIFE SPAN, THE LIFE COURSE, AND THEIR DIFFERENCE

In developing a theory of the role of social structure in cognitive function and the implications of

this relationship for cognitive aging, I take a life span developmental perspective on individual outcomes. This means that I consider cognitive development across the entire life cycle—that is, across all major life stages—namely, childhood, adolescence, early adulthood, midlife, and older age. At the same time, this includes the potential consideration of the influence of life course events and trajectories with respect to individual outcomes that occur within those life stages (see Alwin & Wray, 2005). The *life course* (not to be confused with the life cycle or the life span) is the concept sociologists and demographers use to refer to trajectories of events and transitions that have an impact on development, the focus here being cognitive development (Alwin, 2008).[4] Harris (1987, pp. 21–22) argued that the study of the life course consists of the trajectories of events and transitions, for example, role sequences, which extend across the life span (see Ferraro, 2001). He noted that events occurring in both the historical time and biographical time reflect processes that can be construed as event sequences. It reflects the kind of emphasis that Mills (1959) described as the intersection of history and biography—studying the historical processes that bring social structural elements to the person and the biographic processes that bring the person to positions in the social structure.

In an early article on "Age Differentiation and the Life Course," Elder (1975, p. 186) recognized the "growing acceptance of a life span [in contrast to the life course] framework in studies of human development, socialization and role of status sequences." He observed (1975, p. 167) that "the life span perspective views human development, socialization, and adaptations as lifelong processes." He identified the "social timetable of the life course (e.g., entry into marriage, retirement), which is defined by age criteria in norms and social roles" as a distinct set of considerations (Elder, 1975, p. 165). Consistent with the view of life course as "events, transitions and trajectories," Elder (1975) argued that the sociological literature on age was a useful adjunct to the life span perspective on human development (see also Elder, 1985, 2000).

The life course approach, according to Elder (1975), not only emphasized the sequence of roles that embodied the phenomenon of age differentiation but also targeted the historical location of birth cohorts as an important index of differences in life span development and their potential role in social change (Mannheim, 1927/1952; Ryder, 1965). Elder's (1975) conceptual framework, which drew a distinction between life span development and the content of the life course (as defined by events, transitions, and trajectories) was reinforced in Featherman's (1983) article on life span perspectives in the social sciences, in which he included the life course as embedded in the larger perspective of life span development (see Featherman, 1983, pp. 8–9, 21, 24, 34–39).

The life course perspective has evolved. Elder (1985) developed the concept of "life trajectories" to define what he meant by life course: "Life trajectories can be charted by linking states across successive years . . . each trajectory is marked by a sequence of life events and transitions, changes in state that are more or less abrupt" (Elder, 1985, pp. 31–32). Elder (1985, p. 32) importantly distinguished between the concept of life course and the concept of life cycle, but he linked the two, that "life course dynamics" come about in part from the interplay of trajectories and transitions. He forused on the interdependence and synchronization of sets of trajectories which defined pathways of development. Interdependence, in this sense, refers to the interlocking nature of trajectories and transitions, *within and across life stages* (Elder, 1985, p. 32).

In Elder's early writings on this subject, the concept of life course is defined by trajectories of events and transitions, for example, role sequences, which extend across the life span. Each life-course transition is embedded in a trajectory that gives it specific form and meaning (Elder, 2000; Elder & Johnson, 2003; Elder et al., 2003). Beginning in the 1990s, Elder and his colleagues began to view the life course perspective as a theoretical orientation for the study of individual lives, human development, and aging. Elder (1997, p. 968) offered the following statement on the life course perspective:

> Life course theory offers . . . a fruitful way to think about and investigate the changing environment of the individual and its developmental implications . . . through an evolving concept of age-graded life course that is embedded in a matrix of social relationships, an active view of the individual in shaping the life course, and an approach toward understanding historical influences in lives and developmental processes.

Elder (2000, pp. 1615–1617) argued that beginning in the 1960s this theoretical orientation has diffused across substantive domains and disciplinary boundaries in the social and behavioral sciences. It has built conceptual bridges among developmental processes, the life course, and social change. The recent writings of Elder and his colleagues (e.g., Elder & Johnson, 2003; Elder, Johnson, & Crosnoe, 2003; Elder & O'Rand, 1996; Elder & Shanahan, 2006) have emphasized several *paradigmatic principles* that characterize the life course approach.

According to Elder and his colleagues, life course theory offers a fruitful way to think about and investigate the changing environment of the individual and its developmental implications; however, as with Baltes's (e.g., Baltes & Baltes, 1980, 1990) SOC theory, although the life course perspective offers a general orientation to understanding the individual in relation to society very little guidance is given for producing a research strategy that would investigate the implications of these considerations for changing environments across the entire life span. The study of the life course requires detailed event histories, which document critical events and transitions in people's lives that are relevant to developmental outcomes (see, e.g., Elder, 1974; Scott & Alwin, 1998), and it is not possible in the general case to harness the rich terrain of life course theorizing. We can, however, frame the life course approach within a more general model—a life span developmental perspective—that allows us to consider the entire range of the life span and the potential for environmental effects on cognitive change across the entire range (see Alwin, n.d.; Alwin & Wray, 2005).

COGNITIVE CHANGE OVER THE LIFE SPAN

At the early stages of the life span, the environment promotes change, and differences in the experience with the environment are most potent in terms of producing individual differences during the period of rapid changes at the maturational level. In Figure 26.1, I depict Bloom's (1964, p. vii) developmental curve and the limits of environmental variation. The gradually rising curve of the level of development that changes as a function of age in this figure is intended to represent the average trajectory of the development of cognitive function. This curve exhibits its highest rates of change at the youngest ages and the rate of change, as depicted here, slows as age increases. The shaded area surrounding this curve is intended to represent the potential for differences in environments to affect the rate of change. The two things are interdependent in Bloom's (1964) theory; that is, as the rate of change slows so does the potential influence of the environment. The greater the potential for environmental effects, the less stable are the individual differences in the attributes of individuals, whereas the less potential for environmental change, the more highly stable are individual differences. The theoretical potential for the influence of environmental factors is represented by the wideness of the shaded area in the figure, which in this case narrows with increasing age.

In Bloom's (1964) words, "variations in the environment have greatest quantitative effect on a characteristic at its most rapid period of change and least effect on the characteristic during the least rapid period of change" (p. vii).

This picture of development in the early years is assumed in Bloom's scheme to be very general, in the sense that it applies to aspects of physical development (e.g., height and weight) as well as cognitive abilities and personality. Bloom's curve is also consistent with much theorizing in psychology of intellectual development. In chapter 1 of this handbook, Scott M. Hofer and I discussed Cattell's (1963) distinction between two interrelated components of cognitive abilities—*fluid* and *crystallized*—both of which are subsumed under the general heading of cognitive abilities. Fluid intelligence is conceptualized as "*the capacity for insight into complex relations . . . independent of the sensory or cultural area in which the tests are expressed*" (Cattell, 1971b, p. 13). Crystallized intelligence, on the other hand, has its origins in experience but is not expected to be independent of other capacities because it "arises as the result of the investment of fluid intelligence, over the years, in whatever higher-level cultural skills the individual is exposed to" (Cattell, 1971b, p. 13; see also Cattell, 1971a; Denny, 1982; Horn, 1968, 1976, 1982a, 1982b; Horn & Cattell, 1967; Horn & Donaldson, 1980).[5] Cattell (1971b) argued that the development of these two aspects of cognitive functioning is collinear through adolescence (or age 15), so we can perhaps assume that the depiction in Figure 26.1 describes both aspects of cognitive functioning through to about ages 18 through 20. At present,

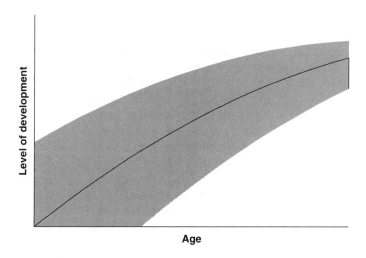

Figure 26.1   Bloom's (1964) Developmental Curve and the Limits of Environmental Variation

little is known about the relative role of environmental change in affecting each of these distinct sets of cognitive function.

Bloom's (1964) empirical work does not go beyond age 18, but he speculated that for most models of cognitive development, in terms an absolute scale, "it is assumed that intelligence remains constant after about age 20" (p. 80), but he conceded that at the time he did his study there was very little evidence available on adult intelligence. It was not clear from his writings whether he was referring to trajectories of levels of functioning, to the stability of individual differences, or both. He speculated that the environments in which people live after young adulthood would likely determine the nature of further intellectual development. He suggested that further development is possible if the forces reflecting environmental change are powerful enough to produce cognitive change, although he surmised from the available evidence that during most of adult life environments are decidedly static and that massive levels of intellectual stability is typical (Bloom, 1964, pp. 80–90). This pattern ultimately is not necessarily normal, or inevitable, because the level of stability is a reflection of the relationship of the person and the environment (Alwin, 1994, pp. 146–147; Ryder, 1965).

With regard to the average trajectory of cognitive abilities, according to Cattell (1971a, 1971b), subsequent to these early periods fluid abilities decline systematically with age, and crystallized abilities increase slightly or otherwise remain relatively stable with age (see Horn, 1982b; Horn & Cattell, 1967). The available literature on cognitive aging generally confirms Cattell's theory with regard to trajectories of aggregate performance. Research shows that there are significant cognitive declines in fluid or process-based abilities (e.g., memory) well past age 65 (Hertzog & Schaie, 1988) and that the declines increase even more rapidly after age 80 (Scherr et al., 1988). By way of contrast, measures of crystallized or education-based abilities, such as vocabulary recognition or verbal reasoning, decline later and less predictably (Park, 1999; Park et al., 1996). Most people agree that there are no pure measures of either component and that any given measure may constitute some combination of both. To the extent that available cognitive measures are dependent upon education, there may be a confounding of age-related trajectories with schooling, given the well-known pattern of intercohort differences in levels of schooling. Note that, in contrast to Bloom's (1964) approach, Cattell's classic prediction about the age-related patterns of fluid and crystallized abilities is about levels and trajectories of cognitive function, and it does not address the question of the relationship between environmental change and individual change. Hence, I return to these issues shortly.

Distinguishing Among Levels, Trajectories, and Rates of Change

There are two ways the social organization of experience via social structural factors can influence cognitive development: via (1) its influence on *levels of cognitive functioning* and (2) its influence on *rates of within-person cognitive change*. A *trajectory* of development is involved as one traces *levels* of functioning through time, and it is therefore linked to within-person change. The vast majority of the research literature on social structure and cognitive function has focused on levels rather than on rates of change. In this chapter, I argue that to understand the nature of the relationship between social structure and life span changes in cognitive function it is important to be highly sensitive to this distinction between average trajectories and average rates of change over the life span, and I have done so in the foregoing discussion of Bloom's (1964) discussion of stability and change. Indeed, I argue that it is because of the earliest influences of social structural factors on cognitive functioning that there may be considerably less of a role on cognitive change later in life.

Finally, from a methodological perspective, cognitive change is typically inferred from either repeated cross-sectional or panel data. It is important to bear in mind that cross-sectional age-related differences reflect the net effects of aging. In the case of longitudinal designs, the focus is on gross age-related changes, where the hypothesis of aging may be only one possible interpretation of age-related within-person change. Generally speaking, neither design can by itself address the foundational assumption of an interaction between the environment and human development, but most people agree that there is a substantial degree of heterogeneity in the nature and degree of cognitive change, which is better studied in a longitudinal design (see chap. 28, this volume). If there were no heterogeneity in age-related levels, trajectories, and levels of stability in cognitive functioning over the life span, then there would be little need to provide the careful examination of social structure and environmental factors as I propose here.

SOCIAL STRUCTURE AND COGNITIVE FUNCTION OVER THE LIFE SPAN

Given U.S. culture and its history, childhood and youth involve life stages that are relatively dense with respect to the occurrence and frequency of life course events in the family, school, community, and workplace that shape early outcomes (see, e.g., Erikson, 1988; Rindfuss, 1991). These early stages are considered particularly important periods for the formation of cognitive capacities. On the basis of the foregoing conceptual framework, in this section I argue that (a) differences in individual experiences organized on the basis of social structures (experiences involving environmentally linked access to resources) contribute to individual differences in cognitive functioning throughout the life span, (b) the potential for structural differences in organized experiences to affect individual differences in cognitive functioning is greatest during periods in which change at a developmental level is the greatest, (c) social structural factors not only help put individual differences into place but also help maintain individual differences throughout most of the adult life span, (d) the potential for change in cognitive functioning is greatest in the early and late periods of the life course. These are the empirical questions to which attention is focused here.

The depiction in Figure 26.2 represents an extension of Bloom's (1964) model, projecting both the age-related levels and potential role of environmental variation throughout the life span—from birth to age 100. Early differences in individual experiences play a critical role in the shaping of these individual differences, and there is a vast literature in behavioral science that shows that such differences exist. There is a growing literature on the stability of individual

differences in cognitive function, which shows high degrees of stability after early adulthood. Some researchers have written that cognitive decline in not inevitable and that individuals can "age successfully" if they promote ameliorative or adaptive health behaviors and avoid critical risk factors associated with deteriorative and chronic diseases normally associated with aging (see chaps. 6 and 18, this volume). This figure projects both absolute level of cognitive development (on a fictitious scale) as well as the range of environmental potential for cognitive change. The latter corresponds loosely to the concept of the "stability of individual differences," in that we expect that the limits of environmental variation is a reflection of the complex relation between the individual and society that results from personological and environmental persistence (see Alwin, 1994, 1995, 1997).

As depicted in Figure 26.2, at the early stages of the life span the environment promotes change and, following Bloom's (1964) line of argument, differences in the experience with the environment are most potent during rapid changes at the maturational level. Variations in the environment have greatest quantitative effect on a characteristic at its most rapid period of change and least effect on the characteristic during the least rapid period of change (Bloom, 1964, p. vii). Later on in midlife, the environment may act to promote stability rather than change, and because of the increasingly stable properties of the environment (Ryder, 1965), efforts aimed at changing the fundamental aspects of individuals through environment change may be doomed to failure (see Musgrove, 1977). Finally, although this is highly speculative at this stage, in older age the experience of the individual may again approximate the "openness to change" characteristic of childhood and youth—and the environmental influences may regain their importance as factors linked to cognitive change (see chap. 6, this volume).

STABILITY AND CHANGE IN COGNITIVE FUNCTION OVER THE LIFE SPAN

There is a great deal of evidence that individual differences in cognitive test scores, among other dimensions of individual differences, are quite

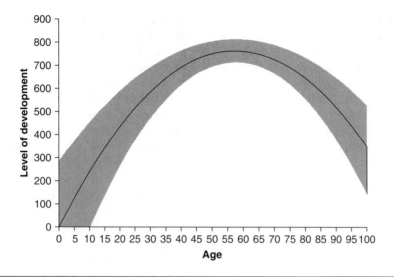

Figure 26.2   Developmental Curve and the Limits of Environmental Variation Across the Entire Life Span

stable over rather lengthy periods of the life span. As is the case with many human traits that reflect both ontogenic and sociogenic influences, individual differences in test scores are relatively less stable in childhood and early adolescence, but with age the differences among persons tend to stabilize, at least through midlife (see Alwin, 1994). In this part of the chapter, I summarize several studies that take a life span approach to examining how much flexibility (or plasticity) there is in cognitive abilities. There is no question that environment plays an important role in cognitive development; it also has a role in the maintenance of individual differences over the life span. No one would likely dispute the possibility that major environmental inputs can contribute to a flexibility and change in older age in a range of abilities, but the findings I introduce here suggests a picture of high degrees of stability in cognitive functioning into old age. It is less clear, however, whether these high levels of stability of individual differences persist among the oldest old, namely, after age 85.

It is well known that individual differences in cognitive abilities are one of the most stable components of human behavior that has been studied. Where the stability of individual differences in human abilities has been taken as problematic, measures of intellective variables are highly stable over most of the adult life span. In Figure 26.3, I present a summary of estimates of

molar stability (using a molar index of 8 years) from 20 longitudinal studies of cognitive functioning spanning a variety of ages (from Alwin, n.d.).[6] These results show that, as predicted on the basis of Bloom's (1964) work, the levels of molar stability are relatively low in the childhood years and increase with age. In Figure 26.3, I have superimposed a best-fitting curve that is described by a polynomial function of the second order, which I take to be a close approximation to the pattern of observed levels of molar stability over the period for which longitudinal data are available.

Stability results for the adult years show there is very little change in the distributional placement of individuals relative to others after the age of 20. For example, the Seattle Longitudinal Study reflects the typical pattern—Hertzog and Schaie's (1986) estimate of the stability of the common factor underlying individual differences in a version of Thurstone's Primary Mental Abilities is .92 over a 14-year period. They also showed that levels of stability increase with age. Similarly, Kohn and Schooler (1978) found a normative stability value of .93 for their concept of "ideational flexibility," assessed over a 10-year period. The entire range of studies indicates that stability grows in magnitude from adolescence onward and from the age of 40 the typical molar stability of intellectual ability is roughly .9.

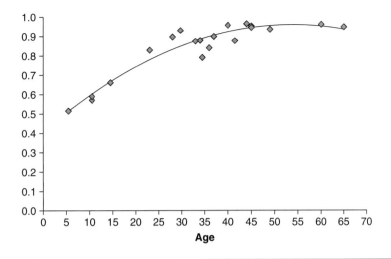

Figure 26.3   Molar Stability Estimates for Cognitive Function From 20 Longitudinal Studies Spanning Various Ages

These results may seem to pose a serious threat to some interpretations arguing that socialization or learning affecting basic intellectual abilities continues well into adulthood. Obviously, some openness to change is possible during adulthood, but if we understand that stability is a function of constancies of person–situation or person–structural linkages, then continuities over time may be viewed as reflections of the stability of socially structured experience, and the proper adjudication of the issue of whether a socioenvironmental interpretation exists for the stability of cognitive abilities would have to focus on the segment of the population that experiences change in social locations at different points in the life cycle, so that life course linkages to changes in socially structured experiences could be determined. Schooler's (1987) analysis of the development of intellectual flexibility over the life span through exposure to changes in the complexity of the environment represents one attempt to apply theories of social structure and personality to human development (see, e.g., Kohn & Schooler, 1983; Kohn & Slomczynski, 1990; Schooler, 1987), but data from this research program have not been adequately organized to reflect life span variations in stability (Alwin, 1995, pp. 250–252). It may be that the greatest change occurs in persons whose environments are changing most rapidly, but those who remain in stable environments are least likely to change (Alwin et al., 1991, 1994; Musgrove, 1977).

The Stability of Cognitive Functioning in Old Age

For the most part, none of the above studies were conducted on persons over age 70, and it is therefore difficult to generalize about levels of stability in the older age ranges as projected in Figure 26.2. To remedy this situation, my colleagues and I examined cognitive measures from the Health and Retirement Study (HRS) to assess the degree of stability roughly from age 50 through 90. The HRS is a set of nationally representative panel surveys of the coterminous U.S. population funded under a cooperative agreement between the National Institute on Aging and the Survey Research Center at the University of Michigan (see Juster & Suzman, 1995). Using these data, we focused on patterns of change in measures of cognitive performance in annual cohorts born from 1904 to 1947, although the availability of data from these cohorts varies with our measure of cognitive functioning. Using data from four waves, 1996–2002, we used four measures of cognitive functioning: (1) a vocabulary test modified from the Wechsler Adult Intelligence Scale—Revised (WAIS–R; Wechsler, 1981) Vocabulary test to capture crystallized intelligence; (2) a serial

7 subtraction test to assess working memory, a key measure of ability; (3) an immediate 10-noun free recall test to measure memory; and a delayed 10-noun free recall test to measure memory (see Herzog & Wallace, 1997).[7] One strength of the HRS data is that they contain a variety of measures—measures of recall, working memory, and vocabulary—but these measures are relatively sparse, compared with many other studies in the gerontological literature. The molar stability estimates for these four measures are shown in Figure 26.4.

The results in Figure 26.4 demonstrate, once again, the high degree of stability in measures cognitive test performance. In general, the measures that are more clearly crystallized in nature—the vocabulary and serial subtraction measures—have the highest levels of molar stability, roughly in the range of .9 or above. In the case of the two memory measures—immediate and delayed recall—the levels of molar stability are substantially lower, in the range of .7 to .8, and one must conclude that levels of stability are not uniform across these different measures. What is not clear from these results is whether environmental changes are becoming increasingly important in older age, in the sense that they promote cognitive change, or whether these different patterns result from the changing nature of the population at the older ages.

LIFE SPAN DETERMINANTS OF COGNITIVE CHANGE

I mentioned earlier that the results presented here and elsewhere regarding the relatively high levels of stability of cognitive test scores over time should perhaps cause some pessimism about the degree to which levels and trajectories of cognitive change are highly volatile in older age. Social scientists often point to fundamental social causes of health disparities, independent of personological or "individual differences" in predispositions toward between-group differences (e.g., see Alwin & Wray, 2005; House et al., 2005; Kaplan et al., 2001; Link & Phelan, 1995; D. R. Williams, 1990). The underlying assumption of these theoretical approaches is that socioenvironmental factors exert a stable impact on health disparities, once the inequality is in place. Some of the same arguments can be made regarding the effects of early individual differences in cognitive functioning (e.g., Gottfredson & Deary, 2004; Kuh & The NDA Preparatory Network, 2007; Richards & Deary,

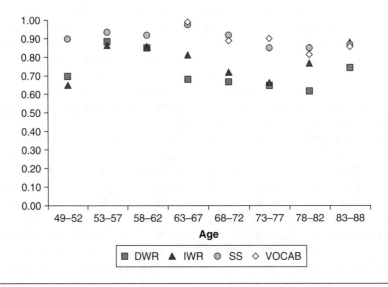

Figure 26.4   Molar Stability Estimates for Four Cognitive Measures From the Health and Retirement Study

NOTE: DWR = delayed word recall score; IWR = immediate word recall score; SS = serial 7 subtraction test score; VOCAB = Vocabulary subtest score.

2005; Snowdon et al., 1996); that is, once they are in place, they exert a lasting influence on developmental outcomes. However, virtually all research showing the power of socioenvironmental effects on health and/or cognitive outcomes assesses the environmental factors only once, presumably on the assumption that the individual's circumstances reflect one's position over a lifetime. As I argued above, however, the question is not *whether* socioenvironmental factors matter, but rather *when* and in *what manner* they contribute to change and stability. It will ultimately be necessary to determine what aspects of environments are likely to change after age 25, to ascertain the extent to which Bloom's (1964) hypotheses about intellectual change in adulthood are correct.

On the other hand, there are several sociological investigations aimed at the examination of levels of cognitive functioning and cognitive change over lengthy periods of the life span. For example, investigations of cohort differences in verbal skills have explicitly found the role of "aging" or "life cycle" contributions to verbal skills beyond early adulthood to be negligible, and there is a great deal of support for the idea that pre-adult levels of individual differences are highly persistent over major portions of the life span (Alwin & McCammon, 1999, 2001; Alwin et al., 2008). In population-based samples of broadly defined populations, what appear to be the most important determinants of individual differences in levels of cognitive function are factors reflecting the environmental influences early in life.

To illustrate some of the important socioenvironmental contributions to cognitive functioning at midlife, I summarize some recent results from an analysis of data from the Wisconsin Longitudinal Study (WLS), aimed at examining the influences of pre-adult functioning and socioeconomic experiences, that is, early differences in environmental exposure, on cognitive functioning at midlife (see Alwin et al., 2008). The WLS is based on a large sample of 1957 high school graduates from the state of Wisconsin (*n* = 8,493), who have been successfully followed over time and whose experiences were assessed on three successive occasions, at (approximately) ages 25, 36, and 52 (Hauser et al., 1992, 1993; Sewell, Hauser, Springer, & Hauser, 2003). The

WLS is one of the first large longitudinal school-based samples of young Americans that has a full set of standard measures of socioeconomic background, cognitive ability in adolescence, high school academic performance, and educational and occupational attainments. The WLS is distinctive in that age variation occurs over time rather than cross-sectionally and because it precedes by about a decade the bulk of the Baby Boom cohorts that were born between 1946 and 1964. Data are available for the WLS sample from approximately age 17 and at ages 24, 37, and 52.

The WLS data permit the assessment of the long-term effects of pre-adult intellectual levels and socioeconomic background on cognitive functioning at midlife. In the WLS, the pre-adult measure of cognitive ability—the Henmon–Nelson Test of Intelligence (see Henmon & Nelson, 1954)—is similar to other standardized measures of general ability, and the WLS measure has been widely used in predicting early socioeconomic attainments (Hauser, Tsai, & Sewell, 1983; Sewell & Hauser, 1975). We assume such a test contains both fluid and crystallized components. Detailed educational, occupational, and income reports are available for parents, such that relatively precise measurement can be made of key socioeconomic background statuses. In addition, the WLS allows us to examine the effect of school performance—in this case, an induced variable made up of rank in high school class and college preparatory curriculum status—as well as educational and occupational attainments subsequent to high school graduation. We make use of detailed educational and occupational data available for respondents at age 35 and age 52. A WAIS-type score involving 10 survey measures of verbal meaning is available in the WLS at age 52.[8]

The WLS is a study of a single cohort, so this controls for age and cohort while looking at the effects of most of the factors listed above. One of the strengths of the WLS data is the rich array of background measures. The main limitation is that it assessed only a WAIS-type verbal score in adulthood and at only one time point; however, the inclusion of the Henmon–Nelson intelligence test score from adolescence allows us to interpret the effects of variables occurring later in the causal sequence on the WAIS score at age 52 in terms of their effects on cognitive change.

To supplement our results from the WLS, we also include results in this summary from an examination of patterns of individual differences in a 10-measure verbal ability score from nationally representative repeated cross-section surveys from the General Social Survey (GSS) over a lengthy period of time, from 1974 through 1998 (Alwin, 1991; Alwin & McCammon, 1999, 2001). These surveys allow us to estimate the contribution of several factors to individual differences in verbal scores, including birth cohort, number of siblings, farm origins, southern residence, intact family background, and aging.

We used a causal model (not shown; see Alwin et al., 2008), using path analysis conventions, which specifies the roles of family background and pre-adult cognitive levels in shaping educational level and high school academic experiences, all of which in turn affect occupational attainment (either directly or indirectly) across the life span. These early factors all help shape socioeconomic attainments and cognitive developments later in life.[9]

Table 26.1 presents findings from our analysis of the WLS and the GSS that estimate the rough relative importance—assessed in terms of the proportion of variance explained by the variable in reduced-form equations reflecting their total effects. The strength of the GSS is that it spans 20+ years; the main weakness is that again it assessed only the verbal dimension and that it relies on repeated cross-sections, studying the same cohorts over time instead of the same people. I note in Table 26.1 that for variables in which our estimates of total effect come from the GSS data, these effects are estimated in a semi-reduced form of our model that does not control for pre-adult levels of cognitive ability.

Another strength of these studies—compared with the existing literature on cognitive functioning—is that they involve a specification of a population of interest and sample from that population. Very few of the data sets on which the literature on cognitive aging is based involves representative sampling of well-specified populations, so it is always difficult to generalize the results. On the other hand, they often involve a rich set of measures assessed longitudinally, often over many occasions of measurement and many years, but there is no strong basis for generalizing to any specific population of interest

Table 26.1 Estimates of Relative Importance of Predictors of Individual Differences in Verbal Ability at Midlife

Relative importance of predictors based on total effects	Variance Explained (%)
Pre-adult intelligence test score	30
Family socioeconomic background	10
Years of schooling completed	5
School success	4
Birth cohort[a]	2.5
Number of siblings[a]	2
Farm origins[a]	2
Southern residence[a]	1
Age[a]	< 1
Nonintact family[a]	< 1
Occupational complexity at age 35	< 1
Maternal employment	0
Birth order	0

[a]Based on semireduced form coefficients that do not control for pre-adult intelligence.

(see, e.g., the studies described in chap. 27, this volume). Hence, I believe that, to the extent to which it is possible to allocate "causal importance" to any set of variables in social research, using representative samples, the findings presented in Table 26.1 reflect generalizations about the factors linked to individual differences in one dimension of cognitive function: verbal ability. The table presents, in their rough order of importance, the determinants of level of verbal ability, evaluated in terms of the variance accounted for by the total effects of each variable.

Because I do not illustrate the causal assumptions of this model, it is perhaps important that I emphasize several things about our analysis of the WLS data that are not reported in detail here. First, the causal ordering is as follows: family background (including family socioeconomic background, maternal employment, and intact family) → pre-adult intellectual functioning → school academic success (including high school rank in class and postsecondary preparatory curriculum) → educational attainment → occupational complexity at age 35 → occupational complexity at age 52 → WAIS score at age 52. Second, the WLS data are from a single cohort of graduating high school seniors; some of the variables of interest are not present (or used) in those data sets, and other models based on the GSS data that are used, in which we assess the effects of birth cohort, number of siblings, farm origins, southern residence, aging and nonintact family, obviously do not control for pre-adult intelligence, so we report results based on semi-reduced form coefficients from the GSS.

In addition, given this causal ordering, and the controls for early or pre-adult cognitive functioning—in the form of the Henmon–Nelson Test of Intelligence score—the effects of schooling and occupational factors are assessed for cognitive change, to the extent that the Henmon–Nelson can act as a proxy for the WAIS content assessed earlier. The Henmon–Nelson test undoubtedly controls for this and more, so we can easily interpret the effects of the schooling and occupational variables on cognitive change in verbal ability.

In rough order of importance, the most important social factors in the WLS data, with respect to explaining variation in WAIS–R score at age 52, are primarily factors associated with the early part of the life cycle: pre-adult test score, family socioeconomic background, school success, and years of schooling completed. The stability parameter for intellectual functioning—that is, the total effect of the Henmon–Nelson score on the WAIS–R score at age 52—is embedded as a parameter in the model we use. It is assessed net of differences in socioeconomic background. This value, in standardized form, is about .55 in our WLS analyses (see Alwin et al., 2008). Recall that this effect coefficient is assessed across the 35-year period from ages 17 to 52. This produces an 8-year *molar stability* estimate of .874 for cognitive ability across the early part of adulthood, net of socioeconomic background (see Alwin, 1994). As I noted earlier in this chapter, this value is quite similar to the levels of stability observed in the Seattle

Longitudinal Study (Hertzog & Schaie, 1986) and to the 10-year stability of .93 that Kohn and Schooler (1983) observed for their measure of ideational flexibility (see Figure 26.3).

These results show that pre-adult cognitive functioning is a powerful predictor of WAIS score at age 52. Nearly one third of the variance in the WAIS score is attributable to the WLS Henmon–Nelson test score, some 35 years later. This is remarkable given the differences between the two tests and the possibility that they are tapping different dimensions of intellectual functioning. In addition, if one considers the fact that only 40% of the variance in the WAIS score is predictable variance then, given our model, the bulk of the prediction is coming from the Henmon–Nelson score. Even after school success, years of schooling and occupational position variables are included in the model as potential mediating mechanisms, the pre-adult test score continues to have a substantial direct effect, and indeed, the largest direct effect. The direct effect accounts for more than 70% of the total effect of pre-adult levels on subsequent levels of intellectual ability. The indirect effect operates primarily through school performance and years of schooling completed. The findings are consistent with an emerging literature on early life experiences and later adult outcomes, which suggests that early cognitive development is predictive of cognitive function and other health outcomes later in life (e.g., Gottfredson & Deary, 2004; Kuh & The NDA Preparatory Network, 2007; Richards & Deary, 2005; Snowdon et al., 1996; Whalley & Deary, 2001).

Another important finding is reflected in the fact that family socioeconomic background has an important effect on the WAIS score, its total effect accounting for 10% of the variance in individual differences in cognitive functioning. These results are consistent with recent research involving nationally representative studies of children indicating that oral language development is strongly influenced by family socioeconomic factors from birth through age 3 (Farkas & Beron, 2004). Childhood socioeconomic position is known to exercise an effect on later cognitive function in adulthood (see, e.g., Kaplan et al., 2001).

Similarly, the importance of successful academic performance and greater amounts of schooling are readily apparent in the analysis of the WLS, their total effects contributing 4% and 5% of the variance in the WAIS score, respectively. Following these factors in rough order of importance are birth cohort (2.5%), number of siblings (2%), farm origins (2%), and southern residence (1%). In the larger scheme of things, factors that are often thought to be important in explaining variation in individual differences in cognitive scores are less important in the present analyses than one might otherwise have expected, including birth order and family intactness (see, e.g., Zajonc, 1976).

Additional findings of interest here concern the effects of occupational levels on intellectual functioning at midlife, once background and pre-adult intellectual differences are taken into account. This involves, first, the effect of occupational position at age 35, and second, net of this, the effect of occupational position at age 52. The latter coefficient reflects the effects of *occupational change* and speaks directly to the learning generalization hypothesis advanced by Kohn and Schooler (see, e.g., 1983). The first thing to note here is that there is a small significant effect of occupational position at age 35. We interpret this to mean that some small amount of variation in intellectual functioning at midlife is attributable to early occupational socialization. The magnitude of this effect is rather small, but it is statistically significant. In addition, there is a small independent effect of occupational position at age 52 net of earlier occupation that is marginally significant. This finding provides weak support for a long line of argument in the sociological literature suggesting that changes in the substantive complexity of the job will result in cognitive shifts (Kohn & Schooler, 1978, 1983; Kohn & Slomczynski, 1990; Schooler, 1987). There is evidence for an effect of occupational change in our analyses of the WLS data, but its importance is relatively small in the larger scheme of factors that influence individual differences in changes in verbal ability from the early adult life span through to midlife.

SCHOOLING FACTORS AND COGNITIVE CHANGE IN OLDER AGE

The results presented above prompted us to review the question of whether some of the socioenvironmental factors investigated in the preceding analyses might affect rates of cognitive change in older age. For example, a literature has developed around the question of whether higher levels of schooling act as a protective factor in cognitive aging by retarding the rate of change in cognitive decline and therefore acting to buffer the processes of aging (e.g., see Anstey & Christensen, 2000; Baltes & Mayer, 1999; Christensen et al., 2001; Dufouil, Alpérovitch, & Tzourio, 2003).

Our own research (Alwin et al., 2008) provides little in the way of support for the effects of schooling on the aging function. Using the cognitive measures from the HRS data referred to above (see also chap. 4, this volume), obtained from a large national sample of community-dwelling respondents between the ages of 50 and 100, our results point to effects of schooling on levels of cognitive functioning These results are based on a set of analyses in which we used latent curve models that permitted us to address the question of whether (a) schooling affects the levels and rates of change in cognitive functioning within cohorts, and (b) the extent to which the effects of schooling on levels of cognitive functioning and the rate of cognitive change varies across birth cohorts. Most importantly, these models addressed the question of whether there are effects on levels and rates of change for *any* cohorts—not simply whether they are equal across cohorts (see Alwin et al., 2008).

In brief, we found that although schooling has salutary effects on levels of cognitive functioning across all measures, there was little evidence that greater amounts of schooling provided a protective impact on the rate of cognitive change. There was some support, among measures of crystallized abilities (vocabulary knowledge and serial subtraction) that greater schooling reduced the rate of decline, but we concluded that there was no strong, consistent support for an effect of schooling on the rate of cognitive change. Moreover, there is no evidence that the effect of schooling on rates of cognitive change varies by cohort for any of the HRS measures, suggesting that birth cohorts do not differ in the extent to which schooling operates to reduce the rate of cognitive decline. To put this conclusion in a more technical context, our results support the formulation of a model for the effects of schooling on the latent factors of the growth model, in which there are effects of schooling on the latent intercepts (individual differences in levels of functioning) but no effects on latent slopes (individual differences in rates of change). This suggests that higher amounts of schooling enhance one's level of cognitive performance, but that age is no kinder to the better educated.

In addition, it appears from our results that the effect of schooling on the intercepts varies by cohort for the more fluid measures, but less so for measures of crystallized abilities (see Alwin et al., 2008). Where there are cohort differences, the values of the coefficients increase from the earlier to later born cohorts, suggesting that the effect of schooling is stronger the more recently it was obtained (see Lorge, 1956). Schooling may be more germane to the tasks used in the measures of crystallized abilities than is the case for the more fluid measures of recall. Thus, the influence of schooling on levels of the crystallized measures (vocabulary and serial subtraction) remains more or less constant with age but, by contrast, schooling's impact on more fluid-based tasks is limited and therefore has even less role with time. Memorization skills associated with schooling (and the effects of schooling) help some, but there is very little in the way of crystallized intelligence directly involved in such recall tasks. Therefore, the weak assistance that schooling provides with respect to memory tasks is more susceptible to fading as biological and neurological processes of aging affecting fluid abilities become more salient in later life.

CONCLUSION

Most people agree that both social and biological factors are at work in developmental (or aging) outcomes involving cognitive function. Indeed, over the past 30 or so years we have witnessed numerous efforts to integrate biological, behavioral (psychological), and social science (sociological and ethnographic) conceptions of human life span development (see Featherman, 1983, and Baltes, 1987). The conceptual sweep of these efforts is often impressive, and a great deal can be learned from sensitizing researchers

to work going on outside their immediate fields. Still, there are differences in beliefs about the causes of (as well as the nature of) cognitive change and stability in older age, especially with regard to the heterogeneity in the nature and extent of cognitive aging. This is in part because of the challenges to verifying existing hypotheses regarding elements of constancy and change in empirical research.

In this chapter, I have focused on the linkage of one set of elements defined as "environmental" factors or as "social determinants" of cognitive aging. I consider the relations between social structure and cognitive function—the link between society and the individual—particularly as it relates to aging. Although the study of social structural factors and cognitive function has been pursued in several disciplines and subdisciplines (e.g., the sociology of education and status attainment processes), this is an area that has until recently been neglected in the study of cognitive aging. I have argued here that to fundamentally understand the relationship between society and the individual one must understand the nature of the social structural inputs into individual differences in cognitive abilities at all ages. Indeed, one theoretical contribution of this chapter is the development of the idea that the role of the social environment potentially changes over the life span.

What I have shown here is that differences in individual experiences organized on the basis of social structures (experiences involving environmentally linked access to resources) contribute to individual differences in cognitive functioning throughout the life span. Early differences in individual experiences play a critical role in the shaping of these individual differences, and there is a vast literature in behavioral science that shows that such differences exist. Borrowing a theme from Bloom's (1964) celebrated work, I have argued that the potential for these differences in experiences to affect between-person differences in cognitive functioning is greatest during periods in which change at a developmental level is the greatest. I have argued, in part on the basis of empirical findings, that social structural factors, especially those experienced during the early stages of the life span, not only assist in putting into place individual differences in cognitive skills but also help maintain individual differences throughout most of the adult life span. I suggested that later on, in midlife, the environment may act to promote stability rather than change, in part because of the increasingly stable properties of the environment. Efforts aimed at changing individuals through environmental change during midlife may be frustrated by the social tendencies toward commitment to roles and overall stability in the course of midlife.

Finally, although there is a growing literature on the stability of individual differences in cognitive function, the potential for change in cognitive functioning may increase in the later periods of the life span. I have argued, following Bloom (1964), that because variations in the environment may have their greatest effects in times of developmental change, and that in older age the experience of the individual may again approximate that of childhood and youth—and the environmental influences may regain their importance as factors linked to cognitive change. Although the best research suggests that level of schooling has little effect on the rate of cognitive change within birth cohorts, I nonetheless believe that environmental conditions may play a potential role in providing opportunities for successful aging. The theoretical framework and the research strategy developed in this chapter have the potential to test whether individual differences in cognitive capacities, if not average levels of functioning themselves, are increasingly influenced by environmental factors in older age.

NOTES

1. To give an example of the present state of theorizing about cognitive aging, a recent primer on cognitive aging (see Park & Schwarz, 2000) makes no mention of variation in environmental factors and their role in cognitive aging. The index, for example, contains no entries under "environment" or under "social" and "social context." The apparent assumption is that cognitive aging is simply an unfolding, in a maturational sense, of cognitive gains and losses over chronological or biological time. This is also true of many other standard sources on cognitive aging (e.g., Craik & Salthouse, 1992). See Baltes (1997, pp. 368–369) for a discussion of this issue.

2. This chapter represents a continuation of a discussion of the conceptualization of issues of life span development and research strategies presented in several related publications, where I develop a synthetic cohort approach to evaluating human change and stability across the life span (e.g., Alwin, 1994, 1995, 1997; Alwin et al., 1991). Crucial to this approach is a strategy for comparing levels of change and stability across the life span using the concept of molar stability.

3. The concept is central not only to the classical and neoclassical structural–functionalist perspectives in sociology but also to virtually all streams of social scientific thought. However, even as sociologists "find it difficult to do without the concept of structure, they also find it nearly impossible to define it in any adequate way ... [sometimes] finding it embarrassingly difficult to define the term without using the word 'structure' or one of its variants in the definition" (Sewell, 1992, p. 2).

4. Some of these contributions use the term *life course* in describing their approach to the study of early life experiences and later developmental outcomes (e.g., Kuh & The NDA Preparatory Network, 2007; Richards & Deary, 2005). It is important to note that this approach is what I here refer to as *life span* development. Of course, the use of terms sometimes differs across disciplines, but in its general use within sociology and demography, the *life course* consists of the trajectories of events and transitions (e.g., role sequences), which extend across the life span. This includes events occurring in both the historical time and biographical time.

5. The distinctions drawn by Cattell have subsequently been mentioned by other authors, which attests in part to their importance. For example, Salthouse (1991, p. 34; see also Salthouse, 1999) distinguished between measures that are more oriented toward *process* abilities and those that tap *product* abilities, and Baltes (1987) distinguished between the *mechanics* and the *pragmatics* of intelligence. Contemporary taxonomies and models of intelligence now include a much more complex array of ability domains (see Carroll, 1996, 1998; Horn, 1985, 1988, 1991; Woodcock, 1994), but the fundamental distinction between fluid and crystallized intelligence continues to guide current thinking (see Flanagan, McGrew, & Ortiz, 2000; McGrew, 1997; McGrew & Flanagan, 1998).

6. The molar stability coefficient is an estimate of the persistence of behavior or behavioral orientations as expressed in age-homogeneous rates of change over specified periods of time. The concept was introduced as a means of organizing empirical

information on human constancy and change and of comparing raw stability estimates across studies having different remeasurement intervals and across different concepts (see Alwin, 1994, pp. 155–158; Alwin, 1995, pp. 233–238). Molar stability is defined as $\beta^{j/k}$, where β is the cohort-specific or age-homogeneous stability estimate observed empirically, k is the number of years over which raw stability is assessed, and j is the number of years selected to express molar stability. In the examples used in this chapter, $j = 8$.

7. More details on these measures, the HRS samples, and the results of these analyses can be obtained from Alwin et al. (2008).

8. The WLS now includes an observation of verbal ability at age 65, based on a more recent follow up of the Wisconsin sample. These data were unavailable at the time this research was completed.

9. We use structural equation methods in this analysis and focus on the total rather than direct effects of variables in a causal model (see Alwin, 1988). The details of our treatment of the WLS data, including the measures and modeling strategies used, are given in Alwin et al. (2008).

REFERENCES

Alwin, D. F. (1988). Structural equation models in research on human development and aging. In K. W. Schaie, R. T. Campbell, W. Meredith, & S. C. Rawlings (Eds.), *Methodological issues in aging research* (pp. 71–170). New York: Springer.

Alwin, D. F. (1991). Family of origin and cohort differences in verbal ability. *American Sociological Review*, 56, 625–638.

Alwin, D. F. (1994). Aging, personality, and social change: The stability of individual differences over the adult life span. In D. L. Featherman, R. M. Lerner, & M. Perlmutter (Eds.), *Life-span development and behavior* (Vol. 12, pp. 135–185). Hillsdale, NJ: Lawrence Erlbaum.

Alwin, D. F. (1995). Taking time seriously: Studying social change, social structure and human lives. In P. Moen, G. H. Elder, Jr., & K. Lüscher (Eds.), *Examining lives in context: Perspectives on the ecology of human development* (pp. 211–262). Washington, DC: American Psychological Association.

Alwin, D. F. (1997). Aging, social change and conservatism: The link between historical and biographical time in the study of political identities. In M. A. Hardy (Ed.), *Studying aging and social change: Conceptual and methodological issues* (pp. 164–190). Thousand Oaks, CA: Sage.

Alwin, D. F. (2008). *Integrating conceptions of the life course*. Unpublished manuscript, Center on Population Health and Aging, Pennsylvania State University.

Alwin, D. F. (n.d.). *The stability of individual differences in cognitive functioning over the life span*. Unpublished manuscript, Center on Population Health and Aging, Pennsylvania State University.

Alwin, D. F., Cohen, R. L., & Newcomb, T. M. (1991). *Political attitudes over the life span: The Bennington women after fifty years*. Madison: University of Wisconsin Press.

Alwin, D. F., et al. (2008). *The aging mind in social and historical context*. Unpublished manuscript, Center on Population Health and Aging, Pennsylvania State University.

Alwin, D. F., & McCammon, R. J. (1999). Aging vs. cohort interpretations of intercohort differences in GSS verbal scores. *American Sociological Review, 64,* 272–286.

Alwin, D. F., & McCammon, R. J. (2001). Aging, cohorts, and verbal ability. *Journal of Gerontology: Social Sciences, 56B,* S1–S11.

Alwin, D. F., & Thornton, A. (1984). Family origins and the schooling process: Early vs. late influence of parental characteristics. *American Sociological Review, 49,* 784–802.

Alwin, D. F., & Wray, L. A. (2005). A life-span developmental perspective on social status and health. *Journal of Gerontology: Social Science, 60B*(Special Issue II), 7–14.

Anstey, K. J., & Christensen, H. (2000). Education, activity, health, blood pressure and Apolipoprotein E as predictors of cognitive change in old age: A review. *Gerontology, 46,* 163–177.

Baltes, P. B. (1987). Theoretical propositions of life-span developmental psychology: On the dynamics between growth and decline. *Developmental Psychology, 23,* 611–626.

Baltes, P. B. (1997). On the incomplete architecture of human ontogeny: Selection, optimization and compensation as the foundation of developmental theory. *American Psychologist, 52,* 366–380.

Baltes, P. B., & Baltes, M. (1980). Plasticity and variability in psychological aging: Methodological and theoretical issues. In G. E. Gurski (Ed.), *Determining the effects of aging on the central nervous system* (pp. 41–66). Berlin, Germany: Schering.

Baltes, P. B., & Baltes, M. (1990). Psychological perspectives on successful aging: The model of selective optimization with compensation. In P. B. Baltes & M. M. Baltes (Eds.), *Successful aging: Perspectives from the behavioral sciences* (pp. 1–34). New York: Cambridge University Press.

Baltes, P. B., & Kliegl, R. (1992). Further testing of limits of cognitive plasticity: Negative age differences in mnemonic skill are robust. *Developmental Psychology, 28,* 121–125.

Baltes, P. B., & Mayer, K. U. (1999). *The Berlin Aging Study: Aging from 70 to 100.* Cambridge, UK: Cambridge University Press.

Baltes, P. B., Staudinger, U. M., & Lindenberger, U. (1999). Lifespan psychology: Theory and application to intellectual functioning. *Annual Review of Psychology, 50,* 471–507.

Bassuk, S. S., Glass, T. A., & Berkman, L. F. (1999). Social disengagement and incident cognitive decline in community-dwelling elderly persons. *Annals of Internal Medicine, 131,* 165–173.

Beckett, M. (2000). Converging health inequalities in later life—An artifact of mortality selection? *Journal of Health and Social Behavior, 41,* 106–119.

Bloom, B. S. (1964). *Stability and change in human characteristics.* New York: Wiley.

Bosworth, H. B., Schaie, K. W., & Willis, S. L. (1999). Cognitive and sociodemographic risk factors for mortality in the Seattle Longitudinal Study. *Journal of Gerontology: Psychological Sciences, 54B,* P273–P282.

Bronfenbrenner, U. (1979). *The ecology of human development: Experiments by nature and design.* Cambridge, MA: Harvard University Press.

Bronfenbrenner, U. (1986). Ecology of the family as a context for human development: Research perspectives. *Developmental Psychology, 22,* 723–742.

Bronfenbrenner, U., & Ceci, S. J. (1994). Nature–nurture reconceptualized in developmental perspective: A bioecological model. *Psychological Review, 101,* 568–586.

Bronfenbrenner, U., & Crouter, A. C. (1983). The evolution of environmental models in developmental research. In P. H. Mussen (Series Ed.) & W. Kessen (Vol. Ed.), *Handbook of child psychology: History, theory and methods* (4th ed., Vol. 1, pp. 357–414). New York: Wiley.

Brookmeyer, R., & Gray, S. (2000). Methods for projecting the incidence and prevalence of chronic diseases in ageing populations: Application to Alzheimer's disease. *Statistics in Medicine, 19,* 1481–1493.

Brookmeyer, R., Gray, S., & Kawas, C. (1998). Projections of Alzheimer's disease in the United States and the public health impact of delaying disease onset. *American Journal of Public Health, 88,* 1337–1342.

Carroll, J. B. (1996). Mathematical abilities: Some results from factor analysis. In R. J. Sternberg and R. Ben-Zeev (Eds.), *The nature of mathematical thinking* (pp. 3–25). Mahwah, NJ: Lawrence Erlbaum.

Carroll, J. B. (1998). Human cognitive abilities. In J. J. McArdle & R. W. Woodcock (Eds.), *Human cognitive abilities in theory and practice* (pp. 5–24). Mahwah, NJ: Lawrence Erlbaum.

Cattell, R. B. (1963). Theory of fluid and crystallized intelligence: A critical experiment. *Journal of Educational Psychology, 54,* 1–22.

Cattell, R. B. (1971a). *Abilities: Their structure, growth and action.* Boston: Houghton Mifflin.

Cattell, R. B. (1971b). The structure of intelligence in relation to the nature–nurture controversy. In R. Cancro (Ed.), *Intelligence: Genetic and environmental influences* (pp. 3–30). New York: Grune and Stratton.

Christensen, H., Hofer, S. M., Mackinnon, A. J., Korten, A. E., Jorm, A. F., & Henderson, A. S. (2001). Age is no kinder to the better educated: Absence of an association investigated using latent growth techniques in a community sample. *Psychological Medicine, 31,* 15–28.

Craik, F. I. M., & Salthouse, T. A. (Eds.). (1992). *The handbook of aging and cognition.* Hillsdale, NJ: Lawrence Erlbaum.

Dannefer, W. D. (1984). Adult development and social theory: A paradigmatic reappraisal. *American Sociological Review, 49,* 100–116.

Dannefer, W. D. (1987). Aging as intracohort differentiation: Accentuation, the Matthew effect, and the life course. *Sociological Forum, 2,* 211–236.

Dannefer, W. D. (1988). What's in a name? An account of the neglect of variability in the study of aging. In J. E. Birren & V. L. Bengtson (Eds.), *Emergent theories of aging* (pp. 356–384). New York: Springer.

Dannefer, W. D. (2003). Cumulative advantage/disadvantage and the life course: Cross-fertilizing age and social science theory. *Journal of Gerontology: Social Sciences, 58B,* S327–S357.

Denny, N. W. (1982). Aging and cognitive change. In B. B. Wolman (Ed.), *Handbook of developmental psychology: Research and theory* (pp. 807–827). Englewood Cliffs, NJ: Prentice Hall.

Dufouil, C., Alpérovitch, A., & Tzourio, C. (2003). Influence of education on the relationship between white matter lesions and cognition. *Neurology, 60,* 831–836.

Duncan, O. D., Featherman, D. L., & Duncan, B. (1972). *Socioeconomic background and achievement.* New York: Academic Press.

Elder, G. H., Jr. (1974). *Children of the Great Depression: Social change in life experience.* Chicago: University of Chicago Press.

Elder, G. H., Jr. (1975). Age differentiation and the life course. *Annual Review of Sociology, 1,* 165–190.

Elder, G. H., Jr. (1985). Perspectives on the life course. In G. H. Elder, Jr. (Ed.), *Life course dynamics: Trajectories and transitions, 1968–1980* (pp. 23–49). Ithaca, NY: Cornell University Press.

Elder, G. H., Jr. (1997). The life course and human development. In R. M. Lerner (Ed.), *Handbook of child psychology, Vol. 1: Theoretical models of human development* (pp. 939–991). New York: Wiley.

Elder, G. H., Jr. (2000). The life course. In E. F. Borgatta & R. J. V. Montgomery (Eds.), *Encyclopedia of sociology* (2nd ed., Vol. 3, pp. 1614–1622). New York: Macmillan Reference USA.

Elder, G. H., Jr., & Johnson, M. K. (2003). The life course and aging: Challenges, lessons, and new directions. In R. A. Settersten, Jr. (Ed.), *Invitation to the life course: Toward new understandings of later life* (pp. 49–81). Amityville, NY: Baywood.

Elder, G. H., Jr., Johnson, M. K., & Crosnoe, R. (2003). The emergence and development of life course theory. In J. T. Mortimer & M. J. Shanahan (Eds.), *Handbook of the life course* (pp. 3–19). New York: Kluwer Academic/Plenum.

Elder, G. H., Jr., & O'Rand, A. M. (1996). Adult lives in a changing society. In K. S. Cook, G. A. Fine, & J. S. House (Eds.), *Sociological perspectives on social psychology* (pp. 452–475). Boston: Allyn & Bacon.

Elder, G. H., Jr., & Shanahan, M. J. (2006). The life course and human development. In W. Damon & R. M. Lerner (Eds.), *Handbook of child psychology* (6th ed., Vol. 1, pp. 665–715). New York: Wiley.

Erikson, E. (1988). Youth, fidelity, and diversity. *Daedalus, 117,* 1–24.

Farkas, G., & Beron, K. (2004). The detailed age trajectory of oral vocabulary knowledge: Differences by race and class. *Social Science Research, 33,* 464–497.

Featherman, D. L. (1983). Life-span perspectives in social science research. In P. B. Baltes & O. G. Brim, Jr. (Eds.), *Life-span development and behavior* (Vol. 5, pp. 1–57). New York: Academic Press.

Featherman, D. L., & Lerner, R. W. (1985). Ontogenesis and sociogenesis: Problematics for theory and research about development and socialization across the life span. *American Sociological Review, 50,* 659–676.

Ferraro, K. F. (2001). Aging and role transitions. In R. H. Binstock & L. K. George (Eds.), *Handbook of aging and the social sciences* (5th ed., pp. 313–330). New York: Academic Press.

Finch, C. E., & Kirkwood, T. B. L. (2000). *Chance, development and aging.* Oxford, UK: Oxford University Press.

Flanagan, D. P., McGrew, K. S., & Ortiz, S. O. (2000). *The Wechsler intelligence scales and Gf-Gc theory: A contemporary approach to interpretation.* Boston: Allyn & Bacon.

Fratiglioni, L., Paillard-Borg, S., & Winblad, B. (2004). An active and socially integrated lifestyle in late life might protect against dementia. *Lancet Neurology, 3,* 343–353.

Gergen, K. J. (1980). The emerging crisis in life-span developmental theory. In P. B. Baltes & O. G. Brim, Jr. (Eds.), *Life-span development and behavior* (Vol. 3, pp. 32–65). New York: Academic Press.

Gottfredson, L. S., & Deary, I. J. (2004). Intelligence predicts health and longevity, but why? *Current Directions in Psychological Science, 13,* 1–4.

Harris, C. (1987). The individual and society: A processual approach. In A. Bryman, B. Bytheway-Allatt, & T. Keil (Eds.), *Rethinking the life cycle* (pp. 17–29). London: Macmillan.

Hauser, R. M., Carr, D., Hauser, T. S., Krecker, M., Kuo, D., Presit, D., et al. (1993). *The class of 1957 after 35 years: Overview and preliminary findings.* CDE Working Paper 93–17, University of Wisconsin–Madison.

Hauser, R. M., Sewell, W. H., Logan, J. A., Hauser, T. S., Ryff, C., Caspi, A., et al. (1992). The Wisconsin Longitudinal Study: Adults as parents and children at age 50. *IASSIST Quarterly, 16,* 23–38.

Hauser, R. M., Tsai, S.-L., & Sewell, W. H. (1983). A model of stratification with response error in social and psychological variables. *Sociology of Education, 56,* 20–46.

Henmon, V. A. C., & Nelson, M. J. (1954). *The Henmon–Nelson test of mental ability: Manual for administration.* Chicago: Houghton Mifflin.

Hertzog, C., & Schaie, K. W. (1986). Stability and change in adult intelligence: I. Analysis of longitudinal covariance structures. *Psychology and Aging, 1,* 159–171.

Hertzog, C., & Schaie, K. W. (1988). Stability and change in adult intelligence: 2. Simultaneous analysis of longitudinal means and covariance structures. *Psychology and Aging, 3,* 122–130.

Herzog, A. R., & Wallace, R. B. (1997). Measures of cognitive functioning in the AHEAD study. *Journals of Gerontology Series B: Psychological Sciences and Social Sciences, 52B,* 37–48.

Horn, J. L. (1968). Organization of abilities and the development of intelligence. *Psychological Review, 75,* 242–259.

Horn, J. L. (1976). Human abilities: A review of research and theory in the early 1970s. *Annual Review of Psychology, 27,* 437–485.

Horn, J. L. (1982a). The aging of human abilities. In B. B. Wolman (Ed.), *Handbook of developmental psychology: Research and theory* (pp. 847–870). Englewood Cliffs, NJ: Prentice Hall.

Horn, J. L. (1982b). The theory of fluid and crystallized intelligence in relation to concepts of cognitive psychology and aging in adulthood. In F. I. M. Craik & S. Trehub (Eds.), *Aging and cognitive processes* (pp. 237–278). New York: Plenum.

Horn, J. L. (1985). Remodeling old theories of intelligence: Gf-Gc theory. In B. B. Wolman (Ed.), *Handbook of intelligence* (pp. 267–300). New York: Wiley.

Horn, J. L. (1988). Thinking about human abilities. In J. R. Nesselroade & R. B. Cattell (Eds.), *Handbook of multivariate psychology* (Rev. ed., pp. 645–685). New York: Academic Press.

Horn, J. L. (1991). Measurement of intellectual capabilities. In K. S. McGrew, J. K. Werder, & R. W. Woodcock (Eds.), *Woodcock–Johnson technical manual* (pp. 197–232). Chicago: Riverside.

Horn, J. L., & Cattell, R. B. (1967). Age differences in fluid and crystallized intelligence. *Acta Psychologica, 26,* 107–129.

Horn, J. L., & Donaldson, G. (1980). Cognitive development in adulthood. In O. G. Brim, Jr. & J. Kagan (Eds.), *Constancy and change in human development* (pp. 445–529). Cambridge, MA: Harvard University Press.

House, J. S., Kessler, R. C., Herzog, A. R., Mero, R. P., Kinney, A. M., & Breslow, M. J. (1992). Social stratification, age, and health. In K. W. Schaie, D. Blazer, & J. S. House (Eds.), *Aging, health behaviors and health outcomes* (pp. 1–32). Hillsdale, NJ: Lawrence Erlbaum.

House, J. S., Lantz, P. M., & Herd, P. (2005). Continuity and change in the social stratification of aging and health over the life course: Evidence from a nationally representative longitudinal study from 1986 to 2001/2002 (Americans' Changing Lives Study). *Journal of Gerontology: Social Science, 60B*(Special Issue II), 15–26.

House, J. S., Lepkowski, J. M., Kinney, A. M., Mero, R. P., Kessler, R. C., & Herzog, A. R. (1994). The social stratification of aging and health. *Journal of Health and Social Behavior, 35,* 213–234.

Juster, F. T., & Suzman, R. (1995). An overview of the Health and Retirement Study. *Journal of Human Resources, 30,* S7–S56.

Kaplan, G. A., Turrell, G., Lynch, J. W., Everson, S. A., Helkala, E. L., & Salonen, J. T. (2001). Childhood socioeconomic position and cognitive function in adulthood. *International Journal of Epidemiology, 30,* 256–263.

Kliegl, R., Mayr, U., & Krampe, R. T. (1994). Time–accuracy functions for determining process and person differences: An application to cognitive aging. *Cognitive Psychology, 26,* 134–164.

Kliegl, R., Smith, J., & Baltes, P. B. (1989). Testing the limits and the study of age differences in cognitive plasticity of a mnemonic skill. *Developmental Psychology, 26,* 894–904.

Kohn, M. L., & Schooler, C. (1978). The reciprocal effects of the substantive complexity of work and intellectual flexibility: A longitudinal assessment. *American Journal of Sociology, 84,* 24–52.

Kohn, M. L., & Schooler, C. (1983). *Work and personality: An inquiry into the impact of social stratification.* Norwood, NJ: Ablex.

Kohn, M. L., & Slomczynski, K. M. (1990). *Social structure and self-direction: A comparative analysis of the United States and Poland.* Cambridge, UK: Basil Blackwell.

Kuh, D., & The New Dynamics of Ageing (NDA) Preparatory Network. (2007). A life course approach to healthy aging, frailty, and capability. *Journal of Gerontology: Medical Sciences, 62A,* 717–721.

Link, B. G., & Phelan, J. (1995). Social conditions as fundamental causes of disease. *Journal of Health and Social Behavior, 36*(Extra Issue), 80–94.

Lorge, I. (1956). Aging and intelligence. *Journal of Chronic Diseases, 412,* 131–139.

Magnusson, D. (Ed.). (1996). *The life-span development of individuals: Behavioral, neurobiological, and psychosocial perspectives.* Cambridge, UK: Cambridge University Press.

Mannheim, K. (1952). The problem of generations. In P. Kecskemeti (Ed.), *Essays in the sociology of knowledge* (pp. 276–322). Boston: Routledge and Kegan Paul. (Original work published 1927)

Marmot, M. G., & Shipley, M. J. (1996). Do socioeconomic differences in mortality persist after retirement? 25 year follow up of civil servants from the first Whitehall Study. *British Medical Journal, 313,* 1177–1180.

Martin, G. M., Austad, S. N., & Johnson, T. E. (1996). Genetic analysis of ageing: Role of oxidative damage and environmental stresses. *Nature Genetics, 13,* 25–34.

McGrew, K. S. (1997). Analysis of the major intelligence batteries according to a proposed comprehensive Gf-Gc framework. In D. P. Flanagan, J. L. Genshaft, & P. L. Harrison (Eds.), *Contemporary intellectual assessment: Theories, tests, and issues* (pp. 151–180). New York: Guilford Press.

McGrew, K. S., & Flanagan, D. P. (1998). *The intelligence test desk reference (ITDR): Gf-Gc cross-battery assessment.* Boston: Allyn & Bacon.

Mead, G. H. (1934). *Mind, self and society.* Chicago: University of Chicago Press.

Merton, R. K. (1949). *Social theory and social structure.* New York: Free Press.

Mills, C. W. (1959). *The sociological imagination.* New York: Oxford University Press.

Musgrove, F. (1977). *Margins of the mind.* London: Methuen.

National Research Council. (2000). *The aging mind: Opportunities in cognitive research.* Committee on Future Directions for Cognitive Research on Aging. Paul C. Stern and Laura L. Carstensen, Editors. Commission on Behavioral and Social Sciences and Education. Washington, DC: National Academy Press.

O'Rand, A. M. (1996). The precious and the precocious: Understanding cumulative disadvantage and cumulative advantage over the life course. *The Gerontologist, 36,* 230–238.

O'Rand, A. M., & Hamil-Luker, J. (2005). Processes of cumulative adversity: Childhood disadvantage and increased risk of heart attack across the life course. *Journal of Gerontology: Social Science, 60B*(Special Issue II), 117–124.

Park, D. C. (1999). Cognitive aging, processing resources, and self-report. In D. C. Park & N. Schwarz (Eds.), *Cognition, aging, and self-reports* (pp. 45–69). Philadelphia: Taylor & Francis.

Park, D. C., & Schwarz, N. (2000). *Cognitive aging: A primer.* Philadelphia: Taylor & Francis.

Park, D. C., Smith, A. D., Lautenschlager, G., Earles, J., Frieske, D., Zwahr, M., et al. (1996). Mediators of long-term memory performance across the life-span. *Psychology and Aging, 11,* 621–637.

Piaget, J. (1970). Piaget's theory. In P. H. Mussen (Ed.), *Carmichael's manual of child psychology* (pp. 703–732). New York: Wiley.

Richards, M., & Deary, I. J. (2005). A life course approach to cognitive reserve: A model for cognitive aging and development? *Annals of Neurology, 58,* 617–622.

Rindfuss, R. (1991). The young adult years: Diversity, structural change, and fertility. *Demography, 28,* 493–512.

Robert, S., & House, J. S. (1996). SES differentials in health by age and alternative indicators of SES. *Journal of Aging and Health, 8,* 359–388.

Rowe, J. W., & Kahn, R. L. (1998). *Successful aging.* New York: Pantheon.

Ryder, N. B. (1965). The cohort as a concept in the study of social change. *American Sociological Review, 30,* 843–861.

Salthouse, T. A. (1991). *Theoretical perspectives on cognitive aging.* Hillsdale, NJ: Lawrence Erlbaum.

Salthouse, T. A. (1993). Speed and knowledge as determinants of adult age differences in verbal tasks. *Journal of Gerontology: Psychological Sciences, 48,* P29–P36.

Salthouse, T. A. (1996a). Constraints on theories of cognitive aging. *Psychonomic Bulletin and Review, 3,* 287–299.

Salthouse, T. A. (1996b). The processing-speed theory of adult age differences in cognition. *Psychological Review, 103,* 403–428.

Salthouse, T. A. (1999). Pressing issues in cognitive aging. In N. Schwarz, D. Park, B. Knäuper, & S. Sudman (Eds.), *Cognition, aging, and self-reports* (pp. 185–198). Philadelphia: Psychology Press.

Schaie, K. W. (1983). The Seattle Longitudinal Study: A 21-year exploration of psychometric intelligence in adulthood. In K. W. Schaie (Ed.), *Longitudinal studies of adult psychological development* (pp. 24–49). New York: Guilford Press.

Schaie, K. W. (1989). Individual differences in rate of cognitive change in adulthood. In V. L. Bengtson & K. W. Schaie (Eds.), *The course of later life: Research and reflections* (pp. 65–85). New York: Springer.

Schaie, K. W. (1990). Intellectual development in adulthood. In J. E. Birren & K. W. Schaie (Eds.), *Handbook of the psychology of aging* (3rd ed., pp. 291–309). San Diego, CA: Academic Press.

Schaie, K. W. (1994). The course of adult intellectual development. *American Psychologist, 49,* 304–313.

Schaie, K. W. (1996). *Intellectual development in adulthood: The Seattle Longitudinal Study.* Cambridge, UK: Cambridge University Press.

Scherr, P. A., Albert, M. S., Funkenstein, H. H., Cook, N. R., Hennekens, C. H., Branch, L. G., et al. (1988). Correlates of cognitive function in an elderly community population. *American Journal of Epidemiology, 128,* 1084–1101.

Schooler, C. (1984). Psychological effects of complex environments during the life span: A review and theory. *Intelligence, 8,* 259–281.

Schooler, C. (1987). Psychological effects of complex environments during the life span: A review and theory. In C. Schooler & K. W. Schaie (Eds.), *Cognitive functioning and social structure over the life course* (pp. 129–147). Norwood, NJ: Ablex.

Scott, J., & Alwin, D. F. (1998). Retrospective vs. prospective measurement of life histories in longitudinal research. In J. Z. Giele & G. H. Elder, Jr. (Eds.), *Methods of life course research: Qualitative and quantitative approaches* (pp. 98–127). Thousand Oaks, CA: Sage.

Sewell, W. H., Jr. (1992). A theory of structure: Duality, agency, and transformation. *American Journal of Sociology, 98,* 1–29.

Sewell, W. H., & Hauser, R. M. (1975). *Education, occupation and earnings: Achievement in the early career.* New York: Academic Press.

Sewell, W. H., Hauser, R. M., Springer, K. W., & Hauser, T. S. (2003). As we age: The Wisconsin Longitudinal Study, 1957–2001. In K. Leicht (Ed.), *Social stratification and mobility* (Vol. 20, pp. 3–111). London: Elsevier.

Snowdon, D. A., Kemper, S. J., Mortimer, J. A., Greiner, L. H., Wekstein, D. R., & Markesbery, W. R. (1996). Linguistic ability in early life and cognitive function and Alzheimer's disease in late life: Findings from the Nun Study. *Journal of the American Medical Association, 275,* 528–532.

Staudinger, U. M., Marsiske, M., & Baltes, P. B. (1995). Resilience and reserve capacity in later adulthood: Potentials and limits of development across the life span. In D. Cicchetti & C. Cohen (Eds.), *Developmental psychopathology: Vol. 2. Risk, disorder, and adaptation* (pp. 801–847). New York: Wiley.

Stern, Y. (Ed.). (2007). *Cognitive reserve: Theory and applications.* New York: Taylor & Francis.

Wechsler, D. (1981). *Wechsler Adult Intelligence Scale—Revised.* San Antonio, TX: The Psychological Corporation.

Whalley, L. J., & Deary, I. J. (2001). Longitudinal cohort study of childhood IQ and survival up to age 76. *British Medical Journal, 322,* 1–5.

Williams, D. R. (1990). Socioeconomic differentials in health: A review and redirection. *Social Psychological Quarterly, 53,* 81–99.

Williams, R. M., Jr. (1960). *American society: A sociological interpretation* (2nd ed.). New York: Knopf.

Woodcock, R. W. (1994). Measures of fluid and crystallized intelligence. In R. J. Sternberg (Ed.), *The encyclopedia of intelligence* (pp. 452–456). New York: Macmillan.

Zajonc, R. J. (1976, April 16). Family configuration and intelligence. *Science, 192,* 227–236.

PART VI

LONGITUDINAL MEASUREMENT AND ANALYSIS

27

INTEGRATIVE ANALYSIS OF LONGITUDINAL STUDIES ON AGING

Collaborative Research Networks, Meta-Analysis, and Optimizing Future Studies

ANDREA M. PICCININ AND SCOTT M. HOFER

Remarkable national and international efforts have produced well over 40 major longitudinal studies of individuals age 50 and older with a significant cognitive assessment component. It is widely recognized that although longitudinal information is time and effort intensive to collect, it is required to address central questions in developmental research relating to intraindividual change and variation and to population inference conditional on attrition and mortality. Given the profound investment of time, energy, and funding that these studies require, it is not uncommon for them to be multidisciplinary in nature. These existing longitudinal studies, therefore, represent an enormous wealth of information on within-person changes in a variety of domains, including cognition, health, personality, affect, lifestyle, and well-being. These studies, coupled with recent developments in statistical analysis and software for analysis of longitudinal data, provide unprecedented opportunities for describing and explaining aging-related changes and cross-process dynamics and for identifying influential factors associated with late life outcomes. Longitudinal studies permit the identification of change from a within-person baseline, thus enabling the identification of characteristics and antecedents that are potentially causally related and amenable to intervention.

As currently practiced, developmental science and theory are largely based on between-person differences, particularly in later adulthood. Given the requirements of data collection in longitudinal research, long intervals often pass until replication or cross-validation of findings. Relative to research reports from cross-sectional age-comparative studies, accumulation of knowledge from longitudinal studies has progressed very slowly. Aggravating this

AUTHORS' NOTE: This chapter, and the Integrative Analysis of Longitudinal Studies on Aging research network, was supported by a grant from the National Institute on Aging and the National Institutes of Health (1R01AG026453) to Oregon State University.

slow process are the complex varieties of measures, covariates, and statistical analyses based on the many decisions that often differ across published findings. The diversity of research interests relative to the number of longitudinal studies has also led to somewhat unique analyses, evaluation of particular models, and limited reporting of results, making comparison of findings difficult. One of the most obvious next steps in the developmental aging field is the evaluation and extension of theoretical and empirical findings in available within-person data. We must maximize what can be learned from existing data and make use of this information in the design of new studies.

The potential knowledge gains from increased collaboration and coordinated analysis of longitudinal data on aging are great. Recent major recommendations for research (Bachrach & Abeles, 2004), including executive summaries published by the National Research Council and commissioned by the National Institute on Aging/National Institutes of Health (NIH) and by the Office of Behavioral and Social Sciences Research/NIH (*The Aging Mind: Opportunities for Cognitive Research* [National Research Council, 2000, pp. 3–5]; *Preparing for an Aging World: The Case for Cross-National Research* [National Research Council, 2001a, pp. 4–7]; *New Horizons in Health: An Integrative Approach* [National Research Council, 2001b, pp. 9–13]) have highlighted the importance of such interdisciplinary, international, and collaborative research making use of longitudinal studies on aging. Butz and Torrey (2006), in *Science*, similarly highlighted the importance of longitudinal research, international replications, and advances in statistical methods to progress in the social sciences.

As we will describe in this chapter, numerous calls have been made for increased collaboration as a means to focus developmental research on within-person processes. We highlight and summarize some examples of collaborative and coordinated research, and we elaborate on some fundamental ideas for implementing strategies for maximizing our understanding of within-person aging-related changes.

We propose a collaborative system that encourages the evaluation and report of both parallel and alternative models on the same data as well as models incorporating individual- and

study-level characteristics to account for disparities across studies. We believe that direct and immediate comparison and contrast of results across independent studies, based on the open availability of analysis protocol, scripts, and results, will result in the most solid accumulation of knowledge based on cross-validated evidence. This is the most powerful way to build our developmental science.

FACILITATING RESEARCH ON LONGITUDINAL STUDIES

Reviews of Longitudinal Research

One approach to encouraging collaboration or cross-validation has been to produce a book or review that brings together work from a number of longitudinal studies. Mednick, Harway, and Finello's (1984a, 1984b) handbook of longitudinal research includes an explicit call for collaboration: "This handbook . . . is also presented to encourage scientists to consider collaborative efforts in which new questions may be put to the existing data banks" (Mednick, Harway, & Finello, 1984b, p. ix). As part of the handbook and central to this collaborative aim, extensive coding of 380 studies was incorporated into a computerized database, facilitating searches according to sample age and selection criteria as well as on antecedent and outcome variables.

Several recent reviews provide information on the number and scope of longitudinal studies on aging in existence with cognitive data. The Canadian Review of Longitudinal Studies on Aging (Health Canada, 2002) consists of a Microsoft Access database with information on 55 studies from more than 11 countries as well as a brief design description (initiation date, sample characteristics, main objective), a more detailed variable list for 51 of the studies (with a brief list for 4 studies not formally reviewed), and a short list of references for each of the studies. Of the studies reviewed, 32 collected both cognitive and objective health data, and an additional 10 contain cognitive and self-reported health. In 2006, Seematter-Bagnoud and Santos-Eggimann reviewed 70 large population-based longitudinal studies on health in individuals age 50 and over, listing them in tabular format according to geographical region. Although these studies more often focus solely on medical issues (e.g., cancer, osteoporosis), 20 overlap with the Canadian review and almost half collected cognitive measures. Seematter-Bagnoud's and Santos-Eggimann's review also includes 9 studies from outside of North America and Europe, compared with the Canadian list, which contains only 1 (which appears in both). Both of these reviews include extensive tables with information on sampling of individuals and measures.

The National Institute on Aging and various data archive (e.g., Inter-University Consortium for Political and Social Research National Archive of Computerized Data on Aging) and Web pages on aging (e.g., AgeNet UK) are also good information sources. AgeNet's review of 55 mainly British studies was conducted in 1999. In 2006, Longview, an independent think tank promoting longitudinal research in the United Kingdom, posted a strategic review (J. Martin et al., 2006) of 92 British panel and cohort studies (many of them social and economic) commissioned by the Economic and Social Research Council. The review discusses priorities, challenges, and opportunities; summarizes the types of studies available; and includes an appendix listing characteristics of each study. One of their main projects addresses "cognitive capital" across the life span, with a recent series of seminars focusing on birth cohort studies from 1946 and 1958.

These resources are similar in format to previous major inventories of longitudinal studies that have listed studies focused on aging. The Social Science Research Council Committee on Life-Course Perspectives on Human Development published an inventory covering middle and old age (Migdal, Abeles, & Sherrod, 1981), listing mainly American (49 of 73) studies. At the request of the Social Science Research Council, Young, Savola, and Phelps (1991) of the Murray Research Center updated the inventory and combined it with parallel documentation of longitudinal studies of childhood and adolescence (Verdonik & Sherrod, 1984). The inventories provided up to several pages of summarized information on the sample, participant attrition, substantive topics, measurement instruments used, representative references, contact information, and current status of the study.

Similarly, Schneider and Edelstein (1990) and a 1995 update (more a supplement, based on its selection criteria) by Zentrum (formerly Zentralstelle) für Psychologische Information und Dokumentation der Universität Trier have focused on European behavioral and medical studies. In these inventories, approximately 30 (from eight countries, with many from Sweden) include collection of data on cognitive function in adults over 50, 6 have life span data, and many also include measures of health. Given the passage of time since publication, 15 additional studies would now include adults over age 50 if it were possible to reconnect with the participants. The information collected includes name(s) of principal investigator(s), title of study, name and address of contact person, abstract, begin and end dates of data collection, computerization of data, size and age range of sample, and relevant publications.

These relatively comprehensive inventories, however, apart from listing representative references, do not describe the scientific contributions of these studies. Published results from these studies currently are largely based on different analytic approaches, limited report of results, and outcomes and covariates that differ in measurement instrument or coding procedure. Such differences hinder direct and quantitative comparison of results across studies and limit attempts to assess generalizability.

Reviews addressing the results from longitudinal studies on aging do exist. For example, Frazier, Hooker, and Siegler (1993) summarized psychological and personality aspects of seven multidisciplinary studies and a handful of additional longitudinal and epidemiological studies, and Schaie and Hofer (2001; see also Hofer & Piccinin, 2007) reviewed current studies that emphasize psychological outcomes. It is interesting to note that both reviews present results from different research questions for each study rather than any indication of consensus, although from the available data comparisons could often be made across studies if comparable analyses were conducted. Anstey and Christensen (2000) reviewed the impact of education, activity, health, blood pressure, and Apolipoprotein E as predictors of cognitive change in older adults and found relatively consistent evidence for education on Mini-Mental

Status Examination (MMSE; Folstein, Folstein, & McHugh, 1975). It is clear, however, that beyond this screening measure it is relatively difficult to find published work that allows straightforward comparisons. Park, O'Connell, and Thomson's (2003) systematic review of cognitive decline in the general elderly population identified 5,990 abstracts, but their selection criteria reduced this number to only 19 articles describing community-based, prospective cohort studies with low attrition. Citing population, country, measure, follow-ups (length and number), and attrition differences, they presented a narrative review rather than their planned meta-analysis. It is also noteworthy that their conclusion—that cognitive decline is almost universal—stands in contrast to recent literature emphasizing individual variability in rate of change and the relative stability of cognitive function for many or most of the individuals in the samples (e.g., Rubin et al., 1998; Wilson et al., 2002).

Combining the utility of the inventory and review formats, the Cognitive and Emotional Health Project (CEHP), funded by the National Institute on Aging, the National Institute of Mental Health, and the National Institute of Neurological Disorders and Stroke has created a searchable database of 67 large-scale ($N > 500$) multidisciplinary longitudinal and epidemiological studies, 42 of which have longitudinal cognitive data on adults age 55 years and older. Queries based on a variety of study characteristics provide a list of the relevant participating studies. Links from this list led to each study's responses to dichotomous questions regarding sample characteristics and construct measurement. For this project, 26 of the studies were selected for further review of findings, and these were summarized, with a focus on risk factors for change, by Hendrie et al. (2006). It is worthwhile to note their comment that aspects of the review were limited by less than complete reporting of the often-complex results. In particular, risk factors were sometimes included as covariates, but the details regarding their impact were not described.

Reflecting on the Herculean efforts devoted to cataloguing, coding and, in the case of CEHP, reviewing such large numbers of longitudinal studies, it is worth considering the value of

ensuring that the details of these products are not lost. This information and these search facilities might best be maintained and disseminated—and perhaps updated—under the aegis of a dedicated centralized repository such as a data archive.

Data Archives

Another approach to encouraging greater use of collected data has been to archive the information in a system that facilitates access. Over the past 60 years, a number of such efforts have been made to increase the accessibility of data for secondary analysis and encourage cross-disciplinary collaborations. The Roper Center is credited as the first to assemble and make available results from polls and other surveys in the 1940s. In 1960, the Zentralarchiv für empirische Sozialforschung was started in Europe (Cologne, France), and over the next few years, the Inter-University Consortium for Political and Social Research (1962) and its National Archive of Computerized Data on Aging (1978), which focuses specifically on aging and health, and the UK Data Archive (1967), were developed. The Henry A. Murray Research Archive (now part of the Harvard–MIT Data Center), a multidisciplinary archive focused on longitudinal data sets, started in 1976 and archives raw data in addition to computerized records.

Also in 1976, an umbrella organization, the Council of European Social Science Data Archives, was set up, with the main goals of cooperation in data archiving and unrestricted exchange of data. One year later, the International Federation of Data Archives/Organizations for the Social Science came into being. It is funded by membership fees and project applications, but some of the country-level archives have more often been funded by national agencies (e.g., Administration on Aging, Economic and Social Research Council, NIH), and in more recent years these agencies have increased the pressure to archive data by requiring investigators to begin the archiving process in order to obtain continued funding.

Data archives are unquestionably of value and are the most secure method for ensuring that data are not lost because of inadequate storage conditions or other problems. The maintaining and dissemination of data on such a large scale is not feasible for individual projects, particularly once funding has ended. However, beyond the straightforward archiving of data, an investigator seeking to maximize a study's data value might also consider collaborative opportunities with external investigators. In particular, such an investigator might seek to work with others holding similar data. Although this might initially appear to go against the competitive spirit that seems to have a hold on everything, including science, it opens up the possibility of building a science based on explicit cross-validation of results. Further advantages of such a cooperative approach are distribution of the work involved, immediate examination of alternative hypotheses and statistical models, and analysis of data by the individuals most familiar with them.

Collaborative Research Networks

How successful have prior calls for cooperation been? Most of us would be hard pressed to name many of them in the social sciences. Collaborative endeavors do exist, however, and are becoming more widespread in many areas inside and outside (e.g., Wikipedia) of academe. Among the successful scientific groups are the Campbell (1999) and Cochrane (1993) collaborations, both independent, not-for-profit, international organizations relying largely on volunteer contributions to produce easily accessible, up-to-date, systematic reviews of social and health care interventions (respectively) and to stimulate high-quality research. The reviews make recommendations for future research; however, data collection and analysis are not part of the mission of these groups.

The MacArthur Foundation and the networks it sponsors are also well known for interdisciplinary work in a variety of areas, including the MacArthur Study of Successful Aging (1988–1996; Rowe & Kahn, 1997), which drew a sample from the top third, based on a set of cognitive and physical criteria, of three of the Established Populations for Epidemiologic Studies of the Elderly programs. This productive set of networks has made use of a range of approaches: collaborative development of a number of related studies (Successful Midlife Development: MIDMAC); implementation of a series of distinct studies addressing key questions

(Early Experience and Brain Development, Successful Pathways through Middle Childhood); addition of measures and waves to ongoing longitudinal studies (Socioeconomic Status and Health); and parallel analyses of data from completed or ongoing longitudinal studies of development (Psychopathology and Development).

With an emphasis on aging, the AgeNet project (1997–2000) aimed to stimulate collaborative, multidisciplinary research and linkages—among academe, industry, and the National Health Service—through a database on longitudinal studies of aging and workshops on aging-related topics. AgeNet and its 1999 workshop on Longitudinal Studies of Aging were precursors of the Longview project and of current efforts for the development of a UK Birth Cohort Collaboration (Kuh & The New Dynamics of Ageing Preparatory Network, 2007). Similarly, CEHP, mentioned earlier, recommended the creation of consortia that would conduct combined analyses across studies but cautioned that this might be severely limited by study compatibility (Hendrie et al., 2006)).

Collaboration becomes a topic in a heady Nobel roundtable discussion on the future of interdisciplinary research and training (Nobel Round Table Discussions, 2006) and is also the focus of the Science of Collaboratories (Wulf, 1993), a National Science Foundation–funded project at the University of Michigan and Howard University. The Science of Collaboratories has ambitious goals of understanding the features required for successful collaborations and ultimately to have collaboration become part of the common infrastructure of science.

Some of the critical tasks in such collaborative research—and, we would argue, to advance the field in the absence of such collaboration—include harmonization of variables for maximal comparability and identification of comparable and noncomparable variables across studies. This could be a role for a data archive as well as a collaborative research network. Two examples of the work involved in harmonization are the Comparison of Longitudinal European Studies on Aging (CLESA) and the Survey of Health, Ageing and Retirement in Europe, which demonstrate the harmonization process from two extremes. CLESA investigators brought together existing measures from independent studies and we describe, below, a variety of their solutions to the obstacles they faced. The Survey of Health, Ageing and Retirement in Europe, on the other hand, started as a multisite study, developing a central questionnaire that was then translated and pretested in all member languages. Its acronym (SHARE) aptly represents the international cooperation and the open data sharing that are central to the project.

Various collaborations have been developed with different structures and levels of linkage among investigators and data. Table 27.1 provides a sampling of some of the main collaborative models and is organized in terms of multisite studies funded as collaborations from the outset and networks of pre-existing studies.

There are clearly many benefits to collaborative endeavors related to longitudinal studies on aging, most notably the opportunity for simultaneous evaluation of longitudinal data to test, replicate, and extend prior findings on aging. Given the key issue of cross-study comparison, harmonization of variables and statistical models are critical aspects, as are the evaluation of alternative models on the same data to permit direct comparison of results across models and the determination of why results might differ. Longitudinal research by itself is challenging, and coordinating analysis across studies is more so given the diversity of study designs, samples, and variables. These challenges are not insurmountable, however, and there is great promise for new collaborations that integrate recent theoretical perspectives for within-person aging (with emphasis on both health and aging), developments in statistical analysis of within-person data, and the remarkable number of completed and ongoing longitudinal studies on aging.

Theoretical, Measurement, and Statistical Issues for Collaborative Research on Aging

In aspiring to a collaborative and accumulative developmental science, it is necessary to consider issues related to comparisons across studies. It is also worth visiting more general issues related to developmental and nonexperimental research quality. We now discuss the importance of addressing developmental questions using within-person information as well as a number of design-related and sample-related issues in quasi-experimental research.

Emphasis on Within-Person Change Related to Aging and Health

Although much previous research in cognitive aging has been performed in the context of relatively healthy aging, there is sufficient evidence in the literature to indicate that changes in cognition and health are related (e.g., Albert et al., 1995; Brady, Spiro, & Gaziano, 2005; Brady, Spiro, McGlinchey-Berroth, Milberg, & Gaziano, 2001; Haan, Shemanski, Jagust, Manolio, & Kuller, 1999; Hassing et al., 2004; Knopman et al, 2001). Theoretical explanations of cognitive aging, however, have rarely taken health into account, or they do so by attempting to exclude major diagnoses such as dementia and so assume that results are based on individuals without health problems (but see Sliwinski & Buschke, 1999). The next steps in cognitive aging and health research are to examine what happens to people as they age by emphasizing the interplay between cognition and health (e.g., Waldstein, 2000) from a multiple-process orientation.

Understanding cognitive aging requires the identification of aging-related changes due to disease processes (morbidity, comorbidity) and mortality (see chap. 16, this volume). Pathological processes (i.e., disease) may be considered distinct but not independent of non-pathological processes of aging (Busse, 1969; Fozard, Metter, & Brant, 1990; Siegler, 1989). In terms of effects on cognition, health can have both direct and indirect effects on cognitive decline. The link between health and cognition may be indirect in that consequences of disease (frailty, level of arousal) impact the level of cognitive reserve, affecting older adults more because of their lower reserve thresholds. Direct effects of health on cognition are those related to pathological changes in the integrity of the neurological, cardiovascular, and cerebrovascular systems. The challenge is to understand aging-related changes in cognition in the context of morbidity and comorbidity and in terms of population inference conditional on survival. Broader changes, such as physical disablement and mental health functioning, also are relevant.

Table 27.1 Examples of Collaborative Research Networks

Collaboration Type and Name/Acronym	Funding	Years	Purpose and Accomplishments
Multisite studies funded as collaborations from the outset			
Nordic Research on Aging (NORA)	National funding agencies and private foundations in each country (e.g., Social Insurance Institution of Finland)	1989–1995	Study health, functional capacity, living habits, and living conditions of 75-year-olds in Denmark, Finland, and Sweden. Summary in Viidik (2002).
Medical Research Council (MRC) Cognitive Function and Ageing Study (CFAS)	MRC	1991–	Estimate prevalence and incidence of cognitive decline and dementia, determine the natural history of dementia, and evaluate service needs. Five sites with identical design; one, established earlier, is different.
International Study of Postoperative Cognitive Dysfunction (ISPOCD)	European Union (EU) BIOMED-1	1994–2001	Investigate cognitive decline after operation and anesthesia. Identified risk factors for long-term postoperative cognitive dysfunction after 3 months: age and use of benzodiazepines before surgery.
International Collaborative of Macronutrients and Blood Pressure (INTERMAP)	U.S. National Heart, Lung and Blood Institute	1995–2005	Multinational, multicenter epidemiologic study of diet impact (especially macronutrients) on blood pressure (ages 40–59).
Cardiovascular Health Study (CHS)	U.S. National Heart, Lung and Blood Institute	1989–1999	Identify risk factors for cardiovascular disease, ages 65+. More than 400 research papers and 120 ancillary studies.
Cross-European Longitudinal Study of Aging (EXCELSA)	EU 5th framework program, BIOMED-2	1998–2002	Study of biobehavioral, psychosocial, and socioenvironmental determinants of competence across the life span.
Advanced Cognitive Training in Vital Elderly (ACTIVE)	U.S. National Institute on Aging	1999–2001	Multisite randomized controlled trial of cognitive interventions.

Collaboration Type and Name/Acronym	Years	Funding	Purpose and Accomplishments
Networks of previously established longitudinal studies			
Berkeley Intergenerational Studies (IGS)	~1960	Initially: Laura Spellman Rockefeller Foundation, Jean MacFarlane; Currently: proposal submitted to National Institute on Aging	Includes the Berkeley Growth Study, the Guidance Study, and the Oakland Growth Study.
Collaborative Alcohol-Related Longitudinal Project	1987–1993	National Institute on Alcohol Abuse and Alcoholism	Interdisciplinary collaborative analysis of longitudinal studies of alcohol; 14 publications.
Quebec Network for Research on Aging	1996–2008	Quebec fund for health research (Fonds de la Recherche en Santé Québec)	Support research on the aging process, from cell to society. Research sections include (among others): cognition, mental health, nutrition, successful aging. Provide infrastructure support, grants, and awards. Sponsor conferences and annual science days. Strategic initiatives include the Canadian Longitudinal Study on Aging, the Longitudinal study of Expressions of Frailty, the Quebec Longitudinal Study on Nutrition and Aging, and sustaining the PRISMA and SOLIDAGE research programs.
The AgeNet project	1997–2000	UK-MRC, BUPA, Research into Ageing, SmithKline Beecham, Westminster Health Care, Office of Science and Technology	Stimulate multidisciplinary and multisector research partnerships relevant to academia, industry, and the National Health Service that would have a beneficial outcome for the health and quality of life of older people. Created database of 55 UK studies, with Web links, ran 21 workshops, initiated e-mail discussion group.
Asia Pacific Cohort Studies Collaboration (APCSC)	1999–	New Zealand Health Research Council, Australian National Health and Medical Research Councils, Pfizer	Focus on stroke, coronary heart disease, and other common causes of death in Asia-Pacific populations. Collaborative meta-analysis. All major cohort studies with blood pressure and cause of death information invited to participate. Database contains over 650,000 participants from 44 cohort studies in mainland China, Hong Kong, Taiwan, Japan, South Korea, Singapore, Thailand, New Zealand, and Australia. It is the largest epidemiological collaboration in the Southern hemisphere and one of the world's five largest medical studies. Published/in press peer-reviewed articles: 35.

(Continued)

Table 27.1 (Continued)

Collaboration Type and Name/Acronym	Years	Funding	Purpose and Accomplishments
Cancer Intervention and Surveillance Modeling Network (CISNET)	2000–	National Cancer Institute (NCI)	A consortium of NCI-sponsored investigators using diverse modeling approaches on a single data set to forecast trends and determine optimal strategies. Collaborative projects on breast, colorectal, lung, and prostate cancers; 76 publications, including general methods, listed on Web site.
European Birth-Lifecourse-Studies (EURO-BLCS; a multinational epidemiological study)	2000–2003	EU 5th framework program	1) Evaluate biological, genetic, clinical, behavioral, and social risk and protective markers for cardiovascular disease over the life course; 2) Consolidate methods of data collection to improve future comparability between countries, and allow data pooling; and 3) Collect new outcome data.
Comparison of Longitudinal European Studies on Aging (CLESA)	2001–2004	EU 5th framework program	Cross-national comparison of determinants of quality of life and health services for the elderly; six countries/institutions from Europe, plus Russia and Israel. Harmonized coding for variables in common across studies. Descriptive comparison of these variables.
Center for Early Diagnosis and Therapy Research for Neurodegenerative Diseases: A Swedish Network	2004–2009	Invest in Sweden, Stiftelsen för Strategisk Forskning, Vårdal Foundation, Stiftelsen för Kunskapsoch Kompetensuteuckling; Knut och Alice Wallenbergs Stiftelse; Vinnova	Early identification and treatment of major neurodegenerative diseases of adulthood through interdisciplinary research. Sponsors twice-yearly thematic workshops to stimulate within-network collaboration.
Australian Research Council (ARC) Research Network in Ageing Well	2005–2010	ARC & National Health and Medical Research Council	Generate innovative, multidisciplinary approaches to understand aging people; relations between age groups; and economic, social, and policy contexts that shape aging experiences.
Dynamic Analyses to Optimize Ageing (DYNOPTA)	2006–2011	ARC Research Network in Ageing Well (see preceding table entry)	Combine data from 9 Australian longitudinal studies of aging to identify key factors for disease prevention and successful aging promotion.

Assuming that aging is a highly complex, dynamic, and multidimensional process, influences that affect the aging rate of multiple systems may differ across individuals, implying that there will be different patterns of biological and psychological aging. Indeed, a useful distinction can be made between *common cause* and *common outcome*, because it is entirely possible that a common cause can lead to different outcomes and that different causes can lead to common outcomes. For example, different aging-related and/or disease-related processes may influence multiple systems within an individual. Age-related environmental influences or health-related changes may be unique to each individual, although different causative "aging" influences may appear to have a common outcome in the population (e.g., Almeida & Horn, 2004; Hofer, Berg, & Era, 2003; Sliwinski, Hofer, & Hall, 2003). This heterogeneity, and increasing disease risk with age, is perhaps the main source of difficulty in differentiating aging-related changes from changes associated with disease processes. In addition, changes in health may result from a complex interaction of life span influences, including education; occupation; and behavioral, health, and genetic risk factors.

Recent work has demonstrated that some of what were once considered normative cognitive aging effects is actually attributable to non-normative processes (e.g., preclinical dementia; Sliwinski, Lipton, Buschke, & Stewart, 1996). Non-normative processes might be very important determinants of cognitive aging, especially in very old age (> 80 years), because recent longitudinal evidence has shown that cognitive loss is strongly linked to disease onset in the case of preclinical Alzheimer's disease and that cognitive function is relatively stable prior to that time (Hall, Lipton, Sliwinski, & Stewart, 2000; Rubin et al., 1998; Sliwinski et al., 2003). Haan et al. (1999) showed that cognitive decline tends to occur primarily in individuals at risk for disease (e.g., Alzheimer's disease, cardiovascular disease) and that cognition is relatively stable in individuals without such diseases. In all of these studies, disease was studied in its preclinical state—meaning that afflicted individuals were ostensibly asymptomatic during the initial study period.

By definition, a normative cause of cognitive loss occurs in most individuals as they age (e.g., Bäckman et al., 2000). However, there is compelling evidence for the operation of processes that cause cognitive loss in a restricted (but not trivial) subset of aging individuals. The development of preclinical dementia (Haan et al., 1999; Hall et al., 2000; Rubin et al., 1998; Sliwinski et al., 2003), and the progression of subclinical cardiovascular disease (Haan et al., 1999) and respiratory dysfunction (Albert et al., 1995) have all been demonstrated to substantially impact estimated rates of cognitive decline. Moreover, these processes, though increasing in prevalence and severity with age, are not strongly correlated with chronological age in cross-sectional analysis. The identification of normative changes may depend on the identification of non-normative changes.

Statistical and Inferential Issues Associated With Sampling Populations, Variables, and Time

The challenges we face in developmental and aging research are traditional ones, involving trade-offs and solutions that are less than optimal. Many of these represent barriers to progress and synthesis in the current literature. Cooperative efforts based on currently available data provide an opportunity to move beyond these limitations.

Sampling People

Generalizations to defined populations of aging individuals must be conditional on historical (birth cohort) and cultural differences. Several major longitudinal studies have obtained multiple sequential cohort samples that permit comparisons across birth cohorts, cross-sectionally and longitudinally (e.g., the Seattle Longitudinal Study). More generally, longitudinal studies on aging often differ from one another in terms of birth cohort or nationality, permitting a basis for historical and cultural comparisons. The issue of population representativeness is also critical to address (see chap. 4, this volume), but there are trade-offs here as well. It may be that we can learn a great deal about basic psychological processes even when our samples are not sufficiently representative (or are of unknown representation) of a population of aging individuals, particularly if we can demonstrate generalizability across studies differing in sampling characteristics (e.g., country, race/ethnicity).

One often-overlooked aspect of inference to defined populations relates to mortality selection. Numerous studies have demonstrated a relatively strong link among age-related outcomes, participant nonresponse, and survival. Studies limited to between-person age differences must generally ignore important population processes associated with attrition and mortality selection. Longitudinal studies with follow-up to age at death, however, permit direct inference to populations defined by both age and survival (Harel, Hofer, Hoffman, Pedersen, & Johansson, 2007; Hofer & Hoffman, 2007). The mortality selection dynamic cannot be understood by single-occasion sampling of different age groups in which selection has already occurred to different degrees and possibly for different reasons. Analyses of longitudinal data provide the opportunity to directly address attrition and mortality selection, which are essential for understanding aging-related changes in health and cognitive outcomes.

A related issue is inappropriate aggregation in the analysis of age-heterogeneous data. The analysis of within-person variability and covariation requires that higher-order levels of between-person differences and within-person change be fully accounted for (i.e., modeled) because unmodeled functions will produce spurious associations. In age-heterogeneous cross-sectional studies, associations among age-dependent processes may arise due to average population age differences and not necessarily from associations between individual "rates of change" (see Hofer, Flaherty, & Hoffman, 2006; Hofer & Sliwinski, 2001, for derivation of cross-sectional covariances from a linear change model). This is one probable reason why between-person estimates of association across age-dependent variables differ from associations based on within-person rates of change. Analysis of age-heterogeneous longitudinal studies may also show upwardly biased correlations among rates of change due to age-based periods of relatively greater change unless between-person age is included in the model (Hofer et al., 2003; Hofer, Sliwinski, & Flaherty, 2002).

Sampling Variables

It is difficult to gauge differences across studies with samples from different birth cohorts or different countries, in large part because the measurements themselves differ. Certainly, measurements used 30 or 40 years ago may not be the ones used today. However, although different studies use different variables to identify particular constructs, most studies permit comparison of constructs at the primary factor level.

A major step in comparing results across studies involves identifying comparable variables or harmonizing the data. The similarity of a measure can vary at a number of levels, and within a single nation large operational differences can be found (e.g., Weiner, Hanley, Clark, & Van Nostrand, 1990). When considering cross-cultural or cross-national data sets these differences can be magnified: Regardless of whether the same measure has been used, differences are inevitably introduced due to language, administration, and item relevance. Furthermore, sampling characteristics can be strikingly different such that results from different studies may reflect different sections of the population. A balance must be found between optimal similarity of administration, similarity of meaning, and significance of meaning—avoiding unreasonable loss of information or lack of depth. These challenges must clearly be addressed in a collaborative endeavor, but in fact they are also critical to general development of the field, because without some means for comparison, research findings lack validation. Recall the common theme in the literature reviews discussed above.

For collaborating studies, the opportunity arises to reach a consensus regarding measurement comparability before, rather than after, the research process, or at least prior to analysis. Two classic methods for harmonizing are use of national or international standards and finding a "common denominator." For example, in CLESA, commercial medication names were converted to generic names and, under supervision of qualified experts, coded according to the Anatomical Therapeutic Chemical classification system. Cause of mortality was coded according to the *International Classification of Disease—9* (World Health Organization, 1977). Addressing the issue of common information, self-reported medical conditions were included if they appeared in at least three of the six countries involved in the project (Minicuci et al., 2003).

CLESA investigator working groups made extensive use of common denominators to harmonize their variables, including the use of algorithms to create comparable variables. Cognitive and depression scores, which were based on different measures or parts of measures in the different studies, were rescored as proportion of total possible score (e.g., see Cohen, Cohen, Aiken, & West, 1999). Challenging situations inevitably arise, and a system for dealing with exceptions must be developed. In CLESA, some levels of a variable were coded as "not applicable" and presumably treated as zero or as missing in analysis (e.g., difficulty in falling asleep "sometimes" was coded "na" [not applicable] for the country that had not provided that response option). Similarly, CLESA investigators coded instrumental activities of daily living according to a single common variable based on the three items held in common across the six countries, each recoded dichotomously in terms of independence. To avoid relying solely on this very simplified coding, however, three further activity variables and a global disability item available in four of the countries were included in the database. The latter could then be used in analyses of the subset of studies with available data (Minicuci et al., 2003).

Continuing with CLESA, which should be commended for provision of excellent detail regarding the harmonization process, it is clear that there will be limits to any such process. For several sociodemographic variables such as occupation category, although a common format was established, the researchers acknowledged that the large cross-country differences reflected unavoidable cultural- and sample-related differences (Minicuci et al., 2003). Although these difficulties might be reduced in collaborations initiated prior to data collection, Nordic Research on Aging investigators have cautioned that "linguistic equivalence does not guarantee semantic equivalence" (Oden, Viidik, & Heikkinen, 2002). CLESA social network and support variables were similarly a challenge to harmonize, because of both wording and categorizing differences in the already collected data (Zunzunegui et al., 2006). As a result, only variables available in at least three countries were harmonized. It is relevant to note, however, that the process of harmonization itself provides valuable insight into study differences that must be considered when comparing results. These can also provide excellent material for follow-up hypotheses in a meta-analytic framework.

In contrast to CLESA, which relied on investigator working groups for the harmonization process, the Collaborative Alcohol-Related Longitudinal Project harmonization was carried out by a core staff and was assessed and refined by the collaborating investigators (Johnstone et al., 1991). The Asia Pacific Cohort Studies Collaboration (APCSC) relies on statistical analysis, writing, and executive committees that interact with principal collaborators in the participating studies.

For studies with ongoing data collection, investigators might agree to add variables that their studies would then hold in common. Members of the European Birth-Lifecourse-Studies project, for example, have handled cohort differences by changing questions where content is culturally dependent (e.g., those regarding types of food eaten) for future waves. Similarly, they, among others, have discussed the addition of items to strengthen their ability to address common outcomes. In the case of data and sampling differences across studies that are difficult to reconcile, new extensions to meta-analysis, which we discuss below, provide exciting possibilities for maximal use of all available data.

Sampling Time

The temporal characteristics of change and variation must be taken into account, because different sampling intervals will likely lead to different results requiring different interpretations for both within- and between-person processes (Boker & Nesselroade, 2002; M. Martin & Hofer, 2004). For example, correlations of change in two variables over time will likely be quite different for short temporal intervals (minutes, hours, days, or weeks), in contrast to change across many years, as is the case for many of the longitudinal studies on aging. Measurement interval is similarly critical for the prediction of outcome variables and for establishing evidence regarding leading versus lagging indicators (Gollob & Reichardt, 1987, 1991).

The selection of intervals between measurements is also critical for separating effects of repeated testing (i.e., learning) from those of development/aging over longer periods of time. Estimates of longitudinal change may be attenuated due to gains occurring as a result of repeated testing, potentially persisting over long intervals (e.g., Willis & Schaie, 1994). Complicating matters is the potential for improvement to occur differentially, which could be related to ability level, age, or task difficulty and which may be due to any number of related influences, including warm-up effects; initial anxiety; and test-specific learning, such as learning content and strategies for improving performance. Differential retest gains such as these confound the identification of differential age-related changes (i.e., in older adults, retest effects may be manifest not as an increase in performance but as an attenuated decrease in performance). In most studies, retest effects are perfectly confounded with age changes and do not permit decomposition of effects at an individual level (see chap. 17, this volume; Thorvaldsson, Hofer, Berg, & Johansson, 2006). Intensive study designs, such as those involving measurement bursts with widely spaced sets of intensive measurements, are required to distinguish short-term learning gains from long-term aging-related changes (e.g., change in asymptotic performance; Sliwinski, Hofer, & Hoffman, 2006).

In addition to sampling time within individuals there are numerous ways to conceptualize and model change over time, and the choice of time process models is critical for the interpretation and understanding of change processes (Hofer & Sliwinski, 2006). Change models typically are based on age, or on time in study with chronological age included as a covariate, making level and rate of change conditional on age. Age- and time-based models are equivalent in single or narrow age cohort samples, but in age-heterogeneous samples the use of age-based models may not be appropriate without tests of the convergence of between-person age differences and within-person age changes (e.g., evaluated in the age-based model by including between-person age at Time 1 as a covariate, as in the time-in-study metric). However, time is better treated more flexibly and directly in terms of other evolving time-dependent processes, such as disease progression (e.g., time prior to or since diagnosis of dementia; Sliwinski et al.,

2003; chap. 28, this volume), measured physiological changes, mortality (see chap. 17, this volume), or events such as retirement or widowhood to understand the effects of stress and psychosocial functions on cognitive outcomes. Such models provide a useful perspective for describing and explaining average change and individual variation in change relative to particular theoretical models for intraindividual change—essentially aligning individuals with common, possibly causal, processes.

Comparing Results Across Studies: Coordinated Analysis, Meta-Analysis, and Evidence Synthesis

Science typically proceeds sequentially, with replication of results often taking years to complete. A key component of collaborative approaches is the potential for immediate cross-validation of research findings. This can be achieved through parallel analysis or reanalysis of data from multiple studies.

Parallel Analysis

In addition to the use of similar measures, the implementation of parallel and of pooled analyses also facilitates comparison of results from unrelated studies. Parallel analyses providing parameter estimates based on the same statistical model (i.e., same method, covariates, control variables, etc.) can more straightforwardly be included in a meta-analytic comparison framework. Such parallel analyses can be conducted independently or can be conducted in a more centralized way by a designated group. For example, Thorvaldsson, Hofer, Skoog, and Johansson (2007) used data from the Gothenburg H-70 study to explicitly replicate terminal decline findings of Sliwinski, Stawski, Katz, Verghese, and Lipton (2006) in Bronx Aging Study data. Using the Sliwinski manuscript as a guide, they found gratifying similar results. In contrast, core staff from the Collaborative Alcohol Project conducted parallel analyses of primary data from relevant subsets of the 39 affiliated studies and combined the results using meta-analysis (Fillmore et al., 1991). Similarly, the APCSC researchers have reported pooled analyses while paying careful attention to participant characteristic differences (e.g., age, gender) across studies.

Independent Versus Centralized Analyses

Having a data analysis core to implement the parallel analyses ensures the availability of resources for implementation of the agreed-upon models, but individual studies can also be encouraged to run their own parallel models. To reduce the impact of constraints and data loss through common denominator problems, each study can also be encouraged to conduct more extensive analyses on the core research questions, making use of more elaborated versions of the key variables and adding relevant variables that might be unique to their own project. In this way, both maximally comparable and maximally rich methods can be applied to each research question.

There are advantages to centralized as well as to distributed approaches to parallel analysis. Whereas centralized analyses facilitate careful scrutiny of sampling and measurement differences across studies, distributed analyses may better protect against capitalizing on chance and overmanipulation of data. As in many situations, a combination of both approaches may be most productive. Centralized analysis, as in the Collaborative Alcohol project, allows the clearest view of the individual study differences, because a single set or group of eyes becomes familiar with the sampling and other idiosyncrasies of each data set. This represents a strength in terms of identifying specific differences that might be due to sampling or other factors and would lead naturally into tests of hypotheses regarding the source of divergent results. It is an open question whether this can be equally well attained if everyone conducted the same exploratory data analysis and a smaller group assembled and evaluated the results. Keeping the analyses completely independent, as did Sliwinski, Stawski, et al. (2006) and Thorvaldsson et al. (2007), may, on the one hand, provide a more powerful cross-validation but may, on the other hand, be more limited in terms of testing hypotheses regarding differences if one has not first taken an interim realigning or harmonizing step.

Although the literature does not currently contain the information necessary to conduct meta-analyses of within-person questions, these methods can be used to evaluate the consistency of the findings produced in such parallel analyses. As in Fillmore's (e.g., Fillmore et al., 1988, 1991; Johnstone et al., 1991) alcohol work, and the APCSC's medical research, it would be possible to estimate average effect sizes, identify inconsistencies across studies, and evaluate the impact of specific cross-study differences (at group and individual levels) on these inconsistencies.

Meta-Analysis and Research Synthesis

The terms *meta-analysis* and *evidence synthesis* refer to approaches for combining data sets and evaluating models. Where parallel analyses of sufficiently similar variables are available, meta-analytic methods can be used to summarize findings and to identify and address variability across studies (Higgins & Thompson, 2002). Differences across studies can be due to study-level (e.g., design features or inclusion criteria) or to individual-level (e.g., education level or age) effects. Pooled raw data analyses, as opposed to pooling of summaries, are required to address questions related to individual-level effects (Stewart & Parmar, 1993).

Comparison of parameters based on models estimated on different variables, different measurement intervals, and different population and sampling characteristics presents another challenge, however. This challenge can be addressed with new methods in which well-developed meta-analytic methods are being extended to permit statistical synthesis of evidence from qualitatively different types of data. For example, various extensions of the basic meta-analysis framework have been used to combine multiple indirect sources of evidence on treatment or exposure effects in what is sometimes termed a *chain of evidence* (Ades, 2003). Bayesian hierarchical models also form the basis of methods for combining data from different types of study (Spiegelhalter, Abrams, & Myles, 2004). This is sometimes termed *generalized evidence synthesis* and requires careful consideration of the relationships between parameters across data sets (Spiegelhalter & Best, 2003). Such ideas extend naturally to the combined analysis of different longitudinal studies on aging with analysis across domains of health, cognition, and personality/affect. Analyses gauging sensitivity to different assumptions about the relationships between parameters across data sets and the likely size and direction of any biases can also be carried out to assess robustness of inference. Bayesian graphical models provide a natural framework for combining a series of local submodels, informed by different data sources, into a coherent global analysis. This approach can be used to carry out analyses that formally combine information from multiple data sets available within a network.

Integrative Analysis of Longitudinal Studies on Aging

Any question can be approached in a variety of ways. An ongoing challenge is to make optimal use of current data resources, while acknowledging their particular strengths and limitations and integrating and synthesizing knowledge based on different designs and approaches, particularly when they are contradictory. It is time to reflect on what we know and how we have come to know it. We must learn as much as possible from existing longitudinal studies, many of which were initiated 20 to 50 years ago and are still actively collecting data. What we learn from these studies should also inform the design new studies, ideally permitting direct comparison across birth cohorts.

We have been working to develop a collaborative research infrastructure for coordinated interdisciplinary, cross-national research aimed at the integrative understanding of within-person aging-related changes in health and cognition. The Integrative Analysis of Longitudinal Studies on Aging (IALSA) project is an open research network currently comprising 25 major longitudinal studies on aging. It serves as a resource for the application of best statistical methods for inference to aging individuals and defined populations. It will encourage the exploration of cross-cultural and cross-cohort effects and direct cross-validation of research findings across independent studies. We use the term *integrative* in several ways: referring to the integration of domains of study (i.e., health, cognition, personality, well-being) that, with notable exceptions, have generally been studied in isolation of one another, as well as to the integration of information across studies and across alternative statistical models. This program of research focuses primarily on explaining aging-related changes in the context of health (i.e., morbidity, comorbidity) and health-related change. We seek explanations that integrate cross-domain information on changes in cognition, health, personality (broadly defined to include well-being), and that also consider the impact of psychosocial characteristics, and contextual factors including sociodemographic characteristics, differences across nations, life events, and stressors. These important issues require macro-level theory and integrative science featuring the analysis of empirical studies that follow individuals over critical life periods.

Studies Involved in the Integrative Analysis of Longitudinal Studies on Aging Network

IALSA membership initially represented, mainly, investigators in the area of cognition and aging with whom we were already collaborating, or at least familiar. For the most part, their studies had a major focus on cognitive aging but also included varying amounts of information on physical and mental health as well as social and demographic variables. This selection strategy admittedly differs from that of, for example, CEHP, which focused on NIH-supported studies and set size, age, and construct criteria. However, we believed that a strong collaborative network could benefit from relying to some extent on existing links.

The 25 studies currently involved in the IALSA network span eight countries and include a total sample size of approximately 70,000. They represent a mix of representative, volunteer, and special population (e.g., veterans, college students, health maintenance organization) samples. Within the network, data have been collected on individuals aged 18 (from birth in one study) to over 100, with birth cohorts ranging from 1880 to 1980 and historical periods from 1946 to the present. Between-occasion intervals range from 6 months to 17 years (the majority are 1–5 years), with between 2 and 32 (mainly 3–5) measurement occasions spanning 4 to 48 years. Education levels vary from samples in which a sizable number have only elementary level education to those reporting mainly high school and beyond. All except one include data on both men and women. Three studies have single-age samples.

Table 27.2   Characteristics of Integrative Analysis of Longitudinal Studies on Aging Network Studies

Study Title and Acronym	Start Year	n (T1)	Age (T1)	Birth Cohorts[a]	Follow-Up (Years)	Intervals	Curr No. Occasions	Type Sample
Australian Longitudinal Study of Aging (ALSA)	1992	2,087	65–103	1891–1927	11	2, 6, 3	4	Stratified sample of community-dwelling individuals and those in residential care
Bonn Longitudinal Study of Aging (BOLSA)	1965	221	62–72	1893–1903	19	Varies	8	Community volunteer sample
Caerphilly Cohort Study of Older Men (CCS)	1979	2,512	45–59	1920–1934	25	4–5	6	Electoral register plus general-practitioner lists, male only
Canberra Longitudinal Study (CLS)	1991	897	70–93	1898–1921	14	3.5	5	Community sample (electoral role), institutional care, oversampling of very old
Cardiovascular Health Study (CHS)	1989	5,888	65+	-1924	10	1	10	Noninstitutionalized Medicare-eligible sample; minorities oversampled
Einstein Aging Studies (EAS)	1980	488	70–90	1890–1910	20	1	20	Volunteer sample
Aging in Women and Men (GENDER)	1995	498	69–81	1914–1926	8	4	3	Opposite-sex twins in Sweden born between 1906 and 1925
Gerontological and Geriatric Population Studies in Göteborg, Sweden (H-70)	1971	1,000	70	1901	29	2–5	12	Representative sample of Gothenberg 70 year olds
Health and Retirement Study (HRS) and AHEAD	1992	12,600	50–60	1932–1942	14	2	7–8	National sample, minorities oversampled
Healthy Older Person Edinburgh Study (HOPE)	1990	603	70+	1900–1918	4	4	3	Medical registry
Interdisciplinary Longitudinal Study of Adult Development (ILSE)	1996	1,384	45, 65	1931, 1951	4	4	2	Former East and West Germany
Long Beach Longitudinal Study (LBLS)	1978	509	55–87	1891–1923	21	2, 14	4	Recruited from health maintenance organization

(Continued)

Table 27.2 (Continued)

Study Title and Acronym	Start Year	n (T1)	Age (T1)	Birth Cohorts[a]	Follow-Up (Years)	Intervals	Curr No. Occasions	Type Sample
Longitudinal Aging Study Amsterdam (LASA)	1991	3,107	55–85	1906–1936	9	3	4	Urban and rural municipal registries
Longitudinal Study of Cognitive Change in Normal, Healthy Old Age (LSCC)	1982 1985	2,050 2,193	49–96	1886–1936	14	1–6	4	Community volunteer sample
National Survey of Health and Development (1946 British Birth Cohort Study) (NSHD)	1946	5,362	birth	1946	60	Varies	39	Nationally representative birth cohort sample
Nordic Research on Aging Study (NORA)	1989	1,204	75	1914	5	5	2	Representative city samples
Normative Aging Study (NAS)	1963	2,280	21–81	1882–1942	42	5	13	Male veterans
Origins of Variance in the Old-Old: Octogenarian Twins (OCTO-Twin)	1990	702	80+	1900–1910	8	2	5	Swedish Twin Registry
Oregon Brain Aging Study (OBAS) and Dementia Prevention Study (DPS)	1989+ 2000	258 214	55–107 85–94	1889–1945 1906–1915	0–18 0–6.5	6 & 12 mo	1–33 (16.5) 1–13	Community volunteers
Seattle Longitudinal Study (SLS)	1956	5,000+ cumulative	22–70	1880–1980	42	7	7	Health maintenance organization
Swedish Adoption Twin Study of Aging (SATSA)	1984	1,500	40–84	1900–1944	6	3	3	Swedish Twin Registry
Swiss Interdisciplinary Longitudinal Study on the Oldest-Old (SWILSO-O)	1994 1999	340 377	80–85	1909–1919	10 5	12 or 18 months	9 5	Stratified (age/sex), initially community-dwelling in an urban and a rural setting
University of North Carolina Alumni Heart Study (UNCAHS)	(1964) 1986 1992	(7,007) 4,989 1,154	(17–25) 40–48	1942–49	(40) 20 14	1.5	– 12 7	• Students—data on file • Joined study • Spouses
Victoria Longitudinal Study (VLS)	1986 1993 2002	484 530 570	55–85 55–85 55–85	1901–1931 1908–1938 1917–1947	15 9 0	3 3 —	6 4 1	Community volunteers
Wisconsin Longitudinal Study (WLS)	1957	10,317	18	1939	48	7–17	5	Random sample high school graduates

NOTES: T1 = Time 1; Intervals = between-occasion intervals; Curr = Current.

a. Computed from reported ages and dates.

Common Outcomes and Predictors

For cross-study analysis and comparison, we consider three levels of linkage: (1) broad construct, (2) narrow construct, and (3) identical indicator. Across most studies, broad conceptual replication (e.g., comparing different measures of verbal ability across studies) is possible in almost all of the domains considered here. In many of the studies, replication on more similar variables—for example, comparing memory for different word lists across studies—is possible. On a smaller subset of studies, opportunities are available for direct comparison of identical measures. Given the generally greater strength of conceptual replications, we consider exact replication necessary mainly because it will allow a more straightforward consideration of country-level differences (although language differences will remain for some comparisons). The types of variables, organized by domain, available in the longitudinal studies on aging that are currently part of the IALSA network are shown in Table 27.3, and we provide additional detail regarding the cognitive measures in this text. This information is available in a searchable database developed for the network.

General Mental Status. The MMSE is used in 12 of the affiliated data sets and will be evaluated in cross-study analysis, with some preliminary details provided here. Because it is a screening device, this measure does not provide good specificity compared with other cognitive assessments (e.g., Royall & Chiodo, 2004). However, analysis of the MMSE in large cross-national surveys will provide important details regarding sensitivity to hypertension-related changes and relative to other cognitive and memory measures. It is also commonly used in medical and epidemiological studies that might not have other cognitive measures and so will provide a good link to this literature.

Verbal/Crystallized Knowledge. Many of the studies use at least one of the Wechsler Adult Intelligence Scales (e.g., Wechsler Adult Intelligence Scale—Revised [WAIS–R]; Wechsler, 1981) Verbal measures, with Vocabulary (seven studies), Synonyms (five studies) and Similarities (eight studies, plus two with AH4 [Heim,

1970]) the most common. In at least three studies, however, idiosyncratic or short forms (e.g., three items) of the measures were used. The National Adult Reading Test (NART; Nelson & Willison, 1991; five studies) and the Mill Hill Vocabulary Scale (Raven & Raven, 1988) are also used.

Reasoning. The WAIS Block Design subtest (in eight studies) is the most commonly used measure of reasoning. Factor-level similarities among matrices tests such as the Cattell Culture Fair Test (Cattell, 1963), the Raven Progressive Matrices (Raven, Raven, & Court, 1958), other matrices tests, and rotation tests such as Thurstone Primary Mental Abilities Spatial Orientation (Thurstone, 1948) (each available in three or fewer studies) will permit conceptual replication of general patterns. Differences between visual–spatial loaded tests and word series measures with a verbal basis can be expected, with the latter showing greater stability.

Speed. Substitution coding (e.g., WAIS Digit Symbol [six studies], Symbol–Digit [two studies], Symbol–Letter Modalities [two studies], and Alphabet Coding [two studies]) and reaction time measures dominate the speed domain.

Memory. With the great interest in age-related memory changes, this domain is well represented in virtually all studies, but with this importance to the research community comes a great variety of measures. Although many of the studies use standard measures such as the WAIS Digit Span subtests (9 studies), the Wechsler Memory Scale Logical Memory Test (Wechsler, 1945, 4 studies), or the memory items from the MMSE, virtually all of the immediate and delayed word list recall tests (12 studies) are based on different words and different numbers of stimuli and exposures. This cross-study mix of similar and different measures, however, will allow us to make best use of the strengths of both conceptual and exact replication approaches.

Attention/Working Memory. WAIS Digit Span Backward (eight studies) and Serial 7s from the MMSE are the most common measures that can be considered to measure working memory.

Table 27.3 Variable Domains by Study in the Integrative Analysis of Longitudinal Studies on Aging Network

Domain Measures	ALSA	BOLSA	CCS	CLS	CHS	EAS	GENDER	H-70	HRS	HOPE	ILSE	LBLS	LASA	LSCC	NSHD	NORA	NAS	OBAS	OCTO-Twin	SATSA	SLS	SWIL SO-O	UNCAHS	VLS	WLS
Biomedical and physical functioning																									
General health																									
Height	x	x	x	x	x	x	x	x	x	x	x	x	x	x	x	x	x	x	x	x	x	x	x	x	x
Weight	x	x	x	x	x	x	x	x	x	x	x	x	x	x	x	x	x	x	x	x	x	x	x	x	x
Self-rated health—																									
Overall	x	x	x	x	x	x	x	x	x		x		x	x	x	x	x	x	x	x	x	x	x	x	x
Relative to age	x	x	x	x	x	x	x			x	x	x	x			x	x	x	x	x		x	x	x	x
Relative to past	x	x			x	x	x	x			x	x	x		x	x	x	x	x			x			x
Health conditions:																									
Self-report	x		x	x	x	x	x	x	x	x	x	x	x	x	x	x	x	x	x	x		x	x	x	x
Records/exam		x			x	x				x	x				x	x	x	x	x	x	x	x	x		
Prescribed meds	x	x	x	x	x	x	x			x	x		x	x	x	x	x	x	x	x	x	x	x	x	
Dental health	x			x				x		x				x	x	x			x	x	x	x	x		
Parents' longevity		x		x	x	x	x				x	x	x	x	x		x	x	x	x	x		x		
Death: Age/cause	x	x	x	x	x	x	x	x	x	x	x	x	x	x	x	x	x	x	x	x	x	x	x	x	x
Sensory																									
Auditory acuity	x	x	x		x	x	x	x	x	x	x		x		x	x	x	x	x	x		x	x	x	x
Visual acuity	x	x		x	x	x	x	x	x	x	x		x		x	x	x	x	x	x		x	x	x	x
Sensory disability	x			x	x	x	x							x	x		x			x					x
Hand grip strength	x			x	x	x	x		x	x	x				x	x	x	x	x	x				x	
Arm flexion					x	x	x									x	x	x	x	x					
Knee extension					x	x	x									x	x	x	x						
Cardiopulmonary																									
Hypertension	x	x	x	x	x	x	x	x	x	x	x	x	x	x	x	x	x	x	x	x	x	x	x	x	x

464

Domain Measures	ALSA	BOLSA	CCS	CLS	CHS	EAS	GENDER	H-70	HRS	HOPE	ILSE	LBLS	LASA	LSCC	NSHD	NORA	NAS	OBAS	OCTO-Twin	SATSA	SLS	SWIL SO-O	UNCAHS	VLS	WLS
Heart attack	x	x	x	x	x	x	x	x	x	x	x	x	x	x	x	x	x	x	x	x	x		x	x	x
Blood pressure	x	x	x	x	x	x	x	x	x	x	x	x	x		x	x	x	x	x	x	x		x	x	x
Heart rate	x		x	x	x	x	x	x					x	x	x	x	x	x	x	x	x			x	
Pulmonary function		x			x	x	x	x			x	x	x		x	x	x		x	x				x	x
Blood samples	x	x	x	x	x	x	x	x	x	x	x	x	x		x	x	x	x	x	x	x		x	x	
Cholesterol	x		x		x			x					x		x	x	x			x			x		
ECG			x	x	x			x					x		x	x	x		x						
Neurological/ neuropsychological																									
Gait					x	x	x	x							x	x	x		x					x	
Balance	x				x	x	x	x						x	x	x	x		x					x	
Tapping Test					x										x	x	x							x	
Finger agnosia						x		x											x						
Clock Test					x			x											x	x					
Other				x														x						x	
Cerebrovascular/ dementia																									
Stroke	x		x	x	x	x	x	x	x				x	x	x		x		x	x	x		x	x	x
Dementia																									
Diagnosis			x	x				x	x								x	x	x	x					
Questionnaires			x					x									x	x	x	x				x	
Genetic risk: ApoE	x			x	x			x						x					x	x	x			x	
Other systemic illness																									
Diabetes	x	x	x	x	x	x	x	x	x	x	x	x	x	x	x		x	x	x	x	x		x	x	x
Cancer	x	x	x	x		x	x	x	x	x	x	x		x	x	x	x		x	x	x		x	x	x
Somatic																									
Fatigue					x	x	x	x			x	x				x						x			x	
Pain	x		x		x	x	x	x	x		x		x			x			x	x		x		x	x
Health behaviors																									
Drug use	x				x	x	x	x			x	x	x	x	x	x	x	x	x	x		x		x	
Alcohol use	x	x	x	x	x	x	x	x	x		x	x	x	x	x	x	x	x	x	x		x	x	x	x
Tobacco use	x	x	x	x	x	x	x	x			x	x	x	x	x	x	x	x	x	x		x	x	x	x
Diet				x	x	x	x	x			x	x	x	x	x	x	x	x	x	x	x	x	x	x	x
Exercise			x	x	x	x	x	x	x		x	x	x	x	x	x	x	x	x	x	x	x	x	x	x

(Continued)

Table 27.3 (Continued)

Domain Measures	ALSA	BOLSA	CCS	CLS	CHS	EAS	GENDER	H-70	HRS	HOPE	ILSE	LBLS	LASA	LSCC	NSHD	NORA	NAS	OBAS	OCTO-Twin	SATSA	SLS	SWIL SO-O	UNCAHS	VLS	WLS
Functional capacity																									
Activities of daily living (ADL)	x			x		x	x	x	x	x	x		x	x	x	x	x	x	x	x		x		x	
Instrumental ADL	x			x		x	x	x	x	x	x		x	x	x	x	x	x	x	x					
ADL (apparatus)			x			x		x						x					x	x					
Activity level	x			x		x	x	x	x	x				x	x	x	x	x		x	x	x		x	
Hobbies				x		x	x	x		x		x		x	x	x	x			x		x			
Home help						x	x	x		x				x	x	x				x		x			
Cognitive functioning																									
Crystallized knowledge																									
NART	x		x	x		x									x										
Vocabulary	x		x	x		x		x				x		x	x	x			x	x	x			x	
Synonyms		x					x																		
Comprehension	x															x									
Information	x					x												x	x	x					
Similarities	x		x	x		x			x				x	x				x	x	x					x
Fluid reasoning																									
Arithmetic	x							x													x				
Series											x										x				
Matrices	x					x		x					x	x	x				x	x				x	
Rotation											x							x							
Block Design	x					x		x			x					x		x	x	x	x			x	
Object Assembly	x										x									x					
Picture	x																								
Arrangement																									
Picture	x									x								x							
Completion																									
General Aptitude																x									x

Domain Measures	ALSA	BOLSA	CCS	CLS	CHS	EAS	GENDER	H-70	HRS	HOPE	ILSE	LBLS	LASA	LSCC	NSHD	NORA	NAS	OBAS	OCTO-Twin	SATSA	SLS	SWIL SO-O	UNCAHS	VLS WLS
Speed																								
Substitution coding	x	x		x	x	x					x		x	x		x		x	x	x			x	x
Number copy task			x			x																		x
Figure identification							x	x											x	x				
Identical pictures						x											x				x		x	x
Number comparison											x													
Finding A/I/O		x	x	x									x	x	x						x	x		
Reaction time		x	x	x		x										x								x
Memory																								
Digit Span		x				x		x	x		x		x	x		x	x	x	x	x				
Free recall			x			x		x	x		x	x	x	x	x	x	x	x	x	x	x			
Delayed						x		x	x		x		x	x	x	x	x	x			x			
Recognition	x		x	x		x	x	x			x	x						x	x	x			x	x
Prose recall			x			x			x		x	x	x			x		x	x				x	x
Cued recall			x			x																		x
MIR Memory Test								x											x					
Incidental memory	x		x						x					x										
Coin Test								x	x										x					
Mental Status Exams																								
Mini-Mental	x	x		x	x	x	x	x	x	x			x			x		x	x	x				x
Blessed					x													x		x	x			

(Continued)

467

Table 27.3 (Continued)

Domain Measures	ALSA	BOLSA	CCS	CLS	CHS	EAS	GENDER	H-70	HRS	HOPE	ILSE	LBLS	LASA	LSCC	NSHD	NORA	NAS	OBAS	OCTO-Twin	SATSA	SLS	SO-O (SWIL)	UNCAHS	VLS	WLS
Attention																									
Serial 7s	x						x	x	x											x					
Backward Span		x				x	x	x								x	x		x						
Other		x	x			x																		x	
Word fluency																									
Category				x		x								x	x		x	x				x		x	
FAS	x	x	x			x						x		x	x	x	x	x			x				
Boston Naming	x					x										x	x	x			x				
Self-rated cognition																									
Cognition					x		x			x								x				x			
Memory				x		x	x	x	x			x	x	x		x	x		x	x		x	x	x	
Metamemory	x						x	x	x		x	x	x		x		x		x	x			x	x	
Psychosocial and demographic																									
Personality																									
Eysenck				x		x					x	x		x	x		x		x	x			x		x
NEO				x							x	x		x						x					x
Type A behavior																	x			x					
Behavioral rigidity		x																			x				
Self-esteem	x	x								x			x	x		x							x	x	
Other		x				x	x						x			x	x						x		

468

Domain Measures	ALSA	BOLSA	CCS	CLS	CHS	EAS	GENDER	H-70	HRS	HOPE	ILSE	LBLS	LASA	LSCC	NSHD	NORA	NAS	OBAS	OCTO- Twin	SATSA	SLS	SWIL SO-O	UNCAHS	VLS	WLS
Interpersonal functioning																									
Social networks	x	x		x	x	x	x	x	x		x	x	x	x	x	x	x		x	x	x	x	x		x
Network history					x	x	x	x								x	x		x	x		x	x		
Support/help	x		x	x	x	x	x	x			x		x	x	x	x	x		x	x		x	x	x	
Loneliness					x	x	x	x			x		x			x			x	x		x			x
Personal control																									
General	x			x			x	x			x		x	x					x	x		x	x		
Health	x						x												x						
Memory/cognitive														x				x							
Mastery																	x							x	x
Life satisfaction/ mental health																									
Mood/depression	x	x	x	x	x	x	x	x	x		x	x	x	x	x	x	x	x	x	x		x	x	x	x
Life satisfaction	x	x	x	x			x	x			x		x		x	x	x		x	x	x	x	x	x	x
Morale	x										x		x			x									
Self-rated emotional health						x	x		x				x			x									
Quality of life	x				x																				
Stress/life events																									
Life events	x			x		x	x				x		x	x	x	x	x		x	x		x	x		
Anxiety/agitation			x								x		x		x		x			x			x		
Perceived stress						x	x				x		x	x		x	x						x		
Illness/handicap related to job							x		x						x			x							x
Demographics																									
Education	x	x	x	x	x	x	x	x	x	x	x	x	x	x	x	x	x	x	x	x	x	x	x	x	x
Occupation	x	x	x	x	x	x	x	x	x	x	x	x	x	x	x	x	x	x	x	x	x	x	x	x	x
Socioeconomic status	x	x	x	x	x	x	x	x	x	x	x	x	x	x	x	x	x	x	x	x	x	x		x	x
Family income	x	x			x	x	x	x	x	x	x	x	x	x	x	x	x					x		x	x
Marital status	x	x	x		x	x	x	x	x	x	x	x	x	x	x	x	x		x	x	x	x	x	x	x
Living arrangement	x	x		x	x	x	x	x	x	x	x	x	x	x	x	x	x		x	x	x	x		x	x
Employment history								x			x				x			x		x			x	x	x

NOTE: Study acronyms are presented in Table 27.2.

Word Fluency. This domain, which does not fit clearly into either verbal ability or memory, is measured mainly by category (seven studies, some using different categories) and first letter (FAS) word fluency (three studies). Category word fluency has also been used as a measure of executive function.

Coordinated Research Process

The coordinated research process begins with a project proposal that delineates the problem, briefly cites relevant research, and details a preliminary protocol for analysis and structure of results.

1. The searchable database is used to identify studies with targeted variables and characteristics that permit implementation of the analysis. Investigators on these studies are alerted to the proposal and collaborate on developing the protocol in terms of available variables (coding differences) and plans for analysis.

2. Preliminary analyses begin by finalizing a protocol for harmonizing variables and development of statistical analysis by the leading project.

3. Parallel analyses will then be performed independently by each group of researchers (or in some cases by the Statistics Core or a single research team) and reported in common format.

4. Results will be combined in tables and figures to identify differences and to permit the discussion of alternative models and follow-up analyses, including pooled, meta-analysis, and evidence synthesis.

5. The process is completed by submission for publication of each study's findings and a summary paper describing the cross-study comparison of results.

Exemplar Analysis

Seven members of the IALSA network have contributed to initial analyses addressing the within-person changes in MMSE with age (Piccinin et al., 2006). Remarkable similarity was found in the rate of change in scores of the MMSE. On average, at age 80 years (85 for the Gothenburg "H-70" study), individuals scored between 25 and 27 on the MMSE and, assuming a linear trend, declined about 0.3 points per year. Consistent with this, older individuals tended to score lower initially (0.1–0.2 point per year) and decline at a faster rate (0.01–0.08 more decline per year). Marked country and birth cohort differences in educational attainment range from an average of 6 or less years in the 1900 birth cohorts in Sweden to 12 in the more recent U.S. birth cohorts. Focusing on studies with similarly coded education, more highly educated participants have higher initial scores (0.2 to 0.4 point) and show less decline (0.02–0.09). Figures 27.1 and 27.2 show expected trajectories for men and women, respectively, of several representative ages (e.g., 75, 80, 85), for the studies with similarly coded education, based on the parameter estimates from the independent analyses.

The IALSA network takes a coordinated and collaborative approach to the integrative understanding of aging, with particular focus on changes in health, cognition, and personality. This approach permits the identification and reconciliation of differences found across studies in terms of measurement; sampling; and demographic, social, and health indicators. The collaboration is broad, with extensive multidisciplinary expertise and interdisciplinary interests. The diversity of perspectives is maintained in the decision-making process and analysis protocol development, ensuring generalizability of results and evaluation of result sensitivity to decisions regarding harmonization of measurements, statistical analysis, and choice of theoretical models. The findings from this program of research will provide a basis for prevention and intervention efforts and inform health policy by identifying premorbid and subsequent changes associated with morbidity and comorbidity as well as the sociodemographic and psychosocial moderators of these changes.

OPTIMIZING FUTURE RESEARCH ON COGNITIVE AGING

What are the possible outcomes of the collaborative research described and proposed here? In addition to the clear potential to make confident strides in knowledge about the aging of cognitive capabilities, the collaborative nature of the

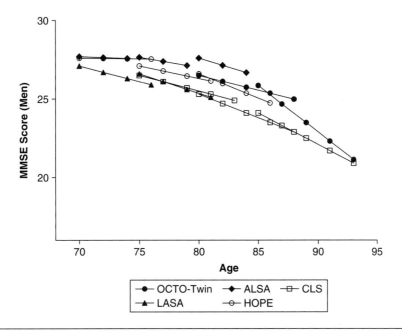

Figure 27.1   Predicted Mini-Mental State Examination (MMSE) Scores for Men From the OCTO-Twin, LASA, CLS, ALSA, and HOPE Longitudinal Studies

NOTE: Study acronyms are presented in Table 27.2.

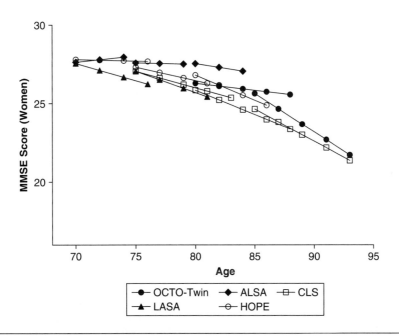

Figure 27.2   Predicted Mini-Mental State Examination (MMSE) Scores for Women From the OCTO-Twin, LASA, CLS, ALSA, and HOPE Longitudinal Studies

NOTE: Study acronyms are presented in Table 27.2.

work may facilitate the future application of what is learned—in terms of both substantive and methodological advances. Focused communications among investigators from different countries will increase the likelihood of the development of sensitive measures of within-person changes, optimally designed for trans-latability across languages and cultures. In addition, careful scrutiny of the variety of measurement intervals and sampling characteristics may lead to principled design recommendations for future longitudinal studies. The interdisciplinary nature of the work will contribute to the development of concrete and more elaborated public health recommendations.

Among the strengths of the proposed network model is the focus on progress of the field rather than individual careers, acceleration of the accumulative research process, and greater ability to study rare events. The benefits of coordinated, collaborative models for the analysis of existing longitudinal studies are many, and include the following:

1. Accelerated generation of knowledge from within-person studies on aging

2. Immediate replication and cross-validation of central hypotheses for development of theories of aging-related changes from a within-person perspective

3. Implementation of advanced statistical models across major studies

4. Training of individuals for state-of-the-art statistical modeling of longitudinal data

5. Opportunities for generalized evidence synthesis making optimal use of available study data and joining studies in ways that will advance knowledge further than possible in any particular study

6. Optimized comparison of measurements and of results from particular studies through harmonization of variables

7. Identification of measures for use in the next assessments or future studies to permit better comparative analysis

8. Cross-national comparison stratified by socioeconomic status, education, and health services

The major challenge in such endeavors remains the balancing of collaborative and competitive forces. Although language, cultural, demographic, design, and measurement differences across studies might also be seen as challenges, these exist in the current literature regardless and so can hardly be seen as a challenge to collaboration, only to cumulative science and understanding. Collaboration is in fact the most powerful tool with which to address the challenge of understanding aging from a within-person perspective.

REFERENCES

Ades, A. E. (2003). A chain of evidence with mixed comparisons: Models for multiparameter evidence synthesis and consistency of evidence. *Statistics in Medicine, 22,* 2995–3016.

Albert, M. S., Jones, K., Savage, C. R., Berkman, L., Seeman, T., Blazer, D., et al. (1995). Predictors of cognitive change in older persons: MacArthur Studies of Successful Aging. *Psychology and Aging, 10,* 578–589.

Almeida, D. M., & Horn, M. C. (2004). Is daily life more stressful during middle adulthood? In O. G. Brim, C. D. Ryff, & R. C. Kessler (Eds.), *How healthy are we? A national study of well-being at midlife* (pp. 425–451). Chicago: University of Chicago Press.

Anstey, K. J., & Christensen, H. (2000). Education, activity, health, blood pressure and Apolipoprotein E as predictors of cognitive change in old age: A review. *Gerontology, 46,* 163–177.

Bachrach, C. A., & Abeles, R. P. (2004). Social science and health research: Growth at the National Institutes of Health. *American Journal of Public Health, 94,* 22–28.

Bäckman, L., Ginovart, N., Dixon, R. A., Robins Wahlin, T.-B., Wahlin, Å., Halldin, C., et al. (2000). Age-related cognitive deficits mediated by changes in the striatal dopamine system. *American Journal of Psychiatry, 157,* 635–637.

Boker, S. M., & Nesselroade, J. R. (2002). A method for modeling the intrinsic dynamics of intraindividual variability: Recovering the parameters of simulated oscillators in multi-wave panel data. *Multivariate Behavioral Research, 37,* 127–160.

Brady, C. B., Spiro, A., III, & Gaziano, J. M. (2005). Effects of age and hypertension status on cognition:

The VA Normative Aging Study. *Neuropsychology, 19,* 770–777.

Brady, C. B., Spiro, A., McGlinchey-Berroth, R., Milberg, W., & Gaziano, J. M. (2001). Stroke risk predicts verbal fluency decline in healthy older men: Evidence from the Normative Aging Study. *Journal of Gerontology, 56B,* P340–P346.

Busse, E. W. (1969). Theories of aging. In E. W. Busse & E. Pfeiffer (Eds.), *Behavior and adaptation in later life* (pp. 11–32). Boston: Little, Brown.

Butz, W. P., & Torrey, B. B. (2006, June 30). Some frontiers in social science. *Science, 312,* 1898–1900.

Cattell, R. B. (1963). *The Cattell Culture Fair Test.* Champaign, IL: Institute for Personality and Ability Testing.

Cohen, P., Cohen, J., Aiken, L. S., & West, S. G. (1999). The problem of units and the Circumstance for POMP. *Multivariate Behavioral Research, 34,* 315–346.

Fillmore, K. M., Grant, M., Hartka, E., Johnstone, B. M., Sawyer, S., Spieflman, R., et al. (1988). Collaborative longitudinal research on alcohol problems. *British Journal of Addiction, 83,* 441–444.

Fillmore, K. M., Hartka, E., Johnstone, B. M., Leino, E. V., Motoyoshi, M. M., & Temple, M. T. (1991). Preliminary results from a meta-analysis of drinking behavior in multiple longitudinal studies. *British Journal of Addiction, 86,* 1203–1210.

Folstein, M. F., Folstein, S. E., & McHugh, P. R. (1975). *Mini-Mental State Examination.* Lutz, FL: Psychological Assessment Resources.

Fozard, J. L., Metter, E. J., & Brant, L. J. (1990). Next steps in describing aging and disease in longitudinal studies. *Journal of Gerontology, 45,* 116–126.

Frazier, L. D., Hooker, K., & Siegler, I. C. (1993). Longitudinal studies of aging in social and psychological gerontology. *Reviews in Clinical Gerontology, 3,* 415–426.

Gollob, H. F., & Reichardt, C. S. (1987). Taking account of time lags in causal models. *Child Development, 58,* 80–92.

Gollob, H. F., & Reichardt, C. S. (1991). Interpreting and estimating indirect effects assuming time lags really matter. In L. M. Collins & J. L. Horn (Eds.), *Best methods for the analysis of change: Recent advances, unanswered questions, future directions* (pp. 243–259). Washington, DC: American Psychological Association.

Haan, M. N., Shemanski, L., Jagust, W. J., Manolio, T. A., & Kuller, L. (1999). The role of APOE [ε]4 in modulating effects of other risk factors for cognitive decline in elderly persons. *Journal of the American Medical Association, 282,* 40–46.

Hall, C. B., Lipton, R. B., Sliwinski, M. J., & Stewart, W. F. (2000). A change point model for estimating onset of cognitive decline in preclinical Alzheimer's disease. *Statistics in Medicine, 19,* 1555–1566.

Harel, O., Hofer, S. M., Hoffman, L. R., Pedersen, N., & Johansson, B. (2007). Population inference with mortality and attrition in longitudinal studies on aging: A two-stage multiple imputation method. *Experimental Aging Research, 33,* 187–203.

Hassing, L. B., Hofer, S. M., Nilsson, S. E., Berg, S., Pedersen, N. L., McClearn, G. E., et al. (2004). Comorbid type 2 diabetes mellitus and hypertension exacerbates cognitive decline: Evidence from a longitudinal study. *Age and Ageing, 33,* 355–361.

Health Canada. (2002). *Review of longitudinal studies on aging.* Retrieved May 5, 2006, from http://www.cihr-irsc.gc.ca/e/10514.html

Heim, A. W. (1970). *AH4: Group Test of General Intelligence.* Windsor, UK: NFER-Nelson.

Hendrie, H. C., Albert, M. S., Butters, M. A., Gao, S., Knopman, D. S., Launer, L. J., et al. (2006). The NIH Cognitive and Emotional Health Project: Report from the critical evaluation study committee. *Alzheimer's & Dementia, 2,* 12–32.

Higgins, J. P., & Thompson, S. G. (2002). Quantifying heterogeneity in a meta-analysis. *Statistics in Medicine, 21,* 1539–1558.

Hofer, S. M., Berg, S., & Era, P. (2003). Evaluating the interdependence of aging-related changes in visual and auditory acuity, balance, and cognitive functioning. *Psychology and Aging, 18,* 285–305.

Hofer, S. M., Flaherty, B. P., & Hoffman, L. (2006). Cross-sectional analysis of time-dependent data: Problems of mean-induced association in age-heterogeneous samples and an alternative method based on sequential narrow age-cohorts. *Multivariate Behavioral Research, 41,* 165–187.

Hofer, S. M., & Hoffman, L. (2007). Statistical analysis with incomplete data: A developmental perspective. In T. D. Little, J. A. Bovaird, & N. A. Card (Eds.), *Modeling ecological and contextual effects in longitudinal studies of human development* (pp. 13–32). Mahwah, NJ: Lawrence Erlbaum.

Hofer, S. M., & Piccinin, A. M. (2007). Longitudinal studies. In J. E. Birren (Ed.), *Encyclopedia of gerontology: Age, aging, and the aged* (2nd ed.). Oxford, UK: Elsevier.

Hofer, S. M., & Sliwinski, M. J. (2001). Understanding ageing: An evaluation of research designs for assessing the interdependence of ageing-related changes. *Gerontology, 47,* 341–352.

Hofer, S. M., & Sliwinski, M. J. (2006). Design and analysis of longitudinal studies of aging. In J. E. Birren & K. W. Schaie (Eds.), *Handbook of the psychology of aging* (6th ed., pp. 15–37). San Diego, CA: Academic Press.

Hofer, S. M., Sliwinski, M. J., & Flaherty, B. P. (2002). Understanding aging: Further commentary on the limitations of cross-sectional designs for aging research. *Gerontology, 48,* 22–29.

Johnstone, B. M., Leino, E. V., Motoyoshi, M. M., Temple, M. T., Fillmore, K. M., & Hartka, E. (1991). An integrated approach to meta-analysis in alcohol studies. *British Journal of Addiction, 86,* 1211–1220.

Knopman, D., Boland, L. L., Mosley, T., Howeard, G., Liao, D., Szklo, M., et al. (2001). Cardiovascular risk factors and cognitive decline in middle-aged adults. *Neurology, 56,* 42–48.

Kuh, D., & The New Dynamics of Ageing (NDA) Preparatory Network. (2007). A life course approach to healthy aging, frailty, and capability. *Journal of Gerontology: Medical Sciences, 62A,* 717–721.

Martin, J., Bynner, J., Kalton, G., Boyle, P., Goldstein, H., Gayle, V., et al. (2006). *Strategic review of panel and cohort studies: Report to the research resources board of the Economic and Social Research Council.* Retrieved March 29, 2007, from http://www.longviewuk.com/pages/publications.shtml

Martin, M., & Hofer, S. M. (2004). Intraindividual variability, change, and aging: Conceptual and analytical issues. *Gerontology, 50,* 7–11.

Mednick, S. A., Harway, M., & Finello, K. (Eds.). (1984a). *Longitudinal research in the United States* (Vol. I). New York: Praeger.

Mednick, S. A., Harway, M., & Finello, K. (Eds.). (1984b). *Longitudinal research in the United States* (Vol. II). New York: Praeger.

Migdal, S., Abeles, R. P., & Sherrod, L. R. (1981). *An inventory of longitudinal studies of middle and old age.* New York: Social Science Research Council.

Minicuci, N., Noale, M., Bardage, C., Blumstein, T., Deeg, D. J., Gindin, J., et al. (2003). Cross-national determinants of quality of life from six longitudinal studies on aging: The CLESA project. *Aging Clinical and Experimental Research, 15,* 187–202.

National Research Council. (2000). *The aging mind: Opportunities for cognitive research.* Committee on Future Directions for Cognitive Research and Aging. Paul C. Stern and Laura L. Carstensen (Eds.). Commission on Behavioral and Social Sciences and Education. Washington, DC: National Academy Press.

National Research Council. (2001a). *Preparing for an aging world: The case for cross-national research.* Panel on a Research Agenda and New Data for an Aging World, Committee on Population and Committee on National Statistics, Division of Behavioral and Social Sciences and Education. Washington, DC: National Academy Press.

National Research Council. (2001b). *New horizons in health: An integrative approach.* Committee on Future Directions for Behavioral and Social Sciences Research at the National Institutes of Health. B. H. Singer and C. D. Ryff (Eds.). Washington, DC: National Academy Press.

Nelson, H., & Willison, J. R. (1991). *National Adult Reading Test (NART): Test manual* (2nd ed.). Windsor, UK: NFER-Nelson.

Nobel Round Table Discussions. (2006). Nobel round-table discussion #1: The future of interdisciplinary research and training. *Society for Experimental Biology and Medicine, 231,* 1225–1239.

Oden, B., Viidik, A., & Heikkinen, E. (2002). NORA—From conception to baseline and follow-up studies. *Aging Clinical and Experimental Research, 14*(Suppl. to No. 3), 1–5.

Park, H. L., O'Connell, J. E., & Thomson, R. G. (2003). A systematic review of cognitive decline in the general elderly population. *International Journal of Geriatric Psychiatry, 18,* 1121–1134.

Piccinin, A. M., Hofer, S. M., Anstey, K. J., Deary, I. J., Deeg, D. J. H., Johansson, B., et al. (2006, November). Cross-national IALSA coordinated analysis of age, sex, and education effects on change in MMSE scores. In S. M. Hofer & A. M. Piccinin (Chairs), *Integrative Analysis of Longitudinal Studies on Aging: Accounting for health in aging-related processes.* Symposium conducted at the annual conference of the Gerontological Society of America, Dallas, TX.

Raven, J. C., & Raven, J. E. (1988). *Mill Hill Vocabulary Scale*. London: HK Lewis.

Raven, J. C., Raven, J. E., & Court, J. H. (1958). *Standard Progressive Matrices*. Oxford, UK: Psychology Press.

Rowe, J. W., & Kahn, R. L. (1997). Successful aging. *The Gerontologist, 37,* 433–440.

Royall, D. R., & Chiodo, L. K. (2004). Executive control and the validity of survey data. *International Journal of Geriatric Psychiatry, 19,* 696–698.

Rubin, E. H., Storandt, M., Miller, J. P., Kinscherf, D. A., Grant, E. A., Morris, J. C., et al. (1998). A prospective study of cognitive function and onset of dementia in cognitively healthy elders. *Archives of Neurology, 55,* 395–401.

Schaie, K. W., & Hofer, S. M. (2001). Longitudinal studies in aging research. In J. E. Birren & K. W. Schaie (Eds.), *Handbook of the psychology of aging* (5th ed., pp. 53–77). San Diego, CA: Academic Press.

Schneider, W., & Edelstein, W. (Eds.). (1990). *Inventory of European longitudinal studies in the behavioural and medical sciences*. Berlin, Germany: Max-Planck-Institut für Bildungsforschung.

Seematter-Bagnoud, L., & Santos-Eggimann, B. (2006). Population-based cohorts of the 50s and over: A summary of worldwide previous and ongoing studies for research on health in ageing. *European Journal of Ageing, 3,* 41–59.

Siegler, I. C. (1989). Developmental health psychology. In M. Storandt & G. R. VandenBos (Eds.), *The adult years: Continuity and change* (pp. 122–142). Washington, DC: American Psychological Association.

Sliwinski, M., & Buschke, H. (1999). Cross-sectional and longitudinal relationships among age, memory and processing speed. *Psychology and Aging, 14,* 18–33.

Sliwinski, M. J., Hofer, S. M., & Hall, C. (2003). Correlated and coupled cognitive change in older adults with and without clinical dementia. *Psychology and Aging, 18,* 672–683.

Sliwinski, M. J., Hofer, S. M., & Hoffman, L. (2006, November). Applying a double negative-exponential model to separate short-term practice gains from long-term cognitive decline. In N. Ram, D. Gerstorf, & J. R. Nesselroade

(Chairs), Innovative Methods for Describing Developmental Change. Symposium conducted at the annual conference of the Gerontological Society of America, Dallas, TX.

Sliwinski, M., Lipton, R. B., Buschke, H., & Stewart, W. (1996). The effects of preclinical dementia on estimates of normal cognitive functioning in aging. *Journals of Gerontology Series B: Psychological Sciences and Social Sciences, 51,* P217–P225.

Sliwinski, M. J., Stawski, R. S., Katz, M., Verghese, J., & Lipton, R. (2006). On the importance of distinguishing pre-terminal and terminal cognitive decline. *European Psychologist, 11,* 172–181.

Spiegelhalter, D. J., Abrams, K. R., & Myles, J. P. (2004). *Bayesian approaches to clinical trials and health-care evaluation*. New York: Wiley.

Spiegelhalter, D. J., & Best, N. G. (2003). Bayesian approaches to multiple sources of evidence and uncertainty in complex cost-effectiveness modelling. *Statistics in Medicine, 22,* 3687–3709.

Stewart, L. A., & Parmar, M. K. (1993). Meta-analysis of the literature or of individual patient data: Is there a difference? *The Lancet, 341,* 418–422.

Thorvaldsson, V., Hofer, S. M., Berg, S., & Johansson, B. (2006). Effects of repeated testing in a longitudinal age-homogeneous study of cognitive aging. *Journal of Gerontology: Psychological Sciences, 61B,* P348–P354.

Thorvaldsson, V., Hofer, S. M., Skoog, I., & Johansson, B. (2007). *Onset of terminal decline in cognitive abilities in non-demented individuals*. Manuscript submitted for publication.

Thurstone, L. L. (1948). *Primary mental abilities*. Chicago: University of Chicago Press.

Verdonik, F., & Sherrod, L. R. (1984). *An inventory of longitudinal research on childhood and adolescence*. New York: Social Science Research Council.

Viidik, A. (Ed.). (2002). NORA studies. Nordic Research on Ageing: The five-year follow-up of the functional capacity of 75-year-old men and women in three Nordic localities [Special issue]. *Aging Clinical and Experimental Research, 14*(Suppl. to No. 3).

Waldstein, S. R. (2000). Health effects on cognitive aging. In P. C. Stern & L. L. Carstensen (Eds.), *The aging mind: Opportunities in cognitive research* (pp. 189–217). Washington, DC: National Academy Press.

Wechsler, D. (1945). A standardized memory scale for clinical use. *Journal of Psychology, 19,* 87–95.

Wechsler, D. (1981). *Wechsler Adult Intelligence Scale—Revised.* San Antonio, TX: The Psychological Corporation.

Weiner, J. M., Hanley, R. J., Clark, R., & Van Nostrand, J. F. (1990). Measuring the activities of daily living: Comparisons across national surveys. *Journal of Gerontology: Social Sciences, 45,* S229–S237.

Willis, S. L., & Schaie, K. W. (1994). Cognitive training in the normal elderly. In F. Forette, Y. Christen, & F. Boller (Eds.), *Plasticité cérébrale et stimulation cognitive* (pp. 91–113). Paris: Foundational National De Gérontologie.

Wilson, R. S., Beckett, L. A., Barnes, L. L., Schneider, J. A., Bach, J., Evans, D. A., et al. (2002). Individual differences in rates of change in cognitive abilities of older persons. *Psychology and Aging, 17,* 179–193.

World Health Organization. (1977). *International classification of diseases—9.* Geneva, Switzerland: Author.

Wulf, W. A. (1993, August 13). The collaboratory opportunity. *Science, 261,* 854–855.

Young, C. H., Savola, K. L., & Phelps, E. (1991). *Inventory of longitudinal studies in the social sciences.* Newbury Park, CA: Sage.

Zentralstelle für Psychologische Information und Dokumentation, Universistät Trier. (Ed.). (1995). *Inventory of European longitudinal studies in the behavioral and medical sciences: Update 1990–1994.* Trier, Germany: University of Trier.

Zunzunegui, M. V., Rodriguez-Laso, A., Otero, A., Pluijm, S. M. F., Nikula, S., Blumstein, T., et al. (2006). Disability and social ties: Comparative findings of the CLESA study. *European Journal of Ageing, 2,* 40–47.

28

TIME-BASED AND PROCESS-BASED APPROACHES TO ANALYSIS OF LONGITUDINAL DATA

MARTIN SLIWINSKI AND JACQUELINE MOGLE

The science of aging seeks to explain why individuals lose, gain, or maintain functioning in different domains (e.g., cognition, health, and emotion) as they transition from young adulthood through middle and into old age (Baltes, Staudinger, & Lindenberger, 1999; Wohlwill, 1973). Although aging research is concerned with how individuals *change* across the adult life span, aging theories are primarily informed by cross-sectional comparisons of how individuals *differ* as a function of their age. Average cross-sectional age differences may approximate the magnitude, on average, of longitudinal age change; however, cross-sectional data cannot unambiguously disentangle effects caused by aging versus stable individual-differences characteristics. Longitudinal data provide a unique opportunity to evaluate aging theories by testing key predictions about how changes in one variable (e.g., processing speed) relate to changes in other variables (e.g., memory). However, before attempting to explain why changes in one variable are associated with changes in another, researchers must accurately describe change on both variables. Providing a theoretically informed and informative

descriptive model of intraindividual change is by no means a trivial task.

The purpose of this chapter is to critically examine different analytic approaches that researchers have used to describe intraindividual change in longitudinal aging studies. The first is a time-based approach that formally represents intraindividual change in some variable (e.g., negative affect, memory) as a function of the passage of time. The second is a process-based approach that formally represents intraindividual change in some outcome as a function of concurrent (or lagged) changes in another variable. We examine some of the assumptions, the flexibility and the limitations of both of these approaches to modeling intraindividual change. This chapter is not intended to address the complexities of fitting specific statistical models to real data. Instead, this chapter addresses epistemological issues that pertain to the type of inferences supported by different approaches to testing hypotheses using longitudinal data. Issues pertaining to centering variables, estimation techniques, and model specification are all critically important for correctly interpreting results from fitting statistical models to longitudinal data. Any of several excellent textbooks (e.g., Diggle, Heagerty, Liang, & Zeger, 2002; Hedeker & Gibbons, 2006; Singer & Willett, 2003) would provide interested readers with guidance on the technical aspects of fitting growth curve models to longitudinal data.

CORRELATED AND COUPLED CHANGE

In their influential chapter on developmental methodology, Baltes and Nesselroade (1979) outlined five rationales or goals for longitudinal life span research:

1. Direct identification of intraindividual change

2. Direct identification of interindividual differences in intraindividual change

3. Analysis of interrelationships in behavioral change

4. Analysis of causes of intraindividual change

5. Analysis of causes of interindividual differences in intraindividual change

These goals clearly distinguish between intraindividual change and interindividual differences in intraindividual change. More specifically, Rationales 4 and 5 explicitly allow for different causal explanations of intraindividual change and interindividual differences in intraindividual change; that is, the reasons why a person sometimes experiences more rapid change than at other times might differ from the reasons why some individuals change differently than other individuals during a given time period. For example, the occurrence of a particular event (e.g., stroke, death of a spouse) might explain a sudden or abrupt change experienced by an individual (i.e., a cause of intraindividual change), whereas the presence or absence of a disease (e.g., diabetes) or stable individual characteristics (e.g., level of education) might account for why some people change differently than others. This distinction is especially salient because the overwhelming majority of longitudinal studies have focused exclusively on Rationale 5 while paying relatively little attention to Rationale 4. In fact, we believe that the literature reflects the view that the best (and perhaps only) way to explain why an individual is changing with advancing age is to identify the reasons why that person is

changing more (or less) than other individuals (i.e., explaining interindividual differences in intraindividual change).

Consider the following example to see how this commonly adopted approach maps onto theoretical predictions regarding causes of age-related cognitive decline. A hypothetical individual, Bob, is experiencing memory decline. The task of a successful aging theory is to explain why Bob's memory is declining. For example, processing speed theory (Salthouse, 1996) predicts that age-related declines in the speed of performing elementary cognitive operations impair higher-order cognitive function. The critical question is how to test this prediction using longitudinal information. The most common approach to answering this question is to compare Bob to other individuals (e.g., Pat and Sally) to identify what about Bob can explain why his memory decline is more (or less) rapid than that of others. Figure 28.1 displays this type of analysis, which in essence examines whether individual differences in the rate of intraindividual change in speed correlate with individual differences in the rate of change in memory. Consistent with the prediction of the speed hypothesis, there is a perfect (positive) correlation between rate of change in speed (on the abscissa) and rate of memory change (on the ordinate). Stated in other words, 100% of the between-person variance in rate of memory change is accounted for by between-person variance in rate of speed change.

The approach described in this example (or more sophisticated variants) is a common approach to testing hypotheses with longitudinal data. Given the strong between-person association in rate of memory and speed change in Figure 28.1 and bearing in mind inherent limitations of inferring causality from observational data, one might interpret this as providing evidence consistent with the claim that Bob's memory is declining because of his decline in processing speed. Alternatively, one might simply conclude that memory and speed are changing together, reflective of a common underlying cause. However, there is another way of analyzing longitudinal data to test aging hypotheses, as illustrated in Figure 28.2, that might lead to a different conclusion. The three plots in Figure 28.2 show the raw data from which the rate of change values plotted in

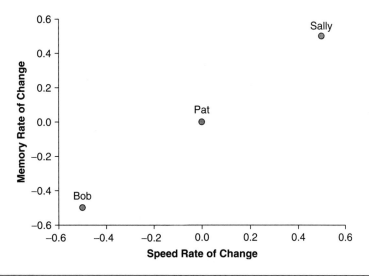

Figure 28.1   Correlated Change in Memory and Speed

Figure 28.1 were calculated: Bob shows average decline on both variables, Pat shows stability, and Sally shows an average increase on both variables. If we were to restrict our analyses to any single individual, however, we would see there is a different relationship between changes in speed and memory than was evident by examining between-person correlation for the average (or rate of) memory and speed change for all the individuals. We see that for any given person an *increase* in speed is accompanied by a concurrent *decrease* in memory, implying a negative association that contrasts with the positive correlation between rates of change; that is, Bob's memory declined by −0.75 between age 75 and 76, and his speed declined by −0.25 during that time. Then his memory declined less (by −0.25) between ages 76 and 77, but his speed declined more (by −0.75) during this time. These data present an interpretive challenge: How can we say that Bob's decline in speed explains his memory decline if his memory declines less when his speed declines more?

For clarity, we refer to the analysis of data in Figure 28.1 as *correlated change* and the analysis of data in Figure 28.2 as *coupled change*. The former describes whether individuals with higher (or lower) than average change in one variable also have higher (or lower) than average change in another variable. The latter describes whether changes in one variable

correspond to changes in another variable for any given individual during a given time interval. Neither approach is always correct or incorrect, but they address different questions. Correlated change can determine whether individuals change consistently on two variables, whereas coupled change can determine whether two variables travel together over time. The likelihood of such extreme disagreement between correlated and coupled change is low, and these two approaches have yielded consistent answers when applied to real data (e.g., Sliwinski & Buschke, 1999; 2004; Zimprich, 2002). However, it is certainly possible that one might obtain evidence of correlated change but not coupled change for two variables, or vice versa. This issue is one of the problems that arise from data aggregation, and interested readers are referred to an excellent discussion by Von Eye and Bergman (2003) of this issue as it pertains to longitudinal research.

The correlated versus coupled change distinction is also relevant for the distinction between time-based and process-based approaches to modeling intraindividual change. This distinction can be further clarified by considering the following models of intraindividual change:

$$\text{memory}_{ti} = a_{1i} + a_{2i}(\text{age}_{ti}) + r_{ti} \qquad (28.1)$$

$$\text{speed}_{ti} = b_{1i} + b_{2i}(\text{age}_{ti}) + r_{ti}, \qquad (28.2)$$

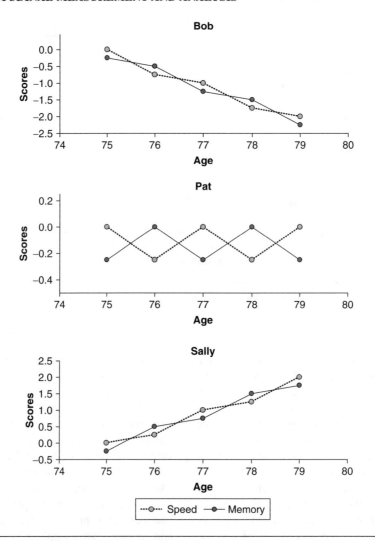

Figure 28.2   Coupled Change in Memory and Speed

which represent performance on memory (or speed) at time t in person i as a function of that person's intercept a_{1i} (or b_{1i}) and that person's rate of change with respect to age, signified by the slope a_{2i} (or b_{2i}) and a residual. Correlated change is then analyzed by examining how the a_2 and b_2 slope parameters covary across individuals. The coupled change approach to modeling intraindividual change is

$$\text{memory}_{ti} = a_{1i} + a_{2i}(\text{age}_{ti})$$
$$+ a_{3i}(\text{speed}_{ti}) + \varepsilon_{ti}, \qquad (28.3)$$

which represents change in memory performance not only as a function of changes in age but also as a function of (intraindividual) changes in speed. The extent of coupling is captured by the a_3 parameter. The two types of models also make different assumptions about how to describe intraindividual change on a given variable. The correlated change approach assumes that intraindividual change can be accurately described with reference only to the passage of time, which is indexed by chronological age in the case of Equations 28.1 and 28.2. In contrast, the coupled change approach assumes that change in the variable of interest is not only a function of the passage of time but also a function of a predictor or mediator that changes over time (e.g., speed). The correlated change model can also accommodate coupled change by allowing the within-person residuals to be correlated. However, this approach to representing coupled change in the residuals does not allow for change in one variable to mediate change in another—only by including a time-varying process variable in the model of intraindividual change can mediation be evaluated. Also, it is important to note that actually fitting these equations to real data would involve sensible decisions about how to center the variables to distinguish between cross-sectional (between-person) and longitudinal (within-person) influences (see Snijders & Bosker, 1999, pp. 80–81, and Sliwinski & Buschke, 2004).

These process-based analyses focus on coupled rather than correlated change. We should mention the recent innovation of the bivariate dual change score model (DCSM; McArdle & Hamagami, 2001) because this approach has also been used to examine the coupling of variables over time and has been used to evaluate theoretical predictions of lead-lag associations between two variables. Ghisletta and Lindenberger (2003) used the DCSM to demonstrate that perceptual speed is a leading predictor of changes in knowledge. This method has also been used to provide evidence that lifestyle activity is a leading predictor of subsequent cognitive change (e.g., Ghisletta, Bickel, & Lovden, 2006). This approach is useful for testing hypotheses regarding how individual differences on one variable (e.g., a measure of activity engagement) predict individual differences in subsequent change on another variable (e.g., cognitive performance). However, it is essential to note that this approach is at the between-person level of analysis and is therefore primarily useful for testing hypotheses that pertain to how people differ from each other, and not to how processes are associated within individuals across time. Because this approach does not focus on within-person relationships, the term *coupling* used to describe results from DCSM analyses means something different than how we have used this term.

The concept of "time" is a critical one in formulating a descriptive model of longitudinal change (for either the correlated or coupled change approach). However, one cannot formulate an appropriate descriptive model of intraindividual change without some theoretical notion of the "change function"; that is, one might ask whether change in memory is a function of age-graded processes or whether it is a function of other progressive processes that are only loosely related to chronological age, such as dementia or cardiovascular disease. Selecting the wrong time basis for this function can distort the true shape of the average intraindividual trajectory of change (Baltes & Labouvie, 1973; Hertzog & Nesselroade, 2003; Sliwinski, Hofer, & Hall, 2003). Therefore it is during the formulation of the descriptive or measurement model of intraindividual change (e.g., Raudenbush, 2002) that researchers must draw on their causal theory of aging. We now discuss how researchers have used various definitions of time to index intraindividual change.

TIME-BASED MODELS OF INTRAINDIVIDUAL CHANGE

Birren (1959) noted that chronological age may be the single most useful variable for characterizing a person's level of functioning but that, despite its utility as an index, it carries little or no explanatory value (Birren & Schroots, 1996). Although chronological age is often used to index change in functioning (e.g., Ghisletta & Lindenberger, 2003; McArdle, Ferrer-Caja, Hamagami, & Woodcock, 2002), other temporal metrics, such as time since baseline (e.g., Sliwinski & Buschke 1999; Wilson et al., 2002), time to study dropout (Sliwinski, Hofer, Hall, Buschke, & Lipton, 2003), time to dementia diagnosis (Hall, Lipton, Sliwinski, & Stewart, 2000), or time to death (Sliwinski et al., 2006; Thorvaldsson, Hofer, & Johansson, 2006; Wilson, Beckett, Bienias, Evans, & Bennett, 2003) have been used as well. The use of some time index for representing intraindividual changes in functioning is the most common approach to the analysis of longitudinal data. However, an important question is which index of time should be used for representing intraindividual psychological change.

If "aging," development, maturation, or senescence is of primary interest, then it seems sensible to represent change as a function of chronological age (e.g., McArdle et al., 2002). This is an especially important consideration if the rate of change varies as a function of age (e.g., decline is a quadratic function of age).

Age-graded increases in the rate of change can be represented either by plotting the observed value of some variable as a function of age (see Figure 28.3, Panel A) or by taking the first derivative of the change function and plotting the slope as a function of age (see Figure 28.3, Panel B). These plots represent the same information regarding change across the age range. Panel A in Figure 28.3 represents the predicted score as a function of age, which shows an accelerating decrease. Panel B shows that instantaneous rate of change (i.e., the slope) is becoming more negative (i.e., accelerating) with increasing age and is implied by the plot of the raw scores as a function of age. However, the situation becomes much more complicated when individuals vary substantially in age at their baseline assessment (Hertzog & Nesselroade, 2003) and when there are relatively little longitudinal data on any individual (i.e., the individuals vary in age by 50 years, but there are only 2 years of follow-up data). When follow-up information is limited, either in terms of duration or the number of testing occasions, then one must combine longitudinal information (i.e., information about intraindividual change) with cross-sectional information (i.e., information about age differences) to produce a composite estimate of change. This approach requires the *convergence assumption*, which postulates the equivalence of longitudinal (within-person) and cross-sectional (between-person) sources of age effects (McArdle & Bell, 2000).

Although this assumption can be tested (e.g., Mehta & West, 2000), in practice such testing is often difficult because the age range is much larger than the duration of follow-up for many longitudinal aging studies. Suppose that Panel A of Figure 28.3 describes the average trajectory from a longitudinal study in which individuals ranged in age at baseline by 20 years but that only 3 years of follow-up information was obtained on any given person. Three such individuals are indicated by the rectangles imposed on the trajectory in Panel A. The trajectory for any given individual would appear relatively linear, with evidence of accelerating change resulting primarily from between-person differences in age. Comparing rate of change across rectangles provides clear evidence that older people are changing more rapidly than younger people. However, examining the trajectories within any given rectangle (i.e., person) reveals very weak evidence that the rate of change was increasing for any given individual as he or she aged.

This situation would make it very difficult, if not impossible, to provide a fair statistical test of the convergence assumption. Data from studies with very wide age ranges and relatively little follow-up may not provide the information necessary to provide statistical evidence in support of convergence if it were to hold in the population.

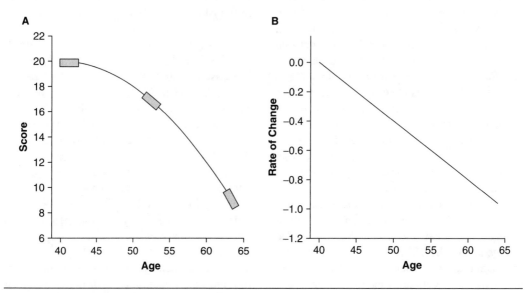

Figure 28.3   Change as a Quadratic Function of Age (A) and Its First Derivative (B)

Faced with such data, a researcher has two options: (1) represent intraindividual change as a (quadratic) function of age and assume convergence holds (e.g., McArdle et al., 2002), or (2) represent intraindividual change as a linear function of age (or time from baseline) and to allow rate of linear change to vary across individuals of different ages (e.g., Sliwinski & Buschke, 2004). A limitation of the first option is that the critical estimate of change (i.e., the acceleration coefficient) would mostly reflect static differences between persons (i.e., older people change more rapidly than younger people) rather than information about intraindividual change (i.e., that a person declines more rapidly as he or she ages). A limitation of the second approach is that it very likely provides an "incorrect" representation of intraindividual change assuming it is constant across a given individual's life span. We can offer no recommendation about which approach should be preferred that applies to all situations. However, we suggest that the first option would be a viable choice if there are strong reasons to believe that convergence holds or one has very specific questions about normative age effects. The second option would be preferred in the absence of strong external evidence of convergence or if the research focuses primarily on intraindividual change.

The choice of how to index time in the representation of intraindividual change matters, and it is critical to understand why. To understand why the choice of the time basis (e.g., chronological age, time from baseline, time to death) matters, consider a simple example of linear change. The data in Table 28.1 show values of a variable (Y) for a given individual obtained across 10 measurement occasions separated by 1 year. The column labeled "Study Time" shows the elapsed time in years relative to the baseline assessment. The column labeled "Age" shows the elapsed time in years relative to the date of this individual's birth, and the column labeled "Death" shows the time in years separating each testing occasion from the date on which the individual died. The bottom row of the table shows the estimated intercept and slope that describe changes in Y as a function of each time basis. This simple exercise shows that the selection of the time basis does not influence the estimate of change *for the individual*; that is, the

slope is invariant across different time indices, which really are all the same index, just centered at different dates (i.e., date of baseline, date of birth, date of death). A similar result would obtain for quadratic change—the acceleration coefficient would be constant across each time basis.

If the characterization of change for any given individual is equivalent regardless of the choice of the time basis for indexing change, why does the selection of the time basis matter? It matters because of how data are aggregated across individuals to estimate a typical or average curve that describes the pattern of intraindividual change. If individuals are misaligned according to a time index that does not reflect the progression of the causal processes driving change, then the estimate of the typical or average curve will be distorted. Baltes and Labouvie (1973) illustrated this effect by describing a circumstance in which change was piecewise linear for each individual, with the first piece reflecting stability in function and the second piece reflecting late life terminal decline (Berg, 1996; Riegel & Riegel, 1972). Aligning people with respect to age produced an average curve that did not describe the shape of the change function for any individual (Baltes & Labouvie, 1973, p. 174). In their review of methods for longitudinal aging research, Hertzog and Nesselroade (2003) pointed out that although such aggregation bias is a critical issue for

Table 28.1 Comparison of Different Definitions of "Time"

Y	Study Time	Age	Death
65	0	70	13
63	1	71	12
59	2	72	11
60	3	73	10
58	4	74	9
55	5	75	8
55	6	76	7
54	7	77	6
53	8	78	5
49	9	79	4
Intercept	64.11	173.14	43.86
Slope	−1.56	−1.56	1.56

longitudinal modeling of developmental change, "it has actually received relatively little attention in the literature describing newer modeling approaches to measuring change" (p. 642). We concur and now discuss some of the few recent studies that have attempted to address this critical issue.

We and our colleagues have described a set of analyses (Sliwinski, Hofer, & Hall, 2003; Sliwinski, Hofer, Hall, et al., 2003) that compared results from different longitudinal models that used different definitions of time to index change: chronological age, time to dementia diagnosis, time to death, and time to study dropout. Results differed substantially depending on the time index used to describe intraindividual change. For example, in a group of individuals with preclinical dementia (i.e., individuals who would develop clinical dementia but had not yet crossed the impairment threshold for diagnosis) we found that the rate of memory loss was not significantly higher compared with a group of nondementing individuals when intraindividual change was indexed using chronological age. There was also the counterintuitive finding of accelerating memory loss as a function of age in the nondemented individuals, but not in the demented individuals (Sliwinski, Hofer, & Hall, 2003). We reasoned that there was an important non-age-graded process driving change in the preclinical dementia group that reflected the progression of their dementing illness. Alternative analyses (Hall et al., 2000; Sliwinski, Hofer, & Hall, 2003) that indexed change relative to the time of clinical diagnosis fit the data substantially better than the age-based model and provided evidence of very rapid acceleration in the rate of memory loss in the preclinical group as their disease progressed. Figure 28.4 (Panels A and B) show raw data for preclinical individuals represented as a function of age and time to diagnosis, respectively. There is much more heterogeneity present in the age-based plot (Panel A) and little visual evidence of accelerating decline (which is counterintuitive given that these individuals were in the preclinical phase of dementia). The dementia-based plot (Panel B) shows less heterogeneity and clear evidence of accelerating memory decline proximal to the time of diagnosis. Using chronological age as the time basis

for representing change in these individuals obscured the true intraindividual trajectory *because individuals of the same age were not at the same stage of their disease process.*

A similar situation may arise when considering the progression of pathologic processes that influence cognitive function and carry an increased risk of mortality. Wilson et al. (2003) investigated the effect of terminal decline in cognitive function and demonstrated a lengthy period of stability in cognitive function with an abrupt onset of decline between 3 and 5 years prior to death. Unfortunately, the situation might in general be more complicated than simply modeling terminal and preterminal decline; that is, there might be both age-graded and non-age-graded processes influencing changes in the same individual. Thus, using a single time index (e.g., age, time to death) to represent change in any individual is likely an oversimplification. Sliwinski et al. (2006) examined terminal cognitive decline using the same analytic approach as Wilson et al. (2003) but represented intraindividual cognitive change as a piecewise function of two different time indices. The first part of this function described memory change as a function of chronological age, and the second part of this function represented change as a function of both age and time to death. Sliwinski et al. found evidence of significant but modest age-based memory decline and evidence of an abrupt acceleration in decline occurring roughly 9 years prior to death. These data provided evidence that intraindividual memory decline was a function of both age-graded and terminal decline processes. Representing change as a function of either terminal decline alone or age alone did not fit the data as well as using both time indices in the same model.

The preceding discussion illustrates why the selection of a time index for representing intraindividual change is important. Selecting age as a time index, for example, makes the assumption that individuals of the same age are at equivalent levels or stages in the causal processes that are driving change in performance. If individuals of the same age differ in terms of the underlying process causing change (as was the case in the analysis of preclinical dementia), then analyzing change as a function of age will produce misleading results, both in terms of the average curve

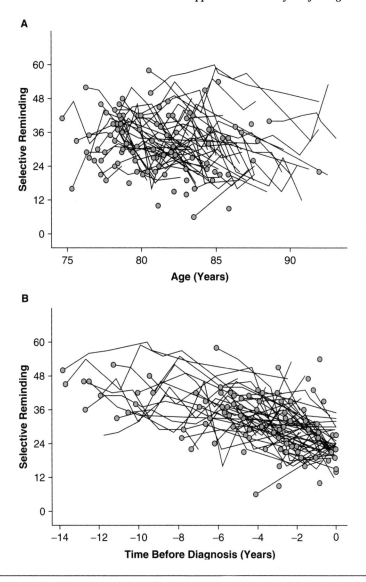

Figure 28.4   Memory Performance as a Function of Age (A) and Time to Dementia Diagnosis (B)

and individual differences in change (Sliwinski, Hofer, Hall, et al., 2003). The problem of selecting a time basis on which to align individuals is critical, because (mis)aligning individuals on an incorrect time index can significantly distort identification of intraindividual change.

So, should selection of a time index for representing intraindividual change be based on a priori considerations (e.g., a researcher is interested in maturation and therefore selects age as the time index), or should selection be data driven (e.g., compare models that use different time indices and select the best fitting one)? There is

no easy answer to this question. We note that Sliwinski, Hofer, and Hall (2003) would have incorrectly concluded that individuals with preclinical dementia exhibited no evidence of accelerated memory loss if they had restricted their analyses to age-based change and not examined memory change indexed by time to diagnosis. This is because individuals of the same age were at different stages of their disease, so representing change as a function of age resulted in a misalignment and type of aggregation bias. We therefore believe that interest in maturational influences is not a sufficient justification to restrict analyses to age-based representation of intraindividual change. However, we also do not believe that the best solution to this problem only involves considering different time indices, as helpful as this may be. Instead, we believe that more informative-descriptive and explanatory longitudinal modeling will require process-based representations of intraindividual psychological change.

PROCESS-BASED MODELS OF INTRAINDIVIDUAL CHANGE

Another, and much less frequently used, approach formally represents change in a variable as a function of concurrent (or lagged) changes in another variable. The rationale for the process-based approach to modeling intraindividual change is that change in the variable of interest is a function not only of the passage of time but also of cognitive, physiological, and psychosocial processes that transpire over time (Birren & Schroots, 1996). Thus, the process-based approach to modeling intraindividual change is focused on coupled change (i.e., how different variables travel together across time within individuals), whereas time-based approaches have tended to focus on correlated change (i.e., whether individuals who change more rapidly on one variable are also changing rapidly on others). The necessity of process-based approaches to theorizing about aging have been recognized (e.g., Li & Schmiedek, 2002), but this recognition has not had a strong influence on how longitudinal data are commonly analyzed.

The essential characteristic of a process-based model of intraindividual change is the inclusion of a time-varying predictor variable that could mediate the effect of time. Equations 28.1 and 28.2 are time-based models because they include only an index of time (i.e., chronological age) in the model of intraindividual change. Equation 28.3 is process based because it includes a time index (age) but also includes a time-varying variable (speed) that could mediate the effect of age. The explanatory logic of process-based models rests on the notion that if intraindividual change in the dependent variable over time is caused by the time-varying process variable, then the effect of time will be reduced. Thus, chronological age

(or any time index) is really a "stand-in" variable that could, in principle, be eliminated by accounting for the cognitive, physiological, and psychosocial processes that actually cause behavioral change in aging individuals.

Very few longitudinal aging studies have adopted such process-based approaches to representing intraindividual change and for theory testing. However, this approach is frequently used in short-term measurement intensive studies, such as daily diary (e.g., Mroczek & Almeida, 2004), experience sampling (e.g., van Eck, Nicolson, & Berkhof, 1998) or measurement burst (e.g., Sliwinski et al., 2006) studies. These studies use process-based models because they express change in behavior (e.g., negative affect or working memory) over time as a function of concurrent (or lagged) changes in a predictor variable (e.g., stressful events). There is little or no concern with explaining trends, because these studies typically encompass very short time periods (a week or two). More traditional longitudinal studies involve more widely spaced intervals between assessments and lengthier follow-up periods, often spanning years rather than hours or days.

Thus, long-term longitudinal studies tend to focus on progressive change, whereas short-term longitudinal studies tend to focus on fluctuations in behavior. However, both long- and short-term longitudinal studies share a common goal of understanding the interrelationships among processes that transpire within individuals across time. Only a handful of studies have used process-based models of intraindividual change to analyze data from long-term longitudinal studies. One set of studies (Sliwinski & Buschke, 1999, 2004) tested the speed hypothesis of cognitive decline by examining whether intraindividual change in memory could be mediated by intraindividual change in measures of perceptual comparison speed. The researchers found that intraindividual change in processing speed mediated the amount of intraindividual change in cued recall (Sliwinski & Buschke, 1999) and free recall (Sliwinski & Buschke, 2004) by 8% and 15%, respectively. MacDonald, Hultsch, Strauss, and Dixon (2003) demonstrated that intraindividual changes in performance variability accounted for between 20% and 37% of the within-person variance in cognitive performance across a 6-year follow-up period. In another analysis, MacDonald, Hultsch, and Dixon (2003) showed that intraindividual declines in basic measures of speed predicted but did not fully account for concurrent intraindividual declines in digit symbol performance. A common feature of these studies that have used process-based approaches to modeling cognitive aging is that explanation involves accounting for intraindividual effects, either in terms of regression coefficients or within-person variance explained.

There are not many examples in the literature that compare process-based and time-based approaches to testing hypotheses using longitudinal data. Therefore, as a final illustration of the differences between a time-based, correlated change approach and a process-based, coupled change approach to explaining longitudinal aging effects, consider a fictitious example of a researcher who postulates that volumetric losses in the hippocampus are the cause of age-related memory declines. One approach to test this hypothesis would be to measure rates of (age-based) change in memory and hippocampal volume and assess how strongly the two are correlated. The other approach would be to test whether intraindividual changes in hippocampal volume are coupled with changes in memory and whether this coupling can (statistically) account for age-based declines.

If one assumes that this causal process (volumetric loss) is very strongly age graded and that the coupling between the measured variables (e.g., memory, hippocampal volume) is invariant across persons, then the correlated change approach would be a viable choice. By *age graded* we mean that for any given individual the association between volume of the hippocampus and age (i.e., the passage of time) is *very* strong; that is, the correlation between the "true" score on a measure of hippocampal volume and chronological age for any given individual should be very high. This does not mean the between-person correlation between age and hippocampal volume in an age-heterogeneous sample needs to be strong but that for any given individual his or her change in age should strongly relate to change in the volume of his or her hippocampus. This relationship could be quadratic or curved or piecewise linear, so long

as there is relatively little systematic within-individual variation in hippocampal volume that is not predicted by the passage of time. In such a circumstance, focusing on consistency among trends in the causal variable and outcome could prove most informative, especially if it could be demonstrated both that the correlation between change in the hippocampus and memory were very strong and that individuals who showed little or no volumetric loss also showed little or no memory loss.

However, if the causal process is not strongly age graded, and if the coupling between the causal process and outcome varies across individuals, then we would not advocate use of correlated change and would instead suggest use of a process-based, coupled change approach. Following on the example introduced in the preceding paragraph, consider two hypothetical individuals who were measured once every 5 years from age 50 to age 65. Table 28.2 displays fictitious data that show a strong association between age and hippocampal volume for both Person 1 ($r = -.95$) and Person 2 ($r = -.90$), consistent with the notion that volumetric loss in the hippocampus is an age-graded process. There is also evidence of a strong within-person association between volume and memory ($r > .95$ for both persons). This high within-person correlation indicates that changes in the hippocampal volume account for most of the within-person variance in memory. The coupling parameter, which is the regression coefficient relating a unit change in hippocampal volume to a unit change in memory, is 2.07 for Person 1 and 0.99 for Person 2. So, these data would be consistent with the prediction that changes in hippocampal volume predict concurrent memory declines but that the strength of this prediction varies between (two) people. Positive coupling in all individuals, however, does not imply a positive correlation between rates of age-based change on the two variables. Person 2 shows the most rapid loss of volume in the hippocampus, with a rate of decline of –0.74/year compared with a rate of –0.50/year for Person 1. However, Person 1 shows more rapid memory decline (at –1.05/year) than Person 2 (at –0.65/year), which indicates a negative association between rate of change in the hippocampus and memory despite a positive coupling between these two variables for each individual.

Table 28.2 Comparison of Coupled and Correlated Change

	Volume		Memory	
Age	Person 1	Person 2	Person 1	Person 2
50	50	50	106.54	73.61
55	45	41	96.17	63.11
60	44	40	97.51	61.33
65	42	38	88.66	63.45
Age Slope	−0.50	−0.74	−1.05	−0.65

This illustration is similar to the point made in Figure 28.2 but extends it by showing that the analysis of correlated change assumes a fixed relationship between the two variables under study. However, if the relationship between the mediator and outcome is random (i.e., varies across individuals), then that would be a case of moderated mediation. An excellent methodological discussion of this type of mediation in the context of multilevel modeling is found in Bauer, Preacher, and Gil (2006). For example, changes in blood pressure might be a stronger mediator of age-related changes in cognition for persons with cardiovascular disease compared with those without. A correlated-change approach to modeling longitudinal aging data cannot easily accommodate the possibility that different causes underlie age-related declines in different individuals. A process-based coupled change analysis can accommodate individual differences in the intraindividual coupling of two or more variables over time. Thus, in principle, process-based modeling could allow for the possibility that different variables mediate declines in different individuals. However, in practice, most longitudinal designs are not well suited to estimation of such variability because they have too few repeated measurements.

EXPLAINING "AGING" IN LONGITUDINAL ANALYSES

Given the complexity of the phenomenon of aging and the different approaches to analyzing

longitudinal data, we would like to conclude with a discussion of the issues one might consider when choosing an analytic approach to test theoretical predictions. To review, time-based analytic approaches represent intraindividual change solely as a function of the passage of time and seek to explain aging by accounting for between-person individual differences in the rates of change (e.g., correlated change). The process-based approach represents intraindividual change as a function of events and processes that transpire over time and seeks to explain longitudinal aging effects by statistical mediation of within-person change. How, then, does one decide whether to test a particular prediction examining correlated or coupled change?

The analysis of correlated change makes the assumption that the time basis used to estimate the rates of change provides a valid representation of the progression of causal processes that produce behavioral change. To the extent that elapsed time (e.g., from baseline or from date of birth) is a fallible index of the progression of the age-related causal processes driving change or there are important causes of change (e.g., disease progression) that are not age-graded, then correlations between estimates of age-based rates of change may be uninformative or even misleading because of misalignment and aggregation bias (see Baltes & Labouvie, 1973; Sliwinski, Hofer, Hall, et al., 2003). Use of time-based approaches to modeling intraindividual change should be informed by an explicit theory regarding whether the underlying cause or causes of change are normative and age graded or whether they are non-normative and not age graded. Even if informed by such an explicit theory, we would advocate considering different time bases (e.g., time to death, time to event) as well as formally testing for convergence should chronological age be selected as the time basis for representing intraindividual change. Also, as discussed in the preceding section, the analysis of correlated time-based change assumes that the association between variables is equivalent across individuals.

A process-based approach does not rely on any index of elapsed time to measure underlying processes that cause change. It instead assumes that elapsed time is a fallible proxy for these processes and seeks to "explain away" the effects of time (e.g., chronological age) by identifying substantive, time-varying variables that directly measure these processes. However, there are assumptions and requirements that can limit the utility of this approach. First, this approach requires that (true) change is not constant, monotonic, or completely time dependent. The process-based approach to modeling intraindividual change makes sense only if we assume that the effects of aging are abrupt, saltatory, and locally reversible. For example, we might hypothesize that age-related memory declines are caused by declining cardiovascular health and predict that changes in cardiovascular function cause concurrent changes in memory. Although there may be trends indicating overall decline in cardiovascular health with increasing age (say, from age 40 to 75), during any given year interval an individual's cardiovascular function may substantially worsen (from age 40 to 41) or decline only a little (from age 74 to 75) in a pattern that is not completely determined by his or her chronological age. The process-based approach would produce evidence of coupled change between memory and cardiovascular function if there was greater memory decline between age 40 and 41 than between age 74 and 75 because there was greater loss of cardiovascular function during the former time period. Thus, identification of coupled change requires that variables be "perturbed" about their overall long-term trajectories. These perturbations ideally would be experimentally induced, but research on developmental and aging processes must usually rely on naturally occurring perturbations.

A second requirement for applying process-based models to the study of intraindividual change is that the frequency of repeated measurements captures the cadence of the processes under study. Unfortunately, most theories of cognitive aging are not very specific regarding the time course of age-related change or, more precisely, the cadence over which changes and fluctuations in performance would reflect the hypothesized causal influences. It seems obvious that measuring changes in processing speed from one day to the next would not be optimal for studying age-graded influences, but it is less obvious whether variability and change in performance from one month to the next (or even one year to the next) would reflect aging effects or other transient influences. It is also possible

that assessments may be so far apart (e.g., follow-up testing every 5 years) that important information could be lost and change would appear smoother and more strongly age graded than it really is. This issue relates to the problem of interval censoring in epidemiological research and aliasing in time series analyses.

A related consideration is that analysis of coupled change using process-based models requires a larger number of repeated measurements than might be normally obtained in conventional longitudinal studies. Many longitudinal studies have fewer than a half dozen repeated measurements, but having a dozen or more observations on individuals might be necessary to accurately model within-person coupled change and individual differences in this coupling (Bauer et al., 2006). Process-based models may not be especially useful when applied to data with relatively few repeated measurements that are spaced according to convenience rather than according to theory.

Conclusion

We have tried to provide a critical examination of different approaches to descriptive and explanatory modeling of longitudinal aging data. Although much of this discussion involved contrasting time-based with process-based approaches, this is somewhat of a false dichotomy. Process-based models of intraindividual change are in fact time-based models with the addition of a within-person mediator added to the representation of intraindividual change. We also contrasted the analyses of correlated and coupled change and demonstrated that they answer different questions and can lead to different conclusions. However, it is very likely that examining both correlated and coupled change would be required for an adequate characterization of developmental and involutional phenomena. Although our view is that analysis of coupled change addresses many interesting and developmentally relevant questions more directly than does the analysis of correlated change, there are some circumstances in which analysis of correlated change is the best available option (e.g., to study strongly age-graded influences and/or when only a few repeated measurements are available).

We have also tried to avoid detailed commentary about particular statistical approaches to analyzing longitudinal data (e.g., structural equation modeling, univariate and multivariate hierarchical liner modeling). There are unique advantages and inherent limitations with all methods commonly used for analyzing longitudinal data. It is likely that none of the methods currently at our disposal will prove optimal for modeling and explaining processes that unfold and interact within aging individuals. However, it is critically important to let theory drive the development of new and innovative analytic methods rather than allow available methodological tools to constrain and direct theory development.

Theorizing about aging has become increasingly process oriented (e.g., Li, 2003), and we believe that analytic models of change should reflect this emphasis. The process-based approach to modeling intraindividual change that we have described in this chapter represents one approach to thinking about longitudinal data that recognizes that behavioral, physiological, and cognitive change is a function not of age but rather of what happens to individuals as they age.

REFERENCES

Baltes, P., & Labouvie, G. (1973). Adult development of intellectual performance: Description, explanation, and modification. In C. Eisdorfer & M. Lawton (Eds.), *The psychology of adult development and aging* (pp. 157–219). Washington, DC: American Psychological Association.

Baltes, P., & Nesselroade, J. R. (1979). History and rationale of longitudinal research. In J. Nesselroade & P. Baltes (Eds.), *Longitudinal research in the study of behavior and development* (pp. 1–39). New York: Academic Press.

Baltes, P., Staudinger, U., & Lindenberger, U. (1999). Lifespan psychology: Theory and application to intellectual functioning. *Annual Review of Psychology, 50,* 471–507.

Bauer, D., Preacher, K., & Gil, K. (2006). Conceptualizing and testing random indirect effects and moderated mediation in multilevel models: New procedures and recommendations. *Psychological Methods, 11,* 142–163.

Berg, S. (1996). Aging, behavior, and terminal decline. In J. Birren, K. W. Schaie, R. Abeles, M. Gatz, & T. Salthouse (Eds.), *Handbook of the psychology of aging* (4th ed., pp. 323–337). San Diego, CA: Academic Press.

Birren, J. (1959). *Handbook of aging and the individual.* Chicago: University of Chicago Press.

Birren, J., & Schroots, J. (1996). History, concepts, and theory in the psychology of aging. In J. Birren, K. W. Schaie, R. Abeles, M. Gatz, & T. Salthouse (Eds.), *Handbook of the psychology of aging* (4th ed., pp. 3–23). San Diego, CA: Academic Press.

Diggle, P., Heagerty, P., Liang, K.-Y., & Zeger, S. (2002). *Analysis of longitudinal data.* Oxford, UK: Oxford University Press.

Ghisletta, P., Bickel, J.-F., & Lovden, M. (2006). Does activity engagement protect against cognitive decline in old age? Methodological and analytical considerations. *Journals of Gerontology Series B: Psychological Sciences and Social Sciences, 61,* P253–P261.

Ghisletta, P., & Lindenberger, U. (2003). Age-based structural dynamics between perceptual speed and knowledge in the Berlin Aging Study: Direct evidence for ability dedifferentiation in old age. *Psychology and Aging, 18,* 696–713.

Hall, C. B., Lipton, R. B., Sliwinski, M. J., & Stewart, W. F. (2000). A change point model for estimating onset of cognitive decline in preclinical Alzheimer's disease. *Statistics in Medicine, 19,* 1555–1566.

Hedeker, D., & Gibbons, R. (2006). *Longitudinal data analysis.* New York: Wiley.

Hertzog, C., & Nesselroade, J. (2003). Assessing psychological change in adulthood: An overview of methodological issues. *Psychology and Aging, 18,* 639–657.

Li, S.-C. (2003). Biocultural orchestration of developmental plasticity across levels: The interplay of biology and culture in shaping the mind and behavior across the life span. *Psychological Bulletin, 129,* 171–194.

Li, S.-C., & Schmiedek, F. (2002). Age is not necessarily aging: Another step towards understanding the "clocks" that time aging. *Gerontology, 48,* 5–12.

MacDonald, S., Hultsch, D., & Dixon, R. (2003). Performance variability is related to change in cognition: Evidence from the Victoria Longitudinal Study. *Psychology and Aging, 18,* 510–523.

MacDonald, S., Hultsch, D., Strauss, E., & Dixon, R. (2003). Age-related slowing of digit symbol substitution revisited: What do longitudinal age changes reflect? *Journals of Gerontology Series B: Psychological Sciences and Social Sciences, 58B,* P187–P194.

McArdle, J., & Bell, R. (2000). An introduction to latent growth models for development data analysis. In T. Little, K. Schnabel, & J. Baumert (Eds.), *Modeling longitudinal and multilevel data: Practical issues, applied approaches, and specific examples* (pp. 69–107). Mahwah, NJ: Lawrence Erlbaum.

McArdle, J., Ferrer-Caja, E., Hamagami, F., & Woodcock, R. W. (2002). Comparative longitudinal structural analyses of the growth and decline of multiple intelligences over the life span. *Developmental Psychology, 38,* 115–142.

McArdle, J., & Hamagami, F. (2001). Latent difference score structural models for linear dynamic analyses with incomplete longitudinal data. In L. Collins & A. Sayer (Eds.), *New methods for the analysis of change* (pp. 139–175). Washington, DC: American Psychological Association.

Mehta, P., & West, S. (2000). Putting the individual back into individual growth curves. *Psychological Methods, 5,* 23–43.

Mroczek, D., & Almeida, D. (2004). The effect of daily stress, personality, and age on daily negative affect. *Journal of Personality, 72,* 355–378.

Raudenbush, S. (2002). Alternative covariance structures for polynomial models of individual growth and change. In D. Moskowitz & S. Hershberger (Eds.), *Modeling intraindividual variability with repeated measures data: Methods and applications* (pp. 25–57). Mahwah, NJ: Lawrence Erlbaum.

Riegel, K., & Riegel, R. (1972). Development, drop, and death. *Developmental Psychology, 6,* 306–319.

Salthouse, T. (1996). General and specific speed mediation of adult age differences in memory. *Journals of Gerontology Series B: Psychological Sciences and Social Sciences, 51B,* P30–P42.

Singer, J., & Willett, J. (2003). *Applied longitudinal data analysis: Modeling change and event occurrence.* New York: Oxford University Press.

Sliwinski, M., & Buschke, H. (1999). Cross-sectional and longitudinal relationships among age, memory and processing speed. *Psychology and Aging, 14,* 18–33.

Sliwinski, M., & Buschke, H. (2004). Modeling intraindividual cognitive change in aging adults: Results from the Einstein Aging Studies. *Aging, Neuropsychology and Cognition, 11,* 196–211.

Sliwinski, M., Hofer, S. M., & Hall, C. (2003) Correlated cognitive change in older adults with and without preclinical dementia. *Psychology and Aging, 18,* 672–683.

Sliwinski, M., Hofer, S. M., Hall, C., Buschke, H., & Lipton, R. (2003). Modeling memory decline in older adults: The importance of preclinical dementia, attrition and chronological age. *Psychology and Aging, 18,* 658–671.

Sliwinski, M. J., Stawski, R. S., Hall, C., Katz, M., Verghese, J., & Lipton, R. (2006). Distinguishing preterminal and terminal cognitive decline. *European Psychologist, 11,* 172–181.

Snijders, T., & Bosker, R. (1999). *Multilevel analysis: An introduction to basic and advanced multilevel modeling.* London: Sage.

Thorvaldsson, V., Hofer, S. M., & Johansson, B. (2006). Ageing and late life terminal decline: A comparison of alternative modeling approaches. *European Psychologist, 11,* 196–203.

van Eck, M., Nicolson, N., & Berkhof, J. (1998). Effects of stressful daily events on mood states: Relationship to global perceived stress. *Journal of Personality and Social Psychology, 75,* 1572–1585.

Von Eye, A., & Bergman, L. (2003). Research strategies in developmental psychopathology: Dimensional identity and the person-oriented approach. *Development and Psychopathology, 15,* 553–580.

Wilson, R., Beckett, L., Barnes, L., Schneider, J., Bach, J., Evans, D., et al. (2002). Individual differences in rates of change in cognitive abilities of older persons. *Psychology and Aging, 17,* 179–193.

Wilson, R., Beckett, L., Bienias, J., Evans, D., & Bennett, D. (2003). Terminal decline in cognitive function. *Neurology, 60,* 1782–1787.

Wohlwill, J. F. (1973). *The study of behavioral development.* New York: Academic Press.

Zimprich, D. (2002). Cross-sectionally and longitudinally balanced effects of processing speed on intellectual abilities. *Experimental Aging Research, 28,* 231–251.

29

CONSIDERATIONS FOR SAMPLING TIME IN RESEARCH ON AGING

Examples From Research on Stress and Cognition

SHEVAUN D. NEUPERT, ROBERT S. STAWSKI, AND DAVID M. ALMEIDA

A *process* is defined as a series of actions or events that are part of development and is often characterized by gradual changes leading to a particular result (Merriam-Webster, 2005). In psychology research, processes are often characterized as explanations or mechanisms for phenomena that unfold within individuals over time. Although there has been a renewed interest in assessing within-person designs (e.g., Molenaar, 2004), in this chapter we highlight the importance of sampling time as it is linked with process. In particular, we highlight research on physiological and psychological processes that account for the association between stress and cognition.

Collecting data at a single point in time, multiple times, and the length between multiple time points all have different consequences for examining an underlying process that is assumed to be captured. When considering processes of change, Nesselroade (1991) identified two kinds of systematic intraindividual (within-person) change that longitudinal researchers should consider. The first is *intraindividual*

variability that identifies short-term, relatively reversible changes or fluctuations. For example, fluctuations in mood would be considered intraindividual variability because people vary around their own average. In contrast, *intraindividual change* designates long-term changes that are usually less reversible. These concepts are especially salient for aging researchers because the characterization of a given individual at any point in time involves his or her status on intraindividual change (e.g., trait change, ontogenetic) and his or her status on intraindividual variability (e.g., state, microgenetic; Nesselroade, 1991). Therefore, differences among persons reflect at least three sources of variance: (1) stable individual differences, (2) intraindividual changes, (3) and intraindividual variability. Combining intraindividual variability and intraindividual change leads to a better representation of the developing individual (Baltes, Reese, & Nesselroade, 1977; Nesselroade, 1991; Nesselroade & Ghisletta, 2000). We assert that the elucidation or detection of mechanisms linking processes may be inextricably linked to the choices of sampling time. One aim of this chapter is to show that daily designs can elucidate short-term processes and mechanisms. A second aim is to show that the repetition of the daily approach (i.e., measurement burst design) can help understand micro-level (daily) effects on behavior as well as contextual (e.g., burst-to-burst) and cumulative/long-term effects. We cast our comments within the context of stress and cognition, an area that has received considerable attention from many disciplines and has great importance for the aging process (e.g., McEwen, 1999).

In laboratory-based studies, stress is typically associated with poorer cognitive performance (e.g., Lupien & Lepage, 2001; Sapolsky, 1996) and has been implicated as a component that may accelerate age-related cognitive decline (McEwen & Sapolsky, 1995; Sapolsky, 1996). Similarly, people who report higher levels of self-reported stress outside the laboratory also tend to experience poorer memory performance (e.g., Vedhara, Hyde, Gilchrist, Tytherleigh, & Plummer, 2000; VonDras, Powless, Olson, Wheeler, & Snudden, 2005). This has led researchers to propose various explanations for the negative effects of stress on memory. Cortisol, a hormone released in response to stress, has been advanced as one important mechanism for explaining the effects of stress on cognition (Kirschbaum, Wolf, May, Wippich, & Hellhammer, 1996; Wright, Kunz-Ebrecht, Iliffe, Foese, & Steptoe, 2005). Longitudinal studies have provided some of the most compelling evidence of a cortisol–cognition link (Lupien et al., 1994, 1998; Seeman, McEwen, Singer, Albert, & Rowe, 1997). These findings suggest that, over time, repeated exposure to heightened levels of cortisol irreversibly damage the hippocampus, one of the consequences of a phenomenon called *allostatic load* (McEwen, 1999).

The evidence supporting the cortisol–cognition link has served to motivate research investigating the effects of short-term acute stressful events on cognitive function. What is not clear, however, is whether the mechanisms that are assumed to underlie the relationship between stressors and long-term changes or differences in cognition are the same mechanisms responsible for short-term changes or decrements in cognition. The long-term effects of cortisol on the hippocampus have been used as a working model for studying the effects of short-term, acute stressful experiences on cognitive function. We propose that the mechanisms that pertain to effects transpiring over longer periods of time (e.g., years), may not be the same as those that operate over shorter periods of time (e.g., days, hours, or even minutes). In this chapter, we highlight the usefulness of daily diary (Bolger, Davis, & Rafaeli, 2003) and measurement burst designs (an extension of a daily diary design; Nesselroade, 1991) for examining both shorter and longer term processes.

THE IMPORTANCE OF SAMPLING TIME

Within the existing stress and cognition literature, time plays an important role for both constructs. Stressors can be short, acute events with short-term effects or ongoing, chronic events with more long-term effects. For example, stressors can take the form of life events (discrete, observable events that stand for significant life changes with a relatively clear onset and offset; Wheaton, 1999), chronic stressors (slowly developing problematic conditions in social environments or roles that typically have a longer time course than life events; Wheaton, 1999), or daily hassles ("the irritating, frustrating, distressing demands that to some degree characterize everyday transactions with the environment"; Kanner, Coyne, Schaefer, & Lazarus, 1981, p. 3). Also, time is important for cognitive aging researchers who may be interested in examining changes in cognition over a long period of time (e.g., Colsher & Wallace, 1991; Evans et al., 1993; Wilson, Beckett, Bennett, Albert, & Evans, 1999), as well as fluctuations in memory ability over shorter periods of time such as from one day to the next (e.g., Neupert, Almeida, Mroczek, & Spiro, 2006; Sliwinski, Smyth, Hofer, & Stawski, 2006). It is important to note that cross-sectional designs do not permit an assessment of the nuances of time, such as the duration of the stressor itself, the duration of its impact, and the changes in cognition. For these reasons, studies that can combine repeated micro-longitudinal designs within the context of a more traditional longitudinal design may be the best suited to address questions of mechanisms between stress and cognition over varying time frames. For example, mechanisms linking an argument on a given day to memory performance the next day could be very different from the mechanisms that link the stress of a chronically toxic relationship to long-term changes in encoding deficits.

The timing of the constructs themselves is important, but the timing in terms of the life course is also crucial to consider. Older adults have been exposed to more stressors throughout their lifetimes compared to younger adults (Pearlin & Mullan, 1992), so the long-term accumulation of stressful events could be an additional context for consideration in the link between a stressful event and cognition in aging. Evidence suggests that older adults, in addition to experiencing more stressors throughout their lifetimes, have poorer memory for activities (e.g., Earles & Coon, 1994; Kausler & Hakami, 1983), slower processing speed (Madden, 1985; Salthouse, 1996), decreased working memory ability (Salthouse, Babcock, & Shaw, 1991), and poorer episodic memory ability (Foos & Sarno, 1998) than younger adults. Longitudinal studies have shown that, on average, cognition declines in old age (e.g., Colsher & Wallace, 1991; Evans et al., 1993; Wilson et al., 1999). Furthermore, there is evidence of age-related atrophy of the hippocampus and frontal lobes (Rosch, 1997). Loss of recent memory, as well as impaired learning and concentrating skills in older adults, is often attributed to smaller hippocampi (Rosch, 1997). Therefore, stress and cognition are important constructs within the aging process. Many of the studies we review in this chapter have been conducted with samples of older adults, further underscoring the importance of changes in stress and cognition and the link between them for aging individuals.

It is also important to consider multiple time frames of stress–cognition processes. For example, the context of micro (daily) events often occurs in the context of more macro (enduring) life situations. It is often the case that daily hassles or stressors occur as a chronic stressor is also unfolding (Serido, Almeida, & Wethington, 2004). Therefore, relatively short-term processes can take place within a context of accumulation, which could compound their effects. For example, continual daily fights with one's spouse could eventually lead to separation and divorce. The ability to concentrate on a day-to-day basis may be impaired by intrusive thoughts about domestic problems, thus impairing cognitive functioning (Sarason, Pierce, & Sarason, 1996). It is also possible that the chronicity of this stress may be associated with impaired cognition because of prolonged stress responses (e.g., Sapolsky, 1992). Daily stressors affect well-being not only by having separate, immediate, and direct effects on emotional and physical functioning, but also by piling up over a series of days to create persistent irritations and overloads that may result in more serious stress reactions, such as anxiety and depression (Lazarus, 1999; Zautra, 2003). We assert that the mechanisms underlying the process of short-term stressors may be distinct from and interact with those related to accumulation and that it is important to design studies that take both into account. In the following sections, we review the literature of chronic and acute stressors and the mechanisms that may tie them to cognition, and then we outline the benefits of daily diary and measurement burst designs.

CHRONIC STRESS

Much of the research linking the effect of chronic stress to cognition has done so by linking cortisol, a hormone released in response to stress, to impaired cognitive function. Glucocorticoids (e.g., cortisol and hydrocortisone) are secreted by the adrenal gland in response to a wide variety of stressors (Heffelfinger & Newcomer, 2001; Sapolsky, 1992). In addition, glucocorticoids are known to regulate various brain functions, including human cognitions (Heffelfinger & Newcomer, 2001). Excessive exposure to glucocorticoids can damage the brain and make neurons more vulnerable to insults (Sapolsky, 1992), and increased glucocorticoid exposure in humans at levels associated with stress can decrease memory and learning function (Heffelfinger & Newcomer, 2001).

In Selye's initial studies (e.g., Selye, 1936), he conceptualized the stress response as having distinct components. In the initial, *alarm* stage, the stressor was noted or experienced. The second stage, *resistance*, consisted of successfully dealing with the short-term physical insult. The third stage was where disease started, when the stressor became chronic. This final stage was termed *exhaustion*, because there were no longer sufficient glucocorticoids to combat the stressor. In Selye's view, then, stress-related disease was due to the stressor itself attacking the undefended body. However, there is little empirical evidence of such a global exhaustion of the hormones of the stress response (Sapolsky, 1992). Chronic stress is not damaging because the body's defenses fail but because, with enough chronic stress, those defenses themselves (i.e., glucocorticoids) become damaging (Sapolsky, 1992, 1996). During an acute stressor, the costs of the stress response can be contained, but with chronic activation they exact a toll on the body (Sapolsky, 1992, 1996).

CORTISOL AND COGNITION: CHRONIC AND ACUTE EFFECTS

There has been considerable interest in understanding how stress affects cognitive function because long-term exposure to cortisol impairs the structural (Brown et al., 2004; Lupien et al., 1998; McEwen, 1999; Sapolsky, 1996; Starkman, Giordani, Gebarski, & Schteingart, 2003) and functional (Brown et al., 2004; Lupien et al., 1994, 1998; Seeman et al., 1997; Starkman, Giordani, Berent, Schork, & Schteingart, 2001) integrity of the hippocampus (Jelicic & Bonke, 2001) and frontal lobe (Lupien & Lepage, 2001). Some of the most compelling evidence suggesting a cortisol–cognition link comes from studies documenting the deleterious effects of long-term exposure to high levels of cortisol (Jelicic & Bonke, 2001). Lupien et al. (1994, 1996) examined how change in older adults' basal cortisol levels over a 4-year period was related to cognitive functioning at the end of that same period. Lupien et al. (1994) examined performance on two tasks as a function of subgroups based on cortisol slope trajectories. Three distinct groups were identified: (1) high increasing slope, (2) moderate increasing slope, and (3) no slope. The increasing-slope groups exhibited reliably poorer recall and slower search times compared with older adults exhibiting no change in cortisol. Furthermore, the older adults exhibiting no change in cortisol did

not differ in cognitive performance from healthy young adults. This suggests that longitudinal increases, over the long term, in cortisol are a sign of hypothalamic–pituitary–adrenal axis dysfunction and that increasing levels of cortisol may impair cognitive performance. Thus, behavioral deficits may be mediated by cortisol-related changes in brain structure (McEwen, 1999; Sapolsky, Krey, & McEwen, 1986).

Seeman et al. (1997) found that change in cortisol over 2.5 years reliably predicted change in delayed recall performance in women, but not in men. Furthermore, changes in recall were found to vary as a function of the change in cortisol. Women who exhibited decreases in cortisol exhibited improved recall over that same time period, whereas women with increasing cortisol levels exhibited a substantial decline in recall performance. Similarly, Seeman et al. (2001) found that baseline levels of allostatic load, of which cortisol is one marker, predicted 7-year changes in general cognitive function. Together, these studies suggest that cortisol is related to changes in cognitive function and that allostatic load may be a risk factor for impaired hippocampal and general cognitive functioning.

Although there is considerable evidence to suggest that cortisol is related to cognitive and brain function, there is reason to suspect it is not the sole mechanism underlying acute stress-related cognitive impairments. First, the evidence suggesting a relationship between changes in endogenous cortisol and cognitive function is inconsistent. Although some studies have shown that stress-related increases in cortisol are associated with lower memory performance (Kirschbaum et al., 1996; Wolf, Schommer, Hellhammer, McEwen, & Kirschbaum, 2001), others have shown no association between cortisol reactivity and memory performance (Domes, Heinrichs, Reichwald, & Hautzinger, 2002; Jelicic, Geraerts, Merckelbach, & Guerrieri, 2004). A number of studies have shown that an increase in cortisol over the course of years is predictive of memory (Lupien et al., 1994, 1998), intellectual deficits (Seeman et al., 1997, 2001), and smaller hippocampal volume (Lupien et al., 1998). Acute increases in cortisol, however, are less predictive of cognitive function (Domes et al., 2002; Jelicic et al., 2004). With longitudinal increases in cortisol linked to the occurrence of stressful events, one cannot rule out factors other than stressful experiences causing such increases in cortisol.

Although it is important to understand how the physiological mediators of stressors impact cognition, it may be equally important to understand the contexts of the triggering stressors themselves. In other words, secretion of cortisol needs to be considered within the context or domain of the stressor. For example, Dickerson and Kemeny (2004) postulated a *social self-preservation theory*: Individuals who might be expected to experience greater threat due to a highly valued ability (e.g., cognitive performance) were the ones who secreted higher amounts of cortisol during the threat. Neupert, Miller, and Lachman (2006) found that older adults with high levels of education secreted the most cortisol over time (i.e., had the steepest slopes of cortisol reactivity) in response to laboratory-based cognitive stressors. In their study, cognitive tests were used as the impetus for changes in cortisol; that is, cognitive testing served as the stressor, and then slopes of change in cortisol were predicted by age and education. In line with Dickerson and Kemeny's ideas, it is possible that cognitive testing is more stressful among individuals with higher education relative to those with lower education because the former are more concerned about decline and have a greater stake in their cognitive performance. In addition, these stressors may be more salient for older adults who could be experiencing some age-related cognitive decline (Neupert, Miller, & Lachman, 2006). This is also consistent with Lazarus's (1999) notion of *primary appraisal*, in which a situation or event must be considered valuable or salient before it can become stressful.

In addition to the domain or context of the stressor, time is also crucial to consider with respect to cortisol studies. Sapolsky, Romero, and Munck (2000) suggested that cortisol can take approximately 1 hour, if not longer, to exert effects on hippocampal function. Thus, the time course for the effects of cortisol on neural function may be at odds with the hypothesis that acute stress-related increases in cortisol mediate cognitive performance decrements observed very proximal to the stressor. Cortisol is typically measured within 10 to 20 minutes after cessation of a laboratory stressor, whereas cognitive assessments are typically conducted within minutes of the stressor. Therefore, cortisol may not have had sufficient time to manifest its effects on the brain, but other components of the physiological stress response could (Sapolsky et al., 2000). Taken together, the results of previous research suggest that cortisol is likely to be implicated in the long-, but not necessarily the short-term effects of stress on cognition. However, as Sapolsky et al. (2000) and Lupien and McEwen (1997) have pointed out, the exact time course for the effects of cortisol on cognition is not known. Future studies examining cortisol and cognition could focus on the time course of the effects and whether they depend on certain situations (e.g., naturalistic vs. laboratory based) and/or individual characteristics.

The sheer accumulation of events and experiences is an important element to understanding time and the stress–cognition links. The cumulative effects of stress hormones are associated with smaller hippocampi (e.g., Heffelfinger & Newcomer, 2001; Starkman, Gebarski, Berent, & Schteingart, 1992; Uddo, Vasterling, Brailey, & Sutker, 1993; Vasterling et al., 2002). Therefore, older adults who have been exposed to more stressors throughout their lifetime compared with younger adults (Pearlin & Mullan, 1992) may have fewer resources (i.e., smaller hippocampi) to combat the negative effects of stressors, thereby resulting in heightened cognitive reactivity (i.e., reduced cognitive performance in response to stressors). It is also possible that resources may never fully develop when traumatic stressful events occur early in life (e.g., Vythilingam et al., 2002). Anderson and Craik (2000) suggested that reductions in hippocampal volume lead to reduced attentional resources and cognitive slowing. Subsequently, these deficits result in reduced cognitive control that then negatively impacts memory performance. Thus older adults, when faced with a stressor, may be more likely to experience lowered cognitive performance because they are unable to tap the same resources available to younger adults. Older adults who have more stressors than younger adults (interindividual difference) may be at greater risk, but the accumulation of stressors across the life course (intraindividual change) is also important.

STRESS AND COGNITION: PSYCHOLOGICAL PERSPECTIVES

Although the physiological view of cortisol has been the predominant view for explaining the effects of stress on cognition, the evidence we have reviewed thus far calls into question whether cortisol is the sole mechanism underlying this relationship. This is particularly important to underscore when examining the short-term effects of stressors, because cortisol appears to exact its toll over extended periods of time (e.g., Heffelfinger & Newcomer, 2001) but may be less influential immediately after a stressor (e.g., Domes et al., 2002). A complementary view of short-term effects is rooted in psychological processes, where mental control, cognitive interference, and resource capacity may be important mechanisms. Mandler (1979) suggested that the experience of stress draws attention away from primary task processing and redirects it toward changes in physical states and the conditions causing such changes. Similarly, Wegner (1988) argued that stress impairs mental control, specifically the ability to concentrate. Consistent with these perspectives, Sarason and colleagues (Sarason et al., 1996; Sarason, Sarason, Keefe, Hayes, & Shearin, 1986), as well as Eysenck and Calvo (1992), have advanced cognitive interference as a mechanism responsible for effects of stress on cognition. Cognitive interference, according to Sarason and Eysenck, can be task-oriented worries (e.g., worrying about performance quality) and off-task thoughts (e.g., thinking about a negative event that may have just happened). The premise of the cognitive interference perspective is that stress-related cognitions create a dual-task situation whereby attention is divided between task performance and coping with the stress. These cognitions in turn limit the capacity to process and store information. Reduced attention to primary-task processing results in decreased performance (e.g., Eysenck & Calvo, 1992). Sarason et al. (1996) stated that this cognitive interference can exist as task-unrelated thoughts (e.g., thoughts about a stressful event that was just experienced) and task-related worries (i.e., self-initiated performance evaluation because of a belief that performance quality is poor after stress). This perspective, then, is concerned with the context of the cognitive testing situation as it pertains to thoughts within the individual at the timing of testing.

Much of the evidence supporting the cognitive-interference hypothesis has come from Klein and colleagues, who have examined how negative life events stress is related to cognitive function. In an interindividual-differences design Klein used negative life events stress as a proxy for a person's proclivity to experience stress-related cognitive interference, such that individuals with higher levels of life stress were (implicitly) those who experience more recurring thoughts about those events (i.e., cognitive interference). Thus, Klein used life events stress to serve as an indirect index of stress-related cognitive interference. Baradell and Klein (1993) and Klein and Barnes (1994) examined how the impact of self-reported negative life events predicted performance on a decision-making task in a sample of college students. Baradell and Klein observed that individuals who reported greater negative life events stress and were more sensitive and aware of bodily states (e.g., heart rate) made more errors, used less efficient decision-making strategies, and made more decisions without examining all options compared with individuals who had low life stress. Similarly, Klein and Barnes observed that high–life-stress individuals who were keenly aware of bodily states and anxious at the time of testing made more errors on a complex reasoning task. These individuals were less efficient in their solving of the analogies, and this inefficiency mediated the effect of life stress on overall problem-solving performance. Klein and Barnes took these findings as evidence that individuals with high life event stress have more (intrusive) thoughts about their previous stressors and focus on bodily states, subsequently devoting less attention to information processing and task performance. One limitation of these studies is that no measure of cognitive interference was included; therefore life events stress is at best an indirect indicator of cognitive interference.

In subsequent studies also using interindividual differences designs, both life events stress and cognitive interference were found to be predictive of cognitive performance. Yee, Edmonson, Santoro, Begg, and Hunter (1996) demonstrated that individuals with higher levels of negative life events stress also exhibited the poorest performance on an analogical reasoning task. Furthermore, individuals reporting higher levels of cognitive interference during the reasoning task took longer to complete the task. Klein and Boals (2001b) conducted three studies examining the relationship among negative life events stress, stress-related cognitive interference, and working memory. They observed reliable negative relationships between negative life events stress and working memory and between stress-related cognitive interference and working memory. Furthermore, the observed relationships between stress and working memory increased as a function of capacity and processing demands, suggesting that cognitive interference is increasingly detrimental when processing and capacity demands are high. Given that these results are correlational, direction of causality cannot be determined. An alternative interpretation is that thought suppression or inhibition is governed by working memory and that individuals with lower working memory capacity are poorer at inhibiting off-task and distracting thoughts (Brewin & Beaton, 2002; Engle, 2002; Rosen & Engle, 1998; Stoltzfus, Hasher, & Zacks, 1996). Furthermore, because event severity and cognitive interference were not examined in the same statistical model, it is not clear whether the experience and impact of stress and the psychological reactivity (intrusive thoughts) about stressful experiences are unique predictors of working memory performance.

Although previous studies cannot provide evidence of directionality or causality, Klein and Boals (2001a) used a within-person design to demonstrate that reducing cognitive interference actually improves working memory. Using a stress reduction technique, they showed that expressive writing (Smyth, 1998) about a stressful life event increased working memory 7 weeks later, compared with writing about a neutral topic. Furthermore, the increase in working memory was mediated by a reduction in stress-related cognitive interference. This study provides the first evidence that stress-related cognitive interference impairs cognitive function, and it is consistent with theories positing such effects when cognitive capacity and attentional resources are limited (Eysenck & Calvo, 1992). In addition, Stawski, Sliwinski, and Smyth (2006) showed that cognitive interference can be especially salient within the context of aging. They found that stress-related cognitive reactivity was predictive of poorer working memory, episodic memory, and processing speed in older adults.

Taken together, the results of these studies indicate that the impact of life experiences and stress-related cognitive interference are important predictors of cognitive functioning in both young and old populations. Furthermore, the impact of negative life experiences may serve as an indirect indicator of stress-related cognitive interference. Given that these studies have demonstrated that a cognitive/psychological component of the stress response is an important factor related to cognitive performance, theories such as processing efficiency theory (Eysenck & Calvo, 1992) and the cognitive interference hypothesis appear tenable. Thus, stress-related cognitive interference may act as a cognitive load and create a situation in which limited capacity and processing resources are divided between task-oriented processing and stress-related cognitive interference. It is possible that cognitive interference could have both acute and long-term effects on cognition. Future studies that incorporate measures of cognitive interference within short time intervals as well as longer time intervals could examine whether cognitive interference acts across varying time frames, much like cortisol. Additionally, because the accumulation of stress can compound the negative effects of daily stressors (e.g., Zautra, 2003), repeated assessments could elucidate whether the effects of stress on cognition are a function of individual trait-like characteristics (e.g., a high-stress individual or someone with high cognitive interference) or a function of the time when the individual was assessed (e.g., a time of particularly high stress or high cognitive interference), or both (e.g., individuals who are assessed at a time of high stress but who typically experience few stressors may react the most).

LIMITATIONS OF THE COGNITIVE INTERFERENCE PERSPECTIVE

Although the literature supporting the cognitive interference hypothesis is small, the results indicate that stress-related cognitive interference is a factor reliably related to cognitive function. However, there are a number of reasons these studies cannot conclusively substantiate the cognitive interference hypothesis. One limitation of the studies providing support for the cognitive interference hypothesis is that cognitive interference is not assessed during concurrent cognitive processing. The cognitive interference hypothesis, and similarly processing efficiency theory (Eysenck & Calvo, 1992), posit impaired cognitive performance when stress-related cognitive interference is experienced simultaneously. Each of the studies reviewed here demonstrated a relationship between stress-related cognitive interference and cognitive performance but did so without evidence of an on-line effect. Thus, at best, these results suggest that people with higher levels of stress-related cognitive interference also exhibit poorer performance across a number of cognitive domains. As stated previously, individuals with a lower level of cognitive function may be increasingly susceptible to the experience of stress-related cognitive dysfunction because of an inability to inhibit off-task thoughts (Hasher & Zacks, 1988; Rosen & Engle, 1998). However, Yee et al. (1996) provided evidence indicating that individuals reporting higher levels of cognitive interference immediately after cognitive assessment exhibited poorer performance. Their findings were observed independent of any experience of stress, so the cause of the cognitive interference cannot be solely attributed to an acute stressful event but may be associated with a dispositional trait (cf. Pierce et al., 1998). To tease apart the influence of states and traits, study designs need to incorporate indicators of intraindividual variability and interindividual differences (Nesselroade, 1991). As we assert in more detail below, designs with frequent repeated assessments over time could be particularly beneficial for examining person- versus context-specific effects.

A second limitation of these studies is that cognitive interference was not measured with respect to a single specific event, proximal to performance on a cognitive task. Therefore, there is no indication that any interference was experienced at the time of, or even proximal to, the cognitive assessment. These assessments of stress-related cognitive interference were inefficient for examining the effect of stress-related cognitive interference during concurrent cognitive performance. Studies that examine both cognitive performance and cognitive interference immediately or even shortly after the experience of a stressful event would provide a better test of the cognitive interference hypothesis as well as provide evidence of direction of causality in the stress–cognition link. It is possible that cognitive interference may have a dynamic effect on memory, but it is also important to note that there could be interindividual trait-like differences in cognitive interference that may act as moderating effects in a dynamic process. We assert that daily diary designs could be beneficial for examining these processes as they occur (or shortly thereafter).

STRENGTHS OF THE DAILY DIARY DESIGN FOR EXAMINING SHORT-TERM EFFECTS

The daily experience paradigm allows researchers to examine within-person covariation between components of daily well-being and daily stressors over time, thereby establishing temporal links between daily stressors and well-being (Shiffman & Stone, 1998; Tennen, Suls, & Affleck, 1991). By studying within-person through-time covariation between daily stressors and well-being one can more precisely establish the short-term effects of concrete daily experiences (Almeida & Kessler, 1998; Bolger, DeLongis, Kessler, & Schilling, 1989; Larson & Almeida, 1999; Lewinsohn & Talkington, 1979; Stone, Reed, & Neale, 1987). Also, the daily diary design reduces retrospective recall bias because participants are asked to recall events that occurred over the previous 24-hour period as opposed to a week or even a year (Kessler, Mroczek, & Belli, 1999). Therefore, a more accurate picture of individuals' daily lives can be captured with this design, and more accurate assessments of stressors and cognitive interference are possible. When conclusions are drawn between people about the relationship between the predictors and outcomes, the covariation that occurs through time is lost. In a within-person design, conclusions can be made about the simultaneous effects of within-person covariation as well as between-person differences. This is especially important when many interindividual differences (e.g., trait-level cognitive interference) may exist in the within-person relationship between stressors and cognition.

In a daily diary study of older adults that examined daily stressors and memory failures over 8 consecutive days, Neupert, Almeida, et al. (2006) found that there was significant within-person covariation between concurrent day stressors and memory failures as well as between stressors and change in memory failures from one day to the next. These associations remained even after controlling for the effects of neuroticism, life event stressors, and health. Life event stressors were also related to the number of memory failures, such that people who reported more life event stressors also reported more memory failures. The general trend in the association between stressors (life events and daily events) and memory failures supports the findings of many laboratory-based studies (e.g., Vedhara et al., 2000) and extends previous work to a more naturalistic setting. Although life event stressors and daily stressors are different types of events (Wheaton, 1999), they are both important when one is examining everyday memory failures. This finding not only shows the association between stressful life events and memory but also underscores the deleterious effects of seemingly minor stressors that most people experience frequently on a daily basis. Therefore, even if someone does not experience any major life event stressors, day-to-day stressors can still negatively affect his or her memory. When participants experienced interpersonal stressors, they experienced more memory failures on that same day as well as an increase in memory failures from one day to the next. It is possible that interpersonal stressors are especially distracting for older adults, who tend to be solution oriented when faced with an interpersonal conflict (Bergstrom & Nussbaum, 1996) and therefore place more effort and attention on finding a solution for emotionally salient goals (Carstensen, Isaacowitz, & Charles,

1999). It is also possible that interpersonal stressors are related to memory failures through cognitive interference, because stressful social situations have been linked with more intrusive cognitions (Sarason et al., 1996). Because effort and attention are directed toward the interpersonal conflict, less attention may be available for tasks requiring memory.

Sliwinski et al. (2006) examined age differences in the effects of naturally occurring daily stressors on cognitive performance. Participants completed a daily diary of stressful events (Almeida, Wethington, & Kessler, 2002) as well as two performance-based cognitive tasks used to assess working memory (the *n*-back [McElree, 2001; Verhaeghen & Basak, 2005] and *n*-count [Garavan, 1998]) for 6 days over the course of 14 days. Participants completed two versions of each task, one with high attentional demands and one without. On days when stress was greater than usual, performance on the attentionally demanding versions of each task was significantly poorer, whereas performance on the nonattentional demanding versions remained unaffected. Furthermore, the stress effect was significantly larger for the older adults on the *n*-count task, suggesting that the effects of stress on cognition may be more detrimental to older adults. These results indicate that stress impairs attentionally demanding cognitive performance and that older adults may be more susceptible to these effects. This study is the first to link naturally occurring stressors to laboratory-based indicators of cognition, but future research that is able to examine stress and cognition on consecutive days could test for lagged effects of the link between stress and cognition from one day to the next. This method and analysis would allow researchers to determine whether the cumulative buildup of stressors over a short period could be important for short-term changes in cognition. It is important to note that daily diary designs could include assessments of cortisol and cognitive interference to examine the saliency of both stress mechanisms. Daily diary studies conducted to date have not empirically determined a mechanism for the observed acute effects of stress on cognition. In addition to identifying possible single mechanisms, future studies could examine whether multiple mechanisms are acting in concert in the dynamic interplay between stress and cognition.

STRENGTHS OF THE MEASUREMENT BURST DESIGN FOR EXAMINING SHORT-TERM AND LONG-TERM EFFECTS

Just as a single assessment of an attribute does not convey information about intraindividual variability, a design with 1 week or 2 weeks of daily assessments does not convey information about change in intraindividual variability transpiring over longer intervals. As Nesselroade (1991) noted, the accurate assessment of intraindividual variability requires repeated assessments over short time intervals, and the assessment of intraindividual change requires repeated measurements over intervals suitable to the subject of inquiry. He proposed that longitudinal research designs be planned around successive "bursts" of measurements rather than just successive measurements. Specifically, each time of measurement within a longitudinal design should provide estimates of intraindividual variability. Researchers have begun to use these suggestions by conducting repeated daily diary assessments over the course of months (e.g., the Cognition, Health, and Aging Project at Syracuse University), years (The VA Normative Aging Study), and even decades (the ongoing National Study of Daily Experiences study within the Midlife in the United States survey). The measurement burst design could be particularly valuable for the study of stress and cognition, because questions regarding the unfolding of short-term effects within longer time periods as individuals and contexts change could be addressed. Specifically, the dynamic processes that occur at and interact over difference cadences (e.g., days, years), between stressors and cognition, such as cortisol, cognitive interference, and developmental changes, could be teased apart with the implementation of this design.

CONCLUSION

We assert that sampling time should be taken seriously, because it has tremendous implications for the underlying process being examined. As others (e.g., Martin & Hofer, 2004) have noted, sampling time will influence analysis and interpretation of intraindividual variability and short-term change. The measurement burst design provides a novel approach for examining the short- and long-term cognitive effects of stressors, but this design can also be applied to other areas of cognitive aging. It is important to note that measurement burst designs can capture short-term processes as they unfold within a more long-term context. By extending the daily diary design to a measurement burst design, researchers will be able to examine long-term changes in short-term covariation within the changing contexts of the individual.

REFERENCES

Almeida, D. M., & Kessler, R. C. (1998). Everyday stressors and gender differences in daily distress. *Journal of Personality and Social Psychology, 75,* 670–680.

Almeida, D. M., Wethington, E., & Kessler, R. C. (2002). The Daily Inventory of Stressful Events: An investigator-based approach for measuring daily stressors. *Assessment, 9,* 41–55.

Anderson, N. D., & Craik, F. I. M. (2000). Memory in the aging brain. In E. Tulving & F. I. M. Craik (Eds.), *The Oxford handbook of memory* (pp. 411–425). New York: Oxford University Press.

Baltes, P. B., Reese, H. W., & Nesselroade, J. R. (1977). *Life-span developmental psychology: Introduction to research methods.* Hillsdale, NJ: Lawrence Erlbaum.

Baradell, J. G., & Klein, K. (1993). Relationship of life stress and body consciousness to hypervigilant decision making. *Journal of Personality and Social Psychology, 64,* 267–273.

Bergstrom, M. J., & Nussbaum, J. F. (1996). Cohort differences in interpersonal conflict: Implications for the older patient–younger care provider interaction. *Health Communication, 8,* 233–248.

Bolger, N., Davis, A., & Rafaeli, E. (2003). Diary methods: Capturing life as it is lived. *Annual Review of Psychology, 54,* 579–616.

Bolger, N., DeLongis, A., Kessler, R. C., & Schilling, E. A. (1989). Effects of daily stress on negative mood. *Journal of Personality and Social Psychology, 57,* 808–818.

Brewin, C. R., & Beaton, A. (2002). Thought suppression, intelligence, and working memory capacity. *Behaviour Research and Therapy, 40,* 923–930.

Brown, E. S., Woolston, D. J., Frol, A., Bobadilla, L., Khan, D. A., Hanczyc, M., et al. (2004). Hippocampal volume, spectroscopy, cognition, and mood in patients recovering from corticosteroid therapy. *Biological Psychiatry, 55,* 538–545.

Carstensen, L. L., Isaacowitz, D. M., & Charles, S. T. (1999). Taking time seriously: A theory of socioemotional selectivity. *American Psychologist, 54,* 165–181.

Colsher, P., & Wallace, R. (1991). Longitudinal application of cognitive function measures in a defined population of community-dwelling elders. *Annals of Epidemiology, 1,* 215–230.

Dickerson, S. S., & Kemeny, M. E. (2004). Acute stressors and cortisol response: A theoretical integration and synthesis of laboratory research. *Psychological Bulletin, 130,* 355–391.

Domes, G., Heinrichs, M., Reichwald, U., & Hautzinger, M. (2002). Hypothalamic–pituitary–adrenal axis reactivity to stress and memory in middle-aged women: High responders exhibit enhanced declarative memory performance. *Psychoneuroendocrinology, 27,* 843–853.

Earles, J. L., & Coon, V. E. (1994). Adult age differences in long-term memory for performed activities. *Journal of Gerontology, 49,* 32–34.

Engle, R. W. (2002). Working memory capacity as executive attention. *Current Directions in Psychological Science, 11,* 19–23.

Evans, D. A., Beckett, L. A., Albert, M. S., Hebert, L. E., Scherr, P. A., Funkenstein, H. H., et al. (1993). Level of education and change in cogni-tive function in a community population of older persons. *Annals of Epidemiology, 3,* 71–77.

Eysenck, M. W., & Calvo, M. G. (1992). Anxiety and performance: The Processing Efficiency Theory. *Cognition and Emotion, 6,* 409–434.

Foos, P. W., & Sarno, A. J. (1998). Adult age differences in semantic and episodic memory. *Journal of Genetic Psychology, 159,* 279–312.

Garavan, H. (1998). Serial attention within working memory. *Memory & Cognition, 26,* 263–276.

Hasher, L., & Zacks, R. T. (1988). Working memory, comprehension, and aging: A review and a new view. In G. H. Bower (Ed.), *The psychology of learning and motivation* (Vol. 22, pp. 193–225). San Diego, CA: Academic Press.

Heffelfinger, A. K., & Newcomer, J. W. (2001). Glucocorticoid effects on memory function over the human life span. *Development and Psychopathology, 13,* 491–513.

Jelicic, M., & Bonke, B. (2001). Memory impairments following chronic stress? A critical review. *European Journal of Psychiatry, 15,* 225–232.

Jelicic, M., Geraerts, E., Merckelbach, H., & Guerrieri, R. (2004). Acute stress enhances memory for emotional words, but impairs memory for neutral words. *International Journal of Neuroscience, 114,* 1343–1351.

Kanner, A. D., Coyne, J. C., Schaefer, C., & Lazarus, R. S. (1981). Comparison of two models of stress measurement: Daily hassles and uplifts versus major life events. *Journal of Behavioral Medicine, 4,* 1–39.

Kausler, D. H., & Hakami, M. K. (1983). Memory for activities: Adult age differences and intentionality. *Developmental Psychology, 19,* 889–894.

Kessler, R. C., Mroczek, D. K., & Belli, R. F. (1999). Retrospective adult assessment of childhood psychopathology. In D. Shaffer & J. Richters (Eds.), *Assessment in child and adolescent psychopathology* (pp. 256–286). New York: Guilford Press.

Kirschbaum, C., Wolf, O. T., May, M., Wippich, W., & Hellhammer, D. H. (1996). Stress- and treatment-induced elevations of cortisol levels associated with impaired declarative memory in health adults. *Life Sciences, 58,* 1475–1483.

Klein, K., & Barnes, D. (1994). The relationship of life stress to problem solving: Task complexity and individual differences. *Social Cognition, 12,* 187–204.

Klein, K., & Boals, A. (2001a). Expressive writing can increase working memory capacity. *Journal of Experimental Psychology: General, 130,* 520–533.

Klein, K., & Boals, A. (2001b). The relationship of life events stress and working memory capacity. *Applied Cognitive Psychology, 15,* 565–579.

Larson, R., & Almeida, D. M. (1999). Emotional transmission in the daily lives of families: A new paradigm for studying family process. *Journal of Marriage and the Family, 61,* 5–20.

Lazarus, R. S. (1999). *Stress and emotion: A new synthesis.* New York: Springer.

Lewinsohn, P. M., & Talkington, J. (1979). Studies on the measurement of unpleasant events and relations with depression. *Applied Psychological Measurement, 3,* 83–101.

Lupien, S. J., de Leon, M., de Santi, S., Convit, A., Tarshish, C., Nair, N. P. V., et al. (1998). Cortisol levels during human aging predict hippocampal atrophy and memory deficits. *Nature Neuroscience, 1,* 69–73.

Lupien, S. J., Lecours, A. R., Lussier, I., Schwartz, G., Nair, N. P. V., & Meaney, M. J. (1994). Basal cortisol levels and cognitive deficits in human aging. *Journal of Neuroscience, 14,* 2893–2903.

Lupien, S. J., Lecours, A. R., Schwartz, G., Sharma, S., Hauger, R. L., Meaney, M. J., et al. (1996). Longitudinal study of basal cortisol levels in health elderly subjects: Evidence for subgroups. *Neurobiology of Aging, 17,* 95–105.

Lupien, S. J., & Lepage, M. (2001). Stress, memory, and the hippocampus: Can't live with it, can't live without it. *Behavioural Brain Research, 127,* 137–158.

Lupien, S. J., & McEwen, B. S. (1997). The acute effects of corticosteroids on cognition: Integration of animal and human model studies. *Brain Research Reviews, 24,* 1–27.

Madden, D. J. (1985). Age-related slowing in the retrieval of information from long-term memory. *Journal of Gerontology, 40,* 208–210.

Mandler, G. (1979). Thought processes, consciousness and stress. In V. Hamilton & D. W. Warburton (Eds.), *Human stress and cognition: An information processing approach.* New York: Wiley.

Martin, M., & Hofer, S. M. (2004). Intraindividual variability, change, and aging: Conceptual and analytical issues. *Gerontology, 50,* 7–11.

McElree, B. (2001). Working memory and focal attention. *Journal of Experimental Psychology: Learning, Memory, and Cognition, 27,* 817–835.

McEwen, B. S. (1999). Stress and the aging hippocampus. *Frontiers in Neuroendocrinology, 20,* 49–70.

McEwen, B. S., & Sapolsky, R. M. (1995). Stress and cognitive function. *Current Opinion in Neurobiology, 5,* 205–216.

Merriam-Webster. (2005). *Medical dictionary.* Retrieved December 8, 2006, from http://www.nlm.nih.gov/medlineplus/mplusdictionary.html

Molenaar, P. C. M. (2004). A manifesto on psychology as idiographic science: Bringing the person back into scientific psychology, this time forever. *Measurement: Interdisciplinary Research and Perspectives, 2,* 201–218.

Nesselroade, J. R. (1991). The warp and woof of the developmental fabric. In R. M. Downs, L. S. Liben, & D. S. Palermo (Eds.), *Visions of aesthetics, the environment & development: The legacy of Joachim F. Wohlwill* (pp. 213–240). Hillsdale, NJ: Lawrence Erlbaum.

Nesselroade, J. R., & Ghisletta, P. (2000). Beyond static concepts in modeling behavior. In L. R. Bergman, R. B. Cairns, L. G. Nilsson, & L. Nystedt (Eds.), *Developmental science and the holistic approach* (pp. 121–135). Mahwah, NJ: Lawrence Erlbaum.

Neupert, S. D., Almeida, D. M., Mroczek, D. K., & Spiro, A. III. (2006). Daily stressors and memory failures in a naturalistic setting: Findings from the VA Normative Aging Study. *Psychology and Aging, 21,* 424–429.

Neupert, S. D., Miller, L. M. S., & Lachman, M. E. (2006). Physiological reactivity to cognitive stressors: Variations by age and socioeconomic status. *International Journal of Aging and Human Development, 62,* 221–235.

Pearlin, L. I., & Mullan, J. T. (1992). Loss and stress in aging. In M. L. Wykle, L. May, & E. Kahana (Eds.), *Stress and health among the elderly* (pp. 117–132). New York: Springer.

Pierce, G. R., Ptacek, J. T., Taylor, B., Yee, P. L., Henderson, C. A., Lauventi, H. J., et al. (1998). The role of dispositional and situational factors in cognitive interference. *Journal of Personality and Social Psychology, 75,* 1016–1031.

Rosch, P. J. (1997). Stress and memory loss: Some speculations and solutions. *Stress Medicine, 13,* 1–6.

Rosen, V. M., & Engle, R. W. (1998). Working memory capacity and suppression. *Journal of Memory and Language, 39,* 418–436.

Salthouse, T. A. (1996). The processing-speed theory of adult age differences in cognition. *Psychological Review, 103,* 403–428.

Salthouse, T. A., & Babcock, R. L., & Shaw, R. J. (1991). Effects of adult age on structural and operational capacities in working memory. *Psychology and Aging, 6,* 118–127.

Sapolsky, R. M. (1992). *Stress, the aging brain, and the mechanisms of neuron death.* Cambridge, MA: MIT Press.

Sapolsky, R. M. (1996, August 9). Why stress is bad for your brain. *Science, 273,* 749–750.

Sapolsky, R. M., Krey, L. C., & McEwen, B. S. (1986). The neuroendocrinology of stress and aging: The glucocorticoid cascade hypothesis. *Endocrine Reviews, 7,* 284–301.

Sapolsky, R. M., Romero, L. M., & Munck, A. U. (2000). How do glucocorticoids influence stress responses? Integrating permissive, suppressive, stimulatory, and preparative actions. *Endocrine Reviews, 21,* 55–89.

Sarason, I. G., Pierce, G. R., & Sarason, B. R. (1996). *Cognitive interference: Theories, methods, and findings.* Mahwah, NJ: Lawrence Erlbaum.

Sarason, I. G., Sarason, B. R., Keefe, D. E., Hayes, B. E., & Shearin, E. N. (1986). Cognitive interference: Situational determinants and traitlike characteristics. *Journal of Personality and Social Psychology, 51,* 215–226.

Seeman, T. E., McEwen, B. S., Rowe, J. W., & Singer, B. H. (2001). Allostatic load as a marker of cumulative biological risk: MacArthur Studies on Successful Aging. *Proceedings of the National Academy of Sciences, USA, 98,* 4770–4775.

Seeman, T. E., McEwen, B. S., Singer, B. H., Albert, M. S., & Rowe, J. W. (1997). Increase in urinary cortisol excretion and memory declines: MacArthur Studies on Successful Aging. *Journal of Clinical Endocrinology and Metabolism, 82,* 2458–2465.

Selye, H. (1936). A syndrome produced by diverse nocuous agents. *Nature, 138,* 32.

Serido, J., Almeida, D. M., & Wethington, E. (2004). Chronic stressors and daily hassles: Unique and interactive relationships with psychological distress. *Journal of Health and Social Behavior, 45,* 17–33.

Shiffman, S., & Stone, A. A. (1998). Ecological momentary assessment: A new tool for behavioral medicine research. In D. S. Krantz & A. Baum (Eds.), *Technology and methods in behavioral medicine* (pp. 117–131). Mahwah, NJ: Lawrence Erlbaum.

Sliwinski, M. J., Smyth, J. M., Hofer, S. M., & Stawski, R. S. (2006). Intraindividual coupling of daily stress and cognition. *Psychology and Aging, 21,* 545–557.

Smyth, J. M. (1998). Written emotional expression: Effect sizes, outcome types, and moderating variables. *Journal of Consulting and Clinical Psychology, 66,* 174–184.

Starkman, M. N., Gebarski, S. S., Berent, S., & Schteingart, D. E. (1992). Hippocampal formation volume, memory dysfunction and cortisol levels in patients with Cushing's syndrome. *Biological Psychiatry, 32,* 756–765.

Starkman, M. N., Giordani, B., Berent, S., Schork, M. A., & Schteingart, D. E. (2001). Elevated cortisol levels in Cushing's disease are associated with cognitive decrements. *Psychosomatic Medicine, 63,* 985–993.

Starkman, M. N., Giordani, B., Gebarski, S. S., & Schteingart, D. E. (2003). Improvement in learning associated with increase in hippocampal volume formation. *Biological Psychiatry, 53,* 233–238.

Stawski, R. S., Sliwinski, M. J., & Smyth, J. M. (2006). Stress-related cognitive interference predicts cognitive function in old age. *Psychology and Aging, 21,* 535–544.

Stoltzfus, E. R., Hasher, L., & Zacks, R. T. (1996). Working memory and aging: Current status of the inhibitory view. In J. T. E. Richardson (Ed.), *Working memory and human cognition* (pp. 66–88). New York: Oxford University Press.

Stone, A. A., Reed, B. R., & Neale, J. M. (1987). Changes in daily event frequencies precede episodes of physical symptoms. *Journal of Human Stress, 13,* 70–74.

Tennen, H., Suls, J., & Affleck, G. (1991). Personality and daily experience: The promise and the challenge. *Journal of Personality, 59,* 313–336.

Uddo, M., Vasterling, J. J., Brailey, K., & Sutker, P. B. (1993). Memory and attention in combat-related post-traumatic stress disorder (PTSD). *Journal of Psychopathology and Behavioral Assessment, 15,* 43–52.

Vasterling, J. J., Duke, L. M., Brailey, K., Constans, J. I., Allain, A. N., & Sutker, P. B. (2002). Attention, learning, and memory performances and intellectual resources in Vietnam veterans: PTSD and no disorder comparisons. *Neuropsychology, 16,* 5–14.

Vedhara, K., Hyde, J., Gilchrist, I. D., Tytherleigh, M., & Plummer, S. (2000). Acute stress, memory, attention and cortisol. *Psychoneuroendocrinology, 25,* 535–549.

Verhaeghen, P., & Basak, C. (2005). Ageing and switching of the focus of attention in working memory: Results from a modified N-Back task. *Quarterly Journal of Experimental Psychology: Human Experimental Psychology, 58A,* 134–154.

VonDras, D. D., Powless, M. R., Olson, A. K., Wheeler, D., & Snudden, A. L. (2005). Differential effects of everyday stress on the episodic memory test performances of young, mid-life, and older adults. *Aging & Mental Health, 9,* 60–70.

Vythilingam, M., Heim, C., Newport, J., Miller, A. H., Anderson, E., Bronen, R., et al. (2002). Childhood trauma associated with smaller hippocampal volume in women with major depression. *American Journal of Psychiatry, 159,* 2072–2080.

Wegner, D. M. (1988). Stress and mental control. In S. Fisher & J. Reason (Eds.), *Handbook of life stress, cognition and health* (pp. 683–697). London: Wiley.

Wheaton, B. (1999). The nature of stressors. In A. V. Horowitz & T. L. Scheid (Eds.), *A handbook for the study of mental health* (pp. 176–197). New York: Cambridge University Press.

Wilson, R. S., Beckett, L. A., Bennett, D. A., Albert, M. S., & Evans, D. A. (1999). Change in cognitive function in older persons from a community population: Relation to age and Alzheimer's disease. *Archives of Neurology, 56,* 1274–1279.

Wolf, O. T., Schommer, N. C., Hellhammer, D. H., McEwen, B. S., & Kirschbaum, C. (2001). The relationship between stress induced cortisol levels and memory differs between men and women. *Psychoneuroendocrinology, 26,* 711–720.

Wright, C. E., Kunz-Ebrecht, S. R., Iliffe, S., Foese, O., & Steptoe, A. (2005). Physiological correlates of cognitive functioning in an elderly population. *Psychoneuroendocrinology, 30,* 826–838.

Yee, P. L., Edmonson, B., Santoro, K. E., Begg, A. E., & Hunter, C. D. (1996). Cognitive effects of life stress and learned helplessness. *Anxiety, Stress, and Coping, 9,* 301–319.

Zautra, A. J. (2003). *Emotions, stress, and health.* London: Oxford University Press.

30

COGNITIVE TESTING IN LARGE-SCALE SURVEYS

Assessment by Telephone

MARGIE E. LACHMAN AND PATRICIA A. TUN

Cognitive functioning is a key indicator of an individual's overall health and well-being, yet large-scale survey studies of aging typically do not examine cognition. Cognitive measures are seldom included in survey instruments, perhaps because it is assumed that reliable and valid assessments are too difficult and time consuming to administer in a survey format by lay interviewers. Assessment of cognitive functioning traditionally is carried out in person, usually in a laboratory or clinical setting by trained testers, using long, time-consuming batteries that include multiple measures of each cognitive domain of interest. Thus, many survey researchers have been reluctant to include cognitive assessment in their batteries even though there is increasing recognition of the importance of cognitive functioning for understanding overall functioning and health, especially in later life.

Psychologists, steeped in psychometric tradition, typically administer lengthy test batteries with multiple items and trials in order to achieve reliable and valid assessments of cognition. This approach to cognitive testing is not feasible for the cutting-edge research that emphasizes multidisciplinary perspectives, including a focus on brain and behavior or mind and body connections, and that must address multiple domains in addition to cognition. Thus, there is a growing demand for shorter cognitive batteries to include in these "big picture" studies. In current research paradigms with a focus on multiple aspects of functioning, it is often not feasible to spend more than 15 minutes on any given domain such as cognition. Thus, it is important to select brief but highly reliable tests that are sensitive to variations and individual differences within the full range of cognitive functioning. Because of rising costs and reluctance of respondents to talk with interviewers in person or in their homes, there has been increasing use of telephone rather than face-to-face data collection. Thus, it becomes critical to develop and validate cognitive batteries

AUTHORS' NOTE: This research was supported by a grant from the National Institute on Aging (PO1-AG020166) to conduct a longitudinal follow-up of the MIDUS (Midlife in the U.S.) investigation. We appreciate Chandra Murphy's valuable assistance with data analysis and manuscript preparation.

that are short enough to be included in national surveys but are also reliable, valid, sensitive to wide age variations, and appropriate for telephone administration. The MacArthur Foundation Research Network on Successful Midlife Development (Brim, Ryff, & Kessler, 2004) has made great strides in developing brief but psychometrically sound instruments for large survey administration in areas traditionally using very long batteries. This trend for brief but reliable and valid measures was begun in the first Midlife in the U.S. National Survey (MIDUS; Lachman & Firth, 2004) for measures of personality, sense of control, and well-being and health, and it was extended to cognition in the second wave, the MIDUS II.

WHY ASSESS COGNITION IN SURVEYS?

Including cognitive measure in epidemiological and longitudinal surveys has multiple benefits. For survey researchers it is useful to describe cognitive functioning of participants and to explore links between cognition and other domains of interest, such as health and economic behavior. Although much of the previous survey work on cognitive aging has used basic measures for dementia screening, there is an increased effort to measure variations of cognitive functioning in the normal range. Even when the primary focus of a study is on other variables, it is important for researchers to verify that participants' cognitive status is adequate to ensure valid responses to their questions. Moreover, there is evidence that age-related cognitive changes can impact several aspects of self-reports of behavior and opinion, including comprehension of questions and effects of question context and response formatting (Schwarz, 1999). It is also beneficial for researchers in the field of cognitive aging to have cognitive assessments with larger, more representative samples than are typically studied in the laboratory.

Understanding cognitive aging involves a focus on more than just age differences. Laboratory samples are often selected to have high education to match college students and to have few or no health problems; even when such samples are not deliberately recruited, the pool of older adults who volunteer to come into the

laboratory are typically high functioning because of self-selection. Such studies typically involve the comparison of young college students and older adults, matched on educational level, using an extreme two-age-groups design. As a consequence, there is little within-group variability in health, socioeconomic status and other key factors. Survey research goes beyond the limits of the laboratory and enables data collection with more representative samples. Thus, inclusion of cognitive batteries in surveys allows for investigation of cognitive aging in relation to a broader range of dimensions, such as disease, education, mental health, and stress.

Effective cognitive functioning throughout adulthood is a key element not only in an individual's quality of life but also in the ability to remain an independently functioning member of society. Although some large-scale surveys have included telephone assessments of cognition, the focus has largely been on screening for dementia (see Table 30.1). Declines in cognitive function can impact older adults' ability to perform instrumental activities of daily living such as managing finances, following medical instructions, and planning sequences of activities, with important implications for health care and both private and public resources (Herzog & Wallace, 1997). Effective functioning in the second half of the life span can be threatened not only by devastating cognitive declines and dementia such as Alzheimer's disease but also by mild cognitive impairment (Petersen et al., 1999) and normative age-related loss.

In the last two decades, a substantial body of research findings from the laboratory and from large longitudinal studies has documented age-related declines in cognitive abilities among adults over age 60 (e.g., Craik & Salthouse, 2000; Salthouse, 1996; Schaie, 1996). To date, much is less known about changes in cognitive abilities during midlife, even though a large proportion of the U.S. population is now entering the mature years with cognitive systems that will undergo age-related changes (Dixon, deFrias, & Maitland, 2001; Sternberg, Grigorenko, & Oh, 2001; Willis & Schaie, 1999). Baby Boomers, who represent some 77 million people born after World War II (between 1946 and 1964), now comprise one third of the American population and are entrenched in the

Table 30.1 Telephone Studies for Assessment of Dementia

Cognitive Battery	Study	No. of Participants	Age of Participants	Cognitive Subtests
Blessed Telephone Information Memory Concentration (TIMC)	Kawas et al. (1995)	49	50–98 years	TIMC administered by phone and in person.
Mini-Mental State Examination (MMSE)	Jorm et al. (1993)		74+ years	
MMSE	Roccaforte et al. (1992)	100		Validity of telephone version of the MMSE; Brief Neuropsychological Screening Test; MMSE as part of the Adult Lifestyles and Function Interview (ALFI–MMSE)
MMSE	Monteiro et al. (1998)	34 (17 women, 17 men)	M = 76.8 (women) M = 77.6 (men)	• Global Deterioration Scale • Functional Assessment Staging • Behavioral Pathology in Alzheimer's Disease Rating Scale • Brief Cognitive Rating Scale • MMSE
Minnesota Cognitive Acuity Screen	Knopman et al. (1999)	228	M = 82.4 years	Orientation, Delayed Word Recall, Verbal fluency, Computation, Judgment
Modified MMSE (3MS)	Norton et al. (1999)	263	63–93 years	3MS and the Telephone Modified MMSE
Short Portable Mental Status Questionnaire (SPMSQ)	Roccaforte et al. (1992)			Tested reliability of telephone version of SPMSQ
Structured Telephone Interview for Dementia	Go et al. (1997)		60–88 years	The National Institute of Mental Health Genetics Initiative: Clinical Dementia Rating Scale
Telephone Interview of Cognitive Status (TICS)	Brandt et al. (1988)	133		

Cognitive Battery	Study	No. of Participants	Age of Participants	Cognitive Subtests
TICS	Desmond et al. (1994)	72	M = 72.1 years	
TICS	Grodstein et al. (2000)	2,138 women	70–78 years	
TICS	Järvenpää et al. (2002)	56	52–80 years	TICS, TELE
TICS Modified (TICS–M)	Buckwalter et al. (2002)	3,681 women	80+ years	
TICS–M Computer Assisted Telephone Interview	Buckwalter et al. (2002)	3,681 women	80+	
TELE self-report interview	Gatz et al. (1997)	65 pairs of twins	55+ years	TELE, including the Mental Status Questionnaire MMSE
	Järvenpää et al. (2002)	56	52–80 years	Compared TELE with TICS and MMSE
	Chumbler & Zhang (1998)	48	65+ years	Validity of a modified telephone screening device (Gatz et al., 1995) against the MMSE
Telephone-Assessed Mental State Exam (TAMS)	Lanska et al. (1993)	30	59–88 years	Compared TAMS with MMSE and Alzheimer's Disease Assessment Scale

middle years (Lemme, 1995). Midlife is a period characterized by myriad tasks (Lachman & James, 1997), including juggling career and family responsibilities (Lachman, 2004). These place heavy stress on the ability to divide attention between multiple concurrent activities, which often becomes more difficult with increased age (Tun & Wingfield, 1995). Nevertheless, there is a paucity of nationally representative data on cognitive functioning in mid- and later life, in part because it is difficult for this age group to come to the laboratory for testing given their busy schedules (Lachman, 2004).

Most major epidemiological surveys, such as the Longitudinal Survey on Aging (M. E. Miller, Rejeski, Reboussin, Ten Have, & Ettinger, 2000) do not measure cognitive function at all. One exception is the Asset and Health Dynamics Among the Oldest Old (AHEAD) study, a telephone survey of 6,500 adults age 70 and over that documented significant changes in mental status and memory function (Herzog & Wallace, 1997). Another is the multisite MacArthur Study of Successful Aging, which examined individuals between the ages of 70 and 79 (Albert et al., 1995). Although longitudinal studies have demonstrated significant changes in midlife for some mental abilities (the Baltimore Aging Study [Shock et al., 1984], Berlin Aging Study [Baltes & Mayer, 1999], Seattle Longitudinal Study [Schaie, 1996], Victoria Longitudinal Study [Hultsch, Hertzog, Dixon, & Small, 1998]), and for some specific groups, such as men (e.g., the Normative Aging Study; Aldwin, Spiro, Levenson, & Bosse, 1989) and postmenopausal women (Women's Health Initiative—Memory Study; Shumaker et al., 1998), no nationally representative, large-scale data have been available specifically for the cognitive functioning of middle-aged men and women until the MIDUS II survey. Results from this study are summarized below.

TELEPHONE TESTING: ADVANTAGES AND LIMITATIONS

In general, cognitive testing is done in person; face-to-face assessment is desirable because it gives the most flexibility in terms of testing equipment and stimuli. It also enables one to establish greater rapport with the participants and personalized treatment in terms of giving breaks and sensitivity to fatigue and understanding of instructions. With face-to-face testing it is possible to include a wider range of tests, including those with visual components, those that require written responses, or those with specialized stimuli or equipment that cannot be administered by phone. Nevertheless, the use of telephone assessment for cognitive testing has a good deal of promise.

Telephone testing offers advantages to both clinicians and researchers, including convenience; low expense; and the opportunity to test a greater number of individuals, including those who are unable or unwilling to be tested in person in a laboratory or clinical setting. Testing by telephone allows researchers to access a wider, more diverse range of respondents who vary in physical mobility and geographical distance from the investigator, as well as in health status, age, socioeconomic status, racial/ethnic background, and educational level. Some respondents may also feel more comfortable with the anonymity of phone testing, because they do not have to face an interviewer if they perform poorly.

There are some limitations associated with telephone testing. It is essential that the respondents can clearly hear the interviewer and test stimuli. Given that increased age is associated with declines in auditory acuity, this can present a challenge. Hearing problems can be exacerbated over the telephone because of variations in the quality of connection, the phone equipment, and technical difficulties. Thus, it is important to include a brief hearing test in telephone batteries to establish the effectiveness of hearing. Fortunately, hearing has not presented a significant problem in previous studies, and one telephone study reported that fewer than 4% of an older sample had hearing difficulties (Lipton et al., 2003).

The use of cell phones is not ideal for telephone testing given that they may introduce variable lags in the signal relating to delays in propagation, transmission, and processing, all of which could affect response latencies. This is especially problematic when timing is critical for a test, as is the case with the Stop and Go Switch Task, which we describe later. Some participants, especially those in the younger age ranges, may have only cell phone service. It may be possible to test these individuals on land line phones in their work setting. Some phones have the push buttons in the head set, which can make it difficult if push-button technology is used for the test responses. Portable phones also can have more interference than other types of phone equipment.

Background noise in the home or work setting also may interfere with the clarity of presentation for cognitive tests by telephone. It may be difficult to monitor background noise or other distractions, which can affect performance and are typically controlled in laboratory settings. However, we have been generally successful in arranging phone interviews at times that are convenient for respondents and that minimize distractions from other people or activities.

Cheating is another potential caveat of telephone testing. Given that the respondent usually cannot be seen by the tester (unless a videophone or webcam is used), it is possible for the respondent to write words down during a memory test, or use paper and pencil to jot down notes. It is also possible for the respondent to get some type of assistance, either from another person or by looking something up in a dictionary or other source. In our experience, we believe the incidence of cheating is low based on the correlations between scores from in-person and telephone administrations in our pilot studies (Tun & Lachman, 2006b), and from the Health and Retirement Study (HRS) reports of concordance between both modes of assessment (Herzog & Rodgers, 1998). In the introduction phase of the survey, we emphasize to participants that no one is expected to be able to answer or complete all of the test questions. We have implemented two procedures to help guard against unwanted writing or cheating. We suggest to our respondents that they close their eyes during the testing and indicate that this can help with concentration and performance. Another strategy we have used is to ask the respondent to hold the phone receiver in one hand and a blank piece of paper in the other hand. We specify that looking at the blank page helps focus and avoid distraction from other sources. It also serves to prevent the respondent from writing. To investigate possible cheating

we examine unusual patterns of performance, such as extreme scores, for example, 100% recall on a word list or scores greater than 2 standard deviations above the age group mean. Other unusual patterns include absence of forgetting between immediate and delayed testing of verbal memory or large improvements in performance with a retest. We also compare level of performance on tests that could be influenced by cheating and those that are less susceptible to cheating. If there is a wide disparity we take this as an indication of potential cheating. The decision as to whether and when to drop data from cases suspected of cheating will depend on the specific research circumstances.

ADMINISTRATION AND SCORING

There are two general administration modes for testing by telephone: (1) a live interviewer or (2) a computer. We have found that participants, especially older adults, prefer to talk with a person rather than a computer. The live interviewer can make sure that the person clearly hears the tests and can verify that the person understands the instructions before beginning the testing and stop the testing if something goes awry or if the respondent has further questions during the test process. Moreover, the live interviewer can detect problems with the interview, including extraneous sounds, such as coughs or false starts, which can interfere and lead to errors or incorrect responses with computerized assessments using voice recognition or sound waves.

A live interviewer can use a computer-assisted telephone interview system or play a standardized recording to control the pace and sequencing of test questions. Entry of some simple responses can be done by the interviewer during the testing. Automated computerized administration, without a live interviewer, usually involves presentation by digitized voice recording, a method that usually cannot be responsive to individual participants' needs. It is possible to have a person listening in on the telephone to make note of invalid trials and make necessary adjustments.

For both live and computer-assisted administrations, we recommend digital recording of the protocol so that it can be reviewed and scored later. Digitized files are ideal so that scoring can be done automatically using computer software such as for latencies; however, analog audio-taping is also useful for reviewing responses and checking accuracy. Processing and scoring can be done by person or computer. Computerized scoring can be applied manually to audio or text files generated by the interviewer, or automatically on line by means of voice recognition, as in the TELECOG battery described below. This works particularly well when response choices are finite and require only a few distinctive responses so accurate responses can be identified more effectively.

Telephone testing can be supplemented and enhanced with mailings. If testing requires stimuli that cannot be delivered orally, it is possible to send the visual materials to the respondents in advance and ask them not to open the envelope until the phone interview session. The interviewer can refer to the test materials and guide participants to look at the stimuli while answering orally administered test questions.

PREVIOUS SURVEYS WITH COGNITIVE ASSESSMENTS

Most large studies collect cognitive data by face-to-face, in-person interview (e.g., Atherosclerosis Risk in Communities [Cerhan et al., 1998], the Cardiovascular Health Study [Haan, Shemanski, Jagust, Manolio, & Kuller, 1999], the Framingham Study [Elias, Elisa, D'Agostino, Silbershatz & Wolf, 1997], Medical Research Council's Cognitive Function and Ageing Study [Medical Research Council Cognitive Function and Ageing Study, 1998]). Attempts to assess cognitive functioning by telephone historically have focused on diagnosis of dementia and other cognitive pathologies. The Mini-Mental Status Examination (MMSE; Folstein, Folstein, & McHugh, 1975) has been adapted for telephone administration in the Telephone Interview for Cognitive Status (TICS; Brandt, Spencer, & Folstein, 1988), which has been used successfully as a screening instrument for dementia. A summary of these and other telephone measures is provided in Table 30.1. The TICS, one of the sources for the HRS/AHEAD battery, is but one of a growing number of telephone assessments of

cognitive status and dementia, including the Telephone Cognitive Assessment Battery, the modified TICS (TICS–M), the MMSE as part of the Adult Lifestyles and Function Interview, Blessed Telephone Information Memory Concentration, the Structured Telephone Interview for Dementia, the Telephone-Assessed Mental State Exam, and the Short Portable Mental Status Questionnaire (see Table 30.1). With relatively simple and brief measures, it is possible to obtain a reasonable estimate of dementia status, but such measures are not sensitive across a wider range of cognitive performance in normal healthy adults.

Nevertheless, as summarized in Table 30.2, a number of studies have demonstrated the efficacy of assessing the normal range of cognition by telephone (Herzog & Wallace, 1997; Kawas, Karagiozis, Resau, Corrada, & Brookmeyer, 1995; Nesselroade, Pederson, McClearn, Plomin, & Bergeman, 1988). The TELECOG (Tennstedt, Lachman, & Salthouse, 2004), a computerized telephone test that uses voice recognition to assess memory and attentional switching in adults, has shown similar performance in person and over the telephone and found few differences across testing mode. The large-scale HRS/AHEAD study (Herzog, Rodgers, & Kulka, 1983; Herzog & Wallace, 1997) has demonstrated the feasibility of a telephone survey of cognitive function in adults over the age of 70. It is important to note that the AHEAD study and the large-scale Nurses' Health Study of 18,000 older women found no significant differences in performance between respondents tested by telephone and face-to-face assessments (Herzog & Rodgers, 1998). Another study that compared phone and face-to-face administration found correlations, adjusted for age and depression, ranging from .71 to .89 for the Age-Related Eye Disease cognitive battery (Petrill, Rempell, Oliver, & Plomin, 2002).

The Karolinska Institute Twins Study in Sweden (Nesselroade et al., 1988) also assessed cognitive functioning in older adults by telephone using reduced versions of standardized tests. They found that shortening the standard versions of established cognitive tests to half the original length and administering them by telephone only minimally compromised the overall reliability and validity of the instrument.

Table 30.2   Telephone Studies for Assessment of Normal Cognitive Functioning

Cognitive Battery	Study	No. of Participants	Age of Participants	Cognitive Subtests
AREDS Telephone Battery	Rankin et al., 2005	1,738	55–80 years	WMS–R Logical Memory I and II, TICS–M, Letter fluency FAS, Animal Category Fluency, digits backward.
BTACT	Tun & Lachman (2006b)	84 in pilot, 4,000 in MIDUS II	23–85 years	Free Recall Immediate and Delayed (15 words), Backward Digit Span, Category Fluency, Number Series, Speed, Task Switching
HRS/AHEAD Study	Herzog & Wallace (1997)	6,500+	70+ years	Immediate free recall test, delayed free recall test, Serial 7s test, counting backwards, naming the day of the week and date, naming objects, naming President and Vice President of the United States, Modified Similarities test from WAIS–R, Self-rating of memory
Nurses Health Study	Grodstein et al. (2000)	2,138 women	70–78 years	East Boston Memory Test: Immediate and delayed recall, TICS, 10-word list for immediate recall, Verbal Fluency
TELECOG	Tennstedt et al. (2004)	120	18–87 years	Free Recall Immediate and Delayed (10 words), Working Memory—N-Back, Task Switching
Telephone-Assessed Cognitive Ability	Nesselroade et al. (1988)	194 pairs of twins	27.5–82 years	Analogies, figure logic (fluid intelligence), Forward and backward digit span (short-term memory, Information, synonyms (crystallized intelligence)
Telephone-Assessed Measure of Cognitive Ability	Petrill et al. 2002	52	6–8 years	Two verbal ability tests, 3 nonverbal ability tests, phonological awareness measure; correlated with Stanford–Binet
Telephone Cognitive Battery	Kent & Plomin (1987)	212	9–15 years	Verbal, spatial, perceptual speed, and memory abilities

NOTE: AREDS = Age-Related Eye Disease; WMS–R = Wechsler Memory Scale—Revised; RICS–M = Telephone Interview of Cognitive Status Modified; BTACT = Brief Test of Adult Cognition by Telephone; MIDUS II = Midlife in the U.S. National Survey; HRS/AHEAD = Health and Retirement Study/ Asset and Health Dynamics Among the Oldest Old; WAIS–R = Wechsler Adult Intelligence Scale—Revised; TICS = Telephone Interview of Cognitive Status.

HRS/AHEAD Study

The HRS/AHEAD study designers (Herzog & Wallace, 1997) recognized the central role of cognitive functioning in relation to functional impairment, disability, and health care utilization among the elderly. They also considered the possible economic consequences of limitations in cognitive abilities, especially involving work and decision making and planning for retirement. Finally, it was recognized that cognitive difficulties needed to be identified, because they could compromise the data quality for the entire survey (Schwarz, 1999).

The HRS/AHEAD cognitive battery (Ofstedal, McAuley, & Herzog, 2002) was designed to be administered by telephone, and it includes measures of memory, mental status, and verbal ability. For respondents who were unable to respond, a proxy informant was asked to rate the respondent's memory, judgment, organization of time, and complete Jorm's 16-item IQCODE (Jorm, Scott, Cullen, & MacKinnon, 1991), which is used to assess dementia.

Many of the items in the HRS/AHEAD cognitive battery were adapted from the TICS (Brandt et al., 1988; Breitner, Welsh, Robinette, & Gau, 1995), or from the Iowa Established Populations for Epidemiologic Study of the Elderly (Purser et al., 2005). Some HRS/AHEAD items were later modified (e.g., the use of four alternate word lists for the recall tasks). The battery is heavily focused on knowledge and orientation items, which are most useful for identifying persons with some degree of cognitive impairment. The immediate and delayed free recall tests, the serial 7s, and the counting backwards test are indexes of episodic and working memory. These are important dimensions to include because there is strong evidence to suggest that these are among the first cognitive functions to decline during healthy aging (Bäckman, Small, & Wahlin, 2000).

TELECOG

TELECOG (Tennstedt, Lachman, & Salthouse, 2004) is a brief, computerized telephone-administered instrument that validly and reliably measures normal cognitive functioning using voice recognition technology. TELECOG focuses on two cognitive domains, memory and cognitive processing speed, which are highly age sensitive and represent basic capacity and processing skills that underlie higher-level cognitive performance and have been related to daily functional activities.

TELECOG includes tests of working memory and episodic memory. Working memory is assessed with the N-Back task (Gevins et al., 1990), which requires the respondent to solve a set of one-digit arithmetic problems and to recall the last addend in each problem. Four different versions of the task are used: 0-Back, 1-Back, 2-Back, and 3-Back. These different trial types allow for increasing the working memory demands without altering the stimulus condition.

TELECOG measures episodic memory with the auditory list learning task, including tests of both immediate and delayed recall. In this task, the respondent hears a list of 10 unrelated words and then is asked to say as many words as he or she can remember (immediate recall). The order in which the words are said is not of concern. Immediately after a respondent is finished with the immediate recall, the 10-word list is presented again but in a different serial order. A total of three trials of the list are presented to the respondent in the immediate word recall task, each in a different order, and the delayed recall is assessed after 20 minutes.

TELECOG measures cognitive processing speed with a switching task (Salthouse, Fristoe, McGuthry, & Hambrick, 1998). The switching task is a test of odd/even or more/less determinations. A respondent hears a string of numbers presented one at a time and is asked to make one of two decisions about each number: (1) "whether the number is odd or even" or (2) "whether the number is more or less than the number five." At random times during the digit presentations, the respondent is told to switch from one type of decision to the other. There were only a few significant within-subject differences in performance between face-to-face computerized testing and telephone assessment, and age patterns were similar across testing modes. One exception is that the older adults were a little faster on the switching tasks by phone than in person, perhaps because the motoric response of key pressing on a computer takes more time than a verbal response.

BRIEF TEST OF ADULT COGNITION BY TELEPHONE

A relatively new telephone measure, the Brief Test of Adult Cognition by Telephone (BTACT), was used in the MIDUS II national survey (Tun & Lachman, 2006b). The range of cognitive domains tested includes key abilities critical to adult functioning based on cognitive aging theory, such as reasoning, executive function, attention, and speed of processing. The BTACT is appropriate for testing a wide range of the population, including well-functioning younger and middle-aged adults as well as older adults. This allows for sensitivity to individual differences in cognition that may be associated with a large array of biological, social, health, and psychological factors. The BTACT requires less

than 20 minutes to administer and includes an optional attention test. We developed an alternative form of the BTACT for studies that involve repeated measures or longitudinal designs, to address retest effects.

The BTACT (see Table 30.3) was designed to tap areas of cognitive function that are sensitive to the effects of aging, including episodic verbal memory (Craik & Anderson, 1999), working memory span and executive function (Baddeley, 1986, 1996), reasoning (L. S. Miller & Lachman, 2000; Schaie, 1996), and speed of processing (Meyerson, Hale, Wagstaff, Poon, & Smith, 1990; Salthouse, 1996; Verhaeghen & Salthouse, 1997). An optional supplementary test records response latencies, which afford a measure of speed of processing, attention, and switch costs. The use of latency data adds an extra dimension to the cognitive measures, providing greater sensitivity to subtle individual differences in speed of processing that may not be revealed by accuracy measures alone (e.g.,

Table 30.3 Midlife in the U.S. National Survey II Brief Test of Adult Cognition by Telephone Tasks and Cognitive Domains

Task	Theoretical Construct(s)	Test Used
Word list recall (immediate and delayed)	Episodic verbal memory	Free recall of a list of 15 words drawn from the Rey Auditory–Verbal Learning Test (Lezak, 1995; Rey, 1964).
Backward digit span	Working memory span	Highest span achieved in repeating strings of digits backwards (Wechsler, 1997).
Category fluency	Verbal fluency: Executive function, semantic memory retrieval	Number of animal names produced in 1 minute (after Borkowski et al., 1967; see also Tombaugh et al., 1999).
Number series	Inductive reasoning	Complete the pattern in a series of 5 numbers with a final number (e.g., 2, 4, 6, 8, 10 . . . 12). Five problems include 3 types of patterns (after Schaie, 1996; Salthouse & Prill, 1987).
Backward counting	Processing speed	Maximum number of items produced counting backwards from 100 in 30 seconds (after AHEAD study; Herzog & Wallace, 1997).
Attention-switching, Stop and Go Task Switch	Reaction time, attention, task switching	Single task or mixed task (task switching; after Cepeda et al., 2001).

NOTE: AHEAD = Asset and Health Dynamics Among the Oldest Old.

Salthouse, 1996). Latencies were calculated by measuring the distance in milliseconds in the speech signal between stimulus onset and response onset using sound editing software. Latencies calculated from recordings of phone interviews have been shown to be similar to those taken from in-person interviews. One possible caveat is that wireless phones may introduce variable delays, and for this reason we caution against testing over cell phones.

The BTACT battery includes *Episodic Verbal Memory*, which includes immediate recall and delayed recall of a 15-word list; *Working Memory Span*, reflecting a system that stores and manipulates information, measured with backward digit span; *Verbal Fluency*, assessed by category fluency, an index of executive function that is linked with frontal lobe function; *Inductive Reasoning*, a measure of fluid intelligence assessed with number series completion; and *Speed of Processing*, measured with a backward counting task requiring rapid generation of a nonautomatic sequence. In addition, an optional Stop and Go Switch Task test yields measures of reaction time and *task-switching* costs, as well as inhibitory control.

Based on factor analysis of the BTACT tests, we found a one-factor solution. On this basis a composite measure can be computed. This is useful for research in which it is suitable to use one general measure, especially if there are not specific hypotheses about differential relationships with the individual subtests or dimensions.

Many of the BTACT tests have been used previously in neuropsychological and laboratory applications. To confirm that our telephone measures yield results similar to the more standard in-person tests, we carried out a validation study on the BTACT both in-person and by telephone, and found no significant effect of mode of testing for any of the subtests (see Table 30.4). We also demonstrated the expected significant correlations between BTACT measures and standardized in-person assessments on other tests of similar cognitive domains administered in person (Tun & Lachman, 2006a, 2006b).

The BTACT and the Stop and Go Switch Task were administered to the MIDUS II nationally representative sample of 4,014 adults ages

Table 30.4 Correlations Between Telephone and Face-to-Face Versions of the Brief Test of Adult Cognition by Telephone (BTACT) Subtests

BTACT Subtest	Correlation Between Phone vs. Face
Word List Immediate	.73**
Word List Delayed	.88**
Backward Digit Span	.57**
Category Fluency	.67**
Number Series	.56**
Backward Counting	.95**
Attention-Switching: Single Task	.82**
Attention-Switching: Mixed Task: Switch	.65**
Attention-Switching: Mixed Task: No Switch	.75**

**p < .01, two-tailed.

32 to 84, with a mean age of 55.26 ($SD = 12.29$). The sample was 54% women, and education ranged from 6 to 20 years (Mean education = 14.23, $SD = 2.6$), with less education in the older age cohorts. Older age cohorts rated their health below the younger groups on a self-report scale, with an overall mean of 3.63 ($SD = 0.96$; 1 = *poor* to 5 = *excellent*). For analysis purposes, the sample was divided into five age groups: G1 (32–44), G2 (45–54), G3 (55–64), G4 (65–74), and G5 (75–85). Results from this sample with the BTACT tests are presented in Figure 30.1. All tests showed significant age differences, with older adults performing more poorly than middle-aged and younger adults. The results for the composite scale are presented in Figure 30.2. Significant differences were found among all age groups.

Switching ability has been assessed primarily in laboratory settings, with typically small numbers of research participants and selectivity bias of the participants who are willing to come into a laboratory. However, innovative methods of testing can provide new insights into this paradigm (Reimers & Maylor, 2005). With the Stop

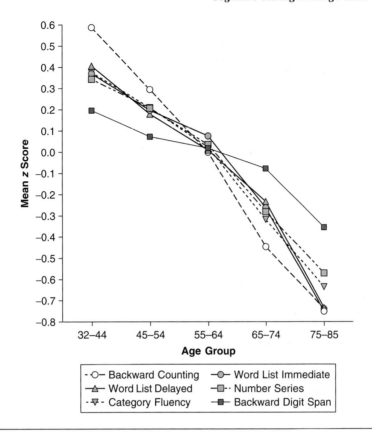

Figure 30.1 Brief Test of Adult Cognition by Telephone Accuracy Scores (*z* Scores) by Age Group

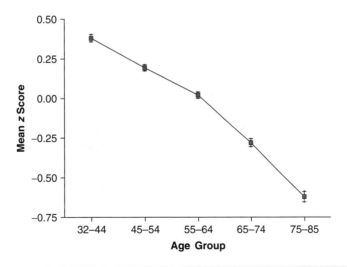

Figure 30.2 Brief Test of Adult Cognition by Telephone Composite Score (*z* Scores) by Age Group (With Standard Errors)

and Go Switch Task, we demonstrated how using a novel method—telephone technology—can expand the range of participants tested and shed new light on individual differences in executive processes.

As shown in Figure 30.3, for all age groups latencies increase with the complexity of the task. In the Stop and Go Switch Task, participants hear the words "red" and "green" and make simple speeded responses of either "stop" or "go," depending on the response rule. The response rule can indicate either a congruent response or an incongruent response that requires inhibitory control of the prepotent response. Latencies are smallest for single-task trials that involve one response rule. On the mixed-task trials that require alternating between two different response rules, nonswitch trials are faster than switch trials. Older adults were slower than young and middle-aged participants on all task conditions, but the magnitude of age differences was greater when switching was involved.

The cost of switching is illustrated in Figure 30.4, which shows age differences in local switch cost across five age groups. Local switch costs (the increase in mixed task latencies on switch trials compared with nonswitch trials) showed robust effects of age, beginning in middle age. We also found age differences in general or global switch costs (the increase in mixed-task latencies compared with single-task

latencies). It is important to note that these age-related increases in both local and general switch costs persisted even after controlling for baseline slowing, suggesting that switching was more difficult with age. In addition, older age groups showed an increase in the effect of congruency (congruent responses relative to incongruent responses), which we take as a reflection of inhibitory control processes (Tun & Lachman, 2006a).

We also found different effects of other demographic variables, which can shed light on the central executive process involved in switching and inhibitory control. Specifically, gender and level of education have different associations with task switching and with inhibitory control. Female gender was associated both with larger switching costs and poorer inhibitory control on incongruent trials; however, education showed a different pattern of effects, such that higher levels of education were associated with smaller switching costs but not with consistently better inhibitory function (Tun & Lachman, 2006a).

CONCLUSION

Given the state of the art of research on cognition and aging, there is a need to incorporate cognitive assessments into large-scale surveys on topic areas such as health and well-being,

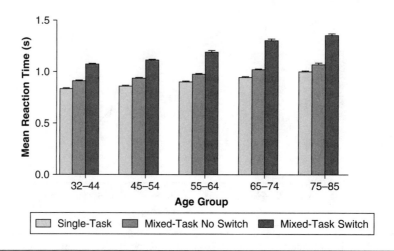

Figure 30.3   Stop and Go Switch Task Reaction Times by Trial Type and Age Group (With Standard Errors)

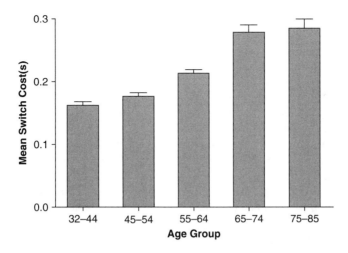

Figure 30.4   Stop and Go Switch Task Local Switch Cost by Age Group (With Standard Errors)

NOTE: Switch costs = median of mixed task switch trials – median of mixed tasks nonswitch trials.

economics, and stress. Testing by telephone greatly increases the range of possible participants, including people who cannot or will not come into the laboratory or clinical settings. Surveys typically cannot accommodate lengthy cognitive batteries even though the studies may benefit from understanding individual differences in cognition and longitudinal changes in cognition in response to time, experimental manipulations, or interventions. Cognition may also be useful as a covariate in studies of health and functional behavior. Another important focus has been to use cognitive data to assess the validity of survey responses, presuming that individuals with cognitive deficits might not provide valid responses to other items in the questionnaire (Knauper, Belli, Hill, & Herzog, 1997).

Many existing telephone batteries in surveys focus on detecting signs of dementia, but there is a need to include cognitive batteries that are more sensitive to the subtle changes associated with normal aging. Given that in adult samples a relatively small proportion of survey participants are expected to have or develop dementia, it is important to focus on those within normal levels of cognitive aging, or those who maintain adequate cognitive function well into their later years. In long-term longitudinal studies, especially with older samples, it may be possible to identify precursors of dementia or diagnostic signs of preclinical conditions. In future studies, we will focus on standardizing and further validating the

BTACT battery, with the goal of establishing norms and diagnostic criteria. Preliminary data look very promising, and we hope to further validate these measures with the in-person data from a subsample of the MIDUS from Boston who were tested with standard in-person cognitive measures. In the MIDUS II survey the cognitive assessment was limited to 15 minutes, but in pilot testing we found that we could also successfully administer paired associate learning and alternating fluency tasks over the phone. Another likely candidate for telephone assessment would be text recall tasks. The use of brief phone batteries may be beneficial for the cognitive aging research field, especially if this assessment approach is associated with less fatigue and anxiety than more traditional long batteries given in person.

Individual differences in cognitive ability have important implications for understanding differences in behaviors and outcomes in multiple domains (e.g., health, economics, social domains). If one is interested in prevention, it becomes important to think about identifying risk factors for cognitive decline, rather than focusing only on the consequences of decline. If individual differences in cognitive functioning for persons in the normal range can be measured well, it would enable tracking over time and identification of predisposing factors associated with decline. This would provide much-needed information about the emergence of cognitive impairments and preclinical status in later life.

Little attention has been given to cognitive functioning as an important resource for later life functioning. For example, cognitive abilities can serve as a moderator of social class differences in health and retirement outcomes. Relationships between cognitive functioning and other important factors, such as health, economic well-being, stress, and depression, need further exploration. Cognitive functioning and changes are interesting outcomes in their own right. There is still a great deal to be learned about predictors of change over time in cognitive functioning, or the transition from normal cognition to cognitive impairment to dementia. All of these and many other potentially important research questions may be more realistically and effectively addressed by including cognitive assessments over the telephone in large-scale surveys.

REFERENCES

Albert, M. S., Jones, K., Savage, C. R., Berkman, L., Seeman, T., Blazer, D., et al. (1995). Predictors of cognitive change in older persons: MacArthur Studies of Successful Aging. *Psychology and Aging, 10,* 578–589.

Aldwin, C. M., Spiro, A., Levenson, M. R., & Bosse, R. (1989). Longitudinal findings from the Normative Aging Study: I. Does mental health change with age? *Psychology and Aging, 4,* 295–306.

Bäckman, L., Small, B. J., & Wahlin, A. (2000). Aging and memory: Cognitive and biological perspectives. In J. E. Birren & K. W. Schaie (Eds.), *Handbook of the psychology of aging* (5th ed., pp. 349–377). San Diego, CA: Academic Press.

Baddeley, A. (1986). *Working memory.* Oxford, UK: Clarendon Press.

Baddeley, A. (1996). Exploring the central executive. *Quarterly Journal of Experimental Psychology, 49A,* 5–28.

Baltes, P., & Mayer, K. U. (1999). *The Berlin Aging Study: Aging from 70 to 100.* New York: Cambridge University Press.

Borkowski, J. G., Benton, A. L., & Spreen, O. (1967). Word fluency and brain damage. *Neuropsychologia, 5,* 135–140.

Brandt, J., Spencer, M., & Folstein, M. (1988). The Telephone Interview for Cognitive Status. *Neuropsychiatry, Neuropsychology, and Behavioral Neurology, 1,* 111–117.

Breitner, J. C. S., Welsh, K. A., Robinette, C. D., & Gau, B. A. (1995). Alzheimer's disease in the National Academy of Sciences–National Research Council Registry of Aging Twin Veterans. III. Detection of cases, longitudinal results, and observations on twin concordance. *Archives of Neurology, 52,* 763–771.

Brim, O., Ryff, C., & Kessler, R. (2004). *How healthy are we?: A national study of well-being at midlife.* Chicago: University of Chicago Press.

Buckwalter, J. G., Crooks, V. C., & Petitti, D. B. (2002). A preliminary psychometric analysis of a computer-assisted administration of the Telephone Interview of Cognitive Status—Modified. *Journal of Clinical and Experimental Neuropsychology, 24,* 168–175.

Cepeda, N. J., Kramer, A., & Gonzalez de Sather, J. C. M. (2001). Changes in executive control across the life span: Examination of task-switching performance. *Developmental Psychology, 37,* 715–770.

Cerhan, J. R., Folsom, A. R., Mortimer, J. A., Shahar, E., Knopman, D. S., McGovern, P. G., et al. (1998). Correlates of cognitive function in middle-aged adults. *Gerontology, 44,* 95–105.

Chumbler, N. R., & Zhang, M. (1998). A telephone screening to classify demented older adults. *Clinical Gerontologist, 19*(3), 79–84.

Craik, F. I. M., & Anderson, N. (1999). Applying cognitive research to problems in aging. In D. Gopher & A. Koriat (Eds.), *Attention and performance XVII* (pp. 583–616). New York: Academic Press.

Craik, F. I. M., & Salthouse, T. A. (2000). *The handbook of aging and cognition* (2nd ed.). Mahwah, NJ: Lawrence Erlbaum.

Desmond, D. W., Tatemichi, T. K., & Hanzawa, L. (1994). The Telephone Interview for Cognitive Status (TICS): Reliability and validity in a stroke sample. *International Journal of Geriatric Psychiatry, 9,* 803–807.

Dixon, R., deFrias, C. M., & Maitland, S. B. (2001). Memory in midlife. In M. E. Lachman (Ed.), *Handbook of midlife development* (pp. 248–278). New York: Wiley.

Elias, M. F., Elias, P. K., D'Agostino, R. B., Silbershatz, H., & Wolf, P. A. (1997). Role of age, education, and gender on cognitive performance in the Framingham Heart Study: Community-based norms. *Experimental Aging Research, 23,* 201–235.

Folstein, M., Folstein, S., & McHugh, P. (1975). Mini-Mental State: A practical method for grading the cognitive state of patients for the clinician. *Journal of Psychiatric Research, 12,* 189–198.

Gatz, M., Pedersen, N., Berg, S., Johansson, B., Johansson, K., Mortimer, J., et al. (1997). Heritability for Alzheimer's disease: The study of dementia in Swedish twins. *Journals of Gerontology, 52A,* M117–M125.

Gatz, M., Reynolds, C., Nikolic, J., Lowe, B., Karel, M., & Pedersen, N. (1995). An empirical test of telephone screening to identify potential dementia cases. *International Psychogeriatrics, 7,* 429–438.

Gevins, A. S., Bressler, S. L., Cutillo, B. A., Illes, J., Miller, J. C., Stern, J., et al. (1990). Effects of prolonged mental work on functional brain topography. *Electroencephalography and Clinical Neurophysiology, 76,* 339–350.

Go, R. C. P., Duke, L., Harrell, L., Cody, H., Bassett, S., Folstein, M., et al. (1997). Development and validation of a Structured Telephone Interview for Dementia Assessment (STIDA): The NIMH Genetics Initiative. *Journal of Geriatric Psychiatry and Neurology, 10,* 161–167.

Grodstein, F., Chen, J., Pollen, D., Albert, M., Wilson, R., Folstein, M., et al. (2000). Postmenopausal hormone therapy and cognitive function in healthy elderly women. *Journal of the American Geriatrics Society, 48,* 746–752.

Haan, M. N., Shemanski, L., Jagust, W. J., Manolio, T. A., & Kuller, L. (1999). The role of APOE ε4 in modulating effects of other risk factors for cognitive decline in elderly persons. *Journal of the American Medical Association, 282,* 40–46.

Herzog, A. R., & Rodgers, W. L. (1998). Cognitive performance measures in survey research on older adults. In N. Schwarz, D. C. Park, B. Knauper, & S. Sudman (Eds.), *Cognition, aging and self-reports* (pp. 327–340). Philadelphia: Psychology Press.

Herzog, A. R., Rodgers, W. L., & Kulka, R. A. (1983). Interviewing older adults: A comparison of telephone and face-to-face modalities. *Public Opinion Quarterly, 47,* 405–418.

Herzog, A. R., & Wallace, R. B. (1997). Measures of cognitive functioning in the AHEAD study. *Journal of Gerontology: Social Sciences, 52B,* 37–48.

Hultsch, D. F., Hertzog, C., Dixon, R. A., & Small, B. J. (1998). *Memory change in the aged.* New York: Cambridge University Press.

Järvenpää, T., Rinne, J. O., Räihä, I., Koskenvuo, M., Löppönen, M., Hinkka, S., et al. (2002). Characteristics of two telephone screens for cognitive impairment. *Dementia and Geriatric Cognitive Disorders, 13,* 149–155.

Jorm, A. F., Fratiglioni, L., & Winblad, B. (1993). Differential diagnosis in dementia: Principal components analysis of clinical data from a population survey. *Archives of Neurology, 50,* 72–77.

Jorm, A. F., Scott, R., Cullen, J. S., & MacKinnon, A. J. (1991). Performance on the Informant Questionnaire on Cognitive Decline in the Elderly (IQCODE) as a screening test for dementia. *Psychological Medicine, 21,* 785–790.

Kawas, C., Karagiozis, H., Resau, L., Corrada, M., & Brookmeyer, R. (1995). Reliability of the Blessed Telephone Information-Memory-Concentration Test. *Journal of Geriatric Psychiatry and Neurology, 8,* 238–242.

Kent, J., & Plomin, R. (1987). Testing of specific cognitive abilities by telephone and mail. *Intelligence, 11,* 391–400.

Knauper, B., Belli, R. F., Hill, D. H., & Herzog, A. R. (1997). Question difficulty and respondents' cognitive ability: The effect on data quality. *Journal of Official Statistics, 13,* 181–199.

Knopman, D., Knudson, D., Yoes, M., & Weiss, D. (1999). Development and standardization of a new telephonic cognitive screening test: The Minnesota Cognitive Acuity Screen (MCAS). *Neuropsychiatry, Neuropsychology, and Behavioral Neurology, 13*(4), 286–296.

Lachman, M. E. (2004). Development in midlife. *Annual Review of Psychology, 55,* 305–331.

Lachman, M. E., & Firth, K. M. (2004). The adaptive value of feeling in control during midlife. In O. G. Brim, C. D. Ryff, & R. Kessler (Eds.), *How healthy are we?: A national study of well-being at midlife* (pp. 320–349). Chicago: University of Chicago Press.

Lachman, M. E., & James, J. B. (1997). Charting the course of midlife development: An overview. In M. E. Lachman & J. B. James (Eds.), *Multiple paths of midlife development* (pp. 1–17). Chicago: University of Chicago Press.

Lanska, D. J., Schmitt, F. A., Stewart, J. M., & Howe, J. N. (1993). Telephone-assessed mental state. *Dementia, 4,* 117–119.

Lemme, B. H. (1995). *Development in adulthood.* Boston: Allyn & Bacon.

Lezak, M. D. (1995). *Neuropsychological assessment* (3rd ed.). New York: Oxford University Press.

Lipton, R. B., Katz, M. J., Kuslansky, G., Sliwinski, M. J., Stewart, W. F., Verghese, J., et al. (2003). Screening for dementia by telephone using the Memory Impairment Screen. *Journal of the American Geriatrics Society, 51,* 1382–1390.

Medical Research Council Cognitive Function and Ageing Study. (1998). Cognitive function and dementia in six areas of England and Wales: The distribution of MMSE and prevalence of GMS organicity in the MRC CFA study. *Psychological Medicine, 28,* 319–35.

Meyerson, J., Hale, S., Wagstaff, D., Poon, L. W., & Smith, G. A. (1990). The information-loss model: A mathematical theory of age-related slowing. *Psychological Review, 97,* 475–487.

Miller, L. S., & Lachman, M. E. (2000). Cognitive performance and the role of control beliefs in midlife. *Aging, Neuropsychology, and Cognition, 7,* 69–85.

Miller, M. E., Rejeski, W. J., Reboussin, B. A., Ten Have, T. R., & Ettinger, W. H. (2000). Physical activity, functional limitations, and disability in older adults. *Journal of the American Geriatrics Society, 48,* 1264–1272.

Monteiro, I. M., Boksay, I., Auer, S., Torossian, C., Sinaiko, E., & Reisberg, B. (1998). Reliability of routine clinical instruments for the assessment of Alzheimer's disease administered by telephone. *Journal of Geriatric Psychiatry and Neurology, 11,* 18–24.

Nesselroade, J. R., Pederson, N. L., McClearn, G. E., Plomin, R., & Bergeman, C. S. (1988). Factorial and criterion validities of telephone-accessed cognitive ability measures. Age and gender comparisons in adult twins. *Research on Aging, 10,* 220–234.

Norton, M. C., Tschanz, J. A., Fan, X., Plassman, B. L., Welsh-Bohmer, K. A., West, N., et al. (1999). Telephone Adaptation of the Modified Mini-Mental State Exam (3MS): The Cache County Study. *Neuropsychiatry, Neuropsychology, and Behavioral Neurology, 12,* 270–276.

Ofstedal, M. B., McAuley, G. F., & Herzog, A. R. (2002, July). *Documentation of cognitive functioning measures in the Health and Retirement Study* (HRS/AHEAD Documentation Report DR-006). Retrieved February 5, 2007, from http://hrsonline.isr.umich.edu/docs/userg/dr-006.pdf

Petersen, R. C., Smith, G. E., Waring, S. C., Ivnih, R. J., Tangalos, E. G., & Kohmen, E. (1999). Mild cognitive impairment: Clinical characterization and outcome. *Archives of Neurology, 56,* 303–308.

Petrill, S. A., Rempell, J., Oliver, B., & Plomin, R. (2002). Testing cognitive abilities by telephone in a sample of 6- to 8-year olds. *Intelligence, 30,* 353–360.

Purser, J. L., Fillenbaum, G. G., Pieper, C. F., & Wallace, R. B. (2005). Mild cognitive impairment and 10-year trajectories of disability in the Iowa Established Populations for Epidemiologic Studies of the Elderly Cohort. *Journal of the American Geriatrics Society, 53,* 1966–1972.

Rankin, M. W., Clemons, T. E., & McBee, W. L. (2005). Correlation analysis of the in-clinic and telephone batteries from the ARES Cognitive Function Ancillary Study (AREDS Report No. 15). *Ophthalmic Epidemiology, 12,* 271–277.

Reimers, S., & Maylor, E. A. (2005). Task switching across the life span: Effects of age on general and specific switch costs. *Developmental Psychology, 41,* 661–671.

Rey, A. (1964). *L'examen clinique en psychologie* [Clinical psychological assessment]. Paris: Presses Universitaires de France.

Roccaforte, W. H., Burke, W. J., Bayer, B. L., & Wengel, S. P. (1992). Validation of a telephone version of the Mini-Mental State Examination. *Journal of the American Geriatrics Society, 40,* 697–702.

Salthouse, T. A. (1996). The processing speed theory of adult age differences in cognition. *Psychological Review, 103,* 403–428.

Salthouse, T. A., Fristoe, N., McGuthry, K. E., & Hambrick, D. Z. (1998). Relation of task switching to speed, age, and fluid intelligence. *Psychology and Aging, 13,* 445–461.

Salthouse, T. A., & Prill, K. A. (1987). Inferences about age impairments in inferential reasoning. *Psychology and Aging, 2,* 43–51.

Schaie, K. W. (1996). *Intellectual development in adulthood: The Seattle Longitudinal Study.* New York: Cambridge University Press.

Schwarz, N. (1999). Self-reports of behaviors and opinions: Cognitive and communicative processes. In N. Schwarz, D. C. Park, B. Knauper, & S. Sudman (Eds.), *Cognition, aging, and self-reports* (pp. 17–44). Philadelphia: Psychology Press.

Shock, N., Greulich, R., Andres, R., Arenberg, D., Costa, P. T., Jr., Lakatta, E. W., et al. (1984). *Normal human aging: The Baltimore Longitudinal Study of Aging* (NIH Publication No. 84–2450). Washington, DC: U.S. Government Printing Office.

Shumaker, S. A., Reboussin, B. A., Espeland, M. A., Rapp, S. R., McBee, W. L., Dailey, M., et al. (1998). The Women's Health Initiative Memory Study (WHIMS): A trial of the effect of estrogen therapy in preventing and slowing the progression of dementia. *Controlled Clinical, 19,* 604–621.

Sternberg, R. J., Grigorenko, H., & Oh, S. (2001). The development of intelligence at midlife. In M. E. Lachman (Ed.), *Handbook of midlife development* (pp. 217–247). New York: Wiley.

Tennstedt, S., Lachman, M. E., & Salthouse, T. (2004). *TELECOG: A brief cognitive telephone assessment.* Unpublished technical report, New England Research Institutes, Watertown, MA.

Tombaugh, T. N., Kozak, J., & Rees, L. (1999). Normative data stratified by age and education for two measures of verbal fluency: FAS and animal naming. *Archives of Clinical Neuropsychology, 14,* 167–177.

Tun, P. A., & Lachman, M. E. (2006a). *Age differences in reaction time in a national telephone sample of adults: Task complexity, education, and gender matter.* Manuscript submitted for publication.

Tun, P. A., & Lachman, M. E. (2006b). Telephone assessment of cognitive function in adulthood: The Brief Test of Adult Cognition by Telephone (BTACT). *Age and Ageing, 35,* 629–632.

Tun, P. A., & Wingfield, A. (1995). Does dividing attention become harder with age? Findings from the Divided Attention Questionnaire. *Aging and Cognition, 2,* 39–66.

Verhaeghen, P., & Salthouse, T. A. (1997). Meta-analyses of age–cognition relations in adulthood: Estimates of linear and non-linear effects and structural models. *Psychological Bulletin, 122,* 231–249.

Wechsler, D. (1997). *Wechsler Adult Intelligence Scale* (3rd ed.). New York: Psychological Corporation.

Willis, S. L., & Schaie, K. W. (1999). Intellectual functioning in midlife. In S. L. Willis & J. D. Reid (Eds.), *Life in the middle* (pp. 233–247). San Diego, CA: Academic Press.

31

Continuous, Unobtrusive Monitoring for the Assessment of Cognitive Function

Misha Pavel, Holly Jimison, Tamara Hayes, Jeffrey Kaye, Eric Dishman, Katherine Wild, and Devin Williams

The ability to assess the cognitive state of an individual is important for both clinical care and for our understanding of the neurological underpinning of cognitive function. Furthermore, understanding changes associated with aging and disease is a critical component of care for the aging populations of the world. Cognitive functioning is one of the key prerequisites for living independently and, as such, it is one of the main determinants of care for elders. Early detection and better prediction of future cognitive decline would enable earlier, perhaps more beneficial treatment as well as preparations for adjustments in care. New methods in unobtrusive monitoring of cognitive performance in a home environment offer the possibility of detecting trends and changes in performance in a natural setting. This reduces the delay and expense associated with current cognitive assessment methods used in clinical practice. The use of frequent, unobtrusive measures would reduce the need to rely on population norms that are confounded by cultural and language differences because we would be able to measure within-individual changes, using individual elders as their own control. This would allow us to detect trends in cognitive performance and potentially offer earlier detection of cognitive decline as well as provide a method for characterizing disease progression. In addition, the routine use of unobtrusive measures of cognition would provide important information for the timely detection and intervention with acute issues, such as the alerting of errors in

AUTHORS' NOTE: This chapter was supported by grants from the National Institute on Aging and the National Institutes of Health (AG024978 and AG024059), and by Intel Corporation to Oregon Health & Science University (OHSU). We are grateful to our colleagues at OHSU, Linda Boise, Nicole Larimer, and our colleagues at Spry Learning, Payton Bissell, and James McKanna, and Dan Blaker for their help with the system development and clinical applications. Holly Jimison, Misha Pavel, and Devin Williams are part-time employees of Spry Learning, a company that may have a commercial interest in the results of this research. This potential conflict of interest has been reviewed and managed by OHSU.

medication management and monitoring the effectiveness of treatments. The practical aspects of care have profound economic and social implications, especially in view of the upcoming challenges due to the rapidly growing demographic of elders and escalating health care costs.

CURRENT APPROACHES
TO COGNITIVE ASSESSMENT

In standard clinical practice, cognitive screenings are usually performed only at advanced age or if there are already patient or family concerns about cognitive dysfunction. These screening tests, such as the Mini-Mental State Examination (Folstein, Folstein, & McHugh, 1975), the Kokmen Short Test of Mental Status (Kokmen, Naessens, & Offord, 1987), and the Memory Impairment Screen (Buschke et al., 1999), can be performed in a physician's office, but they are fairly coarse and not particularly useful for the early detection of problems (Petersen et al., 2001). More complete neuropsychological batteries can be performed to obtain more sensitive diagnostic information. These normally include measures of short-term and working memory, divided attention, motor speed, planning, and general executive function. However, these tests are time consuming, expensive, and performed infrequently, if at all. These tests typically are administered by a trained neuropsychologist and performed in an office setting. The results are interpreted by comparing the patient's scores with population norms.

This current standard process of cognitive assessment of elders is unfortunately plagued by a variety of shortcomings. Time and insurance constraints often force physicians to focus on a single medical problem and thus do not typically lead to timely recognition of cognitive change. Cognitive testing is not a normal part of an elder's visit to a physician, and a single snapshot of a person's cognitive function is often not representative of his or her overall cognitive health. Although self-report may provide a wider view of ongoing changes, patients are often reluctant to admit to problems because of a fear of losing their independence. In fact, fully 50% of people age 75 or older seeing a primary

care practitioner received no diagnosis or evaluation of their memory complaint (Boise, Neal, & Kaye, 2004; Callahan, Hendrie, & Tierney, 1995), and patients and their families report memory problems in only a small percentage of cases where the patient has clinically measurable dementia (Ganguli et al., 2004). Among the most significant issues is the fact that the assessment process is in most cases triggered by noticeable symptoms on the part of the elder or his or her caregiver. Even after the initial symptoms are noted, the first visit to the clinic usually is further delayed because of denial and the fear of a potential loss of independence.

A typical primary care physician has access only to the less sensitive screening instruments, such as the Mini-Mental State Examination, that are likely to detect the more severe cognitive decline in later stages. This process may further delay a visit to a neurologist. Then, once the elder is referred to a neurologist, the neuropsychological tests are highly variable, and the scores must be interpreted with respect to population norms. Although with the norms one can correct for some characteristics, such as age, gender, and sometimes an estimate of educational level, in general these norms only roughly reflect the individual's background and capabilities prior to the decline. For example, scores on many of the neuropsychological tests are influenced by an individual's cultural experiences, language abilities (many are non-native English speakers), and exposure to testing paradigms.

In addition to the issues of delays and infrequent repeated assessments, as well as the cultural confounders, there is another, perhaps more subtle but significant problem: The results of the repeated administration of many of these tests suggest considerable variability over time for an individual respondent (Burton, Strauss, Hultsch, Moll, & Hunter, 2006; Martin & Hofer, 2004; Strauss, MacDonald, Hunter, Moll, & Hultsch, 2002). The variability is likely to arise from multiple components, such as the individual's instantaneous capabilities, state of fatigue, or simply random variation. For example, a coefficient of correlation of 0.5–0.8 between two administrations of the same test (e.g., the Trail Making Test) separated by a couple of months is not unusual. In some cases, the variability may itself be a marker of disease progression (Burton et al., 2006). The infrequent measurements from the standard assessments lead to what are called *aliasing errors*.

Aliasing errors are defined in the signal processing literature as errors that arise during sampling of a continuous function if the sampling frequency is lower than 2fmax, where *fmax* is the maximum frequency in the function (this is also known as the *Nyquist sampling theorem*). In our context, this means that the frequency of administering the tests should match the dynamic of the changes in cognitive function. For example, if we hypothesize that variables of interest vary between mornings and evenings, then we need to test more often than twice a day.

Of course, repeated administration of the traditional tests is complicated by sequential effects, such as learning and forgetting phenomena (Sliwinski, Stawski, & Hofer, 2006), which may be affected differentially in individuals with cognitive impairment (Cooper et al., 2001; Cooper, Lacritz, Weiner, Rosenberg, & Cullum, 2004).

Another shortcoming of the present approaches to clinical cognitive assessment is the common reliance on paper-and-pencil tests. This method generally precludes the assessment of trial-by-trial response times and the processing of dynamic stimuli. As a result, there has been a significant gap between the approaches of experimental cognitive psychologists and those studying adult cognitive development (see chap. 2, this volume).

In summary, traditional neuropsychological assessment methods have difficulties due to the time and expense associated with testing, infrequent measurements, lack of ability to measure dynamic properties of performance, unwanted variability due to culture and language effects, and the need to reference to population norms for each test and for any new innovation in testing.

POTENTIAL BENEFITS OF FREQUENT UNOBTRUSIVE MONITORING IN THE HOME

An obvious remedy for many of the shortcomings of traditional cognitive assessments would be more frequent sampling of the performance on the neuropsychological tests combined with enhancements of these tests by incorporating computer-based stimuli presentations and response recording. The computer-based testing would permit more frequent administration of the tests with similar but different stimuli. To the extent that the respondents comply with the protocol of these studies, it is possible reduce some of the aliasing effects and to examine individual changes over time. Even though this approach is technically feasible, repeated administration of the same tests may change the nature of the test, and this needs to be understood (Sliwinski et al., 2006). In addition, because the tests are not particularly interesting to the test-taker, respondent compliance with the protocol may be an issue.

To obtain frequent measures of cognitive performance, the assessment methods must be inexpensive and minimally intrusive. This naturally implies the importance of being able to make measurements in a home environment. Thus, an alternate approach is to develop assessment techniques that are unobtrusive and based on the activities that elders do in the course of their normal lives. In the following sections, we describe some examples of unobtrusive methods for assessing proxies of cognitive performance, including gait and speed-of-walking assessments; computer typing speed and mouse device motor movements; linguistic complexity measures from computer typing; and, finally, cognitive assessments embedded in enjoyable computer games.

OVERVIEW OF UNOBTRUSIVE MONITORING OF BEHAVIORAL MARKERS OF COGNITION

Although the precise measurement of cognitive function requires well-controlled testing situations, there is anecdotal evidence that everyday activities and behaviors may carry important information. It is not unusual that a skilled clinician can make assessment of a patient's state on the basis of that patient's posture, movements, and answers to matter-of-course questions.

Supporting this anecdotal evidence are empirical results that have emerged during the last decade suggesting significant connections between sensorimotor behaviors, such as gait, and cognitive functions. For example, people's gait velocity has been linked to their cognitive capabilities and, as we illustrate in the next section, a decrease in the speed of walking can be used as a predictor of future cognitive decline.

This connection between frequent, observable behaviors and cognitive functions can be exploited by continuous unobtrusive monitoring of the behaviors and subsequent inference of the cognitive functions.

Many everyday human activities are more or less directly related to the underlying cognitive functions. For example, interactions with simple household devices such as telephones, remote controls, VCRs/DVD players, or computers are by and large controlled by movements reflecting directly cognitive decisions. Monitoring elders' interactions with these devices therefore has the potential to provide information regarding the participants' cognitive functions. We note in passing that there are also examples whereby everyday behaviors are very similar to those used in neuropsychological tests. For example, the speed of dialing has face validity with the speed of finger tapping.

Frequent measurements of cognitive performance offer the primary benefit of being able to view trends and changes in performance, using individuals as their own controls to develop a within-person history of performance. Comparison to norms would still be valuable, but looking at changes for a given individual would alleviate the need to correct for language and cultural experience issues. It would also provide a more sensitive measure for high-performing individuals who "top out" on tests compared with norms and thus have problems detected at much later stages of a decline process (i.e., disease progression). Frequent assessments would also provide us with measures of learning, forgetting, and day-to-day or time-of-day variability in cognitive performance, permitting change at the individual level to be gauged against the full context of the individual's normative functioning.

Monitoring of Gait Velocity: An Example of Unobtrusive Cognitive–Motor Assessment

As noted earlier, recent results suggest that slowing in the motor changes can be predictive of future cognitive decline. This has been shown both generally as overall slowing or gait disturbance measured by clinical signs on motor rating scales (Richards, Stern, & Mayeux, 1993; Verghese et al., 2002; Wilson, Schneider,

Bienias, Evans, & Bennett, 2003), and more specifically related to timed walking (Camicioli, Howieson, Oken, Sexton, & Kaye, 1998; Goldman, Baty, Buckles, Sahrmann, & Morris, 1999; Marquis et al., 2002; Tabbarah, Crimmins, & Seeman, 2002). In an ongoing study of healthy brain aging at the Oregon Alzheimer's Disease Center, several hundred healthy study participants have been monitored for up to 18 years. During their participation, their cognitive state was assessed once or twice a year. In addition to the neuropsychological assessment, participants' speed of walking was measured. Over the years in this retrospective study, a number of participants exhibited cognitive decline and their assessment results can be compared with the results of participants who remained cognitively healthy. One way to compare the progression of the decline is to compare the slopes of linear regression for the individual subjects. The results of this type of analysis are shown in Figure 31.1. We computed the slopes of the control group to the slopes of the patients with mild cognitive impairment prior to the diagnosis. Statistical analysis using the Kolmogorov–Smirnov test confirmed the intuitive interpretation—that the walking speed of participants destined for a diagnosis of mild cognitive impairment declined faster than the walking speed of control group participants.

Gait velocity has also been linked to cognitive function more directly by experiments with dual tasks aimed at the differential diagnosis of neurological problems such as Parkinson's or brain injury. Sheridan (2002) found that stride variability was increased in dual-task experiments in which patients with Alzheimer's disease repeated random digits while walking.

These and similar results motivated a new direction of research in our laboratory: We began to develop approaches to monitor the gait velocity of the elders during their normal everyday activities. To explain our methodology we describe an approach to the unobtrusive measurement of gait velocity and its variability based on continuous monitoring of individual participants in their residences. We have applied the same approach to the monitoring of patients with Parkinson's disease.

We note in passing that the development of the monitoring system had to surmount a

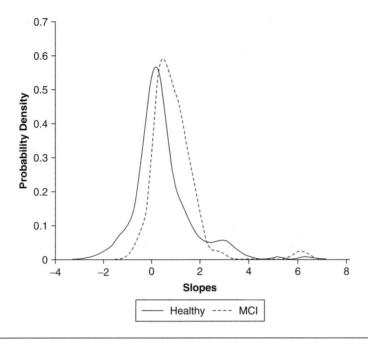

Figure 31.1   Distribution of Slopes of Increasing Time to Walk 30 Feet by Participants With a Future
Diagnosis of Mild Cognitive Impairment (MCI) and a Healthy Group

number of challenges in addition to the obvious need for accuracy and reliability (Hayes et al., 2007). For example, one of our critical objectives was to design the system to be minimally obtrusive. The participants were typically not asked to wear any special devices—except in situations with multiple occupants in a residence. In those cases, we asked the participant to wear a device in form of a watch to enable us to distinguish the individual's activities. Additional challenges that constrain the system design are that the implementation had to be low cost, easy to install and retrofit in existing residences, and not require frequent maintenance. For example, the battery life of any battery-powered device was required to exceed 3 months.

The system we are currently using and deploying experimentally for assessing the participants' gait velocity is based on a combination of wireless motion detectors, in particular, pyroelectric infrared motion sensors (PIR); contact switches; and, when needed, active radio frequency identification (RFID) devices (Hayes, Pavel, & Kaye, 2004). The RFID devices are used for participants who live in a multiperson dwelling (e.g., with a spouse). Each residence is equipped with a client PC that collects data from the various wireless systems and that is connected to the Internet via a high-speed link such as cable modem or, at the minimum, DSL. The data from the local client are collected and sent via a secure link to an SQL database server at the Oregon Health & Science University.

A PIR sensor is designed to generate an event when it detects a movement of an object with a different temperature than the background and when the motion signal exceeds a given threshold. The details of the models of the PIR response mechanisms are presented elsewhere (Pavel, Hayes, Adami, Jimison, & Kaye, 2006), but in general the inference of gait velocity is computed from the time interval required for the participant to move from one location to another. In general, such assessments cannot be made directly; instead, it can be computed using model-based inference, for example, one based on semi-Markov models described by Pavel et al. (2006).

In some residencies, it is possible to assess gait velocity more directly by taking advantage of the layout of the dwelling. For example, whenever a residence has a hall or a corridor, it may be possible to place the motion detectors such that a person walking through the hall would trigger the PIR motion detectors in a sequence whose timing would be proportional to the inverse of his or her gait velocity.

An example of a deployment at a particular residence is shown in Figure 31.2. In this particular application, the gait velocity is measured by using restricted-field PIR motion sensors (±4° field of view, or about ±6.5 centimeters at a distance of 90 centimeters from the sensor) placed along a corridor (see Figure 31.2). By storing the event time at which an individual passes in front of these sensors, in sequence, we can estimate the walking speed along the hall (Hayes et al., 2004) and, to some extent, its variability. The gait velocity is estimated by the time interval between the events ("firings") generated by the first and third motion detectors in sequence.

Although this general approach to the estimation of gait velocity is rather simple, the actual estimates must be derived from those sequences that are generated with high probability by the monitored individual. There are several ways that the "correct" or expected sequence may not correspond to the gait velocity of the monitored individual. Examples of these include spurious firings, firing generated by pets, and those triggered by people other than the monitored individual. We note that the placement of the motion detectors is chosen in such a way as to minimize any intrusion by pets. In any case, these anomalous sequences need to be detected and removed from the estimation process.

If a participant lives alone, the only sequences that need to be discarded are those that might have been generated by his or her visitors or pets. Thus, it is important to spot the potential presence of additional individuals in the residence or the sequence that may be caused by spurious firings. This detection can be generally accomplished by distinguishing sensor activities that are not consistent with a single individual using statistical pattern classification techniques based on probabilistic models of "normal" activities.

Figure 31.2   Example of a Part of a Residence With a Number of Pyroelectric Infrared Motion Sensors, RFID Receiver Stations, and the Hall Used to Measure the Gait Velocity

The probabilistic models work by integrating information from all the sensors, knowledge learned from prior activities with environmental constraints. There are numerous ways of implementing such models, but one of the simplest approach is based on hidden Markov models (HMM; Rabiner, 1989). In this scenario, HMMs are used to represent the location of the monitored individual in terms of discrete states and his or her movements in terms of transition probabilities. One of the simplest examples of an HMM used for this purpose is shown in Figure 31.3 (Pavel et al., 2007). The states represent general locations surrounding the corridor with the motion sensors for the assessment of gait velocity. Note that the HMM embodies some of the constraints of the dwelling architecture (e.g., adjacency of the different locations) by identifying nonzero transition probabilities. Once trained, the model is used to assign the probability of the best matching sequence of states to the data. If the probability of the most likely sequence of states is too low, then the sequence is not used in the assessment process.

This type of modeling of the participant's mobility is even more important when monitoring individuals living in multiple-occupant dwellings (Hayes et al., 2007; Pavel et al., 2007). In those situations it is even more important to distinguish the location of each individual because the frequency of the relevant events triggered by the cohabitant is much higher than by the visitors in the single-occupant case. The models of mobility are applied to both occupants,

and the estimates of locations are used to attribute the gait velocity measurements.

To illustrate this approach, we present sample data from two different studies. In one of our earliest studies, we monitored participants (83.9 ± 2.6 years) in their homes (Hayes et al., 2004). All participants in this study had normal cognitive functions as measured by a set of standard neuropsychological tests, and all had a score of zero on the Clinical Dementia Rating. The participants were monitored in their homes, and the data were transmitted to a server in our laboratory. The resulting time to walk is shown estimated over time in Figure 31.4.

The second example is from a more recent study in which we monitored a home with two occupants: One of the participants was diagnosed with early stages of Parkinson's disease, and the second was the participant's healthy spouse. Using the techniques described above, we monitored the speed of walking of both individuals, each identified by an RFID device (a watch)—a monitoring system developed by HomeFree, Inc. (Milwaukee, WI). The results of the estimated speed of walking are shown in Figure 31.5.

MONITORING MOTOR SPEED FROM COMPUTER KEYBOARD INTERACTIONS

Elders are currently the fastest growing demographic of new computer users. According to a 2004 Pew Internet and American Life survey, 22% of adults 65 and older use the Internet (Pew Internet Project, 2004). However, adults 65 and older are participating at faster rates, and that trend is expected to continue. The survey also showed that 93% of seniors with Internet access have sent or received e-mail and that seniors are more inclined than any other group of Internet users to go online and check e-mail on any given day. This natural use of computers offers a valuable opportunity for assessing motor speed by looking at routine typing and mouse interactions. In recent studies monitoring elders' computer interactions in their home environment, Jimison, Pavel, and McKanna (2007) used keyboard typing speed to approximate the neuropsychological test of finger tapping. The objective was to develop a measure of typing speed that was as reliable and consistent as possible. It is clear

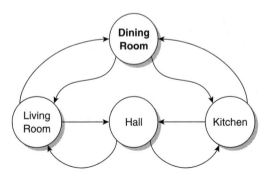

Figure 31.3 Hidden Markov Model Representing the Dynamics of a Patient in His Residence

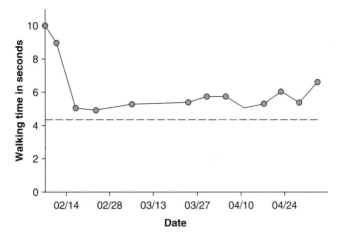

Figure 31.4   Mean Time to Walk a Fixed Distance for 1 of the Participants, Estimated Using a 1-Week Moving Window With 1-Day Overlap

NOTE: Dashed line = walking time for the same distance, estimated from the results of the timed walk test performed during a clinical office visit.

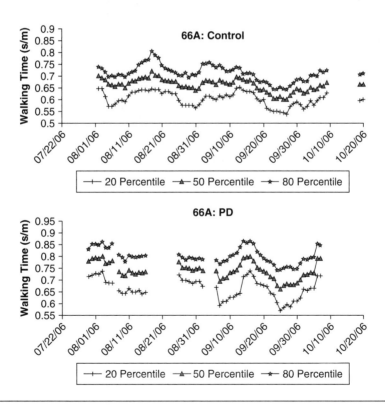

Figure 31.5   Example of Results From One House With a Patient With Parkinson's Disease (Lower Panel) and a Control Participant (Upper Panel)

NOTES: The abscissa is the date of each observation, and the ordinate is the time it takes to walk along the test area. The three different sets of data correspond to the 20th, 50th, and 80th percentiles of walking times. The missing data indicate that the corresponding individual was not in the residence. The data were computed using a 7-day moving window.

that, under normal conditions, a computer user's typing speed will vary, depending on distractions, pausing when thinking of what to type, and so on. In addition, people have varying typing abilities. Our exploration of measures to minimize this unwanted variability has led us to considering speed of typing during consistent periods of word processing and considering repeated keyboard events, such as log-ins.

An advantage of measuring log-in speed is that it is relatively free of contamination with context, distractions, language abilities, and typing abilities. In addition, it is a short, easily distinguishable repeated event that can be quickly selected from the large data files and averaged for mean estimates.

Figure 31.6 shows median interstroke intervals on log-ins for three of the participants in Jimison et al.'s (2007) experiment. A larger interstroke interval is indicative of slower typing speed. Jimison et al. took the median value for log-in speed for each day as the most robust measure of typing speed. Another important variable to consider in predicting cognitive problems is the variability in scores over time. In many cognitive monitoring tests we have performed, we have noticed that respondents with cognitive impairment have both lower scores on average as well as a much higher variability from day to day. In Figure 31.6, the lower two lines represent two cognitively healthy elders

whose data on average are both low (faster typing speed) and stable from day to day. The top line represents data from a participant with mild cognitive impairment (slower typing—i.e., greater interstroke interval and greater variability in performance). The speed of typing for this person is highly variable from day to day and on average slower. Thus, the simple measure of log-in speed seems to be a promising indicator of cognitive performance.

MONITORING WORD COMPLEXITY

In addition to using the speed of keyboard typing as an indicator of cognitive function (a proxy for the finger tap neuropsychological test), we also measure linguistic complexity during naturalistic typing in e-mail and word processing. Our metrics for complexity include word length and frequency of the words in the English language. These measures are calculated on an individual's local computer, and only the statistics are stored for daily encrypted transfer to a secure research server. In this way, the content of an individual's writing remains private. Other researchers' analyses of individuals' writings over time have indicated that word complexity decreases with cognitive decline, long before it can be picked up on standard neuropsychological tests (Garrard, Maloney, Hodges, & Patterson, 2005).

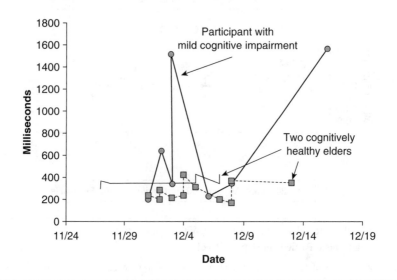

Figure 31.6   Plot of Median Interstroke Interval on Login for Three Elderly Participants

Monitoring Computer Mouse Interactions

Another source of useful sensorimotor information involves interactions with pointing devices, such as a mouse or trackball. These interactions require the user to execute visually guided movements. Our initial investigations are focused on the idea that the trajectories executed by the user may provide useful information regarding his or her cognitive processes.

In a similar manner to the keyboard-based interactions, the context of the interaction may greatly influence the trajectories and their interpretations. We focused our analysis on the interactions with pointing devices during the game of FreeCell. In this situation, it is possible to assess the context of the moves from the state of the game.

The basic data consist of point-to-point movements, where each move is represented by samples in time corresponding to the locations of the cursor on the computer screen. An example of a trajectory of a move is shown in Figure 31.7.

A key question involves how best to represent the trajectories in terms of a small number of parameters that would capture the participants' performance in a way that would most likely relate to their cognitive ability. This representation should, of course, be rotation and scale invariant and capture characteristics such as tremor and inaccurate aiming. In previous research, MacKenzie, Kauppinen, and Silfverberg (2001) used techniques such as the number of "straight" segments, but those parameterizations depend on the scale of measurement and the definition of *straight*. For example, a segment could be deemed straight if the maximum perpendicular distance is less than a given threshold.

To avoid the necessity of making such assumptions, we developed several metrics that are relatively independent of scale. The first of these is the ratio of the lengths of the trajectory to the distance between the endpoints. This metric measures the deviation from a single straight line. A straight line, however, is not necessarily the most efficient way for a human to move from one point to another because of the kinematic and dynamic constraints of human articulated mechanisms of the arm and hand.

For that reason, we developed a novel approach borrowed from machine vision called *Fourier descriptors* (Zahn & Roskies, 1972). Intuitively, Fourier descriptors capture the trajectory in terms of harmonic functions that capture the various rates of deviation from the straight line. Formally put, if the trajectory is described in terms of the coordinates in a complex plane, then

$$u(t) = x(t) + jy(t),$$

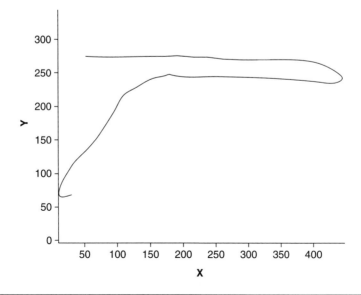

Figure 31.7   A Typical Trackball Movement During a Game of FreeCell

where j designates an imaginary dimension. Given this formulation, it is natural to express the trajectory in terms of its harmonic components using the Fourier representation

$$u(t) = \frac{1}{N} \sum_{k=0}^{N-1} a(k) \exp\left(\frac{j2\pi kt}{N}\right)$$

where the coefficients $a(k)$ are computed

$$a(k) = \sum_{k=0}^{N-1} u(t) \exp\left(\frac{-j2\pi kt}{N}\right).$$

The coefficient corresponding to the $k = 0$ represents the location of the trajectory, and thus we ignore it for the purpose of this analysis. The remaining coefficients represent the trajectory in terms of components that vary with higher frequencies.

For the purpose of the analysis of the pointing device, trajectories were sampled and interpolated so that the sample spacing was approximately 10 pixels along its length. To avoid discontinuities, the paths were extended by their mirror images in each coordinate.

A graph of the first 10 components for the trajectory in Figure 31.7 is shown in Figure 31.8. It is interesting to note that the global characteristics of each move are represented by the low

frequency components, whereas the small deviation (e.g., corresponding to tremor) would be characterized by the higher components. This can be seen by band-limiting the Fourier descriptor representation to the low-frequency components and reconstructing the move. For the purpose of the trajectory characterization, we used the total power in the trajectory and in different sub-bands.

The benefit of this analysis of mouse movements is that the efficiency of moving toward an intended target should correspond to sensor motor performance and thus to cognitive measures.

MONITORING AND ASSESSMENT BASED ON COMPUTER GAMES

Our final example of frequent unobtrusive monitoring of cognition in the home environment has to do with embedded cognitive assessment algorithms in computer games that are enjoyable for elders to play on a routine basis. To make these measurements as unobtrusive as possible, Jimison et al. (2007) performed a needs assessment to define elders' preferences for computer applications, games, and potential barriers to computer use. They used focus groups and surveys to help us define a set of features for an

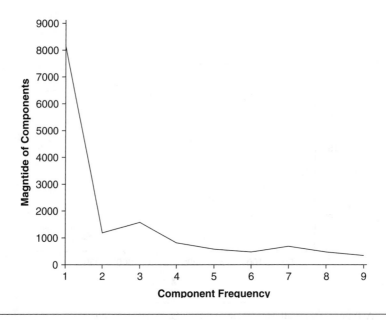

Figure 31.8 First Nine Fourier Descriptors

elder Web portal that could be used as a research environment to collect real-time interaction data. They also defined a set of enjoyable computer games that could be adapted for cognitive monitoring. To select the games for further development, they observed which features were most enjoyable and easily understood by elders and then performed a cognitive task analysis on each of the games to characterize its appropriateness for providing information on one of the cognitive dimensions described in the previous section on standard cognitive tests. They ended up creating and testing a suite of nine adaptive cognitive computer games for elders that measured a variety of proxies for the standard neuropsychological tests. Many of the games were variants of common familiar games, with embedded assessment algorithms. However, Jimison et al. also took standard tests and adapted them to a game format.

By taking this approach to cognitive computer game development, Jimison et al. (2007) were able to obtain fairly frequent measurements across our nine games tested in a 3-month pilot study in the homes of 30 elderly residents of five senior residential facilities in Portland, Oregon. The participants in this study were mostly female (83%), with an average age of

80.4 ± 6.0 years and an average level of 15.2 ± 2.7 years of education. Figure 31.9 shows fairly high usage of the cognitive games in general (three of the games had at least 200 sessions over 3 months, and three others had approximately 150 game sessions over 3 months). However, two of our cognitive computer games had less than optimal routine computer play on average.

Subtle changes in verbal fluency are likely an important behavioral marker of future cognitive decline (Garrard et al., 2005). In addition, measures of verbal fluency are routinely a key component of a standard battery of neuropsychological tests. It is often measured as semantic fluency (e.g., name as many animals as you can within 60 seconds) or letter fluency (e.g., name as many words as you can that start with the letter "f" within 60 seconds). To incorporate this type of measure into an enjoyable activity for elders, we adapted two computer word games to measure speed of word generation and the complexity of word generation.

The left panel of Figure 31.10 shows an example of a word jumble game in which the users are give a set of seven letters and asked to generate as many words from that set as quickly as they can. They are given cues on the right of

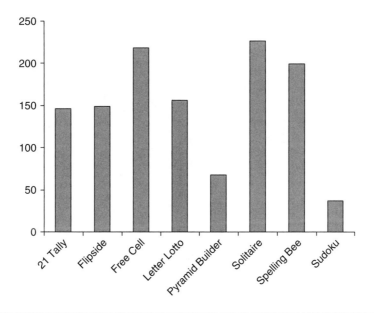

Figure 31.9   Average Number of Games Played per Participant Over a 3-Month Period for Each of Our Cognitive Computer Games

the screen to show how many words are possible. Entering a word that incorporates all seven letters allows the user to go onto the next round. Two basic metrics relating to verbal fluency can be generated from monitoring the user's interactions in this game: (1) speed of word generation and (2) the complexity of the words generated (defined by word length and frequency of use in the English language).

The right panel of Figure 31.10 shows another word game designed to measure verbal fluency, but with the additional task of search and planning. In this game, the user must connect adjacent letters to form words as quickly as possible. A higher score is given for longer words and for using highlighted letters. With the reference abilities of verbal fluency measured in the game shown in the left panel of this figure, we are now able to quantify the increased performance requirements due to search and planning. In each of these games, the difficulty of the board layout is adapted to the skill of the user. Our adaptation algorithms keep the success rate at approximately 60% to 80%, so that users are challenged, but not frustrated. This also gives us the best opportunity to measure performance (i.e., users' scores do not top out when the task is too easy or bottom out when the task is too difficult).

In these games, we rate as having higher verbal fluency users who can create longer and more sophisticated words (against time and difficulty of available letters). We concentrate on monitoring relative performance (with respect to the user's baseline) to look for differences. This is likely to be a more sensitive measure that is less influenced by education and language abilities and more influenced by cognitive changes.

Other standard neuropsychological tests specifically measure aspects of memory. As a close proxy for those tests, we embedded measures of short-term and working memory into a variation of the standard concentration card game on the computer, as shown in Figure 31.11. In this game, users must remember the location of various cards they select and match pairs. Game difficulty is adapted on the basis of the number of cards and the cognitive difficulty of the matches. These range from simple shape and color matches to cognitively more difficult matches, such as matching a digital clock time with the analogue picture equivalent. For this game, we estimate memory ability using a metric describing the effective size of a probabilitstic memory buffer. This metric is defined by estimates of the parameters of a function that describe how long—that is, how many flip-backs—the participant was able to successfully remember seeing a target card. Through repeated play of this game, we are able to estimate an individual's memory "buffer length" for both the card value and location. This measure

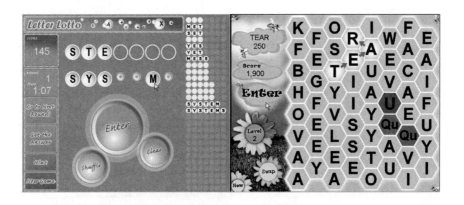

Figure 31.10   Measuring Verbal Fluency With Computer Word Games

Left panel: Word jumble game that measures the user's relative ability to find longer, more complex words from a set of seven letters. Right panel: Word game that measures the user's relative ability to find longer, more complex words in a difficult search environment.

SOURCE: Reprinted with permission of Spry Learning Company.

is referenced to an ideal player's performance (with infinite memory).

We have designed other computer games to specifically test the remaining dimensions of cognition. Figure 31.12 shows a shape and color matching game that provides us with measures of planning (inferring the number of steps ahead a user would have to be able to plan in order to be successful). In this game we can also manipulate difficulty and provide added features to test memory and divided attention.

In addition to the games for which we adapted activities that elders already found to be enjoyable, we also took standard tests, such as the Trail Making Test (Stuss, Stethem, & Poirier, 1987), and adapted it to be fun. In this game, users use the mouse input device to select circles in numerical sequence, letter sequence, and mixed targets. This activity is similar to the Trail Making Test in that it requires several dimensions of cognitive executive function, including visual search, attention, and set switching. Each of these additional components can be extracted and assessed with repeated game use. These more frequent measures allow us to monitor within-subject trends and monitor

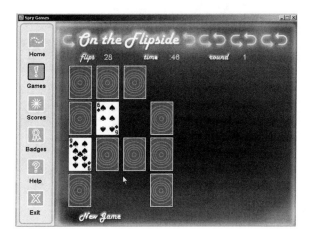

Figure 31.11 Example of a Memory Computer Game

SOURCE: Reprinted with permission of Spry Learning Company.

Figure 31.12 Color and Shape Matching Game That Tests Planning Ability, Memory, and Attention

SOURCE: Reprinted with permission of Spry Learning Company.

performance variability. Both of these features offer promise in being able to detect cognitive problems earlier and potentially more reliably.

Most of our experience and testing of computer games for cognitive monitoring has come from our work with an implementation of the popular Solitaire game of FreeCell, as shown in the top panel of Figure 31.13 (Jimison et al., 2004). We found that this game was by far the favorite with the elders whom we interviewed, and it was the first computer game we adapted for use in cognitive monitoring. In our research

version, we compare user performance to our computer solver. The lower panel of Figure 31.13 shows the game difficulty starting at 82 moves to optimal solution, with the lower line showing the computer solver's direct path to solution. The upper line shows the participant's moves going toward and away from the best solution. We use the slope of the participant's performance as a measure of efficiency of play. In our early pilot work comparing FreeCell performance of cognitively healthy elders with the performance of persons with diagnosed with mild cognitive

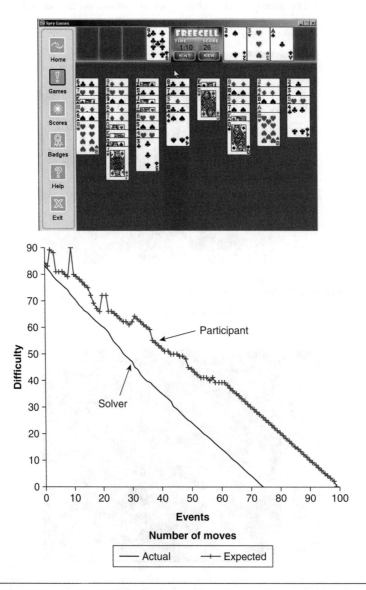

Figure 31.13   Sample Game of FreeCell and a Diagram Showing Participant's Performance Versus a Computer Solver

impairment, we were able to use the efficiency metric to distinguish the two groups.

The results of our early pilot tests to show the feasibility of monitoring computer interactions in the home are presented in Table 31.1. We monitored 12 elders in a local senior residential facility for 3 weeks. Using conventional neuropsychometric tests described earlier, we found that 3 of the elderly participants (mean age 80.2 ± 8.0) had mild cognitive impairment. Using only data from their FreeCell performance, we were able to distinguish cognitively healthy participants from those with mild cognitive impairment. It is interesting that the variability of the measures over time was in itself a useful feature in classifying cognitive impairment.

In summary, the method of using computer games as a vehicle for cognitive monitoring offers us the ability to collect frequent data on motor speed, verbal fluency, working memory, planning, and attention. Early pilot data show promise for the approach in classifying mild cognitive impairment, and ongoing longitudinal studies will test the effectiveness of the approach in its ability to detect early signs of cognitive decline.

CONCLUSION

Cognitive monitoring in the home offers distinct advantages for managing the care of elders. First, it is the most important issue for elders with regard to their quality of life and their ability to maintain independence. Second, real-time and continuous information on cognitive performance offers important feedback on the effectiveness of therapies. In addition, the detection of acute problems due to illness or medication side effects could be made in a much more timely and effective manner. Medication errors due to drug–drug interactions, side effects, and faulty adherence (under- or over-dosing) are extremely common for elders, who often take more than five medications per day.

In addition, understanding cognitive performance over time offers substantial benefits over our current clinical methods for assessing elders. With unobtrusive home monitoring, we are able to make frequent measurements that capture both short- and long-term changes, as well as variability in performance—a key attribute in and of itself. This allows us to use individuals as their own controls and makes the evaluation less susceptible to confounding factors, such as cultural experiences and issues due to assessing a person in a non-native language. By detecting trends in an individual's performance, we have the potential to detect cognitive decline at a much earlier point in time.

Notwithstanding the clinical and care-oriented motivation for understanding the effects of aging and disease, the assessment of the changes associated with aging can provide unprecedented insights into the function of cognitive systems. In a similar manner to researchers using developmental studies (e.g., with toddlers) to determine the acquisition of cognitive skills, one can use the fine-grain analysis of cognitive decline observed using game performance metrics to study underlying cognitive processes. The cognitive changes, such as a decline with aging or disease, will likely be easier to isolate in aging.

Although the goals of this home monitoring approach appear to be attainable, and the preliminary results appear to be encouraging, a real demonstration of this technology-based continuous monitoring strategy will require one or more longitudinal studies focused on the assessment and early detection of cognitive decline. Several such studies are just in their initial stages, and the results will likely be available in several years.

In the meantime, we need to continue intensive analysis of the behavioral markers and the statistical properties of the measured metrics.

Table 31.1 FreeCell Efficiency Cognitive Metric Scores for Nine Cognitively Healthy Elders and Three Elders With Mild Cognitive Impairment (MCI)

Participant	Average of participants' mean efficiency	SD of participants' mean efficiency	Average of participants' SD efficiency
Healthy	0.58	0.12	0.38
MCI	0.27	0.72	0.55

It should be obvious that among the main issues is the question of whether the gain in precision due to the high sampling frequency or continuous measurements would compensate for the additional variability due to the fact that the conditions of measurement are not controlled and subject to contextual, environmental, and motivational variability. The cost–benefit trade-offs will need to be confronted by empirical studies.

REFERENCES

Boise, L., Neal, M., & Kaye, J. (2004). Dementia assessment in primary care: Results from a study in three managed care systems. *Journal of Gerontology: Medical Sciences, 69,* M621–M626.

Burton, C. L., Strauss, E., Hultsch, D. F., Moll, A., & Hunter, M. A. (2006). Intraindividual variability as a marker of neurological dysfunction: A comparison of Alzheimer's disease and Parkinson's disease. *Journal of Clinical and Experimental Neuropsychology, 28,* 67–83.

Buschke, H., Kuslansky, G., Katz, M., Stewart, W. F., Sliwinski, M. J., Eckholdt, H. M., et al. (1999). Screening for dementia with the Memory Impairment Screen. *Neurology, 52,* 231–238.

Callahan, C., Hendrie, H., & Tierney, W. (1995). Documentation and evaluation of cognitive impairment in elderly primary care patients. *American College of Physicians, 122,* 422–429.

Camicioli, R., Howieson, D., Oken, B., Sexton, G., & Kaye, J. (1998). Motor slowing precedes cognitive impairment in the oldest old. *Neurology, 50,* 1496–1498.

Cooper, D. B., Epker, M., Lacritz, L., Weine, M., Rosenberg, R. N., Honig, L., et al. (2001). Effects of practice on category fluency in Alzheimer's disease. *Clinical Neuropsychology, 15,* 125–128.

Cooper, D. B., Lacritz, L. H., Weiner, M. F., Rosenberg, R. N., & Cullum, C. M. (2004). Category fluency in mild cognitive impairment: Reduced effect of practice in test–retest conditions. *Alzheimer Disease and Associated Disorders, 18,* 120–122.

Folstein, M., Folstein, S., & McHugh, P. (1975). Mini-Mental State: A practical method for grading the cognitive state of patients for the clinician. *Journal of Psychiatric Research, 12,* 189–198.

Ganguli, M., Rodriguez, E., Mulsant, B., Richards, S., Pandav, R., Bilt, J. V., et al. (2004). Detection and management of cognitive impairment in primary care: The Steel Valley Seniors Survey. *Journal of the American Geriatrics Society, 52,* 1668–1675.

Garrard, P., Maloney, L. M., Hodges, J. R., & Patterson, K. (2005). The effects of very early Alzheimer's disease on the characteristics of writing by a renowned author. *Brain, 128,* 250–260.

Goldman, W. P., Baty, J. D., Buckles, V. D., Sahrmann, S., & Morris, J. C. (1999). Motor dysfunction in mildly demented AD individuals without extrapyramidal signs. *Neurology, 53,* 956–962.

Hayes, T. L., Pavel, M., & Kaye, J. A. (2004, September). *An unobtrusive in-home monitoring system for detection of key motor changes preceding cognitive decline.* Paper presented at the 26th Annual International Conference of the IEEE Engineering in Medicine and Biology Society, San Francisco.

Hayes, T. L., Pavel, M., Larimer, N., Tsay, I. A., Nutt, J., & Adami, A. G. (2007). Distributed healthcare: Simultaneous assessment of multiple individuals. *IEEE Pervasive Computing, 6*(1), 36–43.

Jimison, H. J., Pavel, M., & McKanna, J. (2007, August). *A Framework for cognitive monitoring using computer game interactions.* Paper presented at the MedInfo Conference, Brisbane, Australia.

Jimison, H., Pavel, M., McKanna, J., & Pavel, J. (2004). Unobtrusive monitoring of computer interactions to detect cognitive status in elders. *IEEE Transactions in Information Technology and Biomedicine, 8,* 248–252.

Kokmen, E., Naessens, J. M., & Offord, K. P. (1987). A short test of mental status: Description and preliminary results. *Mayo Clinic Proceedings, 62,* 281–288.

MacKenzie, I. S., Kauppinen, T., & Silfverberg, M. (2001, March). *Accuracy measures for evaluating computer pointing devices.* Paper presented at the CHI 2001—ACM Conference on Human Factors in Computing Systems, New York.

Marquis, S., Moore, M. M., Howieson, D. B., Sexton, G., Payami, H., Kaye, J. A., et al. (2002). Independent predictors of cognitive decline in healthy elderly persons. *Archives of Neurology, 59,* 601–606.

Martin, M., & Hofer, S. M. (2004). Intraindividual variability, change, and aging: Conceptual and analytical issues. *Gerontology, 50,* 7–11.

Pavel, M., Hayes, T. L., Adami, A., Jimison, H. B., & Kaye, J. (2006, August). *Unobtrusive assessment of mobility.* Paper presented at the presented at 28th Annual International Conference of the IEEE Engineering in Medicine and Biology Society, New York.

Pavel, M., Hayes, T., Tsay, I., Erdogmus, D., Paul, A., Larimer, N., et al. (2007). *Continuous Assessment of Gait Velocity in Parkinson's Disease from Unobtrusive Measurements.* Paper presented at the Third Interantional IEEE EMBS Conference on Neural Engineering, Hawaii.

Petersen, R., Stevens, J., Ganguli, M., Tangelos, E., Cummings, J., & DeKoski, S. (2001). Practice parameter: Early detection. Mild cognitive impariment (an evidence-based review). *Neurology, 56,* 1133–1142.

Pew Internet Project. (2004). Older Americans and the Internet. *Pew Internet and American Life Project.* Available online at http://www .pewinternet.org/ PPF/r/117/report_display.asp

Rabiner, L. (1989). A tutorial on hidden Markov models and selected applications in speech recognition. *Proceedings of the IEEE, 77,* 257–286.

Richards, M., Stern, Y., & Mayeux, R. (1993). Subtle extapyramidal signs can predict the development of dementia in elderly individuals. *Neurology, 43,* 2184–2188.

Sheridan, T. B. (2002). Some musings on four ways humans couple: Implications for systems design. *IEEE Transactions on Systems, Man,* and Cybernetics Part A:Systems and Humans, *32*(1), 5–10.

Sliwinski, M. J., Stawski, R. S., & Hofer, S. M. (2006, April). *Decomposing aging and practice effect in cognitive performance.* Abstract presented at the Cognitive Aging Conference, Atlanta, GA.

Strauss, E., MacDonald, S. W., Hunter, M., Moll, A., & Hultsch, D. F. (2002). Intraindividual variability in cognitive performance in three groups of older adults: Cross-domain links to physical status and self-perceived affect and beliefs. *Journal of the International Neuropsychology Society, 8,* 893–906.

Stuss, D. T., Stethem, L. L., & Poirier, C. A. (1987). Comparison of three tests of attention and rapid information processing across six age groups. *The Clincal Neuropsychologist, 1,* 139–152.

Tabbarah, M., Crimmins, E. M., & Seeman, T. E. (2002). The relationship between cognitive and physical performance: MacArthur Studies of Successful Aging. *Journals of Gerontology Series A: Biological Sciences and Medical Sciences, 57,* M228–M235.

Verghese, J., Buschke, H., Viola, L., Katz, M., Hall, C., Kuslansky, G., et al. (2002). Validity of divided attention tasks in predicting falls in older individuals: A preliminary study. *Journal of the American Geriatrics Society, 50,* 1572–1576.

Wilson, R. S., Schneider, J. A., Bienias, J. L., Evans, D. A., & Bennett, D. A. (2003). Parkinsonianlike signs and risk of incident Alzheimer disease in older persons. *Archives of Neurology, 60,* 539–544.

Zahn, C. T., & Roskies, R. Z. (1972). Fourier descriptors for plane close curves. *IEEE Transactions on Computers, C-21,* 269–281.

PART VII

INTEGRATIVE PERSPECTIVES ON COGNITIVE AGING

32

ANIMAL MODELS OF HUMAN COGNITIVE AGING

GERALD E. MCCLEARN AND DAVID A. BLIZARD

The realm of human cognition is very complex and multifaceted and, in spite of impressive advances since the early 20th century, its description and understanding are still works in progress. An abiding research focus during this time has concerned the changes in cognitive processes that accompany aging. With the dazzling new techniques of neurobehavioral research added to the existing research armamentarium, we can expect very rapid changes in the future in our conceptualization of human cognition in general and in its gerontological manifestations in particular. Animal models will undoubtedly play a large role in these advances. The purpose of this chapter is to offer some observations on the present state of animal models in cognitive science and some suggestions about their future deployment in investigations of age-related cognitive change.

One of our principal points concerns the limitations on generalizability from the specific configuration of variables, both environmental and genetic, that comprise the particular measurement situations of these model systems. Another concern is the special attention that must be given to distinguishing cognitive change from changes in other processes when comparing animals of different ages.

From the present perspective, a key question is: Which subsystems get modeled in animal research? For what aspects (models) of human cognition do we think we can generate a veridical or useful animal model? It's probably fair to say that we do not have rock-solid criteria for answering this question. To a considerable extent, it's a matter of face validity.

Whatever the case, there is no dearth of accumulated information about candidate animal cognitive processes upon which to draw in addressing cognitive aging. In the mid-20th century there was an explosion of creativity in this research domain, and learning theory and empirical research assumed a central position in the field of psychology. An enormous literature was generated, both from research on human beings and on animals (see Hilgard & Bower, 1966, for a view of the status of the area at that time). The names Guthrie, Harlow, Hull, Skinner, Spence, Thorndike, and Tolman may serve as representative of the army of experimental and comparative psychologists who were engaged in the enterprise. They and their coworkers developed an enormously varied and imaginative armamentarium of equipment and techniques to explore this complex domain.

Human cognition covers a broader range than the processes of learning and memory, of course, but these two basic features were most intensively studied in these animal models. There were straight runways, mazes (enclosed, elevated, multiple choice, single choice, radial, temporal, etc.) jump-stands, operant devices, problem-solving situations, discrimination, oddity, matching from sample problems (see Munn, 1950, for a broad sampling of these devices and procedures). From this cornucopia only a small sample has trickled through into the neurobehavioral research of today. It might be thought that this situation satisfactorily reflects the sifting and winnowing over the decades of the apparatus and methods that had proved most fruitful—survival of the most productive.

An alternative, less sanguine, explanation might be suggested for at least some of this filtration. Quite properly in the logic of replication in experimental science, particular apparatuses and procedures that have provided interesting results have been favored for use in subsequent research, and many have cumulated to the status of "gold standard." There is no guarantee of the generalizability of results from these stalwart situations, however. In the following, we review some of the evidence about the particularity of results that may derive from specific measurement situations. As a consequence of such uniqueness or specificity, towering edifices of data may have been built on perilously narrow foundations.

The Measurement Situation

Many decisions are required to translate the abstract notion of a model as isolation of a subsystem within a complex system into the practical world of data collection. In respect to models of learning, these involve such matters as how to induce a state of motivation and arrange for its subsequent alleviation, the particular configuration of the learning problem presented to the animal, the response required of it, and so on. Furthermore, a point of particular importance, which we emphasize later in the chapter, is that the nature of the animal subjects must be decided. This choice refers not only to species but also to genetically identifiable groups within the species.

In the traditional terms of experimental method, a measurement situation comprises all of the manipulated (independent) variables, controlled variables, random variables, and outcome (dependent) variables. Manipulation of the independent variables provides for varied input to the dependent, outcome variable from the subsystem under scrutiny. The identification of a variable as one to be controlled is an implicit recognition that the subsystem of which it is part has the potential to affect the outcome. (Fixing one variable of a subsystem at some controlled value does not, of course, guarantee that the subsystem cannot provide variable input to the outcome; compensatory feedbacks within the subsystem might still permit variable states and thus some differential effect on the outcome. Overall, however, the general expectation is that fixation of an element might reduce the variability of the subsystem of which it is part and, of particular potential importance, its interaction effects with the independent variable[s].)

The broad features of the measurement situation may be identified rather easily. One might wish to compare young and old mice with respect to maze learning, for example—but in the details reside the issues (and they can indeed be diabolical). How should one arrange the situation so that the animal will do something? Should hunger motivation be used? How? Food deprivation for 24 hours? Reduction of body weight to 90% of baseline level? Maybe thirst would be better. What response will be required? Bar pressing, climbing a ladder, swimming through a maze, running through a maze? If the latter, what apparatus? Maybe a Hebb–Williams maze (Rabinovitch & Rosvold, 1951)? Maybe a Lashley III (Lashley & Wiley, 1933)? Maybe. . . With that decision made, how many trials should be given per day? And at what intertrial intervals? And at what time of day? What level of illumination should be provided in the apparatus and in the room in general? How will the reinforcement (the food "reward") be administered? Small pellets administered after each trial or access for a limited time to a food source? Maybe a sugar solution would work better? Should all animals be brought simultaneously from the colony room to the testing room, thus requiring different wait times before testing? How will the effects of odor trails left by the previous mouse be dealt with? How will operational noises from elsewhere in the laboratory be masked or reduced? Will one technician handle all animals, or will there be rotating assignments? What is the microbiological status of the laboratory? Again, a central issue from the point of view of this chapter, what subject animals will be used; what will be their genetic definition? This exercise may appear to be nit-picking, but these nits can matter. Both from theory and from hard experience, it has been shown that features of this sort can massively influence performance in the learning situations we contrive.

A logical admonition, observed long ago but sometimes forgotten or ignored, is that learning and memory cannot be directly assessed, only inferred from observed performance. The performance of an animal in a measurement situation is the product of motivational or emotional state, sensory competence or motor capabilities, among other things, along with (one hopes) some cognitive process or processes of interest. Changes in performance over repeated trials, the basic data of learning investigations, can reflect changes in any of these noncognitive processes as well as in "learning." Thus, "learning" inferred from change in behavior in a highly stressful situation may measure diminution in induced terror over repeated trials. The learning that is accomplished by the animal may be that the situation is not, after all, lethal. The model may be evaluating cognition under conditions of panic, probably a more focused phenomenon than intended by the investigator.

Genetics and Individuality of Cognitive Aging

A commanding aspect of human cognitive aging is the range of individual differences in onset, rate, and pattern of change. Individuality is, of course, the essence of the science of genetics and, as expected, considerable effort has been devoted to exploring the relative contributions of genetic and environmental factors to individuality in cognitive decline.

For the application of animal models to this domain, some very versatile tools have been available. Of particular pertinence to the present topic are inbred strains, systematically derived genetically heterogeneous stocks, and selectively bred lines.

Very briefly described, inbred strains are generated by mating of relatives (usually siblings). After about 20 consecutive generations of such inbreeding, the offspring approach the condition of being genetically uniform. Once this condition has been achieved, the genetic state of the group is relatively stable (it is subject to rare mutational events, of course). Thus, different samples of animals of a particular strain tested at different times and in different laboratories will be genetically (approximately) the same, providing relatively constant reference material. Over the last century, many inbred strains have been developed. These strains differ in genotype, and they have come to constitute basic research material throughout the broad arenas of biomedical research (see Blizard & Darvasi, 1999; Bogue & Grubb, 2004; Lyon, 1995; Silver, 1995).

For some purposes, genetically heterogeneous ("het") stocks have strong interpretational advantages over inbred material (McClearn, Wilson, & Meredith, 1970). This is particularly true in situations where correlations of traits across individuals are a central interest. Correlations within an inbred strain, obviously, can assess only covariances traceable to environmental influences. Systematically derived and maintained het stocks offer covariances attributable to both genetic and environmental sources and constitute a superior research platform for animal models involving multivariate analyses.

One particular use of a het stock is to provide a foundation for the generation of selectively bred animals. Insofar as the location of an animal on a continuous distribution is in part determined by genes, mating of extreme animals will, over successive generations, result in a change in the frequency of variants (alleles) of the trait-relevant genes. Thus, bidirectional selection over generations can result in two lines with greatly differing phenotypic values, based on differences in frequencies of trait-increasing and trait-decreasing alleles that have been brought about by selective mating. We note that the different groups can be used either in the role of manipulated variables or as control variables. (Readers may refer to McClearn and Hofer [1999a, 1999b] for a more extensive general discussion of the merits and limitations of these genetic tools.)

Interactions of genetic factors with design features of the measurement situation can be striking. Warren (1988), for example, showed that mice of the inbred DBA/2 strain made more errors than did inbred C57BL/6 mice in a Lashley III maze when they were hungry and rewarded with food. However, there was no difference at all between the strains when they were thirsty and rewarded with water.

Strain differences in shock avoidance learning have been repeatedly demonstrated in rats and mice, and inferences have been drawn about the motivational basis of these group differences. However, what if the differences reflect differences in the ability of the groups to perform a particular motor response, rather than in a dimension such as "emotionality" or "learning ability"? An elegant study (Mori & Makino, 1994) showed that if mice of four different strains were allowed to rear/jump, or to make a horizontal locomotor response to perform the avoidance, there were major strain differences in the response selected by specific strains. Three strains (C57BL/6, BALB/c, and DBA/2J) all used horizontal locomotion to avoid shock, whereas the C3H/He strain employed rearing or jumping. Thus, differences in avoidance behavior among strains may reflect the chance pairing of the avoidance criterion (selected by the experimenter) with strain-specific response tendencies. A richly detailed study (Wahlsten, Cooper, & Crabbe, 2005) involving these and other strains in water escape tasks revealed a complexity of strain differences in sensory factors, response proclivity, and sensitivity to apparatus design, warranting the conclusion that "no single task can reveal the full richness of spatially guided behavior in a wide range of mouse genotypes" (Wahlston et al., 2005, p. 36).

Tryon's (1940) classical Bright and Dull lines of rats provide further examples. These lines were selectively bred for facility in learning the correct pathway in a 17-unit multiple T maze. Searle (1949) examined the rats' performance in several different situations. In general, the strains performed as their names implied under conditions of hunger motivation and food reward. However, under escape-from-water motivation, the Dulls were brighter than the Brights. Searle also noted that the Dulls were fearful of the movement of the non-retrace doors that were a design feature in the maze in which their ancestors had been selected for poor

performance. Some of the difference between these lines in "brightness," therefore, can likely be attributed to appetitive motivational states and to fear.

The above are not isolated examples; here, they are representatives of a large body of pertinent literature. If not pervasive, such effects are at least sufficiently common to demand extreme caution in generalizing the results from any one configuration of variables that make up a learning situation. Generalizability of results cannot be assumed; it must be demonstrated empirically, and conclusions from the narrow base of a single genotype or a single measurement situation must be regarded as tentative until the demonstration is in hand.

Sprott and Stavnes (1975) reviewed a large number of researches on a particular class of learning situation—avoidance learning—in connection with research on genetic influences on cognitive aging. Their summary emphasized situational dependence: "... in almost any behavioral test, results will depend upon the *interaction* between a given genotype and the situation in which it finds itself" (p. 156). Their succinct conclusion can stand as a summary of the present review of the problems of situational specificity: "One of the more obvious conclusions to be drawn is that studies in which genetically controlled subjects are exposed to a single or limited number of learning environments will produce results that have little or no generality" (p. 162)

These issues would appear to be particularly pertinent to the study of aging of cognitive function. Older animals may respond differently to the standard motivation-inducing operations. Frequently used methods to standardize appetitive motivation include, for example, 20 hours of food deprivation or 23.5 hours of water deprivation. These procedures might have dramatically different metabolic and physiological consequences for an older than for a younger animal, and these differences might affect performance. Indeed, Warren (1986) concluded that a thirst procedure is "contraindicated as a method for investigating learning by old mice." Similarly, older animals may have sensory deficits and, insofar as visual, auditory, or olfactory cues may be pertinent to task performance, may appear to be "cognitively impaired." A recent case in point was provided by Wong and

Brown (2006), who showed that DBA/2 mice experience a loss of visual function between 6 and 12 months of age, accounting substantially for the strain's performance decrement relative to that of a number of other strains.

Age-related differences in sensitivity of pain receptors to footpad shock might affect performance in active or passive avoidance procedures. Furthermore, response requirements that are objectively identical might have quite different consequences for young and old animals. Consider the requirement of locomotion in a maze, particularly where the assessment of performance is related to time of transit. What about arthritis in the older animals? What about the changes in muscle physiology that might affect speed of locomotion with the relevant cognitive processes unimpaired? What about required swimming, which must involve a murine version of panic as well as extraordinary energy expenditure?

A particularly convoluted example, also from research on Tryon's (1940) strains, was provided by McGaugh and Cole (1965), who examined the effect of intertrial interval on performance under hunger motivation (in a simpler maze than that used in the original selective breeding program) of two age groups of these lines of rat. Young rats (29–33 days old) were compared with young adults (142–164 days) under conditions of 30 seconds (massed practice) or of 30 minutes (distributed practice) between successive trials. Samples of both sexes were tested. In the young adult males, an expected result was obtained: Bright animals made fewer errors than Dull animals, and both groups made more errors under the massed condition. In younger males, the massed practice effect was only present in the Brights, and the difference between the lines vanished—the errors of the Dulls (which did not differ between conditions) were midway between the massed and the distributed performance of the Brights. In young adult females, the distribution of practice effect was striking in both Brights and Dulls, but the differences between the groups were nearly identical; that is, the Bright distributed errors were the same as the Dull distributed, and the Bright massed were the same as the Dull massed. In the younger females, the distribution of practice effect did not appear in the Dulls, whose performance was

equivalent to that of the Brights under the massed condition but inferior to that of the Brights under the distributed condition. The effects of the measurement feature of distribution of practice clearly are dependent on the contexts of genotype, sex, and age.

In the remainder of this chapter we address a particularly attractive target for such research: the influence of environmental factors on cognitive decline with age and the efficacy of preventive interventions.

THE ROLE OF ENVIRONMENT IN HUMAN COGNITIVE FUNCTION IN OLD AGE

Research on the deterioration of human cognitive function in late life encompasses a broad range of dysfunction that includes general cognitive decline as well as the devastating deficits associated with Alzheimer's disease (AD). A new dimension in this research field has been added by a number of investigators who have conducted retrospective examinations of cognitive function of AD patients. Individuals destined to develop AD tend to exhibit differences in cognitive function early in life. Scoring of autobiographical essays written by nuns at an average age of 22 showed that individuals with lower density of ideas and lower grammatical complexity were 30 times more likely to perform poorly on a test of mental function administered approximately 60 years later and much more likely to exhibit neuropathological indices of AD in postmortem determinations (Snowdon et al., 1996).

A subsequent study showed a relationship between customary daily activities and the likelihood of developing AD. The intensity and diversity of 26 nonoccupational activities during midlife were significantly higher in 358 healthy control participants than in 193 possible or probable AD patients even when adjusted for age, gender, income adequacy, and education. The increase in time devoted to intellectual activities from early adulthood (20–39 years) to middle adulthood (40–60 years) was furthermore associated with a significant decrease in the probability of developing AD (Friedland et al., 2001). Such studies have stimulated interest in the influence of environment of individuals throughout their life span and its potential contribution to cognitive function in late life. One hypothesis asserts that high levels of engagement in a variety of activities creates a "cerebral reserve" that delays onset of cognitive deterioration in old age. Another interpretation suggests that the level of participation in stimulating activities throughout life is an early indicator of variations in central nervous system function that are predictive of brain function in late life. How to sort out this chicken-and-egg dilemma? It is difficult to resolve it with retrospective studies in humans, and whereas prospective studies of the influence of interventions on late life cognition are being undertaken (e.g.,Willis et al., 2006), the length of human life makes such studies daunting to contemplate and almost prohibitively expensive to support. In such circumstances, it is inevitable that animal models will be attempted.

ENVIRONMENTAL INTERVENTIONS AND RODENT COGNITION

The current interest in the potential contribution of daily activities to the cognitive phenotype in human old age has been briefly discussed above. Animal studies may prove to be especially efficient at testing the impact of alterations in the environment on cognitive function in late life. Much of the preceding discussion has concerned the local and time-limited environmental features of the measurement situation. The impact of longer term environmental factors—rearing conditions and systematic experiential interventions, for example—are perhaps more relevant to this domain; this topic has also been studied for more than 50 years, and the results comprise a rich methodological resource for experimental design and interpretation of results. Some relevant features of these areas are described in the following sections.

Environmental Enrichment and Impoverishment in Rodents: Mimicking Differential Life Experiences in Humans

The earliest studies were stimulated by the theoretical writings of Hebb (1949) and a paper by Forgays and Forgays (1952), who showed that rats raised in environmental enrichment (EE) in early life demonstrated superior learning ability compared with those raised in a standard environment (SE). An EE in these studies consisted of caging animals in groups and providing them with a variety of manipulanda (climbing ramps, swings, etc.) of the kind often used by pet owners. More systematic attempts at enrichment have also been attempted and are described by Davenport (1976). By comparison, a standard environment (SE) consisted of caging animals in their regular housing, usually a clear plastic cage with no additional objects, with the laboratory environment maintained in a uniform manner. An impoverished environment (IE), also used in some experimental designs, more closely approximated SE but was accentuated by further attenuating visual, auditory and other sensory input. Subsequent studies in several species were reviewed by Davenport (1976) and Renner and Rosenzweig (1987), who found that the preponderance of evidence supported the idea that raising animals during development in EE resulted in improved learning ability, particularly in complex tasks. Davenport pointed out as a result of his own studies and those of others (e.g., Henderson, 1970), who conducted large-scale studies of Gene × Environment (GXE) interactions in mice, that disadvantaged groups showed the greatest benefit of being raised in EE.

This finding has been confirmed in more recent investigations of the effects of EE on various kinds of impairments (traumatic brain injury [Passineau, Green, & Dietrich, 2001], lead exposure [Guilarte, Toscano, McGlothan, & Weaver, 2003], cerebral ischemia [Farrell, Evans, & Corbett, 2001]), including those resulting from genetic manipulations (a mouse model of Huntington's disease [Hockly et al., 2002], a genetic model of trisomy [Martínez-Cué et al., 2002], and genetically based cortical ectopias [Schrott et al., 1992]). Davenport (1976) and Renner and Rosenzweig (1987) separately pointed out the importance of being alert to the contribution of motivational influences that might result from EE to differential performance in cognitive tasks. They contrasted studies that found no effect of EE (Davenport, 1976; Domjan, Schorr, & Best, 1977; Henderson, 1972) with those that did (e.g., Van Woerden, 1986). In general, tasks involving aversive motivation were less successful in demonstrating effects of EE than those that used appetitive tasks.

Clear-cut biological effects of EE have also been demonstrated. These were noted first in the early 1960s, when an influential group working at the University of California at Berkeley showed that rats (descendants of Tryon's [1940] selected lines) raised in EE had larger brains than those raised in IE (Rosenzweig, Krech, Bennett, & Diamond, 1962), independently of changes in body weight. This research was then extended to more detailed studies of the thickness of specific brain regions (Bennett, Diamond, Krech, & Rosenzweig, 1964; Bennett, Krech, & Rosenzweig, 1964) and, later, to alterations in the density of dendritic branching (Holloway, 1966). More recently, a number of studies showed that mRNA expression of nerve growth factor and neurotrophin-3 in the hippocampus and/or visual cortex (Torasdotter, Metsis, Henriksson, Winblad, & Mohammed, 1996, 1998) and of brain derived neurotrophic factor in the hippocampus (Falkenberg et al., 1992) were altered by exposure to EE. These neurotrophic factors, which have the potential to influence the neural substrate in a dynamic manner, are intriguing possibilities for examination of the mechanism via which the environment influences the nervous system (reviewed by Mohammed et al., 2002).

Environmental Enrichment
Effects on Cognition in Old Animals

Of particular relevance in the present context are studies showing that EE also exerts an effect in old animals as well as young. Kobayashi, Ohashi, and Ando (2002) first showed that EE improved learning of the Hebb–Williams maze in young (2.5 months), middle-aged (15 months), and old (25 months) F344 male rats (a strain commonly used in aging studies), if it was started at weaning and continued until the time of test. However, the same investigators went on to demonstrate that 3 months of EE significantly improved performance on the Hebb–Williams maze of both adult (11 months) and old (22 months) rats, if it was applied in the period preceding the behavioral test. Although the effects of lifelong EE were much greater on Hebb–Williams performance of the oldest age group than the 3 months exposure to EE, the fact that 3 months of EE improved performance of the oldest age group was consistent with the idea that the aged nervous system is still able to respond to environmental intervention. A similar conclusion was supported by the results of Winocur (1998), who found that old (23 months) rats of the Long–Evans stock showed large effects of EE and IE on Hebb–Williams performance: Three months exposure to IE immediately before the test resulted in a large deterioration in performance among old rats, although EE had a mild positive effect compared with SE. Using a brief exposure type of enrichment (3 hours/day for 14 days and continuing through the period of test), a recent study by Frick and Fernandez (2003) showed that EE administered immediately before the test improved the performance of 27- to 28-month-old female C57BL/6 mice if the test situation provided only distal cues as to the location of a submerged platform in a Morris water maze (MWM) but had no effect if performance required mice only to reach a visible platform to escape from water. A similar result (29 days of EE administered immediately before the test improved spatial but not cued performance of the MWM) was obtained earlier on 18-month-old male and female C57BL/6 mice (Frick, Stearns, Pan, & Berger-Sweeney, 2003). These various findings lend credence to the idea that EE effects on behavior in animals extend throughout the life span and raise the possibility that medium-term and late-onset exposure to EE can have ameliorating effects.

GENE × ENVIRONMENT INTERACTIONS INVOLVING REARING ENVIRONMENT

It will be no surprise to learn that GXE interactions have been found in the rearing environment research literature. Cooper and Zubek (1958) studied rats derived from a selective breeding program (other than Tryon's). Bright and Dull animals from this study were raised in EE, SE, and IE and tested for performance in a Hebb–William maze. It was found that rearing environment had unequal effects in the two strains. The Bright strain outperformed the Dull strain only when the animals were raised in SE.

In EE, both strains performed equally well, and in IE they performed equally poorly. Sex × Environment interactions have sometimes also been seen: Martínez-Cué et al. (2002) noted that EE had opposite effects on MWM performance of males and females, and Wagner et al. (2002) demonstrated a positive effect of EE on MWM spatial performance of male (but not female) rats with brain injuries. In addition to these experiments, which were conducted with a limited number of genetically different groups, Henderson's (1970, 1976) extensive study of the effects of EE on brain and behavior of 36 different genetic groups of mice attests to the importance of GXE interactions

Animal studies clearly can provide a major avenue of research on the role of environment in late life cognitive function. Among other things, experimental designs could evaluate whether environmental manipulations such as enrichment need to be implemented at specific stages of life (early development, adolescence, adulthood, middle age) or even during late life itself. However, the caveats cited above would certainly lead us to expect particularity in the effects of different environments and complex interactions among the environmental variables and between them and genotype. Different kinds of experience should be evaluated: Enrichment, for example, frequently results in greater opportunity for increased motor activity, leading to the question of whether the effects of enrichment may be due to increased exercise. Does social experience (often a component of enrichment) have an effect on cognitive function in late life, in and of itself? The barren environment in which experimental animals are "standardly" raised mimics only too well the kinds of impoverished environments deemed inimical to the appropriate development of human cognition (Beckett et al., 2006). Studies of the effects of enrichment and other environmental interventions on cognitive aging in rodents would constitute an important means of discovering whether the previous literature on cognition in aged rodents, largely based on animals raised in SEs, reflects the idiosyncratic response of animals to institutionalization.

These reviews have provided exemplars of animal model contributions to the study of cognitive processes, to the impact of age on these processes, and to the exploration of environmental influences that might alter such age-related changes. It should be clear that major opportunities abound for a rodent-based approach to the role of environment and genetics and the interaction between the two, in shaping the complex phenotype(s) subsumed under the rubric of "cognitive aging." The earlier narrative also has provided some caveats about the interpretation of outcomes from these model systems.

To repeat, one salient observation has been that results from a single apparatus or situation should be regarded as tentative, if not idiosyncratic. Generalization must be demonstrated, not assumed. Another theme has been that noncognitive aspects of animal performance in learning situations can seriously confound interpretation about cognitive features of the performance. Fortunately, there are some useful strategies and tactics available for approaching these matters.

MULTIPLE ASSESSMENTS

One remedy for many of the identified problems appears to be straightforward: multiple assessments. The use of several configurations of measurement situation intended to assess some latent construct opens possibilities for the whole range of multivariate conceptualizations and analytical procedures that have so enabled the human cognitive research enterprise. As is the case with many matters of high current relevance, there is a long history of interest in this topic. Royce (1950) reviewed studies that obtained intercorrelations among several measures of learning (in rats, mostly, but with one study on mice and one on chicks) beginning in 1920. Despite this decades-old history, the volume of pertinent research has been low (Plomin, 2001). Recently, however, several major studies have combined the perspectives of quantitative genetics, multivariate statistics, and cognitive science with highly promising results.

Galsworthy, Paya-Cano, Monleón, and Plomin (2002) tested genetically heterogeneous mice on a battery of diverse cognitive tasks including different motivations, different apparatus designs, and different response requirements. Analysis of the various measures produced a first principal component that accounted for 31% of the total variance. This result not only gives firm evidence that there is some common process or processes involved in the different tasks but also provides, by the specific factor loadings, a rational basis for task selection in subsequent research.

Matzel et al. (2003) similarly evaluated a sample of genetically heterogeneous mice on a battery of five diverse learning tasks and found a "general" factor accounting for 38% of the total variance. A subsequent study by these investigators (Matzel et al., 2006) found a principal component accounting for 32% of the variance of six learning tasks and found furthermore that several measures of exploratory activity loaded heavily on the same factor.

These studies not only offer data of intrinsic value but also serve as promissory notes for expansion of our understanding of the dimensions and architecture of murine cognition and for provision of powerful tools for application to studies of cognitive aging. Elaboration of the description of murine "g" may provide a fruitful avenue of research concerning which aspects of human cognition can be usefully modeled with an animal system.

Leveling the Noncognitive Playing Field for Old and Young

Galsworthy et al.'s (2002) study, described above, and a later publication that offered a more detailed description of the various protocols (Galsworthy et al., 2005) did not include aged mice, but the researchers attempted to deal directly with the issue that individual differences on cognitive tasks may well reflect variation on dimensions that we would consider noncognitive (differences in emotional behavior; susceptibility to organic deprivations, such as food or water restriction; impaired sensory responsivity, etc.) by selecting protocols that were very different from each other in the kinds of motor demands placed on the animal and that were motivated by different reinforcers. Thus, it was argued that any communality that was found among the tests could not be based on any single noncognitive dimension. Instead, the principles underlying choice of the test battery would tend to reduce or vitiate correlations among tests. Such an approach also seems a

sensible way to formulate a test battery for use with old rodents. Nevertheless, because old rodents are likely to represent even greater extremes of susceptibility to organic deprivations, and whose performance is likely to be impaired to a greater extent by motor instability and diminished sensory responsiveness, even greater care is needed when developing appropriate protocols. This factorial approach offers bright prospects of statistical clarification of issues of noncognitive processes clouding the assessment of cognitive function.

In advance of more detailed exploitation of this approach, there is much opportunity for common-sense innovation in the development of suitable tests for use with old rodents that minimize or reduce dependence on organic deprivations, sensory cues that require an intact auditory and visual system for their detection, as well as a high level of motor performance. A test developed in our laboratory that uses "return to home cage" as a reward may serve as an example. Mice learn the Lashley III maze as rapidly when the reward for traversing the maze is return to a familiar cage, as do mice deprived of food given the traditional pellet in the goal box (Blizard, Cousino Klein, Cohen, & McClearn, 2003). The test is conducted under conditions of dim illumination in an attempt to minimize the importance of visual cues in guiding maze performance. Although time to traverse the maze is recorded, the main performance index reflects not only an animal's speed but also the number of correct choices as a proportion of total entries into defined segments of the maze. Thus, although motor activity is required to move from start to goal box, the test does not require a high level of motor competence. The maze works well for both male and female mice, ranging in age from the early postweaning period to mice aged 750 days or more (Blizard et al., 2006). The fact that the mice are not food deprived to motivate performance on the test is a major advantage because it rules out the potential influence of organic deprivations on performance.

CONCLUSION

It should be clear that there are no perfect solutions to the various concerns repeatedly enunciated above. Furthermore, there never will be, given the complexity of the process(es) being modeled and the finitude of the knowledge base and the pragmatics of the requisite research. However, it is fair to say that the accumulated literature points out ways in which our instruments can be substantially improved. The magnitude and the nature of the empirical data currently available suggest (in spite of our caveats) a truly powerful capability of animal models in addressing the pivotal aspects of cognitive aging.

Many of the genetic tools that are available to provide both independent and controlled variables in various research designs have histories a century old. It is essential to note (particularly in the present context) that their puissance has not suffered from decline with age. They are the same powerful tools that have illuminated the inheritance of continuously distributed phenotypes and have transformed agriculture and medical practice. In addition, newly available molecular genetic methods are available for exploitation.

As a particularly promising prospect, the widespread use of microarray technology now permits exploration of the pattern of gene expression in response to specific environmental interventions. The intriguing potential of this method to the study of EE is illustrated by a recent article reporting the study of gene expression in the cortex of 4-month-old mice derived from a cross of two widely used strains after varying periods of exposure to EE (Rampon et al., 2000). Varying patterns of expression (relative to naïve controls) were found among 60 genes, and their magnitude of expression relative to that seen in control mice after 3 hours was consistent with that seen after 6 hours of exposure to EE. The expression of a larger number of genes (100) changed after exposure to 2 or 14 days of EE, and most of these were different from those that responded to short-term EE. The kinds of genes whose expression was affected by EE were of great interest. In response to short-term exposure, one of the highest levels of induction was in DNA methyltransferase (a tenfold increase). Activity of this enzyme is critical for neurogenesis induced by nerve growth factor. After long-term EE, the expression of a number of genes associated with

N-methyl-D-aspartic acid receptor function (a gene believed to be importantly involved in learning and memorial processes influenced by the neurotransmitter glutamate) increased (relative to controls), providing support for the notion that some of these alterations might influence learning and memory. Backtracking to our discussion of the potential role of daily activities in cognitive function in late life in humans, this use of microarray technology amply illustrates the power that animal studies can bring to this area of research by focusing attention on specific genes and toward specific brain regions that may be activated by various kinds of daily activities.

Each of these general approaches, one based on quantitative genetics and the other on molecular genetics, has its own powerful agenda to serve. However, their objectives are not competitive. Their merger will provide tools of great synergism. If these tools are combined with the burgeoning insights and methods of multivariate analysis, and a reasonable appreciation of the history of development of animal models of cognition, the future looks promising indeed.

REFERENCES

Beckett, C., Maughan, B., Rutter, M., Castle, J., Colvert, E., Groothues, C., et al. (2006). Do the effects of early severe deprivation on cognition persist into early adolescence? Findings from the English and Romanian adoptees study. *Child Development, 77,* 696–711.

Bennett, E. L., Diamond, M. C., Krech, D., & Rosenzweig, M. R. (1964, October 30). Chemical and anatomical plasticity of brain. *Science, 146,* 610–619.

Bennett, E. L., Krech, D., & Rosenzweig, M. R. (1964). Reliability and regional specificity of cerebral effects of environmental complexity and training. *Journal of Comparative & Physiological Psychology, 57,* 440–441.

Blizard, D. A., Cousino Klein, L., Cohen, R., & McClearn, G. E. (2003). A novel mouse friendly cognitive task suitable for use in aging studies. *Behavior Genetics, 33,* 181–189.

Blizard, D. A., & Darvasi, A. (1999). Experimental strategies for quantitative trait loci (QTL) analysis in laboratory animals. In W. E. Crusio & R. T. Gerlai (Eds.), *Handbook of molecular-genetic* techniques for brain and behavioral research (pp. 82–99). Amsterdam: Elsevier Science.

Blizard, D. A., Weinheimer, V. K., Cousino Klein, L., Petrill, S. A., Cohen, R., & McClearn, G. E. (2006). Return to home-cage as reward for maze learning: Extension to young and old genetically heterogeneous mice. Comparative Medicine, 56, 196–201.

Bogue, M. A., & Grubb, S. C. (2004). The Mouse Phenome Project. Genetica, 122, 71–74.

Cooper, R. M., & Zubek, J. P. (1958). Effects of enriched and restricted early environments on the learning ability of bright and dull rats. Canadian Journal of Psychology, 12, 159–164.

Davenport, J. W. (1976) Environmental therapy in hypothyroid and other disadvantaged animal populations. In R. N. Walsh & W. T. Greenough (Eds.), Environments as therapy for brain dysfunction (pp. 71–114). New York: Plenum.

Domjan, M., Schorr, R., & Best, M. (1977). Early environmental influences on conditioned and unconditioned ingestional and locomotor behavior. Developmental Psychobiology, 10, 499–506.

Falkenberg, T., Mohammed, A. K., Henriksson, B. G., Persson, H., Winblad, B., & Lindefors, N. (1992). Increased expression of brain derived neurotrophic factor is associated with spatial learning and enriched environment. Neuroscience Letters, 138, 153–156.

Farrell, R., Evans, S., & Corbett, D. (2001). Environmental enrichment enhances recovery of function but exacerbates ischemic cell death. Neuroscience, 107, 585–592.

Forgays, D. G., & Forgays, J. W. (1952). The nature of the effect of free-environmental experience in the rat. Journal of Comparative & Physiological Psychology, 45, 322–328.

Frick, K. M., & Fernandez, S. M. (2003). Enrichment enhances spatial memory and increases synaptophysin levels in aged female mice. Neurobiology of Aging, 24, 615–626.

Frick, J. M., Stearns, N. A., Pan, J.-Y., & Berger-Sweeney, J. (2003). Effects of environmental enrichment on spatial memory and neurochemistry in middle-aged mice. Learning and Memory, 10, 187–198.

Friedland, R. P., Fritsch, T., Smyth, K. A., Koss, E., Lerner, A. J., Chen, C. H., et al. (2001). Patients with Alzheimer's disease have reduced activities in midlife compared with healthy control-group members. Proceedings of the National Academy of Sciences, USA, 98, 3440–3445.

Galsworthy, M. J., Paya-Cano, J. L., Liu, L., Monleón, S., Gregoryan, G., Fernandes, C., et al. (2005). Assessing reliability, heritability and general cognitive ability in a battery of cognitive tasks for laboratory mice. Behavior Genetics, 35, 661–678.

Galsworthy, M. J., Paya-Cano, J. L., Monleón, S., & Plomin, R. (2002). Evidence for general cognitive ability (g) in heterogeneous stock mice and an analysis of potential confounds. Genes, Brain, and Behavior, 1, 88–95.

Guilarte, T. R., Toscano, C. D., McGlothan, J. L., & Weaver, S. A. (2003). Environmental enrichment reverses cognitive and molecular deficits induced by developmental lead exposure. Annals of Neurology, 53, 50–56.

Hebb, D. O. (1949). The organization of behavior. New York: Wiley.

Henderson, N. D. (1970, August 21). Brain weight increases resulting from environmental enrichment: A directional dominance in mice. Science, 169, 776–778.

Henderson, N. D. (1972). Relative effects of early rearing environment and genotype on discrimination learning in house mice. Journal of Comparative & Physiological Psychology, 79, 243–253.

Henderson, N. D. (1976). Short exposures to enriched environments can increase genetic variability of behavior in mice. Developmental Psychobiology, 9, 549–553.

Hilgard, E. R., & Bower, G. H. (1966). Theories of learning (3rd ed.). New York: Appleton-Century-Crofts.

Hockly, E., Cordery, P. M., Woodman, B., Mahal, A., van Dellen, A., Blakemore, C., et al (2002). Environmental enrichment slows disease progression in R61/2 Huntington's disease mice. Annals of Neurology, 51, 235–242.

Holloway, R. L. (1966). Dendritic branching: Some preliminary results of training and complexity in the rat visual cortex. Brain Research, 2, 393–396.

Kobayashi, S., Ohashi, Y., & Ando, S. (2002). Effects of enriched environments with different starting times on learning capacities during aging in rats assessed by a refined procedure of the Hebb–Williams maze task. Journal of Neuroscience Research, 70, 340–346.

Lashley, K. S., & Wiley, L. E. (1933). Studies of cerebral function in learning. IX. Mass action in relation to the number of elements in the problem to be learned. *Journal of Comparative Neurology, 57,* 3–55.

Lyon, M. F. (1995). *Genetic variants and strains of the laboratory mouse* (3rd ed.). New York: Oxford University Press.

Martínez-Cué, C., Baamonde, C., Lumbreras, M., Paz, J., Davisson, M. T., Schmidt, C., et al. (2002). Differential effects of environmental enrichment on behavior and learning of male and female Ts65Dn mice, a model for Down syndrome. *Behavioural Brain Research, 134,* 185–200.

Matzel, L. D., Han, Y. R., Grossman, H., Karnik, M. S., Patel, D., Scott, N., et al. (2003). Individual differences in the expression of a "general" learning ability in mice. *Journal of Neuroscience, 23,* 6423–6433.

Matzel, L. D., Townsend, D. A., Grossman, H., Han, Y. R., Hale, G., Zappulla, M., et al. (2006). Exploration in outbred mice covaries with general learning abilities irrespective of stress reactivity, emotionality, and physical attributes. *Neurobiology of Learning and Memory, 86,* 228–240.

McClearn, G. E., & Hofer, S. M. (1999a). Genes as gerontological variables: Uniform genotypes. *Neurobiology of Aging, 20,* 95–104.

McClearn, G. E., & Hofer, S. M. (1999b). Genes as gerontological variables: Uses of genetically heterogeneous stocks. *Neurobiology of Aging, 20,* 147–156.

McClearn, G. E., Wilson, J. R., & Meredith, W. (1970). The use of isogenic and heterogenic mouse stocks in behavioral research. In G. Lindzey & D. D. Thiessen (Eds.), *Contributions to behavior-genetic analysis: The mouse as a prototype* (pp. 3–22). New York: Appleton-Century-Crofts.

McGaugh, J. L., & Cole, J. M. (1965). Age and strain differences in the effect of distribution of practice on maze learning. *Psychonomic Science, 2,* 253–254.

Mohammed, A. H., Zhu, S. W., Darmopil, S., Hjerling-Leffler, J., Ernfors, P., Winblad, B., et al. (2002). Environmental enrichment and the brain. *Progress in Brain Research, 138,* 109–133.

Mori, T., & Makino, J. (1994). Response types to shock and avoidance learning in inbred strains of mice [Article in Japanese]. *Shinrigaku Kenkyu, 65,* 295–302.

Munn, N. L. (1950). *Handbook of psychological research on the rat.* New York: Houghton Mifflin.

Passineau, M. J., Green, E. J., & Dietrich, W. D. (2001). Therapeutic effects of environmental enrichment on cognitive function and tissue integrity following severe traumatic brain injury in rats. *Experimental Neurology, 168,* 373–384.

Plomin, R. (2001). The genetics of g in human and mouse. *Nature Reviews Neuroscience, 2,* 136–141.

Rabinovitch, M. S., & Rosvold, H. E. (1951). A closed field intelligence test for rats. *Canadian Journal of Psychology, 5,* 122–128.

Rampon, C., Jiang, C. H., Dong, H., Tang, Y. P., Lockhart, D. J., Schultz, P. G., et al. (2000). Effects of environmental enrichment on gene expression in the brain. *Proceedings of the National Academy of Sciences, USA, 97,* 12880–12884.

Renner, M. J., & Rosenzweig, M. R. (1987). *Enriched and impoverished environments.* New York: Springer-Verlag.

Rosenzweig, M. R., Krech, D., Bennett, E. L., & Diamond, M. C. (1962). Effects of environmental complexity and training on brain chemistry and anatomy: A replication and extension. *Journal of Comparative & Physiological Psychology, 55,* 429–437.

Royce, J. R. (1950). Factorial analysis of animal behavior. *Psychological Bulletin, 47,* 235–259.

Schrott, L. M., Denenberg, V. H., Sherman, G. F., Water, N. S., Rosen, G. D., & Galaburda, A. M. (1992). Environmental enrichment, neurocortical ectopias, and behavior in the autoimmune NZB mouse. *Developmental Brain Research, 67,* 85–93.

Searle, L. V. (1949). The organization of hereditary maze-brightness and maze-dullness. *Genetic Psychology Monographs, 39,* 279–325.

Silver, L. M. (1995). *Mouse genetics.* New York: Oxford University Press.

Snowdon, D. A., Kemper, S. J., Mortimer, J. A., Greiner, L. H., Wekstein, D. R., & Markesbery, W. R. (1996). Linguistic ability in early life and cognitive function and Alzheimer's disease in late life: Findings from the Nun Study. *Journal of the American Medical Association, 275,* 528–532.

Sprott, R. L., & Stavnes, K. (1975). Avoidance learning, behavior genetics, and aging: A critical review and comment on methodology. *Experimental Aging Research, 1,* 145–168.

Snowdon, D. A., Kemper, S. J., Mortimer, J. A., Greiner, L. H., Wekstein, D. R., & Markesbery, W. R. (1996). Linguistic ability in early life and cognitive function and Alzheimer's disease in late life. Findings from the Nun Study. *Journal of the American Medical Association, 275,* 1879.

Torasdotter, M., Metsis, M., Henriksson, B. G., Winblad, B., & Mohammed, A. H. (1996). Expression of neurotrophin-3 mRNAs in the rat visual cortex and hippocampus is influenced by environmental conditions. *Neuroscience Letters, 218,* 107–110.

Torasdotter, M., Metsis, M., Henriksson, B. G., Winblad, B., & Mohammed, A. H. (1998). Environmental enrichment results in higher levels of nerve growth factor mRNA in the rat visual cortex and hippocampus. *Behavioural Brain Research, 93,* 83–90.

Tryon, R. C. (1940). Genetic differences in maze-learning ability in rats. *Yearbook of the National Society for the Study of Education, 39,* 111–119.

Van Woerden, C. J. M. (1986). *Effects of differential experience on brain behavior in the rat.* Nijmegen, The Netherlands: Universiteit te Nijmegen.

Wagner, A. K., Kline, A. E., Sokoloski, J., Zafonte, R. D., Capulong, E., & Dixon, C. E. (2002). Intervention with environmental enrichment after experimental brain trauma enhances cognitive recovery in male but not female rats. *Neuroscience Letters, 334,* 165–168.

Wahlsten, D., Cooper, S. F., & Crabbe, J. C. (2005). Different rankings of inbred mouse strains on the Morris maze and a refined 4-arm water escape task. *Behavioural Brain Research, 165,* 36–51.

Warren, J. M. (1986). Appetitive learning by old mice. *Experimental Aging Research, 12,* 99–105.

Warren, J. M. (1988). Age, incentives, and maze learning in hybrid mice. *Behavior Genetics, 18,* 167–173.

Willis, S. L., Tennstedt, S. L., Marsiske, M., Ball, K., Elias, J., Koepke, K. M., et al. (2006). Long-term effects of cognitive training on everyday functional outcomes in older adults. *Journal of the American Medical Association, 296,* 2805–2814.

Winocur, G. (1998). Environmental influences on cognitive decline in aged rats. *Neurobiology of Aging, 19,* 589–597.

Wong, A. A., & Brown, R. E. (2006). Age-related changes in visual acuity, learning and memory in C57BL/6J and DBA/2J mice. *Neurobiology of Aging, 28,* 1577–1593.

33

GENETIC AND ENVIRONMENTAL INFLUENCES ON COGNITIVE CHANGE

CHANDRA A. REYNOLDS

I am grown old and my memory is not as active as it used to be. When I was younger, I could remember anything, whether it had happened or not; but my faculties are decaying now and soon I shall be so I cannot remember any but the things that never happened. It is sad to go to pieces like this but we all have to do it.

—*The Autobiography of Mark Twain*

The phrase *cognitive aging* evokes the notion of inevitable decline, although it is evident that some individuals decline sooner or more rapidly compared with others. To what extent is cognitive decline genetically programmed, and to what extent are environmental forces important? Human behavioral genetic research has a unique perspective to lend in addressing these questions. In this chapter, I briefly describe findings of twin and adoption studies, highlighting recent work that incorporates latent growth models; contemplate the search for specific gene candidates and environments; and offer some future directions.

ANONYMOUS GENES AND ENVIRONMENTS

General Cognitive Ability

Numerous twin and adoption studies in the last century have indicated strong heritable influences for general cognitive ability (g; e.g.,

Bouchard & McGue, 1981). These studies have relied on the comparison of relatives who differ in genetic (e.g., identical vs. fraternal twins) or environmental relatedness (e.g., siblings reared together vs. those reared apart) to estimate the relative contributions of genes and environments to individual variation in cognitive ability (see Figure 33.1). Heritability and environmentality represent estimates of the *relative* importance of genes and environmental factors on variation in intellectual ability and are contextually bound by both population and time of measurement (Plomin, DeFries, McClearn, & McGuffin, 2001).

An interesting pattern has emerged from cross-sectional comparisons across the life span: Heritability increases with age from approximately 40% in childhood (Plomin et al., 2001) to as much as 80% in late adulthood (Pedersen, Plomin, Nesselroade, & McClearn, 1992), yet with evidence of a subsequent decrease to 62% at 80 years of age and beyond (McClearn et al., 1997). Concomitantly, shared

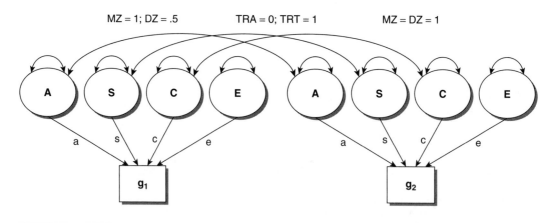

Figure 33.1 Model of Twin Pair Similarity for General Intelligence, *g*

NOTES: A = additive genetic influences, S = shared rearing environmental influences, C = correlated environmental influences, E = nonshared environmental influences; MZ = monozygotic or identical twins; DZ = dizygotic or fraternal twins; TRA = twins reared apart; TRT = twins reared together; g = general intelligence with subscript denoting member of twin pair, 1 or 2. Expected twin correlations for MZ and DZ twins reared together or apart can be obtained using path-tracing rules.

environmental effects diminish in influence after childhood, with nonshared environmental influences explaining the remaining trait variation (McCartney, Harris, & Bernieri, 1990; McGue, Bouchard, Iacono, & Lykken, 1993). These patterns have been confirmed in longitudinal adoption and twin studies, suggesting that it is not an artifact of cross-sectional comparisons (Bartels, Rietveld, Van Baal, & Boomsma, 2002; Bishop et al., 2003; Finkel, Pedersen, McGue, & McClearn, 1995; McGue & Christensen, 2001; Reynolds et al., 2005).

Specific Cognitive Abilities

Specific cognitive abilities representing verbal, spatial, memory, and perceptual speed domains indicate moderate to strong genetic influences, generally 30% to 70%, with generally higher estimates for verbal tasks and lower estimates for memory tasks (e.g., DeFries et al., 1976; McClearn et al., 1997; Pedersen et al., 1992). Heritability ranges widely within a domain, however. For example, heritability for memory traits varies from 32% to 70% (Finkel & McGue, 1993; McClearn et al., 1997; Pedersen et al., 1992; Posthuma, Neale, Boomsma, & de Geus, 2001). Some evidence suggests that heritability for working or short-term memory may be larger than for long-term

memory (Johansson et al., 1999; Posthuma et al., 2001). Similar to the case for general cognitive ability, both cross-sectional and longitudinal studies suggest that shared environmental effects decline after childhood (Plomin, Fulker, Corley, & DeFries, 1997), although findings from the Swedish Adoption/Twin Study of Aging (SATSA) suggest that shared rearing environments may still be influential to a small degree, even into old age (Pedersen et al., 1992). Median cross-sectional heritability estimates from adult twin studies in the last 20 years, including reports from Japan, Holland, Norway, Sweden, and the United States (Bouchard, Segal, & Lykken, 1990; Finkel & McGue, 1998; McClearn et al., 1997; Pedersen et al., 1992; Posthuma et al., 2001; Tambs, Sundet, & Magnus, 1984; Wright et al., 2001) are shown in Figure 33.2 for span memory and perceptual speed measures. Heritability estimates for span memory appear to increase from young to young-old adulthood and then decline afterward. For perceptual speed, as for g, heritability estimates appears to increase into later adulthood (see Figure 33.2).

Patterns of increasing or decreasing heritability estimates with age suggest initial but incomplete answers to the etiology of cognitive aging raised at the outset of this chapter. The pattern of increasing heritability for g into the young-old

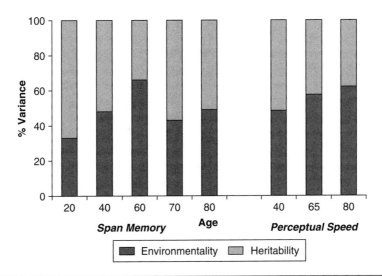

Figure 33.2   Relative Importance of Genes and Environment on Span Memory and Perceptual Speed: Cross-Sectional Twin Studies

age period might suggest support for theories of genetic regulation or programming of aging (McLean & Le Couteur, 2004), for example, inherent biological timers that contribute to senescence or genes associated with longevity. On the other hand, by old-old age genetic variance lessens while person-specific environmental influences strengthen, lending some support for environmental theories of aging. Nevertheless, a focus on relative contributions of genetic and environmental factors (i.e., heritability and environmentality) provides incomplete or even misleading answers when they are compared age by age (e.g., age 50, age 60, age 70, etc., as in Figure 33.2). Heritability and environmentality estimates provide incomplete answers to etiology, not only because they are anonymous but also because they are ratios over the total trait variance that may camouflage the configurations of genetic and environmental variances that occur longitudinally. An important question is whether variance in cognitive performance increases or decreases over the life course (Morse, 1993). Behavioral genetic studies should focus on unscaled genetic and environmental variances when considering developmental processes over age to understand better the direction of genetic and environmental impacts; indeed, this has been emphasized in the SATSA study by Pedersen and colleagues (e.g.,

Finkel, Pedersen, Plomin, & McClearn, 1998; Pedersen, 2004; Reynolds et al., 2005). For example, if both unscaled genetic and environmental variances climb (or fall) in tandem over age, then no change in heritability and environmentality estimates would be observed. Yet the pattern of the increasing unscaled variances would point to new influences emerging or amplification of effects. If both variances decrease, then one might surmise a dissipation of effect by genes and environments that hitherto were important; for example, genotypes associated with cognitive decline and mortality may be "dropping out" of the population. If genetic and environmental variance patterns are complementary over age, then one might observe differences in relative estimates. For example, if heritability decreases, is it because genetic influences are stable but environmental variance increases, or because genetic variance is decreasing and environmental variance is stable? Finkel and colleagues (1998) examined change in phenotypic, genetic, and environmental variances over a 6-year span for general and specific cognitive abilities in the first three waves of cognitive assessments in SATSA. A cross-sequential approach was taken by fitting a biometrical model to covariance matrices for 10 overlapping cohorts. One of the most important findings was that genetic variance decreased substantially over time, whereas environmental variance slightly increased for a measure of g, that is, the first principal component of 13 cognitive tests. This finding supported the lower heritability found for general cognitive ability in participants age 80 years and older in the Origins of Variance in the Old-Old: Octogenarian Twins (OCTO-Twin) study (McClearn et al., 1997).

Intraindividual Change in Cognitive Abilities

Studies of intraindividual change over age are key in effectively addressing the etiology of cognitive aging with the prospect that influences on cognitive change may not be identical to those for cognitive ability level. The extent to which genetic and environmental influences are important for normative cognitive *change* is less well understood than cognitive performance levels. Earlier studies have applied models of continuity and change to covariance information (e.g., simplex models) and suggested that genetic influences explain much of the continuity from age to age, particularly in adulthood (Plomin, Pedersen, Lichtenstein, & McClearn, 1994). However, analyzing covariances across time addresses not intraindividual change but rather the stability or change of rank ordering in ability from one time point to the next. The emergence of latent growth models has provided new tools to assess the contribution of genes and environments to individual trajectories of cognitive change and allows one to consider patterns of change in genetic and environmental variances. In a recent study, my colleagues and I applied quadratic latent growth curve models to cognitive data collected on 798 nondemented twins 50 years and older from SATSA; up to four measurement occasions per twin were available over a span of 13 years (Reynolds et al., 2005; see Figure 33.3). We examined 10 cognitive tests spanning verbal, spatial, memory, and perceptual speed domains as well as a measure of g, the first principal component of the specific cognitive measures. Twin zygosity (identical vs. fraternal) and rearing status (together or apart) allowed us to parse variance of the growth model parameters—intercept, slope and quadratic—into genetic and environmental variances. We observed significant

genetic and nonshared environmental variance for all traits, with small to negligible influences from shared or correlated environments. Across all cognitive tests and g, heritable factors largely explained between-individual variation in ability levels at age 65 (intercept), with heritability estimates ranging from 52% to 91% (median: 78%). Although the linear slope at age 65 exhibited negligible to small heritability estimates across measures, ranging from 1% to 35% (median: 15%), moderate to strong heritability was observed for the quadratic effect, ranging from 9% to 75% (median: 41%). These standardized estimates of variance overshadow the fact that the variability in ability level at age 65 (intercept) well exceeded that for linear slope at 65 years and the quadratic effect (i.e., the biggest difference between individual growth trajectories) is ability level rather than patterns of linear and quadratic change in trajectories. In addition, individual differences in intercept and linear slope, as well as their interpretation, reflect the choice to center the age predictor at age 65 years. To examine changes in genetic and environmental variances over all ages, we plotted expected genetic and environmental variance by 10-year age increments, as a function of intercept, slope, and quadratic variances. The general pattern over most cognitive measures was that genetic variance decreased after age 65 years, whereas nonshared environmental variance increased after age 65 years. This was very clear for g (see Figure 33.4, top panel). If environmental variance rises while genetic influences are stable, this could imply that age-associated environmental events begin to play a larger role in cognitive aging. However, results for two memory measures, Digit Span and Thurstone Picture Memory, suggested that genetic and nonshared environmental variances increase after age 65 years (see Figure 33.4, middle and bottom panels). If genetic variance rises with age, this may imply that certain genes begin to influence cognition only in older adulthood. Such a pattern could be construed as support for genetic influences on aging.

Additional support for nonshared environmental influences on linear cognitive change over time has emerged in studies of Danish twins 70 years and older (McGue & Christensen, 2002) and Swedish twins 80 years and older

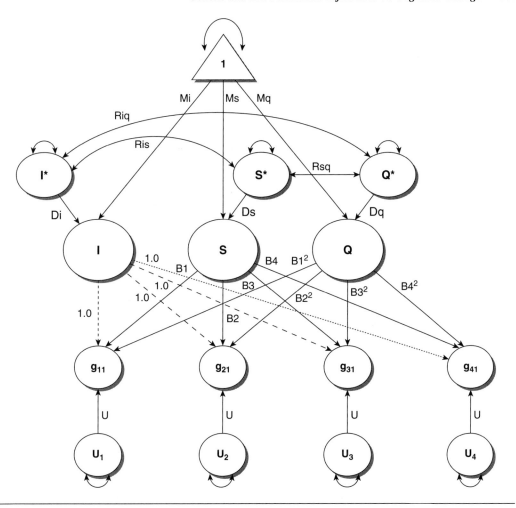

Figure 33.3 Nonlinear Latent Growth Model of Cognitive Change

SOURCE: Adapted from "Quantitative Genetic Analysis of Latent Growth Curve Models of Cognitive Abilities in Adulthood," by C. A. Reynolds, D. Finkel, J. J. McArdle, M. Gatz, S. Berg, and N. L. Pedersen, 2005, *Developmental Psychology, 41*, p. 6. Copyright 2005 by the American Psychological Association. Reprinted with permission.

NOTES: At any timepoint, g is a function of the latent intercept (I), slope (S) and quadratic effect (Q), which is centered at 65 years. The latent means are indicated by the paths from the unit constant (triangle) to the latent I, S, and Q where MI = mean intercept (ability level at 65 years); MS = mean slope (linear rate of change at 65 years); MQ = mean quadric term (twice the acceleration in the trajectory), indicate the average growth model. Deviations from the average growth model are denoted by Di, Ds, and Dq, for intercept, slope, and quadratic terms respectively. In biometrical analyses, the deviations are decomposed into genetic and environmental variance based on differential similarity of MZ and DZ twins, reared together and apart. Correlations between intercept, slope, and quadratic terms are denoted by Ris, Riq, and Rsq. The latent variables U1 to U4 reflect measurement occasion variance. Age basis coefficients for the linear and quadratic portion of the model, B1(t) and B2(t), etc., are directly calculated as the difference between an individual's observed age at each measurement occasion minus the centering age of 65 years.

(Johansson et al., 2004) with negligible evidence of heritability. Among nondemented twin pairs in the OCTO-Twin study, rates of linear change across verbal, reasoning, memory, and perceptual speed measures were often weakly or negatively correlated supportive of a primary role for nonshared environmental influences (Johansson et al., 2004). Given that nearness to death predicted decline in memory, reasoning, speed, and verbal performance in the OCTO-Twin

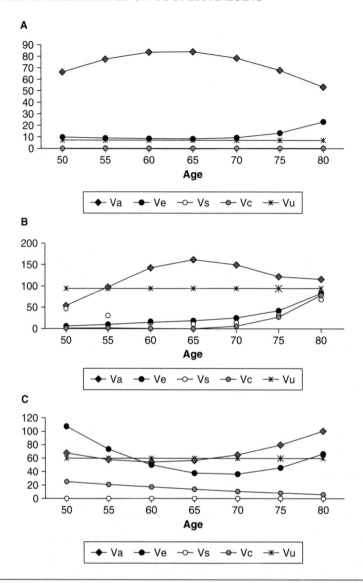

Figure 33.4   Genetic and Environmental Sources of Variance Over Age: (a) First Principal Component (*g*),
(b) Thurstone Picture Memory, (c) Digit Span

SOURCE: From "Quantitative Genetic Analysis of Latent Growth Curve Models of Cognitive Abilities in Adulthood," by
C. A. Reynolds, D. Finkel, J. J. McArdle, M. Gatz, S. Berg, and N. L. Pedersen, 2005, *Developmental Psychology, 41*, p. 12
(data reported in Table 6). Copyright 2005 by the American Psychological Association. Reprinted with permission.

NOTE: Va = additive genetic variance; Ve = nonshared environmental variance; Vs = shared rearing environmental variance;
Vc = correlated environmental variance; Vu = measurement occasion variance.

sample, differential entry into a terminal decline
phase may explain the weak or low correlations
within pairs; for example, downward turns in
trajectories may be of similar shape among
pairs, but the *timing* of the downturn may be due
to environmental factors leading to lessened
similarity. In a combined analysis of SATSA
and OCTO-Twins, accounting for mortality

through imputation techniques reduced intrapair
resemblance for linear change (Pedersen et al.,
2003). The specific health and disease factors
that may lead to differential entry into terminal
decline phase need to be addressed in future
studies.

Although nonshared environmental measures
may appear to have a prominent role in linear

rates of cognitive decline in late adulthood (Johansson et al., 2004; McGue & Christensen, 2002), heritable influences should not be ruled out on the basis of the SATSA latent growth curve analyses. Reynolds et al. (2005) applied nonlinear growth models over age, not time, and found greater heritability for quadratic trends than has been found for linear models. The differences in findings across studies may be due to age structure differences as well as length of follow-up. In addition to a younger age structure in the SATSA sample, change over 13 years rather than 6 years was examined.

A SEARCH FOR SPECIFIC GENES

Most behavioral genetic studies of the 20th century deliberated over the relative contributions of anonymous genes and environments to cognitive performance and, more recently, cognitive change. Meanwhile, molecular genetic studies of cognition addressed single-gene or chromosomal disorders that resulted in mental retardation (Plomin & Spinath, 2004). The emergence of methods to locate genes of modest effect sizes, not to mention breakthroughs from the Human Genome Project (International Human Genome Sequencing Consortium, 2001), and similar undertakings, have led to the union of quantitative behavioral genetics with molecular genetics (Plomin et al., 2001). Thus, the search for quantitative trait loci (QTLs) became possible for complex traits that involve numerous genes with small contributions (Plomin & Spinath, 2004).

In general, there are two approaches to finding QTLs that may be important to cognitive performance and change: (1) linkage and (2) association. Association studies typically make use of particular known gene candidates, whereas linkage is often used to find chromosomal regions where a gene candidate might exist. I describe these approaches here only briefly. More detailed information can be obtained elsewhere (e.g., Plomin et al., 2001).

Linkage

Linkage analysis examines patterns of familial transmission to determine whether a particular disorder or extreme trait value (e.g., accelerated cognitive decline) is linked to a particular gene or DNA marker (Plomin et al., 2001). If the gene or DNA marker is close to the trait-causing gene, then one ought to see that the transmission of the gene or DNA marker is coupled with the transmission of the trait. Linkage studies often make use of siblings or, ideally, fraternal twin pairs (dizygotic [DZ]) to control for age effects. To date, virtually no studies of normative cognitive aging have used linkage to identify potential locations of QTLs. Linkage is more frequently used in studies of Alzheimer's disease (e.g., Goddard et al., 2004).

Association

Association approaches examine whether a particular form of the gene (i.e., allele) is associated with exhibition of a disorder or particular trait value (Plomin et al., 2001), for example, accelerated cognitive decline. For quantitative traits, the association test compares mean differences in a trait given particular candidate alleles or genotypes (combinations of alleles) and is generally considered to have greater power than linkage approaches to identify genes of small to medium influence on an observed trait (phenotype; Risch & Merikangas, 1996). Often, unrelated cases and controls are used for association studies (e.g., the IQ QTL Project; Plomin & Spinath, 2004) in which allele frequencies of candidate genes are compared; for example, high-IQ children versus children with average IQs. Association tests based on sibling within-pair mean differences are especially valuable in that they avoid possible alternative explanations such as population stratification effects (Fulker, Cherny, Sham, & Hewitt, 1999; Neale et al., 1999), where a spurious association arises because cases and controls derive from different subpopulations with different gene frequencies. Both linkage and association approaches can be combined (Posthuma, de Geus, Boomsma, & Neale, 2004). However, association approaches have been used far more frequently in the case of cognitive aging.

Apolipoprotein E and Cognitive Decline

Most association studies of cognition or cognitive decline have focused on the gene coding for apolipoprotein E (APOE), a cholesterol transporter in the brain. For over a decade, the presence of the APOE e4 allele has been confirmed in numerous studies to enhance the risk of late onset AD (Strittmatter et al., 1993). Behavioral hallmarks of AD include memory decline, among other cognitive changes; therefore, APOE has been targeted in studies of normative age-related cognitive decline. A review of eight studies suggested that APOE e4 was not convincingly associated with general cognitive ability level or change (Anstey & Christensen, 2000). More recently, cognitive change across a span of eight decades, (i.e., between 11 and 79 years), was significantly associated with APOE e4 in the Scottish Mental Survey (Deary et al., 2002).

Cognitive decline in a variety of specific cognitive ability measures has been associated with APOE e4 (e.g., Wilson et al., 2002). Poorer memory performance or accelerated memory change in community-based samples has been associated with APOE e4 across multiple studies (e.g., Anstey & Christensen, 2000; Bretsky, Guralnik, Launer, Albert, & Seeman, 2003; Nilsson, Nyberg, & Bäckman, 2002); indeed, when analyses are limited to individuals without even questionable dementia symptoms the APOE e4–memory association remains (Mayeux, Small, Tang, Tycko, & Stern, 2001). However, others have noted no significant effect (e.g., Small et al., 2000). Taken as a whole, APOE appears to be a relevant gene that influences normative memory performance or change.

Is There a Single Pathway for Alzheimer's Disease and Nonpathological Cognitive Aging?

Plomin and Spinath (2004) suggested that given that late onset AD is a complex disorder (i.e., influenced by multiple genes and environments), one ought to consider AD as representing "the extreme of a dimension," for example, representing the low end of cognitive performance. Note that APOE e4 is but one risk allele for AD, with perhaps four to five other major risk alleles remaining to be found (Warwick Daw et al., 2000). APOE e4 is associated with neuropathology that is observed in confirmed Alzheimer's disease patients, i.e., the presence of senile plaques and neurofibrillary tangles (Lahiri, Sambamurti, & Bennett, 2004). Neurofibrillary tangles may be nonspecific to AD and do occur in persons never diagnosed

with AD or with other dementias (e.g., Schmitt et al., 2000). In nondemented elderly people, memory functioning was related to the presence of postmortem "AD-like" neuropathology (Schmitt et al., 2000). Similarly, the Religious Orders Study (Bennett et al., 2003) found that memory, perceptual speed, and visuospatial scores were related to postmortem senile plaque and neurofibrillary tangle pathologies in the cortex in a sample including AD-diagnosed and nondemented individuals.

Given that APOE may be relevant to normative cognitive decline as well as to dementia, it may point to a common pathway, at least in part. A common pathway may explain findings from studies of AD-discordant cotwins in which the unaffected cotwin showed poorer cognitive performance than control participants, particularly for MZ rather than DZ cotwins (Gatz et al., 2005). Other evidence suggests that different biological mechanisms may be at work in normative cognitive aging versus AD. On the basis of animal studies, subtler structural and molecular synaptic changes more aptly characterize mild cognitive change as opposed to AD, which reveals discernible neuroanatomical alterations and neuronal death (Hof & Morrison, 2004). Nonetheless, the neurodegenerative pathways suspected in AD (e.g., amyloid pathway) may still be quite relevant to normative cognitive change because the same cortical and hippocampal circuits are affected in both cases (Hof & Morrison, 2004). Altogether, factors that lead to normative or subclinical cognitive decline may be in part the same or correlated with the factors that lead to dementia or AD.

Other Pathways

Studies of normal memory and attention processes in rats, primates, and humans have suggested other potential pathways and candidates to consider. Synaptic plasticity and early memory-related neural processes may involve serotonin 2A receptors (Kandel, 2001). Hippocampal and prefrontal cortical regions show an age-associated decline in these receptors in cross-sectional studies (Sheline, Mintun, Moerlein, & Snyder, 2002), whereas frontal cortical regions may show lessened RNA expression of serotonin 2A based on postmortem analyses (Lu et al.,

2004). An association study of an HTR2A polymorphism (H452Y) suggested serotonin 2A involvement in episodic memory performance in young adults (de Quervain et al., 2003). Recall performance was higher in participants with the common histidine–histindine genotype than in carriers of the rarer tyrosine allele for both sexes in the case of the verbal task and for men for the figural task.

Age-associated changes in gene expression in frontal cortical regions hint of multiple pathways that may bear relevant QTLs involved in cognitive aging (Lu et al., 2004). Postmortem analysis of RNA expression in frontal cortex of more than 11,000 genes suggested that 4% showed altered expression with age. Genes that support learning and memory processes, including synaptic activity and malleability, such as serotonin receptor 2A, showed decreased expression, while concomitantly genes involved in stress reaction including DNA repair, oxidation and inflammatory pathways showed increased expression (Lu et al., 2004). Cumulative DNA damage, perhaps due to defective mitochondrial functioning and the buildup of free radicals, was evident particularly for those genes showing down-regulated expression, including those supportive of learning and memory processes (Lu et al., 2004). Apart from DNA damage, which points to an environmental aging process, other mechanisms by which gene expression alternations occur with age are not yet clear. Furthermore, the question of whether some genotypes may be less vulnerable to DNA damage remains to be answered. If this is the case, it would suggest the importance of gene–environment interaction.

The hunt for genes relevant to normative cognitive aging intersects with the search for genes for cognitive disorders as well as to those that might influence individual differences in g. Nevertheless, gene candidates for cognitive change may or may not be associated with ability level, and vice versa. For example, a cathepsin D exon 2 polymorphism was associated with a measure of g but not change in g over 15 years in adults 40 to 80 years (Payton et al., 2003), suggesting that the role the cathepsin D gene plays in apoptosis, programmed cell death, may be important to individual differences in general intelligence. Similar findings have been noted for a nicastrin gene polymorphism, which is involved in the preseilin-amyloid pathway (Deary et al., 2005). Five-year change in executive control as well as baseline performance was associated with a polymorphism in the gene encoding catechol-O-methyltransferase, which catabolizes dopamine (de Frias et al., 2005). Few studies have examined candidate gene associations with nonpathological cognitive change beyond two time points, although moving beyond the assumption of linearity may be necessary given the greater heritability of nonlinear change (Reynolds et al., 2005).

Incorporating Genotypes Into Biometrical Latent Growth Models

Apart from APOE, relatively few studies have examined association of genotypes with normative cognitive *change,* and fewer yet have done so in the context of informative biometrical designs (e.g., twin designs). Methods that use twin sibling samples are well suited to address the presence of true specific gene association (Fulker et al., 1999; Neale et al., 1999; Posthuma et al., 2004). My colleagues and I recently replicated and extended a case-control association study of the serotonin 2A receptor gene (HTR2A) with episodic memory (de Quervain et al., 2003), to consider longitudinal memory changes in later adulthood (Reynolds, Jansson, Gatz, & Pedersen, 2006). Specifically we examined the -1438 G/A [dbSNP: rs6311] variant of the gene coding for 5-HT2A serotonin receptors (HTR2A), for association with baseline memory performance as well as longitudinal memory change over 13 years in the SATSA study. Empirical Bayes predictors of individual intercepts, slopes, and quadratic parameters from a nonlinear growth model fit served as the outcomes. The association procedure capitalized on differences between and within twin pairs who differed on HTR2A genotype[1] to establish whether particular HTR2A genotypes predicted worse memory performance than others. We observed differences for the intercept and quadratic change dependent on HTR2A allele status. Participants with the common allele exhibited higher performance longitudinally than those with the less frequent allele for Thurstone Picture Memory, a test of episodic figural recognition.

Genes for What?

Given the positive and moderate manifold of correlations among specific cognitive measures for the sake of efficiency, should we examine change in g in lieu of specific abilities? Indeed, multivariate behavioral genetic studies suggest high genetic correlations among specific cognitive abilities (e.g., Cardon & Fulker, 1994) with perhaps the exception of memory measures (Luciano et al., 2001; Tambs et al., 1984). Plomin and Spinath (2004) argued that if one finds a QTL that is associated with specific cognitive performance, then one ought to find an association with g. However, if one focuses on g to the exclusion of specific traits, it may lead one to miss potentially strong relationships with change in particular cognitive processes (e.g., memory decline) and perhaps conclude that a gene candidate effect is weak because it is not strongly associated with change in g. For example, evidence suggests that APOE e4 may selectively affect episodic memory performance and change compared with other cognitive abilities that showed a weaker association (Wilson et al., 2002). Another level of this discussion is determining what leads from a QTL to cognitive change; that is, what are the intermediate processes? Behavioral geneticists are searching for relevant and heritable neural substrates closely related with cognitive processes to use in linkage and association studies. Such intermediary characteristics are sometimes referred to as *endophenotypes* (Gottesman & Hanson, 2005). Biometrical studies have suggested that correlates of general intelligence or memory and attention, such as processing speed, or electroencephalography measures, such as the P300 event-related potential component, may be reasonable targets for linkage or association analyses (Posthuma, Mulder, Boomsma, & de Geus, 2002; Wright et al., 2002).

Specific Environmental Risk and Protective Factors

Cognitive vitality in old age stems from interconnecting and accumulating biopsychosocial influences over the life course. In particular, positive and negative environmental factors may play an increasingly important role in cognitive change (cf. non-normative influences; Baltes, Reese, & Lipsitt, 1980). However, measured environments have rarely been included in twin and adoption studies despite the growing evidence for the role of nonshared environmental variance in cognitive change (e.g., Reynolds et al., 2005). Epidemiological studies suggest low education, low early-life socioeconomic environment, and head injury as risk factors for cognitive decline and AD (e.g., Anstey & Christensen, 2000; Moceri et al., 2001). Predictors of lessened cognitive decline may include use of estrogen replacement therapy, antioxidant supplements, and nonsteroidal anti-inflammatory drugs (e.g., Baldereschi et al., 1998; Maxwell, Hicks, Hogan, Basran, & Ebly, 2005; Zandi & Breitner, 2001).

Education and Childhood Socioeconomic Status

Rates of cognitive decline may be lessened in individuals with higher levels of education (Anstey & Christensen, 2000). The mechanisms by which education may be protective (and low education a liability) are not fully known: Higher levels of education may act to shore up cognitive reserve, resulting in greater resilience in the face of biological aging processes, or the relationship may be due to genetic influences that mediate intellectual capacity. Empirical findings suggest that the education–cognition relationship is not straightforward, perhaps even bidirectional. A common genetic factor may contribute to the covariation among education level, cognitive ability, and mental status performance (Pedersen, Reynolds, & Gatz, 1996). A common biological factor is indirectly supported by epidemiological studies: Educational attainment predicts cognitive change even when health traits are controlled for, suggesting that education level is not a proxy for health and dietary practices (Lee, Kawachi, Berkman, & Grodstein, 2003). However, environmental factors unique to individuals may also be important: Among MZ twins who were discordant for AD, the affected twin was more likely to have lower levels of education than the unaffected cotwin (Gatz et al., 2006).

Early-life socioeconomic status (SES) and later risk of cognitive decline or AD have been examined in a community-based sample of cases and controls (e.g., Moceri, Kukull, Emanuel, van Belle, & Larson, 2000) and in the Religious Orders Study (Wilson et al., 2005). For example, number of siblings and urban residence before 18 are associated with an increased risk of AD (Moceri et al., 2000). However, family and community socioeconomic standing in early childhood may be predictive not of cognitive decline or increased AD risk but rather overall level of cognitive performance, according to findings from the Religious Orders Study (Wilson et al., 2005).

Head Injury

Head injury is a well-known risk factor for AD. Two studies suggest it may be important as a risk of cognitive decline as well (Corkin, Rosen, Sullivan, & Clegg, 1989; Luukinen, Viramo, Koski, Laippala, & Kivela, 1999). Major head injury was associated with change in cognitive status after more than 2 years among adults 70 years or older (Luukinen et al., 1999). World War II veterans who sustained head injuries with penetration as young adults showed evidence of accelerating decline across all cognitive domains in a 30-year follow-up (Corkin et al., 1989).

Estrogen

Early population-based or community-based studies indicated that estrogen replacement therapy might be protective against or delay the onset of AD (e.g., Baldereschi et al., 1998). However, recent studies, including large-scale randomized clinical trials, have failed to show such a benefit for cognitive decline or for risk of AD, particularly for women 65 years and older (Craig, Maki, & Murphy, 2005; Mulnard, Corrada, & Kawas, 2004). However, on the basis of rodent studies, Hof and Morrison (2004) suggested that there may be an age-sensitive critical period during which estrogen may be beneficial if begun during the perimenopausal period rather than postmenopausal period.

Antioxidant Use

Vitamin E is one of several vitamins (including A and C) that are thought to potentially reduce free radical damage (i.e., reduce oxidative stress) and thus may be protective factors against cognitive decline (Maxwell et al., 2005; Morris, Evans, Bienias, Tangney, & Wilson, 2002). A recent community-based study suggests that vitamin E, via food or supplements, may diminish cognitive change over 18 months in adults 65 to 102 years of age (Morris et al., 2002). Results were significant even when controlling for multiple demographic factors, including education as well as smoking and alcohol consumption. Similar results have been found in a large population-based prospective study with a longer follow-up (Maxwell et al., 2005): Use of vitamin E and C supplements or multivitamin supplements were related to a significantly lower risk of 5-year cognitive change even when controlling for potential demographic or health confounds but were not related to incident dementia or AD risk.

GENE–ENVIRONMENT INTERACTION

Biological systems may interact in complex manners with environmental contexts that are not easily reducible to single gene candidates or environmental contexts (McClearn, 2006). Biometrical models applied to human traits typically do not allow for estimation of gene × environment (GXE) interaction, although the animal and plant literatures suggest it may be a common phenomenon (McClearn, 2006). A GXE interaction suggests one of two possibilities: (1) "genetic control of sensitivity to the environment" or (2) "environmental control of genetic expression" (Kendler & Eaves, 1986, p. 282). The findings from the large population-based Dunedin Multidisciplinary Health and Development Study indicate that GXE interaction may be important to common human behavioral traits (i.e., antisocial behavior and depression; Caspi et al., 2002, 2003).

GXE interactions may change given the passage of time and maturational level of an organism (McClearn, 2006). Over the lifetime there is an accumulation of exposure to social and biological stressors. Some individuals with particular genotypes may be more susceptible to certain environmental conditions and show a greater risk of cognitive decline than under other environmental conditions. Increasing nonshared environmental variance with age may hint at the possible emergence of GXE interaction. In the context of family-based studies, if gene–environment effects are present but are not modeled, the effects will be subsumed under nonshared environmental variance (Falconer, 1989). Thus, the noted increases in nonshared environmental effects with age across specific cognitive abilities, as well as g, may in fact include possible GXE interactions. In the context of identical twins (monozygotic [MZ]), who share the same genes, within-pair differences reflect nonshared environmental influences. Thus, differential sensitivity of particular genotypes to certain environments (or environment-dependent gene expression) should lead to greater within-pair differences for some genotypes than others (Berg, Kondo, Drayna, & Lawn, 1989; Martin, 2000). Genes sensitive to environmental circumstance have been called *variability genes*, as opposed to those genes that are related to mean differences in a trait (i.e., *level genes*; Berg et al., 1989; Martin, 2000).

Although some researchers suggest that variability genes may be of greater importance than level genes (Berg et al., 1989; Martin, 2000), relatively few studies have undertaken such research, particularly using biometric designs. The extent to which APOE may be a variability gene was examined in a Dutch study of identical adolescent twins pairs for several lipoprotein traits (plasma cholesterol, plasma triglycerides, low-density lipoprotein-cholesterol, apoB, and apoE; de Knijff et al., 1993). If within-pair differences varied by genotype (e.g., APOE e4 status), that would indicate the presence of GXE interactions. However, no significant intrapair differences among the different apoE phenotype classes were found. Thus, the authors concluded that APOE might not be a variability gene in adolescence. Recent examinations of MZ twins from SATSA suggest that APOE may be a variability gene for cognitive aging in a verbal task that relies in part on semantic memory, the Information subtest (Central Värnpliktsbyrån Scales [Jonsson & Molander, 1964], a Swedish adaptation of the Wechsler Adult Intelligence Scales Information subtest; Reynolds, Gatz, Berg, & Pedersen, 2007). Furthermore, person-specific environmental influences relevant to depressive symptoms may form part of the environmental aspects that interact with APOE genotype, leading to differential change.

Evidence from the AD literature suggests that APOE–environment interactions should not be overlooked. For example, APOE may interact with factors such as head injury, education, and childhood SES. The combination of a positive APOE e4 status and traumatic head injury history resulted in a tenfold increase in the risk of AD in a community-based sample (e.g., Mayeux et al., 1995), substantially higher than either risk factor alone. APOE predicts recuperation after head injury, where a positive e4 status is associated with poorer memory performance, acquisition, and recall subsequent to the head injury (Crawford et al., 2002).

Education and childhood SES may interact with APOE e4 status. The protective effect of higher education on risk of cognitive decline may be mitigated by the presence of the APOE e4 allele (Seeman et al., 2005). Participants in the MacArthur Studies of Successful Aging, who were 70–79 years old at baseline, with greater than an eighth-grade education and who carried at least one APOE e4 allele, showed steeper declines in memory and general cognitive performance over a span of approximately 6 years (Seeman et al., 2005). Nondemented community-dwelling individuals with two copies of the APOE e4 allele and low education showed steeper decline in measures of cognitive functioning than those who carried one copy of APOE e4 (Shadlen et al., 2005). In terms of childhood SES, AD risk may be greatest among carriers of the APOE e4 allele and those whose fathers worked as unskilled or manual laborers (Moceri et al., 2001).

Epigenetics. Epigenetic mechanisms may in part explain the underlying process by which genes and environments interact to produce differential cognitive change trajectories. *Epigenetic* refers to adaptive processes by which enduring changes in gene expression result from nongenetic sources of influence (Gottesman & Hanson, 2005; Kramer, 2005). As such, epigenetic mechanisms may explain processes by which even genetically identical individuals (MZ twins) may become increasingly different with the passage of time (Fraga et al., 2005). More broadly, they embody GXE interaction as environmentally directed gene expression (cf. Gottesman & Hanson,

2005). Differential gene expression within MZ twin pairs in lymphocytes, epithelial cells, and muscle cells was increasingly observed over age, spanning 3 to 74 years (Fraga et al., 2005), suggesting the importance of epigenetic effects across development. One should expect epigenetic divergence in brain tissue as well, although similar analyses have not yet been undertaken. The extent to which epigenetic processes in neuronal cells may occur and lead to individual differences in gene expression would be of particular interest to consider with respect to cognitive aging. Notable variability in frontal cortex gene expression was observed between persons 45 to 71 years of age in a postmortem RNA analysis (Lu et al., 2004), with support for nongenetic mechanisms underlying altered genetic expression (i.e., free radical damage to gene-promoter regions).

CONCLUSIONS AND FUTURE DIRECTIONS

The forward momentum in behavioral genetic investigations is to move beyond unnamed variance components toward incorporating measured gene candidates in studies of cognitive aging. Behavioral genetic designs are well suited to distinguish true from spurious association with gene candidates and should become more prominent in the search for QTLs for cognitive aging. Measured environments have infrequently been included in twin and adoption analyses, despite the fact that environmental histories are often collected; neither have GXE interactions been routinely addressed, although epidemiological research suggests the importance of specific environmental factors, such as antioxidant use (e.g., vitamin E supplements).

Environmental circumstances are important to gene action (Gottesman & Hanson, 2005; McClearn, 2006). Although we should move toward the inclusion of measured gene and environmental candidates, we must take care to consider multiple contexts of gene–environment coaction and interaction rather than isolated gene candidates and environmental factors (McClearn, 2006). The increasing role of nonshared environment on cognitive aging suggests the possibility of genotype–environment interaction that could be further clarified by considering candidate QTLs and measured environmental factors in longitudinal studies to better understand mechanisms of cognitive change. Despite the importance of understanding of gene–environment interplay, most QTL association studies examine mean differences by allele or genotype rather than associations with variability (Martin, 2000). To date, only one biometrical study of intraindividual cognitive change has examined possible variability genes using identical twins (Reynolds et al., 2007).

Additional longitudinal behavioral genetic studies focusing on cognitive aging are needed to replicate and extend research that has been conducted. Indeed, current cognitive aging research programs focused on individuals can and should be adapted to include additional family members. Including relatives would allow researchers to examine specific gene candidates and specific environmental effects. Using siblings, or other family designs, controls for possible confounds, such as population stratification, a potential problem in case-control studies employing individuals. Apart from behavioral genetic studies, longitudinal studies of cognitive aging have sometimes included spouses (Health and Retirement Study; Hauser & Willis, 2005) or siblings (Wisconsin Longitudinal Study; Hauser & Willis, 2005), but this is the exception rather than the rule. Although expanding designs to include additional individuals is costly, family-based designs are efficient in that one can identify clusters (i.e., families, sibships) and because multi-level modeling techniques can be used to manage the dependencies in such designs. The additional wealth of information in moving from individuals to families is well worth the extra data collection involved. In addition to behavioral genetic hypotheses, the dynamics of social relationships and cognitive change could be examined.

Principally important is the ability to distinguish among normative decline, terminal decline, and dementing disorders, because different genetic and environmental factors may be at play. There may be etiological commonalities as well, if dementia represents the outermost boundary of the continuum of cognitive changes seen with advancing age. Informative longitudinal studies are essential to uncover the possibly independent etiologies of decline in presymptomatic individuals who will go on to be diagnosed with dementia such as AD versus others who will remain cognitively intact. Biometrical studies, particularly twin/adoption designs, are among the most well suited to address possible differences in etiology because they simultaneously account for sources of variance contributing both to complex predictive factors, such as educational attainment, as well as to cognitive decline trajectories (level vs. change). Other nontwin sibling-based designs would be informative, particularly in the case of gene candidate association studies. However, only a handful of longitudinal behavioral genetic studies of cognitive aging exist, with most outside the United States and with virtually no ethnic diversity in the populations studied. Additional investment is warranted to ensure adequate replication of findings cross-nationally and within understudied ethnic groups.

NOTE

1. MZ pairs contributed to between-pair differences only, whereas DZ pairs contributed to both within- and between-pair differences.

REFERENCES

Anstey, K., & Christensen, H. (2000). Education, activity, health, blood pressure and apolipoprotein E as predictors of cognitive change in old age: A review. *Gerontology, 46,* 163–177.

Baldereschi, M., Di Carlo, A., Lepore, V., Bracco, L., Maggi, S., Grigoletto, F., et al. (1998). Estrogen-replacement therapy and Alzheimer's disease in the Italian Longitudinal Study on Aging. *Neurology, 50,* 996–1002.

Baltes, P. B., Reese, H. W., & Lipsitt, L. P. (1980). Life span developmental psychology. *Annual Review of Psychology, 31,* 65–110.

Bartels, M., Rietveld, M. J., Van Baal, G. C., & Boomsma, D. I. (2002). Genetic and environmental influences on the development of intelligence. *Behavior Genetics, 32,* 237–249.

Bennett, D. A., Wilson, R. S., Schneider, J. A., Evans, D. A., Mendes de Leon, C. F., Arnold, S. E., et al. (2003). Education modifies the relation of AD pathology to level of cognitive function in older persons. *Neurology, 60,* 1909–1915.

Berg, K., Kondo, I., Drayna, D., & Lawn, R. (1989). "Variability gene" effect of cholesteryl ester transfer protein (CETP) genes. *Clinical Genetics, 35,* 437–445.

Bishop, E. G., Cherny, S. S., Corley, R., Plomin, R., DeFries, J. C., & Hewitt, J. K. (2003). Development genetic analysis of general cognitive ability from 1 to 12 years in a sample of adoptees, biological siblings, and twins. *Intelligence, 31,* 31–49.

Bouchard, T. J., Jr., & McGue, M. (1981, May 29). Familial studies of intelligence: A review. *Science, 212,* 1055–1059.

Bouchard, T. J., Jr., Segal, N. L., & Lykken, D. T. (1990). Genetic and environmental influences on special mental abilities in a sample of twins reared apart. *Acta Geneticae Medicae Gemellologiae (Roma), 39,* 193–206.

Bretsky, P., Guralnik, J. M., Launer, L., Albert, M., & Seeman, T. E. (2003). The role of APOE-epsilon4 in longitudinal cognitive decline: MacArthur Studies of Successful Aging. *Neurology, 60,* 1077–1081.

Cardon, L. R., & Fulker, D. W. (1994). A model of developmental change in hierarchical phenotypes with application to specific cognitive abilities. *Behavior Genetics, 24,* 1–16.

Caspi, A., McClay, J., Moffitt, T. E., Mill, J., Martin, J., Craig, I. W., et al. (2002, August 2). Role of genotype in the cycle of violence in maltreated children. *Science, 297,* 851–854.

Caspi, A., Sugden, K., Moffitt, T. E., Taylor, A., Craig, I. W., Harrington, H., et al. (2003, July 18). Influence of life stress on depression: Moderation by a polymorphism in the 5-HTT gene. *Science, 301,* 386–389.

Corkin, S., Rosen, T. J., Sullivan, E. V., & Clegg, R. A. (1989). Penetrating head injury in young adulthood exacerbates cognitive decline in later years. *Journal of Neuroscience, 9,* 3876–3883.

Craig, M. C., Maki, P. M., & Murphy, D. G. (2005). The Women's Health Initiative Memory Study: Findings and implications for treatment. *Lancet Neurology, 4,* 190–194.

Crawford, F. C., Vanderploeg, R. D., Freeman, M. J., Singh, S., Waisman, M., Michaels, L., et al. (2002). APOE genotype influences acquisition and recall following traumatic brain injury. *Neurology, 58,* 1115–1118.

Deary, I. J., Hamilton, G., Hayward, C., Whalley, L. J., Powell, J., Starr, J. M., et al. (2005). Nicastrin gene polymorphisms, cognitive ability level and cognitive ageing. *Neuroscience Letters, 373,* 110–114.

Deary, I. J., Whiteman, M. C., Pattie, A., Starr, J. M., Hayward, C., Wright, A. F., et al. (2002, August 29).

Cognitive change and the APOE epsilon 4 allele. *Nature, 418,* 932.

de Frias, C. M., Annerbrink, K., Westberg, L., Eriksson, E., Adolfsson, R., & Nilsson, L. G. (2005). Catechol O-methyltransferase Val158Met polymorphism is associated with cognitive performance in nondemented adults. *Journal of Cognitive Neuroscience, 17,* 1018–1025.

DeFries, J. C., Ashton, G. C., Johnson, R. C., Kuse, A. R., McClearn, G. E., Mi, M. P., et al. (1976, May 13). Parent–offspring resemblance for specific cognitive abilities in two ethnic groups. *Nature, 261,* 131–133.

de Knijff, P., Boomsma, D. I., de Wit, E., Kempen, H. J., Gevers Leuven, J. A., Frants, R. R., & Havekes, L. M. (1993). The effect of the apolipoprotein E phenotype on plasma lipids is not influenced by environmental variability: Results of a Dutch twin study. *Human Genetics, 91,* 268–272.

de Quervain, D. J. F., Henke, K., Aerni, A., Coluccia, D., Wollmer, M. A., Hock, C., et al. (2003). A functional genetic variation of the 5-HT2a receptor affects human memory. *Nature Neuroscience, 6,* 1141–1142.

Falconer, D. S. (1989). *Introduction to quantitative genetics* (3rd ed.). New York: Wiley.

Finkel, D., & McGue, M. (1993). The origins of individual differences in memory among the elderly: A behavior genetic analysis. *Psychology and Aging, 8,* 527–537.

Finkel, D., & McGue, M. (1998). Age differences in the nature and origin of individual differences in memory: A behavior genetic analysis. *International Journal of Aging and Human Development, 47,* 217–239.

Finkel, D., Pedersen, N. L., McGue, M., & McClearn, G. E. (1995). Heritability of cognitive abilities in adult twins: Comparison of Minnesota and Swedish data. *Behavior Genetics, 25,* 421–431.

Finkel, D., Pedersen, N. L., Plomin, R., & McClearn, G. E. (1998). Longitudinal and cross-sectional twin data on cognitive abilities in adulthood: The Swedish Adoption/Twin Study of Aging. *Developmental Psychology, 34,* 1400–1413.

Fraga, M. F., Ballestar, E., Paz, M. F., Ropero, S., Setien, F., Ballestar, M. L., et al. (2005). Epigenetic differences arise during the lifetime of monozygotic twins. *Proceedings of the National Academy of Sciences, USA, 102,* 10604–10609.

Fulker, D. W., Cherny, S. S., Sham, P. C., & Hewitt, J. K. (1999). Combined linkage and association sib-pair analysis for quantitative traits. *American Journal of Human Genetics, 64,* 259–267.

Gatz, M., Fiske, A., Reynolds, C. A., Johansson, B., Fratiglioni, L., & Pedersen, N. L. (2005). Performance on neurocognitive tests by co-twins to dementia cases compared to normal control twins. *Journal of Geriatric Psychiatry and Neurology, 18,* 202–207.

Gatz, M., Mortimer, J. A., Fratiglioni, L., Johansson, B., Berg, S., Reynolds, C. A., et al. (2006). Potentially modifiable risk factors for dementia in identical twins. *Alzheimer's & Dementia, 2,* 110–117.

Goddard, K. A., Olson, J. M., Payami, H., van der Voet, M., Kuivaniemi, H., & Tromp, G. (2004). Evidence of linkage and association on chromosome 20 for late-onset Alzheimer disease. *Neurogenetics, 5,* 121–128.

Gottesman, I. I., & Hanson, D. R. (2005). Human development: Biological and genetic processes. *Annual Review of Psychology, 56,* 263–286.

Hauser, R. M., & Willis, R. J. (2005). Survey design and methodology in the Health and Retirement Study and the Wisconsin Longitudinal Study. In L. J. Waite (Ed.), *Aging, health, and public policy: Demographic and economic perspectives* (pp. 209–235). New York: Population Council.

Hof, P. R., & Morrison, J. H. (2004). The aging brain: Morphomolecular senescence of cortical circuits. *Trends in Neurosciences, 27,* 607–613.

International Human Genome Sequencing Consortium. (2001). Initial sequencing and analysis of the human genome. *Nature, 409*(6822), 860–921.

Johansson, B., Hofer, S. M., Allaire, J. C., Maldonado-Molina, M. M., Piccinin, A. M., Berg, S., et al. (2004). Change in cognitive capabilities in the oldest old: The effects of proximity to death in genetically related individuals over a 6-year period. *Psychology and Aging, 19,* 145–156.

Johansson, B., Whitfield, K., Pedersen, N. L., Hofer, S. M., Ahern, F., & McClearn, G. E. (1999). Origins of individual differences in episodic memory in the oldest-old: A population-based study of identical and same-sex fraternal twins aged 80 and older. *Journals of Gerontology Series B: Psychological Sciences and Social Sciences, 54,* P173–P179.

Jonsson, C.-O., & Molander, L. (1964). *Manual till CVB-skalan* [Manual of the CVB Scales]. Stockholm, Sweden: Psykologi Forlaget.

Kandel, E. R. (2001, November 2). The molecular biology of memory storage: A dialogue between genes and synapses. *Science, 294*, 1030–1038.

Kendler, K. S., & Eaves, I. A. (1986). Models for the joint effect of genotype and environment on liability to psychiatric illness. *American Journal of Psychiatry, 143*, 279–289.

Kramer, D. A. (2005). Commentary: Gene–environment interplay in the context of genetics, epigenetics, and gene expression. *Journal of the American Academy of Child & Adolescent Psychiatry, 44*, 19–27.

Lahiri, D. K., Sambamurti, K., & Bennett, D. A. (2004). Apolipoprotein gene and its interaction with the environmentally driven risk factors: Molecular, genetic and epidemiological studies of Alzheimer's disease. *Neurobiology of Aging, 25*, 651–660.

Lee, S., Kawachi, I., Berkman, L. F., & Grodstein, F. (2003). Education, other socioeconomic indicators, and cognitive function. *American Journal of Epidemiology, 157*, 712–720.

Lu, T., Pan, Y., Kao, S. Y., Li, C., Kohane, I., Chan, J., et al. (2004, June 24). Gene regulation and DNA damage in the ageing human brain. *Nature, 429*, 883–891.

Luciano, M., Wright, M. J., Smith, G. A., Geffen, G. M., Geffen, L. B., & Martin, N. G. (2001). Genetic covariance among measures of information processing speed, working memory, and IQ. *Behavior Genetics, 31*, 581–592.

Luukinen, H., Viramo, P., Koski, K., Laippala, P., & Kivela, S. L. (1999). Head injuries and cognitive decline among older adults: A population-based study. *Neurology, 52*, 557–562.

Martin, N. G. (2000). Gene–environment interaction and twin studies. In T. D. Spector, H. Snieder, & A. J. MacGregor (Eds.), *Advances in twin and sib-pair analysis* (pp. 144–150). London: Greenwich Medical Media.

Maxwell, C. J., Hicks, M. S., Hogan, D. B., Basran, J., & Ebly, E. M. (2005). Supplemental use of antioxidant vitamins and subsequent risk of cognitive decline and dementia. *Dementia and Geriatric Cognitive Disorders, 20*, 45–51.

Mayeux, R., Ottman, R., Maestre, G., Ngai, C., Tang, M. X., Ginsberg, H., et al. (1995). Synergistic effects of traumatic head injury and apolipoprotein-epsilon 4 in patients with Alzheimer's disease. *Neurology, 45*, 555–557.

Mayeux, R., Small, S. A., Tang, M., Tycko, B., & Stern, Y. (2001). Memory performance in healthy elderly without Alzheimer's disease: Effects of time and apolipoprotein-E. *Neurobiology of Aging, 22*, 683–689.

McCartney, K., Harris, M. J., & Bernieri, F. (1990). Growing up and growing apart: A developmental meta-analysis of twin studies. *Psychological Bulletin, 107*, 226–237.

McClearn, G. E. (2006). Contextual genetics. *Trends in Genetics, 22*, 315–319.

McClearn, G. E., Johansson, B., Berg, S., Pedersen, N. L., Ahern, F., Petrill, S. A., et al. (1997, June 6). Substantial genetic influence on cognitive abilities in twins 80 or more years old. *Science, 276*, 1560–1563.

McGue, M., Bouchard, T. J., Jr., Iacono, W. G., & Lykken, D. T. (1993). Behavioral genetics of cognitive ability: A life-span perspective. In R. Plomin & G. E. McClearn (Eds.), *Nature, nurture & psychology* (pp. 59–76). Washington, DC: American Psychological Association.

McGue, M., & Christensen, K. (2001). The heritability of cognitive functioning in very old adults: Evidence from Danish twins aged 75 years and older. *Psychology and Aging, 16*, 272–280.

McGue, M., & Christensen, K. (2002). The heritability of level and rate-of-change in cognitive functioning in Danish twins aged 70 years and older. *Experimental Aging Research, 28*, 435–451.

McLean, A. J., & Le Couteur, D. G. (2004). Aging biology and geriatric clinical pharmacology. *Pharmacological Reviews, 56*, 163–184

Moceri, V. M., Kukull, W. A., Emanuel, I., van Belle, G., & Larson, E. B. (2000). Early-life risk factors and the development of Alzheimer's disease. *Neurology, 54*, 415–420.

Moceri, V. M., Kukull, W. A., Emanuel, I., van Belle, G., Starr, J. R., Schellenberg, G. D., et al. (2001). Using census data and birth certificates to reconstruct the early-life socioeconomic environment and the relation to the development of Alzheimer's disease. *Epidemiology, 12*, 383–389.

Morris, M. C., Evans, D. A., Bienias, J. L., Tangney, C. C., & Wilson, R. S. (2002). Vitamin E and cognitive decline in older persons. *Archives of Neurology, 59*, 1125–1132.

Morse, C. K. (1993). Does variability increase with age? An archival study of cognitive measures. *Psychology and Aging, 8,* 156–164.

Mulnard, R. A., Corrada, M. M., & Kawas, C. H. (2004). Estrogen replacement therapy, Alzheimer's disease, and mild cognitive impairment. *Current Neurology and Neuroscience Reports, 4,* 368–373.

Neale, M. C., Cherny, S. S., Sham, P. C., Whitfield, J. B., Heath, A. C., Birley, A. J., & Martin, N. G. (1999). Distinguishing population stratification from genuine allelic effects with Mx: Association of ADH2 with alcohol consumption. *Behavior Genetics, 29,* 233–243.

Nilsson, L. G., Nyberg, L., & Bäckman, L. (2002). Genetic variation in memory functioning. *Neuroscience and Biobehavioral Review, 26,* 841–848.

Payton, A., Holland, F., Diggle, P., Rabbitt, P., Horan, M., Davidson, Y., et al. (2003). Cathepsin D exon 2 polymorphism associated with general intelligence in a healthy older population. *Molecular Psychiatry, 8,* 14–18.

Pedersen, N. L. (2004). New frontiers in genetic influences on cognitive aging. In R. A. Dixon, L. Bäckman, & L.-G. Nilsson (Eds.), *New frontiers in cognitive aging* (pp. 235–252) New York: Oxford University Press.

Pedersen, N. L., Plomin, R., Nesselroade, J. R., & McClearn, G. E. (1992). A quantitative genetic analysis of cognitive abilities during the second half of the life span. *Psychological Science, 3,* 346–353.

Pedersen, N. L., Reynolds, C. A., & Gatz, M. (1996). Sources of covariation among Mini-Mental State Examination scores, education, and cognitive abilities. *Journals of Gerontology Series B: Psychological Sciences and Social Sciences, 51B,* P55–P63.

Pedersen, N. L., Ripatti, S., Berg, S., Reynolds, C., Hofer, S. M., Finkel, D., et al. (2003). The influence of mortality on twin models of change: Addressing missingness through multiple imputation. *Behavior Genetics, 33,* 161–169.

Plomin, R., DeFries, J. C., McClearn, G. E., & McGuffin, P. (2001). *Behavioral genetics.* New York: Worth.

Plomin, R., Fulker, D. W., Corley, R., & DeFries, J. C. (1997). Nature, nurture, and cognitive development from 1 to 16 years: A parent–offspring adoption study. *Psychological Science, 8,* 442–447.

Plomin, R., Pedersen, N. L., Lichtenstein, P., & McClearn, G. E. (1994). Variability and stability in cognitive abilities are largely genetic later in life. *Behavior Genetics, 24,* 207–215.

Plomin, R., & Spinath, F. M. (2004). Intelligence: Genetics, genes, and genomics. *Journal of Personality and Social Psychology, 86,* 112–129.

Posthuma, D., de Geus, E. J., Boomsma, D. I., & Neale, M. C. (2004). Combined linkage and association tests in Mx. *Behavior Genetics, 34,* 179–196.

Posthuma, D., Mulder, E. J. C. M., Boomsma, D. I., & de Geus, E. J. C. (2002). Genetic analysis of IQ, processing speed and stimulus–response incongruency effects. *Biological Psychology, 61,* 157–182.

Posthuma, D., Neale, M. C., Boomsma, D. I., & de Geus, E. J. C. (2001). Are smarter brains running faster? Heritability of alpha peak frequency, IQ, and their interrelation. *Behavior Genetics, 31,* 567–579.

Reynolds, C. A., Finkel, D., McArdle, J. J., Gatz, M., Berg, S., & Pedersen, N. L. (2005). Quantitative genetic analysis of latent growth curve models of cognitive abilities in adulthood. *Developmental Psychology, 41,* 3–16.

Reynolds, C. A., Gatz, M., Berg, S., Pedersen, N. L. (2007). Genotype-environment interactions: Cognitive aging and social factors. *Twin Research and Human Genetics, 10*(2), 241–254.

Reynolds, C. A., Jansson, M., Gatz, M., & Pedersen, N. L. (2006). Longitudinal change in memory performance associated with HTR2A polymorphism. *Neurobiology of Aging, 27,* 150–154.

Risch, N., & Merikangas, K. (1996, September 13). The future of genetic studies of complex human diseases. *Science, 273,* 1516–1517.

Schmitt, F. A., Davis, D. G., Wekstein, D. R., Smith, C. D., Ashford, J. W., & Markesbery, W. R. (2000). "Preclinical" AD revisited: Neuropathology of cognitively normal older adults. *Neurology, 55,* 370–376.

Seeman, T. E., Huang, M. H., Bretsky, P., Crimmins, E., Launer, L., & Guralnik, J. M. (2005). Education and APOE-e4 in longitudinal cognitive decline: MacArthur Studies of Successful Aging. *Journals of Gerontology Series B: Psychological Sciences and Social Sciences, 60,* P74–P83.

Shadlen, M. F., Larson, E. B., Wang, L., Phelan, E. A., McCormick, W. C., Jolley, L., et al. (2005). Education modifies the effect of apolipoprotein epsilon 4 on cognitive decline. *Neurobiology of Aging, 26,* 17–24.

Sheline, Y. I., Mintun, M. A., Moerlein, S. M., & Snyder, A. Z. (2002). Greater loss of 5-HT(2A) receptors in midlife than in late life. *American Journal of Psychiatry, 159,* 430–435.

Small, B. J., Graves, A. B., McEvoy, C. L., Crawford, F. C., Mullan, M., & Mortimer, J. A. (2000). Is APOE-epsilon4 a risk factor for cognitive impairment in normal aging? *Neurology, 54,* 2082–2088.

Strittmatter, W. J., Saunders, A. M., Schmechel, D., Pericak-Vance, M., Enghild, J., Salvesen, G. S., et al. (1993). Apolipoprotein E: High-avidity binding to beta-amyloid and increased frequency of type 4 allele in late-onset familial Alzheimer disease. *Proceedings of the National Academy of Sciences, USA, 90,* 1977–1981.

Tambs, K., Sundet, J. M., & Magnus, P. (1984). Heritability analysis of the WAIS subtests: A study of twins. *Intelligence, 8,* 283–293.

Warwick Daw, E., Payami, H., Nemens, E. J., Nochlin, D., Bird, T. D., Schellenberg, G. D., et al. (2000). The number of trait loci in late-onset Alzheimer disease. *American Journal of Human Genetics, 66,* 196–204.

Wilson, R. S., Scherr, P. A., Hoganson, G., Bienias, J. L., Evans, D. A., & Bennett, D. A. (2005). Early life socioeconomic status and late life risk of Alzheimer's disease. *Neuroepidemiology, 25,* 8–14.

Wilson, R. S., Schneider, J. A., Barnes, L. L., Beckett, L. A., Aggarwal, N. T., Cochran, E. J., et al. (2002). The apolipoprotein E epsilon 4 allele and decline in different cognitive systems during a 6-year period. *Archives of Neurology, 59,* 1154–1160.

Wright, M., De Geus, E., Ando, J., Luciano, M., Posthuma, D., Ono, Y., et al. (2001). Genetics of cognition: Outline of a collaborative twin study. *Twin Research, 4,* 48–56.

Wright, M. J., Luciano, M., Hansell, N. K., Geffen, G. M., Geffen, L. B., & Martin, N. G. (2002). Genetic sources of covariation among P3(00) and online performance variables in a delayed-response working memory task. *Biological Psychology, 61,* 183–202.

Zandi, P. P., & Breitner, J. C. (2001). Do NSAIDs prevent Alzheimer's disease? And, if so, why? The epidemiological evidence. *Neurobiology of Aging, 22,* 811–817.

34

DOES PARTICIPATION IN COGNITIVE ACTIVITIES BUFFER AGE-RELATED COGNITIVE DECLINE?

BRENT J. SMALL AND CATHY L. MCEVOY

In recent years, there has been considerable interest in the role of lifestyle activities modifying the presence of age-related deficits in cognitive functioning. Indeed, this interest can be seen in both scientific publications (Kramer & Willis, 2002; Stern, 2007) as well as more popular media (Einstein & McDaniel, 2004; Small & Vorgan, 2006). In part, this reflects the fact that it is appealing to believe modifying age-related changes in cognitive performance may be under our own control, often evoking the adage of "Use it or lose it." Although there is much interest in the role of lifestyle activities as mediators of age-related declines in cognitive performance, definitive evidence of this relationship has been mixed.

We begin this chapter by describing two theoretical perspectives that help guide an understanding of how lifestyle activities might impact cognitive performance. We then review evidence for and against a relationship between lifestyle activities and cognitive performance, both cross-sectionally and longitudinally. Next, we describe several critical issues; specifically, we examine evidence for the direction of the effect of cognitive activities on cognitive performance through the use of advanced statistical analysis, describe how the match between types of cognitive activities and domains of cognitive performance may impact the presence or absence of significant effects, and describe possible mechanisms of action.

THEORETICAL PERSPECTIVES

In the literature, there are two theoretical perspectives that are relevant to the study of how lifestyle activities may impact cognitive performance in old age. Although each perspective does not provide specific predictions about the types of lifestyle activities that may provide the most benefit to older adults, and neither do they articulate specific mechanisms of action, they

AUTHORS' NOTE: The support of the National Institute on Aging through a grant to Brent J. Small (R03 AG024082) during preparation of this chapter is gratefully acknowledged.

are nonetheless useful to describe and allow us to put this research in context. Schooler and colleagues (e.g., Schooler, 1984, 1999) have argued that substantive complexity of environments, defined in part as ill-defined contingencies and substantive latitude in decision making, may reward cognitive effort. Furthermore, they contend that this exposure may generalize to other situations, performance on cognitive ability tests being one. By contrast, exposure to relatively simple environments may contribute to decrements in intellectual functioning. Kohn and Schooler (1978) have demonstrated how substantive complexity in work environments (Schooler, 1999) and during leisure time (Schooler & Mulatu, 2001) is related to superior cognitive functioning, after controlling for potentially confounding variables.

Another theoretical perspective that is relevant to the potential for lifestyle activities to influence cognitive functioning is that of *cognitive reserve*. Developed on the basis of the neuropsychological literature, the hypothesis of cognitive reserve was derived in an attempt to explain how similar neurological insults (e.g., stroke) produced different behavioral outcomes across patients, and how neuropathological changes associated with Alzheimer's disease may or may not manifest as clinically significant behavioral deficits (Stern, 2002, 2007). In this theory, "reserve is defined in terms of the amount of damage that can be sustained before reaching a threshold for clinical expression" (Stern, 2002, p. 449). For example, educational attainment has been viewed as an index of cognitive reserve, and several studies have reported that persons with more years of education are at reduced risk for developing Alzheimer's disease (Stern, Tang, Denaro, & Mayeux, 1995). In addition, recent research has also highlighted the role of lifestyle activities as a potentially modifiable factor that can influence cognitive reserve (Wilson & Bennett, 2003).

Empirical Evidence

The literature on participation in lifestyle activities and cognitive performance is somewhat mixed (see Anstey & Christensen, 2000). Several studies have found that participation in lifestyle activities is related to better cognitive performance cross-sectionally (Christensen et al., 1996; Richards, Hardy, & Wadsworth, 2003) and fewer negative changes longitudinally (Hultsch, Hertzog, Small, & Dixon, 1999). For example, Hultsch, Hammer, and Small (1993) reported that active lifestyle was positively associated with a range of cognitive abilities in their sample of adults ages 55 through 85. Moreover, individuals who were in the very old group, classified as 70- to 85-year-olds, received the most benefit from participating in cognitively engaging lifestyle activities. Barnes, Wilson, Mendes de Leon, and Bennett (2006) reported that, among a sample of African American participants, more frequent cognitive activity was related to current cognitive functioning. However, lifelong access to cognitive resources (e.g., books) was not significantly related to cognitive performance.

In terms of evidence from studies that have examined these relationships longitudinally, Schooler and Mulatu (2001) reported that participation in cognitively complex lifestyle activities was related to fewer declines in cognitive performance over a 20-year follow-up period. Similarly, Wilson et al. (2003) reported that across an approximate 5-year follow-up interval, individuals who participated in more cognitive activities (e.g., reading) at baseline experienced reduced cognitive decline longitudinally. Specifically, a 1-point increase in cognitive activity score at baseline was associated with an approximately 19% decrease in annual rate of cognitive decline. Furthermore, Andel et al. (2005) reported a lower risk of Alzheimer's disease for persons who had cognitively complex jobs.

However, other studies have failed to observe a mediating relationship between lifestyle activities and cognitive performance either cross-sectionally (Salthouse, Berish, & Miles, 2002) or longitudinally (Richards et al., 2003). Salthouse and colleagues (2002) examined whether participation in lifestyle activities mediated age-related differences in speed of processing or memory performance in a sample ranging in age from 20 to 91. Their results indicated that age-related differences in cognition were not reduced by taking into account either the frequency of participation in lifestyle activities or the extent to which these activities were rated as requiring cognition.

Mackinnon, Christensen, Hofer, Korten, and Jorm (2003) reported in a longitudinal study that declines in activity frequency were mirrored by a decline in cognitive functioning. However, when participants were dichotomized into those who maintained their level of activity and those who demonstrated significant decline in activity participation over time, no statistically significant differences were observed in terms of the magnitude of the decrements in cognitive functioning between each group. The authors concluded that although decrements in activity frequency and cognitive performance were synchronous, the fact that persons who maintained or declined in activity frequency showed no differences in the magnitude of change in cognitive performance over time indicates that "the naturalistic maintenance of activities offers no protection against cognitive decline" (Mackinnon et al., 2003, p. 225).

There are several possible reasons for the discrepant findings that have been reported. These include variability in the statistical techniques that have been used, including the adequate conceptualization of changes in functioning; differences in the manner by which lifestyle activities are conceptualized; and variation in the cognitive outcome.

METHODOLOGICAL APPROACHES TO THE STUDY OF LIFESTYLE–COGNITION RELATIONSHIP

Past attempts to examine the longitudinal relationship between changes in lifestyle activities and cognitive performance have been limited by a number of factors, including the availability of multiple waves of data as well as the statistical approach to data analysis. These factors also inhibit the ability to specify direction of relationships between lifestyle activities and cognitive performance. For example, although cross-sectional relationships between active lifestyle and cognitive performance are of interest, they tell us very little about whether participation in lifestyle activities generalizes to performance on standardized tests of cognitive ability, as Schooler and colleagues have argued

(Schooler, 1999; Schooler & Mulatu, 2001), or whether individuals who are initially more cognitively able choose to participate in complex lifestyle activities. Furthermore, the longitudinal data that have been used to examine these relationships have often used only two measurement points (Hultsch et al., 1999; Pushkar Gold et al., 1995; Schooler & Mulatu, 2001). As a result, only linear changes in functioning can be specified, and lead–lag relationships—changes in one measure preceding changes over subsequent panels of follow-up intervals—cannot be examined. Thus, there are a number of advantages to having more than two measurement points (Singer & Willett, 2003; Willett, 1989). Finally, the issue of temporal ordering of changes in activity patterns and changes in cognitive performance is a critical one. For example, Hultsch et al. (1999) reported that structural equation models that portrayed changes in lifestyle activities as driving changes in cognitive functioning fit the data just as well as alternate models that portrayed changes in cognitive abilities as resulting in reductions in the participation of cognitive activities. Similarly, Schooler and Mulatu (2001) examined the reciprocal relationship between 20-year changes in activity lifestyle and changes in a composite measure of cognitive performance. They reported that in one model, with their original combination of subjective and objective measures of cognitive performance, the relationship between changes in activity and changes in cognition was larger than the reciprocal effect (βs = .32 vs. .24, respectively). However, when standardized measures of cognitive performance were used to index cognitive functioning, the path from cognitive performance to lifestyle activity was larger (βs = .31 vs. .18, respectively), suggesting that declines in cognitive performance may precede declines in lifestyle activity. At the heart of this issue is the fact that past attempts to link active lifestyle with cognitive performance have been derived from studies that have used correlational or quasi-experimental designs to examine these relationships. Thus, we are unable to make strong conclusions regarding whether change in one variable preceded a change in another.

Attempts to specify the nature of relationships between cognition and lifestyle activities across multiple waves of data poses special problems from an analytic perspective. There are a number of potential solutions, including cross-lagged regression models (Schooler & Mulatu, 2001), latent change structural equation models (Christensen et al., 1996; Hultsch et al., 1999), and multilevel or hierarchical linear models (Bryk & Raudenbush, 1992), each of which has its own advantages and disadvantages. One more recent approach is the application of dual change score models (DCSM) to examine the relationship between changes in lifestyle activities and changes in cognitive performance.

Dual Change Score Models

There are a number of advantages to the DCSM data analytic method (McArdle, 2001). First, these models build upon the general theme of structural equation models for latent growth (Duncan, Duncan, Stycker, Li, & Alpert, 1999). As such, the DCSM models are based upon traditional difference equations; are able to describe trajectories over time; and include separate estimation of measurement errors, which is critical for the adequate analysis of longitudinal data. Second, we are able to use all available data across the follow-up period, not just cases that have complete longitudinal data, assuming that lost data are missing at random (Schafer, 1997). This is an important feature of these types of methods, and it allows all participants to contribute to the relationships that are examined, even if they do not return across all follow-up periods.

Perhaps the most significant advantage of this statistical method is that the DCSM approach allows us to directly pose and test models about longitudinal changes in multiple variables over time. In this case, we can evaluate multiple models corresponding to specific hypotheses, including (a) that there is no relationship between changes in activity lifestyle and changes in cognitive performance; (b) that active lifestyles are a *leading indicator*, such that they precede changes in cognitive functioning; (c) cognitive performance is the leading indicator of changes in activity participation; or (d) a form of *dynamic coupling* exists among both variables, whereby changes in both

variables influence changes in the other, although the magnitude of these effects may be different.

Figure 34.1 illustrates a univariate DCSM model for a single variable (Y; e.g., cognitive performance) measured at multiple times of measurement.

The measured variable (Y) has an error associated with it that is assumed not to change over time or correlate with itself across the measurement period. A latent variable is then derived, and represents a true score, in the sense that it has common variance (e.g., F_{YT1}) and associated error (e.g., e_{T1}). The time series of variables is further extracted into a level factor (Y_0) and a slope (Y_S). The level factor represents a person's score at the beginning of the time series, and the slope represents a person's change scores across the follow-up interval. Both the level and slope latent variables also have variances associated with them that are correlated with one another (not shown in Figure 34.1 for clarity purposes). In each case, the variance components represent individual differences in either baseline scores or individual differences in rate of change over the follow-up period. Finally, the model contains a linear growth (α) and proportional growth (β) parameter.

Using this basic model, one can test whether changes in active lifestyle or changes in cognition can be characterized as linear growth ($\beta = 0$), proportional growth ($\alpha = 0$), or both linear and proportional growth. Figure 34.2 displays a bivariate DCSM model whereby activity lifestyle parameters with change slopes are linked to a cognitive outcome and are used to examine whether rate of change in one variable is related to rate of change in another. Specifically, using these models, we can evaluate whether changes in activity lifestyle precede changes in cognitive performance, thereby suggesting that active engagement may protect cognitive abilities consistent with the work of Schooler and colleagues (Schooler & Mulatu, 2001; Schooler, Mulatu, & Oates, 1999), or whether changes in cognitive abilities precipitate changes in active lifestyle, such that less cognitively able individuals choose to give up challenging lifestyle activities. Finally, we are able to evaluate a model that includes both relationships and in this case differences in the magnitude of the effects can be generated.

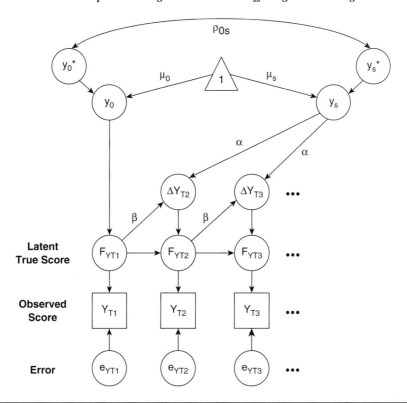

Figure 34.1   Univariate Dual Change Score Model Illustrating Changes in Cognitive Performance (Y)

SOURCE: From *New Methods for the Analysis of Change* (p. 148), by J. J. McArdle and F. Hamagami, 2001, Washington, DC: American Psychological Association. Copyright 2001 by the American Psychological Association. Adapted with permission.

NOTES: Squares represent measured variables, circles are unmeasured or latent variables, and the triangle signifies a constant and indicates that the relationships modeled here are at the mean level (i.e., $\mu 0$, μs), rather than the variance–covariance structure over time. T1 = Time 1; T2 = Time 2; T3 = Time 3.

The main change between the bivariate model depicted in Figure 34.2 and the univariate change model shown in Figure 34.1 is an additional parameter that predicts changes over time (γ); that is, the model for change in the first latent variable (ΔX_{T2}) includes a constant change (α), a proportional effect (β) of the factor (F_{XT1}) upon itself, and a coupling effect (γ_{yx}) of the second factor (Y_{T1}). The same is true for change in the second latent variable (ΔY_{T2}), which includes a constant change (α), a proportional effect (β) of the factor (F_{YT1}) upon itself, and a coupling effect (γ_{xy}) of the second factor (F_{XT1}). In this dynamic model, the predictors of one latent variable are embedded in the outcomes of the other variable, and vice versa.

Given the inclusion of the coupling parameter in the multivariate DCSM, we can test specific hypotheses about the relationship between changes in one factor and their influence on a second. Specifically, for bivariate comparison, four models can be tested. In the first, both coupling measures are constrained to be zero ($\gamma_{XY} = \gamma_{YX} = 0$). In this case, we test the hypothesis that although within-factor changes may be present, there is no dynamic coupling present, inasmuch as the changes are unrelated to each other. In the second model, one factor is a leading indicator of the other (i.e., $\gamma_{XY} > 0$). With this model, we can test whether activity lifestyle is a leading indicator of changes in cognitive ability. The third model posits the reverse relationship,

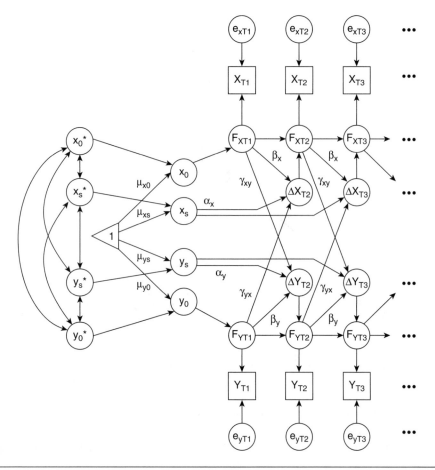

Figure 34.2   Bivariate Dual Change Score Model Illustrating How Changes in Lifestyle Activities (X) May Influence Changes in Cognitive Performance (Y)

SOURCE: From *New Methods for the Analysis of Change* (p. 145), by J. J. McArdle and F. Hamagami, 2001, Washington, DC: American Psychological Association. Copyright 2001 by the American Psychological Association. Adapted with permission.

NOTE: T1 = Time 1; T2 = Time 2; T3 = Time 3.

whereby changes in the other factor are leading indicators of changes in the first (i.e., $\gamma_{YX} > 0$). This model would indicate that changes to cognitive performance precede changes to participation in lifestyle activities. The final model specifies a dynamic coupling relationship such that the cross-factor parameters are both different from zero (i.e., $\gamma_{XY} > 0$ and $\gamma_{YX} > 0$). It should be noted that although the bivariate DCSM illustrated here provides a stronger test of directionality of effects, as compared to correlated latent change models, for example, strict interpretations of causality still cannot be derived from correlational data. In our view, the DCSM

analyses further our ability to derive conclusions regarding whether an active lifestyle positively influences cognitive performance, but a strict test of causal inferences requires random assignment to intervention and control groups.

In the literature, there are now two examples (Ghisletta, Bickel, & Lövdén, 2006; Lövdén, Bergman, Adolfsson, & Lindenberger, 2005) of the application of the DCSM models to the relationship between changes in lifestyle activity participation and changes in cognitive performance. Lövdén et al. (2005) examined the issue of temporality of changes in social participation (e.g., restaurant visits, sports, hobbies) and changes in perceptual speed in a sample of participants from the Berlin Aging Study (Baltes & Mayer, 1999). The results indicated that changes in social participation were related to subsequent changes in perceptual speed but that preceding changes in perceptual speed were not related to changes in social participation. Thus, the results provide evidence that changes in lifestyle activities preceded changes in cognitive performance. Although exciting, one of the limitations of this study has to do with using perceptual speed as the outcome measure. The role of cognitive changes precipitating declines in lifestyle activities may be more salient for those cognitive processes for which change is more easily perceived by participants; that is, it is unlikely that subtle declines in perceptual speed would greatly impact an individual's functioning in everyday life. In contrast, subtle memory declines that manifest as word- or name-finding difficulties may be more noticeable and relevant to common lifestyle activities, such as crossword puzzles or social interactions.

Ghisletta and colleagues (2006) also examined the relationship between changes in participation in lifestyle activities and perceptual speed but also examined verbal fluency as a cognitive outcome over a 5-year follow-up period. Similar to Lövdén et al. (2005), the results indicated that changes in lifestyle activity, measured by frequency of media activities (e.g., reading a book) and leisure activity (e.g., playing a game) were related to subsequent changes in perceptual speed. However, the results also indicated that other categories of lifestyle activities, including manual (e.g., gardening), external–physical (e.g., going for walks), social (e.g., attending cultural events), and religious (e.g., praying), were unrelated to changes in perceptual speed. Moreover, changes in the measure of verbal fluency were unrelated to changes in any of the six lifestyle activity domains.

Taken together, these results suggest that the DCSM statistical approach is relevant to the analysis of the relationship between active lifestyle and cognitive performance. In two studies, the analyses indicated that changes in active lifestyle preceded changes in cognitive performance, whereas the opposite was not true. Although these studies are informative, they also pose questions regarding whether there is

selectivity in terms of the cognitive activity domains that are relevant, as well as questions concerning the generality of effects on the outcome measure; that is, four domains of lifestyle activities were unrelated to cognitive performance in Ghisletta et al.'s (2006) study. Moreover, lifestyle activities were shown to be beneficial to perceptual speed but not to verbal ability in this same study.

OPTIMAL COGNITIVE ACTIVITY

To some extent, the research we have just reviewed questions whether there is an optimal frequency and type of activity that provides the greatest benefit to lessen age-related cognitive decline; that is, it asks whether some activities are more beneficial for cognitive performance than others. For example, it may be obvious that activities that engage cognitive abilities are more likely to result in gains in performance, as compared to less cognitively engaging lifestyle activities, but are there differences among the cognitively engaging activities themselves (e.g., crossword puzzles vs. Sudoku)?

We can broadly disassociate attempts to examine the relationship between activities and cognitive performance into those that focus on training of skills and those that emphasize or examine a broader experience of cognitive activity. The Advanced Cognitive Training for Independent and Vital Elderly trial (ACTIVE; Ball et al., 2002; Jobe et al., 2001) is an example of an intervention that focuses on the training of specific skills in relation to changes in cognitive performance. There are a number of benefits to a targeted intervention such as we see in the ACTIVE research. There is considerable experimental control and as a result, the reason for improvements in cognitive performance can more easily be identified and applied to other individuals. However, the main limitation of this type of intervention is the lack of transfer from the trained cognitive ability domain to other abilities. For example, Willis et al. (2006) reported that at a 5-year follow-up, after training sessions at baseline and Years 1 and 3 the memory, speed-of-processing, and reasoning groups showed cognitive benefits in the domains on which they were trained. However, aside from a significant effect in the speed-of-processing group on reasoning, there were no other cross-domain transfer effects. Furthermore, the reasoning group exhibited benefits in an instrumental activities of daily living measure, but no influence of reasoning, speed-of-processing, or memory training was seen in two tests of everyday cognition. This study suggests that training in these specific skills does improve performance on those trained domains both cross-sectionally (Ball et al., 2002) and longitudinally (Willis et al., 2006), but very little cross-domain transfer was observed.

The implication of this research from the standpoint of understanding the influence of lifestyle activities is that their cognitive benefit may be contingent upon the mental abilities they access during performance. For example, if a person regularly enjoys crossword puzzles, then his or her performance on measures of verbal fluency may be exercised, but it is unlikely that benefits to speed of processing would be realized, unless the crossword puzzle itself is timed. Thus, a systematic deconstruction of the types of cognitive skills that are activated during performance of leisure activities may be necessary to fully understand the source of influence. It is interesting that these types of deconstruction have been seen before in literature on expertise in chess (Ericsson & Charness, 1994), bridge playing (Charness, 1979), and even typing (Salthouse, 1984).

As an example of a controlled broader experiential intervention, we highlight recent work from the Experience Corps project (Fried et al., 2004; Tan, Xue, Li, Carlson, & Fried, 2006). This program is unique in that the intervention places older adults in elementary schools where they participate in a program targeting the academic outcomes of children in kindergarten through Grade 3. The program was designed to increase the participants' physical, social, and cognitive activity, in the hopes that this multipronged intervention would have additive effects on these outcomes. The results of a pilot test of this intervention have shown some effects, but in general they have been relatively modest (Fried et al., 2004). For example, at a 4- to 8-month follow-up, 69 persons were in the intervention group and 57 were in the control group. Results indicated that, relative to the control group, participants in the intervention group rated themselves as significantly more active at follow-up, rated themselves as stronger at follow-up, and experienced decreases in walking time. However, many other physical activity outcomes showed no difference between the intervention and control groups. For social activities, relative to the control group, participants in the intervention group reported contact with more people but did not differ on measures of emotional support. Finally, for cognitive activity, intervention group participants reported reductions in the number of hours of television watched per day but no differences in the participation of cognitively stimulating activities outside of the intervention materials. Taken together, an intervention such as that described by Experience Corps has possibilities to improve functioning, but currently the effects are relatively small in magnitude.

How Does an Active Lifestyle Buffer Age-Related Cognitive Decline?

Even if we are able to establish a relationship between lifestyle activities and cognitive performance, the question remains specifically how an active lifestyle influences age-related changes in cognitive performance. For example, in their conceptual model of the effects of Experience Corps training on cognitive performance, changes in brain structure and function are presupposed (Fried et al., 2004). But is there evidence to substantiate such claims?

The cognitive training literature includes some evidence that systematic training, such as that seen in the ACTIVE study, may result in changes to the brain activation patterns as seen with functional neuroimaging (Jones et al., 2006). For example, Nyberg et al. (2003), using the method of loci mnemonic technique, reported that older adults whose performance improved after learning the technique showed increased activation in the occipito-parietal area, relative to older adults who did not benefit from the training. Similarly, Draganski et al. (2004) reported that, after training on a three-ball juggling task, participants experienced an expansion of gray matter in the mid-temporal brain region.

Both Nyberg et al.'s (2003) and Draganski et al.'s (2004) studies suggest that focal training can result in changes to the structure and function of the brain. However, assessing whether participation in leisure activities results in brain changes is likely to be more difficult. Unlike in training studies, we are unable to randomly assign individuals to varied occupations or varied lifestyle activities. Moreover, the types of activities in which individuals participate likely reflect a lifetime of participation instead of activities that have been done just recently or within a circumscribed point in time. To evaluate a possible mechanism of action for overall activity patterns, information from the animal literature can be very informative (Milgram, Siwak-Tapp, Araujo, & Head, 2006). For example, rodents housed in environmentally enriched conditions have been shown to exhibit multiple structural brain changes, including hippocampal neurogenesis (Kemperman, Gast, & Gage, 2002) and increased dendritic branching and sprouting (Turner, Lewis, & King, 2003).

Arendash et al. (2004) reported that environmental enrichment improved the cognitive performance of aged, memory-impaired Alzheimer's transgenic mice. In a later study, these same investigators reported that environmental enrichment, when begun in young adulthood, protects Alzheimer's transgenic mice from otherwise certain cognitive impairment (Costa et al., 2007). Most recently, Arendash and colleagues examined the aspect of enrichment that resulted in greatest benefits to these Alzheimer's transgenic mice. Specifically, they dissected out the social activity, physical activity, and cognitive activity components of environmental enrichment to determine which exhibit the greatest effect on cognitive performance (Cracchiolo et al., 2007). Only animals in the cognitively enriched condition showed cognitive protection, decreased Alzheimer's neuropathology, and increased hippocampal synaptic formation. The authors concluded that physical and/or social activity are insufficient, in this sample, to result in protection against cognitive impairment in Alzheimer's mice. Although these studies were performed in mice, they nonetheless suggest that a high level of cognitive activity is critical to protecting against or reversing AD-like cognitive impairment.

CONCLUSION

As researchers continue to explore the question of whether participation in cognitive lifestyle activities buffer age-related cognitive decline, it becomes increasingly important to consider the relationships between the activities and the cognitive outcomes. Neither cognitively demanding lifestyle activities nor cognitive outcomes can be thought of as process pure. Completing a crossword puzzle requires access to one's vocabulary, including word meaning and spelling. With more challenging crossword puzzles, the person also has to consider multiple interpretations of the cues to find the intended meaning. Whereas vocabulary access is a relatively stable cognitive skill across the adult life span, using cues in flexible ways to come up with a relatively low-frequency meaning requires more fluid cognitive ability. Likewise, cognitive outcomes, such as memory performance, consist of multiple skills, some of which are relatively stable across the life span and others that show age decrements. Asking whether engagement in cognitively demanding activities can buffer cognitive decline is a fine place to start, but it is likely that results of these inquiries will continue to be mixed until we can more clearly match activities to outcomes. The relatively low rate of generalization observed in cognitive training studies suggests that matching is essential if we are going to observe consistent positive effects of either lifestyle activity changes or formal training on aspects of cognition.

Several issues are important, including whether lower level cognitive constructs, such as speed of processing, underlie higher-level cognitive outcomes, and whether lifestyle activities and occupations can effectively be decomposed into component cognitive skills. Both of these issues have been addressed to some extent in separate literatures, giving us a starting place for this discussion. Many researchers have shown that basic cognitive processes, such as attention or speed of processing, are components of higher-level outcome measures, such as reasoning (Salthouse & Ferrer-Caja, 2003). Much of the training literature is predicated on the notion that cognitive processing, as measured by speed-of-processing tasks, declines with age and that this produces much of the decline in cognitive outcomes. The obvious corollary is that improving speed of processing will improve all cognitive outcomes for which speed of processing is a component. Unfortunately, speed-of-processing training, like other forms of training, has not shown much generalization (although some generalization to driving ability has been observed; Roenker, Cissell, Ball, Wadley, & Edwards, 2003). It is probably reasonable to assume that, if generalization is going to occur across skills, it is most likely to occur at the level of generalizing from a component skill to a higher-level outcome instead of from one higher-level skill to a different higher level outcome skill. Given the current low level of such generalization, research probably needs to be more targeted to individual, matched skills.

This leads to the issue of whether we can effectively decompose lifestyle activities into component skills. This clearly is much more challenging than decomposing laboratory tasks. What are the component skills in a lifetime of accounting, or building design? Can we expect the former to maintain calculation ability and the latter to maintain spatial skills? Should we expect an award-winning architect to maintain calculation ability, or vocabulary access, at a greater level than would be predicted by level of education and other relevant variables? To the extent that generalization has not been easily found in training studies, we might answer "no" to the last question. However, to the extent that cognitive stimulation leads to neurogenesis or dendritic branching in brain regions shared by different cognitive tasks, generalization of the effects of lifestyle activities over long periods of adulthood may be observed. As we learn more about the biological bases of cognitive lifestyle activities and cognitive outcomes, we may be able to make better predictions about the buffering effects of those activities on cognition.

REFERENCES

Andel, R., Crowe, M., Pedersen, N. L., Mortimer, J. A., Crimmins, E., Johansson, B., et al. (2005). Complexity of work and risk of Alzheimer's disease: A population-based study of Swedish twins. *Journal of Gerontology: Psychological Sciences, 60B,* P251–P258.

Anstey, K., & Christensen, H. (2000). Education, activity, health, blood pressure, and aplipoprotein E as predictors of cognitive change in old age: A review. *Gerontology, 46,* 163–177.

Arendash, G. W., Garcia, M. F., Costa, D. A., Cracchiolo, J. R., Wefes, I. M., & Potter, H. (2004). Environmental enrichment improves cognition in aged Alzheimer's transgenic mice despite stable B-amyloid deposition. *Neuroreport, 15,* 1751–1754.

Ball, K., Berch, D. B., Helmers, K. F., Jobe, J. B., Leveck, M. D., Marsiske, M., et al. (2002). Effect of cognitive training interventions with older adults: A randomized controlled trial. *Journal of the American Medical Association, 288,* 2271–2281.

Baltes, P. B., & Mayer, K. U. (Eds.). (1999). *The Berlin Aging Study: Aging from 70 to 100.* New York: Oxford University Press.

Barnes, L. L., Wilson, R. S., Mendes de Leon, C. F., & Bennett, D. A. (2006). The relation of lifetime cognitive activity and lifetime access to resources to late-life cognitive function in older African Americans. *Aging, Neuropsychology, and Cognition, 13,* 516–528.

Bryk, A., & Raudenbush, S. (1992). *Hierarchical linear models in social and behavioral research.* Mahwah, NJ: Lawrence Erlbaum.

Charness, N. (1979). Components of skill in bridge. *Canadian Journal of Psychology–Revue Canadienne De Psychologie, 33,* 1–16.

Christensen, H., Korten, A. E., Jorm, A. F., Henderson, A. S., Scott, R., & Mackinnon, A. (1996). Activity levels and cognitive functioning in an elderly community sample. *Aging and Ageing, 25,* 72–91.

Costa, D. A., Cracchiolo, J. R., Bachstetter, A. D., Hughes, T. F., Bales, K. R., Paul, S. M., et al. (2007). Enriched housing improves cognition in AD mice by amyloid-related and unrelated mechanisms. *Neurobiology of Aging, 28,* 831–844.

Cracchiolo, J. R., Mori, T., Bachstetter, A., Mervis, R., Nazian, S. J., Tan, J., et al. (2007). Enhanced cognitive activity—over and above social or physical activity—is required to protect Alzheimer's mice against cognitive impairment, reduce Aβ deposition, and increase synaptic immunoreactivity. *Neurobiology of Learning and Memory, 88*(3), 277–294.

Draganski, B., Gaser, C., Busch, V., Schuierer, G., Bogdahn, U., & May, A. (2004, January 22). Changes in grey matter induced by training. *Nature, 427,* 311–312.

Duncan, T. E., Duncan, S. E., Stycker, L. A., Li, F., & Alpert, A. (1999). *An introduction to latent growth curve modeling: Concepts, issues, and applications.* Mahwah, NJ: Lawrence Erlbaum.

Einstein, G. O., & McDaniel, M. A. (2004). *Memory fitness: A guide for successful aging.* New Haven, CT: Yale University Press.

Ericsson, K. A., & Charness, N. (1994). Expert performance—Its structure and acquisition. *American Psychologist, 49,* 725–747.

Fried, L. P., Carlson, M. C., Freedman, M., Frick, K. D., Glass, T. A., Hill, J., et al. (2004). A social model for health promotion for an aging population: Initial evidence on the Experience Corps model. *Journal of Urban Health, 81,* 64–78.

Ghisletta, P., Bickel, J.-F., & Lövdén, M. (2006). Does activity engagement protect against cognitive decline in old age? Methodological and analytical considerations. *Journal of Gerontology: Psychological Sciences, 61B,* P253–P261.

Hultsch, D. F., Hammer, M., & Small, B. J. (1993). Age differences in cognitive performance in later life: Relationships to self-reported health and activity life style. *Journal of Gerontology, 48,* P1–P11.

Hultsch, D. F., Hertzog, C., Small, B. J., & Dixon, R. A. (1999). Use it or lose it: Engaged lifestyle as a buffer of cognitive decline in aging? *Psychology and Aging, 14,* 245–263.

Jobe, J. B., Smith, D. M., Ball, K., Tennstedt, S. L., Marsiske, M., Willis, S. L., et al. (2001). ACTIVE: A cognitive intervention to promote independence in older adults. *Controlled Clinical Trials, 22,* 453–479.

Jones, S., Nyberg, L., Sandblom, J., Stigsdotter Neely, A., Ingvar, M., Petersson, K. M., et al. (2006). Cognitive and neural plasticity in aging: General and task-specific limitations. *Neuroscience and Biobehavioral Reviews, 30,* 846–871.

Kemperman, G., Gast, D., & Gage, F. H. (2002). Neuroplasticity in old age: Sustained five-fold induction of hippocampal neurogenesis by long-term environmental enrichment. *Annals of Neurology, 52,* 135–143.

Kohn, M. L., & Schooler, C. (1978). The reciprocal effects of the substantive complexity of work and intellectual flexibility: A longitudinal assessment. *American Journal of Sociology, 84,* 24–52.

Kramer, A. F., & Willis, S. L. (2002). Enhancing the cognitive vitality of older adults. *Current Directions in Psychological Science, 11,* 173–177.

Lövdén, M., Bergman, L., Adolfsson, R., & Lindenberger, U. (2005). Studying individual aging in an interindividual context: Typical paths of age-related, dementia-related, and mortality-related cognitive development in old age. *Psychology and Aging, 20,* 303–316.

Mackinnon, A., Christensen, H., Hofer, S. M., Korten, A. E., & Jorm, A. F. (2003). Use it and still lose it? The association between activity and cognitive performance established using latent growth techniques in a community sample. *Aging, Neuropsychology, and Cognition, 10,* 215–229.

McArdle, J. J. (2001). A latent difference score approach to longitudinal dynamic structural analysis. In R. Cudeck, S. du Toit, & D. Sorbom (Eds.), *Structural equation modeling: Present and future* (pp. 341–380). Chicago: Scientific Software International.

McArdle, J. J., & Hamagami, F. (2001). Latent difference score structural models for linear dynamic analyses with incomplete longitudinal data. In L. M. Collins & A. G. Sayer (Eds.), *New methods for the analysis of change* (pp. 139–175). Washington, DC: American Psychological Association.

Milgram, N. W., Siwak-Tapp, C. T., Araujo, J., & Head, E. (2006). Neuroprotective effects of cognitive enrichment. *Ageing Research Reviews, 5,* 354–369.

Nyberg, L., Sandblom, J., Jones, S., Stigsdotter Neely, A., Petersson, K. M., Ingvar, M., et al. (2003). Neural correlates of training-related memory improvement in adulthood and aging. *Proceedings of the National Academy of Sciences, USA, 100,* 13728–13733.

Pushkar Gold, D., Andres, D., Etezadi, J., Arbuckle, T., Schwartzman, A. E., & Chaikelson, J. (1995). Structural equation modeling of intellectual change and continuity of predictors of intelligence in elderly men. *Psychology and Aging, 10,* 294–303.

Richards, M., Hardy, R., & Wadsworth, M. E. J. (2003). Does active leisure protect cognition? Evidence from a national birth cohort. *Social Science & Medicine, 56,* 785–792.

Roenker, D. L., Cissell, G. M., Ball, K. K., Wadley, V. G., & Edwards, J. D. (2003). Speed-of-processing and driving simulator training result in improved driving performance. *Human Factors, 45,* 218–233.

Salthouse, T. A. (1984). Effects of age and skill in typing. *Journal of Experimental Psychology-General, 113,* 345–371.

Salthouse, T. A., Berish, D. E., & Miles, J. D. (2002). The role of cognitive stimulation on the relations between age and cognitive functioning. *Psychology and Aging, 17,* 548–557.

Salthouse, T. A., & Ferrer-Caja, E. (2003). What needs to be explained to account for age-related effects on multiple cognitive variables? *Psychology and Aging, 18,* 91–110.

Schafer, J. L. (1997). *Analysis of incomplete multivariate data.* New York: Chapman and Hall.

Schooler, C. (1984). Psychological effects of complex environments during the life span: A review and theory. *Intelligence, 8,* 259–281.

Schooler, C. (1999). Social structure and the environment: Some basic theoretical issues. In A. Jasinska-Kania, M. L. Kohn, & K. M. Slomczynski (Eds.), *Power and social structure: Essays in honor of Wlodzimierz Wesolowski* (pp. 37–49). Warsaw, Poland: University of Warsaw Press.

Schooler, C., & Mulatu, M. S. (2001). The reciprocal effects of leisure time activities and intellectual functioning in older people: A longitudinal analysis. *Psychology and Aging, 16,* 466–482.

Schooler, C., Mulatu, M. S., & Oates, G. (1999). The continuing effects of substantively complex work on the intellectual functioning of older workers. *Psychology and Aging, 14,* 483–506.

Singer, J. D., & Willett, J. B. (2003). *Applied longitudinal data analysis: Modeling change and event occurrence.* New York: Oxford University Press.

Small, G. W., & Vorgan, G. (2006). *The longevity bible.* New York: Hyperion.

Stern, Y. (2002). What is cognitive reserve? Theory and research application of the reserve concept. *Journal of the International Neuropsychological Society, 8,* 448–460.

Stern, Y. (Ed.). (2007). *Cognitive reserve: Theory and applications.* New York: Taylor & Francis.

Stern, Y., Tang, M. X., Denaro, J., & Mayeux, R. (1995). Increased risk of mortality in Alzheimer's disease patients with more advanced educational and occupational attainment. *Annals of Neurology, 37,* 590–595.

Tan, E. J., Xue, Q.-L., Li, T., Carlson, M. C., & Fried, L. P. (2006). Volunteering: A physical activity intervention for older adults—The Experience Corps program in Baltimore. *Journal of Urban Health, 83,* 954–969.

Turner, C. A., Lewis, M. H., & King, M. A. (2003). Environmental enrichment: Effects on stereotyped behavior and dendritic morphology. *Developmental Psychobiology, 43,* 20–27.

Willett, J. B. (1989). Some results on reliability for the longitudinal measurement of change: Implications for the design of studies of individual growth. *Educational and Psychological Measurement, 49,* 587–602.

Willis, S. L., Tennstedt, S. L., Marsiske, M., Ball, K., Elias, J., Koepke, K. M., et al. (2006). Long-term effects of cognitive training on everyday functional outcomes in older adults. *Journal of the American Medical Association, 296,* 2805–2814.

Wilson, R. S., & Bennett, D. A. (2003). Cognitive activity and risk of Alzheimer's disease. *Current Directions in Psychological Science, 12,* 87–91.

Wilson, R. S., Bennett, D. A., Bienias, J. L., Mendes de Leon, C. F., Morris, M. C., & Evans, D. A. (2003). Cognitive activity and cognitive decline in a biracial community population. *Neurology, 61,* 812–816.

35

THE ADDED VALUE OF AN APPLIED PERSPECTIVE IN COGNITIVE GERONTOLOGY

MATTHIAS KLIEGEL, PETER RENDELL, AND MAREIKE ALTGASSEN

THE CLAIM

> For older adults, who often have special needs such as remembering to take medication and meeting health-related appointments, prospective memory functioning is of utmost importance. (Einstein & McDaniel, 1990, p. 717)

Einstein and McDaniel's (1990) seminal article laid the ground for a now-booming research area in applied cognitive gerontology: the study of age-related prospective memory performance (see, e.g., Kliegel, McDaniel, & Einstein, 2008; chap. 10, this volume). As with prospective memory, many experts in cognitive gerontology postulate that research on topics such as memory and other cognitive functions is of enormous importance because those processes are essential for everyday life (see Kliegel & Martin, 2003, for another example in prospective memory; see also Baddeley, 1998; Neath & Surprenant, 2003; and Ward & Morris, 2005, for examples in retrospective memory, executive function, attention, or planning). For instance, one of the major textbooks on adult development and aging, by Cavanaugh and Blanchard-Fields (2002), starts its introduction on memory in everyday life with the notion that research on age-related everyday cognitive functioning such as prospective memory is important for three reasons: (1) It may shed some light on the generalizability of findings based on laboratory tasks; (2) new or alternative variables affecting performance may be discovered; and (3) research on everyday cognitive functioning, such as everyday memory, may lead to a reconceptualization of those cognitive constructs.

In this chapter, we examine this claim and argue that although this postulation is ubiquitous in cognitive gerontology, the majority of empirical studies have so far mainly used these three propositions to motivate the laboratory work reported. In contrast, few attempts have been made to properly take its conceptual and methodological consequences into account. Focusing on two major constructs discussed in

AUTHORS' NOTE: Preparation of this chapter was supported in part by a grant from the Swiss National Science Foundation.

the area of applied cognitive gerontology (i.e., planning and prospective memory), we review and present data that demonstrate striking consequences that may emerge when one takes the applied nature of those constructs seriously. We do this in three steps. In the first step, we report evidence initially exploring what we actually know about older adults' everyday prospective memory functioning and how well current research paradigms of prospective memory are mirroring real life aspects of behavior. In the second step, which focuses on planning, we demonstrate that adopting more or less applied scenarios and material in laboratory settings may affect findings of potential age differences in cognitive performance. Moreover, we show that the choice of more or less applied task settings will enable or prevent older adults from utilizing compensatory processes that can be assumed to be of enormous relevance in their everyday functioning. Thus, in line with Cavanaugh and Blanchard-Fields (2002), we argue that using more or less applied paradigms in laboratory research on (applied) cognitive functions such as planning or prospective memory will not only influence the under- or overestimation of age differences but also affect detection of processes possibly underlying (age-related) performance. In a third step, again taking prospective memory as a paradigmatic example, we show that age-related performance—even when analyzing age differences within old age—can strongly depend on whether performance is measured in the laboratory or in real life. In each section we also discuss potential conceptual and methodological consequences of the data presented, and we include some suggestions for future cognitive gerontology. Note that we do not argue against laboratory research in cognitive gerontology because it has most successfully used clearly controlled material over many decades. The (sole) aim of this chapter is to initiate a discussion about the proposal that applied cognitive gerontology should take the applied character of the constructs under investigation even more seriously in order to not miss important aspects of age-related performance in cognitive functions such as planning or prospective memory. In our view, applied aspects of cognitive research (in gerontology) are not to be used only

for matters of justification of basic research or as tests of generalizability or ecological validity of basic research. We review data that we believe show that using more applied material in the laboratory and/or testing performance in real life may reveal novel and important aspects of the phenomena studied that would be missed otherwise.

THE MISSING LINK

Without an intact prospective memory it is scarcely possible to function independently in an everyday life context. An older person living independently must be able to remember to keep appointments, pay bills, take medicine and carry out domestic chores. (Cohen, 1996, p. 54)

Research on prospective memory and aging is seen as being timely and relevant because across the entire life span, but especially in old age, successful performance in real life prospective memory tasks will determine whether a person can lead an independent life. But what do we actually know about level of performance in older adults (and the determining mechanisms) in real life prospective memory tasks?

Surprisingly few studies have actually addressed this question. Three lines of research can be regarded as initially investigating real life prospective memory performance. One line of research uses the diary approach of asking participants to record their daily prospective memory performance. A second line is research on typical prospective memory tasks, such as medication adherence, and a third line assesses participants' self-evaluation of their everyday prospective memory abilities.[1]

Diary studies have mostly been conducted in the early days of prospective memory research and almost exclusively on young adults. Two studies in which young adults had to record their everyday memory failures suggested that prospective memory failures, such as forgetting to make a phone call or forgetting to do an assignment, constitute more than half of everyday memory problems (Crovitz & Daniel, 1984; Terry, 1988). Subsequent studies focused on prospective memory tasks and their characteristics. Ellis (1988) asked seven young adults to report on their everyday intentions for 10 days and then examined the dimensions of naturally occurring prospective memory tasks. Most intentions were revealed to fall in two categories: (1) *pulses*, that is, personally important intentions that can be realized only within a short period of time, and (2) *steps*, that is, less important intentions that may be satisfied over a longer time period. On 5 consecutive days, Ellis and Nimmo-Smith (1993) assessed eight younger adults' performance in real life prospective memory tasks and their spontaneous recollection of the intended activities. They found that intended activities often spontaneously pop into mind when an individual is concentrating less on a concurrent activity or when the concurrent activity is not very attention demanding. In three experiments, Marsh, Hicks, and Landau (1998) finally investigated the nature of and performance in real life prospective memory tasks among younger adults by assessing participants' intention planning and their later report of actual performance 5 or 7 days later. They also investigated whether the use of memory aids improves real life prospective memory performance—which was not the case, possibly because individuals who did not rely on external memory aids had greater memory and attentional capacities. Taken together, these studies reveal important dimensions that may influence prospective memory performance in everyday life. They do not, however, reveal much evidence of potential age differences and/or possible underlying mechanisms of age-related performance, or how well standard prospective memory tests reflect everyday functioning.

Most recently, Kvavilashvili and Fisher (2007) approached this gap using a diary approach to study (age-related) performance in a (experimenter-given) time-based prospective memory task that had to be executed in participants' daily lives. Participants were to remember to make a phone call at a chosen time on the 7th day following their initial meeting with the experimenter. Moreover, while being asked to refrain from using any external memory aids participants had to keep a structured diary throughout the week and were asked to record every instance when they recalled or rehearsed their intention to make the phone call. In one of the three studies described by Kvavilashvili and

Fisher, age differences were explored. Here, 36 younger adults and 38 older adults reported a total of 868 rehearsals during the week with a mean of 12.40 (SD = 6.64, range: 2–26) per person. In terms of accuracy, 2 younger and 1 older adult did not call at all. Seventy-eight percent of the participants called on time, and there was no significant age effect in prospective memory performance. There was also no age effect on number of rehearsals, and both age groups showed a J-shaped pattern, with increasing rehearsal frequency in the final days. Most important for the purpose of the present chapter, this finding is in sharp contrast to many laboratory studies that have revealed substantial age deficits in time-based prospective memory tasks as well as reduced strategic monitoring in older adults (e.g., Einstein, McDaniel, Richardson, Guynn, & Cunfer, 1995; Kliegel, Ramuschkat, & Martin, 2003; Park, Hertzog, Kidder, Morrell, & Mayhorn, 1997). In consequence, Kvavlishavili and Fisher's study seems to indicate that in real life older adults may have many fewer problems in a cognitive task such as time-based prospective memory than what the broad experimental evidence on age-related prospective memory performance implies. We return to the dichotomy of findings from laboratory research and research assessing experimenter-given prospective memory tasks in everyday life later in this chapter. For the moment, one might conclude that in everyday life prospective memory performance is spared from cognitive aging. However, as indicated above, Kvavilashvili and Fisher (2007) did not really assess everyday prospective memory performance, because the task was provided by the experimenter and—more important—participants were asked to refrain from using any external aids or reminders and had to keep a diary; all in all, not really a typical, everyday-like prospective memory situation.

Research on medication adherence has aimed at investigating the naturally occurring prospective memory task of taking medication in time (note that this task is regarded as a central everyday prospective memory task because it is referred to very frequently in introduction sections of empirical articles reporting on age differences in prospective memory as well as in the two quotes cited previously by Cohen, 1996, and Einstein & McDaniel, 1990). Although the pattern is complex, several studies have shown that older adults are not necessarily worse, and sometimes are even better, at remembering to take medication on time. In particular, work by Park and colleagues has demonstrated that the overall rate of medication adherence errors is very low (e.g., Park, Morrell, Frieske, & Kincaid, 1992) and that young-old adults often perform even better than middle-age adults, despite showing the expected decline in basic cognitive resources such as working memory, speed of processing, and long-term memory (e.g., Morell, Park, Kidder, & Martin, 1997; Park et al., 1999). It is interesting that contextual factors such as busyness of lifestyle were the best predictors of this everyday prospective memory task, and Wilson and Park (2008) concluded that in the prospective memory task of medication adherence "context may take precedence over cognition" (p. 399).

Taken together data again seem to indicate that, in contrast to many laboratory results, in everyday life prospective memory performance of healthy older adults seems to be fairly well preserved (e.g., Kliegel, Eschen, & Thöne-Otto, 2004; Kliegel & Jäger, 2006b; Kliegel, Martin, & Moor, 2003; Kliegel, McDaniel, & Einstein, 2000).[2] Thus, one important issue to be targeted in the future is to actually relate laboratory research and the paradigms used to study naturally occurring prospective memory situations. In other words, to what extent does laboratory task performance reflect everyday prospective memory functioning—conceptually and empirically?

A recent approach to relate laboratory task performance to indicators of everyday functioning is to use standardized questionnaires in which participants self-evaluate their everyday prospective memory performance. An instrument that has been given some attention so far is the Prospective Retrospective Memory Questionnaire (PRMQ; Crawford, Henry, Ward, & Blake, 2006; Smith, Della Sala, Logie, & Maylor, 2000). The PRMQ was designed to disentangle self-rated prospective and retrospective memory performance in everyday life, which contrasts with previous self-reports of memory ability that did not differentiate prospective and retrospective memory functioning. Specifically, the PRMQ assesses how often errors in everyday prospective and retrospective memory tasks

occur. Factor analyses revealed that a tripartite structure model best fits the PRMQ scores, that is, a general memory factor and two orthogonal specific factors of prospective and retrospective memory (Crawford, Smith, Maylor, Della Sala, & Logie, 2003). These factors are captured using 16 items that are equally divided between a Prospective Memory subscale and a Retrospective Memory subscale that assess everyday prospective and retrospective errors, respectively.

In two studies, we and our colleagues recently started to test the link between age-related performance in typical laboratory prospective memory tasks and self-rated real life prospective memory performance. What can we learn from performance in laboratory tasks about how a person perceives his or her actual everyday performance? A clear limitation of this line of research is that subjective ratings of everyday memory performance are somewhat different from actual, everyday memory performance; with ratings being influenced by other factors, such as personality and depressive tendencies (e.g., Bolla, Lindgren, Bonaccorsy, & Bleeker, 1991; Kliegel & Zimprich, 2005; Kliegel, Zimprich, & Eschen, 2005; Lane & Zelinski, 2003; Zimprich, Martin, & Kliegel, 2003). However, as long as no study has actually compared both age-related laboratory test performance and performance in a range of real life prospective memory challenges,[3] self-rating data do at least approximate participants' everyday performance (especially when one statistically takes into account potential factors of influence, e.g., depressive tendencies).

In a first study, Kliegel and Jäger (2006a) assessed a life span sample of 87 adults (mean age = 44.11, SD = 18.94). Two laboratory-based tasks were administered as objective prospective memory measures: (1) an event-based task and (2) a time-based task. For both tasks, a two-back working memory task was used as the ongoing activity. Participants were presented with pseudo-random sequences of the Snodgrass and Vanderwart (1980) pictures. By pressing designated keys, participants indicated whether the same picture had occurred two trials before. The dependent variable was the number of correct responses (number of correct rejections plus hits). For the event-based prospective memory task participants were told to press a target key whenever an animal picture was displayed during the *n*-back task. Five prospective cues were presented. Answers were scored as correct if they occurred within 5 seconds after cue presentation. For the time-based prospective memory task participants were instructed to press a target key every 2 minutes as exactly as possible (again five times). Answers were scored as correct if they occurred within a time window of 5 seconds (± 2.5 seconds) around the prospective target times (cf. Kliegel, Jäger, et al., 2005; Kliegel, Martin, McDaniel, & Einstein, 2001). The PRMQ was used as an indicator of subjective everyday prospective and retrospective memory performance. Higher scores on the Prospective and Retrospective subscales point to more reported everyday memory failures.

Analyses of the PRMQ showed that participants reported significantly more difficulties with prospective ($M = 18.16$, $SD = 4.20$) than with retrospective remembering ($M = 16.48$, $SD = 3.84$). In contrast to previous findings (e.g., Crawford et al., 2003), in Kliegel and Jäger's (2006a) sample, higher scores on the Total scale were associated with older age ($r = .23$, $p < .05$), an effect that was mainly due to the Retrospective scale ($r = .27$, $p < .05$) rather than the Prospective scale ($r = .17$, $p = .12$).[4] Correlational analyses were conducted to examine whether laboratory-based tasks may predict self-rated prospective memory performance in the real world as measured by the PRMQ. Laboratory-based prospective memory performance was the only significant predictor for self-rated everyday prospective memory performance (time-based performance: $r = -.22$, $p < .05$; for event-based prospective memory, this relation approached significance: $r = -.19$, $p = .08$) and was not a significant predictor of self-rated retrospective memory performance. Thus, prospective memory performance in the laboratory was able to differentially predict everyday prospective remembering.

In a second study, Zeintl, Kliegel, Rast, and Zimprich (2006) focused on older adults only and used a large-scale sample. Moreover, noncognitive factors, such as depressive symptoms and subjective metamemory beliefs, were assessed to evaluate their influence on subjective memory ability. Three hundred sixty-four older

adults took part (mean age = 73.0 years, $SD = 4.43$). They were recruited as part of Wave 1 of the Zurich Longitudinal Study on Cognitive Aging. Prospective memory performance was assessed with the Red Pencil task (Dobbs & Rule, 1987), in which participants were instructed to repeat the words "red pencil" whenever the experimenter said them during the testing session (three times). The dependent variable was the proportion of correct responses, whereby higher scores point to better performance. As an indicator of self-rated prospective memory performance in everyday life, again the PRMQ was administered. To measure depressive symptoms, the Geriatric Depression scale was applied, and to assess metamemory beliefs the Capacity scale of the Metamemory in Adulthood Questionnaire was administered.

The data showed that, within the sample of older adults, self-rated everyday prospective memory functioning was not related to age. Moreover, the complete sample results did not reveal a significant relation between laboratory-based prospective memory performance and self-rated everyday prospective memory functioning. However, when subdividing the sample according to subjective everyday prospective memory performance, different patterns were found for both subgroups. Laboratory-based prospective memory performance was a significant predictor of everyday prospective memory ratings only for high everyday performers. For low performers (i.e., high complainers about everyday prospective memory problems), subjective everyday performance was significantly related to depressive symptoms and subjective memory capacity, but not with prospective memory test performance.

Consequently, and in line with previous research (e.g., Kliegel & Zimprich, 2005), prospective memory test performance may be related to subjective everyday prospective memory only when there are no depressive symptoms overshadowing memory ratings. Thus, as indicated above, we acknowledge that self-ratings do not reflect most accurately real life performance. However, they provide initial directions and those show that performance in prospective memory laboratory tasks indeed is at least significantly related to older adults' self-perceptions of prospective memory performance in everyday life; note that this relation seems to be more pronounced than in most retrospective memory tasks (Hertzog & Hultsch, 2000). However, the relation is still rather weak (~.22). Hence, current laboratory tasks do not seem to capture features well that reflect everyday prospective memory challenges. It is likely that tasks using more contextualized material might be one way of approaching this issue. So far, no study has systematically tested this assumption in the field of prospective memory. In the next section, therefore, we turn to a related field in which we have addressed this question in more details: planning. Regarding the previous section on current knowledge about everyday prospective memory functioning in old age, one has to conclude that we currently do not know much at all, neither about everyday prospective memory performance per se nor about possible age differences in level of performance or factors that might differentially influence age-related everyday prospective memory functioning. Hence, future research should find ways to assess performance in naturally occurring prospective memory tasks and thus to analyze prospective memory performance in real life and empirically and conceptually relate everyday performance to measures used for research purposes

REALISTIC LABORATORY TESTING MATERIAL CAN UNCOVER NEW INSIGHTS IN BASIC PROCESSING

In this section, we report on two studies that have systematically approached the questions of what influence more or less realistic test material may have on adult age differences in laboratory planning performance and on the processes underlying (age-related) performance.

In the first study, Phillips, Kliegel, and Martin (2006) investigated adult age effects on abstract and more contextualized planning tasks in the same participants. In addition, the role of processing speed and inhibition was assessed. Thirty-nine young (M = 24.8 years, SD = 2.0) and 39 older (M = 69.5, SD = 5.5) adults participated. Both groups completed a computerized version of a traditional laboratory planning task: the Tower of London (TOL; Shallice, 1982). This untimed task requires participants to shift discs with the fewest possible moves from a given

start state to a given end state (see Figure 35.1, left panel). The dependent variable was the difference between the minimum number of moves to solve 10 tasks and the actual number of moves needed by a participant. As a more contextualized laboratory planning measure, the Plan-a-Day test (PAD; Funke & Krüger, 1993) was applied. Here, participants complete errands in a fictitious real life work setting on a computer while considering constraints with respect to errand priority and time course. As a fictitious employee of a company, each participant is required to carry out as many appointments as possible during a day. Participants are presented with a map of the buildings of the company on the computer screen (see Figure 35.1, right panel). Each appointment needs to be completed at a specific time or time window, and distances between locations need to be considered. With the help of certain keys, participants can see the appointments they have to schedule and can delete or modify plan elements. After having correctly completed a practice trial, the test block starts. It comprises 2 days, and for each of them seven tasks need to be planned in 20 minutes of test time. The dependent variable is the number of errands carried out weighted with their priority. In addition, speed of processing was measured with the Digit-Symbol Substitution Test (Wechsler, 1981), and inhibition was measured with the Stroop test (Stroop, 1935).

The results revealed greater age differences in a laboratory-based planning task (TOL) than in the more contextualized planning task (PAD). Young adults showed a significantly better planning efficacy in the TOL task in comparison to older adults. However, most important, no significant age effects emerged on the PAD task despite it being a complex and timed task in which multiple task elements and constraints had to be considered simultaneously. Both planning tasks correlated significantly with processing speed and education. Thus, both tasks seem to be influenced by processing speed, which declines considerably with age. Further analyses showed that age differences in TOL performance might result from a global cognitive change and not from a specific executive function deficit, because processing speed but not inhibition explained age-related variance. In

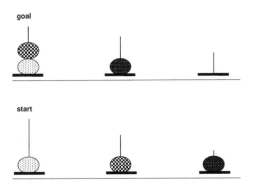

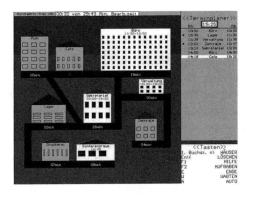

Figure 35.1   Pictorial Examples of the Tower of London (*Left*) and the Plan-a-Day Task (*Right*) as Used in Phillips et al. (2006)

SOURCE: PAD figure reprinted with permission of Dr. Joachim Funke, University of Heidelberg. Copyright © Funke & Krüger.

contrast, in hierarchical regression analyses, age-related PAD performance was mainly predicted by individual differences in crystallized intelligence. In sum, data indicate that age effects on laboratory tasks such as the TOL may not necessarily indicate poor planning ability in more contextualized everyday-like laboratory tasks, because knowledge-based strategies may compensate for older adults' slowed processing on more realistic tasks (Marsiske, Lang, Baltes, & Baltes, 1995).

Because the two planning tasks in Phillips et al.'s (2006) study did of course differ in many aspects besides being more or less contextualized, in a second study, Kliegel, Martin, McDaniel, and Phillips (2007) investigated the role of task familiarity and cognitive resources in adult age differences in planning performance by modifying task familiarity in the same errand planning task. On the basis of the data found by Phillips et al. (2006), Kliegel, Martin, McDaniel, and Fisher (2007) assumed that even though planning is a resource demanding task, older adults may perform as well as young adults under familiar circumstances. Tasks were parallelized on structure, difficulty, and format, and they varied only the surface structure of the tasks to be planned so that they either involved planning a real world shopping tour or an artificial space tour. A total of 104 individuals, 52 young ($M = 25.6$, $SD = 5.3$) and 52 older ($M = 70.9$, $SD = 6.2$) adults participated. Groups did not differ with respect to gender or years of education. A 2 (age: young vs. older adults) × 2 (planning task features: real world vs. artificial) between-subjects design was used, with 26 participants of each age group assigned to one of the two planning conditions.

Following up on a task previously used by Bisiacchi and colleagues (Bisiacchi, 1996; Bisiacchi, Sgaramella, & Farinello, 1998) participants planned a sequence of six activities. For the real world planning task, participants were provided with a town map of the area where they had to complete their six errands: (1) paying an electricity bill, (2) withdrawing money from the bank to pay the bill, (3) visiting a friend in the hospital, (4) getting holiday pictures to show the friend in the hospital, (5) buying a birthday present for a nephew, and (6) getting medicine for oneself. Participants were asked to make a plan for performing as many of the tasks as possible and using the shortest possible route. Thus, individuals had to sequence errands, schedule actions, and logically order goals (e.g., they had to realize that they first need to withdraw money from the bank to later pay the bill). In addition, they had to consider constraints regarding task settings: start time and time when they had to return home, opening hours of shops/offices, and distances between locations. Moreover, irrelevant information was included in the map (i.e., irrelevant places), in the distance information, and the instructions (i.e., why the friend is in the hospital). Participants were given 10 minutes to set up their plan, which they then wrote down on a prepared answer sheet. Scoring of the plan's quality closely followed that of Bisiacchi (1996;

Bisiacchi et al., 1998), taking into account the number of planned errands and avoidance of errors (e.g., paying the bill before obtaining the money or paying no attention to opening hours).

The artificial planning task was matched to the real world task on structure, difficulty, and format. Instructions were analogous those in to the real world condition; however, the setting, errands, and task constraints were put into an unfamiliar, novel setting. Participants were asked to plan a sequence of six errands consisting of paying their taxes at Planet A (real world version: paying an electricity bill), getting gold from Planet B to pay the taxes (real world version: withdrawing money from the bank to pay the bill), visiting a politician at Planet C (real world version: visiting a friend in the hospital), getting documents to show the politician (real world version: getting holiday pictures to show the friend in the hospital), buying a birthday present for the 20th birthday of a nephew (real world version: buying a birthday present for a nephew), and getting medicine plants for oneself (real world version: getting medicine for oneself). Again, participants were given an outer space map of the area and asked to prepare a plan while taking constraints into account and being confronted with irrelevant information (e.g., why the politician is at the specific planet). Participants were given 10 minutes to prepare their plan and to write it down on the same prepared answer sheet as in the real world condition.

In both task conditions memory for relevant versus irrelevant task features was evaluated to assess the allocation of (more or less limited) processing resources to specific aspects of the task. Following Martin and Ewert (1997), participants were asked 10 questions about relevant information (e.g., both versions: "What did you have to buy for your nephew?") and 10 questions about irrelevant information of the planning task (e.g., "Where on the map is the school/Planet P?"). Martin and Ewert showed that resource allocation to task-relevant information in errand planning tasks can be evaluated by the difference between correct answers to irrelevant questions minus correct answers to relevant questions. In addition, memory capacity, inhibition, and speed of processing were assessed.

Groups differed significantly on these three basic cognitive measures and on the two

planning tasks. The age effect on planning was, however, qualified by a significant Age × Task Version interaction. Separate post hoc tests showed that age differences were observed only in the artificial and not in the real world task version. Thus, older adults appeared to be able to compensate for their cognitive deficits in the more familiar planning task but not in the novel task. To initially explore a possible compensatory mechanism, Kliegel, Martin, et al. (2007) analyzed memory for relevant versus irrelevant task features. It is important to note that, in contrast to the traditional measures of cognitive processing resources, there was a significant interaction of memory for relevant versus irrelevant task features with age. Older adults showed better performance than young adults in the familiar task, whereas the opposite pattern emerged in the novel planning task condition.

When the discovered age differences in the assessed variables were interrelated, a striking picture emerged. First, cognitive resources (i.e., speed of processing and inhibition) contributed to the overall age effect in planning performance, which could be expected and is consistent with previous results (e.g., Salthouse, 1993; Zacks & Hasher, 1994). Second, and most interesting, the interaction between age and task familiarity, could be predicted by taking memory for relevant versus irrelevant task features into account. This seems to indicate that older adults may have been able to compensate for their basic cognitive resource deficit by focusing on relevant and ignoring irrelevant information. However, this effect emerged only in the familiar task version. Consequently, selecting relevant information may be seen as a potential compensatory process that could be detected only in the more applied setting.

Taken together, data show three things:

1. The issue of whether older adults will have specific problems with planning tasks will heavily depend on the methodological approach chosen to test this question.

2. When solely relying on traditional laboratory paradigms such as the TOL, besides underestimating older adults' planning performance in real life situations we may also overestimate

the influence age deficits in basic cognitive resources can have on performance in complex real life situations.

3. Compensatory processes that actually support and protect everyday performance—either used consciously or without conscious control—could be masked when research paradigms do not allow these compensatory processes to emerge.

All three of these conclusions strongly argue for the use of more applied task materials in future cognitive gerontology—to explicitly contrast age-related performance in more or less everyday-like materials and to study the mechanisms that potentially differentially underlie performance in both assessment procedures. We expect that this approach will greatly contribute to the understanding of compensatory processes associated with successful cognitive aging.

It is important to note that if these effects are observed by constructing laboratory task procedures as more or less mirroring everyday-like situations, then even stronger effects can be expected when test settings are moved out of the laboratory and into participants' everyday lives. Accordingly, in the next section we show a unique paradox that has been revealed in research on prospective memory and aging that strongly argues for more work on everyday memory functioning to actually take place in everyday life.

THE LABORATORY-NATURALISTIC SETTING AGE-PROSPECTIVE MEMORY PARADOX AND ITS POTENTIAL FOR APPLIED BASIC COGNITIVE GERONTOLOGY

Across all PM [prospective memory] conditions, highly significant effects were revealed, although the direction of the effect was dependent on location. Thus, whereas laboratory locations were associated with substantial age-related deficits . . . , naturalistic locations were associated with substantial age advantages. . . . This suggests that even if aging is associated with a decline in the basic processes involved in PM (which is probable given the greater experimental control associated with laboratory studies), this does not translate to

deficits in everyday life. (Henry, MacLeod, Phillips, & Crawford, 2004, p. 32)

In their influential meta-analysis on age-related prospective memory performance, Henry et al. (2004) observed a consistent pattern of age *advantage* across naturalistic tasks and a less consistent pattern in reverse direction for laboratory studies. This pattern has been described as the *age-prospective memory paradox*: It was demonstrated with the same participants in both settings (Rendell & Thomson, 1999), as well as with parallel tasks in each setting (Rendell & Craik, 2000). Both findings were confirmed in Henry et al.'s meta-analysis, and the age-prospective memory paradox has recently started to attract increasing attention (see Phillips, Henry, & Martin, 2008, for a review).

At face value it seems the paradox appears to be either a watertight case for advocating ecologically valid methods or convincing evidence for controlled laboratory methods. As robust as this starkly contrasting finding appears to be, it seems to point toward the conclusion that older adults are being underestimated in tasks that lack an applied perspective. Alternatively, it may be that in naturalistic studies older adults are using extraordinary means to cover up the difficulty they demonstrate in laboratory studies, pointing to the conclusion that controlled experiments are needed to accurately portray the age-related pattern. As indicated previously, we argue that these alternatives are too simplistic and that the paradox points toward the conclusions not only that basic research can benefit from the inclusion of plausible, more applied tasks but that also the explicit consideration of the context or setting in which a task is embedded will make a difference in uncovering crucial aspects of age-related cognitive performance. In this regard, the paradox demonstrates the need to more frequently include parallel task versions for both settings to ascertain the contribution of the setting. Note that we argue that the contribution of the setting is worth *direct* investigation as an important factor rather than a potential confound to be eliminated or dismissed.

It is interesting that when reporting this paradox, Rendell and Thomson (1999), observed that a frequent initial response to this finding has been to attempt to dismiss or explain it away. Favored

explanations invoked involve age-related disparity in motivation levels and the use of external
aids (which, in our view, per se, constitute important aspects of age-related responses to prospective memory challenges). Accordingly, in their
review on age-related prospective memory performance, Phillips et al. (2008) reported that
these explanations are favored in the literature,
despite the lack of experimental research that has
actually investigated motivation as a potential
factor associated with the paradox (see Kliegel,
Phillips, & Fischer, 2004, for initial evidence that
task importance may indeed be related to this
finding), the limited evidence supporting use of
aids as explanation of paradox, and the mounting
evidence that is contrary to the use-of-aids
explanation (d'Ydewalle & Brunfaut, 1996;
Maylor, 1990; Park et al., 1997; Patton & Meit,
1993; Rendell & Craik, 2000; Rendell &
Thomson, 1999).

In this section, we aim at taking the empirical
and conceptual implications of the paradox one
step further. Including the recent review of the
paradox presented by Phillips et al. (2008), so far,
discussions of the paradox have focused solely on
the comparison of young adults and older adults.
However, as we demonstrate in this section, the
effects of an applied setting extend to age differences *within* the older age range. This novel perspective provides even more striking evidence that
the understanding of age-related prospective
memory performance will greatly benefit from
explicitly targeting the consequences of different
task procedures and settings on performance.
Specifically, we extend the analysis of the paradox by examining contrasting findings between
young-old adults (60s to around mid-70s) and
old-old adults (from around mid-70s up).
Extending the level of analyses to age-related performance within the older age range will thereby
provide some new insights into the effects that the
setting, the time period, and the features of the
tasks applied might have on the level of environmental support and thereby on potential age differences. In this extended level of age-related
analysis we also argue against a substantial
explanatory role of cohort differences in personality, attitude toward punctuality or even lifestyle,
because these possible cohort differences dissi-
pate substantially when the comparisons are made
between older adults barely 10 years apart.

First, we re-examine data and procedures initially reported by Rendell and Thomson (1993,
1999). In sum, they have shown that older adults
were superior to young adults on the task of logging time at set times across their everyday time
course and that older adults were consistently
superior even when daily frequency was varied
(Rendell & Thomson, 1993) and when complexity and regularity of schedules, opportunity to
use external reminders, and conjunction cues
were varied (Rendell & Thomson, 1999).
Another pattern, which is not usually highlighted
but is focused on here, is the equivalent performance of young-old and old-old adults. In
Rendell and Thomson's (1999) Experiment 2, 80
young-old (60–69 years) and 80 old-old (70+)
adults did not significantly differ across the variations in complexity and regularity of the everyday time logging task, but the old-old adults
were significantly worse than young-old adults
on retrospective memory tasks and laboratory
prospective memory tasks (Experiment 3). It is
important to note that although the participants
were the same in each setting, the prospective
memory tasks were not analogous; thus, the
question remains: Which aspects of the setting
could have been associated with this contrasting
finding? One of the laboratory prospective memory tasks required participants to remember to
note the time they finished a questionnaire and
the other task required that they stop a stop-clock
after 7 minutes. From a conceptual perspective,
it appears to be important to note that the stop-
clock task in the laboratory session and the time-
logging task in the naturalistic setting were both
time based, but the laboratory version involved
judging that an arbitrary period of time (7 minutes) had passed, whereas the naturalistic
version had times of day as the set target.
This responding at set times of day is a feature
of many of the naturalistic studies that have
found older adults to be superior to young
adults (Devolder, Brigham, & Pressley, 1990;
Moscovitch, 1982; West, 1988). Although not
explicitly examined in the original studies, we
suggest that these task differences, involving different time-based tasks, are a likely explanation
for the contrasting age-related performance in
each setting (Rendell & Thomson, 1999). The
older adults remembered to log the time on average about 70% of the set times, suggesting that

ceiling effects were not an explanation why old-old adults performed as well as young-old adults. Also, lifestyle—or, more specifically, busyness—is an unlikely explanation for the results including only the older sample, because level of occupation did not significantly affect performance in the time logging task. We acknowledge, however, that those post hoc analyses still remain to be directly tested.

To take those conclusions one step further, we also reanalyzed Rendell and Craik's (2000) data, applying the conceptual perspective described above. Rendell and Craik explicitly addressed the issue of task differences with analogous prospective memory tasks in the laboratory and naturalistic setting with Virtual Week, and Actual Week. Virtual Week is a board game that simulates 7 days of daily activities, and Actual Week involves the replication of Virtual Week over 7 calendar days in real life. As in the previous studies, the typical paradoxical age-related pattern was found, with young adults being superior to older adults in Virtual Week and with young adults being inferior to the older adults in Actual Week. This seems to suggest that the paradox may not reflect the greater structure of older adults' lives. However, at present the evidence for this conclusion is rather limited, because Virtual Week may have initially approximated the structure of daily life with a set of repeated regular "daily" activities that still did not capture what could be key elements in real life: the personal familiarity and predictability of the daily activities for older adults. In addition, participants in Virtual Week discover the pattern of daily events as the virtual day unfolds, but in daily life older adults are probably aware of the likely pattern of activities before the day starts.

More conclusive evidence on possible mechanisms of age-related performance in laboratory and real life settings comes from a conceptual re-examination of Rendell and Craik's (2000) data following up on the previously outlined considerations regarding task features. Again, this reanalysis focuses on the pattern of young-old versus old-old adults and reveals novel and more complex age-related trends for the different settings. As can be seen in Figure 35.2, on one of the types of tasks (the irregular tasks; i.e., tasks that were different on each day [e.g., Today please phone the plumber at 4:00 p.m.]), the older adults showed much better performance in the naturalistic than in the laboratory setting. In addition, the old-old were worse than young-old adults in the laboratory setting but equivalent in the naturalistic setting, which replicates the pattern found by Rendell and Thomson (1999). However, on the other two types of tasks (regular and time check tasks; i.e., tasks simulating medication adherence at set times and a task in which the participant had to inform the experimenter at an arbitrary time, e.g., when the stopclock [which was in full view] showed 2 minutes, 30 seconds in Virtual Week) the performance of the two older groups on Virtual Week matched their performance in Actual Week. A conceptual re-examination of these tasks reveals two possible critical features: (1) whether the prospective memory target is relatively focal to the ongoing activity, in particular having a time of day as target compared with judging the passing of an arbitrary period of time, and (2) the demands of the retrospective memory component, in particular the complexity of the task content (see also chap. 10, this volume, for a conceptual framework generally highlighting the importance of those two features in age-related prospective memory performance).

In a study on prospective memory performance in a clinical context, focalness was recently proposed as a potentially critical feature for time-based tasks in Virtual Week by Rendell, Jensen, and Henry (2007). This distinction between focal versus nonfocal tasks had previously been proposed only for event-based tasks (e.g., Einstein & McDaniel, 2005). In general, tasks in which the target events are focal to the processing required for the ongoing activity are presumed to depend more on automatic processes, and tasks with nonfocal target events are presumed to depend more on strategic processes. Age differences on event-based prospective memory tasks have been reduced when the target event is focal rather than nonfocal (e.g., Rendell, McDaniel, Forbes, & Einstein, 2007). In their clinical study, Rendell, Jensen, and Henry (2007) suggested that the regular time-based task in Virtual Week (simulating medication adherence at set times) is relatively focal and the time check task (informing the experimenter when a specific time has

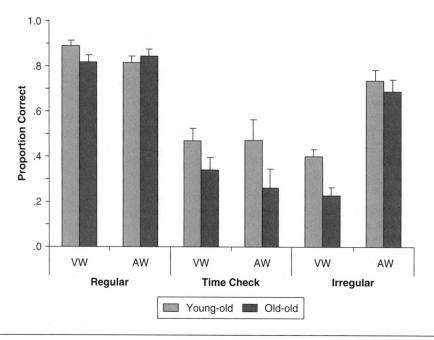

Figure 35.2   Re-Examination of Rendell and Craik's (2000) Prospective Memory Results With a Focus on Young-Old Adults Compared With Old-Old Adults

NOTE: Virtual Week (VW) is the laboratory task, and Actual Week (AW) is the naturalistic task.

elapsed) is relatively nonfocal. Both are regular in that they involve a hypothetical medication task that is the same each day or virtual day. The tasks are distinguished by having time of day or virtual time for the regular focal task and having the elapsing of an arbitrary time period that is independent of the ongoing activity for the regular nonfocal (time check) task. In Virtual Week, as participants circulate the board in simulation of day, the virtual time is cued by activities relevant to the virtual time, and the passing of each hour is marked by passing the squares with the time clearly marked. In daily life, the structured pattern of daily activities also could provide strong cues for the time of day, especially when time targets are neat hourly times (e.g., 1:00 p.m. or 4:00 p.m.).

This re-examination of Rendell and Craik's (2000) data suggests that one element contributing to the paradoxical age-related findings is the use of different time-based tasks in the laboratory compared with naturalistic studies that provide more or less environmental support and thus lead to differential age effects even across

the older age range. Consistent with this line of reasoning, the regular time-based tasks were similar to the typical naturalistic tasks in previous studies that have shown age benefits of older adults being better than young adults (e.g., naturalistic studies requiring participants to phone the experimenter at a set time over several days; Devolder et al., 1990; Moscovitch, 1982; West, 1988). In contrast, the time-check task was more similar to typical time-based tasks in previous laboratory studies that have demonstrated age-related deficits, where participants have to judge the elapsing of an arbitrary time period (e.g., Einstein et al., 1995; Kliegel, Ramuschkat, & Martin, 2003; Park et al., 1997).

The claim that the level of retrospective memory demands may also be a critical feature in this paradox can be addressed by comparing the regular and irregular tasks in each setting. The regular tasks are the same medication tasks each day, whereas the irregular tasks are different each day, for example, phone the plumber at 4:00 p.m. and have a haircut at 2:00 p.m. These tasks differ systematically in relation to the retrospective memory demands of the task content. One could argue that remembering the content of 28 different irregular tasks requires more processing resources than remembering the content of the same two regular tasks 14 times each (note that the latter task demands are quite similar to the task demands in the medication adherence studies described previously). The tasks both have targets that are times and events within the ongoing activity. On the regular tasks, with focal targets and relatively low retrospective memory demands, old-old and young-old adults did not differ, and the older adults were relatively accurate in both laboratory and naturalistic settings. On irregular tasks, with focal targets and relatively high retrospective memory demands, older adults' performance differed in laboratory and naturalistic settings. As noted, the older adults performed much better in the naturalistic setting than in the laboratory setting, and the old-old adults were significantly worse than young-old adults in the laboratory setting but did not differ in the naturalistic setting. So it seems that when the prospective memory tasks have targets that are times of day and events within daily life, then older adults are able to compensate for the difficulties they have on prospective memory tasks that have demanding retrospective memory components. How they compensate should be an interesting variable to directly study in the future rather than a confound inherent to naturalistic studies. A potentially critical feature is the longer time period of naturalistic tasks (several days) compared with laboratory tasks (1 or 2 hours), with older adults making better use of this increased time. In addition, older adults' facilitated performance could be assisted by the opportunity for more self-paced pattern of ongoing activities in naturalistic studies. All of these aspects warrant close empirical examination in the future.

The studies on prospective memory in both laboratory and naturalistic settings have revealed the described paradoxical age-related findings across settings. Testing the same participants in each setting confirmed the paradox (Rendell & Thomson, 1999); however, it is two features of Rendell and Craik's (2000) study that have begun to reveal explanations of this paradox: the development of a laboratory task that simulated naturalistic situation and the development of an analogue to this laboratory task for the naturalistic setting. This route will have to be continued in future research on age differences in prospective memory and most likely in other areas of applied cognitive gerontology.

NOTES

1. Note that the approach of testing participants' prospective memory performance in real life by externally giving them a prospective task to be performed in their daily life is extensively discussed in the section titled "The Laboratory-Naturalistic Setting Age-Prospective Memory Paradox and Its Potential for Applied Basic Cognitive Gerontology."

In the current section, we discuss the available evidence on naturally occurring everyday prospective memory functioning.

2. In pathological aging, there are, however, initial data showing that among patients attending a memory clinic, about 40% report prospective memory problems as their main clinical symptoms (Kliegel & Martin, 2003).

3. Again, we want to stress that this does not comprise studies that give participants tasks to be performed in real life that are activities they would not have done without being instructed to do so.

4. Note that those age correlations were not reported by Kliegel and Jäger (2006a).

REFERENCES

Baddeley, A. (1998). *Human memory: Theory and practice.* Boston: Allyn & Bacon.

Bisiacchi, P. S. (1996). The neuropsychological approach in the study of prospective memory. In M. Brandimonte, G. O. Einstein, & M. A. McDaniel (Eds.), *Prospective memory: Theory and applications* (pp. 297–318). Mahwah, NJ: Lawrence Erlbaum.

Bisiacchi, P. S., Sgaramella, T. M., & Farinello, C. (1998). Planning strategies and control mechanisms: Evidence from closed head injury and aging. *Brain and Cognition, 37,* 113–116.

Bolla, K. I., Lindgren, K. N., Bonaccorsy, C., & Bleeker, M. L. (1991). Memory complaints in older adults: Fact or fiction? *Archives of Neurology, 48,* 61–64.

Cavanaugh, J. C., & Blanchard-Fields, F. (2002). *Adult development and aging.* Belmont, CA: Wadsworth.

Cohen, G. (1996). Memory and learning in normal ageing. In R. T. Woods (Ed.), *Handbook of the clinical psychology of ageing* (pp. 43–58). Chichester, UK: Wiley.

Crawford, J. R., Henry, J. D., Ward, A. L., & Blake, J. (2006). The Prospective and Retrospective Memory Questionnaire (PRMQ): Latent structure, normative data and discrepancy analysis for proxy-ratings. *British Journal of Clinical Psychology, 45,* 83–104.

Crawford, J. R., Smith, G., Maylor, E. A., Della Sala, S., & Logie, R. H. (2003). The Prospective and Retrospective Memory Questionnaire (PRMQ): Normative data and latent structure in a large non-clinical sample. *Memory, 11,* 261–275.

Crovitz, H. F., & Daniel, W. F. (1984). Measurements of everyday memory: Toward the prevention of forgetting. *Bulletin of the Psychonomic Society, 22,* 413–414.

Devolder, P. A., Brigham, M. C., & Pressley, M. (1990). Memory performance awareness in younger and older adults. *Psychology and Aging, 5,* 291–303.

Dobbs, A. R., & Rule, B. G. (1987). Prospective memory and self-reports of memory abilities in older adults. *Canadian Journal of Psychology, 41,* 209–222.

d'Ydewalle, G., & Brunfaut, E. (1996). Are older subjects necessarily worse in prospective memory tasks? In M. Georgas, E. Manthouli, E. Besevegis, & A. Kokkevi (Eds.), *Contemporary psychology in Europe: Theory, research and applications* (pp. 161–172). Göttingen, Germany: Hogrefe & Huber.

Einstein, G. O., & McDaniel, M. A. (1990). Normal aging and prospective memory. *Journal of Experimental Psychology: Learning, Memory, and Cognition, 16,* 717–726.

Einstein, G. O., & McDaniel, M. A. (2005). Prospective memory: Multiple retrieval processes. *Current Directions in Psychological Science, 14,* 286–290.

Einstein, G. O., McDaniel, M. A., Richardson, S. L., Guynn, M. J., & Cunfer, A. R. (1995). Aging and prospective memory: Examining the influences of self-initiated retrieval processes. *Journal of Experimental Psychology: Learning, Memory, and Cognition, 21,* 996–1007.

Ellis, J. A. (1988). Memory for future intentions: Investigating pulses and steps. In M. M. Gruneberg, P. E. Morris, & R. N. Sykes (Eds.), *Practical aspects of memory: Vol. 1. Current research and issues* (pp. 371–376). Chichester, UK: Wiley.

Ellis, J. A., & Nimmo-Smith, I. (1993). Recollecting naturally-occurring intentions: A study of cognitive and affective factors. *Memory, 1,* 107–126.

Funke, J., & Krüger, T. (1993). *Plan-A-Day (PAD).* Bonn, Germany: Psychologisches Institut der Universität Bonn.

Henry, J. D., MacLeod, M. S., Phillips, L. H., & Crawford, J. R. (2004). A meta-analytic review of prospective memory and aging. *Psychology and Aging, 19,* 27–39.

Hertzog, C., & Hultsch, D. F. (2000). Metacognition in adulthood and old age. In F. I. M. Craik & T. A. Salthouse (Eds.), *Handbook of aging and cognition* (2nd ed., pp. 417–466). Mahwah, NJ: Lawrence Erlbaum.

Kliegel, M., Eschen, A., & Thöne-Otto, A. I. T. (2004). Planning and realization of complex intentions in traumatic brain injury and normal aging. *Brain and Cognition, 56,* 43–54.

Kliegel, M., & Jäger, T. (2006a). Can the Prospective and Retrospective Memory Questionnaire (PRMQ) predict actual prospective memory performance? *Current Psychology, 25,* 182–191.

Kliegel, M., & Jäger, T. (2006b). Delayed-execute prospective memory performance: The effects of age and working memory. *Developmental Neuropsychology, 30,* 819–843.

Kliegel, M., Jäger, T., Phillips, L. H., Federspiel, E., Imfeld, A., Keller, M., et al. (2005). Effects of sad mood on time-based prospective memory. *Cognition and Emotion, 19,* 1199–1213.

Kliegel, M., & Martin, M. (2003). Prospective memory research: Why is it relevant? *International Journal of Psychology, 38,* 193–194.

Kliegel, M., Martin, M., McDaniel, M. A., & Einstein, G. O. (2001). Varying the importance of a prospective memory task: Differential effects across time- and event-based prospective memory. *Memory, 9,* 1–11.

Kliegel, M., Martin, M., McDaniel, M. A., & Phillips, L. H. (2007). Adult age differences in errand planning: The role of task familiarity and cognitive resources. *Experimental Aging Research, 33,* 145–161.

Kliegel, M., Martin, M., & Moor, C. (2003). Prospective memory and aging: Is task importance relevant? *International Journal of Psychology, 38,* 207–214.

Kliegel, M., McDaniel, M. A., & Einstein, G. O. (2000). Plan formation, retention, and execution in prospective memory: A new paradigm and age-related effects. *Memory & Cognition, 28,* 1041–1049.

Kliegel, M., McDaniel, M. A., & Einstein, G. O. (Eds.). (2008). *Prospective memory: Cognitive, neuroscience, developmental, and applied perspectives.* Mahwah, NJ: Lawrence Erlbaum.

Kliegel, M., Phillips, L., & Fischer, C. (2004, April). *Importance effects on age differences in performance in event-based prospective memory.* Paper presented at the 10th Cognitive Aging Conference, Atlanta, GA.

Kliegel, M., Ramuschkat, G., & Martin, M. (2003). Exekutive Funktionen und prospektive Gedächtnisleistung im Alter: Eine differenzielle Analyse von ereignis- und zeitbasierter prospektiver Gedächtnisleistung [Executive functions and prospective memory performance in old age: An analysis of event-based and time-based prospective memory]. *Zeitschrift für Gerontologie und Geriatrie, 36,* 35–41.

Kliegel, M., & Zimprich, D. (2005). Predictors of cognitive complaints in old age: A mixture regression approach. *European Journal of Ageing, 2,* 13–23.

Kliegel, M., Zimprich, D., & Eschen, A. (2005). What do subjective cognitive complaints in persons with aging-associated cognitive decline reflect? *International Psychogeriatrics, 17,* 499–512.

Kvavilashvili, L., & Fisher, L. (2007). Is time-based prospective remembering mediated by self-initiated rehearsals? Role of incidental cues, ongoing activity, age and motivation. *Journal of Experimental Psychology: General, 136,* 112–132.

Lane, C. J., & Zelinski, E. M. (2003). Longitudinal hierarchical linear models of the Memory Functioning Questionnaire. *Psychology and Aging, 18,* 38–53.

Marsh, R. L., Hicks, J. L., & Landau, J. D. (1998). An investigation of everyday prospective memory. *Memory & Cognition, 26,* 633–643.

Marsiske, M., Lang, F. R., Baltes, P. B., & Baltes, M. M. (1995). Selective optimization with compensation: Life-span perspectives on successful human development. In R. A. Dixon & L. Bäckman (Eds.), *Compensating for psychological deficits and declines: Managing losses and promoting gains* (pp. 35–79). Mahwah, NJ: Lawrence Erlbaum.

Martin, M., & Ewert, O. (1997). Attention and planning in older adults. *International Journal of Behavioral Development, 20,* 577–594.

Maylor, E. A. (1990). Age and prospective memory. *Quarterly Journal of Experimental Psychology, 42A,* 471–493.

McDaniel, M. A., & Einstein, G. O. (2000). Strategic and automatic processes in prospective memory retrieval: A multiprocess framework. *Applied Cognitive Psychology, 14,* S127–S144.

Morrell, R. W., Park, D. C., Kidder, D. P., & Martin, M. (1997). Adherence to anti-hypertensive medications across the life span. *The Gerontologist, 37,* 609–619.

Moscovitch, M. (1982). A neuropsychological approach to memory and perception in normal and pathological aging. In F. I. M. Craik & S. Trehub (Eds.), *Advances in the study of communication and affect: Vol. 8. Aging and cognitive processes* (pp. 55–78). New York: Plenum.

Neath, I., & Surprenant, A. M. (2003). *Human memory: An introduction to research, data, and theory.* Belmont, CA: Wadsworth.

Park, D. C., Hertzog, C., Kidder, D. P., Morrell, R. W., & Mayhorn, C. B. (1997). Effect of age on event-based and time-based prospective memory. *Psychology and Aging, 12,* 314–327.

Park, D. C., Hertzog, C., Leventhal, H., Morrell, R. W., Leventhal, E., Birchmore, D., et al. (1999). Medication adherence in rheumatoid arthritis patients: Older is wiser. *Journal of American Geriatrics Society, 47,* 172–183.

Park, D. C., Morrell, R. W., Frieske, D., & Kincaid, D. (1992). Medication adherence behaviors in older adults: Effects of external cognitive supports. *Psychology and Aging, 7,* 252–256.

Patton, G. W., & Meit, M. (1993). Effect of aging on prospective and incidental memory. *Experimental Aging Research, 19,* 165–176.

Phillips, L. H., Henry, J. D., & Martin, M. (2008). Adult aging and prospective memory: The importance of ecological validity. In M. Kliegel, M. A. McDaniel, & G. O. Einstein (Eds.), *Prospective memory: Cognitive, neuroscience, developmental, and applied perspectives* (pp. 161–185). Mahwah, NJ: Lawrence Erlbaum.

Phillips, L. H., Kliegel, M., & Martin, M. (2006). Age and planning tasks: The influence of ecological validity. *International Journal of Aging and Human Development, 62,* 175–184.

Rendell, P. G., & Craik, F. I. M. (2000). Virtual and Actual Week: Age-related differences in prospective memory. *Applied Cognitive Psychology, 14,* S43–S62.

Rendell, P. G., Jensen, F., & Henry, J. D. (2007). Prospective memory in multiple sclerosis. *Journal of the International Neuropsychological Society, 13,* 410–416.

Rendell, P. G., McDaniel, M. A., Forbes, R. D., & Einstein, G. O. (2007). Age-related effects in prospective memory are modulated by ongoing task complexity and relation to target cue. *Aging, Neuropsychology, and Cognition, 14,* 236–256.

Rendell, P. G., & Thomson, D. M. (1993). The effect of ageing on remembering to remember: An investigation of simulated medication regimens. *Australian Journal of Ageing, 12,* 11–18.

Rendell, P. G., & Thomson, D. M. (1999). Aging and prospective memory: Differences between naturalistic and laboratory tasks. *Journal of Gerontology: Psychological Sciences, 54B,* P256–P269.

Salthouse, T. A. (1993). Speed mediation of adult age differences in cognition. *Developmental Psychology, 29,* 722–738.

Shallice, T. (1982). Specific impairments of planning. *Philosophical Transactions of the Royal Society of London B, 298,* 199–209.

Smith, G., Della Sala, S., Logie, R. H., & Maylor, E. A. (2000). Prospective and retrospective memory in normal ageing and dementia: A questionnaire study. *Memory, 8,* 311–321.

Snodgrass, J. G., & Vanderwart, M. (1980). A standardized set of 260 pictures: Norms for name agreement, image agreement, familiarity, and visual complexity. *Journal of Experimental Psychology: Human Learning and Memory, 6,* 174–215.

Stroop, J. R. (1935). Studies of interference in serial verbal reactions. *Journal of Experimental Psychology, 18,* 643–662.

Terry, W. S. (1988). Everyday forgetting: Data from a diary study. *Psychological Reports, 62,* 299–303.

Ward, G., & Morris, R. (2005). Introduction to the psychology of planning. In R. Morris & G. Ward (Eds.), *The cognitive psychology of planning* (pp. 1–34). Hove, UK: Psychology Press.

Wechsler, D. (1981). *Wechsler Adult Intelligence Scale—Revised.* New York: Psychological Corporation.

West, R. L. (1988). Prospective memory and aging. In M. M. Gruneberg, P. E. Morris, & R. N. Sykes (Eds.), *Practical aspects of memory: Current research and issues: Vol. 2. Clinical and educational implications* (pp. 119–128). Chichester, UK: Wiley.

Wilson, E. A. H., & Park, D. C. (2008). Prospective memory and health behaviors: Context trumps cognition. In M. Kliegel, M. A. McDaniel, & G. O. Einstein (Eds.), *Prospective memory: Cognitive, neuroscience, developmental, and applied perspectives* (pp. 391–410). Mahwah, NJ: Lawrence Erlbaum.

Zacks, R. T., & Hasher, L. (1994). Directed ignoring: Inhibitory regulation of working memory. In D. Dagenbach & T. H. Carr (Eds.), *Inhibitory processes in attention, memory, and language* (pp. 241–264). San Diego, CA: Academic Press.

Zeintl, M., Kliegel, M., Rast, P., & Zimprich, D. (2006). Prospective memory complaints can be predicted by prospective memory performance in older adults. *Dementia and Geriatric Cognitive Disorders, 22,* 209–215.

Zimprich, D., Martin, M., & Kliegel, M. (2003). Subjective cognitive complaints, memory performance, and depressive affect in old age: A change-oriented approach. *International Journal of Aging and Human Development, 57,* 339–366.

36

SOCIAL RESOURCES AND COGNITIVE FUNCTION IN OLDER PERSONS

LISA L. BARNES, KATHLEEN A. CAGNEY,
AND CARLOS F. MENDES DE LEON

The potential importance of social integration in accounting for individual differences in the physical and mental health outcomes of older adults has received increased attention in the past 20 years. Various constructs have been developed to characterize the social resources that emanate from a person's integration into his or her broader social environment. These resources and their impact on health can be categorized into three major research areas: (1) social networks, (2) social engagement or activity, and (3) social support. The term *social networks* refers to the matrix of social relationships to which individuals are tied (Fischer, 1982; Peek & Lin, 1999). *Social engagement* is designated by participation in socially meaningful or productive activity (Barnes, Mendes de Leon, Bienias, & Evans, 2004; Glass, Mendes de Leon, Marottoli, & Berkman, 1999). *Social support*, arguably the most well characterized of the three, is broadly defined as resources (e.g., instrumental, informational, emotional) provided by other persons (Cohen & Syme, 1985; Lin, 1982, 1986). Although these constructs often overlap, an underlying theme is that they each capture an important aspect of social interaction. Taken together, these lines of research suggest that older adults who have high levels of social involvement tend to enjoy better physical (Bosworth & Schaie, 1997) and mental health (Krause, 1997), and live significantly longer (Liang et al., 1999; Seeman et al., 1993), compared with older people who are not as socially integrated. For example, several studies have shown that older adults who report larger social networks (Mendes de Leon et al., 1999; Seeman et al., 1993); more frequent participation in church, clubs, or social groups (Unger, Johnson, & Marks, 1997); and more frequent productive activity, such as volunteer or paid work (Glass et al., 1999; Musick, Herzog, & House, 1999), have increased longevity, reduced risk for disability, and reduced risk of cognitive decline and Alzheimer's disease.

According to several life span developmental perspectives, individuals actively regulate social resources as they age for the purpose of personal growth and adaptation (Baltes & Lang, 1997; Lang, 2001; Lang, Featherman, & Nesselroade,

1997; Ryff, 1991). This process is modulated in important ways by the social environment that shapes an individual's resources through prevailing norms, values, and expectations and optimizes adaptation in the face of changing goals and capacities (Verbrugge & Jette, 1994). Until recently, most research in this area has focused primarily on resources at the level of the individual, paying little attention to the larger contextual environment. This is in stark contrast to a variety of other research arenas, including childhood development (e.g., Bradley, 1993, 1999; Bradley et al., 1995; Molfese, Modglin, & Molfese, 2003); organizational and industrial psychology (e.g., Kohn & Schooler, 1983); and urban sociology and criminology (e.g., Browning, Feinberg, & Dietz, 2004; Massey & Denton, 1993; Morenoff, Sampson, & Raudenbush, 2001; Sampson, Raudenbush, & Earls, 1997; Wilson, 1987), in which the central importance of the social environment had been extensively documented.

As the emphasis on social determinants of health evolved, a growing body of sociological and epidemiologic research began to show that differences in the social composition of the environment in which people live or work could also have a significant influence on health outcomes (Browning & Cagney, 2003). Consequently, researchers from a broad range of disciplines have attempted to delineate the structural factors, and associated mechanisms, that connect the larger social environment to the individual. Following in the tradition of urban social ecologists (Jacobs, 1961), there is now a resurging appreciation of the overall quantity and flow of social resources that exist in communities or neighborhoods and their impact on health outcomes. In this chapter, we provide a brief overview of what is currently known about the association between social resources and one very important health factor for older adults: cognitive function. We begin by briefly reviewing where the bulk of the research lies in this field—the association between social resources measured at the individual level with cognitive function. This part of the chapter is not meant to be an exhaustive review because there are already many good reviews on this topic in the literature (e.g., Barnes, Mendes de Leon, Wilson, Bienias, & Evans, 2004; Holtzman et al., 2004; Richards, Hardy, & Wadsworth, 2003; Rowe &

Kahn, 1997; Zunzunegui, Alvarado, Del Ser, & Otero, 2003). Instead, we focus more specifically on the much smaller literature on the relation of community-level social resources to cognitive function, using the concept of social capital as a foundation for the discussion. The chapter concludes with a series of challenges for the field of aging. We focus on social resources and their implications for cognitive function and emphasize future research directions in this area.

INDIVIDUAL-LEVEL SOCIAL RESOURCES AND COGNITIVE FUNCTION

Several studies have reported that older adults with a socially more involved lifestyle tend to have better cognitive function (e.g., Arbuckle, Gold, & Andres, 1986; Christensen et al., 1996; Hultsch, Hammer, & Small, 1993). Epidemiologic evidence from population-based studies further suggests that social engagement is protective against cognitive decline (Barnes, Mendes de Leon, Wilson, et al., 2004; Bassuk, Glass, & Berkman, 1999; Beland, Zunzunegui, Alvarado, Otero, & Del, 2005; Holtzman et al., 2004; Zunzunegui et al., 2003). For example, Bassuk et al. (1999) showed that a composite measure consisting of six indicators of social engagement was related to rate of cognitive decline over a 12-year follow-up period. In a population-based study, Barnes, Mendes de Leon, Wilson, et al. (2004) tested a group of 6,102 adults aged 65 and older, for up to three occasions over approximately 5 years, and observed that higher levels of both social contacts and social engagement were found to be associated with a reduced rate of cognitive decline.

Although it is generally thought that social integration is protective against cognitive decline, there are important inconsistencies in this literature (e.g., Aartsen, Smits, van Tilburg, Knipscheer, & Deeg, 2002; Arbuckle, Gold, Andres, Schwartzman, & Chaikelson, 1992; Hilleras, Jorm, Herlitz, & Winblad, 1999), presumably due to differences in how *social integration* is defined and or assessed, variability in how cognitive function is measured, and whether potentially confounding variables are taken into account. For example, frequency of cognitive (Wilson et al., 1999, 2003) and physical

(Dustman, Emmerson, & Shearer, 1994; Weuve et al., 2004) activity is positively related to cognitive function or reduced rate of cognitive decline in older adults, but studies often combine the different indexes of activity into a single measure, and few studies have examined the independent effects of these other types of activities on cognitive function or decline (e.g., Barnes, Mendes de Leon, Wilson, et al., 2004).

SOCIAL CAPITAL AS A CONTEXT FOR UNDERSTANDING COMMUNITY-LEVEL RESOURCES

The concept of social capital has its roots in sociology and economics (Bourdieu, 1986; Coleman, 1988, 1990; Loury, 1977; Portes, 1998; Wall, Ferrazzi, & Schryer, 1998). Defined from a traditionally sociological perspective, it refers to potential or actual resources that are inherent within social networks, communities, or societies (Bourdieu & Wacquant, 1992; Carpiano, 2006), as well as being an emergent property inhered in the network. The first published definition appeared as early as 1920 (Hanifan, 1920, cited in Macinko & Starfield, 2001), and Jacobs (1961) used the term in her work on trust and networks 40 years later, but Bourdieu (1980) is credited as the first to dedicate an entire work to the concept (Macinko & Starfield, 2001). Only within the past 20 years has social capital been brought into the fields of public health and epidemiology (e.g., Putnam, 2000; Wilkinson, 1996), and here the term usually refers to resources accessible to members of a defined group or community through their engagement in various community and social structures that facilitate collective action for mutual benefit and problem resolution (Locher et al., 2005; Seeman & Crimmins, 2001). Central to the various usages of the term is the idea of resources or benefits that accrue as a result of being socially connected (Carpiano, 2006; Portes, 1998; Putnam, 2000). Defined in this way, social capital would include any or all of the following: expectations or obligations of support, resources to information, informal social control (Coleman, 1990), and civic engagement (Putnam, Leonardi, & Nanetti, 1993). The important distinction for social capital is that social connectedness is not merely conceived as a characteristic of the individual but is also conceived as a quality that characterizes a community of individuals (O'Rand, 2001), such as a neighborhood, or an occupational setting.

Recent research has begun to examine the link between social capital and health. Kawachi and colleagues (Kawachi, Kennedy, Lochner, & Prothrow-Stith, 1997) measured the extent of social capital (measured by levels of trust of fellow citizens and their extent of membership in voluntary groups and organizations) in the 50 U.S. states and found that areas with the highest reported levels of social capital had lower mortality rates. Similar relationships have been observed for low social capital and self-rated health (Hyyppa & Maki, 2001; Kawachi, Kennedy, & Glass, 1999) and for psychological distress (Rietschlin, 1998). Although social capital provides a context for understanding how community-level emergent processes are related to health, there has been relatively little research on what those processes might be. It is interesting that the link between social capital and health is analogous to the research on the social disorganization theory of violence. Research in this area focuses on the neighborhood environment in which violence occurs in an attempt to identify community-level determinants of social deviance (e.g., Sampson & Groves, 1989; Sampson et al., 1997). These studies have shown consistently an inverse relationship between community-level factors, such as social cohesion (mutual trust and solidarity), and prevalence of violent crimes. Low levels of social cohesion are thought to undermine residents' ability to collectively regulate behavior within the neighborhood, leading to an increased rate of violent crimes and other types of social problems. Applying this theory to the link between social capital and health, communities with high levels of social capital would be better able to promote healthy behaviors; increase access to health-related resources, services, and amenities; and enhance the emotional support and associated norms of reciprocity in trusting social environments (Berkman, Glass, Brissette, & Seeman, 2000; Kawachi et al., 1999; Locher et al., 2005).

It is possible that social capital influences health by bridging the social resources to which people have access through individual-level social interactions (e.g., an actual exchange of social support) and the totality of community-level resources that exist between people in a community. These might include resources and benefits gained through involvement in broader social or community-oriented organizations or groups, such as community centers, adult day care centers, and religious organizations, among others.

A number of empirical constructs have been created to capture aspects of neighborhood social processes and to demonstrate their role in individual-level health and well-being (D. Cohen, Finch, Bower, & Sastry, 2006; Franzini, Caughy, Spears, & Fernandez Esquer, 2005; Kirtland et al., 2003; Sampson et al., 1997). Findings related to social processes and their effects on health are compelling and have been described elsewhere (Browning & Cagney, 2002; Wen & Christakis, 2005). In the following section, we focus our attention on studies that have examined community-level resources and their influence on cognitive function in older adults.

COMMUNITY-LEVEL SOCIAL RESOURCES

There is an increasing interest in how social factors defined within a broader social context, at the neighborhood or local area level, influence health (Diez Roux, 2001, 2002). A number of studies have found that living in disadvantaged neighborhoods is associated with a range of health outcomes, including self-rated health (Malmstrom, Sundquist, & Johansson, 1999; Patel, Eschbach, Rudkin, Peek, & Markides, 2003), cardiovascular disease (Diez Roux et al., 1999, 2001), depression (Yen & Kaplan, 1999), and mortality (Martikainen, Kauppinen, & Valkonen, 2003; Smith, Hart, Watt, Hole, & Hawthorne, 1998; Waitzman & Smith, 1998). Most research to date has focused on basic social structural features of the neighborhood environment, such as neighborhood socioeconomic status, usually emphasizing the influence of poverty, residential instability, or social disadvantage. These neighborhood structural factors have been consistently shown to be of prime importance in explaining the accumulation of health risks and poor health behaviors by promoting neighborhood organization or social order.

In attempts to further refine the examination of neighborhood structural factors and their impact on health, recent studies have begun to examine more specific social process mechanisms, such as social cohesion and disorder. It is hypothesized that specific indices of neighborhood features will lead to a better understanding of the pathways or mechanisms by which disadvantaged neighborhoods lead to poor health. Although a wide range of health outcomes has been examined, few studies have assessed the relation of community-level resources to cognitive function in old age. Cognitive impairment in old age is common, and the number of people affected is expected to more than triple by 2040 because of a longer life expectancy of older adults (Suthers, Kim, & Crimmins, 2003). It is plausible that community-level social resources may be particularly important for cognition in older adults who have decreased mobility and therefore restrict their daily activities to their local neighborhood areas (Diez Roux, 2002; Glass & Balfour, 2003; Satariano, 1997).

Espino, Lichtenstein, Palmer, and Hazuda (2001) examined whether the proportion of Mexican Americans and European Americans with cognitive impairment differed across three socioculturally distinct urban neighborhoods. Performance on the Mini-Mental State Examination (Folstein, Folstein, & McHugh, 1975), a measure of global cognition, was related to neighborhood type among Mexican Americans, with barrio residents having an approximately threefold greater risk of cognitive impairment compared with Mexican Americans living in transitional neighborhoods and/or suburbs. Espino et al. attributed the disparity to ethnic differences in the prevalence of lower educational levels and types of neighborhood residence. Wight et al. (2006) examined whether educational attainment at the neighborhood level (U.S. census tract), independent of individual-level risk factors and neighborhood-level socioeconomic status, is associated with cognitive function in a nationally representative sample of older adults. They found that cognition was associated with neighborhood-level educational attainment, such that persons living in low-education neighborhoods had, on average, a lower level of cognitive function than persons living in areas with a higher average level of education, and this association appeared to be independent of differences in individual-level education. Both studies focused on basic social structural features of the neighborhood (e.g., educational attainment) measured at the aggregate level. Only one study, to our knowledge, has considered specific neighborhood conditions that may influence cognition in older adults. Barnes and colleagues (2007) examined perceptions of both individual- and community-level social cohesion and neighborhood disorder (e.g., unsafe traffic conditions, inadequate lighting at night), in a population-based study of adults over age 65. They found that both social cohesion and exchange and neighborhood social and physical disorder were associated with greater cognitive function when measured at the individual level. In contrast, when these processes were examined at the level of the community, only neighborhood social and physical disorder was associated with cognitive function, such that higher levels of disorder were associated with lower cognitive function (Barnes et al., 2007).

There may be a number of explanations for the observed relationship between community-level social resources and cognitive function. First, living in a neighborhood characterized by low levels of social capital or high levels of disorder may increase stress for its residents, which may affect cognition through biological pathways involved in the hypothalamic–pituitary–adrenal axis (Issa, Rowe, Gauthier, & Meaney, 1990; McEwen & Sapolsky, 1995). It is also possible that an environment that facilitates interaction and social participation may be cognitively stimulating in and of itself, thereby slowing the progression of cognitive decline (Albert et al., 1995; Barnes, Mendes de Leon, Wilson, et al., 2004; Bassuk et al., 1999; Hultsch, Hertzog, Small, & Dixon, 1999; Wilson et al., 2003). Future studies are needed to examine whether access to resources that provide stimulating cognitive, physical, and social environments (e.g., libraries, parks, fitness centers) can account for the association between neighborhood conditions and cognition. There may also be more indirect effects by which social capital and neighborhood processes promote healthy behaviors, such as by providing the infrastructure to participate in physical activities or increasing cardiovascular fitness, both of which have been linked to better cognitive function and less

cognitive decline (Dik, Deeg, Visser, & Jonker, 2003; Hillman et al., 2006; Lytle, Vander, Pandav, Dodge, & Ganguli, 2004; Newson & Kemps, 2006). More studies that can measure specific neighborhood conditions and their relation to cognitive function in old age are needed to test these and other hypotheses.

In this chapter, we have explored salient issues regarding the impact of social resources in cognitive aging. A growing body of evidence suggests that social resources, at both the individual level and community level, contribute to higher cognitive function. Although the mechanisms remain to be elucidated, they appear to operate in much the same way that social resources contribute to better overall health and well-being. It is expected that with increasing age, and the subsequent decline in access to social resources, changes in social resources will predict future cognitive decline. If this claim is substantiated, social resources may represent a potentially modifiable factor that can influence the cognitive health of a rapidly aging society.

CONCLUSION

The data we have reviewed in this chapter suggest that social context is associated with cognitive function and cognitive decline. Although the majority of the research has focused on social resources measured at the individual level, there is emerging evidence that contextual-level resources may also be an important factor to consider. These results add to a growing literature on the positive health effects of particular lifestyle factors in aging research. Because social resources may be modifiable, these findings have considerable implications for an aging population that will likely face an increasing burden of cognitive impairment. There are at least four unresolved issues that future research can address to gain a more complete understanding of the ways in which social integration at an individual level as well as a contextual level may be related to better cognitive function in old age.

First, as alluded to earlier, the research on community-level or contextual-level factors and cognition is still relatively sparse. Most previous studies have focused on social resources at the individual level, with limited attention to the relation of community-level social resources with cognitive function. Additional studies that include different contextual variables are needed to determine which characteristics of community-level resources are related to cognition. Data gathered by Barnes et al. (2007) suggest that community-level social resources, at least negative neighborhood conditions, can influence the cognitive function of older adults. It may also be important for future research to explore the neighborhood factors that enhance cognitive function.

Second, disparate patterns of social integration exist among older adults and within neighborhoods. Future studies should examine how demographic and other lifestyle characteristics may modify the association of individual- and community-level social resources with cognitive function. It may be the case that healthier or more cognitively intact individuals seek out more favorable neighborhoods and, as a result, may also have higher motivation to maintain neighborhood quality. How these and other factors may influence the association of social resources and cognitive function needs to be further elucidated. It will also be important to model longitudinal changes in social resources and determine their effect on cognition and cognitive decline.

Third, it is not clear from epidemiologic studies what mechanisms may mediate the association of social resources and cognitive function. Understanding the biobehavioral mechanisms, such as depressive symptoms, social support, or health behaviors, through which social resources affect cognition will be a substantial future challenge for researchers. One potential mechanism linking limited social resources with poor cognitive function is stress. Some studies demonstrate that living in a stressful environment is related to health and psychological well-being (e.g., McEwen, 2001). Furthermore, recent evidence suggests that experiences of chronic stress and depressive symptomatology are associated with cognitive decline and risk of Alzheimer's disease in older adults (Wilson, Barnes, et al., 2005; Wilson et al., 2002; Wilson, Bennett, et al., 2005). Studies that link neighborhood conditions, inflammatory biomarkers reflective of a stress process (e.g., interleukin-6, cortisol), and

cognitive function are needed to further examine the extent to which chronic stress may mediate the relation of social resources and cognitive decline in aging.

Fourth, it will be critical to examine the relation of social resources and cognition within a life span perspective. The studies reviewed in this chapter measured individual- and community-level social resources in old age, but these features could be a proxy for early-life social conditions (Hayward & Gorman, 2004); that is, it is possible that older adults who live in socially disadvantaged neighborhoods with limited access to social capital and other socioeconomic resources have generally lived difficult lives punctuated with disadvantage. Perhaps social disadvantage in early life increases the likelihood of being on a trajectory of poor health and cognitive impairment in late life through poorer quality education or fewer occupational opportunities, and measuring social resources in old age is either too late or not sufficient. Future research is needed to understand whether the relationship between individual- and community-level resources and cognition is a long-term process that begins in early life or instead represents an additional risk profile for the adverse mental and physical health outcomes associated with old age. The ultimate challenge for future generations will be to characterize the social environment, not only at the individual level but also at the neighborhood level, and during distinct developmental periods, to determine at what stage of the life course these relationships may manifest.

REFERENCES

Aartsen, M. J., Smits, C. H., van Tilburg, T., Knipscheer, K. C., & Deeg, D. J. (2002). Activity in older adults: Cause or consequence of cognitive functioning? A longitudinal study on everyday activities and cognitive performance in older adults. *Journals of Gerontology Series B: Psychological Sciences and Social Sciences, 57,* 153–162.

Albert, M. S., Jones, K., Savage, C. R., Berkman, L., Seeman, T., Blazer, D., et al. (1995). Predictors of cognitive change in older persons: MacArthur Studies of Successful Aging. *Psychology and Aging, 10,* 578–589.

Arbuckle, T. Y., Gold, D., & Andres, D. (1986). Cognitive functioning of older people in relation to social and personality variables. *Psychology and Aging, 1,* 55–62.

Arbuckle, T. Y., Gold, D. P., Andres, D., Schwartzman, A., & Chaikelson, J. (1992). The role of psychosocial context, age, and intelligence in memory performance of older men. *Psychology and Aging, 7,* 25–36.

Baltes, M. M., & Lang, F. R. (1997). Everyday functioning and successful aging: The impact of resources. *Psychology and Aging, 12,* 433–443.

Barnes, L. L., Cagney, K. A., Bienias, J. L., Wilson, R. S., Scherr, P. A., Evans, D. A., & Mendes de Leon, C. F. (2007). [Unpublished raw data].

Barnes, L. L., Mendes de Leon, C. F., Bienias, J. L., & Evans, D. A. (2004). A longitudinal study of Black–White differences in social resources. *Journals of Gerontology Series B: Psychological Sciences and Social Sciences, 59,* 146–153.

Barnes, L. L., Mendes de Leon, C. F., Wilson, R. S., Bienias, J. L., & Evans, D. A. (2004). Social resources and cognitive decline in a population of older African Americans and Whites. *Neurology, 63,* 2322–2326.

Bassuk, S. S., Glass, T. A., & Berkman, L. F. (1999). Social disengagement and incident cognitive decline in community-dwelling elderly persons. *Annals of Internal Medicine, 131,* 165–173.

Beland, F., Zunzunegui, M. V., Alvarado, B., Otero, A., & Del, S. T. (2005). Trajectories of cognitive decline and social relations. *Journals of Gerontology Series B: Psychological Sciences and Social Sciences, 60,* 320–330.

Berkman, L. F., Glass, T., Brissette, I., & Seeman, T. E. (2000). From social integration to health: Durkheim in the new millennium. *Social Science and Medicine, 51,* 843–857.

Bosworth, H. B., & Schaie, K. W. (1997). The relationship of social environment, social networks, and health outcomes in the Seattle Longitudinal Study: Two analytical approaches. *Journals of Gerontology Series B: Psychological Sciences and Social Sciences, 52,* 197–205.

Bourdieu, P. (1980). Le capital social: Notes provisoires [Social capital: Provisional notes]. *Recherche Science Social, 31,* 2–3.

Bourdieu, P. (1986). The forms of capital. In J. Richardson (Ed.), *Handbook of theory and research for the sociology of education* (pp. 241–258). Westport, CT: Greenwood Press.

Bourdieu, P., & Wacquant, L. (1992). *Invitation to reflexive sociology.* Chicago: University of Chicago Press.

Bradley, R. H. (1993). Children's home environments, health, behavior, and intervention efforts: A review using the HOME inventory as a marker measure. *Genetic, Social, and General Psychology Monographs, 119,* 437–490.

Bradley, R. H. (1999). The home environment. In S. L. Friedman & T. D. Wachs (Eds.), *Measuring environment across the life span: Emerging methods and concepts* (pp. 31–58). Washington, DC: American Psychological Association.

Bradley, R. H., Whiteside, L., Mundfrom, D. J., Blevins-Knabe, B., Casey, P. H., Caldwell, B. M., et al. (1995). Home environment and adaptive social behavior among premature, low birth weight children: Alternative models of environmental action. *Journal of Pediatric Psychology, 20,* 347–362.

Browning, C. R. & Cagney, K. A. (2002). Neighborhood structural disadvantage, collective efficacy, and self-rated physical health in an urban setting. *Journal of Health and Social Behavior, 43,* 383-399.

Browning, C. R., & Cagney, K. A. (2003). Moving beyond poverty: Neighborhood structure, social processes, and health. *Journal of Health and Social Behavior, 44,* 552–571.

Browning, C. R., Feinberg, S. L., & Dietz, R. D. (2004). The paradox of social organization: Networks, collective efficacy, and violent crime in urban neighborhoods. *Social Forces, 83,* 503–534.

Carpiano, R. M. (2006). Toward a neighborhood resource-based theory of social capital for health: Can Bourdieu and sociology help? *Social Science and Medicine, 62,* 165–175.

Christensen, H., Korten, A., Jorm, A. F., Henderson, A. S., Scott, R., & Mackinnon, A. J. (1996). Activity levels and cognitive functioning in an elderly community sample. *Age and Ageing, 25,* 72–80.

Cohen, D. A., Finch, B. K., Bower, A., & Sastry, N. (2006). Collective efficacy and obesity: the potential influence of social factors on health. *Social Science and Medicine, 62,* 769–778.

Cohen, S., & Syme, S. L. (1985). *Social support and health.* Orlando, FL: Academic Press.

Coleman, J. (1988). Social capital in the creation of human capital. *American Journal of Sociology, 94,* S95–S120.

Coleman, J. S. (1990). *The foundation of social theory*. Cambridge, MA: Belknap Press.

Diez Roux, A. V. (2001). Investigating neighborhood and area effects on health. *American Journal of Public Health, 91,* 1783–1789.

Diez Roux, A. V. (2002). A glossary for multilevel analysis. *Journal of Epidemiology and Community Health, 56,* 588–594.

Diez Roux, A. V., Merkin, S. S., Arnett, D., Chambless, L., Massing, M., Nieto, F. J., et al. (2001). Neighborhood of residence and incidence of coronary heart disease. *New England Journal of Medicine, 345,* 99–106.

Diez Roux, A. V., Nieto, F. J., Caulfield, L., Tyroler, H. A., Watson, R. L., & Szklo, M. (1999). Neighbourhood differences in diet: the Atherosclerosis Risk in Communities (ARIC) Study. *Journal of Epidemiology and Community Health, 53,* 55–63.

Dik, M., Deeg, D. J., Visser, M., & Jonker, C. (2003). Early life physical activity and cognition at old age. *Journal of Clinical and Experimental Neuropsychology, 25,* 643–653.

Dustman, R., Emmerson, R., & Shearer, D. (1994). Physical activity, age and cognitive neuropsychological function. *Journal of Aging and Physical Activity, 2,* 143–181.

Espino, D. V., Lichtenstein, M. J., Palmer, R. F., & Hazuda, H. P. (2001). Ethnic differences in Mini-Mental State Examination (MMSE) scores: Where you live makes a difference. *Journal of the American Geriatrics Society, 49,* 538–548.

Fischer, C. S. (1982). *To dwell among friends: Personal networks in town and city*. Chicago: University of Chicago Press.

Folstein, M. F., Folstein, S. E., & McHugh, P. R. (1975). "Mini-Mental State": A practical method for grading the cognitive state of patients for the clinician. *Journal of Psychiatric Research, 12,* 189–198.

Franzini, L., Caughy, M., Spears, W., & Fernandez Esquer, M. E. (2005). Neighborhood economic conditions, social processes, and self-rated health in low-income neighborhoods in Texas: A multilevel latent variables model. *Social Science and Medicine, 61,* 1135–1150.

Glass, T. A., & Balfour, J. L. (2003). Neighborhoods, aging, and functional limitations. In I. Kawachi & L. F. Berkman (Eds.), *Neighborhoods and health* (pp. 303–343). Oxford, UK: Oxford University Press.

Glass, T. A., Mendes de Leon, C. F., Marottoli, R. A., & Berkman, L. F. (1999). Population based study of social and productive activities as predictors of survival among elderly Americans. *British Medical Journal, 319,* 478–483.

Hanifan, L. J. (1920). *The community center*. Boston: Silver, Burdett.

Hayward, M. D., & Gorman, B. K. (2004). The long arm of childhood: The influence of early-life social conditions on men's mortality. *Demography, 41,* 87–107.

Hilleras, P. K., Jorm, A. F., Herlitz, A., & Winblad, B. (1999). Activity patterns in very old people: A survey of cognitively intact subjects aged 90 years or older. *Age and Ageing, 28,* 147–152.

Hillman, C. H., Motl, R. W., Pontifex, M. B., Posthuma, D., Stubbe, J. H., Boomsma, D. I., et al. (2006). Physical activity and cognitive function in a cross-section of younger and older community-dwelling individuals. *Health Psychology, 25,* 678–687.

Holtzman, R. E., Rebok, G. W., Saczynski, J. S., Kouzis, A. C., Wilcox, D. K., & Eaton, W. W. (2004). Social network characteristics and cognition in middle-aged and older adults. *Journals of Gerontology Series B: Psychological Sciences and Social Sciences, 59,* 278–284.

Hultsch, D. F., Hammer, M., & Small, B. J. (1993). Age differences in cognitive performance in later life: Relationships to self-reported health and activity life style. *Journal of Gerontology, 48,* 1–11.

Hultsch, D. F., Hertzog, C., Small, B. J., & Dixon, R. A. (1999). Use it or lose it: Engaged lifestyle as a buffer of cognitive decline in aging? *Psychology and Aging, 14,* 245–263.

Hyyppa, M. T., & Maki, J. (2001). Individual-level relationships between social capital and self-rated health in a bilingual community. *Preventive Medicine, 32,* 148–155.

Issa, A. M., Rowe, W., Gauthier, S., & Meaney, M. J. (1990). Hypothalamic–pituitary–adrenal activity in aged, cognitively impaired and cognitively unimpaired rats. *Journal of Neuroscience, 10,* 3247–3254.

Jacobs, J. (1961). *The death and life of great American cities*. New York: Random House.

Kawachi, I., Kennedy, B. P., & Glass, R. (1999). Social capital and self-rated health: A contextual analysis. *American Journal of Public Health, 89,* 1187–1193.

Kawachi, I., Kennedy, B. P., Lochner, K., & Prothrow-Stith, D. (1997). Social capital, income inequality, and mortality. *American Journal of Public Health, 87,* 1491–1498.

Kirtland, K. A., Porter, D. E., Addy, C. L., Neet, M. J., Williams, J. E., Sharpe, P. A., et al. (2003). Environmental measures of physical activity supports: Perception versus reality. *American Journal of Preventive Medicine, 24,* 323–331.

Kohn, M. L., & Schooler, C. (1983). *Work and personality: An inquiry into the impact of social stratification.* Norwood, NJ: Ablex.

Krause, N. (1997). Anticipated support, received support, and economic stress among older adults. *Journals of Gerontology Series B: Psychological Sciences and Social Sciences, 52,* 284–293.

Lang, F. R. (2001). Regulation of social relationships in later adulthood. *Journals of Gerontology Series B: Psychological Sciences and Social Sciences, 56,* 321–326.

Lang, F. R., Featherman, D. L., & Nesselroade, J. R. (1997). Social self-efficacy and short-term variability in social relationships: The MacArthur successful aging studies. *Psychology and Aging, 12,* 657–666.

Liang, J., Bennett, J. M., Krause, N. M., Chang, M. C., Lin, H. S., Chuang, Y. L., et al. (1999). Stress, social relations, and old age mortality in Taiwan. *Journal of Clinical Epidemiology, 52,* 983–995.

Lin, N. (1982). Social resources and instrumental action. In N. Lin & P. Marsden (Eds.), *Social structure and network analysis* (pp. 131–145). Beverly Hills, CA: Sage.

Lin, N. (1986). Modeling the effects of social support. In N. Lin, A. Dean, & W. M. Ensel (Eds.), *Social support, life events, and depression* (pp. 173–209). Orlando, FL: Academic Press.

Locher, J. L., Ritchie, C. S., Roth, D. L., Baker, P. S., Bodner, E. V., & Allman, R. M. (2005). Social isolation, support, and capital and nutritional risk in an older sample: Ethnic and gender differences. *Social Science and Medicine, 60,* 747–761.

Loury, G. (1977). A dynamic theory of racial income differences. In P. A. Wallace & A. LeMund (Eds.), *Women, minorities, and employment discrimination* (pp. 153–186). Lexington, MA: Lexington Books.

Lytle, M. E., Vander, B. J., Pandav, R. S., Dodge, H. H., & Ganguli, M. (2004). Exercise level and cognitive decline: The MoVIES project. *Alzheimer Disease and Associated Disorders, 18,* 57–64.

Macinko, J., & Starfield, B. (2001). The utility of social capital in research on health determinants. *Milbank Quarterly, 79,* 387–427.

Malmstrom, M., Sundquist, J., & Johansson, S. E. (1999). Neighborhood environment and self-reported health status: A multilevel analysis. *American Journal of Public Health, 89,* 1181–1186.

Martikainen, P., Kauppinen, T. M., & Valkonen, T. (2003). Effects of the characteristics of neighbourhoods and the characteristics of people on cause specific mortality: A register based follow up study of 252,000 men. *Journal of Epidemiology and Community Health, 57,* 210–217.

Massey, D., & Denton, N. A. (1993). *American apartheid: Segregation and the making of the underclass.* Cambridge, MA: Harvard University Press.

McEwen, B. S. (2001). From molecules to mind: Stress, individual differences, and the social environment. In A. R. Damasio, A. Harrington, J. Kagan, B. McEwen, H. Moss, & R. Shaikh (Eds.), *Annals of the New York Academy of Sciences: Vol. 935. Unity of knowledge: The convergence of natural and human science* (pp. 42–49). New York: New York Academy of Sciences.

McEwen, B. S., & Sapolsky, R. M. (1995). Stress and cognitive function. *Current Opinions in Neurobiology, 5,* 205–216.

Mendes de Leon, C. F., Glass, T. A., Beckett, L. A., Seeman, T. E., Evans, D. A., & Berkman, L. F. (1999). Social networks and disability transitions across eight intervals of yearly data in the New Haven EPESE. *Journals of Gerontology Series B: Psychological Sciences and Social Sciences, 54,* S162–S172.

Molfese, V. J., Modglin, A., & Molfese, D. L. (2003). The role of environment in the development of reading skills: a longitudinal study of preschool and school-age measures. *Journal of Learning Disabilities, 36,* 59–67.

Morenoff, J. D., Sampson, R. J., & Raudenbush, S. W. (2001). Neighborhood inequality, collective efficacy, and the spatial dynamics of urban violence. *Criminology, 39,* 517–560.

Musick, M. A., Herzog, A. R., & House, J. S. (1999). Volunteering and mortality among older adults: Findings from a national sample. *Journals of*

Gerontology Series B: Psychological Sciences and Social Sciences, 54, S173–S180.

Newson, R. S., & Kemps, E. B. (2006). Cardio-respiratory fitness as a predictor of successful cognitive ageing. *Journal of Clinical and Experimental Neuropsychology, 28,* 949–967.

O'Rand, A. M. (2001). Stratification and the life course. In R. H. Binstock & L. K. George (Eds.), *Handbook of aging and the social sciences* (pp. 197–213). New York: Academic Press.

Patel, K. V., Eschbach, K., Rudkin, L. L., Peek, M. K., & Markides, K. S. (2003). Neighborhood context and self-rated health in older Mexican Americans. *Annals of Epidemiology, 13,* 620–628.

Peek, M. K., & Lin, N. (1999). Age differences in the effects of network composition on psychological distress. *Social Science and Medicine, 49,* 621–636.

Portes, A. (1998). Social capital: Its origins and applications in modern sociology. *Annual Review of Sociology, 24,* 1–24.

Putnam, R. (2000). *Bowling alone: The collapse and revival of American community.* New York: Simon & Schuster.

Putnam, R., Leonardi, R., & Nanetti, R. (1993). *Making democracy work: Civic traditions in modern Italy.* Princeton, NJ: Princeton University Press.

Richards, M., Hardy, R., & Wadsworth, M. E. (2003). Does active leisure protect cognition? Evidence from a national birth cohort. *Social Science and Medicine, 56,* 785–792.

Rietschlin, J. (1998). Voluntary association membership and psychological distress. *Journal of Health and Social Behavior, 39,* 348–355.

Rowe, J. W., & Kahn, R. L. (1997). Successful aging. *The Gerontologist, 37,* 433–440.

Ryff, C. D. (1991). Possible selves in adulthood and old age: A tale of shifting horizons. *Psychology and Aging, 6,* 286–295.

Sampson, R., & Groves, W. (1989). Community structure and crime—Testing social-disorganization theory. *American Journal of Sociology, 94,* 774–802.

Sampson, R. J., Raudenbush, S. W., & Earls, F. (1997, August 15). Neighborhoods and violent crime: A multilevel study of collective efficacy. *Science, 277,* 918–924.

Satariano, W. A. (1997). The disabilities of aging—Looking to the physical environment. *American Journal of Public Health, 87,* 331–332.

Seeman, T. E., Berkman, L. F., Kohout, F., Lacroix, A., Glynn, R., & Blazer, D. (1993). Intercommunity variations in the association between social ties and mortality in the elderly. A comparative analysis of three communities. *Annals of Epidemiology, 3,* 325–335.

Seeman, T. E., & Crimmins, E. (2001). Social environment effects on health and aging: Integrating epidemiologic and demographic approaches and perspectives. In M. Weinstein, A. I. Hermalin, & M. A. Stoto (Eds.), *Annals of the New York Academy of Sciences: Vol. 954. Population health and aging: Strengthening the dialogue between epidemiology and demography* (pp. 88–117). New York: New York Academy of Sciences.

Smith, G. D., Hart, C., Watt, G., Hole, D., & Hawthorne, V. (1998). Individual social class, area-based deprivation, cardiovascular disease risk factors, and mortality: The Renfrew and Paisley Study. *Journal of Epidemiology and Community Health, 52,* 399–405.

Suthers, K., Kim, J. K., & Crimmins, E. (2003). Life expectancy with cognitive impairment in the older population of the United States. *Journals of Gerontology Series B: Psychological Sciences and Social Sciences, 58,* S179–S186.

Unger, J. B., Johnson, C. A., & Marks, G. (1997). Functional decline in the elderly: Evidence for direct and stress-buffering protective effects of social interactions and physical activity. *Annals of Behavioral Medicine, 19,* 152–160.

Verbrugge, L. M., & Jette, A. M. (1994). The disablement process. *Social Science and Medicine, 38,* 1–14.

Waitzman, N. J., & Smith, K. R. (1998). Phantom of the area: Poverty-area residence and mortality in the United States. *American Journal of Public Health, 88,* 973–976.

Wall, E., Ferrazzi, G., & Schryer, F. (1998). Getting the goods on social capital. *Rural Sociology, 63,* 300–322.

Wen, M. & Christakis, N. A. (2005). Neighborhood effects on posthospitalization mortality: a population-based cohort study of the elderly in Chicago. *Health Services Research, 40,* 1108–1127.

Weuve, J., Kang, J. H., Manson, J. E., Breteler, M. M., Ware, J. H., & Grodstein, F. (2004). Physical activity, including walking, and cognitive function in older women. *Journal of the American Medical Association, 292,* 1454–1461.

Wight, R. G., Aneshensel, C. S., Miller-Martinez, D., Botticello, A. L., Cummings, J. R., Karlamangla, A. S., et al. (2006). Urban neighborhood context, educational attainment, and cognitive function among older adults. *American Journal of Epidemiology, 163,* 1071–1078.

Wilkinson, R. (1996). *Unhealthy societies: The afflictions of inequality.* London: Routledge.

Wilson, R. S., Barnes, L. L., Bennett, D. A., Li, Y., Bienias, J. L., Mendes de Leon, C. F., et al. (2005). Proneness to psychological distress and risk of Alzheimer disease in a biracial community. *Neurology, 64,* 380–382.

Wilson, R. S., Barnes, L. L., Mendes de Leon, C. F., Aggarwal, N. T., Schneider, J. S., Bach, J., et al. (2002). Depressive symptoms, cognitive decline, and risk of AD in older persons. *Neurology, 59,* 364–370.

Wilson, R. S., Bennett, D. A., Beckett, L. A., Morris, M. C., Gilley, D. W., Bienias, J. L., et al. (1999). Cognitive activity in older persons from a geographically defined population. *Journals of Gerontology Series B: Psychological Sciences and Social Sciences, 54B,* P155–P160.

Wilson, R. S., Bennett, D. A., Bienias, J. L., Mendes de Leon, C. F., Morris, M. C., & Evans, D. A. (2003). Cognitive activity and cognitive decline in a biracial community population. *Neurology, 61,* 812–816.

Wilson, R. S., Bennett, D. A., Mendes de Leon, C. F., Bienias, J. L., Morris, M. C., & Evans, D. A. (2005). Distress proneness and cognitive decline in a population of older persons. *Psychoneuroendocrinology, 30,* 11–17.

Wilson, W. J. (1987). *The truly disadvantaged: The inner city, the underclass, and public policy.* Chicago: University of Chicago Press.

Yen, I. H., & Kaplan, G. A. (1999). Poverty area residence and changes in depression and perceived health status: Evidence from the Alameda County Study. *International Journal of Epidemiology, 28,* 90–94.

Zunzunegui, M. V., Alvarado, B. E., Del Ser, T., & Otero, A. (2003). Social networks, social integration, and social engagement determine cognitive decline in community-dwelling Spanish older adults. *Journals of Gerontology Series B: Psychological Sciences and Social Sciences, 58,* S93–S100.

37

SOCIAL CONTEXT AND COGNITION

FREDDA BLANCHARD-FIELDS,
MICHELLE HORHOTA, AND ANDREW MIENALTOWSKI

There is a wealth of research showing that, in comparison to young adults, older adults' performance differs across a wide variety of cognitive tasks. Studies of the basic mechanics of cognition typically find declines in cognitive change and tie this change to physiological decline, especially when tasks are highly resource-dependent (Zacks, Hasher, & Li, 2000). Although this approach is important for identifying changes in basic cognitive processes, these studies may not accurately reflect the potential range of older adults' skills and knowledge. Cognitive studies have traditionally not examined how social knowledge (e.g., beliefs about appropriate behavior in particular situations), emotions, and motivational factors affect cognition and reasoning that are necessary for successful cognitive functioning in an everyday context. However, when such contextual variables are included, researchers find that older adults' cognitive functioning often remains intact and may even improve across the life span (Blanchard-Fields, Jahnke, & Camp, 1995; Carstensen & Mikels, 2005; Hess, 2005). The overarching goal of this chapter is to consider the impact of such contextual factors on cognitive change in adulthood.

Studying adult cognitive change embedded in a social context is an important component of a life span developmental perspective. This perspective views effective development as a lifelong adaptive process that highlights the importance of multidirectionality (including gains and losses), multidimensionality, and multifunctionality (Baltes, Lindenberger, & Staudinger, 2006). When cognition is placed in a social context, important issues are raised for cognitive aging research such as how life experiences, social interactions, beliefs, and emotions influence both our motivations and how we process material. As individuals grow older, they use skills that they have learned and aspects of the environment that will aid them in meeting their selected goals. Thus the role of motivation and processing goals becomes particularly important in studying cognition in a social context. Even as certain basic cognitive mechanisms decline, such as recall or speed of processing, older adults may still possess the social knowledge and skills that allow them to function effectively. In other words, decline in performance in cognitive mechanics does not necessarily translate into how cognition operates or into the types of knowledge that are implemented in a social context. Consequently, along with the mechanics of cognition, cognitive functioning must be examined in terms of individual, social, and cultural variations as well as their interactions (Baltes et al., 2006).

It is not always the case that social context is facilitative, reflecting gains in cognitive performance. Social context can also have a debilitating effect reflecting loss in cognitive performance. Thus, as we consider social context effects on the cognitive functioning of older adults in this chapter, we are interested in identifying the conditions and contexts in which older adults function effectively and the conditions and context in which they do not.

This chapter organizes social context on two broad levels: (1) self-perceived social context and (2) interactive social context. First, at the individual level, we specify *self-perceived social context*, or the internalized representation of and reactions to external social contextual factors. This highlights the importance of social knowledge-based forms of cognition such as an individual's goals, emotion, personal knowledge structures, beliefs, and stereotypes in interpreting a cognitive task. A common way of conceptualizing the importance of self-perceived social context is to examine how this context can facilitate compensatory mechanisms used by older adults to offset cognitive losses. This is exemplified in research demonstrating effective functioning on the part of older adults in knowledge-rich domains such as everyday problem solving (Artistico, Cervone, & Pezzuti, 2003; Berg & Klaczynski, 2002; Blanchard-Fields, 2007), social intelligence (Blanchard-Fields, 1996), and memory in context (Hess, 2005). However, there are also aspects of the self-perceived social context that can be detrimental to cognitive performance, such as the perception of negative age stereotypes in memory testing situations. Both facilitative and debilitating aspects of self-perceived social context are examined in the first section of this chapter.

In the second section of this chapter we address cognition within an *interactive social context*. This type of context is a relational level of analysis that requires consideration of the dynamic interaction within the immediate social context involving the self and an external other. Research in this area primarily includes the social-communicative context of the individual as she performs cognitive tasks collaboratively with another individual. This type of context can also involve social exchanges in which the cognitive outcome variable (e.g., memory) involves communication of information with a partner (e.g., retelling a story to a partner). As with self-perceived context, interactive social contexts

can be either beneficial or detrimental to the effective functioning of the older adult depending upon characteristics of the social context.

SELF-PERCEIVED SOCIAL CONTEXT

Our thoughts and actions are defined by how we perceive and interpret the world around us. Goals, emotions, and social knowledge are motivational factors that color our perceptions and define our self-perceived social context. Because this type of context is highly influenced by one's personal motivations, individuals who are exposed to the same contextual environment can interpret it differently. In turn, such interpretations can impact cognitive outcomes (e.g., memory, attentional focus, reasoning, etc.) both in positive and negative ways.

Developmental theories in the literature propose various trajectories of motivation across the life span and these alternative trajectories result in differential cognitive outcomes. From a cognitive resource perspective, individuals allocate resources to selected domains of personal relevance and importance resulting in adaptive cognitive functioning. For example, *socioemotional selectivity theory* posits a positivity effect such that older adults are increasingly motivated to process positive emotional experiences and down-regulate negative experiences in comparison to younger adults. In terms of cognitive functioning, older adults' attention is deployed toward positive stimuli and away from negatively valenced stimuli when compared to young adults (Carstensen & Mikels, 2005). In this section, we discuss such motivational factors including emotion, personal goals, social knowledge, personal beliefs about the self, and stereotypes that may impact various cognitive outcomes in older adulthood.

Goals

Personal goals play a major role in creating context in our lives. They reflect the underlying motivations of our thoughts and actions, and they are shaped by how we perceive our own ever-changing environmental context. Across the life span, personal goals change to match our needs, with young adults striving mainly for achievement-oriented goals, such as completing a college degree or starting a career, and middle-aged and older adults seeking a balance between functioning autonomously and sharing their lives with others (e.g., children, significant others/spouses). Here we focus on a few instances drawn from the literature that illustrate how goal orientations at different points in the life span influence observed age differences in cognitive functioning.

Selective optimization with compensation is a pervasive theoretical model that posits that development occurs as we continuously update personal goals to match our appraisal of available resources (Baltes & Baltes, 1990). Throughout life we are faced with many choices and each decision we make involves selecting a preference and optimizing our growth along this path. We choose manageable goals based upon both our interests and the physical and cognitive limitations that we are facing. With advancing age, such limitations become more salient and require us to re-evaluate our interests. Therefore in the latter half of adulthood, research suggests that interests shift toward physical health and socioemotional domains (Carstensen & Mikels, 2005; Rowe & Kahn, 1998).

This shift in priorities means that in a given task context the goal of the task may be perceived differently by older and younger adults. A clear example of this shift in goal selection can be seen in research that examines how young and older adults prioritize task performance in a dual-task manipulation. Young and older adults were asked to memorize a list of words while simultaneously maintaining their balance as they navigated an obstacle course (Li, Lindenberger, Freund, & Baltes, 2001). Although age-differences in dual-task costs were larger for the memory task than for the walking task, older adults chose to forgo improving memory performance via external aids (i.e., reduce the speed of stimulus presentation) and instead chose to use the external aid designed to optimize walking performance (e.g., a hand-rail). When deciding which was more important to them, memory performance versus balance, older adults displayed a preference for physical safety even though such a choice might create the appearance of reduced cognitive ability. From this example, we see that life span shifts in personal goals can be both helpful and harmful.

Goal selection requires that we carefully choose where we should invest our limited resources. When faced with cognition tasks in the laboratory, young adults are primarily motivated to achieve maximum performance. Older adults prefer to maintain performance, optimizing their current resources rather than risking loss (Ebner, Freund, & Baltes, 2006). From a motivational standpoint, older adults are less willing than young adults to invest energy into improving their cognitive performance (e.g., training benefits) and instead are more interested in maintaining their abilities at their current level, a level that allows for autonomous functioning. Although the selective investment of resources does not necessarily translate into cognitive gains, it does help older adults optimize their cognitive performance in the domains that they prioritize in their lives (e.g., intergoal facilitation; Riediger, Freund, & Baltes, 2005). Throughout adulthood, we strive to attain those personal goals that are deemed important to us, adjusting these goals when faced with potentially overwhelming demands or with a shrinking pool of cognitive and physical resources. Although we cannot compensate for all of the resource limitations that come with advancing age, we can invest those resources we have into those goals that maximize an independent lifestyle and a positive sense of well-being.

Along these lines, recent work by Carstensen and her colleagues (e.g., Carstensen & Mikels, 2005) suggests that the pursuit of emotionally meaningful interactions becomes a primary motivation that can substantially influence cognition in the latter half of the life span. We therefore turn next to the impact of emotion processing goals on cognition.

Emotion Processing Goals

Emotion and affect may increasingly influence cognitive processes across the life span as emotion processing goals become prioritized in middle-age and older adulthood. This becomes apparent when one considers the number of ways that individuals selectively process emotional information. One form of selective processing that has received much theoretical attention in the aging literature is the positivity effect (Carstensen & Mikels, 2005). This effect reflects a processing priority for positive information on the part of older adults, which, for example, could result in more accurate recall of positive information. A negativity suppression effect has also received attention in the aging literature (Blanchard-Fields, 2006). This form of selective processing prioritizes ways to minimize the processing of negative information.

Carstensen, Mikels, and Mather (2006) operationalized a positivity effect as age differences in the ratio of positive to negative material in information processing. Researchers have found that in directing one's attention to positive or negative stimuli older adults avoid attending to negative stimuli and in some cases attend more to positive stimuli (Mather & Carstensen, 2003, Experiment 1). In memory experiments, older adults recall and recognize more positive images and neutral images than negative ones in comparison to young adults (Charles, Mather, & Carstensen, 2003, Experiment 1), they show better performance in a working memory task for positive emotional stimuli in comparison to negative emotional stimuli (Mikels, Larkin, Reuter-Lorenz, & Carstensen, 2005), remember more positive information when recalling autobiographical information (Kennedy, Mather, & Carstensen, 2004; Levine & Bluck, 1997), and remember their decisions as more positive in emotional valence (Mather, Knight, & McCaffrey, 2005).

An alternative perspective proposes that focusing on negative information is adaptive because it signals danger and vulnerability and thus is important for survival. This emphasis on negativity has been found in both the social and cognitive neuroscience literature for well over a decade (e.g., Lane & Nadel, 2000; Rozin & Royzman, 2001). Within the social cognitive aging literature, some studies demonstrate that older adults spend more time viewing negative stimuli (Charles et al., 2003) and display a negativity effect (Thomas & Hasher, 2006; Wood & Kisley, 2006). With respect to memory, Grühn, Smith, and Baltes (2005) found no evidence for a positivity effect and instead found evidence for a reduced negativity effect in older adults when remembering a list of words with negative, positive, and neutral valence. When incidentally encoding pictures, both young and older adults recalled the central element more than the peripheral elements only for negative scenes.

However, when instructed to attend to this difference, only young adults overcame this encoding bias, whereas older adults could not overcome the memory trade-off (Kensinger, Piguet, Krendl, & Corkin, 2005).

Emotional goals therefore appear to help individuals when they create a supportive context for cognitive processing. The distinctiveness of emotions helps older adults to process information, and, for example, reduces the number of false memories produced (Kensinger & Corkin, 2004; May, Rahhal, Berry, & Leighton, 2005). Conversely, emotions impede information processing when they create interference. For example, situations high in arousal and high in executive control processing demands lead older adults to be poorer at remembering and processing information (Kensinger & Corkin, 2004; Mather & Knight, 2005; Wurm, Labouvie-Vief, Aycock, Rebucal, & Koch, 2004). Second, a focus on only positive information can interfere with decision making by leading to the neglect of important criteria for making a quality decision in some contexts (Löckenhoff & Carstensen, 2004).

Social Knowledge

Self-perceived context is also shaped by the social knowledge that we acquire from life's experiences. While navigating through life's experiences, knowledge and strategies that lead to successful outcomes become engrained in our repertoire of adaptive responses. Because older adults have had more time to refine this social knowledge, they may develop an increased sensitivity to the circumstances surrounding their experiences and thus have the potential to better adapt their strategies to meet the demands of the circumstances than younger adults. For example, when asked to consider multiple sources of information to make a social judgment, older adults are more likely than young adults to base their decision on the information that is most diagnostic to the domain in which the judgment is made (Hess, 2006).

Similarly, research suggests that the conditions under which older adults are tested play a substantial role in their ability to use personal knowledge to offset cognitive decline. When given psychometric tests of planning, older adults perform better when asked to engage in activities that are more similar to their actual personal routines (e.g., planning a day) than to standard neuropsychological laboratory tasks of planning (e.g., Tower of London; Phillips, Kliegel, & Martin, 2006). When performing everyday problem-solving tasks, older adults are more efficacious than young adults at solving problems that are relevant to the later years of life but are less effective when the problem-solving task is a standard psychometric test (Artistico et al., 2003).

The facilitative effect of social knowledge also has been observed in research on attributional reasoning across the life span (Blanchard-Fields, 1996). With advancing age there is a greater tendency to attribute the cause of an event resulting in a negative outcome (e.g., the break up of a marriage) to the dispositional (internal) characteristics of the main or target character. This tendency is coupled with a failure to fully consider situational factors that might also explain the negative outcome (Blanchard-Fields & Beatty, 2005). Some research suggests that the content of relevant social beliefs and values accounts for age differences in such causal attributions (Blanchard-Fields & Hertzog, 2000). Specifically, older adults hold more traditional values and beliefs about relationships and are more likely to make dispositional attributions about individuals whose relationship behaviors violate those beliefs. This research demonstrates that different social contexts evoke differential beliefs and values that underlie one's judgments. Similarly, research finds that the tendency to attribute cause to dispositional characteristics of the target on the part of older adults is eliminated when the situation highlights the plausibility of environmental explanations for the event. Simply heightening the perceptual salience of the situational forces did not influence older adults' judgments about character, whereas highlighting a social-motivational explanation for the behavior did impact older adults' explanations for the behavior (Blanchard-Fields & Horhota, 2005). Thus, although older adults can be prone to biased or misinformed social judgments in some situations, these biases can be ameliorated when older adults make use of their social knowledge structures related to beliefs and their knowledge of social-motivational components of human behavior.

Further evidence that social knowledge can facilitate older adults' reasoning processes is found in research demonstrating that social judgments made by older age groups are more sensitive to the diagnosticity of the information that is available when making that judgment compared with young adults (Hess, 2006). For example, young adults are likely to adjust their impression of a target character if they receive new information about the target that contradicts their original impression. Older adults are more selective in the information that they use in forming judgments, focusing on details that are most relevant to the judgment domain (Hess, Osowski, & Leclerc, 2005), and adjust their initial impression only if the new information is diagnostic (i.e., informative and relevant) for the domain of the social judgment (Hess, Bolstad, & Woodburn, 1999). Additional work also has demonstrated that older adults' use of trait-diagnostic information for social judgments can be motivated by manipulations of personal relevance and social accountability (Hess, Germain, Rosenberg, LeClerc, & Hodges, 2005; Hess, Rosenberg, & Waters, 2001). This suggests that older age groups are willing to invest resources on information processing in social reasoning situations if they are invested in the social context in which the judgment is made.

Despite the positive influence that accumulated social knowledge can have on social cognitive outcomes, when cognitive demands are high an individual's accumulated knowledge structures may not be sufficient for making effective judgments. Contrary to the studies reviewed above, if the social judgment scenario requires that older adults ignore some information and attend to other information, they have difficulty preventing the unwanted information to enter into their judgments and decision making. In this case, older adults display biased judgments when the task required them to consider true information while simultaneously discounting false information about a target (Chen & Blanchard-Fields, 2000). In addition, age-related resource limitations may make it especially difficult for older adults to apply knowledge in time for it to be useful in social reasoning. For example, theory-of-mind research suggests that resource limitations impair older adults' ability to adopt the perspective of characters in hypothetical situations to draw conclusions about a target's behavior (Sullivan & Ruffman, 2004).

Together, these results suggest that older adults may be able to use experience accumulated during life to guide judgments and decision making in contexts that are relevant to daily life and tap into relevant social knowledge structures, but they fail to benefit from experience on narrowly defined tests that focus on one's ability to produce the most ideal (i.e., correct) solution in novel situations. However, there are important caveats to this interpretation of the results. Although older adults might use personal experience to bolster their performance on tasks that are similar to those encountered in their day-to-day activities, experience is seldom manipulated or even measured as an individual-difference variable in research studies. Furthermore, personal experience, or lack thereof in specific testing domains and contexts, can also impair older adult performance on tasks designed to examine social cognition.

Memory Beliefs, Self-Efficacy, and Control

As we have argued thus far, older adults allocate their resources to a cognitive task when they are invested in the task and the context in which the task is occurring. Therefore, beliefs about one's cognitive abilities for a given task should affect individuals' performance and should impact their perception of the performance context in which they find themselves. Much of the literature on beliefs about cognition has focused on the domain of memory and includes work on implicit theories about the memory abilities of people in general. More specifically, this work includes research on stereotypes (Hummert, 1999; Ryan, 1992), perceptions of rates of memory change (Lineweaver & Hertzog, 1998; McFarland, Ross, & Giltrow, 1992), and attributions of performance and control beliefs (Erber, 1989; Hertzog, Lineweaver, & McGuire, 1999; Lachman, Steinberg, & Trotter, 1987), as well as research about one's personal abilities to succeed or self-efficacy on a memory task (Berry, 1999).

Researchers most commonly have found that people of all ages believe in age-based declines in memory abilities (Ryan, 1992). Studies that have differentiated the concept of memory into a series of everyday, specific tasks, such as remembering names or places, have found that implicit beliefs about all of these facets are negatively associated with age (Lineweaver & Hertzog, 1998; McFarland et al., 1992; Ryan, 1992; Ryan & Kwong See, 1993). In addition to beliefs about decline in cognitive domains in general, people also hold beliefs about the causes of declines. Research examining memory failures has found that older targets' forgetfulness is attributed to lack of ability rather than effort (Erber, 1989; Erber & Prager, 1999). Older adults report that they feel less control over their intellectual functioning (Devolder & Pressley, 1992; Lachman, 1986), and have lower memory self-efficacy, than do young adults (Berry & West, 1993; Lineweaver & Hertzog, 1998). These beliefs are based in part on past successes and failures on a task as well as on feedback from others (e.g., social feedback). Therefore, older adults' beliefs in age-related reductions in cognitive functioning may reflect more frequent negative feedback from forgetting episodes rather than positive feedback about success. These beliefs may also reflect social pressure to ascribe failure to age rather than to effort (Cavanaugh, 1996).

Berry and West (1993) suggested that memory self-efficacy and performance relationships should be strongest for older adults because they are more concerned about their memory and potential memory loss than are younger adults. Some recent evidence suggests that the belief–performance correlations do in fact increase with age, at least for some belief constructs (Jopp & Lindenberger, 2003). The evidence further suggests that beliefs about cognition may be facilitative or debilitative depending on the type of belief that is elicited in a person by the performance context.

When a person attributes the cause of task performance to an internal factor (i.e., something about oneself), this leads to increased effort and motivation on the task as well as higher goal setting, both of which can facilitate performance. For example, if a person's perceived self-efficacy is high, then the goals that are set and the person's commitment to those goals will be high (Bandura, 1989). Several studies have shown that participant performance, self-efficacy, and motivation are positively affected by setting goals for both young and older adults (West, Bagwell, & Dark-Freudman, 2005). When efficacy was high, it was reflected in higher goal setting, and subsequently more effort was invested to obtain the goal that was set (West, Welch, & Thorn, 2001). In longitudinal work, Valentijn, Hill, and Van Hooren (2006) found that individuals' memory self-efficacy predicted objective memory performance 6 years later, with higher levels of self-efficacy predicting higher performance levels.

Conversely, beliefs can be detrimental to performance, because participants who make low internal, stable, and global attributions for successful performance show declines in memory performance (Lachman et al., 1987). These findings may relate to a decreased use of strategies, which is a form of effort. Several studies have now shown that participants who make uncontrollable attributions perform less well on memory tasks and report less strategy use for those tasks (Devolder & Pressley, 1992; Hertzog, McGuire, & Lineweaver, 1998).

In sum, negative memory beliefs appear to be detrimental to memory performance, because the belief that one cannot do something may relate to reduced effort on memory tasks, a greater likelihood of retaining ineffective memory strategies, or the failure to correctly analyze the cause of performance. However, positive beliefs can be beneficial to memory performance because they may motivate individuals to compensate for the losses in cognitive abilities commonly experienced by older adults.

Stereotypes and Stereotype Threat

Stereotypes are beliefs about attributes and behaviors of members of a particular group that act as a way to categorize and understand large amounts of information available to a person at any given time (Hilton & von Hippel, 1996). With respect to aging, there is evidence to suggest that traditional cognitive aging studies may underestimate older adults' cognitive performance because of the debilitating context that stereotypes can create; however, the influence of stereotypes cannot wholly account for the observed declines in cognitive performance.

Stereotypes related to age groups are multifaceted, including both negative and positive subcategories in the stereotype (e.g., older adults are perceived as both frail and kind; Hummert, 1999). However, a large body of evidence suggests that the negative components of aging stereotypes tend to dominate thinking (Perdue & Gurtman, 1990, although see Chasteen, Schwarz, & Park, 2002). Relevant to the current discussion is evidence that such negative stereotypes about older adults can be detrimental to subsequent cognitive performance (Andreoletti & Lachman, 2004; Chasteen, Bhattacharyya, Horhota, Tam, & Hasher, 2005; Hess, Auman, Colcombe, & Rahhal, 2003; Levy, 1996).

Some recent work has aimed to link negative stereotypes with cognitive performance directly. Levy (1996) initially found that older adults' memory performance tended to be lower when negative stereotypic traits were activated. Several additional studies have confirmed the detrimental effects of negative age stereotypes on certain kinds of memory performance (Hess, Hinson, & Statham, 2004; Stein, Blanchard-Fields, & Hertzog, 2002). Rahhal, Hasher, and Colcombe (2001) directly examined the effect of a testing situation on older adults' memory performance. They found that age differences were found in a condition emphasizing memory, but in a condition emphasizing learning both young and older adults' performances were equal.[1]

More recently, researchers have tried to measure the stereotype process more rigorously in older adult populations by assessing stereotype activation. Chasteen et al. (2005) explicitly measured participants' perceptions of stereotype threat (i.e., concern about being judged in the testing context based on an age stereotype) and found that young and older adults reported different perceptions of stereotype threat in the testing situation. Older participants perceived higher levels of stereotype threat in the situation, and these perceptions were related to decreased memory performance. Hess et al. (2003) induced negative age stereotypes and showed that such stereotypes led to declines in the memory performance of older adults. Additional research has found that high levels of education may act as a buffer to the influence of stereotypes. Individuals with high levels of education were not affected by stereotypes on a memory task, whereas individuals with lower amounts of education were affected by stereotype manipulations (Andreoletti & Lachman, 2004).

Although the aforementioned studies have focused on young and older adults, there is also evidence that middle-aged adults are susceptible to negative age stereotypes (O'Brien & Hummert, 2006). Middle-aged adults with an older age identity displayed poorer memory performance when they were told that their performance would be compared with older adults' performance. Individuals with more youthful identities did not show differences in memory performance regardless of whether they were told that they would be compared to young or older individuals.

Although the lion's share of the research in this area has focused on the detrimental effects of stereotypes, there is also some mixed evidence for the beneficial effects of positive stereotypes on older adults' cognitive performance (Hess et al., 2004; Levy, 1996; Stein et al., 2002). Cultural groups that hold more positive views of aging have either no significant differences in memory performance between young and older participants (Levy & Langer, 1994) or smaller age differences (Yoon, Hasher, Feinberg, Rahhal, & Winocur, 2000).

In sum, this section on self-perceived social context provides evidence that goals, emotions, and social knowledge differ across the life span and affect our perceptions of the cognitive tasks at hand. The interpretations that we project onto situations can impact cognitive outcomes (e.g., memory, attentional focus, reasoning) both in positive and negative ways. Next, we turn to a discussion of interactive social context.

INTERACTIVE SOCIAL CONTEXT

Our personal interpretations of the world are not limited to thoughts and actions that emerge solely from the self; they also evolve in the dynamic exchanges that we share with other people. As we interact with others, we communicate and take in information about domains that we feel are essential. In the laboratory, social communication is assessed in terms of its value to the listener and in terms of what it indicates about the cognitive status of the speaker. Social communication has also been examined as partners work together to solve problems in a collaborative fashion. In both cases, communication is facilitated by a shared sense of what is important to cognitive performance between partners. This is measured at the level of what is said and in terms of the actual level of cognitive ability demonstrated by the dyad. The key to social interaction is recognizing that social communication and cognitive outcomes assessed via communication (e.g., problem solving, memory) often require the integration of multiple perspectives. In this section of the chapter we address cognition within an interactive social context by discussing cognition at a relational level of analysis in which dynamic interaction between one's immediate social context (self-relevant) and the perspective of an external other is considered.

Collaborative Cognition

Collaborative cognition occurs when two or more people work together to solve a cognitive task. By definition, it is cognition that occurs in an interactive context, and the interactive nature of the context can either provide benefits or hinder an individual's performance (Dixon, 2001). Older adults prefer to solve problems collaboratively when they perceive deficits in their own functioning but prefer to work alone when they perceive themselves as capable of completing the task on their own (Strough, Cheng, & Swenson, 2002). In addition to serving as a means to compensate for one's perceived inadequacies, collaboration also serves to enhance relationships between collaborative partners (Meegan & Berg, 2002). For example, in the case of individuals who are trying to solve a problem or recall a piece of information, it may be helpful if one's collaborative partner acts as a memory aid or has the necessary information to produce a solution. Furthermore, the act of collectively retelling a story or reliving a past event can be a way to positively reflect on one's relationship. However, if the collaborative partner's memory fails when bringing to mind the information she was responsible for remembering, then collectively the partners may do worse at recalling the information than if each had been working individually.

Collaborative cognition frequently occurs in everyday contexts. Researchers have frequently compared the performance of married couples with that of unfamiliar partners using joint decision-making tasks (Berg, Johnson, Meegan, & Strough, 2003), episodic memory tasks (Dixon & Gould, 1998), and everyday problem-solving tasks (Dixon, Fox, Trevithick, & Brundin, 1997; Margrett, 2000). These studies show that collaboration can be equally beneficial to young and older adults when paired performance is compared with individual performance.

Several factors influence whether collaboration will enhance performance or act as a detriment to it. It has been thought that the more one knows her partner, then the more beneficial collaboration with that partner will be. However, findings on this point have been mixed. Some studies show that when collaborators are well acquainted (e.g., married couples), older adults can perform as well as young adults (Dixon & Gould, 1998). Conversely, other studies have shown that familiarity does not aid collaborative recall (Gould, Osborn, & Krein, 2002). Also, the content of the exchange seems to matter. Performance is better when partners engage in cooperative speech acts than when they engage in sequences of controlling speech acts. Moreover, the latter is associated with decisions to divide the tasks rather than working on them together (Berg et al., 2003). When partners interact cooperatively and support each other, outcomes are facilitated and result in more efficient solutions or higher quality decision-making processes. When couples engage in rejecting or countering ways, they show poor performance and suboptimal strategy use when solving problems (Berg et al., 2003). Finally, the type of task and the gender of the interactive partners appears to influence collaborative outcomes. Structured tasks are equally influenced by male or female partners, whereas less structured tasks tend to be more influenced by the male in the dyad (Margrett & Marsiske, 2002).

Collaboration can be detrimental if a partner actually disrupts the other partner's preferred strategy or thought processes. When recalling information alone, individuals typically use different retrieval strategies than when they try to recall information with a partner. For example, collaboration partners may divide up items on a list to be remembered rather than both partners trying to remember all the information. At retrieval, one partner may recall information the other partner has missed, or one partner may act as a cue for the other partner's recall (Dixon, 2001). However, if at retrieval one partner tries to use a retrieval strategy that is different from the strategy to which the other partner is accustomed, then collaborative recall can lead to fewer correctly recalled items than in individual recall (Finlay, Hitch, & Meudell, 2000). Furthermore, cognitive outcomes can also be impaired if group members prevent other members from elaborating on their ideas either at encoding or retrieval. Finally, collaboration is also detrimental when a person feels that she is being forced to work with someone else because others are questioning her ability to effectively perform the task autonomously. Being forced to engage in unwanted collaborative efforts can be related to lowered self-efficacy (Meegan & Berg, 2002).

Reflecting developmental themes across adulthood, potential collaborators change because of changing contexts, such as family or work (Meegan & Berg, 2002). With age, the number of potential collaborators may shrink. However, the shared history with those collaborators increases and therefore can facilitate knowledge of the partner's skills and differential expertise (Meegan & Berg, 2002). Social communication is an integral part of a collaborative context, and social communication in itself also acts as a way to facilitate or impede cognitive performance.

Social Communication

Communication patterns tend to change with age. Differences in older adults' ability to communicate their thoughts may either reflect declines in perceptual abilities, such as hearing loss, or may reflect strategies used to compensate for working memory or attentional difficulties that relate to older age (Garcia & Orange, 1996). Furthermore, social stereotypes that are present in the context of intergenerational and intragenerational communications can affect what an older adult discloses in a given situation (Nussbaum, Hummert, Williams, & Harwood, 1996). These communication-related contextual factors have been shown to impact various measures of cognition.

As we discussed in the "Stereotypes and Stereotype Threat" section, age stereotypes can operate in a detrimental way in situations that require intergenerational communication. Contextual cues, such as a person's appearance, can activate negative stereotypes of aging in a listener whose subsequent treatment of the older adult can have a detrimental impact on the older adult's ability to competently communicate (Nussbaum et al., 1996; Ryan, Giles, Bartolucci, & Henwood, 1986). Listeners often modify their speech toward older adults in a manner known as *elderspeak* or *overaccommodation.* Speech is more comprehensible to older adults when the number of clauses per utterance is reduced in order to simplify syntactic complexity (Kemper & Harden, 1999). However, certain components of elderspeak, such as exaggerated prosody, can be detrimental to older adults' comprehension, thereby making older adults more prone to errors on tasks that require joint communication (Kemper & Harden, 1999).

Alternatively, the communicative context can act in ways to enhance cognition in older adults. When asked to read a story to later recall and retell to a listener, older adults recalled more information when the listener was a child than when the listener was an experimenter (Adams, Smith, Pasupathi, & Vitolo, 2002). This suggests that the communicative context of the recall task has an impact on actual performance. One would presume that the child was given more information because she had never heard the story before, and the task appealed to older adults' sense of generativity. Conversely, retelling the story to an experimenter who presumably already knows the story led to a gist-based, less detailed recalled story.

The fact that older adults tend to speak to young adults by underaccommodating the conversational needs of young adults may reflect older adults' cognitive level of functioning. *Underaccommodation* refers to features such as disclosures of personally painful information, nonlistening behavior, or use of disapproving tones (Bonnesen & Hummert, 2002; Giles, Fox, Harwood, & Williams, 1994). This difference in conversational style is taken as evidence for declines in ability to stay on task and focused attention. However, an alternative perspective is that older and young adults perceive these features of speech differently. Older adults report painful self-disclosures as less painful and more appropriate than do young adults (Bonnesen & Hummert, 2002); that is, older adults feel that disclosing this information is relevant to the task, whereas it is often counted against them as being off topic or overly verbose.

Overall, interactive social contexts can lead to conversational styles between older adults and their communication partners by creating expectations about what an older adult should do in a given situation. These communication styles can enhance or diminish an older adult's performance on a task, depending on the communication partner and the partner's interaction style with the older adult.

Conclusion

There is a growing literature providing evidence that social context factors substantially influence adaptive cognitive functioning in older adulthood. This work stresses the importance for future research to examine cognitive and social cognitive functioning in light of the context of emotions, personal goals, societal and personal beliefs and knowledge, and one's social interactive milieu. Before outlining a number of areas that need further examination and research, we must also acknowledge the sociohistorical and cultural context. This context is more distal in nature when compared to the types of context addressed in this chapter. Development unfolds in the context of a changing social and historical environment (Baltes et al., 2006); therefore, sociohistorical and cultural factors include concepts such as cultural context, education, socioeconomic status, and family networks, all of which can impact cognitive outcomes. Although it is beyond the scope of this chapter, further understanding of cognitive functioning in various cultures and cohorts must be a part of any future research agenda in this area.

With respect to research examining the interface between emotion and cognition and aging, recent work has focused on the positivity effect. It will be important for future research to investigate the appraisal mechanism by which positive emotional stimuli are prioritized over negative stimuli. For example, is this mechanism motivational in nature, or is it tied to biological changes in older adults' reactivity to emotional stimuli? It is possible that a more complex picture will emerge given cohort differences in emotion regulation strategies. One issue is whether the proactive strategies used by today's middle-aged adults (i.e., Baby Boomers) will change to resemble the more passive emotion regulation strategies of Depression-era older adults (Blanchard-Fields, Stein, & Watson, 2004). As social neuroscience researchers begin to explore the influence of emotion on age differences in cognition, the interface between life span shifts in personal goals (i.e., motivation) and biological changes in the connectivity of prefrontal and emotional regions of the brain will become better understood (Knight & Mather, 2006).

The findings that stereotypes influence performance have received increased attention in the literature. As yet, the mechanisms by which stereotypes influence performance outcomes are not understood. The primary mechanism that has been proposed is anxiety; however, there is little support in the literature that anxiety specifically mediates the effect of negative stereotypes on memory performance (Chasteen et al., 2005; Hess et al., 2003; O'Brien & Hummert, 2006). Furthermore, studies have not explained the process by which changes in arousal translate into performance deficits. A second hypothesized mechanism involves self-efficacy and control. More specifically, if stereotypes prime a lack of control for older adults, then effort in the task is suppressed, leading to differences in performance outcomes. As yet, this factor has also not received definitive support. Not only is understanding the mechanisms by which stereotypes and memory beliefs operate on memory important for characterizing when social context is debilitative for older adults, but it also allows for a more rigorous examination of those contexts that might facilitate older adults' cognitive performance.

Finally, the research on social interactive contexts suggests that social engagement in the form of collaborative networks can provide support for adaptive functioning in situations where the aging individual's cognitive resources may be insufficient to effectively negotiate the cognitive task in question. However, questions remain about which characteristics of collaboration reduce age differences in performance and which do not. Also unclear is whether interactive experiences are more beneficial or detrimental for certain cognitive domains over others.

The research reviewed in this chapter highlights the importance of considering the roles that social factors might play in producing age differences in cognitive functioning. It is essential to not limit our explanations of cognitive change to cognitive processing mechanisms. Important social factors, such as schematic beliefs or motivational goals, influence how a person approaches a testing context, how an individual will attend to specific information, and when this information will influence cognitive functioning. Future research holds the promise of further specifying the conditions under which social context may degrade or bolster the cognitive performance of older adults.

NOTE

1. A caveat to this finding is that the pattern of results was driven by changes within the young adult group, because memory performance was boosted in the young adult memory-instruction group. In addition, stereotype activation is inferred by the pattern of results but was not measured.

REFERENCES

Adams, C., Smith, M. C., Pasupathi, M., & Vitolo, L. (2002). Social context effects on story recall in older and younger women: Does the listener make a difference? *Journals of Gerontology Series B: Psychological Sciences and Social Sciences, 57B*, P28–P40.

Andreoletti, C., & Lachman, M. E. (2004). Susceptibility and resilience to memory aging stereotypes: Education matters more than age. *Experimental Aging Research, 30*, 129–148.

Artistico, D., Cervone, D., & Pezzuti, L. (2003). Perceived self-efficacy and everyday problem solving among young and older adults. *Psychology and Aging, 18*, 68–79.

Baltes, P. B., & Baltes, M. M. (1990). Psychological perspectives on successful aging: The model of selective optimization with compensation. In P. B. Baltes & M. M. Baltes (Eds.), *Successful aging: Perspectives from the behavioral sciences* (pp. 1–34). New York: Cambridge University Press.

Baltes, P. B., Lindenberger, U., & Staudinger, U. M. (2006). Life span theory in developmental psychology. In R. M. Lerner & W. Damon (Eds.),

Handbook of child psychology: Theoretical models of human development (pp. 569–664). Hoboken, NJ: Wiley.

Bandura, A. (1989). Regulation of cognitive processes through perceived self-efficacy. *Developmental Psychology, 25,* 729–735.

Berg, C. A., Johnson, M. M. S., Meegan, S. P., & Strough, J. (2003). Collaborative problem-solving interactions in young and old married couples. *Discourse Processes, 35,* 33–58.

Berg, C. A., & Klaczynski, P. A. (2002). Contextual variability in the expression and meaning of intelligence. In R. J. Sternberg & E. L. Grigorenko (Eds.), *The general factor of intelligence: How general is it?* (pp. 381–412). Mahwah, NJ: Lawrence Erlbaum.

Berry, J. M. (1999). Memory self-efficacy in its social cognitive context. In T. Hess & F. Blanchard-Fields (Eds.), *Social cognition and aging* (pp. 69–96). San Diego, CA: Academic Press.

Berry, J. M., & West, R. L. (1993). Cognitive self-efficacy in relation to personal mastery and goal setting across the life span. *International Journal of Behavioral Development, 16,* 351–379.

Blanchard-Fields, F. (1996). Causal attributions across the adult life span: The influence of social schemas, life context, and domain specificity. *Applied Cognitive Psychology, 10,* 137–146.

Blanchard-Fields, F. (2006, April 30). *The two faces of processing: Aging and the interface between emotion and cognition.* Talk given at the Cognitive Aging Conference, Atlanta, GA.

Blanchard-Fields, F. (2007). Everyday problem solving and emotion: An adult developmental perspective. *Current Directions in Psychological Science, 16,* 26–31.

Blanchard-Fields, F., & Beatty, C. (2005). Age differences in blame attributions: The role of relationship outcome ambiguity and personal identification. *Journals of Gerontology Series B: Psychological Sciences and Social Sciences, 60B,* P19–P26.

Blanchard-Fields, F., & Hertzog, C. (2000). Age differences in social schematicity. In U. von Hecker, S. Dutke, & G. Sedek (Eds.), *Generative mental processes and cognitive resources: Integrative research on adaptation and control* (pp. 175–198). Dordrecht, The Netherlands: Kluwer Academic.

Blanchard-Fields, F., & Horhota, M. (2005). Age differences in the correspondence bias: When a plausible explanation matters. *Journals of Gerontology Series B: Psychological Sciences and Social Sciences, 60B,* P259–P267.

Blanchard-Fields, F., Jahnke, H. C., & Camp, C. (1995). Age differences in problem solving style: The role of emotional salience. *Psychology and Aging, 10,* 173–180.

Blanchard-Fields, F., Stein, R., & Watson, T. (2004). Age differences in emotion regulation strategies in handling everyday problems. *Journals of Gerontology Series B: Psychological Sciences and Social Sciences, 59,* P261–P269.

Bonnesen, J. L., & Hummert, M. L. (2002). Painful self-disclosures of older adults in relation to aging stereotypes and perceived motivations. *Journal of Language & Social Psychology, 21,* 275–301.

Carstensen, L. L., & Mikels, J. A. (2005). At the intersection of emotion and cognition: Aging and the positivity effect. *Current Directions in Psychological Science, 14,* 117–121.

Carstensen, L. L., Mikels, J. A., & Mather, M. (2006). Aging and the intersection of cognition, motivation, and emotion. In J. E. Birren & K. W. Schaie (Eds.), *Handbook of the psychology of aging* (6th ed., pp. 343–362). Amsterdam, The Netherlands: Elsevier.

Cavanaugh, J. C. (1996). Memory self-efficacy as a moderator of memory change. In F. Blanchard-Fields & T. M. Hess (Eds.), *Perspectives on cognitive change in adulthood and aging* (pp. 488–507). Boston: McGraw-Hill.

Charles, S. T., Mather, M., & Carstensen, L. L. (2003). Aging and emotional memory: The forgettable nature of negative images for older adults. *Journal of Experimental Psychology: General, 132,* 310–324.

Chasteen, A. L., Bhattacharyya, S., Horhota, M., Tam, R., & Hasher, L. (2005). How feelings of stereotype threat influence older adults' memory performance. *Experimental Aging Research, 31,* 235–260.

Chasteen, A. L., Schwarz, N., & Park, D. C. (2002). The activation of aging stereotypes in younger and older adults. *Journals of Gerontology Series B: Psychological Sciences and Social Sciences, 57B,* P540–P547.

Chen, Y., & Blanchard-Fields, F. (2000). Unwanted thought: Age differences in the correction of social judgments. *Psychology and Aging, 15,* 475–482.

Devolder, P. A., & Pressley, M. (1992). Causal attributions and strategy use in relation to memory performance differences in younger and older adults. *Applied Cognitive Psychology, 6,* 629–642.

Dixon, R. A. (2001). Collaborative memory. In N. J. Smelser & P. B. Baltes (Eds.), *International encyclopedia of the social and behavioral sciences* (Vol. 14, pp. 9570–9572). Oxford, UK: Elsevier Science.

Dixon, R., Fox, D. P., Trevithick, L., & Brundin, R. (1997). Exploring collaborative problem solving in adulthood. *Journal of Adult Development, 4,* 195–208.

Dixon, R. A., & Gould, O. N. (1998). Younger and older adults collaborating on retelling everyday stories. *Applied Developmental Science, 2,* 160–171.

Ebner, N. C., Freund, A. M., & Baltes, P. B. (2006). Developmental changes in personal goal orientation from young to late adulthood: From striving for gains to maintenance and prevention of losses. *Psychology and Aging, 21,* 664–678.

Erber, J. T. (1989). Young and older adults' appraisal of memory failure in young and older adult target persons. *Journals of Gerontology Series B: Psychological Sciences and Social Sciences, 44,* P170–P175.

Erber, J. T., & Prager, I. G. (1999). Age and memory: Perceptions of forgetful young and older adults. In T. M. Hess & F. Blanchard-Fields (Eds.), *Social cognition and aging* (pp. 197–217). San Diego, CA: Academic Press.

Finlay, F., Hitch, G. J., & Meudell, P. R. (2000). Mutual inhibition in collaborative recall: Evidence for a retrieval-based account. *Journal of Experimental Psychology: Learning, Memory, and Cognition, 26,* 1556–1567.

Garcia, L. J., & Orange, J. B. (1996). The analysis of conversational skills of older adults: Current research and clinical approaches. *Journal of Speech-Language Pathology & Audiology, 20,* 123–135.

Giles, H., Fox, S., Harwood, J., & Williams, A. (1994). Talking age and aging talk: Communicating through the life span. In M. L. Hummert & J. M. Wiemann (Eds.), *Interpersonal communication in older adulthood in older adulthood: Interdisciplinary theory and research* (pp. 130–161). Thousand Oaks, CA: Sage.

Gould, O. N., Osborn, C., & Krein, H. (2002). Collaborative recall in married and unacquainted dyads. *International Journal of Behavioral Development, 26,* 36–44.

Grühn, D., Smith, J., & Baltes, P. B. (2005). No aging bias favoring memory for positive material: Evidence from a heterogeneity–homogeneity list paradigm using emotionally toned words. *Psychology and Aging, 20,* 579–588.

Hertzog, C., Lineweaver, T. T., & McGuire, C. L. (1999). Beliefs about memory and aging. In T. M. Hess & F. Blanchard-Fields (Eds.), *Social cognition and aging* (pp. 43–68). San Diego, CA: Academic Press.

Hertzog, C., McGuire, C. L., & Lineweaver, T. T. (1998). Aging, attributions, perceived control and strategy use in a free recall task. *Aging, Neuropsychology, and Cognition, 5,* 85–106.

Hess, T. M. (2005). Memory and aging in context. *Psychological Bulletin, 131,* 383–406.

Hess T. M. (2006) Adaptive aspects of social cognitive functioning in adulthood: Age-related goal and knowledge influences. *Social Cognition, 24,* 279–309.

Hess, T. M., Auman, C., Colcombe, S. J., & Rahhal, T. A. (2003). The impact of stereotype threat on age differences in memory performance. *Journals of Gerontology Series B: Psychological Sciences and Social Sciences, 58B,* 3–11.

Hess, T. M., Bolstad, C. A., & Woodburn, S. M. (1999). Trait diagnosticity versus behavioral consistency as determinants of impression change in adulthood. *Psychology and Aging, 14,* 77–89.

Hess, T. M., Germain, C. M., Rosenberg, D. C., Leclerc, C. M., & Hodges, E. A. (2005). Aging-related selectivity and susceptibility to irrelevant affective information in the construction of attitudes. *Aging, Neuropsychology, and Cognition, 12,* 149–174.

Hess, T. M., Hinson, J. T., & Statham, J. A. (2004). Explicit and implicit stereotype activation effects on memory: Do age and awareness moderate the impact of priming? *Psychology and Aging, 19,* 495–505.

Hess, T. M., Osowski, N. L., & Leclerc, C. M. (2005). Age and experience influences on the complexity of social inferences. *Psychology and Aging, 20,* 447–459.

Hess, T. M., Rosenberg, D. C., & Waters, S. J. (2001). Motivation and representational processes in adulthood: The effects of social accountability and information relevance. *Psychology and Aging, 16,* 629–642.

Hilton, J. L., & von Hippel, W. (1996). Stereotypes. *Annual Review of Psychology, 47,* 237–271.

Hummert, M. L. (1999). A social cognitive perspective on age stereotypes. In T. Hess & F. Blanchard-Fields (Eds.), *Social cognition and aging* (pp. 175–196). San Diego, CA: Academic Press.

Jopp, D., & Lindenberger, U. (2003). *Adults' beliefs about intellectual functioning and aging: Age-based increase in relation to performance.* Unpublished manuscript.

Kemper, S., & Harden, T. (1999). Experimentally disentangling what's beneficial about elderspeak from what's not. *Psychology and Aging, 14,* 656–670.

Kennedy, Q., Mather, M., & Carstensen, L. L. (2004). The role of motivation in the age-related positivity effect in autobiographical memory. *Psychological Science, 15,* 208–214.

Kensinger, E. A., & Corkin, S. (2004). The effects of emotional content and aging on false memories. *Cognitive, Affective & Behavioral Neuroscience, 4(1),* 1–9.

Kensinger, E. A., Piguet, O., Krendl, A. C., & Corkin, S. (2005). Memory for contextual details: Effects of emotion and aging. *Psychology and Aging, 20,* 241–250.

Knight, M., & Mather, M. (2006). The affective neuroscience of aging and its implications for cognition. In T. Canli (Ed.), *The biological bases of personality and individual differences* (pp. 159–183). New York: Guilford Press.

Lachman, M. E. (1986). Locus of control in aging research: A case for multidimensional and domain-specific assessment. *Psychology and Aging, 1,* 34–40.

Lachman, M. E., Steinberg, E. S., & Trotter, S. D. (1987). Effects of control beliefs and attributions on memory self-assessments and performance. *Psychology and Aging, 2,* 266–271.

Lane, R. D., & Nadel, L. (Eds.). (2000). *Cognitive neuroscience of emotion.* New York: Oxford University Press.

Levine, L. J., & Bluck, S. (1997). Experienced and remembered emotional intensity in older adults. *Psychology and Aging, 12,* 514–523.

Levy, B. (1996). Improving memory in old age through implicit self-stereotyping. *Journal of Personality and Social Psychology, 71,* 1092–1107.

Levy, B., & Langer, E. (1994). Aging free from negative stereotypes: Successful memory in China among the American deaf. *Journal of Personality and Social Psychology, 66,* 989–997.

Li, L. Z. H., Lindenberger, U., Freund, A. M., & Baltes, P. B. (2001). Walking while memorizing: Age-related differences in compensatory behavior. *Psychological Science, 12,* 230–237.

Lineweaver, T. T., & Hertzog, C. (1998). Adults' efficacy and control beliefs regarding memory and aging: Separating general from personal beliefs. *Aging, Neuropsychology, and Cognition, 5,* 264–296.

Löckenhoff, C. E., & Carstensen, L. L. (2004). Socioemotional selectivity theory, aging, and health: The increasingly delicate balance between regulating emotions and making tough choices. *Journal of Personality, 72,* 1395–1424.

Margrett, J. (2000). Collaborative cognition and aging: A pilot study (Doctoral dissertation, Wayne State University, 1999). *Dissertation Abstracts International, 61*(01), 565B (AAT 9954531).

Margrett, J. A., & Marsiske, M. (2002). Gender differences in older adults' everyday cognitive collaboration. *International Journal of Behavioral Development, 26,* 45–59.

Mather, M., & Carstensen, L. L. (2003). Aging and attentional biases for emotional faces. *Psychological Science, 14,* 409–415.

Mather, M., & Knight, M. (2005). Goal-directed memory: The role of cognitive control in older adults' emotional memory. *Psychology and Aging, 20,* 554–570.

Mather, M., Knight, M., & McCaffrey, M. (2005). The allure of the allignable: Younger and older adults' false memories of choice features. *Journal of Experimental Psychology: General, 134,* 38–51.

May, C. P., Rahhal, T., Berry, E. M., & Leighton, E. A. (2005). Aging, source memory, and emotion. *Psychology and Aging, 20,* 571–578.

McFarland, C., Ross, M., & Giltrow, M. (1992). Biased recollections in older adults: The role of implicit theories of aging. *Journal of Personality and Social Psychology, 62,* 837–850.

Meegan, S. P., & Berg, C. A. (2002). Contexts, functions, forms, and processes of collaborative everyday problem solving in older adulthood. *International Journal of Behavioral Development, 26,* 6–15.

Mikels, J. A., Larkin, G. R., Reuter-Lorenz, P. A., & Carstensen, L. L. (2005). Divergent trajectories in the aging mind: Changes in working memory for affective versus visual information with age. *Psychology and Aging, 20,* 542–553.

Nussbaum, J. F., Hummert, M. L., Williams, A., & Harwood, J. (1996). Communication and older adults. In B. R. Burleson (Ed.), *Communication yearbook 19* (pp. 1–47). Thousand Oaks, CA: Sage.

O'Brien, L. T., & Hummert, M. L. (2006). Memory performance of late middle-aged adults: Contrasting self-stereotyping and stereotype threat accounts of assimilation to age stereotypes. *Social Cognition, 24,* 338–358.

Perdue, C. W., & Gurtman, M. B. (1990). Evidence for the automaticity of ageism. *Journal of Experimental Social Psychology, 26,* 199–216.

Phillips, L. H., Kliegel, M., & Martin, M. (2006). Age and planning tasks: The influence of ecological validity. *International Journal of Aging & Human Development, 62,* 175–184.

Rahhal, T. A., Hasher, L., & Colcombe, S. J. (2001). Instructional manipulations and age differences in memory: Now you see them, now you don't. *Psychology and Aging, 16,* 697–706.

Riediger, M., Freund, A. M., & Baltes, P. B. (2005). Managing life through personal goals: Intergoal facilitation and intensity of goal pursuit in younger and older adulthood. *Journals of Gerontology Series B: Psychological Sciences and Social Sciences, 60B,* P84–P91.

Rowe, J. W., & Kahn, R. L. (1998). *Successful aging.* New York: Pantheon.

Rozin, P., & Royzman, E. B. (2001). Negativity bias, negativity dominance, and contagion. *Personality and Social Psychology Review, 5,* 296–320.

Ryan, E. B. (1992). Beliefs about memory changes across the adult life span. *Journals of Gerontology Series B: Psychological Sciences and Social Sciences, 47,* 41–46.

Ryan, E. B., Giles, H., Bartolucci, G., & Henwood, K. (1986). Psycholinguistic and social psychological components of communication by and with the elderly. *Language and Communication, 6,* 1–24.

Ryan, E. B., & Kwong See, S. (1993). Age-based beliefs about memory changes for self and others across adulthood. *Journals of Gerontology, 48,* 199–201.

Stein, R., Blanchard-Fields, F., & Hertzog, C. (2002). The effects of age-stereotype priming on the memory performance of older adults. *Experimental Aging Research, 28,* 169–181.

Strough, J., Cheng, S., & Swenson, L. M. (2002). Preferences for collaborative and individual everyday problem solving in later adulthood. *International Journal of Behavioral Development, 26,* 26–35.

Sullivan, S., & Ruffman, T. (2004). Emotion recognition deficits in the elderly. *International Journal of Neuroscience, 114,* 94–102.

Thomas, R. C., & Hasher, L. (2006). The influence of emotional valence on age differences in early processing and memory. *Psychology and Aging, 21,* 821–825.

Valentijn, S. A., Hill, R. D., & Van Hooren, S. A. H. (2006). Memory self-efficacy predicts memory performance: Results from a 6-year follow-up study. *Psychology and Aging, 21,* 165–172.

West, R. L., Bagwell, D. K., & Dark-Freudman, A. (2005). Memory and goal setting: The response of older and younger adults to positive objective feedback. *Psychology and Aging, 20,* 195–201.

West, R. L., Welch, D. C., & Thorn, R. M. (2001). Effects of goal-setting and feedback on memory performance and beliefs among older and younger adults. *Psychology and Aging, 16,* 240–250.

Wood, S., & Kisley, M. A. (2006). The negativity bias is eliminated in older adults: Age-related reduction in event-related brain potentials associated with evaluative categorization. *Psychology and Aging, 21,* 815–820.

Wurm, L. H., Labouvie-Vief, G., Aycock, J., Rebucal, K. A., & Koch, H. E. (2004). Performance in auditory and visual emotional stroop tasks: A comparison of older and younger adults. *Psychology and Aging, 19,* 523–535.

Yoon, C., Hasher, L., Feinberg, F., Rahhal, T. A., & Winocur, G. (2000). Cross-cultural differences in memory: The role of culture-based stereotypes about aging. *Psychology and Aging, 15,* 694–704.

Zacks, R. T., Hasher, L., & Li, K. Z. H. (2000). Human memory. In F. I. M. Craik & T. A. Salthouse (Eds.), *The handbook of aging and cognition* (2nd ed., pp. 293–357). Mahwah, NJ: Lawrence Erlbaum.

38

Dyadic Cognition in Old Age

Paradigms, Findings, and Directions

Mike Martin and Melanie Wight

Dyadic Cognition in Old Adults

In the coming decades, the number of couples who have been married for a long time or couples who have been living together for a long time will rise. In fact, in Switzerland, at the time they retire, 75% of women and 80% of men still live with their spouses, and one third of the 80-year-olds are still married. In addition, women age 65 on average still live 15 more years with their partner (Swiss Federal Statistical Office, 2005). In Germany, from 1996 to 2005, the proportion of old couples rose from 8% to 27% for husbands and from 6% to 21% for wives (German Federal Statistical Office, 2000). As an increasing number of couples grow older and may be able to tackle tasks, responsibilities, and problems jointly, the examination of dyadic cognition in old age requires a fresh view on existing paradigms and studies. In this respect, one key question is to which degree interdyadic differences in dyadic cognitive skills, or the *interactive social context* (see chap. 37, this volume), predict how people manage to overcome everyday difficulties, such as financial, social, health related, and cognitive problems (Meegan & Berg, 2002).

In this chapter, we review findings from research that has examined paradigms that have been used to study cognition in older dyads (i.e., pairs of persons both 60 years or older). We focus on (a) paradigms that have been used to examine dyadic cognition in old age; (b) performance differences in dyadic cognition; and (c) explanatory concepts for performance differences such as dyadic versus individual performance, age, sex, training, relationship characteristics, and communication patterns. The studies included in our review have examined dyadic memory, dyadic planning, dyadic decision making, dyadic reasoning, and dyadic comprehension. We show that relatively few paradigms have been used to study the developmental changes in dyadic cognition performance, and we point to future directions in terms of needs for further paradigm development and empirical research.

To capture the dyadic ability to solve cognitive tasks, a number of different constructs have been proposed in the literature. The most influential ones in recent years have been called *interactive minds* (Baltes & Staudinger, 1996), *transactive memory* (Wegner, Giuliano, & Hertel, 1985), *socially shared cognition*, and *collaborative*

AUTHORS' NOTE: We thank S. Angst Fuchs, D. Bauert, M. Landis Schöning, and F. Luchsinger-Vetter for helpful comments on an earlier version of the chapter.

cognition (Dixon, 1992). All of these constructs see cognition mainly as a social process and therefore examine cognitive performances of social entities such as dyads (see Strough & Margrett, 2002). *Interactive minds* refers to the phenomenon that the acquisition of individual knowledge may be influenced by other people's cognition-related behaviors. This reciprocal influence can lead to a level of performance that may be higher than each person's level of independent individual performance. In the tradition of the interactive minds approach, social interactions during learning, problem solving, and collaborative memory at old age, as well as the cooperative acquisition of expert knowledge, have been studied. It is interesting to note that researchers in this area have pointed out that social interactions can enhance cognitive performance and cognitive development but that social interaction can also have negative consequences on cognitive performance (Baltes & Staudinger, 1996).

The notion of *transactive memory* refers to two or more people encoding, storing, and retrieving information. Transactive memory theory is based on the idea that individuals can serve as external memory aids for others (Wegner, 1986). Partners in close relationships, such as spouses, should typically be relatively well informed about each other's knowledge (Wegner, Erber, & Raymond, 1991). That way, both partners can profit from the couple's memory and have to encode only things that belong to their own knowledge areas. Developing such familiarity with the partner's knowledge takes time, but it eventually has the advantage that couples develop an implicit structure to jointly solve memory tasks. With this implicit structure, couples may have a transactive memory that is better than both partners' individual memories.

Compared with the interactive minds and the transactive memory approaches, *collaborative cognition* and *socially shared cognition* more specifically describe cognitive activities with more than one person present. This cognitive activity is directed toward one or more cognitive tasks, involves collaboration, and is characterized by common goals of the interacting persons (Dixon, 1992). Collaborators are often used as external memory aids, which is why collaboration is often seen as a possibility for enhanced performance and as a compensation for age-related memory decline. People with injury- or age-correlated declines of fundamental memory mechanisms (e.g., processing speed, neuronal integrity) might be able to compensate for these losses through collaboration (Dixon & Gould, 1998).

For the purpose of this review, we consider *dyadic cognition* the general term to indicate whenever two persons work together on the same cognitive task at the same time. When considering specific cognitive abilities, we also use the more specific terms *dyadic memory*, *dyadic planning*, *dyadic decision making*, *dyadic reasoning*, and *dyadic comprehension*. We consider dyadic cognition paradigms when, at least in principle, they allow one to obtain information about the product and the process of particular dyadic cognitive abilities and performances. Although a number of studies with younger dyads have used cognitive tests to manipulate the amount of stress (e.g., Bodenmann, 2000) and to examine dyadic responses to stress (e.g., Bodenmann, 1995; Bodenmann & Cina, 1999; Bodenmann, Pihet, Cina, Widmer, & Shantinath, 2006; Bodenmann & Widmer, 2000), or the relation between cognitive abilities and ratings of emotional well-being (e.g., Kolanowski, Hoffman, & Hofer, 2007), we focus on research that has examined dyadic cognition in old age and in which the dependent variable of interest was cognitive performance. This means that at least one outcome measure in the included studies had to be cognitive performance of an older dyad.

Overall, this review has three goals: (1) to examine which paradigms have been used to study dyadic cognition in old age; (2) to determine whether there is evidence for performance differences in dyadic cognition; and (3) to review the degree to which performance differences can be explained by age, individual versus dyadic cognition, sex, prior training with the materials used, relationship characteristics, and communication patterns of the dyads examined. Finally, we make recommendations for future paradigm development and research directions.

PARADIGMS TO EXAMINE DYADIC COGNITION

To examine age differences in dyadic cognition, experimental paradigms need to fulfill some essential requirements: Paradigms should be appropriate to use with individuals and dyads over a wide age range, sex differences, and hierarchy differences. Paradigms should also allow repeated measurement. This way, paradigms can be used in age comparisons, comparisons between individual versus dyadic performance, longitudinal studies, and in married couples versus professional dyads of different ages. From an experimental point of view, paradigms should allow one to manipulate the causal mechanisms suspected to influence dyadic performance. When examining existing paradigms, we therefore determine the degree to which existing paradigms fulfill these criteria and which areas might need additional paradigm development.

DYADIC MEMORY

Dyadic Memory Paradigms

In the literature on old people's dyadic cognition, dyadic memory has been studied most often. This is probably because collaborating on a memory task may compensate for age-related individual losses in memory performance. In fact, several memory studies with young adults have shown that young individuals can gain by collaborating on memory tasks (Dixon, 2000; Dixon & Bäckman, 1995; Dixon, Fox, Threvithick, & Brundin, 1997; Dixon, Gagnon, & Crow, 1998; Finlay, Hitch, & Meudell, 2000; Stephenson, Kniveton, & Wagner, 1991). However, relatively little is known about old adults' performance in dyadic cognition. In general, the paradigms that have been used to examine old dyads' memory performance are similar to those that have been used to examine individual memory performance (for an overview, see Table 38.1). These paradigms range from recognition for verbal material over recall for verbal and spatial material, to prospective memory, and include typical laboratory tasks as well as tasks using materials familiar from or similar to everyday life.

Dyadic Memory Paradigms: Performance or Process Differences

Summarizing the results of the few studies on dyadic memory tasks is difficult, because the studies focus on different aspects of older dyads'

collaborative memory performance. However, three aspects of dyadic memory in old age have received particular attention. First, with respect to dyadic performance, most studies with older adults report that dyadic performance is superior to individual memory performance (Dixon & Gould, 1998; Johansson, Andersson, & Rönnberg, 2000, 2005; Ross, Spencer, Linardatos, Lam, & Perunovic, 2004); that is, one individual trying to recall items or a story will perform worse than two people working jointly on the same task. This result is the same for naturalistic tasks, such as remembering items from a shopping list, and typical laboratory tasks, such as word or story recall. In comparisons of dyadic memory performance to nominal group performance (i.e., the pooled, nonredundant performance of two individuals), real dyads typically perform worse than nominal dyads (Andersson & Rönnberg, 1995; Basden, Basden, Bryner, & Thomas, 1997; Johansson et al., 2000, 2005; Ross et al., 2004). However, this is true only for episodic memory, not semantic memory. This means that semantic tasks are not negatively affected by collaboration. A difference in the process of achieving memory performance seems that real dyads generate fewer correct answers, but they also make fewer mistakes than nominal pairs (Johansson et al., 2000).

Second, one may wonder whether older, familiar dyads, such as married couples, perform better on memory tasks than unacquainted pairs. Here, the findings are inconclusive. Whereas Dixon and Gould (1998) reported such a familiarity effect on story recall tasks, other studies (Gould, Osborn, Krein, & Mortensen, 2002; Johansson et al., 2000) have found no or only small advantages of familiarity on retrospective verbal tasks, spatial memory tasks, and prospective memory tasks (Johansson et al., 2000). When married couples indicate that they use a transactive memory system, performance levels can be as high as nominal pair performance (Johansson et al., 2005).

Third, studies of dyadic cognition in old age typically compare older adults' collaborative memory performance to young adults' collaborative performance. For this comparison, different results have been reported. Some studies find no story recall performance differences between young and older married couples (Dixon & Gould, 1998), and other studies do report

Table 38.1   Studies That Have Examined Older Adults' Dyadic Memory

Characteristic	Dixon & Gould (1998)	Gould et al. (1991)	Gould & Dixon (1993)	Gould et al. (1994)	Gould et al. (2002)	Johansson et al. (2000)	Johansson et al. (2005)	Ross et al. (2004)
Paradigm(s)	Story recall	Story recall	Vacation description	Story recall	1. Story recall 2. Word recall 3. Referential naming task	1. Prospective event- and time-based tasks 2. Verbal and spatial information recall	1. Episodic memory task (questions about stories) 2. Semantic memory task (questions about famous places, etc.)	1. Verbal recognition 2. Item recall from shopping list
Sample	Experiment 1: 84 young, unacquainted adults (M age = 24.4) and 84 older, unacquainted adults (M age = 67.9). Experiment 2: 10 young (M age = 29.4, M marriage = 3.02 years) and 10 older (M age = 71.6, M marriage = 40.15 years) couples	84 young, unacquainted adults (M age = 24.4) and 84 older, unacquainted adults (M age = 67.9)	10 young couples (M age = 28.5, M marriage = 3 years) and 10 old couples (M age = 70.7, M marriage = 40 years)	20 young dyads (M age = 26.30) and 20 older dyads (M age = 69.52). Half unacquainted, half couples (M marriage [young] = 3 years, M marriage [older] = 40 years)	30 young couples (M age = 26, M marriage = 4 years) and 30 older couples (M age = 67.4, M marriage = 44 years). Worked either with spouse or unfamiliar other-sex partner first	20 married couples (M marriage = 46.5 years), 19 arranged pairs, 36 control persons (M age = 73)	62 couples (M age = 73, M marriage = 43 years)	29 married couples in collaborative condition, 30 married couples in individual condition (M age = 72.8, M marriage = 45.04 years)

Characteristic	Dixon & Gould (1998)	Gould et al. (1991)	Gould & Dixon (1993)	Gould et al. (1994)	Gould et al. (2002)	Johansson et al. (2000)	Johansson et al. (2005)	Ross et al. (2004)
Different couples (age, familiarity, sex, etc.)	Yes; Experiment 1: Young, old, unfamiliar, same sex Experiment 2: Young and older couples	Yes; young, older, unfamiliar, same sex	Yes; young and old	Yes; young, old, married, unacquainted	Yes; young, old, married, unacquainted	Yes; married and unacquainted	No; married and nominal pairs	No
Within-subject design	No	No	No	No	Yes and no; same people in dyads and couples. Not the same in young and old	No	Yes; married couples tested in dyads and individually	No
Causal mechanisms suspected to influence performance	Experiment 1: Age, individual versus dyad Experiment 2: Age, predictions, postdictions	Age, elaboration characteristics, such as denotative and annotative elaborations	Age differences in story structure, story content, interactions of collaborators	Age differences in story-based productions, task discussion, sociability/ support productions	Age, familiarity, tasks	Dyad versus individual, tasks, transactive memory	Dyad versus individual versus nominal pairs, responsibility, agreement	Dyad versus individual, expertise
Individual and dyadic measurements	Experiment 1: Yes Experiment 2: No	Yes	No	No	No	Yes; individual scores used for nominal pairs	Yes; individual scores used for nominal pairs	Yes
Measurement of relationship indicators	Experiment 1: No Experiment 2: Couples' expertise questionnaire (no age difference in knowledge about one's partner)	No	No	No	No	Transactive memory questions	Responsibility and agreement	No

performance differences between older and young married couples (Gould et al., 2002). However, differences in the structure, the content, and the interaction when recalling an experienced event have been observed (Dixon & Gould, 1998; Gould, Kurzman, & Dixon, 1994). Important age differences were found in the referential naming task (Gould et al., 2002), with older dyads communicating less efficiently than young dyads. A reason for this result could be that older adults focus on reducing errors instead of increasing efficiency, that is, they verify and reverify their viewpoints more often to accomplish the task with as few errors as possible. In addition, Gould and Dixon (1993) found that story structure, content, and interaction style differ between older and young married couples when recalling a jointly experienced event. Older adults' strategy of using more words and speaking more slowly could possibly be explained by older adults' word-finding difficulties (Gould & Dixon, 1993). Fewer supportive words from older adults as well as more monologues might be explained by older adults' strategy to decrease the memory demands of the task and the cognitive demands of collaboration (Gould & Dixon, 1993).

Interdyadic Differences in Memory: Explanatory Concepts

In most of the tasks mentioned in Table 38.1, causal mechanisms suspected to influence performance are collaboration, age, and familiarity. What have been examined as potential causes underlying the interdyadic differences in memory performance are familiarity of the dyadic partners (married vs. unacquainted, length of relationship, general dyadic collaboration expertise), closeness of task to everyday experience, communication style (number of words used, number of turns taken), strategy differences (use of transactive memory, division of responsibility, readiness to risk errors, reduction of memory load through monologues), dyadic agreement, intradyadic responsibility distribution, metacognitive skills, memory self-efficacy, age- and gender-typical communication styles (willingness to interrupt, formal vs. informal communication), individual memory skills of partners, interference of individual encoding with partner's explicit encoding, and need for contextual support. Again, the emerging picture is inconclusive. Whereas familiarity,

operationalized through comparisons of married and unmarried couples, did play a role for some areas, such as story recall (Dixon & Gould, 1998), it did not affect performance in a referential naming task (Gould et al., 2002). The effect of familiarity may be explained by characterizing older couples as being experts at working together, meaning that they have excellent knowledge of each other's cognitive skills and knowledge as well as practice in all kinds of collaborative situations (Dixon & Gould, 1998). Also, older couples might have experienced individual cognitive decline and might be more motivated than young couples to compensate for those losses through collaboration (see also chap. 37, this volume). Yet another explanation might be the considerable collaborative metacognitive skills (pre- and postdictions) older couples show (Dixon & Gould, 1998). Their accuracies follow a pattern similar to patterns of young individuals or young couples, suggesting that older couples are dyadic collaboration experts. When the intradyadic agreement and distribution of responsibilities were more specifically examined, indications were found that these factors can contribute to the best possible performance of older dyads, probably because the division of responsibility reduces the required amount of inhibition and enhances the effort the individual puts into the task (Johansson et al., 2005). Responsibility and agreement did not influence dyadic performance on the semantic task, because no new information needs to be encoded, and therefore information overload for the individual is not a problem.

Ross et al.'s (2004) result that collaborating dyads made fewer mistakes than nominal dyads can be explained by the fact that false positives are unique to each person, therefore making it unlikely that one's partner has the exact same wrong memories. This suggests that collaboration can counteract the effects of aging on source monitoring. The reduction of false positives (e.g., when an individual chose item that was on original list but not on a personal shopping list, or chose item that is on no list but is in the supermarket) in collaborative remembering can be very important, because older people tend to have wrong memories more often than young adults. Empirical findings support the importance of the readiness to risk errors and the age and sex differences in communication styles, even when no performance differences could be observed.

A limitation of the existing approaches is the difficulty of comparing individual and dyadic performance in a within-subject design, the lack of individual ability measurements, and the lack of experimental manipulation of the explanatory variables. In fact, most studies use between-dyads designs, age is often taken as a proxy for a general decline in memory performance, and explanatory variables are usually examined through questionnaires. Therefore, the power to detect effects is smaller than in typical experimental paradigms. This suggests that in an ideal situation, experimental paradigms applied within a within-dyad design may help to disentangle the factors contributing to age and interdyadic differences in dyadic cognition. Although it may be argued that most of the existing paradigms might be used for this purpose, more empirical evidence from experimental within-dyad designs, demonstrating feasibility and adequate measurement properties, is clearly needed. The measurements of relationship characteristics also need more attention in future research regarding older dyads' memory. Transactive memory, degree of responsibility and agreement, and couple's expertise (i.e., how well the partners know each other) have been analyzed with a few tasks, but a deeper understanding of these and other characteristics are needed to better understand dyadic memory in old age.

Dyadic Planning

Dyadic Planning Paradigms

Older dyads' planning has not received much attention in the literature. Only three studies have considered the planning abilities of older dyads, and planning typically appears under the heading of everyday problem solving. In the studies reviewed in this section, dyadic planning focused on errand planning and trip planning.

Dyadic Planning Paradigms: Performance or Process Differences?

The few studies that have looked at older adults' dyadic planning abilities have focused on dyadic versus individual performance and on the comparison of older and young dyads. Familiarity aspects have not received much attention on planning tasks, but some studies have looked at sex differences (Cheng & Strough, 2004; Margrett & Marsiske, 2002) and relationship characteristics (Berg, Johnson, Meegan, & Strough, 2003). Unlike for the memory tasks, for planning tasks differences between individual performance and dyadic performance and differences between older and younger dyads are not very clear. Cheng and Strough (2004) found that young adults planned faster and more accurately than older adults, but no age differences were found on most of the primary performance measures. When old adults were instructed to pay attention to important aspects of the planning task, they were able to perform as well as young adults. Berg et al. (2003) expected that older couples would show fewer low-affiliation interactions than younger couples because of the less conflictual nature of long-term marriages (Carstensen, Isaacowitz, & Charles, 1999); surprisingly, however, there was no difference between young and older couples in how they interacted. However, Berg et al. (2003) found that, independent of the dyads' age, collaboration characterized by high affiliation was associated with shorter routes on an errand-running task. Thus, interaction characteristics seem to be important when we look at collaboration outside of the laboratory in everyday life.

In a comparison of collaborators and individuals, Cheng and Strough (2004) did not find differences on most of the performance measures, even though collaborators make fewer planning mistakes than individuals (cf. dyadic memory research). Differences between the planning task in this study and the memory tasks used in other studies might explain the different results when it comes to collaborative performance. Studies that have found collaborative performance to be superior to individual performance have used memory tasks such as story recall (Dixon & Gould, 1998) and remembering digits (Dixon, 1992).

Whether sex differences in dyadic planning exist remains unclear, because one study (Cheng & Strough, 2004) found that women perform worse on planning tasks than men, and one study did not find sex differences (Margrett & Marsiske, 2002). It is interesting to note that even though Margrett and Marsiske (2002) did not find sex differences in planning performance, they did find that men are more influential, that is, more likely to use their own judgment to influence their own collaborative

Table 38.2   Studies That Have Examined Older Adults' Dyadic Planning

Characteristic	Berg et al. (2003)	Cheng & Strough (2004)	Margrett & Marsiske (2002)
Paradigm	Errand planning	Trip planning	Errand planning
Sample	6 young (M age = 29.7) married couples	24 young women, 24 young men (M age = 19.98), 25 older women and 24 older men (M age = 71.14) worked either alone or with same-sex friend	98 older married couples (M age = 72.90, M marriage = 45.81 years); each participant (196) completed the task independently and in dyads (52 with spouse, 46 with stranger of opposite sex)
Different couples (age, familiarity, sex, etc.)	Yes; young and old couples	Yes. Young, old, same-sex, familiar dyads	No, just older couples
Within-subject design	No	No	Yes and no, same task individually and in dyads, but half with spouse and other half with stranger
Causal mechanisms suspected to influence performance	Age differences in interaction style. Coding into high- and low-affiliation interactions	Age, collaboration	Collaboration, sex, and familiarity (actor–partner method), collaborative as well as task-specific expectations, evaluations, and competitiveness
Individual and dyadic measurements	No	Yes	Yes
Measurement of relationship indicators	High- and low-affiliation interactions	No	Open-ended interview to find out about daily collaboration

outcome on the planning task in the collaborative situation.

Interdyadic Differences in Planning: Explanatory Concepts

The fact that collaborating dyads did not outperform individuals on most performance measures (Cheng & Strough, 2004) of trip planning may be explained by the relatively low memory demands of the task. Participants were allowed to use external memory aids, such as maps, instructions, and daily itineraries. In the dyadic memory tasks for which an advantage of collaboration was found, memory demands were higher, and therefore collaboration is more likely to enhance performance (Cheng & Strough, 2004).

Married couples' interaction styles were related to cognitive planning performance (Berg et al., 2003). Constructive elaborations; explorations of the situation; and initiation of joint action instead of commanding, rejecting, and resisting others led to better planning. Berg et al. (2003) stated that this finding is consistent with findings reported in the child development literature (Rogoff, 1998, cited in Berg et al., 2003). One explanation for the worse performance of low-affiliation couples is that they often made two individual plans for the errands. Berg et al. (2003) suggested that these couples find collaboration aversive and try to avoid it in daily life.

Overall, planning seems to be of enormous importance to older dyads' ability to cope with the changing demands of everyday life. The studies we have reviewed are inconclusive with respect to the factors that contribute to optimal planning performance in the laboratory and in everyday life. More studies on elderly dyads' planning abilities clearly are needed. Within-dyad designs as well as larger sample sizes would help us better understand which mechanisms influence dyadic planning performance in old age.

DYADIC DECISION MAKING

Dyadic Decision-Making Paradigms

Margrett and Marsiske (2002) as well as Berg et al. (2003) also used decision-making tasks in the studies mentioned earlier. Another approach to examine decision making in older dyads stems from the wisdom tasks used by Staudinger and Baltes (1996). Again, only very few studies about dyadic decision making in old age exist, and they have used very different types of tasks. For example, whereas wisdom and social dilemma tasks require social competence, vacation decision making is a decision-making task in the traditional sense (see Table 38.3).

Thus far, only three studies on old adults' dyadic decision making have been published. Most of the paradigms do not fulfill the criteria that would allow a wider use in empirical research or comparisons of results between studies. Small sample sizes (Berg et al., 2003) and the lack of within-subject study designs make comparisons between older and young dyads as well as between collaborative and individual performance difficult. Margrett and Marsiske (2002) and Staudinger and Baltes (1996) allowed with their tasks a comparison between individual and dyadic performance, but not between familiar and unfamiliar dyads and older and young dyads. Comparable to the dyadic planning tasks, Berg et al. (2003) were interested in how relationship characteristics influenced dyadic performance and coded speech acts into low- and high-affiliation interactions. Margrett and Marsiske asked about couples' daily collaboration. Staudinger and Baltes varied five causal mechanisms to find out how collaboration can be most effective. Individual and dyadic measurements are possible in all three decision-making tasks, and relationship indicators are measured by all three paradigms.

Dyadic Decision-Making Paradigms: Performance or Process Differences?

As we have mentioned, three studies have looked at older adults' dyadic decision making (Berg et al., 2003; Margrett & Marsiske, 2002; Staudinger & Baltes, 1996). The focus of the three studies is on differences between individual and dyadic decision making, on age differences when it comes to making decisions, and on sex differences as well as relationship characteristics. Important relationship or communication characteristics for making optimal decisions are high- or low-affiliation interactions. High-affiliation interactions were associated

Table 38.3   Studies That Have Examined Older Adults' Dyadic Decision Making

Characteristic	Berg et al. (2003)	Margrett & Marsiske (2002)	Staudinger & Baltes (1996)
Paradigm	Vacation decision making task	Social dilemmas	Wisdom paradigm
Sample	6 young (*M* age = 29.7, *M* marriage = 5.5 years) and 6 older (*M* age = 70.8, *M* marriage = 41.2 years) couples	98 older married couples (*M* age = 72.90, *M* marriage = 45.81 years), each participant (196) completed the task independently and in dyads (52 with spouse, 46 with stranger of opposite sex)	122 participants with partners. Total 244 participants (148 women and 96 men). Half young adults (20–44) and half older adults (45–70)
Different couples (age, familiarity, sex, etc.)	Yes; older and young married couples	No; only older couples	Yes; young and old adults with partners brought along
Within-subject design	No	Yes and no; same task individually and in dyads, but half with spouse and other half with stranger	Yes and no; same task individually and in dyads, but half with young and half with older dyads
Causal mechanisms suspected to influence performance	High- and low-affiliation interactions	Collaboration, sex, and familiarity (actor–partner method), collaborative as well as task-specific expectations, evaluations, and competitiveness	1. External dialogue plus individual appraisal 2. External dialogue 3. Internal dialogue 4. Unconstrained individual thinking time 5. Standard: Individually
Individual and dyadic measurements	No	Yes	Yes
Measurement of relationship indicators	High- and low affiliation interactions	Open-ended interview to find out about daily collaboration	Questions about relationship with person with whom they interacted

638

with better decision-making strategies. This pattern of high-affiliation interactions being related to searching for more information on the particular features of the potential solutions instead of information allowing a fast exclusion of particular alternatives is congruent with the idea that, for feature-based decision strategies, couples need to agree on which features are most important instead of just agreeing on the final choice. Again, affiliation did play a role for dyadic performance, but no age effects were found. The expectation that, because of more high-affiliation interactions, older dyads would be better at collaborative decision making was not supported (Berg et al., 2003).

Margrett and Marsiske (2002) examined sex differences in decision making. Overall, men were more likely to influence their own collaborative performance and their partners'. In the planning task, men were more likely to use their own judgment to influence their own collaborative outcome, and when it came to making decisions about social situations, men were more likely to influence their own collaborative performance and their partners'. This was an unexpected finding, because women performed better on this task than did men. This result, together with the interpersonal nature of the task, which is traditionally seen as being in a more feminine domain, makes it surprising that men were more influential during collaboration.

Another type of decision-making tasks is wisdom tasks. Young and older people perform the best on wisdom tasks when they can discuss the problem with somebody they know, when they have sufficient time for individually pondering the decision, or when they internally think about what a person they know would say to the problem (Staudinger & Baltes, 1996). This means that external and internal dyadic decision making leads to higher-quality wisdom decisions than does individual decision making. The usual focus on the individual when analyzing wisdom might lack ecological relevance, because wisdom can be considered as a prototype of an interactive-minds construct. Two important factors for optimal wisdom-related performance are (1) the interaction with other people's minds and (2) individual thinking to review other people's ideas (Staudinger & Baltes, 1996). The wisdom task showed significant age differences; that is,

older dyads profited more from the "external dialogue plus individual thinking time" condition than did young dyads.

Interdyadic Differences in Decision Making: Explanatory Concepts

The findings we have reviewed show that men have more influence on collaborative outcome when the task is not very structured and allows more than one correct answer (Margrett & Marsiske, 2002). This finding clearly suggests that collaborative performance in decision-making tasks depends more on interpersonal and social factors than on individual cognitive abilities or task familiarity.

One important factor can be individual and dyadic beliefs and knowledge about how an optimal performance can be achieved. To examine this aspect of dyadic cognition, metacognitive questionnaires have been used in several studies on decision making as well as other domains of dyadic cognition (Strough, Cheng, & Swenson, 2002). For example, in Berg et al.'s (2003) study, couples reported that when collaborating in everyday life they often divide and delegate labor. Division of labor occurred because of special interests of couples' members, or because of different abilities (Margrett & Marsiske, 2002), or it was based on a traditional distribution of responsibilities within the older couples that was not reported by younger couples (Berg et al., 2003). Some couples described collaboration as a form of problem solving, whereby one person takes the lead and the other person refines the plan. Most of the individuals said that their partner's and their own problem-solving styles were complementary (Berg et al., 2003) and that they were convinced that working together with a spouse leads to the best outcome in a dyadic cognition task (Feltmate, Gagnon, Kang, & Dixon, 2006), followed by collaborating with a friend, and then by working alone. This is in contrast to the fact that for older adults typically prefer to solve everyday problems alone (Berg, Meegan, & Deviney, 1998; Blanchard-Fields, Jahnke, & Camp, 1995). Only older adults who think that their own cognitive performance is weak prefer to work with others (Strough et al., 2002). Furthermore, Margrett and Marsiske (2002) demonstrated that participants who worked on a task with their spouses rated their expectations of satisfaction with collaborative teamwork more positively than the participants who were assigned to work with strangers. In fact, self- and partner-rated expectations of competitiveness were predictive of collaborative performance on tasks of planning, decision making, and comprehension (Strough, Patrick, Swenson, Cheng, & Barnes, 2003).

One social factor that has been shown to affect performance independent of the age of the dyads examined is the affiliation of the partners. In Berg et al.'s (2003) study, the fact that there were more high-affiliation interactions on the decision-making task than on the planning task may be explained by the fact that the task was presented via computer, which led to more interaction between the couples in general. Another possible explanation is that vacation decisions are seen as very important, regularly occurring in everyday life, and therefore have to be discussed and negotiated intensively. This is different from the wisdom-related decision making that may be optimized through interaction with the minds of other persons (external or in our own head) and individual thinking time to filter and review the different aspects of the decision to be made. The age effects in favor of older dyads may depend on familiarity with the problem domain, the interaction of existing knowledge with good performance conditions that provide an external dialogue, and the time needed for an individual appraisal of the important aspects of the decision to be made.

Overall, the literature on dyadic decision making in old age suggests a differentiation of paradigms to capture different decision-making domains of everyday relevance and to integrate measures of dyadic interaction to analyze the degree to which performance of process differences depend on the age, sex, cognitive abilities, or task characteristics of the particular decision-making paradigm used.

DYADIC REASONING

Dyadic Reasoning Paradigms

Only two studies have looked at dyadic reasoning in old age. It is interesting to note that both studies analyzed reasoning performance in old age and focused on the consequences of a reasoning-training program and the differences between individual and dyadic training on reasoning performance.

Margrett and Willis (2006) and Saczynski, Margrett, and Willis (2004) used a letter series test (Blieszner et al., 1981, cited in Margrett & Willis, 2006), a word series test (Schaie, 1985, cited in Margrett & Willis, 2006), and a letter set test (Ekstrom et al., 1976, cited in Margrett & Willis, 2006) to train and test reasoning abilities in older couples. The main difference between both studies is that Saczynski et al. included a posttest 3 months after the training. In Margrett and Willis's study, the sample size was 49 older couples (mean age = 71.43 years, mean length of marriage = 46.53 years), and in Saczynski et al.'s study the sample size was 47 couples (mean age = 71.6 years, mean length of marriage = 47 years). Couples in both studies were randomly assigned to questionnaire only ($n = 31$ individuals), individual training ($n = 32$ individuals), and collaborative training ($n = 32$ individuals). Within-subject designs were not used in either of the studies. Possible influences, such as individual and dyadic training, were manipulated, and individual and dyadic measurements were possible in both studies. Neither study included measurements of relationship characteristics.

Dyadic Reasoning Paradigms: Performance or Process Differences?

Both Margrett and Willis (2006) and Saczynski et al. (2004) analyzed inductive reasoning in older dyads. Both studies also primarily focused on training this ability through a self-guided strategy training (individual and collaborative) and the question of whether dyadic training is better than individual training. Saczynski et al. found that inductive reasoning training is related to gains in strategic behavior for individual and collaborative training groups on assessments completed alone and with one's spouse. The performance level was maintained until 3 months after the end of the training program. There was no difference in strategy use at immediate posttest between the individual and the dyadic training group (see also Margrett & Willis, 2006). However, collaboratively trained people demonstrated a better maintenance of strategy use than individually trained people at the 3-month follow-up when assessed in a collaborative problem-solving context. This means that collaborative learning alleviates dissipation of training effects observed once intervention is complete, but only in the collaborative context in which they were learned.

Interdyadic Differences in Reasoning: Explanatory Concepts

A reason for the benefit of collaboratively trained people at Saczynski et al.'s (2004) 3-month follow-up could be that collaboratively trained dyads were more likely to apply their training to everyday life, or engaged more in practice and reinforcement with their spouses, than individually trained people. Margrett and Willis (2006) also mentioned the possibility that benefits of dyadic collaboration in their study could have become evident after more time had passed. It is also possible that the benefits of dyadic inductive reasoning training can be found in other aspects of the training, such as subjective experience, transfer of training effects, or at other time points during the training. More research clearly is needed to determine which factors may lead to improved dyadic reasoning skills in old adults, and more paradigms are needed to relate reasoning performance in laboratory tasks to reasoning in everyday tasks.

DYADIC COMPREHENSION

Dyadic Comprehension Paradigms

Only one study used a task to assess older dyads' comprehension of everyday material: Margrett and Marsiske (2002) included a task in their study of older adults' everyday cognitive collaboration to assess older married couples' ability to solve problems concerning everyday printed materials (e.g., health and medication use, financial management, or housekeeping). The sample comprised 98 older married couples (mean age = 72.90 years, mean length of marriage = 45.81 years). Two parallel 14-item forms from the 28-item short-form version of the Everyday Problems Test (Willis & Marsiske, 1993, cited in Margrett & Marsiske, 2002) were

created. The questions were open-ended, to provide enough possibilities for dyadic interaction. The task was unambiguous and highly structured, requiring one solution. Task performance was assessed by the total number of correctly answered items. The same task was completed individually and in dyads, but because half the people worked with their spouse and the other half worked with a stranger, the study did not use a real within-subject design. Manipulated possible influences were collaboration, sex, familiarity (actor–partner method), collaborative and task-specific expectations and evaluations, and competitiveness. To find out about relationship characteristics that might influence collaboration, the authors used an open-ended interview about couples' daily collaboration.

Dyadic Comprehension Paradigms: Performance or Process Differences?

Margrett and Marsiske's (2002) results indicate that men and women equally influenced each other on the experimental task. Most important for collaborative performance was the actor's performance in the work-alone condition, that is, the better the performance when working alone, the better the collaborative performance. There was also a significant influence of the actor's partner, meaning that the better the actor's partner performed when alone, the better the actor's own performance in the collaborative condition.

Dyadic Comprehension Differences: Explanatory Concepts

Margrett and Marsiske (2002) explained their finding by saying that in highly structured tasks both partners are equally influential. However, how the dyadic interaction and the dyadic performance might change when task demands are increasingly more complex remains an open question. Thus, more paradigms and more research are needed to better understand older dyads' comprehension performance.

DISCUSSION

It is clear that dyadic cognition requires different abilities as well as different skills in dyadic ability management depending on the particular cognitive task examined. In addition, task requirements may interact differentially with relationship characteristics before and while working on the cognitive task at hand. Therefore, to summarize the results from studies on dyadic cognition in old age it is necessary to differentiate among dyadic memory, dyadic planning, dyadic decision making, dyadic reasoning, and dyadic comprehension. With respect to dyadic memory performance, empirical findings show that older adults' dyadic performance is superior to their individual memory performances. Compared with the pooled, nonredundant episodic memory performance of two individuals (nominal pairs), real dyads usually generate fewer correct recalls but also make fewer mistakes (e.g. Ross et al., 2004). When the partners know each other (spouses, friends) and use a transactive memory system, they are able to perform better than stranger dyads on memory tasks and sometimes even as well as nominal pairs (e.g., Johansson et al., 2000). Whether older dyads perform worse (Gould et al., 2002) or the same (Dixon & Gould, 1998) as younger dyads on memory tasks remains unclear, although most studies have shown differences in interaction styles between young and older dyads. Results suggest that older adults communicate less efficiently; that is, they tend to use more words, speak more slowly, and use fewer supportive words for their partners (Gould & Dixon, 1993; Gould et al., 1994, 2002).

In regard to dyadic planning and dyadic decision making, Berg et al. (2003) did not find interaction differences between younger and older dyads. Their hypothesis that older adults would show more high-affiliation interactions than younger adults was not confirmed. High-affiliation interactions were associated with better planning and decision making in young and older couples, though. On general planning and decision-making performance measures older dyads performed as well as young dyads. It is interesting to note that, contrary to the results regarding dyadic memory, older adults' dyadic planning does not lead to more efficient plans than individual planning, probably because of the relatively low memory demands of the task. However, dyads make fewer planning errors than individuals (Cheng & Strough,

2004). Whether sex differences in planning exist remains unclear, but Margrett and Marsiske (2002) found that in dyadic planning older men influence their own collaborative outcome more than women. A similar result was found for dyadic decision making: When it came to making decisions about social situations, men aged 70 and older were more likely to use their own judgment to influence their own and their partners' collaborative outcome (Margrett & Marsiske, 2002). This finding is interesting, because older men and women performed equally well on the planning task, and women performed better than men on the decision-making task. On the Everyday Problems Test (a comprehension task), Margrett and Marsiske did not find such sex effects. Men and women were equally influential on this task. What was important for good dyadic performance on this task was the actor's performance in the individual condition and the actor's partner's performance in the individual condition.

With respect to dyadic decision making on wisdom tasks, young and older people perform better when they can collaborate with a familiar partner in a dyad than when they have to make decisions individually. For optimal decisions, people need individual thinking time after the external or internal dyadic discussion (Staudinger & Baltes, 1996). Dyadic-reasoning studies suggest that dyadic and individual inductive reasoning training is associated with better strategic behavior on assessments completed alone or with the spouse. It is interesting that dyadic training led to better strategy maintenance than individual training at the 3-month follow-up when assessed collaboratively (Saczynski et al., 2004). Finally, studies on dyadic comprehension suggest the importance of the individual's performance for the collaborative performance.

CONCLUSION

We began this chapter by defining the requirements of optimal paradigms to examine dyadic cognition and its development in old age. According to these requirements, paradigms should be appropriate to use with individuals and dyads that cover a wide age range, sex differences, and hierarchy differences. Paradigms should also allow repeated measurement to be used in age comparisons, comparisons between individual versus dyadic performance, longitudinal studies, and in married couples versus professional dyads of different ages. From an experimental point of view, paradigms should allow one to manipulate the causal mechanisms suspected to influence dyadic performance.

Despite the relatively large number of studies on dyadic memory in old adults, it is not clear whether the paradigms used do fulfill the criteria that would allow a wider use in empirical research or comparisons of results between studies. For example, with respect to the possible comparison between individual and dyadic performance, only Johansson et al. (2005) use a within-subject design in their episodic and semantic memory tasks. Because of the use of repeated measurements, Gould et al.'s (2002) study allows comparisons between familiar and unfamiliar dyads (story recall, word recall, referential naming task). All other studies have not used within-subject designs to compare performances of different groups. In the studies we have reviewed, comparisons between young and older couples have not used a within-subject design. However, it appears that, except for the referential naming task (Gould et al., 2002), all tasks examined may allow one to compare individual and dyadic performance as well as interdyadic differences in performance. Thus, empirical testing is needed to demonstrate whether the comparison between dyads is possible with all other paradigms.

It is still unclear whether the tasks used in the three studies on dyadic planning in old age (Berg et al., 2003; Cheng & Strough, 2004; Margrett & Marsiske, 2002) fulfill our criteria for experimental paradigms. A within-subject design has been used in part by Margrett and Marsiske (2002), but the other studies did not use such a design. Causal mechanisms suspected to influence dyadic performance include age, sex, and collaboration, as well as relationship characteristics and collaborative expectations. Individual and dyadic measurements are potentially possible in all three planning tasks, but such measurements were not made by Berg et al. (2003). Again, as with the dyadic memory tasks, there is not a lot of information on relationship characteristics. Berg et al.

(2003) coded interactions into low and high affiliation interactions, and Margrett and Marsiske asked about couples' daily collaboration. Thus, more empirical testing is needed to examine the influence of relationship characteristics on dyadic planning.

The inductive reasoning studies and the comprehension studies allow individual and dyadic measurements and, therefore, the manipulation of the suspected causal mechanism (dyadic vs. individual training). Margrett and Willis (2006), Saczynski et al. (2004), and Margrett and Marsiske (2002) examined older adults' learning abilities and therefore did not include young dyads or same-sex dyads. A within-subject design has not been used, and relationship indicators have not been measured. Thus, more data are required to establish potential age effects and effects of dyadic collaboration in reasoning and comprehension tasks and to clarify the influence of relationship characteristics on the quality of reasoning and comprehension performance.

Overall, a number of paradigms have been, or may be, used to examine dyadic cognition in old age. Most paradigms may be used to establish age and dyadic collaboration effects in dyadic cognition and to examine the role of particular explanatory mechanisms but thus far have not been used for this purpose. Therefore, more empirical research is needed to establish and understand the phenomena of dyadic cognition in old age and the potential and adaptive capacities older dyads may possess, and to improve our understanding of which types of tasks and in which dyadic constellations it is preferable to collaborate and which individual efforts are leading to better task performance. With respect to paradigm development, there seems to be a need for standard paradigms to be used to for individual, dyadic, and repeated individual and dyadic testing for each of the domains of cognition reviewed here. In addition, paradigms that clearly dissociate the required abilities would allow us to better understand how dyads manage the abilities and responsibilities to optimize dyadic task performance.

Overall, we strongly believe that the developmental and longitudinal approach to cognition in old age has proven its advantages to understand individual development across the life span (Hofer & Sliwinski, 2006; Schaie & Hofer,

2001). The inclusion of a dyadic partner in the examination and analyses of cognitive development, however, creates a number of new and additional empirical, theoretical, and methodological challenges. For example, if individuals regulate the performance of their partners, this may lead to decreases in the individuals' performance (Hertel, Deter, & Konradt, 2003; Sebanz, Knoblich, & Prinz, 2003). However, this decrease might be highly adaptive in the long run, because it may stabilize the cognitive and emotional well-being of the dyad (Martin & Hofer, 2004) and thus improve openness to new cognitive challenges and well-being. In fact, dyadic cognition might be an ideal means by which to study the regulation of cognition in the sense that it is more obvious in dyads compared with individuals that cognitive performance takes place in the context of social interactions and socially relevant goals (see chap. 37, this volume), and the estimation of a partner's abilities may be seen as a social skill that is needed to regulate the well-being of a dyadic partner. Thus, examining dyadic cognition situates cognition in the context of meaningful exchanges between persons and may still be examined in the laboratory with experimental paradigms. However, adding a dyadic perspective to the examination of individual cognitive development widens our horizon with respect to adaptive capacities and plasticity individuals may possess. It also alludes to the fact that individual performance may be underestimated without including the dyadic perspective, because what may lead to a lower individual performance in one test at one time point may be supporting the best possible developmental trajectory of a dyad's aptitude well into old age. Along similar lines, the performance of an individual within a dyad is typically dependent upon the actions of the partner. Therefore, it is difficult to independently measure an individual's ability for dyadic cognition. Thus, the selection of control groups, or experimental control of the partner's actions (e.g., by using virtual partners or experimenters instructed to follow a limited set of rules in the interaction), may prove useful in the future. With more empirical research on different types of dyadic cognition, and with a similar developmental approach made possible through repeatable testing procedures, we will be increasingly better able to understand the contribution and adaptive capacities of dyadic interactions on the cognitive performances of individual members of social dyads.

REFERENCES

Andersson, J., & Rönnberg, J. (1995). Recall suffers from collaboration: Joint recall effects of friendship and task complexity. *Applied Cognitive Psychology, 9,* 199–211.

Baltes, P. B., & Staudinger, U. M. (Eds.). (1996). *Interactive minds: Life-span perspectives on the social foundations of cognition.* New York: Cambridge University Press.

Basden, B. H., Basden, D. R., Bryner, S., & Thomas, R. L. (1997). Does collaboration disrupt retrieval strategies? A comparison of group and individual remembering. *Journal of Experimental Psychology: Learning, Memory, and Cognition, 23,* 1176–1191.

Berg, C. A., Johnson, M. M., Meegan, S. P., & Strough, J. (2003). Collaborative problem-solving: Interactions in young and old married couples. *Discourse Processes, 35,* 33–58.

Berg, C. A., Meegan, S. P., & Deviney, F. P. (1998). A social-contextual model of coping with everyday problems across the life-span. *International Journal of Behavioral Development, 22,* 239–361.

Blanchard-Fields, F., Jahnke, H. C., & Camp, C. (1995). Age differences in problem-solving style: The role of emotional salience. *Psychology and Aging, 10,* 173–180.

Bodenmann, G. (1995). *Bewältigung von Stress in Partnerschaften. Der Einfluss von Belastungen auf die Qualität und Stabilität von Paarbeziehungen* (S.95f) [Coping in close relationships. The influence of stress on the quality and the stability of close relationships]. Bern, Switzerland: Huber.

Bodenmann, G. (2000). *Stress und Coping bei Paaren* [Stress and coping in couples]. Göttingen, Germany: Hogrefe.

Bodenmann, G., & Cina, A. (1999). Der Einfluss von Stress, individueller Belastungsbewältigung und dyadischem Coping auf die partnerschaftsstabilität: Eine 4-Jahres-Längsschnittstudie [The influence of stress, individual coping, and dyadic coping on relationship stability: A 4-year follow-up]. *Zeitschrift für Klinische Psychologie, 28,* 130–139.

Bodenmann, G., Pihet, S., Cina, A., Widmer, K., & Shantinath, S. (2006). Improving dyadic coping in couples with a stress-oriented approach: A 2-year longitudinal study. *Behavior Modification, 30*, 571–597.

Bodenmann, G., & Widmer, K. (2000). *Stressbewältigung im Alter: Ein Vergleich von Paaren jüngeren, mittleren und höheren Alters* [Coping in old age: A comparison between younger, middle-aged, and older couples]. *Zeitschrift für Gerontologie und Geriatrie, 33*, 217–228.

Carstensen, L. L., Isaacowitz, D. M., & Charles, S. T. (1999). Taking time seriously: A theory of socioemotional selectivity. *American Psychologist, 54*, 165–181.

Cheng, S., & Strough, J. (2004). A comparison of collaborative and individual everyday problem solving in younger and older adults. *International Journal of Aging and Human Development, 58*, 167–195.

Dixon, R. A. (1992). Contextual approaches to adult intellectual development. In R. J. Sternberg & C. A. Berg (Eds.), *Intellectual development* (pp. 350–380). New York: Cambridge University Press.

Dixon, R. A. (2000). Concepts and mechanisms of gains in cognitive aging. In D. Park & N. Schwarz (Eds.), *Cognitive aging: A primer* (pp. 23–41). Philadelphia: Psychology Press.

Dixon, R. A., & Bäckman, L. (Eds.). (1995). *Compensating for psychological deficits and declines: Managing losses and promoting gains.* Mahwah, NJ: Lawrence Erlbaum.

Dixon, R. A., Fox, D. P., Threvithick, L., & Brundin, R. (1997). Exploring collaborative problem solving in adulthood. *Journal of Adult Development, 4*, 195–208.

Dixon, R. A., Gagnon, L. M., & Crow, C. B. (1998). Collaborative memory accuracy and distortion: Performance and beliefs. In M. J. Intons-Peterson & D. Best (Eds.), *Memory distortions and their prevention* (pp. 63–88). Mahwah, NJ: Lawrence Erlbaum.

Dixon, R., & Gould, O. (1998). Younger and old adults collaborating on retelling everyday stories. *Applied Developmental Science, 2*, 160–171.

Feltmate, S. E., Gagnon, L. M., Kang, S. J., & Dixon, R. A. (2006, April). *Exploring metacognitive characteristics of collaborating dyads.* Poster presented at the 11th Cognitive Aging Conference, Atlanta, GA.

Finlay, F., Hitch, G., & Meudell, P. R. (2000). Mutual inhibition in collaborative recall: Evidence for a retrieval-based account. *Journal of Experimental Psychology: Learning, Memory, and Cognition, 26*, 1556–1567.

German Federal Statistical Office. (2000). *Bevölkerungsentwicklung Deutschlands bis zum Jahr 2050. Ergebnis der 9. koordinierten Bevölkerungsvorausberechnung* [Population development in Germany until the year 2050. Results of the 9th Coordinated Population Forecast]. Wiesbaden, Germany: Statistisches Bundesamt.

Gould, O., & Dixon, R. A. (1993). How we spent our vacation: Collaborative storytelling by young and old adults. *Psychology and Aging, 8*, 10–17.

Gould, O., Kurzman, D., & Dixon, R. A. (1994). Communication during prose recall conversations by young and old dyads. *Discourse Processes, 17*, 149–165.

Gould, O., Lee, T., & Dixon, R. (1991). Adult age differences in elaborations produced during prose recall. *Psychology and Aging, 6*, 93–99.

Gould, O. N., Osborn, C., Krein, H., & Mortenson, M. (2002). Collaborative recall in married and unacquainted dyads. *International Journal of Behavioral Development, 26*, 36–44.

Hertel, G., Deter, C., & Konradt, U. (2003). Motivation gains in computer-supported groups. *Journal of Applied Social Psychology, 33*, 2080–2105.

Hofer, S. M., & Sliwinski, M. J. (2006). Design and analysis of longitudinal studies on aging. In J. E. Birren & K. W. Schaie (Eds.), *Handbook of the psychology of aging* (6th ed., pp. 15–37). Amsterdam: Academic Press.

Johansson, O., Andersson, J., & Rönnberg, J. (2000). Do elderly couples have a better prospective memory than other elderly people when they collaborate? *Applied Cognitive Psychology, 14*, 121–133.

Johansson, O., Andersson, J., & Rönnberg, J. (2005). Compensating strategies in collaborative remembering in very old couples. *Scandinavian Journal of Psychology, 46*, 349–359.

Kolanowski, A., Hoffman, L., & Hofer, S. M. (2007). Concordance of self-report and informant assessment of emotional well-being in nursing home residents with dementia. *Journal of Gerontology: Psychological Sciences, 62B*, P20–P27.

Margrett, J. A., & Marsiske, M. (2002). Gender differences in old adults' everyday cognitive collaboration. *International Journal of Behavioral Development, 26,* 45–59.

Margrett, J. A., & Willis, S. L. (2006). In-home cognitive training with old married couples: Individual versus collaborative learning. *Aging, Neuropsychology, and Cognition, 13,* 173–194.

Martin, M., & Hofer, S. M. (2004). Intraindividual variability, change, and aging: Conceptual and analytical issues. *Gerontology, 50,* 7–11.

Meegan, S. P., & Berg, C. A. (2002). Contexts, functions, forms, and processes of collaborative everyday problem solving in older adulthood. *International Journal of Behavioral Development, 26,* 6–15.

Ross, M., Spencer, S. J., Linardatos, L., Lam, K. C. H., & Perunovic, M. (2004). Going shopping and identifying landmarks: Does collaboration improve old people's memory? *Applied Cognitive Psychology, 18,* 683–696.

Saczynski, J. S., Margrett, J. A., & Willis, S. L. (2004). Old adults' strategic behavior: Effects of individual versus collaborative cognitive training. *Educational Gerontology, 30,* 587–610.

Schaie, K. W., & Hofer, S. M. (2001). Longitudinal studies in aging research. In J. E. Birren & K. W. Schaie (Eds.), *Handbook of the psychology of aging* (5th ed., pp. 53–77). San Diego, CA: Academic Press.

Sebanz, N., Knoblich, G., & Prinz, W. (2003). Representing other's actions: Just like one's own? *Cognition, 88,* B11–B21.

Staudinger, U. M., & Baltes, P. B. (1996). Interactive minds: A facilitative setting for wisdom-related performance? *Journal of Personality and Social Psychology, 71,* 746–762.

Stephenson, G. M., Kniveton, B. H., & Wagner, W. (1991). Social influences on remembering: Intellectual, interpersonal, and intergroup components. *European Journal of Social Psychology, 21,* 463–475.

Strough, J., Cheng, S., & Swenson, L. M. (2002). Preferences for collaborative and individual everyday problem solving in later adulthood. *International Journal of Behavioral Development, 26,* 26–35.

Strough, J., & Margrett, J. (2002). Overview of the special section on collaborative cognition in later adulthood. *International Journal of Behavioral Development, 26,* 2–5.

Strough, J., Patrick, J. H., Swenson, L. M., Cheng, S., & Barnes, K. A. (2003). Collaborative everyday problem solving: Interpersonal relationships and problem dimensions. *International Journal of Aging and Human Development, 56,* 43–66.

Swiss Federal Statistical Office. (2005). *Alter und Generationen- das Leben in der Schweiz ab 50 Jahren* [Age and generations—Life from 50 on in Switzerland]. Neuchâtel, Switzerland: Bundesamt für Statistik.

Wegner, D. M. (1986). Transactive memory: A contemporary analysis of the group mind. In M. B. Mullen & G. R. Goethals (Eds.), *Theories of group behavior* (pp. 185–205). New York: Springer-Verlag.

Wegner, D. M., Erber, R., & Raymond, P. (1991). Transactive memory in close relationships. *Journal of Personality and Social Psychology, 61,* 923–929.

Wegner, D. M., Giuliano, T., & Hertel, P. T. (1985). Cognitive interdependence in close relationships. In W. L. Ickes (Ed.), *Compatible and incompatible relationships* (pp. 253–276). New York: Springer.

39

MIDLIFE COGNITION

The Association of Personality With Cognition and Risk of Cognitive Impairment

SHERRY L. WILLIS AND JULIE BLASKEWICZ BORON

A major distinction among life span psychological theories is their differing position on stability versus change in midlife (Lachman, 2004). Trait theories such as those concerned with personality (Costa & McCrae, 1980) or intelligence (Schaie, 2005) have depicted midlife as a period of stability, at least when studied at the aggregate level. By the fourth decade of life, there appears to be considerable stability in personality traits (Costa, Herbst, McCrae, & Siegler, 2000). Caspi and Roberts (2001) concluded that personality consistency increases with age and is more common than change in midlife and old age.

As Costa and McCrae (1999) noted, historically, personality and cognition have been isolated and separated from one another. Reviews of the literature have concluded that there are weak associations between personality and ability (Ackerman & Rolfhus, 1999). Costa and McCrae (1999) went so far as to suggest that intelligence should be conceptualized as a sixth factor in addition to the five personality factors assessed by the NEO Personality Inventory (NEO-PI). However, few longitudinal studies have included adequate measurement of both

personality and abilities such that concurrent and antecedent–consequence relationships could be examined in samples of sufficient size and across lengthy periods of the life span.

If personality traits reach a higher level of consistency in midlife and intellectual abilities also are more stable, then examining the association between personality and intelligence may be of particular interest in midlife. Moreover, research examining early antecedents of cognitive risk in old age have indicated that certain personality dimensions may directly or indirectly have an influence on onset of chronic disease or on neurodegeneration that contribute to cognitive impairment. Specifically, personality characteristics associated with proneness to psychological distress have been reported to be associated with increased cognitive risk (Crowe, Andel, Pedersen, Fratiglioni, & Gatz, 2006). In addition, personality characteristics have been associated with health behaviors associated with chronic diseases (e.g., cardiovascular disease) that are known to impact cognitive functioning (Roberts & Bogg, 2004).

The aim of this chapter is to examine the literature on the association between personality traits and cognitive functioning in midlife and the research findings on the role of certain personality traits in increasing or diminishing the individual's risk of cognitive impairment. Gender differences in association between personality and cognition have been noted in some studies and will be briefly discussed (Feingold, 1994). A criticism of the trait approach to the study of personality has been the lack of theory articulating the mechanisms or processes underlying development and change in personality traits (Endler, 2000). Cognitive or learning styles have been suggested as possible mechanisms underlying the relationship between personality and cognition and thus will be briefly reviewed. The stability of personality traits across the life span is an important issue, because the assumption of long-term disposition to personal distress is critical to the personality–cognitive impairment hypothesis. I briefly review the findings on stability of personality in midlife and the possible mechanisms that maintain continuity in personality in adulthood.

Personality Traits in Adulthood

There is considerable consensus that the structure of the personality traits can be encompassed by the Big Five superordinate dimensions of Neuroticism, Extraversion, Openness to Experience, Agreeableness, and Conscientiousness (Costa & McCrae, 1980). The NEO-PI (Costa & McCrae, 1985) assesses the big five traits and generates facet scores for six facets for each of the five factors. The same basic factor structure has emerged from a broad range of personality assessment derived from a variety of instruments and methodologies (Caspi & Roberts, 2001; Endler, 2000). Considerable convergence between self-reported trait ratings and ratings of others who know the individual have been found; in addition, there is convergence between observer ratings of spouses and peers. Although Costa and McCrae's big five appears to be the prevailing current trait model of personality, a considerable amount of research has used the California Psychological Inventory (CPI) of 20 facets of personality (Jones, Livson, & Peskin, 2003). The CPI facets were designed to measure aspects of personality meaningful to the average person (Gough & Bradley, 1996). The CPI and NEO-PI differ not only in the domains of personality studied but also in the level of analysis (facets, factors) and the manner in which the domains were derived. CPI facets represent dispositions selected for their importance in social life, whereas the NEO-PI measures traits abstracted through factor analysis (Helson, Jones, & Kwan, 2002).

Neuroticism measures emotional instability versus stability (Costa & McCrae, 1985). Individuals who score higher on Neuroticism are characterized as being more anxious, depressed, and emotionally labile (Eysenck & Eysenck, 1985). Extraversion measures the need for stimulation and activity and sociability, as opposed to introversion (reserved, quiet; Costa & McCrae, 1985). Individuals who score high on Extraversion are characterized as being more sociable, lively, active, and venturesome (Eysenck & Eysenck, 1985). Openness to Experience measures curiosity, creativity, and imagination at one pole as opposed to conventionality and not being analytical at the other pole (Costa & McCrae, 1985). Agreeableness measures the quality of a person's interpersonal focus, ranging from being good natured, forgiving, and trusting at one pole to being cynical, uncooperative, and ruthless at the other pole. Conscientiousness measures a person's degree of organization and persistence at one pole and aimlessness, unreliability, and carelessness at the other pole.

Association of Personality Traits and Mental Abilities in Adulthood

Given the voluminous literature on personality traits and on mental abilities, studies examining the relationship between these two trait approaches have been remarkably limited. As Costa and McCrae (1999) noted, historically, personality and cognition have been isolated and separated from one another, and the early studies suggested only weak associations between the two trait approaches. Costa and McCrae (1999) argued that the limited associations between personality and ability may in part be due to differing time dimensions assessed in personality and some cognitive measures. For example, they reported nonsignificant relationships between personality traits such as conscientiousness and cognitive states, such as choice reaction time; somewhat higher correlations were found when personality traits were related to more complex forms of cognition (Costa & McCrae, 1999).

Few longitudinal studies have included adequate measurement of both personality traits and abilities. Likewise, few studies have examined the personality–ability relationship over lengthy periods of the life span, such that concurrent and antecedent–consequence relationships could be examined in sufficiently large samples. Moreover, several of the studies that have examined personality–cognition relationships in adulthood have had predominately male samples, limiting the study of gender differences in the associations (Mroczek & Spiro, 2003). Boron (2003) examined the relation of the NEO-PI factors and Primary Mental Ability (PMA; Thurstone & Thurstone, 1949) scores in young, middle, and late adulthood in the Seattle Longitudinal Study (SLS) and found more consistent and significant relationships in middle and late adulthood, than in young adulthood. Greater consistency and significance in personality–cognition relationships in midlife may be due to an increase in consistency in both personality and cognition during midlife. Moreover, in research within the SLS with adequate samples of men and women, almost four times as many significant personality–cognition relationships were found for midlife women as for men (Boron, 2003).

Costa and McCrae (1999) and others (Boron, 2003; Schaie, Willis, & Caskie, 2004) have concluded that the most meaningful relation is between Openness to Experience and various cognitive abilities. Below, I briefly summarize findings regarding the association of personality traits and mental abilities for middle-age and older adults.

Neuroticism

Neuroticism is the personality trait that most consistently exhibits negative relationships with various cognitive processes and mental abilities. Participants from the Normative Aging Study who were high in anxiety (a facet of Neuroticism) were found to score lower on information-processing ability, manual dexterity,

and pattern analysis capability (Costa, Fozard, McCrae, & Bosse, 1976). In a more recent study with the Normative Aging Study participants, memory complaints predicted the level, but not the rate, of change in both Neuroticism and Extraversion (Mroczek & Spiro, 2003). Men who complained of memory problems had lower Extraversion and higher Neuroticism. Negative relationships between Neuroticism and creativity have also been found (McCrae, 1987).

Boron (2003) examined personality–ability relationships for early (36–49 years) and later (50–63 years) middle-age adults. For early midlife women, Neuroticism was significantly negatively related to performance on inductive reasoning, spatial orientation, verbal ability, and speed; no significant relationships with Neuroticism were found for early midlife men. Education accounted for additional variance on reason and verbal abilities for women. For late midlife women, Neuroticism was significantly negatively related only to verbal ability; however, for late midlife men, Neuroticism was significantly negatively related to reason; in both cases, education accounted for additional variance. In the total SLS sample from young adulthood to old age, Neuroticism was significantly negatively related only to verbal ability (Schaie et al., 2004).

Extraversion

For participants in the Baltimore Longitudinal Aging Study, a positive relationship was reported between creativity and Extraversion (McCrae, 1987). In a recent study with the Normative Aging Study participants, memory complaints predicted the level, but not the rate, of change in both Neuroticism and Extraversion (Mroczek & Spiro, 2003). Boron (2003) found that for early midlife women (36–49 years), Extraversion was negatively related to performance on spatial orientation and verbal ability; no significant relationships were found for early midlife men. Education accounted for additional variance on verbal ability for women. For late midlife women (50–63 years), Extraversion was significantly positively related only to number; however, for late midlife men, Extraversion was significantly negatively related to verbal ability; in both cases, education accounted for additional variance. In the total SLS sample,

Extraversion was related to verbal ability (Schaie et al., 2004)

Openness to Experience

Studies have found Openness to Experience to be the most consistent trait to correlate with cognitive abilities and to have the highest relationships. Costa et al. (1976) suggested that this association may be due in part to the significant relationship among Openness to Experience, education, and socioeconomic status; in addition, cognitive style (i.e., greater tolerance for novel experiences) as a mediator has been hypothesized. Participants from the Normative Aging Study who were high on Openness to Experience and high on Extraversion performed better on some cognitive processes (Costa et al., 1976). A positive relationship among divergent thinking, creativity, and Openness to Experience was found for participants in the Baltimore Longitudinal Aging Study (McCrae, 1987). For middle-age adults, a positive relation of Openness and knowledge of humanities and civics was found (Ackerman & Rolfhus, 1999). Boron (2003) reported that for early midlife women, Openness was positively related to performance on verbal memory, inductive reasoning, spatial orientation, and verbal ability (with the largest effect noted for verbal ability); the only significant relation for early midlife men was verbal ability. Education accounted for additional variance on reason and verbal ability for women. For late midlife women, Openness was positively related to verbal ability; additional variance was accounted for by education. For late midlife men, Openness was positively related to memory, and verbal ability; additional variance was accounted for by education. In the total SLS sample, Openness was related to inductive reasoning, spatial orientation, perceptual speed, verbal ability, and verbal memory (Schaie et al., 2004).

Conscientiousness

Given their more recent addition to the NEO assessment battery, less research has included the factors of Conscientiousness and Agreeableness. For participants in the Baltimore Longitudinal Aging Study, a positive relationship between creativity and Conscientiousness was found (McCrae, 1987). Boron (2003) found no significant associations for early midlife women and men with Agreeableness or Conscientiousness. For late midlife women, a negative relationship of Conscientiousness with reason and verbal ability was reported; education accounted for additional variance. No significant relationships were found for late midlife men. In the total SLS sample, Conscientiousness was related to verbal ability (Schaie et al., 2004).

Agreeableness

Boron (2003) reported a modest positive relationship for late midlife women of Agreeableness with reason and speed ability; additional variance was accounted for by education. No significant relation was observed for late midlife men. In the total SLS sample, Agreeableness was negatively related to inductive reasoning and spatial orientation (Schaie et al., 2004).

Cognitive Style as a Mechanism Linking Personality and Ability

Given the relatively modest associations between personality and abilities, it has been suggested that cognitive or learning styles may be an important link in the cognition–personality relationship. Costa and McCrae (1999) have suggested that there may be stronger associations between personality and cognitive styles than directly with cognitive abilities. Likewise, Sternberg and Grigorenko (1997) suggested that styles may be a bridge between personality and cognition. *Cognitive style* has been defined as characteristic modes of perceiving, remembering, thinking, problem solving, or decision making. In a somewhat similar approach, Langston and Sykes (1997) suggested that individual beliefs and expectancies may be a proximal mechanism whereby personality traits influence behavior.

Neuroticism has been positively related to thinking styles characterized as more simplistic or norm favoring in young adults (Zhang & Huang, 2001). In contrast, reflective learning styles have been negatively associated with neuroticism in midlife adults (Furnham, 1996). Furnham (1996) found that an activist and pragmatic learning style related positively to Extraversion and Openness to Experience in midlife adults. Openness has also been related to thinking styles characterized as involving creativity and complexity in young adult samples (Zhang & Huang, 2001). Conscientiousness was related to thinking styles involving a hierarchical approach in young adults. (Zhang & Huang, 2001).

CUMULATIVE CONTINUITY IN PERSONALITY TRAITS

Much of the recent life span research on personality traits has focused on a discussion of the relative stability of traits across adulthood (Cost & McCrae, 2006; Roberts & DelVecchio, 2000). The issue of stability is particularly relevant to recent findings regarding personality and cognitive risk. Wilson et al. (2003) argued that it is the long-term predisposition to psychological distress, represented by psychological traits such as neuroticism, that may contribute to some individuals' increased risk of cognitive impairment. In the following section, we briefly review the types of stability of concern in studying personality traits and discuss mechanisms that may contribute to continuity in personality, particularly in midlife and old age.

Caspi and Roberts (2001), in their discussion of personality development across the life course, concluded that although there are continuity and discontinuity at all life stages, empirical evidence suggests that personality consistency increases with age and is more common than change in midlife and old age. However, it is important to understand the various types of continuity studied; we discuss several types of continuity below.

Findings on continuity are also impacted by the methods used to study stability. Earlier studies of continuity used a nomothetic approach to examine mean trends in the data via repeated measures analysis of variance procedures and to study bivariate correlations for the sample as a whole. A limiting assumption of the analysis of variance approach is the assumption that the overall pattern of change within a sample generalizes to all subjects. A limitation of simple correlational analysis is that the relationship between two variables is linear (Jones & Meredith, 1996). However, more recent studies (Jones & Meredith, 1996; Mroczek & Spiro,

2003; Small, Hertzog, Hultsch, & Dixon, 2003) have taken an individual-differences approach, focusing on individuals' unique patterns of personality change. The relatively new statistical techniques of hierarchical linear modeling (Bryk & Raudenbush, 1987) and latent curve analysis (Meredith & Tisak, 1990) have been used. These procedures permit examination of nonlinear change and offer options for dealing with missing data.

Types of Continuity

Differential Stability

Rank order continuity indicates consistency in individual differences in a sample across time. This is the most common form of stability studied in personality. Costa et al. (2000) examined both rank order and intraindividual stability over a 6- to 9-year period in middle age; rank order stability in midlife approached retest reliability. Small et al. (2003) also reported uniformly high 6-year stability coefficients in a study involving the Victoria Longitudinal Study participants. In their meta-analysis, Roberts and DelVecchio (2000) concluded that rank order consistency in personality peaks in the 50s. Moreover, there is little variability across different personality domains in rank order consistency.

Absolute Stability

A second type of consistency focuses on intraindividual stability or constancy in amount of an attribute over time. Thus, the argument for stability claims not that personality scores do not vary over time but that individuals retain the same rank order across time. Costa et al. (2000) reported small intraindividual decreases in levels of Neuroticism, Extraversion, Openness to Experience, and Conscientiousness within the 6 to 9 years studied in midlife; decline was more evident for women than for men. Age-related changes were considered modest and over a 10-year period were on the order of less than 0.20 standard deviation units. Women were found to decline on all facets of Neuroticism except anxiety and to decline also on Extraversion.

Many of the more recent studies of personality continuity have focused on the question of absolute stability using hierarchical linear modeling or latent curve analyses (Jones & Meredith, 1996; Mroczek & Spiro, 2003; Small et al., 2003). These longitudinal studies have found reliable individual differences in rates of personality change, although the magnitude of variance was small relative to the total variance between individuals (Helson et al., 2002). Using repeated measures multivariate analyses of variance, Small et al. (2003) reported only a significant decline for Openness over the 6-year interval. However, with latent change analyses, significant individual differences in change were found for all five NEO-PI factors; individuals who were initially lower on the personality dimension exhibited greater increases 6 years later. Likewise, Mroczek and Spiro (2003) found significant variability over a 12-year interval in both level and rate of change for Neuroticism and Extraversion for men in the Normative Aging Study. However, these studies also acknowledge that many participants are well characterized by the overall trajectory for a given trait.

Schaie et al. (2004) estimated age-related changes in the NEO-PI traits from young adulthood to old age; of interest is that middle age marked a shift in trajectories for several of the NEO-PI traits; a plateau or stability beginning in midlife was noted for Neuroticism, Openness, and Conscientiousness. For Neuroticism, there was an increase from young adulthood to midlife, with stability after middle age. Openness showed a modest increase until age 46, a plateau until the late 60s, and a decline thereafter. Extraversion was highest in young adulthood and showed a decline from the 40s. Conscientiousness was highest in young adulthood with a decline until the 50s, followed by a plateau.

Gender Differences

Gender differences in level of personality traits and in rate of change have received relatively little attention (Feingold, 1994). Across studies of gender differences in level of personality traits, the largest gender differences have been found for Neuroticism and Openness, with women scoring higher than men (Costa, Terracciano, & McCrae, 2001; Feingold, 1994;

Small et al., 2003). Gender differences may vary by facet within a domain. In a meta-analysis, Feingold (1994) reported that men scored higher than women on assertiveness, from the Extraversion domain, whereas women scored higher on the Extraversion facet of gregariousness. Women scored higher than men on tendermindedness and trust, from the Agreeableness domain, and on the anxiety facet of the Neuroticism domain. Most studies have examined gender differences only in level of the trait. Small et al. (2003) reported gender differences in rate of change over a 6-year period with an initial age range of 55 to 85 years; women showed greater declines in Neuroticism, but greater increases in Agreeableness.

Structural and Ipsative Continuity

Two additional forms of continuity focus on the interrelationship among traits and have received less attention in the literature. *Structural continuity* refers to the persistence of correlational patterns among a set of variables across time. Some developmental psychologists argue that structural invariance should be established before other kinds of stability are examined (Baltes, Reese, & Nesselroade, 1977). Costa and McCrae (1992) concluded that there do not appear to be qualitative structural shifts beyond adolescence in the NEO personality traits. However, several studies using confirmatory analytic techniques have reported that facets from the NEO-PI do not always adhere to a simple factor structure, with each facet corresponding to one and only one factor (Church & Burke, 1994; Small et al., 2003). Small et al. (2003) chose to reduce the number of facets to examine structural stability over time; considerable structural stability was found for the reduced model.

Ipsative continuity focuses on individual- rather than group-level continuity and denotes continuity in the configuration of variables within an individual across time. Very little longitudinal research within the NEO approach has been conducted using the ipsative view. However, Eysenck (1967) suggested that differing configurations of neuroticism and extraversion within an individual are related to neural systems.

MECHANISMS FOR MAINTAINING CONTINUITY IN PERSONALITY

The finding of relative stability in personality at least from middle age into old age leads to the question of which mechanisms may contribute to continuity. One of the criticisms of a trait approach has been the relatively limited consideration within theory or research in understanding the mechanisms or processes underlying development and change in a trait. The definition of a trait as an enduring disposition may in part account for the limited interest in explanatory variables, other than genetic ones. Langston and Sykes (1997) noted that "the trait area of personality seems to have become stuck in the rut of investigating which traits are fundamental to the exclusion of other important questions, particularly the question, how do traits work" (p. 142). Bandura (1999) observed that what is needed is "an integrated conceptual scheme that not only classified behaviors but specifies their determinants and the key mechanisms through which they operate and the modes by which desired ones can be fostered and undesired ones altered." (p. 166). Caspi and Roberts (2001) proposed the mechanisms described in the following section for the maintenance of continuity in personality. The mechanisms related to stability in environment may be particularly relevant to the personality continuity seen in midlife and old age.

Environmental Influences. Personality characteristics may show continuity because the environment is stable. Warren and Hauser (1997) reported that socioenvironmental conditions show remarkable intragenerational persistence in adulthood. Longitudinal environmental correlations are of approximately the same magnitude as longitudinal personality correlations. However, there has been insufficient research to examine the directionality of the relationship between personality and environment. It is assumed that stable and enduring features of the environment are fostering continuity in personality. However, stable, enduring, and partially heritable personality traits may lead to seeking out or producing consistency in one's environment.

Genetic Influences. Genetic influences on personality continuity have been explored in twin studies. McGue, Bacon, and Lykken (1993) examined in adulthood the genetic and environmental etiology of age-to-age continuity in twins. Monozygotic cross-twin correlations were consistently and significantly larger than the dizygotic cross-twin correlations. The authors estimated that approximately 80% of phenotypic stability may be associated with genetic factors. Although genetic factors may influence continuity, there is the question of the mechanisms by which continuity is maintained. Kagan (1997) suggested that inherited variations in threshold of arousal may contribute to longitudinal consistencies. Alternatively, genetic factors may exert their influence through gene–environment correlations.

Person–Environment Interactions. Three types of person–environment interactions may foster continuity in personality. First, *reactive transactions* occur when different individuals exposed to the same environment experience it, interpret it, and react to it differently. Each person extracts a subjective psychological environment from the objective surroundings, and it is that subjective environment that shapes subsequent personality. Once psychological constructs of the self are well organized, as in midlife, these constructions make individuals selectively responsive to information that is congruent with their expectations and self views (Fiske & Taylor, 1991)

Second, *evocative transactions* occur when individuals evoke distinctive reactions from others on the basis of their personality characteristics. The person acts, the environment reacts, and the person reacts back in a mutually interlocking evocative transaction. Such transactions continue across the life span and promote continuity. Facial expressions of emotion are especially important in evocative person–environment transactional processes; they convey information to others about what the individual is feeling and how the individual is likely to act. Personality traits have been found to be registered in facial expressions and thus may influence continuity by evoking congruent and reciprocal responses from other persons (Keltner, 1996).

Third and last, *proactive transactions* may account for the age-related increase in magnitude of stability coefficients across the life span. The most consequential environments for personality development are interpersonal environments, in particular, friendship and mate selection. Friends and partners tend to resemble each other; empirical studies indicate that members of peer groups are similar because individuals selectively choose to affiliate with similar others. Affiliations with similar others tend to consolidate behavioral patterns over time. Demands of the social environment remain relatively stable over time. Consistency in social network relations may contribute to continuity in how one views and defines oneself. Assortative mating may influence personality continuity because similarities between spouses create an environment that reinforces initial tendencies (Buss, 1984). Caspi and Herbener (1990) found that persons who married a partner similar to themselves were subsequently more likely to show personality continuity over time.

PERSONALITY AND RISK OF COGNITIVE IMPAIRMENT

Personality Traits, Stress, and Neural Impairment

There is increasing evidence that psychological distress may have biological consequences that influence cognitive functioning. Experiencing stress, depression, and anxiety are associated with hormonal and immune system changes; these associations have been implicated in theories of neural degeneration and the development of cognitive impairment (Sapolsky, 1996, 2001). Stress is associated with activation of the hypothalamic–pituitary–adrenal (HPA) axis. Activation of the HPA axis results in the release of glucocorticoid hormones; long-term exposure to these hormones has been found to result in neurodegeneration. Long-term exposure to glucocorticoids appears to have a negative effect on the hippocampus, the brain area associated with memory and learning, in both animals and humans. Higher levels of cortisol, a human glucocorticoid, are often present in depression; people with a history of depression have been found to have less hippocampal volume than matched control participants (Sheline, Wang, Gado, Csernansky, & Vannier, 1996). In addition,

HPA hyperactivity has been found in Alzheimer's disease (AD) patients, who also experience hippocampal damage (Busciglio et al., 1998)

In addition, psychological distress as represented in depression and anxiety has been found to be associated with greater production of proinflammatory cytokine interleukin-6 (IL-6; Kiecolt-Glaser, McGuire, Robles, & Glaser, 2002). IL-6 appears to promote inflammatory neuronal damage, as evidenced in beta-amyloid plaques seen in AD (Papassotiropoulos, Hock, & Nitsch, 2001).

It is the long-term exposure to psychological distress and the associated long-term exposure to glucocorticoids and IL-6 that appear to be likely to lead to neurological damage resulting in risk to cognitive functioning. One approach to studying long-term psychological distress is to study individuals' proneness to psychological distress, as represented by personality traits that have been shown to remain relative stable over much of the adult life span. Neuroticism and, to a lesser extent, extraversion, are the personality traits that have been implicated as predisposing individuals to long-term psychological distress.

Higher levels and more frequent experiences of psychological distress have been found for individuals high in neuroticism. Individuals with higher neuroticism scores report greater distress in response to major life events (Parkes, 1990) and to daily stressful events (Marco & Suls, 1993). Reactivity to stress may be even greater in older adults as compared to younger adults (Mroczek & Almeida, 2004). In addition, people high in neuroticism may have greater exposure to stressors. Study participants high in neuroticism have reported more interpersonal stressors, had more negative appraisals of stressful events, and used less adaptive coping strategies compared with those low in neuroticism (Gunthert, Armeli, & Cohen, 1999).

Although the theory and findings regarding neuroticism and stress have been fairly consistent, findings on the association of extraversion, stress, and neural functioning have been mixed. Eysenck (1967) theorized that extraversion was related to cortical arousal and possible cognitive functioning. In his model, cognitive function may be negatively affected by people high in extraversion or high in introversion. Moderate extraversion reflecting moderate arousal was hypothesized to be optimal for cognitive functioning. Findings regarding higher cognitive functioning in moderate extraverts have been mixed and the hypothesis of high extraversion related to risk of cognitive impairment or neurodegeneration has not be adequately tested.

Studies of neuroticism and extraversion have generally examined these two traits separately (Robinson, 2001). However, in Eysenck's (1967) theory, the neuronal systems underlying neuroticism and extraversion are not assumed to be independent. The cortical arousal linked to extraversion is considered a function of the reticulo-cortical activating system, whereas neuroticism represents the activation of the limbic system. Activation of the limbic system indirectly heightens cortical arousal through its activating influences on the reticulocortical activating system. On the basis of these assumptions, Neuroticism would be considered a moderator of the association between Extraversion and arousal (Robinson, 2001). In part on the basis of these assumptions, Gray (1981) proposed an alternative theory that focused on the dimensions of anxiety and impulsivity that result from rotation of Eysenck's (1967) Neuroticism and Extraversion factors. The dimension of anxiety runs from the High Neuroticism/Low Extraversion quadrant (high anxiety) to the Low Neuroticism/High Extraversion quadrant (low anxiety). The impulsivity dimension runs from High Neuroticism/High Extraversion quadrant (high impulsivity) to Low Neuroticism/Low Extraversion (low impulsivity). It would follow that a combination of high Neuroticism and low Extraversion would be related to greater risk of cognitive impairment. Partial support comes from findings that people with anxiety disorders and with generalized anxiety disorder score higher on Neuroticism and lower on Extraversion compared with control respondents (Gomez & Francis, 2003; Trull & Sher, 1994).

Research on Neuroticism, Extraversion, and Cognitive Risk

Several recent studies have provided some support for an association between the personality traits of Neuroticism and Extraversion and increased risk of cognitive impairment. Crowe et al. (2006) examined the relationship between personality and cognitive impairment in members of the Swedish Twin Registry. Neuroticism and Extraversion scores were obtained in midlife, and cognitive impairment was assessed 25 years later, in old age. Greater Neuroticism was associated with higher risk of cognitive impairment. Moderate Extraversion, as hypothesized by Eysenck (1967), was associated with lower risk of cognitive impairment, as compared to high Extraversion or introversion. The combination of high Neuroticism and low Extraversion was associated with increased risk of impairment, supporting Gray's (1981) hypothesis regarding the effects of anxiety on cognition. An unexpected additional finding was that high Neuroticism/high Extraversion was also associated with cognitive impairment; high Neuroticism/high Extraversion would correspond with high impulsivity in Gray's framework.

Wilson and colleagues have published several articles linking Neuroticism and risk of dementia (Wilson, Barnes, et al., 2005). Wilson et al. (2003) examined the association of distress proneness with incident AD and cognitive decline in the Religious Orders Study. During a 5-year follow-up, participants who were high on distress proneness (90th percentile on Neuroticism) had twice the risk of developing AD of those who were low on distress proneness (10th percentile on Neuroticism). Neuroticism was related to decline in episodic memory but not in other cognitive domains with a greater than tenfold increase in memory decline in participants high on neuroticism. However, Neuroticism was not related to common measures of AD pathology at autopsy. In a second study, Wilson et al. (2006) tested the hypothesis of the association of distress proneness to increased risk of AD in the Rush Memory and Aging Project. Older individuals without dementia completed a neuroticism measure and were followed over 3 years. Persons with high level of distress proneness (90th percentile on Neuroticism) were 2.7 times as likely to develop AD than those not prone to distress (10th percentile on Neuroticism). Neuroticism was associated with more rapid cognitive decline also. In a third study, Wilson, Krueger, et al. (2005) examined the association of Neuroticism and Extraversion in a geographically defined urban sample of elders. In a 6-year follow-up after personality assessment, a high level of Neuroticism was associated with a 33% increase in risk of death compared with a low Neuroticism score. A high level of Extraversion was associated with a 21% decrease in risk of death compared with a low score. The association of Neuroticism and Extraversion with mortality was not substantially changed by taking into account disease conditions, substance use, or body mass. However, adjustment for cognitive, social, and physical activity did reduce the association of both traits with mortality.

PERSONALITY AND HEALTH BEHAVIORS

The preceding section focused on research that has examined the role of a long-term proneness to psychological distress on neurodegeneration and risk of cognitive impairment. An alternative way personality traits may have an indirect effect on health and on cognitive functioning is by their association with health behaviors. Several studies have reported an association between personality traits and health behaviors; these health behaviors have been related to chronic diseases (e.g., cardiovascular disease, diabetes) with onset in midlife and that have been found to be associated with cognitive impairment. Although Neuroticism was the personality trait of primary interest in studying the effect of stress on cognitive functioning, Conscientiousness appears to be an important trait in examining health behaviors (Roberts & Bogg, 2004). *Conscientiousness* refers to individual variability in propensity to follow socially prescribed norms for impulse control, to be task and goal directed, to be planful, to delay gratification, and to follow norms and rules. A number of studies have found an association among Conscientiousness, health, and longevity, in part through the effect of Conscientiousness on health behaviors as well as through its effect on social-environmental factors that contribute to health, such as work, family structure, and socioeconomic status (Roberts, Walton, & Bogg, 2005).

Brummett et al. (2006) examined personality traits as predictors of body mass index (BMI) over 14 years in midlife. Openness and Agreeableness were negatively related to BMI.

Neuroticism was positively related to BMI in women only. Extraversion was positively related to BMI in men. Conscientiousness was negatively related to BMI in both men and women, with a higher negative association in women. Conscientiousness also predicted change in BMI during midlife such that participants lower in Conscientiousness tended to show larger gains in BMI with age.

Most studies that have examined the association of Conscientiousness and health behaviors have been unidirectional, assuming that Conscientiousness was a predictor of subsequent health behaviors. Roberts and Bogg (2004) examined both Conscientiousness as a predictor of health behaviors and the impact of socioenvironmental and substance use behaviors on changes in Conscientiousness over time, within the Mills Longitudinal Study sample of women. Social responsibility, a facet of Conscientiousness, as measured in young adulthood, was negatively related to substance use (tobacco, marijuana) in midlife but positively related to alcohol consumption in midlife. In addition, marijuana consumption at age 43 was negatively related to changes in social responsibility at age 52. Women who admitted to smoking marijuana at age 43 were more likely to decrease in social responsibility between 43 and 52.

Roberts and Bogg (2004) conducted a meta-analysis of the relationship between Conscientiousness-related traits and health behaviors. Conscientiousness was found to predict nine health behaviors: (1) alcohol use, (2) disordered eating habits (including obesity), (3) drug use, (4) physical inactivity, (5) risky sexual practices, (6) risky driving practices, (7) tobacco use, (8) suicide, and (9) violence (Roberts et al., 2005). The Conscientiousness facet with the strongest and most consistent relationship to health behaviors was conventionality. Individuals with a propensity to adhere to society's norms were less like to engage in unhealthy behaviors. Other facets of Conscientiousness related to health behaviors were impulse control and reliability.

CONCLUSION

In this chapter, we have reviewed the literature on the cumulative consistency of personality that peaks in midlife and the association between personality and cognitive abilities in midlife. We have suggested that the greater stability in personality in midlife may have important implications for studying the association between personality and abilities in the second half of the life span. The limited research available suggests that the relationships between personality and abilities in midlife are stronger than earlier in the life span and that midlife personality traits, such as Neuroticism, may be important predictors of cognitive risk in later adulthood.

Examination of the relationship between personality and ability in the latter half of the life span has been limited by the lack of longitudinal studies that include adequate measurement of both personality and ability measures and that cover long periods in adulthood. Several of the longitudinal studies that have reported associations between personality and ability in adulthood have unfortunately had limited numbers of women in their samples. There is evidence that women may show earlier decline on key personality traits beginning in midlife and that the strength of the association between personality and ability may vary by gender. Hence, further research on the role of gender in personality–ability relationships is a high priority.

During the past 5 years, there has been increasing support for the finding that individuals who score higher on personality traits such as Neuroticism may be at increased risk for cognitive impairment. These findings have been reported in the Swedish Twin Registry and in several diverse samples in the United States. Most of these studies have measured personality only over a limited time period, and thus the significance of personality as a long-term risk factor needs further study. Particularly notable are the findings from the Swedish Twin Registry, which found that personality in midlife predicted cognitive risk some 30 years later. Unfortunately, none of these studies have included biomarkers of stress or neural imaging, as well as personality and cognitive risk measures; hence, the directionality and pathways among personality, stress, and cognition have not been adequately examined.

Research findings suggest that a second way in which personality may be associated with risk of cognitive impairment may be indirectly, through the health behaviors. Siegler and others (Brummett et al., 2006) have reported significant relationships between personality and a diverse set of health variables. These health variables, such as BMI, have been shown to be important precursors of onset of chronic disease, such as cardiovascular disease, which is known to impact cognitive functioning. Studies examining the role of health and disease in relation to cognition should consider inclusion of personality traits in their models.

Personality traits have traditionally been examined at the level of the individual trait rather than as configurations. Costa and McCrae (1980, 1995) in their studies of traits have indicated that there is considerable stability in configurations. However, Eysenck's (1967) early theoretical work suggests that configurations of several traits may be of interest in studying the association between personality and neurodegeneration. For example, Eysenck hypothesized that high Neuroticism and low Extraversion would increase one's risk for neurodegeneration, and the Swedish Twin Registry study found support for this hypothesis. Cognitive aging has benefited from the joint study of various abilities, such as fluid and crystallized intelligence. It appears that further exploration of various configurations of personality traits and their joint change would be profitable, particularly in midlife with increased consistency in personality.

Given the strong focus on stability of personality traits, most studies have examined personality in a unidirectional manner, as a predictor. There has been limited study of reciprocal relationships, in which personality has been examined in a bidirectional approach. Roberts and Bogg (2004), however, showed that although Conscientiousness impacts lifestyle and health behaviors, these lifestyles may impact future levels of Conscientiousness. Further study of reciprocal relationships involving personality are thus merited.

As Costa and McCrae (1999; Costa et al., 1976) noted, personality and cognition have traditionally been studied in relative isolation. However, during the past 5 years a number of studies in midlife and old age have suggested the need for further exploration of the association between personality and ability in the latter half of the life span. Both the personality and cognitive literatures would profit from mutual exploration of these domains. An important outcome would be a more integrated understanding of adults in midlife and old age.

REFERENCES

Ackerman, P. L., & Rolfhus, E. L. (1999). The locus of adult intelligence: Knowledge, abilities, and nonability traits. *Psychology and Aging, 14,* 314–330.

Baltes, P. B., Reese, H., & Nesselroade, J. R. (1977). *Lifespan developmental psychology: Introduction to research methods.* Monterey, CA: Brooks/Cole.

Bandura, A. (1999). Social cognitive theory of personality. In L. A. Pervin & O. P. John (Eds.), *Handbook of personality: Theory and research* (2nd ed., pp. 154–196). New York: Guilford Press.

Boron, J. (2003). *Effects of personality on cognitive ability, training gains, and strategy use in an adult sample: Seattle Longitudinal Study.* Unpublished master's thesis, Pennsylvania State University, University Park, PA.

Brummett, B. H., Babyak, M. A., Williams, R. B., Barefoot, J. C., Costa, P. T., & Siegler, I. C. (2006). NEO personality domains and gender predict levels and trends in body mass index over 14 years during midlife. *Journal of Research in Personality, 40,* 222–236.

Bryk, A. S., & Raudenbush, S. L. (1987). Application of hierarchical linear models to assessing change. *Psychological Bulletin, 101,* 147–158.

Busciglio, J., Andersen, J. K., Schipper, H. M., Gilad, G. M., McCarty, R., & Marzatico, F., et al. (1998). In P. Csermely (Ed.), *Annals of the New York Academy of Sciences: Vol. 851. Stress, aging and neurodegenerative disorders: Molecular mechanisms* (pp. 429–443). New York: New York Academy of Sciences.

Buss, D. M. (1984). Toward a psychology of person–environment correspondence: The role of spouse selection. *Journal of Personality and Social Psychology, 53,* 1214–1221.

Caspi, A., & Herbener, E. S. (1990). Continuity and change: Assortative marriage and the consistency of personality in adulthood. *Journal of Personality and Social Psychology, 58,* 250–258.

Caspi, A., & Roberts, B. W. (2001). Personality development across the life course: The argument for change and continuity. *Psychological Inquiry, 12,* 49–66.

Church, A. T., & Burke, P. J. (1994). Exploratory and confirmatory tests of the big five and Tellegen's three- and four-dimensional models. *Journal of Personality and Social Psychology, 66,* 93–114.

Costa, P. T., Jr., Fozard, J. L., McCrae, R. R., & Bosse, R. (1976). Relations of age and personality dimensions to cognitive ability factors. *Journal of Gerontology, 31,* 663–669.

Costa, P. T., Herbst, J. H., McCrae, R. R., & Siegler, I C. (2000). Personality at midlife: Stability, intrinsic maturation, and response to life events. *Assessment, 7,* 365–378.

Costa, P. T., Jr., & McCrae, R. R. (1980). Still stable after all these years: Personality as a key to some issues in adulthood and old age. In P. B. Baltes & O. G. Brim, Jr. (Eds.), *Life span development and behavior* (Vol. 3, pp. 65–102). New York: Academic Press.

Costa, P. T., Jr., & McCrae, R. R. (1985). *The NEO Personality Inventory manual.* Odessa, FL: Psychological Assessment Resources.

Costa, P. T., Jr., & McCrae, R. R. (1992). Four ways five factors are basic. *Personality and Individual Differences, 13,* 653–665.

Costa, P. T., & McCrae, R. R. (1995). Primary traits of Eysenck's P-E-N System: Three- and five-factor solutions. *Journal of Personality and Social Psychology, 69,* 308–317.

Costa, P. T., Jr., & McCrae, R. R. (1999). *Cautions and considerations for the links between cognition and personality.* Paper presented at the 9th Biennial Meeting of the International Society for the Study of Individual Differences, Vancouver, British Columbia, Canada.

Costa, P. T., & McCrae, R. R. (2006). Age changes in personality and their origins: Comment on Roberts, Walton & Viechtbauer (2006). *Psychological Bulletin, 132,* 26–28.

Costa, P. T., Jr., Terracciano, A., & McCrae, R. R. (2001). Gender differences in personality traits across cultures: Robust and surprising findings. *Journal of Personality and Social Psychology, 81,* 322–331.

Crowe, M., Andel, R., Pedersen, N. L., Fratiglioni, L., & Gatz, M. (2006). Personality and risk of cognitive impairment 25 years later. *Psychology and Aging, 21,* 573–580.

Endler, N. S. (2000). The interface between personality and cognition. *European Journal of Personality, 14,* 377–389.

Eysenck, H. J. (1967). *The biological basis of personality*. Springfield, IL: Charles C Thomas.

Eysenck, H. J., & Eysenck, M. W. (1985). *Personality and individual differences: A natural science approach*. New York: Plenum Press.

Feingold, A. (1994). Gender differences in personality: A meta-analysis. *Psychological Bulletin, 116*, 429–456.

Fiske, S. T., & Taylor, S. (1991). *Social cognition*. New York: McGraw-Hill.

Furnham, A. (1996). The FIRO-B, the Learning Style Questionnaire, and the five-factor model. *Journal of Social Behavior and Personality, 11*, 285–299.

Gomez, R., & Francis, L. M. (2003). Generalized anxiety disorder: Relationships with Eysenck's, Gray's and Newman's theories. *Personality and Individual Differences, 34*, 3–17.

Gough, H. G,. & Bradley, P. (1996). *CPI manual* (3rd ed.) Palo Alto, CA: Consulting Psychologists Press.

Gray, J. A. (1981). A critique of Eysenck's theory of personality. In H. Eysenck (Ed.), *A model of personality* (pp. 246–276). New York: Springer-Verlag.

Gunthert, K. C., Armeli, S., & Cohen, L. H. (1999). The role of neuroticism in daily stress and coping. *Journal of Personality and Social Psychology, 77*, 1087–1100.

Helson, R., Jones C. J., & Kwan, S. Y. (2002). Personality change over 40 years of adulthood: Hierarchical linear modeling analyses of two longitudinal samples. *Journal of Personality and Social Psychology, 83*, 752–766.

Jones, C. J., Livson, N., & Peskin, H. (2003). Longitudinal hierarchical linear modeling analyses of California Psychological Inventory data from age 33 to 75: An examination of stability and change in adult personality. *Journal of Personality Assessment, 80*, 294–308.

Jones, C. J., & Meredith, W. (1996). Patterns of personality change across the life-span. *Psychology and Aging, 11*, 57–65.

Kagan, J. (1997). Biology and the child. In W. Damon & N. Eisenberg (Eds.), *Handbook of child psychology* (Vol. 13, pp. 221–241). New York: Wiley.

Keicolt-Glaser, J. K., McGuire, L., Robles, R. F., & Glaser, R. (2002). Psychoneuroimmunology and psychosomatic medicine: Back to the future. *Psychosomatic Medicine, 64*, 15–28.

Keltner, D. (1996). Facial expressions of emotion and personality. In C. Magai & S. H. McFadden (Eds.), *Handbook of emotion adult development and aging* (pp. 385–401). San Diego, CA: Academic Press.

Lachman, M. E. (2004). Development in midlife. *Annual Review of Psychology, 55*, 305–331.

Langston, C. A., & Sykes, W. E. (1997). Beliefs and the Big Five: Cognitive bases of broad individual differences in personality. *Journal of Research in Personality, 31*, 141–165.

Marco, C. A., & Suls, J. (1993). Daily stress and the trajectory of mood: Spillover, response assimilation, contrast, and chronic negative affectivity. *Journal of Personality and Social Psychology, 64*, 1053–1063.

McCrae, R. R. (1987). Creativity, divergent thinking and openness to experience. *Journal of Personality and Social Psychology, 52*, 1258–1265.

McGue, M., Bacon, S., & Lykken, D. T. (1993). Personality stability and change in early adulthood: A behavioral genetic analysis. *Developmental Psychology, 29*, 96–109.

Meredith, W., & Tisak, J. (1990). Latent curve analysis. *Psychometrika, 55*, 107–122.

Mroczek, D. K., & Almeida, D. M. (2004). The effects of daily stress, personality and age on daily negative affect. *Journal of Personality, 72*, 355–378.

Mroczek, D. K., & Spiro, A. (2003). Modeling intraindividual change in personality traits: Findings from the Normative Aging Study. *Journal of Gerontology: Psychological Sciences, 58B*, 153–165.

Papassotiropoulos, A., Hock, C., & Nitsch, R. M. (2001). Genetics of interleukin 6: Implications for Alzheimer's disease. *Neurobiology of Aging, 22*, 863–871.

Parkes, K. R. (1990). Coping, negative affectivity, and the work environment: Additive and interactive predictors of mental health. *Journal of Applied Psychology, 75*, 399–409.

Roberts, B. W., & Bogg, T. (2004). A longitudinal study of the relationships between conscientiousness and the social-environmental factors and substance-use behaviors that influence health. *Journal of Personality, 72*, 325–353.

Roberts, B. W., & DelVecchio, W. F. (2000). The rank-order consistency of personality from childhood to old age: A quantitative review of longitudinal studies. *Psychological Bulletin, 126*, 3–25.

Roberts, B. W., Walton, K. E., & Bogg, T. (2005). Conscientiousness and health across the life course. *Review of General Psychology, 9,* 156–168.

Robinson, D. L. (2001). How brain arousal systems determine different temperament types and the major dimensions of personality. *Personality and Individual Differences, 31,* 1233–1259.

Sapolsky, R. M. (1996, August 9). Why stress is bad for your brain. *Science, 273,* 749–750.

Sapolsky, R. M. (2001). Depression, antidepressants, and the shrinking hippocampus. *Proceedings of the National Academy of Sciences, USA, 98,* 12320–12322.

Schaie, K. W. (2005). *Developmental influences on adult intellectual development: The Seattle Longitudinal Study.* New York: Oxford University Press.

Schaie, K. W., Willis, S. L., & Caskie, G. (2004). The Seattle Longitudinal Study: Relationship between personality and cognition. *Aging, Neuropsychology and Cognition, 11,* 304–324.

Sheline, Y. I., Wang, P. W., Gado, M. H., Csernansky, J. G., & Vannier, M. W. (1996). Hippocampal atrophy in recurrent major depression. *Proceedings of the National Academy of Sciences, USA, 93,* 3908–3913.

Small, B. J., Hertzog, C., Hultsch, D. F., & Dixon, R. A. (2003). Stability and change in adult personality over 6 years: Findings from the Victoria Longitudinal Study. *Journals of Gerontology Series B: Psychological Sciences and Social Sciences, 58B,* 166–176.

Sternberg, R. J., & Grigorenko, E. L. (1997). Are cognitive styles in style? *American Psychologist, 52,* 700–712.

Thurstone, L. L., & Thurstone, T. G. (1949). *Examiner manual for the SRA Primary Mental Abilities Test* (Form 10-14). Chicago: Science Research Associates.

Trull, T. J., & Sher, K. J. (1994). Relationship between the five-factor model of personality and Axis I disorders in a nonclinical sample. *Journal of Abnormal Psychology, 103,* 350–360.

Warren, J. R., & Hauser, R. M. (1997). Social stratification across three generations: New evidence from the Wisconsin Longitudinal Study. *American Sociological Review, 62,* 561–572.

Wilson, R. S., Arnold, S. E., Schneider, J. A., Kelly, J. F., Tang, Y., & Bennett, D. A. (2006). Chronic psychological distress and risk of Alzheimer's disease in old age. *Neuroepidemiology, 27,* 143–153.

Wilson, R. S., Barnes, L. L., Bennett, D. A., Li, Y., Bienias, J. L., Mendes de Leon, C. F., et al. (2005). Proneness to psychological distress and risk of Alzheimer disease in a biracial community. *Neurology, 64,* 380–382.

Wilson, R. S., Evans, D. A., Bienias, J. L., Mendes de Leon, C. F., Schenider, J. A., & Bennett, D. A. (2003). Proneness to psychological distress is associated with risk of Alzheimer's disease. *Neurology, 61,* 1479–1485.

Wilson, R. S., Krueger, K. R., Gu, L., Bienias, J. L., Mendes de Leon, C. F., & Evans, D. A. (2005). Neuroticism, extraversion, and mortality in a defined population of older persons. *Psychosomatic Medicine, 67,* 841–845.

Zhang, L. F., & Huang, J. (2001). Thinking styles and the five-factor model of personality. *European Journal of Personality, 15,* 465–476.

PART VIII

FUTURE DIRECTIONS FOR RESEARCH ON COGNITIVE AGING

THE FUTURE OF COGNITIVE AGING RESEARCH

Interdisciplinary Perspectives and Integrative Science

SCOTT M. HOFER AND DUANE F. ALWIN

We initiated this project with a set of concerns about the future of cognitive aging research and a determination to raise a number of critical questions about the direction the field of cognitive aging is going. We asked a wide range of questions that we and others believe the field should be asking—including questions about the theoretical perspectives that should be brought to bear on understanding processes of cognitive aging, the current state of our knowledge across the broad spectrum of human abilities and functional capacities, the kinds of research strategies and measurement approaches that will be needed in future work, the types of interdisciplinary forms future research will take, the pertinent data resources for understanding cognitive aging processes, and how such data should be modeled and explained (for a detailed overview, see chap. 1, this volume). Addressing these issues provides the essential elements underlying the development of research strategies that will have payoff for the future of research in cognitive aging and related areas. We discuss some of these strategies in this chapter.

The first task in addressing these issues is really one of summarizing the existing knowledge base: What do we know? And what is the basis of this knowledge? The chapters included in this handbook provide succinct summaries of what is known. The overall focus of these chapters and the rationale for this volume are consistent with the knowledge-based strategies for assessing the progress of science, as articulated in the National Research Council report, *A Strategy for Assessing Science* (National Research Council, 2007).

Another aim of this handbook is to seek the guidance of leading researchers by challenging them to think of innovative future directions for research on cognitive aging and promotion of cognitive health. Along with the research summaries, these chapters provide a basis for such future directions by identifying current challenges, unanswered questions, and potential next steps for future research.

We direct attention to three particular issues in this final chapter. First, we want to emphasize the prospects for interdisciplinary research in the field of cognitive aging and note some recent developments. Second, we discuss the need for continued examination of existing data, along with strategies for collaboration and data sharing for comparative and integrative data analysis. Third, we address the question of what new data resources are needed to facilitate future interdisciplinary research on cognitive aging and for making projections regarding population aging. Ultimately, it is through the integration of theory, empirical evidence, and research methods—including new developments in measurement strategies, study designs, and statistical analysis—that future progress will be made.

THE FUTURE OF INTERDISCIPLINARY RESEARCH

Several new initiatives have the potential for enhancing interdisciplinary collaborations. We discuss these and then address the questions of what issues surround the use of data that already exist for examining these new ideas, and what new data resources need to be developed to meet the challenges of the future. We argued in Chapter 1 that the challenge for future research on cognitive aging involves not only coming to terms with the nature of developmental processes, and the social, cultural, and demographic realities of population aging that contribute to these processes, but also the need to foster new interdisciplinary research agendas in the pursuit of knowledge of cognitive aging.

The authors of *The Aging Mind* (National Research Council [NRC], 2000) emphasized the need for interdisciplinary approaches for the development of a comprehensive theoretical framework, incorporating age-related variation in environmental factors, age-related changes in sensory function and health, and the interaction of these factors with neurological changes in development. They introduced a valuable framework for setting the agenda of the future of cognitive aging, by highlighting multiple components of the cognitive aging process and arguing that the ultimate focus of research on cognitive aging should be the conjunction of factors that shape performance of activities of living (NRC, 2000, pp. 9–11). The NRC committee identified three major areas—neural health,

cognition in context, and the structure of the aging mind—in which scientific developments are "creating significant opportunities for breakthroughs," and they urged the National Institute on Aging (NIA) to undertake major research initiatives that would further work in these areas.

Because cognitive aging is the result of a number of factors working in combination, the NRC committee stressed the importance of *interdisciplinary* forms of research. They encouraged the NIA to establish funding mechanisms that would challenge cognitive scientists from a multiplicity of disciplines to work together to solve the problems of understanding how these factors jointly contribute to cognitive aging.

There have been recent efforts to enhance interdisciplinary research on aging, although these developments have been limited in scope and activity. In Chapter 1, we described the 2001 NIA workshop "Cognitive and Emotional Health: The Healthy Brain Workshop," jointly sponsored by the NIA, the National Institute of Mental Health, and the National Institute of Neurological Disorders and Stroke. An international group of approximately 35 senior investigators attended, together with a large number of staff members from the National Institutes of Health (NIH). The workshop participants discussed research concerning determinants of adult cognitive, emotional, and mental health. The workshop brought together selected leaders in the field for substantive discussions about the current status of existing knowledge, the potential value of secondary analyses of existing data, the need for further instrument development to facilitate future studies, and potential designs of large studies that might be undertaken in the future (see Hendrie et al., 2006).[1]

Social scientists (sociology, demography, economics, and anthropology) have become interested in the contributions they can make to the study of cognitive aging. This handbook reflects one example, because many of the chapter authors come from these fields. Another example involves developments in the field of *neuroeconomics*, a branch of behavioral science that combines neuroscience, economics, and psychology to understand how people make choices. Indeed, there are some recent initiatives from the NIA to study the neuroeconomics of aging. The NIA supported a workshop, held in the spring of

2006 at Stanford University, in conjunction with a National Science Foundation–sponsored seminar, which focused on the social and behavioral processes and the neurobiological mechanisms of economic behavior.

The emphasis on interdisciplinary research is clearly the way things are moving, and this is reflected in the 2004 Behavioral and Social Research (BSR) Program Review Committee report of the National Advisory Council on Aging, which explicitly mentions cognitive aging as a priority topic area for BSR program activities (NIA, National Advisory Council on Aging, BSR Program Review Committee, 2004). The program review committee, itself an interdisciplinary group, suggested several future directions for research on cognitive aging:

- Continue to support advances in cognitive aging, especially through the appropriate application of new techniques and analytic methods, such as neuroimaging.
- Because much basic research on cognitive aging within broader sociocultural contexts remains to be done, and given the scope and interdisciplinary nature of these opportunities, encourage greater collaboration with other NIA programs (especially with Neuroscience and Neuropsychology of Aging, which has a large portfolio in cognitive aging) and other offices (e.g., Office of Behavioral and Social Science Research) and institutes at NIH to support investigator-oriented research opportunities, infrastructure needs, and large-scale research initiatives. For instance, we echo the NRC committee's recommendation for a large-scale, multisite, population-based longitudinal study of cognitive aging to better understand the needs of an increasing proportion of the U.S. population.
- Promote research on optimal cognitive aging as well as normal and abnormal cognitive aging to identify those facets of cognition that are improved or sustained into older life. (NIA, National Advisory Council on Aging, BSR Program Review Committee, 2004, pp. 5–6)

Such initiatives can take several forms—and we do not pretend to know how future research on cognitive aging will develop—but one of the most desirable would involve cognitive and developmental psychologists working together with neuroscientists, physicians, epidemiologists, and social scientists (in particular, economists, sociologists, and demographers) to develop a comprehensive longitudinal study of cognitive aging based on large representative samples internationally. Such a study would rigorously assess dimensions of cognitive capabilities, including those typically assessed in laboratory settings, as well as disability status, health, nutrition, and social context across appropriately spaced intervals of time. Such an approach would provide the basis for a greater understanding of the future of cognitive aging in this country and internationally.

THE USE OF EXISTING DATA RESOURCES

Given the increasing breadth of the empirical literature, the complexity of our theories, and the current sophistication of our multivariate statistical tools for modeling age-related growth and decline, cognitive science has never been better poised to understand the nature of the processes that contribute to cognitive aging. Existing longitudinal data from the numerous completed and ongoing studies from around the world will play a major role in understanding processes leading to cognitive aging, for making projections about population aging, and in permitting cross-national comparison and validation of research findings. One of the clearest next steps in the aging field are the evaluation and extension of theoretical and empirical findings in available within-person (i.e., longitudinal) data. We must also learn all we can from current studies in order to optimally design new studies.

Strategies for Data Sharing

One important strategy for the investigation of cognitive aging processes involves the use of existing data to evaluate theory and hypotheses and to provide a basis for identifying gaps in knowledge. Over the past several decades, at least since the 1960s, there have been major changes in the ways in which many of the social and economic sciences have developed data resources for the investigation of social and scientific problems (Alwin, 2004). There are two important trends within the social sciences: (1) the development of large-scale cooperative research projects conducted collectively by experts in various fields of study that pool ideas and resources and (2) a movement toward archiving data resources collected using public funds in centralized, computerized data archives, so that the data are available to all scientists.

These trends are increasing in the behavioral and medical sciences (e.g., psychology, epidemiology, human development, and gerontology), the fields that dominate the study of cognitive aging. In contrast to the economic and social sciences, these fields have less of a tradition of data sharing, and the norm within many fields has been that the data (even though they may have been collected using public funds) are the property of the investigator(s) who gathered them. In recent years, resources have been provided to large-scale studies of aging for preparation and archiving of data for public use, and these are positive indications of changing norms.

The federal government has increasingly played a role in making data resources collected using public funds available to all researchers, although policies appear to be applied somewhat unevenly. At present, the NIH has a policy in place that requires investigators to submit a data-sharing plan and, after a reasonable period of time, make their data available to other investigators. In effect since 2004, the NIH is on record as supporting data sharing as an important research strategy: In 2003, the NIH published a statement on data sharing, which included the following summary statement:

> NIH reaffirms its support for the concept of data sharing. We believe that data sharing is essential for expedited translation of research results into knowledge, products, and procedures to improve human health. The NIH endorses the sharing of final research data to serve these and other important scientific goals. The NIH expects and supports the timely release and sharing of final research data from NIH-supported studies for use by other researchers. (NIH, 2003)

There are several reasons why data sharing in the field of cognitive aging is important (Rockwell & Abeles, 1998). First, data analysis often involves making choices that may affect

the results, and it is often desirable to replicate results conducted by the initial investigators. Given large and complex data structures, it is important that those who collect the data allow other researchers to examine them in order to achieve standards of objectivity. Regardless of the quality of the initial investigation, most scientific discourse requires subsequent extensions in ways not anticipated by the initial investigators. Though rarely performed, it would be desirable for other researchers to examine the data further in order to refine and extend the initial findings and develop tests of alternative hypotheses. Prior findings can often be placed in a new light by adopting innovations, both theoretical and methodological, that were previously unavailable. For example, the application of new developments in data analysis or ways of handling nonresponse in longitudinal studies solve inferential problems that were not earlier possible and permit stronger opportunities for cross-validation.

Strategies for Integrative Analysis

The potential knowledge gains from increased collaboration and coordinated analysis of longitudinal data on aging are great. Numerous calls have been made for increased collaborative efforts as a means to focus developmental research on within-person processes. Recent major recommendations for research (Bachrach & Abeles, 2004), including executive summaries published by the NRC and commissioned by the NIA/NIH or Office of Behavioral and Social Sciences Research/NIH (NRC, 2000, pp. 3–5; 2001b, pp. 4–7; 2001c, pp. 9–13), have highlighted the importance of interdisciplinary, international, and collaborative research making use of longitudinal studies on aging. Butz and Torrey (2006) similarly highlighted the importance of longitudinal research, biology, and international replications, along with advances in statistical methods, to progress in the social sciences.

The use of existing data on within-individual change and between-individual differences is one powerful way to evaluate theory and hypotheses and provide a basis for identifying gaps in knowledge. A mechanism for using existing data, without going so far as to publicly archive the available data, is to collaborate on the coordinated analysis of data and synthesis of research findings. In Chapter 27 of this volume, Andrea M. Piccinin and Scott M. Hofer highlight and summarize some of these efforts for collaborative and coordinated research and elaborate on strategies for maximizing our understanding of within-person aging-related changes. The Integrative Analysis of Longitudinal Studies on Aging[2] is an international research network of 25 longitudinal studies on aging, including substantive and statistical experts associated with each study. Here, *integrative data analysis* refers to the integration of domains of study (e.g., health, cognition) that, with notable exceptions, have generally been studied in isolation from one another, as well as to the integration of information across studies and across alternative statistical models. A coordinated analysis approach can maximize opportunities for reproducible research (e.g., Gentleman & Lang, 2007) through open access to analysis and data harmonization scripts and output for published results. This facilitates modification and evaluation of alternative models related to published papers and the application of these particular models and variable harmonizations to other current and future studies. A major strength of collaborative, coordinated research, as opposed to use of multiple archived data sets, is that the investigators associated with each study are major partners in the analysis and synthesis of particular research questions, bringing essential expertise related to study characteristics. This serves to realize the full potential for maximizing each study's data value while permitting rigorous comparison.

An integration of the life span developmental and demographic approaches is also essential in the analysis of longitudinal data given the selection and mortality dynamics in populations and the bias that results when inferences regarding aging-related change do not take this mortality selection into account (e.g., Alwin, Hofer, & McCammon, 2006; Hofer & Hoffman, 2007; Hofer & Sliwinski, 2006). It is essential that statistical analyses attend to within-individual change as well as make generalizations about specific populations of individuals defined by both chronological age and survival age as well as other population characteristics. It is essential to look to evidence from longitudinal studies on

aging for providing a strong basis for theoretical developments that are firmly grounded from a within-individual change perspective and that take into account the selection and mortality dynamics that can be assessed only in longitudinal designs.

THE DEVELOPMENT OF NEW DATA ON COGNITIVE AGING

Despite the great potential of the current status of the field, including available data, innovative methods, and theoretical perspectives, one can argue that there are limitations with the existing data that pose a major threat to the credibility of our population inferences about age-related differences reported in the social, behavioral, and psychological literatures on cognitive development.

The basic problem is that much of our knowledge about age-related changes in cognitive function is based on cross-sectional designs or on longitudinal studies of relatively unknown or questionable representativeness. There are exceptions to this general characterization of the extant literature, but most scholars would agree that this is a fair description of the state of the current knowledge base. It is therefore critical that we reassess the basis for many of the findings that shape our conclusions about population cognitive aging, the optimal designs for studying age-related change, and the kinds of data we will need for studying cognitive aging in the future.

The NRC committee report on "Future Directions" was quite explicit with regard to the requirements of future research on cognitive aging. The report argued that, to achieve the objectives of the recommended research initiatives,

> It will be necessary to expand the use of large-scale multivariate, longitudinal studies . . . to expand and improve on previous longitudinal research by including variables reflecting high-resolution cognitive and neural measures; indicators of health status and sensory-motor functioning; and measures of relevant life experience. (NRC, 2000, p. 52)

The report went on to argue that it is also "important to examine a broad representative sample of the population, sometimes oversampling in subgroups whose health status or responses to life experiences are expected to illuminate important theoretical questions, and to encompass a wide age range" (NRC, 2000, p. 52). Finally, the report argued that "by following individuals into very old age, promising new findings suggesting the existence of unexpected linkages between cognitive functioning and survival could be investigated" (NRC, 2000, p. 52).

When we survey the recommendations of the NRC report and the chapters in this handbook, we see that several basic problems need to be addressed in any assessment of the current state of knowledge and planning for the future development of knowledge in this area:

- The limitations of cross-sectional designs that focus on between-person age differences and the threat posed by contextual factors to interpretations of age-related cognitive differences.
- The problems with convenience samples of unknown representativeness.
- Confounding of inference in samples with unknown degrees of health and disease.
- The limitations of longitudinal designs with relatively few and widely spaced assessments.
- The paucity of rigorous measurement for understanding the explanatory role of factors that are theoretically linked to cognitive aging, for example, changes in sensory function and morbidity.
- The need to develop integrative research strategies for building on both experimental and individual-differences approaches and for emphasizing cross-validation of key research findings from different methodological perspectives
- The current status of norms and practices for data sharing and for conducting scientific inquiry.

Many of the chapters in this book argue that some of these limitations pose serious threats to the validity of projections about the future of cognitive aging over the next several decades. We comment briefly on some of these issues in the following sections.

The Need for Longitudinal Designs

Most theoretical propositions related to aging in humans are based on evidence from between-person differences in age-heterogeneous samples.

Although the limitations of such designs have long been recognized (e.g. Hofer, Flaherty, & Hoffman, 2006; Kraemer, Yesavage, Taylor, & Kupfer, 2000; Mason & Fienberg, 1985; Wohlwill, 1973), they are pervasive in research on cognitive aging. Cross-sectional designs generally rely on untenable assumptions for the purpose of understanding individual-level change processes as well as for inference to defined populations of aging individuals. Although cross-sectional designs are *not* inherently limited for specific purposes, especially if they involve the replication of cross-sections over time (e.g., the existence of *diachronic* cross-sectional data for the same cohorts can be used as a legitimate basis for separating the effects of aging and cohort effects under certain circumstances; e.g., Alwin & McCammon, 1999, 2001; Duncan & Kalton, 1987), they cannot address within-person change or population mortality selection.

The emerging consensus, therefore, is that the reliance on between-person information needs to be complemented by continued theoretical and methodological progress in longitudinal aging research (see e.g., chaps. 2, 3, 4, 5, 14, 16, 17, 23, 27, 28, 29, 30, 31, 33, and 34, this volume; Alwin & Campbell, 2001; Hofer & Sliwinski, 2006; Schaie & Hofer, 2001). Evaluation and development of theories of aging require that one obtain and analyze data on within-person change. As such, longitudinal studies are essential for our understanding of between-person differences in rates of change and within-person change processes. Longitudinal data can also facilitate an understanding of how between-person differences at any particular age or time period arise through description of the change processes leading to between-person differentiation as distinct from initial between-person variation. Modeling health indicators is especially challenging in cross-sectional studies because the within-person processes associated with health-related changes are likely to be highly selected in such samples (i.e., leading to nonparticipation for persons who have had greater declines in health) and are thus unlikely to be accessible by between-person comparison. Whether the focus is on between-person age differences or within-person age changes, the nature of the inference and confounds related to the sample, design, and statistical analysis must be clarified, in terms of age, birth cohort, survival age, and other effects and their interactions. Indeed, different research designs and levels of analysis (e.g., birth cohort, average population change, correlated and coupled change) provide complementary and necessary perspectives on the dynamics of aging. Each level of analysis provides unique information regarding aging-related change, although the particular inferences and interpretations possible from any single level of analysis have delimited ramifications for theories of aging (Hofer & Sliwinski, 2006).

Very long-term longitudinal studies also represent an important next step in theory development and permit the direct analysis of early life antecedents and long-term health-related influences (e.g., Deary & Batty, 2007; Kuh & The New Dynamics of Ageing Preparatory Network, 2007; Richards, Sacker, & Deary, 2006). More longitudinal research over lengthy periods of time is needed to confirm patterns of cognitive change in middle and old age (see chap. 39, this volume). New longitudinal investigations that implement sampling designs that are adequate for the generalization of findings to populations of interests can take advantage of the significant improvements that have been made in studying *change within individuals as they age.* Combined with the strategy of examining within-person change over lengthy time periods, there is also a strong need for a better understanding of the patterns and processes of within-person change over strategically defined shorter periods of time. For example, the sensitive detection of change early in the decline process has long been of great interest. Analysis of change in existing longitudinal studies, retrospective to knowledge of particular events, such as diagnosis of dementia or death, provides evidence for accelerated change (i.e., inflection point) in functioning up to 7 to 10 years prior to the event (see e.g., chaps. 17 and 28, this volume).

Although significant effort has led to the development of sensitive cognitive and neuropsychological tests for detecting dementia and health-related change, more recent developments for prospective identification of change have occurred in the area of research design, emphasizing time-intensive assessments of cognitive functioning (see e.g., chaps. 5, 29, and 31, this volume). These designs hold great promise for the prospective detection of change because change is identified relative to each individual's baseline level of functioning, provided one has sufficient within-person observations. Such designs also permit direct modeling and separation of retesting effects from longer-term changes due aging or pathology because of the relative independence from short-term gains due to test exposure (i.e., practice, learning) and long-term change processes (i.e., aging, pathology).

Sample Selection and Generalizability

Most studies of cognitive aging—whether cross-sectional or longitudinal—do not use rigorous strategies for sample selection developed on the basis of a clear specification of the population of interest and an explicit design for sampling that population. Instead, the predominant research design used by investigators working in cognitive aging is one that relies on volunteer participant samples. Even the best work in the area of cognitive aging is therefore limited with respect to generalizability, raising concerns about projections that may be made about the future of cognitive aging to defined and representative populations.

There may be some areas of social and behavioral science where population sampling is not critical because the processes involved are so basic that any set of individuals available for study will suffice. However, in order to generalize to a given population of interest, probability sampling of that population is required. Some studies used large, representative samples of the U.S. population—both repeated cross-sectional designs and longitudinal designs—but, generally speaking, these studies are quite limited in their measurement of cognitive performance. Such studies nevertheless have the potential of making an important contribution to the understanding of the nature of cognitive change in adulthood as well as providing information that will be useful in assessing the generalizability of previous findings to the middle-aged and older U.S. population. Longitudinal research based on representative samples of known populations is required to confirm the conclusions developed on the basis of the extant literature. There is clearly a need for greater exchange with researchers whose work is rooted in the demographic tradition of understanding population processes, which puts a great deal of emphasis on probability methods of survey sampling.

There is a need for new longitudinal studies based on true "samples" in the sense that they rely on state-of-the art methods of statistical sampling of well-defined populations. In such studies, the selection of cases is governed by a replicable process such that their presence in the sample has a known probability. Publicly available longitudinal surveys have included cognitive performance measures on the same person repeatedly over time, permitting generalization to known populations. One of the few studies in this category is the Health and Retirement Study, discussed in Chapters 4 and 26 of this handbook.

Comprehensive Measurement of Cognition, Health, and Context

The interrelation of population processes, health status, and biological processes, and cognitive functioning requires comprehensive assessment in an ecologically valid, contextually relevant measurement design in large-scale, community-based samples (see e.g., chaps. 3 and 16, this volume). Knowledge of the relationship of aging to cognitive function is crucial to understanding the linkages between age and cohort-related socioeconomic, racial/ethnic, gender, and health disparities. The NRC's Committee on Future Directions for Cognitive Research on Aging, articulated in *The Aging Mind: Opportunities in Cognitive Research* (NRC, 2000), stressed the importance of the development of an ecologically valid and comprehensive assessment of cognitive function, health status, sensory/motor functioning, and lifestyle/contextual factors in large-scale representative studies.

An optimal measurement instrument might require on-site or mobile intensive assessments of cognitive functioning, clinical evaluations, and biological assays that can be used within the framework of a population-based demographically informed sampling strategy. A measurement battery of this type will be necessary for comprehensive assessments of individual health, cognitive, and psychosocial variables for nationally representative population samples. Measurement-intensive batteries of this magnitude, that include detailed assessment of cognitive abilities, have not, to our knowledge, been developed for large-sample

assessments and are not well represented in large-scale surveys of health. Such research would require instrument development (testing, pretesting, design for retesting effects, minimizing respondent burden, dealing with validity and reliability issues) to collect biological data for use in the context of large, population-based surveys. Design strategies might include intensive within-person assessments and longitudinal measurements planned around closely spaced successive "bursts" of measurements rather than widely spaced successions of single time point assessments as is in common use. Criteria for developing, selecting, and/or modifying measurement instruments include attention to: (a) multidimensional focus, (b) incorporation of broad contextual factors, (c) focus on sensitive periods and optimal intervals for assessing change, (d) individual differences in reactivity, (e) theoretical stability of particular environmental influences, (f) optimal temporal resolution (including serendipitous and non-normative events), and (g) outcome/predictor level of analysis.

In Chapter 30 of this volume, Margie E. Lachman and Patricia A. Tun discuss measurement development in large-scale surveys that permit sensitive assessment of particular types of cognitive functioning. These aims are compatible with the recommendations of the Committee on Population of the NRC's Commission on Behavioral and Social Sciences and Education, summarized in the book *Cells and Surveys: Should Biological Measures Be Included in Social Science Research?* (NRC, 2001a). Given recent critiques of the reliability and validity of survey measurement of health, such goals are highly significant and the proposed developmental work strongly warranted.

Cognitive measures are not often included in large-scale survey data collections because it is assumed that reliable assessments are too difficult and time consuming to administer in an interview format using professional interviewers. Future studies must address the utility and validity of survey measurement of cognitive functioning. If, as we have argued, future research should produce data based on a model of population processes that insists on the use of representative samples of the population, then this changes the question of whether cognitive functioning can be measured in a survey context to whether the survey context must be modified to accommodate the depth of measurement required in psychometric testing. The development of measures of cognitive performance that can be used in survey settings should be given a high priority for research that uses population-based samples.

CONCLUSION

Most current theoretical propositions related to aging in humans are supported by evidence from between-person age differences. However, rigorously testing theories of aging requires obtaining and analyzing data on within-person change to evaluate and complement the existing knowledge gained from data on between-person comparison. Equally important is understanding the impact of health-related change and mortality on changes in cognition with age—incorporating population dynamics in making inferences to individuals conditional on age/cohort, survival, and health. As such, longitudinal studies are essential for our understanding of within-person change processes and between-person differences in these processes, permitting the identification of health and mortality influences on aging-related outcomes and appropriate conditional population inference. Longitudinal data also facilitate an understanding of how between-person differences at any particular age or time period arise, through description of the change processes leading to between-person differentiation as distinct from initial between-person variation.

Although it is generally accepted that varieties of pathological processes (i.e., disease, oxidative damage to cells) are distinct but not independent of processes of aging (e.g., Busse, 1969; Fozard, Metter, & Brant, 1990; Siegler, 1989), it is also the case that the effects of disease can easily be mistaken for changes due to aging given increased morbidity and comorbidity with age and particularly because of changes related to undiagnosed or preclinical phases of disease. In Chapter 16, Avron Spiro III and Christopher B. Brady make the strong case for improving our measures of health as a necessary prerequisite for understanding the relations between health and cognition.

Aging-related changes due to disease processes and mortality are also related to birth cohort and social factors across historical periods, which must also be considered in understanding population aging (see chap. 4, this volume). This integration of a life span developmental perspective with attention to population dynamics related to health and mortality is essential for progress on understanding cognitive declines in aging populations.

From our perspective, knowledge and theory regarding cognitive aging will be enhanced by interdisciplinary research that seeks to integrate research findings across studies that differ in terms of perspective, sampling, measurement, and design. We must make use of existing data resources in ways that not only maximize the value of any particular study but also maximize the comparability of research findings and permit strong evaluation and cross-validation of key hypotheses and theories (see chap. 27, this volume). Such research can focus on identifying better "clocks" by modeling alternative time functions (e.g., disease progression, major stress events) that better account for underlying within-person processes of aging-related change (see chaps. 17, 28, and 29, this volume). Cross-study analysis permits the identification and reconciliation of differences found across studies in terms of measurement, sampling, demographic, social, and health indicators and can provide a basis for making informed decisions regarding optimal or essential test batteries of health, cognition, personality, and other measures for new data collection efforts. In general, we think that it is important that current and future studies permit analytical opportunities for quantitative comparison across samples differing in birth cohort and country given the historical shifts and cultural differences that have an effect on late life processes and outcomes.

The demands for the study of cognitive aging make it an inherently interdisciplinary undertaking involving demography, sociology, psychology, and health sciences. From our perspective, the opportunities for a truly integrative approach for understanding cognitive aging are currently very high given the advanced state of the field, availability of existing long-term longitudinal data, new developments in designs and statistical modeling, and the broad interdisciplinary interest in cognitive processes.

NOTES

1. The Healthy Brain workshop was first held July 9–10, 2001, in Bethesda, Maryland, and has since then held additional meetings (see http://trans .nih.gov/CEHP/workshop.htm).

2. Support for the Integrative Analysis of Longitudinal Studies on Aging research network includes grants from the NIA (1R01AG026453 and 5P30AG024395).

REFERENCES

Alwin, D. F. (2004, March). Developments in data sharing in the social and behavioral sciences. *ASA Footnotes, 32*. Retrieved from http://www2 .asanet.org/footnotes/

Alwin, D. F., & Campbell, R. T. (2001). Quantitative approaches: Longitudinal methods in the study of human development and aging. In R. H. Binstock & L. K. George (Eds.), *Handbook of aging and the social sciences* (5th ed., pp. 22–43). New York: Academic Press.

Alwin, D. F., Hofer, S. M., & McCammon, R. (2006). Modeling the effects of time: Integrating demographic and developmental perspectives. In R. H. Binstock & L. K. George (Eds.), *Handbook of the aging and the social sciences* (6th ed., pp. 20–38). San Diego, CA: Academic Press.

Alwin, D. F., & McCammon, R. J. (1999). Aging vs. Cohort interpretations of intercohort differences in GSS Verbal scores. *American Sociological Review, 64,* 272–286.

Alwin, D. F., & McCammon, R. J. (2001). Aging, cohorts, and verbal ability. *Journal of Gerontology: Social Sciences, 56B,* S1–S11.

Bachrach, C. A., & Abeles, R. P. (2004). Social science and health research: Growth at the National Institutes of Health. *American Journal of Public Health, 94,* 22–28.

Busse, E. W. (1969). Theories of aging. In E. W. Busse & E. Pfeiffer (Eds.), *Behavior and adaptation in later life* (pp. 11–32). Boston: Little, Brown.

Butz, W. P., & Torrey, B. B. (2006, June 30). Some frontiers in social science. *Science, 312,* 1898–1900.

Deary, I. J., & Batty, G. D. (2007). Cognitive epidemiology. *Journal of Epidemiology and Community Health, 61,* 378–384.

Duncan, G. J., & Kalton, G. (1987). Issues of design and analysis of surveys across time. *International Statistical Review, 55,* 97–117.

Fozard, J. L., Metter, E. J., & Brant, L. J. (1990). Next steps in describing aging and disease in longitudinal studies. *Journal of Gerontology, 45,* 116–126.

Gentleman, R., & Lang, T. (2007). Statistical analyses and reproducible research. *Journal of Computational & Graphical Statistics, 16,* 1–23.

Hendrie, H. C., Albert, M. S., Butters, M. A., Gao, S., Knopman, D. S., Launer, L. J., et al. (2006). The NIH Cognitive and Emotional Health Project: Report of the critical evaluation study committee. *Alzheimer's & Dementia, 2,* 12–32.

Hofer, S. M., Flaherty, B. P., & Hoffman, L. (2006). Cross-sectional analysis of time-dependent data: Problems of mean-induced association in age-heterogeneous samples and an alternative method based on sequential narrow age-cohorts. *Multivariate Behavioral Research, 41,* 165–187.

Hofer, S. M., & Hoffman, L. (2007). Statistical analysis with incomplete data: A developmental perspective. In T. D. Little, J. A. Bovaird, & N. A. Card (Eds.), *Modeling ecological and contextual effects in longitudinal studies of human development* (pp. 13–32). Mahwah, NJ: Lawrence Erlbaum.

Hofer, S. M., & Sliwinski, M. J. (2006). Design and analysis of longitudinal studies of aging. In J. E. Birren & K. W. Schaie (Eds.), *Handbook of the psychology of aging* (6th ed., pp. 15–37). San Diego, CA: Academic Press.

Kraemer, H. C., Yesavage, J. A., Taylor, J. L., & Kupfer, D. (2000). How can we learn about developmental processes from cross-sectional studies, or can we? *American Journal of Psychiatry, 157,* 163–171.

Kuh, D., & The New Dynamics of Ageing Preparatory Network. (2007). A life course approach to healthy aging, frailty, and capability. *Journal of Gerontology: Medical Sciences, 62A,* 717–721.

Mason, W. M., & Fienberg, S. E. (1985). *Cohort analysis in social research: Beyond the identification problem.* New York: Springer-Verlag.

National Institutes of Health. (2003, February). Final NIH statement on sharing research data (Notice NOT-OD-03-032). Retrieved August 2007 from http://grants.nih.gov/grants/guide/notice-files/ NOT-OD-03-032.html

National Institute on Aging, National Advisory Council on Aging, Behavioral and Social Sciences (BSR) Program Review Committee. (2004). *BSR Review Committee report* (revised August 10, 2004). Retrieved August 3, 2007, from http://www.nia.nih.gov/ResearchInformation/ExtramuralPrograms/BehavioralAndSocial Research/

National Research Council. (2000). *The aging mind: Opportunities in cognitive research.* Committee on Future Directions for Cognitive Research on Aging. Paul C. Stern and Laura L. Carstensen, Editors. Commission on Behavioral and Social Sciences and Education. Washington, DC: National Academy Press.

National Research Council. (2001a). *Cells and surveys: Should biological measures be included in social science research?* Committee on Population. Caleb E. Finch, James W. Vaupel, and Kevin Kinsella, Editors. Commission on Behavioral and Social Sciences and Education. Washington, DC: National Academy Press.

National Research Council. (2001b). *New horizons in health: An integrative approach.* Committee on Future Directions for Behavioral and Social Sciences Research at the National Institutes of Health. B. H. Singer and C. D. Ryff, Editors. Washington, DC: National Academy Press.

National Research Council. (2001c). *Preparing for an aging world: The case for cross-national research.* Panel on a Research Agenda and New Data for an Aging World, Committee on Population and Committee on National Statistics, Division of Behavioral and Social Sciences and Education. Washington, DC: National Academy Press.

National Research Council. (2007). *A strategy for assessing science: Behavioral and social research on aging.* Committee on Assessing Behavioral and Social Science Research on Aging. Irwin Feller and Paul C. Stern, Editors. Center for Studies of Behavior and Development, Division of Behavioral and Social Sciences and Education. Washington, DC: National Academy Press.

Richards, M., Sacker, A., & Deary, I. J. (2006). Lifetime antecedents of cognitive reserve. In Y. Stern (Ed.), *Cognitive reserve* (pp. 37–52). New York: Psychology Press.

Rockwell, R. C., & Abeles, R. P. (1998). Sharing and archiving data is fundamental to scientific progress. *Journals of Gerontology Series B: Psychological and Social Sciences, 53,* S5–S8.

Schaie, K. W., & Hofer, S. M. (2001). Longitudinal studies in aging research. In J. E. Birren & K. W. Schaie (Eds.), *Handbook of the psychology of aging* (5th ed., pp. 53–77). San Diego, CA: Academic Press.

Siegler, I. C. (1989). Developmental health psychology. In M. Storandt & G. R. VandenBos (Eds.), *The adult years: Continuity and change* (pp. 122–142). Washington, DC: American Psychological Association.

Wohlwill, J. F. (1973). *The study of behavioral development.* New York: Academic Press.

AUTHOR INDEX

Subject Index

ABOUT THE EDITORS

Scott M. Hofer is Professor of Human Development and Family Sciences and Director of the Psychosocial Core in the Center for Healthy Aging Research at Oregon State University. He received his PhD in psychology from the University of Southern California in 1994 and held postdoctoral positions at the Age and Cognitive Performance Research Center at the University of Manchester and the Center for Developmental and Health Genetics at Pennsylvania State University, where he was promoted to Associate Professor. His research examines the role of aging and health on changes in cognitive functioning, in interaction with demographic and psychosocial influences, and on statistical analysis and design issues for understanding developmental and aging processes. He collaborates with national and international researchers on longitudinal studies of development and aging and is associate investigator on research networks in Australia, Sweden, and the United Kingdom. He is currently co-leading the development of an international collaborative research network for the Integrative Analysis of Longitudinal Studies on Aging, funded by the National Institute on Aging.

Duane F. Alwin is the Tracy Winfree and Ted H. McCourtney Professor of Sociology and Demography at Pennsylvania State University, where he currently directs the Center on Population Health and Aging, a National Institute on Aging–funded Demography of Aging center. He received a PhD in sociology and educational psychology from the University of Wisconsin in 1972. He is currently Chair of the Section on Aging and the Life Course of the American Sociological Association. His research interests include a wide range of phenomena concerned with aging and the life course, and he is best known for his innovative work on the connections among human development, social structure, demography, and social change. His research has received continuous support from the National Institute on Aging since 1983. His current scholarship focuses on the implications of population processes for research on cognitive aging, as well as on the linkage between social structures and health inequalities. He has published extensively on these and related topics and is the recipient of numerous prestigious awards, grants, and special university honors.

ASSOCIATE EDITORS

Roberto Cabeza studied at University of Tsukuba, in Japan, and at the University of Toronto. He is currently Associate Professor in Psychology and Neuroscience at Duke University, where he is also core faculty at the Center for Cognitive Neuroscience and Senior Fellow at the Center for the Study of Aging and Human Development. Dr. Cabeza investigates the neural correlates of memory in young and older adults using functional neuroimaging techniques. He has more than 90 scientific publications, and he is the author of an influential model on the effects of aging on hemispheric asymmetries in brain activity. Dr. Cabeza has edited several volumes, including *Cognitive*

Neuroscience of Aging and the *Handbook of Functional Neuroimaging of Cognition.* In 2003, he was conferred the Young Investigator Award by the Cognitive Neuroscience Society, and in 2005, he received the Busse Research Award in the Biomedical Sciences.

Jennifer J. Manly is Associate Professor of Neuropsychology in Neurology at the G. H. Sergievsky Center and the Taub Institute for Research in Aging and Alzheimer's disease at Columbia University. She completed her graduate training in neuropsychology at the San Diego State University/University of California, San Diego Joint Doctoral Program in Clinical Psychology in 1996. After a clinical internship at Brown University, she completed a postdoctoral fellowship at Columbia University. Her research focuses on cognitive and genetic aspects of aging and Alzheimer's disease among African American and Hispanic elders. She is an Associate Editor of the *Journal of the International Neuropsychological Society* and is a consulting editor for several other neuropsychology and neurology journals. She received Early Career Awards from Division 40 of the American Psychological Association and the National Academy of Neuropsychology and is a Fellow of the American Psychological Association.

Mark A. McDaniel is Professor of Psychology at Washington University in St. Louis. He received his PhD from University of Colorado in 1980. His research is in the general area of human learning and memory, with an emphasis on prospective memory, encoding and retrieval processes in episodic memory and applications to educational contexts, and aging and memory. He has served as Associate Editor of the *Journal of Experimental Psychology: Learning, Memory, and Cognition* (1995–2000) and as president of the Rocky Mountain Psychological Association and is a Fellow of Divisions 3 and 20 of the American Psychological Association. He has published over 160 journal articles, book chapters, and edited books on human learning and memory and is coauthor, with Gilles Einstein, of two recent books: *Memory Fitness: A Guide for Successful Aging* and *Prospective Memory: An Overview and Synthesis of an Emerging Field* (Sage, 2007).

Martin Sliwinski is Professor of Psychology and an associate in the Center for Health and Behavior at Syracuse University. His research focuses on the relationships among cognition, health, and affect across the adult life span, particularly on the statistical modeling of intraindividual change and variability in cognition, health, and emotion in older adults. His methodological work using a "burst design" for understanding the nature of short-term variability in functioning has contributed to the understanding of the relationship of stress and cognitive change. He has also collaborated with the longitudinal Einstein Aging Studies, which focuses on the cognitive, physiological, and health markers of preclinical dementia.

Sherry L. Willis is a researcher, professor, teacher, and interventionist in cognitive aging in the Department of Human Development and Family Studies at Pennsylvania State University. Dr. Willis's research has focused on age-related cognitive changes in later adulthood. She is known for her work on behavioral interventions to remediate and enhance cognitive performance in community-dwelling normal elderly persons. She is a Principal Investigator of the Penn State site on the Advanced Cognitive Training for Independent and Vital Elderly (ACTIVE) study, a randomized controlled trial to examine the effects of cognitive interventions in the maintenance of everyday functioning in at-risk community-dwelling elderly persons, funded by the National Institute on Aging. Dr. Willis has conducted programmatic research on changes in everyday problem-solving competence in the elderly and cognitive predictors of competence. She and her colleagues have developed several measures of everyday problem solving. She has served as president of Division 20, Adult Development and Aging, of the American Psychological Association. She was a Fulbright Fellow in Sweden. She received a Faculty Scholar Medal for Outstanding Achievement in 1999 and the Pauline Schmitt Russell Distinguished Research Career Award in 2001 from Pennsylvania State University. She has funding from the National Institute on Aging to examine midlife predictors of cognitive risk in old age and has received a MERIT (Method to Extend Research in Time) award for this research.

ABOUT THE CONTRIBUTORS

Adrienne Aiken Morgan is a doctoral student in clinical psychology at the University of Florida (UF). Adrienne is completing a year-long clinical internship in neuropsychology at the University of Chicago Medical Center, and she will receive her PhD in August 2008. Her academic studies and research foci include normal cognitive aging and cognitive decline and the influence of cardiovascular health and fitness on cognitive performance and decline, particularly in African Americans. She has published work examining and characterizing ethnic group differences in cognitive performance between African American and European American older adults, and she is currently examining the effects of improved physical fitness on executive cognitive function in elders.

David M. Almeida received his PhD in developmental psychology at the University of Victoria and is Professor of Human Development and Family Studies at Pennsylvania State University. His research interests center on the general question of how daily stressful experiences influence individual health and well-being during adulthood. Dr. Almeida directs the National Study of Daily Experiences (NSDE), one of the in-depth studies that are part of the National Survey of Midlife in the United States (MIDUS). The purpose of the NSDE is to examine the day-to-day lives, particularly the daily stressful experiences, of a subsample of 1,484 MIDUS respondents who completed short telephone interviews on each of 8 consecutive nights. Dr. Almeida has adapted this telephone daily protocol to assess daily stress and health in other projects, including the Penn State Initiative on Hotel Work and

Health, the Normative Aging Study, and the Daily Management of Type 2 Diabetes. His work has been funded by grants from the National Institutes of Health, the John D. and Catherine T. MacArthur Foundation, the W. K. Kellogg Foundation, the Johnson & Johnson Foundation, and the Alfred P. Sloan Foundation.

Mareike Altgassen is an Assistant Professor of Psychology at the Developmental Psychology Unit, Department of Psychology, Dresden University of Technology, Germany. She completed her dissertation in September 2007 at the University of Zurich, Switzerland, and received her MA in psychology at the University of Heidelberg, Germany. Her research focuses on prospective memory development across the life span with a special emphasis on clinical populations (autism, schizophrenia, depression, Parkinson's disease).

Kaarin Anstey is Associate Professor and Director of the Ageing Research Unit at the Centre for Mental Health Research, Australian National University. Her interests are in the epidemiological and applied aspects of cognitive aging and well-being, with an emphasis on longitudinal studies. She is currently Principal Investigator on Dynamic Analyses to Optimize Ageing (DYNOPTA), a large study that involves pooling nine longitudinal aging studies, and is Principal Investigator on Wave 3 of the Personality and Total Health (PATH) Through Life Study, involving 7,500 adults from young, middle, and late adulthood. Anstey also leads a study of cognitive aging and hazard perception in older drivers.

Lisa L. Barnes is Associate Professor in the Departments of Neurological Sciences and Behavioral Sciences at Rush University Medical Center and a cognitive neuropsychologist in the Alzheimer's Disease Center. She received her PhD in biopsychology from the University of Michigan and a completed a postdoctoral fellowship in cognitive neuroscience at the University of California, Davis. Her research interests include health disparities among older Blacks and Whites, and psychosocial risk factors for cognitive decline and Alzheimer's disease. Dr. Barnes is also the Principal Investigator of a longitudinal epidemiologic study of cognitive decline in over 400 older African Americans funded by the National Institute on Aging.

Cynthia A. Berg is currently Professor of Psychology at the University of Utah. Her research interests involve contextual variations in the nature of intelligence and everyday problem solving across the life span, especially collaborative problem solving involving chronic health stressors. She serves on the editorial board of *Psychology and Aging*. Her work is funded by the National Institute of Aging and National Institutes of Diabetes and Digestive and Kidney Disorders. She received her PhD from Yale University in 1987.

Fredda Blanchard-Fields is Professor in the School of Psychology at Georgia Institute of Technology. She received her PhD in developmental psychology from Wayne State University in 1983. She is a Fellow of the American Psychological Association (Divisions 3 and 20), the Gerontological Society of America, and the American Psychological Society. She is currently the Associate Editor of *Psychology and Aging*. She has served as chair of the National Institutes of Health grant review study section for social psychology, emotion, and personality research. Her program of research examines adaptive developmental changes in adulthood in various areas of social cognition. She has numerous publications in the general area of social cognition and aging, including causal attributional processing, everyday problem solving, coping, and perceived controllability from adolescence through older adulthood. She has coedited two books, including *Perspectives on Cognitive Change in Adulthood and Aging* and *Social Cognition and Aging*. Her research on causal attributional processing and aging as well as everyday problem solving and aging have been and are currently funded by grants from the National Institute on Aging. She received the 2005 Distinguished Mentor Award from the American Psychological Association, Division 20.

David A. Blizard is Senior Research Scientist in the Center for Developmental and Health Genetics in the College of Health and Human Development at Pennsylvania State University. He trained in physiological psychology and behavior genetics at the University of Wales in Cardiff; the Jackson Laboratory in Bar Harbor, Maine; and Rockefeller University in New York City. His interests lie in elucidating gene–environment interactions using rodent models with regard to a variety of biobehavioral phenotypes. He believes that animal model systems have great potential to illuminate some of the provocative issues limiting our understanding of the role of genes and environment in age-related cognitive decline.

Julie Blaskewicz Boron is Assistant Professor of Psychology, Youngstown State University. She received her PhD in human development and family studies at Pennsylvania State University in 2005 and was a postdoctoral fellow at the Georgia Institute of Technology. Her research interests are in how cognitive change impacts older adults' daily lives and functioning, what strategies older adults use to compensate for cognitive changes, and in examining what and how individual characteristics influence the impact of cognitive change on daily life.

Christopher B. Brady is a Research Health Scientist at the VA Boston Healthcare System and Assistant Professor of Neurology at the Boston University School of Medicine (BUSM). His VA and National Institutes of Health–funded research program focuses on the effects of aging and health on cognition, specifically, whether there are gender differences in the degree to which age-related cognitive decline is associated with vascular disease risk factors. He also collaborates with investigators at BUSM on a study of the effects of age and health on language. He teaches in the BUSM Behavioral Neuroscience program and is a supervisor in clinical neuropsychology in the Boston Clinical Psychology Consortium. He earned his PhD in clinical psychology from Washington University and his master's degree in research methodology from the University of Pittsburgh.

Kathleen A. Cagney is Associate Professor in the Departments of Health Studies and Comparative Human Development at the University of Chicago. Her work examines social inequality and its relationship to health with a focus on neighborhood, race, and aging and the life course. She is Principal Investigator of a study that explores neighborhood social context and its role in the health and well-being of older Chicagoans. She is Co-Director of the Center on the Demography and Economics of Aging. She holds a PhD from Johns Hopkins University and an MPP from the University of Chicago.

John Cerella received his PhD from Harvard University in 1975 and spent the next 20 years as a Research Psychologist at the VA Outpatient Clinic, Boston, studying cognitive aging. In 1995, he joined the Department of Psychology of Syracuse University as a Research Professor. At Syracuse University, he has collaborated with Professor William Hoyer in research on the acquisition of cognitive skills in the elderly, and with Professor Paul Verhaeghen in research on working memory and executive functioning in the elderly.

Neil Charness is William G. Chase Professor of Psychology and an Associate in the Pepper Institute on Aging and Public Policy at Florida State University. He received his undergraduate degree at McGill University and a PhD from Carnegie Mellon University. Neil has published over 100 journal articles and book chapters on the topics of age and expert performance and on age and technology use. Recent books include *Designing for Older Adults: Principles and Creative Human Factors Approaches* (coauthored, 2004), and the *Cambridge Handbook of Expertise and Expert Performance* (coedited, 2006).

Dale Dannefer is Professor and Chair of the Department of Sociology at Case Western Reserve University. His scholarly work focuses on understanding human development and life course patterns as constituted through the interaction of social forces and processes of individual aging. A pioneer in developing cumulative

advantage theory as an explanatory life-course framework, his current research interests also include life-course institutionalization and globalization and efforts to implement "culture change" in long-term care settings. He has been a research fellow at the Max Planck Institute for Human Development and Education in Germany, at the Andrus Gerontology Center at the University of Southern California, and at the Social Control program at Yale University.

Eric Dishman, General Manager and Global Director of Intel's Health Research & Innovation Group, is responsible for driving Intel's worldwide research, new product innovation, and usability engineering activities in Digital Health. His interdisciplinary group, located in the United States and Europe, focuses on developing information and communication technologies across the continuum of health care from hospital to home. He is a Principal Research Scientist for Intel's Digital Health Group and brings an ethnographic approach to Intel's research and product development efforts. He is cofounder and remains involved in collaborations such as the Technology Research for Independent Living Centre in Ireland and the Everyday Technologies for Alzheimer's Care program with the Alzheimer's Association; he also is Co-Director of the Oregon Center for Aging and Technology and serves as National Chair of the Center for Aging Services Technologies, a cross-industry advocacy group to accelerate technology research and development for aging in place.

Gilles O. Einstein received his PhD from the University of Colorado and is Professor of Psychology at Furman University, where he won the Meritorious Teaching Award in 1985 and the Excellence in Teaching Award in 2006. He has served on the editorial boards of the *Journal of Experimental Psychology: Learning, Memory, and Cognition*, *Memory & Cognition*, and *Psychology and Aging*, and he is a Fellow of the American Psychological Association. His research, which focuses on the processes involved in prospective remembering and how these processes are affected by aging, has been supported by the National Institute on Aging, the National Institute of Mental Health, and the National Aeronautics and Space Administration.

Gwenith G. Fisher is an Assistant Research Scientist at the Survey Research Center of the Institute for Social Research at the University of Michigan. She has worked on the Health and Retirement Study (HRS) and the Aging, Demographics, and Memory Study (ADAMS, a supplement to the HRS to study dementia) since 2001. In addition to continuing her work with the HRS and ADAMS, she is working with HRS coinvestigators on a project funded by the National Institute on Aging to assess and develop new cognitive measures in the HRS. In 2003, she was the inaugural recipient of the A. Regula Herzog Young Investigators Award at the University of Michigan. She holds a BA from Pennsylvania State University and MA and PhD degrees in psychology from Bowling Green State University.

Linda B. Hassing is Associate Professor of Psychology at Göteborg University in Sweden. She earned her PhD in 1998 in psychology at the Göteborg University. Dr. Hassing's research focuses on health and cognitive aging, with a special emphasis on terminal decline and cognition and the impact of diabetes and hypertension on cognition. Currently she is working on a project studying the effect of lifestyle factors in middle age and later risk of cognitive impairment and dementia.

Scott M. Hayes earned a PhD in clinical psychology with an emphasis in neuropsychology at the University of Arizona, under the supervision of Drs. Lee Ryan and Lynn Nadel. Dr. Hayes is currently a National Research Service Award postdoctoral fellow, collaborating with Drs. Roberto Cabeza and Kathleen Welsh-Bohmer at the Center for Cognitive Neuroscience at Duke University and the Bryan Alzheimer's Disease Research Center at Duke University Medical Center. His research focuses on studying age-related changes in memory and neural structure and function, using diffusion tensor imaging and functional magnetic resonance imaging. His clinical work has emphasized assessment, diagnosis, and intervention with patients experiencing memory deficits, most commonly as a result of Alzheimer's or cerebrovascular disease, head injury, depression, or posttraumatic stress disorder.

Tamara Hayes is Assistant Professor in the Department of Biomedical Engineering at Oregon Health and Science University. Her research is focused on the use of ubiquitous computing to deliver health care in the home, with the goal of identifying early markers of cognitive impairment. Recently, her research has been focused on the unobtrusive, continuous, in-home assessment of motor activity and walking speed using a system based on wireless motion sensor technology. Other projects include the development of a novel device for tracking medication adherence and use of accelerometry for assessing balance in patients with Parkinson's disease.

Steven G. Heeringa is a Research Scientist in the Survey Methodology Program, the Director of the Statistical and Research Design Group in the Survey Research Center (SRC), and the Director of the Summer Institute in Survey Research Techniques at the Institute for Social Research at the University of Michigan. He has over 30 years of statistical sampling experience directing the development of the SRC National Sample design, as well as sample designs for SRC's major longitudinal and cross-sectional survey programs. He has been actively involved in research and publication on sample design methods and procedures such as weighting, variance estimation, and the imputation of missing data that are required in the analysis of sample survey data. He has been a teacher of survey sampling methods and has served as a sample design consultant to a wide variety of international research programs based in countries such as Russia, the Ukraine, Uzbekistan, Kazakhstan, India, Nepal, China, Egypt, Iran, the United Arab Emirates, and Chile.

Christopher Hertzog is Professor of Psychology at the Georgia Institute of Technology. He received his PhD from the University of Southern California in 1979, working under the supervision of K. Warner Schaie. After a 2-year postdoctoral fellowship at the University of Washington, he became Assistant Professor at Pennsylvania State University before taking residence at Georgia Tech in 1985. He has published widely on adult cognitive development, with emphases on individual differences, intelligence, memory, skill acquisition, and metacognition.

Lesa Hoffman received her PhD in psychology at the University of Kansas and is currently

Assistant Professor in the Department of Psychology at the University of Nebraska—Lincoln. At the core of her research is the integration of advanced quantitative methods (e.g., multilevel, structural equation, and item response modeling) to the examination of psychological and developmental processes, particularly within the study of cognitive aging. Recent projects have focused on the role of visual attention in predicting impairment in older drivers, the methodological barriers to examining longitudinal changes in cognition, and innovation applications of multilevel modeling for within-person designs.

Michelle Horhota is a doctoral candidate in the School of Psychology at the Georgia Institute of Technology. Her research focuses on attributional judgments, stereotypes, and communication across the life span.

Holly Jimison is Associate Professor in the Department of Medical Informatics and Clinical Epidemiology at Oregon Health and Science University. She received her doctorate in medical information sciences at Stanford University, with dissertation work on using computer decision models to tailor patient education materials to individuals. Dr. Jimison has both academic and industry experience in the design and evaluation of medical technologies. Her research is focused on consumer health informatics, with an emphasis on in-home monitoring, multimedia tools for informed consent, medical decision making, and technology for successful aging. Her current projects include cognitive monitoring and remediation using computer games, automated health coaching research, and interactive exercise systems for home-bound elders. Dr. Jimison is a Fellow of the American College of Medical Informatics and Past President of the Oregon Chapter of Health Information Management Systems Society. She currently serves on the Executive Council for Oregon's Roybal Center for Aging & Technology.

Boo Johansson is Professor of Geropsychology at the Department of Psychology, Göteborg University, Sweden, since 2001. He is also Adjunct Professor of Biobehavioral Health at the College of Health and Human Development, Pennsylvania State University. His research focus is on cognition and mental health in late adulthood and aging. For more than 25 years he was

affiliated with the Institute of Gerontology, School of Health Sciences, Jönköping University, Sweden. Dr. Johansson's research is largely based in longitudinal and multidisciplinary population-based aging studies, for example, the normative H70 Study (cohorts of original 70-year-olds followed for more than 30 years), the Origins of Variance in the Old-Old: Octogenarian Twins (OCTO Twin) Study (which uses a twin design to disentangle the relative contributions of genetic and environmental influences for late life biobehavioral functioning by studying identical and fraternal twins ages 80 and older), and the HARMONY Study (which uses the twin design to study risk and protective factors for cognitive impairment and dementia in later life).

Jeffrey Kaye received his MD from New York Medical College and trained in neurology at Boston University, where he served as Chief Resident in Neurology. Following his residency he completed a Fellowship in Movement Disorders. He then was a Medical Staff Fellow at the National Institute on Aging (NIA), National Institutes of Health (NIH), in the Laboratory of Neurosciences. He is currently Professor of Neurology and Biomedical Engineering at Oregon Health and Science University (OHSU). He directs the NIA–Layton Aging and Alzheimer's Disease Center at OHSU and the Portland VA Medical Center. He also directs the Oregon Center for Aging and Technology. Dr. Kaye's research program has focused over the past two decades on the question of why some individuals remain protected from dementia at advanced ages while others succumb at much earlier times. The centerpiece of his studies has been the ongoing Oregon Brain Aging Study, established in 1989. He currently leads a large NIH study using ubiquitous, unobtrusive technologies for assessment of elders in their homes to detect cognitive decline. Dr. Kaye has received the Charles Dolan Hatfield Research Award and serves on many national and international panels and review boards in the field of geriatrics and neurology. He is author of over 200 scientific publications and holds several grant awards from federal agencies, national foundations, and industrial sponsors.

Susan Kemper is the Roy A. Roberts Distinguished Professor of Psychology and Senior Scientist in the Gerontology Center of the

Schiefelbusch Life Span Institute at the University of Kansas, Lawrence. Her research interests cover the life span, focusing on the role of working memory in language processing by young and older adults and language acquisition by children. Her "The Language Across the Lifespan Project" addresses how aging affects the processing of spoken and written language and includes comparative studies of healthy older adults and adults with Alzheimer's disease. She has contributed to work on the use of language abilities as a predictor of late-life cognitive impairment and Alzheimer's disease in the Nun Study. Her work has been supported by a series of grants from the National Institute on Aging, including a Career Development Award. In 2004, she received the Master Mentor Award from the Retirement Research Foundation and the American Psychological Association (Division 20).

Matthias Kliegel is Full Professor of Psychology and Chair of the Developmental Psychology Unit at the Department of Psychology at the Dresden University of Technology, Germany. He received his PhD in psychology from the University of Heidelberg, Germany. Afterward, he worked as a Research Associate at the German Centre for Research on Ageing. In 2002, he was appointed Assistant Professor of Psychology at the Department of Psychology at the University of Zurich, Switzerland, where he teaches life span developmental psychology and leads a research group on development of intentional behavior across the life span. His research focuses on cognitive development across the life span with a major interest in the development of intentional behavior, especially prospective remembering. His research has been supported by the Swiss National Science Foundation as well as the German Research Foundation. In 2003, he received the Vontobel Award for Research on Aging.

Ralf T. Krampe is Professor of Psychology at the Katholieke Universiteit Leuven in Belgium. His research focus is on the development of expert and elite performance throughout the life span. Together with Anders Ericsson he has worked on expert musicians and their deliberate practice. Together with Neil Charness he has studied chess experts between the ages of 20 and 80. More recently, he has become interested in high-level sensorimotor skills such as postural control in young and older people practicing martial arts. Another focus is timing control in young and older musicians, and he has moved to the use of functional magnetic resonance imaging for this work.

Margie E. Lachman is Professor and Chair of Psychology and Director of the Lifespan Developmental Psychology Lab at Brandeis University. She was editor of the *Journal of Gerontology: Psychological Sciences* (2000–2003) and has edited two volumes on midlife development. Dr. Lachman's research is in the area of life span development, with a particular focus on how self-regulatory processes and beliefs such as the sense of control are related to memory, physical activity, and health. Dr. Lachman was a member of the MacArthur Foundation Research Network on Successful Midlife Development and is collaborating on a 10-year longitudinal follow-up of the MacArthur midlife sample (MIDUS). In 2003, she received the Distinguished Research Achievement Award from the American Psychological Association, Division on Adult Development and Aging.

Anna P. Lane is a research assistant in the National Institute of Labour Studies (NILS) at Flinders University in Australia and a research associate with the Australian Research Council/National Health and Medical Research Council Research Network in Ageing Well, where she assists in developing initiatives for research and capacity building in the area of the aging workforce.

Kenneth M. Langa is Associate Professor in the Department of Internal Medicine, the Ann Arbor Veterans Affairs Health Services Research and Development Center, and the Institute for Social Research, all at the University of Michigan. He is a Co-Investigator for the Health and Retirement Study, National Institute on Aging–funded longitudinal study of 20,000 adults in the United States. Dr. Langa received an MD and PhD in public policy at the University of Chicago. He is a practicing general internist, treating adult patients with chronic medical conditions. Dr. Langa's research focuses on the epidemiology and costs of chronic disease in older adults, with an emphasis on Alzheimer's disease and other dementias. He is currently focusing on the relationship of cardiovascular risk factors to cognitive decline and dementia in middle-age and older adults.

Mary A. Luszcz earned a BA from University of Dayton, an MA from George Peabody College, and a PhD from the University of Alabama. Prior to working at Flinders University in Australia, she taught at the University of New Brunswick and Mount Saint Vincent University in Canada. She is a Fellow of the Academy of Social Sciences of Australia, the Gerontological Society of America, the Australian Association of Gerontology, and the Australian Psychological Society. Her cognitive aging research focuses on memory, metamemory, and neuropsychology. As Principal Investigator of the Australian Longitudinal Study of Ageing, she leads a multidisciplinary collaborative effort tracking the lives of Australians over age 70 for the past 15 years. She teaches in the School of Psychology and the School of Medicine, where she is course coordinator for the Program in Applied Gerontology. From 1997 to 2001, she was Secretary General and Vice President of the International Association of Gerontology. She is Editor of the Behavioural Science Section of the journal *Gerontology* and a member of the Editorial Board of the *Australasian Journal on Ageing*. She has served on the Australian Research Council and the National Health and Medical Research Council and is a member of the management committee of the Australia-wide Research Network in Ageing Well and its South Australian Convenor.

Mike Martin is Full Professor of Gerontopsychology and Director of the Center of Gerontology at the University of Zurich, Switzerland. Dr. Martin received his master's degree at the University of Georgia; his PhD in Developmental Psychology at The University of Mainz, Germany; and his habilitation at the University of Heidelberg, Germany. His research focuses on longitudinal and experimental studies of cognitive and social development across the life span, including studies examining predictors of development in childhood, middle adulthood, old, and extreme old age. Recent publications include an encyclopedia of gerontology, a textbook on the psychological aspects of aging, and a coedited volume on midlife development.

Ryan J. McCammon is a research analyst in the Department of Psychiatry and a doctoral candidate in sociology at the University of Michigan. He has coauthored several publications on topics related to aging, birth cohorts, and health and cognitive functioning. His research interests include population health and aging, mental health, and quantitative methods for the analysis of longitudinal data.

Gerald E. McClearn is Evan Pugh Professor of Health and Human Development in the Department of Biobehavioral Health and the Center for Developmental and Health Genetics at Pennsylvania State University. His primary research interest is in the interaction of genetic and environmental influences on aging processes. His research has involved participation in several Swedish Twin Studies and in the use of inbred and heterogeneous stocks of mice as model systems for exploring biogerontological processes.

Joan M. McDowd is Professor and Associate Director for Research in the Landon Center on Aging at the University of Kansas Medical Center. She earned her PhD in psychology from the University of Toronto and her undergraduate degree from Washington University in St. Louis. Her research interests are in the area of cognition and aging, with an emphasis on visual selective attention and inhibitory processes. She has published studies of healthy aging in this area of cognition and has expanded recent work to include people with stroke, Parkinson's disease, and Alzheimer's disease.

Cathy L. McEvoy is Professor of Aging Studies at the University of South Florida. Her research focuses on aging and memory, with an emphasis on the implicit processes underlying recall and recognition. Her work has been funded by the National Institute on Aging and explores how older adults use implicitly activated knowledge to supplement explicit recall of recently experienced events. She has studied interventions for maintaining everyday memory functioning for older adults and has collaborated on research studying the implicit contributions to cognition in deaf adults, to suggestibility in eyewitnesses, to juror bias from pretrial publicity, and to addictive behavior.

Carlos F. Mendes de Leon is a social epidemiologist and Professor of Internal Medicine at Rush University Medical Center in Chicago. He received his PhD in preventive medicine and community health from the University of Texas Medical Branch at Galveston and completed a postdoctoral fellowship at Yale University School of Public Health. He has published extensively on social factors and racial disparities in aging-related health. He was the recipient of the 2001 Ewald W. Busse Research Award from the International Association of Gerontology. He serves on the editorial boards of five peer-reviewed journals in medicine, gerontology, and psychosomatic medicine.

Andrew Mienaltowski is a doctoral candidate in the School of Psychology at the Georgia Institute of Technology. His research examines changes in everyday decision and emotion regulatory processes across the adult life span. Publications from this work appear in *Psychology and Aging* and the *Journals of Gerontology: Psychological Sciences*.

Jacqueline Mogle is currently working on her doctoral degree in experimental psychology at Syracuse University. She received her bachelor's degree in psychology from the State University of New York College at Brockport. Her research focuses on the use of technology for the assessment of cognitive function in older adults, statistical methods for analyzing longitudinal data, and the effects of stress on cognitive functioning. She received the Eric F. Gardner Research Fellowship in 2006.

Peter C. M. Molenaar is Professor of Human Development at Pennsylvania State University. Prior to this, he was Professor of Psychological Methodology, Mathematical Psychology and Psychometrics, and Head of the Methodology Department at the University of Amsterdam. His research involves the application of mathematical–statistical ergodic theory to study the relationships between intraindividual (ideographic) analyses and interindividual (nomothetic) analyses of psychological processes. His areas of special expertise are multivariate time series analysis, brain imaging, quantitative genetics, cognitive development, structural equation modeling, nonlinear dynamics, optimal control, and philosophy of mind.

Moshe Naveh-Benjamin earned his PhD in cognitive psychology from the University of Michigan. He is currently Professor of Psychology at the Department of Psychological Sciences at the University of Missouri—Columbia. His research explores fundamental processes and structures of human memory, including adult-age changes in episodic memory; interactions among attention, encoding, and retrieval processes; and the role of memory processes in real life settings. He has published over 60 journal articles and book chapters, as well as an edited book, *Perspectives on Human Memory and Cognitive Aging* (2002). He is a Fellow of the Psychonomic Society.

Shevaun D. Neupert is Assistant Professor in the developmental psychology program at North Carolina State University. She earned her PhD from the University of Arizona, her MS from Western Washington University, and her BA from Pepperdine University. She also completed a postdoctoral fellowship at Brandeis University. Her research typically incorporates daily diary designs to answer questions regarding the importance of daily stressors, beliefs, appraisals, and sociodemographic characteristics on differences and changes in well-being across the adult life span. In particular, her program of research focuses on the mechanisms linking daily stressors with everyday cognition, daily affect, and daily physical health.

Susan R. Old earned her MA from the University of Missouri–Columbia and continues graduate work in the Cognition and Neuroscience training program within the Department of Psychological Sciences at that institution under the advisement of Dr. Moshe Naveh-Benjamin. Her research interests involve cognitive aging and the effects of divided attention on memory. She was awarded the 2006 Psychological Sciences Outstanding Master's Thesis Award for her work on associative memory and aging.

Denise C. Park is Regents Professor and T. Boone Pickens Distinguished Chair of Clinical Brain Science at the Center for Brain Health at the University of Texas at Dallas. Her research activities are focused on understanding the interplay between neurobiological and experiential forces on cognitive function across the life span. She is currently studying the neural signature associated with a healthy mind across the life span as well as the impact of cultural forces on cognitive and neural aging. She is also conducting intervention work to determine whether sustained intellectual and social activity enhances cognitive function in late adulthood.

Robin Shura Patterson is a doctoral candidate in the Department of Sociology at Case Western Reserve University (CWRU). Her research interests include cumulative dis/advantage and health disparities over the life course, the sociopolitical construction of social problems, and international child trafficking. She is currently project coordinator for *Learning From Those Who Know,* a multimethod action research project on reform efforts in long-term care. She was awarded a National Institute of Aging Fellowship in CWRU's doctoral training program.

Misha Pavel is Professor of Biomedical Engineering with a joint appointment in Computer Science and Engineering at Oregon Health and Science University. Until mid-2003, he spearheaded the establishment of the Department of Biomedical Engineering and served as its first department chair. His previous positions included a position as a Technology Leader at AT&T Laboratories in Menlo Park, California, as Associate Professor at New York University, as Assistant Professor at Stanford University and as a researcher at Bell Laboratories. Dr. Pavel received his PhD in experimental psychology from New York University and an MS in electrical engineering from Stanford University. His main area of research is at the intersection of mathematical modeling of complex behaviors of biological systems, engineering, and cognitive science, with a focus on changes associated with aging and neurological diseases. Dr. Pavel has published in the areas of computational neuroscience, information fusion, pattern recognition, engineering systems, and clinical research.

Andrea M. Piccinin is Research Associate Professor of Human Development and Family Sciences at the Oregon State University and a member of the Center for Healthy Aging Research. Dr. Piccinin received her PhD from the University of Southern California in 1994. Her research interests focus on changes in cognitive function in later life through longitudinal analysis of within-person development, as well as the measurement and design issues that surround such work. She is coleading the Integrative Analysis of Longitudinal Studies on Aging network, funded by the National Institute on Aging, emphasizing integration of health and well-being measures in the study of cognitive function, of results across multiple studies, and of methods for within- and between-person analysis.

Brenda L. Plassman is an Associate Research Professor and the Director of the Program in Epidemiology of Dementia in the Department of Psychiatry and Behavioral Sciences at Duke University Medical Center. Her research has focused on the epidemiology of Alzheimer's disease and other dementias in nationally distributed sample populations. She is Principal Investigator of the Duke Twins Study of Memory in Aging in the National Academy of Sciences–National Research Council Twin Registry of World War II male veterans and the Principal Investigator of the Duke component of the Aging, Demographics and Memory Study (ADAMS), a substudy of the Health and Retirement Study (HRS).

Philippe Rast is a PhD student (dissertation completion: September 2007) in the Department of Psychology at the University of Zurich, Switzerland. He received his MA at the University of Bern, Switzerland. His research focuses on methods of longitudinal research; metacognition and cognitive development across the life span; and experimental studies of learning, cognition, and metacognition. He is also an investigator on the Zurich Longitudinal Study on Cognitive Aging (ZULU), funded by the Swiss National Science Foundation.

Peter Rendell is Associate Professor and Reader in psychology at Australian Catholic University in Melbourne. He completed his PhD in 1995 at Monash University, Melbourne, in the area of aging and prospective memory. His research focuses on aging and memory and is characterized by empirical studies that use novel tasks, including the Virtual Week prospective memory task. He is collaborating with researchers at the University of New South Wales, Australia; the University of Zurich, Switzerland; and Washington University, St. Louis, United States. His current projects include using computer versions of Virtual Week to investigate the impact of aging and individual differences on prospective memory. He has extended his interest in prospective memory in older adults to children and within various groups, including pregnant women, persons with multiple sclerosis, persons with schizophrenia, and substance abusers. His research interest is also on emotional regulation in adults with dementia and adults with schizophrenia.

Chandra A. Reynolds received her PhD in psychology from the University of Southern California in 1994 and subsequently held postdoctoral fellowships at the Institute for Behavioral Genetics at the University of Colorado at Boulder, and the Andrus Gerontology Center, University of Southern California. She is currently Associate Professor in the Department of Psychology at the University of California, Riverside. Her research focuses on the interrelationships between health and cognition across development. In collaboration with colleagues at the Karolinska Institute, Jönköping University, and the University of Southern California, Dr. Reynolds currently directs a National Institute on Aging (NIA)–funded project that considers the genetic and environmental etiology of cognitive change and decline, including candidate genes. Additional projects include an NIA-funded study of the dynamic interrelationships between health and psychosocial trajectories across the life course that may predict longevity.

Willard L. Rodgers is Research Professor in the Institute for Social Research at the University of Michigan in Ann Arbor. Starting in the early 1980s, he has done research on the quality of survey data provided by older respondents. He has been associated with the Health and Retirement Study (HRS), a longitudinal study of the U.S. population over age 50, since its inception in 1991. He has used HRS data to examine secular trends in cognitive abilities. Currently, he is codirecting a study designed to develop an improved battery of measures of cognitive abilities for use in future waves of the HRS. He has a PhD in psychology from the University of Pennsylvania and an MPH in biostatistics from the University of Michigan.

K. Warner Schaie is the Evan Pugh Professor of Human Development and Psychology at Pennsylvania State University. He also holds an appointment as Affiliate Professor of Psychiatry and Behavioral Sciences at the University of Washington. He received his PhD in psychology from the University of Washington; an honorary doctorate in philosophy from the Friedrich-Schiller University of Jena, Germany; and an honorary ScD degree from West Virginia University. He received the Kleemeier Award for Distinguished Research Contributions from the Gerontological Society of America, the Mensa lifetime career award, and the Distinguished Scientific Contributions award from the American Psychological Association. He is author or editor of 52 books, including the textbook *Adult Development and Aging* (5th ed.) and the *Handbook of the Psychology of Aging* (6th ed.). He has directed the Seattle Longitudinal Study of cognitive aging since 1956 and is the author of more than 275 journal articles and chapters on the psychology of aging. His current research interest is the life course of adult intelligence, its antecedents and modifiability, and the early detection of risk for dementia, as well as methodological issues in the developmental sciences.

Brent J. Small is Associate Professor in the School of Aging Studies at the University of South Florida and holds a courtesy joint appointment in the Department of Psychology. He is also Associate Professor in the Health Outcomes and Behavior program and the Biostatistics Resource Core at the H. Lee Moffitt Cancer Center and Research Institute. Dr. Small's research focuses on changes in the cognitive performance of older adults as well as the application of advanced statistical models to understand these changes. More recently, his research has examined genetic correlates of cognitive performance among persons undergoing treatment for cancer.

Avron Spiro III is Senior Research Scientist at the Normative Aging Study, part of the Massachusetts Veterans Epidemiology Research and Information Center (MAVERIC), at the Department of Veterans Affairs Boston Healthcare System. He is also Associate Professor of Epidemiology at the Boston University School of Public Health and Associate Professor of Health Policy and Health Services Research at the

Boston University Goldman School of Dental Medicine. Dr. Spiro is a Fellow of Division 20 of the American Psychological Association and has served on the editorial boards of *Psychology and Health* and the *Journal of Traumatic Stress*. He has published over 150 papers and chapters on aging, health, mental health, and cognition and is a coeditor of the *Handbook of Health Psychology and Aging* (2007).

Robert S. Stawski is a National Institute of Mental Health postdoctoral research fellow at Pennsylvania State University Gerontology Center, where he works and collaborates on numerous studies examining stress, health, and cognition across the adult life span. He earned his PhD in experimental psychology from Syracuse University and his undergraduate degree in psychology from Oklahoma State University. His research interests include biological and psychological links between stressful experiences and cognition; intraindividual variability in cognition, emotion, and health; and cognitive aging.

Valgeir Thorvaldsson is a fourth-year doctoral student at the Department of Psychology, Göteborg University, Sweden. Currently he is involved in several projects that aim to identify factors that contribute to change and variability on functional outcomes and biological aging markers in very old age. His research is mainly conducted within the framework of major Swedish population-based longitudinal studies, such as the Gerontological and Geriatric Population Studies in Gothenburg (H70) and the Origins of Variance in Old-Old: Octogenarian Twins (OCTO-Twin) Study.

Patricia A. Tun earned her PhD from the Georgia Institute of Technology and currently serves as Adjunct Associate Professor of Psychology at Brandeis University and Associate Director of the Memory and Cognition Laboratory. She has carried out extensive cognitive aging research funded by the National Institute on Aging to investigate changes in cognitive function, specifically memory and language, across the life span. Her work has focused primarily on age-related changes in attention and memory in processing spoken materials. She collaborates on the Midlife in the U.S. (MIDUS)

national study of aging, with a special interest in biopsychosocial influences on cognition in midlife and old age, and factors that contribute to successful cognitive aging.

Paul Verhaeghen is currently Associate Professor at the School of Psychology at the Georgia Institute of Technology in Atlanta, interested in working memory, attention, information processing, and aging.

Keith Whitfield received his PhD in life span developmental psychology from Texas Tech University and currently serves as Professor of Psychology and Neuroscience at Duke University. His articles, books, and chapters are on individual development in minority aging with a focus on African Americans. His research on twins and individuals focuses on how health, cognition, and their interactions impact aging among African Americans. He is currently conducting a National Institute of Aging (NIA)–supported longitudinal study of cognition among African Americans in Baltimore, MD. He has been a member of the National Academy of Sciences–National Research Council Aging Mind committee, the Research Agenda for the Social Psychology of Aging committee, and the Institute of Medicine report "Assessing Interactions Among Social, Behavioral, and Genetic Factors on Health." He also serves as a member to the Board of Scientific Counselors for the NIA.

Keith F. Widaman is Professor and Chair of the Department of Psychology at the University of California, Davis. He conducts research on the development of human mental abilities and on statistical methods used in behavioral and social science. He has studied the cognitive processes underlying numerical facility, especially the nature of change from childhood through early adulthood. He also studies the structure and development of adaptive behaviors of persons with mental retardation, particularly how parenting behaviors foster growth of adaptive behaviors. His quantitative work encompasses factor analysis, structural equation modeling, and significance testing in regression analysis. He is a Fellow of the American Psychological Association and a past winner of the Cattell Award from the Society of Multivariate Experimental Psychology.

Melanie Wight is a PhD student and senior researcher in the gerontopsychology program at the University of Zurich, Switzerland. Her research interests are social relationships, marriage, and collaborative cognition across the life span. She holds a master's degree in clinical psychology from the University of Fribourg, Switzerland.

Katherine Wild is Assistant Professor of Neurology at Oregon Health and Science University (OHSU). She received her BA from Williams College and her PhD in health psychology from the Ferkauf Graduate School of Psychology at Yeshiva University. She has been at the OHSU Aging and Alzheimer Disease Center since its inception in 1988. Her research interests include early behavioral changes in dementia, attitudes of the elderly toward technology, and decisions around driving competency. She served on the Older Driver Advisory Committee, which was convened by the Oregon Department of Motor Vehicles (DMV) in response to the Initiative for Safe Mobility of House Bill 3071. She also participated in the DMV Medical Work Group toward implementation of the committee's recommendations. She is collaborating with Spry Learning Company in its development of computer-based cognitive interventions for the elderly.

Devin Williams is the CEO and founder of two companies dedicated to advancing the study and practice of using technology to facilitate elders aging in place and to improve the aging process. She cofounded Spry Learning Company in 2000 to develop game technology for early detection of cognitive decline, and in 2007 founded Mindermast, Inc., to develop comprehensive brain fitness programs to protect and improve brain health. Devin and her companies both collaborate extensively with several research institutions as well as conduct in-house research funded by the National Institute of Standards and Technology Advanced Technology Program. Devin earned her MBA at Harvard Business School and her undergraduate degree at Georgetown University.

Robert S. Wilson is Professor of Neuropsychology in the Department of Neurological Sciences, the Department of Behavioral Sciences, and the Rush Alzheimer's Disease Center at the Rush University Medical Center in Chicago. He came to Rush in 1976 after earning his PhD in psychology from Wayne State University. He is board certified in clinical neuropsychology and has served as a consulting editor on several journals related to neuropsychology or aging. He has extensive experience designing, conducting, and analyzing longitudinal studies of aging and Alzheimer's disease, including clinical–pathologic studies, population-based studies, and behavioral neuroscience studies.

Linda A. Wray, Assistant Professor of Biobehavioral Health and Women's Studies at Pennsylvania State University, received her PhD in Gerontology and Public Policy from the University of Southern California in 1995. Her research agenda and publications focus broadly on investigating the behavioral aspects of the links between the social environment, aging, and health in midlife and older age. Her current studies funded by the National Institute on Aging primarily utilize large nationally representative panel data to examine how spousal relationships influence behavioral and health outcomes in diabetes management and the role of chronic health conditions in cognitive aging.

Daniel Zimprich is Assistant Professor in the Department of Psychology at the University of Zurich, Switzerland. He received his MA (Diplom) at the University of Mannheim, Germany, and his PhD in psychology at the Institute of Gerontology at the University of Heidelberg, Germany. His current research focuses on methods of longitudinal research; cognitive and personality development across the life span; and experimental studies of learning, cognition, and metacognitive skills. He is part of an international network of researchers for the Integrative Analysis of Longitudinal Studies of Aging, and has worked with numerous longitudinal data sets covering development from childhood and adolescence to middle age and old age.